PURĀṆA RESEARCH PUBLICATIONS, TÜBINGEN
edited by
Heinrich von Stietencron

Volume 2

Brahmapurāṇa

Summary of Contents,
with Index of Names and Motifs
by

Renate Söhnen and Peter Schreiner

1989
Otto Harrassowitz · Wiesbaden

Brahmapurāṇa

Summary of Contents,
with Index of Names and Motifs
by
Renate Söhnen and Peter Schreiner

1989
Otto Harrassowitz · Wiesbaden

CIP-Titelaufnahme der Deutschen Bibliothek

Söhnen, Renate:
Brahmapurāṇa : summary of contents, with index of names and motifs /
by Renate Söhnen and Peter Schreiner. –
Wiesbaden : Harrassowitz, 1989
(Purāṇa research publications, Tübingen ; Vol. 2)
ISBN 3-447-02960-9
NE: Schreiner, Peter:; Brahmapurāṇa; GT

Printed with a grant from the Deutsche Forschungsgemeinschaft

Phototypesetting: pagina, Tübingen
Printing and binding: Elektra, 6272 Niedernhausen
Printed in Germany

ISSN 0931-9158

Table of contents

Editor's preface XVII

Introduction XIX

Extent and form of the summary - The conspectus - The Brahmapurāṇa in its relation to other texts - The Gautamīmāhātmya - Introduction to the index - Acknowledgements

Appendices 15–17 (supplement to Vol. I) XXXIX

Concordances of Brahmapurāṇa and Mārkaṇḍeyapurāṇa

Part I: Summaries of chapters 1-246

1: Setting of the recitation of the Purāṇa; creation of the world 1

2: Descendants of Manu Svāyaṃbhuva; creation by Dakṣa 2

Veṇa-episode - Pṛthu-episode - Pracetasas-episode - Origin of Māriṣā

3: Creation of beings; descendants of Dakṣa 4

4: Distribution of sovereignties; Pṛthu-episode 8

Distribution of sovereignties - Story of Veṇa's misbehaviour and Pṛthu as first king - Origin of the bards Sūta and Māgadha - Pṛthu and the milking of the earth

5: Description of Manu-eras 12

Era of Manu Svāyaṃbhū - Era of Manu Svārociṣa - Era of Manu Uttama - Era of Manu Tāmasa - Era of Manu Raivata - Era of Manu Cākṣuṣa - Era of Manu Vaivasvata - Account of the era of Manu Sāvarṇa

6: Story of Vivasvat and Saṃjñā and their progeny 16

7: The solar dynasty 17

Story of Ilā - Manu's sons and their progeny - Ikṣvāku's line up to Satyavrata - Story of Kuvalāśva - Story of Satyavrata (part 1)

8: The solar dynasty (contd) 20

Story of Satyavrata (part 2) - Story of Sagara - Story of Sagara's birth - Birth of Sagara's sons - Descendants of Sagara

9: The origin of Soma, the abduction of Tārā, and the birth of Budha . . . 24

10: The lunar dynasty: Amāvasu branch 25

Story of Purūravas - Story of Jahnu - Story of Satyavatī and the birth of Jamadagni - Viśvāmitra and his sons

11: The lunar dynasty (contd): Branch of Āyu's younger sons 27

Story of Raji - Descendants of Anenas - Descendants of Kṣatravṛddha

12: The lunar dynasty (contd): Story of Yayāti 29

13: The lunar dynasty (contd): The branches of Yayāti's sons 31

Descendants of Puru - The branch of Kakṣeyu, son of Raudrāśva - Descendants of Titikṣu - The branch of Ṛceyu, son of Raudrāśva - Descendants of Turvasu - Descendants of Druhyu - Descendants of Anu - Descendants of Yadu - Story of Arjuna Kārtavīrya

14: The lunar dynasty (contd): Genealogy of Kṛṣṇa 38

Branch of Śvaphalka - Branch of Citraka - Descendants of Bhojyā's sons - Descendants of Vasudeva

15: Genealogy of the Bhojas and the Kukuras 41

Jyāmagha branch - Kukura branch

16: Genealogy of Vṛṣṇyandhakas; story of the Syamantaka-jewel 43

Descendants of Bhajamāna - Descendants of Kroṣṭṛ - Story of the Syamantaka-jewel (part 1) - Descendants of Satrājit - Descendants of Vṛṣṇi

17: Story of the Syamantaka-jewel (part 2) 45

18: Description of Jambūdvīpa 46

Divisions of the earth

19: Description of Bhāratavarṣa 50

List of peoples of Bhāratavarṣa

20: Description of the six outer continents 52

Description of Plakṣadvīpa (Fig-tree-continent) - Description of Śālmaladvīpa (continent of the Silk-cotton tree) - Description of Kuśadvīpa (continent of Kuśa-grass) - Description of Krauñcadvīpa (Crane-continent) - Description of Śākadvīpa (Teak-tree-continent) - Description of Puṣkaradvīpa (Lotus-continent)

21: Description of the nether worlds 56

22: Description of hells 57

Attribution of evil deeds to the different hells

23: Description of the heavenly worlds; Viṣṇu and his Śakti 59
24: Nārāyaṇa as Śiśumāra and the cycle of water 61
25: Places of pilgrimage 62
26: The dialogical setting for Brahman's narration 66
27: Description of Bhāratavarṣa 66
28: Description of Oṇḍradeśa; on worship of the sun and of Rāmeśvara . . . 69
Description of the land sacred to the sun (Koṇārka, Koṇāditya)
29: On worship of the sun 71
30: The sun as highest deity; his twelve-fold shape; Mitra's instruction to Nārada 73
31: Various aspects of the sun; the 12 Ādityas; the 21 names of the sun . . . 76
32: The birth of Vivasvat; story of Saṃjñā and Mārtaṇḍa 77
33: On the origin of the sun; the 108 names of the sun 80
34: Story of Satī; the birth of Umā 81
35: Umā and Rudra: her devotion to Rudra; Śiva as a child and the crocodile 84
36: Umā's self-choice; the wedding of Śiva and Umā 85
37: Praise of Śiva by the gods 87
38: Story of how Kāma was burnt by Śiva; Menā's reproach of Śiva 88
39: Destruction of Dakṣa's sacrifice by Śiva 89
Origin of Fever from Śiva's sweat
40: Dakṣa's hymn of the thousand names of Śiva; the distribution of fever . . 91
41: Description of Ekāmraka; worship of Śiva 93
42: Description of Viraja; description of Utkala 94
43: Story of Indradyumna 95
Holy places in Avantī and the way of obtaining liberation by performing certain rituals there
44: Story of Indradyumna (contd): The journey to the southern ocean 97
Description of Puruṣottamakṣetra
45: Story of Indradyumna (contd): The disappearance of Nīlamādhava . . . 98
Story of the disappearance of Nīlamādhava - Dialogue between Janārdana Vāsudeva and Śrī

46: Story of Indradyumna (contd): Description of Puruṣottamakṣetra 101

47: Story of Indradyumna (contd): Construction of temple; Indradyumna's horse-sacrifice 102

48: Story of Indradyumna (contd): Indradyumna's anxiety 103

49: Story of Indradyumna (contd): Hymn to Viṣṇu 104

50: Story of Indradyumna (contd): Making of the images 105

51: Story of Indradyumna (contd): Boons granted by Viṣṇu 106

52: Mārkaṇḍeya-episode: The end of the cosmic cycle 107

53: Mārkaṇḍeya-episode (contd): The Flood and the child in the fig-tree . . . 108

54: Mārkaṇḍeya-episode (contd): Mārkaṇḍeya's vision 109

55: Mārkaṇḍeya-episode (contd): Mārkaṇḍeya's hymn to Viṣṇu 109

56: Mārkaṇḍeya-episode (contd): Viṣṇu's teachings 110

57: Pañcatīrtha-Māhātmya 112

58: Narasiṃha-Māhātmya 113

59: Śvetamādhava-Māhātmya 115

60: Matsyamādhava-Māhātmya; rules for bathing in the ocean 117

61: Prescriptions concerning worship 119

Prayer-formulas to be used for the ceremony

62: The ocean as holy place (Samudrasnānamāhātmya) 121

63: Pañcatīrtha-Māhātmya (concluded). On auspicious dates 121

64: On the importance of the month Jyeṣṭha 122

65: Bathing festival of Kṛṣṇa, Balarāma, and Subhadrā 123

66: Description of the car festival 125

67: The installation-ceremony and its merit 125

68: Description of Viṣṇu's world 127

69: Puruṣottamakṣetra-Māhātmya 129

70: Puruṣottamakṣetra-Māhātmya; Gautamī-Māhātmya 130

Conclusion to the Puruṣottamakṣetra-Māhātmya - Beginning of the Gautamī-Māhātmya - Classification of holy places - Lists of examples for each of the four kinds of holy places

71: Prehistory to Śiva's marriage with Pārvatī 131
72: Account of the events at the wedding-ceremony 132
73: Story of Bali and Viṣṇu's three steps (Vāmana-Avatāra) 134
74: Gaṇeśa's device to make Gautama bring down the Gaṅgā 135
75: Gautama's hymn to Śiva 138
76: The Gautamī Gaṅgā on earth 139
77: Śiva's account of the Gautamī Gaṅgā 140
78: Descent of the Bhāgīrathī Gaṅgā 141
79: Story of Viṣṇu as boar lifting up the sacrifice 143
80: Story of the pigeon couple and the hunter 144
81: Story of Skanda's lust 146
82: Story of the Kṛttikās and of Skanda's birth 147
83: The completion of Bhauvana's ten horse-sacrifices 147
84: Birth of Hanumat and his half-brother 149
85: Story of Kaṇva's hunger 149
86: Story of Yama neglecting his duty 150
87: Story of Indra and Ahalyā 151

Prehistory of Ahalyā's marriage to Gautama - Ahalyā's seduction by Indra and Gautama's curse - Removal of the curses by Gautamī

88: Varuṇa as teacher of Janaka and Yājñavalkya 153
89: Story of Vivasvat, the surrogated Chāyā, and the birth of the Aśvins . . . 154
90: Story of Garuḍa and the snake Maṇināga 155
91: Story of Jābāli and the cows 156
92: Story of Sanājjāta and his mother Mahī 157
93: Story of Viśvāmitra and Indra 158
94: Story of Śiva's devotee Śveta, who could not be taken away by Death . . 159
95: Śukra (Uśanas) and the science of reviving the dead 160
96: Indra and Brahmin-murder 161
97: How Kubera lost his kingdom and became lord of the north 162

98 : Story of Agni and Jātavedas 163
99 : Story of Pṛthuśravas and his younger brother 164
100: Story of Kaśyapa and his two wives Suparṇā and Kadrū 164
101: Purūravas and Sarasvatī 165
102: Brahman's incest 166
103: Disturbance of Priyavrata's horse-sacrifice 167
104: Story of Hariścandra, Rohita, and Śunaḥśepa 168
105: Story of the (first) purchase of Soma 170
106: Story of the origin and distribution of the nectar of immortality 172
107: Story of Vṛddhagautama and the old maid 174
108: Story of King Ila who became Ilā, the mother of Purūravas 176
109: The destruction of Dakṣa's sacrifice; Viṣṇu's discus swallowed by Śiva . . 179
110: Story of Dadhīci and his son Pippalāda 181
111: The Prince as Serpent 187
112: Śiva and the Mothers fighting against the demons 189
113: The treacherous fifth head of Brahman 190
114: Gaṇeśa and the obstacle at the Sattra-rite of the gods 191
115: Śiva's help to Śeṣa against the demons 192
116: Death as slaughterer at a sacrifice of sages 192
117: Datta Ātreya and Śiva 194
118: Story of the Rākṣasas Aśvattha and Pippala 194
119: The plants and Soma 195
120: The plants and Soma (contd) 196
121: Kaṭha and his special gift to his teacher Bharadvāja 197
122: Stories of Dhanvantari and of Indra regaining his kingdom 198
123: Story of Daśaratha and his dutiful son Rāma 201

Daśaratha's fight with the demons - Daśaratha kills the Brahmin boy - Rāma's adventures - Daśaratha's redemption

124: Story of Indra and Diti 206

Story of Diti and Kaśyapa - Story of Indra and Maya - Indra in Diti's womb - Śiva ends the conflict between Indra and Diti

125: The enmity between Anuhrāda and Ulūka 210

126: Competition between Agni and the waters 212

127: The sacrificer kidnapped by a demon 213

128: Story of Agni and Śiva's semen; the abduction of Suvarṇā 215

129: Stories about Indra 217

Story of Indra and Namuci - Story of Indra and Mahāṣani - Indra, Indrāṇī, and Vṛṣākapi

130: Story of Agastya teaching Āpastamba 221

131: Saramā and the Paṇis 222

132: Story of Pippalā, Viśvāvasu's sister 224

133: The demon born of the smoke at Bharadvāja's sacrifice 224

134: The Rākṣasas and the magic woman Ajaikā Muktakeśī 225

135: Story of Brahman, Viṣṇu, and Śiva's Liṅga 226

136: Maudgalya and Viṣṇu 227

137: Dispute between Lakṣmī and Poverty 228

138: Story of Madhuchandas, family priest of King Śaryāti 230

139: Pailūṣa's »thirst« and the »sword of knowledge« 231

140: Ātreya as Indra 232

141: Pṛthu and the earth 234

142: Meghahāsa and the gods 235

143: Rāvaṇa and Śiva 236

144: Ātreyī, Aṅgiras, and Agni (the fire) 237

145: Discussion about the best way to liberation 238

146: Story of Yayāti 239

147: Viśvāmitra and the Apsarases 240

148: Kāṇva's sacrificial fire getting extinct during the offering 241

149: Viṣṇu as Narasiṃha 242

150: Jīgarti's life after death and his redemption by Śunaḥśepa 243

151: Purūravas and Urvaśī 244

152: The abduction of Tārā 245

153: Prācīnabarhis' long reign and his obtaining a son from Śiva 247

154: The repudiation of Sītā 247

155: The earth as sacrificial gift turning into a lioness and exchanged for a cow 249

156: Viṣṇu's fight with the demons 249

157: Rāma and the Liṅgas 250

158: The Āṅgirasas and their mother's curse; Agastya's teaching 251

159: Kadrū and Vinatā 253

160: Battle between gods and demons 255

161: Creation of the world from Brahman's primordial sacrifice 256

Birth of Brahman - Dialogue between Brahman and the heavenly voice - Preparation of the sacrifice - Performance of the sacrifice

162: Story of Manyu helping the gods against the demons 260

163: Śākalya, a devotee of Viṣṇu, and the Rākṣasa Paraśu 261

164: Story of King Pavamāna and the Ciccika-bird 262

165: Marriage of the sun-god's ugly daughter Viṣṭi 264

166: Story of Saṃpāti and Jaṭāyu 266

167: The young Brahmin and the Rākṣasī 266

168: The performance of King Abhiṣṭut's horse-sacrifice 267

169: The hunter and the Brahmin as devotees of Śiva 269

170: The good merchant and the treacherous Brahmin 270

171: The game of dice between Indra and Pramati 273

172: Confluence of the Gautamī with the ocean 275

173: Viśvarūpa's terrible sacrifice 276

174: Completion of the sacrifice performed by the sages 277

175: Brahman's teachings about *dharma*; on the origin of the Gaṅgā 279

Brahman's teachings about the *dharma* in time and space - Further account of how the Gaṅgā was obtained by Gautama from Śiva - Superiority of the Gautamī Gaṅgā

176: Prehistory of the image of Vāsudeva 283

Story of Rāvaṇa and his brother Vibhīṣaṇa - Summary of Rāmāyaṇa

177: On the greatness of Puruṣottamakṣetra and the merit obtained there . . 284
178: Kaṇḍu-episode 285
179: Introduction to Kṛṣṇacarita 288
Description of the constituents and the development of the human body
180: Manifestations and incarnations of Viṣṇu 290
181: Heavenly prelude to the incarnation of Viṣṇu as Kṛṣṇa 292
182: Birth of Kṛṣṇa 293
183: Kaṃsa's plans and thoughts 294
184: Adventures of the child Kṛṣṇa 294
Pūtanā-episode - Episode of the overturned cart - Episode of Kṛṣṇa being bound to mortar
185: Kālīya-episode 295
186: Dhenuka-episode 296
187: Pralamba-episode; institution of hill-worship by Kṛṣṇa 297
188: Govardhana-episode; encounter of Indra and Kṛṣṇa 298
189: Kṛṣṇa and the cowherds; Ariṣṭa-episode 299
190: Kaṃsa's plans against Kṛṣṇa; Keśin-episode 301
191: Akrūra's devotion to Kṛṣṇa 302
192: Encounter between Akrūra and Kṛṣṇa; Kṛṣṇa's journey to Mathurā . . 302
193: Kṛṣṇa's deeds in Mathurā; killing of Kaṃsa 303
194: Kṛṣṇa's education; Pañcajana-episode 305
195: Jarāsaṃdha-episode 306
196: Kālayavana-episode; Mucukunda and Kṛṣṇa 306
197: Kṛṣṇa and Mucukunda; Baladeva in Gokula 307
198: Balarāma forcing Yamunā to change her course 308
199: Marriage of Kṛṣṇa and Rukmiṇī 308
200: Abduction of Pradyumna and his killing of Śambara 308
201: Marriage of Aniruddha; killing of Rukmin 309
202: Naraka-episode 310

203: Kṛṣṇa and Satyabhāmā in the world of the gods 311

Kṛṣṇa taking away the Pārijāta-tree; opposition of Kṛṣṇa and Indra

204: Reconciliation of Kṛṣṇa and Indra; the Pārijāta-tree on earth 312

205: Descendants of Kṛṣṇa; Bāṇa-episode: Uṣā's dream 312

206: Bāṇa-episode (contd) 313

207: Pauṇḍraka claiming to be Viṣṇu; the burning of Kāśi 314

208: Balarāma's heroic deeds: Release of Sāmba 315

209: Balarāma's heroic deeds: Dvivida-episode 316

210: The destruction of the Yādavas 316

211: Kṛṣṇa's death 318

212: Arjuna's deeds and failures after Kṛṣṇa's death 318

Arjuna's visit to Vyāsa - Vyāsa's consolation of Arjuna - Aṣṭāvakra-episode

213: Manifestations of Viṣṇu 320

Pauṣkara-manifestation - Vāräha-manifestation - Narasiṃha-manifestation - Dattātreya-manifestation - Manifestation as Jāmadagnya - Manifestation as Rāma - Manifestation as Keśava (= Kṛṣṇa) - Manifestation as Kalkin

214: The path to Yama's world; the gates to his city 324

215: Punishment of the wicked in Yama's world; description of hells 326

216: Reward of the righteous in Yama's world 330

217: The fate of the soul after death; retribution for deeds by rebirth 331

218: Merit of giving food to Brahmins 335

219: On ancestral rites 336

220: Prescriptions for ancestral rites; their effects 341

Prescriptions concerning articles to be employed and to be avoided - Prescriptions concerning food forbidden during ancestral rites - Prescriptions concerning special cases of ancestral rites

221: On the proper conduct 349

Prescriptions concerning daily routines - Prescriptions concerning cleaning - Prescriptions concerning ancestral rites

222: Rules for the conduct according to caste and stage of life 356

223: Rise and fall within the caste system (dialogue between Śiva and Umā) 358

224: On the effects of actions (dialogue between Śiva and Umā, contd) . . . 360

225: On rebirth (dialogue between Śiva and Umā, contd) 362

226: Dialogue between Śiva and the sages 363

227: On the destiny of Vaiṣṇavas after death 365

228: Praise of singing while keeping vigil 366

Story of the devoted Cāṇḍāla and the Rākṣasa - Story of the previous and the following rebirths of the Mātaṅga

229: Episodes illustrating the manifestations of Viṣṇu's Māyā. 369

Story of Śuci - Story of Nārada's experience with Viṣṇu's Māyā - Story of Śuci (contd): the sage as Cāṇḍāla girl

230: On the conditions during Kali-Yuga 371

231: The end of a cycle of Yugas and the return of Kṛta-Yuga 374

232: On the dissolution of things 376

233: Description of occasional dissolution (contd) 377

234: On suffering and final release from existence (absolute dissolution) . . 379

235: Description of the practice of Yoga 380

236: On Sāṃkhya and Yoga 381

237: On the opposition of action and knowledge 384

238: On liberation by knowledge 387

239: On the difference between Sāṃkhya and Yoga; on the practice of Yoga 389

240: On Sāṃkhya and Yoga 390

241: Dialogue between Karālajanaka and Vasiṣṭha 393

On the emanation of the world

242: On the worldly bondage and destiny of the soul 394

243: Dialogue between Karālajanaka and Vasiṣṭha (contd) 395

Vasiṣṭha's answer concerning Yoga

244: Dialogue between Karālajanaka and Vasiṣṭha (contd) 398

On knowledge and ignorance - On perishable and imperishable

245: Dialogue between Karālajanaka and Vasiṣṭha (contd) 399

Editor's preface

The second volume in the series of »Purāṇa Research Publications« is designed to make the contents of the Brahmapurāṇa easily accessible to scholars. Its detailed summary of contents seeks to carry all relevant information; it also includes notes on changing levels of dialogue, insertions, parallel passages in other texts, etc. The exhaustive index to the summary will be found useful to sanskritists and non-sanskritists alike for tracing any particular subject in the text. Together with the three word indices (key-word-in-context, index of word forms, and reverse index) and the text itself supplied in the first volume,[1] the index of contents completes the research tools prepared for the Brahmapurāṇa.

The Brahmapurāṇa is the first work in the Purāṇa category - and probably the first in the whole of Indian literature - for which research tools of such a type have been supplied.

In spite of the late additions in its Māhātmya-section, this Purāṇa was considered by W. Kirfel to be one of the oldest extant texts of the entire Purāṇa literature. The two authors' introduction to this volume shows that Kirfel's conclusions may have to be revised and that R. C. Hazra who considered it a late Purāṇa was nearer to the truth. But it is not their age alone which makes Purāṇic texts a worthwhile object of study. This can be proved by the Gautamī-Māhātmya which constitutes the latest major addition to our text, but is by no means without interest to the student of Indian culture since it preserves traditions going back to the vedic period.

Comparative studies are called for in other respects, too. If the Brahmapurāṇa was, in its present shape, compiled in eastern India and most probably in Orissa: what is its relation to the Utkalakhaṇḍa of the Skandapurāṇa, which was compiled in the same region? Both texts refer to Anantavāsudeva. A small shrine of this deity is situated on the southern side of the Jagannātha temple within the inner compound wall (no. 85 in the »Record of Temples« and its »Map of the Temple of Lord Jagannāth of Puri«, attached to the Shri Jagannāth Temple Rules of 1960). The Brahmapurāṇa gives a legendary account of its image in a probably appended chapter. The more important and famous temple of the deity Anantavāsudeva was consecrated in Bhubaneshwar in 1278 A.D. and is referred to in the Skandapurāṇa. An inscription proves that the latter temple was dedicated to Hālin, Cakrin, and Subhadrā (i.e. Balarāma, Kṛṣṇa, Subhadrā), whose original images are now placed at the Bindusarovar tank below the temple. These three gods were representatives of the triad of gods in the Puruṣottama temple of Puri, installed as a symbol of power

[1] Peter Schreiner and Renate Söhnen, Sanskrit Indices and Text of the Brahmapurāṇa, Wiesbaden 1987.

in the Śaiva temple city of Bhubaneshwar. The small shrine in Puri could, in turn, house a representative of the god Anantavāsudeva of Bhubaneshwar and thus be one of many shrines for representatives of major Orissan deities within the compound of the Jagannātha temple. But neither the Brahmapurāṇa's description of the image of Anantavāsudeva in Puri nor its explanation of the name Anantavāsudeva betray any relation between the two gods. We are confronted with a change in the theological concept of »Anantavāsudeva«. The question is: which is the earlier concept of this god? What are the consequences for the chronological sequence of the two texts? Can the shrine of Anantavāsudeva in Puri be dated and thus establish a terminus post quem for the respective chapter in the Brahmapurāṇa?

It is also to be noted that a Brahmapurāṇa was known earlier to Vijñāneśvara and al-Bīrūnī. Narasiṃha Vājapeyin, author of the Nityācārapradīpa, distinguished between two different Brahmapurāṇas, one of which (containing the Puruṣottama-Māhātmya and therefore corresponding more or less to our present text) he considered an Upapurāṇa. Comparisons are called for also with other texts, such as regional Māhātmyas of Orissa and of the Godāvarī basin. And, of course, the parallel passages noticed already by R. C. Hazra and listed in the appendices of the first volume of this series (with additions at the end of the introduction to the present volume) require further detailed investigation. Such tasks and many others would be made much easier if more of the Purāṇa texts were provided with indices of the kind we are now publishing for the Brahmapurāṇa.

It is now for the scholars to try the research tools presented here and, if they find them useful, to encourage us to proceed with other texts. It is particularly hoped that scholars of neighbouring disciplines (history, geography, religious studies, etc.) will now get access to the materials of the Brahmapurāṇa and include them in their respective areas of research.

Tübingen, January 1988 — Heinrich von Stietencron

Introduction

The summary of contents of the Brahmapurāṇa[1] is, primarily, meant as a tool for those who cannot read the Sanskrit original. It should, of course, also prove useful for the indologist who wants to survey larger sections of the text in searching for evidence and material concerning all those topics which are not directly accessible by looking up a particular Sanskrit word. For his convenience, references to verses or groups of verses of the Sanskrit text are printed in the margin of the summary; the index to the summary of contents refers to these references, not to the page numbers of the printed book. It is thus possible to use the same references for looking up a passage in the Sanskrit text, even if one may have to go through a number of verses to find the exact occurrence of a name or a motif.

Though published in Germany, the summary is written in English, for the sake of wider accessibility. This decision created, of course, a number of problems for the authors, especially concerning style and terminology. Many of these problems however were solved with the kind help of Mary and John Brockington, Edinburgh, to whom we wish to express our special thanks.

Extent and form of the summary

It was never intended to prepare a translation of the text;[2] although the summary is, at places, almost as detailed as a translation. Its usefulness for all purposes of research was felt to depend rather on its comprehensiveness regarding details of contents, on its close interrelation with the other materials prepared by the Tübingen Purāṇa Project,[3] and most of all, on the index.[4]

[1] A summary of contents of the BrP was first presented by H. H. Wilson, in: Essays on the Puránas I, JRAS 1839, vol. 5; reprinted in: Analysis of the Purāṇas, ed. by Reinhold Rost, Delhi 1979. The Uttarakhaṇḍa which Wilson mentions (»nothing more than a Mahātmya of the Bālajā river«; Analysis of the Purāṇas, p. 20) is not part of the printed editions, while Wilson's copy did not contain the Gautamīmāhātmya. See also W. Ruben: Purāṇic line of heroes, p. 353-354.

[2] A translation of the BrP, according to the VePr edition, has now been published in the »Ancient Indian Tradition and Mythology Series« (as vol. 33-36, Delhi 1985-86), but our work had already been finished before we had access to this translation.

[3] The Purāṇa Project was established in 1982 under the direction of H. v. Stietencron, with the purpose of providing scholars with research tools, such as indices and concordances to the texts (their Sanskrit wording) and their contents, in order to facilitate access to the Purāṇas. The project was financed by the Deutsche Forschungsgemeinschaft and carried out with the help of the Department of Literary and Documentary Data Processing of the

Concerning scope and manner of presentation we decided for an extended description or paraphrase of contents rather than a concise summary like those which Jacobi presented for the Rāmāyaṇa and the Mahābhārata,[5] mainly because of the index in which *all* names and subjects of interest occurring in the BrP should be included (as an index to the summary of contents it can only contain what is contained in the summary itself - the more the better), on the other hand we felt that difficult passages or words should not be skipped over: freely interspersed question marks, alternative translations, and footnotes document our difficulties in understanding certain passages.

As a summary, this publication should clearly be recognizable as just a tool without literary ambitions. The peculiarities of the text were to remain visible to the reader; all matter which is evaluation rather than presentation had to be made discernible.

Such evaluation is, for instance, contained in our grouping of verses.[6] Criteria for grouping verses are in the first place the contents - verses which relate to the same topic, a specific event in an episode, etc. -; literary criteria like change of speaker, metre, literary genres (e.g. hymns, summaries, dialogues, etc.) were also taken into consideration.

Evaluation is further contained in the footnotes; references to parallels in other texts, problems raised by wording or content, occasional discussions about opinions of other scholars were collected in the course of preparing the summary. Many of them result from chance findings, and we are aware that such notes and references are far from being complete or evenly distributed over the various sections of the BrP. Had we wanted to eliminate all the question marks and all the footnotes indicating that a verse or passage remained unclear (unclear to us, that is), we ourselves would have had to carry out the research for which we only wanted to provide the tools.

Bibliographical references are scarce and often occur in abbreviated form; the reader will find full bibliographical information in the Purāṇic and Epic Bibliography which is intended as an integral part of the material prepared by the project. This bibliography is nearing completion and will give detailed information about secondary literature. The reader is warned not to assume that secondary literature has not more to say about many problems and topics than what has been referred to in our summary.

Computer Centre of the University of Tübingen; its programme package TUSTEP (TUebingen System of TExt-processing Programmes) proved to be an excellent tool for all operations needed.

[4] For these reasons, and for the many footnotes in which problems of understanding the text as well as its connections with other texts are discussed, we think our summary will prove a useful tool, even if the new translation mentioned above is available now.

[5] cf. H. Jacobi: Das Rāmāyaṇa. Bonn 1893 (repr. Darmstadt 1970); Mahābhārata, Bonn 1903 (repr. Hildesheim 1980). His indices of names present of course only those names mentioned in his summary, not all that are found in the Epics.

[6] References to the numbers of the summarized verses are printed in the margin.

The conspectus

In order to give the reader an impression of the topics and the composition of the BrP as a whole,[7] we have provided the following conspectus which does not only present a kind of »table of contents« grouping chapters according to their common subject, but also shows the layers of interlocution (dialogical setting) as well as the »sources« or (more or less literally) parallel texts, as far as we could trace them.[8]

ch.[9]	layer of interlocution	topic	sources, parallel texts
1-17	A. Lomaharṣaṇa - hermits	Purāṇapañcalakṣaṇa	HV 1-10; 20-29
18-24	A.	Cosmography	ViP 2,2-7; 2,9
25	A.	List of Tīrthas	-
26	A.	(transition)	
	B. Vyāsa - sages	(transition)	
	C. Brahman - heavenly sages	(transition)	
27	C.	Bhāratavarṣa	MkP 57
28	C.	Koṇādityamāhātmya	-
29-33	C.	Koṇādityamāhātmya	SāP 38; 2; 4-5; 8-9, 25; 11-12; 14
34-38	C.	Śiva and Umā	-
39-40	C.	Śiva and Dakṣa	MBh 12,274 and App.I,28;[10] VāP 30
41	A. → B. → C.	Ekāmrakamāhātmya	-
42-69	C.	Puruṣottamamāhātmya	
42	C.	Utkalavarṇana	-
43-51	C.	Indradyumna-legend	-

[7] Since we have been working with one Purāṇa, and with one Purāṇa as a whole, it might seem that we have taken a position clearly opposed to that of W. Kirfel who says, »Generally speaking, the Purāṇas, to a great extent, go back to a still traceable basic core, which, of course, is preserved more completely in some of them, less completely in others. This basic core was partly changed in the various Purāṇas, sometimes by revision of certain passages, but mainly it was overgrown, almost past recognition, by insertion or addition of smaller or larger text passages of most heterogeneous contents. This process must have continued for several centuries, and this is the reason why a Purāṇa is *never* to be looked at as a whole, but always section by section, according to the individual texts assembled in any of it.« (Kṛṣṇa's Jugendgeschichte, in: Kleine Schriften, p. 51.)

[8] Kirfel and Hazra gave us the most help here; we were able to add a few new parallels. - For exact concordances, cf. vol. I, Appendices II-XIV and the Appendices XV-XVII (containing the parallels of BrP and MkP) at the end of this Introduction.

[9] According to the ASS edition; for a concordance with the VePr ed. cf. Appendix I of the text volume (PRP 1).

[10] Northern recension (without the Śārada version) and Kumbhakonam edition.

[45	D. Viṣṇu - Śrī	Indradyumna-legend	-]
52-56	C.	Mārkaṇḍeya-episode	MBh 3,186-187
57-63	C.	Pañcatīrthamāhātmya	-
64-69	C.	Holy days and observances in Puruṣottamakṣetra	-
70	C.	(conclusion)	-
70[11]-175	D. Brahman - Nārada	Gautamīmāhātmya	-
176	C.	Anantavāsudevamāhātmya	-
177	B.	Religious merit obtained in Puruṣottamakṣetra	-
178	B.	Kaṇḍu-episode	ViP 1,15
179	A. → B.	The 108 names of Viṣṇu	HV 30
180	B.	Viṣṇu's manifestations	MkP 4
181-212	B.	Kṛṣṇacarita	ViP 5,1-38
213	B.	Viṣṇu's manifestations	HV 31
214-216	B.	*śrāddha*-ritual, hells, etc.	-
217	A. → B.	*karman*, rebirth	MBh 13,112
218	B.	Merit of donations	-
219	B.	Establishment of ancestral rites	-
220-221	B.	Prescriptions for ancestral rites and daily life	MkP 30-35
222	B.	Varṇāśramadharma	ViP 3,8-9
223-225	B. → C1. Śiva - Umā	Retribution of actions	MBh 13,131-133
226[12]	B. → C2. Śiva - hermits	hymn to Kṛṣṇa	MBh 13 App.I,16[13]
227-229	B.	On the worship of Viṣṇu	-
230	B.	Dissolution of the cosmos	ViP 6,1-2.37
231	B.	End of a cosmic cycle	-
232-234	B.	Yugas; end of the world	ViP 6,3-5
235	A. → B.	Yoga	-
236-240	B.	Yoga and Sāṃkhya	MBh 12,231-233; 238-242;
241-245	B. → C3. Vasiṣṭha - Karālajanaka	Yoga and Sāṃkhya	MBh 12,289-296
246	A. Lomaharṣaṇa - hermits	(end of dialogue;) Purāṇapraśaṃsā	

[11] From v. 12 onward.

[12] From this chapter onward, the ASS ed. numbers the remaining chapters by one number fewer, since it uses the number 225 here for a second time.

[13] Northern recension, without ms. D3.

This conspectus is a deliberate attempt to correlate three levels of textual analysis which, from the methodological point of view, need to be distinguished. It may thus raise some of the methodological problems involved in the analysis and interpretation of purāṇic texts.

The first level is the level of textual analysis on a formal, text-immanent basis. Segmentation by dialogical setting is one obvious procedure of such analysis.[14]

A second level is that of contents proper; the order of topics, repetitions, etc., provide a structure which may be interpreted quite independently of formal literary analysis. Possibly it is this level on which the discussion about »Purāṇa« as a genre will have to concentrate, a discussion which will have to take into account that a considerable number of parallels to the BrP are found in MBh and HV, i.e. texts which are traditionally considered to belong to the epic genre. After different levels of textual analysis are distinguished and separately analysed, the task will be to relate those levels to each other.

When looking at the topics treated in the BrP, one will notice immediately that this is not merely a »pañcalakṣaṇa«-Purāṇa. Chapters which deal with the five traditional topics occur[15] but they form a comparatively small part of the text. In trying to find a positively descriptive term, Trivedi calls the BrP a »Tīrtha-Purāṇa«,[16] a name which does not take into consideration the Kṛṣṇacarita and which neglects ch. 213–245.

We suggest that the BrP may contribute to a descriptive rather than a normative definition of what constitutes a Purāṇa. If we assume that the redactors of the BrP indeed wanted to produce a »Mahā-Purāṇa«, then Pañcalakṣaṇa-topics, Tīrtha-Māhātmyas, the Kṛṣṇacarita, and sections on *dharma*, ceremonies, ancestral rites, philosophy and Yoga were all believed necessary in a text which wanted to lay claim on the title »Purāṇa«.

[14] The general structure and outline of the BrP as a whole has been noted by Kirfel, Bhāratavarṣa p. 8f., who says that the passages told by Vyāsa (177–246) are closer to the part related by Lomaharṣaṇa (1–25) than are the chapters told by Brahman (27–176); he considers ch. 177–246 as generally older than ch. 27–176. With regard to the relation between structure of interlocution and content, Surabhi H. Trivedi distinguishes »regular chapters« and »appended chapters« (JOIB 18, 1968–1969, p. 86), i.e. chapters in which the hermits do not put forth some query but in which the reply to previous questions is continued. A third class of chapters is called »irregular«, i.e. those which begin a new topic which is not introduced by a request by the partner to the dialogue (e.g. ch. 4 and 6). Whether and how division by chapters, by dialogical set-up and by contents really interrelate or depend on each other, still needs to be examined. The division of chapters varies in different editions of the text and in different versions of a passage in different texts (e.g. Kṛṣṇacarita in ViP and BrP). It is at least independent of whether a request by the listeners is put forth or not. There are the »appended chapters« noted by Trivedi, but there are also chapters which contain more than one request by the listeners, e.g. 7.35–36 and 56; 178.5 and 113; 217.2–3, 12–13 and 18.

[15] cf. W. Kirfel, PPL; and S. Trivedi, JOIB 18, p. 89.

[16] JOIB 18, p. 94.

It is the last column in the conspectus which presents evidence for a diachronic analysis of the text by pointing out parallels. The analysis of identity or variations in parallel texts may reveal a relative chronology of texts.

When looking at the distribution of these parallels, one may be struck by the fact that the passages for which no literal parallels are known so far in the epics and the other »Mahāpurāṇas« are those of the Gautamīmāhātmya (GM) and most of the Māhātmyas concerning holy places in Orissa.[17] one might search for such parallels in regional Purāṇas and Māhātmyas, such as Ekāmrapurāṇa, Sūryapurāṇa, Nīlādrimahodaya, Utkalamāhātmya, etc. Parallels to Harivaṃśa (HV) and Viṣṇupurāṇa (ViP) are found as belonging to the first as well as to the second layer (A and B) of interlocution, parallels to MBh, however, belong to the second and third layer (B and C) of interlocution, which may be explained by the subject matter involved: for the »classical« Purāṇa topics (Purāṇapañcalakṣaṇa, cosmography, final dissolution as well as the Kṛṣṇacarita) HV and ViP served as sources, whereas sections on *dharma* were mainly drawn from MBh (and MkP).

Concerning the Gautamīmāhātmya, which belongs to a fourth layer (D) of interlocution, there is little doubt that it was incorporated into the BrP at a later stage; one piece of evidence is provided by the dialogical setting: there is no reference to any other layer of interlocution at either the beginning or the end of the GM; this may be interpreted as evidence for the assumption that the GM was added rather mechanically to a text which must have been already complete.[18] In deviation from the other sections of the BrP, the GM draws frequently on vedic sources (see below), but, except for some few quotations of Ṛgvedic verses, does not present a literal parallel to any of the sources used; on the contrary, it freely changes the contexts and gives new versions of the stories (or hints to stories) found in its source.

The Brahmapurāṇa in its relation to other texts

It has been known for some time that the BrP has most of its text in common with several other texts.[19] If Surabhi H. Trivedi says that »as to the chapters common to Vāyu, Harivaṃśa and Brahma Purāṇa, a comparison of them proves the indebtedness of the BrP to Harivaṃśa,«[20] one may agree;[21] yet, it should be noted

[17] This made us suspect that passages not directly concerned with holy places of Orissa may also have parallels elsewhere in epics or other Mahā- or Upapurāṇas. It would not be surprising if there could be found literal parallels to (parts of) the story of Śiva and Umā (ch. 34-38), to the descriptions of hells and punishments (ch. 214-216), or to chapters 226-229 on the path of Vaiṣṇavas after death, on the Mātaṅga-episode and the two intertwined episodes illustrating the workings of Viṣṇu's Māyā.

[18] It may be noted, in this context, that the GM shows far fewer variant readings than other sections of the BrP.

[19] cf. Hazra, Purāṇic records, p. 147-149, who provides a concordance, on which Surabhi H. Trivedi: Brahma Purāṇa, a formal study. In: JOIB 18, 1968-1969, bases hers (p. 79-81). Our concordances (cf. Appendices to the text volume, p. 801 ff.) attempt to be more detailed.

[20] JOIB 18, p. 82.

[21] cf. L. Rocher: »In all these cases the Brahma° is reputed to be the borrower.« (The Purāṇas, Wiesbaden 1986, p. 155.

that scholars who have held this opinion have provided neither the evidence established by such comparisons,[22] nor the arguments which would prove their conclusion. Moreover, there is another school of thought (most notably represented by W. Kirfel and his followers, and shared by W. Ruben) claiming that in those passages common to BrP and HV and BrP and ViP, the BrP has preserved the older text.[23]

Thus, the question of the »older version« and the mutual indebtedness of the texts concerned has to be taken up again; older arguments will have to be examined on the basis of the new text material now available (e.g. the critical editions of the epics) as well as of methodological reflections which may provide new approaches and arguments not only for the question of the »oldest version« but also for the more general controversy about »how should we study Purāṇas?«

The fundamental methodological distinction to be kept in mind concerns the level of textual analysis, on which statements and conclusions like the above-mentioned ones are based. Are we, e.g., talking about »the« BrP as a whole, and consequently about what happened at the time of its composition (layer A-C) or final redaction (with inclusion of layer D); or are we talking about what happened to a particular passage now contained in the BrP, but probably conceived independently and perhaps changed afterwards according to the new context?

In view of the methodological implications it may be worth while briefly to review some of the earlier research into the relationship of the BrP to other texts. S. H. Trivedi's conclusion has already been quoted. Her work relies mainly on the approach of R. C. Hazra who says about the relationship of BrP to other texts: »Though the present apocryphal Brahma-p. is a voluminous work, there is little which it can claim as its own. It is a late conglomeration of chapters mainly borrowed from other sources such as the Viṣṇu-P., Mārkaṇḍeya-P., Vāyu-P., Mahābhārata and Harivaṃśa.«[24]

Concerning the date of the BrP, Hazra clearly distinguishes between dating individual sections and dating the compilation of the text as a whole. »The apocryphal Brahma-p., with its borrowed and non-borrowed chapters, does not seem to have been composed, or rather compiled, earlier than the beginning of the tenth century A.D. Had it been composed earlier, it should have been drawn upon, or at least referred to, by the Nibandha-writers earlier than the middle of the 13th century A.D. It is not that the early Nibandha-writers did not believe in the authoritativeness of the Upapurāṇas. The numerous verses quoted by them from a good number of such works show that they gave almost the same importance to the Upapurāṇas and the Mahāpurāṇas as sources of Dharma. Even after the middle of

[22] Comparison of what, on which level of textual analysis, one may ask; comparison of contents, of outline, of grammar, of style, or interpolations and omissions?

[23] Unfortunately, neither of these schools seems to have taken notice of the other; Ruben could have known Hazra's article on the BrP, but apparently does not know it; Hazra and even more so Trivedi could have known Kirfel but do not refer to his results.

[24] cf. Purāṇic Records, p. 145-157 (quotation on p. 147); a list of »Verses quoted from the Brahma-P. or Brāhma in Nibandhas and commentaries« is printed on p. 321-324.

the 13th century this apocryphal Brahma-P. began to be regarded as an authority only by a comparatively small section of writers consisting mainly of Hemādri, Śūlapāṇi, Vācaspatimiśra and Govindānanda.«[25] According to Hazra, the period in which the compilation of the text might have taken place thus would be 900–1250 A.D.; the same span of time emerges for the date of those chapters which were not obviously borrowed from some other source,[26] excepting the GM which Hazra places »most probably earlier than the tenth century A.D.«[27]

If the non-borrowed chapters provide the point of reference for dating the BrP as a redacted, compiled unit, the chapters containing the Orissa-Māhātmyas deserve special attention. R. Geib, who analysed the chapters which contain the Indradyumna-legend, also studied the parallels in SkP. The SkP version, which he calls a »Neugestaltung« in comparison with the BrP, is dated by him between 1278 and 1310 A.D.[28] The date 1278 refers to the Anantavāsudeva-temple in Bhubaneshwar, which was (according to the SkP version of the Indradyumna-legend) visited by King Indradyumna on his pilgrimage to Puruṣottamakṣetra. According to Geib, this temple was »a branch of the great Viṣṇu-temple at Puri«, which may refer to the older Puruṣottama-temple built by Yayāti I (950–975);[29] it contained stone versions of the three wooden figures in Puruṣottamakṣetra.[30] The name Anantavāsudeva, in this case, is to be interpreted as »Ananta (= Balarāma) and Vāsudeva (= Kṛṣṇa)«. In the BrP, however, this name clearly refers only to Kṛṣṇa »named Endless« (cf. ch. 59.1 and the detailed iconographic description in ch. 176). The prehistory of this image, given in ch. 176, resembles that one of the Nīlamādhava image which had disappeared according to the account given in ch. 45. Like the interpolated dialogue between Viṣṇu and Śrī (ch. 45), ch. 176 is certainly a later addition to the Puruṣottamakṣetra-Māhātmya (for which assumption there is also linguistic evidence),[31] for it is not accounted for in the summary given in ch. 45.77–89. An Anantavāsudeva image is mentioned only between Narasiṃha as described in ch. 58 and Śvetamādhava as described in ch. 59, the first two verses[32] of which mention the Anantavāsudeva image. These verses, however, may be an interpolation of the time when the Anantavāsudeva shrine was established within

[25] Purāṇic Records, p. 151.

[26] Purāṇic Records, p. 155–156.

[27] Purāṇic Records, p. 156.

[28] cf. R. Geib: Indradyumna-Legende, Wiesbaden 1975, p. 134.

[29] Indradyumna-Legende p.107.

[30] cf. Editor's preface to this volume.

[31] The name Indrajit, for instance, appears in the form Indrajita, which shows influence of modern Indian languages.

[32] Strangely enough, v. 2 alludes to the prehistory as given in ch. 176, which integrates the story of the Anantavāsudeva image in the Rāmāyaṇa story. It is difficult to guess why this prehistory should not have been told at its proper place, but was added to the Puruṣottamakṣetra-Māhātmya (probably together with ch. 177) at its end, in one manuscript together with the Gautamīmāhātmya, which is thus inserted in the Puruṣottamakṣetra-Māhātmya. This problem may perhaps be solved after a critical edition of the BrP (with further manuscript evidence) will have been prepared.

the precincts of the Puruṣottama temple. If this shrine could be dated, we would get a terminus post quem for the final redaction of the BrP.

W. Ruben undertook a close comparison of the Kṛṣṇacarita of HV and BrP.[33] The question which he aims to solve is »whether it is possible to reconstruct the archetype of the original supplement to Mbh which certainly was much shorter than our H [i.e. HV] is today, and probably has been better preserved in B [i.e. BrP] than in H. One has to decide whether B is only a recent excerpt of H, without any textual value, or whether our H is an interpolated text of an original, nearly as short as B.«[34]

The »original Kṛṣṇa-story« which Ruben unearths is, in conclusion, described as »nearly as short as it is in B. It was not written in a proper epic style and it was no self-sufficient epic but only a supplement. It was a collection of heroic deeds similar to a chronicle, composed not for aesthetic pleasure but for religious devotion. It was something similar to a guide to the sacred places around Mathurā, in order to instruct the pilgrims in a simple collection of old local tradition.«[35]

With regard to the initial question and the analysis of the length of texts, one has to remember that Ruben was working on the basis of the vulgate of the HV (ed. Bombay, Śāka 1848). In the meantime the critical edition (ed. P. L. Vaidya, Poona 1969) has amply verified Ruben's suspicion that the original text was much shorter than the HV Ruben had at his disposal at the time.

The relation between the Kṛṣṇa episodes of BrP and HV regarding the wording is one of similarity, while that between BrP and ViP is one of near identity. Ruben is not explicit in stating the relationship between BrP and ViP, but he seems to follow Kirfel in considering ViP as secondary, in spite of the fact that he noted a number of readings in ViP which are closer to HV than the corresponding readings of BrP.[36]

Kirfel's argument in that matter also relies almost exclusively on considerations of length. Comparing BrP and ViP he observes that the text of the ViP was expanded by 162 verses which he attributes mostly to »a pious soul«. He notes that the prediction of Kaṃsa's fall is missing in BrP and concludes that »looked at as a whole, the text of the BrP, a short extract of which is presented in the Agnipurāṇa adhy. 12, is thus more original than that of the Viṣṇup., and consequently the form of the legend is here older.«[37]

However, the argument about the length of text would yield different results for the different passages which are parallel in ViP and BrP. In the extant BrP there are five sections which show very close, verbal similarities with passages of the ViP, viz. the cosmological chapters (ch. 18–24), the Kaṇḍu-episode (ch. 178), the Kṛṣṇacarita (ch. 181–212), the section on *dharma* (ch. 222) and the sections on eschatology (ch.

[33] W. Ruben: The Kṛṣṇacarita in the Harivaṃśa and certain Purāṇas. In: JAOS 61, 1941, p. 115–127. And: »On the original text of the Kṛṣṇa-epic«. In: NIA, Extra Series I (A Volume of Eastern and Indian Studies presented to F. W. Thomas), Bombay 1939, p. 188–203.

[34] JAOS 61, p. 115.

[35] JAOS 61, p. 121.

[36] cf. JAOS 61, p. 125 for examples.

[37] Kṛṣṇa's Jugendgeschichte. In: Kleine Schriften p. 52.

230–234). At first glance it is obvious that all these passages belong to the first and the second layer of interlocution in BrP; they do not seem to be linked by any obvious outline or inner coherence.

With regard to the length of the parallel passages, the Kaṇḍu-episode is much longer in BrP than in ViP but seems to have been adjusted to the context of BrP secondarily. To our knowledge ViP and BrP are the only texts which contain this Kaṇḍu-episode.[38]

The passage on eschatology is, in its episodic passages, briefer in BrP than in ViP. In BrP Vyāsa is the narrator; the episode of the sages' visit to Vyāsa as told in ViP has been dropped in BrP.[39] In the didactic passages, on the other hand, BrP has inserted a whole chapter.[40]

The Kṛṣṇacarita is shorter in BrP than in ViP; whereas the differences in the parallel chapter on *dharma* are restricted to variant readings, such as found in all those parallel texts.

With regard to the relationship between BrP and HV Kirfel anticipates in the above-mentioned article the result of the comparisons undertaken for his edition of the PPL-passages, viz. that BrP and HV form a »group« within the corpus of Purāṇic texts, and that they probably derive from a common source, even that »they derive ultimately partly from a single manuscript.«[41]

Kirfel has observed that the passages related by Vyāsa (layer B) are closer to those related by Lomaharṣaṇa (layer A) than are those related by Brahman (layer C).[42] Nevertheless it remains an intriguing problem why the separation of layers of narration or interlocution was introduced (by the redactors or compilators) at all. The hypothesis which offers itself most readily would have to assume that two different redactional activities (by two redactors, at different times, on different occasions, at different places?) used the same source (i.e. the ViP).[43]

To sum up: though neither Hazra, Kirfel nor Ruben attempts to date »the« BrP (they talk about and analyse select passages, i.e. those which the BrP has in common with other texts), the results at which they arrive have implications for the kind of redactional activity, especially for the kind of sources used by the redactors of the BrP as a whole.

A way out of the impasse between either restricting one's attention to isolated passages (as postulated by Kirfel) or looking at individual passages only in the context of whole Purāṇas is possible if both approaches are combined. It can be shown that Kirfel, Hacker, and others have gone wrong in their judgment about the

38 Rm 4,47.10 mentions a Kaṇḍu in a different context; BhP 4,30 seems to presuppose both episodes.

39 One verse (230.82), however, may be regarded as alluding to this episode.

40 Ch. 231, describing Kali-Yuga, possibly from some other source.

41 Kṛṣṇa's Jugendgeschichte. In: Kleine Schriften p. 53.

42 Interestingly enough, there is no parallel to ViP in this layer of interlocution.

43 It may be noted here that the MBh is quoted on layers B and C. Whether the use made of the ViP and of the MBh differs e.g. with regard to the treatment of vocatives, the quality of language, the thoughtfulness of changes, the regularity of metre, etc., will have to be examined.

BrP exactly because they did not take that step of looking at the redactional history of the whole text.

As an example, Hacker's interpretation of BrP ch. 213 may be discussed. This chapter contains a version of the myth of Prahlāda. »In its report of the myth of the man-lion HV has only some insignificant additions to that version which has come down to us in BrP; besides, it has some transpositions. Those passages of BrP and HV can therefore be considered as representing the same recension of that myth. The story about the man-lion, however, is here (i.e. in HV/BrP) just a part of a larger textual unit which concerns several *prādurbhāvāḥ*. Looked at within this larger context, it becomes clear that HV is considerably enlarged and therefore younger.«[44]

If, however, one does not restrict one's attention and analysis to such an isolated unit, if, rather, one looks at the BrP as a whole, one will discover that those verses which made Hacker consider the HV »considerably enlarged and therefore younger« are not missing but are found at a different place in the BrP, viz. as BrP 179.10–66, i.e. at the beginning of the Kṛṣṇacarita. It is worth while having a closer look at the sequence of contents.[45] The question why Kṛṣṇa, who is extolled in the 108 names of Viṣṇu, was born in the house of Vasudeva introduces, in HV as well as in BrP,[46] an account of the life and deeds of Kṛṣṇa. However, HV first narrates the other manifestations of Viṣṇu (briefly, in ch. 31) before telling about Kṛṣṇa extensively (basically for the rest of the HV); this corresponds largely to the frame of the sequence of events on a mythological scale, beginning with the creation of the world and extending to its dissolution. This general frame is the same in BrP, but concerning Viṣṇu's manifestations the sequence is changed: After the introductory question about Kṛṣṇa's birth (including the 108 names of Viṣṇu) taken from HV, a passage on Viṣṇu's manifestations is partly taken from the MkP, then the story of Kṛṣṇa is narrated in the words of the ViP; Viṣṇu's other manifestations as found in the HV are treated at the end of the whole section.

If HV had copied from BrP, then one would have to assume that the redactor had selected two passages, i.e. the introductory question including the 108 names of Viṣṇu and the account of the *prādurbhāvas* other than Kṛṣṇa, in order to form two consecutive chapters which were, in its source, separated by a passage on Viṣṇu's manifestations and the whole Kṛṣṇacarita: a Kṛṣṇacarita which is parallel to that of ViP.

If, on the other hand, BrP copied from HV, one would have to assume that the redactor selected two chapters from HV and separated them by a passage from MkP and the Kṛṣṇacarita from the ViP, using the HV passages as a sort of frame for the whole section, which was connected with the »Māhātmya-section« by the Kaṇḍu-episode from the ViP. A satisfactory explanation for this procedure is not easy to find; the complex relations between anonymous texts obviously require further study.

44 Prahlāda, p. 27–28.

45 For a concordance cf. Appendix 8 to vol. 1.

46 In HV these question are asked by King Janamejaya, in BrP by the hermits; vocatives and imperatives had therefore to be changed in number by the redactors.

By analysing the vocatives in the parallel texts of the Kṛṣṇacarita in ViP and BrP it can be shown[47] that most changes[48] are explicable as necessary or plausible, if the redactor of BrP changed the text of the ViP to suit the new context, while one would have to assume an unusual amount of ingenuity and effort to explain why the redactor of the ViP introduced such a great variety of vocatives in copying his source in cases where a simple change of plural to singular forms would have sufficed.[49]

The identity of results obtained by analysing vocatives in the different passages common to ViP and BrP indicates that it was the ViP on which the BrP has drawn. Otherwise one would have to assume that the Kaṇḍu-episode, the Kṛṣṇacarita, the chapters on *dharma* and eschatology, all of them and each separately nearly identical in wording and dialogue setting to what they are in the ViP, had been independent texts.

Thus it may be accepted as a working hypothesis that BrP is younger than ViP and probably also younger than HV and MkP.[50] The BrP turns out to be a text which clearly came about by some redactional activity; the texts which were first only considered as parallels have to be considered »sources« of the BrP.

One obvious next step in testing this hypothesis would be a comparison of the readings of the BrP with the variants recorded in those of its sources for which critical editions exist, e.g. the MBh.

Ch. 217 in BrP (corresponding to MBh 13,112) may serve as an example:[51]

*544 (= BrP 217.34-36) is an insertion after MBh 13,112.39, found only in the Northern Recension (D3 missing). The same applies to *545 and *546 (BrP v. 42ab and 50-51).

This by itself would provide evidence that the BrP is related to the Northern Recension and not to the Southern Recension of the MBh. Further evidence is provided by variant readings, e.g. MBh 13,112.39 (= BrP 217.33) is read differently in the Southern Recension; BrP follows the variant of the Northern Recension. On

[47] cf. P. Schreiner: Zur Redaktionsgeschichte des Brahmapurāṇa. To be published in the Proceedings of the XXIII. Deutscher Orientalistentag, Würzburg 1985.

[48] In BrP the Kṛṣṇacarita is told by Vyāsa to a number of sages; i.e. vocatives are expected to apply to Brahmins in the plural. In the ViP Parāśara speaks to Maitreya, i.e. vocatives have to apply to a Brahmin in singular form. On the assumption that one text might have copied from the other we can start from the hypothesis that wherever a vocative is found in the original text, some change has necessarily to take place, either by changing the number of the vocative or by substituting the inappropriate vocative.

[49] The result of this examination of vocatives in the Kṛṣṇacarita is confirmed by the chapter on *dharma* which in ViP is told by Aurva to King Sagara. Consequently vocatives in the singular, addressed to a king had to be changed to vocatives in the plural, addressed to Brahmins. Among 19 instances in 116 lines of text in the ViP, only 4 out of 13 different vocatives occur more than once, while BrP has *dvijāḥ* six times, *dvijottamāḥ* four times, *viprāḥ* four times - each substituting for different vocatives in the ViP.

[50] For this section, the parallels between BrP and HV as well as BrP and MkP will to have to be studied more closely.

[51] For longer passages found only in the Northern Recension of the MBh, e.g. MBh 12 App. I,28 (= BrP ch.40) and MBh 13 App. I,16 (= BrP ch.226), cf. the conspectus.

the other hand, after MBh 13,112.32 the Southern Recension has an insertion (*541) which is missing in BrP. Thus, judging from insertions, omissions and variants one may conclude that BrP followed the Northern Recension and not the Southern Recension. This implies a rough regional localization for the redaction of the BrP, which can probably be narrowed down even more. From a number of asterisk passages in the MBh (*558, *561, *562, *565) which the BrP shares with V1 (Maithili ms.) and B (Bengali mss.) one may conclude that it was especially the Bengali version of the MBh which was used as a source by the redactors of the BrP. This regional localization would confirm the suggestion that the redaction of the BrP probably centres around the Māhātmyas of Orissa. Unfortunately, however, the evidence is not always uniform. There is a considerable amount of evidence which does not fit into this model. BrP has additions, omissions, and variants which are not found in any attested variant of the MBh.

One of the main tasks for which the tools provided by the Tübingen Purāṇa Project could be used as a basis is the evaluation of detailed comparisons of text parallels.[52] Detailed special studies will, of course, be needed to solve all the problems raised by the kind of variants found.

A working hypothesis emerging from our preliminary comparison of various parallel texts suggests that the BrP was compiled in the north-east of India, probably Orissa, by drawing on older sources; its redaction seems to have aimed at fulfilling the standards currently set for a »Purāṇa« as a literary genre. Therefore, it is not justified to quote the BrP as a testimony for critically reconstructing an »older« version of those passages which the BrP has in common with MBh, HV or ViP:[53] there never was a »HV-BrP-Kern« (core). Relative chronology leads to the assumption that the BrP is younger than MBh, HV and ViP and secondary to all of them. This implies that the HV must be considered our only and oldest testimony for the transition from Epic to Purāṇa.

The Gautamīmāhātmya

On the fourth layer (D) of interlocution (later additions), the GM[54] forms an independent text with special characteristics that distinguish it from the rest of BrP, the most striking one being perhaps that it draws frequently on vedic sources, which is by no means the case with the rest of the BrP.[55] Thus, literal quotations of whole verses from the RV are found in BrP 140.23 and 174.14–17; in many other cases Ṛgvedic verses are changed and adapted to the purpose of the story, such as in BrP

[52] The computerization of a text of course helps in comparing versions, especially if automatic collation can be used.

[53] As assumed by W. Kirfel and those who followed him.

[54] A short survey of its contents is given by Surabhi Trivedi in her article »Brahma-Purāṇa, a formal study« (JOIB 18, 1968, p. 74–100), p. 94–98.

[55] The only quotation from a vedic source apart from the GM, given by P. V. Kane (Vedic Mantra and legends in the Purāṇas, in: Dr. C. Kunhan Raja Presentation Volume, 1946, p. 5–8), BrP 233.62, is already found in the MBh passage which was used as a source.

98, 119–120, 129, 151, 152, 154, 161, and 171. Another vedic source was the Aitareya-Brāhmaṇa, stories from which appear in BrP 102, 104, 105, 139, and 155.[56] In some cases names occurring in the RV are made the basis of a newly invented story, such as in BrP 125, 127, 162, etc.

Beside vedic sources, the GM obviously also used epic and purāṇic sources, which are far more difficult to identify. For instance, the story of the pigeon couple and the hunter (BrP 79) is a new version of the story told in MBh 12,141–145; the story told in BrP 107 may go back to MBh 9,51; that of Kadrū and Vinatā (BrP 159) to MBh 1,18–22, etc.

An adaptation of the Rāmāyaṇa story is found in BrP 123;[57] other stories, most probably taken from later stages of the tradition of the Rāmāyaṇa are told in ch. 154 (Sītā's banishment), ch. 84 (cf. Rm 4,65.12–19), ch. 97 (cf. Rm 7,9 and 7,15), ch. 108 (cf. Rm 7,78–81); ch. 143 (cf. Rm 7,16); perhaps also ch. 96 (cf. Rm 1,24.18 ff.), or the story of Yayāti and Pūru (Rm SR 7,58–59, transferred to App. I No.8 in the ed. Baroda), though originally belonging to the MBh (1,76–80). Whether the famous story of Indra and Ahalyā (BrP ch. 87) goes back to the Rm, whether that of Dadhīci's bones goes back to one of the versions in the MBh (9,60; 3,98–99; 12,329.13–41), or whether they are taken from a Purāṇic source[58] (or even local oral tradition?) cannot be decided, since nearly all stories adapted from other sources have undergone a considerable change and seem to be furnished with quite genuine traits of narration.

Other characteristics of the GM are the use of Triṣṭubh/Jagatī metre in a rather ancient form (occurrence of »Triṣṭubh A«, of hypermetrical pādas, etc.);[59] lack of more elaborate metres (like Vasantatilakā, Śārdūlavikrīḍita etc.);[60] a tendency to use enjambment,[61] e.g. in ch. 74 v. 1, 24–25, 38, 46–47 (with wrongly inserted inquit-formula!), 49–60; in ch. 104 v. 15, 39–40, 65, 68, 76, etc., which we did not notice in the other sections of the BrP, references to stories told before or to be told later within the GM; the consistent use of the first person for the narrator Brahman,[62] even when a story about him is adapted from an old source, etc.[63]

[56] For an analysis of the use the GM made of vedic sources, cf. R. Söhnen, Das Gautamīmāhātmya und seine vedischen Quellen, in: Festschrift für Ernst Risch, Berlin 1986, p. 176–195.

[57] For a comparison of this version with the original Vālmīki Rāmāyaṇa, cf. J. L. Brockington, Righteous Rāma, Delhi 1985, p. 239.

[58] e.g. Viṣṇudharmottarapurāṇa etc.; the story of Rāma worshipping Śiva-Liṅgas (ch.157) is probably taken from a Śivaite Purāṇa (cf. Brockington, op. cit. p. 238ff.).

[59] e.g. in ch. 105, 107, 110, 112, 125, 128, 129, 140, 150, and 157. For the definition of »Triṣṭubh A« and hypermetrical pādas, cf. H. Oldenberg, Zur Geschichte der Triṣṭubh, repr. in: Kleine Schriften ed. by K. L. Janert, Wiesbaden 1967, vol. II, p.1216 ff.

[60] Exceptions are: Puṣpitāgra in 173.36, and a somewhat corrupt Drutavilambitā in 175.80.

[61] With enjambment we mean syntactical connection of pāda 2 and 3, or pāda 4 and pāda 1 of the subsequent śloka, if a new sentence starts in or after pāda 3 or pāda 1, e.g.

viṣṇur daityāṃś ca danujān gohartṝṃś caiva rākṣasān |
hantuṃ prayatnam akarot; *jagṛhe ca mahad dhanuḥ* |131.17|
śārṅgaṃ, *yal lokavikhyātaṃ daityanāśanam eva ca* |

[62] Exception: 139.25.

[63] There seem to be also quite a number of (pseudo-?) vedic words, e.g. root-nouns like *tvac-*

Introduction to the index

The index of names and motifs should help to make accessible the contents of the Brahmapurāṇa as presented in the Summaries. It is thus meant to supplement the Sanskrit indices and text published as volume 1 of the Purāṇa Research Publications (PRP). We have tried to make it as self-explanatory as possible, adding explanations and identifying names as far as feasible and necessary. A short list of major guidelines is found at its end.

Categories of entries

This index comprises all material which was thought to be of possible interest to a reader of the summaries; it is thus a compound index of heterogeneous entries (which might have been presented in separate indices):

1. Names occurring in the Sanskrit text (which were not specially marked, e.g. by capital letters, in the Sanskrit indices and text), inclusive of geographical names, names of peoples or of castes etc.;
2. catchwords denoting concrete things and their interrelations, as well as narrative motifs, if they are thematic in the passage concerned;
3. terms of linguistic or literary analysis, names of metres employed in the Sanskrit text etc.;
4. names of scholars quoted in the footnotes;
5. titles of other important (Sanskrit) texts referred to in the summaries.

The entries may either consist of one word, as in the case of names, which were directly excerpted from the text, or of a group of words (»multi-word« entries) denoting an interrelation between two or more catchwords, each of which can be looked up in the index (see below); these entries were abstracted from the text.

Names; one-word entries

Since proper names are not specially marked in the Sanskrit text and its indices, the summary and its index are intended to include all names occurring in the text of the Brahmapurāṇa.

Names of individuals (gods, demons, human beings, etc.) may occur in the index without additional information, as far as they are unambiguous. Names which are ambiguous are provided with additional information, usually in brackets (e.g. »Hari [Indra]«, »Campā [city]«, etc.), but without brackets if the entry is to be found also under a different catchword (e.g. »Śunaḥśepa, place of pilgrimage«; cf. below on turn-around entries).

As for the claim to completeness in indexing proper names, a problem arose from the large number of different names and epithets (based on attributes, patronymics, etc.) of an individual. If we had listed all these names or epithets as they occurred in

(*tvak* in the Sanskrit indices), *rāj-* (*rāṭ*), *śuc-* (*śuk*), but aspects of grammar and vocabulary have to be studied more thoroughly, before conclusions can be drawn.

the text, the user of the index would have to search for all occurrences of an individual under a large variety of entries (in the case of Kṛṣṇa, for instance, numbering several hundred). We therefore decided to subsume the occurrences of different names and epithets of an individual under his/her major name(s). Thus, the reader may find all places referring to Kṛṣṇa under the entry »Kṛṣṇa«, but not a reference to each and every occurrence of »Hari«, »Keśava«, »Madhusūdana«, »Dāmodara«, or to whatever other epithets and names may be used, in the Sanskrit text, in referring to Kṛṣṇa. We did, however, attempt to let the summary (and consequently the index) reflect, to some degree, the variety and distribution of names and epithets; and there will be, we hope, no name of Kṛṣṇa actually occurring somewhere in the Brahmapurāṇa, which is not found at least once in the index. For a complete reference to all occurrences of such names or epithets the user must, however, consult the indices to the Sanskrit text in Vol. I.

All names are given in their stem form, e.g. »Hanumat«, »Brahman« (rather than »Brahmā«), »Jyotis«, »Nandin«, »Uṣas« beside »Uṣā«, etc. Plurals are formed by adding »-(e)s«, i.e. according to English grammar. Variants in spelling were retained and indexed because they may be helpful for further research. Thus we included also variants of names which are grammatically incorrect and change the meaning (e.g. »Abhiṣṭuta« beside »Abhiṣṭut«, »Indrajita« beside »Indrajit« etc.).

In cases of names and concepts a word is italicized if the word itself is intended, e.g. »etymology of *Nārāyaṇa*«; in cases of proper names the capitalization is retained.

The summary of contents and its index were planned and prepared as a supplement to the reprint of the text and the accompanying indices of wordforms in the Sanskrit original. Anyone interested in Sanskrit terminology can thus check the occurrence of any word of interest (*nārāyaṇa*, *bhakti, aśvamedha* etc.) in the Sanskrit indices. Against this background it seemed redundant to include Sanskrit terminology in the index to the summary; and consequently we made an attempt to translate wherever this seemed feasible. Thus, »devotion« was chosen for *bhakti*, »quality« for *guṇa*, »profit« and »pleasure« for *artha* and *kāma*, »ancestral rite« for *śrāddha*, »rice-ball« for *piṇḍa*, etc. Exceptions are e.g. *dharma, puruṣa, prakṛti, sattra-*. A few Sanskrit terms are treated as loan words in English, e.g. the names of the four castes, yoga, mantra. The distinction between names and concepts is expressed by capitals and italics, e.g. Brahman (m.) and *brahman* (n.); Dharma (personified as a god) and *dharma* (concept), Prakṛtis (a class of gods) and *prakṛti* (primordial matter).

Multi-word entries (motifs and contexts)

Besides personal names, the index presents other important catchwords from the text of the summary, such as names of concrete things as well as narrative motifs, if they are thematic within the passage concerned. The index does not take account of a more or less incidental occurrence of certain words. Thus, the »birth of Kṛṣṇa« is not indexed, if it is only mentioned but not dealt with. On the other hand, different expressions of (nearly) the same thing or matter are subsumed under one entry; the terminology used in the index is more restricted and standardized than the terminology used in the summary (cf. also below). E.g., »goals of life« and »aims of life« are subsumed under »goals of life« in the index, »shower of flowers« and »rain of flowers« under »rain of flowers«. The reader of the index is requested to look up synonyms, if he does not find the entry expected by him.

Cross-references were created in cases where it could not be decided which expression was more adequate, or when two expressions seemed not to be congruent in all places where they were used (for instance »actions« and »practices«; »retribution«, »effects«, and »reward(s)«), or when we did not want to restrict the terminology represented in the index too rigorously.

Included in the index are also terms of linguistic or literary analysis, such as »etymology of ...«, »explanation of ...«, »simile«, »refrain«, »summary«, »backward reference«, »request by listener(s)«, »quotation from ...«, »conclusion«, »phalastuti«, »first-person narrator«, »hymn«, »maxim«, names of metres, etc. The selection of such terms was of course determined by what we considered important or worth taking account of. The term »announcement« may need some explanation: it refers to passages where, by some kind of stereotyped expression, the narrator announces a new topic (»I shall now tell you about ...«); »abbreviating formula« refers to those passages where a description or episode is characterized as »abbreviation« by saying (e.g.) »I would not be able to complete this description in a hundred years.«

The index should not be expected to give the context of each catchword and the reader is referred to the summary for contexts. But in the case of frequent terms used in different aspects we thought it useful to give additional information, such as »earth as cow«, »earth as goddess«, »son obtained by asceticism«, »adoption of son«, »Rāma as dutiful son«, etc.

The reader should be aware of the structure, variety and repetition of multi-word entries in the index. These consist of two or more catchwords which are all intended to appear in the index at different places in the alphabet. Their multiplication is done automatically by the computer, which cannot change the syntax but can duplicate (or triplicate) an entry and transpose its members at specially marked caesuras. Thus »Indra and Namuci« appears again as »Namuci, Indra and«. The same applies to entries consisting of three and four catchwords connected by particles or prepositions or participle constructions. For instance, »sages existing in body of Vāsudeva« will be also found as »Vāsudeva, sages existing in body of« and »body of Vāsudeva, sages existing in«.

In sorting the entries the order is strictly alphabetical; if the first word of an entry is identical with that of the preceding entry it is replaced by a hyphen.[64]

The mechanics of the so-called »turn-around entries« provide a convenient tool for creating a net-work of relations and cross-references between motifs and names; this by itself helps to minimize the danger that some motif or name is missed by the user of the index altogether, as long as he follows the guidelines mentioned below.

[64] In two cases not only the first word, but the first sequence of words forming an entity, is replaced by a hyphen: »place of pilgrimage« and »prescription(s) concerning«, since the endless repetition of »of pilgrimage« and »concerning« would have looked quite awkward.

Some aspects which might impede the completeness of the index should, however, be mentioned; they concern perspective, the focus of attention, and restrictions of terminology.

Perspective and focus of attention concern the summary itself as much as the index. To find »lotus-flower« in the index does not imply that references to all occurrences of lotuses (theoretically coterminous with the occurrences of the Sanskrit words for »lotus«) are listed. For such completeness the Sanskrit indices are the more appropriate tools. To find »lotus-flowers« does, moreover, not even necessarily imply that all occurrences of the English word »lotus« in the summary are thereby indexed, for the index-words are not extracted mechanically or automatically from the text of the summary, but were specifically marked or, in case of multi-word entries, specifically formulated. Thus, the index entries represent a selection from the materials, selected on the basis of what we considered significant in a particular context. For instance, in the context of »worship of Śiva with lotuses« the mention of lotuses was considered significant; in the context of a description of a hermitage the presence of lotuses may not have been considered relevant (and may have been subsumed under »description of hermitage«). The fact that someone is killed by a blow of fist which split him in two halves was deemed worth mentioning - but we did not list all instances of killing nor all methods of killing.

As for the focus of attention, it may, for instance, be on the narrative, episodic, content; if the episode at hand happens to centre around a curse, »curse of x by y« appears to be an adequate entry. Or the focus may be on literary techniques; then an analogous curse may be seen as containing a forward reference to events told later. Standardizing and regulating all the decisions which were to be taken at the time of formulating any entry has not been attempted.

Finally, the problem of choice of terminology should be mentioned. A certain streamlining of the terminology seemed necessary on the basis of actually occurring variation in the completed and sorted index. »Rebirth« and »reincarnation« needed to be lumped together no less than »battle«, »fight« and »war«. Two techniques were used: Either we decided upon one term and subsumed the other under it - for the sake of completeness we occasionally added a one-way cross-reference (e.g. »*idol* see *image, statue*«). Or, we retained both terms and added a two-way cross-reference (e.g. »*slaying* see also *killing*«, »*killing* see also *slaying*«).

References

As was pointed out above (p. XIX), the references in the index are not to page numbers, but to the numbering of verses or groups of verses as printed in the margin of the summary. The numbers of chapters and verses are those of the Sanskrit text as printed in Vol. I of this series.

In the summary, the verses are grouped together into units and sub-units of contents, according to their common subject. References to these grouped units, when occurring immediately following each other, have not been automatically grouped once more for the index (as is usually done with page numbers), but listed separately. The user of the index will therefore find references like

- 221.77.78.82cd-84.85-86.139cd-140ab.140cd-141ab.141cd-143ab etc., according to the units grouped in the summary, instead of
- 221.77-78.82cd-86.139cd-143ab.[65]

Names that do not occur in the Brahmapurāṇa, but are mentioned in footnotes (inclusive of names of scholars referred to) are also indexed; since all references are not to pages but to chapter and verses of the ASS edition of the Brahmapurāṇa, references are, even in such cases, to the text passage to which the footnote belongs.

Guidelines for using the index

- Read all entries under a catchword. Related motifs and contexts may differ only by additions which, however, lead to different placing according to the alphabetical order.
- Check both singular and plural forms for separate entry.
- Watch out for cross-references at the end of a catchword.
- In a detailed entry check the other components, e.g. after finding »Kṛṣṇa and Aditi« check »Aditi ...«.
- Read, in the summary, the passages referred to in the index with an eye to possible other catchwords and motifs; reading the context may convey ideas about parallel or synonymous or alternative formulations of the same or a related motif which may also be found in the index. And read those passages in their wider context (a whole episode, a chapter, a line of arguments, a literary genre, etc.).

Acknowledgements

As we did in vol. I of the PRP, we wish to thank all those who have contributed to whatever could be achieved during and after the time we worked in the Tübingen Purāṇa Project. Professor H. v. Stietencron continued to accompany our work, as director of the Project and as colleague, with interest and support. The assistance extended to us by John and Mary Brockington, who have already been named at the beginning of this introduction, cannot be over-estimated.

Our special thanks are, once again, due to the Department of Literary and Documentary Computing, its chairman Dr. W. Ott and his team, especially H. Fuchs, who helped us with untiring patience whenever we met with small or big problems during the final setting of the text and its index.

We wish to acknowledge the support of the Deutsche Forschungsgemeinschaft, which has been funding the Purāṇa Project and enabled the publication also of the second volume of the PRP series.

Finally we wish to thank Dr. H. Petzolt of Otto Harrassowitz Verlag, who has been most understanding and lenient with our efforts to prepare the files for photocomposition ourselves, in order to keep the price of the book as low as possible.

[65] The references in the index are grouped according to chapters (the chapter number is only printed once); the figures after a dot are verse numbers.

For reasons beyond our control the publication of this volume has been unduly delayed; it should have been published by 1986. Both authors, however, left the Purāṇa Project during this year, and it was left to R. Söhnen, who at least remained in Tübingen, to carry out the final redaction and to see the volume through the press. It is with a sense of relief that we finally present the results of our efforts to the public.

Appendices 15-17

Supplement to Volume 1

Appendix 15*

Concordance of BrP ch. 27 and MkP (ed. Bibl. Ind.) ch. 57 (description of Bhāratavarṣa)

BrP	MkP
27.1-9	-
.10-13ab	**57**.1cd-4
.13cd	-
.14-58	.5-40
-	.50-51ab
.59-70	.52cd-64ab
.71-80	-

Concordance of BrP ch. 180 and MkP ch. 4 (Viṣṇu's manifestations)

BrP	MkP
180.1-5	**4** .36-40ab
.6-13	(= ViP 1,2.1-8)
.14-29ab	.40cd-55
.29cd-38	-
.39-41	.56-58
.42ab	-
.42cd-ef	.59

*For Appendices 1-14 see vol. I of this series.

Appendix 16

Concordance of BrP ch. 220 (Effects of ancestral rites), MkP 30-33 and MBh 13,87-89

Note: The MBh chapters are parallel only in topic and outline, not in terms of literal identity. As for the sequence of topics, however, MBh and BrP are closer together than BrP and MkP.

BrP	MkP	MBh
220.1-5	-	-
.6	-	**13,92**.(20)
.7-9	-	-
.10	**31**.(20)	-
.11-12	-	-
.13	**30**.(4)	-
.14	-	-
.15-22ab	**33**.1-8ab	**13,87**.(10-17)
.22cd-30ab	**32**.1-8	**13,88**.(3-10)
.30-33ab	-	.(11-14)
.33cd-42	**33**.8cd-16ef	**13,89**.(2-14)
.43-68	-	-
.69-82ab	**30**.12cd-25ef	-
.82cd-100ab	**31**.1-18	-
.100cd	-	-
.101	.23	-
.102-104	-	-
.105-110ab	.30-35ab	-
.110cd-120ab	**32**.29-38	-
.120cd-126	**31**.36-63ab	-
.127-212	-	-

Appendix 17

Concordance of BrP 221 with MkP 34-35

BrP	MkP
221.1-30ab	**34**.1-30ab
-	.30cd
.30cd-40ab	.31-40
.40cd-41	.41cd-42
-	.43ab
.42-43	.43cd-45ab
.44ab	.41ab
.44cd-67ab	.45cd-68ab
-	.68cd-69
.67cd-71ab	.71-73
-	.74ab
.71cd-73ab	.74cd-76ab
-	.76cd-77
.73cd-76	.78-81ab
-	.81cd
.77ab	.82ab
.77cd-78	-
.79-81ab	.82cd-84
-	.85-86ab
.81cd	.86cd
.82ab	-
.82cd-83	.87-88ab
-	.88cd

BrP	MkP
221.84	**34**.(89)
-	.90
.85-86ab	.91-92ab
-	.93
.86cd-94ab	.94-101
-	.102-103ab
.94-102cd	.103cd-111
.102ef-104	.112-114ab
.105-108ab	.115-118ab
.108cd	.114ab
.109ab	.118cd
.109cd-117ab	**35**.1-8
-	.9ab
.117cd-127	.9cd-19
-	.20ab
.128-137	.20cd-30ab
.138-139ab	.31cd-32
.139cd-140ab	.30cd-31ab
.140cd-161	.33-54ab
-	.54cd
.162-165ab	.55-57ef
.165cd-170ef	-

Part I

Summaries of Chapters
1-246

Ch. 1: Setting of the recitation of the Purāṇa; creation of the world[1]

1–2 (VePr ins. homage to Gaṇeśa, an incipit, homage to Vāsudeva, the Jaya-verse.[2]) Maṅgalācaraṇam:[3] Homage to Hari as creator, maintainer, destroyer of the world (*trimūrti*-functions), as highest principle (*puruṣa*), object of meditation, bestower of liberation.

3–9 Description of the Naimiṣa-forest: list of trees; living beings; castes and stages of life; fruits.

10–12 Welcoming of guests on the occasion of a *sattra*-rite.

13–15 Arrival of the bard Lomaharṣaṇa.

16–20 The hermits praise[4] Lomaharṣaṇa's knowledge; they ask about the origin of the cosmos and its inhabitants, and also about the future of the world.[5])

21–29 Lomaharṣaṇa begins with a hymn of praise to Viṣṇu and the teacher.

30 Transmission of the Purāṇa from Brahman to Dakṣa etc.

31–32 Announcement of the recitation; phalastuti.

33–56 *Creation of the world*

33–34 *Puruṣa* (= Brahman = Nārāyaṇa) formed the All out of matter.[6]

35 Sequence of evolution:[7] (Primordial Matter) → the Great (*mahān*) → Ego-consciousness (*ahaṃkāra*) → elements (*bhūta*) → various entities.

36–37ab Invitation to listen to a description of the cosmic constituents in detail.

/cd–38ab Bhagavān Svayaṃbhū wanted to create beings; he created waters in which he deposited his semen.

[1] The first 15(17) chapters of the BrP contain those passages which were collated by W. Kirfel as the PPL. Among the Purāṇas which contain parallel passages, the BrP coincides most closely with the HV and belongs to Kirfel's text-group I. For a concordance of BrP and HV see the Appendix.

[2] cf. MBh 1.1.0.

[3] In Śārdūlavikrīḍitā-metre.

[4] In this summary we use present tense for what belongs to the dialogical setting, in order to indicate that in summarizing or paraphrasing the original we are not intending to reproduce the narrative style of the text (which, of course, has »*uvāca*«, i.e. »said«, etc.). However, we also use present tense for what can be considered to belong to the (fictional, narrative) present of the narrator and the listening sages or hermits, especially in case of all maxims, theological statements, mythological descriptions etc., which may be assumed to have been common to the fictional reality of the narration and the world of belief of those who redacted the text, as well as those for whom it was composed. We use past tense for the episodes reported as belonging to the past from the point of view of Lomaharṣaṇa, Vyāsa, Brahman, or whoever may be the narrator of the episode.

[5] v. 20 duplicates 18–19.

[6] Another translation (and interpretation) also seems possible: The *puruṣa* is the primordial matter; from him the Lord (= Brahman = Nārāyaṇa) formed the All (cf. RV 10.90, Puruṣasūkta, and v. 51cd below).

[7] We abbreviate the description of genealogies or evolutions by using → to indicate descent, + to indicate common parenthood (»marriage« is not always explicitly mentioned).

38cd–39ab Etymology of Nārāyaṇa.

39cd–42 This seed turned into a golden egg; from it Brahman Svayaṃbhū was born. He divided the egg into two halves, heaven and earth; and between them he made the atmosphere. On the water he put the earth, and made the directions tenfold. On it (the earth?) (he put) time, mind, speech, desire, wrath, lust.

43–45ab He created the mind-born Prajāpatis: Marīci, Atri, Aṅgiras, Pulastya, Pulaha, Kratu and Vasiṣṭha. They are known as Brahmins in the Purāṇa.

45cd–46ab Of old Brahman created Rudra (sing.) and Sanatkumāra, who was born before the former ones (?).[8]

46cd From those seven (?) originated the living beings and the Rudras (pl.).

47ab Skanda and Sanatkumāra exist by combining their energy (*tejas*).

47cd–48ab Seven heavenly families originated from them.

48cd–50ab He created lightning, thunder, clouds, rainbow, food, rain, three Vedas, Sādhyas and other gods.

50cd–51ab High and low beings originated from the limbs of the Prajāpati Āpava, who emitted the creation of living beings.[9]

51cd–52 When the beings did not multiply he divided himself into male and female; as such he created beings of two kinds (sexes).

53ab He exists[10] filling heaven and earth with his greatness.

53cd–54 Viṣṇu created Virāṭ, Virāṭ created a man (*puruṣa*), known as Manu, who (presides over) (the first) Manu-era; the second is named that of Mānasa.[11]

55 This *puruṣa* (that stemmed from Virāṭ) created beings. The beings of the Nārāyaṇa-creation were also not born from females (*ayonija*).

56 Phalastuti.

Ch. 2: Descendants of Manu Svāyaṃbhuva; creation by Dakṣa

1–4 Having created living beings (v.l. wanting to create ...) Āpava took Śatarūpā as wife. While Āpava existed, filling the heaven with his greatness, Śatarūpā was born according to *dharma*. After ten thousand years of asceticism she obtained that man (*puruṣa*) as her husband, who is also called Manu Svāyaṃbhuva. The present Manu-era of 71 Yugas is called his.

5 From this man, who had originated from Virāṭ, Śatarūpā bore Vīra. Vīra + Kāmyā → Priyavrata and Uttānapāda.

6 Kāmyā was (the daughter) of Kardama; she had 4 sons: Saṃrāṭ, Kukṣi, Virāṭ, Prabhu.

[8] Interpolation? cf. Hacker, Sāmkhyization, in: Kleine Schriften, p. 167–205.

[9] cf. v. 34 above

[10] Shift to present tense as in the text.

[11] In speaking of the cosmic measurements of time we use »cycle« for *kalpa*, »era« for the Manvantaras, »period« for the (mostly four) »ages« (*yuga*); in the latter case we also use »Yuga« as an English word.

7-8 Uttānapāda was adopted by Atri. Uttānapāda + Sūnṛtā → 4 sons. Sūnṛtā, the daughter of Dharma, was born as a result of a horse-sacrifice and (became) the mother of Dhruva.

9 Uttānapāda + Sūnṛtā → Dhruva.

10-13 Dhruva practised asceticism for three hundred divine years, desiring fame. Brahman gave him a position similar to his own in front of the Seven Sages (Great Bear). About him Uśanas, the teacher of gods and demons, sang a verse, praising Dhruva's asceticism.

14-15 Dhruva + Śaṃbhu → Śliṣṭi and Bhavya. Śliṣṭi + Succhāyā → 5 sons: Ripu, Ripuṃjaya (VePr Puraṃjaya), Vīra (VePr Putra), Vṛkala, Vṛkatejas. Ripu + Bṛhatī → Cakṣus (VePr Cākṣuṣa).

16 He procreated from Puṣkariṇī Vairiṇī, daughter of Vīraṇya (VePr Araṇya), Manu Cākṣuṣa.

17-20ab Manu + Naḍvalā (daughter of Vairāja) → 9 sons: Kutsa, Puru, Śatadyumna, Kavi, Tapasvin, Satyavāk, Agniṣṭuba (VePr Agniṣṭut), Atirātra, Sudyumna, and Abhimanyu as the tenth. Puru + Āgneyī → 6 sons: Aṅga, Sumanas, Svāti (VePr Khyāti), Kratu, Aṅgiras, Gaya (VePr Maya).

20cd Aṅga + Sunīthā → Veṇa (VePr Vena).

21-28 *Veṇa-episode; Pṛthu-episode*

21-24 Because of Veṇa's misbehaviour there was a great upheaval. The sages churned his right hand in order to produce offspring. When his hand was churned a great king originated, for whom the sages prophesied great fame and success. Veṇa's son, Pṛthu, protected (the earth) and is known as the first king.

25-28ab From him (or: afterwards) Sūta and Māgadha were born. By him that cow (i.e. the earth) was milked, together with (i.e. with the help of?) gods and sages etc. for the sake of livelihood for the subjects. The earth gave milk into the vessels of various classes of beings (listed), thereby supporting life.

28cd Pṛthu's 2 sons, Antardhi and Pātin, were born at the end of a sacrifice.

29-30ab Antardhāna (*sic*) + Śikhaṇḍinī → Havirdhāna + Dhiṣaṇā (daughter of Agni) → 6 sons: Prācīnabarhis, Śukra, Gaya, Kṛṣṇa, Vraja, Ajina.

30cd-31ab Prācīnabarhis was a greater Prajāpati than Havirdhāna; by him the beings were increased.

31cd Prācīnabarhis (...) the (beings) who walk on the earth.[1]

32 Savarṇā (daughter of Samudra, i.e. the ocean) → Kṛtadāra.

33 Savarṇā bore 10 Prācīnabarhiṣas, known as Pracetasas and well-versed in archery.

34-49 *Pracetasas-episode; origin of Māriṣā*

34-46 They practised asceticism for 10,000 years by staying in the ocean. In the meantime the sky was covered by trees, which caused the obstruction of living beings and prevented the winds from blowing. For 10,000 years the beings could not move. The

[1] Unclear; syntactically incomplete.

Pracetasas emitted wind and fire from their mouths, uprooting the trees and burning them. Soma (the moon) intervened in their favour by offering to the Pracetasas a girl (daughter of the trees), called Māriṣā, who would be the mother of their future offspring. By combining half of their and half of his (the moon's) brilliance (*tejas*), Dakṣa would be born who would continue the line.

47–49 The Pracetasas restrained their wrath, married Māriṣā, and Dakṣa was born. He created all things and creatures from his mind, and afterwards created women. He gave 10 (of his daughters) to Dharma, 13 to Kaśyapa. To Soma he gave those named Nakṣatras.[2] From them, all classes of living beings were born.

50 From then onwards beings originate from sexual intercourse, while previously it happened by intention, looking or touching.

51–53 The sages ask for clarification of a doubt: 1. They had heard that Dakṣa was born from the (right) thumb of Brahman, and Dakṣa's wife from the left thumb, while Lomaharṣaṇa had explained that he was a descendant of the Pracetasas. 2. How could the grandson of the moon become the moon's father-in-law?[3]

54–56 Lomaharṣaṇa answers: All beings are subject to origination and destruction. »Kings«[4] like Dakṣa etc. come into being in every cosmic period (*yuga*). 2. Previously there was no difference according to age (elder or younger), but asceticism alone was the cause of dignity.[5]

57 Phalastuti regarding Dakṣa's creation.

Ch. 3: Creation of beings; descendants of Dakṣa

1 The sages ask for a more detailed description of the origin of gods, demons, Gandharvas, snakes and Rākṣasas.

2 Lomaharṣaṇa relates that Dakṣa had been ordered by Svayaṃbhū to create living beings, and he calls attention to the following account.

3–7ab The Lord (VePr Prajāpati, i.e. Dakṣa) created mental (mind-born) beings: gods, sages, Gandharvas, Asuras, Yakṣas, Rākṣasas. When his mind-born (offspring) did not increase further, he desired to procreate various offspring by lawful intercourse, married Asiknī, a daughter of Vīraṇa, and begot 5000 sons by her.

7cd–9 When the divine sage Nārada saw that they wanted to procreate he spoke to them, provoking their destruction as well as his own curse.[1] Previously the sage Nārada had been born from Parameṣṭhin as son of Dakṣa's daughter, out of fear of Dakṣa's curse.[2]

[2] cf. v. 3.35, below.

[3] Father-in-law, since some of Dakṣa's daughters were married to the moon.

[4] *Nṛpāḥ* in the sense of *prajāpati*?

[5] If there is no distinction of age, then a grandson can give his daughter to an (ageless) grandfather, especially if he is superior by the standard of asceticism.

[1] Anticipatory explanation, cf. v. 14.

[2] v. 7–15 seem to attempt the reconciliation of different traditions: Nārada was the one responsible for the destruction of Dakṣa's sons. For that he was cursed by Dakṣa. Nārada is

10–14 Later the divine sage procreated him in Asiknī, the daughter of Vīraṇa, like a father. By him (Nārada) Dakṣa's sons, known as the Haryaśvas, were all destroyed according to their fate. Dakṣa resolved to destroy Nārada, with the help of the Brahman-Sages. Dakṣa and Parameṣṭhin made an agreement that Nārada should be born as his (Parameṣṭhin's) son from one of Dakṣa's daughters. Therefore Dakṣa gave his daughter to Parameṣṭhin. Nārada was born from her, out of fear of being cursed.

15 The sages inquire how Dakṣa's sons were destroyed by Nārada.

16–18ab Lomaharṣaṇa answers: The Haryaśvas desired to procreate; Nārada, however, spoke to them[3] that as mere children they should not procreate without knowing the extent of the earth in all directions.

18cd–19ab Upon this advice they left in all directions and never returned, like rivers that have entered into the ocean.

19cd–23 After the destruction of the Haryaśvas Dakṣa procreated another 1000 sons from Vīraṇa's daughter, the Śabalāśvas, who were equally eager to procreate but were sent off by Nārada with the same words. They agreed among each other to follow their brothers' track; they left and have not returned to this day.

24 Ever since, a brother searching for his brother is destroyed; this should not be done by wise people.

25–28 When he came to know that his sons had been destroyed, Dakṣa procreated 60 daughters with his wife Vairaṇī (= Asiknī, Vīraṇaś daughter). Kaśyapa, Dharma, Soma and other great sages took them as wives. Dakṣa gave 10 to Dharma, 13 to Kaśyapa, 27 to Soma, 4 to Ariṣṭanemin, 2 to Bahuputra, 2 to Aṅgiras, 2 to Kṛśāśva.

29–30ab Dharma's wives were called: Arundhatī, Vasu, Yāmī, Lambā, Bālā, Marutvatī, Saṃkalpā, Muhūrtā, Sādhyā, Viśvā.

30cd–33 Descendants of Dharma's wives: Viśvā → All-Gods (Viśvedevas). Sādhyā → the Sādhyas. Marutvatī → the Marutvats. Vasu → the Vasus. Bhānu → the Bhānus. Muhūrtā → the Muhūrtas. Lambā → Ghoṣa. Yāmī → Nāgavīthī. Arundhatī → all the realms of the earth. Saṃkalpā → Saṃkalpa, the soul (self) of everything. Nāgavīthī → Vṛṣala.

34–46ab Soma's wives and their descendants:

34–35ab Dakṣa[4] gave as Soma's wives (those daughters, who) are known by the names of stars in astronomy.[5]

35cd–36 Announcement of a list of the 8 Vasus: Āpa (VePr Aya), Dhruva, Soma, Dhava, Anila (wind), Anala (fire), Pratyūṣa, Prabhāsa.

37–38cd Āpa → Vaitaṇḍya, Śrama, Śrānta, Muni.[6] Dhruva → Kāla (time, or death). Soma → Varcas → Varcasvin. Dhava → Draviṇa, Hutahavyavaha.

also known to have been Dakṣa's grandson, born from Kaśyapa to whom Dakṣa had married some of his daughters. The notion that Dakṣa was also Nārada's father is peculiar to BrP and HV (cf. PPL 157.10/1). The rest is common to Kirfel's text-group I.

[3] Connection to verse 8?

[4] *Rājā*, v.l. *rājan*,cf. PPL 161.34.

[5] cf. v. 2.48, above.

[6] The number of sons is not clear, since *putraḥ* is singular; Kirfel (PPL 161.37) seems to take them as 4 sons.

38ef From Manoharā[7] → Śiśira, Prāṇa, Ramaṇa.

39–40 Anila + Śivā → 2 sons: Manojava, Avijñātagati. Agni → Kumāra, born in a thicket of reeds → Śākha, Viśākha, Naigameya.

41ab As descendant of the Kṛttikās (the Pleiades) he is called Kārttikeya.

41cd–42ab Pratyūṣa → 1 son, a seer, named Devala → 2 sons.

42cd–46ab Bṛhaspati's sister, who knew *brahman* and roamed over the earth unattached as one who had realised Yoga, was Prabhāsa's wife; their son was Viśvakarman, who practised thousands of crafts and promoted the gods(?), made ornaments for them all, as well as their vehicles, and by whose craft human beings live.

46cd–49 Kaśyapa + Surabhi → 11 Rudras: Ajaikapād, Ahirbudhnya, Tvaṣṭṛ, Rudra; Hara, Bahurūpa, Tryambaka, Aparājita, Vṛṣākapi, Śaṃbhu, Kapardin, Raivata, Mṛgavyādha, Śarva, Kapālin.[8]

50 In the Purāṇa 100 Rudras are mentioned who fill the world of plants and animals.

51–52 Announcement of the wives of Kaśyapa: Aditi, Diti, Danu, Ariṣṭā, Surasā, Khasā, Surabhi, Vinatā, Tāmrā, Krodhavaśā, Irā, Kadru, Muni.

53–58 Descendants of Kaśyapa's wives (announcement): In a previous Manu-era the 12 best Suras were called Tuṣitas, who for the well-being of all worlds spoke amongst themselves, when the era of Manu Cākṣuṣa came near, that it would be best for them to enter Aditi, in order to be born in the Manu-era. Thus they were born from Kaśyapa and Aditi in the era of Manu Cākṣuṣa. They are known as the 12 Ādityas: Viṣṇu, Śakra (= Indra), Aryaman, Dhātṛ, Tvaṣṭṛ, Pūṣan, Vivasvan, Savitṛ, Mitra, Varuṇa, Aṃśa, Bhaga. (VePr ins.: Known as Tuṣitas in the Cākṣuṣa-era, they are known as Ādityas in the Vaivasvata-era.[9])

59 The offspring of the 27 wives of Soma were brilliant (stars?).

60 The wives of Ariṣṭanemin had 16 descendants. Among the (descendants of) Bahuputra the 4 Vidyuts are well known.

61ab The Ṛg-verses were honoured in the Cākṣuṣa-era by the Brahman-Sage(s).

61cd (The offspring of) Kṛśāśva are well known as Devapraharaṇas.

62–64ab All these and the 33 gods are born again at the end of 1000 periods (*yuga*). They are subject to origination and destruction like the rising and setting of the sun. Thus the divine embodiments occur in each period.

64cd–70ab Kaśyapa + Diti[10] → Hiraṇyakaśipu, Hiraṇyākṣa, and 1 daughter, Siṃhikā + Vipracitti → Saiṃhikeyas. Hiraṇyakaśipu → 4 sons: Hrāda, Anuhrāda, Prahrāda,

[7] Another of the wives of Dhava?

[8] The list seems to contain 14 names; in the HV (see Kirfel PPL 163.49), a further line is given between 47cd and 48 by which Tvaṣṭṛ is to be understood as father of Viśvarūpa and of those bearing the following 10 names, so that the number 11 is correct when applied to Tvaṣṭṛ's progeny only. This is congruent with MBh 12,208.21f., 13,150.12f. (cf. Hopkins, Epic Mythology, p. 173), where the Rudras are sons of Tvaṣṭṛ, but the names listed partly differ. 12,208.21f.: Viśvarūpa, Ajaikapād, Ahirbudhnya, Virūpākṣa, Raivata, Hara, Bahurūpa, Tryambaka, (Sāvitra, Yayanta, Pinākin). 13,150.12f.: Ajaikapād, Ahirbudhnya, Pinākin, Ṛta, Pitṛrūpa, Tryambaka, Maheśvara, Vṛṣākapi, Śaṃbhu, Havana, Īśvara.

[9] Contradicts v. 53(166) where they were called Tuṣitas in a former Manu-era, who decided to be born as Ādityas in the Cākṣuṣa-era, which is the one dealt with in the present chapter; cf. v. 56.

[10] Continues from v. 58.

Saṃhrāda. Hrāda → Hrada → Śiva and Kāla. Prahrāda → Virocana → Bali → 100 sons, among whom Bāṇa was the eldest, then Dhṛtarāṣṭra, Sūrya (sun), Candramas (moon), Indratāpana (v.l. Candratāpana?), Kumbhanābha, Gardabhākṣa, Kukṣi etc.

70cd-71 Bāṇa was the eldest, most powerful and dear to Paśupati; in a previous cycle he had asked Umā's husband (Śiva, Paśupati) for the boon of becoming his attendant (? *pārśvato vihariṣyāmi*).

72-73ab Hiraṇyākṣa → 5 sons: Bharbhara, Śakuni, Bhūtasaṃtāpana, Mahānābha, Kālanābha.

73cd-74ab Announcement of the 100 sons of Danu.

74cd-78ab Dvimūrdhan, Śaṅkukarṇa, Hayaśiras, Ayomukha, Śambara, Kapila, Vāmana, Mārīci, Maghavan, Ilvala, Svasṛma (VePr Sṛmaṇa) Vikṣobhaṇa, Ketu, Ketuvīrya, Śatahrada, Indrajit, Sarvajit, Vajranābha, Ekacakra, Mahābāhu, Tāraka, Vaiśvānara, Puloman, Vidrāvaṇa, Mahāśiras, Svarbhānu, Vṛṣaparvan, Vipracitti.

78cd-80ab All those were born from Kaśyapa and Danu, and Vipracitti etc. are all Dānavas (demons). To list their offspring is impossible because there are too many.

80cd-83 Svarbhānu → Prabhā (f.); Puloman → Śacī (f.); Hayaśiras → Upadīpti (f.) (VePr Upadānavī); Vṛṣaparvan → Śarmiṣṭhā (f.); Vaiśvānara → Pulomā (f.) and Kālikā (VePr Kālakā), who were married to Marīci. From them he had 60,000 sons, (the Paulomas and Kālakeyas), as well as another 1400 who live in golden cities.

84-86ab The Paulomas and Kālakeyas, strong Dānavas and invincible for the gods, were slain by Arjuna due to Brahman's boon. Afterwards other demons were born from Siṃhikā.[11]

86cd-89ab Vipracitti[12] + Siṃhikā → the 13 Saiṃhikeyas: Vaṃśya, Śalya, Nala, Bala, Vātāpi, Namuci, Ilvala, Sṛmaṇa, Añjika, Naraka, Kālanābha, Saramānas, Svarakalpa. (VePr ins. as v. 201cd-202ab: Hrada → Mūṣaka and Huṇḍa. Tāḍakā (f.) → Mārīca, the son of Sunda.)

89cd-90ab These are the main descendants of Danu; their sons and grandsons are counted in hundreds and thousands.

90cd-92ab Saṃhrāda (VePr adds: + Tāmrā)→ Nivātakavacas, 300 millions of sons who live in Maṇivatī, not to be killed by the gods they were felled by Arjuna.[13]

92cd-93ab Tāmrā had 6 daughters: Krauñcī, Śyenī, Bhāsī, Sugrīvī, Śuci and Gṛdhrikā.

93cd-95ab Krauñcī → the Ulūkas (owls) and Pratyulūkakas. Śyenī → the falcons. Bhāsī → the vultures. Gṛdhrī → the Gṛdhras (vultures). Śuci → aquatic birds. Sugrīvī → horses, camels, asses. The line of Tāmrā is well-known.

95cd-96ab Vinatā → Garuḍa and Aruṇa.

96cd-97ab Surasā → 1000 snakes having several heads and moving in the air.

97cd-98 Kadru → 1000 Nāgas who are dominated by Suparṇa (= Garuḍa), among whom the main ones are Śeṣa, Vāsuki, and Takṣaka.

99-101 Lists of Nāgas: Airāvata, Mahāpadma, Kambala, Aśvatara, Elāpatra, Śaṅkha, Karkoṭaka, Dhanaṃjaya, Mahānīla, Mahākarṇa, Dhṛtarāṣṭra, Balāhaka, Kuhara, Puṣpadaṃṣṭra, Durmukha, Sumukha, Śaṅkha, Śaṅkhapāla, Kapila, Vāmana, Nahuṣa, Śaṅkharoman, Maṇi, etc.

[11] VePr om. v. 84cd-85.

[12] cf. above, v. 64ff.

[13] cf. v. 84-85cd, above.

102ab Their sons and grandsons number hundreds and thousands.

102cd–103 14,000 cruel wind-eaters, a Krodhavaśa-crowd,[14] to whom all beings with tusks also belong: land-animals, birds, and water-animals – they are known as progeny of Dharā.

104–105 Surabhi bore cows and buffaloes, Irā climbing plants, creepers, and grass. Khaśā the Yakṣas and the Rākṣasas, Muni the Apsarases, Ariṣṭā the Gandharvas.

106 Conclusion: The offspring of Kaśyapa have been related. Their sons and grandsons number hundreds and thousands.

107ab This creation is known (to have occurred) in the Svārociṣa-era.

107cd–109ab In the Vaivasvata-era when a great sacrificial rite sacred to Varuṇa was arranged, this creation of living beings is said (to relate to) Brahman performing a sacrifice; on that occasion the 7 sages, who first originated from (Brahman's) mind, were made sons by Brahman himself.

109cd–122 Afterwards, Diti, whose sons had been destroyed in the fight between gods and demons, pleased Kaśyapa, who was satisfied and granted her the boon of having a son who would be capable of killing Indra, on the condition that she observe purity for 100 years. She agreed and conceived from Kaśyapa. On seeing the development of her invincible child Indra kept looking for a breach in her vow. In the last year Diti one night went to bed without having washed her feet. Therefore Indra was able to enter her womb. He cut the embryo into 7 parts. When the child cried Indra told him not to cry, and he divided each part again into 7 parts. Thus were born the 49 Maruts (*marut*, i.e. wind; *mā rodīḥ*, i.e. don't cry), who assist Indra.

123–124 On each group of beings Hari bestowed Prajāpatis[15] and, after that, these (i.e. the following) realms, that of Pṛthu etc., on each group of beings (thus arisen).[16]

125 This Hari is *puruṣa*, hero, Kṛṣṇa, Viṣṇu, Prajāpati, the rain-god, the sun, the endless.[17] To him belongs the whole world.

126 Phalastuti: He who knows this creation of beings becomes free from fear of return (i.e. rebirth) and free from fear of the other world.

Ch. 4: Distribution of sovereignties; Pṛthu-episode

1–17 *Distribution of sovereignties*

1 After anointing Pṛthu as king, Brahman began to distribute dominions.

2–9 He anointed Soma (i.e. the moon) as sovereign over the twice-born castes, the plants, the stars and planets, sacrifices and austerities; Varuṇa over the waters, Vaiśravaṇa (= Kubera) over the kings, Viṣṇu over the Ādityas, Agni (= fire) over the Vasus; Dakṣa over the Prajāpatis, Vāsava (= Indra) over the Maruts (winds), Prahrāda

[14] cf. v. 54b, above.

[15] cf. PPL 173.125: Hari (as) Prajāpati bestowed these realms, starting with Pṛthu, step by step, on each class of beings.

[16] v. 123cd = v. 115cd.

[17] i.e. Ananta, Śeṣa?

over the Daityas and Dānavas; Yama Vaivasvata over the forefathers; Śiva over Yakṣas, Rākṣasas, kings, and all ghosts and goblins (*piśāca*); the Himālaya over the mountains, the ocean over the rivers; Citraratha over the Gandharvas, Vāsuki over the Nāgas, Takṣaka over the serpents, Airāvata over the elephants; Uccaiḥśravas over the horses, Garuḍa over the birds; the tiger over the wild animals; the bull over the cows; the fig-tree[1] over the trees.

10 Having thus distributed sovereignties, Brahman established the guardians of the directions:

11–15 Sudhanvan, son of Vairājya, in the east; Śaṅkhapāda, son of Kardama (v.l. Dardama) in the south; Ketumat, son of Rajas, in the west; Hiraṇyaroman, son of Parjanya, in the north. Even today they protect the earth and her seven continents.

16–17 At the consecration ceremony (*rājasūya*) king Pṛthu was anointed by these kings. The era of Manu Cākṣuṣa having passed, he assigned sovereignty over the earth to Manu Vaivasvata.

18 Announcement that the story of Manu Vaivasvata will be told extensively, if desired by the listening hermits. Its importance in a Purāṇa is great.

19–23 The hermits request to be told more about Pṛthu's birth, about how he milked the earth, and about how the earth was milked by forefathers, gods, sages, demons, snakes, Yakṣas, trees, mountains, Piśācas, Gandharvas, twice-born, and Rākṣasas, and about their respective vessels; about what served as calf, milk and milker. Finally they ask why Veṇa's hand was churned by the irate sages.

24–26 Lomaharṣaṇa continues by announcing Pṛthu's story, by mentioning the necessary qualification of the listeners (purity, education, gratefulness, well-wishing) and by characterizing the story to be told as secret and providing heaven, fame, life, and wealth, and as equal to the Vedas.

27 Phalastuti: Reciting this story causes freedom from harm of (deeds) done or undone.

28–122 *Story of Veṇa's misbehaviour and Pṛthu as first king*

28–34 Aṅga, descendant of Atri, was a protector of *dharma*; his son was Veṇa, whose mother was Sunīthā, a daughter of Death. Because of the maternal grandfather's defect the grandson of Death abandoned his *dharma* and weltered in lust and greed. He broke all boundaries of righteousness, transgressed vedic rules, and enjoyed wickedness. His subjects did not recite or sacrifice, the gods did not receive Soma or oblations, because Veṇa had ordered that no sacrifices must take place. He considered himself the only one worthy to be sacrificed to, the only sacrificer and the only sacrifice; sacrifices should be offered to him alone.

35–41 Marīci and other sages advised him to give up unrighteousness, reminding him of his promise to observe his royal duty. In reply, Veṇa boasted that he was the only creator of *dharma*, and that he could destroy heaven and earth.

42–47 Now the sages became angry, overpowered Veṇa and churned his thigh. A small black man was born, who, looking frightened, was told to sit down (*niṣīda*) by Atri. He became the forefather of the Niṣādas and procreated the Dhīvaras,[2] as well as

[1] *Ficus infectoria* according to Monier Williams.

[2] Name of a mixed caste.

the Tuṣāras, Tunduras and other inhabitants of the Vindhya-mountains, who originated from Veṇa's blemish.

48–52 Then the sages churned Veṇa's right hand, like a fire-stick. From Veṇa's hand Pṛthu originated, looking like Agni himself; he seized the bow Ajagava, heavenly arrows and a radiant armour. When he was born, all beings rejoiced, and Veṇa went to heaven, saved from the hell called »Put« by his righteous son.[3]

53–57 Ocean and rivers endowed Pṛthu with jewels, and all waters were present for his anointment. Brahman, together with gods and Āṅgirasas, animals and plants, anointed Veṇa's son; Pṛthu became overlord of all sovereignties. His subjects, who had been displeased with his father, were delighted by him; and because of this delight (*anurāga*) he was called king (*rājan*).

58–59 Rivers stopped, when he wanted to go to the ocean, mountains gave way to him; there was no defeat, the earth gave fruits without being ploughed, food was cooked by thought only, cows fulfilled all desires, there was honey in every hollow tree.

60–67 *Origin of the bards Sūta and Māgadha*

60 At that time, during a Brahman-sacrifice, Sūta (i.e. bard) was born from the Soma-juice (*sūti*), on the *sautya* day.

61–65 At the same sacrifice the wise Māgadha was born. The two were asked by the sages to praise king Pṛthu. They objected that they did not know the king's deeds, but the sages insisted on praising him on account of his future deeds.

66 Since that time the bards (Sūta, Māgadha, Bandin) employ blessings (*āśirvāda*) in praises.

67 Pleased by their praise, the king gave Anūpadeśa (i.e. marshy country?) to Sūta, and Magadha to Māgadha.

68–95 *Pṛthu and the milking of the earth*

68–73 Pleased with Pṛthu the sages told his subjects that he would provide them with their living. They turned to the king who, eager to help them, took his bow and chased the earth. She turned into a cow; during her flight she even reached Brahman's world, but could not escape Pṛthu's flaming arrows.

74–80 Unable to find refuge anywhere, she turned to him and reminded him of the sin of killing a woman and of the difficulty in maintaining his subjects without her.

81–87 Pṛthu answered her with the maxim justifying the death of one for the sake of many; he ordered her to support his subjects and to become his daughter.

88–89 The earth agreed, asking to be provided with a calf, in order to give milk, and to be made flat.

90 Pṛthu levelled the mountains with the end of his bow.

91–93 In the former creation (*visarga*) there was no division of the earth into cities and villages, no farming or cattle-breeding, no ploughing or commerce, no distinction of truth and untruth, no greed or envy. All that originated in the Vaivasvata-era starting from Pṛthu.

[3] For the etymology of *putra* cf. e.g. Nirukta 2,11, and Rm 2,107.12.

94-95 When the earth was made flat, the subjects began to settle, their means of living being fruits and roots, obtained with great labour.

96-122 The milking of the earth.

96 Turning Manu Svāyaṃbhuva into a calf, king Pṛthu milked the earth. He milked all kinds of grain that serve as food for all living beings (subjects) to this day.

97-98 Then all kinds of beings (see list) milked the earth; milk, calf, and milker were different for each of them:

100-109 List of classes of beings, of respective calves, milkers, milk, and material of milking vessels.

Being	Calf	milker	milk	vessel
sages	Soma	Bṛhaspati	asceticism	metres
gods	Śatakratu	Ravi	*ojaskara*[4]	gold
ancestors	Yama	death	nectar	silver
Nāgas	Takṣaka	Airāvata	poison	gourd
Asuras	Virocana	Madhu	Māyā	iron
Yakṣas	Vaiśravaṇa	Rajatanābha	Antardhāna	unannealed v.
Rākṣasas	Sumālin	Rajatanābha	blood	skull
Gandharvas	Citraratha	Suruci	pure smell	lotus
mountains	Himālaya	Meru	jewels, herbs	rock
trees	fig-tree	Sāl-tree	sprouting	Palāśa-wood

110-111 Thus the earth was the supporter of all, growing all kinds of grain, fulfilling all desires.

112 Since the earth was filled with the grease (*medas*) of Madhu and Kaiṭabha (?), she is called »Medinī«.

113 Thereafter the earth became Pṛthu's daughter, therefore she is called »Pṛthvī«.[5]

114 The earth was divided and purified by Pṛthu.

115-121 Pṛthu was the best of kings, he should be revered by all kinds of beings. The Brahmins who know the Vedas and Vedāṅgas should revere him as being born from Brahman. Kings and those who want to become kings should revere him as the first of kings. Kṣatriyas and those who want to win a battle should revere him as the first of warriors. Warriors who begin a fight after praising Pṛthu obtain wealth and fame. Vaiśyas should revere him as supporter. Śūdras who wait upon the three castes should revere him likewise.

122 Conclusion to the list of calves, milkers, milk, milking vessels. Lomaharṣaṇa asks what else the hermits want to know.

[4] Food of the gods? cf. PPL 245,85d: *vartante yena devatāḥ*.

[5] cf. above, v. 87.

Ch. 5: Description of Manu-eras[1]

1-2 The sages ask for an extensive report about the Manu-eras and the creation previous to these, about the number of Manus and the duration of the Manu-eras.

3 Lomaharṣaṇa, unable to tell all that in hundreds of years, announces a brief version.

4 List of previous Manus: Svāyaṃbhuva, Svārociṣa, Uttama, Tāmasa, Raivata, Cākṣuṣa.

5ab The present Manu is Vaivasvata.

5cd-6ab (The future Manus are:) Sāvarṇi, Raibhya (v.l. Bhāvya[2]), Raucya and four Meru-sāvarṇis.[3]

6cd-7ab Conclusion to the list of past, present, and future Manus.

7cd Announcement of the names of sages, sons of Manu, and classes of gods in each Manu-era.

8-11ab *Era of Manu Svāyaṃbhū*

8-9ab (The sages are:) Marīci, Atri, Aṅgiras, Pulaha, Kratu, Pulastya, Vasiṣṭha, the seven sons of Brahman; they are the »Seven Sages« (Great Bear) in the northern direction.[4]

[1] The account of the so-called Manu-eras (*manvantarāṇi*) has been collated by Kirfel as section 3 of the PPL-materials (cf. p. 254–283). The texts are grouped into three text-groups: 1. BrP, HV, ŚiP (Dharma-Saṃhitā), BḍP, VāP; 2. MtP, PdP; 3. KūP, ViP (cf. concordance, PPL p. XX). Regarding the first text-group, Kirfel notes the following results: »In der ersten Hälfte des Textes der Gruppe I (p. 254–58), die über die Manvantara's der Vergangenheit handelt, finden wir den gleichen Text nur in Br., H. und Śidh., da das Bḍ-Vā an der Stelle, wo wir bei seiner systematisch-chronologischen Stoffanordnung (Bḍ I.36 = Vā 62) eben diesen Text erwarten würden, nur eine lange Liste der schemenhaften Göttergestalten, die während dieser Zeiträume existiert haben sollen, aufweist. Trotz des etwas abweichenden Inhalts finden sich in ihr noch ein paar Anklänge an den Text der genannten drei Purāṇa's, die allein schon den Gedanken nahelegen könnten, daß eben dieser Text dem Diaskeuasten bekannt gewesen und von ihm mit Absicht durch den erwähnten listenartigen Abschnitt ersetzt worden sei. Daß dieses aber tatsächlich der Fall gewesen sein muß, lehrt die zweite Hälfte der Textgruppe I (p. 258 ff.); die von den Manvantara's der Zukunft handelt. Hier weist nämlich das Bḍ-Vā fast den ganzen mit jener älteren Purāṇa-Gruppe übereinstimmenden Text auf, wenn dieser auch durch Zusätze erweitert und die Versfolge stellenweise etwas verschoben ist. Wenn der Diaskeuast des Bḍ-Vā aber die zweite Hälfte dieses Textes benutzt und größtenteils übernommen hat, so muß er, da derselbe ein einheitliches Ganzes bildet, auch die erste gekannt, sie jedoch absichtlich bei Seite geschoben haben. ...« (p. XXXV f.) When considering HV-BrP »the same text« and »a unified whole«, Kirfel neglects the fact that BrP does not contain those passages of HV which narrate about the future Manvantaras (except the one about the Sāvarṇa Manvantara, which seems to be somewhat confused and may have been inserted later in the BrP). Thus the present Manvantara constitutes a border-line, after which the future Manu-eras (except for the first one) are only summarized. HV contains texts about past as well as future eras; BrP contains only the text about past eras (including the first future era), while Bḍ-Vā contain only the text about future eras. Bḍ-Vā do not agree with the older Purāṇa-»group«, but only with the HV.

[2] Later on Bhautya, cf. 52 below.

[3] cf. 49–50ab below.

9cd–10 List of 10 sons of Manu Svāyaṃbhū: Āgnīdhra, Agnibāhu, Medhya, Medhātithi, Vasu, Jyotiṣmat, Dyutimat, Havya, Savala, Putrasaṃjñaka.[5]

11ab Conclusion to (the account of) the first Manu-era.

11cd–15 *Era of Manu Svārociṣa*

11cd–12 Aurva, Vasiṣṭhaputra (or: the son of Vasiṣṭha, epithet to Aurva?), Stamba, Kaśyapa, Prāṇa, Bṛhaspati, Datta, Atriccyavana (VePr Atri, Cyavana), are the great sages, proclaimed by (the) Vāyu(-Purāṇa?).[6]

13ab The gods are said to have been called Tuṣitas in the Svārociṣa-era.

13cd–15ab Havighna,[7] Sukṛti, Jyotis, Āpa, Mūrti, Smṛta (?),[8] Pratīta, Nabhasya, Nabha, Ūrja: these are the sons of Manu Svārociṣa, known as valiant kings.

15cd Conclusion to the account of the second Manu-era.

16–19 *Era of Manu Uttama*

16ab Announcement of the account of the third Manu-era.

16cd Vasiṣṭha had seven sons, known as Vāsiṣṭhas.

17ac Hiraṇyagarbha (i.e. Brahman?) had sons called Ūrjas (or: had a daughter called Ūrjā). Conclusion.

17d–19ab The ten sons of Manu Uttama are: Iṣa, Ūrja, Tanūrja, Madhu, Mādhava, Śuci, Śukra, Saha, Nabhasya, Nabha.

19cd The Bhānavas were the gods. Conclusion.

20–24ab *Era of Manu Tāmasa*

20ab Announcement of the account of the fourth Manu-era.

20cd–21 Kāvya, Pṛthu, Agni, Jahnu, Dhātṛ, Kapīvat, Akapīvat are the seven sages. (Their) sons (and) grandsons are famous in the Purāṇa.

22ab The Tathās (? VePr Satyas) are the gods of the era of Manu Tāmasa.

22cd–24 Dyuti, Tapasya, Sutapas, Tapobhūta, Sanātana, Taporati, Akalmāṣa, Tanvin, Dhanvin, Paraṃtapa are known as the ten sons of Tāmasa, proclaimed by (the) Vāyu(-Purāṇa?).

24b Conclusion.

[4] There are no gods mentioned in the BrP for the Manu-era, whereas in HV the list of sages is followed by an additional half verse, stating that the gods were named Yāmas.

[5] In place of the last two names, there is only one name given in VePr, Manuputra.

[6] If Vasiṣṭhaputra is taken as a name, and the VePr version of two names instead of the last one is accepted, the number of nine sages instead of the expected number of seven would be arrived at.

[7] Probably incorrect for Havidhra.

[8] If there is no name in this place, one name in the list of ten sons would be missing; HV gives the name Ayasmaya.

24cd–28 *Era of Manu Raivata*

24cd–25 List of the seven sages: Devabāhur, Yadudhra, the hermit Vedaśiras, Hiraṇyaroman, Parjanya, Ūrdhvabāhu, son of Soma, Satyanetra Ātreya.

26 The Gods were the Ābhūtarajasas (VePr Abhuktarajasas), the Prakṛtis, the Pāriplavas and the Raibhyas.

27–28 Announcement of sons: Dhṛtimat, Avyaya, Yukta, Tattvadarśin, Nirutsuka, Āraṇya, Prakāśa, Nirmoha, Satyavāk, Kṛtin are the sons of Manu Raivata. Conclusion.

29–33ab *Era of Manu Cākṣuṣa*

29ab Announcement of the sixth Manu-era.

29cd–30ab Bhṛgu, Nabha, Vivasvat, Sudhāman, Virajas, Atināman, Sahiṣṇu are the seven sages.

30cd–31 The gods of the Cākṣuṣa-era are the Ābālaprathitas (VePr Aprabhūtas), inhabiting heaven separately, and the Lekhas: these are the five classes of gods.[9]

32–33ab The sons of the sage Aṅgiras are the ten famous Nāḍvaleyas (i.e. sons of Naḍvalā?), beginning with Ruru. Conclusion to the sixth Manu-era.

33cd–38ab *Era of Manu Vaivasvata*

33cd Announcement of the seventh Manu-era.

34–35 Atri, Vasiṣṭha, Kaśyapa, Gautama, Bharadvāja, Viśvāmitra, and the son of Ṛcīka, named Jamadagni, are the seven sages.

36–37ab The Sādhyas, the Rudras, the All-Gods (Viśvedevas), the Vasus, the Maruts, the Ādityas, and the two Aśvins, known as sons of Vivasvat,[10] are the classes of gods in the Vaivasvata era.

37cd–38ab The sons of those great sages are ten, Ikṣvāku etc.[11]

38cd–39 The sons and grandsons of these were facing (? VePr spread to) all directions, in groups of seven, in each Manu-era, in order to establish *dharma* and to protect the world(s).

40–41 When a Manu-era has passed, these four groups of seven, having performed their function (*karman*), go to the Brahman-world. Others fill their position by practising asceticism, those who lived in the past and those who are still living, one after the other. (?)

42–47 *Account of the era of Manu Sāvarṇa*[12]

42 Announcement of the list of the seven sages in the Sāvarṇa-era:

[9] The text seems to be corrupt, since only two classes of gods are named. The PPL-text (Kirfel p. 257, 31–32) gives a list of five classes of gods: The Ādyas, Prabhūtas, Ṛbhus, Pṛthukas, and Lekhas.

[10] See next chapter.

[11] cf. below, 7.1–2.

[12] This passage, which concerns the first future Manu-era, seems to disturb the connection between the Manu-eras of the past (and present) so far described, and the conclusion to this

43 Rāma, Vyāsa Ātreya, Bhāradvāja, Drauṇi (or: son of Droṇa, referring to the next name), Aśvatthāman.[13]

44–45ab Gautama, Ajara, Śaradvat, Gālava, Kauśika, Aurva, Kāśyapa: these are the seven future (sages).

45cd–46 The future sons of Manu Sāvarṇa are Vairin, Adhvarīvat, Śamana, Dhṛtimat, Vasu, Ariṣṭa, Adhṛṣṭa, Vājin, Sumati.[14]

47 Phalastuti: The man who praises them while getting up in the morning, obtains fame and longevity.

48 Conclusion to the account of the past Manu-eras; announcement of an abridged account of the future Manu-eras.

49–52 Account of the future Manu-eras: there are five Manus called Sāvarṇa, one of them is Vaivasvata and four of them, sons of the Prajāpati Parameṣṭhin, have become Merusāvarṇis.[15] They are grandsons of Dakṣa, and sons of Priyā (f.), practising great asceticism on mount Meru. The son of Prajāpati Ruci is known as Manu Raucya. Born of the goddess Bhūti, another son of Ruci is known as Bhautya.[16]

52 These are the seven future Manus in the present cycle (*kalpa*).

53–54ab This whole earth is to be protected by them for a full thousand of Yugas, and on account of asceticism Prajāpati always (brings about) reabsorption in them (?).[17]

54cd–55ab 70 *yuga*-periods including Kṛta, Tretā etc. are called a Manu-era.

55cd–56 These 14 Manus, who are characterised in all Vedas and Purāṇas as letting glory increase, are powerful lords of the living beings (= Prajāpatis); describing them is auspicious.[18]

57ab In (all) Manu-eras there is reabsorption; at the end of reabsorption there is origination.

57cd–58ab Even in hundreds of years, the end of the creation and reabsorption of beings cannot be told (extensively).

58cd–60 Reabsorption occurs in all Manu-eras. The gods having a remainder (of life as gods) continue to exist, together with the seven sages,endowed with asceticism, chastity

description, contained in v. 48cd–52 below. Moreover, it is the only account of a future Manu-era in the BrP, and as such, might be expected to follow the abridged account of the future Manu-eras v. 48cd–52 below, where it is actually to be found in the HV, and, according to it, in the PPL-text. The phalastuti (which concludes this passage, while in the HV it concludes the description of all future Manu-eras) may lead to the conclusion that either the Manvantara-passage in the BrP ended after the report about Manu Sāvarṇa with the phalastuti, or that this passage was inserted later on, but in the wrong place, i.e. before the abridged account of all future Manu-eras, which, besides, had already been given at the beginning of this chapter, v. 4–6 above (cf. note at the beginning of ch.5.).

[13] If these names are accepted as belonging to the list of sages in the Sāvarṇa-era, together with the names listed in the next verse, the number of sages would be far more than seven.

[14] One should expect ten names, as found in the PPL-text (p. 261, v. 50): Cariṣṇu, Ārya, and Dhṛṣṇu, instead of Ariṣṭa and Adhṛṣṭa.

[15] cf. v. 6ab above.

[16] cf. v. 5cd–6ab above.

[17] cf. v. 57 below.

[18] v. 54cd–55ab as well as v. 55cd–56 seem to interrupt the passage concerned with the topic of reabsorption (at the end of a Manu-era), starting in v. 54ab and continued in v. 57ab.

(*brahmacarya*) and sacred knowledge (i.e. the Veda). It is said that after a thousand *yuga*-periods the cycle (*kalpa*) is without remainder (i.e. finished). Then all beings are burnt by the rays of the sun.

61-62 All beings, with Brahman at their head, together with all Ādityas, merge into the best of gods, Hari Nārāyaṇa, who is the creator of all beings, again and again, in every cosmic cycle. He is the unmanifest, eternal god; to him the whole world belongs.

63 Announcement of the creation in the present era of Manu Vaivasvata.

64 Here, in connection with the genealogies, the old legend of Hari is told, who was born in the family of the Vṛṣṇis.

Ch. 6: Story of Vivasvat and Saṃjñā and their progeny[1]

1ab Lomaharṣaṇa continues: Kaśyapa + daughter of Dakṣa → Vivasvat.

1cd-2 Vivasvat (= Mārtaṇḍa, i.e. the sun) + Saṃjñā, daughter of Tvaṣṭṛ known as Sureśvarī (v.l. A Ureṇu, B Sureṇu).

3-4 Saṃjñā did not like her husband's shape with its glowing limbs.

5 Etymological explanation of the name Mārtaṇḍa.[2]

6 Vivasvat heated up the three worlds by his brilliance (*tejas*).

7-8 The children of Vivasvat and Saṃjñā were Manu Vaivasvata and the twins Yama and Yamunā.

9-14 As she did not like her husband's black shape, she made her shadow (*chāyā*) look like herself (*savarṇa*) and ordered her (the shadow = Chāyā) to take her place in her family but not to tell anybody about it; she herself wanted to return to her father. Chāyā (= Savarṇā[3]) gave her solemn promise.

15-17 After that, Saṃjñā departed for her father's abode. Arriving there, she was scolded by Tvaṣṭṛ and ordered to go back to her husband, but she did not obey and changed herself into a mare grazing in the land of the Northern Kurus (Uttarakurus).

18-20ab Vivasvat + (wrong) Saṃjñā (= Chāyā) → Manu Sāvarṇa (v.l. Sāvarṇya) and Śanaiścara (= Saturn).

20cd-23 Saṃjñā (= Chāyā) loved her own children more than those who had already been born, which Yama would not tolerate; he threatened her with his foot and was cursed by her, that his foot would fall off.

24-30 Frightened by this curse, Yama complained to his father about his mother's behaviour and asked his help against the curse; his father, though he could not make the curse unspoken, promised his son to save him by evasion (*parihāra*).

31-34ab Now Vivasvat turned to his wife and asked her the reason for her unjust preference. First she tried to evade, but Vivasvat came to know the truth by Yoga; when he grasped her by her hair, she confessed the truth.

[1] cf. Bṛhaddevatā 6.162-177, where Saṃjñā, however, is named Saraṇyu (cf. Blau, Purāṇische Streifen).

[2] cf. K. Hoffmann: Martāṇḍa and Gayomart (cf. also below ch. 32.34-36.

[3] This name, however, occurs only in the inquit-formula, outside the metric text.

34cd–40 Full of wrath, Vivasvat hurried to his father-in-law, Tvaṣṭṛ, who tried to calm him, telling him the reason for his daughter's fraud, praising Saṃjñā for her Yoga, and promising him to change Vivasvat's shape into a more beautiful one. Vivasvat had to ascend the (potter's) wheel, and his brilliance was cut off, making him appear far more lovable.

41–43 According to Tvaṣṭṛ's advice, by means of Yoga, Vivasvat came to know about his wife who had changed into a mare. In the shape of a horse he copulated with her through her mouth but she vomited his seed through her nose.

44–45ab By this the Aśvins were born: Nāsatya and Dasra, sons of Mārtaṇḍa.[4]

45cd–46ab Now Vivasvat showed his wife his beautiful shape; Saṃjñā was delighted.

46cd–48ab Yama, however, was distressed by this event. As a righteous king (*dharmarāja*) he pleased his subjects; he became lord of the forefathers and world-guardian (or: guardian of one world-quarter or direction).

48cd–50ab Manu Sāvarṇi[5] was a Prajāpati; he is the future Manu of the Sāvarṇi-era. On Mount Meru he practises asceticism to this day. Śanaiścara became a planet (Saturn).

50cd–51ab From his (Vivasvat's) brilliance Tvaṣṭṛ made Viṣṇu's discus (*cakra*) as a means to destroy the Dānavas.

51cd–52ab Yamī[6] became the river Yamunā.

52cd–53 (The elder son of Savarṇā) was known as Manu and as Sāvarṇa; the second one, Śanaiścara (= Saturn) became a planet.[7]

54 Phalastuti for listening to (this account of the) »birth of gods«.

Ch. 7: The solar dynasty

1–2 The nine sons of Manu Vaivasvata are Ikṣvāku, Nābhāga, Dhṛṣṭa, Śaryāti, Nariṣyanta, Prāṃśu, Riṣṭa, Karūṣa, and Pṛṣadhra.

3–19ab *Story of Ilā*

3–5ab When Manu still had no son, he performed a sacrifice in order to get sons. During that sacrifice, at the offering of an oblation as the share of Mitra and Varuṇa, a beautiful girl named Ilā was born in this share (*aṃśe*).

5cd–8 Manu asked her to follow him (as his daughter), but she refused because, being born in their share, she belonged to Mitra and Varuṇa.

9–14ab After that Ilā turned to Mitra and Varuṇa for advice. The two gods were pleased with her observance of *dharma* and granted her to be known as their daughter, as well as to become a son of Manu, named Sudyumna.

[4] For the birth of the Aśvins cf. also H. Lommel: Vedische Skizzen, Kl. Schriften p. 273.

[5] In v. 19d and v. 52d he was called Sāvarṇa; the story about Chāyā-Savarṇā seems to be told in order to explain the name (Manu) Sāvarṇi.

[6] In v. 8 above she was called Yamunā.

[7] Repetition of v. 48cd–50ab, except for the variation Sāvarṇa/Sāvarṇi.

14cd-16 While returning home to her father (Manu), she met Budha, the son of Soma, on her way, and agreed to have sexual intercourse with him; from this Purūravas was born.

17-19ab After that she became Sudyumna, as predicted by Mitra and Varuṇa. Sudyumna's sons were Utkala, Gaya, and Vinatāśva, to whom belonged Utkalā (in the North), the Eastern region, known as Gayā, and the Western region.

19cd-21ab (Before) entering the sun (i.e. dying), Manu divided the earth into ten parts (for his sons), and the middle region was given to Ikṣvāku.[1] Sudyumna, however, did not get a kingdom, as he was a girl also.

21cd-22 According to the Vasiṣṭha's precept , his stay was in Pratiṣṭhāna; this kingdom Sudyumna handed over to Purūravas.[2]

23 The descendant of Manu showed male and female characteristics; he was known as Ilā as well as Sudyumna.[3]

24-43 *Manu's sons and their progeny*

24 Nariṣyanta's sons were the Śakas; Nābhāga's son was Ambarīṣa.

25 Dhṛṣṭa ruled over the land Dhārṣṭika; Karūṣa's sons were the Kārūṣas, who are Kṣatriyas.[4]

26ab The sons of Nābhāga and Dhṛṣṭa, first Kṣatriyas, later on become Vaiśyas.

26cd-27ab Prāṃśu's son was called Prajāpati; Nariṣyanta's son was king Yama »Daṇḍadhara« (»the bearer of the stick«).

27cd-28ab Śaryāti had twins: a son Ānarta and a daughter, Sukanyā, Cyavana's wife.

28cd-29ab Ānarta's son was Raiva, his country was Ānarta and his capital Kuśasthalī.

29cd Raiva's son was Raivata »Kakudmin«.

30-34 As the eldest son (B,C: the eldest of 100 sons, cf. v. 38cd below), he obtained Kuśasthalī.Together with his daughter, he spent many Yugas - equivalent to one minute of the gods -, listening to music in Brahman's world. Returning to his capital, he found Kuśasthalī changed into Dvāravatī, capital of the Yādavas led by Vasudeva. He gave his daughter, Samudrā (= Revatī) to Baladeva and retired to Mount Meru for asceticism, while Rāma (Baladeva) enjoyed his life with Revatī.

35-36 The hermits inquire, why Kakudmin and Revatī did not grow old during many *yuga*-periods, and how Śaryāti's line was continued, in spite of his ascetic life.

37a-d Lomaharṣaṇa answers that in Brahman's world there is no old age, no hunger, thirst nor death, no cycle of seasons.[5]

[1] Another translation seems to be possible: After Manu's death, Ikṣvāku, who had obtained the middle country, again divided the ruling power (and) the earth in ten parts.

[2] After v. 21cd, VePr (A after v. 22) inserts the following passage in parentheses: Sudyumna reigned in Pratiṣṭhāna, as well as Dhṛṣṇuka, Ambarīṣa, and Daṇḍaka, who made the Daṇḍaka-forest which, by being entered only, delivers from sins. Sudyumna went to heaven, after having procreated Aila (= Purūravas).

[3] To be read after v. 21ab?

[4] cf. v. 42cd below.

[5] cf. KathU 1.12.

37ef–41 When Kakudmin went to heaven, Kuśasthalī was taken by Rākṣasas; his 100 brothers were beaten and fled in all directions, so that now the descendants of Śaryāti, Kṣatriyas named Śāryātas, are spread everywhere.

42 The two sons of Nābhāga and Riṣṭa, who were Vaiśyas, became Brahmins;[6] Karūṣa's sons, the Kārūṣas, are Kṣatriyas.[7]

43 Since Pṛṣadhra hurt his teacher's cow, he was cursed to become a Śūdra.

44ab Conclusion to the account of Manu's sons.

44cd–109 *Ikṣvāku's line up to Satyavrata*

44cd–45ab Ikṣvāku, who was born from Manu's sneezing (*kṣuvat*), had 100 sons.

45cd–46ab The eldest of them was Vikukṣi, who became king of Ayodhyā.

46cd–48ab He had 500 sons, led by Śakuni, who guarded the Northern region; and 58 (?) sons, led by Vaśāti, who guarded the south.

48cd–51ab Vikukṣi, ordered by Ikṣvāku to bring hare-meat for an ancestral rite (*aṣṭakā*), did not act according to his duty but ate the meat of the hare himself; therefore he was called Śaśāda (»Hare-Eater«). Though abandoned by Ikṣvāku, he became king after his father's death, according to the preception of Vasiṣṭha.

51cd–53 Śaśāda → Kakutstha → Anenas → Pṛthu → Vistarāśva (v.l. Virāśva) → Ārdra → Yuvanāśva → Śrāvasta who founded Śrāvasti.

54–55 Śrāvasta → Bṛhadaśva → Kuvalāśva, who was known as Dhundhumāra (= »Killer of Dhundhu«).

56 The hermits ask about Dhundhu's death, and how Kuvalāśva got his name.

57–86 *Story of Kuvalāśva*

57–58ab Kuvalāśva had 100 brave and righteous sons.

58cd–71ab Having handed over the kingdom to his son, Kuvalāśva's father (= Bṛhadaśva) wanted to enter the forest, but was stopped by the sage Uttaṅka, who reminded the king of his duty to protect his subjects. He asked for help against the demon Dhundhu, who lived in the desert Uddālaka, hidden under the sand, and caused earthquakes for seven days by his movements, thus making it difficult for the sage to live in his hermitage and practise asceticism. If the king killed this Rākṣasa, he would be made famous by the sage (v.l. his brilliance would be increased by the sage), in accordance with a boon granted to him by Viṣṇu.

71cd–73 Bṛhadaśva refused to go himself, but gave his son to Uttaṅka.

74–77 Together with his 100 sons, Kuvalāśva set out for his task. With his brilliance (*tejas*) Viṣṇu entered Kuvalāśva; a heavenly voice declared him to be Dhundhumāra (»killer of Dhundhu«), and auspicious signs, such as heavenly garlands, fragrances and music, appeared noted.

78–81 His sons dug up the sandy ocean where the demon was hiding, and attacked him, but they were burnt by his flames, except three.

[6] cf. v. 26ab above.
[7] cf. v. 25cd above.

82-84 After that, Kuvalāśva attacked the monster, extinguished his fire and killed him.
85-86 As reward, Uttaṅka granted him inexhaustible wealth, invincibility, pleasure in *dharma*, an endless stay in heaven, and a place in heaven also for his 97 dead sons.
87-88 Kuvalāśva's remaining three sons were Dṛḍhāśva, Candrāśva and Haryaśva, whose son was Nikumbha.
89 Nikumbha → Saṃhatāśva → Akṛśāśva and Kṛśāśva.
90 His[8] daughter was Haimavatī, whose son was Prasenajit.
91-92 Prasenajit + Gaurī (subsequently the river Bāhudā) → Yuvanāśva → Māndhātṛ.
93-95ab Māndhātṛ + Caitrarathī (= Bindumatī, daughter of Śaśabindu) → two sons, Purukutsa and Mucukunda.
95cd-97 Purukutsa → Trasadasyu + Narmadā → Saṃbhūta → Tridhanvan → Trayyāruṇa → Satyavrata.

98-109 *Story of Satyavrata (Part 1)*[9]

98-99 Satyavrata's evil actions: he disturbed a marriage-ceremony by carrying off the wife of another man, and abducted the daughter of a citizen.
100-102ab His father (= Trayyāruṇa), displeased with his behaviour, sent him away to live with the »dog-eaters« (*śvapāka*).
102cd-104ab According to his father's order, Satyavrata left the city and lived with the dog-eaters; his father, too, set out for the forest.
104cd-105ab Because of this breach of *dharma*, Pākaśāsana (= Indra) did not send rain for twelve years.
105cd-109 Viśvāmitra practised asceticism at the border of the ocean; his wife, being left in this (i.e. Satyavrata's) region, wanted to sell her middle son, in order to maintain the others, for 100 cows. Satyavrata, beholding the child with a rope round his neck (*gala*), released the sage's son and maintained him in order to please Viśvāmitra. Therefore the great sage Kauśika was named Gālava.

Ch. 8: The solar dynasty (contd)

1-23 *Story of Satyavrata (Part 2)*

1-2 Satyavrata maintained Viśvāmitra's family by hunting wild animals and fastening their meat to a tree near the hermitage.
3-4 Observing a secret vow, he underwent religious observances[1] for 12 years, on the command of his father, after the king's departure for the forest; meanwhile Vasiṣṭha protected Ayodhyā, the kingdom and the royal palace as a sacrificer and preceptor.
5-8 Satyavrata, however, bore Vasiṣṭha a deep grudge, because he had not prevented his father from exiling him.[2] As the prayer-formulas (*mantra*) of the marriage-cere-

[8] *tasya*, connection not clear.
[9] For a detailed account see e.g. DBhP 7,10.
[1] *dīkṣām avahat* for *avasat*, cf. v. 11ab and 13ab below, and PPL 320,3.
[2] cf. v. 12ab below.

mony are completed (and valid only) at the seventh step, Satyavrata did not violate (the marriage sacrament) at the seventh step; therefore he was angry with Vasiṣṭha, because he, though knowing the rules (= *dharma*), did not protect him.[3]

9 Vasiṣṭha had acted intentionally, but Satyavrata did not know his intention.

10ab Concerning this (or: with him) his father was dissatisfied.

10cd Therefore Pākaśāsana (= Indra) did not send rain for 12 years.[4]

11–12 Thinking that (by Satyavrata's undergoing)[5] difficult religious observances there would be an atonement (? *niṣkṛti*) for the family, Vasiṣṭha did not stop Satyavrata when being exiled, intending to consecrate his (= Trayyāruṇa's? or Satyavrata's?) son as a king.

13–15b He (= Satyavrata) underwent religious observances for 12 years.[6] Finding no meat, he beheld Vasiṣṭha's cow and, being angry and tired, killed it and, together with Viśvāmitra's sons, ate its meat.

16–18 About that Vasiṣṭha grew extremely angry and told him that he would have removed Satyavrata's sin had he not committed two other sins, making his transgressions threefold: displeasing his father, killing his preceptor's cow, and connection with a girl without sacrament.

19 Seeing the three sins (*śaṅku*), the sage uttered »*triśaṅku*«; therefore Satyavrata was called Triśaṅku.

20–21 Since Triśaṅku (= Satyavrata) had maintained his family, Viśvāmitra granted him a boon; he chose to ascend to heaven with his earthly body.

22 With the fear of the twelve years' drought banished, he (Viśvāmitra) consecrated him king and performed sacrifices for him.

23 Against the will of the gods and Vasiṣṭha, Kauśika (= Viśvāmitra) made him ascend to heaven with his body.[7]

24–28 Genealogy: Satyavrata + Satyarathā (from the Kekaya-family) → Hariścandra (called Traiśaṅkava) → Rohita → Harita → Cañcu → Vijaya (conqueror of the whole earth) → Ruruka → Vṛka → Bāhu.

29–72 *Story of Sagara*[8]

29–30 Bāhu was expelled from his kingdom by the Haihayas and Tālajaṅghas; his pregnant wife sought shelter with sage Aurva; he was not very righteous in the Age of Righteousness (*dharmayuga*).[9] Together with poison (*gara*), Bāhu's son Sagara was born.

[3] For the contents of v. 7, cf. 7.98 above; the marriage-ceremony seems to have been disturbed before the seventh step, thus Satyavrata could think himself not to be guilty of abducting another's wife.

[4] cf. 7.104cd–105ab.

[5] The sentence is incomplete: the following accusative forms cannot be connected with any verb; but cf. HV 10.11, where *vahatā* is read instead of *vihitām*.

[6] cf. v. 3 above.

[7] cf. v. 20–21 above. cf. also Rm (Cr Ed.) 2,102.10–11, where Triśaṅku, however, ascends to heaven because of his truthfulness (*satyavacanāt*); he is son of Pṛthu and father of Dhundhumāra, according to the Rm.

[8] For this story cf. e.g. Rm (Poona Ed.) 1,37–43.

[9] ? Thus according toVePr and Ms. C; ASS reads »he was Nāsatya (?, »not untruthful«)...«.

31-32 Obtaining the fire-weapon from Bhārgava (= Aurva), Sagara conquered the world, defeating the Tālajaṅghas and Haihayas; the Śakas, Pahlavas and Pāradas were deprived of their Kṣatriya-*dharma* by him.

33-34 The hermits inquire why Sagara was born together with poison, and why he deprived the Śakas etc. of their *dharma*.

35-51 *Story of Sagara's birth*[10]

35-37 Being expelled from his kingdom by the Haihayas, Tālajaṅghas, Śakas, Yavanas, Pāradas, Kāmbojas and Pahlavas, Bāhu went to the forest together with his wife; there he died.

38 His wife, Yādavī, was pregnant; her co-wife had previously given her poison.

39-40 She (= Yādavī) was prevented from ascending her husband's funeral pyre by the sage Aurva Bhārgava; in his hermitage Sagara was born, together with the poison (*gara*).

41-42ab After educating him, Aurva gave him the fire-weapon Āgneya.

42cd-43 With that weapon, Sagara slew the Haihayas, like Rudra slaying the animals , thereby obtaining fame.

44-51 Seeing that Sagara wanted to destroy them, too, the other tribes, Śakas, Yavanas, Kāmbojas and Pāradas, prayed for Vasiṣṭha's help; on his order, Sagara spared their lives, but deprived them of their *dharma* and changed their appearance; he shaved the heads of the Śakas halfway and that of the Yavanas and Kāmbojas totally; the Pāradas had to wear their hair loose, the Pahlavas had to wear moustaches. All of them had to give up recitation: the Śakas, Yavanas, Kāmbojas, Pāradas, Koṇisarpas (VePr Kālasarpas), Māhiṣakas, Darvas (VePr Daryas), Colas and Keralas; these Kṣatriyas were deprived of their *dharma* by Sagara, according to Vasiṣṭha's word.

52-53 After that, Sagara wanted to perform a horse-sacrifice. The horse was sent away, but disappeared in the earth near the coast of the south-eastern ocean.

54-57 In order to find the horse Sagara and his sons dug up that region, thereby disturbing Viṣṇu, who slept there in the shape of Kapila. Waking up, Kapila burnt Sagara's sons, by the brilliance issuing from his eyes, except for four, Barhiketu, Suketu, Dharmaratha, Pañcanada,[11] carrying on the family line.

58-59ab Hari Nārāyaṇa granted him (= Sagara) an undecaying family line, indestructible fame, an endless stay in heaven, and that the ocean would be his son, who is, accordingly, called Sāgara (i.e. Sagara's son).

59cd-61 Having obtained the horse from the ocean, Sagara performed 100 horse-sacrifices. The number of his sons was 60,000.

62 The hermits inquire how the 60,000 sons were born.

[10] For the story of Sagara's birth cf. also Rm 2,102.14-19; Sagara's father, however, is named Asita there.

[11] v.l. Pañcajana.

63-73 *Birth of Sagara's sons*

63-64 Lomaharṣaṇa continues: Sagara had two wives, an elder one named Keśinī, daughter of Vidarbha, and a younger, very beautiful one, named Mahatī, daughter of Ariṣṭanemin.

65-68 Aurva allowed Sagara's wives to choose either one son, who would carry on the family line, or 60,000 sons. Both wives made their choice, whereupon one of them (VePr Keśinī) gave birth to Pañcajana,[12] and the other one to a gourd containing 60,000 seeds.

69-72ab These were put into jar with clarified butter, and nurses were given to each of them. After 10 months they came forth as 60,000 sons; thus, the 60 000 sons were born from a gourd.

2cd-73ab One of these sons who had entered Nārāyaṇa's brilliance[13] was Pañcajana, who became king.

73cd-92 *Descendants of Sagara*

3cd-75ab Pañcajana → Aṃśumat → Dilīpa Khaṭvāṅga, who, descending from heaven for one moment of life, put together (?) the three worlds by his truthfulness.

5cd-77ab Dilīpa → Bhāgīratha who made Gaṅgā descend from heaven and led her to the ocean; therefore she is regarded as his daughter and named Bhāgīrathī.

7cd-84ab Bhāgīratha → Śruta → Nābhāga → Ambarīsa → Sindhudvīpa → Ayutājit → Ṛtuparṇa (a friend of Nala) → Ārtaparṇi → Sudāsa (a friend of Indra) → Kalmāṣapāda Saudāsa (a friend of Mitra) → Sarvakarman → Anaraṇya → Nighna → Anamitra and Raghu.

84cd-92 Anamitra → Duliduha → Dilīpa → Raghu, king of Ayodhyā → Aja → Daśaratha → Rāma → Kuśa → Atithi → Niṣadha → Nala → Nabha → Puṇḍarīka → Kṣemadhanvan → Devānīka → Ahīnagu → Sudhanvan → Śala → Ukya → Vajranābha → Nala.

93 There are two persons named Nala, one being the son of Vīrasena, and one belonging to the Ikṣvāku-family.[14]

94 Conclusion: These are the kings belonging to the solar dynasty, starting with Ikṣvāku.

95 Phalastuti: He who recites (this account of) the creation by the Āditya Vivasvat (i.e. the sun), the god presiding over the ancestral rites and bestower of progeny, will have offspring and enter into union with Vivasvat (VePr will reach the same world as Vivasvat).

[12] But cf. v. 57 above, where Pañcajana is named among the four sons spared by Kapila, who carry on the family-line; and v. 72cd-73ab below.

[13] cf. v. 54-57 above.

[14] There seem to be, however, two Nalas in the Ikṣvāku-family: the son of Niṣadha, and the son of Vajranābha, besides Nala, son of Vīrasena, who seems to be alluded to in v. 80ab.

Ch. 9: The origin of Soma, the abduction of Tārā, and the birth of Budha[1]

1 From Brahman's mind Soma's father Atri was born.

2-5 After 3000 heavenly years of asceticism practised by Atri, his seed rose, having become Soma;[2] water flowed from his eyes, illuminating the ten directions. To them the embryo was entrusted, but being unable to keep it, they let it fall to the ground.

6 Seeing it fall Brahman made it mount a chariot.

7-8 Brahman's sons and the gods praised Soma; by that his brilliance was increased.

9-10 Driving round the earth with his chariot 21 times, Soma filled the earth with his brilliance, from which originated the plants.

11 He practised asceticism for ten decades of *padmas*, i.e. 1000 millions (of years?).[3]

12 Sovereignty over seeds and plants, over sages and waters, was bestowed upon him.

13-16 On obtaining his kingdom, he performed a consecration ceremony (*rājasūya*) giving sacrificial gifts of 10,000 (cows?). He gave the three worlds to the participants and to the best of sages. His priests were Hiraṇyagarbha, Brahman, Atri and Bhṛgu, whereas Hari was the supervising priest. Nine goddesses did service: Sinī, Kuhū, Dyuti, Puṣṭi, Prabhā, Vasu, Kṛti, Dhṛti, and Lakṣmī.

17-20 Having obtained his kingdom, Soma became haughty and abducted Tārā, Bṛhaspati's wife; when asked to give her back to (the son of) Aṅgiras (= Bṛhaspati), he refused.[4]

21 Uśanas attacked Bṛhaspati from behind, as did Rudra, taking up his bow »Ajagava«.

22 By him (= Rudra?) was thrown the weapon Brahmaśiras (i.e. »Brahman's head«), which destroyed the fame of the gods.

23 At that time (or: due to that) the famous »Tārakāmaya-battle« between gods and demons arose.

24-25 Asked for protection by the gods, Brahman stopped Rudra and Uśanas, giving Tārā back to Bṛhaspati.

26 Seeing her pregnant, Bṛhaspati ordered her to abort the embryo.

27 As soon as the child was born, his beauty surpassed that of the gods.

28-30 Full of doubt the gods asked Tārā whether her son's father was Soma or Bṛhaspati but she remained silent. Her son wanted to curse her but was stopped by Brahman who asked Tārā himself.

31-32 To Brahman she confessed that the child was conceived from Soma. Soma acknowledged the child as his son by kissing him on his head; he named him Budha. (As a planet) Budha (= Venus) rises to the sky in inverted order (*pratikūlam*).

[1] For a German translation of this chapter see W. Kirfel: Der Mythos von Tārā und der Geburt des Budha, in: Kl. Schriften, p. 92 ff.

[2] Soma in this episode is both a fluid (semen, tears, Soma-juice, nectar of immortality) and a luminous heavenly body.

[3] The reading: *padmānāṃ darśanāya* does not seem to make much sense; it probably arose from a misunderstanding of the word *padma* in the reading *padmānāṃ daśatir daśa*, as found in VePr.

[4] For this story cf. also ch. 152 below.

33-34 His son was Purūravas, son of Ilā; to him seven sons were born by Urvaśī. Conclusion to (the account of) Soma's birth.
35ab Announcement of (the account of) the lunar dynasty.
5cd-36ab Phalastuti concerning (the story of) Soma's birth.

Ch. 10: The lunar dynasty: Amāvasu branch

1-14 *Story of Purūravas*[1]

1-3 Lomaharṣaṇa continues: Budha's son was Purūravas (description of his qualities).
4 Urvaśī, giving up her pride, chose him (as her husband).
5-8 They lived together for 15 years, for 6, 5, 7, 8 and 18[2] years, enjoying themselves in the Caitraratha-forest, on the banks of the Mandākinī, in Alakā (i.e. Kubera's capital) in the Nandana-forest (i.e. Indra's paradise), in the land of the Uttarakurus, at the feet (?) of Gandhamādana, on top (VePr on the northern flank) of Mount Meru, in all these forests that are frequented by the gods.
9-10 He ruled in Prayāga, the most sacred region, and was king in Pratiṣṭhāna, on the northern bank of the Jāhnavī (= Gaṅgā).
11-12 Purūravas had seven sons, known in the world of Gandharvas (VePr born in heaven): Āyu, Amāvasu, Viśvāyu, Śrutāyu, Dṛdhāyu, Vanāyu, Bahvāyu.
13-14 Amāvasu → Bhīma → Kāñcanaprabha → Suhotra + Keśinī → Jahnu.

15-20 *Story of Jahnu*

15-18cd When Jahnu performed a great snake-sacrifice, Gaṅgā, who wanted him to be her husband but was rejected by him, inundated the sacrificial ground. Angrily he cursed her and drank up her water.
8cd-19ab Seeing this, the great sages made her Jahnu's daughter named Jāhnavī.
19cd-20 Jahnu married Kāverī, daughter of Yuvanāśva; due to Yuvanāśva's curse Gaṅgā formed Kāverī, the best of rivers and wife to Jahnu, out of (her) half.[3]
21-23 Jahnu + Kāverī → Sunadya → Ajaka → Balākāśva → Kuśa → Kuśika, Kuśanābha; Kuśāmba, Mūrtimat.
24-28ab Birth of Gādhi: Kuśika grew up with cowherds (VePr with Pahlavas) living in a forest. Wishing to have a son like Indra, he practised asceticism; Śakra (= Indra) watched him for a thousand years. Seeing Kuśika's utmost asceticism, Sahasrākṣa (»having 1000 eyes« = Indra) fulfilled his wish by becoming Kuśika's son, Gādhi Kauśika, himself. His mother was Paurvā (VePr Paurukutsā).

[1] For translation and other versions (HV, ViP) cf. K. F. Geldner: Purūravas und Urvaśī, in: Vedische Studien II, p. 243 ff.; cf. also ch. 151 below (which is not mentioned by Geldner).
[2] The last figure not in VePr.
[3] Thus according to the PPL-text; the reading of this verse seems to be corrupt.

28cd–50ab *Story of Satyavatī and the birth of Jamadagni*

28cd–29ab Gādhi had a daughter named Satyavatī, whom he gave in marriage to Ṛcīka, a descendant of Bhṛgu.

29cd–34ab In order to get a son, Ṛcīka made a pot of gruel, gave it to his wife and told her to keep it for herself, while her mother should have another one, whereupon a fierce warrior, a destroyer of Kṣatriyas, would be born to her mother, and a peaceful, ascetic Brahmin to herself. After that he left for the forest, in order to practise asceticism.

34cd–38ab In the meantime, Gādhi and his wife came to see their daughter, on a pilgrimage. Satyavatī took both pots and gave one to her mother, who, by fate (*daivena*), took the one meant for her daughter, leaving her own with her. Thereupon Satyavatī became pregnant with the embryo that would kill all Kṣatriyas.

38cd–41ab Ṛcīka, having come to know these facts by Yoga, told his wife that she had been deceived by her mother and prophesied that a cruel son would be born to her, whereas her brother would be endowed with *brahman*.

41cd–43 She did not want such a son, but, as it could not be changed, Ṛcīka once more told her she would have a cruel son, due to her parents.

44–46ab Once more she asked for a peaceful son, conceding that her grandson might be cruel.

46cd–49ab Now Ṛcīka agreed and fulfilled her wish by the power of his asceticism; thereafter Jamadagni Bhārgava was born to them. (VePr adds: Previously, when Bhṛgu mixed up the pots of Indra (C Rudra) and Viṣṇu, Jamadagni was born from the offering in Viṣṇu's share.)

49cd–50ab Satyavatī became the river Kauśikī.

50cd–53ab Jamadagni was married to Kāmalī Reṇukā of the Ikṣvāku-family; to them was born the terrible Rāma Jāmadagnya, destroyer of Kṣatriyas.

53cd–54 Ṛcīka + Satyavatī → Jamadagni, Śunaḥśepha and Śunaḥpuccha.

55–68a *Viśvāmitra and his sons*

55–56 Gādhi had a son named Viśvāmitra, who, after obtaining the rank of a Brahman-sage, was called Viśvaratha.

57–60 His sons were Devarāta, Kati, from whom the Kātyāyanas originate; by Śālāvatī he had the sons Hiraṇyākṣa, Reṇu, Reṇuka, Sāṃkṛti, Gālava, Mudgala, Madhucchandas, Jaya, Devala, Kacchapa, and Hārita.[4]

61–62 From these sons arose the following clans (*gotra*) of the Kauśikas: the Pāṇins, Babhrus, Dhyānajapyas, Devarātas, Śālaṅkāyanas, Baṣkalas, Lohitas, Yamadūtas, and Kārūṣakas. (VePr adds: Sauśravas, Kauśikas, and other Saindhavāyanas, Devalas, Reṇus, Yājñyavālkyas,[5] Audumbaras, Āmbubhiṣṇus, Tārakāyaṇas, Cuñculas, Śālavatyas, Hiraṇyākṣas, Sāṃkṛtyas, Gālavas; another son of Viśvāmitra was Nara Nārāyaṇi; many Kauśikas are known as *ṛsyantaravirānta* (?).)

[4] Though the number of sons is said to be ten, 12 names of sons are enumerated.

[5] According to PPL-text.

63 In this family-line, there was the famous connection between Brahmin and Kṣatriya, between Paurava and Kauśika (= Viśvāmitra).

64–65ab Śunaḥśepha is considered the eldest son of Viśvāmitra, for he obtained (membership in) Kauśika's family; he became Viśvāmitra's son.

65cd–67ab At the sacrifice of (king) Haridaśva (VePr Hariścandra), he was used as the sacrificial animal (*paśu*), but given to Viśvāmitra by the gods; therefore he is called Devarāta.[6]

67cd–68 Including Devarāta, Viśvāmitra had seven sons;[7] from Dṛṣadvatī he had an eighth son, whose son was Lauhi. Conclusion to the account of the family of Jahnu; announcement of Āyu's family-line.

Ch. 11: The lunar dynasty (contd): Branch of Āyu's younger sons

1–2 Lomaharṣaṇa continues: Āyu and Prabhā (daughter of Svarbhānu) had five sons: Nahuṣa, Vṛddhaśarman, Rambha, Raji, and Anenas.

3–26 *Story of Raji*

3 Raji had 500 sons, famous as »Rājeya-power«, who caused Indra's fear.

4–7 When the war between gods and demons started, both groups went to Brahman, asking him who would be victorious. Brahman answered that they who could win Raji to fight with them would also win the victory.

8–16 Now the gods as well as the demons asked Raji, who was born from Prabhā as a grandson of Svarbhānu in the lunar dynasty, to fight for them in the war. Raji promised to help the group that was willing to make him their »Indra« (i.e. chief, king). The gods agreed to that condition, whereas the demons told him that their Indra was Prahlāda (VePr Prahrāda).

17–19ab Thereupon Raji took the side of the gods and slew the demons, thus regaining the lost majesty (*śrī*) of the gods.

19cd–21ab Śatakratu (= Indra) granted Raji to be Indra, but said that he himself was Raji's son. Raji agreed, not noticing that he was being deceived by Śakra (= Indra).

21cd–24ab After Raji's death, his 500 sons took the inherited kingdom away from Indra, and repeatedly attacked Śatakratu's abode, the heavenly world called Triviṣṭapa.

24cd–26ab Becoming self-conceited and unrighteous, Raji's sons lost their power; Indra slew them and regained his kingdom (or rank).

26c-f Phalastuti: He who listens to and remembers this (story of the) fall from and regaining of Indra's rank will not come to any mischief.

[6] For this story, cf. ch. 104 below and Ait.Br. 7.13 ff.; transl. by H. Lommel: Brahmanische Legenden; discussed by F. Weller: Die Legende von Śunaḥśepa... Berlin 1956, and by H. Lommel: Die Śunaḥśepa-Legende, ZDMG 114, 1964 (= Kl. Schriften p. 440–479).

[7] cf., however, v. 57–60 above.

27-31 *Descendants of Anenas*

27ab Rambha had no sons; announcement of the lineage of Anenas.

27cd-31 Anenas → Pratikṣatra → Saṃjaya (VePr Sṛñjaya) → Jaya → Vijaya → Kṛti → Haryatvata → Sahadeva → Nadīna → Jayatsena → Saṃkṛti → Kṣatravṛddha. These are the (descendants) of Anenas. (VePr reads: There is another (son ?) of Kṣatravṛddha.)[1]

32-61 *Descendants of Kṣatravṛddha*

32-33ab Kṣatravṛddha → Sunahotra → Kāśa (VePr Kāśya), Śala (VePr Śalla), Gṛtsamada.

33-34ab Gṛtsamada → Śunaka → Śaunaka, Brahmins, Kṣatriyas, Vaiśyas, and Śūdras.[2]

34cd Śala (VePr Śalla) → Ārṣṭisena (VePr Ārṣṭiṣena) → Kāśyapa.

35 Kāśa (VePr Kāśya) → Dīrghatapas (king of Kāśi) → Dhanus → Dhanvantari.[3]

36-38 After a long time of asceticism he (= Dīrghatapas,[4] whose name seems thereby to be explained) obtained the god Dhanvantari (the physician of the gods) as his son. As king of Kāśi he (Dhanvantari), the destroyer of all diseases, obtained the Āyurveda from Bharadvāja, and handed it to his pupils, dividing it into eight parts.

39-40 Dhanvantari → Ketumat → Bhīmaratha → Divodāsa, king of Vārāṇasī.[5]

41-43 At that time Vārāṇasī was uninhabited, due to a curse of Nikumbha. Only the Rākṣasa Kṣemaka lived there, while Divodāsa stayed at the border of this region, in a town on (the bank of the river) Gomatī.

44-48 Previously, Vārāṇasī belonged to Bhadraśreṇya, but was taken from him by Divodāsa, who slew him and his 100 sons, except Durdama, because he was a mere child. Durdama, however, took back his paternal heritage by force, after obtaining the heritage of Haihaya (?), and settled the conflict.[6]

49-50ab Divodāsa + Dṛṣadvatī → Pratardana → Vatsa and Bharga.

50cd Vatsa → Alarka → Saṃnati (VePr Vatsa → Śatrujit → Ṛtadhvaja).

51-53 His (whose?) son was Alarka, who was friendly to Brahmins and true to his promises;[7] a verse on him says that he was endowed with youth for 66,000 years, and that he was granted the utmost duration of life by Lopāmudrā. A very large kingdom belonged to him, who was abounding in youth and beauty.

[1] This Kṣatravṛddha seems to be identical with the second son of Āyu, who was named Vṛddhaśarman in v. 2 above, but unlike Āyu's other sons is not mentioned afterwards. In the second text-group of the PPL-text, however, he is found as the second son of Āyu, while the first text-group, to which the BrP belongs, names him Kṣatravṛddha, the name Vṛddhaśarman being given as a v.l. of the BrP.

[2] cf. below 13.63b-64ab.

[3] cf. below 13.64cd-65ab.

[4] cf. below 13.64cd-65ab.

[5] cf. below 13,.65cd-66.

[6] For this story, cf. also below ch. 13.67-72ab.

[7] These epithets seem to allude to Rm 2,12.43cd and 14.4, where Alarka is quoted as an instance of keeping one's promises and is said to have given away his eyes for a blind Brahmin, a story which is also found among the Jātaka-tales (no. 499), but is told there about the Sivi-king.

54 At the end of the curse,[8] he (who?) slew the Rākṣasa Kṣemaka and lived again in the beautiful city Vārāṇasī.[9]

55–59 Saṃnati → Sunītha → Kṣema → Ketumat → Suketu → Dharmaketu → Satyaketu → Vibhu → Ānarta → Sukumāra → Dhṛṣṭaketu → Veṇuhotra → Bhārga (VePr Bharga).

60ab Vatsa → Vatsabhūmi; Bhārga (VePr Bharga) → Bhārgabhūmi (VePr Bhargabhūmi).[10]

)cd–61ab Conclusion: These are the sons of Aṅgiras, born in the Bhārgava-family, three sons (and ?) thousands of Brahmins, Kṣatriyas, Vaiśyas.[11]

61cd Conclusion to the Kāśyapa-line, announcement of Nahuṣa's line.

Ch. 12: The lunar dynasty (contd): Story of Yayāti[1]

1–2 Lomaharṣaṇa continues: Nahuṣa and Virajā, (his) father's daughter (? *pitṛkanyā*), had six sons: Yati, Yayāti, Saṃyāti (VePr Śaryāti), Āyāti, Pārśvaka (VePr Yāti, Suyāti, of whom Yayāti succeeded as the king.[2])

3 Yati was the eldest son, Yayāti the next one. He married Go, the daughter of Kakutstha, while Yati strove for liberation and became (absorbed in) *brahman*.

4–5ab Yayāti conquered the earth; he married Devayānī, daughter of Uśanas, and the Asura-girl Śarmiṣṭhā, daughter of Vṛṣaparvan.

5cd–6ab Yayāti + Devayānī → Yadu and Turvasu; Yayāti + Śarmiṣṭhā → Druhyu, Anu and Puru (VePr Pūru).

6cd–8 Śakra (= Indra) gave him a heavenly chariot, with whose help he conquered the earth within 6 nights (i.e. 7 days, one week).

9–10 Afterwards the chariot belonged to all Kauravas (A,C Pauravas), but from the Kaurava Janamejaya (it went into the possession) of (the king of Cedi) named Saṃvartavasu.[3] Belonging to (Janamejaya,) the son of Parīkṣit and descendant of Kuru, (VePr oh king!)[4] the chariot was destroyed, due to Garga's curse.

11–17 Janamejaya had hurt Garga's son (VePr Vākrūra) and incurred the guilt of Brahmin-murder. Afflicted with the smell of blood, he was expelled from the land of the Pauras, and did not find shelter anywhere. He approached Śaunaka, who purified him by a horse-sacrifice. The smell of blood disappeared, and Indra, being

[8] cf. v. 42 above.

[9] This verse seems to belong to the story of Divodāsa in v. 41 ff. above, not to the story of Alarka.

[10] This verse probably continues v. 50ab, since only there are Vatsa and Bharga mentioned together.

[11] Seems not to be a conclusion to the present chapter.

[1] For the story of Yayāti cf. e.g. MBh 1,70ff., and Ch. 146, below.

[2] The additional line of VePr is in agreement with the HV, but excluded from the PPL-text by Kirfel.

[3] i.e. the Vasu (cf. PPL-text: *yāvad Vasunāmno vai Kauravāj Janamejayāt*) in v. 15cd below?

[4] The vocative *rājendra*, which does not fit into the context of the BrP, is also found in the HV, which was obviously the source for this passage.

pleased, gave the heavenly chariot to Vasu,[5] the king of Cedi; from him it was obtained by Bṛhadratha, who gave it to his son (= Jarāsaṃdha).The Kaurava-son[6] Bhīma[7] killed Jarāsaṃdha and gave it to Vāsudeva.

18-21 After conquering the whole earth with its oceans and the seven continents, Yayāti divided his kingdom, giving the east to Yadu, the middle to Puru (= Pūru), and the south-east to Turvasu. By them the earth is protected, to this day.

21cd Announcement of a later account of their descendants.

22-23 Putting down bows and arrows, King Yayāti was contented with the five brave men (= his five sons) (v. 22ab,23cd). The king grew old; putting the burden (of kingship?) on his relatives, he laid down his weapons and roamed the earth (v. 22cd-23ab).[8]

24-38 Having divided the earth,[9] Yayāti asked his eldest son Yadu to take upon himself his old age. Yadu refused to do so, because of another obligation towards a Brahmin, which he would have to remove first (?); the inconveniences of old age could not be borne by him. He suggested that another son should be asked. Yayāti became angry and cursed him that his descendants should remain bereft of kingship, since he did not honour the order of his father, the only stage of life and the only *dharma* of a son. The other sons, when asked, refused as well and were similarly cursed. Finally Puru was approached with the same words. He agreed, and Yayāti, endowed with his son's youth, roamed the earth, striving for the fulfilment of his desires and enjoying life together with Viśvācī (an Apsaras). When his desires were fulfilled (VePr Since, however, his desires were never fulfilled), he returned to Puru, gave back his youth to him, and took up his own old age again.

39 On that occasion he recited some verses by means of which one can retract one's desires like a tortoise its limbs.

40-46 Quotation of Yayāti's verses, proclaiming the unquenchability of desires, the endlessness of the hope for life and wealth, and the pleasure of having given up all desires.

47-48 Together with his wives, Yayāti entered the forest, practised asceticism, and, by taking no food, died of starvation at Bhṛgutuṅga.

49 In his line there were five royal sages who spread over the earth.

50 Announcement of Yadu's[10] family-line, in which Hari Nārāyaṇa was born, the descendant of Vṛṣṇi.

[5] Corr. from *vaśaś*, according to A and the PPL-text.

[6] HV: *kauravanandana* (vocative).

[7] = Bhīmasena, brother of Janamejaya and son of Parīkṣit, or Bhīmasena, son of Ṛkṣa and father of Pratīpa, or the brother of Yudhiṣṭhira and Arjuna (who is normally called a Pāṇḍava, but a contemporary of Vāsudeva)? There are 3 Bhīmasenas (cf. ch. 13, v. 112-113, below.

[8] These two verses, which seem to be somewhat confused, obviously disturb the connection between the preceding passage about the division of the earth and v. 24, starting with »Having divided the earth...«.

[9] According to the PPL-text, where »Having grown old« is read in the place of »Having divided the earth«, this story is told before the report on the division of the earth.

[10] cf. below ch. 13.153ff.; first the family-lines of Yadu's younger brothers are reported.

51 Phalastuti: He who listens to the story of Yayāti will be endowed with offspring, life, and fame.

Ch. 13: The lunar dynasty (contd): The branches of Yayāti's sons

1 The Brahmins ask for an account of the family-lines of Puru, Druhyu, Anu, Yadu, and Turvasu.

2 Lomaharṣaṇa announces Puru's family-line.

3-140 *Descendants of Puru*

3-4 Puru → Suvīra → Manasyu → Abhayada → Sudhanvan → Subāhu → Raudrāśva.

5-8 Raudrāśva → ten sons: Daśārṇeyu, Kṛkaṇeyu, Kakṣeyu, Sthaṇḍileyu, Sannateyu, Ṛceyu, Jaleyu, Sthaleyu, Dhaneyu, Vaneyu, and ten daughters: Bhadrā, Śūdrā, Madrā, Śaladā, Maladā, Khaladā, Naladā, Surasā, Gocapalā, and Strīratnakūṭā; they were married to the sage Prabhākara belonging to the family of Atri.

9-12ab Prabhākara + Bhadrā → Soma, by whom light was established, when the sun, hit by Svarbhānu, fell from the sky, and the world became dark; uttering a blessing, this sage (= Prabhākara?) stopped the falling sun; he (= Soma? or Prabhākara?) founded the best families (*gotra*) descending from Atri, and his strength was established by the gods on the occasion of Atri's sacrifices.

12cd-14ab From them (i.e. the ten daughters of Rudrāśva) Prabhākara had ten sons, devoted to asceticism, who founded families, named Svastyātreyas and Tridhanavarjitas.[1]

14cd-49 *The branch of Kakṣeyu, son of Raudrāśva*

14cd-15ab Kakṣeyu → Sabhānara, Cākṣuṣa, and Paramanyu.

15cd-20ab Sabhānara → Kālānala → Sṛñjaya → Puraṃjaya → Janamejaya → Mahāśāla → Mahāmanas → Uśīnara and Titikṣu.

20cd-22ab Uśīnara had five wives: Nṛgā, Kṛmi, Navā, Darvā, and Dṛṣadvatī, and from them five sons, born to him after severe asceticism, when he was old.

22cd-23 Nṛgā → Nṛga; Kṛmi (f.) → Kṛmi (m.); Navā → Nava; Darvā → Suvrata; Dṛṣadvatī → Śibi Auśīnara.

24-25ab The Śibis were (descendants or subjects) of Śibi; the Yaudheyas belonged to Nṛga, Navarāṣṭra to Nava, the city Kṛmilā to Kṛmi, and the Ambaṣṭhas to Suvrata.

25cd-27ab The four sons of Śibi were Vṛṣadarbha, Suvīra, Kaikeya, and Madraka, who ruled over the Kaikeyas, Madrakas, Vṛṣadarbhas, and Suvīras. Announcement of Titikṣu's progeny (or subjects?).

[1] These names seem to have been explained by v. 9-11 above, which disturbed the connection between v. 8 and 12.

27cd-49 *Descendants of Titikṣu*

27cd-29 Titikṣu (B,C Titikṣu's son Uṣadratha) was king of the eastern region. (Titikṣu →) Uṣadratha → Phena → Sutapas → Bali, who, in his former existence, was king Kāñcaneṣudhi, but was born now as a great Yogin.

30-31 Bali's sons were Aṅga, Vaṅga, Suhma, Puṇḍra, and Kaliṅga, called the »Bāleya-power«, who founded families; the Bāleya-Brahmins belonged to his (Bali's) line.

32-35 A boon was granted to Bali by Brahman: To be a great Yogin for the duration of one cosmic cycle (*kalpa*), to be of incomparable strength, to know the true meaning of *dharma* etc., to be invincible in battle as well as in *dharma*, and to constitute the four castes. After that Bali obtained peace (VePr and went to heaven).

36 To them[2] belong the Aṅgas, Vaṅgas, Suhmakas, Kaliṅgas, and Puṇḍrakas; now (follow) the subjects (offspring) of Aṅga (announcement?).

37-39 Aṅga → Dadhivāhana → Diviratha → Dharmaratha (VePr Svargaratha) → Citraratha, whose father (i.e. Dharmaratha, VePr Svargaratha) drank Soma with Indra while sacrificing on Mount Kālañjara.

40-41 Citraratha → Daśaratha Lomapāda, whose daughter was Śāntā;[3] due to the favour of Ṛśyaśṛṅga, Caturaṅga was born to him.

42 Caturaṅga → Pṛthulākṣa → Campa.

43-44 Campa's city was Campā, previously named Mālinī; due to the favour of Pūrṇabhadra, Haryaṅga was born to him, for whom Vaibhaṇḍaki (= Ṛśyaśṛṅga) made Indra's elephant descend on earth by means of magic formulas (*mantra*).

45-48 Haryaṅga → Bhadraratha → Bṛhatkarman → Bṛhaddarbha → Bṛhanmanas → Jayadratha → Dṛḍharatha → Janamejaya → Vaikarṇa → Vikarṇa → 100 sons, who continue the line of the Aṅgas.

49 Conclusion to the lineage of Aṅga.

50-140 *The branch of Ṛceyu, son of Raudrāśva*

50 Announcement of the lineage of Ṛceyu.

51-52 Ṛceyu → Matināra → Vasurodha, Ratiratha, and Subāhu, experts in the Veda, truthful and friendly to Brahmins.

53 He (who? Matināra?) had a daughter named Ilā, who was approached by Taṃsu.[4]

54-55 Taṃsu → Dharmanetra + Upadānavī → Duṣyanta, Suṣmanta, Pravīra, and Anagha.

56-57 Duṣyanta + Śakuntalā → Bharata, after whom the Bhāratas are (v.l. the land Bhārata is) named.

58-61 When Bharata's sons were all destroyed by their mothers' wrath, as reported before (!), Bharadvāja, the son of the Aṅgiras Bṛhaspati, performed extensive rites (for Bharata). In the beginning, they were unsuccessful (*vitatha*) in producing a son, but afterwards a son named Vitatha was born from Bharadvāja. After Vitatha's birth Bharata went to heaven; Bharadvāja anointed his son Vitatha as king and left for the forest.

[2] i.e. Bali's sons named in v. 30-31 above.

[3] Married with Ṛśyaśṛṅga, cf. Rm 1,9-11.

[4] His parentage is not mentioned; in the PPL-text he is Matināra's son, whereas Ilā's parentage is not quite clear there either.

62–63a Vitatha had five sons: Suhotra, Suhotṛ, Gaya, Garga, Kapila.

63b–64ab Suhotra → Kāśika and Gṛtsamati, whose sons were Brahmins, Kṣatriyas, and Vaiśyas.[5]

64cd–67ab Kāśika → Dīrghatapas Kāśeya → Dhanvantari → Ketumat → Bhīmaratha → Divodāsa, king of Vārāṇasī (= Benares),[6] who killed all Kṣatriyas.

67cd–68ab Divodāsa → Pratardana → Vatsa and Bhārgava.[7]

68cd Alarka, however, (was) the king's (which king's?) son, a king of truthful mind.[8]

69ab The lord of the earth[9] took the heritage of Haihaya.

69cd He (= Durdama) took his paternal heritage, of which Divodāsa had bereft him by force.

70ab By the high-minded Durdama, the son of Bhadraśreṇya... .[10]

70cd He (= Durdama) had been spared by Divodāsa, as he was a mere child.

71ab The son of Bhīmaratha was Aṣṭaratha.[11]

71cd–72ab The (?)[12] of this child (= Durdama?) was taken away by the son (of whom?), by the Kṣatriya, who wanted to end the conflict.[13]

72cd–75ab Alarka, however, the king of Kāśi,[14] was endowed with youth and beauty for 66,000 years. Due to the grace of Lopāmudrā he reached the highest age. At the end of (his) life (?), he killed the Rākṣasa Kṣemaka and settled in Vārāṇasī.

75cd–77 Alarka → Kṣemaka (?) → Varṣaketu → Vibhu → Ānarta → Sukumāra → Satyaketu.

78 Vatsa → Vatsabhūmi; Bhārgava → Bhargabhūmi.[15]

79 Conclusion: These are the sons of Aṅgiras, born in the Bhārgava-family, Brahmins, Kṣatriyas, Vaiśyas, and Śūdras.[16]

80ab Announcement of another (?) line originating from Ajamīḍha.[17]

80cd–81ab Suhotra[18] → Bṛhat → Ajamīḍha, Dvimīḍha, Purumīḍha.

81cd–82ab Ajamīḍha had three wives: Nīlī, Keśinī, and Dhūminī.

82cd–87 Story of Jahnu:[19] From Keśinī was born Jahnu, who celebrated a great sacrifice, and whom Gaṅgā approached, desiring a husband. Being rejected she inundated the

[5] cf. 11.32cd–34ab.

[6] cf. 11.35 and 39–40.

[7] cf. 11.49–50ab.

[8] There is no connection to the preceding text; interpolation?

[9] Who? Divodāsa? Alarka? Durdama?

[10] Incomplete sentence.

[11] This half-verse seems to belong to another context.

[12] Object is missing.

[13] The whole passage, 63cd–79, seems to be a slightly shortened and partly confused repetition of 11.32cd–61ab. In particular, the story of Divodāsa and Durdama seems not to have been understood, as the corruptions show; the text as given in v. 68cd–72ab can hardly be presented in a meaningful summary.

[14] The following passage, up to v. 91, is missing in B, v. 92 being connected with 72cd by changing the name Aṣṭaka into Alarka.

[15] cf. 11.60ab.

[16] cf. 11.60cd–61ab.

[17] He has, however, not been mentioned so far. – This half-verse is repeated as v. 92cd below.

[18] cf. v. 62 above.

[19] cf. 10.15–20, above, where Keśinī, however, is the wife of Suhotra, descendant of the Amāvasu-line.

sacrificial ground. The angry Jahnu announced that he would drink her up in order to punish her haughtiness. The great sages, seeing her drunk up by Jahnu, made her Jahnu's daughter. Jahnu married Kāverī (daughter of Yuvanāśva), half of whose body became a river later on, due to Gaṅgā's curse.

88-90 Jahnu[20] → Ajaka → Balākāśva → Kuśika, an enthusiastic hunter, who grew up with the Pahlavas living in the forest. He practised severe asceticism, in order to obtain a son equal to Indra. Out of fear, Śakra (= Indra) himself took birth as Kuśika's son Gādhi Kauśika.[21]

91 Gādhi → Viśvāmitra → Aṣṭaka (VePr and C insert - VePr in parentheses, without counting the verses: Viśvabādhi, Śvajit, and a daughter, Satyavatī. Satyavatī + Ṛcīka → Jamadagni. The sons of Viśvāmitra, starting with Devarāta, were famous in all worlds. Their names are:[22] Devarāta, Kati (father of Kātyāyana), Hiraṇyākṣa (born by Śālavatī), Reṇu (whose daughter is Reṇukā), and the Gālavas and Maudgalyas, born by Saṃkṛti. The well-known clans (*gotra*) of Kuśika's descendants are:[23] the Pāṇins, the Babhrus, the Dhyānajapyas, the Devarātas, the Śālaṅkāyanas, the Sauśravas, the Lohitas, the Yāmabhūtas, the Kārīṣis; another famous clan of the Kauśikas are the Saindhavāyanas. There are many other Kauśikas, originating from other marriages of the sage (= Viśvāmitra). The liaison of this line (i.e. the Kauśika-line) with the Paurava-line is well-known as one between Brahmins and Kṣatriyas.[24] Śunaḥśepha is known as Viśvāmitra's eldest son; he was a Bhārgava, but became a member of the Kauśika-family.[25] The sons of Viśvāmitra are Devarāta etc.; Dṛṣadvatī is the mother of Aṣṭaka.[26])

92ab Aṣṭaka → Lauhi. Conclusion to (the account of) Jahnu's family.

92cd Announcement of another line originating from Ajamīḍha.[27]

93-96 Ajamīḍha + Nīlī (VePr Nīlinī) → Suśānti → Purujāti → Bāhyāśva → five sons: Mudgala, Sṛñjaya, Bṛhadiṣu, Yavīnara, and Kṛmilāśva. As these five (*pañca*) are enough (*alam*) for protection, they are called Pañcālas.

97 Mudgala → Maudgalya + Indrasenā → Vadhnya (VePr Vadhnyaśva). (VePr inserts here:[28] The son[29] called Satyadhṛti was an expert in archery. Once, when he beheld an Apsaras, his semen was spilt, and twins were born in a thicket of reeds. Śaṃtanu, who was hunting there, picked them up, out of pity (*kṛpā*), therefore he (i.e. the male twin) is known as Kṛpa, and Gautamī (his twin sister) as Kṛpī; these are called Śāradvatas (i.e. descendants of Śaradvat) as well as Gautamas. Announcement of

[20] cf. 10.23-28 above.

[21] cf. 10.23-28, above.

[22] cf. 10.57-60.

[23] cf. 10.61-62.

[24] cf. 10.63.

[25] cf. 10.64-65ab.

[26] cf. 10.67cd-68a.

[27] cf. v. 80 above.

[28] This passage is also embodied in the PPL-text, after two further verses containing the following information: Vadhnyaśva + Menakā → twins: Divodāsa and Ahalyā + Śaradvat → Śatānanda.

[29] Whose? According to the PPL-text, he seems to be the son of Śatānanda, the grandson of Śaradvat, and the great grandson of Vadhnyaśva.

Divodāsa's descendants: Divodāsa → Mitrayu → Soma from whom the Maitreyas originated. They were also attached to the Bhārgava-family, though originating from Kṣatriyas.)

98-99 Sṛñjaya → Pañcajana → Somadatta → Sahadeva → Somaka.[30]

100-101 Somaka was born as a descendant of Ajamīḍha, when the family-line was diminished (?). Somaka → Jantu → 100 sons, the youngest of whom was Pṛṣata, the father of Drupada. These are the descendants of Ajamīḍha.

102-105 Ajamīḍha's queen was Dhūminī (i.e. the »smoky« one), who, desiring a son, practised extensive asceticism. Once, having sacrificed to Agni, she slept on the Kuśa-grass of the Agnihotra, when Ajamīḍha begot Ṛkṣa with her, who was of smoky colour.

106-107 Ṛkṣa → Saṃvaraṇa → Kuru, who founded Kurukṣetra, beyond Prayāga; the Kauravas originated from him.

108 Kuru → four sons: Sudhanvan, Sudhanus, Parīkṣit, and Pravara.

109 Parīkṣit → Janamejaya, Śrutasena, Agrasena, and Bhīmasena. (VePr inserts here:[31] Sudhanvan → Suhotra → Cyavana → Kṛtayajña,[32] who, after performing sacrifices, begot Caidyoparivara, a friend of Indra, who was named Vasu, too.[33] Caidyoparivara + Girikā → 7 sons: Bṛhadratha (king of Magadha), Pratyagratha, Kratha (called Maṇivāhaṇa »jewel-bearer«), Śakala, Juhu, Matsya, and Kālin. Bṛhadratha → Kuśāgra → Ṛṣabha. Announcement of Juhu's line:[34] Juhu → Suratha.)

110-111 Janamejaya → Suratha → Vidūratha → Ṛkṣa.

112-113 Another man bearing that name is known as a descendant of Bharadvāja. There are two Ṛkṣas in the lunar dynasty, two Parīkṣits, three Bhīmasenas, and two Janamejayas. The son of the second Ṛkṣa (i.e. the son of Vidūratha) was Bhīmasena.

114 Bhīmasena → Pratīpa → Śāṃtanu (VePr Śaṃtanu), Devāpi, and Bāhlika.

115ab Śāṃtanu's son was Bhīṣma (VePr Śaṃtanu became king.[35])

115cd Announcement of Bāhlika's descendants:

116 Bāhlika → Somadatta → Bhūri, Bhūriśravas, and Śala.

117ab Devāpi became teacher of the gods.

117cd Cyavana's son was Kṛtaka, who was dear to him (or: was sacrificed ?).[36]

118 Announcement of Śāṃtanu's (VePr Śaṃtanu) lineage.

119 Śāṃtanu (VePr Śaṃtanu) + Gaṅgā → Devavrata, famous as Bhīṣma, the »grandfather« of the Pāṇḍavas.

120 Śāṃtanu (VePr Śaṃtanu) + Kālī (= Satyavatī) → Vicitravīrya.

121 With the wives of Vicitravīrya Kṛṣṇa Dvaipāyana procreated Dhṛtarāṣṭra, Pāṇḍu, and Vidura.

30 VePr inserts: Ajamīḍha was the son of Gṛtsamati.

31 In the PPL-text, this passage is given after v. 108, where it seems to fit better; otherwise it destroys the connection between v. 109 and 110.

32 cf. v. 117cd below, where he is named Kṛtaka, however.

33 cf. above 12.9-10 and 15cd-17; he seems to be identical with Uparicara, king of Cedi, in the MBh.

34 Not in the PPL-text.

35 cf. v. 118ab below.

36 Seems to belong to another context, cf. insertion after v. 109 above.

122 Dhṛtarāṣṭra + Gāndhārī → 100 sons, the best of whom was Duryodhana.

123-124 Pāṇḍu → Dhanaṃjaya (= Arjuna) + Subhadrā → Abhimanyu (Saubhadra) → Parīkṣit → Pārīkṣita (= Janamejaya) + Kāśyā (VePr Kāśi) → Candrāpīḍa and Sūryāpīḍa.

125 Candrāpīḍa → 100 sons, called the Jānamejaya-power.

126-127ab Satyakarṇa, the eldest of them, resided in Vārāṇasa (= Vārāṇasī); his son was Śvetakarṇa.

127cd-132ab Having no sons, he left for the forest, in order to practise asceticism. After entering the forest, (too, his wife) Mālinī, a daughter of Sucāru (VePr Subāhu), born in the Yādava-family, conceived a child by him. In spite of that, Satyakarṇa pursued the course once taken; Mālinī followed him and, on the way, gave birth to a boy, Kumāraka. She abandoned the child and followed her husband, as Draupadī had done before.

132cd-137 The boy cried on the flank of a mountain (VePr in a mountain cave); out of pity clouds appeared. Paippalādi and Kauśika, two sons of Śraviṣṭhā, saw (him), and washed him in water. His sides, rubbed on the rocks, were covered with blood; beautifully adorned (? *susamāhitaḥ*) with rubbed sides, he was black like a goat (*ajaśyāma*). Thus, his two sides became black like that of goats, by fate; therefore he was named Ajapārśva (i.e. »having flanks like a goat«). He was brought up by the two Brahmins in Remaka's (VePr Romaka's) house. Remaka's (VePr Romaka's) wife took (adopted?) him, in order to have a son. He became Remakī's (VePr Romakī's) son; these two Brahmins, however, were (his) friends.

138 They (pl.) had sons and grandsons (born) simultaneously, and living for identical periods of time. (?)

139-140 Yayāti, son of Nahuṣa, recited a verse about it, saying that the earth would never be without Pauravas.

141 Conclusion to the Paurava-line; announcement of Turvasu's line.

142-148ab *Descendants of Turvasu*

142-146 Turvasu → Vahni → Gobhānu → Aiśānu (VePr Traiśānu) → Karaṃdhama → Marutta. Another Marutta was mentioned as a son of Āvikṣit.(?) He (= Marutta) had no sons, but a daughter named Saṃyatā, who was given to Saṃvarta as a sacrificial gift; he obtained the Paurava Duṣyanta as son. Thus, due to Yayāti's curse, Turvasu's line joined that of the Pauravas.

147-148ab Duṣyanta → Karūroma → Āhrīda → four sons: Pāṇḍya, Kerala, Kāla (VePr Kola), and Cola (VePr adds: whose realms are the lands of the Pāṇḍyas, Colas, and Keralas).

148-151 *Descendants of Druhyu*

148-150ab Druhyu → Babhrusetu → Aṅgārasetu, the lord of the Maruts, who was killed by Yauvanāśva in a battle that lasted ten months.

148cd-151 Aṅgārasetu → Gāndhāra, after whom the land Gāndhāra is named; the horses from that region are the best.

152–153ab *Descendants of Anu:*

152–153ab Anu → Dharma → Dyūta (VePr Dhṛta) → Vanaduha (VePr Śatadruha) → Pracetas → Sucetas.[37]

153cd–204 *Descendants of Yadu*

153cd–154ab Yadu had five sons: Sahasrāda (VePr Sahasrada), Payoda, Kroṣṭṛ, Nīla, and Añjika.

154cd–155ab Sahasrāda (VePr Sahasrada) had three sons: Haihaya, Haya, and Veṇuhaya.

155cd–156 Haihaya → Dharmanetra → Kārta → Sāhañja, who resided in the city Sāhañjanī.

157–159 Mahiṣmat[38] → Bhadraśreṇya → Durdama → Kanaka → four sons: Kṛtavīrya, Kṛtaujas, Kṛtadhanvan (VePr Kṛtakarman), and Kṛtāgni.

160 Kṛtavīrya's son was Arjuna (Kārtavīrya), who, with 1000 arms, became the ruler of the seven continents; he conquered the earth with a chariot shining like the sun.

161–198 *Story of Arjuna Kārtavīrya*[39]

161–164 After practising asceticism for 10,000 years, striving to obtain the favour of Datta, son of Atri, he was granted four boons: 1. 1000 arms, 2. being prevented by the good, whenever thinking of unrighteousness, 3. pleasing (his subjects) by means of *dharma*, after conquering the earth, 4. death in battle, after killing many enemies.

165 His 1000 arms became visible in battle, due to (the power of) Yoga, as if by the magic of the Lord of Yogins (or: like the arms of the Lord of Yogins that become visible during yogic practice by his magic power).

166–169 Conquering the earth, he completed 700 sacrifices in the 7 continents, with 100,000 (cows) as sacrificial gift, with golden posts and altars, attended by gods, Gandharvas, and Apsarases (as guests).

170–171 At one sacrifice the Gandharva Nārada sang a verse (*gāthā*) saying that no king would reach Kārtavīrya.[40]

172–173 He could be seen as a Yogin, driving over the seven continents in his car, with his weapons. There was no loss of goods, nor grief, nor trouble, since he protected his subjects, according to his duty.

174–176ab He was a universal emperor (*cakravartin*) and a protector of animals and fields; by raining he became Parjanya (the rain-god), due to his being a Yogin. With his 1000 arms, he »shone« like the autumn sun with 1000 rays.

176cd–187ab He defeated the Nāgas, the sons of Karkoṭaka, and settled in their city Māhiṣmatī. He restrained the ocean during the rainy season. Stirred up by his playing, the

[37] In the PPL-text, where Anu's line comprises the genealogy starting with Sabhānara (reported as Kakṣeyu's branch in the BrP, cf. v. 14cd–49 above), this verse is connected with Turvasu's line by naming Dharma as a son of Gāndhāra, not of Anu.

[38] Son of Sāhañja, according to the PPL-text, where there is one half-verse more (PPL p. 411, v. 5cd).

[39] For the episodes contained in this passage cf. A. Gail: Paraśurāma, p. 7 f.

[40] The end of Nārada's verse is not clearly marked; the next two verses might be regarded as belonging to it, too. The perfect tense in v. 174, however, shows that the narrative must have started again.

frightened Narmadā (river) approached him. By beating the ocean he paralyzed the great Asuras. He set (the ocean) in motion, like Mandara the milk-ocean when it was churned by gods and demons; thereupon the great snakes (= Nāgas? Asuras?) submitted to him. He even captured Rāvaṇa, but released him upon the intervention of Pulastya (Rāvaṇa's grandfather).

187cd–189ab By thc Bhārgava Rāma Jāmadagnya Kārtavīrya's arms were cut down like a forest of golden Palmyra-trees.

189cd–197ab Once, when Kārtavīrya was asked for food by hungry Citrabhānu (i.e. the fire), he gave him all the seven continents as alms, which were consequently burnt by Citrabhānu, including the empty hermitage of Varuṇa's son Vasiṣṭha Āpava. Because he had not protected Vasiṣṭha's hermitage, Kārtavīrya was cursed to be killed by the Bhārgava Rāma Jāmadagnya.

197cd–198ab (Slightly varied repetition of v. 173, here disturbing the connection between Vasiṣṭha's curse and its coming true.)

198cd–199ab Thus Kārtavīrya suffered death according to his wish.

199cd–202 He had 100 sons, of whom five were left: Śūrasena, Śūra, Vṛṣaṇa, Madhupadhvaja, and Jayadhvaja, the king of Avanti. Jayadhvaja → Tālajaṅgha → 100 sons, known as the Tālajaṅghas.

203–204 In the family of the Haihayas, the Vītihotras, the Sujātas (VePr Suvratas), the Bhojas, and the Āvantyas are well-known, as well as the Tauṇḍikeras, the Tālajaṅghas, the Bharatas, and the Sujātas, who are so numerous that they cannot be mentioned in detail.

205–207ab A family-line of Yādavas starts with Vṛṣa, whose son was Madhu. Madhu had 100 sons; among them Vṛṣaṇa was the maintainer of the family-line. The Vṛṣṇis originated from Vṛṣaṇa, the Mādhavas from Madhu; they are called Haihayas and Yādavas, after Yadu.

207cd–208ab Phalastuti concerning (the account of) Kārtavīrya's birth.

208cd–209 Conclusion to the five family-lines originating from the five sons of Yayāti.

210–212ab Phalastuti: The king who listens to the (account of the) five offspring (*visarga*) will be lord over five sons. He will obtain five boons: (long) life, fame, sons, rulership, and prosperity, by keeping in mind and listening to the (account of the) group of five.

212cd–213ab Announcement of Kroṣṭṛ's family-line, who continued Yadu's family-line.

213c-f Phalastuti concerning Kroṣṭṛ's line, in which Viṣṇu Hari was born, the descendant of Vṛṣṇi (or: of the Vṛṣṇis).

Ch. 14: The lunar dynasty (contd): Genealogy of Kṛṣṇa[1]

1–2ab Lomaharṣaṇa continues: Kroṣṭṛ[2] had two wives, Gāndhārī and Mādrī. Kroṣṭṛ + Gāndhārī → Anamitra; Kroṣṭṛ + Mādrī → Yudhājit and Devamīḍhuṣa.

[1] The colophon in VePr calls this chapter »Description of the birth of Kṛṣṇa«, which topic, however, is not mentioned at all.

[2] Son of Yadu, cf. 13.153cd–154ab

2cd The line of the Vṛṣṇis became threefold.[3]

3ab Mādrī had two sons: Vṛṣṇi and Andhaka.[4]

3cd Vṛṣṇi → Śvaphalka and Citraka.

4-11 *Branch of Śvaphalka*

4-7 Where Śvaphalka resided, there was no fear of drought. Once, when there was no rain for three years, the king of Kāśi called for Śvaphalka, whereupon Harivāhana (= Indra) sent rain. Śvaphalka married the king's daughter Gāndinī.

8-10 Śvaphalka + Gāndinī → Akrūra, Upamadgu, Madgu, Medura, Arimejaya, Avikṣita, Akṣepa, Śatrughna, Arimardana, Dharmadhṛk, Yatidharman, Dharmokṣan, Andhakaru, Āvāha, Prativāha, and a daughter named Sundarī.[5]

11 Akrūra + Ugrasenā → Prasena and Upadeva.

12-24ab *Branch of Citraka*

12-13 Citraka → Pṛthu, Vipṛthu, Aśvagrīva, Aśvabāhu, Svapārśvaka, Gaveṣaṇa, Ariṣṭanemi, Aśva, Sudharman, Dharmabhṛt, Subāhu, Bahubāhu, and two daughters: Śraviṣṭhā and Śravaṇā.

14ab Asiknī + (?)[6] Śūra and Devamīḍhuṣa.[7]

4cd-20ab (Śūra)[8] + Bhojyā → first Vasudeva, called Ānakadundubhi, because at his birth there was a heavenly sound of drums and kettle-drums as well as showers of flowers; then Devabhāga, Devaśravas, Anādhṛṣṭi, Kanavaka, Vatsavat, Gṛñjama, Śyāma, Śamīka, Gaṇḍūṣa, and five daughters: Pṛthukīrti, Pṛthā, Śrutadevā, Śrutaśravā, and Rājādhidevī. (VePr inserts: Śrutadevā + Āvatya.)

0cd-24ab Account of Bhojyā's daughters: (VePr inserts: Śrutadevā → Jagṛhu (?), descendant of Avata.[9]) Śrutaśravā → Śiśupāla, the king of Cedi, who had previously been Hiraṇyakaśipu, the king of the Daityas. Pṛthukīrti + Vṛddhaśarman → Dantavakra, king of the Karūṣas. Pṛthā was adopted as a daughter by Kunti; Pāṇḍu married her. She had three sons: Yudhiṣṭhira (from Dharma), Bhīmasena (from Vāta, the wind-god), and Dhanaṃjaya (= Arjuna) from Indra.

[3] Does this refer to the three sons of Kroṣṭṛ? It seems rather strange that they should be called Vṛṣṇi-family, if Kroṣṭṛ is understood as son of Yadu. Either the half-verse 2cd does not fit in here, or Kroṣṭṛ cannot be identical with the son of Yadu. Or should Kroṣṭṛ be replaced by another name, such as Vṛṣṇi?

[4] It is not clear who could have been the father of Vṛṣṇi and Andhaka. Should they be two further sons of Kroṣṭṛ? They are also mentioned together below, in 15.30-31, as sons of Sātvata and Kausalyā. In ch. 16, there is a repetition of v. 1-2ab (16.9-10ab) as well as of v. 3 (16.49cd-50ab), which seems to be corrupt, however.

[5] cf. below, 16.50-54.

[6] Citraka? Kroṣṭṛ, whose sons were mentioned above as Yudhājit and Devamīḍhuṣa? or Devamīḍhuṣa (cf. v.l. in HV: *devamīḍhuṣaḥ*)?

[7] HV reads nom. instead of acc.

[8] cf. Vasudeva »Śauri« in v. 28 below.

[9] Or is *āvatyaḥ* a misreading for *āvantyaḥ* »king of Avanti«, which seems probable from the parallels in the following verses (e.g. *caidya*, *karūṣādhipa*)?

24cd-25ab From Anamitra, the youngest son of Vṛṣṇi,[10] Śini was born; Śini → Satyaka → Yuyudhāna.[11]

25cd-34ab *Descendants of Bhojyā's sons*

25cd Devabhāga → Uddhava.
26ab Devaśravas was called the best of the learned.
26cd Anādhṛṣṭi → Aśmakya (VePr Anādhṛṣṭi + Aśmakī → a famous son.[12])
27ab Śrutadevā + Śatrughna.[13]
27cd-28ab Śrutadevā → Ekalavya, known as Naiṣādi, as he was brought up by the Niṣādas.
28c-f To Vatsavat (VePr Vatsāvat), who had no son, Vasudeva Śauri (i.e. descendant of Śūra, cf. v. 14 above) gave (his own) legal son (?) Kauśika.
29-31 To Gaṇḍūṣa, who had no son, Viṣvaksena (= Kṛṣṇa) gave (the following) sons: Cārudeṣṇa, Sudeṣṇa, Pañcāla, Kṛtalakṣaṇa,[14] who never returned without a fight (?), Rukmiṇī's younger son,[15] whom a thousand crows followed wherever he went, wishing to eat the *cārus* (?) slain by Cārudeṣṇa.
32ab Kanavaka → Tantrija and Tantripāla.
32cd Gṛñjima → Vīru and Aśvahanu.
33-34ab Śyāma → Śamīka,[16] who took the kingdom (?); though trying to beware of leading a life of enjoyment (or: of being a Bhoja?), he obtained consecration as king (*rājasūya*) (?); his son was Ajātaśatru.
34cd Announcement of Vasudeva's descendants.
35 Phalastuti, concerning the three branches of the Vṛṣṇis.[17]

36-57 *Descendants of Vasudeva*

36-38 Vasudeva had 14 wives: Rohiṇī, Madirādi, Vaiśākhī, Bhadrā, Sunāmnī, Sahadevā, Śāntidevā, Śrīdevī, Devarakṣitā, Vṛkadevī, Upadevī, Devakī, Sutanu, and Vaḍavā.
39-41 Vasudeva + Rohiṇī (daughter of Bāhlika and main wife of Vasudeva) → 8 sons: Rāma (Baladeva), Śaraṇa (VePr Śāraṇa), Śaṭha, Durdama, Śubhra, Piṇḍāraka and Uśīnara, and one daughter, Citrā, who is famous as Subhadrā.
42ab Vasudeva + Devakī → Śauri (= Kṛṣṇa ?).[18]

[10] But in v. 1 above he was mentioned as son of Kroṣṭṛ. Or are there two Anamitras? cf. also 16.9-11.

[11] The verse seems to be inserted here, in the context of the report on the offspring of Bhojyā's daughters and sons.

[12] Obviously without name, but the next half-verse may be corrupt.

[13] But cf. next half-verse.

[14] Name or epithet?

[15] Most probably referring to Cārudeṣṇa.

[16] He is named as brother of Śyāma and Vasudeva, in v. 19 above.

[17] Seems to fit in better after v. 2cd above, disturbing the context here.

[18] Should be read later, since it disturbs the connection of the preceding and following verses, which deal with Rohiṇī's children.

42cd Rāma (Baladeva) + Revatī → Niśaṭha.
43ab Subhadrā + Pṛthā's son (= Arjuna) → Abhimanyu.
43cd Akrūra[19] + the daughter of (the king of) Kāśi[20] → Satyaketu.[21]
44 Announcement of a short account of Vasudeva's sons from his seven (!) wives.
45-46ab Śāntidevā → Bhoja and Vijaya; Sunāmā → Vṛkadeva and Gada; Vṛkadevī → Agāvaha.
46cd The daughter of the Trigarta-king was Śiśirāyaṇi's wife.[22]
47ab She (or he?) was curious about his virility, but there was no semen.
47cd In the twelfth year, looking like black metal ...[23]
48-50ab Being falsely accused,[24] angry Gārgya approached a Ghoṣa-girl[25] for sexual intercourse; she was the Apsaras Gopālī in the disguise of a cowherdess; she conceived Gārgya's child, who, on the command of Śūlapāṇin (the »spear-handed one«, i.e. Śiva) was born from Garga's (? = Gārgya's) human wife.
50cd-56 Named Kālayavana, he became king; turning to the east,[26] stout like a lion, he was brought up in the house of the sonless Yavana-king; thus he became Kālayavana. Eager to fight, the king (i.e. Kālayavana)[27] asked Nārada (for an adequate enemy), who named the Vṛṣṇyandhaka-family. With an army he went to Mathurā, and sent a messenger to the Vṛṣṇyandhakas, who made Kṛṣṇa their leader; after taking counsel together, they decided to leave Mathurā and settled in Dvāravatī.[28]
57 Phalastuti, concerning the birth of Kṛṣṇa.[29]

Ch. 15: Genealogy of the Bhojas and the Kukuras

1-12ab Lomaharṣaṇa continues: Kroṣṭṛ → Vṛjinīvat → Svāhi → Uṣadgu → Citraratha → Śaśabindu → Pṛthuśravas → Antara → Suyajña → Uṣat (or: Uṣata) → Śineyu → Maruta → Kambalabarhiṣa → Rukmakavaca → Parajit → five sons: Rukmeṣu, Pṛthurukma, Jyāmagha, Pālita, and Hari.

[19] Son of Śvaphalka, cf. v. 8cd above.
[20] Or: a girl from Kāśi?
[21] But cf. v. 11 above.
[22] Is he identical with Gārgya?
[23] Sentence incomplete; should probably be read between v. 50ab and v. 50cd, as explanation of the first part of the name Kālayavana.
[24] Seems to refer to the story told in 196.1-4 below, where Gārgya is called a eunuch by a Yādava called Śyāla, cf. the reading of Ms. A *'bhiśasto gārgyaḥ śālena*.
[25] Wrong reading for *gopa*-girl? (cf. the parallel verse in HV 25.9.)
[26] v.l. »the upper part of his body being (like) that of a bull«; cf. also HV 25.11, where the whole line is to be understood differently, however.
[27] cf. 196.5-8, below.
[28] The whole passage from 46cd-56, which is obviously told in order to explain why Kṛṣṇa and the Vṛṣṇyandhakas settled in Dvāravatī, seems to have replaced the account of Kṛṣṇa's birth, which should be expected in this place; cf. next verse.
[29] This topic has not been mentioned, however.

12cd–13 Pālita and Hari were given to the Videhas by their father; Rukmeṣu became king, together with (or: supported by) Pṛthurukma, whereas Jyāmagha, driven away by these two, lived in a hermitage.

14–29 *Jyāmagha branch*

14–15 Invited by Brahmins, Jyāmagha went to another country, to (the city) Mṛttikāvatī on the bank of the Narmadā-river (VePr to Mekhalā[1]); after conquering the mountain Ṛkṣavat he settled in the city Śuktimatī.

16–21 Jyāmagha's wife was Śaibyā. Though they had no son, he did not marry another wife. Once, when he won a girl in a battle, he took her to his home, but, being afraid of his wife, introduced her as daughter-in-law, i.e. she should be wife to a future son. Due to the girl's asceticism, Śaibyā bore a son, Vidarbha, who was married to the girl and had two sons from her: Kratha and Kaiśika.

22–23 Vidarbha → Bhīma → Kunti → Dhṛṣṭa → three sons: Āvanta, Daśārha, and Viṣahara.

24–28 Daśārha → Vyoman → Jīmūta → Vikṛti → Bhīmaratha → Navaratha → Daśaratha → Śakuni → Karambha → Devarāta → Devakṣatra → Madhu + Vaidarbhī → Purudvat + Aikṣvākī → Satvat.

29 Phalastuti, concerning Jyāmagha's line.

30–31 Satvat (VePr Sātvata) + Kauśalyā → Bhajamāna, Devāvṛdha, Andhaka, and Vṛṣṇi.

32 Bhajamāna had two wives named Sṛñjayī : Bāhyakā and Upabāhyakā.

33 Bhajamāna + Sṛñjayī Bāhyakā → Krimi, Kramaṇa, Dhṛṣṭa, Śūra, and Puraṃjaya.[2]

34 Bhajamāna + Sṛñjayī Upabāhyakā → Āyutājit, Sahasrājit, Śatājit, and Dāsaka.

35–41ab Devāvṛdha practised extensive asceticism; touching the water of the river Parṇāśā, he wished firmly to have a son endowed with all qualities. Being continually touched by him, Parṇāśā started to love him, but did not know what to do (v.l.: and decided finally): »He will not approach any woman who could bear him a son like that; I myself shall be his wife.« She changed into a beautiful young girl, and chose him (as her husband); after ten months Babhru was born, endowed with all qualities.

41cd–45ab The Purāṇa-experts praise Devāvṛdha's (= Babhru's?) qualities: Babhru is the best of men, Devāvṛdha is equal to the gods. 66 and 1007 men have gained immortality from Babhru and Devāvṛdha.[3] His descendants are the Bhojas and the Artikāvatas.

45cd–46ab Andhaka[4] + daughter of Kāśya → four sons: Kukura, Bhajamāna, Sasaka, and Balabarhiṣa.

46cd–61 *Kukura branch*

46cd–48 Kukura → Vṛṣṭi → Kapotaroman → Tiliri (VePr Tittiri) → Vasu → Abhijit → Āhuka and Śrāhuka.

[1] City or river?

[2] Name or epithet?

[3] It is not clear, whether Devāvṛdha should be taken as patronym of Babhru.

[4] cf. v. 30–31 above.

49-50ab About Āhuka there is a traditional verse: He should walk ahead, clad in white. (?)
50cd-51ab He who walks near to a Bhoja[5] (or: He who sets out for (the country of) Bhoja) (?) will never be without sons etc.
51cd-53 Thousands of archers, chariots etc. of Bhoja went into the eastern region of the Nāgas, and as many into the northern region. (?)[6]
54 The Bhojas are rulers of the whole earth; the Andhakas gave their sister to the people of Avanti (?).[7]
55 Āhuka + Kāśyā (or: a girl from Kāśi?) → Devaka and Ugrasena.
56-58ab Devaka → 4 sons, equal to the gods: Devavat, Upadeva, Saṃdeva, and Devarakṣita, and seven daughters, whom he gave to Vasudeva: Devakī, Śāntidevā, Sudevā, Devarakṣitā, Vṛkadevī, Upadevī, and Sunāmnī.[8]
58cd-59 Ugrasena → nine sons, the eldest being Kaṃsa, further Nyagrodha, Sunāman, Kaṅka, Subhāṣaṇa, Rāṣṭrapāla, Sutanu, Anāvṛṣṭi, and Puṣṭimat; their sisters were: Kaṃsā, Kaṃsavatī, Sutanū (or: Sutanu?), Rāṣṭrapālī, and Kaṅkā.
60ab The line of Ugrasena and his descendants is well-known as Kukuras.
60cd-61 Phalastuti concerning the line of the Kukuras.

Ch. 16: Genealogy of Vṛṣṇyandhakas; story of the Syamantaka-jewel

1-8 *Descendants of Bhajamāna*[1]

1-3 Lomaharṣaṇa continues: Bhajamāna → Vidūratha → Rājādhideva → 8 sons: Datta, Atidatta, Śoṇaśva, Śamin, Daṇḍaśarman, Dantaśatru, Śatrujit; and 2 daughters: Śravaṇā, Śraviṣṭhā.
4-6 Śamin → Pratikṣatra (VePr Praticchatra) Svayaṃbhoja → Bhadika (VePr Hṛdīka) → 10 sons: Kṛtavarman, Śatadhanvan, Devānta, Narānta, Bhiṣak, Vaitaraṇa, Sudānta, Atidānta, Nikāśya, Kāmadambhaka.
7 Devānta → Kambalabarhiṣa → 2 sons: Asamaujas, Nāsamaujas.
8 (He - who?) gave 3 sons to sonless Asamaujas: Sudaṃṣṭra, Sucāru, Kṛṣṇa, who were called Andhakas.

9-11 *Descendants of Kroṣṭṛ*

9-11 Kroṣṭṛ + 1. Gāndhārī → Anamitra; Kroṣṭṛ + 2. Mādrī → 2 sons: Yudhājit, Devamīduṣa; Anamitra → 4 sons: Nighna, Nighnata, Prasena, Satrājit.[2]

[5] Bhoja seems to be the name of a clan, cf. ch. 17.1, where Śatadhanvan is introduced as a Bhoja.
[6] The connection of this passage is not clear. Does it refer to the son of Vasudeva and Śāntideva, named Bhoja (cf. 14.45ab)?
[7] This verse should perhaps be read after v. 203 of ch. 13, or after v. 45ab above. The whole passage 49-54 seems to be rather confused.
[8] cf. 14.36-38.
[1] They are now different from those mentioned in ch. 15.32-34.
[2] cf. above, 14.1-2.

12–45ab *Story of the Syamantaka-jewel (part 1)*

12 (Introduction:) Prasena, who obtained the Syamantaka jewel from the sun, lived in Dvāravatī.

13–24 Satrājit was a friend of the sun-god. Once he went to touch water at sunrise and to pay homage to the sun, but could only see his friend as a brilliant circle, when standing before him. He wondered whether he, as the sun's friend, should not (be granted) a special (favour) (or: he asked Vivasvat, what difference should be between both of them). Vivasvat took the Syamantaka jewel from his neck, whereupon his body became visible. Now Satrājit asked him for the jewel, and received it from the sun-god. As he went home he was regarded as the sun himself by the people. At home he gave the jewel to his brother Prasenajit (= Prasena); it effected prosperity and welfare in the house of the Vṛṣṇyandhakas.

25–45ab Govinda (Kṛṣṇa) wanted to have the jewel, but, though capable of taking it, did not do so. One day, when Prasena went hunting, he was killed by a lion because of the jewel. After that the lion himself was killed by a bear who took the jewel to his cave. Meanwhile the Vṛṣṇyandhakas suspected Kṛṣṇa of having slain Prasena because of the jewel. Kṛṣṇa promised to search for the jewel. He followed Prasena's footprints and found his dead body, but not the jewel. Looking around, he saw the lion that had been killed by the bear, and followed the footprints of the bear. When he reached the cave, he heard the voice of the bear child crying and the voice of his nurse calming the child and telling about the jewel. Kṛṣṇa, leaving his brother and his attendants outside, entered the cave and struggled with the bear, named Jāmbavat, for 21 days. Baladeva, believing his brother killed, returned home, but Kṛṣṇa overpowered the bear, got his daughter Jāmbavatī and the jewel, which he took home, to demonstrate his blamelessness, and gave it back to Satrājit.

45cd–49ab *Descendants of Satrājit*

45cd–48ab Satrājit + 10 wives → 100 children, among them 3 sons: Bhaṅgakāra, Vātapati and Vasumedha, and 3 daughters: Satyabhāmā, Vratinī, and Prasvāpinī, who was married to Kṛṣṇa.

48cd–49ab Bhaṅgakāra[3] → Sabhākṣa, Nāveya.

49cd–58ab *Descendants of Vṛṣṇi*[4]

49cd Mādrī → Yudhājit → Vṛṣṇi.[5]

50ab Vṛṣṇi → 2 sons: Śvaphalka, Citraka.[6]

50cd–54ab Śvaphalka + Gāndinī (daughter of the king of Kāśi) → Śrutavat (Atithipriya) → 14 sons: Akrūra, Upamadgu, Madgu, Mudara, Arimardana, Ārikṣepa, Upekṣa, Śatruhan, Arimejaya, Dharmabhṛt, Dharman, Gṛdhrabhojāndhaka, Āvāha, Prativāha, and 1 daughter, Sundarī.[7]

[3] Bhaṅgakāra, corr. for Bhagaṃkāra.
[4] cf. above ch. 14.2–13.
[5] Or: Mādrī → Vṛṣṇi → Yudhājita.
[6] cf. above ch. 14.3cd.

cd-55ab His daughter was Vasuṃdharā, wife of Viśrutāśva.[8]

cd-56ab Akrūra + Ugrasenā → 2 sons: Vasudeva, Upadeva.[9]

cd-58ab Citraka → 11 sons: Pṛthu, Vipṛthu, Aśvagrīva, Aśvabāhu, Supārśvaka, Gaveṣaṇa, Ariṣṭanemi, Dharma, Dharmabhṛt, Subāhu, Bahubāhu, and 2 daughters: Śraviṣṭhā, Śravaṇā.[10]

58cd-59 (Conclusion:) Phalastuti, concerning the story of Kṛṣṇa's false accusation.

Ch. 17: Story of the Syamantaka-jewel (part 2)

1 After Kṛṣṇa had given the jewel to Satrājit, Babhru (= Akrūra) ordered the Bhoja Śatadhanvan to take it (for him).

2 Akrūra (= Babhru) had already asked Satyabhāmā (Satrājit's daughter) for the jewel (but in vain).

3-5 Śatadhanvan slew Satrājit, took the jewel and gave it to Akrūra, who ordered him to keep silent about this transaction, and promised him to help him in fighting, if attacked by Kṛṣṇa.

6-7 Satyabhāmā, full of grief because of her father's death, went to the city of Vāraṇāvat and told her husband (i.e. Kṛṣṇa ?) about Śatadhanvan's deed.

8-11 Kṛṣṇa had performed the death-rites for the Pāṇḍavas[1] and had given their family heritage to Sātyaki. Returning to Dvarakā, he decided to obtain the jewel from Śatadhanvan, since the (lawful) owners, Prasena and Satrājit, were now dead, and told his brother (Rāma Baladeva) to accompany him.

12-16 A battle between Kṛṣṇa and the Bhoja Śatadhanvan ensued. Attacked by Kṛṣṇa, the Bhoja looked for Akrūra's help, but Akrūra, due to a curse (?), did not interfere, though capable of helping. The Bhoja tried to flee, but his horse Hṛdayā was exhausted after running 100 Yojanas, so that Kṛṣṇa could pursue and attack him.[2]

17-23 With his enemy's horse dead, Kṛṣṇa dismounted also, ordering his brother (Baladeva) to keep his horse. Near Mithilā Kṛṣṇa slew his enemy, but could not find the jewel. After returning, he was asked for it by Baladeva who did not believe Kṛṣṇa that the jewel was not with him; he grew angry and left Kṛṣṇa, entering Mithilā.

24-27 At that time Babhru (son of Gāndī) (= Akrūra) performed many sacrifices, spending great riches, because of the Syamantaka jewel; they were called Akrūra-yajñas.

[7] cf. above ch. 14.7-10; there is no corresponding name for Śrutavat (Atithipriya), Mudara corresponds to Medura, Ārikṣepa to Avikṣita, Upekṣa to Akṣepa, Śatruhan to Śatrughna, Dharmabhṛt to Dharmadhṛk, Dharman to Yatidharman, Gṛdhrabhojāndhaka to Dharmokṣakaru.

[8] No correspondence in ch. 14; connection not clear, but perhaps Sundarī (54ab) is epithet to Vasuṃdharā?

[9] cf. above ch.12(14).11; Vasudeva there corresponds to Prasena here.

[10] cf. above ch.14(12).12-13; Dharma corresponds to Sudharman.

[1] Reference to the chronological frame of the MBh?

[2] *śatadhanvānam ārdayat/ardayat*, or: *śatadhanvān amardayat*?

28 Duryodhana[3] went to Mithilā, in order to learn fighting with clubs from Baladeva.

29-31 By the heroes of the Vṛṣṇyandhakas, Baladeva was led towards Dvārakā; Akrūra also went there, together with the Andhakas, out of fear of a split among the relatives, since he had killed Satrājit and his associates in sleep. Kṛṣṇa, however, observed him.

32-34 After Akrūra had left the land, there was no rain. Being entreated by the Kukura-Andhakas, he returned, and Indra sent rain (to the border of the ocean).

34 Akrūra gave his sister (Sundarī) to Vāsudeva (Kṛṣṇa) in marriage.

35-40 Coming to know by Yoga (or: by connecting (his observations), i.e. by inference) that the jewel was with Babhru (Akrūra), Kṛṣṇa entered the assembly and asked him to give him the jewel, in order to be cleared from all suspicion. Babhru did so, and Kṛṣṇa gave it back to him, who put it on and shone like the sun.

Ch. 18: Description of Jambūdvīpa[1]

1-6 The hermits confirm the conclusion of the stories about the creation of various beings and about their deeds.

7-9 They ask Lomaharṣaṇa to inform them about the extent of the earth.

10 Lomaharṣaṇa announces a summary of the subject since it would take more than a hundred years to give the details also.

[3] Reference to the chronological frame of the MBh?

[1] We translate *varṣa* by »region«, *dvīpa* by »continent«, when it refers to the seven-*dvīpa*-theory, and by subcontinent, when it refers to the four-*dvīpa*-theory, since in the latter theory the four *dvīpa*s, being arranged around Mt. Meru, are not independent »islands« or »continents«. For a description of the regions of Jambudvīpa cf. also MBh (Cr.Ed.) 6,7-9. Verses 11-31 are summarized in the introduction to »Das Purāṇa vom Weltgebäude« by W. Kirfel, who does not trace the different views or ideas that are the constituent elements of the cosmography of this chapter. They are discussed to some extent by Lüders in Varuṇa I, pp. 94ff. (about the surrounding oceans), 156ff. (about the heavenly Gaṅgā), 276ff. (about the four rivers, with quotations from Purāṇas) and 288ff. (about the rivers and the *dvīpa*-theory). Lüders comes to the conclusion that there must have been two different theories, one of the 7 continents, the innermost one, Jambūdvīpa, being divided into 7 regions; and one of the 4 *dvīpa*s around Meru, the southern *dvīpa* being Jambūdvīpa, which is also called Bhāratavarṣa. The first theory is regarded as epical by him (except for MBh 6,7.10cd-11), the second one as purāṇic. For the relationship between epic and purāṇic cosmographical accounts, cf. also L. Hilgenberg, »Die kosmographische Episode im MBh und PdP«, Bonn 1934, who considers the MBh-passage to be based on a corresponding passage in the PdP, and S. K. Belvalkar, »The cosmographical episode in MBh and PdP«, who establishes the MBh as the primary source. In the following chapter both theories are represented, the 7-*dvīpa*-theory or 7-*varṣa*-theory constituting a frame (v. 11-21 and 62c-f) around the passages containing the 4-*dvīpa*-theory which is combined with the idea (or metaphor) of the earth-lotus. But even by ascribing the passages of the chapter to one of these theories the difficulties are not settled. For instance, there is no allusion to 4 subcontinents except for the excursus on the name Jambūdvīpa which is connected with the »emblem« (*ketu*) of the southern Viṣkambha-mountain (v. 24cd-25ab).

11-62ef *Divisions of the earth*[2]

11-12 List of 7 continents (*dvīpa*): Jambūdvīpa, Plakṣadvīpa, Śālmaladvīpa, Kuśadvīpa, Krauñcadvīpa, Śākadvīpa, Puṣkaradvīpa,[3] surrounded by 7 oceans of salt, sugar-cane (juice), liquor, butter, curds, milk and water.

13-15 In the centre of Jambūdvīpa there is the golden mountain Meru, 84,000 Yojanas high, 16 (thousand) Yojanas deep below the earth, 32 (thousand) Yojanas above, and at the foot 16,000 Yojanas wide; that mountain is the »pericarp« of the »earth-lotus«.[4]

16-17 The mountain ranges south of Meru are Himavat, Hemakūṭa, and Niṣadha; north of Meru there are Nīla, Śveta and Śṛṅgin. The two in the middle are 100,000 (Yojanas) in measure, the others are 10^5 less (than the previous two); their height as well as their width is 2000 (Yojanas).

18-20 The regions (*varṣa*) are: Bhārata, Kiṃpuruṣa, Harivarṣa (south of Meru), Ramyaka, Hiraṇmaya, Uttarakurū (north of Meru), their extent being 9000. The middle region is Ilāvṛta, where the golden Meru is situated.[6]

[2] Short outline of ch. 18:
11: 7 continents (concentric)
12: 7 oceans (concentric)
13-15: Jambūdvīpa and Meru (central)
16-17: 6 mountain-ranges (linear)
18-19: 6 regions (linear)
20-21: Ilāvṛta and Meru (central)
22: 4 »support-mountains« (*viṣkambaparvata*) (peripheral)
23-24ab: 4 Ketu (peripheral)
24cd-28: excursus on Jambū, Jambūdvīpa, Jambūnadī
29: Ketumāla, Ilāvṛta, Bhadrāśva (linear)
30: 4 groves
31: 4 lakes (peripheral)
32-36ab: 4 times 5 »filament-mountains« (*kesarācala*) (peripheral)
36cd-38ab: Brahman's city (central)
38cd-39ab: Gaṅgā (central)
39cd-44ab: 4 rivers (peripheral)
44cd-45ab: 4 mountains around Meru (peripheral)
45cd-46ab: 4 lotus-leaves (peripheral)
46cd-51: 4 times 2 border-mountains (peripheral)
52-56: Description of the valleys
57-59: Viṣṇu in the four and seven (eight) regions (i.e. »lotus-leaves«).
60-62ab: Continuation of the description of valleys.
62c-f: The mountain-ranges in the 7 regions.

[3] cf. MBh 6,12.2-3: Jambūdvīpa, Śākadvīpa, Kuśadvīpa, Śālmali, Krauñcadvīpa, i.e. only five.

[4] cf. MBh 6,7.9.

[5] Obviously 10 thousands (of Yojanas) are to be understood; cf. Kirfel, Kosmographie, p. 58.

[6] Seven-*varṣa*-theory. cf. MBh 6,7.6: Bhārata, Haimavata, Harivarṣa south of Meru; 35-36: Hairaṇyaka, Airāvata north of Meru, Ilāvṛta in the midst, and two regions in two arcs, i.e. 8 in total (cf. 59 below); MBh 6,8.2: Uttarakuru between Meru and Nīla; MBh 6,9.2: Ramaṇaka between Śveta and Niṣadha; MBh 6,9.5: Hiraṇmaya/Hiraṇmat between Nīla and Niṣadha; MBh 6,9.10cd-11ab: Airāvata in the utmost north.

21-23ab On the four sides of Meru extends Ilāvṛta for 9000, and there are 4 mountains; they support Meru, being 10,000 Yojanas wide: Mandara (east), Gandhamādana (south), Vipula (west), Supārśva (north).[7]

23cd-24ab Each of them has a tree of 111 (Yojanas) as their emblem: Kadamba-tree, rose-apple-tree (Jambū-tree), sacred fig-tree (Pippala-tree), and Banyan-tree (Vaṭa-tree).

24cd-28 The rose-apple-tree provides the name for Jambūdvīpa. Its fruits are as big as elephants, and their juice can be drunk from the river Jambūnadī. Those who drink her water, are free from pain (v.l. sweat), bad smell, old age and decay of senses. The earth of the river banks, drenched with this juice and afterwards dried by pleasant winds, is a kind of gold called Jāmbūnada.

29 Ilāvṛta is situated between Bhadrāśva (east of Meru) and Ketumāla (west of Meru).

30 There are four groves around Meru: Caitraratha (east), Gandhamādana (south), Vaibhrāja (west), Nandana (north).

31 There are four lakes: Aruṇoda, Mahābhadra, Asitoda, Mānasa.

32-36ab In each direction there are five »filament mountains« (*kesarācala*): Śāntavat, Cakrakuñja (VePr. Cakrakumbha), Kurarī, Mālyavat, headed by Vaikaṅka, in the east; Trikūṭa, Śiśira, Pataṅga, Rucaka, Niṣadha in the south; Śikhivāsa, Savaidūrya,[8] Kapila, Gandhamādana, headed by Jānudhi[9] in the west. These, Jaṭhara etc., are close to Meru.[10] Śaṅkhakūṭa, Ṛṣabha, Haṃsa, Nāga, headed by Kālañjara, in the north.

36cd-38ab On the top of Meru is Brahman's city, measuring 14,000 Yojanas, around which the residences of the world-guardians are located in the different directions.

38cd-44ab Brought forth by Viṣṇu's foot, flooding the moon, Gaṅgā falls down to Brahman's city. There she divides into four rivers, flowing into four directions: Sītā joins the ocean after crossing the eastern region Bhadrāśva; Alakanandā flows to the south to Bhāratavarṣa and joins the ocean, divided in seven arms; Cakṣus, after crossing the mountains, flows through the western region named Ketumāla; Bhadrā crosses the northern mountains and joins the ocean after flowing through Uttara(kuru).

44cd-45ab Between Nīla and Niṣadha, there are Mālyavat and Gandhamādana; between them Meru is situated in the shape of a pericarp.[11]

Table of names according to the seven-*dvīpa*- and seven-*varṣa*-theory (v. 11-20):

Lists of names:

7 Dvīpas:	7 Oceans:	7 varṣas:	7 mt. ranges:
Jambū	Salila	Bhārata	Himavat
Plakṣa	Ikṣoda	Kiṃpuruṣa	Hemakūṭa
Śālmala	Surā	Harivarṣa	Niṣadha
Kuśa	Sarpis	Ilāvṛta	Meru
Krauñca	Dadhi	Ramyaka	Nīla
Śāka	Kṣīra	Hiraṇmaya	Śveta
Puṣkara	Jala	Uttarakuru	Śṛṅgin

[7] Four-*dvīpa*-theory?

[8] Epithet?

[9] Jārudhi corr. for Jānudhi, cf. v. 50 below.

[10] Jaṭhara has not been named until now; the name, however, occurs again in v. 46cd-47ab, below.

[11] Duplicate of v. 21cd-23ab above? 44cd cf. with MBh 6,7.7. Four-*dvīpa*-theory and lotus-metaphor.

45cd–46ab Outside of the border mountains (*maryādāśaila*) there are four (lotus) leaves: Bhārata, Ketumāla, Bhadrāśva, Kuru (= Uttarakuru).

46cd–50 Extending north and south towards Nīla and Niṣadha the border mountains are Jaṭhara and Devakūṭa. East and west (of Meru) are Gandhamādana (mountain or forest) and Kailāsa measuring 80 Yojanas and situated in the ocean; from south to north are Niṣadha and Pāriyātra, directed towards Nīla and Niṣadha;[12] as in the western direction of Meru in the same way there are two (border mountains) situated in the east. Extending east and west Triśṛṅga and Jārudhi are mountains of the northern region situated in the ocean.[13]

51 These are the border mountains, two in each of the four directions, near to Meru.[14]

52–55 Between these filament mountains are the valleys Śītānta etc., frequented by Siddhas. There are most charming groves of the gods like Lakṣmī, Viṣṇu, Agni, Sūrya, and Indra, as well as resting-places used by men and Kiṃnaras; Gandharvas, Yakṣas, Rākṣasas, Daityas and Dānavas, who are playing there night and day.

[12] v. 49ab = 47ab.

[13] v. 50d = 48d.
Table according to directions (v. 21–50):

east	south	west	north
viṣkambaparvata:			
Mandara	Gandhamādana	Vipula	Supārśva
Emblems:			
Kadamba	Jambū	Pippala	Vaṭa
Subcontinents (*dvīpa*):			
Bhadrāśva	Jambūdvīpa	Ketumāla	Uttarakuru
Groves:			
Caitraratha	Gandhamādana	Vaibhrāja	Nandana
Lakes:			
Aruṇoda	Mahābhadra	Asitoda	Mānasa
Rivers:			
Śītā	Alakanandā	Cakṣus	Bhadrā
»Filament-mountains« (*kesarācala*):			
Śāntavat	Trikūṭa	Śikhivāsa	Śaṅkhakūṭa
Cakrakuñja	Śiśira	Savaidūrya	Ṛṣabha
Kurāri	Pataṅga	Kapila	Haṃsa
Mālyavat	Rucaka	Gandhamādhana	Nāga
Vaikaṅka	Niṣadha	Jārudhi	Kālañjara
Mountains around Meru:			
Mālyavat	Niṣadha	Gandhamādana	Nīla
»Lotus-leaves«: (seem to be identical with the *dvīpas*)			
Bhadrāśva	Bhārata	Ketumāla	Kurava
Border-mountains:			
Jaṭhara	Gandhamādana	Niṣadha	Triśṛṅga
Devakūṭa	Kailāsa	Pāriyātra	Jārudhi

[14] The concept of »border mountains« remains unclear and difficult to reconcile with the rest of the text.

56 These are the heavens called »earthly« (*bhauma*), the abode of the good where no sinner is allowed to go even in hundreds of births.

57-58 Viṣṇu inhabits Bhadrāśva in the shape of Hayaśiras, Ketumāla in the shape of Vārāha (boar), Bhārata in the shape of Kūrma (tortoise), and (Uttara-)Kuru in the shape of Matsya (fish); in the shape of Viśvarūpa he is found everywhere - Hari who is all and the lord of all.

59 As support of all and identical with all he inhabits the eight (!) regions, Kiṃpuruṣa etc.[15]

60-62ab There is no grief nor weariness, no trembling nor fear of hunger etc.; the beings are free from doubts and all mischiefs living 120,000 years; and no other earthly (things?) are in them, nor hunger and thirst etc. In those places there is no Kṛta-, Tretā-Yuga etc.

62c-f In each of the seven regions there are seven chief mountain ranges (*kulācala*) and rivers that rise from them by hundreds.

Ch. 19: Description of Bhāratavarṣa[1]

1 Lomaharṣaṇa continues: The Bhārata-region (i.e. India) is situated north of the ocean and south of the snow-mountain (i.e. Himālaya).

2 It extends 9000 Yojanas and is the »place for deeds« (*karmabhūmi*) for those who desire heaven or liberation.

3 List of seven chief mountain ranges: Mahendra, Malaya, Sahya, Śuktimat, Ṛkṣa, Vindhya, Pāriyātra.[2]

4 From there (i.e. Bhārata?) one reaches heaven or liberation, or (rebirth as) an animal, or hell.

5 From there heaven and liberation - and to the middle one goes at the end.[3] There is no other place for (meritorious) deeds.[4]

6ab Announcement of the 9 divisions of Bhārata.[5]

6cd-7ab List of the 9 divisions: Indradvīpa, Kasetumat (VePr Kaserumat), Tāmraparṇa, Gabhastimat, Nāgadvīpa, Saumya, Gandharva, Vāruṇa.

[15] Are v. 57-59 a Viṣṇuitic interpolation? v. 57-58 use the four-*dvīpa*-theory, v. 59 the seven-*varṣa*-theory.

[1] The text of this chapter has been collated with parallel purāṇic passages and translated in W. Kirfel: Bhāratavarṣa (Indien). Textgeschichtliche Darstellung zweier geographischer Purāṇa-Texte nebst Übersetzung. Stuttgart 1931. For a description of Bhāratavarṣa cf. also MBh (Cr.Ed.) 6,10.

[2] cf. MBh 6,10.10, where Ṛkṣavat corresponds to Ṛkṣa.

[3] i.e. death? The sentence is asyntactic.

[4] Bharatavarṣa as place for deeds is discussed again in a later chapter (27), where a further, partly parallel, partly more detailed, description of Bharatavarṣa is given (27.14 ff.); for the comparison of both texts see Kirfel, Bharatavarṣa, p. 18 ff.

[5] Note the imperative in the singular.

7cd-8ab This one,[6] the ninth of them, is an island, surrounded by the ocean, extending 1000 Yojanas from south to north.

8cd In the east of it live the Kirātas, in the west the Yavanas.

9 (The four castes), Brahmins, Kṣatriyas, Vaiśyas and Śūdras live in it, distinguished by their professions, viz. sacrifice, fighting, trade etc.[7]

10 List of rivers:[8] Śatadru, Candrabhāgā etc. originate from the foot of Himavat (Himālaya).[9] Vedasmṛti etc. originate on the Pāriyātra.

11-12ab Narmadā, Suramā (VePr Surasā) etc. originate on the Vindhya-mountains; Tāpī, Payoṣṇī, Nirvindhyā, Kāverī etc. originate at the foot of Ṛkṣa. They take away evil.

12cd-13ab Godāvarī, Bhīmarathī, Kṛṣṇaveṇī etc. originate from Sahya, they take away evil and fear (or: fear of evil).

13cd Kṛtamālā, Tāmraparṇī etc. originate on the Malaya.

14 Trisāṃdhyā, Ṛṣikulyā etc. originate from the Mahendra. Ṛṣikulyā, Kumāra etc. originate on Śuktimat.

15ab There are other rivers and streams by the thousand.

15cd-19 *List of peoples of Bhāratavarṣa*

15cd On the banks of these rivers live Kurus, Pañcālas, Madhyadeśas (or: the inhabitants of the middle region);

16 and those living in the eastern region inhabiting Kāmarūpa; the Pauṇḍras, Kaliṅgas, Magadhas inhabiting the whole south;

17 and westerners (*āparāntya*) are the Saurāṣṭras, the Śūdras, Ābhīras, Arbudās; Mārukas and Mālavas inhabiting the Pāriyātra-mountain.[10]

18 Sauvīras have obtained Saindhava (?),[11] Śālvas, inhabitants of Śākala, Madras, Rāmas, Ambaṣṭhas, Pārasīkas etc.

19 These happy and thriving people drink the water of these rivers and live near them.

20 In Bhārata there are (four) Yugas which do not exist anywhere else: Kṛta, Tretā, Dvāpara and Kali.[12]

[6] i.e. the ninth division is not given a name.

[7] Other texts insert a list of mountains; cf. Kirfel, Bhāratavarṣa p. 22, and ch. 27 v. 29cd-24ab below.

[8] A more detailed list of rivers is found in ch. 27, v. 26-39, below.

[9] For identifications of these names cf. Kirfel, Bhāratavarṣa p. 27ff.

[10] »Āparāntyas« could be a proper name; cf. Kirfel, Bhāratavarṣa p. 44 and BrP 27.44f. with p. 48 and BrP 27.59.

[11] Other texts take Saindhava as proper name and insert the Hūṇas which provides a clue for chronology. cf. Kirfel, Bhāratavarṣa p. 7: »An und für sich würde nämlich die nicht einheitlich bezeugte Erwähnung der Hūṇa's in Śl. 15 dazu berechtigen, für denselben das Ende des 5. nachchristlichen Jahrhunderts als 'terminus a quo' anzusetzen, natürlich unter der Voraussetzung, daß der Text ein einheitliches Ganzes bildet. Unsere Ausführungen dürften aber gezeigt haben, daß sich dieser Schluß nur auf einen sekundären Bestandteil, eine spätere Interpolation, gründen und mithin auch nur für diese letztere zutreffen würde. Für den eigentlichen Kern unseres Textes kann diese chronologische Annahme also nicht in Frage kommen, da er offenbar einer älteren Zeit angehört.«

[12] Kirfel's text and translation end here. For the last verse cf. MBh 6,11.3 where *puṣyam* corresponds to Kali.

21 It is the place for asceticism, sacrifices and alms performed for the sake of the world beyond.

22 In Jambūdvīpa Viṣṇu as the personified sacrifice (*yajñapuruṣa*), consisting of sacrifice, is constantly worshipped with sacrifices by men.

23 Within Jambūdvīpa Bhārata is best because it is the only place for actions while other places are for the enjoyment (of the consequences of deeds).

24 After accumulating religious merit for thousands of existences a living being is born as a human being.[13]

25-27 Gods praise those as happy who are born (reborn) in Bhārata as men, the place where heaven and liberation can be effected.[14] Those who renounce the fruits of works in Viṣṇu reach this place of works and finally merge with him (i.e. Viṣṇu, the highest self). »We know that those human beings who are bereft of their senses by Bhārata (*bharatena*, or: not bereft of their senses in Bhārata, *bharate na*) will certainly not obtain bondage to another body if (or: after) deed(s) which bestow heaven have vanished.«[15]

28 Conclusion to the description of Jambūdvīpa.

29 Jambūdvīpa is surrounded by an ocean of milk (v.l. salt-water) extending 100,000 Yojanas.

Ch. 20: Description of the six outer continents[1]

1-2 Jambūdvīpa is surrounded by the ocean of salt-water which is surrounded by Plakṣadvīpa; the extent of Jambudvīpa is 100,000 Yojanas; Plakṣadvīpa extends twice as far (200,000 Yojanas).

3-21 *Description of Plakṣadvīpa (Fig-tree-continent)*

3-5 Medhātithi is the ruler of Plakṣadvīpa. His 7 sons are Śāntabhaya, Śiśira, Sukhodaya, Ānanda, Śiva, Kṣemaka, Dhruva, who rule the 7 regions bearing their names.

6-7 7 border-mountains: Gomeda, Candra, Nārada, Dundubhi,[2] Somaka, Sumanas, Vaibhrāja.

8-9 The inhabitants live together with gods and Gandharvas, without disease or death.

10-11 Announcement of list of rivers (with phalastuti for those who listen to their names): Anutaptā, Śikhā (VePr Śikhī), Viprāsā (VePr Vipāśā), Tridivā, Kramu, Amṛtā, Sukṛtā.

[13] The passage v. 20-24 contains addresses in the singular, inappropriate in the dialogical context of the BrP.

[14] cf. verses 2, 4 and 5.

[15] Translation questionable; the word *kuvayam* has not been translated; it is marked by a question-mark in both editions. v. 25-26 in Upajāti-metre, v. 27 in Indravajrā-metre.

[1] cf. Kirfel, Kosmographie, pp. 110-127; for a collated text of this chapter cf. Kirfel, Weltgebäude, pp. 21-36.

[2] Corrected for Dandubhi in the text.

12-13 These are the mountains and rivers; there are thousands of smaller ones, from which the inhabitants drink water.

14-15 There are no Yugas in Plakṣadvīpa; people live 5000 years without disease.

16-17 The four castes (*varṇa*) are: Āryakas, Kurus, Viviśvas and Bhāvins.

18 In the midst of it there is a fig-tree, hence the name Plakṣadvīpa.

19 In Plakṣadvīpa Hari (= Viṣṇu) is worshipped in the shape of Soma (moon).

20 Plakṣadvīpa is surrounded by the ocean of sugarcane juice.

21 Conclusion to the description of Plakṣadvīpa, announcement of that of Śālmala.

22-34 *Description of Śālmaladvīpa (continent of the Silk-cotton tree)*[3]

22-23 Vapuṣmat is ruler of Śālmala; his sons are Śveta, Harita, Jīmūta, Rohita, Vaidyuta, Mānasa, Suprabha, who rule the 7 regions bearing their names.

24 The ocean of sugarcane juice is surrounded by Śālmaladvīpa extending twice as far (i.e. 400,000 Yojanas).[4]

25-27 7 mountains: Kumuda, Unnata, Balāhaka, Droṇa, Kaṅka, Mahiṣa, Kakudmat.

28 7 rivers: Śroṇi, Toyā, Vitṛṣṇā, Candrā (VePr Cakrā), Vimocanī, Nivṛtti.

29-30 The 7 regions are Śveta, Lohita, Jīmūta, Harita, Vaidyuta, Mānasa, Suprabha, inhabited by four castes.[5]

31 The four castes are: Kapilas, Aruṇas, Pītas , Kṛṣṇas (i.e. light brown, reddish, yellow, and black).

32 Viṣṇu is worshipped by sacrifices in the shape of Vāyu (wind).

33 The gods are present there; a large silk-cotton tree is the reason for the name of the continent.[6]

34 It is surrounded by the liquor ocean having the same extent.

35-45 *Description of Kuśadvīpa (continent of Kuśa-grass)*

35 The liquor ocean is surrounded by Kuśadvīpa, which is twice the size of Śālmala (800,000 Yojanas).

36-38ab Kuśadvīpa belongs to Jyotiṣmat; his sons are Udbhida, Veṇumat, Svairatha, Randhana, Dhṛti, Prabhākara, Kapila.[7] The regions bearing their names are inhabited by Daityas and Dānavas, gods and Gandharvas, Yakṣas, Kiṃpuruṣas etc. together with men.

38cd-40ab The 4 castes are named Damins, Śuṣmins, Snehas, and Māndahas (v.l. Mandehas).[8]

40cd-41ab In Kuśadvīpa they worship Janārdana in the form of Brahman.[9]

[3] This continent seems to be a »colour-continent« since many of the names occurring indicate a colour.

[4] v. 24 should be read before 22; cf. the similar order in v. 1-3 above.

[5] cf. 22-23, above.

[6] cf. MBh 6,13.6cd.

[7] cf. MBh 6,13.12-14: Audbhida, Veṇumaṇḍala, Rathākāra (v.l. Dvairathākāra), Pālana, Dhṛtimat, Prabhākara, Kāpila.

[8] v. 40ab seems corrupt; read *svādhikāra + rakṣāya* for *svādhikāra + kṣayāya*?

[9] v. 41ab unclear.

41cd–42 The 7 mountains are Vidruma, Hemaśaila, Dyutimat, Puṣṭimat, Kuśeśaya, Hari, Mandara.[10]

43–44 The rivers are Dhūtapāpā, Śivā, Pavitrā, Saṃmati, Vidyut, Ambhas, Mahī, who take away all evil, and thousands of smaller ones.

45 Kuśadvīpa is named after a bundle of Kuśa-grass; it is surrounded by an ocean of clarified butter of the same extent.[11]

46–58ab *Description of Krauñcadvīpa (Crane-continent)*

46–47ab The butter ocean is surrounded by Krauñcadvīpa of twice the extent (i.e. 1,600,000 Yojanas).

47cd–49ab In Krauñcadvīpa live Dyutimat's sons; they and the regions are similarly named: Kuśaga, Mandaga, Uṣṇa, Pīvara, Andhakāraka, Muni and Dundubhi.[12]

49cd–51 The mountains are Krauñca, Vāmana, Andhakāraka, Devavrata, Dhama, Puṇḍarīkavat, Dundubhi, each one being double the height of the last.[13]

52ab The mountains of each continent are of the same kind as the continents.[14]

52cd–53ab In the regions and mountains the people live together with gods.

53cd–54ab The castes are Puṣkalas, Puṣkaras, Dhanyas.[15]

54cd–56ab The 7 main rivers are Gaurī, Kumudvatī, Saṃdhyā, Rātri, Manojavā, Khyāti and Puṇḍarīkā.

56cd–57ab The Puṣkaras etc. worship Janārdana here in the shape of Rudra by Yoga of meditation (*dhyānayoga*) (VePr in the shape of Rudra as Yogin).

57cd–58ab Krauñcadvīpa is surrounded by the ocean of curds of equal extent.

58cd–74ab *Description of Śākadvīpa (Teak-tree-continent)*[16]

58cd–59ab The ocean of curds is surrounded by Śākadvīpa of twice the extent (i.e. 3,200,000 Yojanas).[17]

59cd–61 The ruler of Śākadvīpa is Bhavya; his sons are Jalada, Kumāra, Sukumāra, Manīraka, Kusamoda (v.l. Kusumoda), Modaki, Mahādruma. The regions are named accordingly.[18]

[10] cf. MBh 6,13.9–11: Sudhāman (*vidrumaiś citaḥ*), Hemaparvata, Dyutimat, Puṣpavat, Kuśeśaya, Harigiri (6 mountains; Dviguṇa ?).

[11] cf. MBh 6,13.6ab.

[12] cf. MBh 6,13.20ff.: Kuśala, Manonuga, Uṣṇa, Prāvaraka, Andhakārakaka, Muni, Dundubhi.

[13] cf. MBh 6,13.17–19: Krauñca, Vāmanaka, Andhakāraka, Maināka, Govinda, Nibiḍa (6 mountains; Dviguṇa ?).

[14] Read: *dvīpadvīpeṣu ye śailā yathā dvīpāni te tathā.*

[15] The list of castes is incomplete. Kirfel, Kosmographie p. 118, lists Tiṣyas as fourth caste according to VrP. cf. Kirfel, Weltgebäude p. 29.

[16] cf. MBh 6,12.

[17] MBh 6,12.9: 37,200 Yojanas, i.e. twice the extent of Jambūdvīpa.

[18] cf. MBh 6,12.23ff.: Mahāmeru, Mahākāśa, Jalada, Kumudottara, Sukumāra, Kaumāra, Maṇīcaka, Modakin, Mahāpuṃs (i.e. 9 regions).

62-63 The mountains are Udayagiri, Jaladhāra, Raivataka, Śyāma, Ambhogiri, Āstikeya and Kesarin.

64 There is a large teak tree; the wind touching its leaves produces utmost happiness.

65 The people there live without distress or disease in 4 castes.[19]

66-67 The rivers are Sukumārī, Kumārī, Nalinī, Reṇukā, Ikṣu, Dhenukā, Gabhasti and 10 thousands of smaller ones.[20]

68ab There are hundreds and thousands of mountains.

68cd-70 The rivers are drunk by the people living on their banks and, in the regions, by those who pursue the fourth goal (= *mokṣa*?); the rivers come from heaven to the earth and are very pure. There is no neglect of duty in the seven regions, no joy, no suffering.[21]

71-72ab The 4 castes are Magas, Māgadhas, Mānasas, and Mandagas.[22]

2cd-73ab Viṣṇu is worshipped here in the shape of Sūrya (the sun).

3cd-74ab Śākadvīpa is surrounded by the milk-ocean of the same extent.

4cd-95ab *Description of Puṣkaradvīpa (Lotus-continent)*

4cd-75ab The milk-ocean is surrounded by the continent named Puṣkaradvīpa which is of twice the size of Śākadvīpa (i.e. 6,400,000 Yojanas).

75cd-76 Puṣkara belongs to Savana; he has 2 sons, Mahāvīta and Dhātaki, to whom the two regions belong.

77-80ab There is one mountain range named Mānasottara, 500,000 Yojanas high, forming a circle in the middle of the continent, thereby dividing it into two concentric circular regions.

0cd-82ab The people there live 10,000 years without disease and grief, love and hatred; there is neither high nor low, killing or being killed, no jealousy, envy, fear, anger, fault, greed etc.

2cd-83ab Mahāvīta is situated outside, Dhātakī inside of the circle formed by the Mānasottara-mountain.[23]

83cd In Puṣkara there is neither truth nor lie.

84ab There are neither mountains nor rivers in this continent.

84cd People wear the same clothes, looking like the gods.

85-86ab The pair of regions is free from the caste-system and the duties of *dharma*, free from vedic tradition, economics, politics and obedience - an earthly heaven.

6cd-87ab In the two regions of Puṣkara Time (or: Death, *kāla*) grants heavenly joys without aging or diseases.

87cd There is a Nyagrodha-tree in Puṣkaradvīpa.

88ab There Brahman resides.[24]

[19] cf. MBh 6,12.28.

[20] cf. MBh 6,12.29cd-32: Sukumārī, Kumārī, Sītā, Kaverakā, Mahānadī (epithet?), Maṇijalā, Ikṣu, Vardhanakā.

[21] cf. MBh 6.12.36.

[22] cf. MBh 6,12.33-35: Magas, Maśakas, Mānasas, Mandagas.

[23] This verse should be inserted between 80ab and 80cd above.

[24] cf. MBh 6,13.14-15: Brahman's abode is on the mountain Puṣkara.

88cd–89ab Puṣkara is surrounded by the ocean of sweet water of the same extent.

89cd–90ab The 7 continents are surrounded by 7 oceans; each continent and its ocean are of the same extent, but of double the extent of the preceding one.

90cd–91ab The waters are equal in all oceans; there is neither decrease nor increase.

91cd–94ab Like the water in a kettle which rises by contact with fire, the water in the ocean rises by the moon without becoming more or less; together with the rising and setting moon and with the increasing and decreasing of the moon the waters rise and decrease by 510 Aṅgulas.

94cd–95ab Food in Puṣkara is automatically to hand; all people consume what has (one of?) six tastes.

95cd–98ab Around the ocean of sweet water there is a golden area (*bhūmi*) of double (the extent) without any living being; there is the mountain range Lokāloka, 10,000 Yojanas broad and as high.[25] It is covered by darkness which is surrounded by the shell of the cosmic egg.

98cd–99ab Including the shell of the cosmic egg, the continents and oceans, this cosmos has an extent of 500 Koṭis (i.e. 5,000,000,000) of Yojanas.

99c-f (Conclusion:) This cosmos, existing before all beings and qualities, is nurse, mother and support of all creatures.

Ch. 21: Description of the nether worlds[1]

1 Lomaharṣaṇa continues: The extent of the earth has been related. Its height is said to be 70,000.

2–5ab Each nether world is of 10,000: Atala, Vitala, Nitala, Sutala, Talātala, Rasātala, Pātāla. In these nether worlds, where the grounds are black, white, yellow, gritty, rocky, (and) golden, and adorned by palaces, live the Daityas and Dānavas and relatives of the Nāgas.

5cd–6ab Returning from the nether worlds to heaven Nārada proclaimed that they are more pleasant than heaven:

6cd–13ab Brilliant jewels adorn the Nāgas; girls of Daityas and Dānavas arouse pleasure even in liberated persons; the rays of the sun give light but do not burn; those of the moon give light but are not cold; serpents, Dānavas etc. enjoy food and drink and do not know the passing of time; forests, rivers, streams, the sound of cuckoos, ornaments, scented ointments, the sound of musical instruments, all these are enjoyed.

13cd–15 Beneath the nether worlds[2] lies that dark embodiment of Viṣṇu called Śeṣa, whose qualities cannot be told by Daityas and Dānavas, who is called Ananta and is revered by gods and sages.

[25] *āvalo hi*?

[1] For this chapter cf. Kirfel: Kosmographie p. 143–147.

[2] In v. 6cd–13ab *pātāla* is used in the singular only; in v. 3ab it is mentioned as the name of one out of seven nether worlds while in v. 2, 5–6 and 13ff. it is used as a generic term for all nether worlds.

15-27 Description of Śeṣa: He has 1000 heads, a garland of svastikas, illuminating the 4 directions with his 1000 head-jewels; he makes all Asuras powerless for the good of the world, his eyes roll passionately, he always has one ring,[3] is crowned, garlanded, appearing like a flaming mountain, is dressed in blue, impassionate, adorned with a white necklace, comparable to mount Kailāsa, onto which Gaṅgā fell. He holds a plough and a club in his hand. He is worshipped by Kānti, and the embodied Vāruṇī. At the end of a cosmic cycle Rudra the destroyer comes forth from his mouth as flames of a poisonous fire to consume the three worlds. Śeṣa supports the whole sphere of the earth lying at the root of the nether worlds, revered by all gods. Even the gods are incapable of describing his strength and power. The earth rests on him like a garland of lotuses, reddened by the flames of the jewels of his hoods. When he yawns the earth quakes. Gandharvas and other heavenly beings (list) cannot reach the end of his qualities; therefore he is called »Endless« (*ananta*). The sandal-paste applied by the wives of the Nāgas becomes perfumed powder in (for) the directions when stirred up by his breath. After paying homage to him, Garga came to know astrology and the effects of omens; by this Nāga the earth and all on it is supported.

Ch. 22: Description of hells[1]

1 Lomaharṣaṇa continues by introducing an account of the hells which are immediately below (VePr below the water), into which sinners fall.

2-6 List of names of the hells: Raurava, Śaukara (v.l. Śūkara[2]), Rodha, Tāna, Viśasana, Mahājvāla, Taptakuḍya (VePr Taptakumbha), Mahālobha, Vimohana, Rudhirāndha, Vasātapta (VePr Vaitaraṇī), Kṛmīśa, Kṛmibhojana, Asipattravana, Kṛṣṇa, Lālābhakṣa, Dāruṇa,[3] Pūyavaha, Pāpa, Vahnijvala, Adhaḥśiras, Sudaṃśa,[4] Kṛṣṇasūtra, Tamas, Avīci, Śvabhojana, Apratiṣṭhoman (VePr Apratiṣṭha), Avīci etc.; these are the terrible hells in Yama's realm into which fall the people who enjoy doing evil.

7-27 *Attribution of evil deeds to the different hells*[5]

7-8 Raurava is the abode of those who bear false witness or tell other lies, those who kill embryos, towns (v.l. their teacher), cows, and those who stop the breath.

9 Śūkara is the abode of those who drink liquor, who kill a Brahmin, who take away gold, and of those who have contact with these.

[3] Or: is shaped, i.e. lies in the form of one ring.
[1] cf. W. Kirfel: Kosmographie, p. 148-152.
[2] cf. also below, v. 8.
[3] Name or apposition?
[4] Same as Saṃdaṃśa below, cf. v. 26?
[5] For another list of hells, sins and punishments cf. ch. 215.

10 Taptakumbha: Those who kill a Kṣatriya or a Vaiśya, who enter the bed of the teacher, who cohabit with their sister and who kill a messenger.

11 Taptaloha: Those who sell sweet (liquor?), protect a man who should be killed, who sell horses, and who abandon their followers.

12ab Mahājvāla: Those who cohabit with a daughter or daughter-in-law.

12cd-13 Śabala: Those who disregard or abuse the teacher, who spoil or sell the Veda and those who have forbidden intercourse.

14ab Vimoha: Thieves and those who violate borders.[6]

14cd-15a Kṛmibhakṣya: Those who hate the gods, Brahmins and fathers, and who spoil (fake) jewels.

15b Kṛmīśa: Those who perform wrong rites (or, work evil wishes, i.e. sorcerers?).

15cd-16a Lālābhakṣya: Those who eat before fathers, gods and guests.

16b Vedaka: Those who make arrows.

16cd-17ab Viśasana: Those who make missiles with ears (*karṇin*), swords etc.

17cd-18ab Adhomukha: Those who take a wrong (or false) wife, who sacrifice for an outcaste, astrologers.

18cd-20 Kṛmipūya: Those who always eat sweetmeats; Brahmins who sell lac, meat, juice, oil, salt; those who rear cats, cocks, goats, dogs, boars and birds.

21-22 Rudhirāndha: Stage-players, fishermen, those who are supported by the son of an adulteress, who give poison, spies, those who live by the prostitution of their wives, Brahmins who approach their wives on festivals.

23ab Vaitaraṇī: Collectors of honey, those who destroy a village.

23cd-24ab Kṛcchra: Those who swallow semen etc., who break borders,[7] who are impure, jugglers.

24cd Asipattravana: Those who fell trees without need or reason.

25 Vahnijvala: Shepherds, hunters, those who put fire (in)to unbaked (pots?).

26 Saṃdaṃśayātana: Those who break a vow or discard their stage of life.

27 Śvabhojana: Those who though observing chastity have pollutions, those who are taught by their sons.

28-29 Conclusion: There are hundreds and thousands of other hells where the performers of evil deeds are roasted. Evils like that and thousands of others are suffered by those who stay in the hells.

30 Those acting against their caste or stage of life fall into the hells.

31 The inhabitants of the hells look at the gods in heaven with the head downward, and the gods look down to the inhabitants of the hell with the face downward.

32 Vegetables, worms, water-born (beings), birds, animals, human beings, the righteous, the gods, those who strive for liberation ...[8]

34ab There are as many beings in heaven as in hell.

34cd The sinner who turns away from atonement enters hell.

35-36 Atonements are taught by the best Sages according to the sins; they are serious for a serious sin, small for an insignificant sin.

[6] In space or of propriety?

[7] cf. 14ab above.

[8] The meaning of v. 32 is not clear; possibly a description of the sequence of existences to be experienced on the way to liberation.

37–41 To remember and praise Kṛṣṇa (Hari, Nārāyaṇa, Viṣṇu, Vāsudeva) surpasses all other atonements.

42–43 To mutter »Vāsudeva« leads to liberation and prevents a person going to hell.

44–47 Heaven is what pleases the mind, hell is contrary to it. Good and evil are named heaven and hell. The same thing may lead to discomfort or to comfort; it may lead to jealousy, from which wrath arises or to pleasantness: nothing is disagreeable or pleasant by itself; such characteristics depend on the mind.

48–49ab The highest *brahman* is consciousness (*jñāna*); unconsciousness (v.l. consciousness) leads to bondage; everything consists of consciousness, nothing is higher than consciousness. Knowledge and ignorance must be considered as consciousness only.

49cd–50ef Conclusion: The orbit has been (VePr briefly) described; Lomaharṣaṇa asks the sages about what they want to hear now.

Ch. 23: Description of the heavenly worlds; Viṣṇu and his Śakti[1]

1–2 The hermits, after confirming the conclusion of the topic of various worlds, ask Lomaharṣaṇa to tell them about the planets and their distances.

3–4 As far as sun and moon are shining is the circumference of the earth and the circumference of the sky is equally far.

5 The distance from the earth to the sun, and from the sun to the moon is 100,000 Yojanas.

6–10 100,000 Yojanas above the moon is the orbit of the lunar mansions. 200,000 Yojanas above the latter Budha (= Mercury) is situated, and Uśanas at the same distance from Budha; Aṅgāraka (= Bhauma = Mars) at the same distance from Śukra (= Uśanas = Venus); Devapurohita (»priest of the gods« = Bṛhaspati = Jupiter) 200,000 from Bhauma; Sauri (= Saturn) 200,000 from Bṛhaspati; the Seven Sages 100,000 from Sauri; Dhruva (= Pole star) 100,000 from the Seven Sages (= Great Bear).

11 So far the »three worlds« (*trailokya*) have been described in brief; they are the ground for the fruits of sacrifice; the sacrifice is established there.

12–15 10,000,000 Yojanas higher than Dhruva is the Maharloka, the abode of those who live for a cosmic cycle; 20,000,000 Yojanas higher is the Janaloka (VePr Janoloka) where the sons of Brahman, Sananda etc. live; four times higher than Janaloka is the Tapoloka, where the Vairāja-gods live without bodies; and six times higher than Tapoloka is the Satyaloka, also called Brahmaloka, the abode of those who will never be born again.

16–20 Explanation of »*trailokya*«: 1. Bhūrloka, the earth, which is trodden by foot; 2. Bhuvarloka, between earth and sun, where Siddhas etc. dwell; 3. Svarloka, between sun and Polar star, measuring 14,000,000. These three worlds are pronounced to be (characterized by) deeds; while Janaloka, Tapoloka and Satyaloka are not (characterized by) deeds. Between the three worlds and those upper worlds which are not

[1] cf. W. Kirfel: Kosmographie, p. 128f.

characterized by deeds (*akṛtaka*) is Maharloka situated, which becomes empty at the end of any cosmic cycle, but is not destroyed.

21 These are the seven Mahālokas; the 7 nether worlds are of the same extent; (together) they make up the cosmic egg (conclusion).

22–27ab From each side this seed is surrounded by an egg-shell like the seed of a Kapittha-tree; the egg-shell is surrounded by water; the water is surrounded by fire; the fire is surrounded by wind; the wind is surrounded by ether; the ether is surrounded by the Great (*mahat*);[2] the Great is surrounded by primordial matter (*pradhāna*), the endless of Sāṃkhya-philosophers (?), which cannot be measured and is the origin of everything, being the supreme Prakṛti.

27cd–28ab There are thousands and ten thousands of thousands of eggs like that, and billions of ten millions.

28cd–44 *Viṣṇu and his energy as cosmic principles*

28cd–29ab Like the fire in wood, like the oil in oil-seed, the »Spiritual principle« (*puṃs*) is contained in primordial matter, pervading it totally, as an indication (experience) of a spiritual Self (?).

29cd–31ab Primordial matter and spiritual principle are kept linked interdependently by Viṣṇu's energy (*śakti*) which is experienced by every being (v.l. which is identical with, i.e. is »the self of« every being). It is this energy which causes the two (principles) to separate and to inter-depend, and provides the impulse at the time of creation.

31cd–32ab Like the wind which carries the coldness in water that is contained in the (water) drops (blown around by the wind), so Viṣṇu's energy (carries) the world consisting of matter and spirit.

32cd–35 As a tree, consisting of root, stem, branches etc., originates from a seed while other seeds originate from it, and from those seeds other trees, showing the same characteristics, similarly, everything from the Great down to specific beings (?, *viśeṣāntāḥ*) is born from the Unmanifest; then the gods etc. come into existence, and from them sons are born and then sons of the sons.

36–37 As there is no diminution of the tree due to growing of trees from its seeds, there is no diminution of the elements (*bhūta*) by the creation of beings (*bhūta*). Since space and time etc. are causes of the tree just by their presence, so Lord Hari is the cause of all without undergoing change.

38–40 Like root, stalk, leaves, shoots, stems, buds, blossoms, sap, grain, chaff, that are contained in the seed of a rice-plant and become visible when granted the conditions for growing, so the bodies of the gods etc. are »contained« in the different actions and start growing by Viṣṇu's energy.

41–43 Viṣṇu is the highest *brahman* (n.) from whom the world originates, who is the world, in whom (the world) exists, and into whom it is absorbed.[3] He is the highest abode, being and non-being, (and) the highest step, to whom the whole world

[2] The meaning of *daśottara* is not clear; cf. W. Kirfel: Kosmographie p. 55: »Jede äußere Schicht ist zehnmal so dick wie die nächst eingeschlossene.«

[3] For this »theological formula« cf. P. Hacker: Prahlāda p. 80–86.

belongs. He (= Viṣṇu) is »root-matter« (*mūlaprakṛti*) as well as the manifest world; into him it disappears and in him it exists.

44 He is the performer of sacrificial rites , he is performed as sacrifice, and he is the fruit of the sacrifice; there exists nothing whatsoever distinct from Hari.

Ch. 24: Nārāyaṇa as Śiśumāra and the cycle of water

1-7ab There is a form of the Lord made up of stars and called Śiśumāra (i.e. Dolphin). At its tail Dhruva (= the Pole star) is placed. By turning itself it makes the stars circle around it since they are tied to it by strings made of wind. The constellation of stars called Śiśumāra has as its basis in its very heart Nārāyaṇa who (or which) is the highest abode. Dhruva had paid homage to Prajāpati and was placed at the tail of Śiśumāra. The basis of Śiśumāra is Janārdana; Śiśumāra is the basis of Dhruva to whom the sun is attached. On the sun rests the whole world.

7cd Announcement of a further explanation.[1]

8-11 The cycle of water: For eight months the sun absorbs moisture which then falls down as rain upon which depends nourishment and thus the whole world. The sun nourishes the moon, the moon by wind-channels is dispersed by the waters into the clouds. Since the waters do not fall down, clouds are »water-carriers« (*ab-bhra*); instigated by wind the pure waters then fall down from the clouds, having completed the preparation brought about by time.

12 Rivers, and oceans, water from the earth and emitted by living beings, these four kinds of water are taken up by the sun.

13-18 The waters of the heavenly Gaṅgā are taken up by the sun and thrown upon the earth without mediation of clouds.[2] A man purified by the touch of these waters is saved from hell. The waters of the heavenly Gaṅgā are thrown upon the earth without clouds by the rays of the sun.[3] That water which falls from heaven in uneven lunar mansions like the Pleiades etc. after seeing the sun, is known to originate from Gaṅgā, discharged by the elephants of the directions, while that water which falls from heaven in even mansions falls down, after having been taken up by the rays of the sun directly. Both kinds are most beneficial for men.

19-25 Water, however, which rains from clouds, nourishes the plants and provides food for living. By it plants grow, and it is the means by which fruits are eventually produced for living beings. By allowing men to perform the prescribed sacrifices it supports the gods. Thus, all beings, the sacrifices, Vedas and castes are supported by the rain which in turn is brought about by the sun. Dhruva is the support of the sun, Śiśumāra that of Dhruva which again is supported by Nārāyaṇa, who is placed in its heart, being the supporter of all beings as well as their origin.

[1] i.e. v. 8-25, of which v. 24-25 duplicate v. 6.

[2] Possibly a reference to dew? In other contexts the heavenly form of Gaṅgā is identifiable as the Milky Way; cf. H. H. Wilson: »That rain which falls whilst the sun is shining and without a cloud in the sky ...« (Viṣṇupurāṇa, p. 190).

[3] Duplicates verse 13.

26 Conclusion: The cosmic egg has been dealt with.

Ch. 25: Places of pilgrimage

1 The hermits inquire about places of pilgrimage (*tīrtha*).
2 Lomaharṣaṇa answers: A man who is self-controlled and practises asceticism etc. will obtain the merit of a holy place (*tīrtha*).
3 Pure mind, control of senses etc. are »*tīrthas*« leading to heaven.[1]
4–6 An impure man will not become pure by bathing at a holy place, nor by gifts, vows etc.; but wherever a man is self-controlled, there is Kurukṣetra, Prayāga, Puṣkara.
7–8ab Lomaharṣaṇa announces a concise report on the holy places on earth, which cannot be told extensively even in hundreds of years.

8cd–83ab *List of places of pilgrimage*[2]

8cd Puṣkara, Naimiṣa-forest;
9 Prayāga, Dharma-forest, Dhenuka, Campaka-forest, Saindhava-forest;
10 Magadha-forest (VePr Sagara-forest), Daṇḍaka-forest, Gayā, Prabhāsa, Śrītīrtha Kanakhala;
11 Bhṛgutuṅga, Hiraṇyākṣa, Bhīma-forest, Kuśasthalī, Lohākula (v.l. Lohārgala), Kedāra, Mandara-forest;
12 Mahābala (v.l. Himālaya, Mahālaya), Koṭitīrtha, Rūpatīrtha, Śūkarava (v.l. Śuddhikara, Śūkara), Cakratīrtha;
13 Yogatīrtha (v.l. Ghoratīrtha), Vyāsatīrtha, Somatīrtha, Sāhoṭaka (v.l. Sākoṭaka, Śākhoṭaka), Kokāmukha, Badarīśaila;
14 Somatīrtha, Tuṅgakūṭa (v.l. Śaṃbhutīrtha), Skandāśrama (v.l. Skandhāśrama), Koṭitīrtha (v.l. Sūryaprabha), Agnipada (v.l. Dhenusaras), Pañcaśikha (v.l. Saptamāyuṣika, Saptamāyuṣmika);
15 Koṭitīrtha, Gaṅgādvāra (v.l. Gaṅgādhara), Pañcakūṭa, Madhyakesara;
16 Cakraprabha, Mataṅga, Kruśadaṇḍa (v.l. Śatrukuṇḍa), Daṃṣṭrākuṇḍa (v.l. Dṛṣṭakuṇḍa), Viṣṇutīrtha (v.l. Viṣṇukuṇḍa);
17 Matsyatila, Badarī, Suprabha, Brahmakuṇḍa, Vahnikuṇḍa, Satyapada;
18 Catuḥśrotas, Catuḥśṛṅga, Dvādaśadhāraka-mountain (v.l. Dvādaśavāraka-mountain), Mānasa, Sthūlaśṛṅga (v.l. Sthalaśṛṅga), Urvaśī;
19 Lokapāla, Manuvara (v.l. Mesadhara), Somāhva-mountain (v.l. Somātri-mountain), Sadāprabha (v.l. Sūryaprabha), Merukuṇḍa (v.l. Madhukuṇḍa, Mahākuṇḍa), Somābhiṣecana;
20 Mahāsrota (v.l. Mahāśrotra, Mahāsūtra), Koṭaraka (v.l. Kokanada, Kāraka, Koraka), Pañcadhāra, Tridhāraka, Saptadhāra (v.l. Vīradhāra), Ekadhāra, Amarakaṇṭaka;

[1] In Upendravajrā-metre; *tīrtha* literally means »ford«.

[2] The two editions of the text vary considerably in the names given and in their sequence. For a concordance of both texts see the Appendix to the text-volume.

21 Śālagrāma (v.l. Śālīgrāma), Cakratīrtha (v.l. Vajratīrtha), Koṭidruma (v.l. Kadalīhrada), Bilvaprabha (v.l. Bimbaprabha, Vidyutprabha), Devahrada, Viṣṇuhrada (v.l. Viṣṇuprabha);

22 Śaṅkhaprabha, Devakuṇḍa, Vajrāyudha, Agniprabha, Puṃnāga, Devaprabha;

23 Vidyādhara, Gāndharva, Śrītīrtha, Brahmahrada, Sātīrtham (?), Lokapālatīrtha (?), Maṇipura-mountain;

24 Pañcahrada, Piṇḍāraka, Malavya, Goprabhāva, Govara, Vaṭamūlaka;

25 Snānadaṇḍa (v.l. Snānakuṇḍa), Prayāga, Viṣṇupada (v.l. Guhāviṣṇupada), Kanyāśrama (v.l. Kanyākuṇḍa), Vāyukuṇḍa, Jambūmārga;

26 Gabhastitīrtha, Yayātipatana (v.l. Yayātipattana), Koṭitīrtha, Bhadravaṭa, Mahākālavana;

27 Narmadātīrtha, Tīrthavajra (v.l. Tīrthabīja) (?), Arbuda, Piṅgutīrtha (v.l. Pañcatīrtha), Vāsiṣṭhatīrtha, Pṛthasaṃgama (v.l. Priyasaṃjñaka);

28 Daurvāsika (v.l. Vārṣika) Piñjaraka (v.l. Pañjiraka), Ṛṣitīrtha (v.l. Sutīrtha), Brahmatuṅga (v.l. Brahma-Rudratīrtha), Vasutīrtha, Kumārika (v.l. Kanyākumārikā);

29 Śakratīrtha, Pañcanada, Reṇukātīrtha, Paitāmaha(tīrtha), Rudrapāda (v.l. Raudrapāda);

30 Maṇimatta (v.l. Maṇimanta), Kāmākhya, Kṛṣṇatīrtha, Kuśāvila (v.l. Kuliṅgaka), Yajana, Yājana (v.l. Śrīśakrayajana), Brahmavāluka (v.l. Brahmabālukā);

31 Puṣpanyāsa (v.l. Vyāsa), Puṇḍarīka, Maṇipūra (v.l. Mantha), Dīrghasattra (v.l. Dīrghamanta), Hayapada (v.l. Haṃsapāda), Anaśana (v.l. Śayana);

32 Gaṅgodbheda, Śivodbheda (v.l. Daśāśvamedha, Kedāra), Narmadodbheda (v.l. Tamasodbheda), Vastrāpada, Dāruvala (v.l. Barhapada), Chāyārohana (v.l. Lokārohaṇa);

33 Siddheśvara, Mitravala, Kālikāśrama, Vaṭāvaṭa (v.l. Svayaṃvaṭa), Bhadravaṭa (v.l. Bhadrabala), Kauśāmbī (v.l. Kauśāmba), Divākara;

34 Sārasvata-dvīpa, (v.l. Deva), Vijaya, (VePr Ullayāṅgopacāra, Cavarambana, Pūrṇavat ?), Rudrakoṭi, Sumanasa (v.l. Rudrakūpa, Saṃyamanī), Drāvanāmita (v.l. Saṃtrāvanāsika);

35 Syamantapañcakatīrtha, Brahmatīrtha, Sudarśana, Pṛthivī,[3] Pāriplava, Pṛthūdaka;

36 Daśāśvamedhikatīrtha, Sarpija (v.l. Sākṣida), Viṣayāntika (v.l. Vijaya), Koṭitīrtha, Pañcanada, Vārāha, Yakṣiṇīhrada;

37 Puṇḍarīka, Somatīrtha, Muñjavaṭa (v.l. Muñjāvaṭaratha), Badarīvana, Āsīna, Ratnamūlaka (v.l. Babūravana);

38 Lokadvāra, Pañcatīrtha, (v.l. Svarlokadvārakatīrtha), Kapilātīrtha, Sūryatīrtha, Śaṅkhinī (v.l. Varusthāna), Gavāṃbhavanatīrtha (v.l. Bhavābhatrana);

39 Yakṣarājatīrtha (v.l. Rākṣasyatīrtha), Brahmāvarta (v.l. Brahmatīrtha), Sutīrthaka (?), Kāmeśvara, Mātritīrtha (v.l. Mātṛtīrtha), Śītavanatīrtha (v.l. Śātavanatīrtha);

40 Snānalomāpaha (v.l. Bhaumasthāna, Haṃsasthāna), Māsasaṃsaraka (v.l. Sārasa, Sarasa), Daśāśvamedha, Kedāra, Brahmodumbara (v.l. Brahmajña);

41 Saptarṣikuṇḍa, Devītīrtha, Sujambuka (v.l. Susaṃyata), Īṭāspada (?) (v.l. Āspada), Koṭikūṭa (v.l. Koṭikṛta), Kiṃdāna (v.l. Kiṃvāna), Kiṃjapa (v.l. Kiṃjaya);

42 Kāraṇḍava, Avedhya (v.l. Viśva), Triviṣṭapa, Pāṇiṣata (v.l. Paṇikhāta), Miśraka, Madhūvaṭa, Manojava (v.l. Madhukaṇṭa, Manomaya);

[3] i.e. the whole earth?

43 Kauśikī, Devatīrtha, Ṛṇamocana (v.l. Kanyātīrtha), Nṛgadhūma, Viṣṇupada;
44 Amarahrada, Koṭitīrtha, Śrīkuñja, Śālitīrtha, Naimiṣeya;
45 Brahmasthāna, Somatīrtha, Kanyātīrtha, Brahmatīrtha, Manastīrtha, Kārupāvanatīrtha (v.l. Pāvana);
46 Saugandhikavana (v.l. Saugandhika), Maṇitīrtha, Sarasvatī, Īśānatīrtha, Pravara, Pāvana, Pāñcayajñika (v.l. Pañcayajñaka);
47 Triśūladhāra, Māhendra, Devasthāna, Kṛtālaya (v.l. Mahālaya), Śākaṃbharī, Devatīrtha, Suvarṇa, Kila(-hrada) (v.l. Kapīmada);
48 Kṣīraśrava (v.l. Kṣīreśvara), Virūpākṣa, Bhṛgutīrtha, Kuśodbhava, Brahmatīrtha (v.l. Brahmāvarta), Brahmayoṇi, Nīlaparvata;
49 Kubjāmbaka, Bhadravaṭa, Vasiṣṭhapada, Svargadvāra, Prajādvāra, Kālikāśrama;
50 Rudrāvarta, Sugandhāśva, Kapilāvana, Bhadrakarṇahrada, Śaṅkukarṇahrada (v.l. Śakrakarṇahrada);
51 Saptasārasvatatīrtha, Auśanasa, Kapālamocana, Avakīrṇa, Kāmyaka (v.l. Pañcaka);
52 Catuḥsāmudrika, Śataki, Sahasrika, (v.l. Satkāñcanasahasrika), Reṇuka, Pañcavaṭaka (v.l. Pañcakaṭaka), Vimocana, Ojasa (v.l. Ainasa ?)
53 Sthānutīrtha, Kurutīrtha, Svargadvāra, Kuśadhvaja, Viśveśvara, Mānavaka (v.l. Vāmakara), Nārāyaṇāśrama;
54 Gaṅgāhrada, Vaṭa, Badarīpāṭana (v.l. Badarīpāvana), Indramārga, Ekarātra, (v.l. Mārgaṇakeśatra), Kṣīrakāvāsa (v.l. Jirikāvāsa);
55 Somatīrtha, Dadhīca, Śrutatīrtha (v.l. Koṭitīrtha), Koṭitīrthasthalī, Bhadrakālīhrada;
56 Arundhatīvana, Brahmāvarta, Aśvavedī (v.l. Aśvadevī), Kubjāvana (v.l. Kubjavana), Yamunāprabhava;
57 Vīra, Pramokṣa, Sindhūttha (v.l. Vīrapramokṣa, Siddhārtha), Ṛṣakulyā (v.l. Ṛṣikulyā), Kṛttika, Urvīsaṃkramaṇa, Māyāvidyodbhava;
58 Mahāśrama (v.l. Mahāhrada), Vaitasikārūpa (v.l. Vetasikārūpa), Sundarikāśrama, (VePr ins.: Brahmāṇī, Gaṅgōdbhavasarasvatī), Bāhutīrtha, Cārunadī (v.l. Bāhukātīrtha), Vimalaśoka;
59 (VePr ins.: Gautamairāvatītīrtha, Śatasahasrikatīrtha, Bhartṛsthāna, Koṭitīrtha, Varā, Kāpilī), Pañcanadatīrtha, Somatīrtha, Sitoda (?, v.l. Śivoda), Matsyodarī;
60 Sūryaprabha, Sūryatīrtha, Aśokavana (v.l. Somakavana), Aruṇāspada, Kāmada (v.l. Vāmanaka), Śukratīrtha (v.l. Sūryatīrtha), Vāluka;
61 (VePr ins.: Avimukta, Nīlakaṇṭhahrada), Piśācamocana, Subhadrāhrada, Vimaladaṇḍakuṇḍa, Caṇḍeśvaratīrtha (v.l. Caṇḍīśvaratīrtha);
62 Jyeṣṭhasthānahrada (v.l. Śreṣṭhasthānahrada), Brahmasara (v.l. Samudra, Kūpa), Jaigīṣavyaguhā (v.l. Jaigīṣavyavana), Harikeśavana;
63 Ajāmukhasara (v.l. Ajāmukharasa), Ghaṇṭākarṇahrada, Puṇḍarīkahrada, Karkoṭaka-vāpī (v.l. Kāṣṭhaka-vāpikā);
64 Suvarṇodapāna, Śvetatīrthahrada, Ghargharikā-kuṇḍa, Śyāmakūpa, Candrikā;
65 Śmaśānastambhakūpa (v.l. Śmaśānastambha, Kumbha), Vināyakahrada, Kūpa (?), Sindhūdbhava (v.l. Siddhodbhava), Brahmasara (v.l. Brahmasaras);
66 Rudrāvāsatīrtha (v.l. Bhadrāvāsatīrtha), Nāgatīrtha, Pulomaka (v.l. Somaka), Bhaktahrada, Kṣīrasaras, Pretādhāra, Kumāraka;
67 Brahmāvarta, Kuśāvarta, Dadhikarṇodapānaka (v.l. Dadhikarṇodayātmaka), Śṛṅgatīrtha, Mahātīrtha, Mahānadī;

68 Brahmasara (v.l. Brahmasaras), Gayāśīrṣākṣaya-vaṭa (?), Dakṣiṇa (?), Uttara (?), Gomaya, Rūpaśītika (v.l. Hayaśantika[4]);

69 Kapilāhrada, Gṛdhravaṭa (v.l. Gṛdhrakūṭa), Sāvitrīhrada, Prabhāsana, Sītavana (v.l. Gītavana), Yonidvāra, Dhenuka (v.l. Dhainuka);

70 Dhanyaka (v.l. Dhanvaka), Kokila (v.l. Lohika), Mataṅgahrada (v.l. Mātaṅgahrada), Pitṛkūpa, Rudratīrtha (v.l. Kūpa ?), Śakratīrtha (v.l. Matitīrtha), Sumālina (?);

71 Brahmasthāna, Saptakuṇḍa, Maṇiratnahrada, (VePr ins.: Mudgalāśrama, Mudgalahrada, Janakakūpa), Kauśikya (v.l. Śoka), Bharatatīrtha, Jyeṣṭhālikā (v.l. Jyeṣṭhālika);

72 Viśveśvara, Kalpasaras (v.l. Puṇyaśata), Kanyāsaṃvetya (v.l. Kanyāsaṃvedha), Niścīvā (?), Prabhava, (v.l. Nidhirāmabhava), Vasiṣṭhāśrama;

73 Devakūṭa, Kūpa, Vasiṣṭhāśrama (v.l. Kauśikāśrama), Vīrāśrama, Brahmasaras, Brahmavīrāvakāpilī;

74 Kumāradhārā, Śrīdhārā, Gaurīśikhara, Śvakuṇḍa, Nanditīrtha;

75 Kumāravāsa, Śrīvāsa, Aurvīśītārtha (?), Kumbhakarṇahrada (v.l. Kulakarṇahrada), Kauśikīhrada (v.l. Kauśikīdruma);

76 Dharmatīrtha, Kāmatīrtha (v.l. Kāñcana), Uddālakatīrtha (v.l. Auddālakatīrtha), (VePr ins.: Daṇḍātmā (?), Mālinītīrtha, Vanacaṇḍikātīrtha), Saṃdhyātīrtha, Kāratoya (v.l. Kālatīrtha), Kapila, Lohitārṇava (v.l. Kapilālohitārṇava);

77 Śoṇodbhava, Vaṃśagulma, Ṛṣabha, Kālatīrthaka, (v.l. Rāmabhaṅgīkatīrthaka), Puṇyāvatīhrada (v.l. Puṇyāvartahrada), Badarikāśrama;

78 Rāmatīrtha, Pitṛvana (v.l. Vitastā), Virajātīrtha, Mārkaṇḍeyavana, Kṛṣṇatīrtha, Vaṭa;

79 Rohiṇīkūpa, Indradyumnasara (v.l. Indradyumnasaras), Sānugarta (v.l. Avasarga), Māhendra, Śrītīrtha, Śrīnada (v.l. Śrīnadī);

80 Iṣutīrtha, Vārṣabha (v.l. Vārṣika), Kāverīhrada (v.l. Kauberahrada), Kanyātīrtha, Gokarṇa, Gāyatrīsthāna (v.l. Gopatisthāna);

81 (VePr ins.: Saṃvarta, Viśvāsa, Saptagodāvarīhrada), Badarīhrada, Madhyasthāna, Vikarṇaka (v.l. Brahmasthānavivardhana ?), Jātīhrada, Devakūpa (v.l. Devahrada), Kuśapravaṇa (v.l. Kuśaprathana);

82 Sarvadevavrata, Kanyāśramahrada, (VePr ins.: Mahārājahrada, Śakratīrtha, Kundaka, Aṅgāratīrtha, Rudrāraṇyaka, Medhāvina (?), Devahrada, Amaravartanatīrtha, Mandākinīhrada, Kṣama, Māheśvara, Gaṅgātīrtha, Tripuruṣa, Bhīmatāṇḍavavāmukha, Pṛthukūṭa, Śālvakūṭa, Śoṇa, Rohitaka, Kapilāhrada, Mālya, Vāsiṣṭhakapilāhrada), Vālakhilyatīrtha;

83ab Akhaṇḍitahrada.

83cd–86ab Phalastuti: He who takes a bath and offers oblations at these holy places according to the rules will obtain at each holy place the merit of a horse-sacrifice.

86c-f Phalastuti: He who listens to, reads, or makes known, this eulogy of places of pilgrimage (*tīrthamāhātmya*) will be released of all evil.

[4] sic

Ch. 26: The dialogical setting for Brahman's narration

1 The hermits inquire about the best of all holy places.

2 Lomaharṣaṇa answers by telling how his teacher Vyāsa answered this question on a former occasion.

3–17 Description of Vyāsa's hermitage in Kurukṣetra and of the occasion on which the conversation took place.

3–5 Description of the surroundings of the hermitage (list of trees).

6–8 Description of Vyāsa, whom to meet many hermits had come.

9–14 List of names of the visitors.

15 Surrounded by them and other sages Vyāsa looked like the moon surrounded by the Nakṣatras (lunar mansions).

16 After the welcome they told each other stories.

17 At the end of the stories they asked Kṛṣṇa Dvaipāyana, Satyavatī's son (= Vyāsa), about a doubt.

18–25 The hermits' questions to Vyāsa:

18 They praise Vyāsa's omniscience.

19–22 They ask what leads to salvation (*śreyas*) in the ocean of worldly existence (described) (question 1). By Vyāsa's instruction people may be saved.[1]

23–25 2. They ask (question 2) about the »field of actions« (*karmabhūmi*) on earth, where by performing actions a man obtains highest perfection; without acting (or: by acting wrongly) he would obtain hell. In the »realm of liberation« he would obtain liberation.

26 (Lomaharṣaṇa introduces Vyāsa's reply.)

27 Vyāsa announces that he will tell how Brahman answered this question before, when asked by the sages:

28–30 Description of the summit of Mount Meru.

31 Description of Brahman.

32–33 Description of his entourage and their activities.

34–35 Vyāsa introduces the following question of the sages:

36 The sages (i.e. Brahman's audience) asked about the field of actions on earth, the realm of liberation.

37 Vyāsa announces Brahman's answer.

Ch. 27: Description of Bhāratavarṣa[1]

1 Brahman announces[2] a Purāṇa.

[1] Verse 22 uses *lomaharṣaṇa* as attribute of *saṃsāra*, a corrected remnant of a vocative referring to the original narrator?

[1] For this chapter cf. the edition and translation by W. Kirfel: Bhāratavarṣa, Stuttgart 1931.

[2] The dialogical setting of the BrP changes in ch. 26; for the rest of the Purāṇa Lomaharṣaṇa only reports the report of Vyāsa who in turn reports what Brahman said. The actual narrator

2 The field of actions on earth (*karmabhūmi*) is Bhāratavarṣa, while heaven and hell are the field for the fruits of actions.

3-9 Whatever anyone does in this region will bear fruit: The rank of gods, highest perfection (*siddhi*), the four goals of life, liberation, sojourn in heaven are gained by actions performed in this region. Even the gods, therefore, long to stay in Bhāratavarṣa.

10-13 The hermits wish to be told about Bhāratavarṣa in detail, about its mountains and sections.

14-80 *Description of Bhāratavarṣa*[3]

14-16 Bhāratavarṣa is divided into nine parts: Indradvīpa, Kaseru, Tāmravarṇa, Gabhastimat, Nāgadvīpa, Saumya, Gāndharva, Vāruṇa; the ninth part is an island surrounded by oceans, and measures 1000 Yojanas from south to north.

17-19ab In the east of it live the Kirātas, in the west the Yavanas; Brahmins, Kṣatriyas, Vaiśyas and Śūdras stay there, purified by their respective activities: sacrifice, fighting, trade etc., which lead to heaven and final beatitude, and are either meritorious or evil.[4]

19cd-20ab List of the seven main mountains: Mahendra, Malaya, Sahya, Śuktimat, Ṛkṣaparvata, Vindhya, and Pāriyātra.

20cd-24ab There are thousands of other mountains: Kolāhala, Vaibhrāja, Mandara, Dardalācala, Vātaṃdhaya (v.l. Vātādhvaga), Vaidyuta (v.l. Daivata), Maināka, Surasa, Tuṅgaprastha, Nāgagiri, Godhana, Pāndarācala (v.l. Pāṇḍurācala), Puṣpagiri, Vaijayanta, Raivata, Arbuda, Ṛṣyamūka, Gomantha, Kṛtaśaila, Kṛtācala, Śrīparvata, Cakora, and hundreds of other mountains.

24cd Distributed among them are peoples like Mlecchas etc.

25ab Announcement of the rivers providing water for those peoples.

25cd-27 List of rivers originating from the Himālaya: Gaṅgā, Sarasvatī, Sindhu, Candrabhāgā, Yamunā, Śatadru, Vipāśā, Vitastā, Airāvatī, Kuhū, Gomatī, Dhūtapāpā, Bāhudā, Dṛṣadvatī, Vipāśā,[5] Devikā, Cakṣus, Niṣṭhīvā, Gaṇḍikā (v.l. Gaṇḍikī), Kauśikā and Āpagā.

28-29 List of rivers originating from the Pāriyātra-(mountain): Devasmṛti, Devavatī, Vātaghnī, Sindhu,[6] Veṇyā, Candanā, Sudānīrā, Mahī,[7] Carmaṇvatī, Vṛṣī, Vidiśā, Vedavatī (v.l. Vetravatī), Siprā (v.l. Śiprā), Avantī (v.l. Dravantī).

30-32 List of rivers originating from the Ṛkṣa(-mountain): Śoṇā, Mahānadī, Narmadā, Surathā, Kriyā, Mandākinī, Daśārṇā, Citrakūṭā; Citrotpalā,[8] Vetravatī,[9] Karamodā,

thus is Vyāsa. In accordance with this shift we use present tense for what refers to the dialogical frame Brahman-hermits, past tense for the episodes reported; cf. the note to ch. 1.16, above.

[3] cf. ch. 19, above.

[4] Are these four qualifications intended as classification of the activities of the four castes? cf. the v.l. Ms. A »but not evil«.

[5] Occurs twice.

[6] cf. also v. 25cd-27.

[7] Name or adjective?

[8] Or, Citrā and Utpalā?

[9] cf. v. 29.

Piśācikā; Atilaghuśroṇī, Vipāpmā (v.l. Vipāśā), Śaivalā; Sadherujā (v.l. Samerujā), Śaktimatī (v.l. Śuktimatī), Śakunī, Tridivā, Kramu, and Vegavāhinī.

33-34 List of rivers originating from the Vindhya(-mountain): Siprā (v.l. Śiprā[10]), Payoṣṇī, Nirvindhyā, Tāpī, Saridvarā (epithet?); Veṇā, Vaitaraṇī, Sinīvalī, Kumudvatī; Toyā, Mahāgaurī, Durgā, Antaḥśilā.

35-36ab List of rivers originating from the Sahya(-mountain): Godāvarī, Bhīmarathī, Kṛṣṇaveṇā; Āpagā,[11] Tuṅgabhadrā, Suprayogā, Pāpanāśinī.

36cd-37ab Rivers originating from the Malaya(-mountain): Kṛtamālā, Tāmraparṇī, Puṣyajā (v.l. Puṣpavatī), Pratyalāvatī (v.l. Upalāvatī).

37cd-38ab Rivers originating from the Mahendra(-mountain): Pitṛsomarṣikulyā, Vāñjulā, Tridivā,[12] Lāṅgulinī (v.l. Lāṅgalinī), Vaṃśakarā.

38cd-39ab Rivers originating from the Śuktimat(-mountain): Suvikālā, Kumārī, Manūgā, Mandagāminī, Kṣayāpalāsinī (v.l. Kṣayā and Palāśinī).

39cd-41ab Conclusion to the lists of rivers: They are all Sarasvatīs (»full of water«), Gaṅgās (»swift-goer«) and Samudragās (»going to the ocean«); they are all mothers, removing evil. There are thousands of smaller rivers, some flowing only in the rainy season and some flowing in each season.

41cd-42 The inhabitants of the middle region are the Matsyas, Mukuṭakulyas (v.l. Kumudamālyas), Kuntalas (v.l. Kratulas), Kāśis and Kośalas; the Andhrakas, Kaliṅgas, Śamakas (v.l. Maśakas) and Vṛkas.

43-50 List of peoples living north of Sahya at the Godāvarī: Vāhīkas, Rāṭadhānas, Sutīras, Kālatoyadas, Aparāntas, Śūdras, Vāhlikas (v.l. Bāhlikas), Keralas; Gāndhāras, Yavanas, Sindhus, Sauvīras, Madrakas, Śatadruhas, Kaliṅgas (!), Pāradas, Hārabhūṣikas (v.l. Haribhūṣikas); Māṭharas, Kanakas, Kaikeyas, Dambhamālikas; their country is like that of Kṣatriyas; there are Vaiśyas and Śūdras (?); Kāmbojas, Barbaras, Laukikas (?), Vīras, Tuṣāras, Pahlavas, Ādhāyatas; Ātreyas, Bharadvājas, Puṣkalas, Daśerakas, Lambakas (v.l. Lampakas), Śunaśokas, Kulikas, Jāṅgalas; Auṣadhis, Calacandras, and different kinds (clans) of Kirātas, Tomaras, Haṃsamārgas, Kāśīras, Karuṇas; Śūlikas, Kuhakas, Māgadhas.

51ab Conclusions to the northern peoples; announcement of the peoples living in the east.

51cd-53 List of peoples living in the east: Andhas, Vāmaṅkurakas, Vallakas, Makhāntakas, Aṅgas, Vaṅgas, Maladas, Mālavartikas; Bhadratuṅgas, Pratijayas, Bhāryāṅgas, Apamardakas, Prāgjyotiṣas, Madras, Videhas, Tāmraliptakas, Mallas, Magadhakas, Nandas.

54-57 List of peoples living in the south: Pūrṇas, Kevalas, Golāṅgulas (v.l. Golāṅgūlas), Ṛṣikas, Muṣikas, Kumāras, Rāmaṭhas, Śakas (!); Mahārāṣṭras, Māhiṣikas (v.l. Māhiṣakas), Kaliṅgas (!), Ābhīras, Vaiśikyas, Aṭavyas, Saravas; Pulindas, Mauleyas, Vaidarbhas, Daṇḍakas, Paulikas, Maulikas, Aśmakas, Bhojavardhanas; Kaulikas, Kuntalas (!), Dambhakas, Nīlakālakas.

58ab Conclusion to the southern peoples; announcement of the peoples in the west:

[10] cf. v. 29.
[11] cf. v. 27.
[12] cf. v. 32.

58cd Śūrpārakas, Kālidhanas, Lolas and Tālakuṭas.

59ab Conclusion to the western peoples; announcement of those living in the Vindhya(-mountains):

59cd–62ab Malajas, Karkaśas, Melakas, Colakas, Uttamārṇas, Daśārṇas, Bhojas, Kiṣkindhakas; Toṣalas, Kośalas (!), Traipuras, Vaidiśas; Tumbūras, Caras, Yavanas (!), Pavanas; Abhayas, Ruṇḍikeras, Carcaras, and Hotradhartis.

62cd–64ab Announcement of countries at (the foot of) the mountains: Nīhāras, Tuṣamārgas, Kurus, Tuṅganas (v.l. Tuṅgaṇas), Khasas, Karṇaprāvaraṇas, Ūrṇas, Darghas, Kuntakas (v.l. Kuñcakas); Citramārgas, Mālavas, Kirātas, and Tomaras.[13]

64cd Here the four Yugas, Kṛta, Tretā etc., are a rule.

65–66ab This Bhāratavarṣa consists of nine parts. South, west and east of it lies the ocean, north of it the Himavat, like a bow-string.

66cd–68 This Bhāratavarṣa contains the seed of everything: according to good or evil deeds one proceeds to the rank of Brahman, of Indra, of the gods, of the Maruts (winds), or to the wombs of wild animals, Yakṣas and Apsarases, creeping animals or plants; there is no other field of actions in the world.

69–70 Even the gods wish to become human beings; for neither gods nor demons can do what man can do; they are bound by actions.

71–72 There is no land on earth like Bhāratavarṣa, where the four castes obtain what they wish; happy is he who is born in Bhāratavarṣa, for he will obtain the fruit of the four goals of life (*dharma*, *artha*, *kāma*, *mokṣa*).

73–78ab List of actions the merits of which can only be obtained in Bhāratavarṣa: Asceticism, giving alms (gifts), sacrifices, pilgrimages, devotion to the teacher, homage to the gods, vows, study of different branches of knowledge (*śāstra*), non-violence, chastity, life of a householder, living in the forest, renunciation, sacrificial rites (?).

78cd Who could tell all the qualities of Bhāratavarṣa?

79 Conclusion to the report on Bhāratavarṣa.

80 Phalastuti: He who listens to or reads this, practising self-control, will be released from all evil and enter the world of Viṣṇu.

Ch. 28: Description of Oṇḍradeśa; on worship of the sun and of Rāmeśvara

1–9 Brahman reports on Koṇāditya and its inhabitants:

1–2 At the border of the southern ocean the land Oṇḍradeśa[1] is situated, adorned by the qualities of its pure inhabitants.

3–7 Praise of the Brahmins of the land.

8 The other three castes are also self-controlled and righteous in this land.

9 The man who sees the sun called Koṇāditya in this land will be released from all evil.

[13] cf. v. 49–50.

[1] Ed. VePr has *oṇḍa*, a printing mistake?

10 The hermits wish to know more about that abode of the sun.

11–65 *Description of the land sacred to the sun (Koṇārka, Koṇāditya)*

11–18 Description of the abode of the sun-god, located on the banks of the ocean, endowed with various trees (listed), extending one Yojana. The sun-god famed as »Koṇāditya« stays at that place; he grants enjoyment and liberation.

19–36 Description of observances in honour of the sun-god:

19–20 In the month of Māgha, on the 7th day of the bright half, one should go there, fasting and self-controlled, and bathe in the ocean at the end of the night.

21 One should satisfy gods, sages, men and ancestors, take off one's garments and put them on again washed and clean.

22 One should sip water, then sit down on the bank of the ocean at sunrise facing the sun.

23 One should draw (?) an eight-leaved (etc.) lotus, with water mixed with red sandal.[2]

24 One should put water mixed with rice and sesamum, with red flowers and Darbha-grass, into a copper vessel.

25 If there is no copper, one should put it into the hollow of a leaf of the Arka-plant, cover the vessel with another one and put it down.

26 One should touch one's limbs with the hands and think of oneself as identical with the sun.

27 One should worship (the sun) in the middle (zenith), in the south-east, south-west, north-west, north-east and again in the middle.[3]

28–29 One should worship the lotus, after calling down the sun from the sky and placing it on the pericarp; then one should display the (or: a) pose of hands (*mudrā*) while meditating.

30–31 Description of the sun-god: On a white lotus, within a fire-ball, with red eyes, two arms, a reddish garment, well adorned etc.

32 Seeing the sun rising, one should take the vessel and kneel down.

33 One should put the vessel on the head, silently, and present the welcome offering (*arghya*) to the sun, together with the prayer-formula (*mantra*) consisting of three syllables.

34 He who is not initiated properly should offer the welcome offering by his (the sun's) name, for a serious worshipper may win the sun by devotion and trust.

35 One should worship in the different directions,[4] the heart, top of the head, skin (? *varman*), eyes and »weapon« (?).

36 After performing all that, one should remove (everything).

37–54ab Merits obtained by sun-worship.

37–38 All Brahmins, Kṣatriyas, Vaiśyas, women and Śūdras who offer to the sun-god with pure mind will reach the ultimate goal, after enjoying (the fulfilment of) their desires.

[2] i.e. draw a *yantra*?

[3] ? The text names Agni, Nirṛti, Śvasana (= Vāyu?) and Kāmāri (= Śiva), which may indicate the directions of which they are the guardians.

[4] cf. v. 27.

39 Whoever turns to (v.l. remembers) the sun-god will obtain happiness.

40–41 As long as the offering is not given to the sun-god, one cannot worship Viṣṇu or Śiva; therefore one should present flowers etc. to the sun-god every day.

42–45 Whoever presents the offering on the 7th[5] will obtain the desired results: The sick will be free from sickness, those who want to have wealth, knowledge or sons, or whatever else they think of while offering, will obtain it, men as well as women. (VePr adds: Freed from all evil man will go to heaven.)

46 He who enters the sun-temple and worships the sun-god with flowers etc., circumambulating him thrice, will go to the sun's place. (VePr adds: with tantric and vedic prayer-formulas (*mantra*).)

47–53ab By prostrating oneself, by praising etc. one will obtain the merit of ten horse-sacrifices, will be released from all sins, will be endowed with youth and heavenly beauty, will rescue 7 past and 7 future generations and will enter the sun-world with a heavenly chariot, enjoying all kinds of delights up to the end of the world. When his merit is consumed, he will be born again in an excellent family of Yogins. Becoming one with Vivasvat he will gain liberation.

3cd–54ab He who undertakes a pilgrimage in the bright half of the month of Caitra will obtain the same merit.

4cd–56ab Those who undertake a pilgrimage at sunrise, at a solstice or equinox, on Sundays, at new or full moon will enter the sun-world with a heavenly chariot.

6cd–62ab Worship of Śiva as Rāmeśvara: At the border of the ocean there resides also Mahādeva (= Śiva) called Rāmeśvara. Those who worship him with scents, flowers etc. will obtain the merit of a *rājasūya*-sacrifice as well as a horse-sacrifice and utmost perfection. With a heavenly chariot they enter the Śiva-world while Gandharvas sing for them. After enjoying the desired delights until the end of the world, when their merit is consumed, they are born as experts in the four Vedas; they enter union with Śaṃkara (or, follow the Yoga(-techniques) of Śiva) and obtain liberation.

2cd–64ab He who dies at this place of Savitṛ (= sun-god) will enter the sun-world; reborn on earth he will become a righteous king; practising the Yoga of the sun (or, on achieving union with the sun) he will obtain liberation.

4cd–65ab Conclusion to the report on the place Koṇārka.

Ch. 29: On worship of the sun[1]

1–6 The hermits repeat what they have heard and express their delight in Brahman's story. They ask him to tell more about the merits connected with different observances and customs: worship; alms; prostration; praising; circumambulation; offering of lamps and incense; anointing (?); fasting; eating only at night; welcome offering (*argha*). They want to know how and where the offering should be

[5] i.e. the date given above, v. 19, or of every month?
[1] cf. SāP Ch.38.

presented, how devotion (*bhakti*) should be practised, and how the god will be pleased.

7-61 Brahman's answer: Description of, prescriptions for, and effects of sun-worship.

7-8 Announcement of a description of devotion (*bhakti*), faith (*śraddhā*) and concentration (*samādhi*).

9-14 Description of a man devoted to the sun-god: The devotee listens to stories about the god, honours his devotees (v.l. worships him devotedly), thinks of him always, acts for him (?, or: performs (ritual) actions with regard to him). He honours works done for the sake of the gods, is not indignant at his devotees nor slanders another deity;[2] he is devoted to the sun-god and thinks of him always, in any situation.[3] Such devotion should always be practised, with devotion, concentration, and mental praise.

15-17 Discipline (*niyama*) observed with devotion etc., and gifts to Brahmins are accepted by gods, men and ancestors; offerings (flowers etc.) presented with devotion are accepted by the gods who shun unbelievers. Whatever is done with a pure attitude will be successful.

18-19 By praise, prayers, oblations, worship and fasting as well as by touching the earth with the head while greeting (the sun) one is released from all evil.

20-21 By circumambulating the sun the devotee circumambulates the whole earth and similarly all the gods.

22-27ab Merits of worshipping the sun on the 6th and/or 7th day of a half-month: One goes to the world of the sun.

27cd-28 By drinking water proceeding from the hemisphere of the sun for each of 24 (months) one will complete the discipline after two years.[4]

29-31ab If the 7th day of the bright half is a Sunday, it is named Vijayā; every observance practised will destroy the worst crimes.

31cd-32ab Those who perform the ancestral rites (*śrāddha*) on a Sunday and sacrifice to the sun obtain whatever they desire.

32cd-33ab In the family of those who act righteously in the name of the sun no needy or diseased person will be born.

33cd-34ab He who anoints (the sun-god?) with white, red or yellow clay will get the success he thinks of.

34cd-35ab He who worships the sun with fragrant flowers will get all he wants.

35cd-42ab Prescriptions for and effects of offering lamps.

35cd-36 He who lights lamps with ghee or sesamum oil will not lose his eyesight and will shine with knowledge.

37 Praise of sesamum.

38 He who lights lamps in temples and at crossroads will be handsome and happy.

39 The first choice (? *kalpa*) is with burnt offerings, the second with the juice of plants; but one should never use grease etc.[5]

[2] Or: the deity of others.

[3] v. 9-10 and 11-13 with refrains.

[4] v. 27cd-28 not quite clear.

[5] Not clear.

40 The lamp should burn upwards, not downwards; thus the giver will not be born as an animal.

41 Nobody should remove or extinguish a burning lamp; if he does so, he will enter bondage, destruction, wrath and darkness.

42ab The giver of lamps will shine in heaven, like a garland of lamps.

42cd–61 Prescriptions for, descriptions of, and effects of offerings (*arghya*) (to the sun), in particular concerning scents, ointments, flowers; prayers, praises; gifts; places for depositing the offering (listed); the manner of presentation (from in front?); scented offerings, flowers; dates for worship; substances for oblation; the water for bathing; gifts. Whatever is presented to the sun-god will be restored 100,000-fold; whatever evil may be committed by thought, word or body, will be destroyed totally by the grace of the sun. By offering to him one will obtain more than by 100 sacrifices including gifts to Brahmins.

Ch. 30: The sun as highest deity; his twelve-fold shape; Mitra's instruction to Nārada[1]

1–6 The hermits wish to know more about the greatness of the sun-god. (1.) Which deity should be worshipped in the four stages of life, in order to obtain liberation? (2.) How can one reach heaven and liberation, and by what action? And by what action will one not fall from heaven again? (3.) Who is the highest god and father and who creates and absorbs the world?

7–13 Brahman describes the sun-god as highest deity;[2] he absorbs and creates living beings, gives light, heat and rain, but is imperishable himself. At creation the world originates from the sun and at dissolution it enters into him again.

14–18 On liberation by entering the sun through Yoga:[3] At death Yogins become wind and enter the sun, dwelling in the sunbeams like birds in the branches of a tree. Also householders, e.g. kings like Janaka, sages like the Vālakhilyas, others who live in the forest and mendicants like Vyāsa, practised Yoga and then entered the sun-disc. Śuka, the son of Vyāsa, practised Yoga, entered the sunbeams and obtained freedom from rebirth.

19–20 About Brahman, Viṣṇu, Śiva etc. one can only hear through the Veda, since they are invisible, whereas the sun, the destroyer of darkness, can be perceived by the eyes. Therefore one should direct devotion to him.

21–22 Appeal to the hermits to worship the sun, who is father, mother and teacher of the whole world and who, out of benevolence, heats the world.[4]

[1] cf. SāP Ch. 2, 4, and 5.

[2] v. 7–13 seem to answer the third question.

[3] Answer to the first and second question?

[4] The reading of ASS seems to connect v. 22 to the following.

23–44 *The twelve-fold form of the sun-god*[5]

23–26 After Brahman (or: the sun as Brahman) created the continents and oceans, the 14 worlds,[6] he stayed on the banks of the »moon-river« (*candrasarit*)[7] for the benefit of the worlds.

23–26 After creating the Prajāpatis and various creatures, the manifest sun-god made himself »Āditya«, twelve-fold,[8] viz. Indra, Dhātṛ, Parjanya, Tvaṣṭṛ, Pūṣan, Bhaga, Aryaman, Vivasvat, Viṣṇu, Aṃśa (or Aṃśumat, cf. below), Varuṇa and Mitra.

27 With these forms the sun-god permeates the whole world.

28–39 Description of the twelve forms: 1. Indra, king of the gods and destroyer of their enemies; 2. Dhātṛ, lord of creation (*prajāpati*), who creates the different creatures; 3. Parjanya, dwelling in the clouds and sending rain by the sunbeams; 4. Tvaṣṭṛ, present in trees and plants; 5. Pūṣan, present in food and nourishing the creatures; 6. Aryaman, the movements of the wind (?, v.l. cover of the wind?); 7. Bhaga, present in the bodies of the living beings; 8. Vivasvat, present in fire and ripening (cooking) the food of living beings; 9. Viṣṇu, who always manifests himself as destroyer of the enemies of the gods; 10. Aṃśumat, present in wind and refreshing the creatures; 11. Varuṇa, present in water and nourishing the creatures; 12. Mitra, dwelling on the banks of the moon-river for the benefit of the worlds.[9]

40–41 He practised asceticism, staying there with Mitra's eye (i.e. the sun) and favouring his devotees with boons. Thus (his) form (= statue?) had formerly been established, for the sake of the worlds; since Mitra dwells/dwelled there, it is remembered as »Mitra«.[10]

42–43 With these twelve forms the sun-god permeates the world; therefore devoted men should think of and worship him in the twelve forms.

44 Phalastuti: Those who worship the twelve Ādityas like that, always listening and reading (the report about them), will be great in the sun-world.

45–86 *Instruction of Nārada by Mitra*[11]

45 The hermits inquire as to why the sun practised asceticism like an ordinary being wishing for a boon.

46–47ab Brahman announces a report on this utmost secret which was told to Nārada by Mitra.

[5] Cf. SāP ch.4 (translated by H. v. Stietencron, Indische Sonnenpriester, p. 158, who also refers to the parallel version of the BhvP, but not to that of the Brp).

[6] i.e. 7 upper and 7 nether worlds?

[7] For the problem of identifying this river (also called Candrabhāgā in the SāP), cf. Kane, Studies in the Upapurāṇas vol.1, p. 60.

[8] cf. e.g. ŚBr 4,5,7.2: The sun in the 12 months of the year.

[9] v. 39cd repeats 24ab, possibly indicating the boundaries of a manipulation of the text; 39ab corresponds to 42ab.

[10] i.e. Mitravana (as in SāP)? -- cf. Hazra, Studies in the Upapurāṇas vol. 1, p. 62 and 82 f., where he argues that the BrP must have taken these passages from the SāP.

[11] cf. SāP ch. 5.

47cd–48 Among the twelve forms of the sun mentioned above, Varuṇa and Mitra practised asceticism, Varuṇa by living on water.

49–52 Once Nārada left the summit of Mt. Meru named Gandhamādana and roamed all over the world. When he came to the place where Mitra practised asceticism, he grew very curious as to which god or ancestors Mitra, the supporter of the three worlds and father of all other gods, could worship.

53–56 Nārada, describing Mitra's superiority, asked him which god or ancestors he worshipped, being himself father and mother of everything and being worshipped by (members of) all four stages of life.

57–86 Mitra answers by expounding *brahman*.

57 He announces a most profound secret.

58–61 The invisible, immovable etc. *brahman* is the same as the Self and soul of beings, known as »knower of the field« (*kṣetrajña*), (supreme) person (*puruṣa*), golden embryo (*hiraṇyagarbha*), consciousness (*buddhi*), the Great (*mahat*), primordial matter (*pradhāna*), as having three shapes (*trirūpa*), All-self (*viśvātman*), Śarva, and imperishable (*akṣara*).

62–64 He[12] constitutes the unity which supports the three worlds; though bodiless he resides in every body, but is not afflicted by deeds; though present in all he cannot be seized. He is known as »with qualities« as well as »without qualities«, is »All« and »attainable by understanding« (*jñānagamya*).

65–67 He has hands, feet, heads, arms etc. on all sides[13] and is called »knower of the field« (*kṣetrajña*) because all bodies are the »field« (*kṣetra*) which he knows.

68ab He is called *puruṣa*, because he lies (*śeti*) in the unmanifest as his stronghold (*pura*).

68cd He is called Sarvatra, because he is to be known as the manifold All and is called Everywhere.[14]

69ab He is called Viśvarūpa because of his many forms.

69cd–70ab He alone owns greatness (being the Great, *mahat*), and he is the only *puruṣa*; therefore he bears the name Mahāpuruṣa.

70cd–75 He multiplies himself hundred- and thousandfold like water assuming many tastes, like the wind being fivefold in the bodies, like fire in different places. He brings forth thousands of shapes like one lamp lighting 1000 lamps; he assumes various names and forms.

76–77 When thinking of himself he is one; when oneness disappears, plurality arises. In the world nothing is eternal but he who is omnipresent, undecaying, immeasurable.

78–79ab From him originated the manifest, consisting of three qualities,[15] which as primordial matter (*prakṛti*) is the origin of Brahman.

79cd–80 He is worshipped by rites addressed to gods and to ancestors. There is nothing higher than him, neither ancestor nor god. Therefore Mitra worships him. (Answer to Nārada's question.)[16]

[12] The text uses masculine forms, in spite of *brahman* (n.).

[13] cf. RV 10,90.

[14] *sarvatra ucyate*; because of lack of Sandhi this might be understood as »called protector of all«, *sarva-tra*; VePr reads *sarvaḥ sarvatra ucyate*.

[15] The vocative plural, *dvijasattamāḥ*, does not fit the context.

[16] Again the vocative *dvijāḥ* does not fit this narrative level; it might refer to Brahman addressing the hermits, or may betray an ill-adapted source of this passage.

81-84 He is worshipped by every being with devotion and is shelter for all; he is omnipresent; to him all beings go; therefore Mitra worshipped him, too.

85-86 Conclusion to Mitra's report on the *brahman*: The secret has been told. All gods etc. worship the sun.

87-88 Brahman concludes the report of what was told to Nārada, warning not to transmit this secret to anyone not devoted to the sun.

89-91 Phalastuti: He who recites or listens to this will enter the sun; the diseased will recover from sickness by listening to it; etc.; everyone will obtain his desires.

92 Appeal to the sages to meditate on the sun-god.

Ch. 31: Various aspects of the sun; the 12 Ādityas; the 21 names of the sun[1]

1-27 Brahman continues by praising and describing various aspects of the sun:

1-3 Praise of the sun-god as the origin of the world and the gods.

4-6 The oblation poured into fire goes to the sun, from there rain originates, from rain food, and from food the creatures; thus everything is born from and absorbed in the sun; he is liberation.

7-10 He is origin of the different subdivisions of time; without him there would be no seasons, and consequently no blossom, no fruits, no sowing, no plants. Even the absence of action by the beings on earth and in heaven is due to him.

11 Without rain the sun does not burn, nor dry up, nor form a halo; he shines by water. (?)

12-14ab The colours of the sun in the different seasons: Brown in spring, golden in summer, white in the rainy season, yellow in autumn, coppery in the snow-season, blood-red in the cool season.

14cd-16 Report on the twelve names of the sun: Āditya, Savitṛ, Sūrya, Mihira, Arka, Prabhākara, Mārtaṇḍa, Bhāskara, Bhānu, Citrabhānu, Divākara, Ravi.

17-21 Report on the Ādityas who preside over the twelve months:

17-18 List of twelve Ādityas:[2] Viṣṇu, Dhātṛ, Bhaga, Pūṣan, Mitra, Indra, Varuṇa, Aryaman, Vivasvat, Aṃśumat, Tvaṣṭṛ, Parjanya.

19-21 Viṣṇu heats in the month Caitra, Aryaman in Vaiśākha, Vivasvat in Jyeṣṭha, Aṃśumat in Āṣāḍha, Parjanya in the month Śrāvaṇa, Varuṇa in Prauṣṭha, Indra in Āśvayuja, Dhātṛ in Kārttika, Mitra in Mārgaśīrṣa, Pūṣan in Pauṣa, Bhaga in Māgha, and Tvaṣṭṛ in Phālguna.

22-26 Report on the number of sunbeams for each of the Ādityas: Viṣṇu has 1200 beams, Aryaman 1300; Vivasvat has 14, Aṃśumat 15, Parjanya like Vivasvat, Varuṇa like Aryaman; Tvaṣṭṛ like Mitra[3] has 1100, Indra 12, Dhātṛ 1200 (v.l. 11); Mitra has 1000 and Pūṣan 900. When the sun goes to the north, the sunbeams increase; when he goes to the south, they diminish.

[1] cf. SāP Ch. 8 and 19.

[2] cf. ch. 30 v. 23-39 above, and W. Kirfel: Kosmographie, p. 130-137.

[3] cf., however, v. 25 below, where Mitra is said to have 1000.

27 Conclusion to the report on 24 of the names of the One, which are 1000 in total.
28 The hermits inquire about the merit obtained by those who praise the 1000 names of the sun.

29–39 *The 21 names of the sun*[4]

29–30 Brahman announces those names which are secret, pure and auspicious.
31–33ab The 21 names are: Vikartana, Vivasvat, Mārtaṇḍa, Bhāskara, Ravi, Lokaprakāśaka, Śrīmat, Lokacakṣus, Maheśvara;[5] Lokasākṣin, Trilokeśa, Kartṛ, Hartṛ, Tamisrahan, Tapana, Tāpana, Śuci, Saptāśvavāhana; Gabhastihastin, Brahman, Sarvadevanamaskṛta.[6]
33cd–34 This hymn consisting of 21 names is known as Stavarāja (king of praises), which takes away diseases and bestows wealth, growth and fame.
35–36 Phalastuti: He who praises the sun by it at sunrise and sunset will become pure and be released from all evil. All that has resulted from thought, speech, body and action is destroyed in the presence of the sun by one prayer only.
37 (It constitutes) various rituals and prayer formulas.[7]
38 He whose hymns are great is believed to remove all evil when worshipped while giving alms etc., at the presenting of food and gifts, at throwing oneself down and at circumambulating.
39 Conclusion: Appeal to the hermits to praise the sun-god by that hymn.

Ch. 32: The birth of Vivasvat; story of Saṃjñā and Mārtaṇḍa

1–2 The hermits confirm that they have been told about the sun-god as free from qualities and in his twelve-fold form; they wonder how a mass of brilliance could have been born by a woman.

3–47 *Story of Vivasvat's (= Mārtaṇḍa's) birth*

3–6 Brahman continues: Dakṣa had 60 daughters, Aditi, Diti, Danu, Vinatā etc., 13 of whom he gave to Kaśyapa. Aditi gave birth to the gods, Diti to the Daityas, Danu to the Dānavas, Vinatā etc. to the other animate and inanimate beings. Their offspring filled the earth.
7–8 The best of Kaśyapa's sons are gods; others are classified according to the three Qualities (as Sāttvikas, Rājasas and Tāmasas). The creator, Prajāpati Parameṣṭhin, made the gods lords of the three worlds and recipients of sacrifices.

[4] cf. SāP ch. 25 (translated by H. v. Stietencron, Indische Sonnenpriester, p. 148).
[5] SāP reads *graheśvara* (»lord of the planets«).
[6] The number of 21 mentioned in v. 33 forces us to interpret epithets like *śrīmat* or *sarvadevanamaskṛta* (»venerated by all gods«) as proper names.
[7] Construction not clear: list of prayer-formulas in nominative case.

9–11 Out of jealousy the Daityas and Dānavas oppressed them (VePr adds: there was a fierce battle of 1000 divine years in which Daityas and Dānavas were victorious). Their mother Aditi, seeing her sons bereft of food, made efforts to please Savitṛ (the sun-god) by fasting and by praising him.

12–16 Aditi's hymn of praise to the sun, praising various aspects of the sun's form (*rūpa*), e.g. as identical with the three Vedas and as identical with the syllable *oṃ*.[1]

17–31 After a very long time during which she praised him day and night, the sun-god appeared but could not be seen by her because of his great splendour. Disturbed, she asked him to show himself to her and to be merciful to her sons. He became visible to her and granted her a boon. She told him about her sons' bad situation and asked him to become her sons' brother with a part of himself, in order to destroy their enemies. He promised her to enter her womb with one thousandth part of himself and to destroy her sons' enemies immediately. Then he became invisible again.

32–34ab After one year one sunbeam out of 1000, named Suṣumna, lodged in her womb; she observed difficult vows like Cāndrāyaṇa (?), in order to bear the heavenly embryo with purity.

34cd–35ab Her husband Kaśyapa, however, became angry and suspected that she wanted to kill the unborn child by fasting.

35cd–36 She answered that he would not be killed but be the killer of the enemies; she (started to) give birth to him.

37–41ab When Kaśyapa beheld the babe he praised him. Thereupon he emerged illuminating all directions with his brilliance. A heavenly voice was heard naming the child Mārtaṇḍa, as the egg (*aṇḍa*) was said to be destroyed (*mārita*), and prophesying that he would slay the Asuras.[2]

41cd–46 Hearing this the gods were full of joy. Indra summoned them to the fight with the Asuras, who were burnt to ashes by Mārtaṇḍa. The gods got back their shares of the sacrifice and praised Mārtaṇḍa and Aditi.

47a-f Mārtaṇḍa, however, performed his own duty, appearing like a fire-ball with rays up and down, but without distinct shape.

48 The hermits want to know how the sun got his more beautiful shape afterwards.

49–107 *Story of Saṃjñā and Mārtaṇḍa*[3]

49–50 Brahman continues: Vivasvat married Saṃjñā, the daughter of Tvaṣṭṛ. They had two sons and one daughter named Yamunā.

51–55 Mārtaṇḍa's brilliance heated the worlds. Saṃjñā could not bear his brilliance and ordered her shadow (*chāyā*) to take her place, but never to tell Vivasvat about the change, while she herself would go back to her father. Chāyā (shadow) agreed and promised to keep the secret.

56–58ab While staying in her father's house for a thousand years, she was again and again ordered by her father to go back to her husband. Finally she changed into a mare and set out for the land of the Northern Kurus (Uttarakuru) in order to practise asceticism there.

[1] With varied refrain.

[2] cf. ch. 6.3.

[3] cf. SāP ch.11 and 12 (also above, 6.1–40).

58cd–63 Meanwhile, Chāyā stayed with the sun-god who, thinking her to be his wife Saṃjñā, had two sons and one daughter with her. But Chāyā did not treat the first-born children with the same love as her own. Manu tolerated it but Yama was annoyed; due to anger, to childishness, or in order to motivate what was to happen, he threatened her with his foot but did not touch her. Nevertheless she cursed him that his foot should fall off.

64–68 Afraid of the effect of the curse, Yama told his father about the unjust behaviour of his mother, about his reaction and about the curse, asking his father to release him from its effects.

69–72 His father wondered about the reason for Yama's anger. As he could not make the curse ineffective, because it was a mother's curse, he modified it to mean that worms would take the flesh (of Yama's foot) to the earth.

73–75 He inquired from Chāyā the reason for her inequitable treatment of the children and wondered whether she was their mother, since a mother would not curse her children. He seized her; afraid he would curse her, Chāyā confessed the truth.

76–79 He went to his father-in-law, who welcomed him and tried to calm him, explaining that his daughter, who was now practising asceticism, could not tolerate his brilliance. He offered to make the sun's shape more lovable.

80–81 Vivasvat agreed; Viśvakarman Tvaṣṭṛ ordered him to ascend a (potter's) wheel in Śākadvīpa and started to trim his brilliance..

82–87 Through the vibrations resulting of this action the earth with oceans, mountains and forests flew up to the sky, the sky turned downwards, the oceans lost their water, the mountains broke asunder, the stars fell down, heavy clouds were shattered by the winds, roaring terribly, the whole world was upset.

88–95 Seeing the sun whirl around, gods and sages praised the sun-god.

89–90ab Praise of the sun-god by the gods.

0cd–91ab Indra and the gods praised him with »*jaya jaya*« etc.

1cd–92ab The seven sages praised him with »*svasti svasti*«.

2cd–93ab The Vālakhilyas etc. praised him with vedic sayings.

3cd–95ab Hymn to the sun-god (by Aṅgiras etc., according to VePr).

5cd–97ab Vidyādharas etc. bowed to him and prayed that his brilliance should become tolerable.

97cd–103 Description of heavenly music and dance.

7cd–99ab The Hāhās and Hūhūs, Nārada and Tumburu started to sing for him in different musical scales and rhythms.

99cd–100 The seven Apsarases Viśvācī, Ghṛtācī, Urvaśī, Tilottamā, Menakā, Sahajanyā, and Rambhā danced for him.

102–103 List of musical instruments.

103 Thus there was a great noise caused by this singing, playing and dancing.

104–107 While all beings praised and worshipped the sun-god, Viśvakarman cautiously trimmed his brilliance. Up to his knees he was skilfully polished by Viśvakarman, but he did not agree to more and descended from the wheel; his shape was far more beautiful than before.

108 Phalastuti:[4] He who listens to (this account on) how the sun was polished will enter the sun-world at the end of his life.

[4] In Puṣpitāgra-metre.

109 Conclusion to the report on the sun-god's birth and to the description of his highest form.[5]

Ch. 33: On the origin of the sun; the 108 names of the sun[1]

1-2 The hermits, not tired of listening, want to know about the origin of the fiery brilliance.

3-8 Brahman continues: When all the worlds were sunk in darkness and everything was destroyed, consciousness (*buddhi*) at first originated from matter (*prakṛti*); from that originated ego-consciousness, which produced the main elements (*mahābhūta*), viz. wind, fire, water, space and earth. From that (or thereupon) an egg originated, containing the seven worlds, the earth with the seven continents and seven oceans. In it Brahman (the first-person narrator), Viṣṇu and Maheśvara (= Śiva) were contained. All beings (or: all of the three gods), bewildered and in darkness, thought about that lord. Then an great splendour appeared, destroying the darkness, and Brahman, Śiva and Viṣṇu recognised by meditation (*dhyānayoga*) that it was Savitṛ; and they all praised him as the lord.[2]

9-23 Hymn by Brahman, Viṣṇu and Śiva, praising the sun-god:

9-13ab Praise of sun as origin of all beings; as Brahman, Mahādeva, Viṣṇu, Prajāpati, Vāyu, Indra, Soma, Vivasvat and Varuṇa; as Time in its *trimūrti*-function (creation, preservation, destruction); as dissolution and origin, manifest and as unmanifest, eternal.

13cd-14ab Knowledge is higher than Īśvara, Śiva is higher than knowledge, the (sun-?)god higher than Śiva: The sun is the highest Īśvara.

14cd-15ab Description of the sun-god: as having feet, hands, faces etc. on all sides, with a thousand beams.

15cd The sun-god as origin of beings (*bhūtādi*), as the seven worlds (*bhūḥ*, *bhuvaḥ* etc.).

16-21 Praise of the sun's appearance and form, emphasizing his transcendence.[3]

22-23 Praise of the sun's beneficial functions.[4]

24-26 Hearing this praise, the sun granted a boon to the gods. They wished that his brilliance should become tolerable; the god agreed.

27-31 Adherents of Sāṃkhya and Yoga and others striving for liberation meditate on him in their hearts. Even if loaded with all evils and bare of any good quality, one will overcome all evil by taking refuge with the sun-god. Sacrifice, Vedas, offerings, giving of many sacrificial gifts is not worth one sixteenth of worshipping the sun-god; to him one goes as the highest among holy places etc.; by praising him one will be released from all evil and enter the sun-world.

[5] This seems to refer to 30.57-86.

[1] cf. SāP Ch.14 (excerpts are translated by H. v. Stietencron, Indische Sonnenpriester, p.153-155).

[2] Construction of sentence is ungrammatical.

[3] With refrain.

[4] In Triṣṭubh-metre, each line beginning with *namo namaḥ*.

32 The hermits want to know the 108 names of the sun.
33–46 The 108 names of the sun-god.
33 Brahman announces the 108 names as a great secret.
34–45 List of names.[5]
46 Conclusion to the list of 108 names.
47 Devotional submission to the sun-god.[6]
48–49 Phalastuti:[7] Praising with this hymn leads to liberation and fulfilment of all desires.

Ch. 34: Story of Satī; the birth of Umā

1–6 Brahman continues, describing Rudra (= Śiva) on mount Kailāsa, who had destroyed Dakṣa's sacrifice and terrified the gods.
7–8 The hermits want to know why Bhava (= Śiva) destroyed Dakṣa's sacrifice.

9–50 *Story of Satī*

9–12ab Brahman continues: Dakṣa had eight daughters who were married. Once he invited them to his house except for the eldest, Satī, married to Tryambaka (= Śiva), whom Dakṣa did not like, for he never bowed to his father-in-law.
12cd–19 Learning about the invitation to her sisters, Satī went to her father's home without being invited. When she received a welcome inferior to that of her sisters, she grew angry and claimed to be treated better, as she was the eldest and most preferable one. Dakṣa, however, praised the other husbands, Vasiṣṭha, Atri, Pulastya, Aṅgiras, Pulaha, Kratu, Bhṛgu and Marīci,[1] as *dharma*-abiding Brahmins and better sons-in-law than Tryambaka (= Śiva).
20a-d Dakṣa said this to provoke being cursed.
20ef–25 Thereupon Satī announced that she would give up her body and proclaimed her intention to become Tryambaka's legal wife again after rebirth. Then she sat down, concentrated, and fixed her attention on fire till fire sprang from her body and reduced her to ashes.
26–29ab Learnig of Satī's death, Śaṃkara (= Śiva) cursed Dakṣa that, because he had neglected Satī and praised the other daughters and their husbands, those great sages should run away from a second sacrifice in the era of Manu Vaivasvata, after the Brahman-sacrifice had been performed in the era of Manu Cākṣuṣa (?).[2]
29cd–32 After addressing the seven sages, Rudra cursed Dakṣa to be born as a human king, grandson of Prācīnabarhis and son of Pracetas and Māriṣā in the era of Manu

[5] We count 118 names and epithets of the sun in this list, from which v. 38cd at least can be excluded since it lists plural nouns.
[6] In Puṣpitāgra-metre.
[7] In Vaṃśasthavila-metre.
[1] The names are already eight without Śiva!!
[2] Or: (as well as) on the occasion of a Brahman-sacrifice in the era of Manu Cākṣuṣa. v. 29b = 30b; text corrupt?

Cākṣuṣa. He himself would repeatedly disturb Dakṣa's actions concerning the three goals of life (*dharma*, *kāma*, *artha*).

33–38 In reply Dakṣa cursed Rudra that, because he had spoken against the seven sages they would not sacrifice to him (i.e. Rudra) together with the other gods, and that Rudra should live on earth, not in heaven, until the end of the Yuga. Rudra replied that since the gods observed caste divisions and ate together, he would eat separately; he would stay on earth by his own will, not at Dakṣa's command.

39–41 Thus, Dakṣa was born among humans and performed sacrifices as a householder; in the Vaivasvata-era Satī was reborn as Umā, daughter of the king of mountains (= Himavat) and Menā.

42–45ab She who was Satī became Umā: The wife of Bhava does not leave her husband as long as he wishes to become incarnate during various Manu-eras; similarly, Aditi remains with Kaśyapa, Śrī with Nārāyaṇa, Śacī with Maghavan (= Indra), Kīrti with Viṣṇu, Uṣas with Sūrya (i.e. Dawn with the Sun), Arundhatī with Vasiṣṭha.

45cd–48 Likewise, Dakṣa was born again in the era of Manu Cākṣuṣa as Prācetas, grandson of Prācīnabarhis and son of the ten Pracetases by Māriṣā; and the seven sages, Bhṛgu etc., who formerly, at a sacrifice to the great god in the first Tretā period of Manu Vaivasvata, assumed the bodies of sons of Varuṇa (?).

49–50 In their new birth there was the same old enmity between Dakṣa and Tryambaka. Therefore one should never be filled with enmity in his wishes (v.l. towards enemies), because such thought (*khyāti*) does not produce well-being for the person in the next birth. (Ed. VePr inserts: One's nature and sentiments are carried over into new bodies.) This is not done by one who knows.

51–54 The hermits want to know how Satī was born again in the house of the king of mountains, how she met Bhava and conversed with him, how she chose her husband and was married to him.

55–101 *Story of Umā's birth*[3]

55 Brahman announces the auspicious story of Umā and Śaṃkara.

56–57 Once when Kaśyapa visited Himavat, he was asked how to obtain 1. imperishable worlds, 2. highest fame, and 3. venerability among the good.

58–73 Kaśyapa's answer.

58 All that is obtained by means of a son.

59 Announcement of what he had experienced previously.

60–72 Story of how a Brahmin ascetic saved his ancestors from hell: Once when Kaśyapa went to Vārāṇasī he beheld a heavenly palace in the sky, and beneath it he heard some moaning from a hole. A Brahmin ascetic went there and entered that place. Inside he saw hermits hanging on a stalk of grass; he asked them why they were hanging there with their faces downwards. They told him that they were his ancestors, who would fall down to hell the very moment he died without offspring. By no other means, and not by his asceticism, could they be released from their dangerous situation; therefore he should procreate a son as soon as possible. The

[3] The sequence of episodes related to Rudra and Umā extends to ch. 38.20.

ascetic promised to do so, worshipped Śiva, drew his ancestors out of the hole and made them leaders of the hosts (of Śiva?). He himself became Rudra's son Suveśa, a leader of Rudra's hosts.

73 Conclusion to Kaśyapa's answer: Therefore Himavat, too, should practise asceticism and procreate a daughter (!).

74–80 Thereupon Himavat practised asceticism, until Brahman was pleased and granted him a boon. Himavat wished to have a son. Brahman promised him a daughter by whom he would obtain great fame, be honoured by the gods and surrounded by holy places (*tīrtha*). She would be his eldest daughter, followed by others (masc., i.e. sons).

81 In due time, three daughters were born to Himavat and Menā: Aparṇā, Ekaparṇā and Ekapāṭalā.

82 As a homeless one, he (Himavat?) practised asceticism, eating only one leaf (of) the Nyagrodha-tree and only one blossom (of) the trumpet-flower-tree; (thereby he produced) Ekaparṇā.[4]

83–84 Ekaparṇā subsisted on only one leaf; Ekapāṭalā on only one flower; thus, they practised asceticism for 1000 years.

85–86 Aparṇā, however, lived without taking any food; her mother wanted to prevent her and uttered »*u mā*« (»oh, not!« ?), by which name Umā became famous.

87–89 This world that is called Trikumārīka (= having or consisting of three virgins) with movable and immovable beings, is a transformation of their asceticism, as long as the earth lasts (?). They all consist of asceticism, practise Yoga, are endowed with eternal youth, and are mothers of the world, which they support by their asceticism.

90 Umā, the eldest and most excellent of them, was devoted to Mahādeva.

91 Uśanas Bhṛgunandana (?) was his (?) adopted son.[5] To him Ekaparṇā bore a son named Devala.

92–93ab The third of them, Ekapāṭalā, was devoted to Jaigīṣavya, son of Alarka; her sons, Śaṅkha and Likhita, are said not to be (her) naturalborn sons.[6]

93cd–99 By Umā's asceticism the three worlds were filled with smoke; Brahman warned her not to destroy the worlds that had been created by herself. He asked her what she wanted. She replied that Brahman should know without asking. He told her that the Lord of Lords, for whose sake she was practising asceticism, would approach her and woo her.

100–101 The god of the gods, the highest Lord, Svayaṃbhū, would approach her in a terrifying, ugly, incomparable shape.[7]

[4] Conjecture; the text seems to be corrupt. Read:
so ṕi kālena śailendro [aniketas tapo 'carat /
nyagrodham ekaparṇaṃ tu pāṭalaṃ caikapāṭalam /
aśitvā ekaparṇāṃ tu] menāyām udapādayat /
aparṇām ekaparṇāṃ ca tathā caivaikapāṭalām /
The passage in parentheses seems to be an interpolated explanation.

[5] Or: Uśanas, an offspring of Bhṛgu, was his (Himavat's) son received by gift.

[6] Or: Śaṅkha and Likhita are known as her sons by unnatural birth (*ayonija* might mean »born by caesarian«).

[7] In Triṣṭubh-Jagatī-metre; the concluding verses are a repetition of the preceding two verses.

Ch. 35: Umā and Rudra: Her devotion to Rudra; Śiva as a child and the crocodile

1–4ab The gods told (Umā) to stop her asceticism, since the Lord of the gods (v.l. he by whom she had been created) would soon become her husband. Having circumambulated her, they disappeared. Umā returned to her hermitage and stayed there leaning against an Aśoka-tree.

4cd–10 Having assumed an extraordinarily ugly shape, hunchbacked, with his nose smashed etc., Hara (= Śiva) appeared and told her that he wanted her as his wife. Umā, perfect in (or, by) Yoga, knew that Śaṃkara had arrived. She welcomed him with hospitable offerings and replied that she was not independent; he should request the lord of mountains, her father.

11–14 Rudra approached Himavat who recognized him in his ugly shape. Being afraid of his curse he told him that his daughter's self-choice (*svayaṃvara*) had already been planned; Rudra should attend it.

15–21 Rudra reported her father's decision to Umā. He doubted that she would prefer him, who was ugly, to others more beautiful. She assured him that she would choose him. In order to dispel his doubts she made her choice on the spot and placed a bunch of Aśoka-flowers on his shoulder.

22–26ab Rudra blessed the Aśoka-tree, granting it to be immortal and to have its shape, blossoms, fruits according to its own will etc.

26cd–28 He further promised that whoever visits that hermitage named Citrakūṭa will obtain the merit of a horse-sacrifice; whoever dies there will enter the Brahman-world; if accomplished in (yogic) discipline, he will have accomplished Umā's asceticism and become a great lord of hosts (*gaṇapati*).

29 After this Śiva disappeared.

30–31 Umā remained behind, despondent and waiting for the Lord of the world, and she entered a rock.[1]

32–64 *Story of Śiva as child and the crocodile*

32–38 Once Umā heard the screams of a boy from the water of a lake near the hermitage. Śiva himself had assumed the shape of that child, who had been seized by a crocodile. The child cried for help, not for his own sake but for that of his parents, since he was their only son.[2]

39–43 Hearing the distressed voice of that Brahmin, Umā approached the lake and beheld the child in the grip of a crocodile which, seeing Umā, dragged the screaming child to the middle of the lake. Pārvatī ordered the crocodile to release the child.

44–45 The crocodile refused, since Brahman had granted him that the first being he would meet with on each sixth day should be his food; the child happened to come first on the sixth day.

[1] ?, perhaps: sat down on a rock.

[2] cf. the story of Daśaratha and the Brahmin boy whom he shot, Rm 2,57–58,and ch. 123 below.

46–51 Umā offered him (the merit of) her asceticism. The crocodile advised her not to waste all of it but to do what he said. Umā promised to do anything within the bounds of propriety, since Brahmins were dear to her. The crocodile asked for all of her asceticism and Umā gave it away. Consequently the crocodile shone like the sun.

52–59 The crocodile offered to return the asceticism, which was so difficult to obtain and should not be renounced, together with the child. Pleased by her devotion to Brahmins, he granted a boon. She replied that she could easily obtain asceticism again but not a Brahmin.[3] Brahmins are far more valuable than asceticism. What has been given away can never be taken back. The crocodile released the child, greeted her, and disappeared shining like the sun. The released child also disappeared like wealth obtained in a dream.

60–63 Umā, noticing that (the power of) her asceticism had gone, started to practise asceticism anew. Śaṃkara prevented her by informing her that she had given her asceticism to him; therefore it would be hers a thousandfold and imperishable. Having obtained imperishable asceticism as a boon Umā kept looking forward to her self-choice.

64 Phalastuti:[4] He who reads this story about Śaṃbhu assuming the shape of a boy (v.l. about Umā's behaviour) will become a lord of hosts (*gaṇapati*) like Kumāra, if he suffers death before having grown up.

Ch. 36: Umā's self-choice; the wedding of Śiva and Umā

1 Brahman continues: The self-choice (*svayaṃvara*) took place on the extended back of Himālaya.

2–6 Though Himavat knew that his daughter would choose Śiva, he announced the self-choice and invited the guests.

7–24ab Description of the arrival of the guests:[1]

7 As soon as the self-choice had been announced the inhabitants of the world began to gather.[2]

8 Brahman (i.e. the first-person narrator).

9–10ab Sahasrākṣa (= Indra, »with a thousand eyes«).

10cd–11ab Vivasvat.

11cd–12ab Bhaga.

12cd–13ab Kṛtānta (= Death, Yama).

13cd–14ab Samīraṇa (= wind, Vāyu).

14cd–15ab Vahni (= fire, Agni).

[3] i.e. the occasion to save this Brahmin boy.

[4] In Upajāti-metre.

[1] In Upajāti-metre.

[2] Each guest is generally described in two lines, i.e. one verse, though the numbering does not correspond; Indra is described in three lines and is mentioned again in 23cd–24ab.

15cd–16ab Rājarāja (= »king of kings«, Kubera).
16cd–17ab Śaśin (= the moon, Soma).
17cd–18ab Gadādhara (= »bearer of the club«, Viṣṇu).
18cd–19ab Aśvins.
19cd–20ab The king of the Nāgas.
20cd–21ab Sons of Diti (= Asuras).
21cd–22ab The king of the Gandharvas.
22cd–23ab The other gods, as well as Gandharvas, Yakṣas, Nāgas and Kiṃnaras.
23cd–24ab Indra (amongst the beings present in the assembly).
24cd–26 Description of Umā.[3]

27–54 *Report on Umā's svayaṃvara*

27–30 Śiva assumed the shape of a child sleeping in (Umā's ?) lap. Recognizing him, Umā took the child and turned away, having obtained the desired husband.
31–36ab Beholding this, the gods were perturbed. Indra wanted to throw his thunderbolt (*vajra*), but his arm suddenly became paralyzed by Śiva. The same happened to Bhaga, while Viṣṇu, observing the child, shook his head.[4]
36cd–39ab Brahman (i.e. the first-person narrator), recognized Śiva, worshipped his feet, and praised him and Umā.
39cd–42 Hymn by Brahman to Śiva.
43–44ab Brahman requested Śiva to have mercy with the gods and to restore their former condition.
44cd–48 After that Brahman addressed the gods, advised them to recognize Śiva and to seek refuge with him. They mentally bowed to him; Śiva was pleased and restored their former condition.
49–52ab Now Śiva assumed his three-eyed shape. Unable to bear his brilliance, the gods closed their eyes: Śiva granted them eyes by means of which they could look at him. They recognized him as the highest three-eyed Lord.
52cd–54ab Umā chose him by placing a garland on his feet. All gods applauded and worshipped Śiva, together with Umā.
54cd–70 Preparations for the wedding; description of the participants in the wedding ceremony.
54cd–57 In the meantime Brahman turned to Himavat, praised him and admonished him not to delay the wedding. Himavat asked Brahman to arrange the wedding ceremony.
58–59ab Brahman obtained Śiva's approval for arranging the wedding.
59cd–63ab Immediately the city was being prepared for the wedding by the gods. Jewels, pearls etc. came to adorn the city. The place in front of the city gate, measured out for the wedding ceremony, was adorned with emeralds, golden pillars, crystal walls and pearl garlands.
63cd–70 Sun and moon were shining, the winds carried perfumed airs; all classes of beings attended the wedding: The four oceans, the gods led by Śakra, heavenly and great

[3] In Upajāti-metre.
[4] cf. MBh 13,145.30–32.

rivers, Siddhas and hermits; Gandharvas, Apsarases, Nāgas, Yakṣas, Rākṣasas, water animals, birds, Kiṃnaras etc. Tumburu and Nārada, Hāhā and Hūhū came with their instruments; the sages recited stories and vedic songs (or: as sung in the Vedas) and muttered the wedding *mantras*; celestial girls sang. Even the six seasons appeared together, personified as women, in order to attend the wedding of Śiva and Umā.

71–124 Poetical descriptions of the six seasons.

71–79 The rainy season.[5]

80–88 Autumn.[6]

89–94 Winter (= snowy season and cold season).[7]

90–93 Description of the Himālaya.

95–105ab Spring.[8]

105cd–116 All seasons together.[9]

117 Description of Anaṅga (the god of love).[10]

118–123 Summer (hot season).

124 Conclusion to the description of the six seasons.[11]

125–136 Description of the wedding ceremony.

125–126 While the music was playing, Brahman (the narrator) adorned the mountain's daughter and led her into the city.

127–129 Brahman told Śiva that on his command he would pour the offering into the fire, according to the customary ritual. Śiva agreed.

130–134 Brahman put Umā's and Śiva's hands together, bound them with Kuśa-grass, while the fire-god stood by with folded hands. Then Brahman poured the offering into the fire and made (the couple) circumambulate the fire. Their hands were untied and the ceremony was concluded. Brahman, together with all gods and (his) mind-born sons, bowed to Śiva.

135a-f Conclusion to (the report on) Umā's self-choice. Announcement of a (further) miraculous (event) (v.l. of a description of the wedding).

Ch. 37: Praise of Śiva by the gods

1a-f At (or: after) the wedding of Bhava (= Śiva) the gods praised the Great Lord.

2–23 Hymn by the gods to Śiva, referring to Śiva's names, appearance, attributes, functions, deeds and identities (v. 19cd–22 use Sāṃkhya concepts), and to the following mythological events: Paralyzing Śakra's (= Indra) arms (5cd); cutting off

[5] v. 73 in Vaṃśasthavila-metre, 74 in Upendravajrā-metre, 75–76 in Vaṃśasthavila-metre, 77 in Upajāti-metre, 79 in Mālinī-metre (rest in Anuṣṭubh).

[6] v. 88 in Śārdūlavikrīḍitā-metre.

[7] v. 94 in Upajāti-metre.

[8] v. 96a-f and 100–105ab in Upajāti-metre.

[9] v. 105cd–106ab, 108 and 116 in Upajāti-metre, 109 in Vaṃśasthavila-metre.

[10] In Mandakrāntā-metre.

[11] In Upajāti-metre.

the head of the sacrifice; pulling Kṛṣṇa's hair; making Bhaga's eyes fall out; pulling out Pūṣan's teeth (9); killing Yama (?, 11); destroying the Yoga of demons (12); concluding with the request that Śiva's friendly shape may be shown.[1]

24–25 Praised in this manner, Śiva agreed and granted a boon.

26–28 The gods replied that Śiva should keep the boon until they should be in need of it. Śiva agreed and returned to his abode.

29 Phalastuti concerning Śiva's feast.[2]

30 Phalastuti concerning listening to and reciting this hymn.

Ch. 38: Story of how Kāma was burnt by Śiva; Menā's reproach of Śiva

1–13 Brahman continues, relating how Manmatha (= Kāma) was burnt by Śiva:

1–6 After the god had returned home, the cruel Manmatha wished to pierce him with an arrow (list of negative epithets of Kāma). Together with his wife Rati, he approached him, but Śiva looked at him contemptuously with his third eye and burnt him with its fire. Crying out for pity, he fell at Śiva's feet.

7–13 Manmatha became unconscious. Rati lamented pitifully and pleaded with Śiva and Umā. Both consoled her by announcing that her husband would continue his function without his body. When Viṣṇu became a son of Vasudeva, then his son would become her future husband. Pleased by this, Rati left while Śiva and Umā enjoyed each other in the Himālaya-mountains.

14–16 Description of lovely places visited by Śiva and Umā.

17–19 Description of their pleasant life amongst the Gandharvas, Vidyādharas etc.[1]

20 In order to please Umā, Śiva did not leave the mountains.[2]

21 The hermits want to know what Śiva and Umā did there together.

22–40 *Story of Menā reproaching Śiva's conduct*

22–23 Brahman continues: In order to please Umā Śiva and his attendants kept producing entertainments.

24–27 Once Umā paid a visit on her own to her mother Menā, who reproached her for playing with her husband like the poor without resources (?).

28–31 Umā was not very pleased with that but did not answer; she left her mother and approached her husband, asking him for another abode. He was surprised, for until then she had always refused to leave for another abode, and he asked her the reason for her change of mind.

32–34 Umā related her visit to her mother, who had criticized Śiva for sporting like the poor instead of enjoying the entertainments of the gods.

[1] v. 2–22 use *namas* plus datives; v. 23 uses *namas* plus vocative.

[2] In Dodhaka-metre.

[1] In Indravajrā-metre.

[2] In Upajāti-metre.

35-38 Śiva laughed and answered, in order to make his wife laugh too, by explaining that her mother was displeased with his wearing hides or nothing at all, having no house, but living at burial-places, with his roaming in the forest with his naked hosts. Umā's mother had been right, yet Umā should not be angry with her, for the relationship with one's mother is the best in the world.

39 Umā replied that she was not concerned about relationships but that he should do what would make her happy.

40 Thereupon both left for Meru.[3]

Ch. 39: Destruction of Dakṣa's sacrifice by Śiva[1]

1-2 The hermits ask for a detailed report on how Dakṣa's sacrifice was destroyed in the Vaivasvata-era.

3 Brahman announces his description.

4-6 Description of the peak of Meru named Jyotiḥsthala where Śiva and Parvatī lived.

7-17ab List of gods and other beings around Śiva:. Ādityas, Vasus and the two Aśvins; Vaiśravaṇa (king of the Yakṣas) with the Guhyakas; Uśanas, Sanatkumāra and the other sages; Aṅgiras and the other divine sages; the Gandharva Viśvāvasu, Nārada and Parvata and hosts of Apsarases; wind bringing all kinds of scents and flowers; blooming trees; Vidyādharas, Sādhyas, Siddhas and other living beings; Rākṣasas and Piśācas; the god's attendants and Nandīśvara, holding a flaming spear; Gaṅgā.

17cd-18ab Conclusion to the description of Śiva etc. on Meru.

18cd-21 Once upon a time the Prajāpati named Dakṣa was going to perform a sacrifice. On that occasion all gods went to Gaṅgādvāra with their heavenly chariots.

22-27ab Description of the arrival of gods and other beings: All beings that lived on earth, in heaven or in the space between came: Ādityas, Vasus, Rudras, Sādhyas, Maruts came together with Viṣṇu; steam-drinkers, smoke-drinkers, drinkers of melted butter and of Soma; Aśvins, Maruts, and the other various classes of gods; and all the other sorts of beings; the viviparous, the egg-born and the sweat-born beings. The gods together with the women and sages shone like fires, standing on their chariots (concluding simile).

27cd-28 Seeing all these (VePr adds: but not seeing Śaṃkara) the sage Dadhīci angrily told them that (VePr adds: without Śiva the sacrifice would do no good) by worshipping somebody unworthy or by neglecting someone deserving worship one obtains great evil (maxim).

[3] In Upajāti-metre.

[1] The BrP version of the story of the destruction of Dakṣa's sacrifice seems to be based on the text of that story as found in the MBh. The critical edition allows us to distinguish two versions of this story, one printed as MBh 12,274, the second printed as App.I.28 of the Śāntiparvan and found only in the Northern recension of the MBh. As is evident from the concordance (see Appendix to the text-volume), the BrP has intertwined those two versions which in the MBh are consecutive passages.

29–32 Then Dadhīci asked Dakṣa why he did not pay homage to Paśupati. Dakṣa pointed out that eleven Rudras were present; and that he did not know another great god (or: anothei as a great god). Dadhīci repeated that because Śaṃkara, his lord whom he thought to be higher than anyone else, had not been invited, the sacrifice would be fruitless.

33 Dakṣa said again that Viṣṇu, the Rudras and other gods had got their share of the sacrifice; to Śaṃkara, however, he would give no share.[2]

34–39 When the gods had left Mt. Meru, Umā asked her husband where they had gone. Śiva replied that they had left for Dakṣa's sacrifice. Umā wanted to know why Śiva did not go with them. He explained to her that he was not provided with a share in any sacrifice.

40–41 Umā replied by describing Śiva as most powerful and incomparable among gods, stating her unhappiness about his exclusion from the shares of the sacrifice.

42 She asked what she could do (asceticism, alms) in order to secure a share of (VePr one third of) the sacrifice for her husband.[3]

43–45 In reply Śiva describes himself as the one whom Brahmins praise as lord of the sacrifices, to whom they sing *rathaṃtara*-melody, whom they worship with *brahman*-formulas, and for whom a share is provided by the Adhvaryus.[4]

46–47 Umā retorted that he was only boasting, as men commonly do in the company of women. Śiva promised to interfere for the sake of his share.

48–49 From the fire of his wrath a being originated who came forth from his mouth; he was ordered by Rudra to destroy Dakṣa's sacrifice.

50 Thereupon Dakṣa's sacrifice was playfully destroyed by the lion-shaped being which was employed by Rudra on becoming aware of Devī's wrath.

51–52 Wrath's female companion was Bhadrakālī, he himself was named Vīrabhadra.

53–58 From the pores of his skin Vīrabhadra dismissed thousands of terrifying Rudras that filled the atmosphere with cries of joy. By that noise inhabitants of the sky were frightened, the mountains fell to pieces, the earth quaked, fierce winds blew, the waters stirred, fires did not burn, stars, the (seven) sages, gods and Dānavas did not shine.[5]

59–66 In this darkness the Rudras burn the sacrifice: Some tear out the sacrificial posts, some crush the sacrificial vessels, some were seen tearing the sacrificial seats (?) like stars from the sky, some carry away the heaps of sacrificial food (including meat), eat it or throw it around, play about in various shapes and abuse the women of the gods.

67–68ab Thus Vīrabhadra burnt the sacrifice together with Bhadrakālī and the Rudras.

68cd–69ab Others produced a terrifying noise, cutting off the head of the sacrifice.

69cd–73 Then the gods asked Vīrabhadra who he was. He told them his name as well as the name of Bhadrakālī and informed them that they had come to destroy the sacrifice. He advised them to seek mercy from Umā's husband, the god of the gods (= Śiva).

[2] In Upajāti-metre. VePr instead has two verses (in Upajāti-metre) in which Dakṣa says that he gave shares to Viṣṇu (other gods and Rudras are not mentioned), but would not give a share to Śaṃkara; with refrain.

[3] In Upajāti-metre.

[4] In Upajāti-metre.

[5] In v. 57–66 verbs are in the present tense.

74-89 *Origin of Fever from Śiva's sweat*

74-81 Suffering from the posts that were torn out and from the vultures flying about, the sacrifice changed into a wild deer and flew towards the sky. But Śiva took an arrow and his bow, and pursued it. When a drop of sweat fell down to the earth from his forehead, a huge fire appeared. Out of this fire a small man originated with red eyes, a yellow moustache, with his hair standing upright, with hairy limbs and bloody (?) ears; black of colour, wearing red garments. He burnt the sacrifice, like fire burns underwood.

82-83 The gods fled in all directions; the earth trembled.

84-88ab Thereupon Brahman (the narrator) addressed Śiva, announcing that the gods would give him a share; but he should desist from further wrath. As the earth would not be able to bear the unified brilliance of that man who originated from Śiva's sweat and who is »fever«, it should be made manifold.

88cd-89 As he had obtained his share, Śiva agreed and became very glad.

90-91 Now Dakṣa, too, in his mind approached Śiva for shelter, stopping his breath and fixing his sight between (?) his eyes. Śiva smiled at him and asked what he should do for him.

92-95 With the great story made known among gods and ancestors (?),[6] Dakṣa humbly replied that if Śiva felt any sympathy for him he should grant that whatever had been destroyed of his sacrifice should not have been in vain.

96-97 Śiva agreed. Having obtained his wish, Dakṣa knelt down and praised Śiva with his 1008 names (announcement of the next chapter).

Ch. 40: Dakṣa's hymn of the thousand names of Śiva; the distribution of fever

1 Brahman continues: Seeing Śaṃbhu's heroism Dakṣa started to praise him.

2-100 Dakṣa's hymn to Śiva (Sahasranāma-Stotra).[1]

2-3ab Addresses (*namas* + vocatives).

3cd-9 Description (nominatives or sentences).

10-37ab Homage (*namaḥ* or *namo 'stu* + datives).

37cd-40ab Addresses (*namaḥ*, *namo 'stu te* + vocatives).

40cd-41a Homage (*namaḥ* + datives (VePr nominatives).

41b-82 Identifications (nominatives or sentences: *tvam eva ...*, occasionally including vocatives).

[6] *śrāvite mahākhyāne* ... seems to belong to another context.

[1] The following hymn has been analyzed and compared with other Sahasranāma Stotras to Śiva by Eugen Rose: Die Śivasahasranāmastotra's in der epischen und purāṇischen Literatur. Eine textkritische und kulturgeschichtliche Untersuchung. Bonn 1934; more recently: Kornelia Giesing: Rudra-Śiva und Tezcatlipoca, Diss. Tübingen 1984, p. 65-154. - Our distinction of sections within this stotra is made without recourse to comparisons of texts, and based on mostly formal criteria.

83 Statement of the impossibility of knowing Śiva's greatness.

84–85 Request for shelter.

86–96 Description (relative clauses).

97–99 Episodic reference: Excuse for not having invited Śiva to the sacrifice.

100 Request for forgiveness.

101–102 When Dakṣa had finished, Śiva expressed his satisfaction, promising that Dakṣa would reach proximity to him.

103–106 In order to inspire confidence, Śiva said once more that Dakṣa need not be worried about the destruction of his sacrifice; he would enjoy the merit of 1000 horse-sacrifices and 100 Vājapeya-sacrifices.

107–111 He advised Dakṣa to study the Vedas, Vedāṅgas and the Sāṃkhyayogas (pl.) as well as to practise asceticism and promised him the merit of observing Pāśupata observances brought into existence by Śiva. Dakṣa should give up his mental pain (fever). After these words Śiva became invisible.

112–120 *The distribution of fever*

112–113ab Having obtained his sacrificial share, Śiva divided the fever into many parts. (Call for attention to listen.)

113cd–118 List of diseases which are manifestations of »fever« in various beings:[2]

Nāgas (elephants ?)	hood-pain (headache ?);
mountains	bitumen (?);
waters	Nīlika-disease (moss?);
snakes	cast-off skin;
cows	hoof-disease;
earth	*ūkhara*-disease (?);[3]
dogs	blindness;
horses	throat-disease (?);[4]
peacocks	crest-splitting;
cuckoos	redness of eyes;
magnanimous people	hatred;
all people	disharmony;
parrots	hiccup-disease;
tigers	exhaustion;
men	fever at birth and death, and in between.

119 Conclusion: This is Śiva's fiery energy (*tejas*) called »fever« which should be duly respected by all living beings.

120 Phalastuti:[5] He who recites this account on the origin of fever with undepressed spirit will be free from disease and obtain all his wishes.

[2] For translations of this passage cf. e.g. W. D. O'Flaherty: Hindu Myths, p. 122; P. Deussen: Vier philosophische Texte, p. 513–514, both based on a text with considerable variants compared to BrP and again different from the text of the crit. ed. of the MBh.

[3] MBh has *ūṣara*, i.e. salinity.

[4] O'Flaherty translates »constipation«.

[5] In Vaṃśasthavila-metre.

121–134 Phalastutis concerning Dakṣa's hymn.

135 Conclusion to the account[6] given by Vyāsa, the son of Parāśara; it should not be made known.

136–137 Phalastuti: He who hears this secret, though even he be born from an evil womb, though he be Vaiśya, Śūdra or woman, will obtain the world of Rudra; a twice-born who has it recited by Brahmins also obtains Rudra's world.

Ch. 41: Description of Ekāmraka; worship of Śiva

1–5 Lomaharṣaṇa continues: Having heard this evil-destroying story about the rise of Rudra's and Pārvatī's wrath, the origin of Vīrabhadra and Bhadrakālī, the destruction of Dakṣa's sacrifice as well as Śiva's mercy on Dakṣa as told by Vyāsa,[1] the listening hermits ask Vyāsa for the rest of the story. Vyāsa tells them about the place Ekāmraka.

6–9 Vyāsa tells how the sages once asked Brahman for the same topic after having been told about the greatness of Śiva. Brahman answered by giving the desired description.

10 Brahman announces a brief account of that place.

11–50ab Description of the place Ekāmraka.

11–12 Beautiful as Vārāṇasī, endowed with 10,000,000 Liṅgas and 8 holy places, Ekāmraka is named after a »matchless mango-tree« that was there in former times.

13–19 Description of the city.

20–37ab Description of the inhabitants.

20–27 Description of the women living there.

28–29 Description of the men, who perform their duties according to the four castes.

30–34ab Continued description of the women, who are compared to Apsarases (Ghṛtācī, Menakā, Tilottamā, Urvaśī, Vipracitti, Viśvācī, Sahajanyā, Pramlocā are named).

34cd–36 List of unpleasant, ugly or criminal people absent from that city.

37ab Conclusion to the description of the inhabitants.

cd–38ab Description of the landscape.

38cd–44 List of trees and flowers.

45–46 List of birds.

47–49ab Lakes and ponds with lotuses and water-animals.

ab–50ab Conclusion to the description of that place.

cd–54ab There resides Śiva, for the welfare of the whole world, who once took water-drops (*bindu*) from each river, lake, pond etc. in order to make the holy place called Bindusaras.

cd–57ab A pilgrimage to that place on the eighth day of the dark half of Mārgaśīrṣa performed according to the rules has the same merit as a horse-sacrifice.

cd–59ab Presenting gifts to the Brahmins there (on various, listed, dates) is 100 times more meritorious than at another place.

[6] Beginning from 26.27.

[1] This reference back covers only ch. 39–40.

59cd–60ab Whoever offers a rice-ball (*piṇḍa*) to his ancestors at the bank of that water will effect everlasting satiation for them.

60cd–71 Whoever worships Śiva in his temple according to the rules (by circumambulations, ointments, flowers, leaves, recitations, songs, scents etc.),[2] will go to Śiva's world[3] in a golden chariot, will enjoy all delights up to the end of the world, will be reborn in a family of Caturvedin Brahmins and finally, when he has obtained the Pāśupata Yoga (i.e. union with Paśupati?), he will reach liberation.

72–74 Likewise, those who behold the god (Śiva) upon rising from sleep, at the occurrences of a new stellar constellation, at a solstice, on the 8th day of Caitra (called Aśokāṣṭamī), or the 12th day of the light half of Śrāvaṇa (or Āṣāḍha), called Pavitrāropaṇa, will go to Śiva's world, as well as those who behold him always.

75–81 Two Yojanas and a half to the west, east, south and north of the god (i.e. of the Liṅga in his temple) extends the place granting enjoyment and liberation; there is a Liṅga called Bhāskareśvara. Those who behold Maheśvara there will go to Śiva's world in a golden chariot, stay there for one cosmic cycle, then be reborn in an illustrious (Brahmin) family or in the house of Yogins and finally, when they have obtained union with Śaṃbhu (or: The Yoga of Śaṃbhu) will obtain liberation.

82–85 He who beholds the Liṅga in that place or anywhere else, in a forest, in a road, crossroad or burying place, and pays homage to it by bathing, adorning, praising it etc., will go to Śiva's world.

86 Even a woman will obtain the merit described above by confidently worshipping.

87 Who could describe the qualities of that place except Maheśvara?

88–90 Anyone, man or woman, who bathes in the Bindusaras-lake, be it with or without faith, in any month, and look at the ugly-eyed god (= Śiva) and the goddess (= Umā, Pārvatī), their attendants (*gaṇa*), Caṇḍa, Kārttikeya, Gaṇeśa, the bull, the wishing tree and (the) Sāvitrī(-verse), will enter Śiva's world.

91 He who bathes at the holy place named Kāpila will obtain the fulfilment of all his wishes and enter the Śiva-world.

92 He who performs the *stambha* (= suppression of all feelings or needs)[4] there, will rescue 21 generations of ancestors and enter Śiva's world.

93 He who takes a bath at Ekāmraka, which is equal to Vārāṇasī, will surely obtain liberation.

Ch. 42: Description of Viraja; description of Utkala

1–11 *Description of a place sacred to Virajā*

1–2 Brahman continues: In Viraja is the abode of Brahman's wife Virajā, the Mother; he who beholds her releases seven (generations of) ancestors; and he who pays homage to her will enter Brahman's (i.e. the first-person narrator's) world.

[2] cf. the description of a *pūjā*, ch. 61, v. 24–38.

[3] Ed. VePr inserts a list of »lords of the earth« to be visited.

[4] Ed. VePr. reads *tīrtham*, »crossing over«, i.e. dying?

3 There are other mothers of the world who take away all evil and love their devotees.

4 There is also the river Vaitaraṇī; he who bathes in it will be released from all evil.

5 Hari himself dwells there in the shape of a boar (*kroḍa*); he who bows to him will reach Viṣṇu's highest step.

6–8 There are other holy places at Viraja named Kāpila, Gograha, Soma, Ālābu, Mṛtyuṃjaya, Kroḍatīrtha, Vāsuka, Siddhakeśvara; he who bathes in these 8 holy places, with self-control, will be released from all evil and enter Brahman's world.

9 He who offers the rice-balls in Viraja will give everlasting satiation to his ancestors.

10 Those who die at that place will obtain liberation.

11 He who bathes in the ocean, then beholds Hari and the goddess Vārāhī will enter the abode of the gods.

12 There are other places of pilgrimage there, which should be made known.

13–49ab *Description of Utkala*

13–14 On the bank of the ocean there is a most sacred, secret place, all sandy, extending 10 Yojanas; it destroys all evil and grants all wishes but is difficult to reach.

15–19 List of trees.

20–23 Description of the trees: blooming and bearing fruit in every season, populated by various kinds of birds (listed).

24–26 List of flowers and creepers.

27–31 Description of ponds and lakes, covered with different lotuses and populated by various kinds of aquatic birds.

32–33 Description of the inhabitants of that place belonging to the different stages of life, etc.

34 Conclusion: Thus, the place is endowed with all good qualities.

35–36ab There is the abode of the famous Puruṣottama; up to the border of Utkala the place is most sacred due to the grace of Kṛṣṇa.

5cd–38ab Where Puruṣottama resides who is the soul of all and the lord of the world(s) (*jagannātha*), there is the abode of all; Brahman (first-person narrator), Śakra(= Indra) and the (other) gods led by Agni dwell there.

8cd–42ab All classes of beings (listed) stay there, as well as the four Vedas, the Vedāṅgas, the different Śāstras, Itihāsas, Purāṇas and sacrifices, also the various rivers, places of pilgrimage, oceans and mountains.

2cd–46ab This most sacred place is esteemed by everyone; is there a better place than that where Puruṣottama resides? (Rhetorical question). Happy are those who live there and see him: they are in heaven and will never die.

6cd–49ab Their life is successful, who behold the best of gods (description of his beauty).

Ch. 43: Story of Indradyumna

1–13 Brahman continues with a summary account of the story of Indradyumna.[1]

[1] i.e. of what is related ch. 43.24–51.58. A summary and analysis of these chapters is provided

1 (A I 1) In former times in the Kṛta-Yuga there was a king as brave as Śakra (= Indra) named Indradyumna.

2–5 (A I 1) Description of his qualities: truthful, well-versed in every branch of knowledge etc., a Vaiṣṇava, a student of Yoga and Sāṃkhya (v.l. devoted to self-knowledge).

6–9 (A I 2) Wishing to pay homage to Hari Janārdana (= Viṣṇu) he surveyed in his mind all the places of pilgrimage, river-banks and hermitages of the world, to find which of them might be most fitting for that purpose, but discarded all of them.

10–13 (A II 1.1–4) He went to Puruṣottama and performed a horse-sacrifice, built a temple, placed (statues of) Saṃkarṣaṇa (= Balarāma), Kṛṣṇa and Subhadrā there, established (or visited) five places of pilgrimage there, bathed, granted gifts, practised asceticism etc., and devotedly paid homage to Puruṣottama every day, whereupon he obtained liberation.

14 (A II 2) He who beholds the Mārkaṇḍeya(-tree), Kṛṣṇa and Rāma (= Baladeva) and bathes in the ocean named Indradyumna will obtain liberation.[2]

15–21 (A F) The hermits inquire: 1. Why did Indradyumna go to the place Puruṣottama? 2. How did he perform the horse-sacrifice? 3. How did he build the temple? 4. How did he make the three statues? 5. How did he protect that place? 6. How did he place the statues in the temple? All this the hermits want to know in detail; they do not get enough of listening but are very curious.

22–23 (B I 1) Pleased by these questions, Brahman announces that he will tell the story.

24 (B I 1) The city Avantī in Mālava was ruled by that king (= Indradyumna).

25–65ab (B I 1 interpolation) Description of Avantī.

25–29 Description of the streets and buildings.

30–44 Description of the inhabitants.

33–36ab Description of the men.

36cd–44 Description of the women.

45–55 List of trees.

56–58ab List of birds.

58cd–63ab Description of ponds and lakes with lotuses and aquatic animals.

by R. Geib: Indradyumna-Legende, Ein Beitrag zur Geschichte des Jagannātha-Kultes, Wiesbaden 1975, p. 47–78. Geib distinguishes three versions of the Indradyumna-legend, which have been intertwined in our text (each version being complete since it relates Indradyumna's departure, the construction of the temple, the horse-sacrifice, the establishment of the wooden idols). The following summary incorporates Geib's results by indicating as which section of which version (A,B,C) he has classified each passage. Geib writes: »Die Indradyumna-Legende des Br. P. erschien uns als eine Summe schlecht miteinander verbundener Einzellegenden, welche sich ohne Schwierigkeiten voneinander trennen ließen. Wir konnten die folgenden Elemente unterscheiden: 1. die aitiologische Sage vom Indradyumna-See (adhy. 48,27ff.); 2.1. die Geschichte vom Mālava-König, der in Puruṣottamakṣetra den Nīlamādhava-Kult gründet (B I 3–5); 2.2. die Wallfahrt eines nach Erlösung strebenden Königs (A I 1–2 und B I 1–2); 3. als *Verbindungsstück* die Legende vom verschwundenen Nīlamādhava (C I); 4. die Legende vom angeschwemmten Baum und von der Aufstellung der drei Jagannātha-Figuren (B II).« (p. 79)

[2] cf. 69.74–77ab.

3cd-65ab Conclusion to the description of Avantī (summary).

5cd-85ab *Holy places in Avantī and the way of obtaining liberation by performing certain rituals there*

65cd-74 (B I 1) There is the abode of the three-eyed Śiva known as Mahākāla. He who bathes in the pool sacred to Śiva, feeds gods and ancestors, performs worship before Śiva's statue (list of accessories) will enter Śiva's heaven, be reborn in an excellent Brahmin family, obtain Pāśupata Yoga and finally liberation.

75-76 There is the holy river Śiprā (v.l. Kṣiprā); he who bathes there according to the rule, after satisfying ancestors and gods, will enjoy various delights in heaven.

77-82ab There is the abode of Janārdana named Govindasvāmin; he who beholds him obtains liberation. With a golden chariot etc. he enters Viṣṇu's world. Afterwards he is reborn in a family of Brahmins or Yogins; performing the Vaiṣṇava Yoga he will finally obtain liberation.

2cd-83ab There is also (an image of) Viṣṇu named Vikramasvāmin; a man or woman who beholds him will obtain the merits already mentioned.

3cd-85ab Likewise there are (images of) other gods, led by Śakra (= Indra), and mothers; by beholding and worshipping them, according to the rules, a man is released from evil and enters heaven.

85cd-88 Continuation of the description of Avantī: Resembling Indra's city Amarāvatī, Avantī is filled by the noise of arrows and strings, by recitals of the Vedas, Itihāsas, Purāṇas, poems, speeches and stories, by day and night.

89 Conclusion to the description of Avantī.

Ch. 44: Story of Indradyumna (contd): The journey to the southern ocean

1 (B I 1) That city was ruled by a king (i.e. Indradyumna) who protected his subjects like his own children.

2-7 (B I 1) Description of Indradyumna, his pious actions and his wealth.

8-9 (B I 2) Thus residing in Avantī, the king (one day) thought of how to win the favour of Hari.

10-12 (B I 2) He went through all Śāstras, Tantras, Āgamas, Itihāsas, Purāṇas, Vedāṅgas and other sources of knowledge, asked his preceptor and other Brahmins and finally reached his aim by choosing the highest goal.

13 (B I 2) Having perceived the highest truth named Vāsudeva he surpassed all erroneous knowledge and wanted liberation.

14-15 (B I 2) (He reflected) how he could pay homage to the four-armed god, clad in yellow clothes, holding conch, discus, and club, wearing a garland etc.

16-40 (B I 3) He left Ujjayinī, together with a large army, with his servants and his priest.

17-22 Description of the warriors, heroes and soldiers that followed him.

23-27ab Description of the women that accompanied them.[1]

[1] Ed. VePr inserts one line after v. 25ab and 11 lines after 27ab describing the accompanying courtesans (3 lines) and adding to the list of professions.

27cd–40 Description of men of various professions who went with him.

41–43 (B I 3) Thus the king accompanied by his subjects, like a father leaving home accompanied by his children, proceeded slowly until he reached the bank of the southern ocean.

44–47 (B I 3) Description of the ocean (including a list of aquatic animals).

48–53ab (B I 3) Characterization of the ocean as a sacred place where Viṣṇu rests, as means of life for all beings, as cause for the waxing and waning of the moon, etc.

53cd–54 (B I 3) The king was astonished and settled on the bank of the ocean, that holy place endowed with all qualities.

55–79 *Description of Puruṣottamakṣetra*

55–63 List of trees.

64–66ab List of birds.

66cd–69 List of flowers and creepers.

70–72 List of inhabitants (70–71ab supernatural beings; 71cd–72 animals).

73–75 Description of pools and lakes with aquatic birds and lotuses.

76–77 Description of hills.

78–79 (Conclusion:) Thus, the king beheld that place, which extended 10 Yojanas in width and 5 Yojanas in length, and is difficult to reach.

Ch. 45: Story of Indradyumna (contd): The disappearance of Nīlamādhava

1–76 *Story of the disappearance of Nīlamādhava*

1–3 (C I) The hermits ask Brahman why (or: whether) there was no statue sacred to Viṣṇu at that place before that king established the statues of Kṛṣṇa, Rāma (Baladeva) and Subhadrā.[1]

4 Brahman answers by announcing that he will tell them briefly what Hari was once asked by his wife Śrī on the Meru.

5–16ab Description of Mount Meru.

5–7 List of inhabitants.

8–12 List of trees.

13–14ab List of flowers.

14cd–15ab List of birds.

15cd–16ab Summary.

16cd–89 *Dialogue between Janārdana Vāsudeva and Śrī*

16cd–17ef While staying there, Śrī put a question to her husband, the lord of the world (*jagannātha*), called Vāsudeva.

[1] This question could be expected rather after ch. 46.

18-20 Śrī asks, how it is possible in the world of mortals to be released from the succession of births.

21 Brahman introduces Janārdana's reply.[2]

22-25 Janārdana (= Viṣṇu) announces an account of the most sacred place Puruṣottama.

26-28 At the end of a cosmic cycle, when all beings had been destroyed, everything had become dark, and nothing could be perceived; only the Great Lord Hari (= Viṣṇu), named Vāsudeva,[3] whose self is Yoga, was awake.[4]

29 At the end of his yogic sleep he created Brahman, who rose in the midst of the lotus of Viṣṇu's navel like lotus filaments.

30-36 Brahman created the five elements, the movable and immovable beings, the sages, gods, demons, ancestors, Yakṣas etc., rivers, animals, birds, worms and insects, the four castes and the casteless (= Mlecchas).

37-41 He imagined himself as having become twofold, a male in his right and a female in his left half. From that moment onward the creatures in this world have been born from sexual intercourse, the high, low, and middle (creatures), and those that are »my[5] fields«.[6] Having thought thus, Brahman went into meditation, resorting to Vāsudeva's shape. In that very moment (by Brahman's meditation alone), (Janārdana) as Puruṣa came into existence, with 1000 eyes, 1000 heads etc.,[7] and endowed with Śrīvatsa-lock.

42-43 After being welcomed and praised by Brahman, Vāsudeva (now again first person narrator) asked him about the reason of his meditation.

44-46 Brahman replied that he wished to know about the best of all places, better than all other religious observances (Yoga, truthfulness, asceticism, faith, holy places).

47-49 Viṣṇu announced the best of all places to Brahman.

50 From that[8] the »king of holy places« came into existence.

51-52 Explanation of the name »Puruṣottama«, i.e. »best of men« among all beings.

53-56 This place is situated on the bank of the southern ocean, 10 Yojanas in extent, where there is a fig-tree that cannot be destroyed even at the end of a cosmic cycle.[9] Merely by beholding this tree or going into its shade one will be released from all sins, even Brahmin-murder. Those who perform devotional rites there go to the abode of Keśava[10], released from all sins.

[2] The answer extends till v. 76; v. 22-25 are an introduction; v. 26-50 an account of the creation of the world and how Puruṣottamakṣetra came into existence; v. 51-58 a description of Puruṣottamakṣetra; v. 59-76 an account of how the blue statue disappeared.

[3] Third person though Vāsudeva is the narrator.

[4] *jāgarti*: present tense in order to express duration.

[5] i.e. Vāsudeva's or Brahman's (see below)?

[6] v. 38cd not clear; thoughts of Brahman (see the following verse) or insertion of an explanation by Viṣṇu to Śrī?

[7] cf. RV 10,90.

[8] The connection of *tasmāt* ist not clear; probably: »from that dialogue between Viṣṇu and Brahman« (which seems to be finished now). Perhaps v. 50, which contains a kind of conclusion, is here in the wrong place.

[9] cf. ch. 52ff.

[10] Ms. B reads: »to Śiva's (!) abode«, in agreement with ch. 56, v. 66cd-73, below.

57–58 Somewhat to the north of that tree but south of Keśava (?) there is a temple. They who behold the statue inside it will go to Viṣṇu's (i.e. the first-person narrator's) abode immediately.

59–67 Once when Yama saw all the people always going (to imediate liberation), he once went to Viṣṇu (the narrator), bowed to him and praised him.[11]

60–67 Hymn by Yama to Viṣṇu.[12]

68–70 Viṣṇu (i.e. the first-person narrator) asked him for the reason of his hymn.

71–73 Yama replied that he could not fulfil his function (of making people die) as long as all people who had seen the blue statue at Puruṣottama kept going to the house named Śveta (the white one, i.e. Viṣṇu's palace?) free from all desires. Therefore this statue should be taken away by Viṣṇu.

74 Viṣṇu promised to hide the statue with pebbles (sand).

75–76 After that he hid the statue with creepers and Yama went to his own residence in the south.

77–89 (C II) Brahman continues by summarizing the contents of what else Viṣṇu told his wife, all that happened after the hiding of the blue statue:[13] Indradyumna's journey and arrival at that place,[14] description of the place,[15] building of a temple and performing a horse-sacrifice,[16] Indradyumna's dream,[17] the finding of the log on the bank of the ocean,[18] the appearance of Viṣṇu and Viśvakarman,[19] the shaping of the statue,[20] installation of all statues in the temple;[21] the story of Mārkaṇḍeya at the end of the cosmic cycle and the installation of (a statue of) Śaṃkara;[22] the Pañcatīrtha-Māhātmya,[23] consisting of paying homage to Śiva at the Mārkaṇḍeya-lake,[24] to the fig-tree Vainateya,[25] to Saṃkarṣaṇa Baladeva,[26] to Kṛṣṇa,[27] the Subhadrā-Māhātmya;[28] paying homage to Narasiṃha[29] and to Anantavāsudeva;[30]

[11] The vocatives *priye* (v. 59) and *mahābhāge* (v. 69) addressed to Śrī attribute this passage to the dialogue between Viṣṇu and Śrī, not to that between Viṣṇu and Brahman, which was most probably already finished in v. 49 above.

[12] List of epithets in acc., dependent on *namāmi* in verse 67.

[13] Summary in catchwords, covering the Indradyumna-legend (as told before and after this summary) and the subsequent chapters on holy places in Puruṣottamakṣetra.

[14] = ch. 44.1-54.

[15] = ch. 44.54–79; ch. 46.

[16] = ch. 47.

[17] = ch. 50.1-16.

[18] = ch. 50.17–23.

[19] = ch. 50.24–42ab.

[20] = ch. 50.42cd–54.

[21] = ch. 51.48–59.

[22] = ch. 52–56.

[23] = ch. 57.

[24] v. 2–11.

[25] v. 12–19.

[26] v. 20–28.

[27] v. 29–56.

[28] v. 57–61.

[29] = ch. 58.

[30] = ch. 59.1-2; this image is described in detail and provided with a prehistory in ch. 176

the Śvetamādhava-Māhātmya;[31] the visit to Svargadvāra and paying homage to the ocean;[32] bathing and offering food;[33] the Māhātmya of bathing in the ocean and in the Indradyumna(-lake);[34] the merit of (visiting the) Pañcatīrtha; the importance of (the month) Jyeṣṭha;[35] the throne of Kṛṣṇa (and) Halāyudha;[36] the merit of the pilgrimage from place to place (?);[37] the description of Viṣṇu's world;[38] and (the praise) of his place (i.e. Puruṣottamakṣetra).[39]

Ch. 46: Story of Indradyumna (contd): Description of Puruṣottamakṣetra

1 (B I) The hermits want to know the rest of the story, what Indradyumna did at that place.

2 Brahman announces a brief account of the view of that place and of the king's deeds.

3-23 Description of Puruṣottamakṣetra.

4-6ab Description of the river Mahānadī; and of villages and towns.

7cd-10 Description of the inhabitants (castes; especially description of the Brahmins).

11-12 Streets and buildings are full of the sound of recitation of various kinds of texts.

13-22 Description of the women.

23 Description of the holy men.

24-30 (B I 4) Beholding this place, the king (= Indradyumna) made up his mind to please Viṣṇu at that place, known to him as Puruṣottama, where there was the fig-tree and the hidden statue named Indranīla, but no other statue belonging to Viṣṇu. In order to make Viṣṇu appear he decided to observe a vow (*vrata*) by performing sacrifices, giving alms, etc., and to build a temple.[1]

below, which is not referred to in this summary and may, therefore, be eve a later addition to the Puruṣottamakṣetra-Māhātmya than the dialogue between Viṣṇu and Śrī. Some characters of this later prehistory (Rāma, Vibhīṣaṇa) are however mentioned in 59.2.

[31] = ch. 59.

[32] Seems to be missing in the text.

[33] = ch. 60.

[34] = ch. 62-63.8.

[35] = ch. 63.9-64.

[36] = ch. 65.

[37] = ch. 66-67.

[38] = ch. 68.

[39] = ch. 69.

[1] At this point in the text one would expect ch. 45, starting with the question of the hermits about why there was no statue etc.

Ch. 47: Story of Indradyumna (contd): Construction of temple; horse-sacrifice

1-3 (B I 4) Brahman continues: After these reflections, the king started his preparations, by consecrating the place, together with his priests, ministers, (VePr astrologers), etc.

4-6 After deciding upon an auspicious day together with them, he performed the *arghya*-ceremony (i.e. offering of water to a guest).[1]

7-9 He called for the rulers of Kaliṅga, Utkala and Kośala and ordered them to take artisans and stone-cutters along in order to bring the best stones from the Vindhya-mountain (by cart and boat).

10-95 *Indradyumna's horse-sacrifice*

10-12 (B I 5) Then he ordered messengers to invite all the kings of the earth together with their priests and counsellors.

13-17 Upon his call all the kings, from all regions and directions of the world, came with cars and elephants etc.

18-21 After their arrival the king announced that he intended to perform a horse-sacrifice and to build a temple in order to please Viṣṇu; he asked for their help.

22-29ab Willingly the kings brought all sorts of precious stones, elephants, horses, chariots and other riches, all sorts of food and other necessary things.

29cd-34 Beholding all the Brahmins, well-versed in the Vedas and other branches of knowledge, all the sages and teachers, the king asked them to discover the place fitting for the horse-sacrifice.

35-41 Thereupon the main priest, together with the Brahmins, carried out the king's word. He had a place where there were fishermen's villages changed into a sacrificial ground with broad roads and (buildings) with pinnacles, with well-adorned palaces, pillars, doorways, female apartments etc., residences for the kings from the different countries and for the different castes.

42-49 Now the kings with their ladies, the Brahmins with the disciples etc. came to dwell in the different houses assigned to them by the king. On being informed about it the king was full of joy.

50-98 Description of the horse-sacrifice.[2]

50 At the beginning of the sacrifice the orators started their discussions.

51-58ab Description of the sacrificial ground as seen by Indradyumna and the other kings: Doorways, couches and seats, vessels etc., wooden posts adorned with gold; different animals and mountains of grain (?). The kings were astonished.

58cd-61 Day and night the drum was beaten in announcement of diverse foods for the Brahmins; thereby the king's sacrifice was growing. Abundant food was distributed, streams of milk were seen.

62 The whole of Jambūdvīpa with people from different countries and Brahmins were seen at the great sacrifice of the king.

[1] As a welcome for Viṣṇu or the assembly?

[2] Seems to be a passage from a separate source (new chapter?) as »*brahmovāca*« is inserted.

63–67 Thousands of men went around with vessels serving the Brahmins; servants and attendants gave food and drink to the Brahmins and honoured the guests that had come from all countries: kings, inhabitants of big cities, dancers and singers.

68–70 Description of the wives (of the king; *tasya* ?).[3]

71–73 Description of elephants, horses and pedestrians.[4]

74–80ef Seeing the preparations and requisites of the sacrifice, the king was filled with joy and ordered the princes to bring the horse and to take it to graze on the earth, while experts in the religious tradition arranged the sacrifice.[5] Offerings should be made, the construction of Viṣṇu's temple should be carried out, and the Brahmins should receive anything they wanted: women, jewels, villages and towns, landed property and other riches. The sacrifice should go on until the deity appeared to the king at that place.

81–93ab Thereupon the king gave heaps of gold and jewels, 1000 horses, bulls and valuable cows to the Brahmins, as well as rich clothes and various precious stones, 500 beautiful young girls with all adornments, and all sorts of delicious foods so that there was no end to giving.

3cd–95ab Seeing this great sacrifice all gods, Daityas etc. were astonished; the king, the chief priest and the counsellors were full of joy. There was nobody poor, sick etc. seen at the celebration; there was never a sacrifice like that seen by the ascetics and long-living hermits.

95c-f Conclusion: Thus, the king performed a horse-sacrifice and built the Viṣṇu-temple. (Ed. VePr adds 5 verses repeating the gifts of the king to Brahmins and others.)

Ch. 48: Story of Indradyumna (contd): Indradyumna's anxiety[1]

1–2 (B IIa 1) The hermits want to know how the statues were made by Indradyumna.

3 Brahman announces a Purāṇa relating how the statues originated.

4–11 When the sacrifice was performed and the temple built, the king (= Indradyumna) was worried about how he could see the highest god. The king did not sleep nor eat nor bathe and would not by any means be satisfied or consoled; day and night he thought about what material would be most fitting for a statue of Viṣṇu, stone, clay or wood.

12 Finally the troubled king turned to Viṣṇu, worshipped him by the method of Pañcarātra (»five nights«) and praised him in a hymn.

[3] Construction not clear.

[4] Construction not clear.

[5] v. 76cd–77ab consist of a list of accusative forms (enumerating sacrificial animals etc.) that cannot be construed with the surrounding sentences. Ed. VePr prints v. 77–99 as a footnote and adds 5 numbered verses at the end of the chapter.

[1] Ch. 48.1–49.6 are printed in a footnote in ed. VePr.

Ch. 49: Story of Indradyumna (contd): Hymn to Viṣṇu

1–59 (B IIa 1) Hymn by Indradyumna to Viṣṇu.[1]

1–8 Homage and addresses (*namas te* with vocatives and refrain).

9 Simile: Like the earth lifted up by Viṣṇu in the shape of a boar, Indradyumna wants to be saved from the ocean of suffering.

10–20 Though Viṣṇu is praised in all his different forms there is no differentiation in him: He is only one. Even the gods do not know him really, how should Indradyumna? His supreme shape, clad in yellow clothes, four-armed, holding the conch, the discus and the club, wearing his crown, showing the Śrīvạtsa-lock on his breast, adorned with garlands, is worshipped by wise people.

21–22 Viṣṇu should save Indradyumna from the ocean of sufferings, as there is nobody else who could help.

23–47ab Description of all the suffering Indradyumna has experienced during his various births and rebirths.

47cd–50ab But now Indradyumna has taken his refuge in him (Kṛṣṇa) who should save him from the ocean of sufferings as there is no one else to help; having found shelter he is free from fear in all troubles.

50cd–54ab Those who do not praise Viṣṇu, who have no devotion (*bhakti*), or who reproach him will be lost and find no rest.

54cd–56ab But in every birth Indradyumna will be a devotee of Viṣṇu: all the gods, Daityas, etc. obtain bliss by praising Viṣṇu; who would not pay homage to him?

56cd–57ab Since even the gods are not able to praise Viṣṇu, how could he (i.e. Indradyumna) praise him?

57cd–59ab Thus, though Viṣṇu is praised only by someone whose nature is ignorance, he should forgive all faults and transgressions committed by Indradyumna.

59c-f (Conclusion to the hymn:) Wish that the hymn might be completed by means of Indradyumna's devotion.

60 Thus praised, Viṣṇu was satisfied and granted Indradyumna all that he wanted.

61–63 Phalastuti: Whoever praises Viṣṇu with that hymn will obtain liberation and enter Viṣṇu's world.

64–66 But this holy hymn should not be made known to the unbelievers (*nāstika*), to fools, to ungrateful, proud, evil-thinking people or non-devotees; only devotees of Viṣṇu with good qualities should obtain it.

67 Conclusion to the hymn.[2]

68 Phalastuti: He who always thinks of Viṣṇu will obtain liberation.[3]

69 Praise of Viṣṇu's qualities.[4]

70 Uselessness of knowledge, good qualities, sacrifices, gifts, asceticism if there is no devotion to Kṛṣṇa.[5]

[1] After verse 6, i.e. at the beginning of ch. 46 according to ed. VePr, that edition inserts 3 verses describing the king's preparation for his praising and adding one verse to the hymn.

[2] In Upajāti-metre.

[3] In Indravajrā-metre.

[4] In Upajāti-metre.

[5] In Upajāti-metre.

71 Phalastuti: Whoever is devoted to (the god) named Puruṣottama will be endowed with all the good qualities in the world.[6]

Ch. 50: Story of Indradyumna (contd): Making of the images

1–3 (B IIa 2.1) Brahman continues: Having thus praised Vāsudeva, Indradyumna fell asleep wondering how Janārdana could appear before him.

4–6 To the sleeping king Vāsudeva showed himself in his blue shape holding conch, discus and club, bow and arrows (v.l. and sword).

7–15 Vāsudeva told the king that he was pleased with his hymn and his devotion and that the king should not be distressed. Then he gave him instructions concerning the statue: The next morning the king should go to the bank of the ocean; there he would see a big tree washed ashore. With an axe he should cut this tree and make a figure.

16–17 After these words Viṣṇu disappeared, leaving the king in great astonishment and in deep thought for the rest of the night, which he spent reciting Viṣṇuitic verses and hymns.

18–22 (B IIa 2.2) The next morning he got up, carried out his normal duties and then went alone to the ocean. There he found a big tree.

23–24 (B IIa 3.1) He took an axe and thought of cutting it into pieces.

25–28 Suddenly Viśvakarman and Viṣṇu appeared in the shape of Brahmins and asked the king what he was doing there and why he was cutting that tree.

29–32 Seeing the Brahmins the king greeted them respectfully and replied that, in order to please Viṣṇu, he intended to make a statue and that he had received instructions from Viṣṇu in a dream.

33–40 Pleased by these words Viṣṇu smiled and praised him for his intention to please Viṣṇu (v. 34–36 contain a description of the »ocean« of Saṃsāra); because of that he would be wealthy and successful; his task would be carried out by them, as they were great experts in sculpture.

41–43ab Accordingly the king left the bank of the ocean and sat down in the shade of a nearby tree while Viṣṇu in the shape of a Brahmin ordered Viśvakarman to make the statue.

3cd–44ab (B IIb1 3.2) The statue should look like Kṛṣṇa with lotus-eyes, with Śrīvatsa-lock and the Kaustubha-Jewel, holding conch-shell, discus and club.

4cd–46ab The second statue should be of white colour and show the plough-bearer (= Rāma Baladeva) whose end is not known by gods, demons etc. and who is therefore called »Endless« (*ananta*) according to the tradition.

6cd–47ab The third statue should be that of Vāsudeva's sister Subhadrā, in golden colour.

48–54 According to that instruction Viśvakarman made the statues in one moment: One of white colour, with blue garments, very strong, wearing one ear-ring and holding a club (?); the second one of blue colour like a dark cloud, with eyes like lotus-leaves,

[6] In Upajāti-metre.

with white garments, marked by the Śrīvatsa-lock, this statue being Hari; the third one of golden colour, lotus-eyed, with coloured garments, adorned with various jewelry.

55–59 (B IIb1 4.1) Indradyumna, much confused by Viśvakarman's skill and the wonderful statues, wanted to know who the strange Brahmins were, whether gods or men, Yakṣas or Vidyādharas, Brahman and Hṛṣīkeśa or the Aśvins.

Ch. 51: Story of Indradyumna (contd): Boons granted by Viṣṇu

1–8 (B IIb1 4.1) Viṣṇu replied that he was neither god nor Yakṣas nor Daitya nor the king of the gods nor Brahman or Rudra, but that he should be known as Puruṣottama (»the highest of men«). He introduced himself as being Brahman, Viṣṇu, Śiva, Indra, Yama, all elements, Varuṇa, the earth etc. He granted a boon to Indradyumna and informed him that this vision was the result of his firm devotion (*bhakti*).

9 Thereupon Indradyumna sang a hymn in praise of Vāsudeva.

10–16 Hymn to Viṣṇu (v. 10: vocatives describing the god's relation to Śrī; v. 11–12: theological attributes, such as: almighty, endless, without qualities, etc.; v. 13–15: iconographic description; v. 16: description of Viṣṇu as benefactor.)

17–21 After praising Viṣṇu, Indradyumna expressed the wish to go to that place which is thought to be the highest step (*paramaṃ padam*) by all beings (v. 18–20 list of beings) and experts in knowledge.

22–45 Viṣṇu granted Indradyumna's wish:

22–26 Indradyumna should reign 10,900 years; then he would go to that »highest step« (*paramaṃ padam*) obtaining endless bliss and the ultimate goal (description of *paramaṃ padam*).

27–28 (Interpolation a1) His fame on earth shall last as long as sky, moon and sun, the seven oceans and the gods in heaven exist.

29–31 (Interpolation a2) The holy place named Indradyumna-tank arose from the parts of a sacrifice. He who bathes there and presents oblations will release 21 ancestors and go to Indra's world with a golden chariot attended by Apsarases and Gandharvas and will stay there as long as 14 Indras.[1]

32–45 (Interpolation b) South of that lake stands a fig-tree (and) near by a temple.[2]

33–36 Description of the surroundings; list of trees.

37–39 To this temple people will bring the three statues on the fifth day of the bright half of Āṣāḍha, place them there for 7 days, fanned by beautiful courtesans with well-adorned fans and establish them.[3]

40–41 Brahmins, ascetics etc. will recite various hymns for Rāma (= Balarāma) and Keśava (= Kṛṣṇa).

[1] i.e. 14 Manu-eras or one cosmic cycle.

[2] i.e. the Guṇḍīca-Mandapa, cf. Geib.

[3] ?, *maṅgalāḥ* referring to the subject of the sentence?

42-45 A man who visits, praises and reveres devotedly (the three statues there) will live in Hari's residence for 10,000 years, served by Apsarases and Gandharvas, sporting with Keśava as an attendant of Hari; roaming about with a golden chariot etc.; after the consumption of ascetic merit he will be reborn as a wealthy Brahmin knowing the four Vedas.

46-47 (B IIb1 4.2) After promising all that, Viṣṇu and Viśvakarman disappeared, while the king, having reached his goal, was full of joy.

48-53 (B IIb1 5.1) After that the king took the three figures to a pure place, established them there and consecrated them at an auspicious date, according to the precept of the teacher; finally he gave the sacrificial gift (*dakṣiṇā*) to the teacher and riches to the other priests.

54-56 (B IIb2 5.2) The statues were established in the temple and worshipped according to the rules, with flowers, perfumes, jewels etc.; to others he gave landed property.[4]

57-58 (B IIb2 6) After ruling and performing sacrifices according to his duty the king went to the highest abode which is Viṣṇu's highest step.

59 (Conclusion:) Brahman asks the hermits what else they want to hear.

60-62 The hermits[5] are much astonished about Brahman's story and put the following questions to him: 1. At what time should one go to the Puruṣottamakṣetra? 2. How is the (pilgrimage to the) five places to be performed? 3. What is the merit of bathing and giving alms at each of the holy places, at the sight of the deities?

63-71 Brahman answers that the best time is the tenth day of the bright half of Jyeṣṭha; those who perform the pilgrimage to the five holy places and see Puruṣottama at that time will go to Viṣṇu's world and never return. He who beholds Hari's discus on top of the temple will at once be released from all sins.

Ch. 52: Mārkaṇḍeya-episode[1]

1-10 Brahman continues: Once, at the end of a cosmic cycle sun and moon were destroyed, and all beings, including trees and mountains, were struck by lightning and devoured by flames; the waters, rivers and seas were dried up; the whole world was filled by fire and wind which split the earth and destroyed the nether worlds with all its inhabitants, as well as gods and other beings. That fire, called »Kalpa-Agni«, blazed like millions of suns and burnt the three worlds, including gods, demons, and men.

11-15ab In that terrible destruction of the world only the sage Mārkaṇḍeya was left, who was devoted to meditation (*dhyānayoga*). Afflicted by hunger and thirst, his mouth, lips,

[4] v. 55cd-56ab might enumerate the gifts donated by the king rather than objects accompanying the worship.

[5] Ed. ASS attributes the following to Viṣṇu as narrator.

[1] BrP 52.1-56.57 agree largely with MBh 3,186.60-187.47, as pointed out also by a note in MBh (cr.ed.) vol. 4, p. 642. For a concordance of the two versions see the Appendix to the text-volume; for a translation see v. Buitenen: The Mahābhārata, vol. 2, p. 568-569 (summary) and p. 585-593.

and palate dried out; reeling with thirst he roamed the earth for some shelter but could not find anyone to save him.

15cd–19 Concentrating continuously on how to find the god Puruṣeśa (»Lord of Man/Men«), he reached the huge eternal fig-tree called Puruṣeśa and settled at the foot of this tree, where there was no danger of fire, thunderbolts, rains of sparks etc.

Ch. 53: Mārkaṇḍeya-episode (contd)

1–11ab Brahman continues describing the destruction of the world by a great flood.

1–5 Description of different clouds.

6–10ab The clouds filled the whole earth with floods of rain for 12 years.

10cd–11 The oceans transgressed their borders, the mountains split asunder, the earth was submerged in the waters.

12–14ab The clouds were destroyed by wind; the wind was drunk by Viṣṇu, who afterwards fell asleep, while the whole world, with gods, demons etc. was submerged in the huge ocean.[1]

14cd–18ab When Mārkaṇḍeya, after concentrating on the Supreme Person (*puruṣottama*), opened his eyes again he saw nothing but water. The fig-tree, the earth, sun and moon, everything had disappeared. He tried to swim across the huge ocean but did not find any shelter.[2]

18cd–20 Pleased by the hermit's meditation and filled with compassion, the Supreme Person (*puruṣottama*) addressed him as a child that is tired and longs for shelter.

21–24 At first Mārkaṇḍeya grew angry, considering this address an insult to his old age, combined with ascetic power, which even Brahman had acknowledged.

25–26 He wondered whether he had been dreaming or the victim of confusion, and decided to take refuge in the Supreme Person with devotion.

27–30 He again beheld the fig-tree above the waters; on its widely extended branches was a golden palanquin (couch, bed?) beautifully adorned with precious stones, cushions (carpets?) etc.

31–33 On that palanquin he saw Kṛṣṇa as a child, four-armed, lotus-eyed, holding the conch-shell, discus and club, with the Śrīvatsa-lock and garlands on his breast.

34–38 Seeing the child Mārkaṇḍeya uttered his surprise at this fearless child. Though normally knowing past, present and future, he did not recognise the god, being confused by Kṛṣṇa's Māyā. Thus, as he did not recognize him, he considered all his asceticism, his knowledge, his life to be in vain.

39–40 He continued swimming until he reached the fig-tree, but he was unable to look at the child because of the child's immense splendour.

41–43 The child, however, seeing Mārkaṇḍeya come near, told him smilingly to enter his body. Mārkaṇḍeya entered his open mouth without saying a word.

[1] v. 9–14 frequently use the present tense, probably in order to describe how the destruction of the world takes place again and again.

[2] Compare 53.17–18 with 52.14.

Ch. 54: Mārkaṇḍeya-episode (contd): Mārkaṇḍeya's vision

1-3 Brahman continues: He (i.e. Mārkaṇḍeya) saw the world with the seven oceans and the seven continents, all regions, Bhāratavarṣa etc., and all mountain ranges.
4-7 Description of Mount Meru; list of animals; list of beings.[1]
8-11 List of mountain ranges.
12-13 List of lands or peoples.
14 Animals.
15 Towns and villages.
16-17 Gods, Gandharvas, Apsarases, Yakṣas, demons etc.
18-19 He saw everything.
20-21 List of heavens and nether worlds.
22-24 Due to the god's grace Mārkaṇḍeya did not lose his memory. Wandering through this endless world, he did not reach an end of Viṣṇu's body, therefore he took his refuge in the god.
25 Suddenly he was discharged through the mouth of the (Supreme) Person (*puruṣa*).

Ch. 55: Mārkaṇḍeya-episode (contd)

1-3 Brahman continues: After leaving the god's mouth, Mārkaṇḍeya again saw the earth that had become an ocean, and saw the child on the palanquin.
4-6 The child smilingly asked him what he had seen and offered him the favour of being able to see him (i.e. his true form).
7-8 Having obtained a new, purified vision due to the god's grace, Mārkaṇḍeya was able to see the god.
9-10 Bowing to the god's feet Mārkaṇḍeya, full of surprise, began to praise the Supreme Self.
11-35 Mārkaṇḍeya's hymn to Viṣṇu.
11 Addressing the god (vocatives) and asking for help.
12-17 Description of his own miserable condition (thirsty, exhausted, tormented by heat, helpless); refrain.
18-23ab Addresses (*prasīda* plus names and descriptive epithets in vocative).
23cd-31 Identifications of the god with everything: with elements and Sāṃkhya principles; with gods; with other classes of beings (concluded with abbreviating formula).
32ab Identification (of Viṣṇu) with past, present, and future.
cd-33ab Even Brahman etc. do not know the god's supreme form.
33cd-34 List of attributes (qualities).
35ab Who could praise him correctly?
35c-f Request for forgiveness for (inadequate) praising.

[1] v. 5-13ab are printed as a footnote in ed. VePr.

Ch. 56: Mārkaṇḍeya-episode (contd)

1-2 Brahman continues: Pleased by Mārkaṇḍeya's hymn Viṣṇu promised to fulfil all his wishes.

3-8 Mārkaṇḍeya replied that he wished to learn 1. Viṣṇu's most excellent Māyā, 2. Viṣṇu's imperishable form (after v. 5ab ed. VePr inserts, in footnote, 57 lines describing what he had seen in Viṣṇu's belly: Various beings, animals, Meru and other mountains, countries and peoples, holy places, rivers, sun and moon, the earth, members of the twice-born castes); 3. why he assumed the shape of a child after drinking up this world, 4. why the whole world was in his body, 5. how long the god would stay there.

9 Viṣṇu consoled him.[1]

10-11 Viṣṇu announces that he will tell Mārkaṇḍeya what even the gods do not know, and show himself to Mārkaṇḍeya, because of Mārkaṇḍeya's devotion to ancestors and his abstinence (*brahmacarya*).

12 Explanation of the name Nārāyaṇa.

13-15 Identifications of Viṣṇu as Nārāyaṇa, creator, maintainer, and destroyer of all beings; as Viṣṇu, Brahman, Śakra (= Indra), Vaiśravaṇa (= Kubera), Yama, Śiva, Soma, Kaśyapa (= Prajāpati?), Dhātṛ, Vidhātṛ, sacrifice.

16-17ab Description of his body by macro-/microcosmic equivalences: Mouth - fire; feet - earth; eyes - sun and moon; skull - sky; ears - the air, the directions; drops of sweat - waters; trunk of body - sky and directions; mind - wind.[2]

17cd-19ab All people wishing to enter heaven offer sacrifices to him.

19cd-22ab As (the snake) Śeṣa he supports the earth, as the boar he lifted the world out of the water, as the fiery mare he drinks the waters and ejects them.[3]

22cd-23ab The four castes originate from the parts of his body.[4]

23cd-24ab The four Vedas originate from him and enter him again.

24cd-26ab Self-controlled people, who have subdued their passions, always pay homage to him alone.

26cd-27ab He is the world-destroying light, fire, sun and wind.

27cd-30ab The stars are the pores of his skin; the four oceans are his abode; all passions are forms of him.

30cd-35ab He is the cause of whatever (good) people get as result of their actions or religious practices.[5] But he cannot be obtained by those who perform evil actions. Thus Viṣṇu is the reward for the good, but cannot be reached by the evil.

35cd-38ab Whenever great danger arises from evil demons who cannot be killed even by the gods, he takes his birth in a righteous family and, assuming a human shape, restores order.[6]

[1] A »consolation« should be rather expected after Mārkaṇḍeya's speech 53.34-38.

[2] Sky, air and directions appear twice in this description.

[3] cf. ŚiP 2/3,20.2-23.

[4] cf. below ch. 161.43 ff. (and RV 10,90.12).

[5] Construction not clear.

[6] Paraphrase of BhG 4.7-8.

cd-39ab He creates all beings and annihilates them by his Māyā.[7]

39cd-42 At the time of action he assumes a human body to establish limits (of morality). Viṣṇu's *dharma* (or body?) is white in the Kṛta-period, dark blue/green (*śyāma*) in the Tretā-period, red in the Dvāpara-period and black (= *kṛṣṇa*, Kṛṣṇa) in the Kali-period. At that time, three parts (of the world) belong to Unrighteousness (*adharma*). At the end of time, Viṣṇu destroys the three worlds as Death (Kāla).

43-44 Descriptive identifications of Viṣṇu (as omnipresent etc.).[8]

45 Conclusion to (Viṣṇu's) description of himself who is not known by anybody.

ab-48ab All over the world people are devoted to him. All the trouble that had happened to Mārkaṇḍeya will turn out to be for his best. All that he had seen in the world is Viṣṇu's self.[9]

48cd His name is Nārāyaṇa, his attributes are conch-shell, discus, and club.

49-50 For 1000 Yugas he will stay sleeping, the soul of all, bewildering (*mohayan*) all; for all that time he will sit there in the shape of a child, until Brahman awakes.

51-54 Report on what was experienced by Mārkaṇḍeya: He had been granted a boon by Viṣṇu (in Brahman's shape); when everything had become a huge ocean, Mārkaṇḍeya had gone out to see the world; by entering the god's body, he had seen the whole world inside but did not understand. Then he was discharged from the god's mouth, and the god had told him about his self which is difficult even for gods to know.

55 Until Brahman awakes Mārkaṇḍeya may (now) stay here without fear.

56-57 When Brahman awakes, he (Viṣṇu) will again create all beings, space, earth, light (fire), wind, and water, and all movable and immovable beings.

58-60 Brahman continues: At the end of the 1000 Yugas Mādhava (= Viṣṇu) addressed Mārkaṇḍeya again, asking him for the reason why he had praised him, granting him a boon, and bestowing long life upon him as Viṣṇu's devotee.

61-66ab Mārkaṇḍeya, bowing to him, answered that his confusion (*moha*) had now disappeared, at the sight of the god. As a boon he chose that, for the sake of people devoted to Śiva, he might be allowed to establish a temple dedicated to Śiva at this holy place, too, in order to show that Hari (= Viṣṇu) and Īśvara (= Śiva) were actually one.

66cd-73 Viṣṇu agreed to that proposal and ordered Mārkaṇḍeya to build a temple for the veneration of the Liṅga; thereby he would stay in Śiva's world (?). There should be no difference between Rudra/Maheśvara (= Śiva) and himself; confused people, however, would not know that. Therefore Mārkaṇḍeya should build Śiva's temple bearing his (Mārkaṇḍeya's) name. North of it he should establish a place of pilgrimage named Mārkaṇḍeya-lake.

74 Brahman concludes: After these words Janārdana disappeared.

[7] Answer to Mārkaṇḍeya's first question?

[8] Ed. VePr gives v. 40-44 as footnote.

[9] Answer to Mārkaṇḍeya's fourth question?

Ch. 57: Pañcatīrtha-Māhātmya[1]

1 Brahman continues announcing (a report on) the rules concerning how to visit the »Five Places of Pilgrimage« (*pañcatīrtha*), including the merit of observances performed there.

2–11 Observances at the Mārkaṇḍeya-lake.

2–4 The pilgrim should bathe thrice in the lake reciting a special formula of praise (quoted in v. 3–4), applying for Śiva's help.

5 Standing in the water up to his navel he should satisfy gods, sages, and ancestors with sesamum water.

6–8 After that he should go to Śiva's temple, circumambulate thrice (the Liṅga called) »Mārkaṇḍeya's lord«, reciting a (special) formula of praise (quoted in v. 8).

9–11 The merit of these observances equals (that of) ten horse-sacrifices. One will go to Śiva's world, be reborn as a Brahmin, practise Śāṃkara-Yoga and finally reach liberation.

12–19 Paying homage to the »wishing tree« (*kalpavṛkṣa*),[2] i.e. the fig-tree Vainateya.

12–14 The pilgrim should thrice circumambulate the fig-tree, paying homage to it with a (special) formula (quoted in v. 13–14) praising the fig-tree and asking to be freed from sins.

15–16 By that homage all sins will fall away from him like the old skin from a snake; he will even be released from Brahmin-murder.

17–19 By paying homage to Viṣṇu in the shape of the fig-tree, he will obtain more merit than that of a king's sacrifice and a horse-sacrifice together, uplift his ancestors, and go to Viṣṇu's world.

20–28 After that he should go to see Puruṣottama (= Kṛṣṇa), Saṃkarṣaṇa (= Balarāma) and Subhadrā; this will take him to the highest abode. He should enter Viṣṇu's temple, circumambulate Saṃkarṣaṇa thrice reciting a (special) formula (quoted in v. 22–23, addressing and describing Rāma Baladeva). Having thus pleased Balarāma (further description) he will obtain what he wants, will be freed from sin and enter Viṣṇu's world. Born again as a knowledgeable Brahmin he will reach liberation.

29–56 Worship of Kṛṣṇa, the Supreme Person (*puruṣottama*)

29 After that he should pay homage to Kṛṣṇa with the formula consisting of twelve syllables (i.e. *oṃ namo bhagavate vāsudevāya*).

30–31 Those who recite that formula will obtain liberation. This way is not pursued even by gods and ascetics.

32–37 Hymn to Kṛṣṇa (twelve times *jaya* plus a name or epithet of Kṛṣṇa; v. 36–37 request to be saved from the cruel »ocean« of Saṃsāra).

38–41 By paying homage thus to Kṛṣṇa (description, list of attributes) he will obtain the merit of 1000 horse-sacrifices.

42–51 The merit of looking at Kṛṣṇa is compared to the effects of other religious observances, e.g. stages of life (with refrain).

[1] Covering 57.1–63.9 (interrupted by Ch. 58–62?).

[2] Thus the common translation, cf. Monier-Williams. Possibly the name here derives from an identification of that tree with the one which lasts longer than cosmic destruction at the end of a cycle (*kalpa*)? cf. v. 14ab.

52–56 Freed from sin he will enter Viṣṇu's world, saving twenty-one ancestors. Born again in an excellent Brahmin family he will obtain liberation by means of Vaiṣṇava Yoga.

57–61 Worship of Subhadrā:

57–58 Then the pilgrim should please Subhadrā with a (special) formula (quoted in v. 58).

59–61 By pleasing her, the mother of the world (etc.), he will enter Viṣṇu's world in a golden chariot, be born again as a Brahmin, and obtain liberation by means of Hari's Yoga.

Ch. 58: Narasiṃha-Māhātmya

1–7 Brahman continues: By paying homage to Bala(deva), Kṛṣṇa, and Subhadrā one will obtain liberation. After leaving their temple the pilgrim should go to the place where the blue (statue of) Viṣṇu disappeared[1] and pay homage to him. Then he should proceed to Viṣṇupura (i.e. the city of Viṣṇu?); there is (a statue of) the Man-Lion (Narasiṃha). By paying homage to him one will be free of any evil and succeed in the four aims of life.

8–11 The hermits want to learn more about Narasiṃha's power, about the accomplishments (*siddhi*) he will grant to those who please him, and about how to please him.

12–18 Brahman's answer: Announcement of Narasiṃha's power; impossibility of mentioning all of his qualities; mention of accomplishments to be obtained by Narasiṃha's favour (v. 15 mentions unrestricted movement everywhere); announcement of »the king of ordinances« (*kalparāja*, i.e. title of a text?) and of an account on Narasiṃha's true nature.

19–25 Description of observances an adept (*sādhaka*) of Narasiṃha should perform.

19–21ab He should live on a vegetarian diet (specified), wear a loin cloth (only), meditate, stay in an isolated place (specified).

21cd–23 After worshipping and fasting on the 12th night of the bright half of the month he should mutter 2 millions (of a certain formula?); then he will be freed from minor as well as great sins.

24–25 He should circumambulate Narasiṃha, offer him incense etc., put flowers on his head, together with camphor and sandal oil; by that accomplishment will come forth.

26–27 Narasiṃha cannot be defeated even by gods, much less by Gandharvas (etc.) and demons.

28 Those demons to destroy whom other adepts (or: adepts of other (deities)?) use a (spell-)formula will perish at the mere sight (of the adepts of Narasiṃha?) who have the splendour of sun and fire.

29–32ab On the protection effected by murmuring the charm (*kavaca*) once, twice and thrice.[2] Narasiṃha grants protection up to a distance of 12 Yojanas.

[1] cf. above, ch.45.

[2] v. 30 duplicates v. 27.

32cd–49 Visit to the »cave« and its effects.

32cd–34ab After that the adept should fast (or stay) three nights at the door of the (or: a) cave,[3] should ignite a fire and offer 200 pieces of Palāśa-wood (*Butea Frondosa*) consecrated by the three verses beginning with *madhu* (= RV 1.90.6–8) to the fire, thereby uttering *vaṣaṭ*.

34cd–36 Then the door of the cave will become visible to him and he should enter the cave without fear, protected by the spell; when he follows the narrow passage the delusion of darkness will disappear and he will see a royal highway.

37–40 Thinking of Narasiṃha he will enter the nether world (*pātāla*); as he enters he should recite the truth called Narasiṃha. Beautiful maidens will welcome him and offer him an elixir by which he will assume a celestial body. Then he will enjoy himself with the girls up to the final destruction; when his body is destroyed he will dissolve into Vāsudeva.

41–43 When this abode no longer pleases him, he leaves the cave, after taking up a turban (?), a spear, a sword, a dye (for the *ṭīka*, the mark on the forehead?), a jewel, a liquid, a rejuvenating elixir, shoes and ointment (?), a black goat's skin, a beautiful ball (pearl?), a water-jar, a rosary, a life-restoring staff, the knowledge of perfect adepts (*siddhavidyā*?), and books of treatises (?).

44–46 The three-flamed (fire?, amulet?), put into the heart, will destroy the sins of millions of former births; put into poison it will destroy the poison, and leprosy in the body (?). By the celestial (fire?, amulet?) in his body (even) he who committed the sin of embryo-murder will be purified. If one thinks of the flaming (fire) in one's heart in terrible situations (or diseases), these situations will be destroyed immediately.

47 Bound around the necks of children it will protect them and destroy boils, swellings etc.

48 When there is a disease one should offer oblations of fuel as well as of ghee and milk three times a day for one month; then all diseases will be destroyed.

49 Conclusion: There is nothing in the world that cannot be accomplished.

50–59ab Spells connected with Narasiṃha-worship.

50–55ab Spell for rain: After worshipping Narasiṃha 108 times, an adept should stir seven pieces of clay taken from an ant-hill, a cemetery and a crossroad, with red sandal-paste and cow's milk. He should make an image (statue?) of the lion and anoint it, dye it and draw it (or write the spell?) on a leaf of birch bark. Binding it (the amulet) round the neck of Narasiṃha, he should utter (the spell) countless times at a water-tank (or the ocean?). After he has done so for seven days only, the earth will be flooded. Or, if he worships Narasiṃha at a dry tree by uttering the truth of 800 (or, 800 times), he will keep off (or stop) rain.

55cd–56 If he fastens it (the amulet?) to a *piñja*-tree (cotton-plant?) and whirls it around, there will be a great wind; afterwards he should keep it immediately with water (?, VePr over which seven (formulas?) have been muttered).

57 The kin of a man at whose door the devotee buries the statue (or: the lion-image on the amulet?) will vanish; but if he takes it out, then he (the devotee?) will give peace.

[3] Entrance to the nether world?

58–59ab Therefore one should always worship Narasiṃha with devotion (*bhakti*). Freed from all sins one will enter Viṣṇu's world.[4]

59cd–77 Account of the fruits of Narasiṃha-worship:

9cd–64ab Brahmins, Kṣatriyas, Vaiśyas, women, Śūdras, and those of the lowest classes, by worshipping the best of gods in the shape of the lion,[5] will be freed from all evil resulting from millions of (former) births, will obtain all they desire (divinity, lordship over the gods, being a Gandharva, Yakṣa or Vidyādhara). By beholding, praising, paying homage to, worshipping the man-lion they obtain sovereignty, heaven and liberation. The man who beholds Narasiṃha obtains all he wishes; freed from all sins he enters Viṣṇu's world.[6]

4cd–65ab By beholding the god in the shape of a lion once only (a devotee) will be freed from all evil resulting from millions of (former) births.[7]

5cd–68ab In all difficulties or dangers (listed) a man needs only to think of Narasiṃha to be released. Like darkness that fades away at sunrise all misfortunes are destroyed at his sight.

8cd–70ab A collyrium ball, shoes from the nether world (?) as well as a rejuvenating elixir[8] or other wishes will be granted, if Narasiṃha is pleased; whatever one has in mind while worshipping the man-lion will be obtained.

70cd–77 By beholding and worshipping the lord of the gods with devotion (a devotee) will obtain the tenfold merit of ten horse-sacrifices; freed from all sins, endowed with all qualities, all his goals accomplished, free from old age and death, he will go to Viṣṇu's world in a golden chariot beautifully adorned, accompanied by celestial girls, praised by Apsarases etc. He will enjoy all pleasures in Viṣṇu's world, in a four-armed shape, together with Gandharvas and Apsarases, up to the final dissolution; then he will be born into an excellent family as an expert in Veda and its auxiliary lore; by means of Vaiṣṇava Yoga he will reach liberation.

Ch. 59: Śvetamādhava-Māhātmya

1–2 Brahman continues: By seeing and worshipping Vāsudeva named »Endless« (*ananta*) one is freed from all sins and reaches the highest step; even Brahman (first-person narrator), as well as Śakra (= Indra), Vibhīṣaṇa, and Rāma, worshipped him,[9] who would not do so? (Rhetorical question).

3 Whoever, after bathing in the »White Gaṅgā« (Śvetagaṅgā), beholds the »White Mādhava« (Śvetamādhava) and Mādhava called »the fish« (Matsyamādhava) will go to Śvetadvīpa (the »White Island«).

[4] v. 59ab = 64ab.

[5] v. 60a = v. 61a; v. 60b = v. 64d.

[6] v. 64ab = v. 59ab.

[7] v. 65ab almost identical with v. 60cd.

[8] cf. 58.41–43.

[9] cf. ch. 176 below, where the prehistory of this image is told in detail.

4-5 The hermits want to know more about Śvetamādhava, and about who placed the statue of Mādhava called the »White« there.

6-21 Brahman relates the story of king Śveta who revived the child of the sage Kapālagautama: In the Kṛta-Yuga there lived a righteous king named Śveta; in his kingdom people lived for 10,000 years (ed. VePr adds: free from disease), and children did not die. At that time there lived a sage named Kapālagautama whose son died before he had cut his teeth, because of Kāla's power (the power of Time or Death). The sage took him to king Śveta, who promised to bring him back from Yama's abode within one week, otherwise he himself would ascend a pyre. Then he worshipped Śiva (Mahādeva) with hundreds of white lotuses; Śiva announced his satisfaction, and the king saw him: Besmeared with ashes, with deformed eyes, with the moon in his hair, wearing a tiger-skin. Śveta asked him to bring the child back to life. Śiva agreed. He rebuked[10] and subdued Kāla, the executor of Yama's orders, and revived the dead child. Then he disappeared, together with Umā. Conclusion.

22 The hermits inquire about the ultimate truth of the name Śveta (i.e. Śvetamādhava? Or: of him called Śveta).

23-25 Brahman announces a Mādhavamāhātmya which fulfils all wishes and destroys danger and distress.

26-33 After reigning for thousands of years according to the worldly and vedic rules, king Śveta took a special vow concerning worship of Keśava (= Kṛṣṇa) and went to the southern ocean, where he had a wonderful temple constructed, near Kṛṣṇa (i.e. the Jagannātha-temple?), 101 Dhanus (i.e. ca. 182 metres) south of Śiva (= Mārkaṇḍeyeśvara).[1] After that Śveta made a white marble statue of Lord Mādhava that looked like the moon; after consecrating it and bestowing gifts on Brahmins etc., he prostrated himself before Mādhava, worshipping him with the formula consisting of 12 syllables including *oṃ*;[2] after observing a silence of one month without taking food at Viṣṇu's place, he praised the highest god (with the following hymn).

34-72 Hymn by Śveta to Nārāyaṇa (Kṛṣṇa, Vāsudeva).

34 Reverence to the four manifestations (*vyūha*) and to Nārāyaṇa.

35-64 Descriptions, names, and epithets of Viṣṇu (qualities, incarnations (*avatāra*), Vedas, etc., including twelve times *oṃ namaḥ*).

65-72 Description of the devotee's miserable situation in the cycle of existences (with vocatives addressing Kṛṣṇa); appeal for rescue from the ocean of existences.

73-77 Thus praised by Śveta, Hari appeared at the holy place Puruṣottama, surrounded by all gods (description of Viṣṇu's appearance and attributes); he was pleased with that hymn and asked Śveta to choose whatever he desired.

78-80 Bowing to Viṣṇu, Śveta answered that he wanted to be his devotee as long as Brahman existed, and to reach Viṣṇu's pure abode (*pada*).

81-91 Viṣṇu granted that he should reach that highest place to which the hermits do not have access; moreover, Śveta would become famous in the three worlds, and he (Viṣṇu) would always be near to that place praised as Śvetagaṅgā by all gods and Gandharvas; those devotees of Viṣṇu who touch the water of the Śvetagaṅgā with a

[10] Ed. VePr called for.

[1] cf. Geib, Indradyumna-Legende, map on p. VIII.

[2] i.e. *oṃ namo bhagavate vāsudevāya*.

tip of Kuśa-grass will go to heaven. He who pays homage to the white statue called Mādhava will be great in Viṣṇu's (i.e. the speaker's) world. Surrounded by heavenly girls, praised by Siddhas and Gandharvas, he will enjoy all pleasures for several Manu-periods. Then he will be born as a Brahmin who knows Vedas and Vedāṅgas, endowed with long life, wealth, beauty, sons and grandsons; giving up his life at Puruṣottama, below the fig-tree, thinking of Hari,[3] he will reach the place of those who are appeased (*śāntapada*).

Ch. 60: Matsyamādhava-Māhātmya; rules for bathing in the ocean

1-6 Brahman continues: After seeing Śvetamādhava one should think of the Matsyamādhava (Mādhava in the shape of a fish) who formerly, out of consideration for the earth, stayed in the nether world in a red shape in order to snatch the Vedas (i.e. from a demon who had stolen them?).[1] By bowing to (Viṣṇu's) first incarnation (*avatāra*) as a fish, one is released from all discomfort and reaches Hari's abode. After some time one will be reborn on earth as a Vaiṣṇava king and, by means of Hari's Yoga, obtain liberation. Conclusion to the account of Matsyamādhava.

7 The hermits inquire about the merit of cleaning oneself (or: bathing in the ocean, *mārjana*).

8ab Brahman announces prescriptions for bathing.[2]

8cd-10 Bathing in the Mārkaṇḍeya-lake is particularly meritorious on the fourteenth of the first half (of a month); similarly, bathing in the ocean is meritorious at all times, but particularly at full moon; then the merit of a horse-sacrifice is obtained.[3]

11 (The) Mārkaṇḍeya(-lake ?), the fig-tree, Kṛṣṇa, Balarāma, the great ocean and the Indradyumna-tank ...[4] is remembered as the Five-Tīrtha-rule (?).

12-15 At the time of the full moon in the month Jyeṣṭha, (or) at the 16th lunar mansion (?), one should go to the »wishing tree« with one's senses controlled, with pure mind etc., take a bath and circumambulate Janārdana thrice. At the sight of the tree one is released from the sins of seven births, and one obtains all wishes.

16-18 Announcement of the auspicious names of the fig-tree: Vaṭa, Vaṭeśvara, Kṛṣṇa, Purāṇapuruṣa; its extent is one and a half and a quarter Yojanas less one foot (?).[5]

19-21 After worshipping the fig-tree with the formula mentioned before, one should go southward 300 Dhanus (ca. 540 metres) to Svargadvāra where Viṣṇu can be seen. By worshipping the piece of wood that was brought there by the water of the ocean one will be released from all diseases and evils.

[3] Here Viṣṇu's direct speech seems to be neglected.

[1] v. 60cd unclear.

[2] Only the following two and a half verses, however, deal with that topic which does not seem to be taken up until ch. 62 below. The passage following here is partly an additional version of the Pañcatīrtha-Māhātmya dealt with in ch. 57.

[3] Seems to be an addition to 57.2-11, above.

[4] The sentence is incomplete, consisting only of accusative forms without any verb.

[5] Seems to be an addition to 57.12-19.

22–24 After previously (?) seeing Ugrasena and reaching the ocean by Svargadvāra (?) one should meditate on Nārāyaṇa, assigning (*nyāsa*) the formula consisting of 8 syllables[6] to one's hands and body, for there is no better formula than this.

25–33 On Nārāyaṇa's greatness: Etymology of Nārāyaṇa. Everything consists of Nārāyaṇa (v. 27–28 list Sāṃkhya principles; v. 28–32 are characterised by a slightly varied refrain). There is nothing higher than Nārāyaṇa, by whom everything is penetrated.

34–38 As the waters are his abode, one should think of him by the waters. At the time of bathing one should think of Nārāyaṇa, assigning (the syllables of the formula *oṃ namo nārāyaṇāya*) to one's hands and one's body as follows: *oṃ* and *na* should be placed in the thumbs, ...,[7] the rest accordingly in the forefingers (?) etc.

oṃ	should be placed in the left foot,
na	in the right,
mo	in the left hip,
nā	in the right;
rā	in the region of the navel,
ya	in the left arm,
ṇā	in the right, and
ya	in the head.[8]

39–45 After concentrating thus upon Nārāyaṇa from all sides one should start (to recite) the following (v. 40–42ab) spell-formula, asking Viṣṇu/Kṛṣṇa for protection in each direction by using diverse names and epithets (Govinda, Madhusūdana, Śrīdhara, Keśava, Viṣṇu, Mādhava, Hṛṣīkeśa, Vāmana, Varāha, and Trivikrama). After that one should identify oneself with Nārāyaṇa, who is holding conch, disc and club. Then one should speak the following (v. 44–45) formula (identifying Viṣṇu with Agni, praising him as origin and lord of all beings, asking him to take away all sins).

46–48 In this way one should bathe, not otherwise; while sprinkling oneself with water, standing in the water, one should recite the »sin-effacing« hymn (RV 10,190) thrice; this will have the same effect as a horse-sacrifice.

49–53 One should put on freshly washed garments, control one's breath, and pay homage to the sun at dawn, by throwing down flowers and water. Keeping one's arms upwards one should recite the Gāyatrī-verse 108 times as well as other verses (*mantra*) to the sun-god. After that one should do one's repetition of sacred texts (*svādhyāya*); turning to the east one should satisfy the celestial sages, the human ancestors and others with water mixed with sesamum seeds according to the rule.

54–65 Additional prescription and prohibitions concerning the ancestral offering: use of one or both hands (v. 54–56); avoidance of sesamum (which had fallen) on body or limbs (v. 57–58); avoidance of pouring water on the earth while standing in water and vice versa (v. 59–60); it has to be offered on earth.

[6] i.e. *oṃ namo nārāyaṇāya*.

[7] v. 36cd not intelligible.

[8] cf. ch. 61.9–12.

Ch. 61: Prescriptions concerning worship

1–3 Brahman continues: After satisfying gods and ancestors, one should draw a castle (?, *pura*) with four corners and doors and a lotus-flower with eight leaves in the midst of it; after that one should pay homage to Nārāyaṇa with the formula of eight syllables.

4–6 Purification of the body by allocation of a (special) formula (announced in v. 4ab): Thinking of the letter *a* (= Viṣṇu?) together with the line of a circle (i.e. the syllable *oṃ*?) in his heart, as the sin-destroying fire, he should think of the letter *rā* in the midst of the moon disc, as located in his head.[1] By that he will obtain a heavenly body.[2]

7–12 Allocation of the formula of eight syllables to the body:[3] Starting with the left foot he should allocate the formula of eight syllables to his body; starting with the left foot he should place the five parts of the body of Viṣṇu (?) and the four manifestations (*vyūha*). He should clean his hands with the root formula and put separate colours on the fingers (?).

oṃ	white earth	left foot;
na	dark green, blue; belonging to Śiva	right foot;
mo	black (or Time, Death)	left hip;
nā	the seed of everything	right hip;
rā	brilliance	navel;
ya	belonging to the wind	left shoulder;
ṇā	going everywhere	right shoulder;
ya	on which the worlds are rooted	head.

13 Formula (in prose) paying homage to Viṣṇu and identifying oneself with the four manifestations (*vyūha*):

Vāsudeva	white	on the head;
Saṃkarṣaṇa (Garuḍa/fire/brilliance/sun)	red	on the forehead;
Pradyumna (wind/clouds)	yellow	in the neck, throat;
Aniruddha (endowed with entire strength)	black	in the heart.

14–16 Formula for locating Viṣṇu/Kṛṣṇa in all directions:

in front	Viṣṇu;
behind	Keśava;
right side	Govinda;
left side	Madhusūdana;
above	Vaikuṇṭha;
below	Varāha;
intermediate directions	Mādhava, going, standing, awake, and asleep; Narasiṃha is shelter.

17–18 Having thus become identical with Viṣṇu one should start the rite (*karma*), performing the sprinkling with the syllable *oṃ* and ending with *phaṭ*, thus removing all obstacles.

[1] Grammar and meaning uncertain; but cf. 60.44–45.

[2] v. 4–6 seem to be an insertion.

[3] cf. 60.35–38 above.

19 Then he should think of sun, moon and fire and put Viṣṇu in the midst of the lotus-flower (described in v. 1-3 above).

20-22 Thinking of the syllable *oṃ* in his heart he should place the formula of eight syllables on the pericarp of the lotus; having worshipped the god with the formula of twelve syllables(i.e. *oṃ namo bhagavate vāsudevāya*), he should reflect on it in his heart and place it outside on the pericarp.

23 Thinking of the four-armed Great Being he invokes him calling to his mind one formula after the other.

24-38 *Prayer-formulas to be used for the ceremony*[4]

24 Invitation (invoking four forms of Nārāyaṇa, fish, boar, man-lion, dwarf).
25 Offering a seat on the pericarp of the lotus.
26 Respectful reception (greeting formula).
27 Offering water for washing the feet.
28 Offering of honey and milk.
29 Offering water for sipping (taken from the Mandākinī).
30 Bathing the god.
31 Dressing the god with golden garments.
32 Applying ointments on the god's body.
33 Applying the sacred thread.
34 Adorning the god.
35 (Alternative suggestion of reciting *oṃ namaḥ*, the »root formula«.)[5]
36 Offering incense.
37 Offering a burning lamp.
38 Offering of eatables (four kinds of food with the six sorts of taste).

39-40 Location of Viṣṇu's names in the lotus leaves: The four manifestations (*vyūha*) in the main directions (Vāsudeva: east; Saṃkarṣaṇa: south; Pradyumna: west; Aniruddha: north), and four incarnations (*avatāra*) in the intermediate directions: boar, man-lion, Kṛṣṇa (Mādhava), dwarf (Trivikrama).

41-45ab Location of (Viṣṇu's vehicle) Garuḍa (in front of the idol), of discus, bow, sword (left) and conch, club, quiver (right), of (his wives) Śrī (south) and Puṣṭi (north); decoration with garlands, the Śrīvatsa-lock and the Kaustubha-jewel. The weapon (?) should be allocated to the corner (?).

45cd-46 Then he should pay homage with tantric (*tāntrika*) formulas to the ten directions (or their representatives): Indra, Agni, Yama, Nairṛta, Varuṇa, Vāyu, Dhanada (= Kubera), Īśāna (= Śiva), Ananta (= Śeṣa), Brahman.

47-50 Description of merits obtained by paying homage to Nārāyaṇa in the way described (fulfilment of all wishes, approach to Viṣṇu, stay at Śvetadvīpa).

51 His (= Viṣṇu's) name with *oṃ* in the beginning and *namas* in the end is called the »formula of (for) all principles« (*sarvatattvānāṃ mantra*).

52-55 In that way one should offer flowers etc., according to the rule, one for each (syllable?); uttering the »root formula« 28, 8 or 108 times one should perform the

[4] In prose, all ending in *oṃ namo nārāyaṇāya namaḥ*

[5] cf. v. 57 below.

eight symbolic hand gestures (*mudrā*) that symbolize the eight attributes of Viṣṇu (?): lotus, conch, Śrīvatsa-lock, club, Garuḍa, discus, sword, and bow.

56 Formula of farewell to the god.

57 Those who do not know the performance of this ceremony should always pay homage with the »root formula«.

Ch. 62: The ocean as holy place (Samudrasnānamāhātmya)

1-4 Brahman continues: After worshipping Puruṣottama one should bow to the ocean with a formula of praise (quoted in v. 2), addressing the ocean as »king of holy places«. Then one should bathe, pay homage to Nārāyaṇa, Balarāma, Kṛṣṇa, Subhadrā, and the ocean; by that a man will obtain the merit of 100 horse-sacrifices.

5-9 Released from all evil, shining with youth and beauty, he will go to Viṣṇu's world, raising up 21 ancestors. There he will enjoy pleasures for 100 Manu-eras; after that he will be born in an excellent Brahmin family and, performing Vaiṣṇava Yoga, will obtain final liberation.

10-13ab Whoever bestows gifts on Brahmins at the »king of holy places« (*tīrtharāja*) on certain auspicious days (specified), obtains 1000 times the merit of other holy places; offerings to the ancestors will grant them everlasting satiation.

13cd-15 Conclusion to (the account of) the merit of bathing in the ocean along with gifts to Brahmins and offerings to ancestors, all being effects of the qualities of that place.

16ab This Purāṇa should not be told to unbelievers (*nāstika*).

6cd-22ab Praise of the »king of holy places« above all other holy places.

22cd-23 Who could describe the qualities of the »king of holy places« where there are 990 millions of places of pilgrimage? Therefore whatever meritorious deed is done there will bear imperishable fruit.

Ch. 63: Pañcatīrtha-Māhātmya (concluded); on auspicious dates

1-7 Brahman continues: After that one should go to the Indradyumna-lake, sip water, thinking of Hari, and address the water with a (special) formula (quoted in v. 3). Then he should satisfy gods, sages, and ancestors; by that he will obtain the merit of ten horse-sacrifices, will raise up seven preceding and seven subsequent members of his family and go to Viṣṇu's world himself.

8-9 Whoever, performing the Pañcatīrtha-pilgrimage and fasting on the eleventh day, beholds Puruṣottama on the fifteenth day of the bright half of the month Jyeṣṭha will obtain the same merit and reach the place from where there is no return.

10 The hermits want to know why the month Jyeṣṭha should be especially auspicious.

11-16 Brahman announces (an account of) the month Jyeṣṭha: During the week beginning with the tenth day of the bright half of Jyeṣṭha all holy places (lakes, rivers etc.) are present at Puruṣottama; thus, all that is performed there at that time will bear imperishable fruit. The tenth day of the bright half of Jyeṣṭha is named »Daśahāra« (i.e. taking away ten); who then beholds Balarāma, Kṛṣṇa and Subadhrā will go to Viṣṇu's world.

17 He who sees Rāma and Subhadrā on the days of the solstice (?) will go to Viṣṇu's world.

18 He who beholds Govinda swinging in (the month of) Phālguna will go to Govinda's world.

19–20 He who performs the Pañcatīrtha-pilgrimage on the day of the equinox[1] will obtain the merit of all sacrifices and will go to Viṣṇu's world, freed from all sins.

21 He who beholds Kṛṣṇa adorned with sandal-paste on the third day of the dark half of Vaiśākha will go to the house of Acyuta (the Unshakable).

22 He who beholds Puruṣottama on the day of the full moon of the month Jyeṣṭha (*jyaiṣṭhī*), at the conjunction with the lunar mansion (*ṛkṣa* ?) Jyeṣṭhā (sacred to Indra), will raise up 21 ancestors and go to Viṣṇu's world.

Ch. 64: On the importance of the month Jyeṣṭha

1–2 On the (special) night of the full moon during Jyeṣṭha (*mahājyaiṣṭhī*), when there is a conjunction with a zodiacal sign or a lunar mansion, one should go to Puruṣottama and see Balarāma, Subhadrā, and Kṛṣṇa; thereby more merit than that of 12 pilgrimages is obtained.

3–16 The merit obtained by beholding Kṛṣṇa on that day equals that obtained by bathing and bestowing gifts during an eclipse at all holy places on earth (listed in v. 3–14):

3–8ab Places and cities:[1] Prayāga, Kurukṣetra, Naimiṣa, Puṣkara, Gaya, Gaṅgādvāra, Kuśāvarta, confluence of Gaṅgā and ocean; Kokāmukha, Śūkara, Mathurā, Marusthala (desert), Śālagrāma, Vāyutīrtha, Mandara, Sindhusāgara; Piṇḍāraka, Citrakūṭa, Prabhāsa, Kanakhala, Śaṅkhoddhāra, Dvārakā, Badarikāśrama; Lohakuṇḍa, Aśvatīrtha, Kāmālaya, Koṭitīrtha, Amarakaṇṭaka; Lohārgala, Jambumārga, Somatīrtha, Pṛthūdaka, Utpalāvartaka, Pṛthutuṅga, Sukubjaka; Ekāmraka, Kedāra, Kāśi, Viraja.

8cd–9 List of mountains:[2] Kālañjara, Gokarṇa, Śrīśaila, Gandhamādana; Mahendra, Malaya, Vindhya, Pāriyātra, Himālaya, Sahya, Śuktimanta, Gomanta, Arbuda.

10 List of rivers:[3] Gaṅgā, Yamunā, Sarasvatī, Gomatī, Brahmaputra (seven arms).

11–14 Additional list of rivers.[4]: Godāvarī, Bhīmarathī, Tuṅgabhadrā, Narmadā, Tāpī, Payoṣṇī, Kāverī, Kṣiprā, Carmaṇvatī; Vitastā, Candrabhāgā, Śatadru, Ṛṣikulyā, Kumārī, Vipāśā, Dṛṣadvatī; Sarayū, Gaṅgā, Gaṇḍakī, Mahānadī, Kauśikī, Karatoyā, Trisrotā, Madhuvāhinī; Mahānadī, Vaitaraṇī (concluded by an abbreviating formula).

[1] VePr day of Viṣṇu.
[1] In locative case.
[2] In locative case.
[3] In locative case.
[4] In nominative case.

17-20 Therefore one should go to Puruṣottama on the day of the full moon of Jyeṣṭha; by beholding Balarāma, Kṛṣṇa, and Subhadrā one will go to Viṣṇu's world, raising up one's whole family, and will enjoy all pleasures up to the end of the world. Born again as a Brahmin who knows the four Vedas and is devoted to Kṛṣṇa he will obtain liberation by Vaiṣṇava Yoga.

Ch. 65: Bathing festival of Kṛṣṇa, Balarāma, and Subhadrā

1 The hermits want to know at which time and in what way Kṛṣṇa should be bathed.

2 Announcements of Brahman's answer.

3 In the month Jyeṣṭha, at the full moon, in (that) lunar mansion the (presiding) deity of which is the moon (i.e. Mṛga), the bathing of Hari (takes place) (always ?).

4-6 (Then) the well (or a cave ?) (comprises) all holy places; there, Bhogavatī (city of the snakes or snake-nymph?) becomes visible. From this well water is brought for the bathing of Kṛṣṇa, Balarāma, and Subhadrā.

7-9 On a platform adorned with banners, flowers, and fragrances, and covered with a white cloth adorned with strings of pearls, Kṛṣṇa and Nīlambara (= Balarāma) are placed with Subhadrā between them, surrounded by ten thousand people of all castes, men and women, while various musical instruments are playing.

10-11 The householders and those who are entering this stage, the ascetics and the religious students bathe Kṛṣṇa and Halāyudha (= Balarāma) on the platform; likewise do all holy places mentioned above, separately, with their water that is mixed with flowers.

12-16 Thereupon the immense sound of the various kinds of drums, of conch-shells and bells is heard, mixed with the voices of women reciting auspicious formulas and the sound of hymns accompanied by vīṇās and flutes, as well as with the voices of sages reciting vedic hymns and verses made powerful by *sāman*-melodies.[1]

17-18 Balarāma and Keśava are fanned with beautifully adorned Yak-fans by young courtesans clad in yellow and red garments and wearing garlands.

19-20 Different classes of gods and semi-divine beings address Puruṣottama.

21-22 Hymn by the gods to Puruṣottama.

23-26 Gods and demi-gods remain in the air; the Gandharvas sing, the Apsarases dance; instruments play, winds blow, clouds send rains of blossoms down to earth; all beings in the air utter exclamations of »victory«.

27-42 Thereafter all classes of gods assemble, bringing the utensils for the sprinkling ceremony with them.

28-30 List of gods.

31-34 List of semi-gods, sages, and Manus.

35-36 Seasons, stars, rivers, lakes, the earth, the directions and trees.

[1] v. 15-16 are difficult to construe: The instrumental cases would suggest a passive verb, whereas for *stuvanti* a subject in the nominative case is missing. Moreover, the vocative *suraśreṣṭha* seems to be out of place.

37–38ab List of goddesses.
38cd–39ab List of mountains.
39 Measures of time.
40–41 The horse Uccaiḥśravas; the king of snakes named Vāmana; Aruṇa and Garuḍa, trees and plants, Death, Yama, and their attendants.
43–45 All these gods bathe Kṛṣṇa and Balarāma.
46–47 All heavenly chariots assemble.[2]
48–51 Then the gods praise Kṛṣṇa with exclamations of victory (*jaya*).
49–51 *Jaya jaya* plus 75 names of Viṣṇu (in prose).[3]
52–54 Now the gods, demi-gods, sages etc. take leave, bowing to Kṛṣṇa, Balarāma, and Subhadrā.
55–56 All heavenly chariots assemble.[4]
57–58 Those mortals who behold Puruṣottama, Balabhadra, and Subhadrā standing on the platform will go to the imperishable abode where there is no disease.
59–76ab Praise of the merit obtained by beholding Kṛṣṇa on the platform, as compared to the merit of bestowing gifts (listed in v. 60–73, comparing the effects of a particular gift with that of beholding Kṛṣṇa as refrain), concluding with an abbreviating formula: How can the greatness of the god on the platform be described? All merit that can be obtained elsewhere is obtained by beholding Kṛṣṇa, Halāyudha, and Subhadrā.[5]
76cd–77 Therefore a man as well as a woman should behold Puruṣottama; thereby they will gain the merit of all holy places together. By the water left from bathing Kṛṣṇa one is sprinkled oneself.[6]
78–80 Women who are barren or whose progeny died, who are unhappy or obsessed by an evil demon, who are abducted (possessed ?) by demons or others, or who are tormented by diseases, will get all their wishes fulfilled by bathing in the water left from Kṛṣṇa's bath. They will get a son, happiness, freedom from sickness, and wealth.
81–82 All sacred waters on the earth are not worth the sixteenth part of the water left by Kṛṣṇa's bath; therefore one should sprinkle one's limbs with that water.
83–99 Praise of merit obtained by beholding Kṛṣṇa directed towards the south, as compared to the merit of pilgrimage to other places.
83 Those who behold Kṛṣṇa moving towards the south for bathing will be released from all sins including Brahmin-murder.
84–96 Sequence of holy places connected with auspicious dates (as compared to the merit of beholding Kṛṣṇa directed towards the south): Badarī, Gaṅgādvāra, Kurukṣetra, Prayāga, Śālagrāma, Puṣkara, mouth of Gaṅgā (Gaṅgāsāgarasaṃgama), Kurukṣetra, all holy places at Gaṅgā and Yamunā, in Naimiṣa etc. (parallel verses, with refrain).

[2] = v. 55–56, below.
[3] v. 50–51 have *jaya* plus 9 names as Ślokas, while ed. VePr has *jaya jaya*, thus making the text non-metrical.
[4] = v. 46–47 above.
[5] v. 76ab an interpolation?
[6] Connection of sentences not clear.

97-99 Conclusion (abbreviating formula; rhetorical question): Of what use is it to talk more of that topic? The merit that is dealt with in the treatises of the Veda, the Mahābhārata, and the Dharmaśāstras, all that is obtained by beholding Kṛṣṇa directed towards the south.

Ch. 66: Description of the car festival[1]

1-2 Brahman continues: Those who behold Kṛṣṇa, Balarāma, and Subhadrā on their way to the Guḍivā (VePr Guṇḍikā) temple will go to Hari's abode; those who behold them in that temple for seven days will go to Viṣṇu's world.

3-5 The hermits want to know 1. by whom was this procession (*yātrā*) established;[2] 2. what is the merit of that procession; 3. why did Kṛṣṇa, Balarāma, and Subhadrā leave their abode and stay for a week at that place near the (Indradyumna-)lake?

6-7ab Brahman relates: Indradyumna once asked Hari a favour: that he should stay one week on the bank of the Indradyumna-tank, and that this journey should be called by the name Guḍivā (VePr Guṇḍikā[3]).

7cd-13 The boon was granted by Puruṣottama (v. 8-12) who, in addition, granted fulfilment of all wishes to those, including Śūdras and women, who worship Kṛṣṇa (the first-person narrator), Saṃkarṣaṇa, and Subhadrā with flowers, fragrances etc., fasts, circumambulations etc., hymns and music etc.

14 Therefore one should take part in the Guḍivā-procession and see Puruṣottama (Kṛṣṇa) there.

15-17 Description of benefits effected (by taking part in the Guḍivā-procession).

18-23 The man or woman who attends the Guḍivā-procession during the bright half of the month Āṣāḍha and beholds Kṛṣṇa, Balarāma, and Subhadrā will obtain the merit of ten and five (or ten times five) horse-sacrifices. Raising up seven forefathers and seven future generations (the worshipper) will go to Viṣṇu's world in a wonderful chariot, attended by Gandharvas and Apsarases; there he enjoys all pleasures up to the end to the world. Born again as a Brahmin knowing the four Vedas he will reach liberation by Vaiṣṇava Yoga.

Ch. 67: The installation-ceremony and its merit

1 The hermits want to know about the merit of different pilgrimages.

2-5 Brahman announces that he will tell them: He who performs the pilgrimage at the Guḍivā-festival, at (the festival when Viṣṇu) rises from his sleep, at the equinox, in Phālgunī, will gain benefit everywhere and go to Viṣṇu's world until the end of the

[1] cf. Gopinath Mohapatra: The land of Viṣṇu, Delhi 1979, p. 87-102.

[2] Meaning of *dakṣiṇasyām*?.

[3] The reading Guṇḍikā occurs consistently in ed. VePr and has therefore not been explicitly noted each time.

cosmic cycle. As many pilgrimages as one performs in the month of Jyeṣṭha, so many cosmic cycles will one stay in Viṣṇu's world.

6–8 Whoever, man or woman completes the pilgrimage in this holy region during the month of Jyeṣṭha 12 times (?) and performs the »installation-ceremony« (*pratiṣṭhā*), will enjoy all pleasure and obtain liberation at the end.

9 The hermits want to know about the performance and the merit of the installation-ceremony.

10 Brahman announces that he will tell about *pratiṣṭhā* as it is prescribed.

11 (Introduction:) When twelve pilgrimages are finished, one should perform the evil-destroying »installation-ceremony«.

12–14 On the eleventh day of the bright half of Jyeṣṭha a person should go to the ocean, sip water, summon all holy places, and take a bath thinking of Nārāyaṇa according to the rules concerning bathing as taught by the sages.

15–18 Then he should satisfy gods, sages and ancestors. After putting on fresh clothes he should sip water and, turning to the (rising) sun, recite the Gāyatrī 108 times, as well as other verses addressed to the sun-god, and worship the sun by turning around three times (clockwise).

19 Bathing and reciting is taught in the Veda for the three (upper) castes, not for Śūdras and women.

20–23 Then he should go silently and pay homage to Puruṣottama. After washing his hands and feet and sipping water, he should bathe the god with ghee, milk, honey-water, *tīrtha*-water (?) and sandal-water, dress him with two excellent garments, anoint him with saffron etc., and present lotuses and other flowers to him.

24–27 Then he should burn incense, kindle a lamp with ghee and present 12 other lamps with ghee and sesamum oil; as an offering of eatables he should present different cakes (made of milk and rice etc.), sugarcane juice, a bit of sweetmeat, and fruits.

28–29ab Thus honouring Puruṣottama with the five services (*upacāra*), he should utter *namaḥ puruṣottamāya* 108 times and should address the god with the following prayer.

29cd–31ab Prayer to Viṣṇu.

31cd–35ab Prostrating himself before the god, (v. 32: he should honour the teacher, for there is no difference between them)[1] he should make a canopy of flowers. The following night he should spend awake, with stories and songs about Vāsudeva.

35cd–39ab At dawn on the twelfth day he should invite pure Brahmins, who know the Veda, the Itihāsas and Purāṇas; after bathing and putting on washed clothes, he should bathe the god and offer him fragrances, flowers, food, lamps etc. and pay homage to him with oblations, prostrations, circumambulations, and all sorts of praise and hymns.

39cd–45 After thus paying homage to Jagannātha he should honour the Brahmins by giving them twelve cows, gold, a parasol and shoes, riches (money?) and clothes; by generosity is Govinda honoured. Then he should present cows, clothes, gold, another parasol and pair of shoes, and a copper vessel to the teacher (*ācārya*).

[1] Insertion?

Thereupon he should give food to the Brahmins, rice-cakes etc., and twelve jars of water together with sweetmeats. Free from envy he should give the ritual reward (*dakṣiṇā*) to the Brahmins as well as to (his) preceptor, according to his ability.

46–48 After honouring the Brahmins he should pay homage to the Viṣṇu-like teacher by giving him gold, clothes, cows and other goods. Then he should utter a formula (quoted in v. 48) praying that Jagannātha/Puruṣottama may be pleased.

49–51 Then he should accompany the Brahmins and his teacher as far as the boundary to see them off; after his return he should have his meal together with his relatives and poor and hungry persons.

52–80 On the merit of the »installation-ceremony«.

52 A man or woman who acts in that way will obtain the merit of 1000 horse-sacrifices and 100 consecration ceremonies (*rājasūya*).

53–57 Raising up 100 deceased and 100 future members of his family, he will go to Viṣṇu's world in a golden chariot, beautifully adorned etc., praised by Apsarases etc.

58–60ab There he will stay for 100 cosmic cycles, assuming a four-armed shape like Jagannātha, enjoying all pleasures together with the various classes of celestial beings.

cd–64ab At the end of his stay he will go to Brahman's abode; having stayed there for the time of 90 cosmic cycles he will go to Rudra's world, which is adorned with hundred times thousands of chariots and with various celestial beings.

64cd–75 There he will spend 80 cosmic cycles; then he will go to the world of cows. After enjoying pleasures difficult to enjoy in the three worlds for 70 cosmic cycles he will go to Prajāpati's world for 60 cosmic cycles; after that to Indra's abode for 50 cosmic cycles; then to the world of the gods for 40 cosmic cycles;[2] from there to the world of the Nakṣatras for 30 cosmic cycles; then to the world of the moon for 20 cosmic cycles; after that to the world of the sun for 10 cosmic cycles; then to the world of the Gandharvas.

76–80 After one cosmic cycle there, he will be reborn on earth as a mighty king ruling according to the (religious) law (*dharma*) and performing sacrifices; after that he will be born in an excellent Brahmin family and obtain liberation by Vaiṣṇava Yoga.

81 Conclusion to the (account of) merit of pilgrimage; question as to what else the hermits want to know.

Ch. 68: Description of Viṣṇu's world

1–3 The hermits inquire about Viṣṇu's world and in what way it can be approached.

4–5 Brahman announces a report on Viṣṇu's world, the highest step, the best of places in all worlds.

[2] Ed. VePr inserts one line after v. 70.

6-27ab *Description of Viṣṇu's world*

6-11 List of trees.
12-13ab Various flowers, creepers, etc.; various water reservoirs.
13cd-14 List of lotuses.
15-16 List of aquatic birds.
17 Conclusion.
18-22 Description of the chariots in the city of Viṣṇu.
23-27ab Description of the inhabitants of Viṣṇu's world (of the women v. 23-26ab).
27cd-28 This world is reached by those people who have seen the lotus-eyed Lord Kṛṣṇa near the fig-tree on the shore of the southern ocean.
29-32 Description of how those blessed people live in Viṣṇu's world, enjoying themselves with Apsarases, free from all misfortune, four-armed, and endowed with Viṣṇu's attributes; some are dark, some are golden, some look like jewels, etc.
33-35 No world is as shining as Hari's world, where the good stay up to the end of the world, (who) behold Kṛṣṇa, Balarāma, and Subhadrā in Puruṣottama.
36-42 Description of the beautiful temple in the centre of Hari's city: its appearance, material, extent, adornments; its four doors, its seven upper stories (?, *pura*) individually characterised by their material, and its pillars.
43 Here the accomplished adepts (*siddha*) can be seen, illuminating the 10 directions, like the full moon with the lunar mansions.
44-53 Description of Viṣṇu and Lakṣmī in this temple: dark blue, clad in yellow garments, with the Śrīvatsa-lock, the discus Sudarśana and the club Kaumodakī on his right, the conch Pāñcajanya and bow and arrows on his left (v. 50cd-53 contain an additional praising description of Viṣṇu, including mention of his thousand arms, eyes etc.).
54-55 List of celestial beings surrounding and praising Viṣṇu.
56-59ab List of names of female divine beings (partly personifications of abstract nouns, vedic metres, phenomena of nature, etc.): Kīrti, Prajñā, Medhā, Sarasvatī, Buddhi, Mati, Kṣānti, Siddhi, Mūrti, Dyuti, Gāyatrī, Sāvitrī, Maṅgalā, Prabhā, Mati,[1] Kānti, Nārāyaṇī, Śraddhā, Kauśikī, the lightning Saudāmanī, Nidrā (sleep), Rātri (night), Māyā, and other goddesses.
59cd Abbreviating formula: What use of further words? All is present there.
60-67 List of names of Apsarases (Ghṛtācī, Menakā, Rambhā, Sahajanyā, Tilottamā, Urvaśī, Nimlocā, Vāmanā; Mandodarī, Viśvācī, Citrasenā, Pramlocā; Rāmā, Candramadhyā, Sukeśī, Manmathadīpinī; Alambuṣā, Miśrakeśī, Muñjikasthalā, Kratusthalā, Pūrvacitti; Parāvatī, Śaśilekhā, Haṃsalīlā (?); Bimboṣṭhī, Navagarbhā) and description of their appearance and occupations.
68-70 There is no disease, death, heat or cold, hunger or thirst, old age, ugliness and misfortune; rather does it provide highest pleasure and fulfil all wishes. There is no world comparable to Viṣṇu's world.
71 Conclusion to the description of Viṣṇu's city (VePr highest step).
72 List of people who are not able to reach Viṣṇu's world: The unbelievers (*nāstika*), those identifying themselves with worldly objects, the ungrateful and treacherous, thieves, those who are not self-controlled.

[1] For the second time.

73 Those who always worship Vāsudeva will go to Viṣṇu's world.

74–77ab Those who, after seeing Kṛṣṇa, Balarāma, and Subhadrā, give up their lives near the wishing tree on the bank of the Southern ocean will go there, as well as those who think of Nārāyaṇa in (the place) Puruṣottama and who die there.

77c-f Conclusion to (the description of) Viṣṇu's world.

Ch. 69: Puruṣottamakṣetra-Māhātmya

1–9 The hermits confirm what they have heard: The excellences of Viṣṇu's world and the greatness of Puruṣottamakṣetra, where dying leads to Viṣṇu's world.[1] They express their wonder and surprise and observe that Brahman did not praise any other holy place (such as Prayāga, Puṣkara, etc.) as much as he praised Puruṣottamakṣetra again and again.

10–11 Brahman confirms the hermits' words concerning the superiority of Puruṣottamakṣetra above all other holy places. He confirms that there is no holy place comparable to the place called after »Puruṣa«, i.e. »(Supreme) Person«. All the other holy places are not worth even a sixteenth part of that place.

12–43 List of explanatory comparisons to illustrate the supremacy of Puruṣottamakṣetra:[2] Viṣṇu (Lord of all); Viṣṇu (Ādityas); Soma, i.e. the moon (Nakṣatras), ocean (seas and lakes), fire (Vasus), Śaṃkara (Rudras), the Brahmin (castes), Garuḍa (birds), Meru (peaks), Himālaya (mountains), Lakṣmī (beautiful women), Jāhnavī, i.e. Gaṅgā (rivers), Airāvata (kings of elephants), Bhṛgu (Great sages), Skanda (army-leaders), Kapila (Siddhas), Uccaiḥśravas (horses), Uśanas (bards), Vyāsa (hermits), Kubera (Yakṣas and Rākṣasas), mind (senses), earth (elements), *ficus religiosa* (trees), wind (all those moving to and fro),[3] Cuḍāmaṇi (jewels), Citraratha (Gandharvas), axe[4] (weapons), the letter or sound *a* (letters, sounds), Gāyatrī (metres), head (parts of the body), Arundhatī (true wives), knowledge about liberation (all realms of knowledge), the king (men), the wishing-cow (cows), gold (objects of value), Vāsuki (snakes), Prahlāda (Daityas), Rāma (i.e. Rāma Jāmadagnya) (warriors), Makara (fishes), lion (wild animals), milk-ocean (oceans), Varuṇa (inhabitants of the sea), Yama (residents of Yama's city), Nārada (divine sages), gold (metals, minerals), Dakṣiṇā, i.e. ritual reward (means of purification), Dakṣa (Prajāpatis), Kaśyapa (sages), sun (planets), *oṃ* (sacred formulas), horse-sacrifice (sacrifices), grain (plants), vine-palm (grasses), *dharma* (means of crossing the »ocean« of existences).

[1] i.e. reference back to ch. 68 only?

[2] Each verse is construed according to the model: »Like X is above or king of all Y, so Puruṣottamakṣetra is the most excellent of all holy places.« This refrain is slightly changed only in v. 41. There seems to be no principle of composition in the order and combination of beings and things enumerated.

[3] Or reference to Hanumat among those moving, jumping to and fro?

[4] Or Indra's thunderbolt?

Ch. 70: Puruṣottamakṣetra-Māhātmya; Gautamī-Māhātmya

1-11 *Conclusion to the Puruṣottamakṣetra-Māhātmya*

1-3ab Brahman repeats that all other holy places, observations, meritorious deeds etc., are not comparable to Puruṣottamakṣetra.

2cd Abbreviating formula.

3ab Confirming formula.

3cd-8ab Description of the path to liberation. He who has only once seen the place called after »Puruṣa« comes to know *brahman* at once; he will not be born again. He should stay one year or one month in Puruṣottamakṣetra, concentrating upon Hari (= Viṣṇu); all recitations, offerings, and practising of asceticism will be of great power. He will go to the highest abode inhabited by Hari, the Lord of Yoga; having enjoyed all kinds of pleasures he will be reborn, at the end of the cosmic cycle, as an excellent man, devoted to wisdom, in a house of Yogins; by means of Vaiṣṇava Yoga he will obtain Hari's independence (freedom).

8cd-10 Short survey of the subjects reported: The Māhātmyas of the wishing tree, of Balarāma, Kṛṣṇa, and Subhadrā, of Mārkaṇḍeya, of Indradyumna as well as (Śveta-)Mādhava, of Svargadvāra; the rules (for paying homage to) the ocean as well as for cleaning oneself at the correct time; the Māhātmya of Bhāgīrathī (= Gaṅgā). After all this has been told, Brahman asks what else the hermits want to hear.

11 Conclusion to the Indradyumna-Māhātmya, and to the Puruṣottama-Māhātmya, which is to be regarded as a most valuable, holy, secret Purāṇa.

12-41ef *Beginning of the Gautamī-Māhātmya*

12 The hermits ask about the holiest of holy places.

13 Brahman answers by reporting a dialogue he once had with Nārada, who had asked him the same question.

14-15 (Nārada's question:) Since Nārada has heard that pilgrimage is superior to asceticism, sacrifices, or alms, he wants to know 1. how many holy places there are in heaven, on earth and in the nether world; (v.l. which kinds of holy places exist, which merit is connected with them) and 2. which of them is especially excellent.

16-29 *Classification of holy places*

16-19 There are four kinds of holy places: those established by gods (»divine«), by Asuras, by Rishis, and by men. A holy place of the Rishis is superior to those of men; one of the Asuras grants more benefit than those of the Rishis, one of the gods is more sacred than those of the Asuras and grants all that is granted by the other three together. A holy place created by Brahman, Viṣṇu or Śiva is called »divine«. The highest of holy places is one that originates from these three (deities) together.

20-22ab The best »ford« (holy place) among the three worlds is the world of mortals; there again it is Jambūdvīpa; in Jambūdvīpa it is Bhāratavarṣa, as it is the »place for (meritorious) deeds« (*karmabhūmi*, »field of actions«); it is only there that the holy places described by Brahman are situated. (VePr inserts an announcement of names of holy places.)

22cd-23 The six rivers between Himālaya and Vindhya as well as the six rivers between the Vindhya-mountains and the Southern ocean originate from the gods; these twelve are especially famous.

24 As Bhāratavarṣa grants many benefits, it is called »place for (meritorious) deeds« (*karmabhūmi*).

25-29 Sometimes holy places of the gods or Rishis may also be called »belonging to the Asuras«, and those belonging to the gods may be called »belonging to the Rishis«, according to the use that is made of them. Those made by men for their own benefit, are called »belonging to men«. Nobody knows these differences, but Brahman (the first-person narrator) thinks Nārada worthy of coming to know it.

30-32 Nārada asks for a description of the different holy places; for by hearing it, a man would be released from all evil, and there is nothing similar to pilgrimage as a means to achieve desired results by comparatively small efforts.

33-41 *Brahman's answer: lists of examples for each of the four kinds of holy places*

33-35ab List of holy rivers, the holy places of the gods: Godāvarī, Bhīmarathī, Tuṅgabhadrā, Veṇikā, Tāpī and Payoṣṇī are known south of the Vindhya-mountains; Bhāgīrathī, Narmadā, Yamunā, Sarasvatī, Viśokā, and Vitastā originate from the Himālaya.

cd-37ab List of names of demons (i.e. the names of the holy places of the Asuras): Gaya, Kolla (v.l. Kola), Vṛtra, Tripura, Andhaka; Hayamūrdhan, Lavaṇa, Namuci, Śṛṅgaka; Yama, Pātālaketu, Madhu, Puṣkara.

37cd-38 List of names of Rishis (i.e. the names of the holy places established by Rishis): Prabhāsa, Bhārgava, Agasti, Nara, and Nārāyaṇa; Vasiṣṭha, Bhāradvāja, Gautama, Kaśyapa, Manu.

39-40 List of names of kings (i.e. the names of the holy places established by men): Ambarīṣa, Hariścandra, Nahuṣa, Rāma; Kuru, Kanakhala, Bharata, Sagara; Aśvayūpa, Nāciketas, Vṛṣākapi, Ariṃdama (name or epithet?).

41a-f (Conclusion:) These holy places were established with regard to fame or merit, or originated by themselves. (Ed. VePr inserts an explanation of Devakhāta, another conclusion, and a phalastuti).

Ch. 71: Prehistory to Śiva's marriage with Pārvatī

1 Nārada asks for a detailed description of that most excellent of all holy places which originated from the three (main) gods (i.e. Brahman, Viṣṇu, Śiva).

2-3 Brahman relates that no holy place and no religious practice (sacrifice etc.) is equal to the holy river Gaṅgā (VePr adds: Gaṅgā bestows great results derived from observances, fasting, austerities; austerities observed at all other places are nothing but purification of the body; only Gaṅgā destroys evil: by being remembered, seen or touched she fulfils all desires) and announces the story of her origin.

4-6 A long time ago, the gods were suppressed by the demon Tāraka, who was strong due to a boon granted by Brahman. They took refuge with Viṣṇu.

7-12 Hymn by the gods, praising Viṣṇu and asking for protection.

13-15 Asked about the danger by which they felt threatened, they told about Tāraka and requested Viṣṇu to kill Tāraka.

16-18 Viṣṇu replied that neither he nor anyone born from him would be able to do that; only a son of the Lord (= Śiva) could do that. Efforts should be made to obtain a wife for him.

19-23 Viṣṇu and the gods approached Himavat and Menā and prophesied that their daughter Dākṣāyaṇī (= Umā: list of epithets of Umā as deity and mother of the world) would marry Śiva, in order to protect the world.

24-26 The parents agreed. Thereupon Gaurī (= Umā) was born in Himavat's house, and she was always absorbed in thinking of Śiva. The gods asked her to practise asceticism in order to win Śiva as her husband; she acted accordingly.

27-37 The gods conferred with each other about how Śiva could be attracted to Pārvatī; Vācaspati advised employing Kāma (the god of love) to shoot Śiva with his arrow, in order to make him fall in love with Pārvatī; only their son Kumāra (the god of war) would be able to kill Tāraka.[1] On the orders of the gods, Kāma approached Śiva and, in spite of his scruples, released his arrow. By Śiva's fiery eye he was reduced to ashes.

38-40ab The gods appeared, in order to observe what had happened; seeing Śambhu (= Śiva) and the burnt Kāma, they were afraid, praised Śiva, and asked him to marry Pārvatī.

41-42 Śiva, whose mind was pierced (by passion, i.e. Kāma's arrows), agreed. (VePr adds: Great souls do not consider advantage or disadvantage with regard to the purposes of others.) Arundhatī, Vasiṣṭha, Brahman (the first-person narrator), and Viṣṇu were sent to make arrangements.

Ch. 72: Account of the events at the wedding-ceremony

1-4 Description of Himavat, the best of mountains, at the time of the wedding (decorations, classes of beings present, etc.).

5-6 Description of the (wedding) platform.[1]

7 Honoured by the great Viṣṇu, Maināka (= Himavat, the son of Menā) was much delighted.

8 The sages, the guardians of the directions, the Ādityas, and the Maruts constructed the platform.

9ab Viśvakarman Tvaṣṭṛ constructed the sacrificial platform.

9cd-10ab After Surabhi, Nandinī, Nandā, Sunandā, and Kāmadohinī (or: the wishing-cow, i.e. Surabhi?) had adorned Īśānī (= Pārvatī),[2] the marriage took place.

[1] The motif of the killing of Tāraka is not continued after ch. 71; cf. ch. 81.2-3, where the accomplished fact is mentioned, and ch. 82, which relates Skanda's birth.

[1] Ed. VePr adds that it was made by Viśvakarman.

[2] Ed. VePr reads: the bridegroom (*kānta*?).

0cd–11ab List of guests (oceans, rivers, sages, the mothers of the world, etc.).

11cd–14 Description of the ceremonial duties of the various persons present at the wedding: Ilā - preparation of the ground (or: earth-rite?), plants - preparation of food, Varuṇa - preparation of drinking, Kubera - alms-giving, Agni - oblation to the two protectors of the world (VePr reads: to Himavat and Śiva), Viṣṇu - worship (*pūjā*), Vedas and Upaniṣads - singing and laughing (Ed. VePr reads: and reciting), Apsarases - dancing, Gandharvas - singing, Maināka - supplying of fried rice.

15–17 When the auspicious time was announced inside the house, the couple took their seats on the (wedding) platform. Having installed[3] the fire and the stone, and having offered fried rice, he (i.e. Śiva) circumambulated (the fire?). In order to touch the stone, he touched Umā's finger, as well as the toe of her right foot, according to Viṣṇu's advice.

18–19 When Brahman (the first-person narrator), who was the invoker at the sacrifice (*hotṛ*), saw Umā's toe, his semen was spilt. Full of shame, he ground it; from this pounded semen the Vālakhilyas originated.

20–22 Thereupon the gods raised a turmoil, and Brahman, ashamed, rose from his seat, in order to leave the assembly. But Śiva, seeing Brahman leave, told Nandin to call him back, as the good should have pity on those who have failed, for even the wise may be deluded by sense-objects (maxim).[4]

23–25ab Out of compassion for Brahman and the worlds, Śiva (VePr Hara) decided to extract the essence of earth and water as a means of purification.

5cd–27ab Using the earth as a bowl, he put the waters inside. Reciting purifying prayer-formulas, he thought of that energy (*śakti*) which purifies the three worlds.[5]

27cd–34 Then he told Brahman to take this bowl, describing the powerful effects of its contents:[6] the waters are divine mothers, the earth is another mother; both (water and earth) are the cause of origin, existence, and destruction. *Dharma* and the sacrifice, enjoyment and liberation, animate and inanimate beings are founded in it (i.e. the water); all evil committed with mind, speech, or body, is destroyed by bathing in or sprinkling with or drinking water. Remembered or drunk, it fulfils all desires.[7] Water is most eminent among all elements; by touching or thinking of this water (i.e. the water in the bowl presented by Śiva), Brahman, too, would be freed from all evil.

35a-f With these words, Śiva gave the bowl to Brahman, whereupon the gods rejoiced.

36 Concluding summary:[8] Seeing the Mother's (= Umā's) toe, the Unborn (= Brahman)[9] had fallen; the Father (= Śiva), however, gave him the purifying Gaṅgā[10] in the bowl.

[3] Ed. VePr reads: kindled.

[4] This maxim is not found in all Mss.

[5] This sentence is not found in all mss.

[6] The order to take the bowl is used as a refrain in v. 27, 31, 32, 33.

[7] This sentence is not found in all mss.

[8] In Upajāti-metre.

[9] Third person though Brahman is the narrator.

[10] First mention of the name Gaṅgā.

Ch. 73: Story of Bali and Viṣṇu's three steps (Vāmana-Avatāra)[1]

1 Nārada wants to know how Gaṅgā went from the bowl to the world of mortals.

2–69 Brahman answers by telling the story of the descent of the Gaṅgā.

2–6 The great Daitya Bali had become insuperable, due to his virtuous behaviour. Therefore the gods consulted among each other how to subdue him, under whose sovereignty conditions were ideal (no enemies, no diseases, no drought, no bad or unbelieving people, etc.).[2]

7–8 Feeling attacked by Bali, the gods could find no rest, so they went to complain to Viṣṇu.

9–17 Complaint of the gods: they describe their miserable condition, putting the responsibility for it on Viṣṇu, whose power (Lord over everything, etc.) and qualities (e.g. *trimūrti*-functions) they contrast with their being subdued by Bali.[3]

18–20 Viṣṇu explained that (the demon) Bali was his devotee as much as the gods, but promised to take the kingdom from him without a fight.

21–22 The gods returned; Viṣṇu embodied himself in Aditi's womb and was born as dwarf, the »soul of the sacrifice« (*yajñapuruṣa*).

23–26 In the meantime Bali had made preparations for a horse-sacrifice; his family priest (*purohita*) was Śukra.

27–33 When the dwarf in the shape of a Brahmin reached the sacrificial ground, Śukra recognised him as their enemy and turned to Bali, who was meditating on the »soul of the sacrifice« (= Viṣṇu), in order to warn him that the dwarf was the »Lord of the sacrifice«, who had come here for the sake of the gods; before granting him anything he might ask for, Bali should first consult Śukra.

34–40 Bali, however, considered himself blessed by the Lord of the sacrifice coming to his house, in order to put forward a request. He politely approached the dwarf, who asked him for earth measuring three steps; Bali poured water to confirm the donation, witnessed by Śukra and the gods.

41–43cd Blessing Bali, the dwarf again asked for earth extending three steps;[4] Bali agreed. Now the dwarf, being the Lord of the sacrifice and the creator of the world etc., grew till sun and moon (belonging to the intermediate sphere) were between his breasts and the gods (belonging to the heavenly sphere) were at his head.

43ef–45 Bali addressed him as god Viṣṇu and encouraged him to measure out, according to his ability, what Bali had conquered with all his soul (? or: by striving for totality?[5]).[6]

[1] A German summary and brief analysis of this chapter is given by G. C. Tripathi: »Der Ursprung und die Entstehung der Vāmana-Legende in der indischen Literatur.« Wiesbaden 1968, p. 201-205. As to the relative chronology of this version of the Vāmana legend, Tripathi concludes that it is later than MtP, BhP, and PdP (Sṛṣṭikhaṇḍa Ch. 30), but earlier than SkP 7/2,14–19.

[2] v. 5-6 are most probably part of the direct speech of the gods, as the present tense is used in them.

[3] According to the pattern: statement about Viṣṇu + rhetorical question as refrain (»How should we who are protected by Viṣṇu, submit to this Daitya?«).

[4] Ed. VePr inserts a call for attention to listen.

[5] Tripathi reads two sentences instead of one: Bali encourages Viṣṇu to stride out; at the end

46–47 Viṣṇu announced his steps, repeatedly encouraged by Bali.

48–51 Having stepped on the back of the tortoise, Viṣṇu put his first step on Bali's sacrifice. The second step was put in Brahman's world. For the third step there was no more space left.[7] When Hari (= Viṣṇu) asked Bali where he should step now, Bali laughed and answered that not he, but Viṣṇu, had created the world, consequently Viṣṇu was at fault for having made it too small. In order to stick to the truth of his words, however, Bali asked Viṣṇu to put the third step on his back.

52–55 Pleased by this proposal, Viṣṇu granted him a boon. When Bali refused to ask for anything Viṣṇu granted him the lordship over the nether world(s), Indra's position for the future, self-government (or self-control?) and imperishable fame.

56–57ab Having installed Bali and his family in the nether world, Viṣṇu gave the kingdom of the gods back to Indra.

57cd Meanwhile the (i.e. Viṣṇu's) footstep, which is to be honoured even by the gods, had arrived there (i.e. in the world of Brahman).[8]

58–63ab When Brahman beheld Viṣṇu's second step,[9] which had come to his abode, he thought about how to honour it as a guest and decided to offer the best he could think of, the water he had obtained from Śiva (description of its salutary effects and attributes).

63cd–65ab Brahman poured this water on Viṣṇu's foot; from there it fell down on Mt. Meru and flowed to the earth in the four main directions.

65cd–67 The southern branch was caught in Śiva's locks; the western returned to the bowl; Viṣṇu seized the northern waters, whereas gods, ancestors, sages, and the guardians of the directions seized the eastern water.

68–69ab Conclusion: The southern waters are the mothers of the world; belonging originally to Brahman, they were brought forth by Viṣṇu's foot and born (again) when staying in Maheśvara's locks.[10]

69cd Remembering their origin fulfils all desires.

Ch. 74: Gaṇeśa's device to make Gautama bring down the Gaṅgā[1]

1 Nārada asks how the goddess (i.e. Gaṅgā), who stayed in Maheśvara's locks, came down to the world of mortals.

he (Bali) would be the winner at any rate. (p. 203)

[6] Ed. VePr inserts: Śukra repeated that he had warned Bali before.

[7] Viṣṇu's steps go vertically through the cosmos, which is here imagined as resting on the back of a tortoise; Bali's sacrifice supposedly takes place on the earth, i.e. the middle storey of the cosmic egg. Brahman's world is the uppermost of the worlds above the earth.

[8] The narrative about Bali being finished, the thread of narration is taken up again from the point when Viṣṇu's second step reached the world of Brahman, who now introduces his own experiences again.

[9] Brahman refers here to Viṣṇu as his father (cf. also ch. 161 below).

[10] This corresponds to the characteristic of Gaṅgā as *tridaivatyaṃ tīrtham* in 70.19 and 71.1.

[1] For an English summary of this episode see O'Flaherty, Origins of evil (1975), p. 300, where this text is discussed against the background of comparable myths found in other Purāṇas,

2-5 Brahman relates that the waters in Śiva's locks were divided into two parts, since there were two persons to bring them down to the earth: one part was brought down by the Brahmin Gautama, the other by the Kṣatriya Bhagīratha.

6 Nārada wants to know why Gautama, and why Bhagīratha, brought the waters down from Maheśvara's locks.

7 Brahman announces the story of how Gaṅgā was brought down by the Brahmin.

8-12 At the time when Umā became the dear wife of Śiva (the lord of the gods), Gaṅgā became dear to him, too (or: became his beloved). When he thought of how to remove Brahman's fault[2] and looked at the goddess (i.e. Gaṅgā) particularly, together with Umā, he created the most excellent sentiment (*rasa*), as he himself was in the condition of (this) sentiment. Because of (or: with regard to) (his) fondness (for her), (her) being dear, being a woman, and being a means of purification, Gaṅgā was more lovable than all other (women).[3] Maheśvara thought of her continually. When Gaṅgā had, for some reason, come out of his locks, Śambhu hid her there (again).

13-22ab Umā could not tolerate this; she asked Bhava (= Śiva) to give her (viz. Gaṅgā) up, but he refused. So Umā turned to (her children ?)[4] Vināyaka (= Gaṇeśa), Jayā and Skanda[5] and told them that she would return to Himavat (i.e. to her father, or to the mountains), in order to practise asceticism, unless Gaṅgā was asked by pure ascetic Brahmins to come down to earth. Thereupon Gaṇeśa conferred with Skanda and Jayā as to what to do.

22cd-38ab Introduction of Gautama, the »ideal ascetic«, into the story.[6]

22cd-24ab In the meantime there had been a drought of twice twelve years, which destroyed the animate and inanimate world, with the exception of Gautama's hermitage.

24cd-30 Desirous of creating beings, Brahman (first-person narrator) had once performed a sacrifice.[7] At first he had created a mountain known as Brahmagiri,[8] where Gautama had always been living, up to the present.[9] In his hermitage diseases, hunger, fear etc. were not known; only there were sacrifices performed; the gods lived on what they received from Gautama, who was famous as sacrificer, »giver«, and »enjoyer«.[10]

cf. particularly KūP 1,15.95-108; VrP 71.10-46; DevīBhP 12,9.1-97; ŚiP 4,25-27 (references according to O'Flaherty).

[2] As first-person narrator Brahman seems to refer to 72.18-36.

[3] Ed. VePr inserts: »Umā knows that Gaṅgā is in my forehead«, thus ...

[4] This seems to be suggested by the mention of Jayā between Vināyaka and Skanda; Jayā as daughter of Gaurī does not seem to be known otherwise (cf. A. Bock: Der Sāgara-Gaṅgāvataraṇa-Mythus, note 4 on p. 309).

[5] v. 16-17 seem to parallel v. 15.

[6] This passage seems to be an interruption of Brahman's main story, adding the prehistory of Gautama, who is thought to be able to help in this special case.

[7] cf. below ch. 161.

[8] A mountain in the Nasik district, Bombay, near Tryambaka, in which the Godāvarī has its source.

[9] i.e. the time of Brahman's relating the story to Nārada.

[10] In v. 26cd-30 the present tense is used, probably in order to denote the duration of time.

31-37 Attracted by his fame, the hermits of different places went[11] to Gautama's hermitage; he honoured them as guests, feeding them and fulfilling all their wishes; plants grew upon Gautama's order; Brahman, Viṣṇu, and Śiva were satisfied by him. The plants grew and multiplied by the power of Gautama's asceticism. All facilities were provided; for many years, Gautama daily honoured hermits as his guests.[12]

38ab (Conclusion:) Thus Gautama acquired much fame.

38cd-42 Vināyaka (= Gaṇeśa) told his mother, his brother, and Jayā about Gautama's renown, suggesting that he should be won over to bring down Gaṅgā either by means of his asceticism or by worshipping Śiva.

43-55 Accordingly, the »king of obstacles« (Vighnarāṭ, i.e. Gaṇeśa), his brother, and Jayā went to Gautama's place. After some days he persuaded the other hermits to leave for their own hermitages. Gautama tried to stop them by offering his services, but Gaṇeśa made them understand that they had been »bought« by food, so that they were not able to return home by their own will. He asked them whether he should decide the matter, without harming Gautama. They agreed, provided that he was acting for the best of Gautama, of the three worlds, and of all Brahmins. This he promised.

56-58 Having thus convinced the Brahmins, Gaṇeśa became a Brahmin, out of consideration for his mother, and he told Jayā to change herself into a cow, in order not to be recognised, and to go to Gautama's hermitage; she should feed on (his) rice and disfigure her shape; when beaten, she should fall down, crying miserably, and pretend to be neither dead nor alive.

59-67 Vijayā (= Jayā) acted accordingly; when Gautama tried to drive away the disfigured cow with grass, she uttered a cry and collapsed amidst a great hullabaloo. Seeing what Gautama had done, the Brahmins announced that they could not stay in Gautama's hermitage any more. Gautama implored them to stay, but they pointed to the fallen cow, who should be regarded as a goddess, as the mother of Rudras, as purifying, etc.; their observances would be destroyed by living in a place where a cow had been hurt. They would rather live by their asceticism than by the wealth of others.

68-75 Gautama asked the Brahmins to purify him; when Vighnakṛt (= Gaṇeśa) announced a way out, Gautama wanted to know how the unconscious cow could be made to get up. The Brahmins pointed to Gaṇeśa as their authority (*pramāṇa*).

76-77 Thereupon »the king of obstacles« told Gautama to take the water of Brahman's bowl hidden in Śiva's locks, and to sprinkle the cow with it; then he and the Brahmins would stay at Gautama's place again.

78-81 Upon these words it rained flowers, and the shout »victory« was heard. Gautama agreed to the proposal. The Brahmins left for their own abodes; Gaṇeśa and Jayā, having fulfilled their task, left, too.

82-87 Gautama began to practise asceticism; by meditation he came to know that he had not committed any fault, but was to fulfil a divine purpose.[13] Resolved on pleasing Śiva and Umā, he would bring down Gaṅgā.

[11] The narration shifts back to the past tense in v. 31-34.

[12] v. 35-37 seem to take up the topics of v. 31-34 in inverted order, and in the present tense instead of the past.

[13] Ed. VePr inserts: He told his wife about his intention.

88 Gautama left for Mt. Brahmagiri.[14]

Ch. 75: Gautama's hymn to Śiva

1 Nārada asks what kind of asceticism was practised by Gautama, and which hymn of praise he recited.
2-50 Brahman relates how Gautama praised Śiva, and its result of it.
2-3 Gautama prepared himself and his seat on Mt. Kaiḷāsa, and started to praise Śiva. While he praised him, it rained flowers.
4-24 Hymn by Gautama to Śiva and Umā.
4-13 Praise of Śiva and his eight »bodies«.
4 Śiva, who is praised as »moon (Soma) of the peoples«, assumes eight bodies, for the sake of the world.[1]
5 Śiva as earth.[2]
6 Śiva as water.[3]
7 Śiva as fire, sun, and moon.[4]
8 Śiva as wind.[5]
9 Śiva as atmosphere (*vyoman*).[6]
10 Śiva as sound.[7]
11 Śiva as sacrifice.[8]
12 Śiva as All.[9]
13 Śiva is beyond tradition and knowledge.[10]
14-22 Umā's origin, functions, deeds, and epithets.
14 Umā's origin as Śiva's will (*prakṛti*).[11]
15 Umā as Śiva's energy (*śakti*).[12]
16 Umā as Śiva's beloved.[13]
17 Umā as mother of the world.[14]

[14] In Upajāti-metre, 88c Indravaṃśā-metre.
[1] In Indravajrā-metre.
[2] In Upajāti-metre.
[3] In Upajāti-metre, 5c Vaṃśasthavila-metre.
[4] In Upajāti-metre, 7c Indravaṃśā-metre.
[5] Directly addressed to Śiva, in Indravajrā-metre.
[6] Directly addressed to Śiva, in Indravajrā-metre.
[7] In Indravajrā-metre.
[8] Directly addressed to Śiva, in Upajāti-metre.
[9] In Upajāti-metre. According to H. Meinhard: Beiträge zur Kenntnis des Śivaismus, p. 9-14, the eight forms are more usually the five elements plus sun, moon, and sacrifice.
[10] Directly addressed to Śiva, and concluding by *namas te*. In Upendravajrā-metre.
[11] In Upajāti-metre.
[12] In Upajāti-metre.
[13] In Upajāti-metre.
[14] In Upajāti-metre.

18 Umā resembling Soma (i.e. the moon).[15]
19 Umā as Vāgīśvarī (i.e. »Lady of Speech«).[16]
20 Umā brought down Gaṅgā for the sake of the world, and for the purification of the »Four-headed One« (= Brahman).[17]
21 Umā as manifestation (*vibhūti*) of Śiva's power.[18]
22 Umā as the success (*siddhi*) of rituals etc.[19]
23 Praise of »Umā's lord« as liberation for Yogins meditating on the *brahman*.[20]
24 Effects produced by Śiva and Umā.[21]
25–27 Thus praised, Śiva appeared before Gautama and granted him a boon.
28–30 Gautama was overwhelmed with joy and asked for Gaṅgā.
31 Śiva wanted Gautama to wish for something for himself, not only for the benefit of the three worlds.
32 Now Gautama wished that all wishes of those who praise (Śiva and Umā) by this hymn should be fulfilled.
33 Śiva agreed, but granted still more boons.
35–45 Gautama wished (again) that Śiva should let Gaṅgā come down to the Brahmagiri; further, that bathing at all places of pilgrimage along her path to the ocean should purify from all sins; that the merit obtained at all other places of pilgrimage, at all auspicious dates, in all Yugas, by all meritorious acts, should be obtained by thinking of her only; those who approach within a distance of ten Yojanas of her, should be released even from great sins, together with their ancestors; she should be the most distinguished of all holy places in heaven, earth, and the nether world.
46–47 Śiva agreed emphatically, and disappeared.
48 At Śiva's command, Gautama took Śiva's tuft of hair (= Gaṅgā), the »best of rivers«, and returned to Mt. Brahmagiri.[22]
49–50 When Gautama arrived there, together with Śiva's lock, it rained flowers; gods, sages etc. honoured Gautama by shouting »victory«.

Ch. 76: The Gautamī Gaṅgā on earth

1 Nārada asks what Gautama did next.
2–4 Brahman relates that Gautama put down Gaṅgā on the top of the mountain (i.e. the Brahmagiri). He asked her to forgive him, and told her to go and do good.

[15] In Upajāti-metre.
[16] In Indravajrā-metre.
[17] Refers to the story of Brahman's fault, which was told in ch. 72. In Upajāti-metre.
[18] In Upajāti-metre.
[19] In Indravajrā-metre.
[20] In Indravajrā-metre.
[21] Directly addressed to Umā; in Upajāti-metre.
[22] Mixture of Vaṃśasthavila-metre (ab) and Upendravajrā-metre (cd). In the first quarter (48a), read *bhagvati* for *bhagavati*, in order to obtain a correct metre.

5-6 Gaṅgā asked him where to go: back to the gods, to Brahman's bowl, or to the nether world?

7 Gautama told her that she had been obtained by him for the benefit of all three worlds.

8-10 Consequently, Gaṅgā divided herself into three parts, one each for heaven, earth, and the nether world. In heaven she became fourfold, on earth sevenfold, in the nether world fourfold, destroying sins everywhere, even according to vedic tradition.

11 Mortals, however, do not see her lower and celestial forms.

12 She is considered divine all along her course to the eastern ocean.

13-17 Gautama circumambulated her; having worshipped Śiva, he made up his mind to bathe on both of her banks. Śiva appeared before him,[1] and Gautama asked him about the rules for bathing at a holy place.

18-23ab Śiva's first answer.

18ab Announcement of the rules relating to the Godāvarī.[2]

18cd-23ab Rules for bathing at places of pilgrimage: First one should perform the *nāndīmukha*-ceremony for the ancestors, then clean one's body; after that one should honour and serve Brahmins, observing abstinence and without talking to fallen persons, in order to obtain the »fruit« of the holy place. Giving up wicked attitudes, and observing the caste rules (*svadharma*), one should give food, blankets, and clothes to needy Sādhus; by listening to the story of Hari (= Viṣṇu/Kṛṣṇa?) and about the origin of the Gaṅgā, one will certainly obtain the »fruit« of holy places.

Ch. 77: Śiva's account of the Gautamī Gaṅgā

1 Tryambaka (= Śiva) told Gautama the following:

2-9ab There will be ten holy places where Śiva will be present: The river Bhāgīrathī (= Gaṅgā) at Gaṅgādvāra (1), at Prayāga (2), and at her mouth into the ocean (3); the river Narmadā in the Amarakaṇṭaka-hills (4), the Yamunā at her confluence (5), the Sarasvatī at Prabhāsa[1] (6); the Kṛṣṇā, Bhīmarathī, and Tuṅgabhadrā at their confluences (7,8,9), and the Payoṣṇī at her confluence (10); all these places provide liberation, but the Gautamī will grant liberation everywhere; she is the best of them.[2] There will be 350 million of holy places (on the banks of the Gautamī) within 200 Yojanas.

[1] This sentence is not found in all mss.

[2] Here appears, for the first time, in connection with the Gaṅgāvataraṇa, the name Godāvarī, i.e. the river that has its source on the Brahmagiri and goes to the eastern ocean, and the origin of which is here connected with the heavenly Gaṅgā.

[1] In Gujarat.

[2] Ed. VePr inserts here: Bathing for 60,000 years in the Bhāgīrathī (Gaṅgā) is equal to bathing in the Godāvarī once when Bṛhaspati (= Jupiter) is in the constellation Leo. At this time it is difficult for men to come near the Gautamī, as all the other rivers, Bhāgirathī etc., come to the Gautamī. Those who attend to other holy places, leaving out the Gautamī, are stupid and go to destruction.

9cd–13 This Gaṅgā is (known as) Māheśvarī, Gautamī, Vaiṣṇavī, Brāhmī (i.e. relating to, or: originating from, Śiva, Gautama, Viṣṇu, Brahman), as Godāvarī, Nandā, Sunandā, and Kāmadāyinī (i.e. the wish-fulfilling one);[3] brought (down) by Brahman, she destroys all sins, even when only remembered, and is always dear to Śiva. Water is the best among the five elements, but the best water stems from holy places. Among these (waters), the Bhāgīrathī is the best; best of all of them, however, is the Gautamī, who was led down along Śiva's locks; there is no other holy place in the three worlds comparable to her.

14–15 (Conclusion:) Brahman repeats that the Gautamī Gaṅgā is the best of all holy places, and asks Nārada what he wants to hear next.

Ch. 78: Descent of the Bhāgīrathī Gaṅgā[1]

1–2 Nārada recalls that two parts (of the Gaṅgā) were mentioned: one brought down by a Brahmin, and one brought down by a Kṣatriya; he wants to hear, now, about the one brought down by the Kṣatriya.

3–77 Brahman relates the story of how Gaṅgā was made to descend by Bhagīratha.

3–8ab Once upon a time there was a king named Sagara, descended from Vaivasvata and born in the family of Ikṣvāku. He had two wives, but no children. He invited Vasiṣṭha to his house, who advised him to pay special attention to the honouring of sages.

8cd–11 Once a royal sage came to Sagara and was duly honoured as a guest; he granted a boon to Sagara, who wished for sons. The sage promised him he would get one son who would continue the family line, from one wife, and 60,000 sons from the other.[2] The sons were born as promised; and Sagara performed many horse sacrifices.

12–24 During one horse sacrifice, Sagara ordered his 60,000 sons to protect the horse. But at some occasion Śatakratu (= Indra) stole the horse.[3] They followed it, but could not find it, for demons, who could not be seen due to magic (*māyā*), had taken it to the nether world. On their search they roamed the world of the gods and the whole earth, without being able to find it, while the king, prepared for the sacrifice, was much troubled, since he had no sacrificial animal. Searching for the horse, the 60,000 sons finally heard a heavenly voice telling them that the horse was in the nether world. In order to get there, they dug up the earth, feeding upon dry earth.

24–31 When the demons heard them coming near, they hurried to the place in the nether world where the sage Kapila was lying asleep. Once he had performed a very

[3] It is not quite clear whether these are names or epithets; cf. a similar case in ch. 72, v. 9cd–10ab, where Umā is decorated by her friends bearing partly similar names.

[1] For a German summary of Ch. 78 cf. A. Bock: Der Sāgara-Gaṅgāvataraṇa-Mythus, Ch. IX, esp. p. 164–166. Bock concludes that the redactor of this version knew the versions of MBh 3,104–108 and Rm 1,37–43 as well as of BdP 2/3,50.21–2/3,55 and 2/3,56.29–53.

[2] cf. ch. 8, v. 64–68.

[3] cf. Rm 1,38.7, where Indra in shape of a Rākṣasa (!) steals the horse.

difficult task for the gods; exhausted but sleepless, he had asked the gods for a place to sleep without being disturbed; if anyone woke him, he should be reduced to ashes. This place was granted to him in the nether world. The demons knew about this condition and about Kapila's irascibility; therefore they arranged a device to kill the Sāgaras without a fight: they bound the horse near sleeping Kapila's head and hid at a distance.

32-37ab Seeing the horse near Kapila's head, the 60,000 Sāgaras believed him to be the thief. Though some of them warned the others, they beat Kapila, in order to wake him up and kill him; Kapila, however, looked at them angrily and reduced them to ashes.

37cd-44 King Sagara had no information about what had happened until Nārada told him; he did not know what to do. He had another son called Asamañjas; coming to know, however, that Asamañjas used to throw children and citizens into the water, Sagara exiled him. Thus he had lost the 60,000 sons by a Brahmin's curse,[4] as well as the one son, so he did not know what to do.

45-46 Asamañjas had a son named Aṃśumat, whom the king called, in order to transfer the task to him. Aṃśumat paid homage to Kapila and returned the horse to Sagara, whose sacrifice could now be completed.

47-54 Aṃśumat's son was Dilīpa, whose son was Bhagīratha. When Bhagīratha heard about his grandfathers' fate, he inquired from Sagara what could be done for their redemption; Sagara referred him to Kapila. The child went to the nether world, paid homage to Kapila, and told him about his problem. After meditating and practising asceticism, in order to please Śaṃkara (= Śiva), Kapila told Bhagīratha that he should have his ancestors submerged in the water from (Śiva's) lock. Bhagīratha agreed and asked where to go and what to do. He was told to go to Mt. Kailāsa and to praise Maheśvara, practising asceticism.

55 There the child went, resolved to practise asceticism, and addressed Śiva.

56-58 Hymn by Bhagīratha to Śiva, emphasizing his own childishness and ignorance, and addressing Śiva as holding the moon in its form as a child (i.e. the crescent). He praised this moon for the sake of his »benefactors«, i.e. his ancestors, whose wishes Śiva should fulfil.[5]

59-69 Śiva appeared before him and granted him a boon. Bhagīratha chose the river in Śiva's locks to purify his ancestors. Śiva agreed and advised Bhagīratha to praise Gaṅgā; thereby he gained her grace.[6] Thereupon he took her to the nether world, told Kapila what had happened, and put her down, as he was told. Then he circumambulated her, told her about Kapila's curse against his ancestors and requested her to save them.

70-75ab For the sake of the world, in order to purify Bhagīratha's ancestors, in order to fill the ocean that was drunk by Agastya,[7] and in order to destroy sins merely by being remembered, she did as she was told by Bhagīratha, submerging the sons of Sagara[8] and filling up what they had dug out. Then she went to Mt. Meru; being again

[4] A curse, however, was not mentioned in the related episode.

[5] v. 57-58 in Upajāti-metre.

[6] No hymn, however, is quoted in this context.

[7] cf. the introduction of the story in the MBh.

[8] Ed. VePr reads: who had been burnt due to a Brahmin's curse.

requested by the young king, she went to the Himālaya, from there to Bhāratavarṣa, and through Bhārata to the eastern ocean.

75cd-76 Conclusion to the story of the »Kṣatriya Gaṅgā«, the Bhāgīrathī, who is also Māheśvarī, Vaiṣṇavī, and Brāhmī (i.e. being related to, or originated from, Maheśvara, Viṣṇu and Brahman),[9] and has her abode on the peak of the Himālaya.

77 Conclusion to ch. 71-78: Thus the water from Śiva's head came down twice, as Gautamī Gaṅgā south of the Vindhya-mountains, as Bhāgīrathī north of them.

Ch. 79: Story of Viṣṇu as boar lifting up the sacrifice

1-2 Nārada replies that he cannot be satiated by listening to Brahman's stories, and wishes to hear about each of the holy places along the course of the Gaṅgā that was brought down by the Brahmin (i.e. the Gautamī), one after the other, about their origin and the merit obtained by visiting them.

3-5ab Brahman objects that he is not able to tell all about these holy places, nor is Nārada able to listen to it, yet he is prepared to give a brief account of those holy places that have been mentioned above,[1] or that are named in the tradition (*śruti*), having paid homage to the »Three-Eyed One« (Trilocana, i.e. Śiva) before.

5cd-6ab The place where Tryambaka (= Śiva) became visible is called Tryambaka.[2]

6cd-7ab The next holy place is named Vārāhatīrtha, famous in the three worlds; Brahman announces that he will tell how Viṣṇu's name (or: one of Viṣṇu's shapes) became its name.

7cd-19 Account of the origin of Vārāhatīrtha. Once upon a time a Rākṣasa named Sindhusena had overpowered the gods and taken the sacrifice to the nether worlds, so that the gods were left without any sacrifice. With this thought, »neither this nor the other world can exist without the sacrifice« the gods entered the nether world too, but could not defeat the demon. They went to Viṣṇu, the »Primordial Man« (*purāṇapuruṣa*), and told him about it. He assumed the shape of a boar and, holding conch, discus, and club in his hands (!), went to the nether world, promising to kill the demon and bring back the sacrifice; the gods should return to heaven. By the same path along which Gaṅgā had reached the nether world he went there, too, splitting the earth. Then he killed the inhabitants of the nether world, lifted up the sacrifice (*makha*) with his mouth (*mukha*) and returned by the same way, while the gods were waiting for him on the Brahmagiri. Leaving this path, he went to the river Gaṅgā and washed off the blood from his limbs with its water; from that water the holy pond called »Vārāha« came into existence. Viṣṇu placed the sacrifice before the gods and restored it to them; it was born from his mouth (*mukha* → *makha*).

20-21ab From this time onward the chief sacrifial utensil is called »*sruva*« (i.e. the ladle used for pouring melted butter),[3] and thus, for a second reason,[4] (Viṣṇu's) form of a boar came into being. Therefore the place is called »Vārāha«.

[9] A. Bock, op. cit., note 20 on p. 312f., understands that she is here entitled with the names of the three *śaktis* of Śiva, Viṣṇu, and Brahman.

[1] i.e. in ch. 25?

[2] Situated 17 miles from Nasik, near the source of the Godāvarī.

[3] There seems to be an etymological connection between the Gaṅgā-stream (*gaṅgāsravaṇa*)

21cd–22 Bathing there and giving alms bestows the merit of all sacrificial rites. To remember one's ancestors at this place frees them from all evil and leads them to heaven.

Ch. 80: Story of the pigeon couple and the hunter[1]

1–5ab Short account of Kuśāvarta and Nīlagaṅgā.[2]

1–3 Brahman confesses that he is not able to relate the importance of Kuśāvarta, where Gautama had deturned (the Gaṅgā ?[3]), by means of Kuśa (grass), and had led her (to her path?); here the ancestors can be satisfied by bathing and alms-giving.

4–5ab Nīlagaṅgā originates from the Nīla-mountain; all pious actions that are performed here are imperishable and satisfy the ancestors.

5cd–6ab Announcement of a description of the place called »Kapota« (»pigeon«).

6cd–9 On mount Brahmagiri lived a violent hunter, who hurt human beings as well as animals, and whose appearance was extremely ugly and frightening (description).

10–12 His wife and children were like him. His wife sent him to the forest, where he killed many animals and birds; some he caught in a cage and some alive. Hungry and thirsty, after roaming the country, he returned back home.

13–14 One afternoon in spring, he was surprised by a thunderstorm. Exhausted by wind, water, and hail showers, he lost his way.

15–17 Unable to distinguish water or land, ditches or paths, and unable to find any shelter, he reflected about the possible nearness of death for himself who had killed so many beings.

18–21 Finally he came across a large tree (the excellence of which is emphasized by a series of similes); with soaked clothes he sat down, worrying about his family. In the meantime the sun had set.

22–25ab In the same tree, a pigeon had been living with his family for many years; his wife was greatly devoted to him.

25cd–29 On that day, both had gone out for food; by the influence of fate, the female pigeon was caught in the cage of that very hunter. Finding the nest empty, and unaware of his wife's presence in the hunter's cage, the pigeon started lamenting and praising his wife's qualities.

30–36 Lamentation, starting with »Today the good one does not return« (*nādyāpy āyāti kalyāṇī*, which is used as a refrain three more times), and containing the praise of the female pigeon's devotion, as well as her husband's inability to live without her.

37–43 From the hunter's cage, the pigeon's wife answered her husband, expressing her happiness about his praising her,[4] and advising him to think of his duty (*dharma*) and not to grieve.

and the *sruva*.

[4] The first reason for assuming the shape of a boar was the necessity of lifting up the earth when she was submerged under the waters.

[1] cf. MBh 12,141–145.

[2] These verses seem not to belong to the context of the following Tīrtha-description; but these places are obviously passed by before reaching the Kapotatīrtha.

[3] *āvartitam* (n.) in v. 2cd, but *tām* in v. 3ab.

[4] v. 40 contains a »maxim« about the importance of a wife's loyalty towards her husband.

44-45 The pigeon came down from the tree; seeing his wife caught and the hunter motionless, he told her that he would free her.

46-55 She objected, pointing out that the hunter had not committed any fault, as birds were his (normal) food. Moreover, he was their guest. The most respectable person (*guru*) for the »twice-born« (i.e. the three upper castes as well as the birds) is Agni, for the (other) castes it is a Brahmin, for a wife her husband, and for everybody it is a guest. Honouring him with (friendly) words will please the goddess »Speech«, honouring him with food will satisfy Śakra (= Indra, the »guest« at the sacrifice), offering water for washing his feet will please the ancestors, offering food etc. will please Prajāpati; attending him will please Lakṣmī and Viṣṇu, offering a bed will please the All-Gods (*viśvedevāḥ*). Therefore the hunter, too, should be honoured as a guest; for all gods would be satisfied by that.[5] Finally it is particularly meritorious to serve someone who has done wrong.

56-59 The pigeon agreed, but recalled their poverty (in poetic words), wondering how they could honour their guest.

60 She answered him that water, fire, and pleasant words could at least be given.

61-64 Thereupon the pigeon flew to the top of the tree; looking around he saw a fire at some distance. He went there and returned with a piece of charcoal, in order to light a fire in front of the hunter, which the pigeon kept burning by throwing dry wood and grass on it. The hunter warmed his limbs and felt happy.

65-70 Realising that the hunter was hungry, the pigeon's wife asked her husband to free her, so that she could feed the guest with her body; her husband, however, did not agree to that, he rather wanted to sacrifice himself. He circumambulated the fire thrice, meditating on the four-armed god Viṣṇu, and entered the fire. Thereupon the hunter started to abuse himself, for whom the pigeon had died willingly.

71-77 Now the pigeon's wife asked the hunter to release her from the cage. The intimidated hunter did so. Circumambulating the fire thrice, she uttered maxims about the wife's duty to follow her husband everywhere, a »path« already taught in the Veda, and about the reward obtained by a faithful wife.[6]

78-79 Having bowed to the earth, the gods, the Gaṅgā, and the trees, and having comforted her children, she turned to the hunter, informing him about her intention to follow her husband,[7] and asking him to have pity on her children.

80-83 Then she entered the fire; whereupon shouts of »victory« arose. A sun-like vehicle appeared to transport the couple, which they entered, thanking the hunter for being their guest and, by that, allowing them to ascend to heaven.

84-89 Bowing to them, the hunter requested them to tell him how he could achieve expiation. The couple advised him to bathe in the Gautamī, for half a month (*pakṣam*),[8] in order to be purified from his sins; to bathe once more in the Gaṅgā, in order to obtain the merit of a horse-sacrifice; if he bathed a further time in the Gautamī, the best of rivers, which originated from Brahman, Viṣṇu, and Śiva, he would, after giving up his unclean body (i.e. after his death), ascend to heaven.[9]

[5] v. 52 in Upajāti-metre.

[6] v.76-77 contain similes illustrating the reward of a faithful wife.

[7] Ed. VePr inserts, as v. 79, a repetition of v. 77.

[8] Or: »once«.

[9] The last sentence could be interpreted in another way: »When bathing and giving up his

90-91ef The hunter acted as he had been advised; assuming a divine shape, he went to heaven. Thus all three, the pigeon couple as well as the hunter, by the grace of Gautamī, reached heaven.

92-93ab From that time onward, the place is called »Kapota« (»pigeon«); any religious practice performed there leads to infinity.

Ch. 81: Story of Skanda's lust

1 (Brahman continues:) The next holy place is Kārttikeya, famous as »Kaumāra« (related to Kumāra, i.e. Skanda or Kārttikeya); by merely hearing its name, one gets (i.e. is reborn as having) a (noble) family and beautiful shape.

2-3 When the demon Tāraka had been killed[1] and the Triviṣṭapa(-heaven) had regained its natural state, Pārvatī was very pleased with her oldest son and encouraged him to a life full of joys and pleasures.

4-7ab Thereupon Viśākha (= Skanda) made love to the wives of the gods, who enjoyed him as well. The gods, who were not able to keep him away from their wives, informed his mother Pārvatī about it, who, again and again, tried to stop him; but being attached to women, Skanda did not listen to her word.

7cd-12 Afraid of a curse, out of love for her son, and in order to protect the gods' wives, she assumed the shape of those whom Skanda wanted to enjoy, thus keeping him off. Whenever the six-headed Skanda called for, and looked at, e.g. Indra's or Varuṇa's wife, he beheld his mother's shape, and became deeply ashamed. Seeing that the whole world consisted of his mother, the son of Gaṅgā (Skanda) resorted to dispassionate indifference (*vairāgya*).

13-15 Realizing that his mother had done all this in order to counteract his behaviour though she had encouraged him before, he went to the Gautamī and promised her (i.e. the river as his mother) that he would from now on consider any female as like his mother (i.e. he would observe chastity).

16-22ab Śaṃkara (= Śiva) was pleased with his son and granted him a boon. Skanda, however, felt that, being Śiva's son and the army-leader of the gods, he was not in need of boons. Yet he wished, though not for himself, that any sinner who had approached his teacher's (*guru*'s) wife should be purified by bathing at this place (in the Gautamī); animals should obtain the highest rebirth (*jāti*, i.e. the highest caste?), the ugly should get beauty and wealth. Śaṃbhu agreed.

22cf From that time onward, this holy place is known as »Kārttikeya«; by bathing and giving alms there, the merit of all rites is obtained.

impure body in the Gautamī he would ascend to heaven,« thus implying the idea of religious suicide at a holy place. The use of different forms of the future tense, however, suggests that the result of the third bath in the Gautamī will be obtained after a comparatively long time, as the form of the periphrastic future is used in order to express a far remote future.

[1] cf. above, ch. 71.

Ch. 82: Story of the Kṛttikās and of Skanda's birth

1 After Kārttikeya, the next holy place is Kṛttikātīrtha; merely by hearing of it one gets the result of drinking Soma (i.e. immortality).

2-6 Long ago, when the demon Tāraka had to be defeated, Kavi (= Agni) drank Bhava's (= Śiva's) semen. Looking at him, who was pregnant with this semen, the wives of the seven sages desired him and became pregnant with this very semen themselves, except for Arundhatī (Vasiṣṭha's wife), who was pure because of bathing at the end of menstruation. Glowing and shining, and worrying about what to do, they went to the Gaṅgā and aborted their embryos into the water. Having the appearance of foam, the six embryos were united by the wind; from that the six-faced Skanda was born.

7-8 The wives of the sages returned home. Recognizing a disfigurement in them, their husbands abandoned them.

9-10 When Nārada saw their distress, he advised them to go to (Skanda) who is called »Kārttikeya« (»son of the Kṛttikās«), »originating from Hara (= Śiva)«, »Gāṅgeya« (»son of Gaṅgā«), and »originated from Agni«, the conqueror of Tāraka; he would grant them (marital) happiness.

11-14 The Kṛttikās went to the six-headed (Skanda) and informed him about what had happened. Kārttikeya consented and advised them to go to the Gautamī, bathe and worship Maheśvara (= Śiva). He himself would go there, too, and then proceed[1] to the »house of the gods« (*devamandira*).[2]

15-16cf Since then this holy place is called Kṛttikātīrtha. He who bathes there at the conjunction of the full moon and the constellation Kṛttikā (i.e. the Pleiades) will obtain the fruits of all rites, and become a king. Whoever remembers this place, or hears about it, is freed from all evil and will have a long life.

Ch. 83: The completion of Bhauvana's ten horse-sacrifices

1 Announcement of the account of Daśāśvamedhikatīrtha.

2-5 Viśvakarman's son was Viśvarūpa, who had a son named Prathama;[1] his son was Bhauvana,[2] whose chief priest was Kaśyapa. Bhauvana, »who ruled the whole earth« (*sārvabhauvana*), told him that he wanted to perform ten horse-sacrifices simultaneously and asked him where to do it. Kaśyapa replied that the place for a sacrifice could be anywhere, where Brahmins had (once?) performed great rites.

[1] Ed. VePr reads: »lead (them?)«.

[2] Temple or heaven?

[1] VePr Pramati.

[2] Originally, this name is a patronym of Viśvakarman; later on (in v. 24, VePr v. 25) Bhauvana is addressed as son of Viśvakarman. The name Viśvakarman Bhauvana is already mentioned in the Ait.Br. (8,21), in the list of ten famous kings who, after conquering the earth, performed a horse-sacrifice; his priest was Kaśyapa, as in the present story.

6–12 Twice the completion of the simultaneous sacrifices could not be achieved; therefore the king again consulted with his teacher, whether it was a fault of place, of time, or of himself. Together they went to Saṃvarta, the elder brother of the »Lord of Speech« (Gīṣpati = Girīṣa, i.e. Bṛhaspati) and asked him for a suitable place and teacher (!). Saṃvarta advised Bhauvana to ask Brahman.

13–16 Thereupon both went to Brahman,[3] who told them to go to the Gautamī: that place would suit best, and Kaśyapa would be the best teacher. By one horse-sacrifice at that place, or by bathing there, the completion of ten sacrifices would be achieved.

17–22 They went to the Gautamī. When the sacrifice was completed, Bhauvana was about to give away the earth (as the sacrificial gift to the teacher). Suddenly there was a heavenly voice, telling him that by his desire to give the whole earth it had actually been given; he should give food instead, for there was no gift equal to that, especially on the sands of the Gaṅgā.[4] He should not bother about it any longer.[5]

23–29 Bhauvana, however, who wanted to give (the earth), was implored by the earth[6] not to give her away;[7] otherwise she would submerge in the midst of the ocean. Asked by the frightened king, what else he should give, the earth replied that anything given on the banks of the Gaṅgā, even only a morsel, would be an imperishable gift, equivalent to the whole earth.[8] Accordingly, Bhauvana, »who ruled the whole earth«, gave food to the Brahmins.

29 Since then this place is known as »Daśāśvamedhika«.[9] By bathing there one gets the fruit of ten horse-sacrifices.

[3] i.e. the first-person narrator.

[4] The king is addressed here as *muni*.

[5] The interference of the »heavenly voice« seems to be an interpolation, duplicating the advice that is given by the earth shortly afterwards. Why should Bhauvana, after being informed that the earth has already been given away by him, insist upon giving it away once more, acting against the explanation of the heavenly voice? Similarly, after the information given by that voice, i.e. that food should be given instead of the earth, Bhauvana's question (v. 25, VePr v. 26) what else he should give would be quite unnecessary. As the earth itself certainly has more reason to object against her being given away, it is likely that the heavenly voice, which has no connection with the story at all, was introduced in order to stress the authoritativeness of the new prescription that was meant to demonstrate the power of the Gautamī, an authoritativeness, however, that is, in this context, questioned by the events following in the story itself.

[6] Ed. VePr adds: repeatedly.

[7] Ed. VePr inserts: »A morsel of food given on the banks of the Gaṅgā is equivalent to giving the whole earth«; this seems, however, to be an advanced duplication of the information given by the earth below; otherwise, Bhauvana's following question would make no sense.

[8] v. 26–27 (VePr 27–28) with a rhetorical question as refrain: »why should you give me away?«

[9] Probably identical with Daśāśvamedhatīrtha in Nasik, as described in Tīrthāṅka, p. 246; the king who performed the sacrifices, however, is here said to be Janaka.

Ch. 84: Birth of Hanumat and his half-brother

1 Brahman announces an account of Paiśācatīrtha, situated on the right bank of the Gautamī.

2-4 On Mt. Añjana, close to the Brahmagiri, lived an Apsaras named Añjanā, who was cursed to be a monkey. Her husband was Kesarin, who had another wife, Adrikā, an Apsaras, too, who was cursed to be a cat.

5-8 Once, when Kesarin had gone to the southern ocean, Agastya came to Mt. Añjana and was welcomed and served well by the two women; being pleased, he granted them a boon. Both wished to have a son, more powerful than all and beneficial to everybody. Agastya agreed and left for the south.

9-12 One day when the women were enjoying themselves singing, dancing, and joking, they were watched by Vāyu and Nirṛti, who fell in love with them and asked them to be their wives. The women agreed. Thereupon Hanumat was born to Añjanā from Vāyu, and Adri, the king of Piśācas, was born to Adrikā from Nirṛti.

13-15 Now the women wished that their disfigurement, which they owed to a curse by Indra, should be rectified. Vāyu and Nirṛti advised them to bathe in the Gautamī, which would deliver them from the effect of the curse.

16-17 The Piśāca Adri took Hanumat's mother to the Gautamī, for a bath, and Hanumat Adri(kā?).

18 Since then this place, near the Brahmagiri, is called »Paiśāca« as well as »Āñjana«; it fulfils all desires.

19-20 53 Yojanas eastward is (the place named) Mārjāra;[1] beyond Mārjāra, ... Hanumat, Vṛṣākapi[2] ... is the famous Phenāsaṃgama; its peculiarities and appearance are proclaimed there.[3]

Ch. 85: Story of Kaṇva's hunger

1 Brahman announces the account of Kṣudhātīrtha.

2-7 Once there was a sage named Kaṇva who, wandering from hermitage to hermitage, was afflicted by hunger. When he saw Gautama's prosperous hermitage, he observed that it would be unfitting to beg from somebody equal to himself (both being famous Brahmins) and preferred to resort to detachment and indifference. He went to the Gautamī, bathed and praised both the river and Hunger (*kṣudhā*).

8-10 Kaṇva's praise.

8 Praise to both, Gaṅgā and Kṣudhā.[4]

[1] It is mentioned again in ch. 129, v. 9-10, with a reference back to the story told here.

[2] v. 19cd is incomplete, as for the acc. m. *hanūmantam* and *vṛṣākapim* a verb is missing. But cf. ch. 129 v. 1 and 10, where Hanūmata seems to be the name of a holy place at the confluence of Godāvarī and Phenā, beside Indratīrtha, Vṛṣākapa, and Abjaka (in v. 1), situated in the neighbourhood of Mārjāra (v. 10).

[3] i.e. later, in ch. 129, v. 1-8, where the origin of the river Phenā is related.

[4] In Vaṃśasthavila-metre.

9–10 Praise of Gaṅgā, who as river removes afflictions, as Kṣudhā (Hunger) causes affliction.

11 Thereupon a pair of one pleasant and one fierce figure appeared before Kaṇva, who again praised them.

12–14 Kaṇva's hymn to Godāvarī (v. 12–13) and Kṣudhā (v. 14).

15–16 Thus praised, both granted him boons.

16–18 From Gaṅgā he chose long life, wealth, pleasure, and liberation.

19–23 From Kṣudhā he wished that he and his family would never again be afflicted by hunger, thirst, or poverty. The same should be granted to those who recite this hymn of praise, or bathe at this holy place.

24 (Conclusion:) Since that time this place has been called Kāṇvatīrtha, Gāṅgatīrtha, or Kṣudhātīrtha.

Ch. 86: Story of Yama neglecting his duty

1 There is an important place of pilgrimage named »Cakratīrtha«; bathing there leads to Hari's world.

2 Anyone who bathes, after fasting, on the 11th day of the light half of a month, at the »Gaṇikāsaṃgama« (i.e. confluence of the Gaṇikā), will reach the imperishable abode (= heaven).

3ab Announcement of the story about what happened there.

3cd–7 There was a rich Vaiśya, named Viśvadhara; in advanced age he had a pretty son, who died young. Grief-stricken the parents made up their mind to die as well.

8–9ab Impressed by their wailing, Yama left his abode, went to the bank of the river Godāvarī and meditated on Janārdana (= Viṣṇu).

9cd–10ab »Have so many living beings grown old (or: increased) in such a short time? Tell me, due to whom is the earth filled up?«[1]

10cd Nobody died, and the earth was overcrowded.

11–16 The earth went to Indra; bowing to her, he asked her why she had come. She complained that, because there was no killing (*vadha*), she was oppressed by a heavy burden and asked for its reason. When Indra promised to find out, she wanted him to order Yama to do his job.

17–19 Indra sent his attendants (Siddhas and Kiṃnaras) to Yama's abode. They went there, but did not find Yama; so they returned and informed Indra.

20–21 Indra asked the sun, Yama's father, who told him that Yama was practising asceticism at the bank of the river Godāvarī, but he did not know the reason.

22–26 Indra was worried, for he feared that Yama might want to oust him from his sovereignty over the gods. Therefore he planned to send some Apsaras to seduce Yama, but none of them accepted the task.

[1] v. 9cd–10ab seem to be direct speech that can hardly be correct in this context. The words »*iti me pṛthvī kathyatām*« (10ab) are obviously taken by mistake from Indra's speech in v. 12 below.

27–29 Angrily, Indra decided to go himself, together with an army of the gods, to slay the enemy. Hari (= Viṣṇu), however, sent his discus (*cakra*) to protect Yama; therefore the place is called »Cakratīrtha«.

30–34 Then Menakā told Indra that no (Apsaras) was capable of looking at Yama, and that it would be better to be killed by Indra than by Yama. She advised him, however, to send a certain (Apsaras named) Gaṇikā, who was very confident about her youth and beauty. Indra was much pleased and sent Gaṇikā to Yama, telling her that after returning with her task done she would be his beloved one, like Śacī.

35–39 Thereupon Gaṇikā fell from heaven, went to Yama and distracted him by sweetly singing (the Rāga) Hindolaka. Yama opened his eyes full of the fire of love and fixed them on her, the enemy of his benefit. Suddenly she dissolved and became a river. Reaching the Gautamī, Gaṇikā, due to the power of this holy place (i.e. Gaṇikāsaṃgama), went to heaven, praised by (Indra's) attendants.

40–42 Seeing her going to heaven, Yama was much surprised. The sun, his father, however, addressed him and told him to fulfil his duty, like the wind, the creator, he himself (i.e. the sun), and the earth, who were all fulfilling their functions.

43–46 When Yama refused to take up his despicable work, the sun assured him that his work would cause him no harm, and pointed to that Apsaras Gaṇikā who had merely dived into the Gautamī and then gone to heaven, while he (Yama) had practised hard asceticism at that place, with no end in sight; he would do better to return to his abode.

47–49ab First the sun, then Yama bathed at the confluence and returned to their abodes. Indra (the »Destroyer of ghosts«, *bhūtahan*) was freed from his worries. The discus travelled to the place where Govinda stayed.

49c-f Phalastuti: Hearing or reciting this story frees from all afflictions and grants long life.

Ch. 87: Story of Indra and Ahalyā

1 Brahman announces the events relating to the holy place Ahalyāsaṃgama.

2–34ab *Prehistory of Ahalyā's marriage to Gautama*

2–5ab In olden times Brahman (the first-person narrator) had created many beautiful girls, one of whom was especially excellent. He wondered whom he could entrust with bringing up this girl.

5cd–8 Finally he handed her over to the ascetic Gautama, who was a most qualified Brahmin, ordering him to bring her up and to present her before him when she had attained youth.

9–14ab Gautama brought her up and took her, beautifully adorned, back to Brahman. When the gods saw her, all of them wanted to marry her; Indra was especially attracted. Brahman, however, wanted to give her to Gautama, whom he thought the most valuable person.

14cd–15ab The firmness of all was stirred up (or: taken away) by this young girl, who was addressed as »Ahalyā« by Brahman and the sages.[1]

15cd–16 Brahman announced that she would be given to whoever would be the first to complete a circumambulation of the earth.

17–20 When the gods were gone, Gautama made the (following) small effort: At that time, Surabhi, the wishing-cow, was pregnant. Seeing her, Gautama thought that she was *urvī* (»broad« or the »Broad One«, i.e. the earth) and circumambulated her; besides, he circumambulated a Liṅga.

22–24 Thinking that he had circumambulated the earth twice by that, while all the gods had not even completed one circuit, Gautama went to Brahman and told him that he had completed the circumambulation.

25–29 Brahman verified it through meditation (*dhyānayoga*) and confirmed that Gautama's actions amounted to circumambulation of the earth; consequently he gave the girl to him.

30–32 When the gods returned, the marriage had already taken place; so they returned to their abodes, Indra full of jealousy.

33–34ab Brahman gave the Brahmagiri to Gautama, where he happily enjoyed his wife Ahalyā.

34cd–59 *Ahalyā's seduction by Indra and Gautama's curse*

34cd–35 Having heard about their conjugal bliss in his heaven Triviṣṭapa, Indra in the disguise of a Brahmin went to the Brahmagiri to see them.

36–39ab Seeing their residence and Gautama's wife, Indra felt strong desire for her; disregarding all other considerations, he kept thinking how he could gain entry to Gautama's quarter. For some time, he did not perceive any chance.

39cd–41 But one day Gautama left the hermitage with his pupils in order to see (another?) hermitage, the river Gautamī, sages, and various grains; Indra watched him and saw his opportunity.

42–43 Assuming Gautama's shape, he approached Ahalyā, told her, smilingly, that he had been drawn back to the hermitage by the memory of her beauty, and took her inside the hut.

44 Ahalyā did not recognize him; enjoying him, she mistook her lover for her husband, when suddenly Gautama returned with his pupils.

45–48 Gautama was surprised that Ahalyā did not come out to greet him, as she usually did, and so were the guards, when they beheld Gautama, for they thought him to be inside the hut; they could only explain this miracle as an effect of Gautama's powerful asceticism.

49 Gautama entered the hut, asking who was there and why Ahalyā did not answer him.

50–52ab Hearing her husband's voice, Ahalyā recognized that her lover was someone else, and quickly got up, whereas Indra changed into a cat.

[1] Should this verse be understood to present an explanation of the name »Ahalyā«?

52cd-54 Upon Gautama's angry remonstrance Ahalyā kept silent. Looking out for her lover, Gautama saw the cat and threatened to reduce him to ashes, if he did not reveal his identity.

55-58ab Now Indra identified himself, admitted his guilt, but defended himself as having been wounded by the god of love, and appealed to Gautama's forgiveness, since good people should not take revenge, even when offended (maxim).

58cd-59 Gautama, however, cursed Indra to be marked by 1000 vulvas, and Ahalyā to become a dried-up river.

60-71 *Removal of the curses by Gautamī*

60-66ab Ahalyā pleaded innocent, since Indra had assumed Gautama's shape, as confirmed by the guards and by Gautama himself through meditation. Therefore he granted her the boon of regaining her original form after having - as a river - united with the Gautamī; so it happened.

66cd-69 Indra, too, begged for indulgence. Gautama granted that he would be marked by 1000 eyes, after having bathed in the Gautamī, at the confluence of Gautamī and »Ahalyā« (= Ahalyāsaṃgama).

70-71 Brahman confirms that he himself saw both miracles. Since then the place has been called »Ahalyāsaṃgama« or »Indratīrtha«.

Ch. 88: Varuṇa as teacher of Janaka and Yājñavalkya

1 The next holy place is called »Janasthāna«, extending 4 Yojanas and granting liberation to those who remember it.

2-3 Once upon a time there was a king of the Solar Dynasty (a descendant of Vaivasvata), named Janaka, who married the daughter of the lord of waters (= Varuṇa), the »mother« (*janakā*) of the four goals of life, named Guṇārṇavā, because she was an »ocean of good qualities«.

4-7 Janaka's family-priest was Yājñavalkya. One day Janaka talked to him about enjoyment and liberation: both are positive values, differing, however, in that liberation does not lead to disappointment and suffering in the end, but is very hard to obtain. He asked Yājñavalkya how liberation could be obtained from happiness.

8 Yājñavalkya advised to ask Varuṇa, Janaka's father-in-law.

9 Both went to Varuṇa and inquired about the path to liberation.

10-15 Varuṇa instructed them that there are two established paths to liberation, action and non-action; the path of action, however, connected with the four goals of life and defined in the Veda, is far superior. He praised the stage of the householder as best among the four stages of life; from it, liberation is obtainable.

16-19 Having honoured Varuṇa, Janaka and Yājñavalkya asked about the place which would grant both enjoyment and liberation. Varuṇa told them that the best part of the earth was Bhāratavarṣa, the best part of it being Daṇḍaka, bestowing enjoyment and liberation; the best of holy places was the Gautamī Gaṅgā.

20 Janaka and Yājñavalkya took leave and returned home.

21–26 Janaka performed rites, such as horse-sacrifices etc., with Yājñavalkya as his priest; by sacrificing at the bank of the (Gautamī) Gaṅgā he obtained liberation. Since many of Janaka's descendants obtained liberation here, too, this sacrificial ground of the Janakas is named »Janasthāna«. It is four Yojanas in extent; it destroys all evil by merely being remembered. By bathing, giving alms, and satisfying one's ancestors, by thinking of this place or going there and worshipping (it) with devotion one obtains all desires and finally liberation.

Ch. 89: Story of Vivasvat, the surrogated Chāyā, and the birth of the Aśvins

1–2cd Brahman announces the story about the origin of the confluence of Aruṇā and Varuṇā with the Gaṅgā.[1]

2ef–3 Kaśyapa's eldest son was Āditya (i.e. the sun, with a list of epithets), whose wife was Uṣā, daughter of Tvaṣṭṛ.[2]

4 Unable to bear her husband's brilliance, she thought about what to do.

5ac Her children were Manu Vaivasvata, i.e. Yama,[3] and the river Yamunā.

5d Announcement of a »surprising topic«.

6–9ab She made a »shadow« (*chāyā*) of herself in her own shape, and ordered her (i.e. the personified Shadow) to act as if she were herself, to look after the children and husband until she returned, but not to tell anybody. Then she left, longing for a more peaceful shape (for her husband).

9cd–12 She went to her father's house and told him everything; Tvaṣṭṛ, however, did not appreciate her behaviour but ordered her to return to her husband. She refused and went to Uttarakuru, where she practised asceticism in the form of a mare.

13–17ab In the meantime Chāyā (the Shadow) lived together with her (= Uṣā's) husband and bore children: Sāvarṇi, Śani and Viṣṭi, who was a miserable girl.[4] As Chāyā did not treat her own and Uṣā's children equally, Uṣā's son Yama grew angry and kicked her with his foot. Chāyā cursed him that his foot should fall off.

17–21 Accordingly it happened; suffering, Yama went to his father and complained, telling him that she who cursed him could not be his mother; for a mother would not grew angry even when her children were naughty (etymology of *mātṛ*), whereas that woman kept »burning« him, so to speak.

22–25ab The sun thought that she was not his wife Uṣā, and that Uṣā was practising asceticism in the shape of a mare in Uttarakuru, in order to pacify him. He went there, too, in form of a stallion, and ran after her, afflicted by passion.

25cd–33 Not recognizing him and trying to remain faithful to her husband, she fled in the southern direction. He kept running after her. They crossed the Gaṅgā, the

[1] Ed. VePr adds: which bestows more merit than Mānasa, Prayāga and Mandākinī.

[2] For the following story, cf. above, ch. 6 and ch. 32.49–107, where Vivasvat's wife is named Saṃjñā, however.

[3] Or: »the twin«?

[4] For her story, cf. ch. 165 below.

Narmadā and the Vindhya-mountains and reached the Gautamī, where she sought shelter in a hermitage called Janasthāna. Five boys who tried to prevent the stallion entering were cursed to become five fig-trees (*vaṭa*).

34-36 The hermits, however, recognized Uṣā's husband by their insight and praised him. When the sun touched the mare's mouth with his mouth, she recognized her husband. She then emitted his semen through her mouth; from this semen the two Aśvins were born in the (Gautamī) Gaṅgā.

37-40ab Thereupon crowds of gods, Siddhas, hermits, rivers, cows, plants, and planets, the sun's chariot with seven horses and the sun's charioteer, Aruṇa, Yama, Varuṇa, Śani and Manu Vaivasvata, came there, eager to see, as well as Yamunā and Tāpī (the sun's daughters), assuming another shape; finally Tvaṣṭṛ, the sun's father-in-law.

40cd-41 Knowing his (i.e. Tvaṣṭṛ's) intention, the sun asked Tvaṣṭṛ to put him on a device for cutting, in order to cut his splendour according to Uṣā's liking.

42 Tvaṣṭṛ agreed and cut the sun's splendour near Somanātha, at the place which is therefore known as Prabhāsa (i.e. »splendour«).[5]

43-46ab The place where the Aśvins were born is called Aśvatīrtha (»horse-ford«)[6] as well as Bhānutīrtha (»sun-ford«)[7] and Pañcavaṭāśrama (»hermitage of the five banyan-trees«).[8] Where Tāpī and Yamunā came to see their father (in another shape), there is the confluence of Aruṇā and Varuṇā with the (Gautamī) Gaṅgā.[9] There are 27,000 different holy places of the gods, where the gods had come to that region.

46cd Bathing there and giving alms grants undecaying merit.

47 By remembering, reciting, or listening to (the above account) one is freed from all evil and becomes happy.

Ch. 90: Story of Garuḍa and the snake Maṇināga[1]

1 Brahman announces the story about the origin of Gāruḍatīrtha.

2-4 A son of Śeṣa, a snake called Maṇināga, pleased Śaṃkara (= Śiva) with devotion, out of fear of Garuḍa, and was granted »fearlessness«.

5-8ab Consequently he was always roaming around near Garuḍa, who eventually seized him and locked him up.

8cd-12ab Realising that the snake had disappeared, Nandin informed his master, Śiva, who knew what had happened and told Nandin. He ordered him to request the snake's release from Viṣṇu.

[5] Situated at the confluence of the Sarasvatī with the ocean, in Gujarat.

[6] Āśvinatīrtha in Tīrthāṅka p. 245.

[7] i.e. Sūryatīrtha in Tīrthāṅka p. 245.

[8] Perhaps to be connected with Pañcavaṭī on the left bank of the Godāvarī? See Tīrthāṅka p. 245. A place named Pañcavaṭī is also mentioned in the Rm 3,13.3 and 3,14.1-2 (cf. also note on 93.1-2 below).

[9] Aruṇāsaṃgama in Tīrthāṅka p. 245; Varuṇā is not mentioned there. Obviously it must be understood that Tāpī and Yamunā came there in the shape of the rivers Aruṇā and Varuṇā.

[1] cf. VDhP 3,343, where the snake, however, is called Sumukha, and owes its fearlessness to Indra.

12cd–19 Viṣṇu ordered Garuḍa to hand over the snake to Nandin, but Garuḍa refused angrily, complaining of Viṣṇu's ingratitude that, while others bestowed gifts upon their servants, Viṣṇu took away the snake which he had taken hold of. He pointed to the services he had always rendered to Viṣṇu, and boasted of his strength, by which Viṣṇu had gained victory over the demons.

20–30 Viṣṇu jokingly repeated Garuḍa's claim and put his little finger on the bird's head to be carried. Garuḍa was disfigured by its weight: his head was pressed down to his chest, the chest down to his feet. Now Garuḍa realized his fault and begged for forgiveness by praising Viṣṇu and invoking his pity. He also addressed Śrī, asking her for protection; she thereupon intervened and also pleaded Viṣṇu to have mercy on Garuḍa. Viṣṇu ordered Nandin to take Garuḍa and the snake to Śaṃbhu by whose grace Garuḍa would regain his original shape.

31–33 Nandin went to Śaṃkara and told him what had happened. Śiva ordered Garuḍa to bathe in the Gautamī; thereby he would obtain his former shape and all other desires, since this river grants refuge to all afflicted by evil or frustrated in their efforts.

34–35 Accordingly, Garuḍa went to the Gautamī, where he bathed and bowed to Śiva and Viṣṇu. Thereupon he became a golden, powerful, fast bird and returned to Viṣṇu.

36 Ever since, that place has been called Gāruḍatīrtha; all observances performed there will be imperishable and effect Śiva's and Viṣṇu's favour.

Ch. 91: Story of Jābāli and the cows

1–2ab Brahman announces the story about how the evil-destroying Govardhanatīrtha came into existence.

2cd–6ab A Brahmin farmer, named Jābāli, used to treat his two oxen badly: he did not unyoke them even at midday, and he beat them. Seeing this, the wish-fulfilling cow Surabhi told Nandin about it; Nandin informed Śaṃbhu, who granted him the boon that his words would come true. Thus authorized by Śiva, Nandin destroyed the whole bovine race, in heaven as well as on earth.

6cd–11ab The gods complained to Brahman (the first-person narrator) that without cows life would be impossible. Brahman sent them to Śaṃkara, who, in turn, referred them to his bull (i.e. Nandin). Nandin ordered them to perform the »Gosava-sacrifice«; by that they would obtain heavenly as well as earthly cows. Since then the Gosava-sacrifice, which was performed (first) by the gods, has been in existence. After that the cows increased on this side of the Gautamī.

11cd–12 This is the holy place called »Govardhana«[1] (»cow-increasing«); to bathe there grants thousand(s) of cows. The result of giving alms and of other meritorious actions is not known (even to the narrator). (Ed. VePr adds: Having looked at Śaṃkara Gautameśvara there, one obtains heaven as long as Mt. Meru lasts.)

[1] Probably identical with the village Govardhana(pura) 6 miles from Nasik (cf. Tīrthāṅka p. 246); according to the BḍP 2,16.44 it was founded by Rāma, but there is no mention of it in the Rm itself.

Ch. 92: Story of Sanājjāta and his mother Mahī

1 Brahman announces the account of the holy place called »Pāpapraṇāśana« (»destroying evil«).

2-11 A Brahmin, named Dhṛtavrata, had a young wife, Mahī, and a son, Sanājjāta. When Dhṛtavrata died, the young widow, seeing no protector for herself and her small child, went to Gālava's hermitage, entrusted her son to him and started roaming about, running after men. Her son grew up in Gālava's house and mastered all of the vedic lore, but having inherited his mother's inclination, he came under the influence of courtesans; like his mother, he roamed different regions. Finally, he as well as his mother happened to settle in a place called Janasthāna; not recognizing each other, mother and son became involved, due to fate, and lived for a long time spending their nights together.

12-18ab Sanājjāta, however, continued to observe the paternal rules, such as bathing, morning prayer (*saṃdhyā*), paying homage to Brahmins, etc. Without realizing it himself, he looked deformed and putrid on his way to the Gautamī Gaṅgā in the morning, but brilliant and beautiful after his morning bath in the river.

18cd-38 Sanājjāta also used to go to the place at the Gautamī where the ascetic Gālava lived, and paid homage to him. Gālava observed the change in Sanājjāta's appearance and wondered about its cause. One day he called the Brahmin and asked him his name, his abode, his profession, and who was his wife. The Brahmin postponed the answer until the next day. After sleeping with his mistress that night, he asked her name and family, since she was like a faithful wife and he wanted their love to last till the end of their lives. Mahī told him about her Brahminic descent, her own name, as well as the name of her husband and her son, whom she had left behind at Gālava's hermitage. Hearing this, the Brahmin collapsed, as if his heart had been pierced. The courtesan wondered why her words had been objectionable to him. He told her that Dhṛtavrata was his father, and that he himself was her son, named Sanādyata (!);[1] this information made her very miserable, too. At dawn Sanājjāta went to Gālava, told him his identity and asked him for a means of expiation.

39-47ab Gālava told him how he had observed his changing appearance, and that all his actions were destroyed in the Gaṅgā, as he had been purified daily. His mother, too, would be purified, as she had shown repentance. Since in the realm of living beings love was natural, there surely was expiation by meritorious contact with good (people), according to fate. Her repentance was due to the merit she had formerly accumulated; after bathing at this holy place, she would be purified.

cd-48ab Both took a bath, by which their evil disappeared.

cd-49ef Ever since, the place has been called Pāpapraṇāśana,[2] Dhautapāpa (»where the evil is washed off«), or Gālava;[3] it destroys great sins and small.

[1] Inverse Sanskritization?

[2] Probably identical with Pāpanāśanatīrtha, on the way from Govardhana to Nasik (cf. Tīrthāṅka p. 246).

[3] i.e. the second Tīrtha, after Pitṛtīrtha, on the way from Govardhana to Nasik, according to Tīrthāṅka p. 246.

Ch. 93: Story of Viśvāmitra and Indra

1-2 (Ed. VePr starts with the following verse that is not found in the mss. of the Ed. ASS: To the south of it (i.e. the place described in the previous chapter) is a holy place called Pitṛtīrtha (»ford of ancestors«).) The place where Rāma and Sītā satisfied the ancestors is known as Pitṛtīrtha;[1] bathing, alms-giving and offerings to the ancestors are imperishable there.

3-4 The place where Rāma Dāśarathi paid homage to Viśvāmitra is called Viśvāmitratīrtha.[2]

5-11 Once upon a time there was a terrible drought, during which Viśvāmitra, his pupils, his sons and his wife went to the Gautamī. Viśvāmitra, seeing them all hungry, ordered his disciples to collect some food, whatever it might be, as quickly as possible. A dead dog was all they could find. Viśvāmitra accepted it and ordered them to cut it, to wash it, and to boil it, reciting vedic verses. Having offered (some of it) to Agni (the fire), according to the rules, and having offered some of it to gods, sages, ancestors, guests, and teachers, they should all eat the rest.

12-24 The disciples acted accordingly. While the dog's meat was being cooked, Agni, the messenger of the gods, appeared; he informed the gods that they were going to be offered the meat of a dog. Indra turned into a falcon and took away the whole pot with the meat. The disciples told Viśvāmitra about it, who became furious and was about to curse Hari (= Indra), when the latter quickly put back the pot, which was now filled with honey. Viśvāmitra, however, told him to return the dog's flesh and to remove the ambrosia, otherwise he would reduce him to ashes. Indra told him to drink and sacrifice the honey, objecting to the dog's flesh as not fit for sacrifice. But Viśvāmitra refused, unless all beings, not just he alone, were allowed to enjoy the honey; otherwise the gods would get dog-flesh. Indra became afraid; he called the clouds and made them rain immortal water (water that was ambrosia). Thereafter Viśvāmitra first satisfied the gods etc. with oblations of that ambrosia given by Hari (= Indra), and satisfied the three worlds; after that, together with his disciples and his wife, he ate it himself.

25-26 Ever since, this place has been a famous place of pilgrimage; bathing and giving alms at that place effects the merit of all sacrifices.

27 Ever since, this place is called Viśvāmitra(-tīrtha), Madhutīrtha, Aindratīrtha, »Śyena« (i.e. falcon) or Parjanya (»rain«).

[1] The first Tīrtha on the way from Govardhana to Nasik, according to Tīrthāṅka p. 246. In the Rm, however, there is no mention of ancestral rites performed by Rāma on this spot. The funeral rites for Daśaratha were performed at Citrakūṭa; after settling in Pañcavaṭī, by the bank of the Godāvarī, the exiles used only to take their morning bath in the Godāvarī, according to Rm 3, ch. 14-15. In the Gautamīmāhātmya itself, Daśaratha is offered an oblation by Rāma at the bank of the Godāvarī (ch. 123.170-176), where the place is called Śavatīrtha.

[2] According to Tīrthāṅka p. 246, it is situated between Pāpanāśanatīrtha (cf. the preceding chapter) and Śvetatīrtha (cf. the following chapter), on the way from Govardhana to Nasik. In the Rm, the contact between Rāma and Viśvāmitra is restricted to the Bālakāṇḍa, where there is no mention of special homage paid to Viśvāmitra by Rāma.

Ch. 94: Story of Śiva's devotee Śveta, who could not be taken away by Death[1]

1 Brahman announces the famous holy place named Śvetatīrtha, which frees from evil merely by being remembered.

2–14 Once upon a time a Brahmin, called Śveta, a friend of Gautama's, lived on the bank of the Gautamī, intent on honouring guests and devoted to Śiva with mind, word, and deed, meditating on him continuously and worshipping him all his life. When the time of his death approached, the messengers of Death (Mṛtyu) came to take hold of him, but they could not enter his house. After some time Citraka drew Death's attention to that improper delay; now Death himself went to Śveta's house and, seeing his messengers in front of it, asked them what was the matter. They answered that they could not see Śveta, as he was protected by Śiva. Thereupon Death entered the house, without being recognized by Śveta. When Nandin saw him standing by Śveta, he first tried to send him away, but when Death threw his noose, Nandin grew angry and killed him with a stick given to him by Śiva.

15–21 The messengers reported everything, including Mṛtyu's death, to Yama, who went to Śveta's house with his attendants (various diseases, hells, etc.). Nandin called on Skanda and Gaṇeśa for assistance; a terrible battle arose, during which Kārttikeya (= Skanda) killed Yama.

22–26 His attendants informed the sun-god (Āditya, Yama's father) who went to Brahman (the first-person narrator); accompanied by the other gods, Brahman went to where Yama lay dead on the banks of the Gaṅgā.

27–30 Now the gods praised Śiva for his regard for his devotees.[2]

31–36 Śiva appeared before them and asked their wish. They replied that Yama, the ruler over law and order (*dharma*) should be revived, otherwise nothing would go on. Śiva agreed, provided that they would accept his condition that his devotee should not die.

37–42 First the gods refused this condition, since it would eliminate the difference between mortals and immortals. Then Śiva proposed that the gods themselves, and not Mṛtyu (Death) should be lords over his and Viṣṇu's devotees who paid homage to the Gautamī; they should not be overcome by diseases, but be released immediately, when taking their refuge in Śiva. Yama and his attendants should bow before them. To this the gods agreed.

43–45 Now Śiva told Nandin to sprinkle water from the Gautamī on Yama. He and his attendants came back to life and returned to the south.

46–48ab On the northern bank of the Gautamī all deities stood worshipping Maheśvara (= Śiva); there are 80,000 plus 14,000 plus 6000 plus 6 (or 6000) holy places, whereas on the southern bank there are 6 times 30,000 (i.e. 180,000).

3cd–50ab Conclusion to the account of Śvetatīrtha; hearing of it effects a life of 1000 years; bathing there and giving alms destroys all evil.

[1] cf. VDhP 1,126.

[2] v. 28–29 in Indravajrā-metre.

50c-f Phalastuti: To hear or recite (this account) purifies all worlds and bestows enjoyment and liberation.

Ch. 95: Śukra (Uśanas) and the science of reviving the dead

1 Brahman announces the famous Śukratīrtha, which bestows all success desired and destroys all evil and diseases.

2-6 Aṅgiras (= Bṛhaspati) and Bhṛgu had a son each, who were called Jīva and Kavi (= Śukra).[1] The fathers decided that both should be instructed by the same teacher. Aṅgiras volunteered to teach them, and Bhṛgu entrusted his son to him.

7-11 Aṅgiras, however, taught them separately, until Śukra reproached him for unequal treatment of his pupils, unbefitting a teacher, and asked for leave to go to another teacher.

12-15ab Bṛhaspati (= Aṅgiras) agreed. Śukra, however, wanted to return to his father only after having obtained knowledge. He asked the old Gautama to name a teacher who would be teacher of the three worlds. Gautama named Śaṃbhu (= Śiva), the lord of the world.

15cd-17 Asked by Śukra[2] how he should please him, Gautama advised him to praise Śiva with hymns, after purifying himself by bathing in the Gautamī. Consequently Śukra went to the Gaṅgā, bathed there and composed a hymn to Śiva.

18-21 Hymn by Śukra to Śiva, emphasizing that Śukra is only an ignorant child, whereas Śiva is the best and greatest of all teachers.[3]

22-28ab Thus praised, Śiva was pleased and granted a boon. Kavi (Śukra) asked for a science that was not known even to gods, including Brahman, and sages. Thereupon Śiva gave him the science of reviving the dead (*mṛtasaṃjīvinī vidyā*),[4] as well as other worldly and vedic knowledge. After that, Kavi returned to his father.

28cd-30 Kavi (= Śukra) was the teacher of the Daityas. For some reason Kaca, Bṛhaspati's son,[5] once obtained the science from Kavi;[6] from Kaca it was obtained by Bṛhaspati and the gods.

31-32 The place on the northern bank of the Gautamī where Kavi obtained this science is called Śukratīrtha or Mṛtasaṃjīvinītīrtha (»Tīrtha of reviving the dead«); bathing there and giving alms bestows imperishable merit.

[1] In the MBh (1,60.40), Śukra (Uśanas) is the son of Kavi and grandson of Bhṛgu.

[2] Ed. VePr inserts: how he could see Śaṃbhu and...

[3] Each verse ends with the refrain »*namo 'stu te*«, with preceding vocative.

[4] In the MBh(1,71.7), this science is applied by Śukra to the fallen Asuras, whose teacher he is.

[5] The same person as Jīva above?

[6] The story alluded to is told in MBh 1,71.

Ch. 96: Indra and Brahmin-murder

1 Brahman continues by announcing the famous Indratīrtha, which merely by being thought of destroys accumulated sins, especially (the guilt of) Brahmin-murder.

2-5ab In former times, when Vṛtra had been slain, Indra was persecuted by Brahmin-murder, who followed him wherever he went. Finally, Indra hid in a lotus-stalk, in a large pond, having become a lotus-filament. Brahmin-murder waited on the banks of that pond for 1000 divine years.

5cd-7 During that period, the gods were without Indra (i.e. without king); they consulted about what to do. Brahman (i.e. the first-person narrator) advised them to consecrate Indra at the Gautamī, in order to purify him and make him Indra again.

8-10 So the gods took Indra to the Gautamī, bathed him and were about to consecrate him, when suddenly Gautama interfered and threatened to reduce them to ashes if they did it, since Indra had violated a teacher's bed.

11-17 Thereupon the gods took Indra to the river Narmadā, in order to anoint him, but there the sage Māṇḍavya threatened to reduce them to ashes. Now the gods paid homage to Māṇḍavya with hymns and arguments, asking him to remove the obstacle which had arisen wherever Indra was to be anointed, and promising to grant him many boons at the place where Indra would be anointed; this place would fulfil all wishes and be free from droughts and famine.

18-19 Māṇḍavya agreed; the consecration-ceremony was performed, and Indra obtained purification (*malanirvātana*). The place was then called »Mālava«[1] by the gods.

20-22ab The gods led the Gautamī to the place where Indra had been anointed; Vasiṣṭha, Gautama, Agastya, Atri, Kaśyapa and other sages, gods and other beings bathed (Indra or themselves?) and performed the consecration (once more?).

22cd-24ab Brahman again anointed Indra with water from his bowl;[2] this water afterwards became the rivers Puṇyā and Siktā (i.e. »anointed«). Their confluences with the (Gautamī) Gaṅgā are frequented by ascetics.

24cd-25ab Ever since, this holy place has been called Puṇyāsaṃgama (»confluence of Puṇyā«); the holy place at the confluence of the Siktā is called »Aindra« (i.e. »belonging to Indra«).

25cd-26 7000 holy places came into existence there. Bathing and alms-giving at these places provides undecaying merit.

27 Phalastuti: Anyone who reads or listens to this account is freed of all evil committed in thought, word, or deed.

[1] Obviously this name is connected with the word *malanirvātana*. A similar story about Indra is told in the Rm (1,23.17-23), in order to explain the name the name of the tribe of the Maladas.

[2] cf. ch. 72 above.

Ch. 97: How Kubera lost his kingdom and became lord of the north

1 Brahman announces an account of the origin of Paulastyatīrtha, which restores a lost kingdom.

2–5ab In former times, the lord of the north (= Kubera), the eldest son of Viśravas, was king of Laṅkā, too. He had powerful half-brothers, Rāvaṇa, Kumbhakarṇa, and Vibhīṣaṇa, who were Rākṣasas, since their mother was a Rākṣasa-woman. Full of devotion, Kubera used to come to see Brahman (the first-person narrator), together with his brothers, in the chariot given to him by Brahman.

5cd–7 Rāvaṇa's mother, however, incited her sons against Vaiśravaṇa, pointing to the natural enmity between gods and Asuras, who had always tried to kill each other, and reproaching them for their cowardice.[1]

8–13ab The three brothers practised asceticism and obtained boons from Brahman (the first-person narrator). Through their maternal uncle Marīca and their maternal grandfather they laid claim to Laṅkā. Thus a great enmity arose between the two(!) brothers, followed by a battle between gods and Dānavas. Rāvaṇa defeated Kubera and seized Laṅkā; moreover he decreed that nobody should grant shelter to his brother.

13cd–14 When he did not find any refuge, Vaiśravaṇa (= Kubera) went to his grandfather Pulastya and asked what he should do.

15–17 Pulastya advised him to go to the Gautamī and praise Maheśvara (= Śiva) there; Rāvaṇa would not be able to enter the water of the Gaṅgā.

18–19 Together with his family and with Pulastya, Kubera went to the Gautamī Gaṅgā, bathed there and praised Śiva.

20–23 Kubera's hymn to Śiva, referring to his lordship over the cosmos (v. 20), his eight forms (v. 21), the birth of Gaṇeśa from Pārvatī's bodily secretion (*mala*) (v. 22), and Śiva's mercy upon Rati (wife of the burnt god of love) effected by Pārvatī's tears (v. 23).[2]

24–28 Thus praised, Śiva appeared and granted a boon; Kubera, however, remained silent out of joyous excitement. Finally a heavenly voice proclaimed that Kubera should obtain sovereignty over wealth. Expressing the thoughts of Pulastya, Viśravas and Kubera, the voice continued that all that had belonged to Kubera before should belong to him again.

29 After worshipping the Someśvara Liṅga,[3] the defeated Kubera attained sovereignty over wealth and over the northern direction and the unlimited ability to bestow gifts; he also attained wives and sons.[4]

30–32ab Kubera confirmed what the heavenly voice had proclaimed, and Śiva assented to it. After having bestowed boons on Pulastya and Viśravas as well, Śiva left.

[1] cf. Rm 7,9.32 ff., where she only incites Rāvaṇa; MBh 3,259.14 (Rāmopakhyāna) does not mention the mother's intervention at all.

[2] v. 20–23 in Upajāti-metre (21d Jagatī-metre).

[3] Situated between Kṣudhātīrtha and Pāpanāśanatīrtha, according to Tīrthāṅka p. 246.

[4] In Upajāti-metre; v. 27–29 (or at least the last of them) seem to disturb the connection between v. 30 and v. 26 (or v. 28); v. 29 may well belong to a context where there was no intervention of a heavenly voice, or should at least be read at the end of the story.

32cd–33 Ever since, this place has been called Paulastya or Dhanada or Vaiśravasa;[5] bathing there etc. is extremely meritorious.

Ch. 98 : Story of Agni and Jātavedas[1]

1 Brahman announces (an account of) the effects of the Agnitīrtha.[2]

2–5 Agni's brother Jātavedas, whose task it was to transport the sacrificial offerings to the gods, was killed by the demon Madhu, during a *sattra*-rite performed by ascetics at the bank of the Gautamī. Agni became angry and entered the waters of the Gaṅgā.

6–9 Thereupon men, sages, and ancestors, whose lives depend on fire, had to give up life. They went to where Agni had entered the water and appealed to him to transport the offerings for them.

10–13ab Agni refused to take up his brother's task, being afraid that he would suffer a similar fate; he objected that he did not have the power to reach this (world) and (the world) beyond (at the same time?).[3]

13cd–15 The gods promised him (long) life, joy in (doing his) work,[4] the power to extend (everywhere), and the »pre-sacrifice« (*prayāja*) and the »final offering« (*anuyāja*) as his share,[5] in accordance with his function as the »mouth of the gods«.

16–17ab Agni agreed und thus obtained the power to reach everywhere, without any fear.

cd–18ab He is called Jātavedas, Bṛhadbhānu (»having high/deep brightness«), Saptārcis (»having seven flames«), Nīlalohita (»the dark-red one«), Jalagarbha (»germ of water«), Śamīgarbha (»germ of/in the Śamī-wood«), Yajñagarbha (»germ of sacrifice«).

18cd Having drawn Vibhāvasu (= the fire) out of the water and anointed him, the wise (gods) ... .[6]

19ab Living in both realms (in this world and beyond), Agni became omnipresent.[7]

19cd The gods left as they had come.[8] That place is called Agnitīrtha.

20–21ab 700 holy places came into existence there; bathing and alms-giving at these places grants the merit of a horse-sacrifice.

[5] None of these names is mentioned in the Tīrthāṅka, though the Tīrtha(s) in question must be situated near (the Liṅga called) Someśvara Mahādeva (see above).

[1] cf. RV 10.51, where Jātavedas, however, is the name of the hidden Agni himself, who was afraid of becoming exhausted, like his brothers, by the efforts of carrying the sacrificial offerings.

[2] The last Tīrtha on the way from Govardhana to Nasik, according to Tīrthāṅka p. 246.

[3] Or: to extend from here (this world) to (the world) beyond.

[4] cf. RV 10.51.7ab *kurmas ta āyur ajaram yad agne | yathā yukto jātavedo na riṣyāḥ*.

[5] cf. RV 10–51.9a *tava prayājā anuyājāś ca kevalāḥ*

[6] The sentence is imcomplete; ASS corrects: Having drawn him out of the water, the wise (gods) anointed Vibhāvasu..

[7] This sentence should be read after v. 16 or after (or instead of?) v. 17ab.

[8] Continuation of 18cd?

21cd–22 There are also the places Devatīrtha, Āgneya and Jātavedasa, as well as a Liṅga of many colours, which was established by Agni. To behold this god (i.e. Śiva who is present in the Liṅga) grants the merit of all rites.

Ch. 99 : Story of Pṛthuśravas and his younger brother

1 Brahman announces (an account of) Ṛṇapramocanatīrtha,[1] known to Veda-experts.

2–7ab Pṛthuśravas, son of Kakṣīvat, did not marry or pay homage to Agni (i.e. he did not perform the daily rites of a householder), through aversion to the world. His younger brother did not marry or pay homage to Agni, either, as it would have been incorrect to marry before his elder brother. Their ancestors told both of them to marry, in order to discharge their »three obligations« (towards gods, Brahmins, and ancestors), but both refused.

7cd–10 Then the ancestors told them to bathe in the Gautamī, which fulfils all desires, and where restrictions of time, place, caste (birth) etc. do not count.

11 Pṛthuśravas bathed there and satisfied the ancestors, thereby becoming free of his three obligations.

12a-f Ever since, the place has been called Ṛṇamocanatīrtha (»freeing from obligations«); by bathing there and alms-giving one is freed from the obligations taught in the Veda and the *dharma*-literature.

Ch. 100: Story of Kaśyapa and his two wives Suparṇā and Kadrū

1–3 The rivers Suparṇā and Kādravā join the (Gautamī) Gaṅgā where there is (a Liṅga of) Maheśvara (= Śiva) on a sandbank in the midst of the Gautamī; there is also an Agni-pool, and one (a pool or holy place?) of Rudra, Viṣṇu, Sūrya (the sun), Soma (the moon), Brahman, Kumāra (= Skanda), and Varuṇa, as well as the confluence with the river Apsarā; by remembering this holy place a man will accomplish all his duties.

4ab Announcement of (the account of this holy place characterized by) destroying all evil.

4cd–6 Once upon a time the Vālakhilyas had been hurt by Indra.[1] Offering half of their asceticism, they asked Kaśyapa to beget a son who would destroy Indra's pride. The Prajāpati Kaśyapa begot one child on Suparṇā and one on Kadrū, the mother of the snakes.

7–8 Once Kaśyapa wanted to depart from his house, and admonished his wives not to commit any offence and not to go anywhere, since this would result in their being cursed.

[1] Situated on the way from Govardhana to Nasik, between Brahmatīrtha and Kṣudhātīrtha, according to Tīrthāṅka p. 246.

[1] cf. MBh 1,31.

9–13 The two wives, however, went to a *sattra*-rite that was performed by self-realized sages on the banks of the Gaṅgā; though the sages tried to prevent them, – but »who could stop the bad behaviour of women?« (maxim) –, they kept interfering with the rites. Finally, they were cursed to become rivers (*āpagā*), since they were standing on a by-way (*apamārgasthita*).

14–18 When Kaśyapa returned home the sages told him what had happened. When he asked them what to do to regain his wives, the Vālakhilyas advised him to go to the Gautamī Gaṅgā and to praise Maheśvara (= Śiva), who stayed there, in the form of (a Liṅga called) Madhyameśvara, in the midst of the river, out of fear of Brahmin-murder. Kaśyapa acted accordingly.

19–21 Hymn by Kaśyapa to Śiva (each verse setting out Śiva's relationship to one triad: the three worlds, the three kinds of suffering, the three Qualities (*guṇas*)).[2]

22–24 Pleased by this hymn, Śiva granted many boons to Kaśyapa, who wanted his wives back. Śiva told him that they would regain their previous shape by joining the (Gautamī) Gaṅgā, as rivers; by Gaṅgā's grace they would be pregnant again.

25–29ab Having regained his wives, Kaśyapa invited the sages for the ceremony of »parting the hair« (in the 4th to 6th month of pregnancy) of his wives. When the sages had finished eating, Kadrū stepped beside her husband and, looking at them, laughed at them with one eye. Furiously the sages cursed her to lose that evil eye. Thus Kadrū, the mother of snakes, became one-eyed.

29cd–31ab Kaśyapa pacified the sages, who advised him to pay homage to the river Gautamī. Kaśyapa and his wives did so.

31cd Ever since, this holy place has been known as the confluence of both. (Ed. VePr. adds: (From where) Kadrū (joins) up to where Sauparṇikā (joins) extends the Jaṭādharatīrtha, which is one barley grain (a certain measurement?) more (*yavādhikam*) than Vārāṇasī.[3])

31ef It appeases all evil and grants the result of all rites.

Ch. 101: Purūravas and Sarasvatī

1 Brahman announces (an account of) Purūravastīrtha, well-known to Veda-experts, which grants liberation merely by being thought of.

2–9 When Purūravas had reached Brahman's[1] abode[2] he beheld the heavenly river Sarasvatī there, near to Brahman. He asked (his wife?) Urvaśī who that beautiful woman was; Urvaśī told him that she was Brahman's daughter. Purūraravas wanted her to be brought to him and sent Urvaśī to ask her to come. Sarasvatī agreed and went to Purūravas, who enjoyed himself (made love) at the banks of the Sarasvatī for many years; thus a son was born, Sarasvat, whose son was Bṛhadratha.

[2] In Upajāti-metre.
[3] Construction of the first part of the sentence not quite clear.
[1] Third person, though Brahman is the narrator.
[2] i.e., after his death?

10-11ab When Brahman[3] came to know that Sarasvatī continuously went to the king (Purūravas), and that Sarasvat was an indication of it to others (?), he cursed Sarasvatī to become a big river.

11cd-17ab Afraid of the curse, Sarasvatī went to the Gautamī (list of epithets) and told her about Brahman's curse. Gaṅgā intervened with Brahman to free Sarasvatī from the curse, arguing that, being creator of the world he should have known that women lust after men and are fickle by nature, and that love affects everyone. Consequently Brahman freed Sarasvatī from the curse, insisting, however, that she should be visible as well. Thus the invisible Sarasvatī became visible in the world of mortals, due to that curse.

17cd-19ab Purūravas went to the place where the cursed Sarasvatī had met with the Gaṅgā and practised asceticism there; by worshipping Siddheśvara (= Śiva), and because of the grace of Gaṅgā, his desires were fulfilled.

19cd-20 Ever since, this Tīrtha has been named after Purūravas; the confluence of the Sarasvatī, where the god (Śiva is present in the Liṅga named) Siddheśvara, is also called Brahmatīrtha.[4]

Ch. 102: Brahman's incest[1]

1-2ab Brahman continues: Sāvitrī, Gāyatrī, Śraddhā, Medhā, and Sarasvatī are known as five merit-bestowing holy places[2] to Veda-experts; bathing there and drinking (water) releases from all blame.

2cd-5ab Sāvitrī, Gāyatrī, Śraddhā, Medhā, and Sarasvatī were Brahman's (the first-person narrator's) eldest daughters. He made (another) one, more excellent than all of them,[3] who was so beautiful that his mind was turned. When he tried to seize her, she fled, changing into a she-deer; thereupon Brahman pursued her as a he-deer.

5cd Śaṃbhu (= Śiva) became a hunter, in order to protect *dharma*.

6ab The five daughters, afraid of Brahman, went to the (Gautamī) Gaṅgā.

6cd-8ab Maheśvara as a hunter threatened to kill Brahman; by that he made Brahman desist. Brahman gave his daughter to Vivasvat.[4]

[3] Now first-person narrator.

[4] It seems to be mentioned again at the end of the next chapter (102.11); for an account of this (or another) Brahmatīrtha see ch. 113 below.

[1] For the story, cf. Ait.Br. 3.33, where it is Prajāpati, however, who tries to commit the incest, and Rudra who prevents him from doing so by shooting an arrow.

[2] The confluence of these five rivers with the Godāvarī is, according to Tīrthāṅka, p. 245, somewhere between Daśāśvamedhatīrtha (cf. ch. 83 above) and the confluence of Aruṇā (cf. ch. 89 above); instead of Medhā, however, Varuṇā is named as one of the five rivers, there.

[3] Her name is not mentioned throughout the story; in the Ait.Br. it is not certain, whether it was Uṣas (Dawn) or Dyaus (Sky).

[4] A slight hint that it might have been Uṣas (cf. ch. 89 above, and Ait.Br.) and not one of the five daughters named above.

8cd-9ab The five daughters came together as rivers; after that they returned to Brahman's world.

9cd-11ab Where they had joined the goddess (i.e. the Gautamī Gaṅgā), there are five holy places and merit-bestowing confluences (?); five rivers (and) Sarasvatī.[5] Bathing there or giving alms fulfils all desires; combined with giving up actions it leads to liberation.

11c-f There the holy place Mṛgavyādhatīrtha came into existence, which fulfils all purposes; heaven and liberation as well as other things are the effects of Brahmatīrtha.[6]

Ch. 103: Disturbance of Priyavrata's horse-sacrifice

1 Brahman announces an account of Śamītīrtha, which appeases all evil.

2-6 A Kṣatriya named Priyavrata prepared for a horse-sacrifice on the southern bank of the Gautamī; his family-priest was Vasiṣṭha.[1] Suddenly the Dānava Hiraṇyaka approached the sacrificial ground. The gods, being frightened, disappeared; some returned to heaven, Agni hid in the Śamī-tree, Viṣṇu in an Aśvattha-tree, the sun in an Arka-plant, Śiva in a Vaṭa-tree, Soma in the Palāśa-tree, Fire[2] in the water of the (Gautamī) Gaṅgā, the Aśvins, seizing the horse,[3] Yama became a crow (*vāyasa*).

7 Vasiṣṭha took a stick and warded off the demons with a command (?).

8 Thereupon the sacrifice continued; the Daityas went away. These holy places (i.e. where the gods took refuge) would grant[4] the effect of ten horse-sacrifices.[5]

9 The first Tīrtha is Śamītīrtha, the second Vaiṣṇava, (then) Ārka, Śaiva, Saumya, and Vāsiṣṭha, which grants all desires.[6]

10-12ab After the sacrifice the gods and sages spoke to Vasiṣṭha (and) Priyavrata, to the trees (mentioned above) and to the Gaṅgā, full of joy. After the completion of the horse-sacrifice, they went off.[7] They said that the holy places would grant the result of a horse-sacrifice.[8]

[5] Or: five holy places, the merit (obtained at them) being joined (like) the five rivers (and) Sarasvatī. (Construction not quite clear.)

[6] Construction of 11ef not quite clear. In this chapter, two accounts, one of the origin of the confluence of the five rivers with the Godāvarī, and one of Brahman's incest and the origin of Mṛgavyādhatīrtha (not mentioned in the Tīrthāṅka) seem to have been combined (perhaps in order to establish a connection between these five rivers and the tradition of the AitBr?).

[1] This half Śloka (3cd) should be read after 2ab, as it disturbs the connection between 3ab and 4ab.

[2] Mentioned for the second time.

[3] Only absolutive, without verbal predicate.

[4] Optative, as in 12ab.

[5] In Upajāti-metre.

[6] The gods mentioned in 6cd are here not mentioned again.

[7] Should be read after the next half Śloka (12ab).

[8] But cf. 8cd above, where the effect of ten horse-sacrifices is ascribed to these holy places.

12c-f Therefore, by bathing and alms-giving at these holy places, one obtains the meritorious effect of a horse-sacrifice.

Ch. 104: Story of Hariścandra, Rohita, and Śunaḥśepa[1]

1-2 Brahman announces an account of how the following holy places got their names: Viśvāmitra, Hariścandra, Śunaḥśepa, Rohita; Vāruṇa, Brāhma, Āgneya, Aindra, Aindava, Aiśvara; Maitra, Vaiṣṇava, Yāmya, Āśvina, Auśana.[2]

3-4ef Once King Hariścandra, born in the (royal) line of the Ikṣvākus, received Nārada and Parvata as his guests. He asked them why everybody longed for a son so eagerly, what could be gained by means of a son.[3]

5-7ab The two visitors replied that the answer might be manifold, the main thing being, however, that a person without a son was not able to enter heaven.

7cd-9 A man to whom a son is born will obtain, by bathing (only), the merit of ten horse-sacrifices; he will be reborn as the highest god. The gods are immortal by means of ambrosia (*amṛta*), the Brahmins etc. by means of a son. A son frees his father and forefathers from the (three) obligation(s).

10-14ab (Living on) roots and water, (wearing) a beard, and (practising) asceticism[4] are useless, if there is no son; for a son means (access to) the other world, (stands for) the (three) goals of life: righteousness (*dharma*), accumulation of wealth (*artha*), and worldly pleasures (*kāma*). He is (identical with) release (from rebirth) and the highest light for all beings, whereas without a son any religious practice is useless. (Ed. VePr adds two Ślokas (13ef-14ef) containing further praise of a son.[5]) Therefore there is nothing in the world that should be more desired than a son.

14cd-22ab Now Hariścandra wanted to know how he could get a son. His guests advised him to go to the Gautamī, where Varuṇa would fulfil all wishes. Hariścandra acted accordingly, and Varuṇa granted him a son, on the condition that he should be sacrificed to him. Hariścandra agreed. He prepared an oblation for Varuṇa (*vāruṇaṃ carum*) and gave it to his wife; thereupon a son (Rohita) was born to him.

22cd-37ab As soon as the son was born, Varuṇa demanded that he should be sacrificed, but Hariścandra sent him away, promising to sacrifice his son when he was ten days old. When Varuṇa returned, Hariścandra postponed the sacrifice again and again: till his son had teeth, till he had his second teeth, till he had finished his education as a Kṣatriya. Finally, when Rohita had reached 16 years of age and was being made heir-apparent, Varuṇa asked again for him to be sacrificed; Hariścandra agreed and

[1] i.e. Śunaḥśepa-story; cf. Ait.Br. 7,13-18.

[2] The first four names, referring to the actors of the story, are no derivatives like the names derived from the gods involved.

[3] v. 4cd should be exchanged with 3cd.

[4] Obviously a description of the third stage of life, which should not be entered before a grandson is born; 10ab seems to have been taken over directly, only with slight change, from Ait.Br. 7,13.4.

[5] v. 14ab is taken over literally from Ait.Br. 7,13.1.

told his son that he was to be sacrificed now, informing him about what had happened before.

37cd–38 Rohita, however, refused, telling his father that rather he himself would sacrifice Varuṇa as (sacrificial) animal to Viṣṇu.

39–43 Varuṇa grew very angry and inflicted a dropsy on Hariścandra, while Rohita, who had left for the forest, stayed for six years at the place where his father had worshipped Varuṇa. Then he heard of his father's disease and worried what he could do for him.

44–59ab Among the sages on the bank of the Gaṅgā there lived a Brahmin named Ajīgarta, son of (Su)vayas,[6] who had nothing to support his wife and his three sons. Seeing him, Rohita asked him why he looked so miserable. The Brahmin complained that nobody would buy one of them for food to nourish the rest of them. Rohita inquired whom he would be willing to sell. Ajīgarta offered himself, his wife, or one of the three sons; Rohita chose a son, who should serve as sacrificial animal for Varuṇa, in his place. As Ajīgarta did not want to give away the eldest son, and his wife wanted to keep the youngest, he sold the middle one, Śunaḥśepa, for 1000 cows, grain, coins, and clothes.

59cd–60 With him Rohita returned to his father and asked him to sacrifice Śunaḥśepa in his place.[7]

61–65 Hariścandra (first?) agreed,[8] (but then) answered that a king should especially protect the Brahmins among his subjects, as they are venerable even to Viṣṇu, and disrespect would lead to the ruin of the family. (Ed. VePr adds a further verse in praise of the Brahmins.) Therefore he would rather die than use a Brahmin as a sacrificial animal; Rohita should take the Brahmin's son away with him.

66–68 Suddenly an invisible voice intervened, telling Hariścandra to go to the Gautamī and to perform the sacrifice there; there it could be completed without Śunaḥśepa being killed.

69–77 Hariścandra went to the Gaṅgā, together with Viśvāmitra, Vasiṣṭha, Vāmadeva, and other sages, and prepared the sacrificial ground. When Śunaḥśepa had been bound to the pole and sprinkled with water, Viśvāmitra first addressed the gods with a formula asking them to accept Śunaḥśepa as sacrificial animal, then he turned to the assembly present, declaring that the Brahmins should be venerated, should bathe in the Gautamī and praise the gods and be gladly devoted to Śiva; Śunaḥśepa, however, should be protected by the hermits and by the gods who consume the sacrificial food.

78–81ab The hermits and the king agreed; Śunaḥśepa bathed in the Gaṅgā and praised the gods, who declared the sacrifice to be complete; Varuṇa in particular said so to the king.

[6] *tu vayasaḥ* should be read as *suvayasaḥ*, or, with metathesis, *suyavasaḥ* (cf. Ait.Br., where Ajīgarta is called Sauyavasi); cf. also 150.2 below, where the father's name is Suyava.

[7] Up to this point, the story is quite similar to that of the Ait.Br.; Hariścandra's further reaction, however, as well as the solution of the conflict by the »heavenly voice« is totally different.

[8] *tathovāca* only in the ASS-Ed.; ed. VePr has *tadovāca*.

81cd–82 By the grace of the gods, of the hermits and of the holy place, the king's sacrifice was thus completed.

83–86ab Viśvāmitra honoured Śunaḥśepa and adopted him as his eldest son; those of his other sons who did not accept Śunaḥśepa as their elder brother were cursed by Kauśika (= Viśvāmitra), while he honoured those who did so, by granting them a boon.

86cd–87ab Where all this had happened, on the southern bank of the Gautamī, there are sacred places, famous to the gods etc.

87cd–88 Announcement of their names: Hariścandra, Śunaḥśepa, Viśvāmitra, Rohita,[9] and 8014 others.

89ab Bathing and almsgiving there grants the merit of a human sacrifice.

89cd–90 Phalastuti: The man who recites this account, has it recited, or listens to it with devotion, will obtain a son, if he has no son, and everything else he desires.

Ch. 105: Story of the (first) purchase of Soma[1]

1 Brahman announces (an account of) the events at the Somatīrtha.

2 Formerly king Soma, consisting of (the nectar of) immortality, belonged to the Gandharvas, not to the gods, who therefore turned to Brahman (the first-person narrator).[2]

3 Soma, life-giving to the gods, was once taken away by the Gandharvas; (thereupon) the distressed gods and sages pondered about how they were to get him back (again).[3]

4–8ab The gods were answered by (personified) Speech (Vāk = Sarasvatī) who advised them to give herself to the Gandharvas, as they were desirous of women, and to take Soma in return for her. The gods were doubtful about this advice, as they needed Sarasvatī as well as Soma, but Sarasvatī told them that she would come back to them. They should prepare a sacrifice on the right bank of the Gautamī;[4] making the sacrifice a (trading) place, they should come and trade Soma for her, as the Gandharvas were desirous of women.[5]

8cd–11ab The gods acted accordingly; messengers were sent to invite (all gods etc.) to mount Devagiri - therefore Devagiri is the name of this mountain,[6] at which place all classes of gods, Gandharvas, Yakṣas and Kiṃnaras, Siddhas, sages and the eight mothers of the gods assembled.

[9] v. 88ab repeats v. 1ab.

[1] cf. Ait.Br. 1,27.

[2] For 2ab, cf. Ait.Br.; 2cd seems to be an insertion, introducing Brahman into the story, who has nothing to do with it.

[3] v. 3a-d seems to duplicate the preceding verse.

[4] v. 7ab seems to be an interpolation, in order to adjust the story to the context of the Gautamīmāhātmya.

[5] v. 4ab and v. 8ab are taken from the Ait.Br.

[6] Inserted explanation, addressed to Nārada.

11cd–13 While the sages were performing the sacrifice on the bank of the Gautamī ... ,[7] at that place Sahasrākṣa (= Indra), surrounded by the gods, asked the Gandharvas to give them Soma in exchange for Sarasvatī.

14–15 The Gandharvas, being desirous for women, acted accordingly; thus Soma belonged to the gods, Sarasvatī to the Gandharvas, yet she stayed with the gods, too.

16–17ab (She) used always to come secretly; since that time Soma has been acquired by trade, but silence should be observed during the transaction.[8]

17cd–18ab After that Soma as well as Sarasvatī belonged to the gods, neither of them, however, to the Gandharvas.[9]

18cd–19 Thereupon all came to the bank of the Gautamī: cows, mountains, etc. (list of superhuman beings).[10]

20 The place where 25 rivers flow into the (Gautamī) Gaṅgā is where the sacrifice was completed; hence it is called »Pūrṇāhūti«.

21 Announcement of the names of the holy places where these rivers flow into the Gautamī.

22–26ab Somatīrtha, Gāndharva(tīrtha), Devatīrtha, Pūrṇātīrtha, Śāla(tīrtha), Śrīparṇāsaṃgama, Svāgatāsaṃgama,[11] Kusumāsaṃgama, Puṣṭisaṃgama, Karṇikāsaṃgama, Vaiṇavīsaṃgama, Kṛśarāsaṃgama, Vāsavīsaṃgama; (the confluence with) Śivaśaryā, Śikhī, Kusumbhikā, Uparathyā, Śāntijā, Devajā; Aja, Vṛddha, Sura, and Bhadra (rivers or places of pilgrimage?); all these and other numerous rivers met with the Gautamī.

26cd–29ab All holy places on earth, which had gone to the »Mountain of the Gods« (i.e. Devaparvata[12]), and gathered at the sacrifice, for the sake of Soma, assembled in the Gaṅgā, assuming the shape of rivers and streams, lakes and rivulets;[13] all of them are famous.

29cd–30ab Bathing there, muttering prayers, sacrificing and performing ancestral rites grants all desires, enjoyment and liberation.

30cd–31ab (Phalastuti:) He who recites or remembers (the account of) them is freed from evil and goes to Viṣṇu's city. (Ed. VePr. adds: Between Pūrṇā and Pravarā are 20 rivers; but there are 25 godly rivers said to have come forth (?).)[14]

[7] Seems to be inserted, in order to connect the story with the Gautamī.

[8] cf. Ait.Br.: *tasmād upāṃśu vācā caritavyam*.

[9] Here seems to be the »original« end of the story.

[10] In Indravajrā-metre; seems to be an addition meant to be inserted after or to replace 10cd–11ab; it provides here a connecting link to the following list of rivers and rivulets that came to this place, too.

[11] Ed. VePr reads Ilāsaṃgama.

[12] cf. above, v. 8–11.

[13] Thus according to Ed. VePr; ed. ASS reads *stavarūpeṇa* »in the shape of praise(s)«.

[14] Seems to connect this chapter with the following one.

Ch. 106: Story of the origin and distribution of the nectar of immortality[1]

1 Brahman announces (an account of) the confluence of Pravarā, and the best Mahānadī (»great river«),[2] where the god (= Śiva) who helps everybody (is present in the Liṅga named) Siddheśvara.

2 (In former times) there was a fierce battle between gods and Dānavas; but there was also mutual friendship between them.

3-7 They held mutual consultations for each other's sake on Mt. Meru. The gods proposed a joint effort to produce the nectar of immortality (*amṛta*); all should drink it and thus become immortal. Conflict should be put aside; in friendship they would achieve their goals and be happy. Enmity should be forgotten; dominion over the three worlds or even liberation would grant less happiness than freedom from enmity (maxim).

8-10ab Thus gods and demons were united in friendship. Together they churned the ocean, using Mount Mandara as their churning stick and (the snake) Vāsuki as rope. By that the nectar of immortality was produced.

10cd-12 When it had been produced, they agreed that, being exhausted, they would return to their residences, and would distribute the nectar evenly after meeting again at some auspicious time.

13-14 After Daityas, Dānavas and Rākṣasas had left, the gods consulted further and decided that the nectar of immortality should not be given to their enemies.

15-18 Bṛhaspati agreed and encouraged them to drink it without the others knowing about it; this would be the only proper advice (*mantra*) which (would lead to) the defeat of (their) enemies. According to the authorities in political maxims, opponents should be thoroughly hated, should never be trusted or consulted; therefore the Daityas should not be given nectar, since they could never be defeated once they became immortal.

19-22 The gods inquired from Vācaspati (= Bṛhaspati) where they should go to drink (the nectar) and where there would be a charm formula (*mantra*, for overcoming their enemies).[3] Bṛhaspati sent them to Brahman (described as »knower«, »speaker«, »giver«). They went to Brahman (the first-person narrator) and informed him about what had happened.

23-26ab Together with the gods Brahman went to Hari (= Viṣṇu) and informed him and Śaṃbhu (= Śiva). All of them went to a cave on Mt. Meru, without the demons knowing about it; making Hari their protector, they stayed there to drink Soma (i.e. the nectar?), Āditya being the one who knew to whom the Soma(-juice) should be given, Soma (the moon) being the distributor, and Viṣṇu (*cakradhṛk*) the protector.

26cd-30 The demons (i.e. Daityas, Dānavas, and Rākṣasas) did not know about this, except for Rāhu, the son of Siṃhikā, who was able to assume any appearance he wanted. Thus he mingled among the Maruts, holding a drinking vessel in his hand. The sun, however, recognized the Daitya and told Soma about it; Soma, who had already given nectar (*amṛta*) to the demon, informed Viṣṇu, and Viṣṇu cut off the demon's

[1] cf. MBh (Poona ed.) 1,15-1.7.

[2] In nominative case, construction not quite clear.

[3] cf. v. 16 above; the word *mantra* seems to be used in a different sense in both cases.

head with his discus. Having already drunk of the nectar, however, the head became immortal.

31-36 The headless trunk, which fell to earth on the southern bank of the Gautamī, caused an earthquake; having touched the nectar for a moment only, it was immortal, too. (The gods thought that,) as head and body depend on each other, that demon would devour them all, if his head and body were joined; therefore they should destroy the body first. They addressed Śaṃkara (= Śiva), requesting him to destroy the body, so that it could not be joined to the head.

37-38 The Lord (= Śiva) sent his supreme energy (*śakti*), the Goddess, mother of the world, surrounded by the mothers, who went to where the body was, eager to devour it.

39-41 While the gods conciliated the head, the body fought with the Goddess for many years. Rāhu (i.e. his head) told the gods that they should first split his body and extract its best essence;[4] being separated from this essence, the immortal body would be reduced to ashes.

42 Pleased with these words, the gods anointed Rāhu, appointing him as »Graha« (i.e. »seizer of planets«).

43-45ab According to Rāhu's words, Śakti, who is called the Goddess, split his body, extracted that best and most preferable (*pravara*) nectar and established it outside; then Ambikā, who is also called Kālarātrī and Bhadrakālī, devoured the body.

cd-46ab The best of all essences, however, started to flow and became the river Pravarā.[5]

46cd And she (i.e. the Goddess) devoured the nectar of immortality, which had been put aside, as well.[6]

47-48ab Thus, the immortal river Pravarā originated from Rāhu's body, endowed with Rudra's energy (*śakti*). It is the most preferable (*pravarā*) of rivers, known as Amṛtā (»the immortal one«) as well.

cd-49ab There are 5000 holy places; Śaṃbhu established himself there for ever, worshipped by the gods.

cd-53ab Pleased with the Goddess, the gods granted boons to her as well as to the river, telling her that she would be worshipped like Śaṃbhu. She should always reside there for the benefit of the people and should fulfil the wishes of all who praise her.

cd-54ab Since this place became the permanent residence of Śiva and Śakti, it is called »Nivāsapura« (»city of residence«) by the hermits.

54cd-56 Previously, the pleased gods had granted boons to the Pravarā: Her confluence with the Gaṅgā should be known as »Suravallabha« (»darling of gods«). Those who immerse themselves there, should obtain enjoyment and liberation, or whatever they desired.

57-58ab Ever since, the place has been known as »confluence of Pravarā«. The Śakti who was sent by the god of gods (= Śiva), is also famed as »Amṛtā« (»immortal«), likewise the great river (*mahānadī*) Pravarā. [7]

[4] Probably the nectar of immortality, cf. v. 44.

[5] Seems to disturb the connection between 45ab and 46cd.

[6] Seems to be connected with 45ab.

[7] Ed. VePr. adds: Bathing and alms-giving there should be known as everlasting (and) pleasing to the ancestors.

Ch. 107: Story of Vṛddhagautama and the old maid[1]

1 Brahman announces the story (*ākhyāna*) of the place called Vṛddhāsaṃgama (»confluence of Vṛddhā, i.e. the old one«), where Śiva (is present in the Liṅga named) Vṛddheśvara.[2]

2–11 Once there was a hermit called »Gautama the old«. When he, the son of Gautama, was still a child, he had a deformed appearance, since he was born without a nose. Out of disgust (?), he went here and there, from one land or holy place to the other. Full of shame, he did not dare to go to a teacher or to study together with other pupils. Somehow, however, he was initiated with the sacred thread by his father; in that condition he departed from home. For a long time he was without education and did not study any science (or holy text, *śāstra*), yet he attended the fire and recited the Gāyatrī-verse; to that extent he was a Brahmin, since by repeated reciting of the Gāyatrī-verse alone a Brahmin is to be called by this name (maxim). In this way he grew older and older, without taking a wife, and kept wandering around in different forests and staying in hermitages and at holy places.

12–16 Once, while staying on Mt. Śītagiri (»cold mountain«), he came across a cave; making up his mind to stay there, he entered it. Inside he saw an old emaciated ascetic woman. He wanted to pay homage to her, but she stopped him, choosing him as her master (*guru*) and quoting a maxim on the destructive effects of being paid homage by a Guru.

17–18 Gautama, however, questioned her proposal, pointing out his inferiority to her in terms of age as well as knowledge.

19–30 In order to explain the situation, the old woman told him her story (ed. VePr inserts a half Śloka containing an announcement): Once there lived a king named Ṛtadhvaja, son of Ṛṣṭiṣeṇa, who was devoted to the duties of Kṣatriyas. One day he went hunting and rested in that same cave. An Apsaras named Suśyāmā, daughter of the kings of the Gandharvas, saw the handsome young king; both fell in love with each other and sported together. After some time the king took leave and went home, while Suśyāmā gave birth to her (i.e. the old woman who is telling the story). Before departing, too, her mother told her that whoever entered this cave would be her husband. Gautama was the first man to enter. As her father and her brother had died after ruling 1080 and 1010 years, she was now self-dependent. The Brahmin should therefore accept her, for, though she had been observing her vows, she now wanted to be loved by a man.

31–34 Gautama objected that he was only 1000 years old, while she was much older; she assured him that he was destined to be her husband by the creator; she threatened to commit suicide, quoting a maxim that death is preferable to unbearable situations.

35–40 Gautama replied that he, being ignorant and disfigured, was not qualified for marriage. She should first arrange for him to become handsome and knowledgeable. The old woman told him that Sarasvatī, the waters and the fire were pleased with

[1] May be compared to MBh 9,51, where the story is told, however, from the point of view of the old maid, her prehistory is somewhat different, and the name of her husband is Śṛṅgavat, son of Gālava.

[2] cf. Tīrthāṅka p. 269.

her asceticism; Vāgīśvarī (= Sarasvatī) would give him knowledge, Agni would give him beauty. After that she addressed Vibhāvasu (= the fire) with her request, who endowed the hermit with knowledge and beauty.

41 As a learned, fortunate and handsome man, the hermit readily made the old woman his wife and enjoyed life with her in the cave for many years.[3]

42–45 One day, Vasiṣṭha, Vāmadeva, and other sages came to that cave. Gautama recognized them and welcomed them. Some of them, especially the younger ones, laughed at him and his old wife.[4]

46 Speech of the young sages, who speculate about the relation between the old woman and the handsome man, asking her to tell them the truth.[5]

47 They conclude by first quoting the maxim »A young woman is poison for an old man« and then jokingly changing it into »a young man is nectar (*amṛta*) to an old woman«.

48–52 All this was overheard by the couple, who felt miserable and ashamed after the guests had departed. Gautama asked Agastya at which holy place they could quickly find relief. Agastya told them that he had once heard hermits say that the Gautamī would fulfil all desires; therefore he advised them to go there; he would accompany them.

53–54 Gautama went there with his wife, practised asceticism, praised Śambhu (= Śiva) and Viṣṇu, and pleased the Gaṅgā.

55–57 Hymn by Gautama to Śiva, Kṛṣṇa and the Gautamī (one verse each, all of them metaphorically elaborating on the life-giving effect of water)

58–61 Gautamī responded by telling him to sprinkle water from her over his wife, while reciting formulas (*mantras*) and performing rites (*upacāra*); thereby she would become most beautiful, and he too would obtain the desired beauty.[6]

62–63ab The couple complied and obtained beauty, due to the grace of the Gaṅgā; the water that was sprinkled became a river.

3cd–64cd It is known by the name of the old woman, i.e. »Vṛddhā« (»old woman«); likewise, Gautama is called »Vṛddhagautama« (»Gautama the old«) by the sages.[7]

4ef–67ab The old woman expressed her wish to the Gautamī that this river should be known under the name »Vṛddhā«; its confluence with the Gautamī should be an unsurpassable Tīrtha, causing beauty, wealth, and prosperous descendants, and granting long life, health, victory, friendship, and purification of the ancestors. This wish was granted by the Gaṅgā.

[3] In a mixture of Triṣṭubh-metre and Jagatī-metre (41b hypermetrical Triṣṭubh, 42b Jagatī); this verse possibly marks the »original« end of the episode.

[4] Ed. VePr inserts 3 verses that duplicate v. 45, adding a contrasting description of the appearance of both.

[5] v. 46d ends the direct speech of the Brahmins, which, however, continues, thus clearly indicating the composite character of the passage. Ed. VePr adds 16 verses, in which the young sages jokingly praise her asceticism, her attachment to *dharma*, speak ill of the body and of women, and try to »explain« why she has a »son« or »grandson«, by imagining actions she performed in a former birth (honouring guests, worshipping Viṣṇu, etc.).

[6] But cf. v. 40 above, where he has already obtained beauty from Agni.

[7] v. 63cd–64cd seem to be an inserted explanation, possibly they should be read after v. 67ab. (Or should the following request have been added later?)

67cd–68ab The Liṅga established by Gautama is called after the »old woman« (= Vṛddheś-vara: »lord of the old woman«);[8] there the hermit and the old woman together obtained happiness.

68dc–69ab Bathing and alms-giving there grants all wishes. Ever since, the place is called Vṛddhāsaṃgama.

Ch. 108: Story of King Ila who became Ilā, the mother of Purūravas[1]

1 Brahman announces the holy place called Ilātīrtha, which removes even the sin of Brahmin-murder and fulfils all wishes.

2–7 In the line of (Manu) Vaivasvata (i.e. in the Solar Dynasty), there was a great king named Ila. One day he went hunting, accompanied by a large army, and roamed through a thicket full of wild animals. He ordered his ministers to return to the city and to supervise his kingdom; Vasiṣṭha, his family-priest, was also to return, together with the king's wives, whereas he would stay in the forest, together only with a small entourage of men dedicated to hunting.

8–14ab After their departure, the king went to live on the Himālaya-mountain, where he discovered a cave adorned with jewels. It belonged to a Yakṣa called Samanyu and his wife Samā. While the king stayed on the mountain, the Yakṣa and his wife enjoyed themselves in their forest, in the shape of deer. Ila did not know that the cave belonged to the Yakṣa and entered it with his men, in order to stay there.

14cd–17 The Yakṣa became angry, but he thought that he could not defeat Ila, and that the king would not give back the cave, even if begged to do so. Nevertheless he sent his Yakṣas to that place, in order to drive Ila out of the cave.

18–20ab They went to Ila and told him to leave the cave; otherwise he would be driven out. Ila became angry and started a fight; after defeating the Yakṣas he stayed in the cave for ten nights.

20cd–21 The Yakṣa and his wife, however, had to live in the forest, so they consulted about what to do (dialogue between the Yakṣa and his wife). (Ed. VePr adds: The Yakṣa asked his wife how to defeat that powerful, conceited king. She offered her assistance. The Yakṣa told her of a means to humiliate the king. She should show herself to the king in the shape of a deer and attract him to a forest called Umāvana (»Umā's forest«) where he would be turned into a woman.)[2]

22–23ab Considering the king's addiction to his passion (i.e. hunting), the Yakṣa thought of how to lead him to his misfortune, since »the kingdoms of all kings come to an end through evil passions« (maxim).

23cd–24ef He ordered his wife to allure the king in the shape of a deer and to induce him to enter the Umāvana (the »forest of Umā«); thereby he would be turned into a woman. This, however, could only be done by the Yakṣiṇī, for he himself, being a man, could not achieve this.

[8] cf. v. 1 above.

[1] cf. Rm 7,87–90; in the PPL-text (cf. above, Ch. 7, 3–19) Ilā is said to be Manu Vaivasvata's daughter, who afterwards changed into Sudyumna.

[2] The passage duplicates v. 23cd–24ef, below.

25 The Yakṣiṇī asked the reason why he could not go there himself.

26–30 Thereupon the Yakṣa related the story of the Umāvana: When Śiva, surrounded by his hosts and gods, was living happily with Umā, she told him secretly that, since all women prefer a secluded place for making love, he should provide her with such a place; he should give her the forest named Umāvana, where any man who entered except for himself, Gaṇeśa, Kārttikeya, and Nandin would be turned into a woman. So Śiva gave the order, for »a man will do anything to please his beloved« (maxim). Therefore the Yakṣa could not go there himself.

31–36ab Having heard her husband's words, the Yakṣiṇī turned into a deer and approached Ila. When Ila saw her, he mounted a horse and pursued her, alone. She slowly attracted him to the Umāvana, by acting like a fearful, fleeing deer, sometimes hiding, sometimes showing herself to the king.

36cd–47 As soon as the king had entered the Umāvana, the Yakṣiṇī turned into a beautiful woman (description) and, smilingly, asked the king, who kept looking for the deer, what he, a woman in man's dress, was doing there, addressing him as »Ilā«. When the king heard this, he became angry, reproached the Yakṣiṇī and asked her for the deer. Again she addressed him as a woman; when the king angrily took his bow and showed it to her, she asked him to look at himself, before accusing her of lying. Then the king saw that there had grown female breasts. Bewildered he asked her what had happened to him, and who she was.

48–51ef Now the Yakṣiṇī introduced herself; she told him how she and her husband had reacted to the king's occupation of their cave, and explained him the effect of entering the Umāvana.

52–53ef Upon these words the king fell from his horse; the Yakṣiṇī, however, consoled him and taught him all that a woman should know (e.g. dancing, singing, decorating herself), and how she should act.

54–55 Ilā asked who would be her husband, and how she could become a man again.

56–58 The Yakṣiṇī told her about Budha (= Mercury), the son of Soma (= the moon), whose hermitage was located east of this forest; in order to have her wishes fulfilled, she should show herself to him when he passed by on his way to his father.

59–61ab Then the Yakṣiṇī disappeared and returned to her husband, to whom she told everything. King Ila's army left the place, whereas Ilā stayed in the Umāvana, dancing and singing as women do.

61cd–64 Once, when she was dancing, Budha saw her and, giving up his purpose of seeing his father, asked her to become his wife. Ilā agreed, remembering the Yakṣiṇī's words.

65–67 Budha took her to his place and made love with her. She pleased her husband in all respects; thus, after a long time, Budha asked her to choose a boon. Ilā wanted a son.

68–70 Budha predicted the birth of a famous Kṣatriya who would establish the Lunar Dynasty; he would be like the sun in splendour, like Bṛhaspati in wisdom, like Pṛthivī (the earth) in patience, like Hari (i.e. Viṣṇu or Indra?) in strength, and like the fire in his wrath.

71–74 When the son was born, exclamations of »victory« could be heard from the gods' abode; all the gods gathered there, including Brahman (the first-person narrator). Just born the boy cried with a far-reaching (loud) voice (*rāvam akarot pṛthusvaram*), therefore he was named »Purūravas« (»crying loudly«) by gods and sages.

75–76ab Budha taught his son all the knowledge of the Kṣatriyas, especially archery; Purūravas grew as fast as the moon.

76cd–87 When he (i.e. Purūravas) noticed that his mother was unhappy, though she had a husband and a son, he respectfully inquired the reason. Ilā answered that she was remembering former events. Asked to tell everything, she first hesitated, as it was a secret, but then she agreed, as »a son is the only refuge of those submerged in the ocean of grief« (maxim). Upon his insisting[3] she related all the former events that had happened to her.

88–93 Now he asked what he could do in order to make her happy. Ilā told him that she wanted to become a man again, to get her/his kingdom back, to consecrate her/his sons, and to lead a religious life (alms-giving, sacrifices, searching for liberation). Asked about the means by which she could become a man, she sent Purūravas to his father.

94–98 Purūravas went to his father, who told him that he knew all that had happened, including Śiva's order concerning the Umāvana; therefore Purūravas should worship Śiva and Umā, for by their grace Ilā would be freed from her curse. Now Purūravas inquired how he could see the god (Śiva) and the Mother (i.e. Umā), by pilgrimage or by asceticism. Budha told him to go to the Gautamī where Śiva and Umā are always present.

99–102ab Purūravas rejoiced about these words; bowing to the Himālaya, to his mother, and to his father and teacher, he went to the Gautamī Gaṅgā to practise asceticism, desiring that his mother should become a man again. Ilā and Budha followed him. Reaching the Gautamī, they bathed and practised a little asceticism; then they composed a superb hymn of praise.

102cd–103 Announcement of the hymns by which first Budha, then Ilā, and finally Purūravas praised Gaurī and Śaṃkara.

104–108 Hymns to Śaṃkara and Gaurī.[4]

104 Hymn by Budha.[5]

105–106 Hymn by Ilā.[6]

107–108 Hymn by Purūravas.[7]

109–110 Asked about what they wanted, Purūravas uttered his wishes: forgiveness for King Ila, who had entered Umā's forest unwittingly, and restoration of his manhood.

111–112 The goddess agreed, and Śiva told them that the king would regain his manhood simply by bathing at this place:

113–115 While Budha's wife was bathing, all female arts that were taught her by the Yakṣiṇī, such as dancing, singing, and loveliness (*lāvaṇya*), entered the water which flowed down from her body into the Gaṅgā. Thus three rivers came into existence: Nṛtyā, Gītā, and Saubhāgyā (»loveliness«); they flowed into the Gaṅgā. Bathing in them and giving alms bestows sovereignty over the gods.

[3] Ed. VePr and Ms D replace 82cd–83ab with three verses containing Purūravas' motives for insisting, in the form of maxims about the duties of a son and their merits.

[4] Each verse ends with a slightly varying refrain in the fourth *pāda*.

[5] In Upajāti-metre.

[6] In Upajāti-metre (105) and Indravajrā-metre (106).

[7] In Upajāti-metre (107) and Indravajrā-metre (108).

116-118 After Ila had regained manhood, he performed a horse-sacrifice. He summoned his family-priest Vasiṣṭha, his wives and his sons, his ministers, his forces, his treasure etc. and established his kingdom in Daṇḍaka. This city is known by Ila's name. (Ed. VePr adds: ...situated in the valley(?) of Sahya (or: in Sahyadroṇī), more pleasant than the city of great Indra. Having become detached from the pleasures of life in this city...)

119-120 He anointed his previously born sons as kings of the Solar Dynasty; then he anointed Aila (the son of Ilā = Purūravas), who established the Lunar Dynasty; he became the oldest and best of all (?).

121-123 The places where Ila's sacrifices took place, where he obtained manhood again, where his sons assembled, where the three rivers that originated from the arts taught by the Yakṣiṇī joined with the Gaṅgā, all these amount to 1016 holy places on both banks. There Śaṃbhu (is present in the Liṅga named) Ileśvara. Bathing there and giving alms grants the fruit of all sacrifices.

Ch. 109: The destruction of Dakṣa's sacrifice; Viṣṇu's discus swallowed by Śiva

1-3ab Brahman announces Cakratīrtha, which destroys sins such as Brahmin-murder, where the god (Śiva) resides (in the Liṅga named) Cakreśvara, from whom Hari (= Viṣṇu) obtained his discus (*cakra*), and where Viṣṇu worshipped Śaṃkara (= Śiva); to merely hear of this holy place frees from all sins.

3cd-6ab When Dakṣa's sacrifice had begun, when the gods had assembled, when god Śiva (Śarva, Maheśvara) was offended by not being invited, when Dākṣāyaṇī (Dakṣa's daughter, = Satī) heard the reason why Śiva was not invited, as well as (or: from) Ahalyā's words, she (= Satī) became angry, (resolved) to destroy her father, and never to forgive him.

6cd-10 When she heard her father blaming her husband, she thought that »Women who can tolerate having their husbands blamed commit great evil; for a woman there is nothing beyond her husband, no matter what he may be like« (maxim). This would be the more valid concerning her husband Mahādeva, the lord of all and the teacher of the world; therefore she would rather give up her body than listen to his being blamed. Full of wrath, she burnt herself; fixing her thoughts on Śiva, she gave up her body, due to (her) strength and Yoga.

10cd-12 When Maheśvara (= Śiva) heard from Nārada what had happened, he grew angry and asked Jayā and Vijayā, who told him of the (self-)destruction of Dākṣāyaṇī at Dakṣa's sacrifice.[8] Surrounded by his frightful hosts Maheśvara went there.

13-20 They surrounded the sacrifice, which was honoured by gods and Brahmins and protected by Dakṣa, the ritually pure sacrificer, shielded by Vasiṣṭha and other sages, guarded by Indra and other gods, adorned by recitations from the Ṛgveda, Yajurveda, and Sāmaveda, as well as the sounds of *svāhā*, adorned (by the presence

[8] Or: of the destruction of Dakṣa's sacrifice by Dākṣāyaṇī? (Meaning not quite clear.)

of the goddesses) Śraddhā (faith), Puṣṭi (success), Tuṣṭi (satisfaction), Śānti (peace), Lajjā (bashfulness), Sarasvatī (speech), Bhūmi (earth), Dyaus (sky), Śarvarī (night), Kṣānti (forbearance), Uṣas (dawn), Āśā (hope), Jayā (victory), and Mati (intelligence); arranged by Tvaṣṭṛ Viśvakarman; enriched by (the presence of) the wish-fulfilling cows Surabhi, Nandinī and Dhenu; the wish-fulfilling coral tree (*pārijāta*) and wish-fulfilling creepers were also present at the sacrifice, as well as anything else that might be wished for; it was protected by Maghavan (= Indra) himself, by Pūṣan and Hari (= Viṣṇu), and honoured by Dakṣa's orders to give (alms), to eat, to perform (rites), and to stay at ease.

21–26ab At first, Vīrabhadra and Bhadrakālī went there, then the bearer of the trident (= Śiva) with his hosts; surrounding the sacrifice, they destroyed it. There was a great tumult: some fled, some took refuge with Śiva, some praised the lord of the gods (= Śiva), some were angry with Śaṃkara (= Śiva). Pūṣan tried to interfere, but he (Śiva?) broke his teeth and made Indra run away immediately; Vīrabhadra tore out Bhaga's eyes and, after whirling around the sun with his arms, threw him down.

26cd–27 The gods went for shelter to Viṣṇu, complaining that this Viṣṇuite sacrifice was being destroyed by Maheśvara's host, while Hari (= Viṣṇu) was looking on.

28–29 Hari (= Viṣṇu) sent out his discus to kill the lord of beings (= Śiva), who, however, made it fall down and swallowed it. Thereupon the guardians of the directions fearfully left, while Dakṣa, seeing the condition of the gods and the sacrifice, praised Śaṃkara with devotion.

30–35 Hymn by Dakṣa to Śiva.

30 Introduction (*jaya* and vocatives).

31–34 Homage to Śiva (*namas te 'stu* or *namo 'stu te* with vocative or dative forms).

35 Request for shelter, addressing Śiva as Jagannātha.

36–39ab Thus praised, Maheśvara was pleased and asked what to give; Dakṣa requested that his sacrifice should be completed. Śiva agreed, made the sacrifice complete and disappeared. The gods, too, went to their residences.

39cd–40 Later on, there was a fight between gods and demons; being afraid of the demons, the gods turned to Śrī's husband Janārdana (= Viṣṇu) and praised him.

41–42 Hymn by the gods to Viṣṇu.[1]

41 Formula of taking refuge.[2]

42 Request for help, referring to Viṣṇu as Nṛsiṃha (man-lion) and to Tārkṣya (= Garuḍa) as his vehicle.

43–45 The god whose attributes are conch, discus and club asked them why they had come. When they told him that they were afraid of the demons and asked him to help them, Hari replied that his discus had been swallowed by Hara (= Śiva), nevertheless he would think of something to protect them; they should all leave.

46–48 Viṣṇu went to the Godāvarī and began worshipping Śaṃbhu (= Śiva) with 1000 fragrant lotus-flowers. (Ed. VePr inserts two verses: A hymn by Viṣṇu to Śiva, by which prayer-formula (*mantra*) he worshipped Śiva, the darling of Bhavānī.)

[1] In Upajāti-metre.

[2] With verb in 1st person sing.; refers to two wives of Viṣṇu, Lakṣmī and (?) Śrī, and to Viṣṇu as Brahman.

49–50ef When one lotus-flower was lacking to complete the number of 1000, the enemy of the Asuras (= Viṣṇu) tore out his eye and added it to the offering. Meditating on Śaṃbhu, Hari presented the vessel with this offering to Śiva.

51 Hymn by Viṣṇu to Śiva, containing a description of the god as knowing men inwardly and as sure refuge.

52–54 While speaking, with tears coming to his eyes, he became absorbed in the god. Śaṃbhu and Bhavānī appeared before him. Embracing him tightly, Śiva loaded Hari with boons; his discus and his eye were restored as before. Then the gods praised (the unity of) Hari and Śaṃkara, as well as the Gaṅgā, the best of rivers, and the god whose emblem is the bull (= Śiva).

55–57ab Ever since, this holy place has been remembered as Cakratīrtha. To hear of it frees from all sins. Whoever bathes there, gives alms, and satisfies the ancestors, is freed from evil and enjoys heaven together with his ancestors. This holy place, whose special sign is the discus, can be seen even today.[3]

Ch. 110: Story of Dadhīci and his son Pippalāda[1]

1–4 Brahman continues: Next to Cakratīrtha just mentioned, is the holy place called »Pippala«, whose greatness cannot be described; the report given by Brahman is according to what he has seen himself.

5–70 *Story of Dadhīci*[2]

5–9 Dadhīci, a great sage, was married to Gabhastinī or Vaḍavā, a daughter of Prātithi (Prātitheyī) and sister of Lopāmudrā (married to Agastya). She always practised austerities. Dadhīci lived happily together with his wife, like another Agastya (*kumbhayoni*, i.e. »born from a jar«), near the Bhāgīrathī (Gaṅgā). By his (Dadhīci's) power the demons were prevented from entering that area as well as the one where Agastya lived.

10–20 One day, after slaying the demons, the (vedic) gods (Rudras and Ādityas, Aśvins, Indra, Viṣṇu, Yama, Agni), came to visit Dadhīci. After their welcome they told Dadhīci that they were not able to enjoy the fruits of their success bearing their weapons, as they could not see any place to put them where they would not be stolen by the demons.

[3] According to Kane, History of Dharmaśāstra IV, p. 742, it is identical with the Cakratīrtha described in ch. 86 above. This is, however, not very probable, as this second Cakratīrtha is situated near Pratiṣṭhāna, the modern Paiṭhaṇ (cf. also the following chapter).

[1] For the story of Dadhīci, cf. MBh 3,98 and 9,50, PdP 6,148 and 150, and SkP 1,1.16–17 and 7,1.32; for a comparison of these versions, cf. R. Söhnen, Dadhīcis Knochen und Pippalādas Zorn, to be published in the Proceedings of the XXIII. Deutscher Orientalistentag, Würzburg 1985 (ZDMG Suppl.).

[2] v. 5–20 in Ślokas, 21–70 in Triṣṭubhs mixed with Jagatīs.

21–70 (The rest of the story is in Triṣṭubh-metre mixed with Jagatī-metre.)

21–24 They wished to entrust their weapons to Dadhīci, in whose hermitage they would be safe.

25–32 Dadhīci agreed, but his wife tried to prevent him, warning him that the demons would pursue him with hatred if he fulfilled the gods' wish, and that the gods would be angry with him if anything happened to their weapons. Dadhīci, however, pointed out to his wife that he had already given his word to the gods.

33–34 She kept silent; the gods put down their weapons, entrusting them to Dadhīci, and departed.

35–39ab A long time passed during which the gods never asked for their weapons. One day Dadhīci consulted his wife about what to do against the demons, who had become stronger and stronger and were now pursuing him with their hatred. Gabhasti suspected that the demons might steal the weapons. In order to protect the weapons, Dadhīci sprinkled them, reciting magic formulas (*mantra*), and drank the sprinkling-water afterwards, which had taken up the strength and brilliance of the weapons. By that action, the weapons became weaker and weaker and finally disappeared.

39cd–41ab When the gods one day needed the weapons again, they came to Dadhīci and asked him to give them back. Dadhīci told the gods that, since he was afraid of the demons, and since the gods had never wanted their weapons back, he had drunk them; he asked the gods what to do.

41cd–46ab The gods replied that they could not exist anywhere without their weapons, so Dadhīci should give them back now; they would accept no other answer. Dadhīci told them to take (their weapons out of) his bones. But the gods were not satisfied with that, so Dadhīci declared he would give up his life in order to make it possible for the gods to make weapons from his bones. The gods requested him to do so.

46cd–47ab Since Dadhīci's wife was not present at this moment, the gods, afraid of her, wished him to do it quickly.

47cd–50 Thereupon Dadhīci gave up his life, full of kindness, knowing that his bones would be valuable to the gods; seated in the lotus-seat, fixing his eyes on the top of his nose, he united his breath and his body warmth with the ether[3] and, concentrating his mind upon the immeasurable highest principle that is to be worshipped in the form of the *brahman*, he obtained union with the *brahman*.

51–56ab When the gods saw that his body had become lifeless, they went to Tvaṣṭṛ and asked him to make weapons of his bones. First Tvaṣṭṛ refused, being afraid to tear the body of a Brahmin apart. Thereupon the gods turned to the cows and asked them to tear off the flesh from the bones, for it would be for their sake that from the bones (Indra's) thunderbolt (*vajra*) would be made.[4] The cows licked off the flesh and gave the cleaned bones to the gods. Now Tvaṣṭṛ fulfilled the gods' wish and made weapons from the bones.

56cd–60 Meanwhile Dadhīci's wife, who was pregnant, returned from worshipping Umā, a water-jar in her hand. Entering the hermitage, she could not find her husband. When she asked the fire, it told her all that had happened during her absence. Full of grief she fell to the ground; Agni tried to console her.

[3] v. 49 not very clear; it might contain allusions to tantric concept about Yoga.

[4] Allusion to vedic myths that tell of Indra's freeing the cows?

61-66 Restraining herself from cursing the gods, she announced her intention of entering the fire, giving reasons for that decision by means of maxims about the transitoriness of everything in this world and about the merit of giving up one's body for the sake of cows, Brahmins, gods, and the poor; concerning her husband, she regretted that he had acted against her advice, but consoled herself with the unknowability of the creator's will.[5]

67-70 After these words, Prātitheyī, paying homage to the fire, entered (the fire) with the skin and hair of her husband. She tore her womb asunder, took out the child and, bowing to the Gaṅgā, the earth, the hermitage, the trees and plants, entrusted her child to them, as he was without any other relatives.

71-229 *Story of Pippalāda*[6]

71-72 After entrusting her child to the care of Pippala-trees, Prātitheyī circumambulated the fire and entered it; together with her husband, she went to heaven.

73-77 The trees and other beings in the forest, who had been fostered by the couple, wept as if they had lost their parents; they agreed to adopt the child.

78-80cd In order to nourish him, the plants and trees went to Soma (the moon), where they obtained nectar (*amṛta*). With this nectar the boy was brought up; he grew as quickly as the moon in the bright half (of the month). Since he was brought up by the Pippala-trees, he was called »Pippalāda« (»eating pippala-fruits«).

80ef-86 When he had grown up, he wondered how he, as a human being, could be the son of trees. The trees told him what had happened to his parents (summary in catchwords). When Pippalāda heard about his parents' death, he fell to the ground; consoled by the plants and trees, he made up his mind to take revenge and to kill those who had killed his father, according to the duty of a son (maxim concerning inherited friends and enemies).

87-97ef The trees took him to Soma, whom they told what Pippalāda had said. Soma advised him to acquire knowledge, ascetic power, and (the art of) excellent speech, and promised to give him courage, beauty, strength, and mental ability.[7] Pippalāda, however, rejected these proposals and asked when and where, and by the advice of which god he would get his desire fulfilled. After having thought about it for some time, the moon answered him that everything could be obtained from Maheśvara (= Śiva). Asked by Pippalāda how he, who was still a child, could see Maheśvara, the moon told him to go to the Gautamī and worship Hara (= Śiva) as Cakreśvara at the Cakratīrtha, where Viṣṇu had seen Śiva and had been presented with a boon and had been given his discus (reference back); the plants would show him the way.

98-99ef Pippalāda was taken by the plants to the abode of Rudra (= Śiva), the lord of the world (*jagannātha*), who had given the discus (to Viṣṇu); there he praised Śiva.

[5] Should 63-65 rather be understood as the consoling words of Agni and be read instead of v. 61, which would fit better between 66 and 67?

[6] For this part of the story cf. PdP 6.150 and SkP 7,1.32-34 (also SkP 5,42 and 6,174-176: here, however, is Pippalāda not a son of Dadhīci). For the motif of the »mare-fire« cf. W. D. O'Flaherty, The Submarine Mare in the Mythology of Śiva, JRAS 1971, p. 9-27.

[7] v. 88 (Soma's speech) in Upajāti-metre.

100–106 Hymn by Pippalāda to Śiva.[8]

100 Introductory reverence.

101 Request for compassion.

102–103 Reference to Śiva on Mt. Kailāsa, together with Devī (= Umā), who laughed at the Ten-headed (Rāvaṇa), but granted him an unfitting boon (?).

104 Reference to Bāṇa (son of Bali and enemy of Viṣṇu), who cast down the good fortune belonging to (Indra) Sutrāman (*sautrāmaṇīm ṛddhim*) and paid homage to Śiva.

105–106 Reference to Viśākha (= Skanda), who grew angry, seeing Gaṇeśa on Śiva's lap; Śiva, smilingly, took him up, too; since the child, however, would not leave his mother, Śiva had to assume the shape of Ardhanārīśvara (»the Lord being a woman with one half«).

107–111 Pleased by this hymn, Svayaṃbhu (= Śiva) granted him a boon. Pippalāda told Śiva about his parents and about his hatred against the gods and asked for the ability to slay them.

112–114 Śiva agreed, provided that Pippalāda was able to see Śiva's third eye. Pippalāda tried, but could not see it. Śiva advised him to practise austerities.

115–120 Pippalāda practised asceticism for many years (description of yogic exercises). Finally he was able to see Śiva's third eye; he reminded the god of the boon granted to him before, asking him to give him the fire of his third eye (?) for the destruction of the gods.

121–123 The plants tried to persuade him to give up his hatred, quoting the maxim that »people full of hatred will go to hell,« which had been uttered by Prātitheyī; Pippalāda, however, grew still more angry, as »the words of the good are useless, when pride is burning in the heart« (maxim).

124–130 He insisted upon Śiva's gift; from Śiva's eye (a) Kṛtyā came into existence; she had the shape of a mare (*vaḍavā*) and was pregnant with fire, since the Brahmin had been thinking of his mother Gabhastinī (also named Vaḍavā), who had been pregnant with him. Kṛtyā asked Pippalāda what to do and was told to consume the gods. She agreed, but started by seizing him. Asked why, she declared that she had started to consume him, as his body was made by the gods. Frightened, Pippalāda went to Śiva and praised him. Śiva ordered Kṛtyā not to consume any being within the distance of one Yojana from the Pippalādatīrtha.

131–133 Accordingly, Kṛtyā stayed outside this region. She gave birth to a huge, terrible fire; seeing it, all the gods were frightened; they went to Śaṃbhu (Śiva) and praised him.

134–136 Hymn by the gods to Śiva, with reference to Śiva as the refuge for all distressed beings, and with the request to protect them from Kṛtyā.

137–142 Śiva advised them to stay within that very Yojana where Kṛtyā was not allowed to go. The gods objected that they could not give up their abode Triviṣṭapa, which had been assigned to them by Śiva. Śiva replied that they should place Sūrya (the sun) there, since all gods were included in his shape.

143–146ab Accordingly, the gods made the sun from the Pārijāta-tree. Tvaṣṭṛ ordered him (i.e., the sun) to stay in this place and to protect the gods. Within one Yojana from the Cakratīrtha the gods stayed on the banks of the (Gautamī) Gaṅgā.

[8] In Upajāti-metre (104c hypermetrical Triṣṭubh-metre).

146c-f There are 30,000,000 and 500 holy places; who could tell about their splendour?

147-154 Then the gods asked Śiva to appease Pippalāda. So Śiva made Pippalāda understand that he would not get back his parents by destroying the gods, that his parents had obtained great fame and merit by their actions, which could not be equalled by Pippalāda's own actions, and that he should rather protect the gods, who were terribly frightened by him and without home; for there is no better deed than to protect the distressed (maxim).

155-156 As far as one's fame spreads in the world of mortals, so long one stays in the world beyond; one should never feel sorry about generous and good people.[9]

157 By these words of Śiva was Pippalāda finally appeased; he bowed to Śiva.

158-159 Pippalāda asked for boons in favour of the Pippalāda-trees who had brought him up.[10]

160-162 Furthermore he wished that this holy place should surpass all other lands and places of pilgrimage; if this condition were fulfilled, he would forgive the gods.

163 The gods agreed to that beautiful speech.[11]

164 Śiva knew his inner character.[12]

165 He granted a boon provided that it was favourable to the gods, too.

166-167 Now Pippalāda wished that all people who bathe in the (Gautamī) Gaṅgā and behold Śiva's foot should obtain ultimate union with Śiva,[13] like his parents, the Pippala-trees, and the gods.

168-171 Śiva agreed to that; the gods granted Pippalāda a further boon, as he had yet not asked anything for himself.

172-178 First bowing to Śiva and the gods, then to Umā and the Pippala-trees, Pippalāda replied that he had always wanted to see his parents, and that he had never understood why all beings except him were allowed to grow up under the protection of their parents; he wanted to know whether any special guilt of his might have caused his ill fortune of being without parents.

179-182 Having consulted with each other, the gods announced that he should see his parents, who were eager to see him as well.

183-187 Beholding his parents, whose eyes were filled with tears of joy, in a beautiful heavenly chariot, he bowed to them, lamenting that he was an unworthy son, as his mother's womb had been torn asunder because of him. The gods and his parents, however, praised him, since he had let the Three-eyed One (= Śiva) appear and had comforted the gods. With him as a son, the worlds (beyond), meant for the good, would never perish. A rain of flowers fell down on his head from the sky, and the sound of the gods shouting »Hail!« was heard.

188-191ab His parents gave him their blessings and advised him to take a wife, to worship Śiva with devotion, and to pay homage to the Gaṅgā; when he had obtained sons and performed sacrifices, he would have fulfilled his duties and would enter heaven for

[9] In Upajāti-metre; in v. 155a the metre should be corrected by eliminating the word *sphurati*.

[10] In Upajāti-metre.

[11] In Upendravajrā-metre.

[12] In Upajāti-metre.

[13] In Upajāti-metre.

a long time. After Pippalāda had agreed to follow this advice, Dadhīci and his wife went back to heaven.

91cd–194ab Now the gods appealed to Pippalāda to appease Kṛtyā and the fire born from her; Pippalāda, however, was not able to do that, since he could not take back his word given before; he sent the gods to Kṛtyā directly.

94cd–198ab So the gods asked Kṛtyā, but she refused, being created, like her son, to devour everything.

98cd–200cd After consulting Brahman (the first-person narrator), they told Kṛtyā and her son to eat everything, (but) to observe the right sequence. She agreed to that. She became a river, named Vaḍavā, and joined the (Gautamī) Gaṅgā; her son, however, became a big fire.

200ef–201ef The gods told the fire to start its meal with the waters, as the waters, like fire, are known as the first of all beings.

202–210 Now the fire wanted to be taken to the ocean in a golden vessel carried by a virtuous young girl. The gods asked Sarasvatī to take the fire on her head. Sarasvatī replied that she was not able to do that alone, but together with four others she could do it. The gods asked Gaṅgā and Yamunā, Narmadā and Tapatī[14] to accompany her; the fire was put into a golden vessel, carried to the ocean, and placed down at Prabhāsa, where there is (a Śiva-temple called) Somanātha; here it stayed slowly drinking the water of the ocean.

211–214 The gods, however, asked Śiva how they themselves, the cows, and the bones (of Dadhīci) could be purified. Śiva advised them to bathe in the (Gautamī) Gaṅgā, in order to be released from their evil deed, and to sprinkle the bones as well, in order to purify them.

215 The place where the gods were freed from evil is called Pāpanāśana (»destroying evil«); bathing there and giving alms frees from Brahmin-murder.

216 The place where the cows were purified is called Gotīrtha; here the fruit of a cow-sacrifice can be obtained.

217–219cd The place where the Brahmin's bones became pure is called Pitṛtīrtha; it increases the bliss of the ancestors. He whose ashes, bones, nails, and hair come together at this place will stay in heaven as long as sun, moon and stars endure, even if he is a sinner. These three holy places (are higher in rank) than Cakratīrtha.

219ef–224 The gods and cows, being purified, declared thet they would go to their abodes, leaving the sun, in whom all gods were contained and who is thought to be the self of all beings, at that place on (the banks of) the Gaṅgā where Śiva is (present in a Liṅga named) Tryambaka; this place should be called Pratiṣṭhāna (»dwelling-place«), since the gods stayed there, being contained in the sun. Then the gods took leave from Pippalāda; in due time the Pippala-trees went to heaven. Pippalāda himself, having caused the place where the trees grew to become sovereign of all regions, worshipped Śaṃkara.

225 He married Gautama's daughter and obtained sons, good fortune, and fame, and (finally) reached heaven, together with his friends.[15]

[14] i.e. Taptī?

[15] In Upajāti-metre.

226–228 Ever since, this holy place has been called Pippaleśvara; it effects the merit of all sacrifices merely by being remembered. Cakreśvara and Pippaleśa are names of Śiva; the man who knows (them) obtains all his wishes. Pratiṣṭhāna,[16] the abode of the sun and consequently of the gods, is especially dear to them.

229 Phalastuti.[17]

Ch. 111: The Prince as Serpent

1 Brahman announces (an account of) Nāgatīrtha, where the god (Śiva) is present as (i.e. in a Liṅga named) Nāgeśvara.

2–6 In Pratiṣṭhāna there lived a king named Śūrasena, who belonged to the Lunar Dynasty. He made great efforts to get a son; finally a snake of dreadful appearance was born to him. Without anybody except the king and his wife knowing this fact, the son was brought up, though the king often thought that it would be better to have no child rather than a snake.

7–8 The snake, however, talked like a human being. One day he asked his father to perform the tonsure-ceremony for him, the initiation with the holy thread, and to let him study the Vedas, otherwise a »Twice-born« would be like a Śūdra (maxim).

9–16 First the king was embarrassed, but somehow a Brahmin was found, who performed all the ceremonies. When the snake had studied the Veda, he asked his father to arrange his marriage, according to his duty; otherwise he would not escape hell (maxim). When the king objected that nobody would give his daughter to a terrible snake, the snake replied that many marriages were brought about forcibly; he declared he would drown himself in the Gaṅgā, should his father not comply with his wish.

17–25 Frightened by this threat, the king called his ministers and told them that he wanted to arrange his son's marriage, in order to bestow the burden of his kingdom upon his son and to retire to the forest. He ordered all efforts to be made to find a wife for his son »Nāgeśvara« (the »Lord of snakes«). The ministers consented, not knowing that the king's son was a real snake.

26–34 When the king asked which girl would be excellent enough, and which king would be fitting as a future relative, one of the ministers, who was wise, interested in the welfare of the kingdom, and well-versed in signs and gestures (i.e. reading the thoughts of others), told him about King Vijaya of the Eastern Region, who had eight sons and one daughter named Bhogavatī, who was beautiful as Lakṣmī and suitable for the king's son. The king asked how this girl could be obtained for his son, and the old minister, who knew the king's thoughts, told him to leave the task to him. The king honoured him with ornaments, clothes, and words, and sent him forth with a great army.

[16] Modern Paiṭhan, on the left (northern) bank of the Godāvarī, according to Kane, HDhŚ IV, p. 792.

[17] In Upajāti-metre.

35–39ab Arriving in the eastern country, the old minister honoured the king with words and other stratagems according to political wisdom (*nīti*) and negotiated the marriage treaty between the king's daughter Bhogavatī and Śūrasena's son. Honoured with ornaments and clothes etc., the king agreed to give his daughter in marriage. Now the old minister returned to Śūrasena and told him about the negotiations.

39cd–47 After a long time the old minister again set out with a great force, with clothes and ornaments, and accompanied by the other counsellors. Concerning the marriage ceremony, he told King Vijaya that Śūrasena's son »Nāga« (»snake«) would not be present himself, but according to Kṣatriya customs, he would be represented by his weapons and his ornaments. As Kṣatriyas and Brahmins always speak the truth (maxim), the king should agree to the marriage with weapons and ornaments. King Vijaya consented; he married his daughter to the weapons and then sent her off, according to the prescriptions, accompanied by his own ministers, with cows, gold, horses, etc. Having given many things, the king was filled with joy.

48–51 The ministers took the girl, went to Pratiṣṭhāna, and presented her to Śūrasena, together with jewelry, female slaves, clothes, etc. The counsellors of King Vijaya, who had accompanied Bhogavatī, were respectfully welcomed and then sent back to their king.

52–56 Vijaya's beautiful daughter was always obedient to her parents-in-law. Her husband, however, stayed somewhere else at a lonely place, in a house adorned with jewels, perfumes, and flowers. He again and again asked his parents why his wife did not approach him (»creep towards him«). Finally his mother ordered the nurse to tell Bhogavatī that her husband was a snake, and then to listen to what the princess would say.

57–60 So the nurse went to Bhogavatī and told her, secretly, that she knew her husband to be a deity, who could never be addressed by his wife, for a snake was no human being. Bhogavatī replied that, in general, a human husband was obtained according to likeness; why should a divine being not be obtained as husband, too, by special merit (maxim)?

61–63 When this word was reported to the snake and his parents, the king wept, considering the law of actions (*karmaṇo gatim*). (?) Bhogavatī, however, asked her friend to show her husband to her, otherwise her youth would pass in vain.

64–68ab Her friend showed her the terrible snake. When Bhogavatī beheld her frightening husband, lying on a bed adorned with flowers and fragrances, she addressed him respectfully, calling herself lucky for having obtained a deity as her husband. Then she went to his bed and rocked him and pleased him with singing and pressing him to her limbs, as well as with fragrances, flowers, and drinking water.

68cd–79 Due to her kindness, the snake suddenly remembered all that had happened before, according to fate. In the night he asked his beloved one why she had not been afraid of him. She replied that one could not act against one's fate, and that for women their husband is always the only refuge (maxim). Hearing this, the snake rejoiced and told her what had come to his memory: how he had been cursed by Śiva; that he had been a son of Śeṣa and had been the snake in Śiva's hand; that his wife Bhogavatī had laughed at something Umā had said, by which Śiva was pleased; when he himself, however, had started laughing, too, Śiva had grown angry and cursed him to be born in a human family, but as a snake. Appeased by Bhogavatī and the snake, Śiva had added that by worshipping him at the Gautamī the snake would get back his knowledge and would be free from the curse. Therefore, Bhogavatī should take him now to the Gautamī and worship Śiva there, together with him. Freed from the curse, both would then go back to Śiva, for »Śiva is the last refuge for all distressed« (maxim).

80–82 Accordingly they went to the Gautamī, bathed there and paid homage to Śiva. Śiva restored their divine shape. After taking leave from the snake's parents, they wanted to go to Śiva's world; the king, however, implored the snake to stay, as he was his only son, to take over the kingdom, to produce many sons, and to go to Śiva's abode only after the old king's death.

83–85ab The King of snakes agreed and, assuming a shape of his own will, ruled the kingdom, together with his wife, his parents, and his sons. After his father's death, he installed his sons in his own place and went to Śiva's city, together with his wife, the (old) minister, and others.

85cd–86 Ever since, this holy place has been known as Nāgatīrtha, where Bhogavatī had established (a Liṅga named) Nāgeśvara. Bathing there and giving alms grants the merit of all sacrifices.

Ch. 112: Śiva and the Mothers fighting against the demons

1 Brahman announces the famous Mātṛtīrtha (»ford of the Mothers«), which frees from all diseases merely by being remembered.

2–3 Once there was a fierce battle between gods and demons, in which the gods could not defeat the demons. Brahman (the first-person narrator) went to the trident-bearer (= Śiva) and praised him.

4–6 Hymn by the gods to Śiva, praising him as the only one who was able to swallow the poison Kālakūṭa, who took possession of the three worlds by slaying Puṣpa (?), who destroyed the god of love, and who, at the churning of the ocean, gave the best to the gods, and was able, as Nīlakaṇṭha, to keep the poison (in his throat).[1]

7–10 Thus praised, the Three-eyed One asked the gods to utter their wish. The gods told him about the danger caused by the demons and asked him to slay them; for what should all living beings do without Śiva's help?

11–19 Accordingly Śiva went to the demons and fought them. When he was exhausted, he assumed the shape of darkness; beads of perspiration dropped from his forehead. When the demons beheld Śiva's dark shape, they went down from Mt. Meru to the earth. Śiva followed them. They fled from place to place, pursued by Rudra (= Śiva). While he was fighting, beads of perspiration fell down. Where they touched the earth, the Mothers came into existence. They declared that they would swallow the demons. Śiva told them to pursue the demons to the nether world.

[1] In Upajāti-metre.

20–22ab The Mothers cleft the earth and went to where the demons were. They slew them and they returned to the gods, who had stayed on the bank of the Gautamī as long as the Mothers were absent.

22cd–23ab The region from where the Mothers had started their journey and where the gods stayed became »Pratiṣṭhāna« (»place of abode«).

23cd–24ab Each of the places where the Mothers came into existence is called Mātṛtīrtha; there are caves leading to the nether world.

24cd–26ab The gods granted the Mothers to be worshipped, too, wherever Śiva was worshipped. The place where they (i.e. the goddesses) stayed is known as Mātṛtīrtha.[2]

26cd–27 They are to be worshipped even by gods, so much the more by human beings.

28 Phalastuti: Whoever listens to, thinks of, or recites this story about the Mātṛtīrthas, will obtain a long happy life.

Ch. 113: The treacherous fifth head of Brahman

1 Brahman continues: Next to this holy place there is another one, not easily accessible to the gods, called Brahmatīrtha; it bestows pleasure and liberation on men.

2–4 When the armies of the gods stood waiting, after the Daityas had entered the nether world, followed by the Mothers, the fifth head of Brahman (the first-person narrator), which had the terrible shape of a donkey's head, addressed the Daityas, telling them not to flee and promising to devour the gods.

5–8ab Beholding this head, which could not be stopped by Brahman, the gods were frightened and asked Viṣṇu for protection. The discus-bearer, though willing to cut off the head, was afraid that the head might devour everything. He advised them to address the three-eyed one (= Śiva), who would be able to cut off and keep the head.

8cd Accordingly the gods, including Brahman, praised Śaṃbhu.

9 Sacrifice does not produce visible results for the sacrificer; believing Śiva to be the garant of results, people have turned against ritual (*pratikarma*) (?).[1]

10–14 Being pleased, the Lord of the gods (= Śiva) agreed to help them; he cut off the dreadful head with his nails and asked where to put it. Ilā said she was not able to bear it; so did the ocean, and the gods told Śiva that he alone was able to bear that head, which would cause the destruction of the world, be it cut off or not. Hearing this, Someśa (= Śiva) kept the head.

15 Seeing this, the gods went to the Gautamī and praised Śiva.

16 Concluding stanza,[2] summing up Śiva's action.

17 All the gods standing near Brahman praised Śiva on seeing his work.[3]

[2] Seems to be an interpolation, giving a further explanation of Mātṛtīrtha and disturbing the connection between 24ab and 26cd.

[1] In Upajāti-metre.

[2] In Upajāti-metre.

[3] Seems to duplicate v. 15, which, however, might itself have been inserted, to interpret v. 16 as a hymn by the gods in praise of Śiva.

18–21 Ever since, this holy place has been known as Brahmatīrtha; up to the present day, Brahman has (only) four heads. He who beholds Brahman's head will go to Brahman's abode. The place where Rudra (= Śiva) stood cutting off Brahman's head is called Rudratīrtha. There the sun is present, too, including the gods in his shape;[4] therefore the holy place is called Saurya (»belonging to Sūrya«), granting the fruit of all sacrifices. Who beholds the sun there will not be born again.

22–23 Brahman's fifth head, which had been cut off by Śiva, was placed in the region Avimukta; whoever beholds Brahman's head at the Brahmatīrtha or at Avimukta is freed even from Brahmin-murder.

Ch. 114: Gaṇeśa and the obstacle at the Sattra-rite of the gods

1 Brahman announces an account of Avighnatīrtha.

2–5 Once the gods performed a *sattra*-rite on the northern bank of the Gautamī, but it could not be completed, due to some obstacle. The gods asked Brahman (the first-person narrator) and Hari the reason; Brahman meditated and told them that obstacles caused by Vināyaka (= Gaṇeśa) kept the *sattra*-rite from being completed; the gods should therefore praise Gaṇeśa as Ādideva (»first god«), after bathing in the Gautamī.

6–18 Hymn by the gods to Gaṇeśa.[1]

6–8 Taking refuge in Gaṇeśa, to whom even the gods, like Viṣṇu and Śiva etc., pay homage and who was invoked by Śiva when he wanted to destroy the three cities; request to help the gods in completing their rite.

9–12 Reference to events in Gaṇeśa's childhood: Gaṇeśa's birth; protection of the moon in Śiva's locks; how Gaṇeśa got his name »Lambodara« (»potbellied«); consecration as »Gaṇeśa« (»Lord of the hosts«).

13 Description of Gaṇeśa holding the noose of obstacles and bearing an axe on his shoulder (with rhetorical question: »Who could be equal to him?«).

14–18 Homage to Gaṇeśa (each verse ending with a verb-form of homage in 1st person sing.).[2]

19–20 Thus praised, Gaṇeśa granted the boon that the *sattra*-rite was free from obstacles.

21–24 When the *sattra*-rite was completed, Gaṇeśa asked the gods to agree that anyone who praised him with this hymn (*stotra*) should be free from poverty and distress. He who bathed there and gave alms should be successful in his actions. The gods agreed and left for their abode.

25 Ever since, this holy place has been called Avighna(-tīrtha); it grants all wishes and removes all obstacles.

[4] Backward reference to ch. 110?

[1] In Upajāti-metre.

[2] Not plural form, as would be expected (cf. v. 6–8).

Ch. 115: Śiva's help to Śeṣa against the demons

1 Brahman announces an account of Śeṣatīrtha.

2-4 Once the great Nāga (snake) Śeṣa, the lord over the nether world, went to the nether world, surrounded by his snakes; the Rākṣasas, Daityas and Dānavas, however, expelled him from there. He went to Brahman (the first-person narrator), complaining and asking for protection.

5-6ab Brahman (the first-person narrator) advised him to go to the Gautamī and praise (Śiva) Mahādeva; nobody fulfils wishes like him.

6c-f So the Nāga went to the (Gautamī) Gaṅgā, bathed there and praised the lord of the gods.

7-9 Hymn by Śeṣa to Śiva.

7-9ab Formula of paying homage, with epithets of Śiva (in dative case).

9c-f Request to grant the desired protection.

10-12ab Pleased by this hymn, Śiva granted what Śeṣa desired; he gave him a spear for the destruction of the demons. With this spear the Nāga went to the nether world and defeated his enemies.

12cd-15ab After that Śeṣa returned to the place (at the Gautamī) where Hara (= Śiva) is present as (a Liṅga named) Śeṣeśvara. A cave originated where the king of the snakes came out of the nether world to see Śiva; from it Gaṅgā-water flowed and joined the Gaṅgā.

15cd-16 North of the god (i.e. the Liṅga representing Śiva) there is a large water basin. The Nāga performed a sacrificial rite there, where Agni is always present. This made the water become hot; it flowed into the Gaṅgā.

17 Having satisfied Śiva, the pleased Nāga obtained the nether world from Śiva and went there.

18-19ab Ever since, this holy place has been called Nāgatīrtha;[1] it frees from disease and poverty, and bestows long life and prosperity.

19cd-20ab Phalastuti: Who listens to, recites, or remembers (the account of) this holy place, where there is (the Liṅga named) Śeṣeśvara, and where Śiva bestows energy (*śakti*) ...[2]

20c-f There are 2100 places of pilgrimage on both banks (of the Gautamī), which bestow all sorts of good fortune.

Ch. 116: Death as slaughterer at a sacrifice of sages

1-2ab Brahman announces the holy place called »Mahānala« or »Vaḍavānala«, where there is (a Liṅga named) Mahānala and the river Vaḍavā.[1]

[1] But cf. v. 1, where it is called Śeṣatīrtha.

[2] Sentence incomplete.

[1] cf. ch. 110, v. 200cd above, where both names are mentioned for the first time; the story told in the present chapter has little to do with the fire and the mare.

2cd–3ab In former times the sages performed a *sattra*-rite in the Naimiṣa-forest; they employed Death as slaughterer (*śamitṛ*).

3cd–5ab While Death was occupied with his duty as slaughterer during this *sattra*-rite, nobody died; except the cattle all beings became immortal. Consequently, the Triviṣṭapa-heaven was empty, the world of mortals overcrowded.

5cd–9 The gods asked the demons to disturb the *sattra*-rite of the sages. Asked what they would get as a reward, the gods promised them half of the sacrifice. Now the demons went quickly to destroy the *sattra*-rite.

10–13 When the sages saw them, they consulted with Death what to do. They left their hermitage and went to the Gautamī, in order to complete the sacrifice. There they bathed and took their refuge in the Great Lord (= Śiva), praising him with folded hands.

14 Hymn by the sages to Śiva, who as creator, as multiform (*viśvarūpa*) and as Someśvara (»lord of the moon«) had made everything by his play (*līlā*).[2]

15–16 Continuation of the hymn by Death, taking refuge in Śiva, who is able to do everything by his wish alone, and referring to Śiva as Mahānala (»great fire« or »by whom great fire is brought into existence«) and Mahākāya (»having a huge body«), who wears a big snake as adornment.

17–19 Asked by Śiva what he wanted, Death told him about the fear (or danger) caused by the Rākṣasas and asked him to protect the sacrifice. Śiva complied, and the *sattra*-rite was completed.

20–22ab When the oblations were distributed, the gods approached. Since they had incited the Rākṣasas to disturb the sacrifice, the sages cursed them that the Rākṣasas should be their cruellest enemies. Ever since, the Rākṣasas have always been hostile to the gods.

cd–24ab Now the gods addressed the Kṛtyā (in shape of) a mare,[3] asking her to marry Death. From the sprinkling water (at the wedding-ceremony) the river Vaḍavā came into existence.[4] It is said that Death established a Liṅga there, named Mahānala.[5]

cd–25ab Ever since, this holy place has been called Vaḍavāsaṃgama (»confluence of the Vaḍavā«). The place where the Liṅga named »Mahānala« is established grants enjoyment and liberation.

25c-f There are one thousand holy places on both banks of the Gautamī, which grant all wishes and destroy sins simply by being remembered.

[2] In Indravajrā-metre.

[3] She has not been mentioned in the whole story as told in this chapter, but seems to belong to the story told in ch. 110.

[4] cf. ch. 110 v. 200ab, where no explanation is given why the Kṛtyā changed into a river.

[5] Obviously because he had praised Śiva as Mahānala (cf. v. 16 above). The »Great Fire« (*mahānala*), however, has little to do with the story told in this chapter, but seems to belong to ch. 110, like the Kṛtyā in shape of a mare.

Ch. 117: Datta Ātreya and Śiva

1 Brahman announces an account of Ātmatīrtha, where Śiva (is present in the Liṅga called) Jñāneśvara; it bestows enjoyment and liberation.

2-5 The brother of Durvāsas and son of Atri was named Datta; he was knowledgeable and dear to Hara.[1] Once he asked his father how and where he could obtain the knowledge of the *brahman* (*brahmajñāna*). Atri advised him to go to the Gautamī and praise Maheśvara (= Śiva).

6 Datta went to the (Gautamī) Gaṅgā and praised Śaṃkara with devotion.

7-17 Hymn by Datta to Śiva.[2]

7-11 Reference to his own ignorance, defectiveness, and unworthiness, concluding with the request to rescue him.

12 Śiva's incomparable compassion and helpfulness.

13 Reference to his own unworthiness even to praise Śiva.

14 Request to place the word »Soma« in his mind, despite his lack of *dharma* and devotion.

15 Expression of his wish not for sovereignty over the gods, but for Siva to place his foot-lotus into Datta's heart.

16-17 Request to dwell where the name Śiva is heard; repetition of his entreaty in general, addressing Śiva as Gaurīpati, Śaṃkara, Somanātha, Viśveśa, Karuṇānidhi, and Akhilātman.

18-19ab Pleased by this hymn, Bhava (= Śiva) showed himself favourable to the ascetic. Ātreya asked for knowledge of the Self (*ātmajñāna*),[3] for liberation, delight in Śiva,[4] and greatness for this holy place. All this was granted by Śiva, who then disappeared.

20c-f Ever since, this place has been known as Ātmatīrtha to the wise; by bathing there and giving alms one may obtain liberation.

Ch. 118: Story of the Rākṣasas Aśvattha and Pippala

1 Brahman continues, describing Aśvatthatīrtha, Pippalatīrtha, and Mandatīrtha.

2-9 In former times, Agastya was the lord of the southern direction. At the request of the gods, however, he first moved slowly to the Vindhya-mountains (description), accompanied by a thousand hermits; then, having been honoured as a guest, he addressed the Vindhya-mountains, taking leave for a pilgrimage to the South, and asking him to grant hospitality to anybody who wanted it; the mountain was to stay there until Agastya returned. The mountain agreed, and Agastya went south, accompanied by the hermits. He slowly approached the Gautamī, in order to perform a *sattra*-rite there, in which he was involved for one year.

[1] Ms A reads »to Hari«.

[2] In Upajāti-metre.

[3] But cf. v. 3 above.

[4] Ms E reads: »devotion to Śiva«, which may be the correct reading, as *bhakti* may have been changed to *bhukti* in connection with *mukti*.

10–14 There were two Rākṣasas named Aśvattha and Pippala, sons of Kaiṭabha. Wishing to obtain an opportunity to destroy the sacrifice, Aśvattha assumed the shape of a tree, and Pippala the shape of a Brahmin; both oppressed the Brahmins: whoever came near the Aśvattha-tree was devoured by it; likewise Pippala, as a Brahmin chanting the Sāmaveda, devoured all his pupils; he was still more terrible.

15–18 When the hermits saw the Brahmins diminishing, they knew that these two were Rākṣasas, and proceeded to the southern bank. They went to Manda (= Śanaiścara, the planet Saturn), son of the sun, who was practising asceticism, and told him about the matter. Śanaiścara promised to slay the Rākṣasas as soon as his asceticism was completed. The hermits offered him their own asceticism; Śanaiścara agreed.

19–24ab In the disguise of a Brahmin he approached the Aśvattha-tree and circumambulated it. Thinking him to be a Brahmin, the Rākṣasa devoured him, as he usually did. Inside his body, Manda opened his eye, looked at the Rākṣasa's intestines and reduced him to ashes. Then he went, as a pupil, to the other Rākṣasa, who had assumed the shape of a Brahmin. As it was his habit, Pippala devoured his new pupil; Bhānu's son (= Śanaiścara), however, reduced him to ashes, too, by one glance.

24cd–30 His task fulfilled, Bhānu's son asked the hermits what else he should do. Overjoyed, the hermits granted him boons. He wished (1) that those who take hold of an (or: this) Aśvattha-tree on his day (i.e. Saturday) should be successful in their doings and should not be influenced by Saturn; (2) that those who bathe at the Aśvatthatīrtha should be successful in their doings; (3) that those who get up early on Saturdays and touch the Aśvattha-tree should be freed from any bad influence of the planets. (Ed. VePr inserts three lines after v. 29, quoting a formula to counteract evil.)

31–32ef Ever since, this holy place is known as »Aśvattha« (and/or) »Pippala«. There are also holy places called »Śanaiścara«, »Āgastya«, »Sāttrika« (»belonging to the *sattra*-rite«), »Yājñika« (»belonging to the sacrifice«), and »Sāmaga« (»chanting the Sāmaveda«) etc., amounting to the number of 16,000 and 8 (?) in total. Bathing there and giving alms grants the merit of all sacrifices.

Ch. 119: The plants and Soma

1 Brahman continues: Somatīrtha is the name of another holy place taught by great persons; bathing there and giving alms bestows the merit of drinking Soma.

2–4cd Before anything else there were the plants, the »mothers« even of Brahman (the first-person narrator); they were previous to all other beings.[1] *dharma* is based on them, as well as studying (the Veda) and performing sacrifices. The three worlds, including animate and inanimate beings, are sustained by them.

4ef–8 The plants asked Brahman (the first-person narrator) for a husband; Brahman promised them a king as husband. The plants asked him where to go (to find the

[1] cf. RV 10,97.1b: *yā oṣadhīḥ pūrvā jātā devebhyas triyugaṃ purā* ... and v. 4ab: *oṣadhīr iti mātaras tad vo devīr upa bruve* ....

husband); Brahman advised them to go to the Gautamī and praise her; this would get them a king worshipped by the worlds. So the plants went to the Gautamī and praised her.

9–12 Hymn by the plants to the Gautamī.[2]

9 Rhetorical question, what should all the distressed do without the Gautamī.[3]

10 Who could know his fate? Gautamī, however, destroys all evil.

11 Nobody knows the power of her, who is kept on Śiva's head, though he is embraced by Gaurī (?).[4]

12 Homage to Gautamī (*namo 'stu te* with vocatives referring, partly, to events related in ch. 74: Flowing from Viṣṇu's step, flowing from Śiva's matted hair).[5]

13–17 Thus praised, Īśā (= Gaṅgā) asked what they wanted. They expressed their wish for a glorious king as their husband. As Gaṅgā and the plants are immortal, she granted them a similar husband: Soma, whose self is *amṛta* (i.e. the nectar of immortality). Gods, sages, and the plants agreed to her words and went back to their abodes.

18–19 The place where the plants obtained Soma as their husband is called Somatīrtha; it grants the effect of drinking Soma. By bathing and alms-giving there one will reach heaven.

20 Phalastuti: Whoever listens to, recites, or remembers this (account) with devotion will have a long life, and will get sons and wealth.

Ch. 120: The plants and Soma (contd)

1 Brahman continues by describing the holy place named Dhānyatīrtha, which abounds in food, gives rest to men, and removes all misfortune.

2 When the plants had obtained King Soma as their husband, they uttered a speech pleasant to the whole world and the Gaṅgā.

3–7ab Speech of the plants:

3ab There is a vedic *gāthā* known to Veda-experts.[1]

3cd–5 Anyone who gives away fertile ground and the mother (i.e. a cow?) near the (Gautamī) Gaṅgā will obtain all he wishes; who gives fertile ground, cows, and plants to the image of Viṣṇu, Brahman, and Īśa (= Śiva) will come to know all that is imperishable and obtain all his wishes.

6–7ab The *brahman*-expert who gives away plants, knowing that they are Soma's queens and that Soma is their husband, will obtain all his desires and reach Brahman's world.

7cd The plants continue (with a »vedic *gāthā*« addressed to King Soma).

8–14 »Vedic *gāthā*« recited by the plants.[2]

[2] In Upajāti-metre, mixed with Vaṃśasthavila-metre.

[3] Pādas ab in Vaṃśasthavila-metre.

[4] Seems to allude to ch. 74.

[5] Pādas ab in Vaṃśasthavila-metre.

[1] Probably refers to v. 8–14 below?

[2] cf. RV 10,97, especially v. 22, which is quoted literally, except 22c, in v. 9; its last quarter,

8 Introductory verse, starting with both refrains: »Whoever gives us to the twice-born...« »...that one, o king, do we protect«, and continuing with a changed quotation of RV 10,97.23ab, addressing Soma as lord of the plants.

9–13 Representation of the »vedic *gāthā*« (v. 9) and similarly composed verses, containing a statement on the nature and importance of the plants, a relative phrase (»who gives us ... to Brahmins«) and the refrain »that one, o king, do we protect«.

14 Phalastuti: Whoever listens to, remembers, or recites this vedic *gāthā* with devotion, »that one, o king, do we protect.«

15 The place where this »vedic *gāthā*« was recited by the plants, »together with King Soma«,[3] on the bank of the Gautamī, is called Dhāṇyatīrtha.

16–18 Ever since, this (place) has been called »Auṣadhya« (»belonging to the plants«), »Saumya« (»belonging to Soma«), »Amṛta«, »Vedagāthā«, as well as »Mātṛtīrtha«; bathing there, murmuring (prayer-formulas), oblations, giving alms, satiation of the ancestors, and granting food will cause infinite results. There are 1600 holy places on both banks of the Gautamī, which destroy all evil and misfortune.

Ch. 121: Kaṭha and his special gift to his teacher Bharadvāja

1 Brahman announces an account of what happened at the confluence of the Vidarbha and the confluence of the Revatī, which is known to Purāṇa-experts.

2–5 Once there was an ascetic sage, named Bharadvāja, who had a very ugly sister, named Revatī. Seeing her ugly shape, he was worried to whom he should give her in marriage, since nobody would marry a girl who caused only discomfort.

6–9 One day a handsome youth of sixteen years, named Kaṭha, reached the hermitage, paid homage to Bharadvāja, and asked him to be his teacher, as he wanted to study the vedic lore and philosophy.

10–12 Bharadvāja agreed to accept him as his pupil and to teach him all he knew: Purāṇa, Smṛti-literature, Veda, and *dharma*-literature, quoting a maxim about an ideal pupil, who could be obtained only by meritorious deeds. Kaṭha affirmed he was a sinless, obedient, devoted, and truthful pupil of noble family.

13–15 Now Bharadvāja taught him all his knowledge; when the instruction was completed, Kaṭha asked his teacher what he should give him, for: »Those who do not give any reward to their teachers go to hell.«

taṃ rājan pārayāmasi (vedic verbal form, for *pārayāmaḥ*), is used as a refrain in each verse; similarly, the substitute of RV 10,97.22c in v. 9c *yo 'smān dadāti viprebhyas* (for *yasmai kṛṇoti brāhmaṇas*) is, slightly changed, repeated in v. 8–12. RV 10,97.23c *upastir asto so 'smākam* is changed into *upāstir asti sāsmākam*, which makes a totally different sense; one might suspect that the phrase *yo 'smān dadāti viprebhyas* is a metamorphosis of RV 10,23d *yo asmān abhidāsati*, either by misunderstanding or by intentionally re-interpreting the sense. The metrical irregularity in 9b (apparently only 7 syllables) is explained by vedic metrical rules: *rājñā* must be read as *rāj(a)nā* (cf. Oldenberg: Ṛgveda. Textkritische und exegetische Noten II, p. 312).

[3] Repetition of 9b, including the metrical peculiarity.

16–18 Bharadvāja demanded that Kaṭha should marry Bharadvāja's sister. Kaṭha refused, arguing that the relationship between teacher and disciple was like that between father and son; how could there be the bond of marriage? But Bharadvāja insisted; he wanted his order carried out. As his reward (*dakṣiṇā*) Kaṭha should marry Revatī.

19–21ab Now Kaṭha agreed and took Revatī in marriage, according to the rules. After he had seen her, he paid homage to Śaṃkara (= Śiva), in order to obtain a beautiful shape for Revatī and Śiva's favour for himself. Consequently Revatī got a shape of unsurpassable beauty.

21ab–22 The sprinkling-water that flowed into the (Gautamī) Gaṅgā became a river, named Revatī, which grants the charm of beauty.

23 Kaṭha performed a further (ceremony of) sprinkling water with different (sorts of) Darbha-grass (*vividhair darbhaiḥ*), for the sake of an auspicious shape; from this the river Vidarbhā came into existence.

24–25 He who bathes at the confluence of Revatī is freed from all evil and will be honoured in Viṣṇu's world; who bathes at the confluence of Vidarbhā and Gautamī, obtains enjoyment and liberation in that very moment.

26 There are one hundred holy places on both banks, which remove all evil and bestow all sorts of accomplishments.

Ch. 122: Stories of Dhanvantari and of Indra regaining his kingdom

1–2 Brahman continues: On the northern bank of the (Gautamī) Gaṅgā there is a holy place named Pūrṇatīrtha; even a man who bathes there unwittingly, obtains welfare. Who on earth could describe the greatness of this place, where (Viṣṇu) with his discus and (Śiva) with (his spear) Pināka are both present?

3–47 *Story of Dhanvantari*[1]

3–7 In former times, at the beginning of a cosmic cycle there was (a king) named Dhanvantari, the son of Āyus; after performing many sacrifices, bestowing many gifts, and enjoying lovely pleasures, he turned indifferent towards worldly objects. On the top of a mountain, near the seashore, on the bank of the river Gaṅgā, at a temple of Śiva and Viṣṇu, especially at a holy confluence, asceticism, oblations and prayers are indestructible. Knowing this, Dhanvantari went and practised extensive asceticism at the confluence of the Gaṅgā with the ocean.[2]

8–20 Earlier, the king had once defeated a great demon who had hidden in the ocean out of fear. Seeing that Dhanvantari had now left his kingdom to his son and had started to practise asceticism, this Asura, named Tama(s), came out of the ocean and

[1] Seems not to be identical with the physician of the gods, who was reborn in the house of the king of Kāśi (cf. ch. 11.35–40, above).

[2] Seems to refer to the original (Bhāgīrathī) Gaṅgā, not to the Gautamī (= Godavarī).

approached the king, who was absorbed in his observances on the bank of the Gaṅgā. In order to take revenge on his enemy, the demon assumed the form of a beautiful young woman (description), who roamed before the king, singing and dancing, and smiling happily, for a long time. Finally, the king asked her who she was, what she was doing there, and why she looked so happy. She replied that his presence was the reason of her happiness, and that she was Indra's good fortune (*lakṣmī*), which could be obtained only by immense merit. Now Dhanvantari gave up his asceticism, thinking only of her and being totally devoted to her, until she disappeared, consuming his great asceticism.

21–24ab At that moment Brahman (the first-person narrator) came to that place, in order to grant boons to Dhanvantari. Seeing Dhanvantari's grief, he told him that he had been deceived by his enemy Tama(s), and consoled him that »All young women delight and cause pain to men, how much more one formed of illusion?«

24cd–27 Asked by Dhanvantari what he should do, Brahman advised him to praise Janārdana (= Viṣṇu), the creator of the world, who grants success to men.

28 So Dhanvantari went to the Himālaya and praised Viṣṇu.

29–43 Hymn by Dhanvantari to Viṣṇu.

29–42 Acclamations (»Hail« plus vocatives or datives), often with a formula addressing Viṣṇu as granting what he himself is identified with, e.g. *kāmada kāmas tvam*.

43 Request to put his hand on his head.[3]

44–47 Thus praised, the lord who bears the conch, the discus, and the club, granted him a boon. Dhanvantari wished for lordship over the gods. Viṣṇu agreed and disappeared; Dhanvantari became ruler of the gods.

48–99 *Story of how Indra regained his lordship over the gods for ever*

48–49 Indra had already been expelled from his kingdom thrice before, as a result of his deeds, once by Nahuṣa because of slaying Vṛtra,[4] once because of killing Sindhusena,[5] and once because of having violated Ahalyā.[6]

50–54ab Trying to remember why he had been expelled (this time), he turned to Vācaspati (= Bṛhaspati) as the expert of *karman*-knowledge. Bṛhaspati, however, sent him to Brahman, since he knew past, present, and future.

54cd–62 Both went to Brahman (the first-person narrator) and asked him what fault had caused Śacī's husband (= Indra) to lose his kingdom. Brahman replied that it was the fault of incomplete *dharma*, giving a list of faults connected with the sacrifice and a description of the consequent ill fate. Then he informed them about the events that had happened to Dhanvantari (summary in catchwords) and what had happened in (Indra's) former births.

[3] In Upajāti-metre.

[4] cf. ch. 96 above.

[5] This name occurs only in connection with the Vārāhatīrtha (ch. 79 above); there, however, it is Viṣṇu in the shape of a boar, who kills the demon Sindhusena for having taken the sacrifice of the gods to the nether world, and is purified by the Gaṅgā-stream.

[6] cf. ch. 87 above.

63–67ab Now Indra and Bṛhaspati asked Brahman how to counter this fault. Brahman advised them to go to the Gautamī and praise Hari and Śaṃkara (= Viṣṇu and Śiva); except these three there was no other means.

67c-f Both went to the Gautamī, bathed there and praised the two gods.

68–73 Hymn by Indra to Viṣṇu, referring to Viṣṇu's incarnations as fish, tortoise, boar, man-lion, dwarf, horse (Hayarūpa), Trivikrama, Buddha, Rāma, Kalkin, and Jāmadagnya; to his identity with Varuṇa, Indra, Yama, Parameśa, and the three worlds; to his bearing Sarasvatī in his mouth and Lakṣmī on his chest; to his many arms, legs, ears, eyes, and heads, and to his compassion.

74–82 Hymn by Bṛhaspati to Śiva.[7]

74 Theological description of Śiva.

75–80 Description of devotees and devotion to Śiva.

81 Request to Śiva to show favour to Bṛhaspati as Śiva's devotee.

82 Homage to Someśvara, who is the subtle and the gross, father and mother, existent and non-existent.

83–86 Thus praised, the two gods granted them every wish; Indra wished that his unsteady kingdom might become stable.

87–92 Having heard Hari's (= Indra's) words, both gods, who were full of compassion, agreed and told them to go to the place Mahātīrtha, sacred to the three gods, on the bank of the Gautamī, and bathe there; then Bṛhaspati should anoint Indra with a formula of praise to the Godāvarī, for the sake of Indra's welfare (*maṅgala*). Whoever bathes in the Gautamī, remembering this formula, would reach, by the grace of Indra and Bṛhaspati, the completion of his *dharma*, and be freed from faults of former births.

93–94 Indra and Dhiṣaṇa (= Bṛhaspati) acted accordingly; Bṛhaspati anointed Indra. Thereby the holy river Maṅgalā came into existence; its confluence with the (Gautamī) Gaṅgā is especially auspicious.

95–97ab Praised by Indra, Viṣṇu became visible; Indra obtained the three worlds as his domain. This »cow« consisting of the three worlds was given to Hari by Indra; therefore he (i.e. Viṣṇu as: Kṛṣṇa) is named »Govinda« (»finding cows«).[8]

97cd–99 By (the power of) Maheśvara (= Śiva) Indra's rulership became steady. At the place where Bṛhaspati, the teacher of the gods, praised Śiva for the sake of the stability of Indra's kingdom, there is a Liṅga named Siddheśvara.

100–102 Ever since, this holy place has been famous as Govinda(-tīrtha), as Maṅgalāsaṃgama, Pūrṇatīrtha, Indratīrtha, Bārhaspatya (»belonging to Bṛhaspati«), where there is the Liṅga named Siddheśvara and the Viṣṇu (statue named) Govinda. (The merit of) bathing, alms-giving and any other good deed performed there is to be known as imperishable and dear to the ancestors.

103 Phalastuti: Whoever listens to, recites, or remembers the (account of the) greatness of this holy place, to him it restores his lost kingdom.

104 There are 37,000 holy places on both banks of the Gaṅgā, which grant the achievement of all (goals).

[7] In Upajāti-metre.

[8] v. 96ab seems to be interpolated in the wrong place.

105 There is no holy place comparable to Pūrṇatīrtha; the life of a man who does not visit it and pay homage to it is in vain.

Ch. 123: Story of Daśaratha and his dutiful son Rāma

1 Brahman continues with an account of Rāmatīrtha, which destroys even the sin of embryo-murder.[1]

2-33ab *Daśaratha's fight with the demons*[2]

2-7ab Daśaratha, a famous hero, born from the Solar Dynasty, powerful as Śakra (= Indra), ruled his inherited kingdom like Bali. He had three wives, Kauśalyā, Sumitrā, and Kaikeyī. While he was king in Ayodhyā, with Vasiṣṭha as his family-priest, there was no disease, no hunger, no lack of rain; all members of the four castes and stages of life were happy.

cd-14ab During his reign there was a great battle between gods and demons; sometimes one party was victorious, sometimes the other. Brahman (the first-person narrator) tried to intervene, but they did not listen to him, and continued fighting. The gods went to Viṣṇu and Śiva, who told both sides to practise asceticism first and then to fight. Now gods and demons practised asceticism; the gods, however, attacked the demons, out of jealousy, and the battle started again; neither gods nor demons could gain victory.

14cd-22 Suddenly a heavenly voice proclaimed that the party on whose side King Daśaratha fought would be victorious.[3] Immediately both parties set forth. Vāyu (the wind) went hastily to Daśaratha and asked him to join the party of the gods; Daśaratha consented. Shortly afterwards, the demons arrived and also asked Daśaratha to help their king in battle. Daśaratha told them that he had been already asked by Vāyu and had promised his help to the gods.

23-33ab Now the king went to the Triviṣṭapa-heaven and fought against the demons. While the gods were looking on, Namuci's brothers destroyed the axle of Daśaratha's car with their arrows. Daśaratha did not notice it, but Kaikeyī did, who was standing near the king; she made her arm the axle of the car. With that car Daśaratha won the battle. After obtaining many boons from the gods, he returned to Ayodhyā. On the way he noticed what Kaikeyī had done for him; he granted her three (!) boons, but she told him the boons should stay with him. The king presented her with jewels and returned to his city. »What would not be given to dear young women at a fitting occasion?« (maxim)

[1] Ed. VePr and three of the mss. of the ASS-Ed. read: Brahmin-murder, which is, in the special connection of the story told, the preferable reading.

[2] i.e., prehistory of the boons granted to Kaikeyī; cf. Rm 2,9.11-18; 2,11.18-19; 2,18.32; in these allusions, however, Kaikeyī's help is quite different: she removes her wounded husband from the battle-field.

[3] cf. the story of Raji, ch. 11.1-26, above.

33cd-73 *Daśaratha kills the Brahmin boy*[4]

33cd-36ab Once Daśaratha went hunting in the forest at night; he dammed up water though he knew that »kings should be free from the seven passions« (maxim), climbed a stand (or: entered the hole, implying that he hunted from within the water?) and with his arrows killed the animals that came there for drinking.

36cd-43 At the same time an old hermit-couple, Vaiśravaṇa[5] and his wife, who were both blind and deaf, told their son that they were thirsty, and lamented about their troublesome life. The son, who was still a child, tried to console them by pointing out that he at least was there to serve them, and by quoting a maxim on the uselessness of sons who do not remove the sorrows of their parents.

44-48ab He made his parents climb the branch of a tree, took a vessel and went for water. Neither he nor the king recognised each other, when he entered the water and started to take it up with the vessel upside down; the king thought him to be a wild elephant and shot him with sharp arrows, though he knew that kings should not kill wild elephants. But »What does a person not do under the influence of fate?« (maxim).

48cd-61ab Pierced by the king's arrow the boy asked what he, a friendly Brahmin, had done to anyone. Hearing these words the king slowly went to the place; when he saw the Brahmin, he was paralysed as if he also had been struck by an arrow. Controlling himself, however, he asked the Brahmin who he was, and what could be done as an expiation, for »a Brahmin-murderer must not be touched or looked at by anyone, not even by dog-eaters«. The boy replied that he was not sorry for himself but for his blind parents, who had none but himself to look after them. He told the king to take the vessel and go to his parents in his place, otherwise they would die of thirst. With these words he expired.

61cd-68 The king dropped his bow and arrows, took up the vessel and went to the old couple, who were troubled because their son had not returned. When they heard the king's footsteps they addressed him as their son, but wondered why he did not reply.

69-73ab Full of pain, as if struck by an arrow, the king told them to take the water. Recognizing, however, that it was not the voice of their son, the couple refused to drink until they knew what had happened. The king told them that their son was at the water-place; but they insisted that he should tell them the whole truth.

73cd-76 The king reported what had happened. Now they ordered him to lead them to that place, but not to touch them, since the impurity caused by the touch of a Brahmin-murderer could never be removed. The king led them to their deceased son; touching his body, they lamented and cursed Daśaratha that he, too, should die from being separated from his son.

77-81 So saying they died. Daśaratha cremated them together with their son, then he returned to his capital. There he told all that had happened to Vasiṣṭha, as he had always been a refuge for the kings of the Solar Dynasty. Vasiṣṭha took counsel with

[4] cf. Rm 2,63-64.

[5] In both editions, the elements *vai* and *śravaṇa* of this name are written separately, in both places of its occurrence, so that the name seems to be Śravaṇa; it does not occur, however, without preceding *vai*.

the other Brahmins, then he advised the king to call Gālava, Vāmadeva, Jābāli, Kaśyapa, etc. and to perform many horse-sacrifices.

82–83 The king acted accordingly. Finally a heavenly voice stated that the king's body had become pure, that he would get sons, and that, by the grace of his eldest son, he would become sinless.

84–119ab *Rāma's adventures*[6]

84–86ab In due time sons were born to the king, by means of the hermit Ṛṣyaśṛṅga; Kauśalyā gave birth to Rāma, Sumitrā to Lakṣmaṇa and Śatrughna, and Kaikeyī to Bharata. All of them were intelligent, obedient and dear to their father.

86cd–96 One day Viśvāmitra asked the king for Rāma and Lakṣmaṇa to protect his sacrifices against Rākṣasas. At first Daśaratha refused, offering himself and his kingdom in their place, but Vasiṣṭha reminded him that no member of Raghu's family ever rejected a request. Thus the king had to call Rāma and Lakṣmaṇa and to hand them over to Viśvāmitra, ordering them to protect the sage's sacrifice. The boys took leave of their father and went off, together with Viśvāmitra.

97–105ab Viśvāmitra instructed them in all fields of Kṣatriya knowledge: about different weapons, learned traditions, about chariots, elephants, horses, performing and removing spells (*mantra*), etc. When their education was finished, they slew the Rākṣasī Tāṭakā for the sake of the inhabitants of the forest; they freed Ahalyā from the curse by touching her with their feet;[7] they protected Viśvāmitra's sacrifice from the Rākṣasas, slaying them with bow and arrows; finally Viśvāmitra took them to King Janaka for a visit, where they showed their knowledge and experience in archery in the assembly of kings; highly pleased, Janaka gave his daughter Sītā, who was not born from a womb, (to Rāma), as well as (other daughters) to Lakṣmaṇa, Bharata, and Śatrughna. King Daśaratha performed the wedding-ceremony of his four sons according to Vasiṣṭha's precepts.

105cd–109ab After some time, when the king was about to bestow the kingdom upon Rāma, his wife Kaikeyī, who was incited by fate in the shape of Mantharā, and was filled with jealousy, created an obstacle, insisting upon Rāma's exile and Bharata's installation as king. Daśaratha refused, but Rāma, who wanted his father to have spoken the truth, entered the forest, together with Sītā and Saumitri (= Lakṣmaṇa), thus entering the pure minds of good people.

109cd–115 After their departure, King Daśaratha, filled with the utmost grief, gave up his life, remembering them and the curse uttered by the Brahmin couple. According to his deeds, he was led to Yama's abode by Yama's servants: in the various terrible hells, named Tāmisra etc., he was roasted, cut to pieces, ground, bruised, dried up, bitten, burnt and submerged; thus he was tormented in the different hells.

[6] Comprising the events of Rm, Bālakāṇḍa and Ayodhyākāṇḍa.

[7] This allusion does not refer to the Ahalyā-story as told in the Gautamīmāhātmya (ch. 87 above), nor to the version told in the Bālakāṇḍa of the Rm (where she is cursed to become invisible), but to a version where she is cursed to become a stone or a rock, as common to all later adaptations of the Rāma-story.

116–120 Meanwhile Rāma had reached the Citrakūṭa-mountain, where he stayed for three years; after that he turned south, towards the Daṇḍaka-forest, famous in the three worlds. After entering this dreadful forest, which was inhabited by demons but void of hermits, he killed the demons and made the forest habitable for hermits. Until Rāma had approached to within five Yojanas of the Gautamī the king stayed in the hells.

121–186 *Daśaratha's redemption*

121–128ab Yama told his servants that Rāma was approaching the Gautamī, therefore his father should be pulled out of the hells. As long as Rāma was within five Yojanas of reaching the Gautamī, his father should not be tormented in the hells. Anyone who acted against Yama's words would be plunged into a dreadful hell. The Gautamī Gaṅgā, being Śiva's highest energy (*śakti*) in the form of water and being venerable even to Hari (= Viṣṇu), Brahman, and Īśāna (= Śiva), should not be in any way neglected by anyone. Even a sinner's son who merely thought of the Gautamī would be released; could a man who had a son like Rāma, and whose son was now staying at the Gautamī, be tormented in hell by anybody? (Rhetorical question).

128cd–139 So Yama's servants raised the king out of the hell where he was tormented, and told him about his good luck of having such a son. Daśaratha asked them why he had been pulled out of the hells so quickly. They informed him about the beneficial effect of his son's stay at the Gautamī; should Rāma perform the ancestral rites for his father there, Daśaratha would be released from all evil and go to the Triviṣṭapa-heaven. Daśaratha, wishing to go to Rāma and tell him these words, asked Yama's servants for leave. Full of compassion, they allowed him to go; thus he approached his son, in a terrible, tormented shape, and full of shame because of the deed he had committed.

140–146 Meanwhile Rāma had reached the Gaṅgā and settled there with Sītā and Lakṣmaṇa. On this day they did not find anything to eat. Lakṣmaṇa expressed his grief that, though being sons of Daśaratha, and in spite of Rāma's strength, they were deprived of food. Rāma replied that everything happened according to their deeds, and that they had not yet presented an oblation to the Brahmins; those who neglect them are always hungry. When they had bathed, honoured the deities and poured the oblation into the fire, they would surely be provided with food by a god.

147–157 While the brothers were talking to each other, Daśaratha slowly approached that place. Lakṣmaṇa thought him to be a demon and angrily ordered him to leave the place where the truthful king Rāma Dāśarathi stayed, otherwise he would shoot him. Daśaratha, however, called him with a low voice, his face bent down, and told his sons and his daughter-in-law who he was, and that he had been tormented in hell for having committed threefold Brahmin-murder. Rāma, Sītā, and Lakṣmaṇa bowed to him and asked him about the action which had caused this effect. Daśaratha replied that for Brahmin-murderers there was no expiation at all.

158–164 Upon these words, all of them were filled with grief. Remembering the king, the stay in the forest, the parents, the sad events, the falling into hell, etc., the king's son (= Rāma) was confused; seeing that the king (i.e. Rāma ?) lacked clear understanding, Sītā spoke, stating first of all that it was useless to lament, but that one should think about some counteraction; he should give her the sin of murdering the innocent Brahmin boy, who was devoted to his parents; she would perform an expiation for that sin, according to the Śāstras. The second sin would be taken over by Lakṣmaṇa, and the last one by Rāma himself.

65-169 Upon these words that were uttered firmly by Sītā, both brothers consented; Daśaratha replied that he was not surprised by her words, as she was Janaka's daughter and Rāma's wife; it was, however, not necessary for them to undergo any pain, but by their bathing in the Gautamī and performing the ancestral rites for him, he would be released from his threefold Brahmin-murder and enter the Triviṣṭapa-heaven. What Sītā had said was fitting to her noble birth. »Noble young women always let (others) cross the ocean of existence« (maxim). By the grace of the Godāvarī, what would be difficult to obtain? (rhetorical question)

70-172 Now they started to perform the ancestral rites for their father, but they had no food to offer. Lakṣmaṇa suggested preparing an oil-cake from Iṅgudi-fruits; Rāma agreed but was troubled by the poverty of the offering.

73-175 Suddenly a heavenly voice told Rāma to give up his grief; dedicated as he was to the *dharma*-rules without any deceitfulness, his poverty did not matter (?); but one who fulfilled his duties with riches gained by wickedness would fall into hell. Moreover there was an old saying, known from the Śāstras, that »Whatever kind of food a man consumes, the same kind of food is consumed by his deities.«[8]

-177ab As soon as the oil cake fell to the earth, Daśaratha disappeared. The place where the corpse touched the ground became the incomparable Śavatīrtha, which destroys even the accumulation of great sins.

cd-184 Now all guardians of the directions, Rudras, Ādityas, and the Aśvins appeared in their chariots; among them was Rāma's father, standing on an excellent chariot, praised by the Kiṃnaras, and shining as bright as the sun. Beholding these celestial hosts, Rāma did not recognise his father and asked where he was. A heavenly voice told Rāma and Sītā that he was among the gods, released from his threefold Brahmin-murder. The gods, too, addressed Rāma, praising him as a dutiful son and showing him his father, who had attained the splendour of the sun. »Though endowed with all sorts of good fortune, a sinner is like a burnt tree; though needy, a man of good actions looks like Candramauli (= Śiva).«

85-186 Daśaratha, too, gave him his blessings and praised his dutifulness.

87-190 The gods told Rāma to go wherever he liked; Rāma, however, wanted to know what else he could do for his father. The gods replied that no river was like the Gaṅgā, no son like him, no god like Śiva, and no man like one who saves (others from evil). Since Rāma had fulfilled his duty and saved his father, all should go to their abode; Rāma should go wherever he liked.

91-194 Rāma, seeing the greatness of the (Gautamī) Gaṅgā, told Sītā and Lakṣmaṇa that they were lucky to have seen the purifying Gaṅgā. He established a Liṅga and paid homage to the god consisting of 36 parts with 16 offerings. Then he praised Śiva with folded hands.

[8] cf. Rm 2,95.31 (ed. Baroda).

195-206 Hymn by Rāma to Śiva, describing Śiva.[9]

207-213ab When Śiva asked him what he wanted, Rāma replied that whoever recites this hymn will be successful in all his doings; that fathers who are staying in hell should be purified by their sons' offering the oblation for the deceased; that by bathing at this place all evil committed by thought, speech, or body should be destroyed; that the merit of giving anything, albeit small, should be imperishable at this place. Śiva agreed and disappeared. Rāma went slowly to the source of the Gautamī, together with his companions.

213cd-216 Ever since, this place has been called Rāmatīrtha. The place where Lakṣmaṇa dropped his arrow out of pity is called Bāṇatīrtha. Where Saumitri (= Lakṣmaṇa) bathed and paid homage to the Śiva-Liṅga, (the place called) »Lakṣmaṇa« came into existence, likewise (the one called) »Ṣītā« (?).

217 How could the excellence (of the merit) resulting from bathing there be described? (Rhetorical question). There is no holy place like Rāmatīrtha.

Ch. 124: Story of Indra and Diti[1]

1-2ab Brahman announces (an account of) Putratīrtha, which is also called Puṇyatīrtha (v.l. Samyaktīrtha)[2] and fulfils all desires merely by being listened to.

2cd-31 *Story of Diti and Kaśyapa*

2cd-3ab When Diti's and Danu's sons were ruined and Aditi's sons were superior in any respect, Diti went to Danu, jealous (of Aditi) out of grief at being separated from her sons.[3]

3cd-6 She told her that she could not bear seeing their rival's (= Aditi's) sons endowed with well-being and prosperity, and that she would rather die, since »even in dreams a rival's good fortune cannot be looked at« (maxim).[4]

7-8 Parameṣṭhin's son consoled her, telling her that Prajāpati knew an accomplishment and would tell her.[5]

9-11 Danu replied that Diti should please their husband Kaśyapa, in order to obtain her wishes.[6]

12-16 Accordingly Diti pleased Kaśyapa. The progenitor (*prajāpati*) Kaśyapa asked what he should give her. Diti wished for a son endowed with all qualities, who would win

[9] By *namāmi* plus accusatives; v. 201-202 contain relative clauses; v. 205 refers to how Śiva's third eye came into existence; in Upajāti-metre.

[1] cf. above 3.109cd-122 and Rm 1,46-47.10.

[2] Name or characterization as »holy« (»perfect«) place of pilgrimage?

[3] v. 3ab in Upajāti-metre.

[4] Mixture of different types of Triṣṭubh-metre (Triṣṭubh A in 3cd) and Jagatī-metre (4ab).

[5] In Upajāti-metre; insertion or remnant of an older story?

[6] According to manuscript E, which leaves out v. 9-10, the advice is obviously given by Parameṣṭhin's son.

all the worlds and be honoured by them. Kaśyapa replied that he would teach her a vow of twelve years; after that time he would make her pregnant as she desired.

17-18 Diti acted according to her husband's words and performed the vow he taught her; for »how can people obtain their wishes without visiting holy places, bestowing gifts, or performing vows?«

19-28ab Having fulfilled her vow, Diti conceived. Kaśyapa told her to observe very strict rules of purity; especially at dawn and dusk she should not sleep nor go with loose hair, nor eat or sneeze or yawn; she should suppress laughing and not stay outside of the house; she should never neglect her household tools; she should not lie down with her head pointing north, should not tell lies and should not look at any man except her husband. Acting accordingly, she would obtain a son who would be lord over the three worlds. She promised to do what he had told her. Kaśyapa went to the gods; in Diti's womb grew a strong embryo.

28cd-31 All this was known to the demon Maya, by magic power (*māyā*). As there was friendship between Indra and Maya, he went to Indra and told him, secretly, about Diti's and Danu's wish, about Diti's vow, and about the growth and strength of her embryo. »The only house of confidence is friendship, which is without fear of injury and is obtained if various favours (good deeds done for the friend?) have accumulated« (maxim).

32 Nārada asks how there could be friendship between Namuci's brother Maya and Indra, who had killed Maya's brother.

33-48 *Story of Indra and Maya*

33-36ab Brahman relates: In former times, Namuci was the lord of the Daityas. There was enmity between him and Indra. Once, when Śatakratu (= Indra) left the battle, Namuci followed him from behind. Being afraid, Śacī's husband (= Indra) dismounted his elephant Airāvata and entered foam. With foam the wielder of the thunderbolt (*vajrapāṇi*) slew his enemy.[7]

6cd-39ab When Namuci was destroyed, his younger brother Maya practised austerities for the destruction of him who had killed his brother; he obtained magic power, dreadful even for the gods. Having obtained boons from Viṣṇu, he became fond of presenting gifts, paying homage to the fires and to Brahmins; thus he waited for an opportunity to defeat Indra.

39cd-47 Indra, however, learning from Vāyu about Maya's liberality and that he was praised by all bards for his magic power and his readiness to kill him, assumed the shape of a Brahmin, went to Maya and asked him for a gift. Maya thought he was a Brahmin and granted him what he had asked for. Now Hari (= Indra) uttered his wish that he wanted Maya's friendship. Quite astonished Maya asked him why. Indra replied that he wished him not to be his enemy. Asked to tell the truth by Maya, Indra assumed his original shape, which is called the »thousand-eyed one« (*sahasrākṣa*). Maya was very astonished, but Indra embraced him, smilingly, as their friendship was now established. »Clever people succeed in obtaining their wishes by any means« (maxim).

[7] For another account of the story of Indra and Namuci, cf. ch. 129.4-8 below.

48 Ever since, Maya and Indra had been very dear to each other.

49–86 *Indra in Diti's womb*

49–52 Consequently, Maya told Indra everything. Asked by Indra what he should do, Maya gave him his magic power and advised him to go to Kaśyapa's hermitage, wait upon Diti, and finally enter her womb and cut her embryo into pieces.

53–67 Accordingly, Śakra went to Diti and waited upon her. She did not notice that these were the actions of Indra, her enemy, but the being in her womb, Kaśyapa's semen, knew it. The thousand-eyed one (= Indra) waited for a long time, thunderbolt in hand. One day, Diti lay down to sleep with her head to the north, at the time of dusk, and Indra knew that this was his chance. He entered her womb; the embryo was frightened, seeing Indra with his weapon, and addressed him, appealing to him not to slay him, his brother, but to protect him.[8] But if he wanted to fight with him, he should wait until he was born, for only in battle is it no sin to kill a person. Moreover, Indra would gain no fame by killing a mere child; it would be an action in no way fitting for him.

68–73ab Indra, however, cut the embryo with his weapon, for »there is no feeling of shame in those who are wrathful or greedy« (maxim). Yet the embryo did not die; the pieces told Indra that they were his brothers. Again he cut them, but they implored him not to kill them. When Indra saw them crying, now seven times seven, he told them, »Don't weep« (*mā ruta*);[9] thus the Maruts came into existence.

73cd–80 Still staying in Diti's womb, they addressed Agastya, in whose hermitage Diti was living, and informed him that Indra had acted like a dog-eater. Troubled by this news, Agastya informed Diti; then he cursed Indra that in battle his enemies should always see his back, for »it is comparable to death for those who flee, if the enemies see their backs in a battle« (maxim). Likewise, Diti cursed Indra to be humiliated by women, as he had not behaved in a manly way, and to lose his kingdom.

81–82 Meanwhile Kaśyapa returned to the hermitage and was informed by Agastya. Indra addressed him from inside the womb and told him that he would not come out because he was afraid of Agastya and Diti.[10]

83–86 Meanwhile Kaśyapa had come to know what his son (= Indra) had done and how Agastya and Diti had cursed him; he was much distressed. He asked Indra how he could do such a thing, and told him to come out. Full of shame, Indra left Diti's womb and declared that he would do now whatever was best.

87–140 *Śiva ends the conflict between Indra and Diti*

87–93 Thereupon Kaśyapa went to Brahman (the first-person narrator), told him all that had happened and asked him how Diti and Agastya could be appeased, how there could be friendship between Indra and the beings in Diti's womb, and how Indra

[8] cf. RV 1,170.2 (*kíṃ na iṇdra jighāṃsasi bhrā́taeo marútas táva ... mā́ naḥ samáraṇe vadhīḥ*); the story is, however, totally different.

[9] Wrong reading for *mā rudaḥ*, cf. Rm 1,46.20.

[10] Seems to be an anticipated repetition of 83 ff.; insertion?

could be free from Agastya's curse. Brahman replied that they should all go to the Gautamī, bathe there, and praise Śiva. Accordingly Kaśyapa went to the Gautamī, bathed, and praised Śiva, for »there are only two means of repelling difficulties: the holy river Gautamī and compassionate Śiva.«

94–99 Hymn by Kaśyapa to Śiva, asking for protection.[11]

100–107 Praised by Kaśyapa, Śiva appeared to him and granted him a boon. Kaśyapa told him all about Indra. Thereupon Vṛṣākapi (= Śiva) addressed Diti and Agastya, decreeing that the forty-nine Maruts should always be fortunate, that they should have their share in all sacrifices to Indra, and that Indra should never be defeated when with them. But all those who kill a brother, from this day onward, should suffer misfortune and division in their families.

108–109 After that Śambhu (= Śiva) turned to Agastya and asked him to give up his wrath, for the Maruts should be immortal (or gods).

110–122 Now Śiva addressed Diti, who had wished only for one son adorned with the sovereignty over the three worlds, and pointed out that she had got many sons instead, and hence should give up her anger, too. Moreover, she should choose a boon. Diti replied that she was quite satisfied with her powerful sons, but that she, indeed, would like to ask something else from Śiva. Encouraged to speak, she stressed how difficult but important it is to produce progeny, which is most desirable to all beings. Therefore Śiva should be gracious in this respect, from this day onward.

23–136ef Śiva's answer.

123–131 Śiva granted that all evil attaching to the lack of progeny or to barrenness of man or woman should perish by mere bathing: Anyone who bathes, offers fruits and recites this song of praise (*stotra*) will obtain a son; a woman without a son will get a son by bathing at this place. A woman three months pregnant and paying homage to Śiva with fruits and a hymn, will see Śiva and obtain a son like Indra. Those who are sonless because of their parents' fault will obtain a son by offering a ball of rice to their ancestors and giving some gold. The family of those, however, who embezzle deposits, steal jewels, and are without funeral rites, will not flourish. Even for those who did wrong and died there will be a refuge: that the living (members of their family) have praiseworthy progeny by visiting holy places.

32–136ab Whoever bathes at the confluence of Diti and Gaṅgā and pays homage to Śiva Mahādeva (list of epithets) with observances, who praises him with this hymn on the fourteenth and eighth nights (of the lunar fortnights), and gives gold and food to Brahmins according to his ability, will have a hundred sons. Having obtained all he wishes, he will finally enter Śiva's world.[12]

136c-f Whoever praises Śiva at any place with his hymn will obtain a son after six months.[13]

[11] Each *pāda* starts with the imperative *pāhi*, to which a vocative is added; v. 98 ends with *namo 'stu te*, and v. 99 contains the statement that Śiva is the only refuge of all distressed.

[12] This passage does not fit into Śiva's speech, as it names Śiva in the third person, with many praising adjectives.

[13] Conclusion to Śivas's speech, again in the first person.

137–139ab Ever since, this holy place has been called Putratīrtha; by bathing there and bestowing gifts one obtains every wish. Because of (Indra's) friendship (*maitrya*) with the Maruts it is called Mitratīrtha, and because Indra became sinless at this place it is called Indratīrtha. Where he obtained his own (*aindrī*) Śrī (or splendour) is the holy place named »Kamalā«.[14]

139cd–140cd Śiva said that all these holy places would grant anything desired; after that he disappeared. The others, having obtained what they wanted, went to where they had come from.

140ef There are 100,000 merit-bestowing holy places.

Ch. 125: The enmity between Anuhrāda and Ulūka[1]

1–2ab Brahman announces (the account of) Yamatīrtha, which is visited even by heavenly sages.

2cd–8 Once there was a pigeon, named Anuhrāda, whose wife was called Heti;[2] both were grandchildren of Death. They had sons and grandchildren. Anuhrāda's enemy was the king of birds, named Ulūka (»owl«), who also had sons and grandchildren; they were descendants of Agni. The enmity between the two birds lasted a long time. The pigeon lived on the northern bank of the (Gautamī) Gaṅgā, the king of birds named Ulūka on the southern bank. They fought against each other with their sons and grandsons for a long time, but neither of them could win.

9–12 The pigeon satisfied Yama, his grandfather, and obtained the special weapon belonging to Yama from him, whereas Ulūka pleased Agni and obtained the fire-weapon. The battle continued; Ulūka threw the fire-weapon upon the pigeon, whereas the pigeon threw the nooses of Yama upon his enemy; again neither of them was victorious.

13–14 Heti, however, the pigeon's wife, seeing her husband and her sons attacked by the fire-weapon, praised the fire with various verses.

15–17 Hymn by Heti to Agni.

15 Salutation to Agni, by whom the gods enjoy their sacrificial food.[3]

16–17 Characterization of Agni as the first of the gods, their priest and their messenger, who is present inside each living being as breath, and in whom Heti takes her refuge.

18–21 Thus praised, Agni asked her where to put his dangerous weapon to rest. She replied that the weapon should rest upon her, rather than on her son or her husband. Pleased with her words, Agni promised her that his weapon should burn neither her sons, her husband nor herself.

[14] Kamalā is another name of Śrī or Lakṣmī, here obviously connected with Indra (otherwise normally with Viṣṇu).

[1] For the names occurring in this story cf. RV 10.165 (which, however, does not contain even an allusion to any story).

[2] cf. RV 10,165.2–3: *hetíḥ pakṣíṇī* (»winged missile weapon«).

[3] In Upajāti-metre.

22 At the same time, the female owl saw her husband in Yama's nooses, suffering from the blows of Yama's stick (*daṇḍa*). So she went to Yama and, full of fear, praised him.

23-24ef Hymn by Ulūkī to Yama, describing Yama's intimidating influence on the behaviour of living beings.[4]

25-32 Thereupon the lord of the southern direction granted her a boon. She wished that her husband and her sons should be protected against Yama's nooses and stick. Yama asked her where his weapons should rest. She replied that they should rest upon her, but Yama showed pity on her and promised that they should all live without any harm.

33-43 Now Yama as well as Agni stayed their weapons. The pigeon and the owl made friendship with each other. Though granted a boon by the two gods, they wished for nothing for themselves, considering a selfish wish to be futile; even fire, water, sun, earth, different sorts of grain etc. act for the sake of the worlds; they agreed that both gods should have a resting-place on both sides of the (Gautamī) Gaṅgā, and that anyone, be he a good man or a sinner, who bathes, bestows gifts, murmurs prayers, and satisfies his ancestors, should obtain an everlasting result of his activities.

44-49 The gods agreed to this; Yama added that in seven families (or: generations? *vaṃśa*) of those who recite a hymn to Yama on the northern bank of the Gautamī, there will be no untimely death. Whoever regularly recites a praise of Death, will always be happy and safe from the 88,000 diseases. At this holy place a pregnant woman should bathe after three months (abl. ?), a barren one after six months (abl. ?), for seven days, then she would bear a hero who would live hundred years, splendid and sensible, and would increase (the number of) sons and grandsons. Offering a rice-ball to the ancestors will cause their liberation; by bathing there a man will be freed from all sins committed in thought, word, or deed.

50-53 After Yama, Agni told the two birds that by reciting a hymn to Agni on the southern bank (of the Gautamī) people would be free from harm caused by fire, even when staying in a designated (? *likhita*) house. A pure man who bathed at the Agnitīrtha and bestowed gifts would obtain the merit of performing an Agniṣṭoma-sacrifice.

54-56 Ever since, this holy place has been known as belonging to Yama and Agni, as »Kapota« (pigeon), »Ulūka« (owl), and »Hetyulūka«.[5] There are 3390 holy places; people who bathe there and bestow gifts will obtain sons and wealth and finally go to heaven.

[4] In Triṣṭubh-metres, mainly of the »A-type« (cf. H. Oldenberg: Zur Geschichte der Triṣṭubh, 1915/1916), nearly each *pāda* beginning with the expression *tvadbhītāḥ* (»being afraid of you«), which must be read in four syllables for the sake of the metre. In two cases, v. 23a and 24a, the metre is, even then, not correct. v. 23a may be corrected by replacing *anu-* (in *anudravante*) by a monosyllabic preverb and *janās* by the older form *janāsas* (cf. the refrain of RV 2,12 *sa janāsa indraḥ*, quoted below in ch. 140, v. 22). In v. 24a, one would have to accept a double *saṃdhi* (*t(u)vadbhītānāśakam* ...), in order to obtain a normal Triṣṭubh without caesura.

[5] Or: is named »Hetyulūka« after the pigeon (*kapota*) and the owl (*ulūka*).

Ch. 126: Competition between Agni and the waters

1-2 Brahman announces that he will tell what happened at the holy place named Tapastīrtha, which increases asceticism, grants all things desired and increases the joy of the ancestors: the discussion among the sages about Agni and the waters.

3-11 One party of sages believed the waters to be the more important, the other party the fire.

4-8 Arguments for the superiority of Agni: There is no life without Agni, for he is the soul of life (i.e. the breath), the self (*ātman*) and the offering (*havya*); by him everything is born. He supports the universe, he is the world consisting of light; nothing is beyond (or higher than) him.[1] He is the semen placed by a man into the »field«, the woman. From him the gods obtain their power (*śakti*); he is the mouth (or first, *mukha*) of the gods, hence there is nothing beyond him.

9-11 Arguments for the superiority of the waters: Food originates from the waters as well as purity; everything is supported by them; they are regarded as the Mothers. Water is the life of the three worlds, as it is said by those who know the former events; the waters are the origin of the nectar of immortality (*amṛta*) as well as of the plants.

12-16ab Thus discussing both points of view, both sides, those representing the Veda and those who contradicted them, went to Brahman (the first-person narrator) and asked him about the matter. Brahman replied that water and fire should be regarded as equally important, for the world was born from both, there was no difference.

16cd-19ab The sages, however, were not satisfied by this answer. They went to Vāyu, the wind, and asked him the same question. Vāyu decided that the fire should be regarded as superior, everything being founded on him.

19cd-22 Again the sages did not agree. They went to the earth and asked her, as the supporter, for the truth. The earth regarded the waters as the most important, for everything was born from the waters.

23 Being dissatisfied once more, the sages turned to him who lies in the milk-ocean (= Viṣṇu) and praised the wielder of conch, discus and club with various hymns (*stotra*).

24-27 Hymn by the sages to Viṣṇu, describing him as omniscient, as abode of the whole universe after the end of one cosmic cycle, as imperishable and immeasurable, as truth etc. He is the inner soul of each being that has a body; he is all, and all is in him. However, there are still some people who do not know him, who is inside, outside, everywhere.[2]

28-29 Thereupon a heavenly voice was heard, advising them to pay homage to both, fire and water, in order to see for whom a result occurred first; thus the superior being could be recognized.

30-32ab The sages, who were very tired and quite indifferent, went to the mother of all worlds, the Gautamī, to practise austerities. There they paid homage, the advocates of the waters to the waters, the defenders of the fire to Agni.

[1] This phrase is repeated (like a refrain) one and a half verses later and, with a slight change, at the end.

[2] In Upajāti-metre, 26b showing A-type Triṣṭubh.

32cd–35 Sarasvatī, however, the heavenly voice, again addressed them, deciding the case with the following arguments: Agni is born from the waters, without water even Agni could not be worshipped; water establishes purity, without bathing in clear, cold water, nobody, be he Veda-expert or not, is worthy to perform his rites. Therefore the waters should be regarded as superior.

36 Having heard these arguments, the sages agreed to the superiority of the waters.

37–39 The place where this *sattra*-rite of the sages had been performed is called Tapastīrtha, Sattratīrtha, or Agnitīrtha; some know it as belonging to Sarasvatī (*sārasvata*). By bathing there and bestowing gifts one obtains all things desired. There are 1400 holy places; by bathing there etc. one attains heaven and liberation.

Ch. 127: The sacrificer kidnapped by a demon

1 Brahman continues: On the northern bank of the (Gautamī) Gaṅgā there is a holy place called Devatīrtha; (the account of) its origin destroys all sins.

2–4ab There was a virtuous king named Ārṣṭiṣeṇa; his wife Jayā was like a second Lakṣmī. He had a son named Bhara, skilful in archery and knowing the Veda; his wife was called Suprabhā.

4cd–9ab King Ārṣṭiṣeṇa, having bestowed his kingdom upon his son, prepared himself to perform a horse-sacrifice on the bank of the river Sarasvatī, together with his chief priest. When he was consecrated by the best of priests, well-versed in the Vedas and Śāstras, the Dānava king Mithu disturbed the sacrifice and carried off the sacrificer, his wife and his priest to the nether world. Thereupon the gods and the priests returned to their abodes.

9cd–15 The son of the king's chief priest, named Devāpi, was still a child; he wondered about the absence of his father and asked his mother where he had gone, stressing that he could not live without his father; if she did not tell him, he would enter fire or the waters. His mother replied that his father had been carried off, together with the royal couple, by a Dānava. The child insisted upon being told the details: where they had been carried off, how and by whom, during which action, who had been witness, and what was the Dānava's abode. His mother told him that the demon Mithu had abducted them to the nether world during a sacrifice, while the gods, the fire, and the Brahmins had been looking on.

16–22 Now Devāpi made up his mind to go to the gods, the fire, the priests, or the demons, in search for his father. He went to Bhara, the king's son, and informed him of his intention of bringing back the abducted by any means (list of religious practices), for »of what use is a person who does not respond, when destruction is arising?« (maxim). King Bhara should rule his kingdom and protect Devāpi's mother, until he returned. Bhara told him not to worry and wished him best luck.

23–28 First Devāpi, concentrating upon the foot of the lord of the gods, went to the priests, bowed to them and complained that they should have protected the sacrifice, the sacrificer, his priest and his wife; but the king etc. had been carried off by a demon in their presence. Therefore they should restore the abducted persons safe and sound, otherwise they would be cursed. The priests replied that Agni was the most venerable deity of the sacrifice; therefore they, as servants of Agni, were not responsible.

29-34 Leaving the priests, Devāpi went to Jātavedas (= Agni), paid homage to him and told him everything. Agni explained to him that he himself as well as the priests were servants of the gods, who consume the oblations and protect the sacrifice. Now Devāpi summoned the gods through their messenger Agni. When they came, he bowed to them and informed them of the words of the priests and Agni and of the curse (he would utter against them). The gods told him that they were called by hymns and vedic prayer-formulas to the sacrificial offering; thus they were not independent, but obedient to the Vedas.

35-47 After purifying himself, Devāpi summoned the Vedas by meditation and asceticism. When they appeared, he bowed to them and told them about the words of the priests, the fire, and the gods. The Vedas informed him that they, too, were not independent, but subordinate to the Lord Mahādeva (= Śiva), the supporter of the whole universe, the abode of all powers and all perfection. Being, however, the *brahman* consisting of words, they knew all that he had asked for: name, abode, etc. of the demon who had carried off his father; they knew that the abducted persons were not hurt, and what he should do in order to reach his goal. Asked by Devāpi for all the details, the Vedas advised him to go to the Gautamī and praise Śiva there, who would be pleased and grant him all he wanted. King Ārṣṭiṣeṇa, his wife Jayā, and Devāpi's father Upamanyu were safe and sound in the nether world; Devāpi should slay the demon with Śiva's help, it would not be possible otherwise. According to the Vedas' words, Devāpi went to the Gautamī, bathed there, and praised Śiva.

48-53 Hymn by Devāpi to Śiva, first pointing to the fact that Devāpi is only a child and cannot praise Śiva correctly; then stating Śiva's unknowability, even by gods and sages, by Brahman and Vaikuṇṭha (= Viṣṇu); Śiva's compassion towards the poor and afflicted, even towards sinners; Śiva as distributor of the reward that is given by the gods to those who praise them, etc.

54-59 Thus praised, the three-eyed one (= Śiva) granted him a boon; Devāpi asked for the return of the king, his wife, and his own father, and for his enemy's death. All this was granted by Śiva. He sent Nandin to the nether world, who killed Mithu and the other chiefs of the demons and brought back the abducted persons to Devāpi.

60-63 Now the horse-sacrifice could be completed. All beings that were present, the fire, the priests, the gods, the Vedas and the sages, proclaimed that the place where Śiva had shown himself to Devāpi had come into existence as Devatīrtha (i.e. »holy place of the gods«) destroying all sins and granting all accomplishments; Devāpi's fame would last for ever. The gods granted boons to those present; finally they bathed in the (Gautamī) Gaṅgā and went to heaven.

64a-f Ever since, there have been 15,800 holy places on both sides of the Gautamī; bathing there and bestowing gifts is extremely meritorious.

Ch. 128: Story of Agni and Śiva's semen; the abduction of Suvarṇā[1]

1-2 Brahman continues: On the southern bank of the Gautamī, there are the holy places called Tapovana (»forest of asceticism«), Nandinīsaṃgama (»confluence of Nandinī«), Siddheśvara, and Śārdūla (»tiger«); by listening to the story of their origin, one is freed from all evil.

3-6 In former times, Agni was the priest of the gods; he married the beautiful Svāhā, a daughter of Dakṣa. However, she was without offspring. When she practised severe asceticism in order to obtain a son, her husband told her to stop her austerities and predicted that she would have children. She complied, for »there is nothing like their husbands' words for fulfilling wishes of women« (maxim).

7-15 Some time later, when danger had arisen from the demon Tāraka, but Kārttikeya had not yet been born, and Śiva and Pārvatī had retreated, the gods, full of fear, came together and implored Agni to tell Śiva about the danger that had arisen. Agni replied that this was against the rule which prohibits disturbing any couple being together in privacy, the more so in the case of Śiva, the Lord of the world. The gods, however, insisted upon Agni's mission, since there was an exception to that rule in the case of great danger; assuming another shape, he should help them and approach Śiva. For that he should obtain the homage of both worlds.

16-23 Agni assumed the shape of a parrot and approached the place where Śiva and Umā were enjoying themselves together. As he could not enter through the door, he flew to the window and sat there, trembling, with bent head. Seeing him, Śiva laughed and told Umā to look at the parrot, who was Agni in disguise; but Pārvatī was very ashamed. Śiva called the bird, told him to open his beak and to take up Śiva's semen. With Śiva's semen inside, Agni could not move on; he stopped, exhausted, at the bank of the river of the gods and passed the semen to the Kṛttikās, from whom Kārttikeya originated.

24-28 What was left of Śiva's semen in his body, Agni gave to his wife Svāhā, who had been consoled by him before (reference back). She gave birth to twins, Suvarṇa and Suvarṇā, who were extremely beautiful and increased their parents' happiness. Agni married his daughter to Dharma and his son to Saṃkalpā.

29-37 Because of the fault of the exchange (mixing of) semen, both of the twins behaved accordingly: Suvarṇa approached the wives of the chief gods, like Indra, Varuṇa, Vāyu, and Kubera, and of the sages, assuming their husbands' shape and enjoying love with them. Similarly, Suvarṇā, Dharma's wife and Svāhā's daughter, behaved as if she were independent; she appeared to whomever she liked in the shape of his consort; thus she enjoyed men, demons, gods, sages, and even ancestors. Finally the gods and demons found out and got very angry with Agni's son and daughter; they cursed the twins to have intercourse with everybody born in any caste.[2]

38-43 Coming to know about this curse, Agni was very frightened. He went to Brahman (the first-person narrator) and asked for a remedy. Brahman advised him to go to the Gautamī, praise Śiva there and tell him everything; he would protect his

[1] For the story of Agni and Śiva's semen, cf. Rm 1,36 and MBh 9,44.
[2] In Triṣṭubh-metre.

children. So Agni went to the Gautamī and praised Śiva with hymns and words equal to those of the Veda.

44-45 Hymn by Agni to Śiva, referring to Śiva as supporter of the world and as self-originated creator, as well as to his forms connected with his functions: fire - destruction, water - creation, sun - protection. (Ed. VePr. adds two verses referring to Śiva's (or Viṣṇu's ?) forms as sacrificer for satisfying the gods, and as wind for animating the beings; to Hari in the form of Śiva for protecting, etc.)

46-49 Pleased by Agni, Śiva granted him a boon. Agni told Śiva what had become of his semen, about the twins' transgressions, and how they had been cursed by the gods. Śiva should avert evil from them.

50-61 Śaṃbhu answered him that Suvarṇa, i.e. gold, which had come out of Agni from Śiva's semen, should be the foundation of all prosperity; he praised gold as a means of purification for the three worlds, as an immortal substance in this world and as dear to the gods, as granting pleasures as well as liberation, as a sacrificial gift. Semen is the best (substance), the highest of which is Śiva's semen, which is, in this case, especially excellent because of having been put into Agni, the fire. Without gold nothing is possible, people are dead even while living. Even a man without good qualities is respectable, if he is wealthy, but not a man with good qualities, who is poor. Likewise Suvarṇā, excellent, but unsteady, will complete everything incomplete she sees. She is obtainable by austerities, prayers, or sacrifices;[3] anything is praised as the excellence of her power. (?) Wherever she stays, she will be present as Kamalā (= Lakṣmī) and as a means of purification. Both will always be independent from now onward, but they will never be connected with merit.

62-63ab With these words Śiva showed himself in the shape of a Liṅga. Agni was glad about the fulfilment of his wishes; Suvarṇā lived happily with her husband Dharma, Suvarṇa with his wife Saṃkalpā.

63cd-70ab Story of Suvarṇā's abduction: One day Śārdūla, the lord of the Dānavas, defeated Dharma and carried Suvarṇā off to the nether world. Dharma and Agni went to Viṣṇu, praised him and asked him to do something for them. Viṣṇu cut off Śārdūla's head with his discus, took Suvarṇā and led her to Śiva, who embraced her again and again.

70cd-72ab The place where the discus was cleaned from Śārdūla's blood is called Cakratīrtha, as well as »Śārdūla«; the place where Viṣṇu brought back Suvarṇā to Śiva is famous as »Śāṃkara« (belonging to Śaṃkara/Śiva) and as »Vaiṣṇava« (belonging to Viṣṇu).

72cd-76 Where Agni and Dharma reached happiness, tears of joy dropped from Agni's eyes, which became the rivers Ānandā and Nandinī. Their confluence with the (Gautamī) Gaṅgā is a holy place where Śiva is present; Suvarṇā is also present, who is known as Dākṣāyaṇī, Śivā, and Āgneyī (daughter of Agni), adorning both banks; as the mother who holds the world, as Kātyāyanī, etc.; who grants all wishes. The place where Agni practised austerities is called Tapovana.

77-81 There are many holy places like these on both banks of the Gautamī, 14,000 on the northern bank, 16,000 on the southern bank; they all have separate names, but are summed up here. The man who listens to them (i.e. to their names) or recites them,

[3] v.l.: She is not obtainable by austerities etc.

will be successful in all his aims. Who, knowing about the events that happened here, bathes etc. will be reborn endowed with prosperity as well as with righteousness.

83-84 The holy place named »Śārdūla« is situated west of (the one named) Abjaka[4] and is more valuable than all holy places in Vārāṇasī. Who bathes there and satisfies his ancestors will be freed from all evil and will enter Viṣṇu's world. Between Śārdūla and Tapovana there are other holy places, the greatness of which cannot be described by anybody.

Ch. 129: Stories about Indra

1-2 Brahman continues: At the Phenāsaṃgama (confluence of the Phenā) there is the famous Indratīrtha, the Vṛṣākapa(-tīrtha), the Hanūmata(-tīrtha), and the Abjaka(-tīrtha), where there is (a statue of) Trivikrama (= Viṣṇu); bathing there and bestowing gifts ends the cycle of rebirth.

3 Brahman announces he will tell what happened at these places on the southern bank of the (Gautamī) Gaṅgā, as well as about (the Liṅga called) Indreśvara, on the northern bank.

4-8 *Story of Indra and Namuci*[1]

The strong Namuci was Indra's enemy. There was a fight between them, in which Indra cut off Namuci's head with a thunderbolt (*vajra*) that was made from the foam of water. This foam fell down on the southern bank of the (Gautamī) Gaṅgā, split the earth and entered the nether world. The water that flowed on the earth along the way shown by Indra's weapon became the river Phenā, named after the foam. Its confluence (with the Gautamī) is a famous holy place, destroying all evil, like the confluence of Gaṅgā and Yamunā.

9-10 The place where Hanūmat's stepmother (*upamātṛ*) was freed from being a cat by Viṣṇu's and Gaṅgā's grace, is called »Mārjāra« (»cat«); its story and the one about the Hanūmata(-tīrtha) has been told before.[2]

11ab Announcement of (the account of) Vṛṣākapa(-tīrtha) and Abjaka(-tīrtha).

11cd-41 *Story of Indra and Mahāṣani*

11cd-16 The first-born of the Daityas was the powerful Hiraṇya, invincible by the gods because of his austerities. He had a very strong son named Mahāśani, whose wife was Parājitā. There was a battle between him and Indra, lasting a long time; finally

[4] cf. the following chapter.

[1] For another account of this story, see ch. 124.33-36ab above; cf. also RV 8,14.13 and Jaim.Br. 1.97.

[2] In ch. 84 above.

Mahāśani defeated Śakra, together with his elephant, bound him and took him to his father. Seeing, however, his sister,[3] he gave up his cruelty; he reported (the events) to Hiraṇya, who kept Indra guarded in the nether world.

17-20ab Now Mahāṣani wanted to defeat Varuṇa, too. Varuṇa, however, gave his daughter in marriage to him, together with the ocean as his abode. Thus he made friends with Mahāśani, whose dear wife was Varuṇa's daughter and whose strength, power, and fame were beyond comparison in the three worlds.

20cd-29 As the world was without Indra (that is, without a powerful sovereign and protector) the gods took counsel among themselves whether to go to Viṣṇu, the slayer of Daityas, to get Indra back, or whether to get another Indra. They went to Viṣṇu, who, however, told them that he could not kill Mahāśani. Instead he went to Mahāśani's father-in-law Varuṇa and asked him to influence his son-in-law so that Indra would come back. Accordingly Varuṇa went to Mahāśani, who honoured him and asked him why he had come. Varuṇa requested him to release his prisoner Indra, the respectable king of the gods, for »releasing a captured enemy leads to great renown for the good« (maxim). Mahāśani agreed and handed Indra over to Varuṇa, together with the elephant.

30-37 In the midst of the Daityas, Mahāśani addressed Hari (= Indra) in the presence of Varuṇa; after greeting him respectfully, however, he taunted him in the worst way, asking how he could claim to be Indra, how he could be proud of his strength, etc. Normally it was fitting only for a woman to be unbound by her lord. How could Indra desire all the things worthy of being enjoyed by a king of the gods, after having been defeated and deprived of them? Life without good reputation is death; thus Indra should be full of shame, not deserving all the epithets attributed to him. Why did Brahman, the creator of those like Indra, who, though humiliated, enter the world (again) and continue living, not suffer from heartbreak?[4]

38-41 With these words Mahāśani gave Indra back to Varuṇa, telling Indra that he should be Varuṇa's pupil and obedient servant. Should he not be submissive to Varuṇa, he would be thrown into the nether world again as a prisoner. Thus Mahāśani scornfully sent Indra to Varuṇa.

42-125 *Indra, Indrāṇī, and Vṛṣākapi*

42-48 Returning home full of shame, Indra told everything that had happened to his wife Paulomī, especially how he had been humiliated by his enemy, and asked how he could purify himself (?). Paulomī consoled him, telling him that she knew all about the demons, their origin, magic power, boons, defeat, and death; thus she would inform him how to defeat them, in order to please him. He should not be surprised or distressed because of his enemy's success,[5] since this was due to a boon granted by Brahman. The means to counter it would be the following.[6]

[3] i.e. Indra's wife Paulomī, see below v. 46.

[4] In Triṣṭubh-metre mixed with Jagatī-metre.

[5] In v. 46, Paulomī speaks of Mahāśani, her uncle's son, as of her »brother«; cf. v. 15 above.

[6] Here Paulomī's speech is interrupted by the narrator, who introduces the second part of it separately.

49–64 Paulomī's advice to Indra (referring to the importance of women in general and in particular): There is nothing that cannot be accomplished by austerities, sacrifices, or devotion to Viṣṇu and Hara (= Śiva). As women's true nature is known only to women, Paulomī knows that there is nothing that cannot be accomplished by the earth and the waters (both females), upon which austerities and sacrifices are founded. For that reason Indra should go to a Tīrtha, where the earth had become a holy place, and praise Viṣṇu and Śiva to have all his wishes fulfilled. In the midst of the earth and its essence is the Daṇḍaka-forest as well as the (Gautamī) Gaṅgā; there Indra should satisfy Viṣṇu and Śiva, since Hari, Hara, and the Gaṅgā are the only refuge for those submerged in the ocean of suffering.[7] Furthermore, faithful wives know everything, hence men should perform their actions together with their wives, for by knowledge the effect of actions is multiplied a hundredfold; without their wives, however, men do not succeed even in small actions. An action done by one alone has only half of its effect; as it is said in the Vedas, »the wife is one half (of the man)«.[8] Since Gautamī in the Daṇḍaka-forest is the best of rivers, removing all faults and granting all wishes, Indra should go there together with his wife; then he would be able to kill his enemies in battle and obtain happiness.

65–67 Accordingly Indra, together with his wife and his teacher (= Varuṇa?), went to the Gautamī in the Daṇḍaka-forest, resolved to practise asceticism; after bowing to the Gaṅgā and bathing, he recited the following hymn, taking his refuge to Śiva.

68–81 Hymn by Indra to Śiva (and Umā).[9]

68–69 Asking Śiva's favour, with reference to Śiva's three functions (to create, support, and devour the world), his independence and unknowability.

70–71 Account of how Śiva created Brahman and cut off his terrible head with his nails; how the »three conditions« (*trivarga*, i.e. goals of life ?) came into existence, as well as all negative qualities (e.g. evil, poverty, greed, error, misfortune) that characterise all that is born.

72–74 Account of how Śiva, seeing all this, asked his wife to protect the World.

75–78 Account of how from the sweat of the Goddess, who, embracing Hara, had clung to him, originated all good entities, first *dharma* (law and religion, foundation of righteousness), then Lakṣmī (good fortune, splendour), gifts, good rain, etc.; ponds, grains, flowers, fruits, etc.; dance and music, holy texts, politics, eating and drinking; weapons, sciences, utensils of the household, holy places and groves, etc.

79–80 Prayer to the Goddess, who had caused the creation to get rid of evil, and who should protect him (Indra), too.

81 Praise of the unity of Śiva and Śakti.

82–93 Thus praised, Śiva asked Hari (= Indra) what he wanted. Indra told him what he had suffered from his powerful enemy, especially by his words, and asked for strength to defeat him or for something else that would help him to defeat his enemy and regain his fame. Śiva replied that he (i.e. Śiva) alone was not able to kill that enemy; Indra and Paulomī should also praise Viṣṇu. He continued by advising

[7] The contents of v. 55–58 are a more detailed repetition of v. 52–53; v. 54 belongs to the context following v. 58.

[8] cf. TS 6.1.8.5; ŚB 5.2.1.10.

[9] v. 68–80 in Upajāti-metre; 68a and c in Jagatī-metre.

Indra to go to the confluence of Gautamī and Phenā, since a confluence is especially effective;[10] on the southern bank he would find Āpastamba,[11] the best of hermits and a devotee of Viṣṇu; together with him and with his own wife, he should praise Viṣṇu.

94-99ab Accordingly Indra bathed at the sacred confluence of (Gautamī) Gaṅgā and Phenā and praised Janārdana (= Viṣṇu) on the southern bank, together with Āpastamba. Viṣṇu asked him what he wanted, and Hari (= Indra) asked for a killer of his enemy; this was granted by Viṣṇu. Thereupon a man was born from the water, who combined Śiva's and Viṣṇu's appearances, holding a discus as well as a spear. He went to the nether world and slew Indra's enemy Mahāśani.

99cd-100ef This Abjaka (man born from the waters) became Indra's friend Vṛṣākapi; even in heaven Indra always accompanied him. Indrāṇī, however, seeing her husband attached to somebody else, grew angry, since she loved him. Indra, however, smiled and consoled her.

101-124 Indrā's speech, starting with the slightly changed quotation of RV 10,86.12: »Without Vṛṣākapi, whose (offerings of) water and sacrificial food are dear to Agni, I am no refuge.«[12] Indra assured his wife that she was wrong in suspecting him, that she was most dear to him, and that he was not thinking of any other woman than her, who had herself advised him to please Śiva and Viṣṇu at the (Gautamī) Gaṅgā. Because of Śiva's favour and because of this friend Abjaka, who was born from the water, he himself had been saved from his grief and had been made »Indra« again, for »what could not be achieved together with a wife supporting her husband?« (maxim). The best friend (of a man) is his wife. On the other hand, there is nothing like the Gaṅgā for being released from evil, and nobody like Śiva and Viṣṇu for reaching the four goals of life. The stability of his rank as »Indra«, however, he owes to his friend Vṛṣākapi. Indrāṇī is his best friend, the Gautamī Gaṅgā the best of holy places, and Hari (= Viṣṇu) and Śaṃkara (= Śiva) the best of gods. Since he obtained his wishes because of their grace, he wants this holy place to become famous. All gods and sages staying on both sides of the Gaṅgā, at the Indreśvaratīrtha and the Abjaka-tīrtha, as well as the Gaṅgā, Śiva on the northern bank and Viṣṇu, who is present as Trivikrama on the southern bank, should agree that all holy places in between should grant liberation merely by bathing; that even the greatest sinner should obtain liberation here; that everything given to the poor should become imperishable merit for the donor, supposing he knows the story of Viṣṇu and Śambhu. Whoever listens to or recites the glorification of this holy place should enjoy its merit. Remembrance of Śiva and Viṣṇu will abolish all sins.

125-127 The gods and sages agreed to that. There are 7000 holy places on the northern bank of the Gautamī and eleven on the southern bank. (The) Abjaka(-tīrtha) is called the heart of the Godāvarī; it is the resting-place of Śiva, Viṣṇu, and Brahman.[13]

[10] v. 90-91, addressing a Brahmin (*vipra*), instead of Indra, seem to be interpolated from another context.

[11] His story is told in the next chapter. Should this allusion to Āpastamba be regarded as a connecting link between this and the following account?

[12] RV *rārana*: »I did not rejoice«, which obviously was no longer understood, is replaced by *śaraṇam*, perhaps due to a reading mistake.

[13] The colophon to this chapter mentions, beside the names of holy places described in this

Ch. 130: Story of Agastya teaching Āpastamba

1 Brahman gives an account of Āpastambatīrtha, famous in the three worlds, able to destroy all evil merely by being remembered.

2-6 Āpastamba, a famous sage, was married to Akṣasūtrā; their son was named Karki. Once his hermitage was visited by Agastya. Āpastamba honoured him as his guest, then he asked him six questions: (1) Who of the three gods is most venerable? (2) By whom or by which means are enjoyment and liberation obtained? (3) Who is without beginning and without end? (4) Who is the deity of the gods? (5) Which god is honoured by the sacrifices? (6) Who is praised in the Vedas?

7-14 Agastya's answer: The authority for the four goals of life is the word (*śabda*); among words the word of the Vedas is the highest authority (*pramāṇa*).[1] The Supreme Person (*puruṣa*), who is mortal and material in his inferior, immortal and immaterial in his superior existence, is praised in the Vedas.[2] Due to the difference of (the three) Qualities (*guṇas*), his material form is threefold. Being Brahman, Viṣṇu, and Śiva, he is but one. He who knows this really knows; but whoever teaches a difference among these three will find no expiation. The Vedas are authority everywhere concerning the individual forms; the one which is without form is believed to be above them (i.e. above the individual forms).

15-16 Interrupting Agastya,[3] Āpastamba wants to know the secret without any doubt or alternative.

17-21 Agastya answers that though there is no difference between these three (i.e. Brahman, Viṣṇu, and Śiva), all accomplishments are best obtained from Śiva, who is the cause of manifestation and the highest light. For this reason Āpastamba should praise Hara (= Śiva) with devotion; in the Daṇḍaka-forest, at the Gautamī, Śiva takes off all evil. Hearing this, Āpastamba was delighted.[4] (Agastya continues:) He (= Śiva) grants enjoyment and liberation to men,[5] he is material as well as immaterial; he creates, supports, and destroys everything. The shape of Brahman is that of the creator, the shape of Viṣṇu that of support, the shape of Rudra is annihilation, so it is taught in all Vedas.[6]

22 Āpastamba went to the (Gautamī) Gaṅgā, bathed there and praised Śiva with the following hymn.

chapter, the Āpastambatīrtha and the Someśvaratīrtha, the account of which is given in the next chapter.

[1] Seems to answer none of Āpastamba's questions.

[2] Answer to question no. 6.

[3] Should these two verses be read at the end of Āpastamba's former speech, including the following sentence that introduces Agastya's answer, or should all following verses be understood as a Śivaite addition to Agastya's teaching that had so far been impartial between the three gods?

[4] This sentence interrupts Agastya's speech, which is continued in the following verses, without the editor's noticing it, as he inserts the usual announcement of speech *agastya uvāca* between v. 20 and 21.

[5] Answer to Āpastamba's question no. 2.

[6] v. 19cd-21 seem to be an explanatory addition to v. 18ab.

23-31 Hymn by Āpastamba to Śiva, who is praised as the essence in all beings, the fire in wood, the fragrance in blossoms, the seed in trees etc., the gold in mountains; to him Āpastamba takes refuge.[7] He who is the creator of all, whom all distressed remember, by whom the gods were urged to *dharma* (?), to whom the oblations go first, before being distributed among the gods; in comparison with whom nothing is praiseworthy, subtle, and great; according to whose order everything exists; in whom is power, sovereignty, greatness, kindness, fame, welfare, and *dharma*, in him Āpastamba takes refuge; he is always the refuge for anyone.

32-33 Being pleased, the Lord (Śiva) addressed Āpastamba, (granting him a boon). For his own sake and the sake of others, Āpastamba wished that everybody who beholds Śiva should obtain all his desires. Śiva agreed.

34 Ever since, this holy place has been called Āpastamba(-tīrtha), which is able to remove even a mass of ignorance and darkness.

Ch. 131: Saramā and the Paṇis[1]

1-2ab Brahman announces an account of the events that happened at the Yamatīrtha and that were told in a traditional narrative (*ākhyāna*, *itihāsa*).[2]

2cd-4ab The watchdog of the gods was a bitch called Saramā; she had two sons, with four eyes, who were dear to Yama and always followed her. She guarded the cows that were used as sacrificial animals.[3]

4cd-6ab Once, when she was watching the cows, the demons approached and bribed her with soft words and gifts, so that they could lead away the cows.

6cd-9 Saramā went to the gods and told them that she had been bound and beaten by the demons, who had led away the cows belonging to the gods. Bṛhaspati, however, did not believe her; he told the gods that she only pretended to be good but was in reality false, and had consented to the abduction of the cows.

10-15 When the teacher of the gods had spoken thus, Śakra (= Indra) kicked Saramā with his foot,[4] and milk flowed from her mouth. Śacī's husband (= Indra) guessed that this milk had been given to her by the Rākṣasas, so that they might be able to lead away the cows; Saramā, however, denied being guilty. Finally, the teacher of the gods (= Bṛhaspati) came to know, by meditation, that Saramā had sided with the enemies of the gods. Consequently Śakra (= Indra) cursed her to be born in the world of mortals as a dog doing evil unwittingly. (?) Accordingly, she was born in the world of men, dreadful because of the evil she had done.

[7] In Upajāti-metre. The formula »in him, the Lord of the moon, I take my refuge«, is repeated as a refrain at the end of all following verses; v. 24-30 start with a relative pronoun referring to Śiva, which is put in all seven cases, according to the grammatical order.

[1] cf. Bṛhaddevatā 8.24-36; VrP 16; for a discussion of the story see H. L. Hariyappa: Rigvedic Legends (the BrP version, however, is not mentioned there).

[2] Possibly refers to the »Ākhyāna-hymn« 10,108 in the RV, which, however, differs considerably from later versions of the story such as the story here.

[3] cf. the version of VrP 16, where the gods want to perform a sacrifice.

[4] cf. Bṛhaddevatā 8.34.

16–24 In order to get back his cows, the Lord of the gods (= Indra) turned to Viṣṇu, who made efforts to kill the demons. He took his famous bow named Śārṅga and went to the place in the Daṇḍaka-forest where the Lord of the world (= Viṣṇu) is present as Śārṅgapāṇi (i.e. as a statue showing Viṣṇu holding the bow Śārṅga in his hand) and where the Rākṣasas had led the stolen cows. Being afraid of Viṣṇu, the demons fled southward, but Viṣṇu pursued them. When he had reached them, with (the help of) Garuḍa, he destroyed the enemies of the gods with his sharp arrows, on the northern bank of the (Gautamī) Gaṅgā.

25 The place where the cows were recovered by the gods is called Bāṇatīrtha; it is a place of pilgrimage sacred to Viṣṇu and also known as Gotīrtha.

26–28 The cows destined for the gods' sacrifice had gathered on the southern bank of the (Gautamī) Gaṅgā; they were brought to an island in the midst of the river. There the gods' sacrifice was performed; hence the island of the cows (Godvīpa) is called Yajñatīrtha; it fulfils all wishes.

29–30 The power (*śakti*) of the Gaṅgā became manifest as Yogamāyā (»whose magic power is Yoga«), the sovereign over all (*viśveśvarī*); on the southern bank there is the holy place named »Gorakṣa« (»shelter of the cows«).

31–39ab The two dogs, Saramā's sons, who had four eyes and were dear to Yama, told all that had happened to Yama and asked for a means to free their mother from the curse. He (i.e. Yama) went to Sūrya, his father, together with the dogs; Sūrya advised his son to bathe in the Gautamī in the Daṇḍaka-forest and to praise Brahman, Viṣṇu, Sūrya, and Īśa (= Śiva), one after the other, then his servants (= the two dogs) would gain (the gods') favour. Accordingly Yama praised the best of the gods at the Gautamī; together with the dogs, the lord of the southern direction (= Yama) pleased Brahman[5] and Bhānu (= the sun) on the southern bank and Īśāna (= Śiva) and Viṣṇu on the northern bank (of the Gautamī).

39cd–51 The gods granted him his foremost wish that Saramā should be free from the curse; (additionally,) Yama expressed many wishes for the sake of the worlds: that whoever bathes at the Bāṇatīrtha and thinks of (Viṣṇu) holding (the bow) Śārṅga should not suffer from poverty or grief in one Yuga after the other; that whoever pays homage to Brahman, after having bathed at the Gotīrtha or Brahmatīrtha, should, by circumambulating the island, have circumambulated the earth with its seven continents. He who offers only a little to a Brahmin or to the fire, should obtain the merit of a horse-sacrifice etc. Whoever recites the Gāyatrī-verse there only once should thereby have studied the Vedas. By bathing on the southern bank and by paying homage to the Goddess, the Energy (*śakti*) of Brahman, Viṣṇu, and Maheśvara (= Śiva), consisting of the three (Vedas), a man should obtain all desires. He who, after bathing, beholds the sun on the southern bank, should, by that, have performed sacrifices with various donations. He who beholds the conqueror of demons (= Viṣṇu) on the northern bank, should reach Viṣṇu's highest step (or abode). Whoever beholds (the Liṅga named) Yameśvara at Yamatīrtha should thereby increase the merit of his ancestors. Even sinful ancestors should reach liberation by (their sons') bathing, bestowing gifts, praying and praising.

[5] Third person, though Brahman is the narrator.

52–53ab There are 8003 holy places; the merit obtained there by bathing and bestowing gifts is inexhaustible. Remembering them destroys the evil accumulated during many lives.

53cd–54ab On account of Brahman's order, listening (to their names or to that account?), together with one's ancestors, or reciting, together with one's family, frees them even from most evil deeds.

54cd–57ef By bathing, giving something, offering a rice-ball to the ancestors, and bowing to the gods, one will be prosperous, famous, brave, sound and happy, will obtain sons, grandsons, and a wife, and not be separated from his relatives, will rescue ancestors in hell and purify his family, and finally, remembering Viṣṇu and Śiva, reach liberation, according to the words of the gods.

Ch. 132: Story of Pippalā, Viśvāvasu's sister

1–2 Brahman continues: There is a holy place named Yakṣiṇīsaṃgama, where the god (Śiva) is present as Yakṣeśvara, granting enjoyment and liberation on being seen; by bathing there the merit of sacrifice and pilgrimage is obtained.

3–5 Viśvāvasu's sister, named Pippalā, used to laugh at teachers; once she went to a *sattra*-rite performed by the sages on the bank of the Gautamī and laughed at the sight of their emaciated bodies, using the exclamations »*vauṣaṭ*« and »*śrauṣaṭ*«.[1] The sages cursed her to become a river; thus the river named »Yakṣiṇī« came into existence.

6 Viśvāvasu, however, paid homage to the sages and freed his sister from the curse upon (her) flowing into the Gautamī.

7–9ef Ever since, this holy place has been known as Yakṣiṇīsaṃgama (»confluence of Yakṣiṇī«); by bathing there and bestowing gifts all wishes are obtained. The place where Śaṃbhu was favourable to Viśvāvasu, is a most holy place; it is sacred to Śiva, known as Durgātīrtha, and destroys all evil and misfortune. This holy place is the essence of all the most holy places and bestows success in any respect upon men.

Ch. 133: The demon born of the smoke at Bharadvāja's sacrifice

1 Brahman continues with a description of Śuklatīrtha, which grants all wishes merely by being remembered.

2–4 There was a hermit called Bharadvāja, whose wife, named Paiṭhīnasī, stayed at the bank of the Gautamī, dedicated to her husband. She arranged the rice-cake (*puroḍāśa*) for Indra and Agni in the Agniṣoma-rite; when it was being baked, somebody whose appearance terrified the three worlds was born from the smoke and ate up the rice-cake.

[1] cf. RV 1,139.1 *astu śrauṣaṭ* ...; *vauṣaṭ* does not occur in the RV (only *vaṣaṭ*), but seems to be a later formation (e.g. Ait.Br. 3.6) rhyming with *śrauṣaṭ*.

5-8 Angrily Bharadvāja asked him who he was. The demon answered that he was called Havyaghna (»destroying the oblations«), the son of Saṃdhyā and Prācīnabarhis, who had been granted by Brahman the boon of consuming the sacrifices according to his wish. His younger brother Kali as well as the whole of his family were black. He himself would destroy the sacrifice and cut the pole to pieces.

9-12 Bharadvāja requested the Rākṣasa not to destroy his sacrifice. Now Yajñaghna[1] told him that he had once been cursed by Brahman, but he had satisfied Brahman and had been granted freedom from the curse after Brahmins had sprinkled him with the nectar of immortality. Therefore Bharadvāja should do the same for him, then he would obtain all he wanted.

13-17 Bharadvāja, addressing him as his friend, asked him how he would be able to do that; for the nectar of immortality had been obtained only by the combined efforts of gods and demons. He should therefore tell him an easier means. The demon replied that the (term) »nectar of immortality« could be applied to the water of the Gautamī, to gold, to the products of the cow, to melted butter, and to the Soma-juice; with one of these or, even better, with the triad of water of the Gautamī, gold, and melted butter, Bharadvāja should sprinkle him. The best »nectar of immortality« would be the water from the Gautamī.

18-23ab Bharadvāja gladly took water from the Gautamī and sprinkled it upon the Rākṣasa, then upon the post, the sacrificial animal, the priests, and the sacrificial ground; thereby everything became bright, including the demon, who had been black before, but in a moment turned bright. When the sacrifice was completed, Bharadvāja dismissed the priests and threw the sacrificial post into the water of the (Gautamī) Gaṅgā. This post can still be seen today, in the midst of the Gaṅgā, as a token (of the things that had happened there).

23cd-25 At that holy place the demon told Bharadvāja that, since he had become bright at this place, anyone who bathes and performs rites here would obtain all wishes that are fulfilled by a sacrifice. Even merely by being thought of it would destroy all evil.

Ch. 134: The Rākṣasas and the magic woman Ajaikā Muktakeśī

1 Brahman announces an account of Cakratīrtha,[1] which destroys evil merely by being remembered.

2-8ab Once the famous Seven Sages, Vasiṣṭha etc., performed a *sattra*-rite at the Gautamī, but it was disturbed by demons. The sages went for help to Brahman (the first-person narrator), who created, by magic power, a beautiful young woman, at whose sight the Rākṣasas would be destroyed. The sages took her, who was named Ajaikā and is present even today in the shape of Muktakeśī (i.e. »loose-haired«), went to the Gautamī and prepared once more for the sacrifice.

8cd-11 Again the Rākṣasas approached; when they saw this (woman filled with) magic power near a fig tree, they started to dance and to sing, to laugh and to weep. Among

[1] Thus in the introductory formula to his speech.

[1] There seem to be four different Cakratīrthas; cf. ch. 86, 109, and 128 (v. 71) above.

them was the lord of Daityas, named Śambara; he devoured the beautiful young woman, her magic power included, which astonished those who had experienced this magic power.

12–14 Since the sacrifice was destroyed again, the gods turned to Viṣṇu for protection. He gave them his discus, which cut the demons to pieces; they died from sheer terror. The *sattra*-rite of the sages was completed; Viṣṇu's discus was cleansed with water taken from the (Gautamī) Gaṅgā.

15–16 Ever since, this holy place is called Cakratīrtha; by bathing there and bestowing gifts one can obtain the merit of all sacrifices. There are 500 places of pilgrimage that take away all evil; each of them grants liberation by bathing and bestowing gifts.

Ch. 135: Story of Brahman, Viṣṇu, and Śiva's Liṅga

1–2ab Brahman continues: The place where Hara (= Śiva) is present as Vāgīśvara is called Vāṇitīrtha, which releases from all evil, even from the sin of Brahmin-murder.

2cd–5ab When Brahman and Viṣṇu disputed with each other about which of them should be regarded as superior, Mahādeva (= Śiva) became visible between them in the form of light. A heavenly voice addressed the two disputants, proposing that whoever would see the end of it/him (i.e. the light/Śiva), should be regarded as superior.

5cd–10ab Thereupon Viṣṇu went down, and Brahman (now the first-person narrator) went up. Viṣṇu hurriedly entered by the side of the light. Brahman, not seeing the end, went farther and farther; finally he returned, wanting to see the Lord. Suddenly it occurred to him that (if) he had seen the end, he would be superior to Viṣṇu. But his truthful four heads would not let him tell a lie, as »there is, among all sins, no sin more deserving hell than a lie« (maxim). How could he, then, manage to tell a lie?

10cd–13cd Thus he created a fifth head, in the shape of a donkey, thinking that he could tell a lie with this one; he said to Viṣṇu that he had seen the end (of Śiva) and hence should be regarded as superior. While he was speaking, Hari and Śaṃkara appeared from the side (of the light that was Śiva), forming one shape, like sun and moon together. Seeing them, Brahman was frightened and praised them.[1]

13ef–14 The two protectors of the world (*jagannāthau*) angrily cursed Speech to become a river, as there is no sin like telling lies.

15–16 Accordingly Speech became a river. When Brahman (the first-person narrator) saw that, he was frightened and cursed her, too, to become invisible, because of her wickedness.

17–19 Being thus cursed, she bowed to the two gods and praised them, in order to be released from the curse. Hari and Hara, being pleased, announced that she should regain her shape after joining the Gaṅgā.

20–24 Accordingly the goddess (i.e. Speech) joined the Gaṅgā, the Bhāgīrathī as well as the Gautamī, and recovered her former shape, which is inaccessible even to the gods. At

[1] Here there seems to be a break in the story.

the confluence with the Gautamī she is known as Vāṇī, at the confluence with the Bhāgīrathī, she is called Sarasvatī. Both confluences are famous and highly esteemed in the worlds. As Vāṇī, Vācā, Sarasvatī the Goddess Speech joined the Gaṅgā. There is a famous place of pilgrimage, since Speech had paid homage to Śiva there and had been freed from the curse.

5-27ab Having removed the depravity of Speech and his own, Brahman[2] returned to his abode. Therefore, anyone who purifies himself, bathes at the confluence and beholds (the Liṅga named) Vāgīśvara will obtain liberation at that moment. He who performs any rite there will not enter the circle of rebirth (*saṃsāra*) again.

27c-f There are 119 places of pilgrimage on both banks, which effect the destruction of sins accumulated in several births.

Ch. 136: Maudgalya and Viṣṇu

1ab Brahman announces (an account of) the events at Viṣṇutīrtha.

cd-3ab The son of Mudgala was the sage Maudgalya, whose wife was named Jābālā. His old father Mudgala, a famous sage, too, was married to Bhāgīrathī.

d-14ab Maudgalya used to bathe every morning in the Gaṅgā; according to his teacher's instructions, he used to invite Viṣṇu (to sit) on the lotus in his own mind (*svamānasasaroruhe*?), by (presenting offerings of) Kuśa grass, earth lumps, and flowers from the Śamī-tree. Lakṣmī's husband (= Viṣṇu) used to come on Vainateya (= Garuḍa), holding conch-shell, discus, and club. Being honoured by Maudgalya, Viṣṇu told him wonderful stories. In the afternoon, Viṣṇu sent him back home and went to his own abode. On the way home, Maudgalya collected something and gave that self-acquired wealth to his wife. She took the rice, roots, or fruits he had given her and prepared a meal for the guests, the children, and her husband, and she herself ate after them. When all had finished, Maudgalya used to tell the wonderful stories he had heard from Viṣṇu on that day.

4cd-16 After a long time, Jābālā told her husband, secretly, that the next time Viṣṇu visited him he should ask Viṣṇu why they had to live in such misery, in spite of Maudgalya's being visited by Viṣṇu, by thinking of whom old age, rebirth, disease, and death would by destroyed.'

17-26 Accordingly Maudgalya asked Viṣṇu why he had to live in bad circumstances though he could see Viṣṇu. Viṣṇu replied that everything that happened to anybody was caused by his own actions, not by anybody else. »The fruit will be according to the sowing« (maxim). Those who do not visit the Gautamī, nor honour Hari (= Viṣṇu) and Śaṃkara (= Śiva), and do not give anything to the Brahmins, how could they enjoy happiness?[1] Maudgalya had not given anything to Brahmins, or to Viṣṇu. By (offering) earth-lumps, Kuśa-grass, water and holy formulas, as well as by drying up one's body, one purifies only oneself, but one can never expect prosperity

[2] Third person, though he is the narrator.

[1] Sentence is incomplete, lacking the verb.

without giving something. By pure conduct of life one can reach liberation while still living (*jīvanmukta*). Liberation (*mukti*) can be easily obtained by devotion to Viṣṇu; enjoyment (*bhukti*), however, can only be obtained by removing the troubles of others by giving (alms) etc., by no other means.

27–31 Maudgalya was confused as he had always thought that liberation was far more difficult to obtain than enjoyment and that, after having reached liberation, there was no more use for enjoyment. For him, liberation was the most desirable goal. Viṣṇu informed him that everything given to Brahmins or to the poor with devotion to Viṣṇu, was imperishable. Without thinking on Viṣṇu one would only obtain the merit of the act of giving, but not get anything back. Therefore Maudgalya should give some food to Viṣṇu or to some Brahmins on the bank of the Gautamī.

32–35ab Maudgalya replied that he had nothing he could give. Now Viṣṇu ordered Garuḍa to bring an ear of corn that could be offered by Maudgalya. Maudgalya put the ear of corn into Viṣṇu's hand.

35cd–36ef Meanwhile Viṣṇu instructed Viśvakarman that there should always be cows, gold, grain, clothes, and jewels as much as would be desired in Maudgalya's family, up to the seventh generation.

37–40 Whatever jewel he wanted was obtained by Maudgalya because of Viṣṇu's and the Gaṅgā's power.[2] Viṣṇu told him to go home and disappeared. At his hermitage, the sage saw the prosperity and was greatly astonished; he praised the power of bestowing gifts and of remembering Viṣṇu as well as that of the Gaṅgā. With his wife, sons and grandsons he enjoyed all (worldly) pleasures and (finally) reached liberation.

41–42 Ever since, this place of pilgrimage is (called) »Maudgalya« and sacred to Viṣṇu; bathing there and bestowing gifts leads to enjoyment as well as liberation. Whoever remembers, or listens to, the account of this holy place, will be dear to Viṣṇu and be released from sins.

43 There are 11,000 holy places on both banks, which grant the fulfilment of all aims to anybody who bathes there, offers gifts, and mutters prayers.

Ch. 137: Dispute between Lakṣmī and Poverty

1 Brahman announces (an account of) Lakṣmītīrtha, which destroys all misfortune.

2–3 Once there was a dispute between Lakṣmī (prosperity) and Poverty. They used to be in contradiction in every respect; (for) »there is no object not concerned with these two« (maxim). Both claimed to be superior; (Poverty) said she had originated first.[1]

4–7 Lakṣmī replied that she is good family, good character, and good life for everybody; without her beings are as if dead, though still living. Poverty, however, argued that

[2] v. 35cd–37 seem to be an interpolation interrupting the connection of the story, in order to stress the blessing of Maudgalya and the power of Viṣṇu and the Gaṅgā, which are mentioned below.

[1] As Śrī is mentioned in the accusative case, it must be Poverty who speaks, though she is not mentioned.

liberation is based on her and that all vices like lust, wrath, greed, intoxication, jealousy etc. do not exist in her presence.

8–14 Lakṣmī said that a man adorned with her is honoured; without prosperity he is despised. With the word »please give!« the five goddesses Dhī (thought), Śrī (splendour), Hrī (modesty), Śānti (calmness of mind), and Kīrti (fame) leave the body. A good and noble character can only be sustained by somebody who does not (need to) ask for anything else; how can a needy person have good qualities or authority? As long as a person does not ask for another thing, he is endowed with qualities and is honoured. Being without property is a great evil, for nobody esteems, addresses, or touches a poor man. Therefore she was superior.

15–24 Poverty, however, reproached her for saying so, arguing that Lakṣmī stays with sinners who give up the Supreme Person (*puruṣottama*), that she betrays the confident, that the pleasure of obtaining her does not counterbalance the repentance afterwards, that (even) the intoxication caused by liquor does not equal that caused merely by being near to wealth, even for knowledgeable persons. Contrary to Lakṣmī, who likes sinners, Poverty stays with qualified, righteous persons, with those devoted to Śiva or Viṣṇu, delighted in a good conduct of life, those who are thankful, great, calm, obedient to their authorities, knowledgeable etc.; therefore she is superior. While she stays with Brahmins, with those dedicated to a vow, with mendicants, and fearless persons, Lakṣmī stays with Kṣatriyas, with sinful, cruel, mischievous, treacherous persons, with hunters etc., with mean and ungrateful persons, with those who neglect the *dharma* rules or betray a friend (*mitradrohin*) etc.

25–28ab Disputing thus, both went to Brahman (the first-person narrator), who told them that the earth existed prior to himself; still prior, however, were the waters - »only women understand the dispute between women« (maxim) - especially those (waters) that originated from (Śiva's) bowl.[2] Gautamī was (therefore) able to decide the case.

cd–30ab Both went to the Gautamī, together with the earth and the waters, who informed the Gautamī about what had happened.

cd–39ab Standing between Lakṣmī and Poverty, Gautamī addressed Poverty in the presence of the guardians of the directions, the earth and the waters, praising Lakṣmī as the splendour of Brahman, of austerities and sacrifices, of wealth and fame, as knowledge and intelligence, as Sarasvatī, as enjoyment and liberation, as patience, accomplishment, etc. (list of abstract nouns); as the earth and the waters, as the plants and the sky, etc.; as Māyā, Uṣas, and Śivā. Everything and every being is pervaded by Lakṣmī; she is the delightful principle in Brahmins, in wise, forgiving, and good people. Everything consists of Lakṣmī, nothing is without her. Poverty should be ashamed of attacking this beautiful goddess. With these words Gautamī sent Poverty away.

cd–40ab Ever since, the water of the (Gautamī) Gaṅgā is hostile to poverty; poverty is mighty only as long as the Gaṅgā is not honoured (by a visit).

cd–41ab Ever since, this holy place has destroyed poverty, by bathing there and bestowing gifts one will gain prosperity and merit.

[2] cf. ch. 72 above.

41c-f There are 6000 places of pilgrimage at this holy place, which grant all accomplishments that are desired by gods, sages, and men.

Ch. 138: Story of Madhucchandas, family-priest of King Śaryāti

1 Brahman announces an account of the events at Bhānutīrtha, which grants all perfections to men.

2–3 Once there lived a famous king named Śaryāti, who was married to Sthaviṣṭhā, a woman of incomparable beauty. His family-priest was Madhucchandas, the son of Viśvāmitra.

4–7 The king went to conquer the earth, together with his priest. On their way (back), he asked his priest why he looked so depressed, in spite of being most honoured in his kingdom, being full of knowledge and free from sins. Having conquered the earth, they had reason to feel glad rather than to feel depressed; he should tell him the truth. Madhuchandas[1] gave the king an explanation about his beloved one:[2]

8–9ef He told him that he was thinking on his dear wife, who had uttered words especially dear to him.[3] »We are following our path, the night is half gone; the mistress of this body is expecting me, full of love,« thinking of this word, he felt great pain, as his beloved was as his life to him.

10–13 The king asked him, smilingly, how he, his teacher and friend, could utter such a word, and how noble-minded people could care for delights that are most unstable. Madhucchandas replied that wherever there is harmony between husband and wife, the three goals of life (*trivarga*) prosper; it should not be overestimated, either as a fault or as an adornment. (?)

14–19 Returning to his own land, the king wanted to test (their wives); he sent messengers to the capital, who spread the news that the king and his priest had been slain by a Rākṣasa. Hearing this news, the king's wives came to a decision (?); the priest's wife, however, immediately fell to the ground dead. The messengers returned to the king and told him about what had happened. Astonished and full of grief, the king sent them back to the capital, to guard the corpse of the priest's wife and announce his arrival.

20–21 Suddenly a heavenly voice addressed the sorrowful king, informing him that the Gautamī would fulfil all wishes.

22–27 Hearing this, Śaryāti went to the banks of the Gautamī, where he bestowed gifts upon Brahmins, satisfied his ancestors, and sent his priest off with riches to be given to the poor at another holy place. When Madhucchandas, who did not know what had happened, had left, the king dismissed his army and entered the pyre, on the

[1] Ed. ASS reads Chandomadhu, probably in order to obtain a normal Pāda in Indravajrā-metre.

[2] In Upajāti-metre; Madhucchandas' following speech, however, is in normal Ślokas.

[3] One would expect a quotation of these words in 8cd–9ab, which are full of assonances (*anuprāsa*); the sentence, however, is obviously not uttered by a woman, but by Madhucchandas himself.

banks of the Gautamī, addressing the Gaṅgā, the sun, and the gods with (the truth-spell) that if he had bestowed gifts, performed sacrifices, and protected his subjects, then by this truth his life should enter the dead body of the priest's faithful wife. As soon as he had entered the fire with these words, the priest's wife was brought back to life.

28–32 When Madhucchandas heard that the king had entered the fire, that his own wife had died and had been brought back to life, and that the king had given up his life for this purpose, he pondered what he should do now, whether he should enter the fire, too, or return to his beloved, or practise asceticism. Finally he decided that he should first (try to) bring the king back to life and then return to his wife. He praised the sun-god, for »there is no other god who fulfils wishes like Ravi (the sun).«

33–34 Hymn by Madhucchandas to Sūrya (*namas* + epithets in dative case, ascribing the *trimūrti*-functions to the sun-god.)

35–38 Asked by Sūrya what he wanted, Madhucchandas wished for the return of the king as well as his own wife, splendid (*śubha*) sons for himself and splendid boons for the king. Thereupon the Lord of the world (Jagannātha) presented him King Śaryāti, adorned with jewels, as well as Madhucchandas' wife and granted him other boons. Full of joy Śaryāti[4] went back to his country, together with his priest; this (spot), however, is remembered as a splendid holy place.

39ab There are 3000 holy places, endowed with good qualities.[5]

39cd–40 Ever since, this holy place has been called Bhānutīrtha (Bhānu – sun), Mṛtasaṃjīvana (bringing the dead back to life), Śāryāta (connected with Śaryāti), or Mādhucchandasa (connected with Madhucchandas), which merely by being remembered destroys all evil.

41 Bathing there and bestowing gifts grants the merit of all sacrifices; it can bring the dead back to life, increases life-time and grants freedom from disease.

Ch. 139: Pailūṣa's »thirst« and the »sword of knowledge»[1]

1–2ab Brahman announces an account of what happened at the Khaḍgatīrtha, situated on the northern bank of the Gautamī; by bathing there and bestowing gifts a man may enjoy liberation.

2cd–7ab There was a Brahmin named Pailūṣa, son of Kavaṣa, who roamed about everywhere, in order to obtain some means of support for his family; but he did not find anything. Then he turned to indifference towards worldly objects, thinking that »when fate is unfavourable, when human effort has failed, there is no other resort for the wise than indifference« (maxim). But then he sighed, for he had not

[4] Read *śaryātiḥ* for *yātaḥ*; as the finite verb is *yayau*, *yātaḥ* can hardly be used as verb here.

[5] Should be read after v. 40 or 41.

[1] For »Pailūṣa's thirst«, cf. Ait.Br. 2.19, where the main figure, however, is named Kavaṣa, son of Ailūṣa, and the thirst is not used in the metaphorical sense of »desire, greed« (like *taṇhā* in Buddhist philosophy), but is taken literally as »longing for water« (*pipāsā*).

inherited anything and had to support many (family-members). He tried different professions, but he could not obtain any property by these activities, and again he turned to indifference.

7cd–11 He pondered how hard it was to understand which practices are forbidden and how difficult austerities were to perform; that he was drawn everywhere to evil action by »thirst« (*tṛṣṇā*); finally, that evil-doing due to desire (»thirst«) existed because of ignorance; »therefore, Thirst, may you be honoured!« (homage to »Thirst«). Then he thought of how this thirst could be destroyed and turned to his father, asking him by which »sword of knowledge«[2] anger and desire could be destroyed and the circle of rebirth be transgressed. Kavaṣa answered his son that one should strive for the knowledge of Īśvara (= Śiva), according to the vedic tradition; therefore he should pay homage to Īśāna (= Śiva), then he would obtain knowledge.

12 So Pailūṣa praised Īśvara, who was pleased and granted him knowledge. Having obtained knowledge, Pailūṣa composed the (following) verses (*gāthā*s).

13–17ef Verses composed by Pailūṣa, listing five »enemies« that should be destroyed by the »sword of knowledge«: anger, thirst (*tṛṣṇā*), (worldly) attachment (*saṅga*), doubt, and hope.

18 Having received knowledge on the bank of the Gautamī, and being freed from illusion by means of the »sword of knowledge«, Pailūṣa obtained liberation.

19 Ever since, this holy place has been known as Khaḍgatīrtha (*khaḍga* = sword), Jñānatīrtha (»ford of knowledge«), Kavaṣa(-tīrtha), and Pailūṣa(-tīrtha); it fulfils all desires.

20 There are 6000 holy places, mentioned by the great sages, which destroy all evil and fulfil all wishes.

Ch. 140: Ātreya as Indra

1 Brahman announces (an account of) the origin of the holy place called »Ātreya« or »Anvindra«,[1] which restores a lost kingdom.

2–3ab On the northern bank of the Gautamī the sage Ātreya once undertook *sattra*-rites, together with priests and hermits; his main priest was Agni, who carries the oblations (to the gods).

3cd–5ab When the *sattra*-rite was completed and the oblation for Maheśvara (= Śiva) offered, Ātreya obtained the power of going everywhere, to Indra's abode as well as to the nether world, due to the power of his asceticism.

5cd–6ef Once he went to Indra's world in heaven and beheld the Thousand-Eyed One (*sahasrākṣa* = Indra) there, surrounded by the gods, praised by Siddhas and Sādhyas, watching the superb dancing and listening to the sweet singing of the Apsarases.

[2] The »sword of knowledge« appears as *paññākhaggaṃ* in the commentary of gāthā 68 in the Lomasakassapajātaka (no. 433, cf. ed. Fausboell III p. 519), which may be a further hint to the adaption of Buddhist thought in this story.

[1] Or: »situated near Indra(-tīrtha)« (*anvindram*)?

7-11 When he saw the great Indra, honoured by the gods, holding his son Jayanta in his lap and enjoying love with Śacī, the protector of the good and granter of boons, the Brahmin was infatuated by Indra's splendour and wished to obtain Indra's kingdom. Honoured by the gods, he went back to his hermitage, but comparing Indra's beautiful city and his own hermitage without any splendour, gold and jewels, Atri's son (= Ātreya) became restless and told his wife that he was unable to enjoy fruits and (edible) roots, though they were pure, when thinking of the nectar of immortality that was consumed there and of the wonderful seats, the hymns and gifts, the splendid assembly, the weapons and clothes, the city and the groves.[2]

12-13 By the power of his asceticism, the hermit called Tvaṣṭṛ and told him that he wanted to become like Indra and that Tvaṣṭṛ should construct Indra's abode for him, otherwise he would reduce him to ashes.[3]

14-18ab Accordingly, Tvaṣṭṛ made the Mt. Meru and the city of the gods, the wishing-tree, the wishing-creeper (*kalpalatā*), and the wishing-cow, the houses adorned with diamonds, the beautiful Śacī, the pleasure-house of the god of love, the assembly hall of the gods and the Apsarases, the elephant Uccaiḥśravas,[4] the weapons and all the gods. Against the will of his consort, Atri's son (= Ātreya) made the imitated Śacī his wife; he made the thunderbolt his weapon and imitated all the things he had seen in Indra's city.[5]

8cd-19ab Having attained all this, the »Indra of the hermits« was exceedingly happy; for »who does not appreciate objects, even if they are enjoyed only by accident« (?) (maxim)[6]

9cd-21cd Coming to know (about Indra's city on earth), the Daityas, Dānavas, and Rākṣasas assembled, full of anger and unable to understand why Hari (= Indra) had left heaven and had come to earth; they decided to fight against the slayer of Vṛtra immediately. The demons went to besiege the city which bore the name of Indra's city, but was brought into existence by Atri's son.[7]

21ef-25 Afflicted by their weapons, Atri's son fearfully praised Hari (= Indra) with the (vedic) hymn »He who, as the first intelligent being, shortly after his birth, filled the gods with power, at whose roaring heaven and earth trembled, frightened because of the greatness of his manly strength: he, o ye peoples, is Indra!« (= RV 2,12.1)[8] Then he addressed his enemies, trying to explain to them that he was not Indra, that Śacī was not his wife, and that the city and forest did not belong to Indra. Only the real Indra was the slayer of Vṛtra, with the thunderbolt as his weapon, the Thousand-Eyed One (*sahasrākṣa*) etc. (list of epithets); he himself, however, was only a Brahmin living on the bank of the Gautamī, who due to ill fate had done something that caused him no well-being, either now or in the future.[9]

[2] In Upajāti-metre.

[3] In Upajāti-metre.

[4] This name usually denotes Indra's horse, whereas his elephant is called Airāvata.

[5] In Upajāti-metre; v. 15 in Upendravajrā-metre.

[6] Meaning not quite clear. In Upajāti-metre.

[7] In Upajāti-metre, mixed with Jagatī metre (20a).

[8] The vedic plural form *janāsas* seems to have been no longer understood, for in both editions the words are divided wrongly *sajanā sa indraḥ* (instead of *sa janāsa indraḥ*).

[9] In Triṣṭubh-metre, partly of the old vedic type, 24c being hypermetrical.

26–30 The Asuras demanded that he should destroy this imitation of (things belonging to) Indra, otherwise he would have no peace. Ātreya promised it, touching fire, and told Tvaṣṭṛ to destroy all that he had made in imitation of Indra's abode, and to give him back his old place, with his hermitage, animals, trees and water, for »all (things) obtained against the (proper) order (*akramam*) do not cause well-being to understanding people« (maxim).

31–34 Thereupon Tvaṣṭṛ destroyed everything, and the Daityas went back to their abode. Tvaṣṭṛ, too, went laughingly to his abode. Ātreya stayed at the Gautamī, together with his wife and his pupils. During a sacrifice he proclaimed, full of shame, the greatness of his confusion to have done such a thing.

35–38 The gods consoled him, announcing that he would be famous. All people who bathed at the Ātreyatīrtha, would become »Indra«, enjoying all pleasures. There would be 5000 places of pilgrimage, famous by the names »Anvindra«, »Ātreya«, and/or »Daiteya«; bathing there and bestowing gifts would effect imperishable merit.

39 After these words the gods left, and the hermit was very delighted.

Ch. 141: Pṛthu and the earth[1]

1 Brahman announces the highly auspicious story about the holy place named Kapilāsaṃgama, which is famous in the three worlds.

2–5 Once there was a famous hermit named Kapila, kind as well as cruel, and dedicated to asceticism. To him, who stayed on the bank of the Gautamī, practising austerities, Vāmadeva and others went and asked him.... After the killing of Vena by the curses of Brahman (or, of Brahmins ?), the kingdom was without *dharma*, so the hermits asked Kapila what they should do now that Veda and *dharma* had been lost.[2]

6–9 Kapila advised them to churn Vena's thigh; something would come out. The hermits did so; from Vena's thigh a black, cruel sinner came into existence. Being afraid, the hermits told him to sit (or calm) down (*niṣīdasva*); thus he became a Niṣāda, from whom the Niṣādas originated.

10–13 Then the hermits churned Vena's right hand; thereby king Pṛthu originated. All the gods went to him, granted him boons, and gave him weapons and spell-formulas. Then they and Kapila requested him to give the plants swallowed by the earth to the living beings as support of life.

14–20 Pṛthu took his bow and told the earth to give him the plants she had swallowed, for the sake of all beings. The earth, however, replied that she could not do so, as she had already digested the plants. Now Pṛthu threatened to slay her, but she reminded

[1] cf. above Ch. 4, where a detailed account of Vena's misbehaviour, Pṛthu's birth, and the milking of the earth is given.

[2] v. 3 and 4 seem to exclude each other as an introduction to the following question; v. 4 presents more detailed information about the reason for the hermits' question, which is mentioned in the question itself, whereas v. 3 shows no special connection with the story told later on; Vena is not mentioned.

him that it was not proper to kill her, as she was a woman, and that he could not support his subjects without her.

21-22 Pṛthu answered her with the maxim justifying the death of one for the sake of many.[3]

23-25 Now the gods and sages pacified the king and advised the earth to assume the shape of a cow and to give the plants to Pṛthu in form of milk, so that he could protect the subjects, and there would be peace. She turned herself into a cow in the presence of Kapila, and the king milked the plants out of her.

26-28 Where (= wherever?) the gods and Gandharvas, the sages together with Kapila reached the earth at the Narmadā, the Sarasvatī, the Bhāgīrathī (Gaṅgā) and the Godāvarī, he milked plenty of milk at these rivers.[4] Milked by Pṛthu, she (?) became the river Puṇyatoyā (or: a river with holy water), which joined the Gautamī.

29-30 Ever since, this holy place has been called Kapilāsaṃgama (»confluence of the Kapilā«).[5] There are 88,000 places of pilgrimage, with purifying effect by merely being remembered.

Ch. 142: Meghahāsa and the gods

1 Brahman announces (an account of) the origin of the holy place named Devasthāna.

2-4 Long ago, in the Kṛta Yuga, at the time of the battle between gods and demons, there was a beautiful Daitya-woman, named Siṃhikā, whose son was the strong demon Rāhu. When the nectar of immortality had been obtained and Siṃhikā's son destroyed,[1] his son Meghahāsa was very grieved and started to practise austerities when he heard about his father's death.

5-6ef The gods and sages went to Rāhu's son, who stayed on the bank of the Gautamī, and asked him to stop his austerities, for he could obtain everything he wanted by the grace of Śiva and the Gaṅgā; what is difficult to obtain by the grace of these two? (Rhetorical question).

7-8ef Meghahāsa replied that he wanted to take revenge for his beloved father, who had been defeated by the gods; for this was the duty of a loving son. But if the gods appealed to him (*prārthayante ced* ...), he would consider his wishes to be fulfilled.

9-10ab Thereupon the hosts of gods made Rāhu a companion of the planets and Meghahāsa the lord of the Rākṣasas; Rāhu's son became the ruler of the south-western direction (or: of the realm of the demons).

10cd-12ab Furthermore he wished that this place should become efficacious according to his own fame. This was granted by the gods, and the place is now famous by the name of the lord of the demons (i.e. by the name »Meghahāsa«).

12cd-13 The place where the gods stayed is called »Devasthāna«; it is difficult to reach for the gods. The place where the god (Śiva) is present as Deveśvara (a Liṅga named »Lord of the gods«) is called Devatīrtha.

[3] cf. above ch. 4, v. 82 ff.

[4] v. 27 may have been inserted in order to bring the Godāvarī into the story.

[5] This river has not yet been mentioned.

[1] cf. the story told in ch. 106 above.

14 There are eighteen holy places, honoured by the Daityas; bathing there and bestowing gifts destroys great sins.

Ch. 143: Rāvaṇa and Śiva[1]

1 Brahman announces (an account of) the origin of Siddhatīrtha, where Hara (= Śiva) is present as (a Liṅga named) Siddheśvara.

2–5 After conquering all regions (of the earth), Rāvaṇa, who was born into the family of Pulastya, went to the world of Soma. When he was fighting with Soma, Brahman (the first-person narrator) told the Ten-Headed One (= Rāvaṇa) to desist from the fight and gave him the formula (*mantra*) of the one hundred and eight names of Śiva for pleasing (Śiva); for »Śiva is the only protection of all unfortunate or suffering people in this world.«

6 Returning from the world of Soma, Rāvaṇa, accompanied by (two) ministers, immediately went back to the (human) worlds with his (chariot named) Puṣpaka, full of pride after gaining the victory.[2] (?)

7–11 He saw the sky, the intermediate sphere, and the earth, snakes, elephants, and Brahmins, and finally the huge mountain Kailāsa, the abode of Śiva and Umā. Very surprised, Rāvaṇa addressed his two ministers, asking who lived there and expressing his intention to take this mountain with him to (his capital) Laṅkā, which would gain in splendour by it. The ministers advised him not to do so, but he did not heed their words. He stopped the Puṣpaka-chariot, jumped at the foot of the mountain and shook it; Śiva, however, noticed it and did the right thing:[3]

12–13 Together with Umā, he laughed at Rāvaṇa, who was haughty because of having conquered the guardians of the directions, who had shaken Mt. Kailāsa and had gone to the nether worlds etc. because of (being pressed down by Śiva's) toe, and who had had his heads cut off. He (i.e. Śiva) granted him a boon; for »Śaṃbhu (= Śiva) bestows (even) unfitting gifts (or, gifts to undeserving people).«[4]

14–16 After obtaining boons from Bhava (= Śiva), Rāvaṇa went to the flower-chariot.[5] On his way to Laṅkā, he stopped at the (Gautamī) Gaṅgā, which had originated from Śiva's matted hair. He paid homage to Śaṃbhu with various prayer-formulas (*mantras*)[6] and with water from the Gaṅgā and obtained a sword from Śiva,[7] as well as all the success and prosperity he wanted. By paying homage to Śiva, he used the formula obtained from Brahman for the protection of the moon. Then he returned happily to Laṅkā.[8]

[1] cf. Rm 7.16.
[2] In Upajāti-metre.
[3] In Upajāti-metre.
[4] In Upajāti-metre.
[5] *kusuma* = *puṣpaka*, Rāvaṇa's chariot.
[6] Does this refer to the formula obtained by Rāvaṇa from Brahman (cf. v. 4 above)?
[7] cf. Rm 7,16.45.
[8] In Upajāti-metre.

17 Ever since, this holy place has been very efficient, granting great success and destroying accumulated sins; it is visited by all Siddhas.[9]

Ch. 144: Ātreyī, Aṅgiras, and Agni (the fire)

1 Brahman announces an account of the holy place called »Paruṣṇīsaṃgama« (»confluence of the Paruṣṇī«), which is famous in the three worlds.

2–4 Once Atri pleased Brahman, Viṣṇu, and Śiva and wished that they should be born as his sons and that he should have a beautiful daughter as well. So it happened: he begot a daughter named »the beautiful Ātreyī«, whereas the three gods became his sons Datta, Soma, and Durvāsas.

5–8ab Aṅgiras originated from the charcoals (*aṅgāra*) of Agni Aṅgiras; therefore (?) Atri gave his daughter to Aṅgiras in marriage. Since Aṅgiras had originated from fire, he always talked in a very rough way (*paruṣaṃ vādīt*) to Ātreyī, though she was always obedient to her husband. The Āṅgirasas were born from her; whenever their father was harsh to their mother, they tried to calm him.

8cd–10 Once, when she was much bewildered by her husband's violent speech, she went to her father-in-law, the fire, told him about the unjustified harshness of her husband, and asked him to tell her (or: her husband) what to do.

11–14 Agni suggested the use of a stratagem in order to calm Aṅgiras; when her husband assumed the (form of) fire she should assume the shape of water and flood him. Ātreyī, however, replied that she would rather bear her husband's harshness than do any harm to him; she would only like him to soften his words.

15–16 Agni replied that fire was in everything, it resided in her husband as well as in him, her father; knowing this, she should not worry. Moreover, the waters were (her or his) mothers, and Agni her father-in-law.[1]

17–19 She argued that, since the waters were the mothers and she herself was the wife of Agni's son, she could not assume the form of the waters, as suggested by him, for it was not possible to be mother and wife simultaneously. Agni replied that she was many things at one time: basically she was *patnī* (i.e. having a husband as her lord), then *bhāryā* (i.e. the one supported by him), then *jāyā* because of bearing children (*jan-*), and *kalatra* because of her qualities. Therefore she should do what he had said. He who is born from her is her son, and she is his mother; there is an old saying that after a birth of a son a woman is no longer a *yoṣit* (i.e. a young woman, apparently before she becomes a mother).[2]

20–22 Convinced by her father-in-law, she acted according to his words; she flowed over her husband, who had assumed the form of fire, with water. Both, husband and wife, merged with the water of the (Gautamī) Gaṅgā; they obtained a placid shape and stayed together like Viṣṇu and Lakṣmī, like Umā and Śaṃkara (= Śiva), like Rohiṇī and the moon.

[9] In Upajāti-metre.

[1] Meaning of the argument not quite clear.

[2] In Triṣṭubh-metre, 17d hypermetrical. The meaning of the argument seems to be that she actually is mother and wife at the same time, after having born sons.

23-24 When she flowed over her husband, her form consisted of water, which was called »Paruṣṇī«[3] and joined the (Gautamī) Gaṅgā as a river. By bathing in the Paruṣṇī one obtains the merit of offering a hundred cows. The Āṅgirasas performed sacrifices there, with many sacrificial gifts.

25-27 There are 3000 holy places on both banks of the Gautamī, with the effect of a special pilgrimage.[4] Bathing there and bestowing gifts is more (valuable) than a horse-sacrifice. Especially at the confluence of the Paruṣṇī and the (Gautamī) Gaṅgā merit can be obtained that cannot be described.

Ch. 145: Discussion about the best way to liberation

1-2ab Brahman announces (a report of) the power of the holy place Mārkaṇḍeya, which grants the merit of all sacrifices and averts all evil.

2cd-5ab Once the sages Mārkaṇḍeya, Bharadvāja, Vasiṣṭha, Atri, Gautama, Yājñavalkya, Jābāli, and others, who were conversant with Vedas and Vedāṅgas, Purāṇas, and philosophical systems, discussed among themselves whether liberation is obtained by knowledge or by action.

5cd-7 Discussing their views, they asked Brahman (the first-person narrator) for his opinion. On learning it, they went to (Viṣṇu) holding discus and club, asked for his opinion, discussed the matter again and went to Śaṃkara (= Śiva). Greeting him and the Gaṅgā, they told him about their dispute.

8-11ab Śiva proclaimed the superiority of action, arguing that knowledge has the form of action and actually is action (*kriyā*);[1] therefore all beings are successful only by acting. Action permeates everything; there is nothing besides acting. Studying knowledge (v.l. the Vedas), performing sacrifices, practising Yoga or paying homage to Śiva, all is action, and no living being exists without it. Only the doings of madmen are something else.

11cd-13 At the place where the sages had their discussion and where Śiva decided the matter everything can be obtained by men through action. Particularly because of Mārkaṇḍa, this place of pilgrimage on the northern bank of the (Gautamī) Gaṅgā, frequented by many hermits, is called Mārkaṇḍa; it purifies one's ancestors merely by being thought of.

14 There are 98 places of pilgrimage, as is said by the One in whom the world is contained. This is taught by the Veda,[2] and the sages accepted it.[3]

[3] This name was obviously understood as being based on the word *paruṣa* (»harsh, rough«); thus the story of Aṅgiras' »harsh words« provides an explanation of the name Paruṣṇi.

[4] Or: causing the effect of a pilgrimage, each. (?)

[1] Meaning of the argument not quite clear.

[2] v.l. »by the god (i.e. Śiva)«.

[3] i.e. Śiva's decision concerning the best way to liberation?

Ch. 146: Story of Yayāti[1]

1 Brahman announces an account of what happened at the next holy place, named »Yāyāta« (belonging to Yayāti), where Śiva is present as (a Liṅga named) Kālañjara.

2–8ab King Yayāti, Nahuṣa's son, who was like another Indra, had two wives, the daughter of Śukra, named Devayānī, and Śarmiṣṭhā, the daughter of Vṛṣaparvan.[2] Devayānī was a Brahmin woman who was given to Yayāti by the favour of Śukra.[3] Devayānī gave birth to two sons, Yadu and Turvasu, who looked like Śukra, whereas Śarmiṣṭhā had three sons, Druhyu, Anu, and Pūru, resembling Śakra (= Indra), Agni, and Varuṇa.

8cd–10 One day Devayānī went to her father Śukra and complained that she had only two sons from Yayāti, whereas her slave (Śarmiṣṭhā) was favoured with three sons. She would rather die than tolerate this offence, for »death is better than loss of honour« (maxim).

11–14 Incited by these words, Śukra went to Yayāti and angrily cursed him to become an old man who is able neither to enjoy nor to give up sensual delight. »Old age is death, in spite of being alive, for those endowed with a body« (maxim).

15–18 Yayāti, honouring Śukra, who had cursed him, replied that he had always acted in accordance with the law, and that he should not have been cursed simply because of the wrong testimony of Devayānī. If knowing people were erroneously angry with an innocent person, then there was nothing wrong with foolish persons burning with hatred.

19–25 Remembering that his daughter, when furious, had done harm more than once, Kāvya (Uśanas, i.e. Śukra) gave up his anger and admitted that Devayānī had done wrong; but since he could not make his curse a lie, he softened it by admitting that Yayāti could exchange his old age with the youth of one of his sons. Yayāti wished that whichever of his sons was willing to take up his old age should become king, and those who would refuse should be cursed; Śukra should agree to this.[4]

26–27 Śukra consented. Now Yayāti called his eldest son, Yadu, and asked him to take over his old age, for »a man is made a *putrin* (i.e. endowed with sons) by (a son) who is obedient to his father« (maxim).

28–31 Yadu, however, refused; Yayāti cursed him and asked Turvasu to fulfil his wish. Turvasu, too, refused and was cursed. Yayāti asked Druhyu and Anu; both refused as well. Having cursed them, Yayāti finally asked Pūru, who willingly took the old age from his father.

32–34 For one thousand years Yayāti was happy and enjoyed all the pleasures that are associated with youth. Then Nahuṣa's son was satiated with all the enjoyments. He called Pūru and told him to take back his youth and return the old age to him.

[1] cf. MBh 1,76–80 and Rm (Bomb. ed.) 7,58–59 (= ed. Bar. 7, App. I, no. 8).

[2] In the MBh-story, Śarmiṣṭhā is, of course, not Yayāti's wife, but Devayānī's royal servant (as is hinted at in v. 9 below), whom Yayāti was forbidden to touch by Devayānī's father.

[3] v. 4–5ab seem to duplicate v. 3.

[4] For 24d, cf. MBh 1,78.39d.

35-37 Pūru, however, refused, since old age cannot be bartered,[5] and the change of (different) states (of the body) cannot be escaped. How could old age be given up, if it had been taken up for the sake of a venerable person? Death is better than the sin of giving up something previously accepted. Besides, he could destroy the old age by means of asceticism.

38-41 After these words he went to the Gaṅgā and practised asceticism on the southern bank of the Gautamī. After a long time Śiva was pleased with Pūru and asked him what he should give him. Pūru replied that the god should destroy the old age that originated from the curse against his father and free his brothers from the curses uttered by their father. Accordingly the Lord of the world destroyed the old age and freed Pūru's brothers from their curses.

42-45 Ever since, this holy place has destroyed old age and disease; untimely old age is destroyed by its merely being remembered. It is renowned by the names Kālañjara, Yāyāta, Nāhuṣa, Paura, Śaukra, and Śārmiṣṭha. These and others are 108 holy places in total, which bestow any kind of success. Bathing there and bestowing gifts destroys all evil and grants enjoyment and liberation.

Ch. 147: Viśvāmitra and the Apsarases

1-3 Brahman continues: On the southern bank is (the place called) Apsaroyuga (i.e. »pair of Apsarases«) and Apsarāsaṃgama (»confluence of Apsarā«); by thinking of it one will obtain good fortune; by bathing there etc., a man will be released. A faithful woman who bathes there after menstruation will bear a son, even if she is barren, by bathing there and giving alms for three months, in the company of her husband.

4 Brahman announces that he will tell why this holy place is called Apsaroyuga.

5-7 Once there was a great enmity between Viśvāmitra and Vasiṣṭha. Menakā was sent by Indra to Gādhi's son (= Viśvāmitra) who was practising austerities at Gaṅgādvāra in order to become a Brahmin, to disturb his asceticism. Accordingly Menā deprived Viśvāmitra of his asceticism, gave him a daughter, and went back to Indra's city.

8-9ab When she had left, Viśvāmitra remembered all he had done. He left this region and went to the holy place at the southern Gaṅgā (i.e. the Gautamī/Godāvarī), where Śiva is present as Kālañjara.[1]

9cd-13 Again Indra spoke about him first to Urvaśī, then to Menā, to Rambhā, and to Tilottamā, but they all refused (to do what Indra wanted). Finally he asked Gambhīrā and Atigambhīrā, who were proud of their youth and beauty and claimed that they could easily divert Gādhi's son from his austerities with dancing and singing, for »who cannot be subdued by those in whose side-glances, laughing, coquetry etc. the god of love resides?« (maxim).

[5] *krīyate* instead of *kṣīyate*, which cannot be constructed syntactically.

[1] cf. the preceding chapter, v. 43.

14–17ab They went to the great river where Viśvāmitra had been practising asceticism for 1000 years, more dangerous than Death, like Śiva staying on earth; they were not able to look at him. When he saw them, dancing and singing and flattering, he grew very angry; for »who is not be filled with anger, seeing actions performed against him?« (maxim).

cd–20ab Though free from desire, Viśvāmitra, laughing at Indra, since he was »freed« of these two Apsarases, cursed them to become fluids (*drava*), since they had tried to »melt« him (*dravitum*). When they pleaded with him, he told them that they would be released from the curse and regain their heavenly shape as soon as they flowed into the (Gautamī) Gaṅgā.

cd–23ab The two Apsarases immediately became two rivers, known as »Apsaroyuga« (i.e. »pair of Apsarases«) The place where they joined each other and joined the Gaṅgā is famous in the three worlds as bestowing enjoyment and liberation. Śiva is present here, granting success. Bathing there and beholding Śiva frees from all fetters.

Ch. 148: Kāṇva's sacrificial fire getting extinct during the offering

1–3ab Brahman announces (an account of) the Koṭitīrtha on the southern (v.l. northern) bank of the (Gautamī) Gaṅgā, by thinking of which one is freed from all evil. Where the god (Śiva) is present as Koṭīśvara, everything is multiplied by 10 millions. There are 20 million holy places.

3cd–7 Kaṇva's eldest son was Bāhlīka, generally known as Kāṇva, who was well-versed in Vedas and Vedāṅgas. Together with his wife, he used to prepare the bricks (for the sacrifice) of the days of new and full moon and of the solstices, while staying on the bank of the Gautamī. In the morning he and his wife used to pour oblations into the fire; one day he had poured one oblation into the ignited fire and was taking the substance for the second oblation in his hand, when the fire went out.

8–14ab Kāṇva, not knowing what to do now, grew very distressed. While he was pondering where to pour the second oblation and deciding to start a new fire, a heavenly voice addressed him, advising him not to start a new fire; rather he should pour (the second oblation) on the half-burnt logs near (to the fire ?). First Kāṇva refused, but the heavenly voice argued that gold is the son of Agni and that son and father are identical; hence what is given to please the son also pleases the father; moreover the pleasure would be multiplied by ten millions.[1]

cd–18ab Thus spoke the heavenly voice; the sages acted accordingly, knowing that what is given to the son is given to the father, too; that there is nothing as pleasing to a father as what is done for the benefit of his son, that the merit of it would be multiplied by ten millions, the weariness of mind would cease, and happiness arise.

18cd–20 Again the heavenly voice addressed Kāṇva, telling him that this had become[2] a great holy place, more effective than all places of pilgrimage in the three worlds; by

[1] Argument not quite clear, since gold has not yet been mentioned in the story.

[2] Past tense instead of normally used optative or future tense.

anything performed here with devotion, he would gain its merit multiplied by ten millions.[3]

21-26 Since the merit of everything done here is multiplied by ten millions (*koṭi*), the place is called Koṭitīrtha. Where this event took place, there is (the place called) Kāṇva, Pautra, Hiraṇyaka, Vāṇī, and the Koṭitīrtha, the greatness of which cannot be described here even by Vācaspati or any other god, and where anything that is performed is multiplied by ten millions, due to the grace of the Godāvarī. Whoever gives one cow to a Brahmin at the Koṭitīrtha, will, by the greatness of this holy place, obtain the merit of ten million (cows given to Brahmins); the same is valid for giving of land.

27a-f Everywhere on the banks of the Gautamī, bestowing of gifts is excellent for the ancestors, but at the Koṭitīrtha in particular its effect will be without end. There are 49 places of pilgrimage known to the hermits.

Ch. 149: Viṣṇu as Narasiṃha

1 Brahman announces that he will tell the origin of the Nārasiṃhatīrtha on the northern bank of the (Gautamī) Gaṅgā.

2-4ab Once there was (a demon named) Hiraṇyakaśipu, invincible for the gods because of his asceticism and strength. Distressed by the demon's hatred against his own son, who was a devotee of Hari (= Viṣṇu), (Viṣṇu) showed himself, stepping out of a pillar in the assembly hall; as Narasiṃha (»man-lion«) he killed him and his army.

4cd-9ab After killing all Daityas in battle, the great beast (i.e. the man-lion) went to the nether world, in order to kill the demons there, then to heaven, then to the earth, and he killed the demons in the mountains, in the ocean and in the rivers, in the villages and the forests, in the air and in the world of light; his nails being more dreadful than thunderbolts, his huge mane blowing in the wind, his roaring and glances being like the fire at the destruction of the world, he bruised the demons, slapping them with his hand and scattering their limbs.

9cd-12 Having destroyed the demons, Hari (= Viṣṇu) went to the Gautamī, which had originated from the water from his own foot. A fierce warrior, named Ambarya, invincible to the gods, an enemy of the lord of the Daṇḍaka-region lived there. Between him and Hari a terrible fight took place; Hari defeated him on the northern bank of the Gautamī Gaṅgā.

13-16ab At that place there is the holy place named Nārasiṃha. Bathing there and bestowing gifts will turn away all evil, grant protection, and keep away old age and death. As no god is comparable to Hari, similarly no holy place is comparable to this one. A man who bathes there and worships Hari will easily obtain anything in the three worlds.

[3] Accepting the separation of words as in VePr (*kāṇva-* as member of a compound, not as vocative), one may doubt that v. 19-20 are actually uttered by the heavenly voice, since the past tense *abhavat* (19a) seems strange enough in direct speech, and the vocative *mune* might well be used by Brahman addressing Nārada, the listener of the story.

16cd–19 Including this one, there are eight prominent places of pilgrimage there, each of which is said to effect merit multiplied by ten millions. Who could describe the effects of a pilgrimage to this holy place, the name of which, being remembered even without faith, destroys all evil, and where Narasiṃha himself is always present? Just as there is no god superior to Nṛhari (i.e. Viṣṇu in the shape of Narasiṃha), similarly there is nowhere a place equal to the Nṛsiṃhatīrtha.

Ch. 150: Jīgarti's life after death and his redemption by Śunaḥśepa[1]

1ab Brahman continues with (the account of) the holy place named Paiśāca.

1cd–4ab In former times a Brahmin named Jīgarti, the son of Suyava, was freed from being (born as) a Piśāca; troubled by the burden of his family and afflicted by hunger, he had sold his middle son Śunaḥśepa to a Kṣatriya to be killed (as a sacrificial animal). »What evil will even a knowledgeable man fallen into misfortune not commit?« (maxim).

4cd–5 For performing the act of slaughtering (at the sacrifice) he obtained further wealth, as well as for performing the act of tearing apart (the sacrificial animal). He was tortured by a great incurable disease.[2]

6–9 At the time of his death he was thrown into the hells; later on he was reborn as a terrible Piśāca and was thrown by Yama's servants among dry pieces of wood in a jungle at the time of heat and forest fire; for »those who sell their daughters and sons, land, horses, and cows do not return from hell up to the end of the world.«

10–14 Beaten and roasted by Yama's servants and remembering the evil he had done, he cried bitterly. The voice of the Piśāca, who had sold his son and was a Brahmin-murderer, was heard again and again by his son, who was on the way (through the same forest). Śunaḥśepa asked who he was. Jīgarti replied that he was Śunaḥśepa's father and described how he was being tormented in the hells, for this was the fate of all sinners.

15–20 Śunaḥśepa told him that he himself was the son whom he had sold; he promised to do something for his liberation. He thought of the Gaṅgā that had originated from Viṣṇu's step as the only means of being freed from the ocean of grief for all distressed; therefore he went to the Gautamī, wishing to pull his father out of hell, bathed there, thinking of Śiva and Viṣṇu, and presented the offering of water to his father in the shape of a Piśāca, who was very distressed. Immediately Jīgarti was

[1] Continuation of the story told in Ch. 104; there Śunaḥśepa's father is named Ajīgarti.

[2] These one and a half verses are not found in two of the mss. of the ASS-edition. Their content is not mentioned in the story told in ch. 104 above, but seems to be partly in agreement with the version of the Ait.Br., where Ajīgarta is paid for binding his son to the sacrificial pole (here not mentioned) and for slaughtering him (= 4cd). However, here it cannot be his son who is slaughtered (and torn apart!), since Śunaḥśepa is not killed at all. Only slaughtering and tearing apart of animals can be meant here; Śunaḥśepa's father is obviously punished not only for selling his son, an act which is regarded as »Brahmin-murder«, but also for slaughtering animals.

purified and obtained an auspicious appearance; he reached Viṣṇu's abode in a chariot, surrounded by the gods, due to the grace of his son, of the Gaṅgā, and of Hari and Śaṃbhu.[3]

21–22 Ever since, (this place) has been (famous as) destroying all that belongs to Piśācas and (as) a great remedy, by thinking of which great sins are immediately destroyed. Thus has been proclaimed the greatness of this holy place (conclusion), where there are 300 other places of pilgrimage which grant enjoyment and liberation.[4]

23 (Summary of 21–22 in Śloka-metre:) There are 300 places of pilgrimage, visited by hermits, which grant any success and anything desired merely by being remembered.

Ch. 151: Purūravas and Urvaśī[1]

1–2 Brahman continues: On the northern bank of the (Gautamī) Gaṅgā there is a holy place named »Nimnabheda« (»destroying depression«), famous in the three worlds; by thinking of it one will be freed from all evil. There is also (an island called) Vedadvīpa (»Veda-island«); by visiting it one will become well-versed in the Veda(s).

3–5ab King Aila fell in love with Urvaśī, for »who is not intoxicated by the sight of a beautiful woman?« (maxim). She followed the king to his abode, eating one drop of melted butter (every day),[2] until she should see him naked; agreeing to this condition, he possessed her again and again.

5cd–7ab Once, when she was sleeping, Purūravas got up in the night, without clothes, looking around in surprise.[3] When she saw him naked, she disappeared; for »how can there be constancy with young women, whose mind is fickle like lightning?« (maxim).

7cd–9 Meanwhile the king fought against his enemies; after defeating them, he went back to the world of the gods. From Vasiṣṭha, his family-priest, he learned about Urvaśī's disappearance and he was very distressed; he did not perform rituals, nor eat, look or listen.

10–16 Finally, seeing the king nearly dead with grief, Vasiṣṭha consoled him informing him about the true nature of women (»their hearts are like those of jackals«),[4] who, being of evil character, always delude men and never make anybody happy. Who is

[3] In Triṣṭubh-metre, among which there are two hypermetrical pādas (15b and d) and one Jagatī pāda (18b).

[4] In Upajāti-metre.

[1] cf. RV 10,95.

[2] cf. RV 10,95.16.

[3] v. 7ab should obviously be read before 6ab, as Purūravas must have departed for battle, before Urvaśī left him; otherwise it would make no sense that Vasiṣṭha informs him about her leaving at his return.

[4] cf. RV 10,95.15cd, where this truth, however, is uttered by Urvaśī herself; v. 11 seems partly to reflect RV 10,95.15ab: *mā mṛthā(ḥ)* → *sā mṛtā*; the wolves, however, are not mentioned here, only the epithet *aśivāsa(ḥ)* → *aśivāḥ*.

not struck down by Time (*kāla*), who does (not) gain importance as long as he is wealthy? Who is not deluded by beauty, who is not shattered by young women? (maxim). Therefore he should give up his grief, regarding her as dead, and should not be depressed any longer. Moreover, there is no better refuge for all who are distressed than Śaṃkara (= Śiva), Viṣṇu, or the Gautamī.

17–22ab Upon these words the king suppressed his grief by force; standing in the midst of the Gautamī, he praised Śiva, Janārdana (= Viṣṇu), Brahman, the sun, the Gaṅgā, and other deities. »The man who does not pay homage to holy places and deities, to what stage will he go at the end of his life?«[5] Taking refuge only in the Lord (= Śiva), and being eager to pay homage to the Gautamī, dedicated to faith and turned away from the ocean of life, he performed many sacrifices with many gifts to the priests; thereby came into existence Vedadvīpa (the »Veda-island«), which is also called Yajñadvīpa (the »island of sacrifice«).

22cd–24ab The man who circumambulates this island[6] will have circumambulated the whole earth. Whoever thinks of Vedas and sacrifices there will obtain their merit.

24cd–27ab This place should be known as Ailatīrtha, Purūrava(-tīrtha), Vāsiṣṭha (»belonging to Vasiṣṭha«), and Nimnabheda (»destroying depressions«). As the depression caused by Urvaśī in Purūravas was destroyed by Vasiṣṭha and the (Gautamī) Gaṅgā, this place of pilgrimage came into existence, granting visible and invisible success.

27cd–29 There are 700 holy places; bathing and bestowing of gifts, there, brings about the effect of all sacrifices. He who, having bathed at the Nimnabheda(-tīrtha), beholds these gods, will get rid of depressions in this world and the world beyond; obtaining a high rank, he will rejoice in heaven like Śakra (= Indra).

Ch. 152: The abduction of Tārā[1]

1 Brahman announces an account of the holy place Nandītaṭa, known to Veda-experts.

2–4 Candramas (i.e. the moon) was the son of Atri; when he had learnt all the Vedas including archery etc. from Jīva (= Bṛhaspati), he told him that he wanted to pay homage to his spiritual preceptor. Joyfully Bṛhaspati told his pupil to ask his wife Tārā (for her orders).

5–9ab So Candramas went into the house to ask her. When he saw Tārā, whose face was like a star (*tārā*), he took her hand and led her into his own house, full of desire. A man is wise and self-controlled only as long as he is not trapped by the eyes etc. of a lovely woman; who is not subdued by the power of desire, especially at seeing a beautiful woman privately? Therefore a woman belonging to a noble family should never see any other man (than her husband) privately. (Maxims)

9cd–14 Recognizing what had happened, Bṛhaspati immediately left his company and, full of anger, cursed Candramas with disagreeable words; for »who can bear to see his

[5] Direct speech by Purūravas or maxim inserted by the narrator?

[6] *dīpa* misprint for *dvīpa*?

[1] This story is alluded to in RV 10,109.2; cf. also above Ch. 9.

beloved in the power of somebody else?« (maxim). Jīva (= Bṛhaspati) also fought with him, but Candramas could not been defeated, either by curses, or by weapons consecrated by the gods, or by spell-formulas etc. Candramas settled Tārā in his house and enjoyed her for many years without fear, for he could not be defeated, either by gods, or kings, or sages.

15-17 When the teacher (of the gods) saw that he could not get back his wife, he thought of a stratagem; for a wise man knows »the end justifies the means«. To lose sight of one's aim is stupid; the wise should adopt any means to achieve their goals; those who only value their reputation soon perish quickly.

18-20 Thus deciding he went to Śukra and had himself announced. Kavi (= Śukra) pleased his guest and asked the reason of his coming. »Even enemies do not turn away from somebody who has come to their house« (maxim). Bṛhaspati told him about the abduction of Tārā from the beginning in all detail.

21-23 Upon these words, Kavi grew furious; he swore not to eat or to drink or to sleep until he had brought back Bṛhaspati's wife, paying homage to Bhava (= Śiva), and cursing the moon.

24-25 Consequently, the teacher of the Daityas (= Kavi Śukra) pleased Śiva and obtained many boons from him; for »what is there difficult to obtain by Śiva's favour?«

26-28 Then Śukra went with Jīva (= Bṛhaspati) to the place where Candramas lived with Tārā and cursed the moon to become leprous. Burnt by Kavi's curse, the moon bears the mark of a wild animal; for »have those who cheat their teachers, masters, or friends not (always) been destroyed?«

29-30 The moon gave Tārā to Śukra, who called for all gods, sages, ancestors, rivers, and plants, and asked them about an expiation for Tārā's conduct.

31-32 Śruti (the vedic tradition personified) told the gods that Tārā should bathe in the Gautamī, together with her husband; the secret, however, that the Gautamī is a refuge in all conditions should not be made public.

33 Tārā bathed in the Gautamī; there was a rain of flowers and voices shouting »hail!«

34-37ab Gods and men, kings who had kept their promises, gave back the wife of a Brahmin; after she was given back, purified from her flaw by the gods,[2] ... there was peace; thereby this holy place came into existence, which destroys all sins and grants all wishes. Bliss and peace was there with gods and demons, especially with Bṛhaspati, Śukra, and Tārā.

37cd-39ef Filled with utmost joy, the teacher (i.e. Bṛhaspati) predicted that the Gautamī would be especially purifying at a conjunction of himself (i.e. the planet Jupiter) with the constellation Leo; at this time all holy places in the three worlds would come to bathe in the Gautamī.[3]

40 This holy place named Ānanda (»bliss«) bestows any kind of bliss: long life, wealth, fame, happiness, etc.

41 There are 5000 places of pilgrimage, according to Gautama; by being thought of or (an account of them) being recited they fulfil all wishes.

[2] V.34 is a literal quotation of RV 10,109.6, v. 35ab a slightly changed version of RV 10,109.7ab.

[3] cf. above ch. 78.

42a-d While Śiva settles there, Nandin roams about on the bank of the (Gautamī) Gaṅgā, therefore it is called Nandītaṭa (»bank of Nandin«).

42ef This place is also called Ānandatīrtha, because it increases bliss (*ānanda*).

Ch. 153: Prācīnabarhis' long reign and his obtaining a son from Śiva[1]

1-2ab Brahman announces (an account of) Bhāvatīrtha, where Bhava (= Śiva), the Self in everything, whose shape is existence and thought, is himself present.

2cd-3 The founder of the Solar Dynasty, Prācīnabarhis, ruled for 35,000,000 years, devoted to the rules of *dharma*.

4-6ab He vowed to renounce his kingdom as soon as he had lost his youth or been deprived of his wife, his sons, or his riches, according to the rule taught by wise and noble people that those who are disaffected should stay somewhere in the desert.

6cd-7 During his reign there was no loss anywhere, no disease nor drought nor quarrel among relatives; nobody was deprived (of anything).

8-11 He performed a sacrifice to obtain a son. Pleased with him, the Lord (= Śiva) granted him a boon; he wished for a son. Bhava (= Śiva) told him to look at his third eye. The king did so; by the brightness of Śiva's eye a son came into existence, known as Mahiman (»magnitude«), by whom the famous Mahimnastuti was composed.

12 What is unattainable, if the Lord (Śiva) is pleased, who is worshipped even by Hari (Viṣṇu or Indra?), Brahman and the other gods?[2]

13-15ab Having obtained a son, the king next asked for the superiority of this holy place. This was granted by Bhava (= Śiva), for the sake of sinful, sick, distressed, and unfortunate people; therefore this place is called Bhāvatīrtha. By bathing there and bestowing gifts one obtains everything desired.

15cd-16ab Due to Bhava's grace, Prācīnabarhis got a son (named) Mahiman, on the bank of the Gautamī; this place is called Bhāvatīrtha.[3]

16cd There are 70 holy places, which grant everything.

Ch. 154: The repudiation of Sītā[1]

1 Brahman continues by describing the holy place named Sahasrakuṇḍa, known to Veda-experts; by remembering it a man will obtain happiness.

2-4 In former times, when Rāma, the son of Daśaratha, had built the bridge across the ocean, had burnt Laṅkā, slain Rāvaṇa, and regained Sītā, he said to her who had

[1] In this chapter, allusions to different stories or motifs seem to have been mixed together, without continuous narrative.

[2] Abridged contents of the Mahimnastuti?

[3] Seems to be an abridged version of v. 8-15ab.

[1] Contents of Rm Yuddhakāṇḍa and Uttarakāṇḍa, with a newly inserted episode.

been purified by the fire, in the presence of the guardians of the directions and his preceptor, that he accepted her again.[2]

5–8ab At this very moment Aṅgada and Hanumat protested that Sītā should not be re-accepted until they had reached Ayodhyā and repeated the fire-ordeal in public; then there could never be any doubt about her purity among the people.

8cd–11ab Without paying heed to their words, however, Lakṣmaṇa, Vibhīṣaṇa, Rāma, and Jāmbavat called Sītā, who mounted Rāma's lap, being hailed by the gods. Then they went to Ayodhyā with the Puṣpaka-chariot; Rāma obtained his kingdom, and they lived happily together.

11cd–14ab After some time, however, having heard some evil gossip, Rāma abandoned her, though she was pregnant, since »even false rumour cannot be tolerated by the high-born« (maxim). Lakṣmaṇa, himself weeping, left the innocent Sītā near Vālmīki's hermitage, since he had to obey his elder brother's order.[3]

14cd–21ab After some time, when Rāma was consecrated (*dīkṣita*) for a horse-sacrifice, together with Saumitri (= Lakṣmaṇa), Rāma's two sons Lava and Kuśa, famous bards like Nārada, arrived at the sacrificial ground, reciting the Rāmāyaṇa with Gandharva-like voices; by certain signs, they were recognised as sons of the king and Vaidehī (= Sītā) and were led to Rāma, who acknowledged them by taking them on his lap and embraced them again and again, since »for those who are afflicted by the griefs of the ocean of rebirth it is the highest relief to embrace their sons« (maxim).[4]

21cd–26 Meanwhile Rākṣasas from Laṅkā, with Sugrīva, Hanumat, Aṅgada, and other monkeys, and all Vibhīṣaṇa's attendants went to king Rāma. Not seeing Sītā, Hanumat and Aṅgada asked where she was. The door-keeper told them that Rāma had abandoned her. Wondering how Rāma could abandon Sītā, who had been purified in the presence of the guardians of the directions, of his own free will, merely because of some rumour, they decided to die; they left (the court) and went back (?) to the Gautamī.

27–30ab Following them, Rāma, too, went to the Gautamī, together with the inhabitants of Ayodhyā, in order to practise severe austerities, always thinking of Sītā (as) the mother of the world, indifferent to the condition of the world, but eager to worship the Gautamī. The Lord of the three worlds (= Rāma) and his younger brother bathed in the Gautamī and strove to please Śiva; finally he gave up his remorse, surrounded by a thousand (attendants and friends).

30cd–31 The place where this happened is called Sahasrakuṇḍa. There are ten other places of pilgrimage, granting everything wished for. Bathing there and bestowing gifts grants thousandfold results.

32–34 Where (Rāma) had the sin-destroying sacrifice performed by Vasiṣṭha etc., with a stream of gifts (?) into a thousand vessels, he obtained all wishes by the grace of the Gautamī, the mother of streams; there the holy place named Sahasrakuṇḍa (»characterised by a thousand vessels/holes«) came into existence.

[2] Contents of Rm Yuddhakāṇḍa.

[3] Contents of Rm 7,43–49.

[4] Contents of Rm 7,94–95.

Ch. 155: The earth as sacrificial gift turning into a lioness and exchanged for a cow[1]

1 (Brahman continues:) The holy place called Kapilātīrtha is also known as Āṅgirasa, Āditya and Saiṃhikeya.

2–3ab Once the Aṅgirasas worshipped the Ādityas by performing a sacrifice on the southern bank of the Gautamī; the Ādityas gave them the earth as a sacrificial gift. The Aṅgirasas practised austerities.

cd–10ab The earth became a lioness and devoured the people. Being very frightened, they informed the Aṅgirasas, who found out that this lioness was the earth. They went to the Ādityas and told them to take the earth back. The Ādityas refused, because it is impossible to take back a sacrificial gift. A person doing so will be reborn as worm living in excrement for 60,000 years. There would be no greater sin than taking back land that was given by oneself or by others; hence they could not possess the earth again. Yet they would take back the sacrificial gift by exchange. The Aṅgirasas agreed to that, and the gods gave them an auspicious brown cow in exchange for the earth.

0cd–11ab Viṣṇu, who grants enjoyments and liberation, is present (there) himself,[2] and the confluence of Kapilā destroys all sins.[3]

11cd The water used for consecrating the donation became a river named Kapilā (»brown cow«).[4]

12–13ab By this exchange of a gift of cows instead of the gift of fruitful land, the hermits protected the people; the place where this took place is called Gotīrtha (»cow-ford«).

3cd–14ab There are a hundred holy places; by bathing there and bestowing gifts one obtains the merit of donating the earth.

14cd It (the river Kapilā) joined the Gaṅgā; and this is (the place) known as Kapilāsaṃgama.[5]

Ch. 156: Viṣṇu's fight with the demons

1–2ab Brahman announces an account of the holy place named Śaṅkhahrada (»conch-shell lake«), where there is (a statue of Viṣṇu) holding conch-shell and club. By bathing there and beholding it one is freed from all fetters.

2cd–3 At the beginning of the Kṛta-Yuga, when Brahman[1] was singing the Sāmaveda (or: *sāman*-melodies), the Rākṣasas, who had originated from the house of Brahman's egg (?), wanted to devour Brahman.

[1] cf. Ait.Br. 6.35.

[2] Connection with the story not clear.

[3] Seems to be inserted in the wrong place, as it destroys the connection of 10ab and 11cd or 12.

[4] Explanation of 11ab?

[5] Should be read after 11cd; v. 10cd–11ab, which seemed to be out of place above, would fit better after 14cd. Whether the sequence of 11cd, 14cd, 10cd–11ab would fit better before or after 12–14ab cannot be decided.

[1] Third person, though he is the narrator.

4-6 Brahman (now first-person narrator) asked Viṣṇu for protection, and he started to slay the demons with his discus. When he had cut them to pieces, he blew his conch-shell. After removing all opposition (all opponents?) on earth and in heaven, Hari blew his conch-shell, full of joy;[2] then all demons perished.

7-9ab The place where this took place is called Śaṅkhatīrtha; it bestows peace upon men, grants all wishes, effects long life and freedom from disease, and increases wealth and (the number of) sons. By remembering it or reciting (an account of) it one obtains all wishes.

9cd-11ab There are myriads of places of pilgrimage, destroying all evil;[3] the great Lord (= Śiva?) knows how to describe their greatness. There is no (holy place) like this anywhere.

Ch. 157: Rāma and the Liṅgas

1-2ab Brahman announces an account of the holy place named Kiṣkindhātīrtha, which grants all wishes and destroys all sins; Bhava (= Śiva) is present there.

2cd-7 In former times Rāma, the son of Daśaratha, together with the inhabitants of Kiṣkindhā, slew Rāvaṇa in battle. After killing him and regaining Sītā with the help of his brother Saumitri, the monkeys, Vibhīṣaṇa, and the gods, he went back to Ayodhyā in the Puṣpaka-chariot, which moved according to one's wishes and had once belonged to Kubera. On his way he beheld the Gautamī Gaṅgā, granting all wishes and removing all grief.

8-9 Stepping on to her bank, he joyfully told the monkeys how the Gaṅgā had released his father from all sins, allowing him to enter the Triviṣṭapa-heaven.[1]

10-14 Glorification of the Gautamī Gaṅgā by Rāma:[2]

10 Gautamī as Mother, bestowing enjoyment and liberation and removing all evil; which river is comparable to her?

11-12ab By her grace, even enemies become friends, like Vibhīṣaṇa; Sītā was won back, Laṅkā destroyed, and Rāvaṇa killed.

12cd-13ab She whom Gautama obtained by paying homage to Śiva[3] causes all desired auspiciousness and destroys all inauspiciousness.

13cd-14 She who alone is able to purify the world, who is the producer of rivers, is now met by Rāma taking refuge in her in body (i.e. deeds), words, and thoughts.

15-18cd Upon these words, the monkeys came leaping (to the Gautamī) and worshipped her with flowers. Rāma worshipped Śarva (= Śiva) and praised (him). The monkeys danced and sang; thus Rāma spent the night happily, surrounded by those dear to him, and he gave up all grief; for »what cannot be obtained by worshipping the Gautamī?« Surprised he looked at his attendants, but praised the Godāvarī, honoured his attendants (?), and attained delight.[4]

[2] v. 5cd-6ab seems to duplicate v. 5ab.

[3] v. 10ab seems to duplicate v. 9cd.

[1] Reference back to ch. 123 above.

[2] In Upajāti-metre.

[3] Reference back to ch. 75 above.

18ef–21ab The next morning Vibhīṣaṇa told him how much they all enjoyed this holy place and that they should like to spend four further nights there. The monkeys agreed; Rāma worshipped Śiva for four further nights and then went to the holy place dear to his brother (?), named Siddheśvara, where the Ten-Headed One (= Rāvaṇa) had become powerful, due to Śiva's grace.[5]

21cd–25ab They stayed there for five days, paying homage to the Liṅgas which each of them had established. Hanumat, who always obeyed the king, followed King Rāma. On the way Rāma told him to tear out (*visarjayasva* ?) all Liṅgas which had been established by himself and by other servants of Śaṃkara.[6] Those who live without respect for Śaṃkara will be reborn in the »Khaḍgapattra« (i.e. »sword-leaved« scil. forest) or in other hells; those who do not worship Śiva's Liṅgas will be cooked by Yama's servants.[7]

25cd–27ab Hanumat tried to carry out Rāma's order, but he could not tear out the Liṅgas, either with his arms or with his tail; this seemed very strange to the kings of the monkeys and to Rāma. »What sensible person would (try to) move a Liṅga of Śiva?«[8]

27cd–28 Seeing the Liṅgas immovable, Rāma called for Brahmins and paid homage (to Śiva), by circumambulating the Liṅgas and by bowing to them with pure heart.[9]

29 This holy place was then visited by all the inhabitants of Kiṣkindhā; even sins (which last) up to the end of the world are destroyed here.[10]

30 Then he (= Rāma) bowed devotedly to the Gautamī Gaṅgā, asking for her favour.[11]

31 Ever since, this most holy place has been called Kiṣkindhātīrtha; it destroys the sins (of anybody) who only recites, remembers, or listens to (an account of it) full of devotion; how much more (is effected) by bathing and bestowing gifts?[12]

Ch. 158: The Āṅgirasas and their mother's curse; Agastya's teaching

1 Brahman continues with (an account of) Vyāsatīrtha and Prācetasa, as a means of purification unsurpassed by anything.

2–3 Brahman (the first-person narrator) relates that he had ten spiritual sons, the progenitors of the world; they went off, in order to find the end of the earth. Brahman created others, who followed those that had disappeared; none of them returned.[1]

[4] In Triṣṭubh-metre, 15d and 17b being hypermetrical; 17c Jagatī-metre.

[5] Reference back to ch. 143 above. v. 18ef–21ab in Upajāti-metre, 20a Jagatī-metre.

[6] Meaning of this order not quite clear. The following half verse (23cd) cannot be understood properly; its reading is obviously corrupt.

[7] In Upajāti-metre.

[8] In Upajāti-metre.

[9] In Upajāti-metre.

[10] In Upajāti-metre.

[11] In Upajāti-metre.

[12] In Upajāti-metre.

4–7 Then Brahman created the Āṅgirasas, experts in the Veda, Vedāṅgas, and various other fields of knowledge (*śāstra*). They bowed to their teacher and started to practise asceticism, but they had not asked their mother before, though »a mother surpasses all other venerable persons in importance« (maxim). Consequently, she grew angry and cursed them never to achieve the completion of their austerities, since they had neglected her.

8–15ef They searched through various regions but could not obtain completion (of their austerities); hindrance (*vighna*) followed them everywhere, caused either by demons, by men, by beautiful women, or by flaws of their bodies. Finally, they went to Agastya, who was born in a water-jar, the best of ascetics and lord of the southern direction; after paying homage to him, the Āṅgirasas, who had been born in the family of Agni,[2] asked him what fault was preventing them from completing their austerities whatever they tried; what they should do? – for they knew him as the best expert in asceticism (praise of Agastya's qualities). Evil people did not know his true nature.

16–21 Agastya thought about it and consoled them; they had controlled their senses, they were progenitors (*sraṣṭāraḥ*) created by Brahman, though they had not yet completed their austerities. They should remember the past: those created by Brahman before, who had gone away, were now happy;[3] those who had followed them, had become the Āṅgirasas (?).[4] After they and those (former sons) had gone, other (sons of) Prajāpati would doubtlessly come about (?). They should go to the Gaṅgā and practise austerities there, for there is no other means than the Gaṅgā, the beloved of Śiva; in this holy region they should pay homage to the »imparter of knowledge« (*jñānada*), who destroys all doubts. There is no accomplishment without a good teacher.

22–27ef Now they asked him for the name of that »imparter of knowledge«, whether he was Brahman, Viṣṇu, or Maheśa (= Śiva), the sun or the moon, Agni or Varuṇa. Agastya replied that the waters could be called Agni (fire), fire might be called sun, the sun might be called Viṣṇu and vice versa; Brahman could be called Rudra, who could be called »all« (*sarva*). Whoever knows all this is praised as »imparter of knowledge«. There are many venerable persons (*gurus*), among whom the most important one is the »giver of knowledge«. »Knowledge« is defined as that by which differentiation is overcome. Śambhu (= Śiva) is only one, without any second; he is named differently, as Indra, Mitra, Agni (etc.),[5] for the sake of the confused (i.e. of those who are still deceived by the variety of outward appearances).

28–29 Upon these words, five of them went to the northern Gaṅgā and five to the southern Gaṅgā (i.e. the Godāvarī), singing (vedic) verses (*gāthās*) and praising all the gods mentioned by Agastya, sitting in particular postures (*āsana*) and meditating about true reality.

[1] cf. the story of Dakṣa's sons in ch. 3.17–24 above.

[2] Allusion to ch. 144 above? Here (i.e. 158.4 above and 158.17 below) they were created by Brahman.

[3] *edhate*: wrong singular instead of plural form (because of the metre?).

[4] Connection not clear.

[5] cf. RV 1,164.46a and c.

30-35ab All the gods were pleased with them and predicted that they would obtain »the rank of progenitors« (*sraṣṭṛtva*, *prajāpatitva*), which was established at the beginning of the Yuga to procure the disappearance of people without *dharma*, to establish the Vedas, to accomplish the three goals of life, and to ascertain the meaning of Purāṇas, Epics, and the Vedas, as well as of the Dharmaśāstra. When *dharma* was neglected and the Veda forgotten, they would re-establish the Vedas, as future »Vyāsas« (»redactors«) and benefactors (of the world).[6]

cd-37ab At the place of their asceticism, on the northern bank of the Gautamī, Śiva, Viṣṇu, and Brahman (the first-person narrator), the sun, fire, the waters, i.e. the »all«, are established; there is no better means of purification than those.

cd-39ab Whatever has assumed different appearances is the highest *brahman* alone; Śiva, whose self is the »all«, permeates all, full of compassion for all beings, especially at this place of pilgrimage, surrounded by all gods, and causing their benefit.

cd-40ef They (i.e. the Āṅgirasas) are known as »redactors« of *dharma*(-knowledge) and of the Vedas; their holy place is named Vyāsatīrtha; by its water all dirt of sins is washed away destroying confusion, darkness, and intoxication and granting every success.

Ch. 159: Kadrū and Vinatā[1]

1 Brahman continues with (an account of) the place called Vañjarāsaṃgama (»confluence of Vañjarā«).

2-4 Once Garuḍa was subordinate to the snakes, because his mother was a slave (of Kadrū, the snakes' mother). Full of distress, he thought how fortunate people are who are independent of others and he deplored his situation.

5-11 He went to his mother and asked her due to whose fault she had become a slave. She replied that it was her own fault and told him that there had been an agreement between Kadrū and herself that she whose word turned out wrong was to become slave of the other; by deceit Kadrū had won against Vinatā,[2] for »fate is strong, which movement does it not make?« (maxim). As she was Kadrū's slave, her son Garuḍa naturally was a slave, too. After these words Garuḍa was sad, but made no reply, thinking about the inevitability of fate.

12-16 Once Kadrū, wishing for her sons' benefit and her own power, started to talk to Vinatā, pointing out how lucky Vinatā was, since her son could visit the sun-god and worship him. Hiding her grief Vinatā asked why Kadrū's sons did not do the same. Now Kadrū ordered Vinatā to take her and her sons to the abode of the snakes near the ocean, where there was a cool lake.

17-21 Accordingly Vinatā and Suparṇa (= Garuḍa) carried Kadrū and the snakes (to that place). Now Kadrū said to Vinatā[3] that Garuḍa should take her sons to the abode of

[6] v. 33cd-34ab and 34cd-35ab have parallel contents, 34cd being a slightly changed quotation of BhG 4.7ab.

[1] cf. MBh (crit. ed.) 1,18-21; 23-24.

[2] It is apparently assumed that the story as told in MBh 1,18 is known to the audience.

[3] The following verse (18), mentioning Garuḍa, does not fit into the context of the dialogue

the gods. She told him[4] that her sons wanted to pay homage to the sun, the teacher (*guru*) of the three worlds; she ordered Vinatā to take them to the orbit of the sun and then bring them back to her, every day. Trembling, Vinatā replied that she was not able to carry Kadrū's sons; her son would undertake the task in her place.

22-24cd Vinatā told her son about Kadrū's order; he agreed to the task and told the snakes to mount him. They did so, and Garuḍa carried them up, nearer and nearer to the sun.

24ef-25ef When the heat of the sun started to burn them, they became disturbed and told Garuḍa to return to the earth.

26-27 But Garuḍa said he would show them the sun and continued flying towards the sun. Burnt by the heat, the snakes fell to the ground on the island Vīraṇa.

28-31ab (Hearing) the lamentations of her burnt sons, Kadrū, perturbed, went to console them; then she turned to Vinatā and accused Garuḍa because of his evil deed; there was no possibility of alleviating her sons' pains. The lord (i.e. father) of the snakes, Kāśyapa (Kadrū's and Vinatā's husband), would not come now because of keeping his master's word;[5] if he were there, there could be health (for her sons). How could there be release from pains for her sons now?

31cd-35 Hearing Kadrū's accusations, Vinatā turned to her son as if she were frightened, and reproached him for having committed this improper deed; he should have shown propriety of conduct, for »one should not commit dishonesty against anybody, even an enemy; the moon shines for a Brahmin as well as for a low-born man« (maxim). Only those who dare not act openly achieve evil things by means of deceit (maxim).

36-39cd Then Vinatā asked Kadrū what she could do, in order to heal the burnt snakes. Kadrū replied that they should be sprinkled with water from the nether world. So Vinatā went to the nether world, brought the water from there and sprinkled Kadrū's sons.

39ef-41ab Garuḍa turned to Maghavan (= Indra) and asked for rain for the sake of the three worlds. Accordingly Parjanya sent rain, and welfare originated for the snakes.[6]

41cd-46ab This Gaṅgā-water from the nether world is (called?) »reviving the snakes« (41cd/44cd). The place where the snakes had been sprinkled is called »Nāgālaya« (»abode of the snakes«) (42cd). Since Garuḍa had brought the water from the nether world to the southern bank of the Gautamī to destroy old age, this water belonged to the Gaṅgā, destroying all evil (45ab, 43). The water that was brought by Garuḍa for destroying old age and by which the snakes were healed (42ab, 44ab) became the river Vañjarā, a transporter of the nectar of immortality, taking away all pains of old age and poverty.[7]

46cd-48ab How can the confluence of that Gaṅgā which originated in the nether world with the one of the world of mortals be described? Merely by thinking of it all

between Kadrū and Vinatā; it is Vinatā, who suggests, in v. 21, that her son should carry out this task.

[4] In the following direct speech, however, Vinatā is addressed and not Garuḍa.

[5] Unclear; allusion to which story?

[6] Seems to be inserted, in order to bring the story in accordance with the one told in the MBh, where the snakes are cured by Indra sending rain, not by water from the nether world.

[7] The sequence of verses seems to be disturbed; repetitions of phrases make the passage seem corrupt.

accumulations of evil are destroyed; who is able to describe the merit obtained by bathing and bestowing of gifts at this place?

48cd–49ef There are 125,000 holy places accumulated at this place, granting all kinds of good fortune and taking away all evil. There is no place (equal to) Vañjarāsaṃgama; by thinking of it all calamities disappear.

Ch. 160: Battle between gods and demons

1–2ab Brahman announces (an account of) the place named Devāgama, which bestows enjoyment and liberation for men and satiation for the ancestors.

2cd–6ab Once there was a battle between gods and demons for the sake of riches. Heaven belonged to the gods, the earth (*ilā*) to the demons, who, having seized the region of religious actions (*karmabhūmi*), prospered in every respect. They killed the people who presented offerings to the gods; hence the gods were without their sacrificial share. They went to Brahman (the first-person narrator) and asked him what to do. Brahman told them that after defeating the demons in battle they would gain the earth, religious actions, sacrificial gifts, and glory.

6cd–9 So the gods went to earth for battle. Daityas, Dānavas, and Rākṣasas assembled there, too: Ahi (the »Snake«),[1] Vṛtra, Bali, Tvaṣṭṛ's son (= Viśvarūpa), Namuci, Śambara, Maya, and many others, all eager to fight. The gods were: Agni, Indra, Varuṇa, Tvaṣṭṛ, Pūṣan, the two Aśvins, the Maruts, and the guardians of the directions, all endowed with various weapons.

10–12 The Dānavas, who stayed in the southern ocean, made a great effort in the south. The mountain Trikūṭa formerly belonged to the Rākṣasas; they, too, met them at the southern ocean. The place of their coming together (*melana*) was the mountain Malaya;[2] this region belonged also to the enemies of the gods.

13–16ef The gods assembled on the bank of the Gautamī, (since a Liṅga of) Śiva was established there; they mounted their chariot(s) and gathered here and there, on a small island in the midst of the Gautamī, the mother of streams, who grants to the ancestors all they desire. Then all the gods praised the god Maheśvara (= Śiva)[3] thinking of a means to subdue their enemies, for only one thing would be the best for them, either victory or death, since »life is miserable for thinking beings who are overpowered by their rivals« (maxim).

17–19 Suddenly there was a heavenly voice, advising the gods to go to the Gautamī[4] and to praise Harihara (= Viṣṇu and Śiva) there; for what cannot be achieved by the favour of the Godāvarī and these two gods?

[1] Does this refer to the following Vṛtra, or is it a name of its own (cf. Ahir Budhnya)?

[2] Obviously an attempt at an etymological explanation of the name Malaya.

[3] v.l. »praised Viṣṇu and Maheśvara«; probably this verse was originally connected with v. 20 below, and the thoughts of the gods (15ef–16) as well as the interference of the heavenly voice (17–19) were inserted later, in order to stress the importance of the Gautamī, against the logic of narration; for one would expect that, after being praised by the gods, Śiva would grant a boon.

[4] Does not fit with the passage 13–15ab above, where it was told that the gods were already staying at the Gautamī.

20 From Hari (= Viṣṇu) and Īśa (= Śiva), who were pleased (by the gods), the gods obtained the desired victory and went in all directions.

21–22ab The place where the gods had assembled is called Devāgama (»arrival of the gods«); it is praised by the hermits perceiving the truth. There are 80,000 Liṅgas of Śiva.

22c-f The mountain Devāgama is also called Priya (»dear«); ever since, this holy place has therefore been known as Devapriya (»dear to the gods«).[5]

Ch. 161: Creation of the world from Brahman's primordial sacrifice

1–6ab Introduction:

1–2ab Brahman announces a description of the holy place named Kuśatarpaṇa as well as Praṇītāsaṃgama, which grants enjoyment and liberation in all worlds.

2cd–4ab At the southern flank of the Vindhya-mountains there is a high mountain called Sahya; from its foot, where Viraja (a place?) and Ekavīrā (a river?) are situated, spring the rivers Godā(varī), Bhīmarathī etc. Its greatness cannot be described.

4cd–6ab Brahman announces that he will tell Nārada the greatest secret about the sacred region on this mountain, which was told in the Veda by himself and which is not known to sages, gods, ancestors, or demons.

6cd–11ab *Birth of Brahman*

6cd–9 The highest principle is the *puruṣa* who is unmanifest and imperishable. From this incorporeal (principle) an inferior and perishable *puruṣa* was born with limbs, being combined with the principle of matter (*prakṛti*). From him (i.e. the second *puruṣa*) the waters originated, from the waters the *puruṣa* (i.e. a third *puruṣa*, viz. Viṣṇu?), from both the lotus, in which Brahman (the first-person narrator) was born.

9–11ab Earth, wind, ether, water, and light were prior to Brahman; he could see only them, nothing else, either movable or immovable (i.e. animate and inanimate) beings, not even the Vedas nor (the principle) from which he originated.

11cd–26 *Dialogue between Brahman and the heavenly voice*

11cd–12 While he thus remained silent, he heard an excellent voice ordering him to procreate the immovable and movable beings.

13–16 Brahman asked how, where, and by which means he should create the world. The heavenly voice, called »Prakṛti«, who was sent by Viṣṇu, the mother consisting of the world, replied that he should perform a sacrifice; then he would obtain the necessary energy (*śakti*). According to eternal tradition, Viṣṇu is the sacrifice.[1] What could not be accomplished by a person who performs a sacrifice, in this world and in the world beyond?

[5] Name or description?

[1] For 15c (*yajño vai viṣṇuḥ*), cf. ŚB 1.1.2.15.

17-20 Again Brahman asked where and with whom (or: by which means) the sacrifice should be performed; the voice, who was the Goddess in the form of the sound »*oṃ*«, replied that he should worship the Lord of the sacrifice in the land of religious actions (*karmabhūmi*) with the Soul of the sacrifice (*yajñapuruṣa*), for he would be the means to be used by Brahman. Everything that belongs to the sacrifice, the exclamation »Svāhā!«, the libation (*svadhā*), ritual formulas (*mantra*s), the Brahmins, and the oblation (*havis*), all is Hari (= Viṣṇu); by (using) him (as means) everything could be obtained from Viṣṇu.

21-23ef Now Brahman asked where the »field of religious actions« should be; for at that time there were neither rivers, such as Bhāgīrathī, Narmadā, Yamunā, Tāpī, Sarasvatī, and Gautamī, nor oceans nor lakes nor streams. The Energy (*śakti*, i.e. the heavenly voice) defined this land as lying south of Mt. Sumeru, of the Himālaya, of the Vindhya-mountains, and of the Sahya-mountains.

24-26 Accordingly Brahman left Mt. Meru and went in that (i.e. the southern) direction, wondering where to stay. Again Viṣṇu's incorporeal voice addressed him, directing him where to go and assigning a place to him in which to prepare the sacrifice; after the preparations he should create all the Vedas.

27-39ab *Preparation of the sacrifice*

27-29 The Itihāsas and Purāṇas and other texts came into Brahman's mouth and became the body of sacred tradition (*smṛti*); at the same moment the complete meaning of the Vedas became known to him. He knew by heart the famous Puruṣasūkta[2] and prepared the sacrificial implements as taught (in that hymn).[3]

30-33ab The region where Brahman purified himself for the sacrifice is named after him; the place of Brahman's sacrifice to the gods is named Brahmagiri;[4] its circumference was 84[5] Yojanas, and it was situated east of Brahman's mountain (i.e. Mt. Brahmagiri). In the midst there was the sacrificial platform, (around it) the Gārhapatya(-fire), the southern (fire),[6] and the Āhavanīya(-fire); thus Brahman created the sacrificial fire(-place)s.

3cd-35ab As it is taught in the Vedas that »without a wife the sacrifice cannot be completed«, Brahman divided himself into two halves, the front (*pūrva*) part (of his body) became his wife, the other one (*uttara*) he himself, in accordance with the vedic statement »One half (of the man) is his wife.«[7]

5cd-39ab Now Brahman made spring-time the melted butter, summer the fuel (for the sacrificial fire), autumn the oblation,[8] and the rainy season the sacrificial grass. The metres (*chandaṃsi*) became the seven sticks for the enclosure (*paridhi*); the three time measurements (divisions of time) are thought of as fire wood,[9] sacrificial

[2] i.e. RV 10,90.
[3] cf. 35cd-39ab below.
[4] cf. above ch. 74, v. 24cd seq.
[5] v.l. 24.
[6] Thus according to ed. VePr; ASS has »south of it«, which does not make sense.
[7] cf. ŚB 5.2.1.10 *ardho ha vā eṣa ātmano yaj jāyā.*
[8] cf. RV 10,90.6cd.
[9] Remote similarity to RV 10,90.15ab.

vessels, and Kuśa-grass, whereas Time (or death) became the sacrificial post, the Yoktra (?)[10] became (the implements of) the animal sacrifice, the three principal qualities (*guṇas*) became the ropes for binding the sacrificial animal. But there was no sacrificial animal (*paśu*).

39cd–58 *Performance of the sacrifice*

39cd–43ab Brahman addressed the incorporeal voice that belonged to Viṣṇu, stating that no sacrifice was possible without a sacrificial animal. The voice advised him to praise the supreme *Puruṣa* with the Puruṣasūkta (the hymn about the *puruṣa*). When Janārdana, the progenitor, was being praised devotedly by Brahman the Goddess (i.e. the voice) told Brahman to use her as sacrificial animal.[11]

43cd–50cd Now Brahman recognised the *puruṣa*, his progenitor, who had entered the ropes at the sacrificial pole, standing on the sacrificial grass, and he sprinkled him.[12] At this moment everything in this world originated from him:[13] the Brahmins from his mouth, the Kṣatriyas from his arms;[14] Indra and Agni were born from his mouth, Vāyu (wind) from his breath;[15] the directions from his ears, the sky from his head,[16] the moon from his brains, the sun from his eye;[17] the intermediate space originated from his navel, the Vaiśyas from his thighs,[18] the Śūdras and the earth from his feet.[19] From the pores of his skin the seers came into existence, the plants from his hair, domestic and wild animals from his nails;[20] worms and insects from his anus and organs of generation; everything, movable and immovable, visible and invisible, originated from him; even the gods originated from him (?).

50ef–53 Again the heavenly voice addressed Brahman, stating that creation had been completed now, and ordered Brahman to pour (the oblation) into the fire and to let forth the sacrificial vessels and the *sāman*-melodies (?),[21] the sacrificial pole, the water used in the sacrifice, and the Kuśa-grass, the shape of the officiating priests and the shape of the sacrifice, what should be explained and what should be meditated about; Brahman should (further) let forth the sacrificial ladle, the *puruṣa*, and the ropes.

54–58 With these words, and while Brahman was pouring (the oblation) into the three fires, the Gārhapatya, the southern and the eastern fire, naming (calling upon ?) the

[10] = Yojana, space measurement?

[11] As this voice belonged to Viṣṇu, who is also the supreme *puruṣa*, the contents of her words also refer to Viṣṇu (or the supreme *puruṣa*) himself.

[12] cf. RV 10,90.7ab.

[13] cf. RV 10,90.12–14.

[14] cf. RV 10,90.12ab.

[15] cf. RV 10,90.13cd.

[16] cf. RV 10,90.14c and b.

[17] cfṚV 10,90.13ab.

[18] cf. RV 10,90.14a; 12c.

[19] cf. RV 10,90.12d; 14c.

[20] cf. RV 10,90.8cd?

[21] Read *sāmāni* for *samāni*?

puruṣa, the origin of the world, he himself, that god of the sacrifice, the lord of the world (*jagannātha*), showed himself as Viṣṇu in white shape in the Āhavanīya-fire, in black shape in the southern fire, and in yellow shape in the fire of the householder (Gārhapatya). In these regions (places ?) Viṣṇu is always present; nothing is devoid of him.

59 Murmuring sacred formulas, Brahman fetched the sacrificial water (*praṇītā*); from that water the river Praṇītā came into existence...[22]

60–61ab He sent forth the sacrificial water, having cleaned it with Kuśa-grass. The water drops that fell to the ground, during the purification, became holy places.

61cd–62 ...which grants the merit of a sacrifice to a man who bathes in it, and which is adorned with (the presence of) the god of gods, characterised by his bow (= Viṣṇu); it is (like) a flight of steps for climbing up to the Vaikuṇṭha paradise (Viṣṇu's heaven).

63–64ab The place where the cleaned Kuśa-grass fell to the ground is called Kuśatarpaṇa,[23] granting much merit; by Kuśa-grass all are satisfied (*tarpita*), (hence) it is called Kuśatarpaṇa.

cd–65ab Later, for some other reason (?), the Gautamī merged with (lit.: in) the Praṇītā,[24] and (the place called) Praṇītāsaṃgama (»confluence of the Praṇītā«) came into existence.

65cd–67 In the Kuśatarpaṇa-region (i.e. at the place of satisfaction by Kuśa-grass) is the holy place called Kuśatarpaṇa; here, north of the Vindhya-mountains (?), Brahman had made the sacrificial post to which Viṣṇu was bound, it became the imperishable Banyan-tree, which is eternal, in the shape of Time (*kāla*), and grants the merit of a sacrifice by being thought of.

68–71 Brahman's sacrificial ground is called Daṇḍaka-forest. When the sacrifice was over, Brahman devotedly satisfied Viṣṇu, who is called »Virāṭ« in the Vedas,[25] from whom the formed (*mūrta*) was born, who was the origin of Brahman and to whom the world belongs. Having paid homage to the lord of gods (= Viṣṇu), Brahman created the place for worshipping the gods, extending 24 Yojanas.[26] Hence there are still today three water basins, according to the three forms of Viṣṇu as Lord of the sacrifice.[27]

72–78 Ever since, this has been called the place of Brahman's worshipping the gods. Even a worm or insect that lives there will obtain liberation in the end. The Daṇḍaka-forest is called »germ of law« (*dharmabīja*) and »germ of liberation« (*muktibīja*). The region adjacent to the Gautamī is especially holy; whoever bathes at the confluence of the Praṇītā or at Kuśatarpaṇa, goes to the highest abode. Thinking of, reciting, or listening to (an account of it) grants all wishes to men, enjoyment as well as liberation. There are 86,000 holy places on both banks of the Gautamī; the merit obtained there was told above (?). Kuśatarpaṇa is superior even to Vārāṇasī; there is

[22] The sentence is continued in 61cd.
[23] Seems to continue the passage 60–61ab above.
[24] Or: at (the place of) the Praṇītā(-ceremony)?
[25] cf. RV 10,90.5ab?
[26] The same place as in v. 30–33ab?
[27] cf. v. 57 above.

no holy place comparable to it, which even destroys sins like Brahmin-murder by being merely thought of. This holy place is called »door to heaven« (Svargadvāra) on earth.

Ch. 162: Story of Manyu helping the gods against the demons[1]

1–2ab Brahman announces (an account of) Manyutīrtha, which grants all wishes to men and destroys all evil.

2cd–6ab In former times there was a battle between gods and demons, in which neither gods nor demons could gain the victory. Discouraged and dejected, the gods went to Brahman (the first-person narrator) and asked for a means to remove their fear. Brahman advised them to go to the Gautamī and praise Maheśvara (= Śiva) there; by that they would obtain the cause of victory.

6cd–10ab Accordingly the gods praised Maheśvara; some practised austerities, some danced, some bathed, and some worshipped him. Pleased by them Maheśvara told them to choose whatever they wanted. They asked for a strong man who could lead them to victory in battle.

10cd–12 Śiva agreed. Somebody was produced from his (Śiva's) brilliance. The thirteen (gods) bowed to him, who was named Manyu (»wrath«) and was the leader of their army, and bowed to Śiva; then they joined Manyu and formed up for battle.

13–19 Standing there, ready for the battle with Daityas and Dānavas, the gods told Manyu that they would fight after having seen his ability of fighting; he should show himself to them. Manyu smiled and told them about his progenitor, the lord of gods (= Śiva), who knows everything about everybody, and permeates everything, but cannot be perceived by anybody. Since Manyu had originated from him, how could the gods be able to perceive him? But he agreed to show himself to them.

20–27ab Then Manyu showed them his huge shape, which had originated from Bhava's (= Śiva's) third eye and which is called »all«, manhood in men, the ego in living beings, the wrath that will cause the end (of the world). Seeing Śaṃkara's representative, flaming with brilliance, and holding all (sorts of) weapons, the trembling gods bowed to him and asked him to be their leader in battle; they praised him as Indra, Varuṇa,[2] and the guardians of directions and asked him to enter them to procure victory for them. Manyu replied that there is nothing without him (i.e. without wrath), that he stays in everything, but nobody perceives him.

27cd–30 Then the Lord Manyu became differentiated: in the shape of Rudra he became Śiva. Everything movable and immovable is permeated by him. By obtaining him the gods gained victory in battle. Victory, wrath, and heroism originate from the brilliance of the Lord (Śiva). Having gained victory by means of »wrath« (*manyu*) in the battle against the demons, the gods went to where they had come from, protected by Manyu.

[1] Seems to be based on RV 10,83 (hym to Manyu), but there are no literal congruencies.

[2] Compare *tvam indras tvaṃ ca varuṇo lokapālās tvam eva ca* to RV 10,83.2ab *manyúr índro manyúr evā́sa devó / manyúr hótā váruṇo jātávedaḥ*.

31-33ef The place on the bank of the Gautamī where the gods pleased Śiva and obtained Manyu as well as victory is called Manyutīrtha. The man who thinks of the origin of Manyu will be victorious and will never be subdued. There is no means of purification comparable to Manyutīrtha, where Śaṃkara (= Śiva) is always present in the shape of Manyu. Bathing there and bestowing gifts as well as thinking of (that place) bestows all things desired.

Ch. 163: Śākalya, a devotee of Viṣṇu, and the Rākṣasa Paraśu

1-2 Brahman announces that he will tell about the events at the holy place named Sārasvata(-tīrtha), which grants all desires, enjoyment and liberation, destroys all evil and diseases, and conveys success to all actions.

3-6 In the northern part of the Puṣpotkaṭa(-range) there is Mt. Śubhra, famous in the (three) worlds, situated at the southern bank of the Gautamī. On that mountain a hermit named Śākalya practised severe asceticism. All beings bowed to him and praised him, who was devoted to Agni and to studying the Veda, on that mountain, which was visited by sages, gods, and Gandharvas.

7-12ab On the same mountain lived a Rākṣasa named Paraśu, frightening the heavenly Brahmins, hating sacrifices and killing Brahmins; he used to roam the forest in different shapes, sometimes as a Brahmin, sometimes as a tiger, sometimes as a god, sometimes as a beautiful woman, sometimes as a domestic or wild animal, sometimes even as a child; thus he approached the wise Śākalya again and again, but he could neither subdue nor kill him.

12cd-16 Once Śākalya had worshipped the gods and was about to eat, when Paraśu, in the shape of a Brahmin, approached him, together with a young girl, and told him that they were hungry and wanted to be his guests; by showing hospitality he would have fulfilled his duties, for »happy in this world and the world beyond are those from whose house guests depart satiated« (maxim). Whoever offers food prepared for himself to guests bestows the earth as a gift.

17-22 Śākalya agreed and offered Paraśu a seat, without recognising him; he honoured him as a guest and gave him food, according to the rules. Paraśu took the water and the food and explained to his host that someone exhausted from a long journey is accompanied by the gods, who are satisfied together with the guest. A guest and a reviler are friends of all: the reviler takes away the evil, a guest is a passage to heaven. But he who looks upon an exhausted guest with disgust is deprived of righteousness, renown and wealth at that very moment. Therefore Paraśu asked him whether he would therefore give him, as his guest, all the food he wanted.

23-25 Śākalya consented. Now Paraśu told him that he was a Rākṣasa, no Brahmin, and that he had watched Śākalya for many years. Being dried up like water in summer, he would lead him away and eat him.

26-31 Śākalya replied that noble and learned people never change a promise; the Rākṣasa should do what he wanted, but he should first listen to him, for those who are about to kill somebody should first be warned. As a Brahmin Śākalya possessed a body like a diamond, and Hari (= Viṣṇu) was his protector. He then prayed that his feet should be protected by Viṣṇu, his head by Janārdana, his arms by Vārāha (the Boar), his back by the king of tortoises, his heart by Kṛṣṇa, his fingers by the beast (i.e. Narasiṃha), his mouth by the Lord of Speech,[1] his eyes by (the god) who rides on the bird (Garuḍa), his ears by the Lord of wealth,[2] everything else by Bhava (= Śiva). The god Nārāyaṇa himself is the only refuge in all kinds of calamities.

32–39 After this (prayer) Śākalya invited the Rākṣasa to take him off and eat him. The Rākṣasa prepared to do so, for »there is not even a grain of pity in the hearts of evil-doers« (maxim). Approaching the Brahmin with terrible tusks and mouth, he looked at him and now recognised the Brahmin's shape as that of Viṣṇu holding conch, discus and club, with thousand feet, heads, eyes, and ears, the only refuge of all beings; he begged for his forgiveness. Then he asked him to tell him a sin-destroying holy place, since »meeting (*darśana*) with great people, be it because of hatred or ignorance, by chance or out of carelessness, is never without (good) result; the contact of iron with (gold?) will lead to the state of a golden ornament«[3] (maxim).

40–42 Śākalya replied that Sarasvatī would soon fulfil the Rākṣasa's wishes; he should praise Janārdana, for nothing else leads to the fulfilment of wishes. Sarasvatī would be satisfied with him because of the Brahmin's words.

43–46 Paraśu agreed and went to the Gaṅgā, the means of purification of the three worlds, and bathed there. Turning towards the Gaṅgā, he beheld Sarasvatī, the mother of the world, who had been in Śākalya's words, in her divine shape, and addressed her, telling her that Śākalya had advised him to praise the Mother's husband and asking her to bestow the ability (for doing so) upon him.

47–49 Sarasvatī agreed; by her favour Paraśu praised Janārdana. Pleased with him, Hari granted him a boon.

50–51 Due to the grace of Śākalya, of the Gautamī, of Sarasvatī, and of Narasiṃha, that extremely evil Rākṣasa Paraśu went to heaven; this was also due to the grace of the owner of the bow Śārṅga (= Viṣṇu).

52–53 Ever since, this holy place is famous as »Sārasvata«; by bathing there and bestowing gifts a person will be famous in Viṣṇu's world. Many holy places, originating from Vāk (Goddess »Speech« = Sarasvatī), from Viṣṇu, from Śākalya, and from Paraśu, came into existence there, on the Śveta-mountain (»White Mountain«).

Ch. 164: Story of King Pavamāna and the Ciccika-bird

1–2 Brahman announces an account of Ciccikātīrtha which removes all diseases and sorrows and grants alleviation (of pains) to all; it is situated on Mt. Śubhra, on the northern bank of the (Gautamī) Gaṅgā, where the god (Viṣṇu) is present, holding the club.

[1] Vāgīśa = Brahman, or in this case Viṣṇu? cf. above 161.39cd–48.

[2] Vitteśa = Kubera or, in this case, Viṣṇu?

[3] *sparśasaṃsparśa* »contact with touch« does not make much sense.

3–6 A Ciccika-bird, named Bheruṇḍa, feeding upon flesh, lived on this Śveta-mountain, which abounded in trees blossoming and bearing fruits at the same time and visited by twice-born (i.e. birds) and all sorts of superhuman beings (Siddhas, Gandharvas etc.). Nearby there was a tree, which was an abode of two-legged or four-legged beings, but not (*na bhājanam*) of disease, pain, hunger, thirst, sorrow, and death. On this mountain, which was endowed with qualities...[1]

7–9ab A king of the eastern region, named Pavamāna, who was devoted to the Kṣatriya-rules and a protector of gods and Brahmins, went into the forest, together with a huge army, and enjoyed himself with his wives and with the pleasures of dancing and music, or he went hunting, a bow in his hand, surrounded by others devoted to hunting.

9cd–13 Once, roaming the forest and being quite exhausted, he approached a tree that grew on the bank of the Gautamī and was crowded with birds, like a householder who is visited by (persons belonging to) all stages of life. Reaching that tree, King Pavamāna saw a big bird with two beaks, absorbed in deep thoughts; he asked him who he was and why he looked so sorrowful, though all other beings at that place seemed to be free from sorrows.

14–16 The Ciccika-bird replied that nobody was afraid of him and he was not afraid of anybody. But he would like to see this mountain void of all these (happy) beings, that is why he felt sorry for himself, not reaching satiation, unable to sleep or to find any consolation.

17–28 The king asked him once more who he was, what evil he had done, why he wanted the mountain to be void of beings, and why he could not be satiated, though he had two beaks. Now the bird told him that in his former birth he had been a Brahmin of noble family, well-versed in Vedas and Vedāṅgas, but neglecting his duty and addicted to dice-playing. He had been »two-faced« (double-dealing), speaking differently in the presence and the absence of a person, had been envious and had cheated everybody by his magic power, had been ungrateful, insincere, eager to blame others, delighting in harming others, had troubled a lot of people in thoughts, deeds, and words, had disunited things and people that belonged together, etc. There had been no sinner like him in the three worlds; for that reason he had been reborn with two mouths; because of having caused pain to others he had now to suffer pain and (wanted) the mountain to be void of beings.

29–37 Then the bird informed the king about sins comparable to Brahmin-murder; for instance a Kṣatriya killing somebody who was fleeing from battle, a (student) not remembering the things he had learnt or disrespecting his teachers; people being friendly on the surface, but secretly blaming others, their feelings, words, and deeds not being congruent; people cursing their teachers or blaming Brahmins, the Vedas or the Supreme Spirit: all these are like Brahmin-murderers. The bird had been similar, hence he had been reborn as a bird; but because of the good he had done in some respects he could remember his former actions.

[1] Sentence incomplete; the passage might be better understood, if the order of (half-)verses were slightly changed, e.g. 4, 5ab, 6cd, 3, 5cd–6ab: »On this mountain, which abounded of ... (description, comprising 4, 5ab, and 6cd), lived a Ciccika-bird ... (3); nearby was a tree ... (5cd–6ab.«

38-46 Now the king wanted to know by what means the bird could be released. The bird told him that there was a holy place named Gadātīrtha, situated on the northern bank of the Gautamī, on (the flank of) that mountain; this holy place destroys all sins. Only Viṣṇu and the Gautamī are destroyers of calamities; for that reason the bird had always striven to see this holy place, but all his efforts had been in vain, he could not reach it by himself. For that reason he liked to ask the king to enable him to see (the statue of) Gadādhara (= Viṣṇu holding his club), the »ocean of compassion«; after after beholding this god, he would (be able to) ascend to heaven.

47-50ef According to this request, the king showed the bird this (statue of the) god (Viṣṇu) as well as the (Gautamī) Gaṅgā. The bird bathed in the Gaṅgā, addressing her with a prayer, praising her again as the only refuge for all sinners and asking her to take away his sins.

51-53ab After having bathed, with pure mind and utmost belief in the Gaṅgā, keeping in mind the formula »Gaṅgā, protect me!«, the bird then bowed to Gadādhara (= Viṣṇu holding the club), took leave of King Pavamāna, and went to heaven. Pavamāna returned to his own capital.

53cd-54 Ever since, this holy place has been known as Pāvamāna and Ciccika,[2] as Gadādhara and as Koṭitīrtha. The effect of everything that is done here will be multiplied by ten million times of ten million.

Ch. 165: Marriage of the sun-god's ugly daughter Viṣṭi

1 Brahman continues with (the description of) Bhadratīrtha, which wards off everything that is unwelcome, destroys all evil and grants peace.

2-4 Āditya's (the sun's) dear and faithful wife was Uṣā, the daughter of Tvaṣṭṛ;[1] he had another wife, Chāyā, whose son was Śanaiścara (= Saturn). His sister, whose shape was dreadful and ugly, was named Viṣṭi. Savitṛ (the sun-god) worried about who he could give her to in marriage; whoever was offered her hand refused, calling her dreadful.

5-17 Therefore Viṣṭi was much distressed and told her father that it is a father's duty to give his daughter in marriage as long as she is still a child, at an age between four and ten years; her bridegroom should be young, of good family, knowledgeable, renowned, etc. (list of good qualities). A father who does not fulfil this duty will go to hell. For the wise a daughter is a (means for the) accomplishment of *dharma*, for the foolish of hell. On one side there is the whole earth, on the other a good daughter, well-adorned and without deception (both are equal in value). A father who sells his daughter, a horse, a cow, or sesamum seed, will not escape Raurava and other hells.[2] The sin committed by a father who neglects (his duty to give his daughter in) marriage cannot be described. She is to be given away as long as she

[2] Or: Ciccikā, as in the beginning of this chapter? The compound *saciccikam* allows both possibilities.

[1] cf. ch. 89 above.

[2] cf. above ch. 150, V.9.

does not yet know shame (*lajjā*) and still plays with dust.[3] A son is for a father like his self; who does not care for one's own self? But what a father does for his daughter is a really good action, the merit of which is imperishable. Who does not do good to sons and grandsons? But by doing so to a daughter a man will become a receptacle of happiness.

18–22 Thus instructed by his daughter, the sun asked her what he should do: nobody would take her as his wife, for it is expected that the qualities of both partners (concerning family, appearance, age, wealth, knowledge, conduct, good character) should match each other. To whom should he give her, with her special qualities? If she agreed to be given to no matter whom, then she should be married that very day.

23–26 Viṣṭi replied that, after all, every condition and relation in this life was predetermined by the deeds committed in a former birth; the father should avoid making (new) mistakes, for the fruit is according to the conduct. Therefore a father acts in accordance with the tradition of his family concerning marriage; the rest happens according to fate.

27–30ab Upon this answer, he gave his formidable daughter to Viśvarūpa, Tvaṣṭṛ's son, who was as terrible and ugly as Viṣṭi; both lived together in harmony as well as in disharmony. Their sons were Gaṇḍa, Atigaṇḍa, Raktākṣa, Krodhana, Vyaya, and Durmukha (all names signifying a bad quality).

30cd–36 Their youngest son Harṣaṇa (»causing joy«) was endowed with good qualities; he was pure, of peaceful mind, etc. Once he went to the house of his maternal uncle (i.e. Yama), where he beheld many (deceased) people, those staying in heaven and those suffering (in hell). He asked Dharma (i.e. Yama, the »king of *dharma*«) who these people were. The »king of *dharma*« replied that those who never transgress the traditional rules never see hell, but those who do not respect the holy texts and prescriptions go to hell.

37–44 Now Harṣaṇa asked his uncle by what action his parents and brothers could attain a beautiful, flawless, auspicious form; such an action he wanted to do, otherwise he would not return to them. The King of *dharma* stated first that Harṣaṇa was really »causing joy« (*harṣaṇa*); there might be many sons in a family, but only one who supports the family is a real son, likewise a son who does good to his parents and his brothers. Since Harṣaṇa had spoken what was agreeable to him (i.e. Yama), he should go to the Gautamī, bathe there and praise Viṣṇu, the origin of the world; when pleased, Viṣṇu would grant everything.

45–47ab Accordingly Harṣaṇa went to the Gautamī and praised Hari, the Lord of the gods, who was pleased and granted Harṣaṇa the welfare of his family, preceded by the appeasement of all that was inauspicious; he concluded with the words »blessing to thee (*bhadram astu te*)!« Thereupon Viṣṭi got the name Bhadrā, and Harṣaṇa's father was called Bhadra.

47cd–48ef Ever since, this holy place has been called Bhadratīrtha, granting auspiciousness to men. Hari (= Viṣṇu) is present there as »Lord of Welfare« (*bhadrapati*). All men who visit this holy place are granted success in all their doings; Janārdana (= Viṣṇu), the god of gods and only receptacle of auspiciousness, is present (there).

[3] Quotation?

Ch. 166: Story of Saṃpāti and Jaṭāyu[1]

1 Brahman continues with the description of the Patatritīrtha, by thinking of which a man has fulfilled his (religious) duties.

2-4ab Kaśyapa had two sons (named) »the two Aruṇas« (i.e. Aruṇa and Garuḍa), whose descendants were Saṃpāti and Jaṭāyu. The two sons of the Prajāpati (named) Tārkṣya were Aruṇa and Garuḍa; in this lineage was born Saṃpāti, the best of birds, as well as his younger brother Jaṭāyu.[2]

4cd-6ab Contending with each other, both flew up to the sun, in order to pay homage to the sun-god. When they reached near the sun, their wings were burnt, and they fell down on the top of a mountain.

6cd-8ab Seeing his relatives motionless, Aruṇa told the sun what had happened and asked him to alleviate their pains; otherwise they would die. The sun-god resuscitated the two birds.

8cd-11ab Garuḍa and Viṣṇu had also heard about the condition of the two birds; they also came, in order to alleviate their pains. Then all of them, Jaṭāyu, Aruṇa, Saṃpāti, Garuḍa, Sūrya, and Viṣṇu went to the (Gautamī) Gaṅgā, to the merit-bestowing holy place named Patatritīrtha, which destroys poison and grants all wishes.

11cd-13 Sūrya and Viṣṇu himself, as well as Suparṇa (= Garuḍa) and Aruṇa are present at the bank of the Gautamī, likewise he, whose emblem is the bull (= Śiva). Because of the presence of the three gods, this holy place is especially excellent; a man who, after bathing and purifying himself, pays homage to these gods, will be free from all sorts of disease and attain the highest bliss.

Ch. 167: The young Brahmin and the Rākṣasī

1 Brahman announces that he will tell a surprising story about the holy place named Vipratīrtha or »Nārāyaṇa«.

2-3 In Antarvedī[1] there lived a Brahmin, well-versed in the Vedas, whose sons were learned, virtuous, and handsome. The youngest son was called Āsandiva; he was endowed with many good qualities.

4-7 At the time when his father wanted to marry him, one night a terrible Rākṣasī, who could assume whatever shape she wanted, took Āsandiva, who had fallen asleep without having thought of Viṣṇu, and carried him to the southern bank of the Gautamī. On the northern side of (Mt.) Śrīgiri was a city, which was visited by many Brahmins, an abode of righteousness and prosperity, ruled by King Bṛhatkīrti, who was endowed with all royal qualities.

8-14 To this city, where there was peace and abundance of food, the Rākṣasī took the Brahmin's son. In different shapes she roamed the earth with him; on the southern

[1] cf. Rm 4,58.2-7.

[2] v. 3-4ab seem to be a more elaborate repetition of v. 2.

[1] The district between Gaṅgā and Yamunā.

bank of the Godāvarī she assumed the shape of an old woman and told him that this (river) was the Gaṅgā; the *saṃdhyā*-prayer should be performed (here) by the Brahmins, according to the rules, but the Brahmins did not observe it correctly; hence they were regarded as low-born by the gods (?). He should call her »mother«, otherwise she would destroy him; if he did what she wanted, she would make him happy and re-unite him with his people. He asked her who she was. Assuring him with several oaths, she replied that her names was Kaṅkālinī, renowned throughout the world. Now he promised her to do whatever she wanted.[2]

15–17 Having heard these words, the Rākṣasī assumed the shape of an old but handsome woman and took him everywhere, introducing him as her gifted son. Thus, people thought him to be an excellent Brahmin, endowed with beauty, youth, good fortune, and knowledge, and her to be his mother, (likewise) endowed with good qualities.

18–21ef An excellent Brahmin gave his daughter in marriage to the young man, after having honoured the Rākṣasī. The bride was happy to be married to him, but he, seeing her good qualities, was much distressed, fearing that the Rākṣasī would devour him and his beautiful and virtuous young wife; he did not know what to do.

22–25 His wife, however, who was devoted to her husband and had noticed that he was distressed, one day asked him in private, while the Rākṣasī was absent, the reason for his sorrow. He told her everything in detail, for »what can not be entrusted to a dear friend and to a noble woman?« (maxim).

26–28 His wife consoled him, stating that there is fear of danger everywhere, even at home, for those who do not control their senses, but not for those who are composed, even less for those who stay at the Gautamī and are devoted to Viṣṇu; therefore he should bathe in the Gautamī and praise the god free from all disease (i.e. Viṣṇu).

29 Accordingly the Brahmin bathed in the (Gautamī) Gaṅgā and praised Nārāyaṇa.

30 Hymn by Āsandiva to Nārāyaṇa, praising him as inner self of the world, as creator, destroyer, and protector, and asking him why he did not protect him.[3]

31–32 Having heard these words, Nārāyaṇa killed the evil Rākṣasī with his thousand-spoked flaming discus Sudarśana, granted boons to Āsandiva, and re-united him with his father.

33 Ever since, this holy place is called Vipra(-tīrtha) and Nārāyaṇa(-tīrtha), where by bathing, bestowing gifts, worshipping (Viṣṇu) etc. every wish is fulfilled.

Ch. 168: The performance of King Abhiṣṭut's horse-sacrifice

1 Brahman continues with the description of Bhānutīrtha, a place of pilgrimage sacred to Tvaṣṭṛ, Maheśvara (= Śiva), Indra, Yama, and Agni, which destroys all evil.

2–5 Abhiṣṭuta[1] was the name of a king agreeable to look at;[2] he wished to worship the gods with a horse-sacrifice. His sixteen priests, among them Vasiṣṭha and Atri,

[2] In Upajāti-metre.
[3] In Upajāti-metre.

[1] In the second half of the story, he is called Abhiṣṭut.
[2] Or: King Priyadarśana was famous as Abhiṣṭuta.

discussed among themselves how to get a place for the sacrifice, since a Kṣatriya was the sacrificer. If a Brahmin was consecrated (for the sacrifice), the king could give the sacrificial ground, but if a king himself was consecrated, who should give, and who should ask for a gift? »Begging is the evil-shaped mother of non-protection; it should not be practised, especially not by Kṣatriyas« (maxim).[3]

6-9 Finally Vasiṣṭha suggested asking the sun-god for land to serve as sacrificial ground, quoting a prayer-formula by which the king should address Savitṛ (= Sūrya) as identical with heavenly power; he would grant to the king whatever he asked for.

10-12 Accordingly the king addressed Ravi (= the sun), who is (identical with) Hari (= Viṣṇu), Īśa (= Śiva), and the Unborn One (= Brahman), with a prayer, asking for a place of sacrifice for the gods. As the sun represents royal power among the gods (*kṣatraṃ daivam*) Sūrya granted land to the king.

13-14 Whoever acts similarly will not experience damage to his sacrifice. The place where, at the horse-sacrifice of King Abhiṣṭut,[4] Ravi appeared to the king, in order to grant him ground for his sacrifice, is called Bhānutīrtha.

15-18ab The splendid horse-sacrifice for the gods (took place), attended by the gods. But the Daityas and Dānavas and other destroyers of sacrifices also approached in the shape of Brahmins, chanting like those who know the Sāmaveda, without being prevented. They spoiled the sacrificial instruments, defamed the ritual actions, and derided the king and the priests.

18cd-21 Nobody knew about their way of conduct except Viśvarūpa, who told his father Tvaṣṭṛ that these were demons. Tvaṣṭṛ advised the gods to take water and Darbha-grass and sprinkle it around, uttering a special spell-formula for destroying those who despise the sacrifice and its implements.

22-24 The gods and Tvaṣṭṛ did so and the demons were reduced to ashes and made to run away. Uttering the spell, Tvaṣṭṛ sprinkled water upon them, and they went off, their lives coming to an end. The place where he did so is called Tvaṣṭṛtīrtha.

25-26ab The place where Yama, upon Tvaṣṭṛ's words, slew the Daityas with his stick of death, his discus, and his noose is called Yamatīrtha.

26cd-28ab Where the sacrifice was completed, where streams of Amṛta were poured into the fire, where the fire was satiated by King Abhiṣṭut, that place is called Agnitīrtha; it grants the merit of a horse-sacrifice.

28cd-29 Indra and the Maruts declared the king to be an emperor of the two worlds, who would be Indra's dear friend.

30 A man will have reached his goal, having satisfied his ancestors at Indratīrtha, especially at Yamatīrtha.

31-35 This holy place is also called Maheśvaratīrtha. Śiva was devotedly worshipped there by Abhiṣṭut, together with Brahmins who knew all (religious) actions. He worshipped Maheśvara with vedic and other prayer-formulas, with dancing, singing and playing instruments, with different observances, with prostrating himself, with fragrance, flowers, lamps, etc. he worshipped both, Viṣṇu and Śambhu. Both were pleased and granted King Abhiṣṭut boons as well as enjoyment and liberation and the special greatness for this holy place.

[3] The presupposition of this passage seems to be a rule saying that the sacrificer himself cannot grant the part of land where the sacrifice is to be performed.

[4] From here onward, he is called Abhiṣṭut instead of Abhiṣṭuta.

36 Ever since, this place of pilgrimage has been sacred to Śiva and Viṣṇu; bathing there and bestowing gifts fulfils every wish.

37 Whoever remembers or recites (the account of) these holy places is released from all sins and will enter the city of Śiva or Viṣṇu (phalastuti).

38 Especially at Bhānutīrtha, bathing grants success in all affairs; at this holy place, there are 100 places of pilgrimage which grant much merit.

Ch. 169: The hunter and the Brahmin as devotees of Śiva

1–2ab Brahman announces the story of the (origin of) Bhillatīrtha, which destroys diseases and sins and bestows devotion to the pair of foot-lotuses of Mahādeva (= Śiva).

2cd–3 On the southern bank of the Gautamī and the northern flank of Mt. Śrīgiri Mahādeva is present in the shape of a Liṅga called Ādikeśa, fulfilling all wishes, worshipped by the sages.

4–6ab A hermit named Sindhudvīpa lived there, whose brother, an excellent sage, too, was called Veda. He used to worship the enemy of Tripura (= Śiva) in the shape of Ādikeśa every noon; then he went collecting alms in the village.

6cd–15 When the Brahmin had disappeared, a hunter always entered that region to hunt. When he had roamed about and killed animals, he put the meat at the curved end of his bow and went to the Ādikeśa-Liṅga and put the meat down outside; then he went to the Gaṅgā, took water and returned to Śiva; drinking-vessels in one hand, and the meat in the other, he went to the Ādikeśa-Liṅga, pushed away with his foot what Veda had offered before, bathed the Śiva-Liṅga with water that he had taken in his mouth, worshipped Śiva with leaves and prepared the meat for him, with the words »May Śiva love me!« He only knew this impure (kind of) devotion to Śiva. Then he went home with the meat. Thus he did every day, and Śiva was pleased with him; for the addiction to Śiva is manifold. When the hunter (*bhilla*) did not come, Śiva was not quite happy; who knows Śaṃbhu's compassion for his devotees?

16–22ab Thus he worshipped Śiva and Umā every day; after some time, however, Veda, the Brahmin, got very angry with that evil-doer (whom he did not know but) who always destroyed his offerings to Śiva; he decided to kill him, for a man who injures a teacher, god, Brahmin, or his lord deserves death, all the more a man who injures Śiva. Considering that this man had destroyed his offerings of beautiful flowers etc. and offered meat and leaves, he was resolved to punish him by killing him; he hid himself, in order to watch him.

22cd–24ef When the hunter came as usual to worship the god, Ādikeśa addressed him, telling him how much he was pleased with the hunter's devotion, who had come from afar (though) being exhausted.

25–32 When Veda heard these words of the god, he grew very angry but said nothing. The hunter worshipped Śiva as usual and went home. Now Veda came forth and addressed the Lord furiously, complaining about that cruel hunter, who was without knowledge about offerings, without caste, without teacher, enjoying evil actions, etc.; to this man Śiva had shown himself, whereas he had never talked to him, the

Brahmin, who had worshipped Śiva according to the rules, dedicated only to him, having neither wife nor sons. It was very strange that Śiva should prefer the defiled meat offered by this hunter; but he was going to kill this hunter by dropping a stone on his head.

33–35 Śiva laughed and told him to wait behind him (i.e. behind the statue) the next day, then the Brahmin might drop the stone. Veda agreed, put the stone away, suppressing his anger, and promised to come the next day.

36–39ab The next morning Veda went there, bathed etc. and started to worship the Liṅga, when he suddenly beheld on its top a terrible wound, red with blood. He wondered what had happened to the Liṅga and what this great portent signified; but he worshipped it, as usual, with earth and cow-dung, with Kuśa-grass and water from the Gaṅgā.

39cd–43ab Meanwhile the hunter came to that place. When he saw the wound on the top of Śaṃkara's Liṅga (named) Ādikeśa, he pierced himself with sharp arrows, reproaching himself that this should have happened as long as he was alive.

43cd–45ef Seeing this, Mahādeva was much surprised; he turned to Veda and told him to look at the hunter who was filled with devotion; while the Brahmin had only touched his head with Kuśa-grass, water, and earth, the hunter had experienced Śiva's very self; devotion exists where love, energy, and reflection are found (?). For that reason he would grant boons to the hunter, and then to the Brahmin, too.

46–47 Thus the god granted a boon to the hunter, who chose the stainlessness of Śiva('s Liṅga), and that this place of pilgrimage should be named after him and should grant the merit of all sacrifices merely by being remembered.

48–49cd This was granted by the Lord of the gods (= Śiva); thus the holy place (named) Bhillatīrtha came into existence, which destroys all accumulations of sins, which establishes great devotion to Mahādeva's feet, and grants enjoyment and liberation for bathing there and bestowing gifts.

49ef Śiva also granted many boons to Veda.

Ch. 170: The good merchant and the treacherous Brahmin

1 Brahman continues by giving an account of Cakṣustīrtha, which grants beauty and happiness, where the god is (present as) Yogeśvara,[1] on the southern bank of the Gautamī.

2–5 On the top of a hill lies Bhauvana, the capital of king Bhauvana, who was dedicated to the *dharma* of Kṣatriyas. In this city lived a Brahmin, named Vṛddhakauśika (or: Kauśika the Old), whose son, a great Veda-expert, was called Gautama; due to a fault of his mother's thinking, however, he was perverted. His friend was a merchant named Maṇikuṇḍala; the friendship between these two, the Brahmin and the Vaiśya, the rich one and the poor one, was unequal.

[1] In this chapter, it is most probably not Śiva, present in a Liṅga (as in other chapters), but Viṣṇu present in a statue (cf. *yogeśvaro hariḥ* in v. 63 below).

6–7ef One day Gautama secretly suggested to the rich merchant that they should travel through the world in order to acquire wealth, for »youth is vain without friendship; but what is it without wealth?« (maxim). A poor man is miserable.

8a-d The merchant replied that his father had wealth enough; what should he do with still more riches?

8ef–13 The Brahmin addressed Maṇikuṇḍala again, doubting that anybody well-versed in the three goals of life can be satiated with wealth; acquisition of gold is always dear to living beings. Better to live on riches acquired by oneself than on wealth given by others. A real son, appreciated by his ancestors, does not »smear« (the things) belonging to the ancestors with words (?). He should live on what he has earned himself and not touch his father's riches. Only he who acquires wealth and gives it to his father and friend is called a son; else he is only a »womb-insect« (*yonikīṭaka*).

14–17ab Hearing this argument, the merchant's son agreed to the Brahmin's suggestion, took jewelry and showed Gautama his riches which were to meet their travelling expenses. He always spoke the truth, but the Brahmin was a deceiver, with evil intentions that were not known to the merchant.

17cd–22 After consulting each other they departed for other countries without their parents knowing. The Brahmin, greedy for the merchant's riches, pondered about how to get hold of them, imagining the beautiful young women in the different cities who could be bought with wealth and would grant him any pleasure he wanted; but how could he get hold of the Vaiśya's riches?

23–25 Thus pondering, Gautama smilingly addressed Maṇikuṇḍala, stating first that people reach prosperity and happiness by unrighteousness, while those who are firm in righteousness are unlucky in this world; hence righteousness is useless.

26a-f Maṇikuṇḍala protested, claiming that, on the contrary, happiness rests upon righteousness, whereas uneasiness, fear of danger, grief, poverty, and affliction are concomitant with evil. Righteousness and liberation belong together; why should one destroy one's own *dharma*?

27–28 Thus they disputed with each other; finally they decided that he whose opinion was proved right should get the property of the other; they would ask people whether supremacy lies with the righteous or with those lacking righteousness.

29–31 Accordingly they asked all sorts of people, and always got the answer that people observing the *dharma*-rules suffer, and those doing evil are happy. Thus the Brahmin won all the wealth belonging to the merchant.

32–36 Maṇimat, however, continued to praise righteousness. The Brahmin was astonished that the Vaiśya was not ashamed, after losing his wealth and after righteousness had been defeated. But the Vaiśya continued to cling to the opinion that people without *dharma* are like empty or bad grain (*pulāka*) or like white ants among winged animals, that *dharma* (righteousness) is the first of the four (?) goals of life, *artha* (acquisition of wealth, profit) and *kāma* (love and enjoyments) coming afterwards.[2] How could the Brahmin claim that he had defeated righteousness?

37–38cd Again they made a bet, the stake now being their hands. Again they asked the people about righteousness, and again the Brahmin won. So he cut off the Vaiśya's hands and asked him what he thought now about righteousness.

[2] For *catūrṇām* one should probably read *trayāṇām*, since only two further goals of life (*puruṣārtha*) are mentioned; cf. also above v. 9.

38ef-39 The Vaiśya replied that he still regarded righteousness as superior, even to his last breath; *dharma* is mother, father, and friend for beings.

40-43 Thus they disputed, the Brahmin being wealthy now, and the Vaiśya bereft of his arms and his wealth. Meanwhile they had reached the (Gautamī) Gaṅgā and Hari Yogeśvara (= Viṣṇu as Lord of Yoga). The Vaiśya praised the Gaṅgā, the Lord of Yoga, and *dharma*, but the Brahmin got very angry and announced that he would cut off the Vaiśya's head, if he did not change his opinion.

44-46 Again the Vaiśya clung to his opinion that righteousness was the best for him; whoever despises Brahmins, preceptors, gods, the Vedas, *dharma*, and Janārdana (= Viṣṇu) should be regarded as an evil-doer and untouchable.

47-48 Full of anger, the Brahmin suggested a further bet, the stake being their lives. The merchant agreed, and again they asked the people and got the same answer as before.

49-50ef Now the Brahmin threw the Vaiśya to the ground, before the »Lord of Yoga« on the southern bank of the Gautamī, and tore out his eyes. Then he addressed him for a last time, pointing to the terrible conditions the Vaiśya owed to *dharma*, and took leave.

51-53 Being deserted by the Brahmin, Kuṇḍala stayed at the same place, without property, without eyes and arms, troubled about his fate, but still thinking of righteousness, though submerged in an ocean of grief.

54-63 When night came, the eleventh night of the bright half of the month, Vibhīṣaṇa came to that place with his son and other Rākṣasas in order to worship the Lord of Yoga. His son, who was called Vibhīṣaṇa too, heard the Vaiśya's voice and showed him to his father. The king of Laṅkā told his son that Rāma was his preceptor and Hanumat his friend, who on another occasion had fetched a big mountain covered with all sorts of plants, including the herbs Viśalyakaraṇī (causing the removal of arrows) and Mṛtasaṃjīvanī (reviving the dead). These he had given to Rāma as a remedy; then he had joined him in his action (i.e. the fight with Rāvaṇa and his army). Afterwards Hanumat had taken back the mountain of the gods; on the way, however, the herb Viśalyakaraṇī had fallen onto the bank of the Gautamī, where there is (a statue of) Hari Yogeśvara (= Viṣṇu, the Lord of Yoga). He (i.e. Vibhīṣaṇa's son) should take this herb and put it on the poor merchant's heart, thinking of Hari, then he would regain all he wanted.[3]

64-68 Vibhīṣaṇa's son wanted to be shown this herb immediately; Vibhīṣaṇa showed him a tree that had grown on the place where the herb had fallen;[4] he should break a branch from this tree and put it on the merchant's heart, then he would regain his former shape. So Vibhīṣaṇa's son cut a branch from the tree and put a piece of it on the Vaiśya's heart, and he immediately regained his eyes and his hands. »Who does not realise the power of jewels, formulas, and plants?«

[3] v. 62 and 63 must be read in reverse order; probably v. 62 should be deleted here altogether, since it anticipates things told later (v.66a-f).

[4] The following verse (65c-f), containing a quotation from the TS (*iṣe tvā* TS 1.1.1.1) and telling how Vibhīṣaṇa's son cut the branch, seems to be out of place, before Vibhīṣaṇa's words in v. 66a-f.

69–74ab The Vaiśya took the branch, thinking of *dharma*; he bathed in the Gautamī, worshipped Hari, the Lord of Yoga, and then departed, taking the branch with him. Wandering around he reached a king's capital, named Mahāpura (»great city«); a great king, called Mahārāja (»great king«), lived there, who had no son, but only one daughter who had lost her eyesight. He had proclaimed that whoever, be he a god or a demon, a Brahmin, Kṣatriya, Vaiśya, or Śūdra, be he with or without qualities, should give eyes (to her), should have her in marriage along with the kingdom.

74cd–76 Day and night the Vaiśya heard this proclamation; finally he said he would offer eyes to the king's daughter. He was taken to the king; here he merely touched the princess with his branch, and she could see immediately.

77–80ef The king was surprised and asked him who he was; the Vaiśya told him all that had happened and praised Brahmins, righteousness, and asceticism, bestowal of gifts and performance of sacrifices, as well as the heavenly plant, by the favour of which he had such powers. Again the king was surprised and thought how noble-minded and excellent this Vaiśya was, and that he could not have obtained such power otherwise; thus the king decided to give him his daughter as well as his kingdom.

81–83 The king acted accordingly and went where he wished, for pleasure; the merchant's son, however, thinking always of his Brahmin friend, was much depressed, for »there is no kingdom without a treaty, there is no happiness without a friend« (maxim).[5] This is the true characteristic of noble people that their minds are always full of compassion, even towards those who harm them (maxim).

84–88 The great king left for the forest, and Maṇikuṇḍala became king. During his reign, he once saw the Brahmin Gautama, who had been robbed by gamblers. Recognizing his friend, he honoured the Brahmin and explained to him the great power of the *dharma*-rules. Then he made him bathe in the (Gautamī) Gaṅgā, in order to remove his sins. Together with the Brahmin, surrounded by the members of his own family and by those of the Brahmin's family, Vṛddhakauśika etc. he performed sacrifices in the presence of Yogeśvara, worshipped the gods and finally went to heaven.

89a-f Ever since, this holy place has been known as Mṛtasaṃjīvana (reviving the dead) and Cakṣustīrtha, which, together with the Lord of Yoga, bestows merit by being thought of only; it creates tranquillity of mind and destroys all evil powers.

Ch. 171: The game of dice between Indra and Pramati

1–2ab Brahman continues with (an account of) Urvaśītīrtha, which grants the merit of a horse-sacrifice; the god Maheśvara (= Śiva) is present there, as well as Hari holding the bow Śārṅga.

2cd–6cd Once there was a king named Pramati, who ruled over the whole earth. When he had subdued his enemies he went to Indra's world, where he saw the Lord of the

[5] v. 81cd–83 disturb the connection between 81ab and 84ab; possibly they were inserted later, in order to stress the nobility of mind of the merchant, who, though having been deceived and hurt, still feels strong friendship for the treacherous Brahmin.

gods, together with the Maruts. He laughed at Indra, who held a noose (for playing at dice) in his hand. Hari (= Indra) invited the king to play with him. Dominated by passion, the king agreed and asked about Indra's stake.

6ef–9ef Indra replied that his stake was Urvaśī and asked for the king's stake. Pramati left it to Indra, and Indra chose Pramati's right hand, including its armour and arrows.

10–13 Having agreed about the stake, both threw the dice. Pramati won and gained Urvaśī, the heavenly woman. He wanted to play once more and again asked Indra for his stake. Now Indra staked his thunderbolt (*vajra*), in exchange for Pramati's hand, and, without hesitation, took a new noose which was adorned with jewels, but again Pramati laughingly won the game.

14–15 Meanwhile Viśvāvasu, the lord of the Gandharvas, who was well-versed in the game of dice, approached and suggested the Gandharva-knowledge as stake. Pramati agreed and won again.

16–17ef Having defeated them both, Pramati, out of foolishness, mocked Indra, how had it been possible for him to become king of the gods, since he was as unable to win in battle as in the game; now he should worship him (i.e. king Pramati).

18–19 Pramati turned to Urvaśī, ordering her to work as his servant. Urvaśī refused, claiming the same position for herself as she had possessed among the gods. But Pramati again scornfully ordered her to work.

20–24 Now Citrasena, Viśvāvasu's son, suggested playing dice with Pramati, both staking kingdom and life. Pramati agreed, but this time Citrasena won, and Pramati was bound by the Gandharvas and lost Urvaśī and the other stakes he had won before; his kingdom, treasury, power, and everything else he possessed now belonged to Citrasena.

25–26 Pramati's son, who was still a child, once asked their family-priest Madhucchandas, a son of Viśvāmitra, what his father had done, where he was imprisoned, and how he could obtain his former position and be free from bondage.

27–39 Madhucchandas pondered for a while and then told what had happened to Pramati: he was imprisoned in the world of the gods after losing his kingdom playing at dice; then he spoke to the king's son of the disadvantages and dangers of the vice of gambling, not only for the gambler himself, but also for his people; the gambler's wife always worries and the gambler himself, too, at the sight of a young woman.[1] A gambler is never happy, being ashamed, without *dharma*, and with no real profession such as agriculture, cattle-breeding, or commerce. He who wants to earn money by playing at dice loses manliness along with the three goals of life and his family. Such action, which was already despised in the Veda,[2] had been taken up by Sumati's father; what should they do? Which wise man would overstep the path explained to Sumati and established by the creator?

40–43 Sumati asked what could be done (by himself) for his father to regain his kingdom. Madhucchandas advised Sumati to go to the Gautamī and pay homage to Śiva, Aditi (v.l. Āditya, i.e. the sun), Varuṇa, and Viṣṇu, then his father would get rid of his bondage.

[1] v. 32 is a metrically adapted version of RV 10,34.10a and 11a.

[2] Allusion to the Gambler's song (RV 10,34), a small part of which is used above.

44–46 Sumati agreed; he went to the (Gautamī) Gaṅgā, bowed to Janārdana, worshipped Śaṃbhu (= Śiva) and practised austerities; thus he freed his father, who had been bound by the gods for 1000 years but now regained his kingdom, because of Śiva and Īśa (= Viṣṇu?) and his own son; he also possessed the Gandharva-knowledge and was dear to Śatakratu (= Indra).

47–49ef Ever since, this holy place has been known as Śāṃbhava (sacred to Śaṃbhu), Vaiṣṇava (sacred to Viṣṇu), as Urvaśītīrtha and as Kaitava (connected with the gambler). What cannot be obtained by the grace of Śiva, Viṣṇu, river(s), and mother(s)? (Rhetorical question). Bathing there and bestowing gifts grants abundant merit, releases from the bondage of evil and destroys all misfortune.

Ch. 172: Confluence of the Gautamī with the ocean

1 Brahman announces that he will give a description of the holy place called Sāmudra, which grants the merit of all holy places.

2–3 The Gaṅgā created by Gautama went to the Eastern ocean, destroying all evil for the sake of the world; she was kept in Brahman's (the first-person narrator's) bowl and held by Śaṃbhu's head.[1]

4–7ab When the ocean (*sindhu*) saw her who had been brought from Viṣṇu's step to the world of mortals by the Brahmin (i.e. Gautama), he thought he should go to meet her, for »there is no protector for someone who does not honour a great person on his/her arrival« (maxim).

7cd–14 Accordingly the lord of jewels, the husband of the rivers etc. (i.e. the ocean) addressed the Gaṅgā respectfully, inviting the water in the nether world, the earth and the sky to enter him, and giving a description of himself as containing jewels, the nectar of immortality,[2] mountains, demons, etc.; at his end Viṣṇu is sleeping, together with Kamalā (= Lakṣmī). Whoever does not greet a person respectfully upon arrival goes to hell (maxim).[3] All these could be easily held by him, but the Gautamī was more in weight and importance than all these; for that reason, she should make herself equal to him before joining him; he could only meet her, after she had divided herself.

15–17ab Hearing these words, the Gautamī Gaṅgā ordered him to fetch the seven sages together with their wives, Arundhatī etc.: then she would reduce herself before joining the ocean.

17cd–19ab The ocean complied; she divided herself into seven parts and joined the ocean in this sevenfold shape, the seven Gaṅgās bearing the names of the seven sages.[4]

19cd–20ef Bathing there, bestowing gifts, as well as listening, reciting, and thinking of (this account) with devotion grants all wishes concerning destruction of evil, enjoyment and liberation, and happiness of mind. There is no holy place in the three worlds superior to the ocean.

[1] Reference back, cf. ch. 72 and 74.
[2] *pīyūṣa* is obviously here to be taken in this sense, not in the sense of »beestings«.
[3] Interrupts the connection between 10 and 12.
[4] cf. the following chapter (173.3–4).

Ch. 173: Viśvarūpa's terrible sacrifice

1–2 Brahman announces that he will tell what happened at (the place) named Ṛṣisattra, where the seven sages sat down (for a *sattra*-rite), and where Śiva is present as (a Liṅga named) Bhīmeśvara.

3–6ab The seven sages divided the Gaṅgā into seven parts; the Vāsiṣṭhā in the south, the Vaiśvāmitrī north of it, then the Vāmadevī, the Gautamī in the midst, then the Bhāradvājī, the Ātreyī, and the Jāmadagnī. Afterwards the sages started a great *sattra*-rite.

6cd–8ef At the same time a powerful enemy of the gods (i.e. a demon), named Viśvarūpa, came to the *sattra*-rite of the hermits. He approached them respectfully, pleasing them with chastity and asceticism, and he asked them how to obtain a powerful son, irresistible even for the gods, by sacrifices or by austerities.

9–25 Viśvāmitra replied, instructing him about the connection between »fruit« and action (*karman*); about the three »causes« (*kāraṇa*), the foremost of which is action; about the twofold »fruit« of action, existence and non-existence; about twofold action (what is being done and what is already finished); about the determination of actions by intentions (*bhāvanā, bhāva*); about the three kinds of intentions, influenced by the three principal Qualities (*sattva*, *rajas*, and *tamas*); about the importance of intentions for obtaining any kind of result of one's actions; etc. Finally he advised Viśvarūpa to perform his actions according to his intentions; accordingly he would obtain his wishes.

26–28 Having heard Viśvāmitra's instructions, Viśvarūpa practised austerities, adopting the intention influenced by *tamas* (darkness, ignorance). Though the sages tried to prevent him, he performed a terrible rite, dreadful for the gods, with a terrible sacrificial hole (*kuṇḍa*), and a terrible sacrificial fire (Jātavedas).

29ab ... thinking on the terrible »Raudrapuruṣa« (cruel individual self or characterisation of Śiva?) hidden in himself.[1]

29cd–33ab Seeing him, who practised austerities, a heavenly voice said ...[2] (The heavenly voice seems to advise Viśvarūpa to think of Śiva in his terrible shape, praising him as Indra, as Varuṇa, and as all;[3] then he would obtain the terrible son he desired, who is called Vṛtra in the Veda.) Who knows the greatness of the terrible Lord of the world (= Śiva?)? He (= Śiva) creates everything but is not affected by attachment.

33cd–34ab Thus the heavenly voice praised him (= Śiva?); the hermits paid homage to Bhīmeśvara and went to their hermitages.

34cd–35ef Viśvarūpa, whose shape, actions, and intentions were terrible, thought of himself as having a terrible body and sacrificed. Therefore Bhīmeśvara as (name or shape of) the god (Śiva) is mentioned in the Purāṇa. Bathing there and bestowing gifts grants liberation.

[1] The last phrase, as well as the following three line (29cd–30), are not found in two of the manuscripts.

[2] The following passage, up to 32ab, shows relatively frequent variants; the sequence of sentences seems to be disturbed, direct speech and narration seem to alternate.

[3] cf. also ch. 158, v. 22–27 etc.

36 Phalastuti:[4] Whoever reads, or listens to, this account of Śiva in terrible shape, with devotion, ... this is known as taking away all sins; by being thought of, or his feet being touched, (he, i.e. Śiva?) grants liberation.[5]

37–39 Praise of the Godāvarī as destroyer of all sins and bestower of the highest meaning (of life), especially at her confluence with the ocean. Whoever bathes at this confluence, will tear all his ancestors out of any hell and go to Purāri's (= Śiva's) city (*puram*). What is known and worshipped in the Vedānta, the *brahman*, is manifest as Bhīmanātha; having seen him, living beings will not enter the circle of rebirth[6] again.[7]

Ch. 174: Completion of the sacrifice performed by the sages[1]

1 The (Gautamī) Gaṅgā, venerable even for the gods, joined the eastern ocean, worshipped by all gods and praised by hermits and the Maruts.[2]

2–5ab All sages, Vasiṣṭha, Jābāli, Yājñavalkya, Kratu, Aṅgiras, Dakṣa, Marīci, and Vaiṣṇava;[3] Śātātapa, Śaunaka, Devarāta, Bhṛgu, Agniveśya, Atri, Marīci[4] etc.; Manu, Gautama, Kauśika, Tumbaru[5] and Nārada; Agastya, Mārkaṇḍeya, Pippala; Gālava, etc., dedicated to Yoga; Vāmadeva, the Āṅgirasas, and the Bhārgavas, well-versed in the sacred tradition; they all, who knew the meaning of the Purāṇas, went to the Gautamī, the river of the gods, and praised[6] (her?)[7] joyfully with prayer-formulas and traditional verses from the Veda.[8]

5cd–6ab Seeing them all assembled, Śiva and Hari (= Viṣṇu) showed themselves to them; gods and ancestors praised these two gods, who, by being seen, take away all distress.[9]

7 All classes of gods, Ādityas, Vasus, Rudras, Maruts, and the guardians of the directions praised Hari (= Viṣṇu) and Śaṃkara (= Śiva).

[4] In Puṣpitāgra-metre.

[5] Sentence is difficult to construe. The editions, neglecting the end of the third quarter, read a compound connecting the third and the fourth quarter; this, however, makes it impossible to construe the remainder of the sentence.

[6] Read *saṃsṛti* (= *saṃsāra*) instead of *saṃsmṛti* »remembrance«.

[7] In Upajāti-metre. These three verses seem not to belong to the story told before, in which the Gautamī was not mentioned.

[1] Probably continuation of the preceding chapter, perhaps rather of Ch. 172?

[2] In Upajāti-metre.

[3] Name or attribute of all preceding sages? v.l. *-viṣṇavaḥ*, i.e. »(and) Viṣṇu (= name of a sage).«

[4] Occurs for the second time.

[5] Error for Tumburu?

[6] Lit.: »will praise«.

[7] Or Indra and Soma at the vedic sacrifice?

[8] In Upajāti-metre, mixed with Jagatī-metre (2b, 3a, 4a).

[9] In Upajāti-metre, mixed with Jagatī-metre (6b).

8–12ef At each of the seven confluences of the (Gautamī) Gaṅgā and the ocean both gods are present. Where there is (the Liṅga named) Gautameśvara, Mādhava (= Kṛṣṇa/Viṣṇu) is also present, together with Ramā (= Lakṣmī); Brahmeśvara is (the name of the Liṅga) established by Brahman (the first-person narrator) for the sake of the worlds and himself. Praised by Brahman and the gods, Viṣṇu is present as Cakrapāṇi, together with gods and Maruts. Aindratīrtha is also called Hayamūrdhaka, since Viṣṇu is present as Hayamūrdhan (i.e. Hayaśiras), at the head (*mūrdhani*) of the gods. Somatīrtha is the name of the place where Śiva is present as (a Liṅga called) Someśvara.[10]

13–17 Recital of the priests at their sacrifice in honour of Indra.[11]

13 Introductory verse to the following quotation of verses from the Rigveda, explaining that in the beginning (of the sacrifice?) Soma was besought by gods and sages with the refrain »*indrāyendo parisrava*«.[12]

14 (= RV 9,114.3:) Seven are the directions, seven the priests, seven the Ādityas, by whom Soma should protect the sacrificers.

15 (= RV 9,114.4:) Request for protection, by the oblation offered to King Soma, against somebody filled with enmity.[13]

16 (= RV 9,114.2:) Request to the sage Kaśyapa (the presumed author of RV 9,114) to increase the hymns of praise and to pay homage to King Soma, who was born as Lord (or husband) of the plants.

17 (= RV 9,112.3:) Self-characterisation of the poet(s) striving to acquire wealth.[14]

18 With these words the sages presented the Soma to the Wielder of the Thunderbolt (= Indra), and Śatakratu's sacrifice was completed.

19–25ab This place is called Somatīrtha; east of it there is Āgneya(-tīrtha), where Agni performed many sacrifices, pleased Brahman (the first-person narrator), and obtained what he desired; Brahman is always present there. Viṣṇu and Śiva are also present there.[15] Therefore it is called »Āgneya« (belonging to Agni); nearby there is (the place called) Āditya(-tīrtha), where Āditya (i.e. the sun) always appears in a different shape, at noon, in order to pay homage (or to be paid homage?) and to see Brahman, Śaṃkara, and Hari (= Viṣṇu). For that reason, i.e. because of the uncertainty in which shape Savitṛ (= the sun-god) will appear, everybody should be honoured there at noon. Hence it (this place) is called Āditya(-tīrtha); next to it is (the place called) Bārhaspatya(-tīrtha). Due to this holy place, Bṛhaspati was

[10] v. 5cd–12ef, the contents of which concern Viṣṇu and Śiva, seem to disturb the connection between 5ab, mentioning the »traditional verses from the Veda,« and v. 13–17, which actually contain a quotation of verses from the Rigveda.

[11] It consists of an introductory verse and four verses quoted from the *pavamāna*-hymns at the end of the ninth book of the Rigveda, characterised by the refrain *indrāyendo parisrava*, i.e. »flow around for Indra, o Soma-juice!«

[12] In this verse, the refrain is part of the Śloka (13d), whereas in the following quotation it is added to each Anuṣṭubh.

[13] *arātīvā* (old ending of nom. sg. of *arātīvan-*), is obviously no longer understood; both editions print *arātī vā* separately.

[14] Meaning or function in this context not clear.

[15] Seems to be inserted, as it disturbs the connection with the following sentence.

honoured by the gods, and he performed many sacrifices, hence it is thought of as belonging to him; merely by thinking of it the planets will be propitiated.

cd–27ab Next to it, on the excellent mountain (named) Indragopa, a great Liṅga was established for some reason; this place is called Adritīrtha because of (its connection with) the Himālaya (?); bathing there and bestowing gifts fulfils all wishes.

27cd–28 Conclusion to Brahman's account of the Gautamī-Māhātmya, stating that all the holy places, even the secret ones, that are found at the Gautamī Gaṅgā from her source on the Brahmādri (= Brahmagiri) up to the confluence with the ocean have been described by Brahman, in an abridged version.

29–30 How could anyone give a total account of the Gautamī who is celebrated by the sages in Veda(s) and Purāṇa(s)? But if someone does something with devotion, no fault or doubt attaches (to him). Therefore Brahman has tried to give a hint of her (greatness), for the sake of the world (?).[16]

31–33 Who could describe the greatness of each holy place at the Gautamī, be it even the husband of Lakṣmī (= Viṣṇu) or Śiva Someśvara? There are many holy places, here and there, bound to time; but the Gautamī is always and everywhere merit-bestowing for men. Who can praise her good qualities? The only adequate thing is to honour her.

Ch. 175: Brahman's teachings about dharma; on the origin of the Gaṅgā

1–2ef Nārada affirms that Brahman has told him about Gaṅgā, who originated from the three gods and was taken (to the earth) by the Brahmin (Gautama), from the beginning to the end; now he wants to come to know a short account of her, who is permeated by Viṣṇu, Īśa (= Śiva), and Brahman.

3–9ef Brahman once more stresses the eminent power of Gautamī Gaṅgā, who first stayed in his bowl, then followed Viṣṇu's step, then stayed in Śiva's locks, then was led to the excellent mountain (i.e. the Brahmagiri) by the Brahmin's power, then flowed towards the eastern ocean, granting all wishes. There is no holy place which surpasses her; by her power all things imagined become real. Nobody can describe the greatness of her who is taught as (identical with) the *brahman*. She excels all other holy places. After listening to Brahman's account, why should not everybody desist from worldly actions?[1] This seemed strange to Brahman.

10–13 Nārada states that Brahman knows and teaches the four goals of life; in telling all he knows about Vedas and Upaniṣads (*chandāṃsi sarahasyāṇi*), about Purāṇas and other sacred traditions, about sacrifices, holy places, austerities etc., he can never tell too much. Now he should explain how everything can be accomplished by devotion.

[16] In Upajāti-metre.

[1] Or perhaps rather: »why should not everybody be delighted with her?« (*uparati* as synonymous with e.g. *abhirati*?

14–32ab *Brahman's teachings about the* dharma *in time and place*

14ab Brahman announces that he will tell the highest secret *dharma*.

14cd–16 There are four kinds of holy places, four Yugas, three principal qualities, three kinds of souls (*puruṣa*?) and of gods, four Vedas, four goals of life, and four kinds of speech;[2] the qualities are also said to be four, because of equality (?).

17–24 *dharma* permeates all; therefore it is called »eternal« (*sanātana*), yet it becomes manifold by being the means of accomplishment (?). Its abode (*āśraya*) is twofold, in time and place. In (the dimension of) time, it always decreases or grows. According to the Yugas, it decreases by one quarter after another. At (special) places, however, it does not decrease; otherwise there would be a total loss of *dharma*. Hence, in places, *dharma* stands firm on four quarters (lit. »feet«), it exists in the form of holy places. In the Kṛta-Yuga, the (total) *dharma* rests in time and place, in the Tretā-Yuga it is diminished by one quarter, in the Dvāpara-Yuga it is only half, and in the Kali-Yuga it moves dangerously on one »foot« (i.e. quarter). Whoever knows this will not lose his *dharma*.

25–28 According to the Yugas, the different castes (*jāti*) are established by the principal qualities and their producers (*guṇakartṛ-* ?); according to the Qualities there is rise and disregard of holy places, castes, and the Vedas, of heaven and liberation (?). Time is said to be (the) manifesting (principle), place is called what is to be manifested (?). ...[3]

29–32ab The Yugas also determine the vedic (?) shape of the gods, of the sacrifices (or actions in general?), of the holy places, of the castes and stages of life. Holy places are sacred to three gods in the Satya-Yuga (= Kṛta-Yuga), to two gods in the Tretā-Yuga, to one god in the Dvāpara-Yuga, and to none in the Kali-Yuga (?). Holy places are known to have been established by the gods in the Kṛta-Yuga, by the Asuras in the Tretā-Yuga, by the sages in the Dvāpara-Yuga, and by men in the Kali-Yuga.[4]

32cd–75 *Further account of how the Gaṅgā was obtained by Gautama from Śiva*

32cd–33ab Brahman announces, as a further topic, a detailed account of the origin of the Gaṅgā, which has been asked for by Nārada.[5]

33cd–35 When Gaṅgā had reached Śiva's head, she became dearer to him (i.e. than Umā). Learning of this, Umā, the mother of the world, who is called »Śruti« (sacred tradition) and bestows enjoyment and liberation, talked to Gaṇeśa.[6]

36–41ef Gaṇeśa asked what was to be done. Umā replied that Gaṅgā should be removed from Śiva's matted locks. Wherever Śiva stays, there the gods, the Vedas, sages, men and ancestors will stay, too. For that reason Gaṇeśa should turn Śiva away from Gaṅgā, then all those will be turned away as well.

[2] cf. also RV 1,164.45 *catvāri vāk parimitā vadāni....*

[3] The meaning of this and of the next sentence is unclear.

[4] cf. the classification of holy places in ch. 70 above.

[5] Obviously referring to the question at the beginning of ch. 74, the account of which seems to be paralleled by the present chapter.

[6] The contents of her speech, however, are not given. cf. above ch. 74.13–22ab, where this story is told with more details.

42–72 Gaṇeśa's answer.

42–46ab On hearing his mother's words, Gaṇeśa replied that he was not able to divert Śiva from Gaṅgā; without this the gods could not be diverted from her, either. There was, however, another reason: Gaṅgā had already been brought down before, by the famous Brahmin Gautama, who had pleased Śiva with asceticism and hymns.[7]

46cd–68 Dialogue between Gautama and Śiva.[8]

46cd–47 Pleased with Gautama, Śiva granted him many boons.

48a-f Thus addressed by Śiva, in the presence of Gaṇeśa (the first-person narrator), Gautama asked only for the Gaṅgā, together with the tuft of Śiva's hair.

49–50 Śiva objected that Gautama had not asked anything for himself; he should choose something difficult.[9]

51–53 Gautama said that Śiva's presence was very difficult to obtain, yet he had succeeded in seeing Śiva, for »by only thinking of Śiva's feet wise people reach their goal.« Blessed by Śiva's presence, he had no further wish.

54–55ab Śiva, full of joy, replied that Gautama had wished something for the benefit of the three worlds,[10] but he should wish something for himself.

5cd–59ef Gautama, however, pondered a little and addressed Śiva, again wishing the same for the sake of all worlds; with the guardians of the directions listening, he said to Śiva that Śiva should dwell everywhere at the Gautamī Gaṅgā, from her source to her confluence with the ocean, fulfilling all wishes. There are other holy places, but those where Śiva is present are especially auspicious. At the place where the Gaṅgā was given by Śiva all holy places should be (assembled?).

60–68 Full of joy, Śiva granted that whoever performs any religious action at the Godāvarī, full of devotion, ...[11] All merit obtained by donating the whole earth with seven continents, with mountains and oceans etc., results from (merely) thinking of the Gautamī. Likewise, by giving the libation called »Ilā« at auspicious dates in Śiva's presence, by always thinking of Viṣṇu, the bearer of the earth, by giving beautiful cows at a famous confluence, the merit of all that will be obtained by bathing and bestowing gifts at the Gautamī. For that reason the Godāvarī should be brought down to the earth by Gautama, destroying all evil and granting all wishes.[12]

69–72 Conclusion to Gaṇeśa's story: All that which had been told by Śiva to Gautama was overheard by Gaṇeśa. This is the reason why Śiva is always present at the (Gautamī) Gaṅgā. Who would be able to stop Śiva? (Rhetorical question). Nevertheless Gaṇeśa promised to prevent people from visiting the Godā(varī) and from worshipping Śiva, in order to please his mother; she should forgive his words.

73–74 Ever since, Gaṇeśa causes some obstacles (*vighna*) for human beings. But he who pays homage to him and regardless of the obstacle goes to the Gautamī, full of devotion, has fulfilled all his duties in this world.

[7] Summary of 74.82–75.24.

[8] cf. ch. 74, v. 25–47 above.

[9] cf. 75.26ef *yācasva devānām api duṣkaram* »... difficult even for the gods.«

[10] v. 54cd is identical with 75.31ab above.

[11] Sentence incomplete.

[12] Construction of the whole passage not quite clear; often nominative case instead of the accusative forms one would expect. For the contents, cf. also ch. 75.35–45 above.

75 There are many obstacles for a sinner who leaves his home; he who, carrying them on his head, goes to the (Gautamī) Gaṅgā, what fruit can he not obtain?[13]

76–77 Who can describe her power, be it even Śiva? Brahman has presented a summary according to the Itihāsa-tradition, where all accomplishments concerning each of the four goals of life are taught in detail.

78 What is said in the Veda (and) in the secret tradition (*śruti*), is a proclamation causing the good (or: the real/true); it is perceived totally and told for the sake of the world as a Purāṇa, endowed with many *dharma*-rules.[14]

79 Phalastuti: Whoever listens to or recites one verse or even one quarter of a verse of this (account),[15] or the name »Gaṅgā, Gaṅgā« will obtain merit.

80 Conclusion:[16] This auspicious and excellent (story) concerning the Gaṅgā (*gāṅga*) is told, destroying all stains of the Kali-Yuga and granting any success, venerable in this world and fulfilling all wishes.

81–85 *Superiority of the Gautamī Gaṅgā*[17]

81ab Hail to Gautama, to whom nobody is comparable.[18]

81cd–82 Whoever goes to the Gautamī Gaṅgā in the Daṇḍaka-forest and utters the name »Gaṅgā, Gaṅgā«, even (at a distance of) a hundred Yojanas, will be released from all evil and enter Viṣṇu's world.

83–84 There are 350 million holy places in the three worlds, which all come to bathe in the (Gautamī) Gaṅgā when Bṛhaspati (= Jupiter) is in the constellation Leo. Bathing for 60,000 years in the Bhāgīrathī (Gaṅgā) is equal to bathing once in the Godāvarī at the conjunction of Bṛhaspati and the constellation Leo.[19]

85 This is the Gautamī, which, by the order of Brahman (the speaker),[20] grants liberation for bathing at each place.[21]

86–90 By remembering it[22] one will obtain the merit of 1000 horse-sacrifices and 100 Soma-sacrifices (*vājapeyas*). In a house where this Purāṇa is available there will be no fear of the Kali-Yuga. It should not be told to all, but to a pious and self-controlled devotee of Viṣṇu; merely by listening to it a man will have fulfilled his duties. He who writes down this book and gives it to a Brahmin will be freed from all sins and will not be born again.

13 In Upajāti-metre.

14 Mixture of Vasantatilakā-metre (a,b) and Indravajrā-metre (c,d), the first quarter, however, is not quite correct; the eighth syllable should be long instead of short.

15 Or Māhātmya, or Purāṇa?

16 The metre seems to be Drutavilambitā, at least in b and c; the first quarter would be metrically correct if the penultimate syllable could be dropped, whereas in the last quarter the first long syllable should be read as two short syllables. There is, however, no possibility of correcting the text accordingly.

17 Passage not found in two of the mss.

18 Addressed to Gautama; seems to belong to another context.

19 cf. above ch. 77.8a and the passage inserted by ed. VePr.

20 Ed. VePr reads »of Śiva«.

21 v. 85 is nearly identical with 77.6cd–7ab.

22 i.e. (obviously) the account of the Gaṅgā (*gāṅga*) mentioned in v. 80.

Ch. 176: Prehistory of the image of Vāsudeva

1-2 The hermits are not yet satiated by listening to the story about Bhagavat.[1] Since the »endless« (*ananta*) Vāsudeva[2] has not been properly described they want to hear of him extensively.

3 Brahman announces a report on the greatness of the »endless« Vāsudeva.

4-7 Brahman previously, in the first cosmic cycle, had told Viśvakarman to make a stone image of Vāsudeva on earth. Seeing it the devotees, Indra and human beings, not knowing fear of demons, reaching the summit of Sumeru and, worshipping Vāsudeva, should live without fear.[3]

8-10 Thereupon Viśvakarman made a statue with conch, discus, and club, lotus-eyes, Śrīvatsa-lock, garlands, crown, yellow garments, broad shoulders, ear-rings.

11 This image was consecrated with prayer-formulas by Brahman.

12-15ab Śakra (= Indra) worshipped this image repeatedly with ablutions and gifts and returned to his residence (VePr adds: taking it along). By worshipping it Indra defeated his enemies, Vṛtra, Namuci etc., and enjoyed (sovereignty over) the three worlds.

15cd-34 *Story of Rāvaṇa and his brother Vibhīṣaṇa*

15cd-19ab In the second Yuga, the Tretā-Yuga, lived the heroic Daśagrīva (= Rāvaṇa); he practised asceticism by fasting for ten thousand years. Brahman granted him a boon; he could not be killed by gods, demons, the messengers of death or by a curse. This Rākṣasa (i.e. Rāvaṇa) defeated the Yakṣas and the lord of riches (= Kubera).

19cd-20 He set out to defeat Indra, starting a fierce battle. For defeating Indra his son Meghanāda obtained the name »Indrajita«.[4]

21-25 When he (= Rāvaṇa) reached Amarāvatī (i.e. Indra's city) he saw Vāsudeva's image (iconographic description) and took it to Laṅkā.

26-32 Rāvaṇa's younger brother (i.e. Vibhīṣaṇa), who was his minister and a devotee of Nārāyaṇa, was thrilled when he saw the image and he venerated it. He asked Rāvaṇa to give it to him. Rāvaṇa had no objections since he was going to conquer the three worlds by venerating the self-born god (VePr Mahādeva), the origin of all beings.[5]

33-34 Vibhīṣaṇa worshipped the image for 108 years and obtained freedom from old age and death, together with the qualities of smallness etc.,[6] and lordship over Laṅkā.

[1] A slight variant of this verse begins the Gautamī-Māhātmya which in ed. ASS and ed. Prayāga is inserted here.

[2] cf. above ch. 59.1-2.

[3] Read *ye na* instead of *yena*; the construction as well as the episodic, narrative references are not clear.

[4] The name should be »Indrajit«, i.e. »defeating Indra«, whereas »Indrajita« means »defeated by Indra«; cf. the comparable »Hanumāna« (derived from the nom. »Hanumān«) for »Hanumat« in modern Indian publications.

[5] i.e. Śiva, though the epithets mentioned could indicate Brahman too.

[6] i.e. probably the eight supernatural powers (*siddhi*) known as effects of the practice of Yoga.

35–36 The hermits express their astonishment and want to hear extensively about the greatness of this god, the endless Vāsudeva, and his origin on earth.

37–51 *Summary of Rāmāyaṇa:*

Brahman continues: The Rākṣasa (= Rāvaṇa) defeated all gods, Gandharvas etc. and abducted the women. He was infatuated by Sītā and deceived Rāghava (i.e. Rāma) in the form of a golden deer. Then Rāma and Saumitri (i.e. Lakṣmaṇa) killed Vālin, anointed Sugrīva as king, and made Aṅgada crown-prince. Then Rāma and a great army of monkeys, Hanumat, Nala, Nīla, Jāmbavat, Panasa, Gavaya, Gavākṣa, and others constructed a bridge (causeway) in the ocean; and they fought the Rākṣasa. Rāma killed Yamahasta, Prahasta, Nikumbha, Kumbha, Narāntaka, Yamāntaka, Mālāḍhya, Mālikāḍhya, Indrajit, Kumbhakarṇa, and Rāvaṇa; he purified Sītā by fire, gave the kingdom to Vibhīṣaṇa, took (the image of) Vāsudeva along, and mounted the »Puṣpaka«-chariot. Returning to Ayodhyā, he made Bharata and Śatrughna king. Venerating his own original shape (i.e. the statue), Hari (i.e. Rāma/Viṣṇu) ruled over the whole earth for 11,000 years and reached Viṣṇu's »step« (or abode) (*vaiṣṇavaṃ padam*). The image he gave to the lord of the ocean.

52–56 When the Dvāpara-Yuga had begun the god, upon the request of the earth, descended in the family of Vasudeva in order to kill Kaṃsa and others with the help of Saṃkarṣaṇa. At that time the ocean himself lifted the image out of the water to the place Puruṣottama (VePr: he himself lifted that image from the ocean at the place Puruṣottama). Ever since, it has been there.

57–62 Those who take refuge in the eternal Lord go to the highest step (*paramaṃ padam*); those who look at and prostrate themselves before the Eternal (*ananta*) get ten times the merit of a royal consecration ceremony (*rājasūya*) and horse-sacrifice. After saving 21 generations one is transported by a celestial vehicle endowed with all pleasures to Viṣṇu's city. One enjoys all pleasures till the end of a (cosmic) cycle, then becomes a Brahmin learned in the four Vedas; after practising the Vaiṣṇava Yoga (or: after obtaining union with Viṣṇu) one is liberated.

63 Thus, the Eternal has been praised; all his qualities cannot be mentioned even in hundreds of years.

Ch. 177: On the greatness of Puruṣottamakṣetra and the merit obtained there

1–2 Brahman repeats that he has described the greatness of the Eternal and of the place Puruṣottama where the Lotus-eyed (= Kṛṣṇa) (list of iconographic attributes) resides, the enemy of Kaṃsa and Keśin.

3 Those who see Kṛṣṇa, Saṃkarṣaṇa and Subhadrā are blessed.

4 Those who always meditate on Kṛṣṇa are liberated;

5 Those who remember Kṛṣṇa day and night enter him when they die.[1]

[1] In Upajāti-metre.

6 Therefore those who desire liberation should always look at Kṛṣṇa in this place.

7 Those who look at the three when lying down and when getting up go to Hari's place.

8 Those who look at the three continuously go to Viṣṇu's world.

9–15 Those who stay there for four months during the rainy season obtain more merit than from travelling to all places of pilgrimage on earth; those who stay there all the time obtain the merit of asceticism; the merit obtained by years of asceticism at other places is obtained here during one month; here one immediately obtains the merit of asceticism, abstinence, and detachment; here one obtains the merit of bathing and alms obtained at all other places. The merit of pilgrimage, observance(s) and discipline is obtained here daily. The merit of all kinds of sacrifices is obtained here daily.

16–19 Merit of death at Puruṣottama: Those who die near the Kalpa-tree attain liberation; those who die between the tree and the ocean are saved; even those who die there involuntarily are saved; even worms and other animals which die there obtain the highest goal.

20 The hermits are told to consider the folly of the world with regard to other places of pilgrimage.

21 By looking once with faith at Puruṣottama one becomes the best among thousands of men.

22–23 Since Puruṣottama is above the material and the spiritual principle (*prakṛti* and *puruṣa*) he is (considered) the »highest Person« (*puruṣottama*) in Veda and Purāṇas; he is the Highest Self as proclaimed in Purāṇas and Vedānta (= Upaniṣads).

24–25 To die there under any circumstance or at any place (listed) grants liberation.[2] Therefore those who desire liberation should attempt to die there.

26 The greatness of (the place named after) Puruṣa is unsurpassed (VePr cannot be adequately described); by dying there one obtains liberation (VePr seeing the fig-tree frees even from Brahmin-murder).

27 (Conclusion:) Only some of the qualities have been praised now (by Brahman); who could name all the qualities of this place even in hundreds of years?

28 If the hermits desire liberation they should live there. (End of Brahman's account of Puruṣottamakṣetra.)

29–30 Vyāsa concludes:[3] Upon Brahman's word the hermits went there, and they reached the highest step; his listeners should live there, too, if they desired liberation.

Ch. 178: Kaṇḍu-episode

1–4 Vyāsa continues by mentioning that at this superb place (the attributes of which are listed) Kaṇḍu, a most qualified sage (whose qualities are listed), and others had obtained the highest perfection (*siddhi*) by worshipping Puruṣottama.

[2] In Upajāti-metre.

[3] Vyāsa continues to be the main narrator till the end of the Purāṇa.

5 The hermits ask who Kaṇḍu was and how he reached the ultimate goal.

6 Vyāsa announces the story of Kaṇḍu.

7–11 At a secluded place on the banks of the river Gomatī,[1] endowed with fruits, trees, flowers, birds, and animals, Kaṇḍu had a hermitage where he practised severe asceticism; he stood between five fires in summer and stayed submerged in water in winter.

12–18 Gods and other heavenly beings were astonished at his asceticism;[2] by his brilliance he heated the earth, the atmosphere and heaven. The gods became afraid; they conferred with Indra as to how to obstruct Kaṇḍu's asceticism. Indra told Pramlocā (whose female attributes are listed) to distract Kaṇḍu's mind and upset his asceticism.

19–24 Pramlocā objected that she feared for her life, that Kaṇḍu might burn or curse her and that there were other experienced Apsarases for the task: Urvaśī, Menakā, Rambhā, Ghṛtācī, Puñjikasthalā, Viśvācī, Sahajanyā, Pūrvacitti, Tilottamā, Alambuṣā, Miśrakeśī, Śaśilekhā, Vāmanā.

25–27 Brahman continues:[3] Indra confirmed that she was qualified; he assigned Kāma (the god of love), Vāyu (wind), and Spring to assist her. Thereupon she left for Kaṇḍu's hermitage.

28–42 *Description of Kaṇḍu's hermitage*

28–31 She saw the hermit and a beautiful forest, endowed with flowers, trees, animals, pleasant sounds, and trees bearing fruit at all seasons.

32–37 List of trees.

38–42 List of birds, aquatic plants and animals.

43–53 Seeing this forest Pramlocā was astonished and told Wind, Love, and Spring to assist her. She announced her intention to let loose the bridled horses of Kaṇḍu's senses (v. 48 names Brahman, Janārdana (= Viṣṇu), and Nīlalohita (= Śiva) in a truth-spell). She went to Kaṇḍu's hermitage and began to sing while Spring made cuckoos sing and Wind carried pleasant scents and Love upset Kaṇḍu's mind by passion.

54–58 When Kaṇḍu heard the singing he went near Pramlocā; thrilled by the sight of her he asked her who she was and told her about his infatuation. She asked for his orders and he took her by the hand and led her to his hermitage.

59–60 Love, Wind, and Spring left and told Hari (= Indra) about Pramlocā's successful undertaking; Indra and the gods were pleased.

61–64 Kaṇḍu, by the power of his asceticism, changed his physique into that of a sixteen year old youth; Pramlocā was astonished and pleased.

65–69 Kaṇḍu gave up all religious practices (listed); engrossed by pleasure he neither noticed that his asceticism was destroyed nor how time was passing. Thus, Kaṇḍu lived with Pramlocā for more than 100 years in Mandaradroṇī.

[1] In VePr: Gaumatī; in ed. Prayāga: Gautamī.

[2] cf. above ch. 2.13, where a similar exclamation about Dhruva is presented as »*śloka* sung by Uśanas«.

[3] Vyāsa was re-introduced as narrator at the end of ch. 177. Mention of Brahman as narrator is out of place here, as well as before verse 46; Vyāsa is named again before verse 58.

70–72 When Pramlocā asked his permission to leave he requested her to stay for a few days longer; she shared enjoyment with him for another 100 years.

73–79 Pramlocā asked repeatedly, but was refused Kaṇḍu's permission to leave for heaven; she stayed on for hundreds of years, their love being always renewed.

80–89 Once, however, Kaṇḍu left the hut in a hurry and, when asked for the reason, told Pramlocā that he was going to perform the evening rites since the day had come to an end. She laughed and asked why only this day had come to an end, whereas previous ones never had. He inquired about her surprise, since she had come to his hermitage in the morning and now the day had come to a close. She told him that hundreds of years had passed and, when asked by Kaṇḍu, specified that they had stayed together for 907 years, six months and three days. Kaṇḍu doubted the truth of her words since to him it appeared like one day but she confirmed it.

90–98 Kaṇḍu blamed himself and deplored the loss of his religious merit due to his passion. He dismissed Pramlocā who had served Indra's purpose; he recognized that he had lived with her as if in marriage and that he himself, not she, was to blame.

99–104 At Kaṇḍu's words Pramlocā began to shake and to sweat. As she left through the air she wiped the drops of her sweat on the leaves of trees. The embryo which had come out of her body in the form of sweat was put together by the trees and nourished by the moon. It grew to become Māriṣā, the wife of the Prācetasas and mother of Dakṣa.

105 Kaṇḍu, his asceticism spent, went to Viṣṇu's place named »Puruṣottama«.

106–111 He saw that pleasant and efficacious place which had previously been frequented by Bhṛgu and other beings desirous of liberation; and he saw Hari (= Viṣṇu) served by gods, Brahmins and others; he considered his objectives achieved.

112 He worshipped Hari (= Viṣṇu) with concentrated mind, muttered the prayer consisting of »Brahmapāra« and remained there as a Yogin with uplifted arms.

113 The hermits want to hear the »Brahmapāra-(hymn)« with which Kaṇḍu worshipped Keśava.

114–117 Vyāsa quotes Kaṇḍu's prayer.

114–116 Description of Viṣṇu's transcendence, (with different combinations of the words *para* and *pāra*), his being cause and effects, and his being *brahman*.[4]

117 Concluding request (in form of a »truth-spell«: According to the truth that Puruṣottama is the eternal *brahman*, Kaṇḍu's faults, his passion etc. should perish.

118–121 When Madhusūdana (= Kṛṣṇa, Puruṣottama) heard this prayer and saw Kaṇḍu's devotion he approached him on Garuḍa and addressed him, asking him for his wish.

122–127 When Kaṇḍu heard the voice he opened his eyes and saw Hari - four-armed etc. (iconographic description); he prostrated himself before him, considered his life and asceticism successful and began to praise the deity.

128–177 Hymn by Kaṇḍu to Viṣṇu:

128–136 Vocatives plus *namo 'stu te* as refrain. (133–136 play with repetitions of one word or concept, viz. *bhūta* (133), *yajña* (134), *kṣetra* (135), and *guṇa* (136).[5]

[4] In Upajāti-metre.

[5] Ed. VePr inserts two verses after verse 131.

137-157 Identifications (*tvam* plus nominatives, naming personifications, e.g. Rudra, functions, e.g. *viśvabhṛt*, attributes, e.g. *acyuta*).[6]
158-165 Theological description of Viṣṇu (as origin (*tvattaḥ* ...), as all, etc.[7]
166ab Request to be saved.
166cd-176 *namas te ('stu)* plus vocatives and datives.[8]
177 Concluding verse in Vasantatilakā-metre.
178 Vyāsa continues: Pleased by this praise Mādhava (= Kṛṣṇa/Viṣṇu) asked Kaṇḍu to choose a boon quickly.
179-183 Kaṇḍu wished to be released from Saṃsāra (list of attributes) and to attain the »highest step«.
184-186 The god told Kaṇḍu to worship him; by god's grace he would obtain liberation. Devoted people of all castes, women and even people of low caste (*śvapāka*, »dog-eaters«) would attain highest perfection, why not Kaṇḍu?
187-190 Viṣṇu disappeared; Kaṇḍu gave up all passion, concentrated on Puruṣottama and obtained liberation.
191 Phalastuti: He who listens to or reads Kaṇḍu's story is freed from evil and goes to heaven.
192 Vyāsa concludes his account of the »field of action« (*karmabhūmi*) and the place for liberation and of the god Puruṣottama.
193-194 Looking at, praising, meditating on Puruṣottama grants all pleasures on earth and Hari's highest place thereafter.[9]

Ch. 179: Introduction to Kṛṣṇacarita

1 Lomaharṣaṇa states that the hermits who listened to Vyāsa where pleased.
2-75 Request of the hermits concerning Viṣṇu's incarnation as Kṛṣṇa and its theological implications.
2-3 The hermits (i.e. Vyāsa's audience) confirm that they had been told about Bhāratavarṣa and about the place named »Śrī-Puruṣa«, the greatness of which astonishes and pleases (in VePr rhetorical question).
4-5 They express a doubt and inquire concerning the origin of Baladeva, Kṛṣṇa and Subhadrā[1] on earth.
6-10ab They ask why Kṛṣṇa and Saṃkarṣaṇa (= Baladeva) were born in Vasudeva's house and how they could take interest in this miserable world of mortals (list of

[6] v. 155-158ab contain allusions to the Puruṣasūkta, RV 10,90.

[7] Mention of the manifestations (*vyūha*) Aniruddha and Pradyumna in v. 165.

[8] Verse 167 contains the epithet *kamalālaya* which may be understood to refer to »him who rests on a lotus« (*kamala*), or to »him who is the resting place of Kamalā, i.e. Śrī, Lakṣmī«. Both versions might have chronological implications when compared to iconographic evidence. v. 172-175 refer to Viṣṇu as fish, as Aśvaśīrṣan (»having a horse's head«), tortoise, boar.

[9] In Śārdūlavikrīḍitā-metre.

[1] Ed. ASS reads Bhadrā instead of Subhadrā.

attributes) and in existence in a womb. They request to be told extensively about their (Kṛṣṇa's and Baladeva's) deeds.[2]

cd-16ab They request to be told how the Lord of gods became »Vāsudeva« by being born in Vasudeva's house; how he came to the world of mortals and for what purpose; how he thought of becoming a human being - he who shepherds the world;

cd-18ab he, who conquered the world with three steps, who established the wordly values (*trivarga*, i.e. *dharma, artha, kāma*), who in the end drank up the world making it one ocean;

cd-22ab he, who first of all as the boar lifted up the earth, who for the sake of Puruhūta (= Indra) conquered the earth (as the dwarf) and gave it to the gods, who as the man-lion tore up Hiraṇyakaśipu, who as the Aurva-fire drank up the ocean;

22cd-26 he, who is called Brahman with a thousand heads etc., from whose navel originated the lotus which is Brahman's residence, who killed the demons in the Tārakāmaya-battle, who killed Kālanemi, who lies in Yoga-sleep in the milk-ocean;

27-28 he, who protected Śakra (= Indra) in Aditi's womb from the demons; who banished the demons to the ocean and made Indra lord of gods;[3]

29-37 he, who made the fire and other constituents of domestic ritual; who made gods and ancestors recipients of offerings; who made the constituents of sacrifice (listed); who made the worlds according to the Yugas; who made the divisions of time (listed); who made the triads of worlds, knowledge, gods, fires, times, deeds, castes, and qualities (*guṇa*);

38-43ab he, who is immanent in all beings; who guides past and future and is fate; who is the goal for the righteous, the lack of goal for the unrighteous; origin of the four castes and their protector; who knows the four (kinds of) knowledge and supports the four stages of life; who is the directions, the elements, sun, moon etc., light and asceticism (or heat); who is transcendent;

cd-44ab he, who is, as god of the Ādityas, the destroyer of demons; who is the destroyer of the worlds in the end;

cd-47ab he, who is the limit (*setu*) of limits, the pure of those whose deeds are pure; the one to be known by those who know the Vedas; the lord of the lordly, Soma for the people of Soma (i.e. the friendly ?), fire of those who glow like fire, lord of Śakras (i.e. Indras), asceticism of ascetics, discipline of the disciplined, brilliance of those endowed with brilliance, quarrel for those who deserve quarrel, the goal of those who have a goal.

47cd-61 *Description of the constituents and the development of the human body*[4]

cd-48ab Development of breath/wind and (digestive ?) fire from ether/sky; identification of breath/fire/Madhusūdana (?).

cd-50ab Development of the embryo: essence → blood → flesh → marrow → bone → *majjan*[5] → semen → embryo.

[2] up to v. 10ab the hermits inquire about Kṛṣṇa and Baladeva, in what follows only about Kṛṣṇa. v. 10cd-66ab are nearly identical with HV 30.3-57.

[3] In Upajāti-metre.

[4] Possibly meant to show which way Viṣṇu had to take, being born as a human being.

[5] Meaning not clear.

50cd–51ab Discrimination of two *rāśis* (?)[6]

51cd–55ab Union of Soma (= semen) and fire (= blood) in the embryo; semen belongs to phlegm, blood to bile; phlegm is situated in the heart, bile in the navel; the heart is in the midst of the body and contains the mind (*manas*); between navel and stomach the (digestive) fire is situated. Prajāpati is the mind, Soma (moon or fluid?)[7] the phlegm, and Agni (fire) is the bile; thus a living being consists of Soma and Agni.

55cd–56ab That embryo was entered by mind, together with the highest soul.[8]

56cd–57ab The wind stays in the body as the five vital breaths.

57cd–58 Explanation of the five vital breaths.

59–61 Obtaining a body is within the range of the senses: the five elements entered its senses and produced their respective parts, viz. earth the body, wind the breath or soul, ether the holes of the body, water the flow within the body, the light of the sky the eyes and vital power (*tejas*); the mind is the soul (VePr ruler) of them all.

62–64 The hermits repeat their question how Viṣṇu from whose manly power (*vīrya*) all these collections (of senses etc.) and fields had originated, could become man in such a world subject to death.

65–72ab They want to hear about his strange origin and the reality of Viṣṇu, who is omnipresent, creates, maintains, and destroys; who is eternal etc. (list of epithets in v. 67–70ab); who is known as being pure Hari (VePr Viṣṇu and Hari) in the Kṛta-Yuga, Vaikuṇṭha among gods, Kṛṣṇa among men; and about the past and future course of his deeds.

72cd–75 Why did Hari come into this world of mortals, in the clan of Yadu – he who is unmanifest, who is eternal, is Nārāyaṇa, Hari, Rudra etc. (list of epithets and identifications).

Ch. 180: Manifestations and incarnations of Viṣṇu

1–12 Vyāsa praises Viṣṇu, mainly by epithets which describe his relation to the world (as four manifestations (*vyūha*); as transcendent; as creator; in identity with other beings; as foundation, etc.).[1]

13–16ab Vyāsa announces an account of what Brahman who revealed the Vedas and *dharma* had been asked by Yakṣas, hermits etc.

[6] Meaning not clear.

[7] Soma as principle or origin of fluid, in contrast to fire.

[8] Thus according to VePr; ASS reads »of the highest soul«, which may refer to the wind as the breath of Viṣṇu taking birth in the embryo.

[1] Verses 1–5 are a list of epithets in dative and relative clauses construed with absolutives; they correspond to MkP 4.36–40; v. 6–9 are taken out of this syntactic context and list epithets in dative (and a relative clause) with *namas*; v. 10–12 construe epithets in accusative with the absolutive *praṇamya* (v. 10), which connects to the following. v. 6–13 correspond to ViP 1,2.1–8.

6cd-17ab Etymology of Nārāyaṇa.

7cd-42ab Characteristics and functions of the four aspects of Nārāyaṇa.[2]

7cd-18ab This Nārāyaṇa permeates everything; he has four aspects; and he is Brahman (m.) with and without attributes.

8cd-21ab Description of the indescribable first form of Nārāyaṇa, called Vāsudeva, which is pure, the fiery, highest foundation for Yogins, beyond the Qualities etc.

1cd-22ab The second form, called Śeṣa, supports the earth and is characterized by the quality of Darkness (*tamas*).

2cd-23ab The third form is active, protects the beings, is characterized by a predominance of Beingness (or Brightness), *sattva*, establishes *dharma*.[3]

3cd-24ab The fourth (form) rests on a snake in water, Energy (*rajas*) being its quality, and produces the creation.

24cd-38 Description of the functions of the third form: It protects beings, establishes *dharma*, kills demons who violate *dharma*, protects gods and *dharma*, creates its own self whenever *dharma* suffers;[4] previously it dug up the earth in the shape of a boar; as man-lion it killed Hiraṇyakaśipu; it killed Vipracitti and other demons; it subdued Bali in the shape of a dwarf and conquered demons by striding through the three worlds; he[5] killed the Kṣatriyas as Jāmadagnya (i.e. Paraśurāma) to revenge his father's death; as Dattātreya he proclaimed the Yoga of eight parts to Alarka; as Rāma he killed Rāvaṇa in battle; when he lies sleeping on the ocean in yogic sleep, having swallowed the three worlds and being praised by the inhabitants of Janaloka, from his navel originates the lotus which is Brahman's residence;[6] when Brahman came into existence, Madhu and Kaiṭabha tried to kill Brahman, but he (Viṣṇu/Nārāyaṇa) slew them.

39ab The (incarnations) cannot all be enumerated.

39cd The present incarnation (*avatāra*) is called Māthura (belonging to Mathurā).

40-42ab Thus, that form characterized by Beingness (i.e. the third aspect of Nārāyaṇa, cf. above) descends; it is called Pradyumna;[7] its task is to protect. It assumes divine, human or animal forms according to Vāsudeva's wish. When revered it grants wishes.

42c-f Conclusion to an account of how Viṣṇu becomes a human being; announcement of a continuation.

[2] The term *vyūha* is not used (rather *mūrti* and *avatāra*), but the four aspects described correspond to what is otherwise called *vyūha*. This passage (except 29cd-38) corresponds to MkP 4.43-59.

[3] For the name of this form cf. below, v. 40-42.

[4] v. 26cd-27ab is a paraphrase of BhG 4.7.

[5] Masculine forms are used, i.e. reference to *mūrti* (f.) as the subject of these statements is forgotten, and the god himself becomes the subject.

[6] Ed. VePr inserts one line after 36ab.

[7] *pradyumna* is used as an adjective in this passage and might be translated as e.g. »pre-eminently mighty«.

Ch. 181: Heavenly prelude to the incarnation of Viṣṇu as Kṛṣṇa

1 Vyāsa announces a summary account of Hari's descending (on earth) for the purpose of alleviating the weight (on earth).

2-4 Whenever *adharma* increases and *dharma* declines Janārdana descends on earth; he is born in each Yuga, dividing his body into two parts, in order to suppress the wicked and to protect the righteous.[1]

5-6 Formerly the Earth, suffering from her heavy burden, went to mount Meru, and prostrated herself before the assembled gods.

7-14 The Earth proclaimed her respect for Nārāyaṇa as a teacher and told (the gods) that Kālanemi and other demons had come to the world of mortals, obstructing the beings; Kālanemi had been killed by Viṣṇu; he became Kaṃsa, son of Ugrasena; Ariṣṭa, Dhenuka, Keśin, Pralamba, Naraka, Sunda, and Bāṇa, son of Bali, and innumerable others, also originated. Their armies were also upon Earth, who could not bear the burden. The gods should do something to unburden her; otherwise she would sink to the nether worlds.

15-19 The gods turned to Brahman who confirmed what the earth had said: All the gods consist of Nārāyaṇa whose various manifestations (*vibhūti*) exist in such a way as to check and balance each other. The gods should go to the milk-ocean and pay homage to Hari who, being identical with the world, would descend on earth and establish *dharma*, even with only a small part of his.

20 Brahman went there together with the gods and praised the god whose emblem is Garuḍa.

21-25 Hymn by Brahman to Viṣṇu.[2]

26-31 Thus praised, the god pulled out a black and a white hair from his head and told the gods that these hairs would be born on earth and abolish her burden. All gods should also partially take birth on earth and fight the demons. His hair would become the eighth child of Devakī, wife of Vasudeva, and kill Kaṃsa, formerly Kālanemi.

32 Viṣṇu disappeared; the gods returned to mount Meru and took birth on earth.

33-35 Nārada prophesied to Kaṃsa that Devakī's eighth child would kill him. Kaṃsa imprisoned Devakī and Vasudeva who handed over each new-born child to Kaṃsa as he had previously said.[3]

36 The sons of Hiraṇyakaśipu, known as »six embryos«, were transferred to Devakī's womb by Nidrā (= Yoganidrā), according to Viṣṇu's instruction.

[1] Paraphrase of BhG 4.7-8.

[2] In Upajāti-metre. Only v. 21-22 are verses of praise mentioning the god's thousandfold appearance, the *trimūrti*-function, and his identity with everything (in Sāṃkhya terms); v. 23-25 inform about the Earth's plight and about the presence of all the gods and ask for instructions.

[3] The last clause might refer to an episode not told in BrP, which does, however, constitute the beginning of the Kṛṣṇacarita in ViP (cf. ViP 5,1.5-11); some such text as preserved in ViP would then be presupposed by BrP, which appears to have abbreviated its source. Within the present text of BrP, the phrase could refer to Nārada who announced each new-born child to Kaṃsa.

37 Yoganidrā, Viṣṇu's great Māyā by whom - as ignorance - the whole world is bewildered was instructed by Viṣṇu:

38–53 (Viṣṇu's speech:) Nidrā should lead the »six embryos« one after the other to Devakī's womb; after they had been killed by Kaṃsa, Śeṣa would partially descend as her seventh child; at the time of birth, he should be transferred to Rohiṇī, Vasudeva's other wife; people would think that Devakī had miscarried out of fear of Kaṃsa, while the child would be known as Saṃkarṣaṇa (»extraction«) because he had been extracted. Then Viṣṇu himself would take birth in Devakī while Yoganidrā should enter Yaśodā's womb. On the eighth day of the dark half in the month of rains, at night, he would be born, while Yoganidrā would be born on the ninth. Vasudeva would exchange the children; Kaṃsa would throw her down to the rocky ground, but she would obtain a place in the sky, Indra would bow before her and make her his sister; she would kill demons, Śumbha, Niśumbha, and others, and would adorn the earth at various places; by Viṣṇu's grace she would fulfil the wishes of those people who praised her (as Bhūti, Saṃnati, Kīrti, Kānti, Pṛthivī, Dhṛti, Lajjā, Puṣṭi, Umā, Āryā, Durgā, Vedagrabhā, Ambikā, Bhadrā, Bhadrakālī, Kṣemyā, Kṣemakarī) or offered her wine and meat.

Ch. 182: Birth of Kṛṣṇa

1–3 Vyāsa continues: According to Viṣṇu's instructions the »support of the world« (= Yoganidrā) transferred the six embryos to (Devakī's) womb one after the other; when the seventh had reached Rohiṇī's womb Hari himself entered Devakī's womb, while Yoganidrā entered that of Yaśodā.

4–6 When Viṣṇu had come to earth the planets and seasons showed auspicious signs. Nobody could bear to look at Devakī because of her brilliance. Devakī who could not be seen by men or women (i.e. lived in seclusion?) was praised day and night by the gods.

7–8 Hymn by the gods to Devakī, identifying her with Svāhā, Svadhā, Vidyā, Sudhā, and with light, stating that she had descended to earth for the protection of the worlds, asking for her favour (grace) and begging her to bear him who bears the whole world.

9–11 Thus praised, she carried the god in her womb. He was born before dawn; at his birth the clouds grumbled softly and the gods showered flowers.

12–13 Seeing his divine attributes (four arms, Śrīvatsa-lock) Ānakadundubhi (= Vasudeva) praised him.[1]

14–15 Vasudeva, afraid of Kaṃsa, prayed to Kṛṣṇa to hide his divine appearance because of Kaṃsa, who would trouble him if he came to know that the lord of the gods had been born in his house.

16 Devakī, too, prayed for his grace, addressing him as supporter of the world, who had appeared as a child.[2]

[1] No hymn is quoted.

[2] In Upajāti-metre.

17 She requested him to withdraw his four-armed appearance so that Kaṃsa would not learn of his incarnation.

18 The god told Devakī that he had been born from her because she had praised him, when she was longing for a son.[3]

19-26 The god grew silent; Vasudeva took him outside, the guards being benumbed by Yoganidrā. Śeṣa shielded him against rain; Yamunā let him pass through knee-deep water. He met Nanda and the cow-herds who had come to deliver the taxes to Kaṃsa. At that time Yaśodā was benumbed by Yoganidrā; Vasudeva exchanged the boy for the daughter to whom she had given birth, and returned. When Yaśodā awoke she was happy with the boy whom she believed to be her child.

27-30 Vasudeva delivered the girl to Devakī's room; when the guards heard the baby's voice they informed Kaṃsa, who seized the child in spite of Devakī's entreaties and threw her down on a rock. But she attained a place in the sky (the intermediate sphere) and assumed her eight-armed form. Mockingly she addressed Kaṃsa:

31 Yoganidrā informed Kaṃsa that his enemy lived and that he should take precautions.

32 Thereupon she left before Kaṃsa's eyes, praised by Siddhas.

Ch. 183: Kaṃsa's plans and thoughts

1-7 Vyāsa continues: Kaṃsa called Pralamba, Keśin, and other demons (Pralamba, Keśin, Dhenuka, Pūtanā, Ariṣṭa are addressed), told them about the gods' intention to kill him, mocked the gods' efforts and told the demons that some counteraction should be taken, for the girl had told him about the birth of his enemy, and that any boy with excessive strength should be killed.

8-11 Thereupon he went inside, told Vasudeva and Devakī that he had killed their children in vain and that he would not kill their children in future. He dismissed them (from their imprisonment) and returned to his residence.

Ch. 184: Adventures of the child Kṛṣṇa

1-6 Vyāsa continues: Set free, Vasudeva went to Nanda, who told him about the birth of his son (i.e. Kṛṣṇa). Vasudeva advised him to leave immediately, since the purpose of coming there had been fulfilled (delivering the taxes); he told him to protect Rohiṇī's son as his own. Thereupon the herdsmen left.

7-20 *Pūtanā-episode*

7-13 While they were staying in Gokula, Pūtanā seized Kṛṣṇa at night and gave him her breast; by that method she used to kill children. But Kṛṣṇa grabbed her breast and

[3] No such praise or episode is mentioned in BrP or ViP.

sucked out her life. She fell with a roar; hearing it, the inhabitants of Vraja came running and found Kṛṣṇa in the lap of the dead Pūtanā. Yaśodā took him and waved the tail of a cow around him while Nanda put cow-dung on his head and pronounced the following protective prayer.

14–19 Nanda's prayer invoking Viṣṇu as Hari, as Keśava in the form of a boar,[1] as Janārdana, Viṣṇu, Govinda in the form of a dwarf, as Nārāyaṇa, Madhusūdana and Hṛṣīkeśa for protection of different parts of the boy's body.

20–28 *Episode of the turned cart*

After this blessing the boy was laid (to rest) under a cart; eager for the breast he cried and kicked with his legs against the cart, turning it over and breaking all the pots. People came running and were informed by the other children that nobody but the boy had turned the cart over. Everybody was amazed; Yaśodā venerated potsherds and cart with curds, flowers etc.

29–30 At Nanda's prompting Garga performed the name-giving ceremony for the two boys in secret, naming them Rāma and Kṛṣṇa.

31–42ab *Episode of Kṛṣṇa being bound to mortar*

After some time the children started crawling; Yaśodā and Rohiṇī could not prevent them from playing with the calves. Yaśodā bound Kṛṣṇa to a mortar; while she was engaged in her work Kṛṣṇa pulled the mortar; it got stuck between two Arjuna-trees which were consequently pulled down by Kṛṣṇa. Hearing the cracking sounds people came running only to find the fallen trees and the smiling boy. Ever after, his name was Dāmodara (»having a rope around the waist«).

42cd–52ab The herdsmen consulted among each other, reviewing the inauspicious past events and decided to leave Vraja. After a hasty departure they settled in Vṛndāvana, which was made green as in the rainy season by Kṛṣṇa's thoughts only.

52cd–57ab Description of the plays, activities, attire of the two children; they grew to be seven years old.

57cd–60 Description of rainy season.

Ch. 185: Kālīya-episode

1–4 Vyāsa continues: One day Kṛṣṇa and others, but without Rāma (i.e. Balarāma), roamed the forest and came to Kālindī (= Yamunā). Nearby was the pool where Kālīya lived whose venom had even poisoned the trees along the bank.

5–10 Madhusūdana (= Kṛṣṇa) saw that Yamunā was polluted by that Kālīya who had been defeated by him but then had been spared. He reflected that it was his duty to kill him, since it was the purpose of his incarnation on earth to punish the wicked; he decided to jump into the pool from a nearby Kadamba-tree.

[1] And in the form of the man-lion. Ed. VePr adds one verse after v. 15.

11–17 When Kṛṣṇa jumped down the splashing water immediately burnt those trees which were touched by it. Kṛṣṇa stirred up the waters with his arms; hearing the noise the king of Nāgas (= Kālīya), surrounded by other snakes and hundreds of his wives, angrily rushed forth. Kṛṣṇa was bound and bitten by them.

18–27 The other boys ran back and shouted, informing the herdsmen and women, who were thunder-struck, started to lament and hurried to the pool. They saw Kṛṣṇa motionless and overpowered by the snake(s). Yaśodā and the other women wanted to enter the water also, rather than return to Vraja[1] without Kṛṣṇa, since he belonged to the *vraja* like the sun to the day (etc.).

28–29 Seeing Nanda and the others dismayed and Yaśodā in a faint, Rauhiṇeya (= Balarāma) pronounced Kṛṣṇa's greatness:

30–33 (Balarāma's words:)He reminded Kṛṣṇa of his divine nature (e.g. *trimūrti*-function), of the fact that the cowherds had become their relatives by their (i.e. Kṛṣṇa's and Balarāma's) having been born amongst them; urging Kṛṣṇa to subdue Kālīya.

34–38 Thus reminded, Kṛṣṇa freed himself, bent down Kālīya's middle hood, stepped on it and started dancing. The snake became unconscious and vomited blood; his wives took refuge with Madhusūdana (= Kṛṣṇa).

39–42 The snake-wives' prayer to Kṛṣṇa, acknowledging Kṛṣṇa's divinity and their own inability to praise and describe Kṛṣṇa of whom the whole cosmos is but a part of a part; asking to be granted their husband's life.

43 Thereupon Kālīya also asked Kṛṣṇa to be gracious.

44–49 Kālīya's prayer to Kṛṣṇa, acknowledging his divinity[2] and arguing that, since he had been created by Kṛṣṇa, punishment for acting according to his (snake-)nature was not justified; admitting his defeat and begging that his life be spared.

50–51 Kṛṣṇa's answer: Kālīya should leave Yamunā and live in the ocean, where he would be protected against Garuḍa by the marks of Kṛṣṇa's feet on his head.

52–53 Vyāsa continues: Hari (= Kṛṣṇa) set free Kālīya who left his pool and moved to the ocean with his whole clan.

54–56 The cowherds embraced Kṛṣṇa and returned to Vraja,[3] singing his praise.

Ch. 186: Dhenuka-episode

1–3 Vyāsa continues: While grazing the cows, Balarāma and Keśava (= Kṛṣṇa) came to a forest of *tāla*-trees where a demon called Dhenuka stayed in the shape of an ass; he lived on the meat of men and cows.

4–5 The cowherds told Rāma and Kṛṣṇa that they wanted the fruits of those trees.

6–13 Kṛṣṇa threw the fruits down; upon hearing the noise the demonic ass came running angrily; when he kicked the two on their chests with his hind legs, he was seized,

[1] Here to be understood as »cattle-shed«, since the move from Vraja to Vṛndāvana has already taken place.

[2] v. 44–45 may be considered a hymn of praise with the admission of Kālīya's inability to praise as a refrain.

[3] cf. note to v. 18–27, above.

whirled around till he was dead, and thrown with great force into the tree, so that many fruits fell down. Other demonic asses that came running were also thrown into the tree as if it was only a game. The earth was adorned by ripe Tāla-fruits and by the bodies of the asses. Thereafter the cattle could graze in that forest without impediment.

Ch. 187: Pralamba-episode; institution of hill-worship by Kṛṣṇa

1 Vyāsa continues: The Tāla-grove looked lovely to the cowherds.

2–7 Description of the two boys' appearance, activities, games.[1]

8–30 *Pralamba-episode*

8–18 A demon called Pralamba assumed human shape and mingled with the herdsmen. When the boys paired up for a game called Bālakrīḍanaka, Govinda played against Śrīdāman, Balarāma against Pralamba; Kṛṣṇa and Balarāma won. Carrying each other on their shoulders they ran up to a Bhāṇḍīra-tree and back. The demon threw Balarāma onto his shoulders and ran on; unable to carry Balarāma's weight he increased the size of his body and assumed a fearsome appearance (described in v. 31–32). As he was carried away Saṃkarṣaṇa (= Balarāma) addressed Kṛṣṇa:

19–20 Balarāma told Kṛṣṇa that he was being carried away, asking what he should do.

21 Vyāsa introduces Kṛṣṇa's answer:

22–25 Kṛṣṇa reminded Balarāma of his nature as the Self of all; he and Kṛṣṇa, being the one cause of the world, had only divided for the sake of the world. Balarāma should kill the demon and act for the benefit of his companions or relatives.

26–28 Vyāsa continues: Thus reminded by Kṛṣṇa, Balarāma hit Pralamba on the head with his fist, so that his eyes came out, he vomited blood, fell down and died.

29–30 The cowherds praised Balarāma and returned with Kṛṣṇa.

31–61 *Institution of hill-worship by Kṛṣṇa*

31–34 Vyāsa continues: After the rainy season Kṛṣṇa noticed eager preparations for an Indra-festival and asked the older cowherds about it.

35–40 Nanda explained that Indra was the lord of rains, upon which the cowherds' existence and welfare depended; therefore he was worshipped with a sacrifice.

41 Dāmodara (= Kṛṣṇa), however, wishing to provoke Indra's wrath, answered Nanda with the following speech.

42–54 Kṛṣṇa's arguments and advice: As cowherds, they lived not by agriculture or trade but by roaming with their cows. Of the fourfold knowledge, i.e. (philosophical) inquiry, »threefold« (sacred science), (practical) knowledge concerning livelihood,

[1] Ed. VePr adds two lines after v. 187.2ab, containing the information that they went to a Bhāṇḍīra-grove.

and science of government, that one concerning livelihood could be divided into three branches: agriculture, trade, and cattle-breeding. The cowherds' means of livelihood being the cows, that branch of knowledge should be esteemed by them as their deity. »Someone who enjoys the fruits of something different from what he worships will not attain welfare in this world and the world beyond« (maxim). Boundaries (of the fields) should be revered, beyond them the forests, and beyond these the mountain hills as the highest refuge (for the cowherds). Hills and cows should be worshipped, not Indra. The herdsmen should, therefore, venerate the hill by a cow-sacrifice; since they depended not on mantras or ploughs (venerated Brahmins and farmers). They should venerate the Govardhana-hill by killing an animal fit for sacrifice, by the milk-products of the whole settlement, and by feeding Brahmins and others. The decorated cattle should go around the hill; thus they would gain the favour of the cows and of the hill.

55–59ab The inhabitants of Vraja were pleased with Kṛṣṇa's advice and performed a sacrifice in honour of the Govardhana-hill; they offered curds, milk, meat etc., and fed hundreds and thousands of Brahmins; the cows circumambulated the hill.

59cd–61 Kṛṣṇa was present on top of the hill, pronouncing himself to be embodied in the hill and enjoying the food brought by the herdsmen; as Kṛṣṇa he ascended the hill along with the herdsmen and venerated his other embodiment, the peak of the hill. When that had disappeared and the herdsmen had obtained boons, the mountain-sacrifice was finished and they returned to their settlement.

Ch. 188: Govardhana-episode; encounter of Indra and Kṛṣṇa

1 Vyāsa continues: Indra was angry at the obstruction of (his) sacrifice; he called the Saṃvartaka-clouds (clouds of doomsday).

2–5 (Indra's words:) He told the clouds that Nanda etc. had stopped performing sacrifices for him, relying rather on Kṛṣṇa; the clouds should torment the cows; he (Indra) would help them.

6–10 Thereupon the clouds flooded the earth; some cows died; others lowed for their calves; the calves seemed to call upon Kṛṣṇa to save them.

11–13 Hari saw everybody's affliction, recognized Indra's doing, and decided to save the settlement by uprooting a hill and holding it up as an umbrella.

14–16 Accordingly, Kṛṣṇa lifted up Govardhana playfully with one hand and told the people to enter underneath fearlessly for protection.

17–19 People, cattle, carts etc. took refuge underneath the hill supported by Kṛṣṇa whose deeds were praised by the people.

20–23 After pouring down rain for seven nights and days Indra called back the clouds. People returned to their houses; Kṛṣṇa put the hill back in its place.

24–28 Vyāsa continues:[1] Pākaśāsana (= Indra) became interested in meeting Kṛṣṇa; he mounted his elephant Airāvata, went to Govardhana and saw Kṛṣṇa, the »cowherd

[1] The insertion of *vyāsa uvāca* at this point is not required by the course of the narration; the parallel text of ViP, however, begins a new chapter after v. 23, which normally starts by mentioning (repeating) the name of the narrator. The text of BrP seems to have retained

of the world«, as one cowboy amongst others. He saw Garuḍa hidden high up shielding Kṛṣṇa. Indra dismounted his elephant and talked to Madhusūdana (= Kṛṣṇa) in private.

29–35 Indra's words, announcing that he would give the reason for his coming; explaining that Kṛṣṇa had been born on earth to alleviate her burden; expressing his satisfaction with Kṛṣṇa who had protected the cows against the rains by lifting up the mountain, and had thereby served the purpose of the gods; now the cows had urged him (Indra) to come and anoint Kṛṣṇa as Vice-Indra (*anvindra*) and lord (*indra*) of cows, thus making him »Govinda«.[2]

36–37 Indra anointed Kṛṣṇa with water which he had brought along with him. During this ceremony milk dripping (from the udders of the cows) moistened the earth.

38 Śacīpati (= Indra) again addressed Kṛṣṇa:

39–41 Indra's words, repeating that he had acted upon the word of the cows; expressing his desire to unburden (the earth); telling him that one part of him had become incarnate as Arjuna, who should be protected by Kṛṣṇa and would help him in unburdening (the earth).

42–47 Kṛṣṇa replied by promising to protect Arjuna as long as he (Kṛṣṇa) lived on earth. After Kaṃsa, Ariṣṭa, Keśin, Kuvalayāpīḍa, Naraka, and others had been killed, there would be a great battle achieving the unburdening (of the earth); for Arjuna's sake he (Kṛṣṇa) would hand over Yudhiṣṭhira etc. to Kuntī at the end of the battle (i.e. allow them to return to their mother).

48–49 Indra embraced Kṛṣṇa; Indra returned to heaven, Kṛṣṇa to Vraja.

Ch. 189: Kṛṣṇa and the cowherds; Ariṣṭa-episode

1–13 *Kṛṣṇa's human nature questioned by the cowherds*

1 Vyāsa continues: After Śakra (= Indra) had left the herdsmen addressed Kṛṣṇa:

2–8 The herdsmen expressed their astonishment at Kṛṣṇa's wonderful feats (references back to Kāliya, Pralamba, Govardhana-episode) and doubted whether he was a human being.

9 Kṛṣṇa pretended to be angry and answered:

10–12 He asked to be treated like a kinsman, being neither god nor Gandharva, nor Yakṣa, nor demon.[1]

13 The herdsmen left.

such a beginning of a new chapter even though it has changed the division of chapters, thus possibly indicating its dependence on a text like that of ViP.

[2] This explanation seems to presuppose an intermediate form »*gav-indra*«, which would then have been changed to »*govinda*«.

[1] v. 11 is corrupt (*arghā* f. ?); cf. ViP 5.13.11.

14–45 *The love-play of Kṛṣṇa and the Gopīs*

14–17 Seeing the autumn-moon etc. (description of nature) Kṛṣṇa wanted to make love with the herdswomen. Together with Rāma (= Balarāma)[2] he sang sweet songs; upon hearing these sounds the women were attracted.

18–20 Description of the women's different reactions showing their love for Kṛṣṇa.

21 Surrounded by the Gopīs, Kṛṣṇa appreciated the autumn-night, eager to start the dancing (or love play, *rāsa*).[3]

22–25 Description of the Gopīs searching for Kṛṣṇa; they assembled on the bank of the Yamunā and kept singing the song about his deeds (*caritam*).

26–29 Description of the women's actions and gestures of love at Kṛṣṇa's approach.[4]

30–33 Mādhava started to lead the Gopīs to the dancing circle (*rāsamaṇḍala*).[5]

34–35 Description of the sounds of tinkling of ornaments in the dance and of the women's singing.

36–38 Description of erotic gestures and love-play with Kṛṣṇa.

39 Antiphony of Kṛṣṇa and the Gopīs.

40–41 Description of the love-play with Kṛṣṇa; one moment without him appeared to the women to be like 10 million years.

42–43 The women came to Kṛṣṇa every night, though they were hindered from leaving the house by their relatives, and Kṛṣṇa enjoyed love-play with them.

44–45 Theological conclusion: The Lord exists in those women and their husbands and in everything just like the five elements; he is everything.

46–58 *Ariṣṭa-episode*

46–58ab Vyāsa continues:[6] One night, while Kṛṣṇa was engaged in love-play, Ariṣṭa came and scared the cattle (v. 47–50 describe the fierce appearance of this bull-shaped demon); the herdsmen called upon Kṛṣṇa, who roared like a lion. The bull came running towards Dāmodara (= Kṛṣṇa) who seized the horns and knocked his knee against the bull's chest. He tore out one horn and beat the demon till he vomited blood and died.

58c-f The herdsmen praised Janārdana (= Kṛṣṇa) just as the gods praised Indra after he had slain Vṛtra.

[2] Balarāma is, however, not mentioned again in the following description.

[3] According to the following verses, however, they have not yet found him.

[4] cf. v. 18–20, above, where the women go to Kṛṣṇa; here he comes to them.

[5] Ed. VePr prints v. 32–33 in a footnote.

[6] The text inserts a *vyāsa uvāca* which may be a trace of the beginning of a new chapter, a division of the text as preserved in ViP 5,13–14.

Ch. 190: Kaṃsa's plans against Kṛṣṇa; Keśin-episode

1–5 Vyāsa continues: After the killing of Ariṣṭa, Dhenuka, and Pralamba, after the lifting of Govardhana, the subjugation of Kāliya (= Kālīya), the breaking of the two trees, the killing of Pūtanā, the turning of the cart,[1] Nārada told Kaṃsa about these events, which he knew by his divine eye, as well as about the exchange of Yaśodā's and Devakī's children. Kaṃsa became extremely angry at Vasudeva. He scolded the Yādavas and reflected upon what to do.

6–8 Kaṃsa thought that Balarāma and Kṛṣṇa should be killed while they were still boys. He decided to invite them for an archery competition and for a wrestling match with Cāṇūra and Muṣṭika, two powerful wrestlers.

9 Thus Kaṃsa made up his mind to kill Rāma (= Balarāma) and Janārdana (= Kṛṣṇa); he turned to Akrūra and addressed him.

10–19 Kaṃsa's words to Akrūra, asking him the favour of inviting Vasudeva's sons for the archery competition and a wrestling match, since he wanted to get those two partial incarnations of Viṣṇu killed by the elephant Kuvalayāpīḍa. After that he would kill Vasudeva and Nanda as well as his father Ugrasena and carry off their cattle and wealth. All Yādavas who had wished for his death should be killed except Akrūra, who should go and persuade the herdsmen to bring milk etc.

20–21 Akrūra was happy since he was going to meet Kṛṣṇa; he agreed and left.

22–38 *Keśin-episode*

22–25 Vyāsa continues:[2] At the same time Keśin was sent as Kaṃsa's messenger. Seeing this demonic horse the people took refuge with Kṛṣṇa.

26–28 Kṛṣṇa reassured the people and challenged the demon to come, announcing that he would knock his teeth out (like the wielder of the trident (= Śiva) did those of Pūṣan).

29–37 The demon came running towards Kṛṣṇa with gaping mouth. Kṛṣṇa forced his arm into Keśin's mouth and broke his teeth; the arm swelled and tore asunder the demon, who fell in two parts like a tree hit by lightning while Kṛṣṇa stood there smiling.

38 The people praised Kṛṣṇa.

39–47 Nārada came along on a cloud, applauded Kṛṣṇa for playfully killing this demon who had troubled the gods,[3] and expressed his satisfaction at Kṛṣṇa's deeds, who by killing Keśin earned the epithet Keśava. Nārada announced that he would be present at the killing of Kaṃsa, by which the earth's burden would be alleviated, wished Kṛṣṇa well and bid him farewell.

48 After Nārada had left Kṛṣṇa returned to Gokula.

[1] Summary list of Kṛṣṇa's deed reported in ch. 185–189.

[2] The following episode is introduced by *vyāsa uvāca* which indicates a division of chapters as in ViP, cf. ViP 5,15–5,16.

[3] VePr inserts one verse after v. 40: Because he had been desirous of the death of the man-stallion (i.e. Kṛṣṇa?), he (i.e. Keśin?) went to heaven, since he was killed by Kṛṣṇa.

Ch. 191: Akrūra's devotion to Kṛṣṇa

1 Vyāsa continues: Akrūra set out for Nanda's abode, full of joy in anticipation of seeing Kṛṣṇa soon.

2-17 Akrūra's thoughts.[1]

2-3 Nobody is more fortunate than he is himself, for he can see Kṛṣṇa, the partial incarnation of Viṣṇu; now his birth is successful.

4-12 Description of Viṣṇu's/Kṛṣṇa's divine functions and attributes: Akrūra will see Viṣṇu, who takes away evil; from whom originated the Vedas; in whom rest the gods; who is the sacrificial *puruṣa*; by performing sacrifices for whom Indra attained lordship over the gods; whose original shape is not known even to Brahman and the (vedic) gods (list of names: Indra, Rudra, the Aśvins, Vasus, Ādityas, and Maruts); who is in all beings and permeates all; who has taken the forms of fish, tortoise, boar, lion, and produced Yoga from Yoga (?); who is now present in human form and stays with the cowherds; who supports the earth, but has now come on earth.

13-17 Akrūra bows to Viṣṇu, who has become a relative of mortals, whose Māyā the world cannot eradicate, by keeping whom in their hearts the mortals overcome ignorance; who is the sacrificial *puruṣa* for sacrificers, Vāsudeva for Śāśvatas, and who is called »Viṣṇu« by the Vedāntins; in whom the world rests, who truly is and is not; who distributes blessings on those who think of him - in him Akrūra takes his refuge.

18-25 Thus thinking Akrūra reached Gokula just before sunset; he saw Kṛṣṇa (described in v. 19-23ab) and Balarāma (described in v. 23cd-24) and was overwhelmed.

26 Akrūra's thoughts describing the two as the supreme abode, the highest step, Vāsudeva divided into two.

27-33 Akrūra's thoughts anticipating his welcome by Kṛṣṇa, contrasting his human behaviour with his divine majesty, and his own unworthiness with Kṛṣṇa's divine omniscience and benevolence.[2]

Ch. 192: Encounter between Akrūra and Kṛṣṇa; Kṛṣṇa's journey to Mathurā

1-4 Vyāsa continues: Upon meeting Kṛṣṇa Akrūra introduced himself, was embraced by Kṛṣṇa and taken to his house, properly welcomed and fed.

5-10 After hearing the account of Kaṃsa's maltreatment of Devakī, Vasudeva, and Ugrasena, and about Kaṃsa's intentions, Kṛṣṇa reassured Akrūra that he knew everything and that Kaṃsa was as good as dead, that he (Kṛṣṇa), Rāma and the herdsmen would go to Mathurā and that Kaṃsa would be killed within two days.

[1] In v. 2-12 nearly every verse culminates in a varying refrain, such as »Him I shall see (v. 2, 3, 4, 6, 7, VePr 8), and »He will touch/see/address me« (v. 8, 9, 10, 12), whereas v. 13-17 end in expressions of devotion.

[2] v. 27 in Indravajrā-metre, v. 28 in Upajāti-metre; after v. 28 VePr inserts three verses in Jagatī-metre; v. 29-33 in Upajāti-metre).

11–13 The next morning the men got ready for departure while the women were watching.

14–31 (The women's words:) They describe Kṛṣṇa's departure, lamenting their misfortune, congratulating the women of Mathurā, and blaming Akrūra for taking away Kṛṣṇa.

32–42 As the party reached the Yamunā at midday, Akrūra wanted to perform his worship; while meditating on *brahman* (n.) he had a vision of Balarāma as Śeṣa and, in his lap, of the four-armed Kṛṣṇa with his divine attributes (described with iconographic details in v. 36–42).

43–47 Recognizing Kṛṣṇa and Balarāma, Akrūra wondered how they could have reached there so quickly but he was prevented from talking by Janārdana; he returned to the chariot where he saw them again in their human appearance; he entered the water again and had the same vision. Now he recognized the true state of affairs and started to praise the Lord with the following hymn:

48–58 Hymn by Akrūra to Viṣṇu, emphasizing that the god is beyond the reach of (human) knowledge, concepts and words, yet is the one essence (»self«) of everything, addressed by various names, and identical with the other (vedic) gods such as Brahman, Paśupati, Aryaman, Vidhātṛ, Dhātṛ, Indra, Agni, Varuṇa, Kubera, and Yama.[1] Akrūra praises (v. 58) the four manifestations (Vāsudeva, Saṃkarṣaṇa, Pradyumna, Aniruddha[2]).

59–61 After praising Kṛṣṇa thus,[3] he worshipped him mentally with flowers and incense and remained in deep concentration for a long time before returning to the chariot.

62–66 Kṛṣṇa, seeing Akrūra's astonishment, asked about what he had seen; Akrūra replied by identifying the Kṛṣṇa of his vision, identical with whole world, with the Kṛṣṇa before him and urged him to continue the journey to Mathurā.

67–68 They reached Mathurā at dusk. Akrūra told Kṛṣṇa and Balarāma to enter the city on foot and not to go to Vasudeva who would be harrassed by Kaṃsa.

69–70 As the two entered Mathurā and walked along the main road people were pleased by the sight.

71–74 The two came across a dyer who worked for Kaṃsa and reviled Rāma and Keśava (= Kṛṣṇa) when they asked for clothes. Kṛṣṇa beheaded him with his hand; having taken away yellow and blue clothes the two went to a garland-maker.

75–86 The garland-maker considered them gods, praised himself as fortunate and offered his choicest garlands. In return, Kṛṣṇa, before leaving, granted him and his family blessings, wealth, long life, and attainment of heaven by thinking of Kṛṣṇa at the hour of death.

Ch. 193: Kṛṣṇa's deeds in Mathurā; killing of Kaṃsa

1–12 Vyāsa continues: On the main road Kṛṣṇa met Kubjā, a humpbacked woman, who introduced herself (v. 4–5) as employed to anoint Kaṃsa. Kṛṣṇa asked for the ointment and received it from her. In return Kṛṣṇa healed her disfigurement by

[1] v. 55–57 in Praharṣiṇī-metre.

[2] Without calling them *vyūha*.

[3] NB.: Balarāma/Śeṣa, though mentioned as part of the vision, is not praised.

straightening her. When invited by the infatuated woman to visit her, Kṛṣṇa promised to come and laughed, (looking) at Balarāma's face.

13–16 Fully adorned the two went to where the bow was kept; Kṛṣṇa lifted the bow and, drawing it, broke it. The bow breaking made a great noise, which filled Mathurā. The two defeated the guards and left the place.

17–22 Informed about Akrūra's arrival and the breaking of the bow, Kaṃsa addressed Cāṇūra and Muṣṭika (v. 18–20) ordering them to kill the two boys by any means and promising appropriate rewards. He further ordered the elephant Kuvalayāpīḍa to be stationed near the gate of the stadium in order to kill the boys as they entered.

23 With everything prepared, Kaṃsa, whose death was imminent, waited for the next day.

24–78ab *Killing of Kaṃsa*

24–31 The citizens had assembled, the kings had taken their seats, the wrestlers were ready; Kaṃsa, the women, the herdsmen, Akrūra, and Vasudeva were present, as well as Devakī, who was hoping to see her son at least at the hour of his death. Cāṇūra and Muṣṭika warmed up; instruments were sounded, people shouted as Baladeva (= Balarāma) and Janārdana (= Kṛṣṇa) entered the stadium, besmeared with blood and holding in their hands as weapons the teeth of the elephant whom they had killed.

32–40 People hailed Kṛṣṇa reporting his past deeds: that he had killed Pūtanā, turned the cart, felled the two trees, danced on Kāliya (= Kālīya), held up Govardhana, killed Ariṣṭa, Dhenuka, and Keśin. He was destined to save the Yādavas; as a part of Viṣṇu he had descended on earth to alleviate her burden. Devakī's breasts started to produce milk; Vasudeva forgot his old age in his joy.

41 The women of the royal harem and of the city gazed without ceasing at the two boys.

42–49 (The women's words:) Description of Kṛṣṇa's appearance (body; attributes, e.g. Śrīvatsa-lock), Balabhadra (= Balarāma), the preparations for the wrestling match with Muṣṭika and Cāṇūra, and the unjust inequality of the contenders.[1]

50–57ab Kṛṣṇa and Balabhadra (= Balarāma) started jumping around (narrator's comment: it was surprising that the earth did not split under their steps); Kṛṣṇa fought against Cāṇūra, Baladeva (= Balarāma) against Muṣṭika; they fought punching and kicking their enemies. Cāṇūra's strength failed while Kṛṣṇa fought playfully.

57cd–60ab When Kaṃsa saw his party falter, he stopped the music; but immediately heavenly music was sounded in the skies and the gods hailed Kṛṣṇa, requesting him to kill Cāṇūra.

60cd–63ab After fighting playfully for a long time Kṛṣṇa whirled Cāṇūra around and killed him.

63cd–65ab Similarly Baladeva (= Balarāma) fought with and killed Muṣṭika.

65cd–67ab Kṛṣṇa threw Tośalaka, the king of wrestlers to the ground; the other wrestlers fled.

67cd–76ab While Kṛṣṇa and Saṃkarṣaṇa (= Balarāma) joyfully jumped around with other cowherds, the furious Kaṃsa ordered his men to remove the two from the stadium,

[1] Ed. VePr inserts one verse after v. 44.

to fetter Nanda and Vasudeva, to seize the herdsmen's cows and property. Kṛṣṇa laughed at him, jumped up at him, pulled him by the hair, threw him down and killed him by falling upon him with the weight of the whole world. Then he dragged the dead body by the hair to the stage.[2]

cd-78ab Kaṃsa's brother Sunāman came running and was defeated by Balabhadra (= Balarāma). People started lamenting.

78cd-79 Kṛṣṇa and Baladeva (= Balarāma) touched the feet of Vasudeva and Devakī, who remembered what was said at the time of Kṛṣṇa's birth,[3] and bowed to them.

80-87 Vasudeva's words, begging for Kṛṣṇa's grace and describing him as the god born on earth to kill the wicked, as identical with everything, as all the gods and as the sacrifice; apologizing for any wrong notion he (Vasudeva) might have had about him due to (parental) love for him; attributing the contrast between Kṛṣṇa's divinity (*trimūrti*-function; identity with all) and his human birth to Māyā;

88-90 (Vāsudeva's words continued[4]) begging for grace; describing Kṛṣṇa as Viṣṇu and lord of the world; describing his own behaviour ln exchanging the children as due to illusion.

Ch. 194: Kṛṣṇa's education; Pañcajana-episode

1-5 Vyāsa continues: Whereas Vasudeva and Devakī had come to know the truth, Kṛṣṇa spread Viṣṇu's Māyā over the Yadus by addressing Vasudeva and Devakī as parents, apologizing for their troubles and stating (v. 3cd-5ab) that only the birth of somebody who honours his parents is meaningful.

6 Thereafter Kṛṣṇa greeted his elders among the Yadus.

7-8 When Kaṃsa's wives lamented the death of their husband, Hari (= Kṛṣṇa) regretted his deed and himself consoled them.

9 Madhusūdana (= Kṛṣṇa) freed Ugrasena and anointed him king.

10 Ugrasena performed the last rites for his son (Kaṃsa) and the others.

11-12 Kṛṣṇa paid reverence to the king asking for his orders and reminding him that due to Yayāti's curse his line was not supposed to rule but that with Kṛṣṇa's support he might even give orders to gods.

13-17 Kṛṣṇa ordered the wind to demand Indra's hall Sudharmā for the Yadus. Informed of Kṛṣṇa's command Puraṃdhara (= Indra) gave the hall.

18-22 Though omniscient Baladeva (= Balarāma) and Janārdana (= Kṛṣṇa) went to live with and be taught by Sāṃdīpani from Kāśi, who lived in Avanti; they learned the whole lore of arms (*dhanurveda*) within 64 days. Sāṃdīpani considered them to be the sun and moon.

[2] *kṛtā* in v. 76 cannot be construed and seems to presuppose the reading *purīkhā tena* (for *pāṃpatena*) in the preceding line which is found in ViP (ed. B).

[3] cf. above, ch. 182.

[4] In Vasantatilakā-metre, repeating the main themes of the preceding Ślokas.

23-31 *Pañcajana-episode*

23-31 When asked to wish for something as a gift (*dakṣiṇā*), the teacher demanded the life of his son who had died at Prabhāsa in the ocean. The ocean told Kṛṣṇa that the boy had been seized by the demon Pañcajana who had the shape of a conch. Kṛṣṇa entered the waters and killed Pañcajana. From his »bones« was made Kṛṣṇa's conch-shell the sound of which scared demons and destroyed *adharma*. Baladeva (= Balarāma) defeated Yama Vaivasvata; the boy was restored to his former body and handed over to his father.

32 Back at Mathurā Rāma (= Balarāma) and Janārdana (= Kṛṣṇa) were a joy to men and women.

Ch. 195: Jarāsaṃdha-episode

1-4 Vyāsa continues: Kaṃsa had married two of Jarāsaṃdha's daughters, Asti and Prāpti; that king of Māgadha besieged Mathurā with a large army in order to kill Hari (= Kṛṣṇa). Kṛṣṇa and Balarāma fought against him by (making) sorties with small forces.

5-7 Then they decided to call upon their ancient weapons; the discus, bows with quivers and arrows, the club Kaumodakī and Balabhadra's (= Balarāma's) ploughshare and club Sunanda came through the air.

8-12 Jarāsaṃdha was defeated, but his life was spared; he resumed the battle 18 times but was always defeated before he retreated.

13-18 This was the effect of the presence of Viṣṇu's part among the Yadus; it is a sport of the creator of the world to wield weapons, to act according to human conventions and make politics (treaties, punishment etc.).

Ch. 196: Kālayavana-episode; Mucukunda and Kṛṣṇa

1-4 Vyāsa continues: The Brahmin Gārgya had been publicly called a eunuch by Śyāla and had been laughed at by the Yādavas. Angrily he went south, practised asceticism and ate powdered iron to obtain a son for the destruction of the Yādavas. After 12 years Mahādeva (= Śiva) granted him a boon. Gārgya fathered a son for the sonless king of the Yavanas, the illustrious Kālayavana.

5-8 After that king had anointed his son and withdrawn to the forest, Kālayavana asked Nārada who were the most powerful kings; Nārada named the Yādavas. Surrounded by a huge army Kālayavana moved towards Mathurā.

9-15 Kṛṣṇa reflected on the weak position of the Yādavas on two fronts against Jarāsaṃdha and Kālayavana; he decided to construct a fort which could be defended even by women and without him, requested land from the ocean, constructed Dvārakā and led the inhabitants of Mathurā there while he himself returned to Mathurā.

16-20 When Kālayavana's army had settled outside Mathurā, Govinda (= Kṛṣṇa) left the city unarmed. The king recognized him and followed him whom not even the thoughts of Yogins can follow. Kṛṣṇa entered a large cave where king Mucukunda was sleeping. Yavana thought him to be Kṛṣṇa, woke him up with a kick and was burnt to ashes by a look from Mucukunda.

21-22 Mucukunda had been victorious in the battle between gods and demons and had chosen the boon of sleeping for a long time. The gods had granted that whoever woke him up would be reduced to ashes.

23-29 Seeing Kṛṣṇa, Mucukunda asked him who he was; Kṛṣṇa introduced himself as Vasudeva's son. Mucukunda fell down before Hari (= Kṛṣṇa) and addressed him as Viṣṇu's partial incarnation, remembering Gārgya's words who had prophesied Kṛṣṇa's birth among the Yadus at the end of the Dvāpara-Yuga, for the benefit of mortals.[1] Therefore he (Mucukunda) was not able to bear Kṛṣṇa's brilliance.[2]

30-45 Mucukunda's prayer, asking for Kṛṣṇa's grace, praising him as refuge of those afflicted by the circle of existences (*saṃsāra*); describing him as identical with the earth etc., as transcendent, as origin of all beings, as everything and asking to be delivered from the afflictions of the circle of existence; describing Mucukunda's painful experiences and people's inability to cut through their confusion and its miserable effects (hells etc.) without worshipping Kṛṣṇa; and repeating his (Mucukunda's) disgust with the world.[3]

Ch. 197: Kṛṣṇa and Mucukunda; Baladeva in Gokula

1-3 Vyāsa continues: Thus praised, Hari (= Kṛṣṇa) granted Mucukunda the desired heavenly existences,[1] unimpeded lordship, rebirth with memory of previous existences and liberation.

4-5 Mucukunda fell down before Kṛṣṇa, came out of his cave, recognized from the people's small size that the Kali-Yuga had come, and left for Gandhamādana, the place of Naranārāyaṇa, to practice asceticism.

6-7 Kṛṣṇa captured Kālayavana's army and took it to Ugrasena in Dvāravatī (= Dvārakā).

8-21 *Baladeva's visit to Gokula*

8-18 Baladeva wanted to visit his relatives and went to Gokula (the settlement of Nanda). Description of his hearty welcome. The Gopīs inquired about Kṛṣṇa and the effect of the urban women on him (v. 12-18 quote the Gopīs' questions).

19-21 Thus, Balarāma made merry with the Gopīs and inhabitants of Vraja.

[1] This reference to a prophecy by Gārgya was not mentioned above.

[2] v. 25-29 contain Mucukunda's words, which refer to the present situation and explain it by reference to previous events not explicitly related in BrP.

[3] v. 45 in Praharṣiṇī-metre.

[1] Which were actually not desired by Mucukunda.

Ch. 198: Balarāma forcing Yamunā to change her course

1–3 Vyāsa continues: While Śeṣa in human form (= Balarāma) stayed with the herdsmen, Varuṇa told Vāruṇī to be available (as liquor) for Balabhadra's (= Balarāma's) enjoyment.

4–6 Balarāma smelled the liquor, saw it flow from a Kadamba-tree and drank it, singing and playing.

7–11 When he felt hot and tired he ordered Yamunā to come to him. The river disregarded his order as the words of a drunken man. Balarāma grew angry and forced the river to come his way by means of his ploughshare.

12–14 The river in human form begged for grace; Balarāma first threatened to disperse her in a thousand (directions) but then let her go.

15–17 After his bath, Kānti presented him with a flower as an ear-ornament and an (ear-)ring; Lakṣmī with a garland which did not wither and with two blue garments. Thus adorned, Rāma (= Balarāma) was happy there and returned to Dvārakā after two months.

18 He married Revatī, Raivata's daughter, from whom Niśatha and Ulmaka were born.

Ch. 199: Marriage of Kṛṣṇa and Rukmiṇī

1–4 Vyāsa continues: Bhīṣmaka was king in Kaṇḍina in the region of Vidarbha; Rukmin was his son, Rukmiṇī his daughter. Kṛṣṇa and Rukmiṇī were in love with each other, but Rukmin, prompted by Jarāsaṃdha, promised her to Śiśupāla since he hated the bearer of the discus (= Viṣṇu).[1] On the occasion of the marriage all the kings went to Kuṇḍina.

5–10 Kṛṣṇa and the Yadus also went there; on the day before the marriage Hari (= Kṛṣṇa) abducted the girl. The infuriated kings, Pauṇḍraka, Dantavaktra, Vidūratha, Śiśupāla, Jarāsaṃdha, Śālva, etc., were defeated by Rāma (= Balarāma) and the Yadus. Rukmin pledged that he would not return to Kuṇḍina unless he had killed Kṛṣṇa; Kṛṣṇa, however, playfully destroyed his forces and defeated him.

11–12 Kṛṣṇa married Rukmiṇī according to the Rākṣasa way; Rukmiṇī bore Pradyumna, who was abducted by Śambara, but who killed him.

Ch. 200: Abduction of Pradyumna and his killing of Śambara

1 The hermits inquire about Pradyumna's abduction and the killing of Śambara.

2–10 Vyāsa answers: On the sixth day the new-born Pradyumna was abducted from the confinement room by Kālaśambara who believed that Pradyumna would kill him.

[1] *cakrin* might refer to Kṛṣṇa; if it refers to Viṣṇu, Śiśupāla would be characterized as non-Vaiṣṇava, his enmity against Kṛṣṇa thus being religiously motivated.

Pradyumna was thrown into the ocean, where he was swallowed by a fish, which was afterwards caught and presented to Śambara. His wife Māyāvatī, supervising the preparation of that fish, found the boy, and was astonished. Nārada told her about the boy's identity and advised her to bring him up.

11-16 She brought him up and fell in love with him when he had become a young man; she gave him all her magic powers (*māyā*). Seeing her attachment Pradyumna asked her why she did not behave like a mother any longer. Māyāvatī told him who he really was and how he had got there.

17-19 Pradyumna challenged Śambara to fight, counteracted seven of his magic feats, and defeated him by means of the eighth. Then he went with Māyāvatī to his father's town.

20-22 When they entered the inner appartment Kṛṣṇa's wives rejoiced; Rukmiṇī remembered her son and marvelled at Pradyumna's resemblance to Kṛṣṇa.

23-28 In the meantime Nārada entered with Kṛṣṇa; he told[1] Rukmiṇī that this was her son Pradyumna and his wife Māyāvatī, who had not really been Śambara's wife but was Kāma's wife reborn, while Pradyumna was an incarnation of Kāma (= the god of love).

29-30 Rukmiṇī and Keśava (= Kṛṣṇa) rejoiced and everybody in Dvārakā marvelled at the lost son, who had returned to his mother.

Ch. 201: Marriage of Aniruddha; killing of Rukmin

1-2 Vyāsa continues: Cārudeṣṇa, Sudeṣṇa, Cārudeha, Suṣeṇa, Cārugupta, Bhadracāru, Cāruvinda, Sucāru, and Cāru were Rukmiṇī's sons, Cārumatī her daughter.

3-5 Kṛṣṇa had seven[1] other wives, Kālindī, Mitravindā, Nāgnajitī, Jāmbavatī, Rohiṇī, Śīlamaṇḍalā, Satyabhāmā (daughter of Satrājit), Lakṣmaṇā; further he had 16,000 other women.

6-9 Pradyumna won Rukmin's daughter during a self-choice ceremony; Aniruddha was their son; for him Kṛṣṇa chose Rukmin's granddaughter, to which Rukmin in spite of his rivalry agreed. Balarāma, Hari (= Kṛṣṇa), and the other Yādavas went to Bhojakaṭa, Rukmin's residence.

10-22 When the wedding was over the (vassal) kings led by the king of Kaliṅga, suggested to Rukmin that he should contest »the one with a ploughshare« (= Balarāma) in a game of dice. They played for 1000 coins and, when Balarāma lost, for another 1000, then for 10,000. The king of Kaliṅga laughed at Balarāma, showing his teeth, and Rukmin called him (Balarāma) ignorant. The bearer of the ploughshare became angry.[2] He staked 100,000 coins; Rukmin threw the dice but Balarāma won. Rukmin also claimed the victory and argued that he had not explicitly accepted the stake. To this a heavenly voice replied that he had accepted not by words but by his action.

[1] According to v. 23 it is Nārada who speaks; the introduction to the direct speech, however, attributes the following words to Kṛṣṇa.

[1] The list contains at least eight names.

[2] There is a misplaced or superfluous *vyāsa uvāca* after v. 17.

23-26 Bala got up, slew Rukmin with the gaming board and knocked out the teeth of the king of Kaliṅga. He tore up a golden pillar and slew the (vassal) kings. Everybody fled.

27 Kṛṣṇa did not say anything about Rukmin's death, as he was afraid of Rukmiṇī as well as of Balarāma.

28 The Yadus returned to Dvārakā, together with Keśava (= Kṛṣṇa) and the newly-married Aniruddha.

Ch. 202: Naraka-episode

1-2 Vyāsa continues: In Dvāravatī Śakra (= Indra) approached Śauri (= Kṛṣṇa) and addressed him.

3-12 (Indra's words:) He reminded Kṛṣṇa of the deeds he had performed to alleviate suffering (killing of Ariṣṭa and Dhenuka, of Pralamba and Keśin, of Kaṃsa, Kuvalayāpīḍa and Pūtanā) and told about Naraka Bhauma (i.e. the descendant of Bhūmi, the earth), the lord of Prāgjyotiṣa, who had locked up the daughters (girls) of gods, kings etc., had stolen Pracetas! (= Varuṇa's) water-giving umbrella, the top of the mountain Mandara, the nectar-dropping ear-rings of Indra's mother (= Aditi), and who now desired the elephant Airāvata; Kṛṣṇa should take action against Naraka.

13-15 Vyāsa continues: Kṛṣṇa clasped Vāsava's (= Indra's) hand, then, along with Satyabhāmā, he mounted Garuḍa (called to service by thinking of him) and went to Prāgjyotiṣa, while Indra returned to heaven.

16-21 He severed the loops (or snares?) around this city by means of his disc; he slew Mura and his 7000 sons. After slaying the »horse-necked« (*hayagrīva*) Mura[1] , and Pañcajana, he slew the forces of Naraka and split Naraka with his discus into two halves.

22 The earth approached the lord of the world (= Kṛṣṇa) and brought Aditi's ear-rings.

23-29 Hymn by the earth to Kṛṣṇa (as Viṣṇu), relating that she had conceived Naraka from being touched by the boar when he had lifted her up; requesting protection for her son's descendants; stating that the lord had become partially incarnated for the sake of alleviating her burden; describing him by his divine functions (*trimūrti*-functions) and attributes (identity with the world, omnipresence, transcendence, making it impossible to praise him[2]); requesting forgiveness for Naraka's deeds, who had been killed by Kṛṣṇa.

30-35 Vyāsa continues: The lord (*bhagavat*) agreed. He took the jewels from Naraka's residence, obtained the 16,100 girls and Naraka's army (elephants with four tusks, and horses),[3] loaded Varuṇa's umbrella and the mountain on to Garuḍa and travelled to heaven in order to give the ear-rings to Aditi.[4]

[1] Or, Hayagrīva (as proper name) and Mura.

[2] Refrain in v. 26-27.

[3] cf. below, 204.13cd-18.

[4] cf. above, v. 3-12.

Ch. 203: Kṛṣṇa and Satyabhāmā in the world of the gods

1-24 Visit of Kṛṣṇa to Aditi.

1-5 Vyāsa continues: Garuḍa carried his load playfully. Kṛṣṇa blew his conch, the gods welcomed him and he went to Aditi's residence, which appeared like the summit of a white mountain; together with Śakra (= Indra) he returned the ear-rings and told her of Naraka's death. The mother of the world praised Hari (= Kṛṣṇa) as creator of the world.

6-19 Hymn by Aditi to Kṛṣṇa, addressing him by epithets describing his identity with everything, his transcendence, and his freedom from all conceptual limitations or worldly conditions;[1] identifying him with the elements etc., and, by the *trimūrti*-functions, with Brahman, Viṣṇu, Śiva, and other forms of cosmic illusion (*māyā*) (v. 9-10); reflecting on the effects of Māyā (ignorance of the real Self, attachment to the world) which can only be counteracted by worshipping Viṣṇu; reflecting on the mistake of worshipping Viṣṇu for the sake of worldly boons instead of for the sake of liberation and asking Viṣṇu's forgiveness for her own mistakes (v. 11-18ab); praising him by iconographic attributes (discus, conch, club, lotus; v. 18cd-19ab); admitting lack of knowledge of anything beyond Viṣṇu (VePr reads: »the highest reality«).

20-21 Thus praised, Viṣṇu asked the mother of the gods to be gracious and to grant boons.

22 Aditi granted that Kṛṣṇa should be invincible in the world of mortals.

23 Then Satyabhāmā along with Śakrāṇi (= Indra's wife) asked Aditi[2] to be gracious.

24-25 Aditi granted her freedom from old age. ; the king of gods (= Indra) paid homage to Kṛṣṇa (or: honoured Kṛṣṇa as guest).

26-73 *Kṛṣṇa taking away the Pārijāta-tree; opposition of Kṛṣṇa and Indra*

26-32 Kṛṣṇa visited the celestial gardens together with Satyabhāmā. When she saw the Pārijāta-tree (description) she asked Kṛṣṇa to transfer this tree to Dvārakā, reminding him of his declarations of love for her.

33-37 Kṛṣṇa smilingly loaded the tree on Garuḍa. The guards reminded him that the tree belonged to Indra's wife, having originated during the churning of the ocean for her adornment, and warned him that Indra would not tolerate the robbery.

38-44 Satyabhāmā replied angrily that Indra's wife should test her husband's love by getting him to prevent the robbery.

45-62 When Śacī was informed about Satyabhāmā's words she incited Indra to fight, together with the gods, against Kṛṣṇa. Kṛṣṇa blew his conch and showered arrows on Indra, whereupon the gods hurled their weapons. Kṛṣṇa playfully eliminated each one of them (Varuṇa's loop; Yama's stick; Kubera's palanquin (?, a weapon?). Sun and moon were obliterated, Agni (fire) dispersed, the Rudras thrown down on earth, the Sādhyas, All-Gods, Maruts, Gandharvas scattered in the air. Garuḍa

[1] v. 6-8 vocatives; VePr inserts one line after v. 7ab.

[2] The text reads *śakrāṇīsahitaṃ ditim* »(Satyabhāma asked) Diti and Śakrāṇī«, which has to be emended to *śakrāṇīsahitāditim* by omitting the incorrect Anusvāra; cf. also ViP (ed. Bombay) 5,30.26 (ed. VePr of ViP reads *śakreṇa sahitāditim*, which is still more probable.)

fought with his beak and wings and defeated Airāvata. When all (other) weapons had been eliminated Vāsava (= Indra) caught hold of his thunderbolt and Kṛṣṇa of his discus, which caused an outcry throughout the three worlds. When Indra threw the thunderbolt Kṛṣṇa caught it.

63 Satyabhāmā told the disarmed and fleeing Indra

64–69 that fleeing was unworthy, offering to return the Pārijāta-tree, and asking him not to feel ashamed, explaining that her challenge arose from her feminine pride in her husband, for »which woman would not be proud of beauty and fame?«

70–73 Indra replied that he did not feel ashamed at being defeated by Kṛṣṇa, praising him as performer of the *trimūrti*-functions, as being all, as unborn and eternal etc. (theological description); who would be able to defeat him?[3]

Ch. 204: Reconciliation of Kṛṣṇa and Indra; the Pārijāta-tree on earth

1–4 Vyāsa continues: Thus praised, Keśava smilingly addressed Indra as »king of gods«, whereas he himself was only a mortal man, asking for forgiveness, and explaining why he had seized the Pārijāta-tree; then he returned the thunderbolt to Indra.

5–7 Indra answered by recalling Kṛṣṇa's divinity, who, though being the lord of the world, pretended to be a mortal, and his beneficial action for the sake of the world; the tree should remain in the world of mortals as long as Kṛṣṇa stayed there.

8–13ab Hari (= Kṛṣṇa) returned to Dvārakā where he planted the tree, the scent of which made people remember their former existence. Thus, the Yādavas saw the superhuman connections of their (present) bodies.[1]

13cd–18 Kṛṣṇa captured Naraka's army, wealth, and women,[2] whom he married at an auspicious moment. He multiplied himself so that each of the 16,100 women thought that Kṛṣṇa was with her alone.

Ch. 205: Descendants of Kṛṣṇa; Bāṇa-episode

1–6 Vyāsa continues by mentioning Kṛṣṇa's descendants: Rukmiṇī's sons, Pradyumna etc., have already been mentioned; Satyabhāmā bore Bhānu etc.; Rohiṇī bore Prapakṣa etc.; Jāmbavatī bore Sāmba etc.; Nāgnajitī bore Bhadravinda etc.; Śaibyā's sons were Saṃgrāmajit etc.; Vṛka etc. were Mādrī's sons; Lakṣmaṇā had Gātravat etc., Kālindī Śruta etc.; from his other wives Kṛṣṇa had 88,100[1] sons. Pradyumna was the eldest (»first«); his son was Aniruddha, whose son was Vajra.

[3] v. 72 in Uddharṣiṇī-metre, v. 73 in Mālinī-metre.

[1] *dehabandhān* instead of *devagandhān*, »the heavenly scents«, which may have intruded because of the preceding line (*vāsyate yasya puṣpānāṃ gandhenorvī triyojanam*); the ViP has the correct reading.

[2] This has already been narrated above, ch. 202.30 ff.

[1] According to Wilson, transl. of ViP, 180,000, according to the Hindī translation in BrP ed. Prayāga 80,000,100, according to the Gītāpress translation of the ViP 88,800.

7-8 Aniruddha married Bali's granddaughter and Bāṇa's daughter Ūṣā (= Uṣā);[2] in this connection there was a fight between Hari (= Kṛṣṇa) and Śaṃkara (= Śiva) and Bāṇa's thousand arms were cut off.

9-10 The hermits request to be told about the fight between Hara (= Śiva) and Kṛṣṇa and about how Hari destroyed Bāṇa's arms.

11-22 *Bāṇa-episode: Uṣā's dream*

11-14 Vyāsa continues: Uṣā, Bāṇa's daughter, once saw Pārvatī and Śaṃbhu (= Śiva) playing together and felt desire herself. Gaurī (= Pārvatī), who knew her thoughts, promised her a husband; Uṣā inquired when and who, and Pārvatī told her that she would marry the man who subdued her in her dream on the 12th day of the light half of Vaiśākha.

15-22 It happened accordingly. When Uṣā awoke from her dream she called out for the man. After some hesitation she told her companion, Citralekhā, daughter of Bāṇa's minister Kumbhāṇḍa, about what had happened and ordered her to find the man. Citralekhā drew protraits of gods, demons, Gandharvas, and humans, among them also the Vṛṣṇyandhakas. On beholding Kṛṣṇa, Balarāma and Pradyumna, she was ashamed and looked away, but at the sight of Aniruddha she lost her shyness; thus she identified him. Her companion went to Dvāravatī by her yogic powers.

Ch. 206: Bāṇa-episode (contd)

1-4 Vyāsa continues: Bāṇa had previously told the Three-eyed One (= Śiva) that he felt oppressed by his 1000 arms unless he could use them in fighting. Śaṃkara (= Śiva) promised him a fight when his peacock-banner was broken (without obvious reason). When Bāṇa reached home he saw that his flag had broken and rejoiced.

5-9 In the meantime Citralekhā had brought Aniruddha by her yogic powers to the girl's quarter, where he made love to Uṣā. The guards informed Bāṇa. After Aniruddha had slain an army of Bāṇa's men, Bāṇa himself was defeated by Aniruddha; he then used magic (*māyā*) and bound Aniruddha with snakes.

10-13 When Aniruddha was missed in Dvāravatī, Nārada informed the Yadus that he had been imprisoned by Bāṇa in Śoṇitapura. Hari (= Kṛṣṇa), Rāma (= Balarāma) and Pradyumna went on Garuḍa to Bāṇa's city. Kṛṣṇa defeated the Pramathas.

14-19 Śiva's three-headed and three-footed (or: threefold) fever affected Kṛṣṇa and Balarāma but was expelled by Viṣṇu's fever. The divine grandfather (= Brahman) asked for mercy for Śiva's fever; Hari (= Kṛṣṇa) consequently promised freedom from affliction by fever to those who remember his fight with the fever.

20 Then Viṣṇu playfully extinguished (the) five fires and defeated an army of demons.

21-23 Then Bāṇa and his army, Śaṃkara (= Śiva) and Kārttikeya fought with Śauri (= Kṛṣṇa). A terrible fight between Hari (= Kṛṣṇa) and Śaṃkara ensued; the gods thought that the dissolution of the world was imminent.

[2] Both spellings of the name are used in this episode, perhaps for metrical reasons.

24–30 Govinda (= Kṛṣṇa) used yawning as a weapon against Śaṃkara (= Śiva) and defeated the Pramathas. Śaṃkara was overpowered by yawning; Guha (= Kārttikeya) fled, wounded by Garuḍa and Pradyumna and made powerless by Kṛṣṇa's pronouncing »*huṃ*«. Then Bāṇa joined the battle on his chariot. Balabhadra (= Balarāma) and Pradyumna defeated Bāṇa's army with arrows and the (i.e. Balarāma's) ploughshare.

31–38 Then Kṛṣṇa fought against Bāṇa; they intercepted each other's weapons. Then Hari (= Kṛṣṇa) decided to kill Bāṇa and seized the discus Sudarśana. The knowledge of the Daityas (and mother of Bāṇa) named Koṭarī appeared as a naked woman before Hari. With his eyes closed he slung his discus, which cut off Bāṇa's arms.

39–44 When the enemy of Tripura (= Śiva) learned that Kṛṣṇa was going to throw the discus Sudarśana again he addressed Kṛṣṇa, acknowledging him as highest god and self, and the destruction of demons as Kṛṣṇa's play, asking for mercy for Bāṇa out of regard for his (Śiva's) boon to Bāṇa.

45–48 Kṛṣṇa was appeased and granted to Umā's husband (= Śiva) that Bāṇa should live, since he (Kṛṣṇa) and Śaṃkara (= Śiva) were really one and were considered different only by those confused by ignorance.

49–50 Kṛṣṇa freed Aniruddha; Garuḍa destroyed the snakes which had bound him. Then Dāmodara (= Kṛṣṇa) took Aniruddha and his wife on Garuḍa to Dvārakā.

Ch. 207: Pauṇḍraka claiming to be Viṣṇu; the burning of Kāśi

1–2 The hermits confirm that Śauri (= Kṛṣṇa) defeated Śakra (= Indra), Śarva (= Śiva), and all other gods; they request to hear other feats which he performed.

3 Vyāsa announces the account of how Kṛṣṇa burnt Vārāṇasī.

4–7 Vāsudeva Pauṇḍraka was told by ignorant people that it was he who was Viṣṇu incarnated as Vāsudeva; he believed it, assumed Viṣṇu's emblems and sent a messenger to Kṛṣṇa, demanding that he should abandon his discus and the name Vāsudeva, and submit to him.

8–12 Kṛṣṇa smilingly told the messenger to return to Pauṇḍraka with the following message: that he would discharge his discus before (or: upon!) him and that he would seek his protection (or: having come together with him, would grant protection), so that there would be no fear (or: danger) of him (or: from his side) any more.[1]

13–24 When the messenger had left, Kṛṣṇa mounted Garutmat (= Garuḍa) and hurried to Pauṇḍraka's city. Hearing of Keśava's efforts the king of Kāśi mobilized his army; with these and his own forces Pauṇḍraka confronted Keśava (= Kṛṣṇa). Seeing Pauṇḍraka from a distance, (adorned with discus, conch, club, and lotus, garland, bow, and with Suparṇa (= Garuḍa) as emblem, with Śrīvatsa-lock, crown, earrings, dressed in yellow, Hari (= Kṛṣṇa) laughed. Janārdana (= Kṛṣṇa) destroyed his army and that of the king of Kāśi in a moment; telling Pauṇḍraka that he would

[1] Kṛṣṇa's speech is ambiguous and can be interpreted as a submission as well as a challenge.

now do as the messenger had demanded, he discharged the discus which tore up Pauṇḍraka, while Garuḍa broke his banner.

25-27 Then the king of Kāśi fought against Vāsudeva (= Kṛṣṇa) who severed his head with arrows and threw it into the city; then he enjoyed himself in Dvāravatī.

28-43 *The burning of Kāśi*

28-43 The people of Kāśi marvelled at who had thrown the king's head; when his son learned that it was Vāsudeva (= Kṛṣṇa), he and his priest pleased Śaṃkara (= Śiva) who granted them a boon. The prince chose a Kṛtyā (a »Fury«) who should kill the murderer of his father. From the fire arose Kṛtyā with fiery mouth and hair, who went to Dvāravatī calling for Kṛṣṇa. The people took refuge to Madhusūdana (= Kṛṣṇa) and asked him to kill her. Kṛṣṇa, who was playing dice, discharged his discus Sudarśana. The spirit fled and entered Vārāṇasī. The army of Kāśi and of the Pramathas was destroyed by the discus which then burnt the whole city before returning to Viṣṇu's hand.

Ch. 208: Balarāma's heroic deeds: Release of Sāmba

1-2 The hermits request to be told more of Rāma's (= Balarāma's) deeds.

3 Vyāsa announces an account of what was done by (Balarāma, the incarnation of) the immeasurable Śeṣa, Ananta.

4-7 Sāmba, Jāmbavatī's son, had abducted Duryodhana's daughter during a self-choice ceremony. Karṇa, Duryodhana, Bhīṣma etc. defeated and imprisoned him. The Yādavas, learning of this, made preparations to kill Duryodhana; Bala (= Balarāma), however, stopped them, offering to go alone to the Kauravas, who would free Sāmba upon his word.

8-18 Balarāma went to Hastināpura and settled outside the city; Duryodhana sent the welcoming gifts (cow, water etc.). Balarāma told the Kauravas to free Sāmba upon Ugrasena's order. Bhīṣma, Droṇa, Karṇa, Duryodhana, etc. angrily replied (v. 12-18) that the Yadus did not deserve royal sovereignty and that no Yādava could give them orders; the honour shown to Balarāma did not extend to the clan.

19-31 When the Kauravas did not free Sāmba, Balarāma hammered the earth with his heel (*jaghāna pārṣṇyā* ?),[1] and challenged the Kauravas for their unjustified pride (v. 22-31), reminding them that Ugrasena resided in the hall Sudharmā, that even gods obeyed his orders, that the Pārijāta-tree was with the Yādavas and that he would free the earth of Kauravas (list of names including Karṇa, Duryodhana, Droṇa Bhīṣma, Bāhlika, Duḥśāsana, Bhūri, Bhūriśravas, Somadatta, Śala, Bhīma, Arjuna, Yudhiṣṭhira, the twin sons of Yama, i.e. Nakula and Sahadeva) and that he would throw Hastināpura into the Bhāgīrathī (= Gaṅgā).

[1] VePr reads »seized his ploughshare«

32-35 Then Balarāma angrily put his ploughshare to the rampart round the city and ploughed it. When Hastināpura rocked violently (? *āghūrṇita*), the Kauravas begged Rāma (= Balarāma) for mercy, promising to free Sāmba.

36-37 They handed over Sāmba and his wife, and Bala (= Balarāma) granted mercy.

38 Even today this city is tilted as visible proof of Rāma's (= Balarāma's) power.

39 The Kauravas bade farewell to Balarāma, Sāmba, and his wife.

Ch. 209: Balarāma's heroic deeds: Dvivida-episode

1 Vyāsa announces an account of another of Balarāma's feats.

2-11ab The ape Dvivida was an ally of the demon Naraka;[1] he opposed the gods because Kṛṣṇa had killed Naraka. He destroyed sacrifices, violated the limits of propriety, burnt cities and villages, threw rocks, caused floods.

11cd-21ab Once Halāyudha (= Balarāma, »he whose weapon is the ploughshare«) was drinking and enjoying himself together with Revatī and others in the garden on Mt. Raivata like Kubera on Mt. Mandara, when Dvivida came and aped Balarāma, broke the vessels, etc., and mocked at the women. Balarāma seized his pestle; Dvivida threw a rock which Balarāma intercepted; he then slew the ape with his fist. When Dvivida fell the top of that mountain (Raivata?) burst.

21cd-22 The gods showered flowers and praised Rāma for killing the wicked ape.

23 Vyāsa concludes the account of such deeds of Śeṣa (= Balarāma).

Ch. 210: The destruction of the Yādavas

1-4 Vyāsa concludes the account of how Kṛṣṇa and Baladeva (= Balarāma) slew demons and wicked kings, thus alleviating the burden on the earth. On the pretext of the Brahmins' curse he annihilated his clan, then left Dvārakā and, abandoned his human nature, returned to Viṣṇu's abode.

5 The hermits inquire about further details.

6-10 Vyāsa continues: Yādava-boys met Viśvāmitra, Kaṇva, and Nārada at the holy place Piṇḍāraka. Driven by their youthful folly and by what was to happen they dressed up Sāmba like a woman and asked the sages what (or whether) this woman who was desirous of a son would give birth to. The sages of divine insight felt offended by the boys and cursed them: The woman would bear a pestle which would annihilate the Yādavas.

11-14 The boys informed Ugrasena. From Sāmba's belly a pestle was born; Ugrasena reduced it to powder which was thrown into the ocean. The lance-like tip could not be powdered; when thrown into the ocean a fish swallowed it. The fish was caught. From its belly Jarā[1] obtained the tip.

[1] cf. above, ch. 202.

[1] The hunter who will kill Kṛṣṇa unintentionally; cf. below 211.5-6. His name should be Jaras, nom. *jarāḥ*, but is given as *jarā* in this verse.

15 Though Kṛṣṇa knew what was really happening and though he was omnipotent, yet he did not interfere with fate.

16–21 The gods sent a messenger who secretly met Kṛṣṇa and told him that Śakra (= Indra) and the other (vedic) gods (listed) wanted to remind him that more than 100 years had passed since he had been born on earth, that the demons had been killed, the burden on the earth had been alleviated; they wanted him to return to heaven if it pleased him; otherwise he should stay on with his (mortal) dependents.

22–27 Kṛṣṇa answered that he knew what the messenger had wanted to say, that he had already begun the destruction of the Yādavas, who were still a burden and would be annihilated by him within seven days, that he would abandon Dvārakā and then return to heaven with Saṃkarṣaṇa (= Balarāma); the messenger should tell the gods that, after adding the burden caused by the Yādavas to all other burdens on earth that had been already alleviated, Kṛṣṇa would return to heaven.

28 The messenger returned to heaven.

29–30 Kṛṣṇa saw ill omens in Dvārakā and sent the Yādavas to Prabhāsa.

31–32 Uddhava, a great Bhāgavata, asked Kṛṣṇa what he should do, since Kṛṣṇa was obviously going to annihilate his clan.

33–35 Kṛṣṇa answered that he should go to the hermitage Badarī on the mountain Gandhamādana, the place of Naranārāyaṇa where he would obtain perfection. He himself would annihilate the clan and return to heaven; Dvārakā would be flooded by the ocean.

36 Uddhava left.

37–43 The Yādavas along with Kṛṣṇa and Balarāma left for Prabhāsa, where they started drinking alcohol with Kṛṣṇa's consent; a mutual quarrel ensued which ended in fighting; they slew each other, and when their weapons were spent they seized Erakā-(grass), which seemed like a thunderbolt, and they slew each other. Pradyumna, Sāmba, Kṛtavarman, Sātyaki, Aniruddha, Pṛthu, Vipṛthu, Cāruvarman,[2] Sucāru,[3] Akrūra, etc. slew each other with Erakā.

44–46 Hari (= Kṛṣṇa) tried to prevent them, but the Yādavas thought he was helping, and continued slaying each other. Then Kṛṣṇa angrily took up Erakā and slew all the Yādavas, while they were killing each other.

47–48 Viṣṇu's chariot Jaitra was drawn by horses out of the ocean while Dāruka looked on; discus, club, bow, quiver, conch, and sword circumambulated him (Kṛṣṇa) and left by the path of the sun (i.e. for heaven).

49 Within a moment all Yādavas were destroyed, except Kṛṣṇa and Dāruka.

50–52ab Balarāma's death: The two saw Rāma (sitting) beneath a tree; a great snake came out of his mouth and went to the ocean, honoured by Siddhas and snakes. The ocean offered the welcoming gifts and the snake entered the waters.

52cd–58 Keśava told Dāruka to report everything to Vasudeva and Ugrasena. He (Kṛṣṇa) would give up his body while remaining in Yoga. Dvārakā would be submerged; therefore the people should wait for the arrival of Arjuna and go with him. Arjuna should be told to guard the people. Vajra should become king.

[2] v.l. Cārudeṣṇa

[3] v.l. Subhāhu

Ch. 211: Kṛṣṇa's death

1-2 Vyāsa continues: Dāruka circumambulated Kṛṣṇa and left, brought Arjuna to Dvārakā and made Vajra king.

3-4 The lord Govinda (= Kṛṣṇa) imposed the highest *brahman*, which is Vāsudeva, on himself and concentrated on all the elements. Remembering what Durvāsas had said,[1] he was completely concentrated (*yogayukta*), his foot upon his knee.

5-10 The hunter Jaras, who had fixed the left-over iron of the pestle on his lance[2] arrived there; he mistook the foot for a deer and pierced it with his lance. Coming near he beheld a man with four arms; he fell down and repeatedly asked for mercy. Kṛṣṇa consoled him and granted that he should go to heaven. A chariot arrived, on which the hunter ascended to heaven.

11-12 Then Kṛṣṇa united himself within his self which was *brahman*, imperishable, (and which was) Vāsudeva, the self of all (etc.), left his human body and reached the threefold goal (v.l. the third heaven).

Ch. 212: Arjuna's deeds and failures after Kṛṣṇa's death

1-4 Vyāsa continues: Arjuna performed the last rites for Kṛṣṇa and Rāma (= Balarāma) and the others. The eight wives of Kṛṣṇa entered the funeral pyre along with Kṛṣṇa, Revatī along with Rāma. Ugrasena, Ānakadundubhi (= Vasudeva), Devakī, and Rohiṇī also burnt themselves.

5-6 Taking Vajra and the people as well as the other thousands of wives of Kṛṣṇa along, Arjuna left Dvāravatī.

7 The hall Sudharmā and the Pārijāta-tree returned to heaven.

8 On the same day that Hari (= Kṛṣṇa) went back to heaven, Kali descended on earth.

9-11 The ocean flooded Dvārakā except for Kṛṣṇa's house, which even today is spared since the lord Keśava (= Kṛṣṇa) is present there. To see this place of Viṣṇu's play frees from all sins.

12-17 Pārtha (= Arjuna) settled with the people in the region of Pañcanada (»of five rivers«). Seeing Arjuna, only one man, with thousands of women, the Ābhīras became desirous of these women. They reflected (v. 15-17) that Arjuna was proud because he had killed Bhīṣma, Droṇa, Jayadratha, Karṇa, etc., but that he despised other, rural people.

18-20 When they attacked Arjuna's people with sticks Arjuna threatened to kill them. But the Ābhīras seized wealth and women.

21-24 Arjuna tried to lift his bow Gāṇḍīva but was not able to do it. In spite of his efforts the string remained loose and he could not remember his (other) weapons. His

[1] Allusion to an episode which has not been told in the BrP; cf. MBh 13,143, where the story is told how Kṛṣṇa became invulnerable, except for his feet.

[2] cf. above 210.14.

arrows did no harm; even the arrows given by Agni disappeared; Arjuna was defeated.

25-28 Then Kaunteya (= Arjuna) remembered that all his powers and victories had depended on Kṛṣṇa. Before his eyes the Ābhīras dragged away the women. He hit the Dasyus with his bow, but they laughed at his blows and left with the women.

29-33 Jiṣṇu's (= Arjuna's) lamentation describing the powerlessness of his arms, his weapons, of himself, due to Kṛṣṇa's absence.

34 With these thoughts Arjuna went to Indraprastha where he made Vajra king.

35-94 *Arjuna's visit to Vyāsa*

35-41 Then Phālguna (= Arjuna) visited Vyāsa[1] who lived in the forest. Arjuna only looked at his feet and Vyāsa inquired about the reason for his lack of lustre (v. 36cd-41 are a sequence of rhetorical questions and list possible offences).

42-53 Arjuna sighed and told Vyāsa what had happened, attributing his powerlessness to Kṛṣṇa's departure and relating his defeat and the abduction of the women, admitting his shame.

54 Vyāsa[2] answered him trying to console him.

55-92 *Vyāsa's consolation of Arjuna*

55-58 Arjuna should not be dejected, for everything originates and perishes due to the power of Time.

59-62 Arjuna was right regarding Kṛṣṇa's importance (*māhātmya*), who had descended in order to alleviate the burden on the earth, who had previously gone to the gods. That purpose was fulfilled; all kings were killed, the clan was annihilated; therefore Kṛṣṇa had left.

63 The »god of gods« (= Kṛṣṇa as Viṣṇu) was the one who creates, maintains, and destroys (*trimūrti*-function).

64-65 Therefore Arjuna should not feel qualms because of his defeat. Bhīṣma, Droṇa, etc., had also been defeated by him, due to time.

66-70 Arjuna's victories and his defeat were due to Viṣṇu's influence,[3] entering other bodies, maintaining the world, and bringing about the destruction of all beings in the end. That Arjuna had killed all Kauravas and was defeated by Ābhīras was only Hari's play.

71 Now he (= Vyāsa) would also tell him why the women had been seized by the Dasyus.

72-85 *Aṣṭāvakra-episode*

72-85 In former times the Brahmin Aṣṭāvakra[4] lived in water for many years, praising *brahman*.[5] Celestial women, Rambhā, Tilottamā, etc., who went to Meru on the

[1] One would expect Vyāsa to speak as first-person narrator; cf., however, below, v. 54-58.

[2] Here first-person narrator; not so, however, in v. 35.

[3] *anubhāvena*? ViP reads *prabhāvena*.

[4] cf. MBh 3,132-134; the present story seems to be a continuation of the MBh-story.

[5] VePr »the god«, i.e. Viṣṇu?

occasion of a celebration of a victory over the Asuras, praised and lauded him who was submerged in eightfold deformity. The hermit angrily cursed them that though they would still obtain »the most eminent man« (*puruṣottama*) as husband, they would also fall into the hands of Dasyus. When asked for mercy he added that they would afterwards return to heaven.

86 Thus the women had obtained Keśava (= Kṛṣṇa) as husband but had also fallen into the hands of Dasyus.

87-88 The Pāṇḍava (= Arjuna) should not grieve. The protector of all had taken everything away, even Arjuna's power.

89-90 Maxims: What is born will die, what has risen will fall, union ends in separation, what is collected will be spent (?); the wise do not grieve nor rejoice, and others learn from their conduct.

91-92 Arjuna and his brothers should forsake the kingdom and practise asceticism; he should inform Dharmarāja (= Yudhiṣṭhira) and leave the next day, together with his brothers.

93-94 Vyāsa continues:[6] Arjuna informed Dharmarāja (= Yudhiṣṭhira) of what he had seen, experienced and heard. According to Vyāsa's words, they made Parīkṣit king and left for the forest.

95 Vyāsa concludes his narration of Vāsudeva's deeds.

Ch. 213: Manifestations of Viṣṇu[1]

1-9 The hermits repeat that they have been told about Kṛṣṇa's and Rāma's (= Balarāma's) greatness (v.l. manifestation, *prādurbhāva*); they now want to hear of another manifestation and mention the boar of which the Purāṇas tell and whose actions, appearance, etc., they want to know; how Nārāyaṇa as a boar lifted the earth. And they want to hear about the nature and actions of (the) other manifestations.

10-11 Vyāsa praises their question as difficult and announces his account of Viṣṇu's manifestation.

12-20 The Lord, whom Veda-experts identify with the various constituents of ritual and sacrifice (v. 12-18 are a list of such nouns in accusative) had thousands of manifestations in the past, and more will occur in future.

21-24 Vyāsa announces a salutary story in reply to the hermits' question, the importance (*māhātmya*) and acts of Vāsudeva who for the sake of gods and mortals manifests himself.

[6] Strictly speaking there is no change of speaker here which would necessitate the mention of the narrator; there is, however, a change in the level of narration; in v. 94 Vyāsa refers to himself again in the third person.

[1] BrP 213 is closely, though not literally, parallel to HV 30-31; cf. the concordance printed in the Appendix to the text.

25–31 *Pauṣkara-manifestation:*

25–26 The god (Viṣṇu), who slept for 1000 Yugas, was manifest as Brahman, Kapila, the Three-eyed (= Śiva), the Thirty (gods), the Seven Sages, snakes, and Apsarases.

27 (He was manifest) as Sanatkumāra and Manu; the primordial god (*purāṇadeva*), fiery like Vaiśvānara, made bodies (*purāṇi*) for himself.[2]

28–29 He who remained in the middle of the ocean when gods, demons, men etc. were destroyed slew Madhu and Kaiṭabha, after granting them a boon.

30–31 Formerly, when he whose navel is a lotus (= Viṣṇu) slept in the ocean, gods and sages originated in Puṣkara; that is the »Pauṣkara-manifestation« of which the Purāṇa tells.

32–42 *Vārāha-manifestation:*

32–42 When Viṣṇu assumed the boar-shape this boar had the Vedas as mouth, etc. (14 lines[3] of further identifications of parts of the body with components of vedic ritual) and lifted the earth from the ocean with his tusk. Thus, the earth was lifted by the boar who is the sacrifice (*yajñavarāha*).

43–79 *Narasiṃha-manifestation:*[4]

43 He is called »Vārāha« and »Nārasiṃha«,[5] who, as the lord of the wild animals, killed Hiraṇyakaśipu.

44–52 That demon (Hiraṇyakaśipu) practised fierce asceticism in a (the) previous Kṛta-Yuga for 10,115 (or 11,500, or 11,005?) years. Brahman was pleased, visited him in his chariot (v. 41–43 list accompanying beings) and granted a boon.

53–57 Hiraṇyakaśipu wished not to be cursed by any being, to be killed only by a being who could kill him and his forces by one stroke of the hand, to be sun, moon, wind, fire, water, atmosphere, space, wrath, passion, Varuṇa, Vāsava (= Indra), Dhanada (= Kubera, the lord of Kiṃpuruṣas).

58–59 Brahman granted all these boons and returned to his residence.

60–65 Gods, Nāgas, Gandharvas, and hermits told Brahman that they were afraid of the effects of these boons; he should think of how Hiraṇyakaśipu could be killed. Brahman answered that Hiraṇyakaśipu would certainly enjoy the fruits of his asceticism, but that he would finally be killed by Viṣṇu. The gods were pleased and returned.

66–71 After he had obtained his boon Hiraṇyakaśipu oppressed the living beings, especially hermits and gods, whom he bereft of sacrifices (which were directed to the demons). The gods (Ādityas, Vasus, Sādhyas, All-Gods, Maruts) took refuge with Viṣṇu (described in v. 71 by a list of epithets).

[2] In Triṣṭubh-Jagatī-metre.

[3] In VePr printed as a footnote.

[4] For a German summary of v. 44–79 cf. P. Hacker, Prahlāda, p. 27–28.

[5] For lengthening of the vowel in the first syllable of a name addressing a god, cf. P. Thieme in MSS 44 (Festgabe für Karl Hoffmann Teil 1), p. 329ff.

72–73 Hymn by the gods to Viṣṇu, praising him as the highest god and asking for his help.

74–79 Vāsudeva (= Viṣṇu) comforted the gods and promised them to slay the haughty demon. He assumed the shape of half a man and half a lion; like a cumulation of dark clouds he came over the demon and slew him with one stroke of his claw.

80 Conclusion to the account of the man-lion; announcement of the dwarf-shape.

81–104 At the mighty Balin's sacrifice the mighty[6] Viṣṇu upset the Asuras with three steps. (v. 82–90ab give a list of names of Asuras, viz. Vipracitti, Śiva, Śaṅku, Ayaḥśaṅku, Ayaḥśiras, Aśvaśiras, Hayagrīva, Vegavat, Ketumat, Ugra, Ugravyagra, Puṣkara, Puṣkala, Aśva, Aśvapati (mentioned twice), Prahlāda, Kumbha, Saṃhrāda, Anuhlāda, Harihaya, Vārāha, Saṃhara, Anuja, Śarabha, Śalabha, Kupatha, Krodhana, Kratha, Bṛhatkīrti (epithet?), Mahājihva, Śaṅkukarṇa, Mahāsvana, Dīptijihva, Arkanayana, Mṛgapāda, Mṛgapriya, Vāyu, Gariṣṭha (epithet?), Namuci, Śambara, Viskara (v.l. Vikṣara), Candrahantṛ, Krodhahantṛ, Krodhavardhana, Kālaka, Kālakopa, Vṛtra, Krodha, Virocana, Gariṣṭha (mentioned for the second time), Variṣṭha, Pralamba, Naraka, Indratāpana, Vātāpī, Ketumat (mentionted for the second time), Asiloman, Puloman, Bāṣkala, Pramada, Mada, Svamiśra, Kālavadana, Karāla, Keśin, Ekākṣa, Candramas, Rāhu, Saṃhrāda (mentioned for the second time), Sambara, Svana; v. 90cd–99 are a list of what kind of weapons they held, and what kind of animal faces they had.) The Asuras attacked Hṛṣīkeśa as he took the steps which wiped them all out; sun and moon were consecutively at his breast, at his navel and at his knee; having gained the earth Viṣṇu gave it to Śakra (= Indra).

105 Conclusion to the dwarf-manifestation; Viṣṇu's fame is told by Brahmins who are conversant with the Veda.

106–112 *Dattātreya-manifestation*

106–112 Announcement of Viṣṇu's manifestation as Dattātreya. When the Vedas, sacrifices and *dharma* had vanished and *adharma* and untruth prevailed he brought back the Vedas and established the four castes. Dattātreya granted a boon to Kārtavīrya, the king of Haihayas, that the should have 1000 arms and protect the earth.

113ab Conclusion to this glorious (*śrīmat*) manifestation.

113cd–123 *Manifestation as Jāmadagnya*

113cd Announcement of the manifestation as Jāmadagnya.

114–122 Rāma slew Arjuna and cut off his 1000 arms with his axe; 21 times he freed the earth of Kṣatriyas, performed a horse-sacrifice in which he gave the earth as a sacrificial gift (*dakṣiṇā*) to Mārīca Kaśyapa, along with elephants,[7] horses, and chariots, and with a golden indestructible bow and elephants. Even today he practises asceticism on the mountain Mahendra for the benefit of the worlds.

[6] Possibly a play on words (Bali, *balavat*, *balin*).

[7] *Vāraṇān*, perhaps wrong reading for *vāruṇān* (as in HV), i.e. »(horses) belonging to Varuṇa«), since elephants are mentioned in the next half verse.

123 Conclusion to the manifestation called Jāmadagnya.

124–158 *Manifestation as Rāma:*

124–126 In the 24th Yuga Daśaratha's son Rāma was born after the Lord had made himself fourfold. He was born to grant mercy to the world, to kill Rākṣasas and to let *dharma* grow.

127–135 He is said to have cared for the welfare of all beings (*sarvabhūtahite rataḥ*); he stayed in the forest for 14 years accompanied by Lakṣmaṇa. Practising asceticism ... (His wife Sītā, formerly named Lakṣmī, accompanied her husband.)[8] ... he stayed in Janasthāna and performed the work of the gods. Following Sītā's trails he slew his assailant Paulastya (= Rāvaṇa), the invincible, cruel, along with his ministers and army (v. 124cd–128 describe Rāvaṇa's fearsome attributes).

136–140 He slew Vālin and anointed Sugrīva king; he slew Lavaṇa, Madhu's son; he slew Mārīca and Subāhu who had disturbed sacrifices; he slew many others, (e.g.) the Rākṣasas Virādha and Kabandha, who were Gandharvas under a curse.[9]

141 Rāma slew many enemies in battle.[10]

142–144 Viśvāmitra gave him weapons; during Janaka's sacrifice he playfully broke the bow; after performing such deeds he arranged for ten horse-sacrifices.

145–153ab Description of Rāma's rule and its ideal conditions: no untruth, no theft, pleasant climate, no untimely deaths, observance of caste hierarchy, no illnesses, etc.[11]

153cd–154 Description of Rāma who ruled for 10,000 years.

155 Under his reign Ṛgveda, Sāmaveda and Yajurveda were continuously recited and alms were offered.

156 Rāma's lustre surpassed that of sun and moon.

157 After performing hundreds of sacrifices he left Ayodhyā and went to heaven.

158 Thus, that great descendant of Ikṣvāku went to heaven after killing Rāvaṇa.

159–163 *Manifestation as Keśava (= Kṛṣṇa):*

A further manifestation is that of Keśava in the Māthura cycle, where he killed Śālva, Caidya, Kaṃsa, Dvivida, Ariṣṭa, Keśin, Pūtanā, Kuvalayāpīḍa, Cāṇūra, and Muṣṭika in his human body; he cut off Bāṇa's arms, slew Naraka and Yavana, stole the king's jewels, deposed wicked kings.

164–165ab *Manifestation as Kalkin:*

There is further the manifestation of Kalkin Viṣṇuyaśas in the village Śambhala for the benefit of all worlds.

165cd–168ab These and other manifestations are sung about in the Purāṇas; even the gods are confused with regard to the account (*anukīrtana*) of his manifestations, about which

[8] Inserted explanation.

[9] Construction? In HV the names are in the accusative and the verses are transposed.

[10] In Upendravajrā-metre.

[11] *Rāme rājyaṃ praśāsati* is repeated four times as a refrain.

the Purāṇa deals, established by vedic authority; this account of (Viṣṇu's) manifestations (has been) presented as brief statement only (*uddeśamātreṇa*).

168cd–169ab The ancestors of one who listens to the proclamation of the manifestations are pleased.

170 By listening to these yogic feats of the lord of Yoga one is freed from all evil and obtains wealth and success.[12]

171 Conclusion to the account of Viṣṇu's manifestations.

Ch. 214: The path to Yama's world; the gates to his city

1–2 The hermits are not yet satisfied with listening; they praise Vyāsa's knowledge.

3–8 They want to hear about the way to Yama's world, its tortures, its distance; further, how people can avoid these tortures; how much distance there is between the worlds of men and of Yama; by which deeds people go to heaven and to hell; how many heavens and hells there are; and what is their appearance and extent.

9 Vyāsa announces that he will speak of the wheel of existences.

10–11ab He announces that he will speak of the way to Yama beginning from dying, as none else can speak, and of its nature.

11cd–103 *The path leading to Yama's world*

11cd–12ab The distance between the world of men and that of Yama is 86,000 Yojanas.

12cd–13ab The path is hot like glowing copper; every being has to walk it.

13cd Those who have done good go to good (places).

14–17 There are 22 (*sic*) hells: (1) Raurava, (2) Raudra, (3) Śūkara, (4) Tāla, (5) Kambhīpāka, (6) Mahāghora, (7) Śālmala, (8) Vimohana, (9) Kīṭāda, (10) Kṛmibhakṣa, (11) Nālābhakṣa (v.l. Lālābhakṣa), (12) Bhrama, (13) rivers of pus and (14) of blood, (15) Agnijvāla, (16) Mahāghora (cf. no. 6), (17) Saṃdaṃśa, (18) Śunaḥbhojana, (19) Ghorā, (20) Vaitaraṇī, (21) Asipattravana.

18–20ab (Continuation of the description of the path:) There are no trees, no water, no shelters.

20cd–27ab Every being has to walk that path alone, irrespective of the hour of death or of age, of walk of life or place of sojourn.

27cd–31 After experiencing the appointed life-span beings die by some means or other (listed in v. 28cd). One assumes another body, born from one's deeds, for the purpose of being tormented; through it one suffers or enjoys the effects of one's deeds.

32–33 Description of dying: Heat loosens the central points (*marmasthāna*); the »upward breath« (*udāna*) moves upwards and stops the movement of food and drink.

34–41ab Enumeration of good deeds (giving of water, giving of food, truthfulness, devotion to gods and Brahmins, observation of *dharma*, etc.), which lead to a pleasant death. According to their actions, dying people overcome disagreeable conditions.

[12] In Indravajrā-metre.

1cd–42ab Those who have lied etc., or abused the Vedas, suffer confusion in death.

42cd–45 Arrival of Yama's messenger causes terror; one shouts for relatives but the voice is indistinct; the eyes turn, one coughs and sighs and leaves the body.

46–51 One gets a similar body to suffer the results of one's deeds; one is bound by Yama's messenger. When the wind has reached the throat, the soul is separated from the body and, as wind, leaves this body of six layers while the relatives look on.

52–54 The (souls) are pulled and beaten along the dark and terrible path (list of adjectives in v. 52–53) by Yama's attendants.

55–69 When Yama's messengers see that life has ceased they want to lead that being away. (v. 56–68 describe their fantastic vehicles, attributes, faces, bodies, by lists of nominatives and instrumentals.)

70–88ab By that passive body[1] the being is led to Yama's palace, bound and beaten, stumbling and crying, pierced and scolded, pulled along that path. Fearful and tortured the being has to walk that path.

88cd–96 Attribution of various tortures to particular sins (not giving alms, killing, eating meat, breach of loyalty, abduction of others' wives, theft of clothes, grain, gold etc., theft of a Brahmin's property, beating Brahmins, etc.).

97–99 Description of the terrors of that path (or of the hell Raurava).

100–103 Everyone has to walk that path being led and tortured by Yama's attendants.

04–107ab One finally enters the city of Yama, which extends for 100,000 Yojanas, is adorned with jewels, has four gates and is populated by fierce gods, demons, etc. (listed).

07cd–128 *Description of the gates to the city of Yama:*

07cd–109 By the beautifully equipped eastern gate (with different jewels, singing and dancing Apsarases and Gandharvas) enter gods, sages, Yogins, Gandharvas, Siddhas, Yakṣas, Vidyādharas, and snakes (?).

10–114ab By the northern gate (endowed with bells, lutes, flutes, vedic recitation, etc.) enter those who know *dharma*, adhere to truth, offer water in heat, fire in cold, transport those who are tired, speak in a friendly way, give alms, serve parents and Brahmins, honour guests.

14cd–119 By the jewel-bedecked western gate (endowed with the sounds of drums and conches) enter those devoted to Śiva, who have bathed at holy places, attended to the five fires, died a voluntary death (by walking north), by dying on the mountain Kālañjara, by entering fire or by fasting, by being killed in a fight for the sake of one's sovereign, of friend(s), of the public or of a cow).

120–128 By the southern gate, which lies in darkness and is surrounded by sharp weapons (listed) and wild animals (listed), enter those who have done evil, those who have killed a Brahmin, a cow, a child or an old person, one who sought shelter, a woman, a friend, or one who was unarmed; those who have had intercourse with a woman not to be approached; who have stolen, embezzled a deposit, have given poison or fire, stolen land, house, bed, clothes, ornaments; those who were cruel about others' faults, spoke untruths, caused suffering to village(s), kingdom, city, those who have

[1] cf. above v. 30 and v. 46.

given false witness, sold girls (or: their daughters), eaten forbidden food, had intercourse (?) with (their) daughter or daughter-in-law, or spoken harshly to parents (?).[2]

Ch. 215: Punishment of the wicked in Yama's world; description of hells

1 The hermits want to know how the wicked enter that city by the southern gate.

2-3 Vyāsa announces that he will speak about that terrible gate which resounds with the howling of jackals, is surrounded by wild animals, demons, ghosts, etc.

4-23 Seeing it the wicked faint, they are bound, dragged, beaten etc., they stumble toward the southern gate, cut by thorns and stones, bitten, burnt, frozen; the way is endowed with ditches, fires, waters, etc., fierce animals (listed), illnesses, dusty wind, rain of stones or sparks, lightning, cold winds, etc.

24-28 Thus the wicked are led by Yama's messenger, alone, regretting their deeds, with dried up mouth, emaciated, burnt, some with their heads downwards.

29-38 Seeing delicious food and drink they beg for it, but Yama's men scold them, reminding them (v. 32-38) that they did not sacrifice or give to Brahmins; this food is for those who have sacrificed and honoured Brahmins.

39-44 Beaten, pierced, bitten by Yama's men and animals they are led before Yama.

45-55ab Led before Yama they see his fierce, fiery etc. appearance with 18 arms (v. 46-50ab describe Yama), next to him Death (*mṛtyu*, described in v. 50cd-51ab), Mahāmārī (daughter of Marīci?) and Kālarātrī, various afflictions and numerous servants of Yama with various weapons (listed), and Citragupta.

55cd-64 Yama scolds the evil-doers; Citragupta addresses them (v. 57-64), listing some of their offences (theft, pride, adultery), explaining their suffering as the effect of their own deeds, addressing (for instance) kings (v. 60-64) who have misused their powers and are now alone and powerless.

65-67 Those kings regret their deeds and stand silent; Yama gives orders for their purification ordering Caṇḍa and Mahācaṇḍa to lead them into the fire of hells.

68-69 The servants of Yama seize them by the legs and whirl them around, throw them into the air, grab them and throw them against rocks.

70-71 Then the bleeding soul[1] becomes unconscious; it is revived by wind and then thrown into the ocean of hells.

72-77 Yama's messengers announce other evil-doers, naming their offences (greed, violence, intercourse with a woman not to be approached, theft, selling of daughters, giving false witness, ungratefulness, deceit of friends, abusing *dharma*) and ask for orders.

78-80 Having put the evil-doer in front of Yama and in thousands and hundreds of hundred thousands and ten millions of hells[2] Yama's servants go to seize the next one, while Yama orders others to execute the punishment taught by Vasiṣṭha and others.

[2] Read *pāruṣyam* for *pauruṣam*?

[1] v. 60-69 concern kings; here the subject of the sentence changes to singular.

[2] cf. below v. 82cd.

81-83ab Yama's men accordingly torment with their weapons (listed) in order to destroy the evil.[3]

cd-84ab Announcement of the nature of hells.

d-136ab *List of hells and punishments:*

	Name	torture, characteristic of hell	offence	duration of stay	extension of hell
cd-86ab	Mahāvīci	blood, thorns	killing of Ccows	100,000 years	10,000 Yojanas
cd-88ab	Kumbhīpāka	glowing copper pots, sand, sparks	Brahmin-murder, annexation of land, embezzling of trust	till end of cosmos	10,000,000 Yojanas
cd-90ab	Raurava	burning arrows	false witness	-	60,000 Yojanas
cd-91ab	Mañjūṣa	burning iron	robbery	-	-
cd-92ab	Apratiṣṭhā	(head downwards in) pus, urine, faeces	tormenting a Brahmin	-	-
cd-93ab	Vilepaka	burning lac	drinking alcohol	-	-
cd-94ab	Mahāprabhā	glowing lances	separating husband and wife	-	-
cd-95ab	Jayantī (?)	iron and rocks	adultery	-	-
cd-98ab	Śālmala	glowing spikes, tearing of tongue, piercing of eyes	having several men (for women), looking lustfully at other women	-	-
9-100ab	Mahāraurava	garlands of fire	murdering women, children, old people	14 Manuantaras	14,000 Yojanas
00cd-101	Tāmisra	burning	arson	till end of Kalpa	100,000 Yojanas
102-103	Mahātāmisra	swords, etc.	theft	300 Kalpas	double the prec.
4-105ab	Nirāloka	water-snakes	murder of parent, breach of confidence	till end of earth	-

[3] v. 82cd = 78cd.

105cd–107ab	Asipattravana	flaming swords	murder of friend	till end of cosmos	10,000 Yojanas
107cd–109ab	Karambha-vālukā	glowing pebbles, sand thorns	tormenting by deceit	300 x 100,000 x 10,000 years (?)	10,000 Yojanas
109cd–110ab	Kākola	worms, pus	eating sweets alone	-	-
110cd–111ab	Kuḍmala	urine, faeces, blood	not performing sacrifices	-	-
111cd–112ab	Mahābhīma (?)	flesh, blood	eating forbidden food	-	-
112cd–113ab	Mahāvaṭa	worms, insects corpses	selling of daughter	-	-
113cd–114ab	Tilapākā	being crushed like sesamum	afflicting others	-	-
114cd–115ab	Tailapāka	burning oil	murder of friend or refugee	-	-
115cd–116ab	Vajrakapāṭā	adamantine chain	selling milk	-	-
116cd–117ab	Nirucchvāsa	darkness, windlessness	no alms to the twice-born	-	-
117cd–118ab	Aṅgāropacaya	glowing sparks	no alms to the twice-born	-	-
118cd–119ab	Mahāpāyin	falling (head downwards)	untruthfulness	-	100,000 Yojanas
119cd–120ab	Mahājvālā	flames	thinking of evil	-	-
120cd–121ab	Krakaca	saws	intercourse with woman not to be approached	-	-
121cd–122ab	Guḍapākā	ponds of heated molasses	mixing of castes	-	-
122cd–123ab	Kṣuradhārā	sharp knives	annexation of land of Brahmins	till end of Kalpa	-
123cd–124ab	Ambarīṣa	fire of doomsday	theft of gold	10x10 mill. Kalpas	-
124cd–125ab	Vajrakuṭhārā	thunderbolts (*vajra*)	hurting of tree (v.l. piercing of parasols)	-	-

5cd-126ab	Paritāpa	fire of doomsday	poisoning, stealing honey	-	-
6cd-127ab	Kālasūtra	adamantine threads, being cut while whirling	stealing grain	-	-
7cd-128ab	Kaśmala	slime, snot	addiction to meat (Ve. adds alcohol)	one Kalpa	-
8cd-129ab	Ugragandha	urine, faeces	performing no ancestral offering	-	-
9cd-130ab	Durdhara	water animals scorpions	accepting bribes	10,000 years	-
0cd-136ab	Vajramahā-	being cut to pieces	theft of gold, grain,	till end of Kalpa	-
	-	being eaten	killing, eating like crows and vultures	-	-
	-	being split with clubs and axes	theft of furniture and clothes	-	-
	-	burning in fire of dry grass	theft of fruits, leaves	-	-
	-[4]	piercing of heart	thinking of another's property or wife	-	-
	(VePr adds 22 lines after v. 133, numbered 134–144:				
	[134 c-f] Āyāsa	burning iron	abusing Vedas and Smṛtis	-	-
	[136] Parilumpa	vultures, dogs, wolves	removing children and angry people (?)	-	-
	[137] Karāla	ghosts	afflicting Brahmins	-	-
	[138] Vilepana	heated lac	drinking alcohol	-	-
	[139] Mahāpīḍā	glowing lances	separating husband and wife	-	-
	[140] Mahāghorā (?)	flaming iron slabs	loving another's wife	-	-

[4] The punishments of v. 130cd–136ab (in VePr beginning with v. 142) are not attributed to hells but are inflicted by Yama's men, repeatedly mentioned.

[141]	Śālmalī	(embracing) glowing spikes	enjoying others' faults	-	-
[142]	-	cutting out of tongue	speaking untruths; violating vital spots	-	-
[143]	-	burning with glowing coal	incest	-	-
[144ab]	-	piercing with spears	theft of *dharma* (?), house, gold)	-	-

136cd–137ab Any turning away from *dharma* leads to severe suffering in Yama's world.

137cd–138ab Thus, there are hundreds of thousands and ten millions of hells.

138cd–142 For even a small wicked deed one suffers in Yama's worlds. People do not listen to the proclamation of *dharma*; they object because it cannot be seen; they commit evil day and night. Those who enjoy the results (of their deeds) here (in this world) and turn away from the world beyond fall into terrible hells. Staying in hell is miserable; staying in heaven is pleasant; both are reached according to a man's deeds.

Ch. 216: Reward of the righteous in Yama's world

1–2 The sages inquire whether there is a means by which one can reach Yama's residence in comfort, avoiding the tortures of Yama's path, the hells, and the gate.

3–4 Vyāsa announces how those who follow *dharma* (non-violence, honouring the teacher, gods, Brahmins) walk that path.

5–63 In celestial chariots, adorned and attended by Apsarases,[1] are transported those who give gifts and food to Brahmins; who present cows; who present sandals, parasol etc.; who give drink (sugarcane juice) and food; who give milk, clarified butter, curds, molasses, honey to Brahmins; who give fruits and flowers; who give cows made of sesamum and clarified butter; who (construct?) ponds, lakes, wells etc.; whose temples are adorned by jewels; who give water; who give wooden sandals etc. to the twice-born; who establish groves for the benefit of others; who give gold, silver, corals, pearls; who give land; who give a daughter (girl); who give scents to the twice-born; who give lamps; who give a dwelling; who give water-pots and bowls; who give ointment; who give rest to tired twice-born; who welcome a twice-born; who venerate Hari; who eat (only) after (others have been fed); who are free from conceit and live on one meal a day; who live, with their senses controlled, on one meal every fourth (day or meal); who eat only on every third day; who eat on every sixth day; who fast for half a month; who fast for one month; who die voluntarily (*mahāprasthāna*, »the great departure«); who cultivate their body by

[1] Mention of these chariots, of the attendant women and of ornaments etc. is variously repeated in this section.

their inner self consisting of Viṣṇu (?); who enter fire while intent on Nārāyaṇa; who fast to death while thinking of Viṣṇu; who die by entering water; Vaiṣṇavas who abandon their body to vultures; who die in battle; Vaiṣṇavas who go on pilgrimage; who sacrifice munificently; who do not make others and servants suffer; who are forbearing, free from anger etc.; who concentratedly (exclusively?) worship Viṣṇu, Brahman, the Three-Eyed (= Śiva), the sun; who do not eat meat and are truthful and pure.

64-66 There is no tastier food than meat; therefore one should avoid it; no pleasure comes from tasty (food); those who give 1000 cows and those who do not eat meat have been declared by Brahman to be equal; the merit of all places of pilgrimage, of all sacrifices accrues to him who does not eat meat.

67-72 Thus, those who are intent on gifts and observances travel in comfort; they are welcomed by Yama and invited to ascend to heaven in a chariot attended by celestial women, to enjoy pleasures there, and then to atone for the few negative effects which may be left. Such people experience Yama like a father.

73-80 Therefore one should pursue *dharma*; from it (originate) profit, pleasure, and liberation (i.e. the other goals of life); it saves from fear and brings about (rebirth as) god or twice-born. Consciousness (*buddhi*) shares in *dharma* (only) after the evil has been destroyed; after thousands of rebirths one is born as a human being. He who does not pursue *dharma* is indeed misguided. Despised, poor, ill, stupid, etc., are those who have not (in their previous lives) adhered to *dharma*, while those who live long, are learned, wealthy, healthy, etc. have formerly practised *dharma*.

81 Thus, those devoted to *dharma* go to the ultimate goal, while the others are reborn as animals.

82-86 Yama has no power over those who are devotees (*anuvrata*) of Vāsudeva; those who continuously revere him do not encounter Yama; over those who take refuge in Acyuta by deeds, thoughts, and words Yama has no power; those who always bow to Nārāyaṇa go to Viṣṇu's world; those who revere Viṣṇu do not see those messengers, the path, Yama, that city, or the hells.

87-89 Even those who commit much evil will not go to hell if they bow to Hari, who takes away all evils; even those who think of Janārdana (motivated) by deceit will go to Viṣṇu's world after death; even a most wrathful person who at some time praises Hari will obtain liberation.

Ch. 217: The fate of the soul after death; retribution for deeds by rebirth[1]

1 Lomaharṣaṇa introduces the next question of the hermits to Vyāsa after they had heard of Yama's path and of the tortures in the hells.

2-3 The hermits inquire (from Vyāsa), whose knowledge they praise, as to who accompanies a person after death into the next world.

[1] This chapter is largely parallel to MBh 13,112; for a concordance see Appendix 10 to the text-volume.

4–11 Vyāsa's answer: Man is born alone and dies alone; nobody follows the dead except *dharma* only. When accompanied by *dharma* a living being goes to heaven, connected with *adharma* one approaches hell. *dharma*, profit and pleasure (i.e. three of the four goals of life) constitute the rewards for a living being; this triad should be pursued, its opposite avoided.

12–13 The hermits want to know how *dharma* can follow a body which is subtle, unmanifest and invisible.

14–17 Vyāsa's answer: The five elements (listed), mind, Consciousness (*buddhi*) and Self always see *dharma*; they are witnesses of a living being in this world; *dharma* follows the soul along with them; skin, bones, flesh, semen, blood are left behind. Connected with *dharma* the soul achieves well-being. Vyāsa asks what else he should tell.

18 The hermits ask how semen comes about.

19–21 Vyāsa's answer: The five elements (listed) are gods who eat food while staying in the body; when they and the mind are satisfied the pure self produces semen. From it (or: then) the slime of man and woman becomes an embryo. Vyāsa asks what else they want to hear.

22 The hermits inquire how a man comes to be born.

23–24 Vyāsa's answer: A man is (at birth) immediately overpowered by the elements; when separated from them he goes on (i.e. assumes another existence). He lives only when joined with the elements; therefore the gods who stay in the elements (?) see his good and bad actions. Vyāsa asks what else they want to hear.

25 The hermits inquire where a soul experiences pleasure and pain after abandoning skin, bones and flesh and separated from the elements.

26 Vyāsa's answer: A soul accompanied by (the effects of) his actions goes to semen; having reached the menstrual flux of women in due course of time (he is born).[2]

27 (There is) affliction by Yama's messengers, (there is) death and the suffering (of) the cycle of rebirths. (Thus,) a man obtains affliction.[3]

28 In this world a living being from birth onwards enjoys the results of his good deeds and of Dharma.

29–31 If he has clung to *dharma* he is reborn as a man and is happy; if he has followed *dharma* and then *adharma* he experiences suffering after pleasure; if united with *adharma* he goes to Yama's region, suffers fiercely and is then reborn as an animal.

32 Vyāsa announces that he will tell which deed leads to which existence.

33–35 In Yama's world, of which the learned tradition (*śāstra*) and narratives (*itihāsa*) tell, there are (also) godlike, pleasant places; they (exist) besides birth as animals; in Yama's world, which is equal to Brahman's world, a being suffers in accordance with (his) specific (*niyata*) actions.

36–110 *Retribution of sins by rebirth as animals*

36 Announcement of which deed leads to which existence.

[2] Sentence incomplete.

[3] Construction unclear.

37-39 He who, after studying the four Vedas, in a confused state accepts (gifts) from a »fallen« person (i.e. who has been excommunicated?) is reborn as a donkey, lives as such for 15 years, then 7 years as a buffalo; is then born as a brahminical demon for 3 months and may then be born as a Brahmin.

40-42 If one has sacrificed for a »fallen« person, one is born as a worm, lives for 15 years, is born as ass, lives 5 years as a pig, 5 years as a cock, 5 years as a jackal, 1 year as a dog and is then born as a human being (male).[4]

43-44 The pupil who commits a sin against his teacher undergoes three rebirths, as a dog, as a beast of prey (»corpse-eater«), as a donkey; then he may be born as a Brahmin.

45-47 The pupil who approaches his teacher's wife even in his thoughts lives for three years as a dog, one year as a worm, then he is reborn as a Brahmin.

48 A teacher who kills a pupil becomes a beast of prey (*hiṃsra*).

49-50 The son who despises his parents is reborn first as a donkey for ten years; after one year as a crocodile he is born as a human being.

51-52 A son with whom parents and teacher are angry is reborn as a donkey, after 10 + 14 months (i.e.two years) he is born as a cat for seven months; then he is born as a human being.

53-54 He who scolds his parents is born as a Sārīka (a bird?); if he beats them he is reborn as a tortoise, after ten years he becomes a porcupine for three years, a snake for six months, then a man.

55-56 He who accepts food from a master (but) serves the enemy of this king is reborn as a monkey for ten years; then he lives for seven years as a mouse and for six months as a dog; then he is reborn as a human being.

57-58 He who embezzles a trust goes to Yama's realm, undergoes 100 rebirths and is then born as a worm for fifteen years; then he is reborn as a man.

59-61 A discontented man becomes a Śārṅgaka (a bird?); one who commits a breach of trust is born as a fish, after eight years he becomes a wild animal (deer) for four months, then a he-goat for one year, then an insect, then a man.

62-65 One who steals grains and seeds (listed) is born as a rat, then as a pig; after dying immediately of an illness one is born as a mute dog, after five years as a man.

66 One who has contact with another's wife becomes a wolf, a dog, a jackal, then a donkey, a snake (?), a heron, a crane.

67 He who violates a brother's wife becomes a he-cuckoo for one year.

68-71ab He who violates the wife of a friend, of a teacher or the king is born as a pig; after five years he becomes a crane for ten years, an ant for three months, then a worm for fourteen months.[5] After the destruction of his *adharma* a man then is born as a human being.

cd-73ab He who gives a girl (daughter) who had been given to one man to a second one (in marriage)[6] is also reborn as a worm for thirteen years; after destruction of his *adharma* he is born as a man.

cd-75ab He who does not perform the rites for gods and ancestors is born as a crow; after 100 years he is born as a cock, then as a serpent (? *vyālaka*) for a month, then as a man.

[4] Ed. Veṅk. continues with what is v. 59 in ed. ASS.

[5] After BrP v. 70 MBh inserts 4 lines, 13,112.71-72ab.

[6] Here VePr inserts v. 43-58 (as v. 56/71), thus leaving the sentence incomplete.

75cd–77ab He who despises his eldest brother, who is like a father, lives as a curlew for ten years, then as a pheasant (? *jīvaka*), then he obtains human nature.

77cd–80ab A man who approaches a Brahmin woman is reborn as a worm, then as a pig which dies by illness immediately after birth; further he is born as a dog, then as a man. Having procreated offspring he dies and becomes a mouse.[7]

80cd–86 The ungrateful goes to Yama's realm and suffers there. Daṇḍaka, Mudgara, Śūla, Agnidaṇḍa, Dāruṇa, Asipattravana, Vālukā, Kūṭaśālmalī (i.e. hells) belong to Yama's realm. Those who have suffered there fiercely are reborn as worms for fifteen years; then one dies as an embryo; then obtains hundreds of rebirths, then is reborn as an animal; after many years of suffering one is reborn as a tortoise.

87–99 Rebirth as an animal for particular thefts:[8]

For stealing ...	one becomes ...
curds	crane and *plava* (aquatic bird?)
fish	bee
fruit, roots, bread	ant
straw (chaff)	»fruit-rat« (?, Hindī *gilaharī*)
milk	partridge
cake mixed with flour	owl
water	crow
brass	pigeon (*hārīta* ?)
silver vessel	dove
golden vessel	worm
(woven) silk	osprey
silk-worms	dancer (?)
cloth	parrot
dukūla-raiment	goose
cotton-cloth	curlew
woollen cloth or linen	hare
powder (? *cūrṇa*)	peacock
red clothes	pheasant
colours, scents	musk-rat; as such he lives for fifteen years, then he is born as a human being
milk	crane
sesamum-oil	an animal which drinks sesamum-oil

100–104 He who kills an unarmed person for wealth becomes a donkey which lives for two years and is then slaughtered; then he becomes a wild animal (deer) which is killed after one year; he becomes a fish which is caught in a net after four months; then he lives as a dog for ten years, for five years as a tiger before becoming a man.

105–108ab Rebirth as an animal for particular thefts (contd.):

musical instrument	sheep (ram)
food containing oil-cake	rat which continuously bites men
clarified butter	crow (?), diver-bird (?)
fish	crow
salt	Cirikāka-crow (?)

[7] v. 78–79, which duplicate v. 64–65 above, are not found in MBh 13,112.

[8] cf. MBh 13.112.95cd–103, the sequence of verses being partly changed, however.

8cd–110ab He who refuses to return what has been entrusted to him is reborn as a fish, then as a short-lived man.

111ab He does not recognize *dharma* as his own guideline.[9]

1cd–113ab Men who commit evil and remove it by observances experience pleasure and pain and are of ill health. As Mlecchas (people living outside India and outside the frame of castes and stages of life) are born those who lead a wicked life.

3cd–114ab Those who do not commit evil are free from illness, are beautiful, and wealthy.

4cd–115ab Women obtain evil (effects) in the same manner; they become wives of such evil (men or animals?).

115cd–116 Conclusion: Thus, the faults with regard to stealing have all been proclaimed. All this has been only briefly told; the hermits should hear more.

117–118 What had formerly been told by Brahman to the heavenly sages has now been told by Vyāsa. The hermits should keep *dharma* in mind.

Ch. 218:Merit of giving food to Brahmins[1]

1–2 The hermits confirm the conclusion of the effects of *adharma* and request to be told about good deeds.

3–5 Vyāsa answers: A man who deliberately commits evil goes to hell; he who by confusion does not realize *dharma* (but) repents should, with concentration of mind, not continue this evil conduct.

6 If one[2] tells (about his *adharma*) among Brahmins who know the *dharma*, one is immediately freed from an offence.

7–8ab If a man confesses (his) *adharma*, he is freed from it. If one's mind disregards evil, correspondingly the body is freed from (the effects of) *adharma*,[3] like a snake that abandons its cast-off skins.

8cd–9ab By giving various gifts to Brahmins a man with concentration of mind goes to heaven.

9–32 *On the importance and merit of giving food to Brahmins*

9cd–10ab Announcement of the gifts by which a man gains *dharma* even if he has acted improperly.

10cd–13ab Among all donations food is the best, since it sustains life, supports the world, is praised by gods, sages, ancestors, and people, and is the means by which one reaches heaven.

[9] Unclear; in MBh (crit.ed.) vol. 17, p. 1104, the phrase »*(yeṣāṃ) ātmanaḥ pramāṇaṃ te*« is translated as »those who follow their own whims (who do not recognise any *dharma*).«

[1] A chapter praising the donation of food is MBh 13,62, which contains occasional brief parallels (e.g. BrP 218.23c = MBh 13,62.7a) but apparently no longer parallels.

[2] *Viprāḥ* in the text.

[3] VePr reads v. 7 after v. 4.

13cd–16ab One should give lawfully obtained food to the twice-born; then one is not reborn as an animal; by feeding 10,000 Brahmins even the man who has enjoyed wickedness is freed from (the effects of) *adharma*.

16cd–21ab A Brahmin who gives food obtained by begging to a Brahmin devoted to recitation will gain happiness. A Kṣatriya who protects the property of Brahmins and gives food to them destroys his bad deeds. A Vaiśya who gives the sixth part of his produce to Brahmins is freed from evil. A Śūdra who gives to Brahmins food collected under danger of life (?) is freed from evil.

21cd–22ab A violent person who gains food by force does not suffer evil (consequences) if he gives (it) to Brahmins.

22cd–23 By giving food to Brahmins one is freed from evil; by giving invigorating food one becomes vigorous oneself.

24–28ab By turning to the path of the good one is freed from evil – the path made by those who know about gifts, walked by the wise among whom are givers of food; for them, justly collected food which is the foundation of everything (is) eternal *dharma* (?). Compared to one's (normal) duty (giving of) food is the highest path (*paramā gatiḥ*). By giving food one reaches the highest goal (*paramā gatiḥ*), has wishes fulfilled, enjoys happiness after death, is freed from evil. Therefore one should give food, except any which has been unjustly obtained.

28cd–29ab A householder who eats after (or: considering it an) offering to the life-forces makes the day fruitful by giving food.

29cd–31ab By always feeding the 100 best of those who know the Vedas, law, *dharma* and traditional narratives, a man does not go to hell and is not born again. He enjoys happiness here and after death.

31cd–32ab He who is attached to such deeds enjoys himself, is beautiful, famous, and wealthy.

32c-f Conclusion: The merit of giving food has been told, which is the root of all *dharma* and gifts.

Ch. 219: On ancestral rites

1 The hermits inquire how the ancestral offering is to be given to those who have gone to the world beyond and stay in the places of their deeds (i.e. according to their deeds).

2–3 After venerating the Lord of the world as a boar, Vyāsa announces the rules of ancestral rites (*śrāddhakalpa*) as they were performed by the Lord after he had lifted the ancestors from the waters of Kokā.

4–5 The hermits ask why the ancestors were submerged in Kokā, and how they were lifted by the boar at the Kokāmukha-tīrtha.

6–12 Vyāsa answers: Previously, at the dawn between Tretā- and Dvāpara-Yuga, the ancestors stayed as divine humans on the top of Meru together with the All-Gods. Soma's daughter Kāntimatī appeared before them with folded hands. The ancestors asked her who (*kā*) and whose (*prabhuḥ ko*) she was. She introduced herself as part (*kalā*) of the moon ready to accept the ancestors as her masters (husbands). Her name was first Ūrjā and then Svadhā; now she had just been named Kokā.[1] The ancestors could not stop looking at her. When the All-Gods recognized that the ancestors had forsaken Yoga by looking at the girl they went to the third heaven.

13-17 The moon, missing his daughter, learned that she had gone to the ancestors out of lust and had been accepted by them. Angrily he cursed the ancestors that having fallen from Yoga (*yogabhraṣṭa*) they should fall down, because they had desired his daughter who had not been given to them. And because she had taken a husband on her own initiative she should become a river on the Himālaya (*śiśirādri*), called Kokā.

18-24 Thus cursed, the ancestors fell at the feet of Himavat and Ūrjā fell on its back, establishing a holy place deriving from the seven oceans (?), as the river Kokā with hundreds of holy places, submerging the top of the mountain, known as *sarit* (»stream«) because of her winding course (*sarpaṇa*). The ancestors saw the river but, without Yoga, did not recognize her. Then the king of mountains gave Badarī (jujube), a cow which produced honey, and the water of Kokā to the famished ancestors. Thus nourished, the ancestors spent 10,000 years like one day.

25-29 Thus, in the world without ancestors and without Svadhā (i.e. Soma's daughter, *svadhā*-calls personified) the Daityas and Yātudhāna-Rākṣasas became powerful; they attacked the ancestors, who, upon seeing the demons, grabbed a rock-slab while Kokā concealed them by flooding the Himācala (= Himālaya). The demons climbed on a Vibhūtaka-tree and, being without food, disappeared.

30 The ancestors were hungry and thirsty in the water; they sang to Janārdana Hari for protection.

31-35 Hymn by the ancestors to Viṣṇu,[2] asking to be lifted from the waters and to be protected against the demons who flee from mention (praise) of the god's names.

36 The god was satisfied and saw the ancestors in the water holding the slab on their heads.[3]

37-39 The god decided to lift them up in the form of a hog; with his tusk he threw the slab down and lifted the ancestors, who clung to the body of the boar, to the mouth of Kokā.[4]

40-41 At the Viṣṇutīrtha Viṣṇu gave them water in a iron pin (? *lohārgala*); Keśava took Kuśa-grass, which originated from his hair, sesamum, originated from his sweat, and a fire-brand.

42-47ab Thus he made a sun-like light, a vessel, and a desired holy place (i.e. Viṣṇutīrtha); he took pure water containing the Gaṅgā (?) from beneath 10,000,000 fig-trees, sacrificial herbs, honey, milk,juices, scents, flowers, ointments; he took a cow from a lake (?), jewels from the ocean, drew (lines) on the earth with his tusk and sprinkled water, which originated from the *gharma*-oblation (consisting of hot milk), he again drew (lines) with Kuśa-grass, and led her (i.e. the earth) around by

[1] Probably meant to echo the questions of the ancestors.

[2] In Triṣṭubh-Jagatī-metre; mainly addressing the deity with epithets in the vocative; v. 33 lists iconographic attributes; v. 34 addresses *śambhu*, i.e. Śiva?

[3] In Vasantatilakā-metre.

[4] A different version of the foundation of ancestral rites with rice-balls (*piṇḍas*) by Viṣṇu as a boar is found in MBh 12,333.11-23.

the fire-brand,[5] sprinkling her again and again; spreading out the Kuśa-grass, which existed in the pores of his body-hair, he asked the sages[6] whether to perform the offering to the ancestors; they told him to do so.

47cd–48 He called the All-Gods with formulas, offered them seats, and achieved the protection of the gods by means of unhusked barley-corns.

49–51 The barley-corns, originating from the share of all gods, protect the directions; they are made for the purpose of protection. They cannot be destroyed by gods, demons, Yakṣas etc.; hence they are called »*akṣata*« (»uninjured«, »unbreakable«); they were first used by Viṣṇu for the protection of the gods.

52–60ab Calling and welcoming the ancestors: Having welcomed the All-Gods he asked them[7] whether to call the ancestors and was told to do so. He knew (?) the Kuśa-grass with roots and tops connected[8] and the sesamum (and) offered them a seat with the left hand having put his hand[9] on his knee. The boar recited the »*āyāntu naḥ*«-formula (»They should come to us ...«) and then the »*apahata*«-formula (»Driven off ...«), making protection from right to left.[10] Then he called the ancestors by name and *gotra*[11] reciting »By the years ...« («*saṃvatsaraiḥ* ...«) he then deposited the welcome-offering. Reciting the immortal words »What of me ...« («*yan me* ...«) for each father, and »What of me, oh grandfather, ...«, the Grandfather[12] offered the welcome-offering. (With the words) »What of me, oh great-grandfather, ...« he gave to the great-grandfather – Kuśa, scents, sesamum and flowers, from right to left. Janārdana followed the same procedure for the mothers and grandmothers.

60cd–65ab Offerings to the ancestors: After honouring them with scents and incense etc., the Lord of the world called upon the Ādityas, Vasus, Rudras (or: he recited the »Āditya-, Vasu-, Rudra-formula«); then he took food together with clarified butter, sesamum and Kuśa-grass, put it in a vessel and asked the hermits whether to sacrifice it into the fire. They told him to do so. One should offer thrice, to Soma, Agni, and Yama, should recite the seven formulas (starting with) »Those of mine ...«.[13] What was left he gave to each ancestor by mentioning name and *gotra*. Therefore one should throw the leftovers into the vessel for the rice-balls (*piṇḍa*).

65cd–71ab Feeding of Brahmins: Then he gave tasty food made of milk, fresh, with few vegetables (?), (but) many fruits, of six tastes; what he gave to Brahmins that he gave (also) to the ancestors in the *piṇḍa*-vessel; food for the ancestors conforms to the Veda,[14] is covered by clarified butter and sprinkled with honey; the formula »the

[5] *Pariṇī* could also imply »marrying« by leading around the fire.

[6] The apposition »existing in the pores of his body-hair« might equally refer to »sages«.

[7] The sages, as above, or the All-Gods?

[8] i.e. bound to form a ring?

[9] Which one?

[10] ? *apasavyataḥ*. According to the Hindī paraphrase this means »putting the sacred thread on the right shoulder«.

[11] According to ed. Veṅk. by reciting »It shall make full ...«.

[12] Here epithet of the Varāha-Viṣṇu?

[13] v. 63 changes over to the style of prescription rather than report (optative instead of perfect tense).

[14] ? *vedapūrvam*; v.l. *devapūrvam*.

earth ...« is recited over it; (then) he sang the triple verse »*madhuvātā* ...«. While the Brahmins ate he recited the five prayer-formulas, beginning with »*yat te prahāram* ...«. Then he sang »*nādhikam te* ...« and the *Trimadhu-*, *Trisuparṇa-*, and *Bṛhadāraṇyaka*-(texts). He murmured the hymn to the sun (? *sūktam sauram*) and the *Puruṣa*-hymn. When the Brahmins had finished eating he asked them whether they were satisfied. They said »yes« and he offered them water, dismissing them in silence (?).

1cd–86 Distribution of rice-balls to the ancestors: He took the *piṇḍa*-vessel and offered it to Chāyā (»shade«) who divided the food into two and then each one into three (parts). The boar scratched the earth and covered it with Kuśa-grass, making its tops point to the south, and he prepared a seat on it with sesamum, with Kuśa-grass with roots (or: with roots and Kuśa-grass). He added scents, flowers etc. to a rice-ball and offered it, reciting »*pṛthivī dadhīr* ...«. The grandfathers and the great-grandfathers and the great-great-grandfathers consented from the air. The boar gave rice-balls also to the grandmothers. (v. 76:) What remained of the food he gave to those ancestors who eat the remnants,[15] reciting the formula »This is for you, oh father ...«. He gave new cloth measuring two fingers, scents, flowers, etc., and he circumambulated them. By sipping water he made the ancestral Brahmins and the gods sip. Then he sprinkled the earth and offered unhusked grain and sesamum-water to ancestors murmuring »Imperishable for us ...«, and »May it please the ancestors ...«. Having pleased them and turning away one should murmur thrice the (formula which) wipes off sins. Then he should recite »What of me ...«, and »Ancestors, give us houses filled with riches and grains.« (?) Having put down the pots for the rice-balls and the Kuśa-grass (? *sapavitraka*), he murmured »They carry vigour ...« and gave water from the river Kokā and ice-milk (?) and sesamum with honey for the satisfaction of the ancestors. After »*svasti*« had been said, satisfying them[16] with ancestral rites on a Sunday. After giving silver as a sacrificial gift to the Brahmins, the wielder of the club (= Viṣṇu) gave a share to the human beings; and they said »*svat*« (?). (v. 84cd:) Asking »Has it been achieved?«[17] and receiving their reply[18] he told them to be comfortable. He asked for the left-over food ...[19] Taking the ancestral Brahmins in his hand, he should put them outside the sacrificial platform, reciting »*vāje vāje* ...«.

87–91ab By the water of ten millions of holy places, throwing his untied full hair (tail?) to the right, he asked a blessing, saying: »Donors shall accrue to us ...«, circumambulated them, revered (their) feet, gave seats to them and spread them out. (He told them) to rest while he entered and seized the middle *piṇḍa* (?). Chāyāmayī, the earth, was his wife; to her the Lord gave the rice-ball. Saying »The ancestors shall make (me) pregnant«, she took the rice-ball and revered the feet of the Brahmins.

[15] i.e. ancestors of the fourth, fifths and sixth degree who are offered food collected by wiping the vessel.

[16] Thus VePr; v. 83b in ASS seems to be more corrupt.

[17] According to ed. Veṅk.

[18] i.e. that of the ancestral sages?

[19] v. 85d unclear.

91cd–98ab (Then) the boar wanted to dismiss the ancestors. Kokā and the ancestors addressed him, telling him (v. 92cd–98ab) that they had been cursed by the moon for having fallen from Yoga. They had been saved from entering the nether world (*rasātala*), but wanted the All-Gods to protect them again, to ascend to heaven, Soma (the firm foundation of Yoga) to be their godhead and saviour, their dwelling because of Yoga (according to Yoga ?) to be in heaven, on earth, or in the intermediate space; some of them (?) to prosper for a month, and Ūrjā, called Svadhā, who had ascended to (was endowed with ?) Yoga, the mother of Yoga, moving in the air, to be their wife.[20]

98cd–107ab Thus addressed, Viṣṇu replied (v. 99cd–113ab) that everything would happen as they had said: Yama would be their deity, Soma (= moon) should be called their Veda-recitation (?), Agni their sacrifice (?); fire, wind and sun their places; Brahman, Viṣṇu, Rudra their superiors (*adhipuruṣa*); they would assume the forms of Ādityas, Vasus and Rudras; they would be Yogins with Yoga-bodies, carrying Yoga, would move at will, allot effects (of actions) to beings (?) in heavens, in hells, on earth; they would fulfil themselves by their Yoga-power; Ūrjā would become Dakṣa's daughter Svadhā and as such be their wife; as Kokā she would be extremely pure with ten millions of holy places (or: as holy as ...), where he (i.e. Viṣṇu) would reside.

107cd–109ab From this time onwards to look at Varāha (the boar) and worship (him) would grant enjoyment and liberation; Kokā's water would destroy grave sins; bathing at the holy places and fasting would grant heaven; giving alms would destroy birth, death, old age.

109cd–113ab The ancestors should stay at the mouth of Kokā for five days during the light half of the month Māgha. He who performed the ancestral rites at that time would receive the above-mentioned fruit. On the 11th and 12th day he himself would stay there; any who fasted (or: dwelt) there would obtain the above-mentioned fruit. The ancestors should go there; he himself would stay there. After these words he (the boar) disappeared.

113cd–115 When the boar had left, the ancestors also went away; Kokā and her place(s) of pilgrimage stayed on the Himālaya (king of mountains). Chāyā, the sow which is the earth, was pregnant from the boar; the demon Naraka Bhauma (i.e. son of Bhūmi, earth) was born from her; the city Prāgjyotiṣa was given to him by Viṣṇu.

116 Conclusion to (the account of) Viṣṇu's appearance as the divine boar at the mouth of Kokā; phalastuti: he who listens to it is freed from evil and obtains the merit of ten horse-sacrifices.[21]

[20] The meaning of »Yoga« in this context is not altogether clear.

[21] In Upajāti-metre.

Ch. 220: Prescriptions for ancestral rites; their effects[1]

1 The hermits request to be told more extensively about the Śrāddhakalpa (i.e. rules for ancestral rites), how, where, when, in which places and by means of which (substances) (the rites should be performed).

2 Vyāsa announces his reply exactly to their questions.

3–4 Śrāddha is to be performed along with (vedic) prayer-formulas by Brahmins, Kṣatriyas and Vaiśyas[2] who follow their family customs. By women, low castes and Śūdras it is to be given according to the instructions of the twice-born, without (vedic) prayer-formulas and without offerings into fire.

5–7 Places for ancestral rites: Places of pilgrimage like Puṣkara etc., mountain tops, rivers, confluences, the seven oceans, one's own house, under trees, in sacrificial ponds.

8–10ab Forbidden places: Among the Kirātas, Kaliṅgas, Koṅkanas, among the Kṛmis, among the Daśārṇas, the Kumārīs, Taṅgaṇas and Krathas; on the northern shores of the ocean, on the southern bank of the Narmadā, east of Karatoyā.

0cd–11ab Recommended times: Each month at new moon; at full moon, in (a new?) lunar mansion.

11cd–13 Kinds of ancestral rites: Obligatory (*nitya*) (with human being, without gods); occasional (*naimittika*, with gods); optional (*kāmya*, performed annually, with twice-born); *vṛddhiśrāddha* (on the occasion of birth rites etc., for which an even number of Brahmins are to be called)

14–22ab Effects of ancestral rites during the 15 days when the sun is in Virgo (*kanyā*):[3]

1st day:	wealth
2nd day:	bipeds
3rd day:	sons
4th day:	destruction of enemies
5th day:	good fortune, beauty (*śrī*)
6th day:	honour
7th day:	lordship over troups (perhaps Śiva's entourage)
8th day:	intelligence
9th day:	women
10th day:	fulfilment of all desires
11th day:	all Vedas
12th day:	victory
13th day:	growth of progeny, cattle, wisdom, independence, prosperity, long life, sovereignty
14th day:	satisfaction for ancestors who have died young or have been killed with a weapon
15th day (new moon):	all desires, endless stay in heaven

[1] For a concordance of this chapter with parallel and comparable texts, cf. Appendix 16 at the end of the introduction to this volume.

[2] *svavaraṇoditam*?, for *svavarṇa-uditam* »prescribed for their own castes«.

[3] For v. 15–22ab, cf. MkP 33.1–8ab.

22cd–31ab Duration of satiation of ancestors:[4]

22cd–23ab Announcement of what is to be given to please the ancestors.

23cd–28ab

Duration of satiation:	Substance offered:
1 month	sacrificial food
2 months	meat of fish
3 months	deer meat
4 months	hare meat
5 months	bird meat
6 months	pork
7 months	goat meat
8 months	meat of black antelope
9 months	meat of *ruru*-antelope
10 months	cow meat (beef)
11 months	mutton
12 months, one year	cow's milk, milk-rice

28cd–29 Rhinoceros-meat ... ,[5] spinach (*kālaśāka* ?), honey and Rohita-meat (horse, deer, fish?) provide everlasting satisfaction and sons.[6]

30–31ab Performance of ancestral rites at Gayā; he who gives sesamum mixed with molasses, honey or (food) mixed with honey – all that is indestructible.

31cd–32ab (Words of the ancestors?)[7] Is there perhaps someone born in our family who would give us a handful of water, milk-rice with honey during the rainy season and in the (Nakṣatra) Maghā?

32cd One should wish for many sons so that one at least may go to Gayā.[8]

33ab One (of them) should offer a virgin Gaurī (female of *bos gaurus*) or let loose a blue bull.[9]

33cd–42 Effects of ancestral rites in the (28) different lunar mansions:[10]

name of mansion:	effect:
Kṛttikā	heaven
Rohiṇī	offspring
The »auspicious one«[11]	brilliance

[4] For v. 22cd–30ab, cf. MkP 32.1–8.

[5] ASS *loham*; VePr *salloha*; the passage is corrupt; one syllable is missing in *vārdhrīṇa* (for *vārdhrīṇasa*).

[6] cf. MBh 13,88.9–10.

[7] cf. MBh 13,88.12.

[8] cf. MBh 13,88.14ab.

[9] For the whole verse cf. MtP 207.40; other texts read *yajeta vāśvamedhena* in place of *gaurīṃ vāpy udvahet kanyām*; cf. Kane, HDhŚ IV, p. 539.

[10] For this section, cf. MkP 33.8cd–16; the corresponding passage in MBh 13.89 deviates in wording, construction and contents.

[11] *Saumya*, i.e. Mṛgaśiras = Orion.

Ārdrā	heroism
Punarvasu	fields
Puṣya	wealth
Āśleṣa	long life
Maghā	offspring (subjects), prosperity
Phālgunī	good fortune (*saubhāgya*)
Uttarā-(Phālgunī)	offspring, munificence (?)[12]
Hasta	learning
Citrā	beauty, brilliance, offspring
Svātī	profit in business
Viśākhā	son(s)
Anurādhā	political power, imperial rule (*cakravartitām*)
Jyeṣṭhā	sovereignty
Mūla	health
Āṣāḍhā	fame
Uttarā-(Āṣāḍhā)	freedom from grief
Śravaṇa	pleasant worlds
Dhaniṣṭhā	wealth
Abhijit	knowledge of the Vedas
Vāruṇa (= Śatabhiṣaj)	perfection in medicine
Prauṣṭhapadyā	sheep and goats
Uttarā-(Prauṣṭhapadyā)	cows
Revatī	metal
Aśvinī	horses
Bharaṇī	life

42 Conclusion: These are the results obtained in the various lunar mansions; therefore optional ancestral rites (offerings) should be given according to the rules.

43–60 Auspicious dates for ancestral rites:[13]

43–48ab Appraisal of ancestral rites when the sun is in Virgo (*kanyā*);[14] it should be performed for the Nāndīmukha-ancestors[15], at full moon as the boar had said. The ancestors then desire rice-balls;[16] those 16 days Nārāyaṇa proclaimed to be equal to (?) sacrifices. Whoever desires the results of a royal consecration ceremony (*rājasūya*) and horse-sacrifice should offer water, vegetable, roots etc. to the ancestors at that time.

8cd–49ab Worship of ancestors when the sun is in Uttarāhasta grants sojourn in heaven.

9cd–50ab When the sun is in Hasta the city of ancestors is empty by order of the king of ancestors (= Yama ?) as long as Scorpio (*vṛścika*) appears.

0cd–51ab When Scorpio has passed the ancestors sigh and return with the gods (?) giving a hard curse.

[12] Ve. *pradānaśīla*, ASS *pradhāna-*.

[13] This passage (up to v. 67) seems to have no parallel in MkP or MBh.

[14] cf. above, v. 14.

[15] cf. below, v. 67.

[16] Construction not clear.

51cd–54 Ancestral rites are to be performed on the eighth days and on the Manvantarā-days (?), on the ninth days (?) it is desirable for the mothers; it is to be performed on the days when the sun passes to a new constellation (*saṃkrānti*); at those times ancestral rites are to be performed without (offering of) rice-balls.

55 On the 3rd of Vaiśākha and the 9th of Kārttika (during the bright halves) ancestral rites should be performed as on passage-days (*saṃkrānti*).

56 On the 13th of Bhādrapada and on the new-moon day of Māgha ancestral rites should be performed with milk-rice as when (the sun is) on its southern course.

57 When a qualified Brahmin enters the house, ancestral rites should be performed by him.

58 When one obtains the required substances one should perform ancestral rites as on Parvan-days (change of phases of moon).

59 They should be performed for mother and father, sonless paternal uncle, and elder brother on the anniversary of their death.

60 Ancestral rites on Parvan-days include (rites for the) gods (?), the individual rites are without gods: Two when with regard to gods, three at ancestral rituals, or one each in both cases.[17]

61ab By analogy everything has also been explained for the female ancestors (or, ancestors on the mother's side?).

61cd–62ab The rice-ball, water, sesamum, Kuśa-grass for the deceased should be put on the earth, outside, near water.

62cd On the third day the bones of the deceased should be collected by Brahmins.

63 Brahmins are purified on the 10th day, Kṣatriyas on the 12th, Vaiśyas on the 15th, Śūdras after one month.

64–66 At the end of the period of impurity the individual ancestral rite (i.e. for one individual recently deceased, *ekoddiṣṭa*) is prescribed, on the 12th day, after (?) a month, three fortnights, and then every month for one year; afterwards the investiture to the line of ancestors (lit. »making them share the Piṇḍa«) is performed. Afterwards the deceased is called Pārvaṇa; then the »deceased« (*preta*) has become an »ancestor« (*pitṛ*).

67a-f There are two kinds of ancestors, with form and without form; the formless are Nāndīmukha-ancestors, the ones with form Pārvaṇa; those who eat the individual ancestral rite are (called) »deceased« (*preta*); thus the ancestors are threefold.

68 The hermits want to know how the ancestral investiture-ceremony is to be performed.

69ab Vyāsa announces the topic.[18]

69cd–70 Brief characterization of the ceremony: Without gods, with one welcoming oblation(-vessel ?) (*argha*), one grass-ring (?, *pavitraka*), not to be given into fire, without invocation (*āvāhana*), while wearing the sacred thread upon the right shoulder (*apasavyam*), including feeding of an uneven number of Brahmins.

71 There is another peculiarity relating to the monthly rite to which the hermits should listen (announcement).

[17] Probably referring to the number of Brahmins to be invited on those occasions.

[18] For the passage 220.69–100ab cf. MkP 30.18cd–31.18.

72-73 One should prepare four pots with sesamum, scents, waters, three for the ancestors, one for the deceased; one should pour the offering from the pot of the deceased into the other three, reciting »those who are the same ... »; the rest is performed as before.

74 The individual ancestral rites (*ekoddiṣṭa*) are the same for women; however, there is no ancestral investiture ceremony if there is no son.

75 For a woman the rite is to be performed by men every year; for the ancestors it is to be performed on the anniversary of death.

76 If there is no son (the rite) should be performed by those entitled to share the rice-balls (i.e. the father); if there are none, by brothers (of the deceased person), or by sons of sons, and by their sons.

77-78ab For the maternal grandfather the sons of their daughters may equally perform it; one who is descended from two[19] may honour maternal and paternal ancestors even by »occasional« ancestral rites (on special occasions).

8cd-80ab If all those are lacking, women may perform the rite without recitation of vedic verses for their brothers. If they are lacking, the king should have all the rites[20] performed for those without family by men of the same caste (*jāti*); because the king is related to all castes (*varṇa*).

80cd Conclusion to obligatory (*nitya*) and occasional (*naimittika*) ancestral rites.

81ab Announcement of another obligatory and occasional rite (?).[21]

1cd-82ab The New-Moon-offering (*darśa*) one should know to be a special rite; it is connected with the vanishing of the moon. Obligatory (*nitya*) means a particular (determined) time at which one should act as described.[22]

82cd-86 After the investiture-ceremony of the father, his great-grandfather goes to (the state of one) eating the remnants and disappears from (participation in) the ancestral rice-balls, for always the fourth of those (i.e. the ancestors), being different from them, becomes a »remnant-eater«. Those beginning with the grandfather of the grandfather share the remnants. Those mentioned in the beginning are three, the »sacrificer« (*yajamāna*) being the seventh.

87-89ab Beyond that range from »sacrificer« to »eaters of remnants« are all others born before, living in hells, born as animals or ghosts, etc. Announcement regarding the offerings by which they prosper.

9cd-97ab Food strewn on earth benefits Piśācas; spilled washing water benefits trees; spilled particles of perfume benefit ancestors reborn as gods; water fallen on earth when the rice-balls are lifted up benefits animals; water dripping from Brahmins who rinse the mouth or wash their feet benefits toothless children, who are excluded from rites and Yoga (*kriyāyoga* ?), and all those bereft of their rights due to affliction. Thus, anything spilled while giving food or water to Brahmins, pure or defiled, benefits those of the family who have been reborn.

7cd-98ab From offerings by means of unlawfully collected wealth Cāṇḍālas, Pulkasas, etc. benefit.

[19] i.e. by adoption?

[20] i.e. beginning from the carrying (of the corpse to the funeral pyre), *vāhādyāḥ*?

[21] After this announcement MkP starts the new ch. 31.

[22] Construction of this passage is unclear.

98cd–100ab Thus, satisfaction of many is achieved by sprinkling water; therefore ancestral rites should be performed devotedly even with potherbs; no-one perishes in a family where ancestral rites are performed.

100cd–101ab The ancestral offering is to be given (i.e. deposited?) among Brahmins (i.e. by feeding them?) who are self-controlled, maintain the sacred fires, are clean and knowledgeable.

101cd–102ab List of qualifications of a Brahmin or enumeration of such qualified Brahmins:[23] One who has thrice kindled the Nāciketa-fire; one who knows the three Madhu- and the three Suparṇa-verses;[24] one who knows the six branches (of vedic science); one who is devoted to the parents; a nephew (sister's son); one who knows the Sāmaveda.

102cd One should feed a sacrificial priest, a family priest, a scholar (*ācārya*), a teacher (*upādhyāya*).

103–104 List of Brahmins to be employed in the ancestral rites (continued from above): Maternal uncle, father-in-law; son-in-law; brother-in-law, Droṇapāṭhaka (?), a Brahmin well-versed in *maṇḍalas* (? *maṇḍalabrāhmaṇa*), one experienced in the meaning of Purāṇas, one who is without and one who is delighted with *kalpa* (sacred precepts concerning the ritual) (*akalpa*, *kalpasaṃtuṣṭa*), one without a wife.

105 Those mentioned above should be invited a day in advance; one should employ them in rites relating to gods as well as ancestral rites (?).[25]

106–109ab Ancestral rites are to be performed by those who are restrained (i.e. abstinent). The ancestors of one who has sexual intercourse before performing the rites or after (while?) offering it or eating (at it)[26] will lie in his semen for one month; the ancestors of one who eats at an ancestral rite after approaching a woman and of one who goes (to a woman afterwards?) live on semen and urine for one month. Therefore the invitation should (v.l. not) be carried out in advance (first) by the prudent. As long as (?) the day has not passed, those who have contact with women are to be avoided.

109cd–112ab One should feed those ascetics who come begging, also Yogins;[27] they are to be honoured because the ancestors have Yoga as their basis (i.e. are connected with Yoga).[28] If among thousands of Brahmins there is one Yogin, he saves the sacrificer and the guests like a boat.

112cd–116ab A traditional verse of the ancestors of Aila,[29] inquiring when a son would be born in their family who would feed them with balls of foods made of leftovers from what a Yogin has eaten, and who would offer a ball of food and rhinoceros-meat at Gayā, since potherbs, butterfat with sesamum and mixed grain (*kṛsara*) serve for their satisfaction, and since they desire rhinoceros-meat (without horn), which is the best offering in connection with the All-Gods and Soma.

[23] cf. MBh 13,90.20–21ab, and MkP 31.23cd and 25ab.

[24] RV 1,90.6–8; 10,114.3–5.

[25] For the passage 220.105–110ab cf. MkP 31.30–35ab.

[26] i.e. the restriction is valid for those who perform the rite as well as those who are invited to attend it?

[27] For the passage 220.110cd–120ab, cf. MkP 32.29–38.

[28] cf. 219.92ff.

[29] cf. MBh 13,88.11–12.

16cd–117ab One should offer ancestral rites on the 13th of Māgha during the southern course (of the sun, i.e. in winter) with honey, butterfat, milk-rice.

17cd–118ab Therefore one should honour one's ancestors devotedly when desiring all (kinds of) wishes (and) freedom from evil.

18cd–120ab Ancestors who are satisfied please the Vasus, Rudras, Ādityas, lunar mansions, planets, and stars. They grant life, offspring, wealth, knowledge, heaven, liberation etc.

120cd With regard to ancestors, the afternoon excels the first half of the day.[30]

121–123 One should formally welcome the Brahmins and dismiss them after the rite and the meal with kind words, accompanying them to the door. Then one should perform the obligatory (daily) rites, and serve the guests.

124–125ab Points of disagreement among authorities: Some demand the obligatory rites for the ancestors, some do not; the rest is the same. Some demand (the rite) separately, some as described above.

125cd Then a man should eat together with his dependants etc.

126 Conclusion: A man knowing *dharma* should perform the ancestral rites in such a way that the Brahmins are content.

127ab Announcement (of an account) of disqualified Brahmins who are to be avoided:

127cd–135 List of physical and moral defects which make a Brahmin a »defiler of the row« (i.e. of invited guests eating at an ancestral rite).[31]

136–138 Negative effects of serving unsuitable guests.

139–140 Admonition to donate clothes on the occasion of an ancestral rite.

141–145 The food given to Brahmins reaches the deceased soul (*jantu*) just like the calf finds its mother. Name and lineage and formulas direct the food given (?). Satisfaction follows them even after death. By threefold repetition of a (special) prayer-formula (quoted as v. 143) the ancestors come and the demons flee; this formula saves.

146–147 List of kinds of cloth to be given and not to be given.[32]

148 If any one of the ancestors is still alive, he is not offered a food-ball (*piṇḍa*) but is served food.

149–151 The food-ball is to be put into fire; the middle one should be given to the wife by someone who desires offspring. Somebody wishing for lustre should give the food-ball to cows; someone wishing offspring (or subjects), fame and renown should put it in water; for long life it is to be given to crows, for a house (full of?) boys to cocks.

152 Some Brahmins teach the lifting up of food-balls at the beginning; it is (at least) permitted to do so by the Brahmins.

153 One should perform the rite as taught by the sages. Otherwise it is a mistake and does no good to the ancestors.

[30] For the passage v. 120cd–126, cf. MkP 31.36–63ab.

[31] For the contents, cf. MBh 13,90.5–17 and MkP 31.27–29 (there are, however, no literal parallels).

[32] Continued from v. 140?

154–188 *Prescriptions concerning articles to be employed and to be avoided*

154–167 List of grains, pulses, fruits, sweets, milk products, spices, flowers, scents to be employed in the rite.

168–177 List of pulses, kinds of milk, fruits, kinds of meat, spices, vegetables to be avoided.

178–185ab Unpleasant, tasteless etc. food should not be given; delicious, tasty, moderately spiced etc. food should be given.

185cd–188ab Kinds of meat to be employed, partly on Manu's authority.

188cd Conclusion.

189ab He who eats what has been forbidden (by Vyāsa, the first-person narrator) will go to the hell Raurava.

189cd–204 *Prescriptions concerning food forbidden during ancestral rites*

189cd–190ab Announcement of what has been forbidden by the boar; it should neither be eaten by Brahmins, nor be given to the ancestors.

190cd–193ab List of animals whose meat is forbidden.

193cd–195ab He who provides that (food, meat) will go to the hell Raurava; he who offers it to the ancestors makes them fall from heaven into hell.

195cd–197 List of forbidden meat, vegetables, fruits.

198–200ab He who gives those to the ancestors goes to the hell Pūyavaha. Therefore one should not eat what has been forbidden by the boar; rather one should eat one's own flesh.

200cd–203ab If one has eaten something forbidden unknowingly or by mistake, one should expiate for it by eating a mixture of fruit, root(s), curds, milks, buttermilk mixed with water, cow urine, and barley every day for seven days; this purifies the body, especially in the case of devotees of Viṣṇu.

203cd–204 Thus, one should avoid what is forbidden and perform the ancestral rite according to one's ability; thereby one pleases the whole world.

205–209 *Prescriptions concerning special cases of ancestral rites*

205 The hermits want to know how the ritual is to be performed as long as the father is still alive.

206 Vyāsa replies that the son should offer to the same three generations as the father.

207 The hermits request to know about ancestral rites in the case where the father has died before the grandfather.

208–209 Vyāsa answers that one should offer a food-ball (*piṇḍa*) to the father and the great-grandfather but food to the grandfather. There is no ancestral investiture ceremony and no Pārvaṇa ceremony.

210 He who performs the ancestral rites will prosper in life, wealth and sons.

211 Phalastuti: The ancestors of him who reads this text (»the nectar of ancestral offering«, according to VePr) during an ancestral rite eat his food for three Yugas.

212 Conclusion and instruction to listen to and recite this text during ancestral rites.[33]

[33] In Indravajrā-metre.

Ch. 221: On the proper conduct[1]

1-3 Vyāsa concludes his report on how a good householder should honour gods, ancestors, and living beings (guests, beggars, animals, etc.) with offerings and food. By neglecting these rites one will experience evil.

4-5 The hermits confirm that they have been told about the three kinds of actions (obligatory, occasional, voluntary); they want to hear about the proper conduct by which one achieves happiness in this world and the next.

6-7 Vyāsa begins by commending proper conduct for the householder; sacrifices, alms-giving, asceticism are of no avail without proper conduct.

8ab A man of bad conduct does not live long (ed. Veṅk.: A man of proper conduct lives as long as Brahman).

8cd The characteristic of proper conduct is the observance of *dharma*.

9 Announcement of a description of proper conduct.

10 The householder should pursue the three goals of life.

11-16 On the pursuit of profit (*artha*) and pleasure (*kāma*):

11-12 With one quarter one should further one's well-being in the other world; half one should spend on one's support and on the obligatory and occasional rites; with one quarter one should increase one's capital. By such conduct one's wealth is secured.

13 Similarly a wise man should observe *dharma* for the sake of avoiding evil. Another duty is the profit of others, which may also grant success.

14-15 Pleasure and the other (goals of life) do not contradict (each other), except when there is fear of offence (?); pleasure which does not contradict the three goals of life is of two kinds. One should consider all the mutual connections (among the goals of life; *anubandha*?).

16 *Dharma* grants profit in connection with *dharma*; it does not hurt one's own interests. Concerning both (i.e. the two motifs?), pleasure (*kāma* n. ?) is twofold; and by that again those two (i.e. *dharma* and *artha*) are twofold (?).[2]

17-112 *Prescriptions concerning daily routines*

17 One should get up early in the pursuit of *dharma* and wealth, sip water, and bathe.

18 The morning worship (*saṃdhyā*) should be performed before the stars fade, the evening worship before the sun sets.

19 Untruth should be avoided.

20 One should pour a libation (*homa*) in the morning and in the evening. One should not look at the sun while it is rising or setting.

21 Combing of hair, cleaning of teeth, applying of ointment, offerings to the gods should be done before noon.

22 List of places forbidden for defecating and urinating.

[1] For this chapter (the last six verses excepted), cf. MkP Ch. 34-35; for a concordance see Appendix 17 at the end of the introduction of this volume.

[2] The passage v. 13-16 is not quite clear; allusions to the necessity of considering one's own as well as the other's profit?

23 One should not look at someone else's wife naked, nor at one's own excrements; one should not look at, touch or speak with a woman during her menstrual period.

24ab One should not defecate or have intercourse in water.

24cd–25 One should not step on urine, feces, hair, ashes, ... (*sapālikāḥ* ?), on spread out chaff of grain or coal, nor on ropes or cloth etc.; not on cloth (clothes) spread out on the path or the ground.

26–30 The householder may eat after offering to ancestors, gods, humans, and (other) beings. One should eat facing east or north, after sipping water, (putting the food) between the knees (i.e. sitting cross-legged on the floor?). One should not find fault with the food; one should avoid too much salt, and leftovers. One should not urinate or defecate while walking or standing up. One should never eat leftovers. After eating (before cleansing properly) one should not speak, recite, look at the sun, the moon, the stars.

31 A broken seat, bedstead or vessel are to be avoided; one should offer a seat to the teacher, honouring him by standing up etc.

32 A wise man should speak (to the teacher?) agreeably, accompany him, do nothing disagreeable.

33 One should not eat or worship dressed in just one garment, nor invite twice-born nor offer into fire.

34 A man should never bathe or lie down naked; he should not scratch his head with both hands.

35 One should not continously wash one's head; one should not touch any limb with oil after washing the head.

36 Among all those who are uneducated one should avoid reciting (sacred texts); one should never despise Brahmins, fire, cows, or the sun.

37 Urinating and defecating should be done facing north during the day, facing south during the night; in distress as one likes.

38 One should not talk about a teacher's wrongs, should appease his wrath and not listen to others maligning him.

39–40ab One should yield the path to Brahmins, a king, a distressed person, a knowledgeable person, a pregnant woman, a rich, deaf, blind, mute or drunken and intoxicated (or insane) person.

40cd–41ab One should circumambulate a temple, a Caidya-tree (?),[3] an intersection of roads, and a knowledgeable teacher.

41cd One should not wear clothes etc. used by others.

42 On the 8th, 14th and 15th day of each half-month one should not apply oil to the body, and should avoid sexual intercourse.

43 One should never stand with raised legs or arms, nor with feet spread apart or with one foot upon the other.

44 One should abstain from scolding and calumny, and from striking the vulnerable points (*marman*) of a courtesan,[4] of a child who has accomplished something, or of someone fallen (?).

[3] Error for *caityataru*, cf. MkP 34.41, »a fig-tree standing on a sacred spots.«

[4] MkP reads v. 44ab after 40ab.

45ab One should not display haughtiness or severity (sharpness).

cd–46ab One should not mock at fools, insane or addicted persons, at the ugly, the disfigured, or the poor.

46cd One should not take the stick to another's pupil or son for the sake of teaching.

47ab One should not sit down after pulling the seat with one's foot.

47cd One should not prepare wheat cake, *kṛśara* (a dish consisting of sesamum and grain) or meat for oneself.

ab–49ab One should eat in the morning and in the evening, after honouring one's guests. Facing east or north, silently, one should always clean one's teeth. One should avoid plants which are to be avoided.

cd–50ab One should never sleep with one's head pointing north or west, but pointing east[5] or south[6]

50cd–52 One should not lie (ed. Veṅk. »bathe«) in perfumed water, and not at dawn; on an eclipse only daytime is mentioned for bathing (?). One should not wipe the limbs with the ends of one's garment; one should not shake hair or one's garments (?) with the hands; one should not remove both garments (at a time). The wise never apply ointment except after bathing.

53–54 One should never wear red garments nor many-coloured or black ones; one should not change around the two garments or the two ornaments. To be avoided are garments without border, ragged, full of insects or hairs, or gazed at by dogs.

55 To be avoided is meat licked by a dog, spoilt by taking out the sap (?), taken from the back, taken at random, or meat which is to be avoided (*sic*).

56 One should not eat visible (?, *pratyakṣam*) salt; to be avoided is what has been stored for a long time, what has dried up or become stale (or: been kept over night).

57 Some kinds (preparations?) of what has been ground, of vegetables, of sugarcane, and milk, and some kinds of meat need not be avoided even if stored for a long time.

58ab One should not lie down at sunrise or sunset.

cd–60ab A man should not eat unbathed, not after resting, not while thinking of something else, not sitting on a bed, nor on the earth, not while speaking, not until the servants have been given (their share). One should eat after bathing, in the mornings and evenings, as prescribed.

cd–62ab A prudent man should not approach another's wife; this destroys life and all religious merit; there is nothing more detrimental to life.

cd–64ab Rites involving a god, fire, or ancestors, and salutation of the teacher should be performed after sipping water; similarly eating. One should respectfully sip only pure water while facing east or north.

cd–65ab (For cleaning oneself) one should avoid earth from inside water, from a dwelling, an ant-hill, a mouse-hole, and what was left after cleaning (by others?).

cd–67ab After washing and sprinkling oneself one should sip three or four times holding the hand between the knee (i.e. in squatting position); having cleansed (wiped) the apertures (of the body) and the head twice by turning it twice (?), having properly sipped water, one may then perform actions (or rites) as one who is pure.

[5] i.e. »Indra's direction«.

[6] »Agastya's direction«; cf. e.g. BrP 118.2; Pargiter, however, seems to ascribe the north-eastern direction to Agastya (translation of MkP, p. 175).

67cd–69 After sneezing, licking (*avalīḍhe*), breaking wind, spitting etc., one should perform sipping; after touching what should not be touched[7] (one should) look at the sun. Or one should seize the right ear; for this is within everyone's capacity; the latter applies in case the former is absent; and if the first-mentioned is not available, attainment of the latter is acceptable (?).

70 One should not gnash the teeth, nor beat one's own body; in sleep, on the way, or while eating one should avoid recitation (*svādhyāya*).

71 At twilight (one should avoid)[8] sexual intercourse and departure; and in the afternoon one should satisfy the ancestors.

72 Bathing of the head, and ancestral and divine (rites?) one should perform facing east and north. One should let (others) do the beard (the shaving?).

73 One should avoid a disfigured girl; rather one should marry a healthy girl of good family who is seventh and fifth from father and mother (i.e. by degree of relation?).

74 One should protect one's wife, avoid jealousy, sleep, intercourse during the day; avoid action which makes others suffer and avoid all pain to living beings.

75 Women of all castes in their menstrual period are to be avoided for four nights, for the sake of preventing the birth of a girl for a fifth (night).

76 On the sixth night one should approach (a woman), preferably on even nights;[9] on even nights sons are conceived, girls on uneven nights.

77 The wise should avoid those without *dharma* at the beginning of a half-month, eunuchs at twilight, a destitute woman[10] during shaving.

78 One should not listen to those who speak ill-mannered things. One should not offer an eminent seat to one who is not eminent.

79 On the occasion of shaving, of a death (*anta* ?),[11] of enjoying a woman, the wise should bathe with his clothes on at a secluded place.

80–81ab One should not reproach or ridicule gods, Vedas, Brahmins, good and truthful people, the teacher.

81cd–82ab One should wear white, auspicious clothes and white flowers as ornament.

82cd–84 A learned man (*paṇḍita*) should not keep friendship with (e.g.) fools, people of improper birth (*jāti*), those without property, or intent only on dispute.

85–86 One should stand up in the company of friends, initiated people, kings, etc.; one should honour them when they come to one's house; those who visit every year should be honoured according to their status.

87–88 One should worship and offer into the fire first to Brahman, then to Prajāpati; thirdly to those connected with the house (i.e. the ancestors?), then to Kaśyapa; then to Anumati, then the domestic oblation (*gṛhabali*).

89–94 One should perform the worship of the All-Gods as previously mentioned; indicating the gods separately one should give to Parjanya, the waters and the earth, to Vāyu (= wind) and to all directions, to Brahman, to the intermediate space, and

[7] The MkP reads »one should touch a cow's back.«

[8] If v. 71ab is construed with 71cd rather than with v. 70cd, it would contain a prescription rather than a prohibition.

[9] Construction?

[10] ?, *riktā* may mean the 4th, 9th, 14th day of the lunar fortnight.

[11] Or: at the end of shaving and enjoying a woman.

to Sūrya (= the sun), to the All-Gods, all beings, to Uṣas (?), to the Lord of beings towards the north; uttering *svadhā* one should give to the ancestors towards the south. Turning towards the north-west one should say: »This illness is for you« (?) and give water mixed with leftover grain (or food). Then one should bow to gods and Brahmins.

95-100 The line above the thumb of the right hand is called »holy place of Brahman« for sipping; the line between thumb and forefinger is known as »holy place of ancestors«; with that one should give to ancestors except those of the Nāndīmukha category. In front[12] of the thumb[13] is the »holy place of gods«. At the root of the little finger is the body of Prajāpati. Respective rites should be performed only with those holy spots (*tīrtha*). For the Nāndīmukha-ancestors one should perform the Piṇḍa-ceremony.

101 One should not carry fire and water simultaneously. One should not stretch out one's feet towards teachers, gods, ancestors, Brahmins.

102 One should not call a drinking cow, nor drink water from folded hands; one should not tarry at any pure periods of time; one should not blow at fire.

103-108 One should dwell only where there are: a payer of debts,[14] a doctor, a Brahmin learned in vedic lore, and a water-bearing river; a powerful king intent on *dharma*; law-abiding citizens; peaceful people; cultivators of the soil; all kinds of plants; not where there are people desirous of conquering, former enemies, or (people) continuously feasting; rather (one should dwell) where the king is unassailable, the earth fertile.

109 All this has been told by Vyāsa; he announces rules concerning food.

110 Food stored in oil for some time is edible; (?); in the case of wheat, barley and milk products, without oil (?).

111 List of edible animals (hare, tortoise, alligator, porcupine, fish); cock and pig are forbidden.

112 By eating meat that is left over from (rites directed towards) gods or ancestors, at a Brahmin's bidding, meat that is consecrated, or as medicine one is not polluted.

113-131ab *Prescriptions concerning cleaning*

113-114 List of materials and things to be cleaned with water (e.g. shell, stone, gold, ropes, clothes, fruits, hides, vessels, etc.).

115 Things made of stone are cleaned with water or by rubbing on stone, oily vessels with hot water.

116-117ab Things cleaned with mud and water (e.g. winnowing baskets, skins, mortar and pestle, clothes, things collected from consecration (?), and bark).

7cd-120ab Woollens and hair are cleaned with dregs of white mustard or with dregs of sesamum; damaged material and cotton is cleaned with water and ashes; wood,

[12] The location of these spots on the palm is not very obvious from what the text says (*uttarataḥ, antaḥ, agre*).

[13] *Aṅguli*, possibly to be distinguished from *aṅguṣṭha*.

[14] Or, a money-lender; the debts to be paid, however, might be those debts which regulate the orthodox life-style, viz. debts to the seers, the ancestors, the gods, human beings, etc.

teeth, bones, horns are cleaned by abrading. The uncleanness of earthen pots (is removed) by baking.

120cd–122 Pure things are alms, the hand of an artisan, articles of trade, the face (mouth) of a woman are pure;[15] knowledge of approach by road (?); what was prepared by servants; what has been formerly acclaimed; what is long past; what is easily entered by many; what is originated inside (?), what is young, what was performed by another old person; houses and dwellings at the end of a ritual; the two breasts of a woman.[16]

123–125ab Flowing waters without smell are pure; earth is purified in the course of time by burning, wiping, or a herd of cattle. After besmearing, scraping, sprinkling by wiping etc. a house is cleaned by sweeping etc. If there is a hair or an insect in the food, if it has been smelled by a cow or if flies have sat on it, earth, water and ashes should be thrown for purification.

125cd–127ab What is (made) of Udumbara(-wood) is purified by means of acid (vinegar?); tin or lead with water; brass by water and ashes; what is besmeared is cleaned with water and earth, and by removing the smell; from other substances as well one should remove colours and smells.

127cd–129ab Meat is pure if killed by a beast of prey or a Cāṇḍāla. Oil etc. which has come from the road,[17] and milk which has satisfied the cow are pure. Dust, fire, the shadow of horse or cow, wind, earth, drops, flies etc. are not affected by touching something polluted.

129cd–131ab Goat and horse are pure from in front, but not the face of a cow or calf.[18] Pure is what flows[19] from the mother; a bird is pure at the time fruits fall down (?); a seat, a bed, a vehicle, rivers at their banks, and grass are purified by wind and the rays of sun and moon, like articles of trade.

131cd–132ab Occasions for sipping: Leaving the road, eating (sneezing ?) and drinking; getting dressed.

132cd–133ab Purity of what has been touched (is achieved) by touching upon water and mud of two roads; a building of baked bricks by contact with wind.

133cd–134ab Of food which has been affected one should throw away the top, sip water and sprinkle the rest with water and mud.

134cd–135ab One who has eaten of what has been polluted (or been shared by someone polluted) should fast for three nights, if it happened unknowingly; if (it happened) knowingly, there is no way of compensating for such a fault.

135cd–136ab If one touches a woman in her menstrual period, of low caste, or in childbed, one should bathe; the same (is prescribed) for those who have carried a corpse.

136cd–137ab If one touches a moist (*sasneham* ?) human bone, one should bathe; one should sip, seize a cow or look at the sun if it was not moist.

137cd–138ab One should not leap over saliva or expectorations (*udvartana* ?); excrement and foot-water should be thrown out of the house.

[15] Or: the mouth of a venal young woman.

[16] Meaning and construction of this passage are quite unclear.

[17] i.e. was obtained from commercial producers or dealers?

[18] cf. Böhtlingk, Indische Sprüche, 2nd ed., no. 4508, quoted from Bṛhatsaṃhitā.

[19] Read *prasravaṇam* as in VePr.

3cd-139ab One should not bathe in the water of another, without having set aside five food-balls (*piṇḍa*). One should bathe in natural ponds, in the water of the Gaṅgā and in (other) large rivers.

cd-140ab One should not stand in gardens etc. at improper times; one should not talk to those hated by the people and to women without husband (*vīrahīna*).

cd-141ab If one touches or talks to those who repudiate gods, to blasphemers of ancestors, holy texts, sacrificers, renouncers etc., one is purified by looking at the sun.

cd-143ab The same is to be done by one who looks at a woman in her menstrual period, at an abandoned corpse, at one without *dharma*, a woman in childbed, a eunuch, persons without clothes, of low caste, or those who have carried a corpse, also those who have enjoyed another's wife.

3cd-146ab Bathing purifies one who has touched what must not be eaten; (one who has touched) a beggar, a heretic, a cat, donkey or dog; food of a dead person, of a Cāṇḍāla, of someone fallen or rejected (or, of a fallen or rejected Cāṇḍāla), or a woman in her menstrual period, and a village pig. The same with two men (dual!) who have been polluted by a woman in childbed.

6cd-149ab One should never omit the obligatory rites. Not performing them is taught only in case of stillbirth. A Brahmin should remain without offerings for ten days; a Kṣatriya should not do his work for twelve, a Vaiśya for half a month, a Śūdra for a month.

9cd-155ab *Prescriptions concerning ancestral rites*

9cd-152ab To a deceased person (*preta*) members of the same family (*gotra*) should give water outside on the 1st, the 4th, 7th and 9th day. The bones should be collected on the 4th day. After the collection touching of limbs (bodily contact) is prescribed (allowed?) (i.e. the period of pollution ends?). All rites after the collection (of bones) have to be performed by members of the same family. Touching of those sharing the food-balls (*piṇḍa*) on the day of death and two ...(?)

152cd-154 In the case of voluntary death, by hanging, burning, taking poison, by tormenting oneself (or burning, *pratāpa*), as well as in the case of death by fasting, in childhood, in a foreign country or after renunciation, purity is immediate. Impurity lasts for three days for relatives (*sapiṇḍa*) if a relative dies (also) after the death of the other (*mṛte anyasmin*)

155ab The purity of before (?) has been mentioned (reference back?); daily rites have to be performed thereafter.

155cd-158 Prescriptions concerning pollution due to childbirth. The same rule applies in the case of a birth for close and distant relatives. After the birth of a son the father should bathe with his clothes. If (one child) follows after the other, purity is by the days (counting) from the (birth of) the (child) born first; after 10 or 12 days, half a month or a month the castes may take up their respective duties again.

159-160 With regard to a deceased person the individual ancestral rite (*ekoddiṣṭa*) is then to be performed. Alms are to be given to Brahmins; one should give what one desires most, or cherishes most, to a qualified (Brahmin) if one wishes it to be imperishable.

161-169ab After completing the (respective number of) days, touching water with weapons and vehicles, giving rice-balls (*piṇḍas*) and water to the deceased, all castes have done their duty. They should act for their welfare here and in the world beyond; the triple sacred science (*trayī*) should be studied, wealth be acquired justly; sacrifices should be performed. One should do what is not disagreeable to oneself and what need not be hidden. To behave thus is the secret (granting) all good things in this world and the next. All castes follow these rules for reaching heaven. By knowing and observing them one is freed from all sins.

169cd Conclusion to this »extract of an extract« (?).

170a-f This teaching should not be given to everybody; excluded are unbelievers (*nāstikas*), evil-minded people, hypocrites, fools, and those who spread fallacious arguments.

Ch. 222: Rules for the conduct according to caste and stage of life[1]

1 The hermits want to hear specifically about the *dharma* of castes and stages of life (*āśrama*).

2–21 On caste regulations.

2 Vyāsa announces the topic of caste duties.

3–6 Duties of a Brahmin: He should be intent on alms-giving, compassion, asceticism, gods, sacrifices, recitation; he should always be supplied with water and guard the fire. For a living he should perform sacrifices and teach, and accept gifts. He should act for the benefit of all and keep friendship with all. He should consider as the same (i.e. be unconcerned about) a cow and the jewel belonging to someone else;[2] he should approach his wife only during her fertile days (*ṛtu*).

7–10 Duties of a Kṣatriya and king: He should give alms to Brahmins, should sacrifice and recite (vedic texts). He lives on his arms preferably by protecting the earth. By protecting the earth kings fulfil their duty; the protection of sacrifices etc. is incumbent on the king. He attains the worlds desired by chastising the wicked and guarding the good; the king maintains the castes.

11–12 Duties of a Vaiśya: Brahman assigned cattle-raising, trade, and agriculture as a living to the Vaiśya; he is entitled to study (vedic texts), sacrifice, alms-giving and *dharma*, and the observance of the obligatory and occasional rites.

13–14 Duties of the Śūdra: Work relating to the twice-born and subsistence thereby, as well as by wealth gained through trade or handicraft.[3] The Śūdra may give alms, sacrifice cooked food, and perform ancestral rites.

15–17 Duties common to all castes: Earning for the maintenance of dependents, intercourse with one's wife during her fertile days; compassion for all beings; forbearance; lack of self-conceit; truth; purity; a relaxed attitude, felicity; speaking pleasantly; friendliness; lack of envy, avarice, spite; equanimity.

[1] BrP 222.1–55 has a close parallel in ViP (ed. Veṅk.) 3,8.20–3,9.32; the dialogue there is between king Sagara and Aurva.

[2] ViP makes the point more clearly by reading *grāvṇi* for *gavi*, i.e. he should consider a stone and the jewel the same.

[3] The expected genitive reference to Śūdras is missing except in a verse found only in the VePr of ViP.

18 These qualities apply to all stages of life as well. Announcement of secondary duties.

19–20 In distress Brahmins may perform the work of Kṣatriyas or Vaiśyas, Kṣatriyas that of Vaiśyas; that of Śūdras is allowed to both (Kṣatriyas and Vaiśyas). If possible they should give it up; mixing of duties is to be avoided, except in distress.

21 Conclusion to the description of caste-duties and announcement of prescriptions for the stages of life.

22–27 Rules for the stage of a student (*brahmacārin*):[4] After initiation (sacred thread ceremony) a boy should live in the house of a teacher, serving the teacher, leading a pure life, learning the Veda, attending upon sun and fire at dusk and dawn, acting like the teacher, learning what he is told to learn, eating food he has begged, bathing in water in which the teacher has previously bathed, bringing fuel etc. every morning.

28–38 Rules for the stage of the householder:

28–31 When one has grasped the Veda, with the permission (of the teacher), one should enter the stage of a householder, obtain a wife as prescribed, earn money by one's work, worship the ancestors with offerings, the gods with sacrifices, guests with food, hermits with recitation, the Lord of beings with offspring, (other) beings with tributes, the whole world by speaking the truth.

32–35 The stage of the householder is supreme because those wandering celibates who live on alms depend on it. They learn the Veda, bathe at places of pilgrimage, wander around to see the earth, without house or food they stay where evening overtakes them. The householder is their support. When they come to his house he should offer welcome-gifts, speak pleasantly, offer seat and bed.

36 A guest who turns away from someone's house disappointed gives his own bad deeds to him and takes the other's merit.

37–38 In the house of a good householder there is no disrespect, selfishness, pride, quarrel or beating, misgivings. By acting accordingly the householder obtains the highest worlds.

39–44 Rules for the stage of the forest-dweller (*vanaprastha*): Towards the end of his life the householder who has fulfilled his duties may entrust his wife to their sons or may go with her to the forest. He should live on leaves, roots, and fruit, wear his hair and beard long, sleep on the ground, be everybody's guest, be dressed in hides and grass; he should perform three ablutions (at dawn, noon, and sunset), worship the gods and welcome all who come to him; begging and tributary offerings are prescribed; he may anoint his limbs with unguents from the forest; his austerity is the endurance of cold and heat. By this conduct he burns all his faults and gains eternal worlds.

45–54 Rules concerning the renouncer (*saṃnyāsin*):

45 Announcement.

46–54 He should give up all attachment to family and property, and all selfishness, all comforts of the three castes;[5] he should be friendly to all beings in words, thoughts and actions, and being restrained (*yukta*) give no offence. He may spend one night in a village, five nights in a town, in order to prevent the arising of likes and

[4] ViP begins a new chapter (3,9) here.

[5] In ViP »relating to the three goals of life.«

dislikes. For the maintenance of life he may beg at a time when the fire is extinguished and people have not eaten.[6] He should not be dejected if he gets nothing, nor rejoice if he gets something; his measure should be what suffices to continue life, while he should beware[7] of obtaining too much respect by which even a liberated ascetic is fettered. Lust, wrath, pride, greed, confusion etc. are to be abandoned; since he has given fearlessness to all, beings need not fear anything after his death.

55-56 The sage who sacrifices to the fire in his body through his mouth with oblations (i.e. the food) obtained as alms goes with the funeral fire to the worlds (beyond). If he follows this stage of liberation (*mokṣa*), and is restrained by resolved intellect (*saṃkalpitabuddhiyukta*), the twice-born will go to the world of Brahman, being at peace like a fire without fuel.[8]

Ch. 223: Rise and fall within the caste system (dialogue between Śiva and Umā)[1]

1-3 The hermits praise Vyāsa as omniscient; they want to know by what action one rises or falls in the range of castes.

4-6 Vyāsa relates that the same question was formerly put by the »daughter of the king of mountains« (= Umā) to Mahādeva (= Śiva) on a pleasant peak of the Himālaya.

7-22 On the change of castes:

7-11 Umā addresses Śiva (list of epithets) and asks how a Vaiśya becomes a Śūdra or a Kṣatriya, how a Brahmin becomes a Kṣatriya or the reverse, how a Brahmin and a Kṣatriya are reborn as a Śūdra, how the three (lower) castes can reach Brahminhood.

12-65 Śiva's answer.

12 Membership of the castes is by nature.

13-18 A Brahmin falls from his rank by wrong deeds. If a Kṣatriya or Vaiśya observes the *dharma* of Brahmins and takes over the functions of a Brahmin, he will thus become a Brahmin in the next birth. But if he gives up his Brahminhood and observes the *dharma* of Kṣatriyas he will be born as a Kṣatriya; similarly he becomes a Vaiśya, while as a Vaiśya he eventually becomes a Śūdra.

19-20 A Kṣatriya or a Vaiśya who gives up his own duties and observes those of Śūdras falls from his position and undergoes a mixing of castes; he becomes a Śūdra.

[6] According to ViP »have eaten.«

[7] Thus according to VePr; v. 51-52 have no parallel in ViP.

[8] In Upajāti-metre.

[1] With this chapter cf. MBh 13,131 and Viṣṇudharma, ed. Grünendahl, Ch. 57. In the MBh, this dialogue is transmitted only in the Northern recension (MBh 13,127-134; the Southern recension substitutes a different text). The chapter in ViDh is parallel in topic and outline, much less in terms of literal identity. For a concordance of the passages concerned, see Appendix to the text-volume.

21–22 The Śūdra who knowingly observes his duties obtains the fruit of *dharma*, as was mentioned by Brahman: the supreme Self and firm accomplishment are pursued by those whose desire is *dharma*.

23–27 Forbidden food and its effects: Hot food (or: food of a cruel person, of an Ugra), food prepared for a group, food from a death- or birth-rite (?), food announced (for someone else), food of a Śūdra must not be eaten. The latter has been censured by Brahman; it leads to rebirth as a Śūdra if one dies while it is in the stomach; one is reborn among those by whose food one has lived.

28–65 On the change of castes.

28–31 A Brahmin who eats forbidden food loses his rank; also one who (e.g.) drinks liquor, kills a Brahmin, steals, breaks his vows, is impure, gives up recitation, is lecherous, supports a courtesan, is supported by an adulterous woman, sells Soma, sleeps with the wife of his teacher, hates the teacher.

32–36 Śūdras may reach Brahminhood by being hospitable, by eating what is left by others.[2] He reaches the rank of Vaiśya by serving the higher castes, by honouring the gods, by approaching his wife only during her fertile days, by not eating meat lightly.

37–40 A Vaiśya becomes a Brahmin by speaking the truth, by not being egotistic, by equanimity, by skill in conciliation (*sāma-*),[3] by sacrificing and reciting, by honouring Brahmins, by lack of spite against other castes, by being a householder, eating (only) twice a day, by eating leftovers (i.e. after serving guest and god), by not being lustful or egotistic, by offering libations, by hospitality, by eating what is left over by others, by arranging three fires only.[4]

41–52ab Reborn as a Kṣatriya he becomes a Brahmin, if he undergoes the sacramental rites from birth onwards. He should perform generous sacrifices; should guard the three fires; should help the afflicted; protect the subjects; be truthful; strive to achieve the three goals of life; be bound by his duties (?); fix the sixth part as tribute; not support vulgar customs (*grāmyadharma*); be skilled in economic matters (*artha*); sleep with his wife only during her fertile days; fast regularly, recite, sleep always ...(*vahiskāntarite* ?) in his house; be hospitable, feed Śūdras; not act for his own gain or lust; serve ancestors, gods, guests, mendicants; offer libations to the fire twice a day. After dying in battle for the benefit of cows or Brahmins and entering the (world beyond), purified by the three fires and sacred formulas, he becomes a learned Brahmin. By his proper actions a Vaiśya becomes Kṣatriya.

cd–54ab Thus, by actions performed in a lower birth, a Śūdra may become a Brahmin; similarly, a Brahmin becomes a Śūdra if he behaves untruthfully, eats indescriminately.

cd–55ab Brahman proclaimed that a Śūdra purified by his actions should be honoured like a Brahmin.

cd–56ab Where a Śūdra rises above his proper nature and actions (or, steps up by acting according to his proper nature), he should be recognized as pure by the Brahmin (according to the opinion of the narrator, i.e. Śiva).

[2] This half Śloka is missing in MBh; it is repeated in 223.40 for Vaiśyas, its last *pāda* in 223.36 for Śūdras.

[3] cf. also ms. C, which reads *śama-*, like MBh 13,131.30b.

[4] *-mātra-* for *-mantra-*; cf. MBh 13.131c.

56cd–65 On the distinctions of Brahminhood:

56cd–58ab Conduct is the cause for Brahminhood, not birth, sacramental rites, revelation, lineage. When established in (a Brahmin's?) conduct even a Śūdra becomes a Brahmin.

58cd–60ab A Brahmin should be like the *brahman*; he in whom the *brahman* exists, which is everywhere the same, without qualities, pure, he is a Brahmin. Those who are pure have been told by Brahman to be instructors by rank and nature.

60cd–61ab A Brahmin is (like) a field walking the earth; the seed falling on it will bear fruit only after death.

61cd–64ab Following the path of the *brahman* (or of Brahmins) one should be content, cling to the proper conduct (»the path of the good«), study the collections of vedic hymns (*saṃhitā*), and perform the domestic sacrifices; be devoted to private recitation but not live on teaching. He who thus follows the true path is prepared to become *brahman*.

64cd–65ab Brahminhood once obtained should be protected, by taking up the birth-privilege of receiving gifts (?), and by actions.

65c-f Conclusion: The secret of how a Śūdra becomes a Brahmin and vice versa has been told.

Ch. 224: On the effects of actions (dialogue between Śiva and Umā, contd)[1]

1–3 Umā addresses Śiva (list of epithets) and asks (1.) what are the bondages of threefold action (by deeds, thought, and speech) and how one can get rid of them; (2.) by what qualities and actions one goes to heaven.

4–16 Śiva's reply.

4 Announcement.

5–8 Answer to the first question: Those who are devoted to truth and *dharma* (or, the *dharma* of truth), are pacified, free from all attributes (*liṅga*),[2] whose doubts are removed, are not bound by *dharma* and *adharma*; those who know about origination and dissolution, are omniscient, are free from passions, do not injure by actions, thoughts or words, do not get involved anywhere, who have stopped taking life (i.e. killing, slaughtering), are well-behaved and compassionate, to whom pleasant and unpleasant (experiences) are the same, those are freed from the bondage of their actions.

9–14 Answer to the second question: Those men go to heaven (refrain) who have compassion, are trustworthy, do not injure; who have no attachment to their own or others' property, avoid another's wife; enjoy only wealth which has been gained according to *dharma*; who behave to wives of others as towards mother, sister, daughter; who approach their wives only during her fertile days and do not enjoy vulgar pleasure; who do not steal, are content with what they have; who guard their eyes and senses and are intent on proper conduct with the wives of others.

[1] This chapter corresponds to MBh 13,132.

[2] Perhaps the karmic residues which, as »subtle body«, are carried over to the next existence.

15-16ef This divine path is to be followed and not to be transgressed. It is connected with alms-giving, rites, asceticism, and it consists of (proper) conduct, purity, compassion; no path beyond that (?) should be followed by those who desire heaven.

17 Umā asks by what speech one is bound and by what one is freed again.[3]

18-26 Śiva's reply:

18-25 Those men go to heaven (refrain[4]) who never speak anything connected with *adharma*; who never tell an untruth for any reason; who speak pleasantly; who do not speak harshly or crudely; who do not speak slanderously, avoid separating of friends, and afflicting pain; who treat all beings equally; who have stopped rascally talk and opposition and speak pleasantly; who do not speak heart-rending words in anger, but calm down their wrath.

26 Conclusion: This *dharma* concerning speech should be followed; telling lies is to be avoided.

27 Umā addresses Śiva (list of epithets) and asks by what thoughts a man is fettered.

28-38 Śiva's reply.

28-29 Announcement: The man whose mind is fixed on *dharma* goes to heaven, but he is fettered if his thinking is misguided.

30-37 Those men go to heaven (refrain[5]) who in their thoughts do not seize another's property deposited in an uninhabited place;[6] who in their thoughts do not injure another's wife even when encountered in secret; who think the same of friends and enemies; who observe the revealed tradition, are compassionate, pure, true to agreements, content with their own property, who are free from enmity and strife, intent on friendship, compassionate; who are knowledgeable, active (or, observing rituals), forgiving, loved by friends, and know about *dharma* and *adharma*; who are indifferent towards the results of good or bad deeds; who avoid the wicked, serve gods and Brahmins.

38 Conclusion; request for further questions.

39-45 Umā inquires about the reasons for long or short life, for the effect of actions that might explain why people are different (regarding their fortune, their looks, intelligence, etc.).[7]

46-56 Śiva's answer:

46 Announcement.

47-52 One who slaughters (other beings), a great Yogin (*yogīndro*),[8] one who has a stick in his hand or one who raises a weapon (and) kills beings, without compassion, causing excitement, not offering shelter even to insects - such a man goes to hell, while he who does not injure goes to heaven. When rising from hell and becoming a human being he lives only briefly.

[3] v. 17 and v. 27 partially repeat what was asked above in Umā's first question.

[4] Same refrain as in v. 9-14.

[5] Same refrain as in v. 9-14 and 18-25.

[6] VePr (like MBh) adds one verse of the same content.

[7] cf. MBh 13,107, where a whole chapter of 148 verses, amounting to a collection and summary of what constitutes »proper conduct«, is devoted to answering this question.

[8] Probably misreading for *yo raudro*, cf. MBh 13,132.48.

53–56ab By pleasant action, free from slaying living beings, without weapon, without stick, causing no harm, without killing or assenting to it, being attached to all beings, to others as to himself, such a man reaches divinity and all available pleasures when he is born among men.

56c-f Conclusion: This path of those who live long and act well was proclaimed by Brahman as connected with the avoidance of injury to living beings.

Ch. 225: On rebirth (dialogue between Śiva and Umā, contd)[1]

1 Umā inquires by what actions and donations man reaches heaven.[2]

2–41 Śiva's reply.

2–8 He who honours Brahmins, gives food, drink, clothes to the afflicted, constructs rest-houses and water-places, performs the obligatory rites, offers seat, bedstead, vehicle, house, jewels, money, grain, fields, women, with calm mind, such a man is reborn in the world of gods. After staying there and enjoying supreme pleasures, one is reborn in a wealthy family, endowed with desirable qualities, pleasures, wealth, etc.

9 Such generous people have formerly been declared by Brahman to be fondly regarded (*priyadarśana*) by all.

10–16 Other people are misers, they do not give grain though they have it, they turn away beggars, guests etc., they do not give money, clothes, etc.; such greedy unbelievers (*nāstika*) go to hell. When after some time they are reborn as human beings they obtain birth in a poor family, are pained by hunger and thirst, are turned out by everybody, have little to enjoy.

17–23ab There are others who are proud and do not offer a seat, do not yield the way, do not present the welcome offering nor foot-water nor water for sipping to those who deserve it, who do not greet their teacher, disrespect respectable persons or who slight old people. Such people go to hell; and when they rise again they are reborn in a rejected family of Śvapākas, Pulkasas, etc. Into such families is born a man who torments his teacher or old people.

23cd–29 He who is not proud, worships gods and guests, who responds with bowing when honoured by people, who speaks sweetly, does good and is dear to all, does not hate, does not injure, who welcomes those who come to him, yields the way, honours his teacher and guests, such a man goes to heaven and, when reborn as a man being, is born in a distinguished family; there he has pleasures and wealth and is generous and devoted to *dharma*, respected by all.

30 Conclusion: A man earns the results of his deeds; this *dharma* has been told as it was proclaimed by the creator (= Brahman).

31–35 He who is of fierce conduct, who scares all beings, oppresses them (list of instruments), injures them, upsets them, such a man goes to hell, and when in the

[1] This chapter corresponds to MBh 13,133.

[2] Question partially similar to 224.3.

course of time he becomes a human being, he is born in a low and greatly afflicted family. One is low and hateful among men as a result of one's own deeds; as such he is to be regarded (also) among his relatives.

36-41 Another one looks compassionately and in a friendly way upon all beings, like a father, is free from animosity, is restrained, trustworthy, does not upset or terrify (list of means); such a man is reborn in heaven; when after living there for a long time like a god he is reborn as a mortal, he lives at ease, enjoys pleasures and comforts. Conclusion: This is the path of the good.

42-45 Umā inquires by what deeds the difference in intelligence among people is caused; and she wants to know the reason for physical disabilities (listed).

46-52 Maheśvara's answer:

46-48 Those who inquire daily from qualified Brahmins about right and wrong, who perform good actions and avoid evil, such a man goes to heaven and becomes intelligent when reborn as a human being, where his well-being is effected by vedic sacrifices.

49 Those who direct lascivious looks at another's wife are born blind.

50 Those who look with evil thoughts at a naked woman are afflicted by illness.

51 Homosexuals (?) are born as eunuchs.

52 Those who fetter animals, violate the teacher's bed or are promiscuous are reborn as eunuchs.

53 Umā inquires which deed is recommended for a man to obtain the bliss of liberation.

54-55 Śiva's answer: By consulting Brahmins one reaches heaven, and is reborn as an intelligent human being, endowed with concentration (*dhāraṇā*).

56 Conclusion: This is the *dharma* of the good, told for the benefit of men.

57-59 Umā inquires what deeds make some people not like to approach Brahmins, why some observe vows while others do not, why some perform sacrifices while others are without oblations.[3]

60-63 Śiva's answer:

60-62 Some keep their vows and the previously established conventions; others call the wrong conduct (*adharma*) »*dharma*« and break the conventions; when reborn as men they are without sacrifices.

63 Conclusion: This »ocean of *dharma*« has been explained by Śiva in order to dispel Umā's doubts.

Ch. 226: Dialogue between Śiva and the sages[1]

1-3 Vyāsa continues: At these words »the mother of the world« (= Umā) was much pleased; the sages present bowed to Śiva, asking a further question.

[3] Read *nirhoma* for *nirmoha*; cf. MBh 13,133.59.

[1] In the crit. ed. of the MBh the dialogue between Śiva and Umā is continued for a further chapter (13.134, in which Maheśvara puts questions to Umā); after that most mss. of the Northern Recension read a passage (App. I, No. 16, l. 1-123), parallel to BrP 226.10ff.; the passage is found in the mss. V1 B Dn D1.2.4-9.

4–6 The sages praise Śiva, mention that people wander in the cycle of worldly existence for a long time, and inquire about the means for deliverance from rebirth.

7–9 Maheśvara (= Śiva) recommends worship of Vāsudeva.

10 The sages address Śiva (list of epithets) and want to hear the glorification of Vāsudeva (i.e. the Vāsudeva-Māhātmya).

11–67 Śiva's answer: Vāsudeva-Māhātmya.

11–12 Hari, the eternal Puruṣa, is superior even to the »Grandfather« (= Brahman); he is also called Kṛṣṇa, Hṛṣīkeśa, great *puruṣa*, ten-armed, etc.

13–14 Brahman, Śiva (i.e. the narrator), stars, gods, sages, etc. originate from his body.

15–17 He is creator and destroyer of the world, lord of gods, omniscient, etc.

18 In human shape he will slay kings (future tense).[2]

19–20ab He is the leader of the gods.

20cd–22ab Brahman resides in his navel; Śiva and all the gods in his body.

22cd–23ab He is associated with Śrī; list of iconographic attributes (sword, etc.).

23cd–25 He is endowed with good qualities (power, beauty, etc.).

26–29 He is favourable to his friends and to the afflicted, respected by all, terrible to his enemies.

30–41 Govinda will be born in Manu's family;[3] his genealogy: Manu → Aṃśa → Antardhāman → Havirdhāman → Prācīnabarhis → Pracetas and 9 other sons (Prācetasas), among them Dakṣa; Dākṣāyaṇī → Āditya → Manu[4] → Ilā and Sudyumna. Budha → Purūravas → Āyus → Nahuṣa → Yayāti → Yadu → Kroṣṭṛ → Vṛjinīvat → Uṣaṅgu → Citraratha and Śūra, a valiant Kṣatriya, whose son will be Ānakadundubhi called Vasudeva. His son will be the four-armed Vāsudeva who honours Brahmins.

42–45ab He will defeat Jarāsaṃdha and release the captive kings; he will rule over all kings and the whole earth, residing in Dvārakā.

45cd–48ab Śiva tells the sages to revere him like Brahman; to see Vāsudeva implies seeing Brahman or Śiva (the speaker); Vāsudeva is Brahman (the »Grandfather«).

48cd–50ab The man by whom the »Lotus-eyed One« (= Vāsudeva) is loved, will be loved by all gods; to take refuge in Vāsudeva entails fame and heaven.

50cd–51 He (Vāsudeva) will be a teacher about *dharma*, which exists where he is revered.

52–53 For the sake of *dharma* he created innumerable sages who, led by Sanatkumāra, reside on mount Gandhamādana.

54–55 The god returns the honour etc. which he receives.

56–57ab This is Viṣṇu's highest asceticism (?),[5] which is always observed by him; he is revered even by the gods.

57cd–58 Devakī's son is to be revered with deeds, thought and words; he should be looked at and attended upon.

59–61 This path was established by Śiva (i.e. the speaker). By looking at the Lord of gods the gods themselves are looked at. Śiva reveres him as the Great Boar; the triad (of worlds or gods?) will be visible in him; all gods live in his body.

[2] v. 17cd–18ab corresponds to an insertion of mss. V1 B Dn3 in MBh, while the same mss. omit line 15 of the text of MBh.

[3] Future tense; cf. above v. 18.

[4] Mentioned for the second time.

[5] MBh reads »vow«.

2–65ab His elder brother will be the plough-bearer, Bala(rāma); with three heads he is looked at as Ananta; the bird (i.e. Garuḍa) could not see the end of the son of Kaśyapa (i.e. the snake Śeṣa, the »bed«) of the god; who encompasses the earth with his body.[6]

d–67ab Viṣṇu and Ananta, i.e. Hṛṣīkeśa and Balarāma, are the same; both should be looked at.

67c-f Conclusion; the sages should worship Vāsudeva, »the best among Yadus«.

Ch. 227: On the destiny of Vaiṣṇavas after death

1–4 The sages state that they have heard the wonderful and auspicious »Greatness of Kṛṣṇa«; they inquire about the fruit of worshipping Vāsudeva – liberation or heaven or both?

5–50 Vyāsa's answer.

5 Announcement.

6–7 Even by initiation alone (concerning Kṛṣṇa-worship) liberation is reached; those who worship Kṛṣṇa with devotion reach liberation and heaven easily, as well as (fulfilment of) all other desires.

8–9 Kṛṣṇa grants wishes (like the wishing-tree etc.).

10–14 All wishes are fulfilled for those, including women and the lowest castes, who worship Vāsudeva (stated repeatedly).

15 Announcement: The way (destiny) of Vaiṣṇavas after death.

6–32ab After leaving the human body (described negatively), Vaiṣṇavas go by heavenly chariot (described) to the residence of the world-guardians. After one Manu-era they continue to stay in ...

the world of:	duration of stay:
intermediate space	10 Manu-eras
Gandharvas	20 Manu-eras
sun	30 Manu-eras
moon	40 Manu-eras
stars (*nakṣatra*)	50 Manu-eras
gods	60 Manu-eras
Indra	70 Manu-eras
Prajāpati	80 Manu-eras
Brahman	90 Manu-eras

4

d–37ab Then they are reborn as learned Yogins into a family of Brahmins and ascend to the heavenly worlds again. In each life they live for 100 years. After ten rebirths they ascend from the world of Brahman to the world of Hari, enjoying all pleasures for 100 Manu-eras.

[6] v. 63ab seems to be corrupt; MBh ins. 3 ślokas between v. 63a and b.

37cd–41 They spend in the world of ...

Varāha	10,000 x 10 million years
Narasiṃha	myriads of tens of millions of years
Viṣṇu	myriads of years.

42–47 They return to the world of Brahman for hundreds of tens of millions of years; then they proceed to the residence of Nārāyaṇa for 10 million times 10 million years; to the residence of Aniruddha for 14 times thousands of tens of millions of years (?); to the residence of Pradyumna for 300 times 10 millions of years; to the residence of Saṃkarṣaṇa for a long time.

48–49 Having remained there for a long time the Yogins enter into Vāsudeva; having gone there they are delivered from death and old age.

50 Conclusion: Thus those who worship Vāsudeva attain pleasures and liberation.

Ch. 228: Praise of singing while keeping vigil

1–5 Vyāsa continues: He who worships Viṣṇu, as prescribed, on the 11th day of each half-month (by offerings, praises, keeping vigil all night, singing about Viṣṇu), such a man reaches Viṣṇu's highest abode.

6 The sages inquire about the effects of singing while keeping vigil.

7–152 Vyāsa's answer.

7 Announcement.

8–91ab *Story of the devoted Cāṇḍāla and the Rākṣasa*[1]

8–14 In Avantī resided Viṣṇu (i.e. an idol of Viṣṇu) holding conch, disc and club. At the outskirts of the city lived a Cāṇḍāla who was a good singer and a wealthy devotee of Viṣṇu; he observed a fast and sang songs (containing the names of Viṣṇu, relating to his manifestations, using five notes) and verses during his nocturnal vigil. In the morning he served food to his sons-in-law, his sisters' sons and daughters, then he ate with his family. This way he had grown old.

15–21 Once he went to the forest to collect wild flowers for Viṣṇu; on the bank of the river Kṣiprā he was seized by a Rākṣasa in order to be devoured. The Cāṇḍāla asked to be eaten the next morning; he would truly return but should not be prevented from keeping the nocturnal vigil. The Rākṣasa replied that he had not eaten for ten days and would not let him go.

22–38 The Mātaṅga (as the Cāṇḍāla is called in the sequel) swore (with a truth-spell) that he would come back. He called upon sun, moon, fire etc. as witnesses. He listed all kinds of evils and sins (v. 24–38) which he would incur if he did not return.

39 The Rākṣasa was surprised and let him go.

[1] A similar story is told in VrP 139.28–90; there are, however, only a very few literal parallels (e.g. *satyamūlam jagat sarvam*). The story seems to be told more exactly in the BrP, but there is no certainty about the connection between the two versions.

40–43 The Śvapāka (i.e. the Cāṇḍāla, alias Mātaṅga) took his flowers, went to the temple and gave them to the Brahmin. He (i.e. the Brahmin) worshipped Viṣṇu by sprinkling (the image) with water and went home. The Mātaṅga fasted during that night and sang, standing outside (the temple?). In the morning he bathed and went to keep his promise.

44–46 On the way he met a man to whom he told everything and who tried to persuade him not to risk his life, asking him whether he did not know the truth that everything, including liberation, can be gained only while living.[2]

47–49 The Mātaṅga appealed to truth, but the man again asked him whether he did not know what Manu had taught:[3]

50 There are five occasions where untruth is no sin.[4]

51 Occasions where speaking in accordance with *dharma* does not apply (maxim).

52–55 The Mātaṅga replied by pointing out that the world is based on truth (*satya*) and operates by truth.

56–59 The Rākṣasa, who was a Brahmin himself, was surprised at his return, praised his truthfulness, declared him a Brahmin, and asked him what he had done during the night in the temple of Viṣṇu.

60–61 The Mātaṅga told him that he had kept vigil and had chanted songs about Viṣṇu.

62–73 The Rākṣasa inquired for how long he had been doing this. When the Mātaṅga told him that he had done it for 20 years at each 11th day, the Rākṣasa requested by thrice invoking truth to be given (the merit of) one night; he would then release his victim. But the Mātaṅga insisted that the Rākṣasa should eat him. The Rākṣasa reduced his request to two night-watches (six hours), and was refused. He admonished the Mātaṅga, whom he considered protected by (his) action according to *dharma*, that the good should show pity on the afflicted, etc., and he asked for one night-watch but was refused. Laughingly he asked for the fruit of the one song sung at the end of the night for amusement (*kautuhāśraya*?).

74–75 The Mātaṅga in return asked him what evil he had formerly committed for him to have been born as a Rākṣasa.

76–85 The Rākṣasa told him that he had formerly been a Brahmin, Somaśarman by name,[5] son of Devaśarman. He had been excluded from vedic lore but performed the kindling of the fire at a sacrifice of a king, out of greed and confusion. When it was complete, the Brahmin (i.e. the narrator) began a great sacrifice of twelve days during the course of which he developed a colic in the stomach. After ten days, but before the rite was complete, while offering to Virūpākṣa (= Śiva), at a demonic moment, he died. Through this fault of sacrificing ignorantly, without prayer-formulas (*mantra*), he had been born as a brahminical Rākṣasa. The Rākṣasa

[2] The metre of v. 46 seems to be a slightly defective Āryā (11, 18, 12, 16 *mātras* instead of 12, 18, 12, 15), which could be corrected by reading *jīvan* instead of *jīva-* in the beginning (which would anyway make better sense) and *na* instead of *kā* in the last line (which would not change the meaning of the sentence and might be the original reading, changed because of the popularity of rhetorical questions).

[3] The verses are not found in Manu.

[4] In Upajāti-metre.

[5] This name is also given in the version of the VrP.

concluded by asking to be pulled out of the ocean of evil and to be given the fruit of the last song.

86–91ab The Cāṇḍāla agreed on the condition that the Rākṣasa should give up slaying living beings. After receiving the fruit of half a *muhūrta* of waking the Rākṣasa went to the eminent place of pilgrimage Pṛthūdaka[6] (»with abundant water«). He died by fasting. By the effect of the singing and of Pṛthūdaka he went to the world of Brahman for 10,000 years. Then he became a Brahmin.

91cd Vyāsa announces that he will tell his further story.

92ab Vyāsa announces the rest of the story about the Mātaṅga.

92cd–96 Remembering the fate of the demon he entrusted his wife to their sons and offered circumambulation to the earth, beginning from Kokāmukha until he saw (the image of) Skanda (?). After seeing Skanda he went to circumambulate, following the circle of rivers. He reached the Vindhya-mountains and visited the holy place Pāpapramocana (i.e. »releasing from evil«). Having performed the bath he was freed from evil and remembered his former births.

97–151 *Story of the previous and the following rebirths of the Mātaṅga*

97–100ab Formerly he had been a learned beggar who once discarded alms (offered) by robbers; due to this fault he was reborn as a Cāṇḍāla. He bathed in the river Narmadā and became a foolish Brahmin in Vārāṇasī.

100cd–127ab There he met a »perfected person« (*siddhapūruṣa*) whom he asked for fun where he had come from. The Siddha told him that he had come from heaven. The fool inquired whether the Siddha knew Urvaśī (originated from Nārāyaṇa's thigh) and told him to speak to Urvaśī in his favour. The Siddha did so; upon his return to Vārāṇasī he reported to the fool that Urvaśī had denied knowing him. He sent the Siddha back to heaven to inquire what he should do that she might know him. She demanded any kind of restrictive observance (*niyama*). The fool announced that from that day onwards he would not eat a carriage. From this Urvaśī recognized that he was a fool making fun of her. She went to Vārāṇasī and bathed in the river Matsyodarī. The fool saw her bathing and his passion was aroused. When Urvaśī recognized him and asked him what he wanted, he asked her to give herself to him. She told him to wait for a moment.

127cd–145 When she returned after one month he was still standing in the river without food. She made a carriage from butter and honey covered with sugar and offered it to the fool as a gift, explaining that this would acquit her at the end of a severe vow which she had observed for the sake of conjugal felicity. Though tormented by hunger he refused, repeating his pledge not to eat a carriage. She reminded him that his pledge had been taken with regard to a wooden carriage, but he denied any such specification. She told him to go home and give it to his family. He refused, saying that he was waiting for the return of the woman who had told him to wait for a moment. Thereupon Urvaśī revealed her proper form and identified herself; she advised him to go to Śūkarava,[7] famous as Rūpatīrtha; he would obtain perfection and then her.

[6] On this place cf. MBh 3,81.122–130.

[7] v.l. *sūkarava*, which could be a misreading for *sūkaraka* (cf. Kane, HDhŚ IV, p. 803, and

146–151 After giving up his body at Rūpatīrtha the fool went to the world of Gandharvas. After 100 Manu-eras he became a king who sacrificed lavishly. Entrusting the kingdom to his sons he again went to Śaukarava;[8] after his death he attained the world of Indra. After 100 Manu-eras he was reborn in Pratiṣṭhāna as Budha's son Purūravas for the sake of uniting with Urvaśī.

152 Conclusion: Thus the twice-born obtained pleasures and liberation at Rūpatīrtha.[9]

Ch. 229: Episodes illustrating the manifestations of Viṣṇu's Māyā

1–2 The sages confirm the conclusion to the preceding chapter; they want to hear by what asceticism and by what action devotion to Viṣṇu comes about.

3–13 Vyāsa's answer.

3 Announcement.

4–7 The difficulty of attaining devotion: After many rebirths a creature may be born as a human being; after that as a Brahmin. Brahminhood leads to (the power of) distinction, from which consciousness of *dharma* (*dharmabuddhi*) arises, leading to welfare. Devotion to Vāsudeva arises only after the evil accumulated during rebirths has been destroyed.

8–13 Devotion to sacrificing arises from devotion to other gods (except Kṛṣṇa). After devotion to sacrificing one practices devotion to Agni (fire), then to Sūrya (the sun), then to Śaṃkara (= Śiva), finally to Keśava (= Kṛṣṇa). By worshipping him (the Lord of the world, called Vāsudeva) one attains enjoyment and liberation.

14 The sages want to know the reason why those who are not Vaiṣṇavas do not revere Viṣṇu.

15–18 Vyāsa's answer: Formerly Brahman effected two creations of beings, one demonic, one divine. Those (beings) of divine nature worship the imperishable (*acyuta*, i.e. Viṣṇu), those of demonic nature malign Hari. Being bereft of insight by Viṣṇu's Māyā, they follow a degraded path. This Māyā (»illusion«) is difficult to know and hard to overcome.

19 The hermits want to know that illusion (*māyā*).

20–88 Vyāsa's answer.

20 Nobody can know Hari's Māyā except Keśava himself.

21 Announcement of an account of what happened to the Brahmin and Nārada (or, of the explanation given to Nārada; cf. below, v. 43cd–66).

22–87 *Story of Śuci*

22–30 Formerly there was a king, Āgnīdhra, who had a son, Śuci, who did not want to be married, since in accordance with his name (»pure«) he had taken refuge in Viṣṇu's

the next footnote); Sūkarava/Saukarava, a region situated on the bank of the Gaṅgā and sacred to Viṣṇu as boar (*sūkara*), is described in VrP 137–139.

[8] Ms. A reads *śūkarakam*.

[9] In Upajāti-metre.

manifest protective (aspect, power?[1]). At the father's insistence and admonitions regarding the pleasures and necessity of marriage he told him about his former existences.

31–86ab Śuci's report to his father.

31–36ab He had been through hundreds and thousands of rebirths as various plants, animals, human and superhuman beings, in various cosmic cycles, because of living together with a wife and family.

36c-f Announcement of (an account of) what happened in his third birth.

37–88 Story of Śuci, continued.[2]

37–43ab After many existences he was reborn as a great sage with firm devotion to Janārdana. Viṣṇu, satisfied, appeared to him on Garuḍa and granted him a boon. He wished to know his highest Māyā. Viṣṇu tried to make him choose something else but the sage insisted on seeing his Māyā.

43cd–67ab *Story of Nārada's experience with Viṣṇu's Māyā*

43cd–55 Viṣṇu replied that nobody had come to know nor would ever come to know his Māyā. Once Nārada, refusing any other boon, had wanted to see it; Viṣṇu told him to submerge in water; Nārada did so and appeared as the daughter of the king of Kāśi; she was married to the son of the king of Vidarbha; the great sage (i.e. Nārada) experienced immense pleasures (as woman)[3] After the king's death his son took over the kingdom of Vidarbha. There was a battle between him and the king of Kāśi in which both kings and their descendants perished. Suśīlā went to the battle-field and witnessed the great slaughter in both armies. She took the corpses to her mother, cremated them and burnt herself in the fire deploring her son. Then she again became the hermit Nārada, while the fire turned into the water and Viṣṇu stood in front of him. The four-armed god[4] asked him who his son was and why he was mourning; Nārada felt ashamed.

56–58 Viṣṇu repeated to Nārada that his Māyā cannot be known. Thereupon Nārada wished for devotion, for (the ability) to remember (Viṣṇu?) at the hour of death, and for eternal vision of Viṣṇu. The place where he had ascended the funeral pyre should become a place of pilgrimage presided over by Keśava. This was granted.

59–63 Viṣṇu prophesied that Maheśvara (= Śiva) would come there to be freed from the head of Brahman attached to him. The place would be famed as Kapālamocana. He whose vehicle is clouds (= Śiva?) would not leave this place of pilgrimage; as long as he would not leave it, the gods would praise it as Vimukta.[5]

64–67ab A sinner is freed from evil there, and if he keeps thinking of Viṣṇu (first-person narrator) he attains liberation. Even a Rudra or Piśāca is reborn in a Brahmin family after many years. At the time of death Rudra announces the saving (formula)

[1] Read *māyā* for *mayā*?

[2] The rest of this chapter is in epic Triṣṭubhs, i.e. Upajāti-metre mixed with Jagatī-lines.

[3] cf. MBh 13,12, the story of the royal sage Bhaṅgāsvana, who has a similar experience.

[4] Viṣṇu as the speaker refers to himself in the third person.

[5] The separation of words in the editions used results in this name, though the context would suggest »Avimukta«, being a well-known name of Kāśi-Vārāṇasī.

to him. After these words Viṣṇu returned to the ocean of milk, while the great sage (i.e. Nārada) went to heaven.

cd–68ab Conclusion to Viṣṇu's answer, repeating that his Māyā cannot be known, except by submerging in water.

68cd–87 *Story of Śuci, continued: The sage as Cāṇḍāla girl*

68cd–71 According to Viṣṇu's advice, the sage submerged in water at Kokāmukha; he became a beautiful Cāṇḍāla girl, married to an ugly, poor Cāṇḍāla who loved her, though she did not love him (?). They had two blind sons and a deaf daughter. The mother always wept when she went to the river.

72–86ab Once she left her pitcher at the bank and entered the river to bathe. She became a Brahmin again. Her husband, who went to the river looking for her, saw only the pitcher. He cried, and the children cried with him. He asked Brahmins at the bank whether they had seen the woman; they confirmed that she had entered the water but had not emerged again. The Cāṇḍāla cried even more. Seeing them the Brahmin (formerly the Cāṇḍāla's wife) felt pity and remembered that he had been that Cāṇḍāla woman. He/she tried to console the husband who lamented that he was not able to console or nourish the children. Eventually the Brahmin told the man what had happened; thereupon the Cāṇḍāla entered (the water of) Kokāmukha together with his children. By the power of that place of pilgrimage he was freed from evil and ascended to heaven. Thereupon the Brahmin became sad, entered the water and went to heaven. He was reborn as a Vaiśya; again he went to Kokāmukha, let his body wither away and ascended to heaven. After that he became the son of Āgnīdhra, remembering his former births by Hari's grace, and abandoning all desire regarding the pleasant or unpleasant.

86cd–87 He (i.e. the son of Āgnīdhra, Śuci) saluted the father, left for Kokāmukha, worshipped Viṣṇu as boar and attained perfection.

88 Conclusion to (the stories about) the Māyā of Murāri (= Viṣṇu) which is like a dream or like magic.

Ch. 230: On the conditions during Kali-Yuga[1]

1–2 The hermits confirm the conclusion to the preceding chapter (Viṣṇu's Māyā). They want to know about the »great dissolution« at the end of a cosmic cycle.

3–7 Vyāsa's answer.

3 Announcement of (an account of) how dissolution of primordial matter comes about.

4–7 Excursus on the divisions of time: One month (among humans) is one day and night of the ancestors. One year (among humans) is (one day and night) of the gods. Four

[1] This chapter corresponds to ViP 6,1–6,2.37. For a concordance to Ch. 230–234, cf. Appendix to the text-volume.

cosmic periods, i.e. Kṛta, Dvāpara, Tretā, Kali, which consist of 12,000 divine years, make one day of Brahman. At the beginning of a Kṛta-Yuga Brahman creates; at the end of a Kali-Yuga he withdraws.

8 The hermits want to hear extensively about the Kali-Yuga when the *dharma* of four quarters (»feet«) becomes defective.

9–59 Vyāsa's answer: Description of the conditions during Kali-Yuga.

9 Announcement (of a summary).

10–27 Castes and stages of life are not observed; vedic injunctions are not observed; marriage, initiation, scriptures, gods, stages of life, observances like fasting, all will be arbitrary; there will be waste of wealth and pride of wealth even if a person has only a little; women have nothing but their hair for ornaments; they will leave their husbands if they become poor; the wealthy will be husbands and be acknowledged as owners; thinking is directed to wealth, wealth spent on enjoyment; women are independent, fond of love and of men who have become rich by foul means; people become selfish even when begged by a friend;[2] cows are respected only for giving milk; people live in fear of drought and famine; they live on roots and fruits etc., kill each other, suffer afflictions. They eat without bathing, do not honour gods and guests, do not offer to the ancestors.

28–31 Women have small bodies, many children; they scratch their head with both hands; they do not respect the orders of husbands or elders; they think only of feeding themselves, are irascible, do not speak the truth. They are of bad conduct.

32–33 Mares[3] without observances receive the Veda; householders do not sacrifice or give alms; hermits receive regular food; sons, even though they are beggars, effect bondage by affection.

34–37 Kings do not protect people's property, but take it away; anyone who can sit on an elephant, carriage or horse may be king, while those who are weak become subjects. Vaiśyas pursue the jobs of Śūdras; Śūdras live as beggars or follow heresies.

38–43 People emigrate in search of grain; when the vedic path disappears and people follow heresies they become short-lived. They practise asceticism which is not according to the injunctions; children will die due to the fault of the king; women will have children at the age of five or seven, men at the age of eight or ten. Men will be old at the age of twelve; and no one will live longer than twenty. People are of little intelligence and perish soon.

44–48 Kali can be recognized as growing whenever heresies become current, whenever those who follow the Veda disappear, when undertakings of men who observe the *dharma* fail, whenever the Lord is not venerated with sacrifices, when the Veda becomes unpopular and heresies attractive.

49–58 In the Kali-Yuga people do not revere Viṣṇu; they disregard gods, Brahmins, Veda, purity; there is little rain and grain, fruits have little sap. Clothes reach to the knees,[4] trees are mostly Śamī-trees; among the castes Śūdras prevail; grain is tiny; milk comes mainly from goats, ointment from Uśira-plants; the parents-in-law will be regarded as authorities; wives[5] who steal houses etc. will be friends; people will

[2] v. 23ab not clear; *vipre* for *vipra*, as voc. sg. would be out of place here? cf. ViP *vipreṣu*.

[3] *vaḍavāḥ* (*sic*); Ve Pr *vāḍavāḥ*, ViP *baṭavaḥ*, i.e. (young) Brahmins.

[4] ViP: are made of hemp.

[5] ViP: rogues etc.

disregard parents and follow the parents-in-law; they daily commit evil; there are hardly any Brahmins.

59 In a short time one gathers as much merit as by practising asceticism in the Kṛta-Yuga.

60 The hermits inquire at what time a little *dharma* produces great results.

61–82 Vyāsa's answer.[6]

61 In the blessed Kali-Yuga great results can be produced at little inconvenience. Furthermore, women and Śūdras are blessed.

62–65 The blessings of Kali-Yuga.

62–63 What is achieved by asceticism, continence and murmuring in ten years in the Kṛta-Yuga takes one year in Tretā, one month in Dvāpara, one day and night in Kali; therefore Kali is to be called good.

64 What is achieved by meditation in Kṛta, by sacrifices in Tretā, by worship in Dvāpara, is achieved by praising Keśava in Kali.

65 Excellence in *dharma* may be achieved with little effort.

66–71 The blessings of being a Śūdra.

66–69 Formerly Brahmins observant of their vows first had to receive the Vedas; then they had to sacrifice spending justly acquired wealth. All their reciting, eating, wealth was vain and led to their down-fall since they could commit mistakes in everything; eating and drinking for them did not mean the quenching of desires. In everything Brahmins are dependent, gaining their worlds by sacrificing with great inconvenience.

70–71 The more fortunate Śūdra, who is entitled to sacrifice cooked food, gains his world by serving Brahmins; he need not pay heed to what is edible or not. Therefore he is called good.

72–76 The blessings of being a woman.

72–74 Men have to earn wealth without violating *dharma*, have to spend it on those who are worthy, have to sacrifice. There is inconvenience in collecting wealth, in protecting it, and in using it properly. By such inconveniences men gain their worlds, i.e. the world of Prajāpati etc.

75–76 A woman reaches this goal by serving her husband without much inconvenience. Therefore women are said to be good.

77 Conclusion to the topic the Brahmins had come to hear. Announcement of an answer to their question(s), which they are told to put.[7]

78–81 In Kali-Yuga *dharma* is observed by little effort; by men who have washed away their sins with the waters of their own qualities, by Śūdras who are intent on serving the twice-born, and by women who serve their husbands. Therefore this triad is considered most blessed. In the Kṛta-Yuga etc. the inconvenience in honouring *dharma* is great for the twice-born, while at the end of (a round of) cosmic periods privileged people reach perfection and follow *dharma* with little effort.

[6] v. 62–82 correspond to ViP 6,2.15–37.

[7] This verse is out of context in BrP since there is no mention of the hermits »coming« in order to put questions to Vyāsa (unless one assumes a reference back to 26.8 and 26.25). The verse is adequate, however, in the context of ViP which consequently appears to have been abbreviated here by the redactor(s) of BrP in an inconsistent way.

82 Conclusion: Without being asked, Vyāsa has given this answer to a question posed only in intention.[8]

Ch. 231: The end of a cycle of Yugas and the return of Kṛta-Yuga

1-2 The hermits wish for the end of the Dvāpara-Yuga (in which they are living); they want to obtain great *dharma* by doing little.

3 They want Vyāsa to speak about the frightening end of a cosmic period.

4-41 Vyāsa answers by describing the conditions at the end of a cosmic period. Kings do not protect, but take away the share of the sacrifice; those who are not Kṣatriyas are kings; Brahmins live like Śūdras while Śūdras behave like Brahmins. Brahmins are soldiers, they all eat together; men are uneducated, fond of drink and meat; they make love to their friend's wife; thieves behave like kings; kings are thieves; servants eat without being told; wealth is respected; the behaviour of the good is not honoured and there is no reproach for the fallen; people have their noses destroyed, they are bald; women are emaciated before (the age of) sixteen.[1] All Vājasaneya-Brahmins (i.e. belonging to the school of the White YV) will teach the *brahman* (?); they appear like Śūdras and live on the outskirts. Śūdras who are rogues pronounce the *dharma*; wild beasts abound, cows disappear, the good turn away from knowledge; those who used to live in the centre (of a city) exchange places with those on the outskirts; people are shameless; Brahmins sell the merit of asceticism and sacrifices; the seasons are upset; animals tamed for the plough are (or become) two years (old) (?); rainfall is erratic; those born in heroic families are compassionate (or pitiable?), just as all people are mean, sons will obtain what should be given to their fathers (?); nobody follows *dharma*; the land is mostly waste; roads are infested by robbers; most people live by trade (?); the sons divide (the heritage) given by the father; they try to take away from one who is opposed to them. Women lose their beauty and jewels even in youth and are decorated only by their hair. The love of a householder will lack virility. Most people are ignoble; women outnumber men. People do not give to each other even when implored; they are weakened by punishments, fire, thieves, kings etc.; grain does not bear fruit; the young behave like the old; the ill-behaved prosper; diverse winds blow in the rainy season, raining stones (?); the world beyond is called in question; noblemen (Kṣatriyas) live like Vaiśyas; relations do not count; treaties and oaths are not kept, debts not honoured; friendliness is ineffective but anger works; even goats stop giving milk; sacrifices are not performed according to the rules; men who are deemed learned do what is not authorized and do not speak as the books say. Everyone knows everything without regard for their elders; there is none who is not a poet; the stars are out of joint (?); the twice-born do not perform rites; kings are thieves; adultery is normal; those who teach the Veda are drinkers; Brahmins perform the horse-sacrifice,

[8] This conclusion only fits the context of ViP, but not that of BrP where the hermits did ask a question (v. 60).

[1] v. 11 unclear.

sacrifice what must not be sacrificed, eat what must not be eaten; they thirst for wealth. Women have just one conch-shell and are dressed in straw (?); the stars are without lustre; the ten directions are upset; sons send their fathers on errands, women their mothers-in-law. Brahmins eat without offering to the fire; men eat without giving offerings or alms. Women deceive their sleeping husbands even though they are not ill, disfigured, etc.; no one requites for what he has done.

42–43 The hermits inquire in which region people, oppressed by taxes, will live while *dharma* is suspended; what will be their actions, their size, their span of life; and after what troubles they will reach the (next) Kṛta-Yuga.

44–93 Vyāsa's answers.

44–46 (First answer:) The downfall of *dharma* leads to lack of qualities in people, which entails degeneration of conduct, lack of vigour and strength, lack of lustre, illness and disgust. Disgust leads to self-knowledge and practice of *dharma*. Thus people attain the Kṛta-Yuga.

47–93 (Second answer.)

47–79 Conditions at the end of or during Kali-Yuga.

47 Some follow *dharma* by advice; some are indifferent, others excite curiosity (?).

48–50 Only perception and syllogism are recognized as means of valid knowledge; some people say that everything (i.e. any statement ?) is without any authority (i.e. there is no means of proof) (?). Fools are respected as learned Brahmins. People trust only in the present and have given up knowledge.

51 When *dharma* has been shaken, (only) people who are honoured by the best do good and are intent on giving alms.

52–55 Signs of degeneration are that people eat everything, are secretive, cruel and shameless. Success is reached in little time; people of low caste behave like Brahmins; there is excessive war, rain, wind, heat.

56–59 Demonic kings (*karṇavedinaḥ*?) rule the earth, who do not heed the sacred prayer-formulas, eat raw flesh, look like Brahmins, are fools, greedy, mean, fallen from *dharma*, who take away the jewelry from others, do violence to others' wives, and are fraudulent.

60–67 Many people who are not prepared for it become hermits. Distinguished men are honoured only with conversation. There will be theft of grain, clothes, and baskets; thieves steal from thieves, murderers kill murderers. People oppressed by taxes take refuge in the forests; when sacrifices have stopped, demons, wild animals, insects etc. trouble people.[2] Thieves band together in different areas.

68–71ab People are driven from their native places. They cross the river Kauśikī and take refuge among the Aṅgas, Vaṅgas, Kaliṅgas, Kāśmīris, Kośalas, and in the mountains and valleys bordering on the Ṛṣīkas (?), the Himālaya and the shore of the ocean.

71cd–78 People dress in leaves and bark, live in the forests among barbarians (*mleccha*). The earth is not empty. Kings are protectors who do not protect. People live on wild animals, fish, snakes, insects, fruits, etc. They dress in bark or hides like hermits. ...[3] People raise goats, sheep, camels, and donkeys; they will stop rivers to get water. They trade with cooked food. (They leave) their hair as it has grown (?). They have many children and lack offspring (i.e. their children die?).

[2] v. 66 not clear; no verb.

[3] v. 76ab not clear.

79 Conclusion: Thus people, being deficient, follow a deficient *dharma*.

80–88 Return of the Kṛta-Yuga. The span of life is more than 30; (people) are weak, overcome by the afflictions of old age; their senses are affected by illness; consequently they will give up attachment to worldly things and serve the good. Because they have ceased with their activities they fall back on truth; because their desires have not been fulfilled they observe *dharma*; threatened with destruction they practise the funeral rites for themselves (?). Thus they attend to alms-giving, truth, protection of living beings. With one quarter of *dharma* in force, well-being comes about. After turning to (proper) qualities and questioning the real values they follow only *dharma*. In the order of their decay they rise again. Having accepted *dharma* they will see (the next) Kṛta-Yuga. The Kṛta-Yuga is like the moon emerging from darkness.

89–92 The meaning of the Veda is known as being the highest *brahman* and is kept as an inseparable, unknowable heritage. For obtaining wishes (one should practise) asceticism; asceticism (*tapas* m.??) is made firm by means of qualities resulting from action; qualities are purified by means of action. Blessing (or: the collection of prayers of the Veda) is present in space and time because of being pronounced by the sages at a certain time in each cosmic period, after they have seen the *puruṣa*. Attending to the four goals of life and to the gods, holy prayers (blessings) as well as (long) life (is present) in each cosmic period.[4]

93 Conclusion: Thus the cosmic periods change; the world of living beings never stands still alternating between destruction and origination.[5]

Ch. 232: On the dissolution of things[1]

1–2 Vyāsa continues: The dissolution of things is of three kinds, »occasional« (*naimittika*), »natural« (*prākṛtika*), »absolute« (*ātyantika*). Occasional dissolution is that kind which occurs at the end of a cosmic cycle and is attributed to Brahman. The absolute dissolution is liberation, while the natural one occurs after two Parārdhas.

3 The hermits want to know more about that natural dissolution.

4–40 Vyāsa's answer.

4–5 Counting positions by the factor of 10, a Parārdha is called what has 18 digits (i.e. 10 to the power of 18); the natural dissolution occurs after twice that much. Then everything manifest dissolves in the unmanifest.

6–12 Divisions of time:

15 *mātrās* (= *nimeṣas*)	= 1 *kāṣṭhā*
30 *kāṣṭhās*	= 1 *kalā*
15 *kalās*	= 1 *nāḍikā* (defined in v. 7–8)
2 *nāḍikās*	= 1 *muhūrta*

[4] The meaning of v. 89–92 is not clear.

[5] In Upendravajrā-metre.

[1] This chapter corresponds to ViP 6,3.

30 *muhūrtas*	= 1 day and night
30 days	= 1 month
12 months	= 1 year
360 days of gods	= 1 year of gods
12,000 years of gods	= 4 cosmic ages
1,000 periods of 4 ages	= 1 day of Brahman
1 day of Brahman	= 1 *kalpa* (= 14 Manu-eras).

At the end of a day of Brahman occurs the occasional dissolution.

13 Announcement of (an account of) the atrocities of such a dissolution; forward reference to the later description of natural dissolution.

14–40 Description of occasional dissolution.

14–23 At the end of 1000 periods of 4 Yugas the earth is nearly destroyed. There is a drought of 100 years which eliminates the feeble beings on earth. Kṛṣṇa in the shape of Rudra makes an effort to absorb all beings into himself. Then Viṣṇu, entering into seven rays of the sun, drinks up all waters, even those in living beings, and dries up the whole earth, all rivers, etc., and all nether worlds. Increased by those waters, he originates seven suns which burn the whole triple world. After all trees etc. have been burnt the earth is like the shell of a tortoise.

24–27 Then that Rudra who is the fire of Time burns the nether worlds by the heat of Śeṣa's breath; when he has burnt the earth he burns the heavens. The three worlds seem like a frying pan.

28–29 The inhabitants of the two worlds retreat to Maharloka, then due to the turn of conditions to Janaloka.

30–40 Janārdana as Rudra then creates from his mouth seven lightning and thundering clouds, of different colours and shapes (listed). By raining for 100 years they extinguish the fire and inundate earth and heaven; then they continue to rain for another 100 years.

Ch. 233: Description of occasional dissolution (contd)[1]

1–4 Vyāsa continues: After the waters have risen to the Seven Sages (i.e. the Great Bear) the whole triple world is an ocean. Then a wind, originating from Viṣṇu's breath, destroys the clouds for 100 years. After drinking up the wind, the Lord who consists of everything rests in this ocean on Śeṣa as his bedstead; Hari lies there assuming the shape of Brahman.

5–6 He is praised by the perfected beings, Sanaka etc., in Janaloka. Those who, desiring liberation, have gone to Brahman's world (*brahmaloka*, might mean the world or state of *brahman*) meditate on him. The Lord himself is engrossed in yogic sleep (»sleep of absorption«) which consists of his own Māyā, meditating on himself in his aspect as Vāsudeva.

[1] This chapter corresponds to ViP 6,4.

7 Conclusion: This is the occasional (*naimittika*) dissolution, when Hari as Brahman, the cause (*nimitta*), rests there.

8 The world is active when he is awake. Everything disappears while he lies on his bed for his (sleep of) Māyā.

9 The night during which the world is an ocean is as long as a day of Brahman, comprising 1,000 periods of 4 ages.

10 At the end of the night Viṣṇu in the shape of Brahman awakes and creates, as told above.

11 Conclusion to the report on the occasional dissolution at the end of a cosmic cycle. Announcement of (an account of) natural dissolution.

12–49 *Description of natural dissolution*

12–29 When (everything) has been achieved (?, ViP: washed away) by drought, fire, etc., in all worlds and the evolution, from Mahat to the specific evolutes, has been destroyed, when the dissolution has been started by the will of Kṛṣṇa, then the waters first swallow the quality of earth, viz. smell etc. Everything is filled with water. Light drinks up the quality of water; the waters disappear along with taste into fire. Everything is filled with fire. It is swallowed by wind; the quality of form disappears; there is only wind in all directions. Ether swallows touch, the quality of wind, which disappears. Then only ether and sound remain. The quality of sound is swallowed by the »origin of beings« (*bhūtādi*) in which senses and their objects coexist. »Origin of beings« is characterized by pride and known as belonging to *tamas* (the principle of Darkness). It is swallowed by »Great Consciousness« (*mahābuddhi*). Earth and the Great are the inner and outer limits; these are the seven productive forces (*prakṛtayaḥ*) in their sequence.[2]

30–33ab They enter into each other; the all-surrounding egg along with all its worlds, mountains, continents etc. dissolves in water. The cover (layer) of water is drunk up by fire; fire dissolves in wind which enters into ether which is swallowed by the »origin of beings« and that in turn by the Great. Primordial matter swallows it along with the others.

33cd–35ab Primordial Matter is called the ultimate cause, being an equilibrium of the (three) Qualities (*guṇa*). It comprises all manifest and unmanifest forms.

35–38ab Further there is one pure, eternal, imperishable (principle)[3]. This in turn is part of the Supreme Self in which all figments of name and class etc. perish,[4] which is pure being, consists of knowledge, is above the Self. It is *brahman*, the highest Self, the highest Lord; it is Viṣṇu from where one does not return.

[2] Thus according to ViP; the reading of BrP looks like a corruption of it caused by a misunderstood vocative *mahābuddhe* which probably also explains *mahābuddhi* in v. 28 in place of a principle *mahat* which is *buddhi* or is characterized by *buddhi* (as in ViP). The sequence of constituents is as follows: earth - smell; water - taste; fire - visibility, form; wind - touch; ether - sound; *bhūtādi*; *mahābuddhi*.

[3] BrP omits the word *pumān* which might be expected here as in ViP.

[4] ViP: In which all figments of name and class etc. do not exist.

38cd–40ab Primordial Matter (*prakṛti*) and *puruṣa* both dissolve in the Supreme Self which is the support of everything, which is praised as a name of Viṣṇu in Vedas and Upaniṣads.[5]

40cd–43ab Vedic action is of two kinds, actively engaged and disengaged; in both ways (Viṣṇu, one of) whose forms is the sacrifice, is worshipped by men: as Lord or Soul of the sacrifice he is worshipped according to the methods taught in the three Vedas (listed); being identical with knowledge (*jñānātman*), he is worshipped by means of Yoga.

43cd–46ab Viṣṇu is everything that can be described and that cannot be named, manifest and unmanifest; in him, in Hari, Primordial Matter dissolves as well as the Supreme Person (spiritual principle; *puruṣa*).

46cd–49ab The span of time of two Parārdhas is called one day of Viṣṇu. The period of dissolution is of the same length. Day and night can be attributed to the supreme Self only in a figurative sense.

49cd Conclusion to the account on natural dissolution.

Ch. 234: On suffering and final release from existence (absolute dissolution)[1]

1–8 Vyāsa continues. Classification of suffering:

1 A man reaches absolute dissolution after experiencing threefold suffering (personal, caused by other beings, and cosmic-supernatural),[2] and after insight and detachment have arisen in him.

2–4 Personal suffering is twofold, bodily and mental. Announcement and list of physical diseases.

5–6 Announcement and list of mental afflictions.

7 Suffering caused by other beings arises from animals, demons, other people.

8 Suffering caused by nature or fate arises from cold, heat, lightning, etc.

9–42 Description of the sequence of sufferings in human life: The discomforts of the embryo, the suffering of birth (including loss of memory), the helplessness of infancy, the ignorance regarding duties and obligations which leads to hell, the infirmity and disgrace of old age, the process and pain of dying.

43 Conclusion; announcement of the sufferings in hell.

44–49 The torments of hell.

50–54ab There is suffering even in heaven, because there is fear of falling down again. One is reborn, and may die at an early age; whatever is pleasurable also contains the seed of suffering.

[5] Taken together, the above passages result in the following steps of dissolution: cosmic egg – water – light, fire – wind – ether – *bhūtādi* – *mahat* (m.) – *prakṛti* *avyakta* (= Brahman, *puruṣa*, Viṣṇu ?, cf. 35–38ab) – Supreme Self (*paramātman*, = Viṣṇu, *parameśvara*, etc.).

[1] This chapter corresponds to ViP 6,5.

[2] cf. e.g. SāṃkhyaKā 1.

54cd–57 Only the tree of release (liberation) can grant shade against the »heat of the sun« of worldly suffering. The only medicine against all-pervading suffering is to obtain God (*bhagavatprāpti*).

58–60ab The means to that are knowledge and action. Knowledge is of two kinds, that acquired by tradition and that arising from discernment. The *brahman* consisting of words is approached through tradition; the highest *brahman* is born from discernment. Ignorance is like darkness; like a lantern is that knowledge which arises from the senses, while knowledge arising from discernment is like the sun.

60cd–61ab Announcement of what Manu said with regard to the Veda.

61cd–63ab There are two *brahmans*, *brahman* as word and an absolute one; one approaches the second via the first. The Atharvaveda says that there are two kinds of knowledge; by the highest, the imperishable (*akṣara*) is reached; the other one consists of Ṛgveda etc.

63cd–66ab The absolute, unmanifest, causeless origin of beings etc. (list of epithets) is seen by the sages (*sūri*); it is the highest *brahman* upon which those meditate who desire liberation; it is Viṣṇu's highest step.

66cd–68ab He who knows origin and dissolution, coming and going of all beings, knowledge and ignorance, he is to be called »Bhagavat«, which indicates all positive qualities.

68cd–69ab He is Vāsudeva since all beings reside (*nirvasanti*) in him and he in all beings.

69cd–70ab Announcement of an explanation of »*Vāsudeva*« as given by Prajāpati to sages.

70c-f Vāsudeva resides (*vasate*) in beings, and they in him; he is the creator.

71–75 He is Primordial Matter; comprises all Qualities and transcends all qualities and faults; he transcends all »covers«[3] and covers the whole earth. He incorporates all good qualities; assumes bodies for the benefit of the world; he is free from afflictions; he is the manifest and the unmanifest; he is omniscient, omnipotent, pure, etc.

Ch. 235: Description of the practice of Yoga

1 The hermits request to know about that Yoga which is medicine against suffering and which leads to union with the highest *puruṣa*.[1]

2 The bard (*sūta*, i.e. Lomaharṣaṇa) introduces Kṛṣṇa Dvaipāyana as a Yogin.

3–29 Vyāsa's answer.

3 Announcement of that Yoga the practice of which leads to liberation.

4–5 One should listen to the teachings of Yoga, to Vedas, Purāṇas, etc., revere the teacher and practise Yoga with due consideration of food, time and place, faults.

6 The diet of the practitioner (grains, fruit, milk, etc.).

7–9 List of conditions (exhaustion, hunger, cold, etc.) and places (noisy; crossings; cremation places; etc.) forbidden for Yoga.

10 Announcement of faults occurring when the proper place is not observed.

[3] cf. above, v. 233.30–33.

[1] cf. above, BrP 234,55cd–57.

11-12 Deafness, loss of memory etc. ensue. Therefore the Yogin should take protective measures. The body is the means for achieving all goals of life (listed).

13-20 Description of the proper practice, with regard to place, time, lotus-position (*padmāsana*), attitude, direction of eyes to the tip of the nose, breath control, restriction of senses, extent of (pronouncing) the syllable *om* (*praṇava*). The motionless Yogin covers *tamas* (the principle of Darkness) with *rajas* (the principle of Passion) and that with *sattva* (the principle of Goodness); he unites with the highest *puruṣa* who is hidden in the heart-lotus.[2]

21-25 First he should fix organs, senses and elements in the »knower of the field« (*kṣetrajña*); this knower of the field is to be united with the absolute.[3] When the mind comes to an end in the Supreme Self, perfection of Yoga appears. Having given up objects and attachment, by dissolving in *brahman*, the Yogin reaches the highest step, *nirvāṇa*, the »fourth state«, and is liberated.

26-27 If the Yogin is free from desires he is liberated. By not attending to the senses, and by detachment the Yogin is liberated.

28 Yoga does not result from lotus-position (*padmāsana*) or from looking at the tip of the nose; the union of senses and mind is called Yoga.

29 Conclusion to the teaching of the liberating Yoga.

30 Lomaharṣaṇa concludes by mentioning that the hermits praised Vyāsa and were intent on asking more.

Ch. 236: On Sāṃkhya and Yoga[1]

1-2 The hermits have not drunk enough from the nectar of Vyāsa's words. They request to know more about Yoga and about Sāṃkhya.

3-5 They want to know how a properly qualified man (intelligent, truthful, etc.) reaches *brahman*, by which means unity of mind and senses can be achieved.

6-69 Vyāsa's answer, describing Sāṃkhya and Yoga.

6 Nobody reaches perfection except by knowledge and asceticism, by curbing the senses, by renouncing everything.

7-8 The »Great Elements« are the first emanation of the Self-born (= Brahman); they enter into embodied living beings, the body being constituted from earth, fluid from water, the eyes from light (fire), the vital breaths from wind, cavities from ether.

9 Viṣṇu is in the feet, Indra in the strength, fire in the belly, the directions are in the ears, Sarasvatī is in the tongue.

[2] *sarvavyāpi*, as in the text, would have to refer to some neuter noun, but could refer to *puruṣottamam* if taken as first member of the compound *sarvavyāpi-nirañjanam*.

[3] VePr inserts three lines on the supernatural perception of Yogins in meditation: They can see the highest step which is characterized as being as small as the 100th part of the tip of a hair.

[1] BrP Ch. 236-245 have parallels in the Śāntiparvan of MBh; for a concordance, cf. Appendix to the text-volume. BrP 236.3-35 corresponds to MBh 12,231.2-34.

10–11 There are ten senses (the five senses of perception are listed), and their separate domains: sound, touch, form, taste, smell.

12 The mind bridles the senses like horses;[2] while the Elemental Self (*bhūtātman*), which rests in the heart, bridles the mind.

13 The mind is master over the senses; the Elemental Self is master over the mind.

14 Constituents of a living being: (5) senses, (5) domains of senses, (1) selfness (*svabhāva*), (1) consciousness (*cetanā*), (1) mind, (2) vital breaths, (1) soul (*jīva*) (making 16 constituents).

15 Consciousness is not called a Quality; *sattva* has no foundation but creates *rajas*, but never the qualities (?).[3]

16ab 16 qualities[4] cover the body[5] which is 17th.

16cd–19 The self which the wise perceive cannot be seen with the eyes but with an enlightened mind. That imperishable[6] is without sound etc., without body but in the body; he who perceives it is ready to become *brahman* after death.

20 The wise look with indifference at a Brahmin, a cow, an elephant, a dog, or an outcaste.

21–23 On the identity of individual and universal self: The Great Self resides in all beings. When the Elemental Self (or, created self?) sees itself in all beings and all beings in itself, then it attains *brahman*. He who is continuously aware that the self in himself is of the same size as in the supreme self, he is ready for immortality.

24–25 Even the gods are confused about the way of that self in all beings, which shows no traces; the way of those who know is like that of a fish in water, of a bird in air.

26 Time »cooks« all beings; but nobody knows wherein time is »cooked«.

27–31 Description of the highest self (i.e. Great Self, cf. v. 21): It has no directions, nothing is outside of it; one cannot reach the end of this cause of everything, even if moving at the speed of thought like an arrow. There is nothing more subtle, nothing more massive; it has hands, feet, eyes etc. on all sides and surrounds everything.[7] It is smaller than atoms, larger than the large. It exists inside all beings but is not perceived.

32 This Self exists in two conditions, perishable in all beings, and imperishable and divine.

33 As a »goose« (*haṃsa*) he is in the body, the »city with nine gates«, restrained, powerful with regard to everything created.[8]

34 Those who see beyond speak of the goose-nature of the unborn.[9]

[2] According to MBh; *rājinaḥ* is obviously a misreading for *vājinaḥ*.

[3] Possibly the text applies the term *guṇa* on two levels, that of metaphysical principles (Goodness, Passion, Darkness), and that of the characteristics or constituents of particular things, cf. v. 16.

[4] i.e. the constituents named in v. 14?

[5] MBh reads *dehe*, »in the body«.

[6] Neuter; while »self« would be masculine.

[7] cf. RV 10,90.

[8] cf. e.g. ŚvetUp 3.18.

[9] v. 34ab unclear.

35 The perishable called »goose« is imperishable when standing aloof (*kūṭastha*); the knowing person who reaches it leaves life and (re-)birth.

36-37ab Vyāsa continues:[10] Conclusion of the answer to the question regarding Sāṃkhya; announcement of (an account of) what has to be done for Yoga.

7cd-40ab The highest knowledge is that of the all-pervading Self (achieved by) unity of senses, mind, and Consciousness (*buddhi*). It can be recognized by someone who is restrained, akin to the Self, etc., who has exterminated the five faults of Yoga (lust, anger, greed, fear, sleep).

0cd-43ab How to conquer the faults of Yoga: Anger by restraint, lust by avoiding desire; sleep by attending to the principle of Beingness; eating and sex by perseverance (firmness); hands and feet are controlled by the eyes; ear and eyes by the mind; mind and speaking by (proper) action; fear is avoided by sobriety; conceit by serving the wise.

3cd-44ab Prescriptions for the proper behaviour of a Yogin: To bow to fire, Brahmins, gods; to avoid harsh, violent speech.

4cd-45ab (The principle of) semen (*śukra*) consists of the brilliance of *brahman*; from it originates the whole world; animate and inanimate beings are regarded as originating from it, the »being of beings« (?).

45cd-46 Meditation, recitation, giving alms, truthfulness, purity etc. increase brilliance and abolish evil.

47-48ab Prerequisites for attaining the rank of Brahman: Equanimity, light food, control of senses, etc.

8cd-49ab Having concentrated mind and senses, one should fix the mind in the self at the beginning and end of the night.[11]

49cd-53 Need to control mind and senses, which are to be fixed in the mind. After the extinction of desires the mind is to be fixed in the Self (metaphorical illustrations). This accomplished, *brahman* shines forth.

54-56ab Prudent (etc.) Brahmins see the Self in the self like a smokeless fire, etc., omnipresent.

6cd-57ab He who observes this strictly, sitting in a secluded place, becomes like the imperishable.

7cd-59ab List of distracting experiences which the Yogin has to disregard: Confusion, giddiness, visions, voices, etc.

59cd-66 A hermit should gain experience in Yoga on the summit of a mountain etc.; control of the mind is foremost; he should live in isolation, maintain equanimity; after six months the sound of *brahman* arises.

67 He must not be distracted by seeing others suffer.

68 Even an outcaste or a woman may reach the ultimate goal by that way.

69 Those who have seen the unborn, eternal, etc., become identical with the highest (principle) (and) do not return.[12]

[10] This repetition of the mention of the speaker (*vyāsa uvāca*) is superfluous in the context of BrP; it is explicable as a remnant of the context of MBh where a new chapter begins here. BrP 236.36-69 corresponds to MBh 12,232.1-34.

[11] cf. also 237.32 below.

[12] In Vaṃśasthavila-metre.

Ch. 237: On the opposition of action and knowledge[1]

1-2 The hermits request clarification regarding the two incongruous injunctions, either to engage in activity or to renounce actions for the sake of knowledge.

3-20 Vyāsa's answer.

3-4 Announcement of an explanation of both positions.

5 To affirm the existence of *dharma* is appropriate; to deny it is (the view) of a Yakṣa.[2]

6 There are two paths, on which the Vedas have taken their stand: the *dharma* of active involvement, and the disengaged *dharma*.

7-14 Action binds, knowledge liberates; ascetics therefore do not act; by actions one is reborn as constituted by the 16 constituents; by knowledge one becomes unmanifest, imperishable. Men of small intelligence (*buddhi*) praise action, but those who have reached the highest consciousness (*buddhi*) do not praise action which leads to further fruition, while knowledge leads beyond suffering, birth, death, and old age, to the highest, eternal, etc., *brahman*, where everyone is free from opposites and is friendly.

15-16 There are two kinds of men, men of knowledge and men of action, comparable to the moon ...[3]

17-19 The self of 11 evolutes brought together by parts (?) should be known as possessing shape and consisting of qualities and actions. The god in it is (like a) drop of Consciousness (*buddhi*) in a lotus, to be known as the »knower of the field«, as that which is conquered by Yoga. The three Qualities make up the qualities of the soul (*jīva*); the soul has the quality of the self, the self (that) of the supreme Self.

20 The conscious quality of the soul moves everything; beyond that is the »knower of the field«, according to those who imagine seven worlds.[4]

21-42 Vyāsa continues:[5]

21-22 The transformations of Primordial Matter are called »knowers of the field«;[6] they do not know him, but he knows them;[7] with the senses and the mind he performs actions, like a charioteer does with horses.

23-25 Senses, their objects (domains), mind, Consciousness (*buddhi*), the »Great Self«, the Unmanifest, the immortal, each stand higher than the one before; the immortal

[1] v. 1-20 of this chapter correspond to MBh 12,233.1-20.

[2] In MBh the contradiction is not demonized.

[3] The references to the moon and the »bent thread« (the first sixteenth of the new moon looks like a bent thread) are not clear; Nīlakaṇṭha refers to BĀUp 1,5.14.

[4] »Who made the seven worlds revolve«, according to MBh; in Upendravajrā-metre.

[5] The repeated mention of the speaker indicates the beginning of a new section, as in MBh. BrP 237.21-42 corresponds to MBh 12,238.1-20. The intervening chapters in MBh are concerned with prescriptions for the ways of life of a Brahmacārin (12,234), of a householder (12,235), of the hermit (12,236), and with the (yogic) practices of a renouncer (12,237).

[6] According to MBh: »The transformations of Primordial Matter surround the »knower of the field«; this reading seems to be presupposed by the second line.

[7] According to MBh; BrP reads: »nor does he know them;« it is not clear, however, to whom this »he« refers.

is the highest limit, the highest refuge. The hidden self in beings is perceived by that subtle, foremost Consciousness.[8]

26–27 After merging mind, senses, etc., in the inner Self and endowing the mind with knowledge, one goes to the highest position (or, takes the last step), now having no superior (*anīśvara*).

28 The mortal whose self is subject to the senses, whose memory is unstable, reaches death.

29–31 One should give up all desires and let the mind enter into Goodness (*sattva*); by settling the mind the ascetic reaches absolute happiness. The characteristic of this settling is like the happiness of sleep, like a flame in a windless place.

32 Thus uniting the Self in the self during the night, eating light food, one will see the self in the Self.

33–40 Characterization of the above teaching as secret, as essence of all knowledge, which must not be given to unqualified persons (e.g. who lack self-control, vedic education, etc.), which is worth more than the whole earth.

41–42ab Announcement of an even greater secret from the Upaniṣads (*vedānta*).

42c-f Conclusion of the answer to the hermits' doubt.

43 The hermits request to be told again about the Self.[9]

44–45 Vyāsa's answer.

44 Announcement.

45 He who (is) the five great elements (earth, water, fire, wind, ether) in all beings, (is) the creator of beings (or elements).

46a-f The hermits inquire: How can one describe what may have a shape (but) in which one does not see a body? The senses have some qualities; how are they recognized?[10]

47–89 Vyāsa's answer.

47 Announcement.

48–50 The qualities of elements:

ether:	sound, hearing, cavities;
wind:	breath, movements, touch;
fire:	shape, sight, digestion;
water:	fluid, taste, sweat;
earth:	odours, smelling, body.

51 Touch relates to wind, taste to water, shape to fire (light), sound to ether, smell to earth.

52 Mind, Consciousness (*buddhi*), selfness (*svabhāva*) are self-originated qualities and transcend the (above) qualities.[11]

[8] For v. 23–25 cf. KaṭhaUp 1,3.10–12.

[9] This question marks the beginning of MBh 12,239. MBh 12,239–241 have a close parallel in MBh 12,187 and in MBh (ed. B) 12,286; the variants of this last version are given in MBh (crit. ed.) 12 AppII,1 (vol. 16, p. 2113–2119).

[10] MBh attributes the line corresponding to 46ab to Vyāsa; meaning and structure of the argument are thus different in BrP.

[11] *Svabhāva* seems to take the place of what is called *ahaṃkāra* in classical Sāṃkhya-terminology.

53 He to whom Consciousness means the most withdraws the senses like a tortoise withdraws its limbs.

54 Highest Consciousness functions in the whole body (?).

55 Consciousness is led by the Qualities and leads the senses including the mind; without Consciousness there would be no qualities.[12]

56 People speak of five senses, mind as the sixth, Consciousness as the seventh, the »knower of the field« the eighth.[13]

57 Sight is for looking, mind deliberates, Awareness determines, the »knower of the field« functions as witness.

58–61 The principles of Passion, Darkness and Goodness are self-originated;[14] they are the same in all beings (or elements); they are the »Qualities«. Anything pleasant, tranquil relates to *sattva* (Goodness); anything connected with affliction (excitement) is indicative of *rajas* (Passion); anything confused, unclear, unintelligible relates to *tamas* (Darkness).

62–64 Characteristics of the Qualities: *sattva* is characterized by joy, pleasantness, self-content; *rajas* by pride, lying, greed, confusion, impatience; *tamas* by confusion, carelessness, fatigue, sleep.

65 Impulse to action is threefold: The mind produces a disposition (*bhāva*); consciousness determines (it); the heart (experiences it as) pleasant.

66 The things are above the senses, mind above things, Consciousness above mind, the highest Self above Consciousness.[15]

67–72 Consciousness is the self of man, it leads the self. When it evolves some condition it becomes the mind. Being separate from the senses, it evolves accordingly: When hearing it become (the sense of) hearing etc.; it differentiates according to sense functions. It obtains pleasure or pain but remains unperturbed. It is identical with the conditions (*bhāva*)[16] and transcends the three of them, as the ocean holds (absorbs) the great floods of the rivers.

73–75 When it (Consciousness) strives for something it becomes the mind;[17] the senses are nevertheless independent and separate. Consciousness (appropriates) the undivided mind; a »disposition« exists (only) in the mind. Prevailing Passion, however, surpasses even the *sattva*-Quality.

76 Those (i.e. the senses?) which come about due to the disposition (*bhāvena*)[18] (exist) in the three (Qualities); they follow their objects like the spokes the felly.

77 The mind should function as lantern along with the senses, which are infused by Consciousness and which may move out or remain indifferent.

[12] Thus according to VePr and MBh.

[13] *Viddhi* does not fit the dialogical setting in BrP. It is not found, however, in the MBh parallels, which have *punar*.

[14] cf. above, v. 52.

[15] cf. KaṭhaUp 1,3.10, and v. 23 above.

[16] i.e. created by mind and senses; or, the emotional states of pleasantness, suffering and perturbation (being indications of the three Qualities).

[17] cf. above, v. 67.

[18] MBh reads »All dispositions which come about«.

78 Nobody should be confused by knowing this.

79-81 The self cannot be perceived by the senses; but when they are curbed by the mind, as if darkness had approached for all beings and everything was light, it shines forth like an illumined form.

82-86ab The liberated Yogin is not affected by the faults of the Qualities (or, by faults and good qualities) like an aquatic bird which is not affected by water; a wise man is not attached and is not affected; if he renounces his former actions and becomes the Self of all beings, being attached (only) by the bond of Qualities,[19] the Self by itself bears fruit, sometimes even among the qualities. The Qualities do not know the Self, but the Self knows them.

86cd-89 One should recognize the difference between the principle of Goodness and the »knower of the field«. One emanates (creates) Qualities, the other does not. Both are separated by the principle of Matter and yet always joined, like gold with stone, like fly and leaf, like cane and shaft, separate yet mutually supportive.

Ch. 238: On liberation by knowledge[1]

1-14 Vyāsa continues.

1 *Sattva* creates the qualities, the »knower of the field« stands above, indifferently, as Lord.

2 Everything is bound to (or, by) selfness (*svabhāva*); when creating the qualities it (*sattva*) creates them like a spider its thread.

3-4 Once in function they do not return, (but) their functioning is not perceived, say some; others (postulate) a return. One should settle this, otherwise there may be great doubt.

5-6 A man should remain without anger or rejoicing after having perceived the Self which has neither beginning nor end.[2]

7-11 Self-knowledge liberates: One should cross this unsteady (world) like a river.[3] He who knows the truth walks on firm ground, for he has contemplated about the only self-knowledge. A man who has recognized the created world as a coming and going of beings obtains highest quietude. To be dedicated to this is a privilege (?) of the twice-born, especially of Brahmins. Those who know the truth are liberated.

12-14 Those who know have no fear; they reach the ultimate goal. Man is discontent with (his) mother and suffers, not seing the god; he who knows what has been done and not done, does not suffer. He blames (VePr »burns«) what was done previously, without intention; what is pleasant and not unpleasant originates for him who acts.[4]

[19] Possibly one should rather read *guṇasaṅge na sajjataḥ*.

[1] BrP 238.1-14 correspond to MBh 12,241.1-14.

[2] v. 6 seems corrupt.

[3] Corrupt wording?

[4] A comparison of this passage with MBh invites a number of textual conjectures. v. 12 is in Jagatī-metre, v. 13-14 in Rathoddhatā-metre, irregular in BrP, regular in MBh.

15 The hermits inquire about the highest *dharma*.[5]
16-39 Vyāsa's answer.
16 Announcement.
17-19 To restrain the senses by Consciousness and unite mind and senses is highest asceticism and highest *dharma*. Thus he was content with the self.[6]
20-23 When the senses are withdrawn the highest Self is seen; the Great Self, identical with the self of all, looks like a smokeless fire. The self does not know its origin or goal (comparison with a tree). There is another, inner self which sees everything.
24-25 Having seen the self by the self one becomes free of passions, free from evil, like a snake which has cast off its skin.
26-30 Allegorical description of the world of senses and passions as a river to be crossed by self-knowledge.
31-33ab By standing firm on Consciousness (*buddhi*) one becomes prepared to become *brahman*, looks at all beings indifferently and sees their origin and end.
33cd-34ab Conclusion: This is the best of *dharmas*.
34cd-35ab The teaching that the selves are all-pervading must only be told to a restrained, friendly person.
35cd-36ab Conclusion: The most secret self-knowledge has been spoken about.
36cd-37ab *Brahman* is above genders, etc.
37cd A man or a woman who knows this is not born again.
38 Conclusion: All existing and non-existing opinions have been told.
39 If asked by a son one should tell him what was said above.[7]
40 The hermits request to know the means for liberation.[8]
41-57 Vyāsa's answer.
41 Vyāsa declares his competence.
42-43 There are different notions (*buddhi*) and paths ...[9]
44-51 Hindrances on the way to self-control and self-knowledge and how to conquer them (anger by forbearance, lust by avoiding desires, etc.).
52 The five faults in Yoga: Lust, anger, greed, fear, sleep.
53-56ab Avoiding those one should practice meditation, recitation, giving alms, truth, modesty etc., which increases brilliance and provokes knowledge; one thus enters the state (or rank) of *brahman*.
56cd-57 The pure path of liberation consists of lack of confusion, anger, excitement etc.

[5] BrP 238.15-39 corresponds to MBh 12,242.1-25, i.e. this question marks the beginning of a new chapter in MBh.

[6] BrP reads *sa evāsīd* for *ivāsīta* in MBh.

[7] In Indravajrā-metre.

[8] BrP 238.40-57 corresponds to MBh 12,266.1-19; the intervening chapters in MBh concern related topics (elements and qualities; yogic vision; control of senses and desires) in chapters 243-247 and, in chapters 248-265, teachings and episodes related to non-violence (*ahiṃsā*). cf. Peter Schreiner: Gewaltlosigkeit und Tötungsverbot im Hinduismus, in: H. v. Stietencron (ed.): Angst und Gewalt: Ihre Präsenz und ihre Bewältigung in den Religionen. Düsseldorf 1979, p. 287-308.

[9] Unclear, with unclear comparison to the making of a pot.

Ch. 239: On the difference between Sāṃkhya and Yoga; on the practice of Yoga[1]

1 The hermits praise Vyāsa's omniscience and inquire about the difference between Sāṃkhya and Yoga.

2-9 Vyāsa's answer.

2 Adherents of Sāṃkhya and Yoga each praise their own position.

3 Adherents of Yoga question the liberation of one who does not believe in God (*īśvara*).

4-5 Adherents of Sāṃkhya proclaim their view as the system leading to liberation (*mokṣadarśana*) due to knowledge and detachment.

6 One must stick to one's position but (also) accept the opinion of the learned.

7-9 Yoga is grounded in direct experience,[2] Sāṃkhya is ascertained by learned traditon; both are true and can lead to the ultimate goal. Purity, compassion and maintaining observances is common to both; the theory (*darśana*) is different.

10 The hermits inquire why, practices being identical, the theory is the same.[3]

11-41 Vyāsa's answer.

11-23 Having overcome the faults of Yoga (passion, confusion, attachment, lust, anger) those who have the strength are purified and liberated (metaphorical illustrations comparing the Yogin with an animal caught in a net, with a fire, with an elephant).

24-28 The powers of Yoga provide access to supernatural beings, protect against death, etc., allow the Yogin to multiply himself, to obtain everything, even Viṣṇu who dispenses liberation.

29-30 Conclusion; and announcement regarding subtle illustrations of absorption and concentration.

31-38 Comparisons of the Yogin approaching the ultimate goal (i.e. when dying?) with an archer, with someone carrying a full vessel upstairs, with the helmsman on a boat, with a charioteer, with a fish.

39-41 Unification of the subtle self with various parts of the body (listed) leads to destruction of action (*karman*) and to liberation at will.

42 The hermits inquire about what the Yogin eats and what he conquers in order to obtain his powers.

43-62 Vyāsa's answer: On the yogic way of life and on the perils of concentration.

43-46 The diet of the Yogin:[4] The Yogin obtains power(s) by grains and oil-cake, but no oil, by barley, water mixed with milk, by fasting for a month.

47-49 By conquering lust, anger, heat and cold, fear, sorrow, sleep, etc., the Yogin lets his self shine.

50-52 Illustration of the difficulty of the path of Yoga (compared to a forest beset with dangers).

[1] This chapter corresponds to MBh 12,289.1-62. The intervening chapters in MBh contain a number of independent episodes and dialogues.

[2] Thus according to MBh.

[3] Sic; MBh has »not the same« as required by the context.

[4] Ed. Veṅk. prints v. 43 as footnote.

53 He who leaves this path commits a grave fault.

54-56 Illustrations of the precarious nature of concentration (*dhāraṇā*), compared to standing on a razor's edge, to steering a ship); when properly practised it leads beyond birth and death.

57 Conclusion (with reference to several teaching traditions, *nānāśāstreṣu*).

58-61 List of beings (e.g. gods like Brahman, Viṣṇu, Bhava (= Śiva), Siddhi (Varuṇa's wife) etc., supernatural beings like Gandharvas, and realms of being (e.g. the three Qualities, mountains, rivers, etc.), which the liberated Yogin reaches and »enters«.[5]

62 Conclusion;[6] mortals who have experienced all Yogas reach Nārāyaṇa.

Ch. 240: On Sāṃkhya and Yoga.[1]

1-2 The hermits applaud Vyāsa for having taught the path of Yoga.[2] They confirm Vyāsa's omniscience and inquire about the prescription of *dharma* in Sāṃkhya.

3-49 Vyāsa's answer.

3-4 Announcement of (an account of) what was put down by Kapila and other sages, in which some see many errors (but) in which there are many qualities and singular lack of faults.

5-16 The realms[3] (specified, e.g. of human and supernatural beings, of animals, demons, gods) and objects (specified, e.g. duration of the world or of suffering in hells; the qualities or attributes of heaven; advantages and disadvantages of vedic teachings, of the Yoga of knowledge, of knowing Sāṃkhya; the various aspects of the Qualities (*tamas, rajas, sattva*) and of Consciousness[4]), which are mastered through knowledge by those who reach liberation.

17-49 Realms and objects of knowledge.[5]

17-19 Senses and their domains (eyesight: form etc.); delusion is based on Darkness, greed on delusion. Viṣṇu, Śakra (= Indra), fire, the Goddess preside over parts or functions of the body.

20-22ab Sequence of dependent constituents: Wind - fire - ether - the Great - *tamas*;[6] *rajas* - *sattva* - Self - Nārāyaṇa - liberation, which depends on nothing else.

[5] In Upajāti-metre; v. 60c has 12 syllables, but in ed. ASS only.

[6] v. 62ab not clear.

[1] This chapter corresponds to MBh 12,290.1-100.

[2] They say »to this student here« (sing.) which may be said by Yudhisthira in the context of MBh, but obviously has not been adjusted to the dialogical frame of the BrP.

[3] cf. 239.4, where *sarvā gatīḥ* may mean e.g. the realms listed here.

[4] One line, corresponding to MBh 290.15bc, is missing, as is evident from the interruption of the series of decreasing numbers of aspects which jumps from six to three.

[5] Regarding the construction of these passages, v. 16 contains the only main clause (»they reach ... liberation«) which is placed between two series of absolutives (v. 5-16 and v. 17-49).

[6] The sequence is corrupted by the omission of one line corresponding to MBh 12,290.21d-22a.

22cd–26 The body (constituted) by 16 qualities; selfness (*svabhāva*); realization (*bhāvanā*); the self; work; senses and sense-objects; the difficulty of attaining liberation; the seven vital breaths;

27–32 Lords of beings; sages, creations; those who have fallen; the sufferings of those fallen in the river Vaitaraṇī, of those variously reborn; the unpleasantness of embryonic existence;

33–34 various Yogas; the ways of human beings dominated by Darkness or Goodness blamed by great adherents of Sāṃkhya;

35–37 the upheaval of sun, moon, and stars; the separation of pairs; the mutual devouring among beings; delusion;

38–44 the difficulty of attaining liberation (aimed at by one among a thousand men;[7] the attitudes of indifference; the body of the dead; rebirth among various families; the suffering (even) of the good; the fate of sinners (Brahmin-murderers; drinkers; offenders against their teacher's wife; those who behave improperly against their mothers, against the heavenly worlds); the effects of evil deeds; the fate of those reborn as animals;

45–49 Vedic teachings; the change of seasons; the passing of time; the phases of the moon; the arising and vanishing of oceans, wealth, relationships, cosmic periods; the deficiencies of the body.

50 The hermits inquire about faults which arise from portents.[8]

51–75 Vyāsa's answer.

51–52 Announcement: Knowers of Sāṃkhya, adherents of Kapila teach five faults: Lust, anger, fear, sleep, breathing.

53–54ab How to conquer these faults: Anger by forbearance (forgiveness), etc.; breathing by eating little.

54cd–68 Those who recognize the worthlessness and the dangers of the world which is Viṣṇu's Māyā (metaphorically described as a lake or ocean) by Sāṃkhya-knowledge thereby cross that lake.

69–75 The path of the liberated: They enter ether; the sun transports them by its rays; wind picks them up and leads them to auspicious worlds, to the highest reach of ether; ether leads them to the highest reach of the principle of Passion (*rajas*), which transports them to the ultimate reach of Goodness (*sattva*); Goodness leads to Nārāyaṇa who leads to the supreme Self; there they become ready for immortality and do not return.

76 Conclusion: This is the ultimate goal of those who are beyond dualities, devoted to truth, endowed with pity for all beings.

77–80 The hermits inquire whether those who have reached the highest stage enjoy it till birth or death or not;[9] they praise Vyāsa's competence; and they point out that liberation would be faulty if, after reaching those sages who attained perfection, one remained in (worldly) knowledge;[10] they consider the *dharma* of involvement

[7] v. 38cd is closely parallel to v. 25ab.

[8] The answer confirms the reading of MBh: »which arise from one's body«.

[9] The line 77cd is probably corrupt, as indicated by thrice *vā*; the point of the question in MBh is whether they remember (*smaranty uta* for *ramante tatra*) or not.

[10] *Vijñāne*, as opposed to *pare jñāne* in v. 80.

(*pravṛtti*) the highest, while for one who is immersed in highest knowledge it might be another (form of) suffering.

81–112 Vyāsa's answer.

81 Vyasa praises the question raised.

82 Announcement of the answer as to where the highest Consciousness (*buddhi*) (exists) according to the adherents of Kapila.

83–84 The senses perceive the body; they are organs for the subtle self and they are powerless without it (metaphorically illustrated).

85–92ab Experience of sleep and dream: The subtle self roams about with the senses, while they are powerless in their respective places in the body. The self, the »knower of the field«, penetrates all qualities (of the three Qualities, of Consciousness, mind, ether, of the five elements) with (his) qualities and roams about.

92cd The senses are like pupils to him (?).

93–94 Having transcended the principle of Matter (*prakṛti*) he (goes to) Nārāyaṇa, the highest Self.[11]

95 Like pupils, mind and senses approach this best one.[12]

96–112 Praise of Sāṃkhya.

96–97 It is possible to reach peace and the Qualities in a short time by the Sāṃkhya-Yoga thus described. The adherents of Sāṃkhya reach the highest goal. There is no knowledge equal to that.

98–103 Sāṃkhya knowledge is the highest; it is called the imperishable eternal *brahman* without beginning and end, etc. (list of epithets), from which all creation and dissolution stems, which is taught in the learned traditions (*śāstra*), the God whom all Vedas aim at and talk about. It is formless; Sāṃkhya is (its) form according to revelation; there are great proofs for it.

104 Among the two kinds of beings on earth, mobile and immobile (animate and inanimate), the mobile is distinguished (?).[13]

105–112 Conclusion.[14]

105 Sāṃkhya is the epitome of all knowledge contained in Vedas, Sāṃkhya, Yoga, and in the Purāṇa.

106–111 Sāṃkhya is the epitome of all knowledge contained in historical tradition (*itihāsa*) and Arthaśāstra; it teaches strength, knowledge, liberation, asceticism; its opposite is always beneficial (?); adherents of Sāṃkhya enjoy pleasures and are reborn as Brahmins. ... ;[15] they reach liberation after death; they are (not?) reborn among animals or sinners, even though they are not eminent among the twice-born. Sāṃkhya is (like) a vast pure ocean which the hermits should concentrate upon (as existing) in Nārāyaṇa.

112 Conclusion: The highest truth has been told; Nārāyaṇa creates and dissolves the world.

[11] Some attributes of the Self in MBh are transformed by BrP to apply to Nārāyaṇa, which leaves the construction unclear.

[12] Construction?

[13] cf. 241.21f.??

[14] In Upajāti-metre.

[15] v. 108 does not make sense according to the reading of BrP.

Ch. 241: Dialogue between Karālajanaka and Vasiṣṭha[1]

1-2 The hermits inquire about that imperishable (*akṣara*) from where one does not return, and about the perishable, as well as about the manifestation of both.

3-4 They praise Vyāsa and his knowledge.

5 Vyāsa announces a report on the dialogue between Vasiṣṭha and Karālajanaka.

6-8 King Janaka asked Vasiṣṭha (who is characterized as skilled with regard to the highest self and certain about the goal of the self) about the highest knowledge.

9-10 Janaka asked about the highest *brahman* and about that which is called perishable.

11-48 Vasiṣṭha's answer.[2]

11-36 *On the emanation of the world*

11 Announcement regarding the perishing of the world.

12-16ab The extent of a cosmic period, cosmic cycle, and day and night of Brahman; at the end of a night of Brahman, he (called e.g. Śaṃbhu and Svayaṃbhu, »Self-originated«) creates the »Great Being« (described e.g. as Lord, light, as having hands, feet, eyes, etc. on all sides[3]).

16cd-19ab Various traditional names (of that first created being?): Golden embryo (*hiraṇyagarbha*), Consciousness (*buddhi*), the »Great« (*mahat*) in Yoga; Viriñci in Sāṃkhya. It has various forms, is all, is the one syllable (*om*?), has all forms (or, the all as its form, *viśvarūpa*).

19cd-20 Undergoing transformations he emanates himself by himself - the principle of Matter (*pradhāna*) originated from contact with him - as the principle of Ego (*ahaṃkāra*).

21-22 What is made manifest from the unmanifest is also called »creation by knowledge«; while the Great, the principle of Ego (is called) »creation by ignorance«. Both, mobile and immobile (animate and inanimate), originated from the One and are called »knowledge and ignorance«.

23-25 The third (step of creation?) is the creation of elements from the principle of Ego; the fourth concerns what is transformed within the principle of Ego: The five elements and their respective qualities (domains, e.g. wind - sound etc.) and simultaneously the group of ten (i.e. senses and organs of action). The fifth is the elementary creation (creation of beings, or, creation from elements).

26-27 The ten organs of perception and of action (listed) originate simultaneously with the mind.

28 This manifest universe consists of 24 principles; those who know it are no longer pained.

29-32 Thus the triple world originated; this should be known regarding ocean(s) and hell(s) and all living beings (specified in a list); evidence is everywhere (?).

[1] This chapter corresponds to MBh 12,291; the dialogue extends from Ch. 241 to Ch. 245 (MBh 12,291-296).

[2] Vasiṣṭha's uninterrupted answer extends till the end of the next chapter, BrP 242.58.

[3] cf. RV 10,90.

33 Embodied beings are found only in water, on earth, and in the air.

34–36ab On every day (of Brahman?) he who is called the manifest perishes totally, (who is) what has originated (*bhūtātman*) and is called imperishable.[4] It is called perishable because it perishes like the world, which is said to be a delusion (*mohātmaka*). The Great is eternally imperishable.

36cd Conclusion: That from where there is no return has been told.

37–44 On the 25th principle: The 25th principle is unmanifest, is called Goodness (*sattva*), creates the manifest, resides in the heart of all beings, animates them; endowed with the principle of Matter it (the 25th principle) transforms itself in creations and dissolutions; it is combined with the three Qualities in various beings and gets absorbed according to what people think of themselves, in accordance with the three Qualities.

45–47 All forms are white, red, or black; the king is told to give them up; by (the principle of) Darkness (*tamas*) one goes to hell; by Passion (*rajas*) one goes to the world of human beings; by Goodness (*sattva*) one enjoys pleasures in the world of the gods. By committing only sins one is reborn as an animal; in the case of both sins and merits, as a human being; in the case of merits only as a god.

48 Thus the wise said that liberation concerns the unmanifest; the 25th principle (i.e. the *puruṣa*) operates due to knowledge.

Ch. 242: On the worldly bondage and destiny of the soul[1]

1–3 Vasiṣṭha continues: Not being awakened (the embodied soul)[2] wanders through thousands of bodies – animals, human beings, gods.

4–5ab He who is free from Qualities gets bound by the threads of the Qualities like a larva in its chrysalis; he enters into opposites (*dvaṃdva*).

5cd–7 List of diseases which arise from the physical body and which the self ascribes to itself.

8–15ab It also (ascribes) good deeds to itself: modes of dressing (v. 8 and 12–14); various kinds of (ascetic?) resting places or postures;[3] foods and gems.

15cd–20ab Various modes of periodic fasting and restricted eating.

20cd–21ab Observances relating to the stages of life, *dharma* and *adharma*, various heresies.

21cd–22 Places of sojourn.

23–24 Religious observances (e.g. ascetic practices, sacrifices); castes; generosity.

25–26ab (The self) further ascribes to itself various qualities (attributes): The three Qualities (listed), the goals of life (listed); it divides itself according to (the conditions of) the principle of Matter (*prakṛti*).

26cd–27 Mention of sacrificial, ritual constituents and actions.

[4] Sic; MBh differently.

[1] BrP 242.1–52ab corresponds to MBh 12,292.1–48.

[2] Subject could be »the 25th« mentioned at the end of the last chapter.

[3] E.g. *vīrāsana*, which also belongs to the Haṭhayoga-postures.

28 The fear of good and bad (deeds) is eternal - through birth and death and by slaughter (?).

29–33 The goddess Prakṛti creates fear and dissolution. The One remains at the end of a day (of Brahman), surpassing the Qualities; it ascribes all that to itself for the sake of play (comparison to the sun and its rays) and attaches itself to action; the world is blinded by the principle of Matter.

34–39 Thoughts of the (deluded) embodied soul (first-person references), regarding the inevitability of suffering, the promise of enjoyment as the result of good deeds, and the chain of rebirths.

40–43ab From human existence (the soul) may go to hell; even the self of the twice-born is surrounded by the Qualities. Thereby (rebirth in) hell occurs among men and gods.

43cd–48ab *Prakṛti* acts and reaps in the various embodiments. The three states (of animal, man, god) belong to *prakṛti*. *Prakṛti* is to be inferred from its characteristics;[4] similarly the characteristic of *puruṣa* is based on inference; but assuming the characteristics of *prakṛti* (the *puruṣa*) ascribes actions and senses to himself, while the senses, emotions etc., are operating.

48cd–52ab Thoughts of the deluded embodied soul, ascribing to itself senses, sins, attributes, time etc., though being (really) free from all that.

52cd–55ab Thus, due to lack of insight, he undergoes thousands of births and deaths (comparison with moon).[5]

55cd–58ef Explanation of the above comparison of the man (or soul) without insight with the moon.[6]

Ch. 243: Dialogue between Karālajanaka and Vasiṣṭha (contd)[1]

1–10 Janaka explained the relation of *puruṣa* and *prakṛti* as one of man and woman who depend on their respective qualities to reproduce the (human) form. Some constituents stem from the father, e.g. bones, sinews, marrow, others stem from the mother, e.g. skin, flesh, blood. This is supported by Veda and learned tradition and, thus, eternally proved. On the basis of their eternal relatedness Janaka considered liberation impossible; he requested Vasiṣṭha to explain this and expressed his desire for liberation.

11–18 Vasiṣṭha replied by making some remarks on the proper understanding and use of books: They have not only to be learned but also understood; they have to be explained before being defended in disputes.

19 Announcement of an explanation according to the views of adherents of Yoga and Sāṃkhya.

[4] Construction?

[5] v. 52cd–58ef correspond to MBh 12,293.1–11.

[6] Not clear; the invisible 16th part of the moon is compared to the unchanging soul (cf. above, 237.15–16). The passage corresponding to MBh 12,293.7cd–11ab is missing in BrP.

[1] BrP 243.1–40 corresponds to MBh 12,293.12–50.

20 Sāṃkhya and Yoga are one, they aim at the same insight.

21–31 The bodily constituents (bone, flesh, blood, etc.) relate only to the senses; qualities (attributes) cannot originate from the great self which has no qualities (rhetorical question); they originate in the principle of Matter. The eight bodily constituents (listed) are also material. (There is) only *puruṣa* and non-*puruṣa*; the feminine is material. *Puruṣa* is the wind (breath?), called »sap« (i.e. »essence«, *rasa*) (?). *Prakṛti* is without characteristics but is perceived due to characteristics which originate from her, as with flowers and fruits (?); similarly the formed and the formless. Equally the 25th is by inference perceived as a characteristic (*liṅga*, »subtle body« ?); being without beginning and end it is only by (wrong) attribution (of material qualities) called or seen as a quality among qualities.

32–34 It is that which the wise according to Sāṃkhya and Yoga (?), due to lack of insight, claim to be above Consciousness (*buddhi*); they call it the Lord with attributes (?) who is unawakened like something manifest. Those who are well-versed in Sāṃkhya and Yoga know the Lord to be without attributes and as the 25th principle standing above the principle of Matter and the Qualities.

35 When they (people) do not recognize him as awakened, unmanifest, (and) in the process of awakening, they consider him/it the same (?).

36 This illustration is correct; the view (of Janaka?) was not correct. They recognize (him) in the process of awakening as different from both (?).

37–40 The illustration of the perishable and the imperishable has been declared by mutual (dependence ?); unity is called imperishable, plurality perishable. He who stands firm in the 25th principle sees both, unity and plurality. This illustration of reality and its knower as separate is correct (?). (Some) wise people speak of this principle (*tattva*) as a reality, (others) proclaim the unreality (or, the not being a principle) of the 25th as the highest. To be avoided is the conduct of one who is to be avoided; reality (springs) from reality eternally (?).

41–45 Janaka admitted to doubts, due to his intellectual limitations, regarding plurality and unity, regarding the reality of the unawakened,[2] the awakened and the one in the process of awakening, regarding the cause of the imperishable and the perishable. He requested to be told about seeing plurality and unity, about polarity, about the uninterrupted, and about the one in the process of awakening,[3] knowledge and ignorance, the imperishable and the perishable, Sāṃkhya and Yoga, the lack of Consciousness in the awakened.[4]

46–65 *Vasiṣṭha's answer concerning Yoga*[5]

46 Announcement.

[2] Read *abuddha*.

[3] According to MBh and to BrP 242.42ab the question should concern the awakened, the unawakened, and the one in the process of awakening.

[4] BrP 243.41–90 corresponds to MBh 12,294.1–49.

[5] Vasiṣṭha's answer extends to the end of the dialogue, BrP 245.41. The following sections referring to Janaka's questions can be identified:
243.46–65: Yoga

47-48 Among Yoga-practices meditation (*dhyāna*) is most powerful; it is of two kinds, concentration of the mind and breath control.

49 Occasions forbidden for Yoga: Urinating, voiding bowels, and eating.[6]

50-53 Turning away from the objects of the senses one should not stimulate the self, which stands above the 24th principle; it should be known continuously by one whose mind is not deficient. Being free from attachments, eating only light food, one should fix the mind in the heart during the night.

54-57 Description of firm concentration (immobility, no sense perceptions, no thoughts).

58 He does not get sexually aroused and moves in all directions.[7]

59-65 He sees the self in his heart as the subject and object of knowledge, which is luminous like a smokeless fire, like the sun, etc.; he is seen by Brahmins, is called most subtle and yet greatest, exists in all beings invisibly, is said to exist beyond Darkness, is pure, without attributes. There is no other indication of Yoga (rhetorical question). He who has such vision sees the highest self.

66 Conclusion (of the vision of Yoga) and announcement (of Sāṃkhya-knowledge).

67-90 On Sāṃkhya.

67-70 The sequence of origination: The unmanifest principle of Matter → the Great → the Ego-principle → five elements (the above eight are procreative, the following sixteen are only products) → five attributes[8] → five senses. So far the enumeration of principles.[9]

71-73 The process of absorption (dissolution) works in the reverse order; creation and absorption concern Matter which is one during absorption, manifold during creation.

74-81 The wise should discriminate the unmanifest (and that)[10] which stands above; the latter is one or many according to the condition of Matter; it lets Matter procreate; (Matter) is the field, the Great Self as the 25th stands above and knows it; thus it is called *puruṣa* because it lies in the unmanifest city (*pure śete*). The field, i.e. as unmanifest, and its knower are different. The unmanifest is knowledge (*jñānam*), the 25th is what is to be known (*jñeya*).[11] The unmanifest is also called Goodness (*sattva*) and Lord; the 25th is neither a principle nor Lord.

82-83 Sāṃkhya goes only so far; there is no complete enumeration; having enumerated 40, 24, by making the number 1000-fold ... the 25th is no principle.[12]

243.67-90: Sāṃkhya
244.1-9: Knowledge and ignorance
244.11-42: imperishable and perishable
245.1-30: Awakened, unawakened, in the process of awakening.

[6] According to MBh; BrP makes little sense.

[7] Corrupt.

[8] i.e. the qualities characteristic of the elements and perceived as their respective domains by the senses.

[9] One would expect mention of the five senses of action plus mind to arrive at sixteen.

[10] Thus with Deussen; cf. v. 78.

[11] Thus the terminology and literal meaning; one might expect rather that the 25th principle be described as subject of knowledge (Deussen translates accordingly); however, the process of cognition as well as its organs («*jñāna*«) are clearly material, and the self has been, in the Yoga-passage, described as that which is seen («*jñeya*«) as pure light.

[12] Corrupt passage.

84 The 25th is the awakened Self which is (yet) being awakened; when it awakens the self it becomes isolated (liberated).

85-90 Conclusion: Those who distinguish become like that (»go to sameness«); the correct illustration thus (is) direct perception of (the principle of) Matter ...[13] Those who remain thus do not return; the perishable is known not to be the highest, the imperishable the highest (?). Those who do not see correctly become manifest again and again, because they consider this (i.e. the material world) to be all and do not know the (real) all. The unmanifest is all; the 25th is no part of this all. There is no fear in those who know thus.

Ch. 244: Dialogue between Karālajanaka and Vasiṣṭha (contd)[1]

1 (Vasiṣṭha continues:) Conclusion of the topic of Sāṃkhya and announcement of the topic of »knowledge and ignorance«.

2-9 *On Knowledge and ignorance*[2]

3 Announcement of knowledge according to the view of Sāṃkhya.

4-9 The sense of perception is »knowledge« for the senses of action; the specific attributes (domains, cf. 243.67-70) (are knowledge) for the senses of perception; mind for (those) domains; the five elements for the mind; the Ego-principle for the elements; consciousness (for) the Ego-principle; *prakṛti* for consciousness; the highest Lord for all principles. Knowledge is to be known.[3] The unmanifest is not the highest; (real) knowledge is the 25th, called the »all in all«, beyond knowledge and object(s) of knowledge. The unmanifest is called »knowledge«, the 25th (n.) »object of knowledge« (*jñeya*); equally the unmanifest is »knowledge« and the 25th (m.) the »knower«.

10 Conclusion of the topic »knowledge and ignorance« and announcement of the topic »perishable and imperishable«.

11-42 *On perishable and imperishable*

11-14ab Both are called »perishable« and »not imperishable«, both have neither beginning nor end and are believed to be »Lord«; both are called »principles«. The unmanifest is called imperishable because it creates and dissolves (absorbs), producing for the creation by the Qualities; it brings about the mutual dependence of Qualities, the Great, etc.

[13] v. 86 seems corrupt.

[1] This chapter corresponds to MBh 12,295.

[2] v. 2 is corrupt; according to MBh: The unmanifest is called »ignorance«, the 25th »knowledge«.

[3] *jñeya*, i.e. *vidyā* is object of knowledge; cf. 243.80 and 244.9.

14cd–16 The 25th is called field when it (i.e. the unmanifest?) throws the net of the Qualities over the manifest self[4] ... it disappears in the 25th.[5] When the Qualities are absorbed into each other the principle of Matter is alone; then the »knower of the field« is led together ... .[6]

17–19 Matter attains the imperishable and (becomes) free from Qualities when, in the body,[7] it turns away from the Qualities. Similarly the »knower of the field« becomes free from Qualities when this knowledge directed to the field stops. He becomes perishable when he knows matter; freedom from Qualities (belongs) to the self (to him?) (?).

20–22 Then he becomes pure, recognizing that he and matter are different; he does not become enmeshed again. On rejecting the net of Qualities, one sees.

23–39 Thoughts of the awakened person (soul), who compares himself in his unredeemed condition to a fish in the water knowing nothing but the water; who blames his lack of insight which made him pursue ever new existences; who praises (the self) to which he became similar; who questions how, out of delusion and ignorance, he had remained in contact with time; who vows to remain detached; who blames himself rather than Matter; who ascribes his many rebirths to selfishness (*mamatva*) which he has now overcome; who wants to become equal to that (self).

40–41 By such insight the 25th is awakened; it/he attains imperishability. Having seen that the unmanifest has the characteristics of the manifest and that which has Qualities is without Qualities, and that what has no Qualities comes first, one becomes like it.

42 Conclusion of the illustration of »imperishable and perishable«.

43 Announcement of the »subtle, pure« as topic.

44–48 On the relation of Sāṃkhya and Yoga. Both have been demonstrated to be two learned traditions, but the view(s) of Yoga are also taught in Sāṃkhya. Sāṃkhya is knowledge which aims at awakening. In that learned tradition is taught also that reality of (which) adherents of Yoga (speak), which is connected with rebirth and is above the 25th (?). The highest principle of Sāṃkhya has been described as awakened, unawakened, and in the process of being awakened. Awakening and the process of being awakened are called illustrations of Yoga.

Ch. 245: Dialogue between Karālajanaka and Vasiṣṭha (contd)[1]

1–30 (Vasiṣṭha continued:) On awakening.[2]

[4] Or, reading *vyaktā ātmani*, »when the manifest (f.) throws the net over the self«.

[5] v. 15 corrupt.

[6] Corrupt.

[7] *vai dehe*, misunderstood vocative *vaideha* applying to Janaka.

[1] This chapter, up to v. 51, corresponds to MBh 12,296.1–50.

[2] Much of the ambiguity of the text derives from the use of the root *budh-* and its derivatives in a context which does not allow the reader to decide whether forms are transitive or intransitive (cognize/awaken), middle or passive (*budhyate*); cf. 243.41–45.

1 The unawakened unmanifest creates ...[3]

2-3 The unborn undergoes transformation for the sake of play and multiplies himself; while transforming he is in the process of awakening (but) does not awaken. He creates and moves the Qualities.

4-5ab Because of the cognition of the unmanifest he is also called cognizing (or, in the process of awakening, *budhyamāna*). The unmanifest does not cognize what has Qualities (or) what is without Qualities; sometimes it is called »known« (?, *pratibuddhaka*).

5cd-6 The 25th, when it cognizes the unmanifest, becomes cognizing. By being mutually cognized the unshakeable is called unmanifest (?).

7 Because of the cognition (*bodhana*) of the unmanifest they call the Great Self, the 25th, »cognizing«; but it does not cognize.

8-10ab The pure, eternal etc. 26th cognizes the 25th and the 24th; being isolated he cognizes the visible and the invisible, the unmanifest and *brahman*.

10cd-14ab When he (m.) cognizes himself, he thinks of himself as different. Then he becomes material when viewing the unmanifest; he cognizes the highest pure consciousness (*buddhi*); then, as awakened, he (i.e. the 25th?) becomes the 26th, abandons the unmanifest and remains in isolation and reaches the liberated Self.

14cd-16 This is called a »principle« (*tattva*) (though) it is not a principle, being free from old age and death. By hearing about the principles one knows them. The wise proclaim 25 principles. He who is endowed with principles (i.e. the 26th?) does not become immersed in wordly existences; he approaches their principles.

17-23ab That 26th is to be grasped; by that single strength he (i.e. the 25th?) becomes similar to it. Even when cognized by the awakened 26th, he (the 25th?) remains without consciousness (cognition, *buddhi*). This is called plurality according to Sāṃkhya and revelation. For the 25th endowed with insight (*cetana*), unity arises when cognized/awakened by consciousness (*buddhi*). It becomes similar to that awakened cognizing (i.e. the 26th). Being unattached it becomes attached; as unattached the 26th arises from action(s). The Lord (i.e. the 25th) abandons the unmanifest (the 24th) when it is cognized due to cognition of the 26th; he (i.e. the 25th) is not cognized and yet cognizing; as demonstrated by tradition it is also called cognized.

23cd-24 Two illustrations of the difference and unity, viz. fly and fig-tree, fish and water.

25-26 This is the liberation of the 25th existing in a body; it is said that it must in this way be liberated from the realm of the unmanifest.

27-30 By going near the highest, the pure, the liberated etc., one becomes the highest, pure, liberated, etc.

31-41 Conclusion: This illuminating teaching may be handed on only to those who stand firm in the Veda but not to the untruthful etc., to those who have faith and other qualifications (listed), but not to one who lacks them even if he should offer the whole earth. Karālajanaka is reminded that he need not fear anything now, since he has heard about the highest *brahman* (described). Vasiṣṭha received this teaching from Hiraṇyagarbha, i.e. Brahman.[4]

[3] ... the Qualities? Corrupt.

[4] In Triṣṭubh-Jagatī-metre.

42–53 Vyāsa continues.[5]
42–43 Conclusion: The highest *brahman* from where there is no return has been told. Those who do not know the highest knowledge truly return.
44–47 Conclusion: The liberating knowledge has been related as heard from the divine sage. Vasiṣṭha received it from Hiraṇyagarbha, Nārada from Vasiṣṭha, Vyāsa from Nārada. The hermits should not fear, as the result of this knowledge.
48–51 Those who do not have this knowledge are reborn a thousandfold in the ocean of existences from which the hermits have been saved.
52 Conclusion: Liberation has been truly taught.
53 This teaching must not be transmitted to unbelievers, to non-devotees, etc.

Ch. 246: Conclusion to Brahmapurāṇa

1–5 Lomaharṣaṇa resumes: Having told this Purāṇa (characterized e.g. by the adherence to dialectic style) to the hermits, Vyāsa stopped; having heard this first Purāṇa named after Brahman they were pleased and praised Vyāsa.
6–12 The hermits confirm the conclusion of this Purāṇa and praise Vyāsa's omniscience, who explained the meaning of the Vedas in his Mahābhārata, studied all four Vedas and subsidiary disciplines, filled the lamp of knowledge with the oil of the Mahābhārata,[1] and opened the eyes of those blinded by ignorance.
13–15 Lomaharṣaṇa continues: The hermits left. He rounds off his own recitation.
16–17 List of persons who may hear this Purāṇa.
18–19 Phalastutis: Specific results for the four castes of hearing this Purāṇa.
20 This Vaiṣṇava Purāṇa is distinguished among all traditions of learning and brings about the goals of life.
21–35 Phalastutis:
21–27 The merit obtained by hearing or reading this Purāṇa is equal to various other meritorious deeds (specified, e.g. fasting at Prayāga, Puṣkara, Kurukṣetra, Arbuda; bathing in the Yamunā; seeing Kṛṣṇa at Mathurā, etc.).
28–29 A Brahmin who recites this Purāṇa (to which fame, long life, etc. attach) at auspicious times (11th and 12th day of each half-month) goes to Viṣṇu's world.
30–33 Hearing this story (*ākhyāna*) fulfils all desires, frees from diseases, etc., effects remembrance of former existence, etc., fulfilment of the four goals of life.
34–35 He who devotedly listens to it enjoys happiness, here and in heaven, and then reaches Hari's step (*pada*). Therefore everyone desiring liberation, members of all four castes, should listen to it.[2]
36 Admonition to the listeners to pay attention to *dharma* which alone accompanies a person to the other world.[3]

[5] i.e. end of the dialogue between Karālajanaka and Vasiṣṭha.
[1] v. 11 in Upajāti-metre.
[2] In Śārdūlavikrīḍitā-metre.
[3] In Vasantatilakā-metre.

37–38 By *dharma* a man may gain power, heaven, fame, etc.; *dharma* is parents and friend to a man.[4]

39 This secret Purāṇa must not be transmitted to an unbeliever.

40 Conclusion: Recitation of the Purāṇa is complete; Lomaharṣaṇa asks permission to leave.

[4] In Upajāti-metre.

Part II

Index
to the Brahmapurāṇa

Ābālaprathitas **5**.30cd-31
abandoning of child **13**.127cd-132ab
- of follower, punishment for **22**.11
- of wife **82**.7-8; **154**.11cd-14ab
- of Yoga **219**.13-17; **239**.53
abbreviating formula **3**.78cd-80ab .89cd-90ab .102ab .106; **5**.3 .57cd-58ab; **13**.203-204; **14**.44; **18**.10; **21**.15-27; **25**.7-8ab; **27**.78cd; **41**.87; **45**.4; **46**.2; **54**.18-19; **55**.23cd-31; **64**.11-14; **65**.59-76ab .97-99; **68**.59cd; **70**.2cd; **79**.3-5ab; **174**.27cd-28; **175**.76-77; **176**.63; **177**.26 .27; **180**.39ab; **213**.165cd-168ab; **217**.115cd-116; **230**.9
abduction of Brahmin **167**.4-7
- of Pradyumna **199**.11-12
- of Rukmiṇī **199**.5-10
- of sacrificer **127**.4cd-9ab
- of Suvarṇā **128**.63cd-70ab
- of women **7**.98-99; **9**.17-20; **152**; **202**.3-12; **208**.4-7; **212**.18-20 .25-28 .42-53
- , punishment for **214**.88cd-96
Abhayada **13**.3-4
Abhayas **27**.59cd-62ab
Abhijit **15**.46cd-48
Abhimanyu **2**.17-20ab; **13**.123-124; **14**.43ab
Ābhīras **19**.17; **27**.54-57; **212**.12-17 .18-20 .66-70
Abhiṣṭut, horse-sacrifice of **168**
- , Śiva worshipped by **168**.31-35
Abhiṣṭuta **168**.2-5
abhra, etymology of **24**.8-11
Abhuktarajasas **5**.26
Ābhūtarajasas **5**.26
Abjaka, place of pilgrimage **128**.83-84; **129**.1-2
- [Vṛṣākapi] **129**.99cd-100ef .101-124
- [Vṛṣākapi], Mahāśani slain by **129**.94-99ab
Abjakatīrtha, place of pilgrimage **129**.11ab .101-124 .125-127
abode, highest **23**.41-43; **24**.1-7ab
- of Brahman **20**.88ab
- of Nārāyaṇa, water as **60**.34-38
- of sun, Pratiṣṭhāna as **110**.226-228
- of Yama **123**.109cd-115
abode see also *city, residence, world*
absence of bad conditions of life **18**.24cd-28 .60-62ab; **20**.8-9 .65 .80cd-82ab .86cd-87ab; **68**.68-70; **164**.3-6
- of bad people **41**.34cd-36
- of bridegroom in wedding-ceremony **111**.39cd-47
- of castes **20**.85-86ab
- of *dharma*, punishment for **215**.136cd-137ab
- of diseases **65**.57-58
- of enmity, maxim about **106**.3-7
- of Yugas **18**.60-62ab; **20**.14-15
absence of see also *freedom from*
absolute in simile, subtlety of the **235**.21-25
- , liberation by vision of the **236**.69
- , Puruṣottama as the **177**.22-23
- , Viṣṇu as the **23**.41-43; **233**.35-38ab
absolute see also *highest transcendence, brahman*
absorption in Consciousness **238**.31-33ab
- in Vāsudeva **58**.37-40
- , liberation by **237**.26-27
- of cosmos in Hari **5**.61-62
- of senses **237**.53; **238**.17-19
- of water by sun **24**.8-11
- of Yogin in beings **239**.58-61
absorption see also *concentration, meditation, union*
- see also *destruction, dissolution*
abstinence during ancestral rites, prescription(s) concerning **220**.106-109ab
abstinence see also *chastity*
abuse, »eunuch« as **196**.1-4
- , »womb-insect« as **170**.8ef-13
abuse see also *offence, reproach*
abusing of Veda(s), punishment for **215**.130cd-136ab
acceptability of meritorious practices **29**.15-17
acceptance of pupil **121**.10-12
accomplishment of *dharma*, daughter as **165**.5-17
accomplishments, list of **58**.12-18
accusation, false **16**.25-45ab
acid, cleaning with **221**.125cd-127ab
acknowledgement of son **9**.31-32; **154**.14cd-21ab
action and intention **173**.9-25
- and knowledge **145**.2cd-5ab; **237**; **238**.12-14
- and non-action **88**.10-15
- , knowledge and **145**.8-11ab
- , omnipresence of **145**.8-11ab
- , superiority of **88**.10-15; **145**.8-11ab

- , ten senses and organs of **241**.26-27
- , three impulses of **237**.65
actions ascribed to illusion **193**.88-90
- , auspicious **214**.110-114ab; **216**.5-63
- , Bhāratavarṣa as field of **19**.2 .5 .21 .23 .25-27; **27**.2 .66cd-68; **70**.20-22ab .24
- , earth as field of **160**.2cd-6ab
- , effect(s) of **214**.27cd-31; **217**.113cd-114ab .114cd-115ab; **224**; **225**
- , effect(s) of auspicious **218**.31cd-32ab
- , elements as witness of **217**.23-24
- , gods bound by **27**.69-70
- in Bhāratavarṣa, effect(s) of **27**.3-9
- in former existences, effect(s) of **165**.23-26
- increased by knowledge, effect(s) of **129**.49-64
- , liberation by **26**.23-25
- , location of field of **161**.21-23ef
- , maxim about effect(s) of **123**.177cd-184; **136**.17-26
- , Puruṣottamakṣetra as field of **178**.192
- , rebirth determined by **217**.29-31; **223**.52cd-54ab
- , renunciation of **237**.82-86ab
- , retribution of **27**.69-70; **123**.140-146; **215**.55cd-64 .78-80 .138cd-142; **217**.4-11 .28 .33-35; **218**.3-5
- , reward(s) for auspicious **214**.13cd
- , three kinds of **125**.44-49; **157**.13cd-14; **164**.17-28
- , three qualities of **173**.9-25
- , transfer of bad **222**.36
- , two kinds of **173**.9-25; **233**.40cd-43ab
actions see also *conduct, deeds, practices*
actors, punishment for **22**.21-22
Acyuta **216**.82-86
adept of Narasiṃha, prescription(s) for **58**.19-25
adepts in heaven of Viṣṇu **68**.43
- of Narasiṃha, equipment of **58**.41-43
adepts see also *Siddhas*
Adhaḥśiras **22**.2-6
adharma, deceased accompanied by *dharma* or **217**.4-11
- in Kali-Yuga **56**.39cd-42
Ādhāyatas **27**.43-50
Adhomukha **22**.17cd-18ab
Adhṛṣṭa **5**.45cd-46
Adhvarīvat **5**.45cd-46
Adhvaryu **39**.43-45
Ādideva, Gaṇeśa as **114**.2-5
Ādikeśa, Liṅga named **169**.2cd-3 .6cd-15 .39cd-43ab
- , Śiva as **169**.4-6ab .22cd-24ef
Aditi **3**.51-52 .53-58; **32**.3-6 .9-11; **34**.42-45ab; **73**.21-22; **124**.3cd-6; **171**.40-43; **203**.23
- , ear-rings of **202**.3-12; **203**.1-5
- , Indra in womb of **179**.27-28
- , Kṛṣṇa and **203**.1-24
- , sun appearing to **32**.17-31
- to Kṛṣṇa, boon by **203**.22
- to Kṛṣṇa, hymn by **203**.6-19
- to Satyabhāmā, boon by **203**.24-25
- to sun, hymn by **32**.12-16
Āditya **31**.14cd-16; **89**.2ef-3; **94**.22-26; **106**.23-26ab; **165**.2-4; **171**.40-43; **174**.19-25ab; **226**.30-41
- , place of pilgrimage **155**.1
Āditya see also *sun*
Ādityas **5**.36-37ab .61-62; **39**.7-17ab .22-27ab; **69**.12-43; **72**.8; **110**.10-20; **123**.177cd-184; **174**.7; **179**.43cd-44ab; **191**.4-12; **213**.66-71; **219**.60cd-65ab .98cd-107ab; **220**.118cd-120ab
- , Aṅgirasas and **155**.3cd-10ab
- and months **31**.19-21
- , number of sunbeams of **31**.22-26
- , seven **174**.14
- , twelve **3**.53-58; **30**.23-26; **31**.17-18
- , Viṣṇu as lord of **4**.2-9
- worshipped by Aṅgirasas **155**.2-3ab
Ādityatīrtha, place of pilgrimage **174**.19-25ab
admonition of listener(s) **177**.29-30
adoption **220**.77-78ab
- of daughter **4**.113; **14**.20cd-24ab
- of seven sages **3**.107cd-109ab
- of son **2**.7-8; **10**.64-65ab; **11**.19cd-21ab; **13**.132cd-137; **14**.28c-f .29-31 .50cd-56; **104**.83-86ab
- of sons **16**.8
adorning of cattle **187**.42-54
Adri [Piśāca], birth of **84**.9-12
Adrikā **84**.2-4 .9-12
Adritīrtha, place of pilgrimage **174**.25cd-27ab
adulterine, punishment for support by **22**.21-22
adultery, prohibition of **221**.60cd-62ab
- , punishment for **215**.94cd-95ab

.130cd-136ab; **217**.66 .67 .68-71ab
advice by Agastya **158**.16-21
- by Agni **144**.11-14
- by Bṛhaspati **106**.15-18
- by Brahman **11**.4-7; **83**.13-16; **119**.4ef-8; **122**.24cd-27; **124**.87-93; **128**.38-43; **181**.15-19
- by Brahmin **163**.40-42
- by Danu to Diti **124**.9-11
- by Gaṇeśa **74**.38cd-42
- by gods and sages **141**.23-25
- by Kapila **78**.47-54; **141**.6-9
- by Kṛṣṇa **210**.33-35
- by Kṛṣṇa to Balarāma **187**.22-25
- by Kṛṣṇa to Nanda **187**.42-54
- by Madhucchandas **171**.40-43
- by Marīci **4**.35-41
- by Maya **124**.49-52
- by Nārada **3**.7cd-9 .16-18ab .19cd-23; **14**.50cd-56; **82**.9-10; **200**.2-10
- by Paulomī **129**.49-64
- by Rāhu **106**.39-41
- by Śiva **110**.137-142 .211-214; **129**.82-93
- by Śruti **152**.31-32
- by Sarasvatī **105**.4-8ab
- by servants of Yama **123**.128cd-139
- by Sītā **123**.158-164
- by Soma **110**.87-97ef
- by Sūrya **131**.31-39ab
- by Tvaṣṭṛ **6**.41-43; **168**.18cd-21
- by Vasiṣṭha **78**.3-8ab; **123**.77-81 .86cd-96; **151**.10-16; **168**.6-9
- by Vasudeva **184**.1-6
- by Veda(s) **127**.35-47
- by Viṣṇu **72**.15-17; **113**.5-8ab; **136**.27-31
- by Viśvāmitra **173**.9-25
- by Vyāsa **212**.91-92
- by wife **167**.26-28
- by Yama **165**.37-44
Ādyas **5**.30cd-31
affliction by hunger and thirst **52**.11-15ab
afflictions, mental **234**.5-6
afflictions see also *diseases*
Āgamas **44**.10-12
Agasti **70**.37cd-38
Agastya **78**.70-75ab; **96**.20-22ab; **110**.5-9; **124**.87-93 .108-109; **174**.2-5ab
- , advice by **158**.16-21
- as lord of the south **118**.2-9; **158**.8-15ef
- as teacher **158**.16-21
- as teacher of Āpastamba **130**
- , boon by **84**.5-8
- , Indra cursed by **124**.73cd-80
- , *sattra*-rite of **118**.2-9
Āgastya, place of pilgrimage **118**.31-32ef
Agāvaha **14**.45-46ab
age, distinction by **2**.54-56
- of marriage, prescription(s) concerning **165**.5-17
age see also *old age*
Āgneya, place of pilgrimage **98**.21cd-22; **104**.1-2
Āgneyatīrtha, place of pilgrimage **174**.19-25ab
Āgneyī **2**.17-20ab; **128**.72cd-76
Agni **3**.39-40; **5**.20cd-21; **13**.102-105; **18**.52-55; **28**.27; **36**.14cd-15ab; **42**.36cd-38ab; **61**.45cd-46; **72**.11cd-14; **80**.46-55; **82**.2-6 .9-10; **93**.5-11 .12-24; **103**.2-6; **107**.35-40; **110**.10-20; **128**.38-43 .62-63ab .72cd-76; **160**.6cd-9; **192**.48-58; **219**.60cd-65ab .98cd-107ab
- , advice by **144**.11-14
- Aṅgiras **144**.5-8ab
- and Ātreyī, discussion between **144**.17-19
- and Jātavedas [brother of Agni] **98**
- and Śiva, gold originated from **128**.50-61
- and Svāhā **128**.24-28
- and waters, competition between **126**
- and Yama, boon by **125**.33-43
- , arrows presented by **212**.21-24
- as deity of the sacrifice **127**.23-28
- as father of gold **148**.8-14ab
- as father-in-law of Ātreyī **144**.8cd-10 .15-16
- as lord of Vasus **4**.2-9
- as messenger of gods **93**.12-24; **127**.29-34; **128**.7-15
- as name of Śiva **158**.22-27ef
- as parrot **128**.16-23
- as priest of Ātreya **140**.2-3ab
- as priest of gods **128**.3-6
- , boon by Śiva to **128**.46-49
- born from waters **126**.32cd-35
- , Brahman pleased by **174**.19-25ab
- , consecration of **98**.18cd
- , devotion to **229**.8-13
- , functions of **125**.16-17
- , Heti and **125**.18-21
- hidden in water **98**.2-5

- , homage to **126**.30-32ab
- , hymn by Heti to **125**.15-17
- in simile **146**.2-8ab
- , Jātavedas **127**.29-34; **173**.26-28
- , Liṅga established by **98**.21cd-22
- , names of **98**.17cd-18ab
- , origin of **161**.43cd-50cd
- , place of pilgrimage sacred to **168**.1
- , praise of **126**.4-8
- , priests as servants of **127**.23-28
- , rice-cake for Indra and **133**.2-4
- , superiority of **126**.4-8
- to Śiva, hymn by **128**.44-45
- , Viṣṇu as **60**.39-45
- , Viṣṇu praised by Dharma and **128**.63cd-70ab
- , weapon of **125**.9-12

Agni see also *brilliance, burning, fire*
Agnibāhu **5**.9cd-10
Agnidaṇḍa **217**.80cd-86
Āgnīdhra **5**.9cd-10; **229**.22-30
Agnihotra **13**.102-105
Agnijvāla **214**.14-17
Agnipada, place of pilgrimage **25**.14
Agni-pool **100**.1-3
Agniprabha, place of pilgrimage **25**.22
Agniṣoma-rite **133**.2-4
Agniṣṭoma-sacrifice **125**.50-53
Agniṣṭuba **2**.17-20ab
Agniṣṭut **2**.17-20ab
Agnitīrtha, merit of bathing at **125**.50-53
- , place of pilgrimage **98**.1 .19cd; **126**.37-39; **168**.26cd-28ab

Agniveśya **174**.2-5ab
Agrasena **13**.109
Ahalyā **13**.97; **109**.3cd-6ab; **122**.48-49
- , education of **87**.5cd-8
- , Indra and **87**
- , marriage of **87**.25-29
- redeemed by Rāma **123**.97-105ab
- , seduction of **87**.42-43

Ahalyāsaṃgama **87**.1 .66cd-69
- , place of pilgrimage **87**.70-71

Āhavanīya-fire **161**.30-33ab .54-58
Ahi **160**.6cd-9
Ahīnagu **8**.84cd-92
Ahirbudhnya **3**.46cd-49
Āhrīda **13**.147-148ab
Āhuka **15**.46cd-48 .49-50ab .55
Aikṣvākī **15**.24-28

Aila **7**.21cd-22; **108**.119-120; **220**.112cd-116ab
Ailatīrtha, place of pilgrimage **151**.24cd-27ab
Ainasa, place of pilgrimage **25**.52
Aindava, place of pilgrimage **104**.1-2
Aindra, place of pilgrimage **104**.1-2
Aindratīrtha, place of pilgrimage **93**.27; **174**.8-12ef
Aindratīrtha see also *Indratīrtha*
air, movement through **3**.96cd-97ab
Airāvata **3**.99-101; **18**.18-20; **69**.12-43; **124**.33-36ab; **188**.24-28; **202**.3-12
- as lord of elephants **4**.2-9
- , fight between Garuḍa and **203**.45-62

Airāvatī **27**.25cd-27
Aiśānu **13**.142-146
Aiśvara, place of pilgrimage **104**.1-2
Aitareyabrāhmaṇa **102**; **104**; **139**; **150**.4cd-5; **155**
- , Kavaṣa [son of Ailūṣa] in **139**

Aja **8**.84cd-92
- , place of pilgrimage **105**.22-26ab

Ajagava, bow named **4**.48-52; **9**.21
Ajaikā created by Brahman **134**.2-8ab
Ajaikapād **3**.46cd-49
Ajaka **10**.21-23; **13**.88-90
Ajamīḍha **13**.80ab .80cd-81ab .81cd-82ab .92cd .93-96 .98-99 .102-105
Ajāmukharasa, place of pilgrimage **25**.63
Ajāmukhasara, place of pilgrimage **25**.63
Ajapārśva **13**.132cd-137
Ajapārśva, explanation of **13**.132cd-137
Ajara **5**.44-45ab
Ajātaśatru **14**.33-34ab
Ajīgarta **104**.44-59ab
Ajīgarti [son of Suyava] **150**.1cd-4ab
Ajina **2**.29-30ab
Akalmāṣa **5**.22cd-24
Akapīvat **5**.20cd-21
Akhaṇḍitahrada, place of pilgrimage **25**.83ab
Ākhyāna-hymn in Ṛgveda **131**.1-2ab
Akṛśāśva **7**.89
Akrūra **14**.8-10 .11 .43cd; **16**.50cd-54ab .55cd-56ab; **17**; **193**.24-31; **210**.37-43
- , Kṛṣṇa appearing to **192**.32-42 .43-47
- to Kṛṣṇa, devotion of **191**
- to Viṣṇu, hymn by **192**.48-58
- welcomed by Kṛṣṇa **192**.1-4

Akrūra-yajña **17**.24-27
Akṣasūtrā [wife of Āpastamba] **130**.2-6

akṣata, explanation of **219**.49-51
Akṣepa **14**.8-10
Ālābu, place of pilgrimage **42**.6-8
Alakā **10**.5-8
Alakanandā **18**.38cd-44ab
Alambuṣā **68**.60-67; **178**.19-24
Alarka **11**.50cd .51-53; **13**.68cd .72cd-75ab .75cd-77; **34**.92-93ab; **180**.24cd-38
alcohol, punishment for drinking of **22**.9; **215**.92cd-93ab.127cd-128ab.130cd-136ab
all, *brahman* as **211**.11-12
- , Nārāyaṇa as **60**.25-33
- , Nārāyaṇa as supporter of **24**.19-25
- , Rudra as **158**.22-27ef
- , Śiva as **75**.12; **158**.37cd-39ab
- , Viṣṇu as **18**.57-58 .59; **55**.23cd-31; **56**.46ab-48ab; **126**.24-27; **181**.21-25; **189**.44-45; **191**.4-12; **193**.80-87; **196**.30-45; **202**.23-29; **203**.6-19 .70-73
- , Viṣṇu as supporter of **18**.59
- , waters as origin of **72**.27cd-34
all see also *omnipresence*
all-comprehensiveness of fire **126**.4-8
of Puruṣottama **42**.36cd-38ab .38cd-42ab
- of Śiva **130**.17-21
- of Viṣṇu **54**
allegorical description of world **238**.26-30
alleviation of burden on earth **188**.29-35 .39-41; **193**.32-40; **202**.23-29; **210**.1-4 .16-21 .22-27; **212**.59-62
All-Gods **3**.30cd-33; **5**.36-37ab; **80**.46-55; **203**.45-62; **213**.66-71; **219**.6-12 .47cd-48; **220**.112cd-116ab; **221**.89-94
allies of Rāma **157**.2cd-7
alliteration **138**.8-9ef
allocation of deities to the body **163**.26-31
- of forms of Viṣṇu to the body **184**.14-19
- of prayer-formula **60**.22-24 .34-38; **61**.4-6 .7-12
- of Viṣṇu to directions **61**.14-16
alms, rejection of **228**.97-100ab
- to Sādhus **76**.18cd-23ab
alms-giving **213**.155
- at wedding **72**.11cd-14
- , merit of **219**.107cd-109ab
- , prescr. conc. **221**.159-160
altars, golden **13**.166-169
Amarahrada, place of pilgrimage **25**.44
Amarakaṇṭaka, place of pilgrimage **25**.20; **64**.3-8ab
Amarakaṇṭaka-hills **77**.2-9ab
Amaravartanatīrtha, place of pilgrimage **25**.82
Amarāvatī [city of Indra] **176**.21-25
- [city of Indra] in simile **43**.85cd-88; **196**.9-15
Amāvasu **10**.11-12 .13-14
Ambarīṣa **7**.21cd-22 .24; **8**.77cd-84ab; **70**.39-40
- [hell] **215**.123cd-124ab
Ambarya defeated by Viṣṇu **149**.9cd-12
Ambaṣṭhas **13**.24-25ab; **19**.18
Ambhas **20**.43-44
Ambhogiri **20**.62-63
ambiguity of message **207**.8-12
Ambikā **106**.43-45ab; **181**.38-53
Āmbubhiṣṇus **10**.61-62
Amṛta, place of pilgrimage **120**.16-18
amṛta see also *immortality, nectar of immortality*
Amṛtā **20**.10-11
- as name of Pravarā **106**.57-58ab
- as name of Śakti **106**.57-58ab
- [river] **106**.47-48ab
amṛta as food of Pippalāda **110**.78-80cd
- as oblation **168**.26cd-28ab
- , immortality caused by **104**.7cd-9
- , waters as origin of **126**.9-11
Amṛtā, explanation of **106**.47-48ab
Aṃśa **3**.53-58; **30**.23-26; **226**.30-41
Aṃśumat **8**.73cd-75ab; **30**.23-26 .28-39; **31**.17-18 .19-21 .22-26; **78**.45-46
amulet, burial of **58**.57
- , protection by **58**.44-46 .47
Anādhṛṣṭi **14**.14cd-20ab .26cd
Anagha **13**.54-55
Ānakadundubhi **14**.14cd-20ab; **182**.12-13; **212**.1-4; **226**.30-41
Anala **3**.35cd-36
Anamitra **8**.77cd-84ab .84cd-92; **14**.1-2ab .24cd-25ab; **16**.9-11
Ānanda **20**.3-5
- , place of pilgrimage **152**.40
Ānandā [river] **128**.72cd-76
Ānandatīrtha, explanation of **152**.42ef
Anaṅga **36**.117
Ananta **3**.125; **21**.13cd-15; **61**.45cd-46; **208**.3; **226**.65cd-67ab
- , identity of Viṣṇu and **226**.65cd-67ab
- , merit of devotion to **176**.57-62

- , three heads of **226**.62–65ab
Ananta, explanation of **21**.15–27; **226**.62–65ab
Anantavāsudeva **45**.77–89
- , greatness of **176**.3
Anantavāsudeva-Māhātmya **176**
Anaraṇya **8**.77cd–84ab
Ānarta **7**.28cd–29ab; **11**.55–59; **13**.75cd–77
- and Sukanyā as twins **7**.27cd–28ab
- [country] **7**.28cd–29ab
Anaśana, place of pilgrimage **25**.31
Anāvṛṣṭi **15**.58cd–59
ancestors and Yoga **220**.109cd–112ab
- attacked by demons **219**.25–29
- , boon by Viṣṇu to **219**.98cd–107ab
- , boons by **220**.118cd–120ab
- , city of **220**.49cd–50ab
- , classification of **220**.64–66 .67a–f .82cd–86
- , curse by **220**.50cd–51ab
- , destiny of **220**.87–89ab
- , donation(s) of food to **219**.18–24
- , duration of satiation of **220**.22cd–31ab
- , effect(s) of offerings to **220**.149–151
- fallen from heaven **219**.18–24; **220**.193cd–195ab
- , investiture ceremony for **220**.69cd–70
- , liberation for **125**.44–49; **131**.39cd–51
- , liberation of **79**.21cd–22
- lifted from waters **219**.37–39
- , offerings to **219**.52–60ab .60cd–65ab
- , pleasing of **213**.168cd–169ab
- , pregnancy due to offerings to **219**.87–91ab
- , prescr. conc. offerings to **60**.54–65
- , punishment for hatred against **22**.14cd–15a
- , release of **41**.92
- released by son **34**.60–72
- , remnant-eaters as class of **220**.82cd–86
- , request of **220**.31cd–32ab
- , satisfying of **80**.1–3 .4–5ab; **93**.1–2; **168**.30
- , seduction of **219**.6–12
- , Soma as deity of **219**.91cd–98ab
- taking refuge to Viṣṇu **219**.30
- to Viṣṇu, hymn by **219**.31–35
- , Yama as lord of **4**.2–9; **6**.46cd–48ab
- , Yoga and **219**.13–17 .91cd–98ab .98cd–107ab
ancestral offerings, methods of deposition of **220**.149–151
- rites **7**.48cd–51ab; **29**.31cd–32ab; **41**.59cd–60ab; **42**.9; **219**
- rites as expiation for Brahmin-murder **123**.165–169
- rites at Gautamī, effect(s) of **123**.128cd–139
- rites, auspicious date(s) for **220**.10cd–11ab .43–60 .64–66 .75 .116cd–117ab
- rites, auspicious hours for **220**.120cd
- rites, Brahmins qualified for **220**.103–104
- rites, classification of **220**.11cd–13 .64–66
- rites, constituents of **219**.42–47ab
- rites, effect(s) of **220** .117cd–118ab .203cd –204 .210
- rites, effect(s) of sexual intercourse during **220**.106–109ab
- rites for women **220**.61ab .74 .75
- rites, forbidden places for **220**.8–10ab
- rites, importance of Yogin at **220**.109cd–112ab
- rites, invitation of Brahmins for **220**.105
- rites, merit of **220**.43–48ab .48cd–49ab
- rites performed at Gayā **220**.30–31ab
- rites, person(s) entitled to performance of **220**.76 .77–78ab .78cd–80ab
- rites, places for **220**.5–7
- rites, prayer-formulas during **219**.52–60ab .71cd–86
- rites, prescr. conc. **221**.149cd–155ab .159–160 .161–169ab
- rites, prescr. conc. forbidden ingredients of **220**.168–177
- rites, prescription(s) concerning **220**
- rites, prescription(s) concerning abstinence during **220**.106–109ab
- rites, prescription(s) concerning ingredients of **220**.154–188
- rites, prescription(s) concerning special cases of **220**.205–209
- rites, prescription(s) concerning **221**.71 .95–100
- rites, qualification(s) of food for **220**.178–185ab
- rites, Vivasvat as lord of **8**.95
ancestral rites see also *funeral, offerings*
Andhaka **14**.3ab; **15**.30–31; **70**.35cd–37ab
Andhakāraka **20**.47cd–49ab .49cd–51
Andhakārakaka **20**.47cd–49ab
Andhakaru **14**.8–10
Andhakas **15**.54; **16**.8; **17**.29–31
Andhas **27**.51cd–53

Andhrakas **27**.41cd-42
androgynous Brahman **1**.51cd-52; **45**.37-41; **161**.33cd-35ab
- Śiva **110**.105-106
Anenas **7**.51cd-53; **11**.1-2 .27cd-31
- , descendants of **11**.27-31
Aṅga **2**.17-20ab .20cd; **4**.28-34; **13**.30-31 .36 .37-39
Aṅgada **154**.5-8ab .21cd-26; **176**.37-51
Aṅgāraka **23**.6-10
Aṅgārasetu **13**.148-150ab .148cd-151
Aṅgāratīrtha, place of pilgrimage **25**.82
Aṅgāropacaya **215**.117cd-118ab
Aṅgas **13**.36 .45-48; **27**.51cd-53; **231**.68-71ab
anger, maxim about **147**.14-17ab
- of Indra **188**.1
- of Kaṃsa **190**.1-5
- pretended by Kṛṣṇa **189**.9
anger see also *Manyu, wrath*
Aṅgiras **1**.43-45ab; **2**.17-20ab; **3**.25-28; **5**.8-9ab .32-33ab; **9**.17-20; **11**.60cd-61ab; **13**.79; **34**.12cd-19; **39**.7-17ab; **174**.2-5ab
- as teacher of Śukra **95**.2-6
- , Ātreyī and **144**.11-14 .20 22
- , Ātreyī married to **144**.5-8ab
- , Bṛhaspati **13**.58-61; **95**.2-6
- , fire as father of **144**.15-16
- originated from charcoals **144**.5-8ab
- to sun, hymn by **32**.93cd-95ab
Āṅgirasa, place of pilgrimage **155**.1
Aṅgirasas and Ādityas **155**.3cd-10ab
- at Gautamī, sacrifice of **155**.2-3ab
- , Ādityas worshipped by **155**.2-3ab
Āṅgirasas **4**.53-57; **174**.2-5ab
- as Prajāpatis **158**.16-21
- as Vyāsas **158**.39cd-40ef
- as Vyāsas of the future **158**.30-35ab
- born from Ātreyī **144**.5-8ab
- , Brahman as creator of **158**.4-7 .16-21
- pursued by hindrance **158**.8-15ef
- , vedic verse(s) sung by **158**.28-29
Anila **3**.35cd-36 .39-40
animal, Apsarases cursed to be an **84**.2-4
- faces of demons **213**.81-104
- , *puruṣa* as sacrificial **161**.39cd-43ab
- , rebirth as **27**.66cd-68; **29**.40; **216**.81; **217**.33-35 .36-110 .55-56; **220**.87-89ab; **229**.31-36ab; **240**.38-44 .106-111; **241**.45-47
- , Śunaḥśepha as sacrificial **10**.65cd-67ab
- , theft of sacrificial **78**.12-24
animals, aquatic **43**.58cd-63ab; **44**.44-47
- at city of Yama, wild **214**.120-128; **215**.4-23
- at water-place, killing of **123**.33cd-36ab
- , edible **221**.111
- , liberation for **177**.16-19
- , list of **54**.4-7 .14; **178**.38-42; **220**.190cd-193ab
- , origin of **3**.102cd-103
- , origin of domestic and wild **161**.43cd-50cd
- , punishment for rearing of forbidden **22**.18cd-20
- , sacrifice of **187**.42-54
- , sacrificial **47**.74-80ef
- , tiger as lord of wild **4**.2-9
Aniruddha **61**.39-40; **178**.158-165; **192**.48-58; **205**.1-6; **210**.37-43
- and Bāṇa, fight between **206**.5-9
- and Uṣā **206**.5-9
- as form of Nārāyaṇa **180**.23cd-24ab
- imprisoned by Bāṇa **206**.5-9
- , marriage of **201**.6-9
- , world of **227**.42-47
Añjana [mountain] **84**.2-4
Añjanā **84**.2-4
Āñjana, place of pilgrimage **84**.18
Añjika **3**.86cd-89ab; **13**.153cd-154ab
annexation of land, punishment for **215**.86cd-88ab .122cd-123ab
announcement **1**.31-32 .36-37ab; **3**.2 .35cd -36 .51-52 .53-58 .73cd-74ab; **4**.18 .24-26; **5**.3 .7cd .16ab .20ab .27-28 .29ab .33cd .42 .48 .63; **9**.35ab; **10**.67cd-68; **11**.27ab .61cd; **12**.21cd .50; **13**.2 .25cd-27ab .36 .50 .80ab .92cd .97 .109 .115cd .118 .141 .212cd-213ab; **14**.34cd .44; **18**.10; **19**.6ab; **20**.21; **22**.1; **24**.7cd; **25**.7-8ab; **26**.27 .37; **27**.1 .25ab .51ab .58ab .59ab .62cd-64ab; **29**.7-8; **30**.46-47ab .57; **31**.29-30; **33**.33; **34**.55 .59; **36**.135a-f; **39**.3 .96-97; **41**.1-5 .10; **42**.12; **43**.22-23; **45**.4 .22-25 .47-49; **46**.2; **48**.3; **56**.10-11; **57**.1; **58**.12-18; **59**.23-25; **60**.8ab; **61**.4-6; **63**.11-16; **65**.2; **67**.2-5 .10; **68**.4-5; **71**.2-3; **74**.7; **79**.6cd-7ab; **80**.5cd-6ab; **83**.1; **84**.1; **86**.3ab; **87**.1; **89**.1-2cd .5d; **90**.1; **91**.1-2ab; **92**.1; **94**.1; **95**.1; **96**.1; **97**.1; **98**.1; **99**.1; **100**.4ab; **101**.1; **103**.1; **104**.1-2; **105**.1 .21;

106.1; **107**.1 .19-30; **108**.1 .102cd-103; **109**.1-3ab; **111**.1; **112**.1; **114**.1; **115**.1; **116**.1-2ab; **117**.1; **121**.1; **124**.1-2ab; **125**.1-2ab; **129**.3 .11ab; **131**.1-2ab; **134**.1; **136**.1ab; **137**.1; **138**.1; **139**.1-2ab; **140**.1; **141**.1; **142**.1; **143**.1; **144**.1; **145**.1-2ab; **146**.1; **147**.4; **149**.1; **152**.1; **153**.1-2ab; **156**.1-2ab; **157**.1-2ab; **160**.1-2ab; **161**.1-2ab .4cd-6ab; **162**.1-2ab; **163**.1-2; **164**.1-2; **167**.1; **169**.1-2ab; **173**.1-2; **175**.14ab .32cd-33ab; **176**.3; **178**.6; **180**.13-16ab .42c-f; **181**.1; **207**.3; **208**.3; **209**.1; **212**.71; **213**.10-11 .21-24 .43 .80 .106-112 .113cd; **214**.9 .10-11ab; **215**.2-3 .83cd-84ab; **216**.3-4; **217**.32 .36; **218**.9cd-10ab; **219**.2-3; **220**.2 .22cd-23ab .69ab .71 .81ab .87-89ab .127ab .189cd-190ab; **221**.9 .109; **222**.18 .21 .45; **224**.4 .28-29 .46; **227**.5 .15; **228**.7 .91cd .92ab; **229**.3 .21 .36c-f; **230**.3 .9 .61 .77; **233**.11; **234**.2-4 .5-6 .43 .60cd-61ab .69cd -70ab; **235**.3 .10; **236**.36-37ab; **237**.3-4 .41-42ab .44 .47; **238**.16; **239**.29-30; **240**.3 -4 .51-52 .82; **241**.5 .11; **243**.19 .46 .66; **244**.1 .3 .10 .43
- of voluntary death **110**.41cd-46ab .61-66
announcement of suicide see *threat of suicide*
anointing, colours for **29**.33cd-34ab
- of Kṛṣṇa **193**.1-12
- of Kṛṣṇa by Indra **188**.36-37
-, prescr. conc. **221**.21
-, prescription(s) concerning **221**.42
anointing see also *consecration*
Antaḥśilā **27**.33-34
Antara **15**.1-12ab
Antardhāman **226**.30-41
Antardhāna **2**.29-30ab
Antardhi **2**.28cd
Antarvedī **167**.2-3
anticipating summary **43**.1-13; **45**.77-89; **210**.1-4 .22-27 .33-35 .52cd-58
Anu **12**.5cd-6ab; **13**.152-153ab; **146**.2-8ab .28-31
Anuhlāda **213**.81-104
Anuhrāda **3**.64cd-70ab
- and Ulūka, battle between **125**.9-12
- and Ulūka, enmity between **125**.2cd-8
Anuja **213**.81-104
Anumati **221**.87-88
Anūpadeśa **4**.67
Anurādhā **220**.33cd-42
Anutaptā **20**.10-11
Anvindra, place of pilgrimage **140**.1 .35-38
anxiety, symptoms of **48**.4-11
Āpa **3**.35cd-36 .37-38cd; **5**.13cd-15ab
Āpagā **27**.25cd-27 .35-36ab
āpagā, etymology of **100**.9-13
Apamardakas **27**.51cd-53
Aparājita **3**.46cd-49
Aparāntas **27**.43-50
Āparāntyas **19**.17
Aparṇā **34**.81 .85-86
Āpastamba **129**.94-99ab
-, Agastya as teacher of **130**
- as devotee of Viṣṇu **129**.82-93
- to Śiva, hymn by **130**.23-31
Āpastambatīrtha, place of pilgrimage **129**.125-127; **130**.1 .34
Āpava, Prajāpati **1**.50cd-51ab; **2**.1-4
-, Vasiṣṭha **13**.189cd-197ab
ape, demon as **209**.2-11ab
applause by Nārada **190**.39-47
Aprabhūtas **5**.30cd-31
Apratiṣṭha **22**.2-6
Apratiṣṭhā **215**.91cd-92ab
Apratiṣṭhoman **22**.2-6
Apsaras, ascetic seduced by **147**.5-7; **178**.43-53 .54-58
-, Ārṣṭiṣeṇa and the **107**.19-30
-, Yama seduced by **86**.35-39
Apsarāsaṃgama, place of pilgrimage **100**.1-3; **147**.1-3
-, Śiva at **147**.20cd-23ab
Apsarases **13**.166-169; **32**.99cd-100; **36**.63cd -70; **39**.7-17ab; **54**.16-17; **140**.5cd-6ef; **213**.25-26; **214**.107cd-109; **216**.5-63
-, boon by Aṣṭāvakra to **212**.72-85
- cursed by Brahmin **212**.72-85
- cursed to be an animal **84**.2-4
- cursed to be rivers **147**.17cd-20ab
-, description of **68**.60-67
-, Indra and **147**.9cd-13
-, list of **32**.99cd-100; **41**.30-34ab; **68**.60-67; **178**.19-24
-, occupations of **68**.60-67
-, origin of **3**.104-105
-, rebirth as **27**.66cd-68
Apsaroyuga, origin of **147**.20cd-23ab
-, place of pilgrimage **147**.1-3 .4
aquatic animals **43**.58cd-63ab; **44**.44-47

- birds **42**.27-31; **68**.15-16
- plants **178**.38-42
Araṇya **2**.16
Āraṇya **5**.27-28
Arbuda **27**.20cd-24ab; **246**.21-27
- , place of pilgrimage **25**.27; **64**.8cd-9
Arbudās **19**.17
archery **2**.33
archery competition **190**.6-8
Ardhanārīśvara, Śiva as **110**.105-106
Ardhanārīśvara see also *androgynous Śiva*
Ārdra **7**.51cd-53
Ārdrā **220**.33cd-42
area, golden **20**.95cd-98ab
Ārikṣepa **16**.50cd-54ab
Arimardana **14**.8-10; **16**.50cd-54ab
Ariṃdama **70**.39-40
Arimejaya **14**.8-10; **16**.50cd-54ab
Ariṣṭa **5**.45cd-46; **181**.7-14; **183**.1-7; **188**.42-47; **190**.1-5; **193**.32-40; **202**.3-12; **213**.159-163
- , fight between Kṛṣṇa and **189**.46-58ab
Ariṣṭā **3**.51-52 .104-105
Ariṣṭa episode **189**.46-58
Ariṣṭanemi **14**.12-13; **16**.56cd-58ab
Ariṣṭanemin **3**.25-28; **8**.63-64
- , wives of **3**.60
Arjuna **3**.90cd-92ab; **14**.43ab; **208**.19-31; **210**.52cd-58; **211**.1-2; **212**
- and Vyāsa **212**.35-94
- as partial incarnation of Indra **188**.39-41
- , consolation of **212**.55-92
- , defeat of **212**.21-24
- , dejectedness of **212**.35-41
- dependent on Kṛṣṇa **212**.25-28 .42-53
- , Dhanaṃjaya **13**.123-124; **14**.20cd-24ab
- , Kārtavīrya **3**.84-86ab .90cd-92ab; **13**.160 .161-198
- Kārtavīrya as ideal king **13**.172-173
- Kārtavīrya, boon by Dattātreya to **13**.161-164; **213**.106-112
- Kārtavīrya, deeds of **13**.176cd-187ab
- Kārtavīrya, snakes submitting to **13**.176cd -187ab
- Kārtavīrya, thousand arms of **13**.160
- Kārttavīrya **213**.114-122
- , Kṛṣṇa and **188**.42-47
- , lament of **212**.29-33
- , pride attributed to **212**.12-17
- , weakness of **212**.21-24
Arjuna-trees felled by Kṛṣṇa, two **184**.31-42ab; **190**.1-5
Arka **31**.14cd-16
Ārka, place of pilgrimage **103**.9
Arkanayana **213**.81-104
Arka-plant **28**.25; **103**.2-6
- , sun in **103**.2-6
arm as axle of car **123**.23-33ab
arms of Arjuna Kārtavīrya, thousand **13**.160; **213**.106-112
- of Bāṇa, thousand **205**.7-8; **206**.1-4
- of devotee, four **67**.58-60ab; **68**.29-32
- of Kṛṣṇa, four **192**.32-42; **211**.5-10
- of Vāsudeva, four **226**.30-41
- of Viṣṇu, ten **226**.11-12
- of Viṣṇu, thousand **68**.44-53
- of Yoganidrā, eight **182**.27-30
army, capturing of **197**.6-7; **202**.30-35; **204**.13cd-18
- , description of **44**.17-22; **47**.71-73
arrow of Kāma, Śiva shot by **71**.27-37
arrows presented by Agni **212**.21-24
- , punishment for making of **22**.16b:
- , Viṣṇu killing with **131**.16-24
arson, punishment for **215**.100cd-101
Ārṣṭiṣeṇa **127**.2-4ab .4cd-9ab
- and the Apsaras **107**.19-30
Ārṣṭiṣena **11**.34cd
Ārṣṭisena **11**.34cd
art of club-fighting **17**.28
Ārtaparṇi **8**.77cd-84ab
artha see *goals of life, profit*
Arthaśāstra **240**.106-111
artificial Śacī fabricated by Tvaṣṭṛ **140**.14-18ab
Artikāvatas **15**.41cd-45ab
Aruṇa **3**.95cd-96ab; **65**.40-41; **89**.37-40ab; **166**.6cd-8ab .8cd-11ab .11cd-13
- and Garuḍa, Tārkṣya as father of **166**.2-4ab
- [caste] **20**.31
Aruṇā **89**.1-2cd .43-46ab
Aruṇāspada, place of pilgrimage **25**.60
Aruṇāvaruṇāsaṃgama, place of pilgrimage **89**.1-2cd
Arundhatī **3**.29-30ab .30cd-33; **34**.42-45ab; **69**.12-43; **71**.41-42; **82**.2-6; **172**.15-17ab
Arundhatīvana, place of pilgrimage **25**.56
Aruṇoda **18**.31
Ārya **5**.45cd-46

Āryā **181**.38-53
Āryaka [caste] **20**.16-17
Aryaman **3**.53-58; **30**.23-26 .28-39; **31**.17-18 .19-21 .22-26; **192**.48-58
Āśā **109**.13-20
Āṣāḍha **31**.19-21; **41**.72-74
Āṣāḍhā **220**.33cd-42
Asamañjas **78**.37cd-44
Asamaujas **16**.7 .8
Āsandiva **167**.2-3
- and Brahmin girl, marriage of **167**.18-21ef
-, boon by Viṣṇu to **167**.31-32
- to Viṣṇu, hymn by **167**.30
ascension of Budha as planet **9**.31-32
- to Brahman-world **5**.40-41
- to city of Viṣṇu **176**.57-62
- to heaven **4**.48-52; **7**.21cd-22; **8**.20-21 .23; **41**.60cd-71; **43**.77-82ab; **51**.29-31; **57**.59-61; **58**.70cd-77; **66**.18-23; **67**.53-57; **80**.80-83 .90-91ef; **86**.35-39; **110**.71-72; **150**.15-20; **211**.5-10; **216**.67-72; **227**.32cd -37ab; **229**.72-86ab
ascetic, conduct of **222**.32-35
-, Gautama as ideal **74**.22cd-38ab
-, gods afraid of **178**.12-18
-, householder and **222**.32-35
-, king rewarded by **7**.85-86
-, offence of **53**.21-24
- power(s) of Gautama **74**.31-37
- seduced by Apsaras **147**.5-7; **178**.43-53 .54-58
- seduced by demon **122**.8-20
-, self-accusation of **178**.90-98
asceticism, Badarī as place for **210**.33-35
- between five fires **178**.7-11
- by fasting **34**.83-84; **176**.15cd-19ab
- by standing in ocean **2**.34-46
- by standing in water **178**.7-11; **212**.72-85
- consumed by demon **122**.8-20
- destroyed by pleasure **178**.65-69
-, distinction by **2**.54-56
- disturbed by demon **7**.58cd-71ab
- disturbed by mother **158**.8-15ef
-, duration of **213**.44-52
- for becoming a Brahmin **147**.5-7
- for fame **2**.10-13
- for obtaining a son **13**.102-105; **128**.3-6; **196**.1-4
- for the benefit of others **213**.114-122
-, Gaṅgādvāra as place for **147**.5-7
-, Gandhamādana as place for **197**.4-5; **210**.33-35
-, husband obtained by **2**.1-4; **15**.16-21; **71**.24-26
-, magic power(s) obtained by **124**.36cd-39ab
-, Mahendra as place for **213**.114-122
-, merit of **177**.9-15
-, Meru as place for **5**.49-52; **6**.48cd-50ab; **7**.30-34
-, ocean as place for **7**.105cd-109
- of three virgins **34**.87-89
- of Umā **34**.93cd-99
- of Viśvāmitra **147**.14-17ab
-, places for **242**.8-15ab
-, power(s) of **10**.46cd-49ab; **87**.45-48; **140**.3cd-5ab
- practised by Mitra **30**.47cd-48
- practised by Varuṇa **30**.47cd-48
- practised by Yama **86**.43-46
- practised in Vaivasvata-era **5**.40-41
-, rejuvenation by **178**.61-64
-, son(s) obtained by **9**.2-5; **10**.24-28ab; **13**,20cd-22ab .88-90; **15**.35-41ab
-, transfer of **35**.46-51 .60-63; **100**.4cd-6; **118**.15-18
ashes and water, cleaning with **221**.117cd-120ab
-, threat of reducing someone to **87**.52cd -54; **96**.8-10 .11-17; **140**.12-13
Asiknī **3**.3-7ab .10-14 .25-28; **14**.14ab
Asiloman **213**.81-104
Āsīna, place of pilgrimage **25**.37
Asipattravana **22**.2-6 .24cd; **214**.14-17; **215**.105cd-107ab; **217**.80cd-86
Asita **8**.35-51
Asitoda **18**.31
Āśleṣa **220**.33cd-42
Aśmakas **27**.54-57
Aśmakī **14**.26cd
Aśmakya **14**.26cd
Aśoka-flowers **35**.15-21
Aśokāṣṭamī **41**.72-74
Aśoka-tree **35**.1-4ab
-, boon by Rudra to **35**.22-26ab
Aśokavana, place of pilgrimage **25**.60
Āspada, place of pilgrimage **25**.41
aspects of Nārāyaṇa, four **180**.17cd-18ab
- of Viṣṇu, four **213**.124-126
aspects see also *incarnation, manifestation*

ass, demon as **186**.1-3
assembly of gods and demons **160**.6cd-9
- of places of pilgrimage **105**.26cd-29ab; **152**.37cd-39ef; **175**.83-84
- of water-drops **41**.50cd-54ab
asses, origin of **3**.93cd-95ab
Aṣṭaka **13**.91 .92ab
Aṣṭaratha **13**.71ab
Aṣṭāvakra, eightfold deformation of **212**.72-85
- to Apsarases, boon by **212**.72-85
Aṣṭāvakra-episode **212**.72-85
Asti **195**.1-4
Āstikeya **20**.62-63
astrologers, punishment for **22**.17cd-18ab
astrological omen(s) **182**.4-6
astrology, knowledge of **21**.15-27
Asuras **3**.3-7ab; **13**.176cd-187ab; **36**.20cd-21ab
-, holy places established by **70**.16-19
Aśva **14**.12-13; **213**.81-104
Aśvabāhu **14**.12-13; **16**.56cd-58ab
Aśvadevī, place of pilgrimage **25**.56
Aśvagrīva **14**.12-13; **16**.56cd-58ab
Aśvahanu **14**.32cd
Aśvapati **213**.81-104
Aśvaśiras **213**.81-104
Aśvaśīrṣan, Viṣṇu as **178**.166cd-176
Aśvaśīrṣan see also *Hayagrīva, Hayaśiras*
Aśvatara **3**.99-101
Aśvatīrtha, place of pilgrimage **64**.3-8ab; **89**.43-46ab
Aśvattha, place of pilgrimage **118**.31-32ef
- [Rākṣasa] **118**.10-14
Aśvatthāman **5**.43
Aśvatthatīrtha, place of pilgrimage **118**.1 .24cd-30
Aśvattha-tree **103**.2-6
-, circumambulation of **118**.19-24ab
-, Rākṣasa as **118**.10-14
-, touching of **118**.24cd-30
Aśvavedī, place of pilgrimage **25**.56
Āśvayuja **31**.19-21
Aśvayūpa **70**.39-40
Āśvina, place of pilgrimage **104**.1-2
Aśvinī **220**.33cd-42
Aśvins **5**.36-37ab; **36**.18cd-19ab; **39**.7-17ab .22-27ab; **50**.55-59; **103**.2-6; **110**.10-20; **123**.177cd-184; **160**.6cd-9; **191**.4-12
-, birth of **89**.34-36
-, origin of **6**.44-45ab
Atala **21**.2-5ab
Aṭavyas **27**.54-57
Atharvaveda **234**.61cd-63ab
Atidānta **16**.4-6
Atidatta **16**.1-3
Atigambhīrā **147**.9cd-13
Atigaṇḍa **165**.27-30ab
Atilaghuśroṇī **27**.30-32
Atināman **5**.29cd-30ab
Atirātra **2**.17-20ab
Atithi **8**.84cd-92
Atithipriya **16**.50cd-54ab
Ātmatīrtha, place of pilgrimage **117**.1 .20c-f
atmosphere, Śiva as **75**.9
atonement see *expiation*
Ātreya **5**.43; **140**
-, Agni as priest of **140**.2-3ab
-, effect(s) of *sattra*-rite of **140**.3cd-5ab
- in heaven of Indra **140**.5cd-6ef
-, Indra imitated by **140**.14-18ab
-, place of pilgrimage **140**.1 .35-38
-, remorse of **140**.31-34
-, *sattra*-rite of **140**.2-3ab
-, Satyanetra **5**.24cd-25
- to Indra, hymn by **140**.21ef-25
Ātreya see also *Dattātreya*
Ātreyas **27**.43-50
Ātreyatīrtha, place of pilgrimage **140**.35-38
Ātreyī **173**.3-6ab
-, Agni as father-in-law of **144**.8cd-10 .15-16
- and Aṅgiras **144**.11-14 .20-22
- as water **144**.20-22
-, Āṅgirasas born from **144**.5-8ab
-, discussion between Agni and **144**.17-19
- married to Aṅgiras **144**.5-8ab
Atri **1**.43-45ab; **2**.7-8; **4**.28-34 .42-47; **5**.8-9ab .11cd-12 .34-35; **9**.1 .2-5 .13-16; **13**.5-8 .9-12ab; **34**.12cd-19; **96**.20-22ab; **117**.2-5; **145**.2cd-5ab; **168**.2-5; **174**.2-5ab
-, moon as son of **152**.2-4
-, triad of gods born as sons of **144**.2-4
Atriccyavana **5**.11cd-12
attainment of *brahman* **237**.7-14; **238**.53-56ab
- of Nārāyaṇa **239**.62
attempt of killing of infant(s) **182**.27-30; **200**.2-10
attendant(s) of Indra **3**.109cd-122

- of Śiva **3**.70cd-71; **41**.88-90
attitude towards mother **81**.13-15
attraction of music **189**.14-17
attractiveness of women, maxim about **147**.9cd-13; **151**.3-5ab; **152**.5-9ab
attribute of Śiva, snake as **111**.68cd-79; **116**.15-16
attributes, concealing of divine **182**.14-15 .17
- , female **178**.12-18
- of Balarāma, iconographic **57**.20-28
- of Gaṇeśa, iconographic **114**.13
- of Kṛṣṇa, iconographic **50**.43cd-44ab; **53**.31-33; **57**.38-41; **192**.32-42
- of Nārāyaṇa **56**.48cd; **240**.93-94
- of Śeṣa, iconographic **21**.15-27
- of Self **240**.93-94
- of sun, iconographic **28**.30-31; **33**.14cd-15ab
- of Vāsudeva, iconographic **44**.14-15; **50**.4-6; **207**.13-24
- of Viṣṇu **55**.33cd-34; **56**.43-44
- of Viṣṇu, iconographic **49**.10-20; **51**.10-16; **59**.73-77; **61**.41-45ab .52-55; **68**.44-53; **79**.7cd-19; **109**.43-45; **122**.44-47; **126**.23; **136**.3cd-14ab; **145**.5cd-7; **156**.1-2ab; **163**.32-39; **176**.8-10 .21-25; **177**.1-2; **178**.122-127; **203**.6-19; **210**.47-48; **219**.31-35; **226**.22cd-23ab; **228**.8-14
attributes see also *description, epithets, shape*
Audbhida **20**.36-38ab
Auddālakatīrtha, place of pilgrimage **25**.76
Audumbaras **10**.61-62
Aurva **5**.11cd-12 .44-45ab; **8**.29-30 .31-32 .39-40 .41-42ab .65-68
Aurva-fire, Viṣṇu as **179**.18cd-22ab
Aurvīśītīrtha, place of pilgrimage **25**.75
Auṣadhis **27**.43-50
Auṣadhya, place of pilgrimage **120**.16-18
Auśana, place of pilgrimage **104**.1-2
Auśanasa, place of pilgrimage **25**.51
Auśīnara, Śibi **13**.22cd-23
auspicious actions **214**.110-114ab; **216**.5-63
- actions, effect(s) of **218**.31cd-32ab
- actions, reward(s) for **214**.13cd
auspicious actions *see also* dharma, righteousness
auspicious colour, white as **221**.81cd-82ab
- date(s) **28**.19-20 .42-45 .53cd-54ab .54cd-56ab; **29**.22-27ab .29-31ab .42cd -61; **41**.57cd-59ab .72-74; **51**.63-71; **58**.21cd-23; **60**.8cd-10 .12-15; **62**.10-13ab; **63**.8-9 .11-16 .17 .19-20 .21 .22; **64**; **65**.3 .84-96; **67**.12-14; **86**.2; **124**.132-136ab; **148**.3cd-7; **152**.37cd-39ef; **219**.109cd-113ab; **228**.1-5; **246**.28-29
- date(s) for ancestral rites **220**.10cd-11ab .43-60 .64-66 .75 .116cd-117ab
- date(s), pilgrimage at **41**.54cd-57ab
- date(s), prescription(s) concerning **221**.102
- hours **221**.21
- hours for ancestral rites **220**.120cd
- omen(s) **7**.74-77
auspiciousness of Jyeṣṭha **45**.77-89; **63**.8-9 .11-16; **64**
- of Phālguna **63**.18
author of Mahimnastuti, Mahiman as **153**.8-11
- of Purāṇa, Brahman as **1**.30
authority, Brahman as **180**.13-16ab
- , Brahmins as **220**.152
- on *dharma*, Brahman as **216**.64-66; **217**.117-118; **223**.21-22 .54cd-55ab; **225**.30
- on *dharma*, Vāsudeva as **226**.50cd-51
- on donation(s), Brahman as **225**.9
- on expiation, Śāstras as **123**.158-164
- on *karman*, Bṛhaspati as **122**.50-54ab
- on knowledge of Śiva, Veda(s) as **139**.7cd -11
- on meat, Manu as **220**.185cd-188ab
- on non-violence, Brahman as **224**.56c-f
- on punishment, Vasiṣṭha as **215**.78-80
- on Sāṃkhya, Brahman as **245**.31-41
- on truthfulness, Manu as **228**.47-49
- on Veda(s), Manu as **234**.60cd-61ab
- , sages as **220**.153
- , Veda(s) as **130**.7-14
autumn **36**.80-88
- as oblation in sacrifice **161**.35cd-39ab
- , description of **36**.80-88; **189**.14-17
Āvāha **14**.8-10; **16**.50cd-54ab
Avakīrṇa, place of pilgrimage **25**.51
Āvanta **15**.22-23
Avanti **13**.199cd-202; **15**.54; **194**.18-22
Avantī **27**.28-29; **43**.24; **228**.8-14
- , description of **43**.25-65ab .85cd-88
- , holy places in **43**.65cd-85ab
Āvantyas **13**.203-204
avarice, effect(s) of **225**.10-16
avarice see also *greed*

Avasarga, place of pilgrimage **25**.79
avatāra see *incarnation(s)*
Āvatya **14**.14cd-20ab
Avedhya, place of pilgrimage **25**.42
Avīci **22**.2-6
Avighna, place of pilgrimage **114**.25
Avighnatīrtha, place of pilgrimage **114**.1
Avijñātagati 3.39-40
Avikṣita **14**.8-10
Avimukta, place of pilgrimage **25**.61; **113**.22-23; **229**.59-63
Avimukta, explanation of **229**.59-63
Avyaya **5**.27-28
awaking of Viṣṇu **67**.2-5
axe of Gaṇeśa **114**.13
axle of car, arm as **123**.23-33ab
Aya **3**.35cd-36
Ayaḥśaṅku **213**.81-104
Ayaḥśiras **213**.81-104
Āyāsa **215**.130cd-136ab
Ayasmaya **5**.13cd-15ab
Āyāti **12**.1-2
Ayodhyā **7**.45cd-46ab; **8**.3-4 .84cd-92; **123**.2-7ab .23-33ab; **154**.5 8ab .8cd-11ab .27-30ab; **157**.2cd-7; **176**.37-51; **213**.157
Ayodhyākāṇḍa of Rāmāyaṇa **123**.84-119ab
Ayomukha **3**.74cd-78ab
Āyu **10**.11-12
- , descendants of **11**
Āyurveda, tradition of **11**.36-38
Āyus **122**.3-7; **226**.30-41
Ayutājit **8**.77cd-84ab
Āyutājit **15**.34
Babhru **15**.41cd-45ab; **17**
Babhrus **10**.61-62; **13**.91
Babhrusetu **13**.148-150ab
Babūravana, place of pilgrimage **25**.37
backward reference **13**.58-61; **41**.1-5; **43**.82cd-83ab; **69**.1-9; **70**.8cd-10; **74**.8-12; **78**.1-2; **79**.3-5ab; **108**.76cd-87; **110**.87-97ef; **113**.18-21; **119**.12; **122**.48-49; **128**.24-28; **129**.9-10; **157**.8-9 .12cd-13ab .18ef-21ab; **172**.2-3; **175**.32cd-33ab; **185**.5-10; **189**.2-8; **190**.1-5; **193**.78cd-79 .88-90; **196**.23-29; **212**.59-62; **221**.89-94; **227**.1-4; **230**.77; **233**.10
bad actions, transfer of **222**.36
- conditions of life, absence of **18**.24cd-28 .60-62ab; **20**.8-9 .65 .80cd-82ab .86cd-87ab; **68**.68-70; **164**.3-6
- men, women as wives of **217**.114cd-115ab
- omen(s) **210**.29-30
- people, absence of **41**.34cd-36
- people, exclusion of **56**.30cd-35ab
- qualities, list of **137**.4-7
- qualities of Brahmin **164**.17-28
- qualities of renouncer **222**.46-54
- qualities, origin of **129**.70-71
bad see also *evil sin, vice*
Badarī **219**.18-24
- as place for asceticism **210**.33-35
- , place of pilgrimage **25**.17; **65**.84-96
Badarīhrada, place of pilgrimage **25**.81
Badarikāśrama, place of pilgrimage **25**.77; **64**.3-8ab
Badarīpāṭana, place of pilgrimage **25**.54
Badarīpāvana, place of pilgrimage **25**.54
Badarīśaila, place of pilgrimage **25**.13
Badarīvana, place of pilgrimage **25**.37
Bāhlika **13**.114 .116; **14**.39-41; **208**.19-31
Bāhlīka, Kāṇva **148**
Bāhlikas **27**.43-50
Bāhu **8**.24-28 .29-30 .35-37
Bahuḅāhu **14**.12-13; **16**.56cd-58ab
Bāhudā [river] 7.91-92; **27**.25cd-27
Bāhukātīrtha, place of pilgrimage **25**.58
Bahuputra **3**.25-28 .60
Bahurūpa **3**.46cd-49
Bāhutīrtha, place of pilgrimage **25**.58
Bahvāyu **10**.11-12
Bāhyakā, Sṛñjayī **15**.32 .33
Bāhyāśva **13**.93-96
baking, cleaning by **221**.117cd-120ab
Bala **3**.86cd-89ab; **208**.4-7 .36-37
Bālā **3**.29-30ab
Balabarhiṣa **15**.45cd-46ab
Balabhadra **65**.57-58; **193**.42-49 .50-57ab .76cd-78ab; **195**.5-7; **198**.1-3; **206**.24-30
Balabhadra see also *Baladeva, Balarāma*
Baladeva **193**.24-31; **194**.18-22; **210**.1-4
- as foster-child of Nanda **184**.1-6
- as teacher of Duryodhana **17**.28
- , birth of Kṛṣṇa and **179**.6-10ab
- in Gokula **197**.8-21
- , Kuvalayāpīḍa killed by Kṛṣṇa and **193**.24-31
- , pestle as weapon of **209**.11cd-21ab
- , ploughshare as weapon of **195**.5-7; **208**.32-35
- , Subhadrā, Kṛṣṇa **179**.4-5

- , Yama Vaivasvata defeated by **194**.23-31
Baladeva see also *Balabhadra, Balarāma*
Balāhaka 3.99-101; **20**.25-27
Bālakāṇḍa of Rāmāyaṇa **123**.84-119ab
Balākāśva **10**.21-23; **13**.88-90
Bālakrīḍanaka **187**.8-18
Balarāma **14**.39-41 .42cd; **16**.25-45ab; **17**.8-11; **43**.14; **62**.1-4; **189**.14-17; **190**.6-8 .9; **195**.1-4; **199**.5-10; **201**.6-9; **205**.15-22; **206**.10-13; **208**.1-2; **210**.37-43; **226**.65cd-67ab
- , advice by Kṛṣṇa to **187**.22-25
- and Dvivida **209**
- and Dvivida, fight between **209**.11cd-21ab
- and Gopīs **197**.19-21
- and Kauravas **208**
- and Muṣṭika, fight between **193**.50-57ab .63cd-65ab
- and Yamunā **198**
- as partial incarnation of Viṣṇu, Kṛṣṇa and **190**.10-19
- as Śeṣa **198**.1-3
- as Śeṣa, description of **192**.32-42
- asking for help from Kṛṣṇa **187**.19-20
- , blue clothes of **192**.71-74; **198**.15-17
- , death of **210**.50-52ab
- , description of **191**.18-25
- , divinity of **187**.22-25
- , divinity of Kṛṣṇa and **191**.26
- , drunkenness of **198**.7-11; **209**.11cd-21ab
- , education of Kṛṣṇa and **194**.18-22
- , iconographic attributes of **57**.20-28
- , looking at Kṛṣṇa and **193**.41
- , ornaments of **198**.15-17
- , praise of **187**.29-30; **209**.21cd-22
- , Rukmin killed by **201**.23-26
- , snake leaving from mouth of **210**.50-52ab
- , statue of **50**.44cd-46ab .48-54
- , Subhadrā, Kṛṣṇa **65**
Balarāma see also *Balabhadra, Baladeva*
Bāleya-Brahmins **13**.30-31
Bali 3.64cd-70ab; **13**.27cd-29; **73**; **160**.6cd-9; **180**.24cd-38; **181**.7-14; **205**.7-8
- as Yogin **13**.32-35
- , boon by Brahman to **13**.32-35
- , boon by Viṣṇu to **73**.52-55
- in simile **123**.2-7ab
- , invincibility of **13**.32-35; **73**.2-6
Bāṇa 3.64cd-70ab .70cd-71; **110**.104; **181**.7-14; **213**.159-163
- , Aniruddha imprisoned by **206**.5-9
- , boon by Śiva to 3.70cd-71; **206**.1-4 .39-44
- , fight between Aniruddha and **206**.5-9
- , fight between Kṛṣṇa and **206**.31-38
- , Śiva and **110**.104
- , thousand arms of **205**.7-8; **206**.1-4
Bāṇa-episode **205**.11-22; **206**
Bāṇatīrtha, place of pilgrimage **123**.213cd-216; **131**.25 .39cd-51
banner, breaking of **206**.1-4; **207**.13-24
Banyan-tree **18**.23cd-24ab
- , eternal **161**.65cd-67
Barbaras **27**.43-50
bard, Nārada as famous **154**.14cd-21ab
bards, blessing by **4**.66
- , origin of **4**.60-67
Barhapada, place of pilgrimage **25**.32
Bārhaspatya, place of pilgrimage **122**.100-102; **174**.19-25ab
Barhiketu **8**.54-57
barley **220**.200cd-203ab
- , origin of **219**.49-51
- , protection by **219**.47cd-48 .49-51
barrenness removed by bathing **65**.78-80; **124**.123-131; **125**.44-49; **147**.1-3
Bāṣkala **213**.81-104
Baṣkalas **10**.61-62
bathing at Agnitīrtha, merit of **125**.50-53
- at Ekāmraka, merit of **41**.93
- at holy places, merit of **214**.114cd-119
- at places of pilgrimage, prescription(s) concerning **76**.18cd-23ab
- at Viraja, merit of **42**.6-8
- , barrenness removed by **65**.78-80; **124**.123-131; **125**.44-49; **147**.1-3
- , expiation by **92**.47cd-48ab; **170**.84-88
- festival **65**
- in Gautamī **111**.80-82
- in Gautamī, merit of **80**.84-89
- in Indradyumna-tank **43**.14
- in Kokā, merit of **219**.107cd-109ab
- in Vaitaraṇī, merit of **42**.4
- , merit of **228**.92cd-96
- of Hari in Jyeṣṭha **65**.3
- of statue **67**.20-23
- of sun and Yama in Gautamī **86**.47-49ab
- , prescr. conc. **57**.2-11; **60**.34-38 .46-48; **67**.12-14; **221**.138cd-139ab
- , prescription(s) concerning **221**.50cd-52
- , purification by **81**.16-22ab; **221**.79

.135cd-136ab
- , restoration of male sex by **108**.113-115
- , substances for **67**.20-23
bathing festival, merit obtained at **65**.57-58
battle between Anuhrāda and Ulūka **125**.9 -12
- between Daityas and Dānavas **162**.13-19
- between gods and demons **3**.109cd-122; **9**.23; **11**.4-7; **32**.9-11 .41cd-46; **97**.8-13ab; **106**.2; **109**.39cd-40; **112**.2-3; **123**.7cd-14ab; **142**.2-4; **160**; **162**.2cd-6ab
- between Jarāsaṃdha and Kṛṣṇa **195**.1-4
- between the kings of Kāśi and Vidarbha **229**.43cd-55
- , death in **216**.5-63
- , help by Kṣatriya-woman in **123**.23-33ab
- , killing permissible in **124**.53-67
- , maxim about fleeing in **124**.73cd-80
- of Mahābhārata, reference to **188**.42-47; **212**.12-17 .64-65
- of ten months **13**.148-150ab
- , promise of help in **123**.14cd-22
battle see also *fight*
bear and Kṛṣṇa, fight between **16**.25-45ab
- , lion killed by **16**.25-45ab
beard, prescription(s) concerning shaving of **221**.72
bearer of earth, Viṣṇu as **175**.60-68
beating, killing by **189**.46-58ab
- of one's parents, punishment for **217**.53-54
beautiful woman, demon as **122**.8-20
- woman, description of **122**.8-20
becoming a Śūdra, curse of **7**.43
beef, eating of **8**.13-15b:
begging not allowed for Kṣatriyas **168**.2-5
beginning of Kali-Yuga **212**.8
- of settlement **4**.94-95
being and non-being **23**.41-43
beings, body of Viṣṇu as origin of **226**.13-14
- , classes of **2**.25-28ab; **4**.100-109; **39**.22-27ab; **55**.23cd-31; **72**.1-4
- , classes of divine **65**.19-20
- , classes of supernatural **3**.3-7ab
- , classification of **32**.7-8
- , classification of living **241**.33
- , earth oppressed by **86**.11-16; **116**.3cd-5ab
- , heavenly **68**.54-55
- , life-span of **18**.60-62ab
- , list of **1**.3-9; **22**.32; **39**.7-17ab; **42**.38cd-42ab; **45**.30-36; **51**.17-21; **54**.4-7; **56**.3-8; **89**.37-40ab; **105**.18cd-19; **152**.29-30; **214**.104-107ab .107cd-109; **241**.29-32
- , offerings to various classes of **220**.89cd-97ab
- , origin of **2**.47-49; **32**.3-6
- , plants as first of **119**.2-4cd
- , rain as support of **24**.19-25
- , Śiva as epitome of **130**.23-31
- , sun as origin of **33**.9-13ab
- , superhuman **54**.16-17; **65**.31-34; **105**.8cd -11ab; **164**.3-6; **239**.58-61
- , supernatural **3**.1; **18**.52-55; **21**.15-27
- , two kinds of **229**.15-18
- , Viṣṇu as origin of **196**.30-45
- , Viṣṇu identical with **196**.30-45
- , waters as first of **110**.200ef-201ef
- worthy of respect **221**.36
beings see also *human beings*
beloved, maxim about pleasing one's **108**.26-30
- of Śiva, Gaṅgā as **74**.8-12; **175**.33cd-35
beneficial effect(s) of noble women **123**.165-169
benefit of the world, Purāṇa told for the **175**.78
benumbing by Yoganidrā **182**.19-26
bet between Brahmin and Vaiśya **170**.27-28
- , hands as stake at **170**.37-38cd
- , life as stake at **170**.47-48
Bhadika **16**.4-6
Bhadra as name of Viśvarūpa **165**.45-47ab
- , place of pilgrimage **105**.22-26ab
Bhadrā **13**.5-8 .9-12ab; **14**.36-38; **18**.38cd-44ab; **179**.4-5; **181**.38-53
- as name of Viṣṭi **165**.45-47ab
Bhadrabala, place of pilgrimage **25**.33
Bhadracāru **201**.1-2
Bhadrakālī **39**.51-52 .67-68ab .69cd-73; **106**.43-45ab; **109**.21-26ab; **181**.38-53
Bhadrakālīhrada, place of pilgrimage **25**.55
Bhadrakarṇahrada, place of pilgrimage **25**.50
Bhādrapada **220**.56
Bhadrapati, Viṣṇu as **165**.47cd-48ef
Bhadraratha **13**.45-48
Bhadraśreṇya **11**.44-48; **13**.70ab .157-159
Bhadrāśva **18**.29 .38cd-41ab .45cd-46ab .57-58
Bhadratīrtha, place of pilgrimage **165**.1 .47cd-48ef

Bhadratuṅgas **27**.51cd-53
Bhadrāvāsatīrtha, place of pilgrimage **25**.66
Bhadravaṭa, place of pilgrimage **25**.26 .33 .49
Bhadravinda **205**.1-6
Bhaga **3**.53-58; **30**.23-26 .28-39; **31**.17-18 .19-21; **36**.11cd-12ab .31-36ab; **37**.2-23; **109**.21-26ab
- , tearing out of eyes of **109**.21-26ab
Bhagavadgītā **56**.35cd-38ab; **158**.30-35ab; **180**.24cd-38; **181**.2-4
bhagavat, explanation of **234**.66cd-68ab
Bhāgavata **210**.31-32
Bhagīratha **74**.2-5; **78**.47-54
- , boon by Śiva to **78**.59-69
- to Gaṅgā, prayer by **78**.59-69
- to Śiva, hymn by **78**.56-58
Bhāgīratha **8**.75cd-77ab .77cd-84ab
Bhagīrathī see also *Gaṅgā*
Bhāgīrathī **8**.75cd-77ab; **70**.8cd-10 .33-35ab; **77**.2-9ab .9cd-13; **78**.75cd-76 .77; **110**.5-9; **135**.20-24; **141**.26-28; **161**.21-23ef; **175**.83-84; **208**.19-31
- [wife of Mudgala] **136**.1cd-3ab
Bhajamāna **15**.30-31 .32 .33 .34 .45cd-46ab; **16**.1-3
Bhaktahrada, place of pilgrimage **25**.66
Bhānavas **5**.19cd
Bhāṇḍīra-tree **187**.8-18
Bhaṅgakāra **16**.45cd-48ab .48cd-49ab
Bhānu **3**.30cd-33; **31**.14cd-16; **131**.31-39ab; **205**.1-6
Bhānu see also *sun*
Bhānus **3**.30cd-33
Bhānutīrtha, place of pilgrimage **89**.43-46ab; **138**.2-3 .39cd-40; **168**.1 .13-14 .38
Bhara [son of Ārṣṭiṣeṇa] **127**.2-4ab .16-22
Bharadvāja **5**.34-35; **11**.36-38; **13**.58-61 .112-113; **121** .2-5; **133**; **145**.2cd-5ab
Bhāradvāja **5**.43; **70**.37cd-38
Bharadvājas **27**.43-50
Bhāradvājī **173**.3-6ab
Bharaṇī **220**.33cd-42
Bharata **13**.56-57 .58-61; **70**.39-40; **123**.84-86ab .97-105ab
Bhārata **18**.18-20 .45cd-46ab .57-58
Bharatas **13**.203-204
Bhāratas **13**.56-57
Bharatatīrtha, place of pilgrimage **25**.71
Bhāratavarṣa **18**.38cd-44ab; **54**.1-3; **70**.20-22ab .24; **78**.70-75ab; **88**.16-19; **179**.2-3
- as field of actions **19**.2 .5 .21 .23 .25-27; **27**.2 .66cd-68; **70**.20-22ab .24
- , description of **19**; **27**.14-80
- , effect(s) of actions in **27**.3-9
- , location of **27**.65-66ab
Bharbhara **3**.72-73ab
Bharga **11**.49-50ab .55-59 .60ab
Bhārga **11**.55-59 .60ab
Bhargabhūmi **11**.60ab; **13**.78
Bhārgabhūmi **11**.60ab
Bhārgava **8**.31-32; **13**.67cd-68ab .78; **70**.37cd-38
- , Jamadagni **10**.46cd-49ab
Bhārgava-family **11**.60cd-61ab; **13**.79 .97
Bhārgavas **174**.2-5ab
Bhartṛsthāna, place of pilgrimage **25**.59
Bhāryāṅgas **27**.51cd-53
Bhāsī **3**.92cd-93ab .93cd-95ab
Bhāskara **31**.14cd-16 .31-33ab
Bhāskareśvara, Liṅga named **41**.75-81
Bhauma, Naraka **202** .3-12; **219**.113cd-115
Bhaumasthāna, place of pilgrimage **25**.40
Bhauṭya, Manu **5**.49-52
Bhauvana **83**.2-5; **170**.2-5
- [city] **170**.2-5
Bhava **34**.7-8 .42-45ab .51-54; **37**.1a-f; **74**.13-22ab; **82**.2-6; **117**.18-19ab; **143**.14-16; **152**.21-23; **153**.1-2ab .8-11 .13-15ab; **157**.1-2ab; **162**.20-27ab; **163**.26-31; **239**.58-61
Bhava see also *Śiva*
Bhavābhatrana, place of pilgrimage **25**.38
Bhavānī **109**.46-48 .52-54
Bhāvatīrtha, place of pilgrimage **153**.1-2ab .13-15ab .15cd-16ab
Bhāvins [caste] **20**.16-17
Bhavya **2**.14-15; **20**.59cd-61
Bhāvya, Manu **5**.5cd-6ab
Bheruṇḍa [Ciccika-bird] **164**.3-6
Bhillatīrtha, place of pilgrimage **169**.1-2ab .48-49cd
Bhīma **10**.13-14; **15**.22-23; **208**.19-31
- , Kaurava **12**.11-17
Bhīma-forest, place of pilgrimage **25**.11
Bhīmanātha, Śiva as **173**.37-39
Bhīmaratha **11**.39-40; **13**.64cd-67ab .71ab; **15**.24-28
Bhīmarathī **19**.12cd-13ab; **27**.35-36ab; **70**.33-35ab; **77**.2-9ab; **161**.2cd-4ab

- , place of pilgrimage **64**.11-14
Bhīmasena **13**.109 .112-113 .114; **14**.20cd-24ab
Bhīmatāṇḍavavāmukha, place of pilgrimage **25**.82
Bhīmeśvara **173**.33cd-34ab
- , Liṅga named **173**.1-2
- , Śiva as **173**.34cd-35ef
Bhiṣak **16**.4-6
Bhīṣma **13**.115ab .119; **208**.4-7 .8-18 .19-31; **212**.12-17 .64-65
Bhīṣmaka **199**.1-4
Bhogavatī **65**.4-6; **111**.26-34 .35-39ab .48-51 .52-56 .57-60 .61-63 .64-68ab .85cd-86
Bhoja **14**.33-34ab .45-46ab; **15**.50cd-51ab
Bhojakaṭa **201**.6-9
Bhojas **13**.203-204; **15**.41cd-45ab .54; **27**.59cd-62ab
- and Kukkuras, genealogy of **15**
Bhojavardhanas **27**.54-57
Bhojyā **14**.14cd-20ab
Bhrama **214**.14-17
Bhṛgu **5**.29cd-30ab; **9**.13-16; **10**.46cd-49ab; **34**.12cd-19 .45cd-48; **69**.12-43; **95**.2-6; **174**.2-5ab; **178**.106-111
- , Kavi [Śukra] as son of **95**.2-6
Bhṛgunandana **34**.91
Bhṛgutīrtha, place of pilgrimage **25**.48
Bhṛgutuṅga **12**.47-48
- , place of pilgrimage **25**.11
Bhūmi **109**.13-20
Bhūri **13**.116; **208**.19-31
Bhūriśravas **13**.116; **208**.19-31
Bhūrloka **23**.16-20
Bhūtasaṃtāpana **3**.72-73ab
Bhūti **5**.49-52; **181**.38-53
Bhuvarloka **23**.16-20
Bilvaprabha, place of pilgrimage **25**.21
Bimbaprabha, place of pilgrimage **25**.21
Bimboṣṭhī **68**.60-67
Bindumatī **7**.93-95ab
Bindusaras-lake **41**.88-90
- , origin of **41**.50cd-54ab
bird feeding upon flesh **164**.3-6
- , Garuḍa as golden **90**.34-35
- , rebirth of Brahmin as **164**.29-37
birds, aquatic **42**.27-31; **68**.15-16
- burnt by sun, healing of **166**.6cd-8ab
- , Garuḍa as lord of **4**.2-9
- , list of **41**.45-46; **42**.20-23; **43**.56-58ab; **44**.64-66ab; **45**.14cd-15ab; **178**.38-42
- , origin of **3**.93cd-95ab .102cd-103
- , punishment for rearing of **22**.18cd-20
birth by caesarian **110**.67-70
- , caste membership by **223**.12
- from mouth **89**.34-36
- from nose **6**.44-45ab
- from sneezing **7**.44cd-45ab
- from sweat **178**.99-104
- from third eye of Śiva **153**.8-11
- from thumbs of Brahman **2**.51-53
- from water-jar **158**.8-15ef
- , loss of memory during **234**.9-42
- of a pestle **210**.11-14
- of Adri [Piśāca] **84**.9-12
- of Aśvins **89**.34-36
- of Dakṣa **2**.47-49 .51-53
- of daughter **34**.74-80
- of fire from mare **110**.131-133
- of Gaṇeśa **97**.20-23; **114**.9-12
- of gourd **8**.65-68
- of Hanumat **84**.9-12
- of human being **217**.23-24
- of Jamadagni **10**.28cd-50ab
- of Kālayavana **14**.48-50ab
- of Kṛṣṇa **182** .9-11
- of Kṛṣṇa and Baladeva **179**.6-10ab
- of Kumāra **3**.39-40
- of Māriṣā **178**.99-104
- of Mārtaṇḍa **32**.37-41ab
- of Nārada **3**.10-14
- of Pāṇḍavas **14**.20cd-24ab
- of Purūravas **7**.14cd-16
- of realms **3**.30cd-33
- of Sagara **8**.35-51
- of Sarasvat **101**.2-9
- of Skanda **82**.2-6
- of sons of Daśaratha **123**.84-86ab
- of sons of Sagara **8**.63-73
- of twins **128**.24-28
- of Umā **34**.55-101
- of Vivasvat **32**.3-47
- , prescr. conc. pollution by a **221**.155cd-158
birth see also *creation, origin*
black and white **133**.18-23ab
- and white hair of Viṣṇu **181**.26-31
- shape of sun **6**.9-14
- shape of Viṣṇu **161**.54-58
- sinner **141**.6-9
blessing by bards **4**.66

- by Viṣṇu **165**.45-47ab
- , formula of **13**.9-12ab
blessings by parents **110**.188-191ab
- of Kali-Yuga **230**.62-65
- of Śūdras **230**.66-71
- of women **230**.72-76
blind princess **170**.69-74ab
blindness cured with branch of tree **170**.74cd-76
blood, boar cleansed from **79**.7cd-19
- , discus cleansed from **128**.70cd-72ab
- , rivers of **214**.14-17
- , smell of **12**.11-17
blowing at fire, prohibition of **221**.102
- of conch **156**.4-6; **203**.1-5
blue bull, letting loose of **220**.33ab
- clothes of Balarāma **192**.71-74; **198**.15-17
- clothes of Śeṣa **21**.15-27
- neck of Śiva **112**.4-6
- statue of Viṣṇu **58**.1-7
boar and earth, marriage of **219**.42-47ab
- as sacrifice **213**.32-42
- cleansed from blood **79**.7cd-19
- , earth lifted by **202**.23-29
- in simile, Viṣṇu as **49**.9
- , Nārāyaṇa as **213**.1-9
- , Viṣṇu as **18**.57-58; **42**.5; **56**.19cd-22ab; **79**.7cd-19; **179**.18cd-22ab; **180**.24cd-38; **191**.4-12; **213**.32-42; **219**.37-39; **226**.59-61
- , world of **227**.37cd-41
- , worship of Viṣṇu as **229**.86cd-87
- worshipped by gods **226**.59-61
boars, punishment for rearing of **22**.18cd-20
boasting of men **39**.46-47
Bock, A. **78**
body after death, special **214**.27cd-31 .46-51 .70-88ab
- and soul **214**.46-51
- and soul in simile **242**.29-33
- as city of nine gates **236**.33
- as means for goals of life **235**.11-12
- , concentration on **239**.39-41
- , Consciousness and **237**.54
- , constituents of **243**.21-31
- constituted from elements **236**.7-8
- , deities existing in human **236**.9
- , deities presiding over **240**.17-19
- , development of human **179**.47cd-61
- , negative description of **227**.16-32ab
- of Vāsudeva, Śiva existing in **226**.59-61
- of Vāsudeva, sages existing in **226**.59-61
- of Viṣṇu **56**.16-17ab
- of Viṣṇu as origin of beings **226**.13-14
- of Viṣṇu, colours of **56**.39cd-42
- of Viṣṇu, division of **181**.2-4
- of Viṣṇu, entering of **53**.41-43; **56**.51-54
- of Viṣṇu, gods residing in **226**.20cd-22ab
- , parts of **239**.39-41
- protected by Viṣṇu **163**.26-31
- , purification of **61**.4-6
body see also *embodiment, forms, incarnation, manifestation, shape*
bondage by Qualities **242**.4-5ab
bones, collecting of **220**.62cd
- of Brahmin, purification of **110**.217-219cd
- of Dadhīci, weapons made from **110**.51-56ab
- , pollution by touching of **221**.136cd-137ab
book, Purāṇa as written **175**.86-90
books, proper use of **243**.11-18
boon by Aditi to Kṛṣṇa **203**.22
- by Aditi to Satyabhāmā **203**.24-25
- by Agastya **84**.5-8
- by Agni and Yama **125**.33-43
- by Aṣṭāvakra to Apsarases **212**.72-85
- by Brahman to Bali **13**.32-35
- by Brahman to crocodile **35**.44-45
- by Brahman to Havyaghna **133**.5-8
- by Brahman to Himavat **34**.74-80
- by Brahman to Hiraṇyakaśipu **213**.44-52 .58-59
- by Brahman to Kārtavīrya **3**.84-86ab
- by Brahman to Rāvaṇa **97**.8-13ab; **176**.15cd-19ab
- by Brahman to Tāraka **71**.4-6
- by crocodile **35**.52-59
- by Dattātreya to Arjuna Kārtavīrya **13**.161-164; **213**.106-112
- by Gaṇeśa **114**.19-20
- by Gautamī **85**.15-16
- by gods to Goddess **106**.49cd-53ab
- by gods to Mucukunda **196**.21-22
- by gods to Pippalāda **110**.168-171
- by gods to Pravarā **106**.54cd-56
- by hermits **118**.24cd-30
- by Hunger **85**.15-16
- by Kaśyapa to Diti **3**.109cd-122
- by Kṛṣṇa to garland-maker **192**.75-86
- by Kṛṣṇa to Mucukunda **197**.1-3
- by Kṛṣṇa to Śiva **206**.45-48

- by Mitra and Varuṇa **7**.9-14ab
- by Pārvatī to Uṣā **205**.11-14
- by Puruṣottama to Indradyumna **66**.7cd-13
- by Rudra to Aśoka-tree **35**.22-26ab
- by Śiva **37**.24-25; **75**.33; **81**.16-22ab; **95**.22-28ab; **97**.24-28; **100**.22-24; **112**.7-10; **124**.100-107; **130**.32-33; **152**.24-25; **153**.8-11; **162**.6cd-10ab; **169**.46-47 .49ef; **175**.46cd-47; **207**.28-43
- by Śiva to Agni **128**.46-49
- by Śiva to Bāṇa **3**.70cd-71; **206**.1-4 .39-44
- by Śiva to Bhagīratha **78**.59-69
- by Śiva to Dakṣa **39**.90-91; **109**.36-39ab
- by Śiva to Dattātreya **117**.18-19ab
- by Śiva to Devāpi **127**.54-59
- by Śiva to Diti **124**.110-122
- by Śiva to Gautama **75**.25-27
- by Śiva to Gārgya **196**.1-4
- by Śiva to Pippalāda **110**.107-111 .165
- by Śiva to Pūru **146**.38-41
- by Śiva to Rati **38**.7-13
- by Śiva to Rāma **123**.207-213ab
- by Śiva to Rāvaṇa **143**.12-13
- by Śiva to Śveta **59**.6-21
- by Śiva to Umā **35**.60-63
- by Śiva to Viṣṇu **109**.52-54
- by sage **78**.8cd-11
- by sun **32**.17-31; **33**.24-26
- by Sūrya to Madhucchandas **138**.35-38
- by Uttaṅka **7**.85-86
- by Viṣṇu **7**.58cd-71ab; **8**.58-59ab; **124**.36cd-39ab; **163**.47-49; **165**.45-47ab
- by Viṣṇu and Śiva **160**.20; **168**.31-35
- by Viṣṇu to ancestors **219**.98cd-107ab
- by Viṣṇu to Āsandiva **167**.31-32
- by Viṣṇu to Bali **73**.52-55
- by Viṣṇu to Dhanvantari **122**.44-47
- by Viṣṇu to Indradyumna **49**.60; **50**.33-40; **51**.1-8 .22-45
- by Viṣṇu to Kaṇḍu **178**.178
- by Viṣṇu to Madhu and Kaiṭabha **213**.28-29
- by Viṣṇu to Mārkaṇḍeya **56**.1-2 .51-54 .58-60
- by Viṣṇu to Nārada **229**.56-58
- by Viṣṇu to Śuci **229**.37-43ab
- by Viṣṇu to Śveta **59**.73-77
- by Viśvāmitra **8**.20-21
- by Yama to Ulūkī **125**.25-32
- , postponement of **37**.26-28

boons by ancestors **220**.118cd-120ab
- by gods **127**.60-63; **141**.10-13
- , five **13**.210-212ab
- , four **13**.161-164
- granted to Kaikeyī, three **123**.23-33ab
- , request for **203**.20-21

border mountains **18**.45cd-46ab .51
borders, punishment for violation of **22**.14ab .23cd-24ab
bow broken by Kṛṣṇa **193**.13-16
- broken by Rāma **213**.142-144
- , golden **213**.114-122
- named Ajagava **4**.48-52; **9**.21
- of Rudra **9**.21
- of Viṣṇu **131**.16-24; **163**.50-51; **171**.1-2ab
- see also ARCHERY **190**.6-8

bowl, earth as **72**.25cd-27ab
- of Brahman **172**.2-3
- of Śiva, Gautamī originated from **137**.25-28ab

boys, education of **222**.22-27
Brāhma as place of pilgrimage **104**.1-2
- , place of pilgrimage **100**.1-3

Brahmabālukā, place of pilgrimage **25**.30
brahmacārin see *student*
Brahmādri **174**.27cd-28
Brahmagiri **74**.24cd-30 .88; **75**.35-45 .48; **76**.2-4; **79**.7cd-19; **80**.6cd-9; **84**.2-4 .18; **87**.33-34ab; **161**.30-33ab; **174**.27cd-28; **175**.3-9ef
Brahmahrada, place of pilgrimage **25**.23
Brahmajña, place of pilgrimage **25**.40
Brahmakuṇḍa, place of pilgrimage **25**.17
Brahmaloka **23**.12-15
Brahman **1**.33-34; **2**.10-13; **3**.84-86ab; **4**.1 .10 .53-57 .115-121; **5**.17a-c .61-62; **9**.1 .6 .7-8 .13-16 .24-25 .28-30 .31-32; **18**.36cd -38ab; **30**.19-20; **31**.31-33ab; **33**.3-8 .9-13ab; **34**.74-80; **36**.36cd-39ab .54cd-57 .58-59ab .125-126 .127-129; **39**.84-88ab; **51**.1-8; **56**.13-15; **61**.45cd-46; **70**.16-19; **71**.41-42; **75**.20; **95**.22-28ab; **96**.22cd-24ab; **106**.23-26ab; **113**; **151**.17-22ab; **168**.10-12; **178**.43-53; **192**.48-58; **203**.6-19; **206**.14-19; **219**.98cd -107ab; **221**.87-88 .89-94; **222**.11-12; **226**.13-14; **236**.7-8; **239**.58-61
- , abode of **20**.88ab
- , advice by **11**.4-7; **83**.13-16; **119**.4ef-8; **122**.24cd-27; **124**.87-93; **128**.38-43;

181.15-19
- , Ajaikā created by **134**.2-8ab
- and heavenly voice, dialogue between **161**.11cd-26
- and Śiva **129**.70-71
- and Viṣṇu, competition between **135**.5cd-10ab
- and Viṣṇu, dispute between **135**.2cd-5ab
- and Viṣṇu, Śiva as **130**.17-21
- and Viṣṇu, Śiva unknowable to **127**.48-53
- , androgynous **1**.51cd-52; **45**.37-41; **161**.33cd-35ab
- as author of Purāṇa **1**.30
- as authority **180**.13-16ab
- as authority on *dharma* **216**.64-66; **217**.117-118; **223**.21-22 .54cd-55ab; **225**.30
- as authority on donation(s) **225**.9
- as authority on non-violence **224**.56c-f
- as authority on Sāṃkhya **245**.31-41
- as creator **45**.30-36; **229**.15-18; **230**.4-7; **241**.12-16ab
- as creator of Āṅgirasas **158**.4-7 .16-21
- as creator of gods **161**.43cd-50cd
- as creator of Indra **129**.30-37
- as deer **102**.2cd-5ab
- as first-person narrator **33**.3-8; **36**.8 .36cd -39ab .125-126; **39**.84-88ab; **42**.36cd-38ab; **59**.1-2; **72**.18-19; **73**.57cd .58-63ab; **83**.13-16; **87**.2-34ab; **91**.6cd-11ab; **94**.22-26; **96**.5cd-7; **97**.2-5ab; **101**.10-11ab; **106**.19-22; **108**.71-74; **110**.198cd-200cd; **112**.2-3; **113**.2-4; **115**.2-4; **119**.2-4cd; **122**.21-24ab .54cd-62; **123**.7cd-14ab; **124**.87-93; **126**.12-16ab; **128**.38-43; **134**.2-8ab; **135**.5cd-10ab .15-16; **137**.25-28ab; **143**.2-5; **145**.5cd-7; **156**.4-6; **158**.2-3 .35cd-37ab; **160**.2cd-6ab; **162**.2cd-6ab; **174**.8-12ef .19-25ab; **176**.4-7 .15cd-19ab
- as manifestation of Viṣṇu **213**.25-26
- as narrator **41**.10; **45**.77-89
- as priest at wedding-ceremony **72**.18-19
- as Rudra **158**.22-27ef
- , birth from thumbs of **2**.51-53
- , bowl of **172**.2-3
- , city of **18**.36cd-38ab
- , constituents of sacrifice originated from **161**.50ef-53
- , cosmic sleep of **56**.55
- , curse by **101**.10-11ab; **133**.9-12
- , day of **230**.4-7
- , destruction by **230**.4-7
- , discharge of semen of **72**.18-19
- , donkey head of **113**.2-4
- , earth and waters as prior to **137**.25-28ab
- , entourage of **26**.32-33; **213**.44-52
- , epithets of **26**.31
- , five daughters of **102**.2cd-5ab
- , five elements prior to **161**.9-11ab
- , five heads of **113**.2-4 .22-23; **135**.10cd-13cd
- , four heads of **113**.18-21
- , functions of **106**.19-22
- , gods taking refuge to **181**.15-19
- , halves of **161**.33cd-35ab
- , Hari as **233**.1-4
- , homage to **131**.39cd-51
- , incest committed by **102**
- instructed by Viṣṇu **161**.24-26
- , lotus as residence of **179**.22cd-26; **180**.24cd-38
- , names of **241**.12-16ab
- , Nārāyaṇa as **180**.17cd-18ab
- , omniscience of **34**.93cd-99; **122**.50-54ab
- , origin of wife of **161**.33cd-35ab
- originated from lotus **161**.6cd-9
- originated from primordial matter **30**.78-79ab
- originated from sacrifice, energy of **161**.13-16
- , place of pilgrimage sacred to wife of **42**.1-11
- , plants as mothers of **119**.2-4cd
- pleased by Agni **174**.19-25ab
- , prophecy of future events by **213**.60-65
- , *puruṣa* as creator of **161**.43cd-50cd
- , rank of **2**.10-13; **236**.47-48ab
- , Rākṣasas originated from egg of **156**.2cd -3
- , rebirth as **27**.66cd-68
- residing in navel of Viṣṇu **226**.20cd-22ab
- , Śiva freed from head of **229**.59-63
- , Śiva worshipped by Viṣṇu and **153**.12
- , *sāman*-melodies sung by **156**.2cd-3
- , sons of **5**.8-9ab; **23**.12-15
- , Speech cursed by **135**.15-16
- , statue consecrated by **176**.11
- to Bali, boon by **13**.32-35
- to crocodile, boon by **35**.44-45

- to Havyaghna, boon by **133**.5-8
- to Himavat, boon by **34**.74-80
- to Hiraṇyakaśipu, boon by **213**.44-52 .58-59
- to Kārtavīrya, boon by **3**.84-86ab
- to plants, promise by **119**.4ef-8
- to Rāvaṇa, boon by **97**.8-13ab; **176**.15cd-19ab
- to Śiva, hymn by **36**.39cd-42
- to Tāraka, boon by **71**.4-6
- to Viṣṇu, hymn by **181**.21-25
- , truthfulness of **135**.5cd-10ab
- , Viṣṇu as **56**.51-54; **109**.41; **233**.10
- , Viṣṇu as creator of **45**.29
- , Viṣṇu as father of **73**.58-63ab
- , Viṣṇu as origin of **161**.68-71
- , Viṣṇu praised by **161**.39cd-43ab
- , Viṣṇu, Śiva **33**.9-23; **74**.31-37; **123**.121-128ab; **129**.125-127; **130**.7-14; **131**.39cd-51; **144**.2-4; **158**.35cd-37ab; **175**.1-2ef; **213**.25-26; **219**.98cd-107ab; **226**.20cd-22ab .45cd-48ab
- , Viṣṇu, Śiva, statue of **120**.3cd-5
- , Viṣṇu superior to **226**.11-12
- , Viṣṇu unknowable to **55**.32cd-33ab; **191**.4-12
- , Viṣṇu worshipped as **20**.40cd-41ab
- with thousand heads, Viṣṇu as **179**.22cd-26
- , world of **4**.68-73; **7**.30-34 .37a-d; **42**.1-2 .6-8; **67**.60cd-64ab; **73**.48-51; **102**.8cd-9ab; **120**.6-7ab; **222**.55-56; **227**.16-32ab .32cd-37ab; **228**.86-91ab; **233**.5-6
- , worship of **131**.31-39ab; **216**.5-63

brahman see also *absolute*

brahman as all **211**.11-12
- as highest step of Viṣṇu **234**.63cd-66ab
- as word **234**.58-60ab
- , attainment of **237**.7-14; **238**.53-56ab
- , Brahmins similar to **223**.58cd-60ab
- , classification of **234**.61cd-63ab
- consisting of words, Veda(s) as **127**.35-47
- , description of **245**.31-41
- , epithets of **234**.63cd-66ab; **238**.36cd-37ab; **240**.98-103
- , exposition of **30**.57-86
- , Gautamī as **175**.3-9ef
- , knowledge of **3**.42cd-46ab; **70**.3cd-8ab; **117**.2-5
- , Kṛṣṇa as **192**.32-42
- , liberation by becoming **12**.3
- , liberation by knowledge of **245**.42-43
- , names of **30**.58-61
- , path of **223**.61cd-64ab
- , Śiva as **158**.37cd-39ab; **173**.37-39
- , Sāṃkhya as knowledge of **240**.98-103
- , sound of **236**.59cd-66
- , two levels of **234**.61cd-63ab
- , union with **10**.38cd-41ab; **110**.47cd-50
- , Vāsudeva as **211**.3-4 .11-12
- , Viṣṇu as **23**.41-43; **178**.117

brahman-expert **120**.6-7ab

brahman-formulas **39**.43-45

Brahmāṇī, place of pilgrimage **25**.58

Brahman-sacrifice **4**.60; **34**.26-29ab

Brahman-Sages **3**.10-14
- , Ṛgveda honoured by **3**.61ab

Brahman-world, ascension to **5**.40-41

brahmapāra-hymn, Kaṇḍu as author of **178**.112

Brahmapurāṇa, characteristics of **246**.1-5
- , superiority of **246**.20

Brahmaputra, place of pilgrimage **64**.10

Brahma-Rudratīrtha, place of pilgrimage **25**.28

Brahmasara, place of pilgrimage **25**.62 .65 .68

Brahmasaras, place of pilgrimage **25**.65 .68 .73

Brahmaśiras, weapon named **9**.22

Brahmasthāna, place of pilgrimage **25**.45 .71

Brahmasthānavivardhana, place of pilgrimage **25**.81

Brahmatīrtha, place of pilgrimage **25**.35 .39 .45 .48; **101**.19cd-20; **102**.11c-f; **113**.1 .18-21 .22-23; **131**.39cd-51

Brahmatuṅga, place of pilgrimage **25**.28

Brahmavāluka, place of pilgrimage **25**.30

Brahmāvarta, place of pilgrimage **25**.39 .48 .56 .67

Brahmavīrāvakāpilī, place of pilgrimage **25**.73

Brahmayoṇi, place of pilgrimage **25**.48

Brahmeśvara, Liṅga named **174**.8-12ef

Brāhmī **77**.9cd-13; **78**.75cd-76

Brahmin addicted to dice-playing **164**.17-28
- , advice by **163**.40-42
- and field in simile **223**.60cd-61ab
- and Vaiśya, bet between **170**.27-28
- and Vaiśya, friendship between **170**.2-5

.81-83
- , Apsarases cursed by **212**.72-85
- as bird, rebirth of **164**.29-37
- as devotee of Śiva **169**.43cd-45ef
- as fool **228**.97-100ab
- as proxy of king **8**.3-4
- as Rākṣasa, rebirth of **228**.76-85
- , asceticism for becoming a **147**.5-7
- , Cāṇḍāla acknowledged as **228**.56-59
- , description of sinful **164**.17-28
- , Gaṇeśa disguised as **74**.56-58
- girl, marriage of Āsandiva and **167**.18-21ef
- , greedy **170**.17cd-22
- , hunter and **169**
- , Indra disguised as **87**.34cd-35; **124**.39cd -47
- kidnapped by Rākṣasī **167**.4-7
- , only son of **35**.32-38
- , punishment for afflicting a **215**.130cd-136ab
- , punishment for tormenting a **215**.91cd-92ab
- , purification of bones of **110**.217-219cd
- , Rākṣasa as **118**.10-14; **163**.12cd-16
- , Rākṣasī as surrogate mother of **167**.8-14 .15-17
- , rebirth as **41**.60cd-71 .75-81; **43**.65cd-74 .77-82ab; **51**.42-45; **57**.9-11 .20-28 .52-56 .59-61; **58**.70cd-77; **59**.81-91; **62**.5-9; **64**.17-20; **66**.18-23; **67**.76-80; **176**.57-62; **227**.32cd-37ab; **228**.86-91ab .97-100ab; **229**.64-67ab
- reborn as Rākṣasa **228**.76-85
- , Śanaiścara disguised as **118**.19-24ab
- , Śiva laughing at **169**.33-35
- , Śiva scolded by **169**.25-32
- , Śūdra regarded as **223**.54cd-55ab .56cd-58ab
- , Sarasvatī in the words of a **163**.43-46
- , treacherous **170**.14-17ab
- , Viṣṇu as **50**.25-28; **163**.32-39
- , Viśvakarman as **50**.25-28
- , Viśvāmitra becoming a **10**.55-56

Brahminhood based on conduct **223**.56cd-58ab
- , inconvenience(s) of **230**.66-69
- , loss of **223**.28-31
- , maxim about **107**.2-11

Brahmin-murder **96**; **100**.14-18; **109**.1-3ab; **110**.215; **113**.22-23; **135**.1-2ab; **161**.72-78
- , ancestral rites as expiation for **123**.165-169
- , expiation for **65**.83; **177**.26
- , horse-sacrifice as expiation for **12**.11-17; **123**.77-81
- , punishment for **22**.9; **150**.10-14; **215**.86cd-88ab
- , sins comparable to **164**.29-37
- , threefold **123**.147-157 .165-169
- , untouchability caused by **123**.73cd-76

Brahmin-murderer, prescription(s) concerning untouchability of **123**.48cd-61ab

Brahmins **11**.33-34ab; **13**.63b-64ab .79; **34**.12cd-19
- and Kṣatriyas **10**.63; **13**.91
- and Kṣatriyas, maxim about truthfulness of **111**.39cd-47
- as authority **220**.152
- , conduct of **223**.61cd-64ab
- , curse by **210**.1-4 .6-10
- , demons as **168**.15-18ab
- , description of **46**.7cd-10
- despised by gods **167**.8-14
- , disqualified **220**.127cd-135
- , disrespect against **167**.8-14; **170**.44-46; **196**.1-4; **210**.6-10; **212**.72-85
- , distinction of **223**.56cd-65
- , duties of **222**.3-6
- , education of **107**.2-11
- , expiation by feeding of **218**.13cd-16ab
- fed by Śūdras **230**.70-71
- , feeding of **47**.58cd-61 .63-67; **67**.39cd-45; **187**.42-54 .55-59ab; **219**.65cd-71ab
- , food for **216**.5-63; **219**.65cd-71ab
- for ancestral rites, invitation of **220**.105
- , gift to **47**.74-80ef .81-93ab .95c-f; **67**.39cd-45; **218**.8cd-9ab
- , honouring of **216**.3-4
- , importance of feeding of **123**.140-146
- , instruction by **225**.54-55
- , Mantras as deity of **187**.42-54
- , merit of feeding of **218**.9-32
- , number of invited **220**.60 .69cd-70
- , origin of **161**.43cd-50cd
- , praise of **28**.3-7
- , prescr. conc. honouring of **76**.18cd-23ab
- , punishment for disrespect against **215**.29-38
- , punishment for hatred against

22.14cd-15a
- , qualification(s) of **67**.35cd-39ab; **107**.2-11; **220**.100cd-101ab .101cd-102ab .102cd .103-104
- qualified for ancestral rites **220**.103-104
- , respect for **35**.46-51 .52-59
- , satisfaction of **220**.126
- , seven **1**.43-45ab
- similar to *brahman* **223**.58cd-60ab
- , truthfulness as distinction of **228**.56-59
- , Vaiśyas turning into **7**.42
- , venerability of **104**.61-65

Brahmodumbara, place of pilgrimage **25**.40
branch of tree as remedy **170**.64-68
- of tree, blindness cured with **170**.74cd-76

breach of chastity, punishment for **22**.27
- of confidence, punishment for **215**.104-105ab; **217**.59-61
- of *dharma* **7**.104cd-105ab
- of vow **3**.109cd-122
- of vow, punishment for **22**.26

breach see also *trangression, violation*
breaking of banner **206**.1-4; **207**.13-24
- of bow **193**.13-16; **213**.142-144
- of teeth of Pūṣan **109**.21-26ab
- of teeth of Rukmin **201**.23-26

breasts, milk oozing from **193**.32-40
breath of Śeṣa **232**.24-27
- of Viṣṇu, wind originating from **233**.1-4
- , *puruṣa* as **243**.21-31
- , vital **214**.46-51

breath control **39**.90-91; **60**.49-53; **235**.13-20; **243**.47-48
breaths, five vital **179**.56cd-57ab .57cd-58
- , seven **240**.22cd-26

Bṛhadāraṇyaka **219**.65cd-71ab
Bṛhadaśva **7**.54-55 .58cd-71ab .71cd-73
Bṛhaddarbha **13**.45-48
Bṛhaddevatā **6**; **131**
Bṛhadiṣu **13**.93-96
Bṛhadratha **12**.11-17; **13**.109; **101**.2-9
Bṛhanmanas **13**.45-48
Bṛhaspati **3**.42cd-46ab; **5**.11cd-12; **9**.17-20 .21 .24-25 .26 .28-30; **23**.6-10; **77**.2-9ab; **95**.12-15ab; **106**.19-22; **108**.68-70; **131**.6cd-9 .10-15; **152**.34-37ab
- , advice by **106**.15-18
- , Aṅgiras **13**.58-61; **95**.2-6
- and Śukra **152**.18-20
- and the planets **174**.19-25ab
- as authority on *karman* **122**.50-54ab
- as planet **175**.83-84
- as teacher of Candramas **152**.2-4
- , curse by **152**.9cd-14
- , Indra and **122**.63-67ab .87-92
- , Indra anointed by **122**.93-94
- to Śiva, hymn by **122**.74-82

Bṛhat **13**.80cd-81ab
Bṛhatī **2**.14-15
Bṛhatkarman **13**.45-48
Bṛhatkīrti **213**.81-104
- [king] **167**.4-7

Bṛhatsaṃhitā **221**.129cd-131ab
bribes, punishment for accepting of **215**.129cd-130ab
bricks for sacrifice **148**.3cd-7
bride, decoration of **72**.9cd-10ab
- , prescription(s) concerning selection of **221**.73

bridegroom in wedding-ceremony, absence of **111**.39cd-47
brilliance, killing with **8**.54-57
- of Devakī during pregnancy **182**.4-6
- of Kṛṣṇa **196**.23-29
- of Śiva, Manyu born from **162**.10cd-12
- of sun, cutting of **6**.34cd-40; **32**.80-81 .104-107; **89**.42
- , origin of **33**.3-8

brilliance see also *Agni, burning, fire*
broken things, prescr. conc. **221**.31
brother, maxim about search for **3**.24
- , punishment for disrespect against **217**.75cd-77ab
- , punishment for killing of one's **124**.100-107
- , search for **3**.19cd-23

brothers, conflict between **17**.17-23
- of Namuci **123**.23-33ab
- , women performing ancestral rites for **220**.78cd-80ab

brown cow, earth exchanged for a **155**.3cd-10ab
Buddha as incarnation of Viṣṇu **122**.68-73
Buddhi **68**.56-59ab
buddhi see *consciousness*
Budha **7**.14cd-16; **9**.31-32; **10**.1-3; **23**.6-10; **108**.56-58 .61cd-64 .65-67 .68-70 .94-98 .99-102ab .102cd-103 .104; **226**.30-41
- as planet, ascension of **9**.31-32

buffaloes, origin of **3**.104-105

bull as attendant of Śiva **41**.88-90
- as emblem of Śiva **109**.52-54; **166**.11cd-13
- as lord of cows **4**.2-9
- , description of demon as **189**.46-58ab
- , letting loose of blue **220**.33ab
burden on earth **86**.11-16; **116**.3cd-5ab; **181**.5-6 .7-14
- on earth, alleviation of **188**.29-35 .39-41; **193**.32-40; **202**.23-29; **210**.1-4 .16-21 .22-27; **212**.59-62
burial of amulet **58**.57
burning by looks **8**.54-57; **38**.1-6; **71**.27-37; **78**.32-37ab; **118**.19-24ab; **196**.16-20
- of demons by Mārtaṇḍa **32**.41cd-46
- of Kāma **38**.1-13; **71**.27-37
- of Kāśi **207**.28-43
- of Rākṣasas **118**.19-24ab
- of Sāgaras **78**.32-37ab
- of snakes by sun **159**.24ef-25ef
- of three worlds by Rudra **232**.24-27
- of widow **8**.39-40; **110**.67-70; **212**.1-4; **229**.43cd-55
burning see also *Agni, brilliance, fire*
butter and honey, food with **219**.65cd-71ab
- as offering **219**.60cd-65ab
- , cows made of sesamum and **216**.5-63
- in sacrifice, spring as **161**.35cd-39ab
- , ocean of **18**.11-12; **20**.45 .46-47ab
butter see also *ghee*
butter-drinker **39**.22-27ab
caesarian, birth by **110**.67-70
Caidya **213**.159-163
Caidyoparivara **13**.109
Caitra **28**.53cd-54ab; **31**.19-21; **41**.72-74
Caitraratha **10**.5-8
- [forest] **18**.30
Caitrarathī **7**.93-95ab
Cakrā **20**.28
Cakrakumbha **18**.32-36ab
Cakrakuñja **18**.32-36ab
Cakrapāṇi, Viṣṇu as **174**.8-12ef
Cakraprabha, place of pilgrimage **25**.16
Cakratīrtha, place of pilgrimage **25**.12 .21; **86**.1 .27-29; **109**.1-3ab .55-57ab; **110**.1-4 .87-97ef .143-146ab .217-219cd; **128**.70cd-72ab; **134**.1 .15-16
Cakreśvara, Liṅga named **109**.1-3ab
- , Śiva as **110**.87-97ef .226-228
Cakṣus **2**.14-15; **18**.38cd-44ab; **27**.25cd-27
Cākṣuṣa **2**.14-15; **13**.14cd-15ab
- , Manu **2**.16; **3**.53-58; **5**.4; **34**.26-29ab .29cd-32 .45cd-48
Cākṣuṣa-era **3**.53-58 .61ab; **4**.16-17; **5**.29-33ab
Cakṣustīrtha, place of pilgrimage **170**.1 .89a-f
Calacandras **27**.43-50
calamity caused by flood **188**.6-10
- , duties of castes in **222**.19-20
calamity see also *danger, misfortune*
camels, origin of **3**.93cd-95ab
Campa **13**.42 .43-44
Campā [city] **13**.43-44
Campaka-forest, place of pilgrimage **25**.9
Cañcu **8**.24-28
Caṇḍa **41**.88-90; **215**.65-67
Cāṇḍāla **221**.127cd-129ab .143cd-146ab
- acknowledged as Brahmin **228**.56-59
- as devotee of Viṣṇu **228**.8-91ab
- as musician **228**.8-14
- as prey of Rākṣasa **228**.15-21
- girl, sage as **229**.68cd-87
Cāṇḍālas **220**.97cd-98ab
Candanā **27**.28-29
Caṇḍeśvaratīrtha, place of pilgrimage **25**.61
Caṇḍīśvaratīrtha, place of pilgrimage **25**.61
Candra [mountain] **20**.6-7
Candra [moon] *see* Candramas
Candrā **20**.28
Candrabhāgā **19**.10; **27**.25cd-27
- , place of pilgrimage **64**.11-14
Candrahantṛ **213**.81-104
Candramadhyā **68**.60-67
Candramas **3**.64cd-70ab
- afflicted with leprosy **152**.26-28
- , Bṛhaspati as teacher of **152**.2-4
- [demon] **213**.81-104
- , invincibility of **152**.9cd-14
- , Tāra abducted by **152**
Candramas see also *moon, Soma*
Candramauli, Śiva as **123**.177cd-184
Candrāpīḍa **13**.123-124 .125
Candrāśva **7**.87-88
Candratāpana **3**.64cd-70ab
Cāndrāyaṇa **32**.32-34ab
Candrikā, place of pilgrimage **25**.64
Cāṇūra **190**.6-8; **193**.17-22 .24-31 .42-49; **213**.159-163
- , fight between Kṛṣṇa and **193**.50-57ab
- killed by Kṛṣṇa **193**.60cd-63ab
capturing of army **197**.6-7; **202**.30-35;

204.13cd-18
car, arm as axle of **123**.23-33ab
car see also *cart, chariot*
Caras **27**.59cd-62ab
Carcaras **27**.59cd-62ab
car-festival **66**
Cariṣṇu **5**.45cd-46
Carmaṇvatī **27**.28-29
 - , place of pilgrimage **64**.11-14
carrying of fire and water, prescription(s) concerning **221**.101
cart turned over by Kṛṣṇa **184**.20-28; **190**.1-5
 - , veneration of potsherds and **184**.20-28
cart see also *car, chariot*
Cāru **201**.1-2
Cārudeha **201**.1-2
Cārudeṣṇa **14**.29-31; **201**.1-2; **210**.37-43
Cārugupta **201**.1-2
Cārumatī **201**.1-2
Cārunadī, place of pilgrimage **25**.58
Cāruvarman **210**.37-43
Cāruvinda **201**.1-2
cases represented in hymn, grammatical order of **130**.23-31
caste, change of **7**.26ab .42; **223**.7-22 .28-65
 - , duration of pollution according to **220**.63; **221**.146cd-149ab .155cd-158
 - , liberation for members of low **178**.184-186
 - membership by birth **223**.12
 - , merit according to **28**.37-38
 - , observance of *dharma* of **76**.18cd-23ab
 - , punishment for transgression of **22**.30
 - regulations among gods **34**.33-38
casteless people, creation of **45**.30-36
castes **1**.3-9; **24**.19-25; **56**.3-8
 - , absence of **20**.85-86ab
 - , classification of reward(s) according to **218**.16cd-21ab
 - , creation of four **45**.30-36
 - during Kali-Yuga **230**.34-37
 - , duties common to all **222**.15-17
 - , establishment of four **213**.106-112
 - , four **4**.115-121; **27**.71-72; **41**.28-29; **46**.7cd-10; **58**.59cd-64ab; **123**.2-7ab; **170**.69-74ab; **213**.145-153ab; **246**.18-19
 - in calamity, duties of **222**.19-20
 - in Yugas **175**.25-28
 - , mixing of **223**.19-20
 - of Krauñcadvīpa, four **20**.53cd-54ab
 - of Kuśadvīpa, four **20**.38cd-40ab
 - of Plakṣadvīpa, four **20**.16-17
 - of Śākadvīpa, four **20**.65 .71-72ab
 - of Śālmaladvīpa, four **20**.31
 - , origin of four **13**.32-35; **56**.22cd-23ab
 - , prescr. conc. **222**.2-21
 - , professions of four **19**.9; **27**.17-19ab
 - , punishment for mixing of **215**.121cd-122ab
 - , Soma as lord of **4**.2-9
 - , sons belonging to four **11**.33-34ab; **13**.79
 - , sons belonging to three **11**.60cd-61ab; **13**.63b-64ab
 - , wish-fulfilment for women and low **227**.10-14
cat, Indra as **87**.50-52ab
cats, punishment for rearing of **22**.18cd-20
cattle, adorning of **187**.42-54
Catuḥsāmudrika, place of pilgrimage **25**.52
Catuḥśṛṅga, place of pilgrimage **25**.18
Catuḥśrotas, place of pilgrimage **25**.18
Caturaṅga **13**.40-41 .42
causes [*kāraṇa*], three **173**.9-25
Cavarambaṇa, place of pilgrimage **25**.34
cave as entrance to nether world **112**.23cd-24ab; **115**.12cd-15ab
 - of Narasiṃha **58**.32cd-49
Cedi, king of **12**.11-17; **14**.20cd-24ab
celestial gardens **203**.26-32
ceremonial functions at wedding-ceremony **72**.11cd-14
ceremonies, maxim about twice-born without **111**.7-8
ceremony of parting the hair **100**.25-29ab
ceremony see also *festival, ritual*
challenge of Kṛṣṇa to Pauṇḍraka **207**.8-12
 - of Satyabhāmā to Śacī **203**.38-44
Chandomadhu **138**.4-7
change of caste **7**.26ab .42; **223**.7-22 .28-65
 - of colours **133**.18-23ab
 - of cosmic periods **231**.93
 - of dog-meat into honey **93**.12-24
 - of habitation **231**.68-71ab
 - of sex **108**.20cd-21 .113-115; **229**.43cd-55 .68cd-71
 - of shape **187**.8-18
changing into mare **6**.15-17; **32**.56-58ab
chanting of Sāmaveda **118**.10-14; **156**.2cd-3
characteristics of Brahmapurāṇa **246**.1-5
 - of Kali-Yuga **197**.4-5; **230**.44-48

- of Qualities **237**.58-61 .62-64
- of Sāṃkhya **239**.4-5
- of Self **236**.27-31
- of the manifestations of Viṣṇu **180**.17cd-42ab
- of Vaiṣṇavas in heaven **68**.29-32
- of Yoga **239**.3
charcoals, Aṅgiras originated from **144**.5-8ab
chariot, heavenly **12**.6cd-8 .11-17; **58**.70cd-77; **65**.46-47 .55-56; **66**.18-23; **67**.53-57; **68**.18-22; **110**.183-187; **227**.16-32ab
- of Viṣṇu **210**.47-48
chariot see also *car, cart*
charioteer in simile **237**.21-22
chastity, punishment for breach of **22**.27
- , vow of **81**.13-15
chastity see also *abstinence*
Chāyā **6**.9-14 .18-20ab .20cd-23; **32**.51-55; **89**.6-9ab .13-17ab; **219**.71cd-86 .113cd-115
- , Śanaiścara as son of **165**.2-4
- , Yama cursed by **6**.20cd-23; **32**.58cd-63
Chāyāmayī **219**.87-91ab
Chāyārohana, place of pilgrimage **25**.32
child, abandoning of **13**.127cd-132ab
- as devotee **95**.18-21; **110**.87-97ef; **127**.48-53
- , invincible **3**.109cd-122
- , Kṛṣṇa as **184**
- , Mārkaṇḍeya addressed as **53**.18cd-20
- , revivification of **59**.6-21; **194**.23-31
- , Śiva as **35**.32-64; **36**.27-30
- swallowed by fish **200**.2-10
- , Viṣṇu as **56**.49-50
child see also *infant*
children, description of **184**.52cd-57ab; **187**.2-7
- , king without **78**.3-8ab
- , play of **187**.8-18
- treated unequal by stepmother **32**.58cd-63
choice of teacher **107**.12-16
- of wrong wife, punishment for **22**.17cd-18ab
choice see also *selection, self-choice*
chorus of gods **65**.23-26; **108**.71-74; **110**.183-187; **193**.57cd-60ab; **209**.21cd-22
churning of ocean **106**.8-10ab; **203**.33-37
- of ocean of milk **13**.176cd-187ab; **112**.4-6
- of right hand **2**.21-24; **4**.48-52; **141**.10-13
- of thigh **4**.42-47; **141**.6-9
Ciccika, place of pilgrimage **164**.53cd-54
Ciccikā **164**.53cd-54
Ciccika-bird **164**
- , release of **164**.51-53ab
- to Gaṅgā, prayer by **164**.47-50ef
Ciccikātīrtha, place of pilgrimage **164**.1-2
circumambulation **41**.60cd-71; **57**.20-28; **60**.12-15; **72**.15-17
- of Aśvattha-tree **118**.19-24ab
- of earth **87**.15cd-16; **131**.39cd-51
- of earth, pilgrimage as **228**.92cd-96
- of fire **36**.130-134; **80**.65-70
- of Gaṅgā **76**.13-17; **78**.59-69
- of hill **187**.42-54 .55-59ab
- of island instead of earth **151**.22cd-24ab
- of Liṅga **57**.6-8; **87**.17-20
- of Liṅgas **157**.27cd-28
- of sun **29**.20-21
- of tree **57**.12-14
- of wishing-cow **87**.17-20
- , prescription(s) concerning **221**.40cd-41ab
circumference of earth **23**.3-4
- of sacrificial ground **161**.30-33ab .68-71
- of sky **23**.3-4
circumstances forbidden for Yoga **243**.49
- of death **214**.20cd-27ab .34-41ab .41cd-42ab
circumstances see also *conditions*
cities destroyed by Śiva, three **114**.6-8
- , golden **3**.80cd-83
Citrā **14**.39-41; **27**.30-32; **220**.33cd-42
Citrabhānu **13**.189cd-197ab; **31**.14cd-16
Citragupta **215**.45-55ab .55cd-64
Citraka **14**.3cd .12-13; **16**.50ab .56cd-58ab; **94**.2-14
Citrakūṭa **35**.26cd-28; **123**.116-120
- , place of pilgrimage **64**.3-8ab
Citrakūṭā **27**.30-32
Citralekhā **205**.15-22; **206**.5-9
Citramārgas **27**.62cd-64ab
Citraratha **13**.37-39 .40-41; **15**.1-12ab; **69**.12-43; **226**.30-41
- as lord of Gandharvas **4**.2-9
Citrasena [son of Viśvāvasu] **171**.20-24
Citrasenā **68**.60-67
Citrotpalā **27**.30-32
city, decoration of **36**.59cd-63ab
- , description of **41**.13-19
- of ancestors **220**.49cd-50ab
- of Brahman **18**.36cd-38ab

- of Indra **140**.7-11; **147**.5-7
- of Indra duplicated by Tvaṣṭṛ **140**.14-18ab
- of Śiva **168**.37; **173**.37-39
- of Viṣṇu **68**.68-70; **105**.30cd-31ab; **168**.37
- of Viṣṇu, ascension to **176**.57-62
- of Yama **214**.104-107ab
- of Yama, gate(s) to **214**.107cd-128; **215**.2-3
city of see also *heaven, world*
clans of Kauśikas **10**.61-62; **13**.91
clarification of doubt **136**.27-31
classes of beings **2**.25-28ab; **4**.100-109; **39**.22-27ab; **55**.23cd-31; **72**.1-4
- of beings, offerings to various **220**.89cd-97ab
- of divine beings **65**.19-20
- of gods **5**.8-9ab .13ab .19cd .22ab .26 .30cd -31 .36-37ab; **213**.66-71
- of supernatural beings **3**.3-7ab
- of texts **44**.10-12
classes see also *classification, kinds of*
classification of ancestors **220**.64-66 .67a-f .82cd-86
- of ancestral rites **220**.11cd-13 .64-66
- of beings **32**.7-8
- of *brahman* **234**.61cd-63ab
- of dissolution **232**.1-2
- of holy places **70**.16-29; **175**.29-32ab
- of human beings **237**.15-16
- of knowledge **234**.58-60ab .61cd-63ab
- of living, beings **241**.33
- of meat **220**.23cd-28ab
- of reward(s) according to castes **218**.16cd-21ab
- of sins **218**.3-5
- of suffering **234**.1-8
classification see also *classes, kinds of*
clean things, list of **221**.120cd-122
cleaning by baking **221**.117cd-120ab
- by rubbing **221**.117cd-120ab
- of house, prescr. conc. **221**.123-125ab
- of metals, prescr. conc. **221**.125cd-127ab
- of teeth, prescr. conc. **221**.21 .48ab-49ab
- , prescription(s) concerning earth for **221**.64cd-65ab
- , prescription(s) concerning **221**.113-131ab
- with acid **221**.125cd-127ab
- with ashes and water **221**.117cd-120ab
- with dregs **221**.117cd-120ab
- with mud and water **221**.116-117ab
- with water **221**.115
- with water and earth **221**.125cd-127ab
cleaning see also *purification*
clever people, maxim about **124**.39cd-47
clothes, donation(s) of **220**.139-140 .146-147
- during Kali-Yuga **231**.71cd-78
- , kinds of **242**.8-15ab
- of Balarāma, blue **192**.71-74; **198**.15-17
- of Kṛṣṇa, yellow **192**.71-74
- of Śeṣa, blue **21**.15-27
- of Vāsudeva, yellow **176**.8-10; **207**.13-24
- , prescription(s) concerning **221**.33 .41cd .53-54 .81cd-82ab
clouds, description of **53**.1-5
- destroyed by wind **53**.12-14ab
- instructed by Indra **188**.2-5
- of doomsday **188**.1; **232**.30-40
- , origin of **1**.48cd-50ab
- raining water of immortality **93**.12-24
club as emblem **21**.15-27
club-fighting, art of **17**.28
cocks, offerings given to **220**.149-151
- , punishment for rearing of **22**.18cd-20
cognition, *puruṣa* and **245**.7
coins as stake at game **201**.10-22
Cola **13**.147-148ab
Colakas **27**.59cd-62ab
Colas **8**.44-51; **13**.147-148ab
colic **228**.76-85
collecting of bones **220**.62cd
- of flowers for worship **228**.15-21
- of honey, punishment for **22**.23ab
colour, white as auspicious **221**.81cd-82ab
colours and fingers **61**.7-12
- , change of **133**.18-23ab
- for anointing **29**.33cd-34ab
- of body of Viṣṇu **56**.39cd-42
- of manifestations of Viṣṇu **61**.13
- of nether worlds **21**.2-5ab
- of Qualities **241**.45-47
- of statues **50**.48-54
- of sun according to seasons **31**.12-14ab
- of Viṣṇu, three **161**.54-58
combing of hair, prescr. conc. **221**.21
commander-in-chief of gods, Manyu as **162**.10cd-12
comment by listener(s) **69**.1-9
comparison of merit **25**.83cd-86ab; **28**.47-53ab .56cd-62ab; **29**.42cd-61; **33**.27-31; **41**.54cd-57ab .93; **57**.9-11 .17-19 .38-41 .42-51; **58**.70cd-77;

60.46-48; **62**.16cd-22ab; **63**.1-7; **64**.1-2 .3-16; **65**.59-76ab .81-82 .83-99; **66**.18-23; **67**.52; **75**.35-45; **79**.21cd-22; **80**.84-89; **89**.1-2cd; **93**.25-26; **98**.20-21ab .21cd-22; **103**.8 .12c-f; **104**.89ab; **110**.216 .217-219cd .226-228; **111**.85cd-86; **118**.31-32ef; **119**.1; **128**.83-84; **132**.1-2; **134**.15-16; **138**.41; **144**.23-24 .25-27; **145**.1-2ab; **148**.18cd-20; **151**.27cd-29; **155**.13cd-14ab; **161**.61cd-62; **163**.12cd-16; **168**.26cd-28ab; **171**.1-2ab; **175**.60-68 .83-84 .86-90; **176**.57-62; **177**.9-15; **216**.64-66; **219**.116; **220**.43-48ab; **230**.59 .62-63; **246**.21-27
- of merit in Yugas **230**.64
- of places of pilgrimage **43**.6-9; **69**.10-11; **70**.1-3ab; **75**.35-45; **77**.9cd-13; **88**.16-19; **149**.13-16ab; **161**.72-78; **177**.20
- of religious practices **49**.70; **230**.64
- of sins **164**.29-37
- of Yugas **230**.62-63 .78-81

comparison see also *hierarchy, superiority*
comparison of merit see also *multiplication of merit*
compassion of Śiva **72**.23-25ab; **127**.48-53; **158**.37cd-39ab; **169**.6cd-15
- of Viṣṇu **122**.68-73; **164**.38-46
- of Viṣṇu and Śiva **122**.87-92

competition between Agni and waters **126**
- between Brahman and Viṣṇu **135**.5cd-10ab
- between gods and demons **11**.8-16

competition see also *conflict, dispute, enmity, opposition, rival*
complaint by Garuḍa to Viṣṇu **90**.12cd-19
- by gods **73**.9-17

completion of sacrifice **104**.78-81ab; **174**.18
- of sacrifice of Dakṣa **109**.36-39ab
- of *sattra*-rite **114**.19-20

concealing of divine attributes **182**.14-15 .17
concentration, dangers of **239**.54-56
- , description of **243**.54-57
- , devotion and **29**.7-8
- during worship **192**.59-61
- in simile **239**.54-56
- of mind **243**.47-48
- of Yogin **239**.31-38
- on body **239**.39-41
- on Nārāyaṇa **240**.106-111

concentration see also *absorption, meditation, union*
conception after vow **124**.19-28ab
- by touching **202**.23-29
- of a hero, observances for **125**.44-49
- , oral **6**.41-43; **82**.2-6
- , prescription(s) concerning date(s) for **221**.76

conch, blowing of **203**.1-5
- , demon as **194**.23-31
- , demons destroyed by sound of **156**.4-6
- of Kṛṣṇa, origin of **194**.23-31
- of Viṣṇu **68**.44-53

concluding summary **41**.1-5; **43**.63cd-65ab; **56**.51-54; **69**.1-9; **70**.1-11 .8cd-10; **72**.36; **113**.16
conclusion **3**.106; **4**.122; **5**.6cd-7ab .11ab .15cd .17a-c .19cd .24b: .27-28 .32-33ab .48; **7**.44ab; **8**.94; **9**.33-34; **10**.67cd-68; **11**.60cd-61ab .61cd; **13**.49 .79 .92ab .100-101 .141 .208cd-209; **18**.1-6; **19**.28; **20**.21; **21**.1; **22**.28-29 .49cd-50ef; **23**.1-2 .21; **24**.26; **27**.39cd-41ab .51ab .58ab .59ab .79; **28**.64cd-65ab; **30**.85-86 .87-88; **31**.27 .39; **32**.109; **33**.46; **34**.73; **36**.135a-f; **39**.17cd-18ab .22-27ab; **40**.119 .135; **41**.37ab .49ab-50ab; **42**.34; **43**.89; **44**.78-79; **47**.95c-f; **51**.59; **56**.74; **58**.49; **59**.6-21; **62**.13cd-15 .22cd-23; **65**.59-76ab .97-99; **67**.81; **68**.17 .71 .77c-f; **70**.11 .41a-f; **77**.14-15; **78**.75cd-76 .77; **94**.48cd -50ab; **150**.21-22; **174**.27cd-28; **177**.29-30; **178**.192; **179**.2-3; **180**.42c-f; **209**.23; **212**.86 .95; **213**.80 .105 .113ab .123 .158 .165cd-168ab .171; **217**.115cd-116 .117-118; **218**.1-2 .32c-f; **219**.116; **220**.42 .80cd .126; **221**.1-3 .109 .169cd; **222**.21; **223**.65c-f; **224**.26 .38; **225**.30 .56; **226**.67c-f; **227**.50; **228**.152; **229**.1-2; **230**.1-2 .77 .82; **231**.79 .93; **233**.7 .11 .49cd; **234**.43; **235**.29 .30; **236**.36-37ab; **237**.42c-f; **238**.33cd-34ab .38; **239**.29-30 .57 .62; **240**.76 .105-112; **241**.36cd; **243**.66; **244**.1 .10 .42; **245**.31-41 .42-43 .44-47 .52
condemnation of self-choice of husband **219**.13-17
conditions at end of cosmic periods **231**.4-41
- during Kali-Yuga **230**; **231**.47-79
- forbidden for Yoga **235**.7-9
- of life, absence of bad **18**.24cd-28 .60-62ab; **20**.8-9 .65 .80cd-82ab .86cd-87ab; **68**.68-70; **164**.3-6
- of life, explanation for various **216**.73-80

- of life, good **152**.40
- of life, ideal **74**.24cd-30; **153**.6cd-7
- on earth, heavenly **20**.85-86ab
conditions see also *circumstances*
conduct, Brahminhood based on **223**.56cd-58ab
- , definition of **221**.8cd
- , difference among people caused by **224**.46-56
- , effect(s) of **221**.8ab .161-169ab; **225**.23cd-29 .36-41
- leading to heaven **224**.9-14 .15-16ef
- leading to liberation **224**.5-8
- , maxim about **159**.31cd-35; **221**.161-169ab
- of ascetic **222**.32-35
- of Brahmins **223**.61cd-64ab
- of householder, effect(s) of **222**.37-38
- of Kṣatriyas **223**.41-52ab
- of Śiva **38**.35-38
- of Śūdras **223**.32-36
- of the wise, maxim about **212**.89-90
- of Vaiśyas **223**.37-40
- of Yogin **236**.45cd-46 .47-48ab
- of Yogin, prescription(s) concerning **236**.43cd-44ab .59cd-66
- , prescr. conc. **224**.4-16
- , superiority of **221**.6-7
conduct see also *action, observances, practices, prescriptions*
confession of sins, expiation by **218**.6 .7-8ab
confidence, punishment for breach of **215**.104-105ab; **217**.59-61
confirmation, formula of **70**.3ab
conflict between brothers **17**.17-23
- of traditions **2**.51-53; **3**.7cd-9
confluence of Diti and Gaṅgā **124**.132-136ab
- of five rivers **102**.9cd-11ab
- of Gaṅgā and Yamunā **129**.4-8
- of Gaṅgā with ocean **65**.84-96; **122**.3-7
- of Gaṅgā [world of mortals] and Gaṅgā [nether world] **159**.46cd-48ab
- of Gautamī with ocean **172**
- of Kapilā and Gautamī **155**.10cd-11ab
- of Phenā and Gautamī **129**.82-93
- of Revatī and Gautamī **121**.1 .24-25
- of Vidarbhā and Gautamī **121**.1 .24-25
confluences, list of **105**.22-26ab
conformity to tradition **220**.153
congruence of qualities of husband and wife **165**.18-22
conjugal privacy, prescription(s) concerning **128**.7-15
conjunction of Jupiter and Leo **152**.37cd-39ef; **175**.83-84
conqueror of Tāraka, Skanda as **82**.9-10
Consciousness, absorption in **238**.31-33ab
- and body **237**.54
- and senses **237**.67-72
- , constituents of **237**.52 .56 .66
- , functions of **237**.55 .57 .67-72 .73-75
- , reality as **22**.48-49ab
consciousness see also *knowledge*
consecrated water, effect(s) of **65**.78-80
- water, sprinkling with **65**.81-82; **110**.35-39ab
consecrated see also *holy sacred*
consecration by vedic verses **58**.32cd-34ab
- of Agni **98**.18cd
- of Gaṇeśa **114**.9-12
- of Indra **122**.93-94
- of Indra, obstacle(s) to **96**.8-10
- of king **4**.16-17; **8**.22; **9**.13-16; **14**.33-34ab
- of Kṛṣṇa as Vice-Indra **188**.36-37
- of Pṛthu **4**.53-57
- of Purūravas **108**.119-120
- of sacrificial gift **155**.11cd
- of statue **51**.48-53
- of Ugrasena **194**.9
- with prayer-formulas **176**.11
- with water **155**.11cd
consecration see also *anointing*
consolation by sons, maxim about **154**.14cd-21ab
- of Arjuna **212**.55-92
- of Indra **129**.42-48
constituents leading to liberation **240**.20-22ab
- of ancestral rites **219**.42-47ab
- of body **243**.21-31
- of consciousness **237**.52 .56 .66
- of cosmos **1**.36-37ab
- of *dharma* **216**.3-4
- of embryo **243**.1-10
- of human being **217**.14-17
- of human being sixteen **236**.14; **237**.7-14; **240**.22cd-26
- of human beings **237**.23-25
- of meditation **243**.47-48
- of sacrifice **161**.35cd-39ab; **179**.29-37; **213**.12-20 .32-42; **242**.26cd-27

- of sacrifice originated from Brahman **161**.50ef-53
- of worship **41**.60cd-71; **66**.7cd-13; **67**.24-27 .35cd-39ab; **228**.1-5
- of worship of Śiva **43**.65cd-74
- of worship of statue **61**.24-38
constituents see also *ingredients*
constitution of body from elements **236**.7-8
construction of Dvārakā **196**.9-15
- of temple **43**.10-13; **47**.7-9; **56**.61-66ab .66cd-73; **59**.26-33
consultation among gods **106**.13-14
- among gods and demons **106**.3-7
contact, prescr. conc. **221**.139cd-140ab .140cd-141ab .141cd-143ab
- , prescription(s) concerning **221**.77 .78 .82cd-84 .85-86
- with fallen persons, punishment for **217**.37-39
- with good people, maxim about **163**.32-39
- with sinners, punishment for **22**.9
continents, seven **4**.11-15; **12**.18-21; **13**.160 .166-169 .172-173 .189cd-197ab; **18**.11 -12; **33**.3-8; **54**.1-3; **131**.39cd-51; **175**.60-68
contradictions among goals of life **221**.14-15
conventions, observance of **225**.60-62
copper, vessel **28**.24
corn, gift of ear of **136**.32-35ab
corpse abandoned to vultures **216**.5-63
- , dragging of **193**.67cd-76ab
- eaten by cows **110**.51-56ab
cosmic cycle **5**.52 .58cd-60 .61-62; **23**.16-20
- cycle as life-span **23**.12-15
- cycle, flood at end of **232**.30-40
- disorder **32**.82-87; **39**.53-58; **53**.10cd-11
- egg **20**.95cd-98ab; **23**.21 .22-27ab; **33**.3-8
- egg, halves of **1**.39cd-42
- eggs, number of **23**.27cd-28ab
- layers of elements **23**.22-27ab
- night, duration of **233**.9
- periods **56**.39cd-42; **230**.4-7
- periods, change of **231**.93
- periods, conditions at end of **231**.4-41
- sleep of Brahman **56**.55
- sleep of Viṣṇu **53**.12-14ab; **56**.49-50; **213**.25-26 .30-31
- water **1**.37cd-38ab
cosmography **18**; **20**; **21**; **22**; **23**; **24**
cosmos as part of Kṛṣṇa **185**.39-42
- by fire, destruction of **21**.15-27; **52**.1-10
- by sun, destruction of **5**.58cd-60
- , constituents of **1**.36-37ab
- , extent of **20**.98cd-99ab
- from golden egg, origin of **1**.39cd-42
- in Hari, absorption of **5**.61-62
- , origin of **1**.16-20; **33**.3-8
- , *puruṣa* as origin of **161**.43cd-50cd
cosmos see also *world*
counteraction, maxim about importance of **127**.16-22
countries, list of **27**.62cd-64ab
couple, mocking at unequal **107**.42-45
couples, divine **34**.42-45ab
courtesans, description of **44**.23-27ab
cow as earth **87**.17-20
- as mother of Rudras **74**.59-67
- , earth as **2**.25-28ab; **4**.68-73 .96-122; **141**.23-25
- , earth exchanged for a brown **155**.3cd-10ab
- , gift of **155**.12-13ab; **208**.8-18
- , holy **74**.59-67
- , hurting of **7**.43
- , killing of **8**.13-15b:
- of Vasiṣṭha **8**.13-15b:
- , punishment for killing of **22**.7-8; **215**.84cd-136ab
- , purification by **221**.136cd-137ab
- , substitution of land and **155**.12-13ab
- , urine of **220**.200cd-203ab
- , waving the tail of a **184**.7-13
cowardice, curse of **124**.73cd-80
cow-dung **169**.36-39ab
- smeared on head **184**.7-13
cowherds, cows as deity of **187**.42-54
- , hill as deity of **187**.42-54
- , Kṛṣṇa entrusted to **182**.19-26
- shifting to Vṛndāvana **184**.42cd-52ab
cowherds see also *Gopīs*
cows as deity of cowherds **187**.42-54
- as sacrificial gift **13**.166-169
- , bull as lord of **4**.2-9
- , corpse eaten by **110**.51-56ab
- , destruction of **91**.2cd-6ab
- , Kṛṣṇa as lord of **188**.29-35
- made of sesamum and butter **216**.5-63
- , merit measured by sacrifice of **110**.216
- , offerings given to **220**.149-151
- , origin of **3**.104-105

- , prescription(s) concerning treatment of **221**.102
- , sacrifice of **131**.26-28; **187**.42-54
- , theft of **131**.4cd-6ab
- , world of **67**.64cd-75
creation and destruction, cycle of **2**.54-56; **3**.62-64ab; **5**.57ab
- as play of Śiva **116**.14
- , five steps of **241**.23-25
- from mind **1**.43-45ab; **2**.47-49; **3**.3-7ab; **9**.1
- from semen in water **1**.37cd-38ab
- from thoughts **45**.37-41
- of Brahman by Viṣṇu **45**.29
- of casteless people **45**.30-36
- of desire **1**.39cd-42
- of four castes **45**.30-36
- of lust **1**.39cd-42
- of mind **1**.39cd-42
- of sacrificial fire **161**.30-33ab
- of *sāman*-melodies **161**.50ef-53
- of seasons for sacrifice **161**.35cd-39ab
- of speech **1**.39cd-42
- of time **1**.39cd-42
- of women **2**.47-49
- of wrath **1**.39cd-42
creation see also *birth, emanation, evolution, origin*
creator and destroyer, Viṣṇu as **56**.38cd-39ab
- , Brahman as **45**.30-36; **229**.15-18; **230**.4-7; **241**.12-16ab
- , Hari as **23**.36-37
- of Āṅgirasas, Brahman as **158**.4-7 .16-21
- of Brahman, *puruṣa* as **161**.43cd-50cd
- of Brahman, Viṣṇu as **45**.29
- of *dharma*, king as **4**.35-41
- of evil things, Śiva as **129**.70-71
- of gods, Brahman as **161**.43cd-50cd
- of Indra, Brahman as **129**.30-37
- of sacrifice, Viṣṇu as **179**.29-37
- of sages, Viṣṇu as **226**.52-53
- , responsibility of **185**.44-49
- , sun as **30**.7-13; **31**.1-3
- , Viṣṇu as **56**.56-57; **179**.29-37 .62-64; **233**.10
cremation of hermits **123**.77-81
cremation see also *ancestral rites, funeral*
crocodile, boon by **35**.52-59
- , Umā and the **35**.32-64
crossing of Yamunā, miraculous **182**.19-26
crow, Yama as **103**.2-6
crows, offerings given to **220**.149-151
Cuḍāmaṇi **69**.12-43
Cuñculas **10**.61-62
curds, ocean of **18**.11-12; **20**.57cd-58ab
curse against gods, threat of **127**.29-34
- against mother, threat of **9**.28-30
- against priests, threat of **127**.23-28
- because of wrong testimony **146**.15-18
- by ancestors **220**.50cd-51ab
- by Bṛhaspati **152**.9cd-14
- by Brahman **101**.10-11ab; **133**.9-12; **135**.15-16
- by Brahmins **210**.1-4 .6-10
- by Chāyā **32**.58cd-63
- by Dakṣa **34**.33-38
- by Diti **124**.73cd-80
- by Gaṅgā **13**.82cd-87
- by Garga **12**.9-10
- by Gautama **87**.58cd-59
- by gods and demons **128**.29-37
- by Indra **84**.13-15; **131**.10-15
- by Kavi [Śukra] **152**.26-28
- by mother **32**.73-75; **158**.4-7
- by Nikumbha **11**.41-43
- by Śiva **34**.26-29ab .29cd-32; **111**.68cd-79
- by sages **116**.20-22ab; **132**.3-5
- by sun **89**.25cd-33
- by surrogate mother **6**.20cd-23; **89**.13-17ab
- by Vasiṣtha **13**.189cd-197ab
- by Viṣṇu and Śiva **135**.13ef-14
- by Viśvāmitra **104**.83-86ab; **147**.17cd-20ab
- by Yayāti, reference to **194**.11-12
- , fear of **3**.10-14; **35**.11-14; **178**.19-24
- , killing with **141**.2-5; **176**.15cd-19ab
- , modification of **6**.24-30; **32**.69-72; **146**.19-25; **147**.17cd-20ab; **212**.72-85
- of becoming a demon **213**.136-140
- of becoming a Śūdra **7**.43
- of being an animal **84**.2-4
- of cowardice **124**.73cd-80
- of leprosy **152**.26-28
- of old age **146**.11-14
- of one-eyedness **100**.25-29ab
- of pregnancy with pestle **210**.6-10
- , provocation of **34**.20a-d
- removed by Śiva **146**.38-41
- , restraining from **110**.61-66
cutting of brilliance of sun **6**.34cd-40; **32**.80-81 .104-107; **89**.42

Cyavana **5**.11cd-12; **7**.27cd-28ab; **13**.109
cycle as life-span, cosmic **23**.12-15
- , cosmic **5**.52 .58cd-60 .61-62; **23**.16-20
- of creation and destruction **2**.54-56; **3**.62-64ab; **5**.57ab
- of rebirth **216**.73-80; **242**.1-3 .34-39; **244**.23-39; **245**.48-51
- of seasons **7**.37a-d
- of water **24**.8-11; **31**.4-6
Dadhīca, place of pilgrimage **25**.55
Dadhīci **39**.27cd-28; **110**.5-70 .188-191ab
- , weapons made from bones of **110**.51-56ab
Dadhikarṇodapānaka, place of pilgrimage **25**.67
Dadhikarṇodayātmaka, place of pilgrimage **25**.67
Dadhivāhana **13**.37-39
daily libation(s), prescr. conc. **221**.20
- routines, prescription(s) concerning **221**.17-112
Daiteya, place of pilgrimage **140**.35-38
Daityas **18**.52-55; **20**.36-38ab; **21**.2-5ab; **106**.13-14 .26cd-30; **115**.2-4; **124**.33-36ab; **140**.19cd-21cd .31-34; **160**.6cd-9; **168**.15-18ab
- and Dānavas, battle between **162**.13-19
- and the Mothers **113**.2-4
- , Kavi [Śukra] as teacher of **95**.28cd-30
- killed by Yama **168**.25-26ab
- , personification of knowledge of **206**.31-38
- , places of pilgrimage honoured by **142**.14
Daityas see also *Dānavas, demons, Piśācas, Rākṣasas*
Daivata **27**.20cd-24ab
Dakṣa **1**.30; **2**.34-46 .54-56; **3**.2 .34-35ab; **5**.49-52; **6**.1ab; **32**.3-6; **34**.1-6 .7-8 .9-12ab .12cd-19 .29cd-32 .45cd-48 .49-50; **39**.90-91; **69**.12-43; **109**.13-20 .28-29; **174**.2-5ab; **178**.99-104; **219**.98cd-107ab; **226**.30-41
- as father of Nārada **3**.7cd-9
- as father-in-law of moon **2**.51-53
- as grandson of moon **2**.51-53
- as lord of Prajāpatis **4**.2-9
- , birth of **2**.47-49 .51-53
- , boon by Śiva to **39**.90-91; **109**.36-39ab
- , completion of sacrifice of **109**.36-39ab
- cursed by Śiva **34**.26-29ab .29cd-32
- , destruction of sacrifice of **39**
- , destruction of sons of **3**.7cd-9; **158**.2-3
- , marriage of daughters of **2**.47-49; **3**.25-28
- , Nārada as grandson of **3**.7cd-9
- , rebirth of **34**.39-41 .45cd-48
- , Śiva cursed by **34**.33-38
- , sacrifice of **109**.3cd-6ab .13-20
- , sons-in-law of **34**.12cd-19
- , Svāhā as daughter of **128**.3-6
- to Śiva, hymn by **40**.2-100; **109**.30-35
Dākṣāyaṇī **71**.19-23; **109**.3cd-6ab; **128**.72cd-76; **226**.30-41
Dakṣiṇa, place of pilgrimage **25**.68
Dakṣiṇā **69**.12-43
dakṣiṇā see *donation, gift, reward*
Dambhakas **27**.54-57
Dambhamālikas **27**.43-50
Damin [caste] **20**.38cd-40ab
Dāmodara **187**.41; **189**.46-58ab; **206**.49-50
Dāmodara, explanation of **184**.31-42ab
Daṃṣṭrākuṇḍa, place of pilgrimage **25**.16
Dānavas **3**.74cd-78ab .78cd-80ab .84-86ab; **18**.52-55; **20**.36-38ab; **21**.2-5ab; **106**.13-14 .26cd-30; **115**.2-4; **140**.19cd-21cd; **160**.6cd-9; **168**.15-18ab
- , battle between Daityas and **162**.13-19
Dānavas see also *Daityas, demons, Piśācas, Rākṣasas*
dance and music, origin of **129**.75-78
- , heavenly **32**.99cd-100
- of Kṛṣṇa on Kālīya **185**.34-38
- , worship with **162**.6cd-10ab
dancing, worship of Śiva by **168**.31-35
Daṇḍaka **7**.21cd-22
- [city] **108**.116-118
- [hell] **217**.80cd-86
Daṇḍaka-forest **7**.21cd-22; **123**.116-120; **129**.65-67; **130**.17-21; **131**.16-24 .31-39ab; **149**.9cd-12; **161**.68-71; **175**.81cd-82
- , importance of **161**.72-78
- , place of pilgrimage **25**.10
- , superiority of **88**.16-19; **129**.49-64
Daṇḍakas **27**.54-57
Daṇḍaśarman **16**.1-3
Daṇḍātmā, place of pilgrimage **25**.76
danger, prescription(s) transgressed in **128**.7-15
danger see also *calamity*
dangers of concentration **239**.54-56
- of gambling **171**.27-39
- of Yoga **239**.50-52

Dantaśatru **16**.1-3
Dantavakra **14**.20cd-24ab
Dantavaktra **199**.5-10
Danu **3**.51-52 .78cd-80ab; **32**.3-6; **124**.2cd-3ab
- , hundred sons of **3**.73cd-74ab
- to Diti, advice by **124**.9-11
Darbha-grass **28**.24; **121**.23; **168**.18cd-21
Darbha-grass see also *grass*
Dardalācala **27**.20cd-24ab
Dardama **4**.11-15
Darghas **27**.62cd-64ab
darkness, destruction of **33**.3-8
- , Śiva as **112**.11-19
Dāruka **210**.47-48 .49 .52cd-58; **211**.1-2
Dāruṇa **22**.2-6; **217**.80cd-86
Dāruvala, place of pilgrimage **25**.32
Darvā **13**.20cd-22ab .22cd-23
Daryas **8**.44-51
Daśagrīva **176**.15cd-19ab
Daśahāra **63**.11-16
Dāsaka **15**.34
Daśaratha **8**.84cd-92; **15**.24-28; **123**.2-33ab .33cd-73 .105cd-109ab .121-186; **213**.124 -126
- and demons, fight between **123**.23-33ab
- and Viśvāmitra **123**.86cd-96
- , birth of sons of **123**.84-86ab
- cursed by hermits **123**.73cd-76
- , hermit killed by **123**.48cd-61ab
- in hell, sojourn of **123**.109cd-115
- , Lomapāda **13**.40-41
- , wedding of sons of **123**.97-105ab
Dāśarathi see *Rāma*
Daśārha **15**.22-23 .24-28
Daśārṇā **27**.30-32
Daśārṇas **27**.59cd-62ab
Daśārṇeyu **13**.5-8
Daśāśvamedha, place of pilgrimage **25**.32 .40
Daśāśvamedhatīrtha, place of pilgrimage **83**.29
Daśāśvamedhikatīrtha, place of pilgrimage **25**.36; **83**.1
Daśerakas **27**.43-50
Dasra **6**.44-45ab
Dasyus **212**.71 .72-85
date(s), auspicious **28**.19-20 .42-45 .53cd-54ab .54cd-56ab; **29**.22-27ab .29-31ab .42cd-61; **41**.57cd-59ab .72-74; **51**.63-71; **58**.21cd-23; **60**.8cd-10 .12-15; **62**.10-13ab; **63**.8-9 .11-16 .17 .19-20 .21 .22; **64**; **65**.3 .84-96; **67**.12-14; **86**.2; **124**.132-136ab; **148**.3cd-7; **152**.37cd-39ef; **219**.109cd-113ab; **228**.1-5; **246**.28-29
- for ancestral rites, auspicious **220**.10cd-11ab .43-60 .64-66 .75 .116cd-117ab
- for conception, prescription(s) concerning **221**.76
- , inauspicious **221**.42
- , pilgrimage at auspicious **41**.54cd-57ab
- , prescription(s) concerning auspicious **221**.102
date(s) see also *hours, Kāla, moment, time*
Datta **5**.11cd-12; **16**.1-3
Dattātreya **117**; **144**.2-4
- as teacher of Yoga **180**.24cd-38
- , boon by Śiva to **117**.18-19ab
- to Arjuna Kārtavīrya, boon by **13**.161-164; **213**.106-112
- to Śiva, hymn by **117**.7-17
- , Viṣṇu as **180**.24cd-38; **213**.106-112
daughter, adoption of **4**.113; **14**.20cd-24ab
- and earth, equivalence of **165**.5-17
- as accomplishment of *dharma* **165**.5-17
- as sacrificial gift **13**.142-146
- , birth of **34**.74-80
- born from sacrifice **7**.3-5ab
- , duty towards **165**.5-17
- obtained by means of horse-sacrifice **2**.7-8
- of Brahman as deer **102**.2cd-5ab
- of Dakṣa, Svāhā as **128**.3-6
- of Gautama, Pippalāda married to **110**.225
- , prescr. conc. marrying one's **165**.23-26
- , punishment for selling of **165**.5-17; **214**.120-128; **215**.72-77 .112cd-113ab
- , punishment for sexual intercourse with **22**.12ab
- , wish for **144**.2-4
daughter-in-law **15**.16-21
- , punishment for sexual intercourse with **22**.12ab
daughters of Brahman, five **102**.2cd-5ab
- of Dakṣa, marriage of **2**.47-49; **3**.25-28
- of Himavat, three **34**.81
Daurvāsika, place of pilgrimage **25**.28
day of Brahman **230**.4-7
- of Viṣṇu **233**.46cd-49ab
days, rain of seven **188**.20-23
- , sacrifice of twelve **228**.76-85

dead king, lament for **193**.76cd-78ab; **194**.7-8
- pollution by the **221**.135cd-136ab
dead see also *deceased*
Death **36**.12cd-13ab; **65**.40-41
- , announcement of voluntary **110**.41cd-46ab .61-66
- as result of instability of meditation **237**.28
- as slaughterer at sacrifice **116**.2cd-3ab
- at holy places **35**.26cd-28
- at inauspicious moment **228**.76-85
- at place of pilgrimage **42**.10; **59**.81-91; **68**.74-77ab
- at place of pilgrimage, voluntary **228**.146-151
- at Puruṣottamakṣetra, liberation by **177**.24-25
- at Puruṣottamakṣetra, merit of **177**.16-19
- at sun temple, merit of **28**.62cd-64ab
- by drowning, voluntary **216**.5-63; **229**.72-86ab
- by fasting, voluntary **12**.47-48; **216**.5-63; **228**.86-91ab; **229**.72-86ab
- by means of Yoga **30**.14-18; **34**.20ef-25; **109**.6cd-10; **110**.47cd-50; **211**.3-4 .11-12
- , circumstances of **214**.20cd-27ab .34-41ab .41cd-42ab
- , destiny after **214**
- , destiny of renouncer after **222**.55-56
- , destiny of Vaiṣṇavas after **227**
- , destiny of Yogin after **214**.107cd-109; **240**.69-75
- , existence in sunbeams after **30**.14-18
- , freedom from 7.37a-d; **45**.59-67; **176**.33-34
- in battle **216**.5-63
- , Kṛṣṇa remembered at hour of **192**.71-74 .75-86
- , Liṅga established by **116**.22cd-24ab
- , marriage of Kṛtyā and **116**.22cd-24ab
- , maxim about voluntary **107**.31-34
- , merit of voluntary **110**.61-66
- , messengers of **94**.2-14
- , methods of voluntary **214**.114cd-119; **216**.5-63; **221**.152cd-154
- of Balarāma **210**.50-52ab
- of king, voluntary **138**.22-27
- of Kṛṣṇa **211**
- of one for the sake of many **4**.81-87; **141**.21-22
- of parents of Kṛṣṇa **212**.1-4
- of Rāma **213**.157
- of Satī, voluntary **34**.20ef-25
- of widow, voluntary **110**.67-70
- , remembering of Viṣṇu at hour of **229**.56-58 .64-67ab
- , special body after **214**.27cd-31 .46-51 .70-88ab
- , threat of voluntary **154**.21cd-26
- to Śiva, hymn by **116**.15-16
- , untimely **35**.64; **59**.6-21; **86**.3cd-7; **217**.80cd-86
death see also *dying*
- see also *Kāla, time, Yama*
death, voluntary see *voluntary* death
death-rites **17**.8-11
debts see *obligations*
decapitation of king of Kāśi **207**.25-27
- of sacrifice **37**.2-23; **39**.68cd-69ab
- with hand, killing by **192**.71-74
deceased accompanied by *dharma* **217**.14-17; **246**.36
- accompanied by *dharma* or *adharma* **217**.4-11
- , torments of the **214**.52-54 .70-88ab .97-99; **215**.4-23 .39-44 .70-71 .81-83ab
deceased see also *dead*
deceit, punishment for **215**.72-77 .107cd-109ab
decoration of bride **72**.9cd-10ab
- of city **36**.59cd-63ab
deeds of Arjuna Kārtavīrya **13**.176cd-187ab
- of Kṛṣṇa **193**.32-40; **202**.3-12
- of Kṛṣṇa, summary of **226**.42-45ab
deeds see also *actions, conduct*
deer, Brahman as **102**.2cd-5ab
- , daughter of Brahman as **102**.2cd-5ab
- , sacrifice as **39**.74-81
defeat of Arjuna **212**.21-24
- of demons **212**.72-85
- of guardians of directions **143**.12-13
- of Indra **129**.11cd-16; **176**.19cd-20; **203**.45-62
- of Kālīya **185**.34-38
- of Kṛṣṇa **185**.11-17
- of righteousness **170**.29-31
defeat see also *victory*
defeats of Jarāsaṃdha, eighteen **195**.8-12
defecating in water, prohibition of **221**.24ab
- , prescr. conc. urinating and **221**.22 .26-30; **243**.49

- , prescription(s) concerning urinating and **221**.37
deficiency of *dharma* **231**.79
definition of conduct **221**.8cd
- of obligatory rites **220**.81cd-82ab
- of Parārdha **232**.4-5
- of Yoga **235**.28
deformation by birth **107**.2-11
- of Aṣṭāvakra, eightfold **212**.72-85
degrees of relation, prescription(s) concerning **221**.73
deities existing in human body **236**.9
- , female **65**.37-38ab; **68**.56-59ab; **109**.13-20
- hiding in trees **103**.2-6
- in simile **108**.68-70
- , maxim about food of one's **123**.173-175
- , mocking at **73**.48-51
- of others, respect for **29**.9-14
- , perceptibility of **30**.19-20
- presiding over body **240**.17-19
deities see also *gods*
deity, Mitra as highest **30**.49-52 .53-56
- of ancestors, Soma as **219**.91cd-98ab
- of Brahmins, Mantras as **187**.42-54
- of cowherds, cows as **187**.42-54
- of cowherds, hill as **187**.42-54
- of farmers, plough as **187**.42-54
- of the sacrifice, Agni as **127**.23-28
- , Śiva as highest **36**.44cd-48 .49-52ab
- , sun as highest **30**.7-13; **33**.13cd-14ab
dejectedness of Arjuna **212**.35-41
delight, Lakṣmī as principle of **137**.30cd-39ab
delivery of taxes **182**.19-26; **184**.1-6
delusion, maxim about failure due to **72**.20-22
demon as ape **209**.2-11ab
- as ass **186**.1-3
- as beautiful woman **122**.8-20
- as bull, description of **189**.46-58ab
- as conch **194**.23-31
- as devotee of Viṣṇu **73**.18-20; **149**.2-4ab
- as horse **190**.22-25
- as human being **187**.8-18
- , ascetic seduced by **122**.8-20
- , asceticism consumed by **122**.8-20
- , asceticism disturbed by **7**.58cd-71ab
- born from smoke **133**.2-4
- , curse of becoming a **213**.136-140
- , sacrifice disturbed by **127**.4cd-9ab
- , sacrificer abducted by **127**.4cd-9ab
demons, ancestors attacked by **219**.25-29
- and gods, opposition of **209**.2-11ab
- , animal faces of **213**.81-104
- as Brahmins **168**.15-18ab
- , assembly of gods and **160**.6cd-9
- , battle between gods and **3**.109cd-122; **9**.23; **11**.4-7; **32**.9-11 .41cd-46; **97**.8-13ab; **106**.2; **109**.39cd-40; **112**.2-3; **123**.7cd-14ab; **142**.2-4; **160**; **162**.2cd-6ab
- burnt by Mārtaṇḍa **32**.41cd-46
- , competition between gods and **11**.8-16
- , consultation among gods and **106**.3-7
- , curse by gods and **128**.29-37
- defeated by Viṣṇu **206**.20
- destroyed by sound of conch **156**.4-6
- detected by Viśvarūpa **168**.18cd-21
- , earth oppressed by **181**.7-14
- , enmity between gods and **97**.5cd-7
- , fight between Daśaratha and **123**.23-33ab
- , fight between Śiva and **112**.11-19
- , friendship between gods and **106**.2
- , gods seeking help from **116**.5cd-9
- killed by Mothers **112**.20-22ab
- killed by Rāma **123**.116-120; **213**.136-140
- killed by Tvaṣṭṛ **168**.22-24
- killed by Viṣṇu **131**.16-24
- , killing of **7**.82-84; **149**.4cd-9ab; **181**.38-53; **190**.29-37; **202**.16-21; **213**.136 -140
- , list of **70**.35cd-37ab; **181**.7-14; **188**.42-47; **213**.81-104
- , magic of **78**.12-24
- , nectar of immortality obtained by gods and **133**.13-17
- , Prahlāda as Indra of **11**.8-16
- , Prahrāda as lord of **4**.2-9
- , promise by gods to **116**.5cd-9
- reigning over the earth **160**.2cd-6ab
- , sacrifices directed to **213**.66-71
- , Saramā bribed by **131**.4cd-6ab
- , *sattra*-rite disturbed by **116**.5cd-9
- , strategem of **78**.24-31
- , victory of gods over **212**.72-85
- , weapons of **213**.81-104
demons see also *Daityas, Dānavas, Piśācas, Rākṣasas*
demoralising effect of misfortune, maxim about **150**.1cd-4ab

denial of food and drink **215**.29-38
departure for forest **7**.58cd-71ab .102cd-104ab; **8**.35-37; **10**.29cd-34ab; **12**.47-48; **13**.58-61 .127cd-132ab; **212**.93-94
- of Kṛṣṇa **192**.14-31
- of weapons of Kṛṣṇa **210**.47-48
deposit, weapons as **110**.21-24
deposition of offerings **29**.42cd-61
descendants of Anenas **11**.27-31
- of Āyu **11**
- of Dharā **3**.102cd-103
- of Druhyu **13**.148-151
- of Ikṣvāku **7**.44cd-109
- of Kadru, Nāgas as **3**.97cd-98
- of Kakṣeyu **13**.14cd-49
- of Kṛṣṇa **205**.1-6
- of Kṣatravṛddha **11**.32-61
- of Puru **13**.3-140
- of Ṛceyu **13**.50-140
- of Sagara **8**.73cd-92
- of Siṃhikā **3**.86cd-89ab
- of Titikṣu **13**.27cd-49
- of Turvasu **13**.142-148ab
- of Vasudeva **14**.36-57
- of wives of Kaśyapa **3**.53-58
- of wives of Soma **3**.34-46ab
- of Yadu **13**.153cd-204
descendants see also *offspring*
descent of Gaṅgā **8**.75cd-77ab; **73**.2-69; **78**.3-77
- of Gaṅgā caused by Umā **75**.20
- of gods to earth **160**.6cd-9
description of Apsarases **68**.60-67
- of army **44**.17-22; **47**.71-73
- of autumn **36**.80-88; **189**.14-17
- of Avantī **43**.25-65ab .85cd-88
- of Balarāma **191**.18-25
- of Balarāma as Śeṣa **192**.32-42
- of beautiful woman **122**.8-20
- of Bhāratavarṣa **19**; **27**.14-80
- of body, negative **227**.16-32ab
- of *brahman* **245**.31-41
- of Brahmins **46**.7cd-10
- of children **184**.52cd-57ab; **187**.2-7
- of city **41**.13-19
- of clouds **53**.1-5
- of concentration **243**.54-57
- of courtesans **44**.23-27ab
- of demon as bull **189**.46-58ab
- of dying **214**.32-33 .42cd-45 .46-51
- of Ekāmraka **41**.11-50ab
- of Gautamī, Gautamī-Māhātmya as abridged **175**.76-77
- of hells **22**
- of hermitage **74**.24cd-30; **178**.7-11 .28-42
- of hermitage of Vyāsa **26**.3-17
- of hills **44**.76-77
- of Himālaya **36**.90-93; **72**.1-4
- of holy men **46**.23
- of horse-sacrifice **47**.50-98
- of hunter **80**.6cd-9; **169**.25-32
- of Indradyumna **44**.2-7
- of Kṛṣṇa **44**.14-15; **57**.38-41; **179**.2-75; **191**.18-25; **193**.42-49
- of Mahānadī **46**.4-6ab
- of Manyu **162**.20-27ab
- of Meru **26**.28-30; **45**.5-16ab
- of messengers of Yama **214**.55-69
- of mountain **164**.3-6
- of Mṛtyu **215**.45-55ab
- of Naimiṣa **1**.3-9
- of nether worlds **21**
- of ocean **44**.44-47 .48-53ab; **172**.7cd-14
- of Pārijāta-tree **203**.26-32
- of ponds **41**.47-49ab; **42**.27-31; **43**.58cd-63ab; **44**.73-75
- of *puruṣa* **241**.37-44
- of Puruṣottama **42**.46cd-49ab
- of Puruṣottamakṣetra **44**.55-79; **46**.3-23
- of rainy season **36**.71-79; **184**.57cd-60
- of Rāvaṇa **213**.127-135
- of Śeṣa **21**.15-27
- of Śiva **123**.195-206
- of Saṃsāra **26**.19-22; **49**.23-47ab; **50**.33-40; **59**.65-72; **178**.179-183; **179**.6-10ab; **196**.30-45
- of sacrifice **109**.13-20
- of sacrificial ground **47**.51-58ab
- of sinful Brahmin **164**.17-28
- of splendour of Indra **140**.7-11
- of spring **36**.95-105ab
- of summer **36**.118-123
- of temple **68**.36-42
- of trees **42**.20-23
- of Utkala **42**.13-49ab
- of Vindhya-mountains **118**.2-9
- of Viṣṇu **126**.24-27; **178**.158-165; **179**.65-72ab; **191**.4-12; **196**.30-45; **202**.23-29

- of Vyāsa **26**.6-8
- of winter **36**.89-94
- of women **41**.20-27 .30-34ab; **43**.36cd-44; **44**.23-27ab; **46**.13-22; **47**.68-70; **68**.23-27ab
- of world, allegorical **238**.26-30
- of worship of Śiva **169**.6cd-15
- of Yakṣiṇī **108**.36cd-47
- of Yama **215**.45-55ab

description see also *attributes, epithets, shape*

descriptionof, heavenly worlds **23**

desire, creation of **1**.39cd-42

destiny after death **214**
- of ancestors **220**.87-89ab
- of renouncer after death **222**.55-56
- of Vaiṣṇavas after death **227**
- of Yogin after death **214**.107cd-109; **240**.69-75

destiny see also *fate*

destroyer, Rudra as **21**.15-27
- , Viṣṇu as **56**.26cd-27ab .39cd-42; **179**.16cd-18ab .43cd-44ab
- , Viṣṇu as creator and **56**.38cd-39ab

destruction by Brahman **230**.4-7
- by wrath of mother **13**.58-61
- , cycle of creation and **2**.54-56; **3**.62-64ab; **5**.57ab
- of clouds by wind **53**.12-14ab
- of cosmos by fire **21**.15-27; **52**.1-10
- of cosmos by flood **53**.1-11ab
- of cosmos by sun **5**.58cd-60
- of cows **91**.2cd-6ab
- of darkness **33**.3-8
- of imitated world of Indra **140**.31-34
- of old age **159**.41cd-46ab
- of sacrifice **116**.5cd-9; **127**.4cd-9ab; **134**.8cd-11; **168**.15-18ab; **209**.2-11ab
- of sacrifice of Dakṣa **39**
- of sons of Dakṣa **3**.7cd-9; **158**.2-3
- of village, punishment for **22**.23ab
- of Yādavas **210**

destruction see also *absorption, dissolution*

detachment due to knowledge of Self **238**.5-6
- in simile **237**.82-86ab

detachment see also *indifference, renunciation*

Deussen, P. **40**.113cd-118

Deva, place of pilgrimage **25**.34

Devabāhur **5**.24cd-25

Devabhāga **14**.14cd-20ab .25cd

Devāgama, place of pilgrimage **160**.1-2ab .21-22ab .22c-f

Devagiri **105**.8cd-11ab

Devahrada, place of pilgrimage **25**.21 .81 .82

Devajā **105**.22-26ab

Devaka **15**.55 .56-58ab

Devakhāta **70**.41a-f

Devakī **14**.42ab; **15**.56-58ab; **181**.26-31 .33-35; **183**.8-11; **190**.1-5; **192**.5-10; **193**.24-31 .78cd-79; **194**.1-5; **212**.1-4
- and Vasudeva, imprisonment of **181**.33-35
- during pregnancy, brilliance of **182**.4-6
- , hymn by gods to **182**.7-8
- to Kṛṣṇa, prayer by **182**.16 .17

Devakṣatra **15**.24-28

Devakuṇḍa, place of pilgrimage **25**.22

Devakūpa, place of pilgrimage **25**.81

Devakūṭa **18**.46cd-50
- , place of pilgrimage **25**.73

Devala **3**.41cd-42ab; **10**.57-60; **34**.91

Devalas **10**.61-62

Devamīḍhuṣa **14**.1-2ab

Devamīduṣa **16**.9-11

Devānīka **8**.84cd-92

Devānta **16**.4-6 .7

Devaparvata **105**.26cd-29ab

Devāpi **13**.114; **127**.9cd-15 .16-22 .23-28 .29-34 .35-47 .60-63
- as teacher of gods **13**.117ab
- , boon by Śiva to **127**.54-59
- to Śiva, hymn by **127**.48-53

Devaprabha, place of pilgrimage **25**.22

Devapraharaṇas **3**.61cd

Devapriya, place of pilgrimage **160**.22c-f

Devapurohita **23**.6-10

Devarakṣita **15**.56-58ab

Devarakṣitā **14**.36-38; **15**.56-58ab

Devarāta **10**.57-60 .65cd-67ab .67cd-68; **13**.91; **15**.24-28; **174**.2-5ab

Devarātas **10**.61-62; **13**.91

Devaśarman **228**.76-85

Devasmṛti **27**.28-29

Devaśravas **14**.14cd-20ab .26ab

Devasthāna, place of pilgrimage **25**.47; **142**.1 .12cd-13

Devatīrtha, place of pilgrimage **25**.43 .47; **98**.21cd-22; **105**.22-26ab; **127**.1 .60-63

Devavat **15**.56-58ab

Devavatī **27**.28-29

Devavrata **13**.119; **20**.49cd-51

Devāvṛdha **15**.30-31 .41cd-45ab
- and Parṇāśā [river] **15**.35-41ab
Devayānī **12**.4-5ab .5cd-6ab; **146**.2-8ab
- and Śukra **146**.8cd-10
- , Śarmiṣṭhā as slave of **146**.8cd-10
development of embryo **179**.48cd-50ab
- of human body **179**.47cd-61
Deveśvara, Liṅga named **142**.12cd-13
Devī, names of **181**.38-53
- , worship of Yoganidrā as **181**.38-53
- , Yoganidrā as **182**.27-30
Devībhāgavatapurāṇa 7.98-109
Devikā **27**.25cd-27
Devītīrtha, place of pilgrimage **25**.41
devotee, child as **95**.18-21; **110**.87-97ef; **127**.48-53
- , four arms of **67**.58-60ab; **68**.29-32
- identified with Viṣṇu **61**.13 .17-18
- , Liṅga talking to **169**.22cd-24ef
- of Śiva **94**.37-42; **122**.75-80
- of Śiva, Brahmin as **169**.43cd-45ef
- of Śiva, hunter as **169**.6cd-15 .39cd-43ab .43cd-45ef
- of Viṣṇu, Āpastamba as **129**.82-93
- of Viṣṇu, Cāṇḍāla as **228**.8-91ab
- of Viṣṇu, demon as **73**.18-20; **149**.2-4ab
- of Viṣṇu, Vibhīṣaṇa as **176**.26-32
- , self-castigation of **169**.39cd-43ab
- , unworthiness of **49**.57cd-59ab; **55**.35c-f; **117**.7-11 .13; **191**.27-33
devotee of Viṣṇu see also *Vaiṣṇava*
devotees, Poverty as friend of **137**.15-24
devotion and concentration **29**.7-8
- , importance of **29**.15-17
- of Akrūra to Kṛṣṇa **191**
- , progression of **229**.8-13
- to Agni **229**.8-13
- to Ananta, merit of **176**.57-62
- to Kṛṣṇa, liberation by **227**.6-7
- to Kṛṣṇa, superiority of **49**.70
- to Śiva **56**.61-66ab; **122**.75-80
- to Śiva, effect(s) of **214**.114cd-119
- to Śiva, liberation by **94**.37-42
- to sun **29**.9-14; **229**.8-13
- to Vāsudeva **229**.4-7
- to Vāsudeva established by Śiva **226**.59-61
- to Viṣṇu, effect(s) of **216**.82-86 .87-89
- to Viṣṇu, liberation by **136**.17-26
- , wish for constant **59**.78-80
devotional, singing **228**.8-14

Dhainuka, place of pilgrimage **25**.69
Dhama **20**.49cd-51
Dhanada **61**.45cd-46; **213**.53-57
- , place of pilgrimage **97**.32cd-33
Dhanada see also *Kubera*
Dhanaṃjaya **3**.99-101
- , Arjuna **13**.123-124; **14**.20cd-24ab
Dhaneyu **13**.5-8
Dhaniṣṭhā **220**.33cd-42
Dhanurveda **194**.18-22
Dhanus **11**.35
Dhanvaka, place of pilgrimage **25**.70
Dhanvantari **11**.35 .39-40; **13**.64cd-67ab; **122**.3-47 .8-20
- as lord of gods **122**.44-47
- as son of king of Kāśi **11**.36-38
- , boon by Viṣṇu to **122**.44-47
- to Viṣṇu, hymn by **122**.29-43
Dhanvin **5**.22cd-24
Dhanya [caste] **20**.53cd-54ab
Dhanyaka, place of pilgrimage **25**.70
Dhānyatīrtha, place of pilgrimage **120**.1 .15
Dharā, descendants of **3**.102cd-103
Dharma **2**.7-8 .47-49; **3**.25-28; **14**.20cd-24ab; **128**.72cd-76
- and Agni, Viṣṇu praised by **128**.63cd-70ab
- [son of Anu] **13**.152-153ab
- [son of Citraka] **16**.56cd-58ab
- , Suvarṇā and **128**.62-63ab
- , Suvarṇā married to **128**.24-28
- , wives of **3**.29-30ab
dharma see also *auspicious actions, duty, goals of life, righteousness*
dharma **5**.38cd-39
- as father and mother **170**.38ef-39
- as friend and parents **246**.37-38
- as means of liberation **69**.12-43
- as source of other goals of life **216**.73-80
- based on plants **119**.2-4cd
- , Brahman as authority on **216**.64-66; **217**.117-118; **223**.21-22 .54cd-55ab; **225**.30
- , breach of **7**.104cd-105ab
- , constituents of **216**.3-4
- , daughter as accomplishment of **165**.5-17
- , deceased accompanied by **217**.14-17; **246**.36
- , deficiency of **231**.79
- , dispute about effect(s) of **170**.26a-f
- during Kali-Yuga, observance of **230**.78-81

- , effect(s) of **216**.73-80; **221**.13; **246**.37-38
- , four quarters of **175**.17-24; **230**.8
- in time and place **175**.14-32ab
- , incompleteness of **122**.54cd-62
- , involvement as highest **240**.77-80
- , king as creator of **4**.35-41
- , kingdom without **141**.2-5
- maintained at holy places **175**.17-24
- , neglect of **213**.106-112
- , observance of **7**.9-14ab
- of caste, observance of **76**.18cd-23ab
- of Kṣatriyas, loss of **8**.31-32 .44-51
- or *adharma*, deceased accompanied by **217**.4-11
- protected by Viṣṇu **56**.35cd-38ab
- , protection by **228**.62-73
- , punishment for absence of **215**.136cd-137ab
- , punishment for disrespect against **215**.72-77
- , rejection of **237**.5
- resulting from knowledge of self **231**.44-46
- , return to **231**.80-88
- , Śiva as **130**.23-31
- , Śiva as protector of **102**.5cd
- spread by sons of seven sages **5**.38cd-39
- , superiority of **170**.77-80ef .84-88
- , two kinds of **237**.6
- , untouchability due to disrespect against **170**.44-46
- , Vāsudeva as authority on **226**.50cd-51
- , waters as origin of **72**.27cd-34
- , Yama as lord of **94**.31-36; **165**.30cd-36

dharma-literature **121**.10-12
dharma-rules in Purāṇa **175**.78
Dharmabhṛt **14**.12-13; **16**.50cd-54ab .56cd-58ab
Dharmadhṛk **14**.8-10
Dharma-forest, place of pilgrimage **25**.9
Dharmaketu **11**.55-59
Dharman **16**.50cd-54ab
Dharmanetra **13**.54-55 .155cd-156
Dharmarāja **212**.91-92 .93-94
Dharmaratha **8**.54-57; **13**.37-39
Dharmaśāstra **65**.97-99; **158**.30-35ab
Dharmatīrtha, place of pilgrimage **25**.76
Dharmokṣan **14**.8-10
Dhārṣṭika [country] 7.25
Dhātaki **20**.75cd-76
Dhātṛ **3**.53-58; **5**.20cd-21; **30**.23-26 .28-39; **31**.17-18 .19-21 .22-26; **56**.13-15; **192**.48-58
Dhautapāpa, place of pilgrimage **92**.48cd-49ef
Dhava **3**.35cd-36 .37-38cd .38ef
Dhenu **109**.13-20
Dhenuka **181**.7-14; **183**.1-7; **190**.1-5; **193**.32-40; **202**.3-12
- , place of pilgrimage **25**.9 .69

Dhenukā **20**.66-67
Dhenuka-episode **186**
Dhenusaras, place of pilgrimage **25**.14
Dhī **137**.8-14
Dhiṣaṇa **122**.93-94
Dhiṣaṇā **2**.29-30ab
Dhīvaras **4**.42-47
Dhṛṣṇu **5**.45cd-46
Dhṛṣṇuka **7**.21cd-22
Dhṛṣṭa **7**.1-2 .25 .26ab; **15**.22-23 .33
Dhṛṣṭaketu **11**.55-59
Dhṛta **13**.152-153ab
Dhṛtarāṣṭra **3**.64cd-70ab .99-101; **13**.121 .122
Dhṛtavrata **92**.2-11
Dhṛti **9**.13-16; **20**.36-38ab; **181**.38-53
Dhṛtimat **5**.27-28 .45cd-46; **20**.36-38ab
Dhruva **2**.7-8 .9 .10-13 .14-15; **3**.35cd-36 .37-38cd; **20**.3-5; **23**.6-10 .12-15; **24**.1-7ab
Dhūminī **13**.81cd-82ab .102-105
Dhundhu **7**.58cd-71ab
- , fight between Kuvalāśva and **7**.82-84

Dhundhumāra **7**.54-55 .74-77
Dhūtapāpā **20**.43-44; **27**.25cd-27
Dhyānajapyas **10**.61-62; **13**.91
dialogue between Brahman and heavenly voice **161**.11cd-26
- between Karālajanaka and Vasiṣṭha **241**; **243**; **244**; **245**
- between Śiva and sages **226**
- between Śiva and Umā **223**; **224**; **225**
- between Viṣṇu and Śrī **45**.16cd-89

dialogue see also *discussion, dispute*
diamond in simile **163**.26-31
dice, game of **164**.17-28; **171**; **201**.10-22; **207**.28-43
diet of Yogin **235**.6; **239**.43-46; **243**.50-53
- , prescr. conc, vegetarian **58**.19-21ab

difference among people caused by conduct **224**.46-56
- between Sāṃkhya and Yoga **239**.7-9

- in simile, unity and **245**.23cd-24
- of intelligence of people **225**.46-52
- of opinions **220**.124-125ab; **238**.3-4; **239**.2 .6; **240**.3-4; **243**.36 .37-40; **244**.44-48
differentiation destroyed by knowledge **158**.22-27ef
- in simile **30**.70cd-75
- of *puruṣa* **30**.70cd-75
differentiation see also *plurality*
Dilīpa **8**.73cd-75ab .75cd-77ab .84cd-92; **78**.47-54
- , truthfulness of **8**.73cd-75ab
Dīptijihva **213**.81-104
direction of ancestors, south as **219**.71cd-86
directions, allocation of Viṣṇu to **61**.14-16
- , elephants of **24**.13-18
- , four **73**.63cd-65ab; **214**.107cd-128
- , guardians of **4**.10; **6**.46cd-48ab; **18**.36cd-38ab; **28**.27; **61**.45cd-46; **72**.8; **123**.177cd-184; **154**.2-4; **160**.6cd-9; **162**.20-27ab; **174**.7; **175**.55cd-59ef
- , homage to guardians of **61**.45cd-46
- , origin of **161**.43cd-50cd
- , prescr. conc. **124**.19-28ab; **221**.37
- , prescription(s) concerning **221**.48ab-49ab .62cd-64ab .72 .89-94
- , seven **174**.14
- , ten **1**.39cd-42; **9**.2-5
directions see also *east, north, south*
Dīrghamanta, place of pilgrimage **25**.31
Dīrghasattra, place of pilgrimage **25**.31
Dīrghatapas **11**.35 .36-38; **13**.64cd-67ab
Dīrghatapas, explanation of **11**.36-38
disabilities, list of physical **225**.42-45
disappearance of Nīlamādhava **45**.1-76
- of Veda(s) **213**.106-112
discharge of semen **13**.97
- of semen of Brahman **72**.18-19
discus cleansed from blood **128**.70cd-72ab
- , killing with **128**.63cd-70ab; **207**.13-24
- of Hari, merit of looking at **51**.63-71
- of Viṣṇu, Kāśi burnt by **207**.28-43
- of Viṣṇu, origin of **6**.50cd-51ab
- of Viṣṇu, Rākṣasas killed by **134**.12-14; **156**.4-6
- of Viṣṇu, Rākṣasī killed by **167**.31-32
- of Viṣṇu swallowed by Śiva **109**.28-29
- of Viṣṇu, Yama protected by **86**.27-29
- of Yama **168**.25-26ab
discussion about means of liberation **145**
- about sacrificial ground **168**.2-5
- among sages **126**.3-11
- between Agni and Ātreyī **144**.17-19
discussion see also *dialogue, dispute*
diseases, absence of **65**.57-58
- , eighty-eight thousand **125**.44-49
- , list of **40**.113cd-118; **94**.15-21; **234**.2-4; **242**.5cd-7
diseases see also *afflictions*
disguise as Brahmin **74**.56-58; **87**.34cd-35; **118**.19-24ab; **124**.39cd-47
- as woman **210**.6-10
disgust, knowledge of self resulting from **231**.44-46
disloyalty, punishment for **217**.55-56
disobedience of wives **100**.9-13
disorder, cosmic **32**.82-87; **39**.53-58; **53**.10cd-11
- of nature **231**.4-41 .52-55
displacement of sun **109**.21-26ab
disposing of excrements, prescr. conc. **221**.137cd-138ab
dispute about effect(s) of *dharma* **170**.26a-f
- between Brahman and Viṣṇu **135**.2cd-5ab
- between Lakṣmī and Poverty **137**
dispute see also *competition, conflict, enmity, opposition, rival*
- see also *dialogue, discussion*
disqualified Brahmins **220**.127cd-135
- guest(s), effect(s) of feeding of **220**.136-138
- people **221**.170a-f
disrespect against Brahmins **167**.8-14; **170**.44-46; **196**.1-4; **210**.6-10; **212**.72-85
- against Brahmins, punishment for **215**.29-38
- against brother, punishment for **217**.75cd -77ab
- against *dharma*, punishment for **215**.72-77
- against *dharma*, untouchability due to **170**.44-46
- against father-in-law **34**.9-12ab
- against Kṛṣṇa **192**.71-74
- against parents, punishment for **217**.49-50
- against Śiva, punishment for **157**.21cd-25ab
- against teacher **170**.44-46
- against teacher, punishment for **22**.12cd -13
- against Veda(s) **170**.44-46; **214**.41cd-42ab; **231**.4-41

- against Veda(s) during Kali-Yuga **230**.10-27
- against Viṣṇu **49**.50cd-54ab; **170**.44-46
- due to poverty **137**.8-14
- , effect(s) of **225**.17-23ab
- , prohibition of **221**.36

disrespect see also *enmity, hatred, opposition, rival*

dissolution, absolute **234**
- , classification of **232**.1-2
- , duration of **233**.46cd-49ab
- in *prakṛti* **243**.71-73
- , natural **232**.4-5; **233**.12-49
- , occasional **232**.14-40; **233**
- of elements **233**.30-33ab
- of elements and qualities **233**.12-29
- of *prakṛti* and *puruṣa* in Viṣṇu **233**.38cd-40ab .43cd-46ab
- of the world in simile **206**.21-23

dissolution see also *absorption, destruction*

distance of heavenly worlds **23**.12-15
- of moon **23**.5
- of planets **23**.6-10
- of sun **23**.5
- to world of Yama **214**.11cd-12ab

distinction by age **2**.54-56
- by asceticism **2**.54-56
- of Brahmins **223**.56cd-65
- of Brahmins, truthfulness as **228**.56-59
- of several concept(s) of self **238**.20-23

distractions of Yogin **236**.57cd-59ab .67

distractions see also *enemies, faults, obstacles*

distressed, maxim about protection of the **110**.147-154

distribution of fever **40**.112-120
- of offerings, prescription(s) concerning **221**.89-94
- of realms **3**.123-124
- of sovereignties **4**.1-17

disturbance of asceticism **7**.58cd-71ab; **158**.8-15ef
- of sacrifice **100**.9-13; **103**.2-6; **114**.2-5
- of wedding-ceremony **7**.98-99

disturbance see also *destruction*

Diti **3**.51-52 .64cd-70ab; **32**.3-6
- , advice by Danu to **124**.9-11
- and Gaṅgā, confluence of **124**.132-136ab
- and Kaśyapa **124**.2cd-31
- , boon by Kaśyapa to **3**.109cd-122
- , boon by Śiva to **124**.110-122
- , Indra and **124**.87-140
- , Indra cursed by **124**.73cd-80
- , Indra in womb of **124**.49-86

Divākara **31**.14cd-16
- , place of pilgrimage **25**.33

divine and human nature of Kṛṣṇa **193**.80-87
- attributes, concealing of **182**.14-15 .17
- beings, classes of **65**.19-20
- couples **34**.42-45ab
- eyesight **36**.49-52ab; **55**.7-8
- messenger sent to Kṛṣṇa **210**.16-21
- sages **39**.7-17ab

divinity of Balarāma **187**.22-25
- of Kṛṣṇa **203**.70-73
- of Kṛṣṇa and Balarāma **191**.26
- of Vāsudeva **234**.71-75

Diviratha **13**.37-39

division of body of Viṣṇu **181**.2-4
- of earth **7**.19cd-21ab; **12**.24-38
- of Gaṅgā **76**.8-10
- of kingdom **12**.18-21
- of ritual food **219**.71cd-86

divisions of time **31**.7-10; **65**.39; **179**.29 .37; **230**.4-7; **232**.6-12; **241**.12-16ab
- of time, three **161**.35cd-39ab

Divodāsa **11**.39-40 .41-43 .44-48 .49-50ab; **13**.64cd-67ab .67cd-68ab .69cd .70cd .97

Dodhaka-metre **37**.29

dog, eating of meat of **93**.5-11

dog-eater **124**.73cd-80

dog-eaters **7**.100-102ab .102cd-104ab; **123**.48cd-61ab

dogs dear to Yama, four-eyed **131**.2cd-4ab .31-39ab
- , impurity of **221**.53-54
- , punishment for rearing of **22**.18cd-20

Dolphin [stellar constellation] **24**.1-7ab

domains of knowledge **240**.5-16 .17-49
- of senses **236**.10-11; **237**.51; **240**.17-19

domestic and wild animals, origin of **161**.43cd-50cd

donation of lamps, effect(s) of **29**.35cd-42ab

donation(s), Brahman as authority on **225**.9
- confirmed by water **73**.34-40
- , effect(s) of **225**.2-8
- , merit of **41**.57cd-59ab; **120**.3cd-5
- of clothes **220**.139-140 .146-147
- of earth **155**.13cd-14ab; **175**.60-68
- of food, effect(s) of **218**.24-28ab

- of food, praise of **218**.10cd-13ab
- of food to ancestors **219**.18-24
- of land, effect(s) of **120**.3cd-5
- of plants, merit of **120**.6-7ab
- , praise of **216**.5-63
- , qualification(s) of recipients of **218**.29cd-31ab
- , retribution of **216**.5-63
donation(s) see also *dakṣiṇā, gift, reward*
donations, merit of **65**.59-76ab
donkey head of Brahman **113**.2-4; **135**.10cd-13cd
doomsday, clouds of **188**.1; **232**.30-40
doomsday see also *dissolution*
double-faced, punishment for being **164**.17-28
doubt, clarification of **136**.27-31
dowry of princess **111**.48-51
dragging by the hair **193**.67cd-76ab
- of corpse **193**.67cd-76ab
Drauṇi **5**.43
Draupadī **13**.127cd-132ab
Drāvanāmita, place of pilgrimage **25**.34
Dravantī **27**.28-29
Draviṇa **3**.37-38cd
drawing of *maṇḍala*, prescr. conc. **61**.39-45ab
- of *yantra* **28**.23; **61**.1-3
Dṛḍharatha **13**.45-48
Dṛḍhāśva **7**.87-88
Dṛḍhāyu **10**.11-12
dream as prophecy of future **205**.11-14 .15-22
- in simile **35**.52-59
- , Māyā of Viṣṇu as **229**.88
- , sleep and **240**.85-92ab
- , vision of Vāsudeva in **50**.4-6
dregs, cleaning with **221**.117cd-120ab
dress see *clothes*
drink, denial of food and **215**.29-38
- , origin of food and **129**.75-78
drinking of alcohol, punishment for **22**.9; **215**.92cd-93ab .127cd-128ab .130cd-136ab
- of Soma **13**.37-39; **82**.1
- of Soma, merit of **119**.1
- of water, prescription(s) concerning **221**.102
- of water, purification by **72**.27cd-34
Droṇa **20**.25-27; **208**.8-18 .19-31; **212**.12-17 .64-65
Droṇapāṭhaka **220**.103-104
drought **17**.32-34
- of hundred years **232**.14-23
- of three years **14**.4-7
- of twelve years **7**.104cd-105ab; **8**.10cd
- of twenty-four years **74**.22cd-24ab
drowning, voluntary death by **216**.5-63; **229**.72-86ab
Dṛṣadvatī **10**.67cd-68; **11**.49-50ab; **13**.22cd-23 .91; **27**.25cd-27
- , place of pilgrimage **64**.11-14
Dṛṣṭakuṇḍa, place of pilgrimage **25**.16
Druhyu **12**.5cd-6ab; **13**.148-150ab; **146**.2-8ab .28-31
- , descendants of **13**.148-151
drums, list of **65**.12-16
- , sounding of **14**.14cd-20ab
drunkenness of Balarāma **198**.7-11; **209**.11cd-21ab
- of Yādavas **210**.37-43
drunkenness see also *intoxication*
Drupada **13**.100-101
Drutavilambitā-metre **175**.80
Duḥśāsana **208**.19-31
Duliduha **8**.84cd-92
Dundubhi **20**.47cd-49ab .49cd-51
- [mountain] **20**.6-7
duplication of city of Indra **140**.14-18ab
duration of asceticism **213**.44-52
- of cosmic night **233**.9
- of dissolution **233**.46cd-49ab
- of fasting **216**.5-63
- of Manu-era(s) **5**.54cd-55ab
- of pollution according to caste **220**.63; **221**.146cd-149ab .155cd-158
- of pollution, prescr. conc. **221**.152cd-154
- of practices of Yoga **236**.59cd-66
- of reign of Indradyumna **51**.22-26
- of reign of Rāma **213**.153cd-154
- of satiation of ancestors **220**.22cd-31ab
- of sojourn in heaven **67**.52-80; **110**.155-156; **227**.16-32ab .32cd-37ab .42-47; **228**.86-91ab .146-151
Durdama **11**.44-48; **13**.69cd .70ab .70cd .71cd-72ab .157-159; **14**.39-41
Durdhara **215**.129cd-130ab
Durgā **27**.33-34; **181**.38-53
Durgā see also *Devī, Gaurī, Goddess, Pārvatī, Umā*
Durgātīrtha, place of pilgrimage **132**.7-9ef

Durmukha **3**.99-101; **165**.27-30ab
Durvāsas **211**.3-4
- [son of Atri] **117**.2-5; **144**.2-4
Durvāsas-episode in Mahābhārata, reference to **211**.3-4
Duryodhana **13**.122; **208**.4-7 .8-18 .19-31
- , Baladeva as teacher of **17**.28
Duṣyanta **13**.54-55 .56-57 .142-146 .147-148ab
duties common to all, castes **222**.15-17
- common to all, stages of life **222**.18
- of Brahmins **222**.3-6
- of castes in calamity **222**.19-20
- of householder **221**.1-3; **222**.28-38
- of king **4**.35-41; **7**.58cd-71ab; **222**.7-10
- of Kṣatriyas **222**.7-10
- of renouncer **222**.45-54
- of Śūdras **222**.13-14
- of son, maxim about **108**.76cd-87
- of student **222**.22-27
- of third stage of life **222**.39-44
- of Vaiśyas **222**.11-12
dutiful son, Rāma as **123**.177cd-184 .187-190
duty of father, maxim about **111**.9-16
- of son, revenge for father as **142**.7-8ef
- of wife, maxim about **80**.71-77
- of women, service as **230**.75-76
- towards daughter **165**.5-17
duty see also *dharma, righteousness*
Dvādaśadhāraka-mountain, place of pilgrimage **25**.18
Dvādaśavāraka-mountain, place of pilgrimage **25**.18
Dvaipāyana, Kṛṣṇa **13**.121; **26**.17; **235**.2
Dvairathākāra **20**.36-38ab
Dvāpara-Yuga **19**.20; **175**.17-24 .29-32ab
Dvārakā **17**.8-11 .29-31; **197**.6-7; **201**.28; **203**.26-32; **204**.8-13ab; **206**.49-50; **210**.1-4 .22-27 .29-30; **211**.1-2; **226**.42-45ab
- , construction of **196**.9-15
- , place of pilgrimage **64**.3-8ab
- , submersion of **212**.9-11
Dvāravatī **7**.30-34; **14**.50cd-56; **16**.12; **197**.6-7; **202**.1-2; **205**.15-22; **206**.10-13; **207**.25-27 .28-43; **212**.5-6
Dvimīḍha **13**.80cd-81ab
Dvimūrdhan **3**.74cd-78ab
Dvīpa see *continents*
Dvivida **213**.159-163
- , Balarāma and **209**
dwarf, Viṣṇu as **73**; **179**.18cd-22ab; **180**.24cd-38; **184**.14-19
Dyaus **109**.13-20
dyer killed by Kṛṣṇa **192**.71-74
dying, description of **214**.32-33 .42cd-45 .46-51
- , means of **214**.27cd-31
dying see also *death*
dynasty, lunar **10**; **11**; **12**; **13**; **14**; **108**.68-70 .119-120; **111**.2-6
- , Prācīnabarhis as founder of solar **153**.2cd-3
- , solar **7**; **8**; **108**.119-120; **123**.2-7ab
Dyūta **13**.152-153ab
Dyuti **5**.22cd-24; **9**.13-16; **68**.56-59ab
Dyutimat **5**.9cd-10; **20**.41cd-42 .47cd-49ab
ear of corn, gift of **136**.32-35ab
ear-rings of Aditi **202**.3-12; **203**.1-5
earth, alleviation of burden on **188**.29-35 .39-41; **193**.32-40; **202**.23-29; **210**.1-4 .16-21 .22-27; **212**.59-62
- and island, substitution of **151**.22cd-24ab
- and Pṛthu **141**.14-20
- and waters as prior to Brahman **137**.25-28ab
- as bowl **72**.25cd-27ab
- as cow **2**.25-28ab; **4**.68-73 .96-122; **141**.23-25
- as field of actions **160**.2cd-6ab
- as lioness **155**.3cd-10ab
- as lotus **18**.13-15
- as mother **72**.27cd-34
- as sacrificial gift **155**.2-3ab; **213**.114-122
- as sow **219**.113cd-115
- as support **126**.19cd-22
- by trees, obstruction of **2**.34-46
- , circumambulation of **87**.15cd-16; **131**.39cd-51
- , circumference of **23**.3-4
- , cleaning with water and **221**.125cd-127ab
- , cow as **87**.17-20
- , demons reigning over the **160**.2cd-6ab
- , division of **7**.19cd-21ab; **12**.24-38
- , donation(s) of **155**.13cd-14ab; **175**.60-68
- , equivalence of daughter and **165**.5-17
- , equivalence of sun and **29**.20-21
- exchanged for a brown cow **155**.3cd-10ab
- , extent of **3**.16-18ab
- , five kinds of **221**.64cd-65ab
- , flooding of **188**.6-10

- for cleaning, prescription(s) concerning **221**.64cd-65ab
- , gods descending on **160**.6cd-9
- , heavenly conditions on **20**.85-86ab
- , hospitality equivalent to gift of **163**.12cd-16
- lifted by boar **202**.23-29
- , livelihood granted by **2**.25-28ab; **4**.74-80
- , lords of the **41**.60cd-71
- , marriage of boar and **219**.42-47ab
- milked at rivers **141**.26-28
- milked by Pṛthu **141**.23-25 .26-28
- , milking of **2**.25-28ab; **4**.96-122
- , offering of water on **60**.54-65
- oppressed by beings **86**.11-16; **116**.3cd-5ab
- oppressed by demons **181**.7-14
- , origin of **161**.43cd-50cd
- , patience of **108**.68-70
- , pilgrimage as circumambulation of **228**.92cd-96
- , plants swallowed by **141**.10-13
- , Pramati as king of the **171**.2cd-6cd
- , pregnancy of **219**.113cd-115
- , prescription(s) concerning purification of **221**.123-125ab
- , purification by water and **72**.23-25ab; **221**.132cd-133ab
- resting upon water **1**.39cd-42
- , Śeṣa as support of **21**.15-27
- , Śiva as **75**.5
- , threat of submersion of **83**.23-29
- to Viṣṇu, hymn by **202**.23-29
- , Viṣṇu as bearer of **175**.60-68

earth see also *country, land, region*

earth-lotus **18**

earthquake **7**.58cd-71ab
- , explanation for **21**.15-27

east, inhabitants of **27**.51cd-53

eastern ocean **172**.2-3

eating as sacrifice **218**.28cd-29ab; **222**.55-56
- before superiors, punishment for **22**.15cd-16a
- of beef **8**.13-15b:
- of forbidden food, effect(s) of **223**.23-27
- of forbidden food, expiation for **220**.200cd-203ab
- of forbidden food, punishment for **215**.111cd-112ab .130cd-136ab; **220**.189ab .198-200ab
- of human flesh **186**.1-3
- of meat of dog **93**.5-11
- of meat, prescription(s) concerning **221**.55 .111 .112
- of meat, punishment for **214**.88cd-96; **215**.127cd-128ab
- of powdered iron **196**.1-4
- , prescription(s) concerning **221**.26-30 .48ab-49ab .56 .58cd-60ab
- sweets, punishment for **215**.109cd-110ab

eclipse **221**.50cd-52

edible animals **221**.111

education of Ahalyā **87**.5cd-8
- of boys **222**.22-27
- of Brahmins **107**.2-11
- of Kṛṣṇa and Balarāma **194**.18-22
- of Kṣatriyas **104**.22cd-37ab; **123**.97-105ab
- of women **108**.52-53ef
- of Yogin **235**.4-5

education see also *preceptor, teacher*

effect(s) of actions **214**.27cd-31; **217**.113cd-114ab .114cd-115ab; **224**; **225**
- of actions in Bhāratavarṣa **27**.3-9
- of actions in former existences **165**.23-26
- of actions increased by knowledge **129**.49-64
- of actions, maxim about **123**.177cd-184; **136**.17-26
- of ancestral rites **220** .117cd-118ab .203cd-204 .210
- of ancestral rites at Gautamī **123**.128cd-139
- of auspicious actions **218**.31cd-32ab
- of avarice **225**.10-16
- of conduct **221**.8ab .161-169ab; **225**.23cd-29 .36-41
- of conduct of householder **222**.37-38
- of consecrated water **65**.78-80
- of devotion to Śiva **214**.114cd-119
- of devotion to Viṣṇu **216**.82-86 .87-89
- of *dharma* **216**.73-80; **221**.13; **246**.37-38
- of *dharma*, dispute about **170**.26a-f
- of disrespect **225**.17-23ab
- of donation of lamps **29**.35cd-42ab
- of donation(s) **225**.2-8
- of donation(s) of food **218**.24-28ab
- of donation(s) of land **120**.3cd-5
- of eating of forbidden food **223**.23-27
- of expiation **217**.111cd-113ab
- of feeding of disqualified guest(s) **220**.136-138

- of feeding of forbidden food 220.198-200ab
- of forbidden sexual intercourse 225.52
- of giving forbidden food 220.193cd-195ab
- of ignorance 206.45-48
- of knowledge of Self 238.24-25
- of looks 225.49
- of Māyā 203.6-19
- of noble women, beneficial 123.165-169
- of non-violence 224.47-52 .53-56ab
- of offerings to ancestors 220.149-151
- of place of pilgrimage, Yama stopped by 45.59-67 .71-73
- of praise of Viṣṇu 216.87-89
- of recitation of hymn 75.32
- of religious practices 125.33-43
- of religious practices in Kali-Yuga 230.62-63
- of righteousness 170.77-80ef
- of sacrifice 225.46-48
- of *sattra*-rite of Ātreya 140.3cd-5ab
- of sexual intercourse during ancestral rites 220.106-109ab
- of thoughts 34.49-50; 215.119cd-120ab .130cd-136ab, 216.87-89; 217.45-47; 224.28-29; 225.50
- of time 212.55-58 .64-65
- of violence 224.47-52
- of worship of Kṛṣṇa 227.6-7
- of worship of Puruṣottama 178.1-4
- of worship of sun 28.42-45; 159.12-16
- of worship of Vāsudeva 227.50

effect(s) see also *punishment, retribution, reward*

egg, cosmic 20.95cd-98ab; 23.21 .22-27ab; 33.3-8
- , halves of cosmic 1.39cd-42
- of Brahman, Rākṣasas originated from 156.2cd-3
- , origin of cosmos from golden 1.39cd-42

eggs, number of cosmic 23.27cd-28ab

Ego-consciousness 1.35

eight arms of Yoganidrā 182.27-30
- forms of Śiva 75.4-13; 97.20-23
- leaves, lotus of 61.1-3
- mothers of gods 105.8cd-11ab
- pose(s) of hands 61.52-55
- syllables, prayer-formula of 60.22-24; 61.1-3 .7-12 .20-22
- Vasus 3.35cd-36

eighteen defeats of Jarāsaṃdha 195.8-12

eightfold deformation of Aṣṭāvakra 212.72-85

eighty thousand Liṅgas 160.21-22ab

eighty-eight thousand diseases 125.44-49

Ekacakra 3.74cd-78ab

Ekadhāra, place of pilgrimage 25.20

Ekākṣa 213.81-104

Ekalavya 14.27cd-28ab

Ekāmraka 41.1-5
- , description of 41.11-50ab
- , extent of 41.75-81
- , merit of bathing at 41.93
- , place of pilgrimage 64.3-8ab

Ekāmraka, etymology of 41.11-12

Ekaparṇā 34.81 .83-84 .91

Ekapāṭalā 34.83-84 .92-93ab

Ekarātra, place of pilgrimage 25.54

Ekavīrā [river?] 161.2cd-4ab

Elāpatra 3.99-101

elements and qualities, dissolution of 233.12-29
- as witness of actions 217.23-24
- , constitution of body from 236.7-8
- , cosmic layers of 23.22-27ab
- , dissolution of 233.30-33ab
- , five 33.3-8; 56.56-57; 179.59-61; 217.19-21
- , identity of Self and 237.45
- prior to Brahman, five 161.9-11ab

elephant, killing of 123.44-48ab; 193.24-31
- of Indra 13.43-44

elephant's teeth as weapon(s) 193.24-31

elephants, Airāvata as lord of 4.2-9
- of directions 24.13-18
- with four tusks 202.30-35

eleven Rudras 3.46cd-49; 39.29-32

elixir, rejuvenation by 58.37-40

emanation from *sattva* 238.2
- of world 241.11-36

embezzlement of trust, punishment for 215.86cd-88ab
- , punishment for 217.57-58

emblem, club as 21.15-27
- , fig-tree as 20.18
- , Garuḍa as 181.20
- , Kuśa-grass as 20.45
- , Nyagrodha-tree as 20.87cd
- of Śiva, bull as 109.52-54; 166.11cd-13
- , plough as 21.15-27

- , silk-cotton tree as **20**.33
- , teak tree as **20**.64
- , tree as **18**.23cd-24ab
emblem see also *attributes*
emblems of Viṣṇu, usurpation of **207**.4-7
embodiment as play of *puruṣa* **242**.29-33
- in simile **242**.4-5ab
- of gods 3.62-64ab
- of soul, process of **217**.26
embryo, constituents of **243**.1-10
- , development of **179**.48cd-50ab
- , origin of **217**.19-21
- , suffering of **240**.27-32
embryo-murder, expiation for **58**.44-46; **123**.1
- , punishment for **22**.7-8
embryos, exchange of **181**.38-53; **182**.1-3
- , six **181**.36; **182**.1-3
emergence of image from ocean **176**.52-56
enclosure sticks in sacrifice, metres as seven **161**.35cd-39ab
ends, maxim about means and **152**.15-17
enemies killed by Kṛṣṇa **213**.159-163
- , maxim about inheritage of friends and **110**.80ef-86
- , maxim about refuge of **152**.18-20
- of knowledge, five **139**.13-17ef
enemies see also *obstacle(s), faults*
enemy, maxim about release of **129**.20cd-29
- , warning of **182**.31
energy, Goddess as **131**.39cd-51
- of Brahman originated from sacrifice **161**.13-16
- of triad of gods **131**.39cd-51
- of Viṣṇu **23**.28cd-44 .29cd-31ab .31cd-32ab .38-40
energy see also *Śakti*
enjoyment and liberation **88**.4-7; **136**.27-31 .37-40
- and liberation granted by Śiva **130**.17-21
- , maxim about **140**.18cd-19ab
- more difficult to obtain than liberation **136**.17-26
enjoyments, heavenly **68**.29-32
- , list of **21**.6cd-13ab
enmity between Anuhrāda and Ulūka **125**.2cd-8
- between gods and demons **97**.5cd-7
- between Kaṃsa and gods **183**.1-7
- between Kaṃsa and Yādavas **190**.10-19
- between Rākṣasas and gods, origin of **116**.20-22ab
- between Śiśupāla and Kṛṣṇa **199**.1-4
- between Vasiṣṭha and Viśvāmitra **147**.5-7
- , maxim about absence of **106**.3-7
enmity see also *opposition, rival*
entering of body of Viṣṇu **53**.41-43; **56**.51-54
entertainment of Umā **38**.24-27
entourage of Brahman **26**.32-33; **213**.44-52
- of Viṣṇu **68**.54-55
- of Yama **215**.45-55ab
entrance to nether world **58**.37-40
- to nether world, cave as **115**.12cd-15ab
Epics, Purāṇa and **158**.30-35ab
epigram see *subhāṣita*
epithets of Brahman **26**.31
- of *brahman* **234**.63cd-66ab; **238**.36cd-37ab; **240**.98-103
- of first evolute **241**.16cd-19ab
- of Indra **140**.21ef-25
- of Kāma **38**.1-6
- of Śiva **115**.7-9ab; **122**.74; **124**.132-136ab; **223**.7-11; **224**.1-3 .27; **226**.10
- of Umā **71**.19-23
- of Viṣṇu **45**.60-67; **55**.18-23ab; **180**.1-12; **213**.66-71; **219**.31-35; **233**.35-38ab
epithets see also *attributes, description, shape*
epitome of beings, Śiva as **130**.23-31
- , Viṣṇu as **179**.44cd-47ab; **192**.48-58
equinox **63**.19-20; **67**.2-5
equipment of adepts of Narasiṃha **58**.41-43
equivalence of daughter and earth **165**.5-17
- of fire and water **126**.12-16ab; **158**.22-27ef
- of self-control and pilgrimage **25**.4-6
- of sun and earth **29**.20-21
equivalences, macro-microcosmic **56**.16-17ab .27cd-30ab
Erakā-grass as weapon **210**.37-43
- , killing with **210**.44-46
establishment of four castes **213**.106-112
- of holy places **70**.16-19
eternal Banyan-tree **161**.65cd-67
- fig-tree **45**.53-56; **52**.15cd-19
- youth **11**.51-53; **34**.87-89
ethics see *conduct*
etymology of *abhra* **24**.8-11
- of *āpagā* **100**.9-13
- of *Ekāmraka* **41**.11-12
- of *gālava* **7**.105cd-109
- of *ikṣvāku* **7**.44cd-45ab

- of *marut* **3**.109cd-122
- of *mārtaṇḍa* **6**.5; **32**.37-41ab
- of *mātṛ* **89**.17-21
- of *medinī* **4**.112
- of *Nārāyaṇa* **1**.38cd-39ab; **56**.12; **60**.25-33; **180**.16cd-17ab
- of *niṣāda* **4**.42-47
- of *Pañcāla* **13**.93-96
- of *pṛthivī* **4**.113
- of *puruṣa* **30**.68ab
- of *Purūravas* **108**.71-74
- of *putra* **4**.48-52
- of *rājan* **4**.53-57
- of *śaśāda* **7**.48cd-51ab
- of *sagara* **8**.29-30 .39-40
- of *sarit* **219**.18-24
- of *sāgara* **8**.58-59ab
- of *sūta* **4**.60
- of *triśaṅku* **8**.19
- of *Umā* **34**.85-86
- of *Vāsudeva* **234**.68cd-69ab .70c-f

etymology see also *explanation*

»eunuch« as abuse **196**.1-4

eunuch, rebirth as **225**.51

evening worship, prescr. conc. **221**.18

evil things, Śiva as creator of **129**.70-71
- thoughts, punishment for **215**.119cd-120ab .130cd-136ab; **217**.45-47

evil see also *bad sin, vices*

evil-doers, liberation for **216**.87-89
- , maxim about **163**.32-39
- , punishment of **215**
- thinking of Viṣṇu **216**.87-89

evil-doers see also *wicked*

evolution in simile **23**.32cd-35
- , sequence of **243**.67-70

evolution see also *creation, emanation, origin*

exchange of embryos **181**.38-53; **182**.1-3
- of infant(s) **182**.19-26; **190**.1-5
- of sacrificial gift **155**.3cd-10ab
- of Soma and Sarasvatī **105**.4-8ab

exclamations of victory **108**.71-74; **110**.183-187; **152**.33

exclusion of bad people **56**.30cd-35ab
- of unbelievers **49**.64-66; **62**.16ab; **68**.72; **221**.170a-f; **245**.53
- of women and Śūdras **67**.19

excommunication see *fallen persons*

excrements, prescr. conc, disposing of **221**.137cd-138ab

exile of Rāma **123**.105cd-109ab
- of son **7**.100-102ab; **78**.37cd-44

existence and non-existence **173**.9-25
- and thought, Śiva as **153**.1-2ab
- in sunbeams after death **30**.14-18

existences, effect(s) of actions in former **165**.23-26
- , memory of former **111**.68cd-79; **164**.29-37; **197**.1-3; **204**.8-13ab; **228**.92cd-96; **229**.22-30 .72-86ab; **246**.30-33

existences see also *rebirth*

expenditure of wealth, prescription(s) concerning **221**.11-12

expiation by bathing **92**.47cd-48ab; **170**.84-88
- by confession of sins **218**.6 .7-8ab
- by feeding of Brahmins **218**.13cd-16ab
- by praising of Viṣṇu **22**.37-41
- by remembering of Viṣṇu **22**.37-41
- , effect(s) of **217**.111cd-113ab
- for Brahmin-murder **65**.83; **123**.77-81; **177**.26
- for Brahmin-murder, ancestral rites as **123**.165-169
- for Brahmin-murder, horse-sacrifice as **12**.11-17
- for eating of forbidden food **220**.200cd-203ab
- for embryo-murder **58**.44-46; **123**.1
- for pollution by eating **221**.134cd-135ab
- for sexual intercourse with teacher's wife **81**.16-22ab
- for sins **22**.35-36; **218**.16cd-21ab
- for violence **218**.21cd-22ab
- , repentance and **92**.39-47ab
- , Śāstras as authority on **123**.158-164

expiation see also *purification*

explanation for earthquake **21**.15-27
- for poverty **225**.10-16
- for various conditions of life **216**.73-80
- of *Ajapārśva* **13**.132cd-137
- of *akṣata* **219**.49-51
- of *Amṛtā* **106**.47-48ab
- of *Ananta* **21**.15-27; **226**.62-65ab
- of *Avimukta* **229**.59-63
- of *Ānandatīrtha* **152**.42ef
- of *bhagavat* **234**.66cd-68ab
- of *Dāmodara* **184**.31-42ab
- of *Dīrghatapas* **11**.36-38
- of *Govinda* **122**.95-97ab; **188**.29-35

- of *Indrajita* **176**.19cd-20
- of *Jāhnavī* **10**.18cd-19ab
- of *Kālayavana* **14**.50cd-56
- of *Keśava* **190**.39-47
- of *Kokā* **219**.6-12
- of *Koṭitīrtha* **148**.21-26
- of *Kṛpa* **13**.97
- of *Kṛpī* **13**.97
- of *kṣetrajña* **30**.65-67
- of *Kuśatarpaṇa* **161**.63-64ab
- of *makha* **79**.7cd-19
- of *Malaya* **160**.10-12
- of *Maṅgalā* **122**.93-94
- of *Mitratīrtha* **124**.137-139ab
- of *Nandītaṭa* **152**.42a-d
- of *Nivāsapura* **106**.53cd-54ab
- of *Pippalāda* **110**.78-80cd
- of *prajāpati* **5**.55cd-56
- of *Pratiṣṭhāna* **110**.219ef-224; **112**.22cd-23ab
- of *Pravarā* **106**.47-48ab
- of *puruṣottama* **45**.51-52; **177**.22-23
- of *Sahasrakuṇḍa* **154**.32-34
- of *sahasrākṣa* **87**.66cd-69
- of *Saptagodāvarī* **173**.3-6ab
- of *sruva* **79**.20-21ab
- of *Vāsudeva* **179**.10cd-16ab
- of *Vidarbhā* **121**.23
- of *Vighna* **175**.73-74
- of *Vitatha* **13**.58-61

explanation see also *etymology*
exposition of *brahman* **30**.57-86
extent of Bhāratavarṣa **27**.14-16
- of cosmos **20**.98cd-99ab
- of earth **3**.16-18ab
- of Ekāmraka **41**.75-81
- of fig-tree **60**.16-18
- of Ilāvṛta **18**.21-23ab
- of Meru **18**.13-15
- of mountains **18**.16-17
- of Puruṣottamakṣetra **44**.78-79
- of Utkala **42**.13-14

extinguishing of sacrificial fire **148**.3cd-7
eye of Mitra, sun as **30**.40-41
- of Śiva, fire from third **110**.115-120
- of Śiva, invisibility of third **110**.112-114
- of Śiva, Manyu originated from third **162**.20-27ab
- of Śiva, origin of third **123**.195-206
- of Śiva, son born from third **153**.8-11
- , offering of **109**.49-50ef

eyes of Bhaga torn out by Vīrabhadra **109**.21-26ab
- of Indra, thousand **87**.66cd-69; **124**.39cd-47
- of Śiva, three **110**.183-187
- of Viṣṇu, thousand **68**.44-53
- , tearing out of **170**.49-50ef

eyesight, divine **36**.49-52ab; **55**.7-8
failure due to delusion, maxim about **72**.20-22
faithfulness of wife in simile **80**.71-77
- of wife, merit of **80**.71-77
- of wife, test of **138**.14-19

faking of jewels, punishment for **22**.14cd-15a
falcon, Indra as **93**.12-24
fall from heaven **219**.18-24; **220**.193cd-195ab
fallen persons, prohibition of speaking to **76**.18cd-23ab
- persons, punishment for contact with **217**.37-39
- persons, sacrificing for **217**.40-42

false accusation **16**.25-45ab
- witness, punishment for **22**.7-8; **214**.120-128; **215**.72-77 .88cd-90ab

fame, asceticism for **2**.10-13
family life, prescription(s) concerning **221**.74
fanning of statue **65**.17-18
farmers, plough as deity of **187**.42-54
fasting, asceticism by **34**.83-84; **176**.15cd-19ab
- , duration of **216**.5-63
- , merit of **219**.107cd-109ab
- , observances of **242**.15cd-20ab
- of Yogin **239**.43-46
- , purification by **221**.134cd-135ab
- , voluntary death by **12**.47-48; **216**.5-63; **228**.86-91ab; **229**.72-86ab

fate, Kṛṣṇa submitting to **210**.15
- , maxim about **123**.44-48ab; **159**.5-11; **171**.27-39
- , predetermination by **165**.23-26
- , unknowability of **119**.10
- , Viṣṇu as **179**.38-43ab

fate see also *destiny*
father and mother, *dharma* as **170**.38ef-39
- and mother, procreation by **243**.1-10
- and mother, sun as **30**.21-22
- and son, identity of **148**.8-14ab; **165**.5-17
- and son, resemblance of **200**.20-22

- , king as **44**.1
- , king compared with **44**.41-43
- , maxim about duty of **111**.9-16
- of Aṅgiras, fire as **144**.15-16
- of Brahman, Viṣṇu as **73**.58-63ab
- of Indra, Kaśyapa as **124**.83-86
- of Nārada, Dakṣa as **3**.7cd-9
- of Yama, sun as **94**.22-26
- , son on lap of **140**.7-11; **154**.14cd-21ab
- , Yama experienced as **216**.67-72
father-in-law, disrespect against **34**.9-12ab
- of Ātreyī, Agni as **144**.8cd-10 .15-16
- of Mahāśani, Varuṇa as **129**.20cd-29
- of moon, Dakṣa as **2**.51-53
faults of sacrifice **83**.6-12; **122**.54cd-62
- of Yoga **235**.11-12; **236**.40cd-43ab; **238**.44-51 .53-56ab; **239**.11-23 .47-49; **240**.53-54ab
- of Yoga, five **236**.37cd-40ab; **238**.52; **240**.51-52
faults see also *distractions, enemies, obstacles*
fear, freedom from **245**.44-47
- of curse **3**.10-14; **35**.11-14; **178**.19-24
- of one's wife **15**.16-21
fearlessness, gift of **222**.46-54
- granted by Śiva **90**.2-4
- , wish for **162**.2cd-6ab
feeding of Brahmins **47**.58cd-61 .63-67; **67**.39cd-45; **187**.42-54 .55-59ab; **219**.65cd-71ab
- of Brahmins by Śūdras **230**.70-71
- of Brahmins, expiation by **218**.13cd-16ab
- of Brahmins, importance of **123**.140-146
- of Brahmins, merit of **218**.9-32
- of disqualified guest(s), effect(s) of **220**.136-138
- of forbidden food, effect(s) of **220**.198-200ab
- of relatives **228**.8-14
feeding see also *food*
feet on hood of snake, marks of **185**.50-51
- , prohibition of stretching out of **221**.101
felling of trees, punishment for **22**.24cd
female attributes **178**.12-18
- deities **65**.37-38ab; **68**.56-59ab; **109**.13-20
festival see *auspicious date(s), bathing festival, bow festival, car festival, Daśaharā, swinging festival*
fetters, snakes as **206**.5-9 .49-50
fever as weapon **206**.14-19
- , distribution of **40**.112-120
- of Śiva **206**.14-19
- of Viṣṇu **206**.14-19
- , origin of **39**.74-89
- , personification of **39**.74-81
- , three heads of **206**.14-19
fickleness of women, maxim about **151**.5cd-7ab
field in simile, Brahmin and **223**.60cd-61ab
- of actions, Bhāratavarṣa as **27**.2 .66cd-68; **70**.20-22ab .24
- of actions, earth as **160**.2cd-6ab
- of actions, location of **161**.21-23ef
- of actions, Puruṣottamakṣetra as **178**.192
»field«, woman as **126**.4-8
fight between Aniruddha and Bāṇa **206**.5-9
- between Balarāma and Dvivida **209**.11cd-21ab
- between Balarāma and Muṣṭika **193**.50-57ab .63cd-65ab
- between bear and Kṛṣṇa **16**.25-45ab
- between Daśaratha and demons **123**.23-33ab
- between Garuḍa and Airāvata **203**.45-62
- between Garuḍa and Kārttikeya **206**.24-30
- between Garuḍa and snakes **206**.49-50
- between Goddess and Rāhu **106**.39-41
- between Ila and Yakṣas **108**.18-20ab
- between Kṛṣṇa and Ariṣṭa **189**.46-58ab
- between Kṛṣṇa and Bāṇa **206**.31-38
- between Kṛṣṇa and Cāṇūra **193**.50-57ab
- between Kṛṣṇa and gods **203**.45-62
- between Kṛṣṇa and Indra **203**.45-62
- between Kṛṣṇa and Keśin **190**.29-37
- between Kṛṣṇa and Pauṇḍraka **207**.13-24
- between Kṛṣṇa and Rukmin **199**.5-10
- between Kṛṣṇa and Śiva **205**.7-8; **206**.21-23
- between Kuvalāśva and Dhundhu **7**.82-84
- between Pradyumna and Śambara **200**.17-19
- between Rāvaṇa and Soma **143**.2-5
- between Śiva and demons **112**.11-19
- between Viṣṇu and Ambarya **149**.9cd-12
- by means of magic power(s) **200**.17-19; **206**.5-9
- by means of plough-share **206**.24-30
fight see also *battle*
fighting as play of Kṛṣṇa **193**.50-57ab

.60cd-63ab; **199**.5-10; **206**.39-44
- as play of Viṣṇu **206**.20
fig-tree **18**.23cd-24ab; **46**.24-30; **69**.12-43
- as emblem **20**.18
- as lord of trees **4**.2-9
- , eternal **45**.53-56; **52**.15cd-19
- , extent of **60**.16-18
- , looking at **177**.26
- , merit of homage to **57**.17-19
- , merit of praise of **57**.15-16
- , names of **60**.16-18
- , prayer-formula addressed to **57**.12-14
- , Vainateya **57**.12-19
- , Viṣṇu as **57**.17-19
filament mountains **18**.52-55
filament mountains **18**.32-36ab
fingers, colours and **61**.7-12
fire, all-comprehensiveness of **126**.4-8
- and water, equivalence of **126**.12-16ab; **158**.22-27ef
- and water, husband and wife as **144**.15-16 .20-22
- and water, prescription(s) concerning carrying of **221**.101
- and water, purification by **158**.35cd-37ab
- as father of Aṅgiras **144**.15-16
- as mouth of gods **126**.4-8
- as offering **126**.4-8
- as origin of all **126**.4-8
- as semen **126**.4-8
- as son of mare [Vaḍavā] **110**.198cd-200cd
- as witness of promise **140**.26-30
- carried in golden vessel **110**.202-210
- , circumambulation of **36**.130-134; **80**.65-70
- , creation of sacrificial **161**.30-33ab
- , destruction of cosmos by **21**.15-27; **52**.1-10
- , extinguishing of sacrificial **148**.3cd-7
- , freedom from harm by **125**.50-53
- from mare, birth of **110**.131-133
- from third eye of Śiva **110**.115-120
- , gold identical with **148**.8-14ab
- in simile, wrath and **108**.68-70
- , Kṛtyā originated from sacrificial **207**.28-43
- , mare pregnant with **110**.124-130
- , meditation on **61**.19
- , ocean drunk by **110**.202-210
- of wrath **39**.48-49
- , offerings put in **220**.149-151
- , omnipresence of **144**.15-16
- produced from thoughts **34**.20ef-25
- , prohibition of blowing at **221**.102
- , ritual **58**.32cd-34ab
- , Śiva as **75**.7
- , sun as **158**.22-27ef
- , superiority of **126**.16cd-19ab
- , weapon of **8**.31-32 .41-42ab
fire see also *Agni, brilliance, burning*
fire-ordeal of Sītā **154**.2-4
fires, asceticism between five **178**.7-11
- , five **206**.20
- , three sacrificial **161**.54-58
first king **2**.21-24
- king, Pṛthu as **4**.115-121
- of beings, plants as **119**.2-4cd
- of beings, waters as **110**.200ef-201ef
first-person narrator, Brahman as **33**.3-8; **36**.8 .36cd-39ab .125-126; **39**.84-88ab; **42**.36cd-38ab; **59**.1-2; **72**.18-19; **73**.57cd .58-63ab; **83**.13-16; **87**.2-34ab; **91**.6cd-11ab; **94**.22-26; **96**.5cd-7; **97**.2-5ab; **101**.10-11ab; **106**.19-22; **108**.71-74; **110**.198cd-200cd; **112**.2-3; **113**.2-4; **115**.2-4; **119**.2-4cd; **122**.21-24ab .54cd-62; **123**.7cd-14ab; **124**.87-93; **126**.12-16ab; **128**.38-43; **134**.2-8ab; **135**.5cd-10ab .15-16; **137**.25-28ab; **143**.2-5; **145**.5cd-7; **156**.4-6; **158**.2-3 .35cd-37ab; **160**.2cd-6ab; **162**.2cd-6ab; **174**.8-12ef .19-25ab; **176**.4-7 .15cd-19ab
- narrator, Lomaharṣaṇa as **246**.13-15
- narrator, Śiva as **223**.55cd-56ab; **226**.20cd -22ab
- narrator, Viṣṇu as **45**.42-43 .68-70
- narrator, Vyāsa as **212**.54; **220**.189ab
fish, child swallowed by **200**.2-10
- , iron tip of lance swallowed by **210**.11-14
- , Mādhava as **60**.1-6
- , Viṣṇu as **18**.57-58; **191**.4-12
fist, killing with **187**.26-28; **209**.11cd-21ab
five boons **13**.210-212ab
- daughters of Brahman **102**.2cd-5ab
- elements **33**.3-8; **56**.56-57; **179**.59-61; **217**.19-21
- elements prior to Brahman **161**.9-11ab
- enemies of knowledge **139**.13-17ef
- faults of Yoga **236**.37cd-40ab; **238**.52; **240**.51-52

- fires **206**.20
- fires, asceticism between **178**.7-11
- food-balls **221**.138cd-139ab
- heads of Brahman **113**.2-4 .22-23; **135**.10cd-13cd
- kinds of earth **221**.64cd-65ab
- musical notes **228**.8-14
- occasions for untruth permitted **228**.50
- passions **56**.27cd-30ab
- places of pilgrimage at Puruṣottamakṣetra **43**.10-13
- rivers **212**.12-17
- rivers, confluence of **102**.9cd-11ab
- senses **179**.59-61; **236**.14
- services of worship **67**.28-29ab
- steps of creation **241**.23-25
- vital breaths **179**.56cd-57ab .57cd-58

flaming spear **39**.7-17ab
fleeing in battle, maxim about **124**.73cd-80
flesh, bird feeding upon **164**.3-6
- , eating of human **186**.1-3
- of dog changed to honey **93**.12-24

flesh see also *meat*
flood at end of cosmic cycle **232**.30-40
- , calamity caused by **188**.6-10

flooding of earth **188**.6-10
flowers as ornaments **221**.81cd-82ab
- for worship, collecting of **228**.15-21
- , kinds of **220**.154-167
- , list of **42**.24-26; **45**.13-14ab
- , rain of **14**.14cd-20ab; **65**.23-26; **74**.78-81; **75**.2-3 .49-50; **110**.183-187; **152**.33; **182**.9-11; **209**.21cd-22

flying to sun **159**.22-24cd; **166**.4cd-6ab
foam as weapon **124**.33-36ab
- , weapon made of **129**.4-8

follower, punishment for abandoning of **22**.11
food and drink, denial of **215**.29-38
- and drink, origin of **129**.75-78
- as sacrificial gift **83**.23-29
- , division of ritual **219**.71cd-86
- during Kali-Yuga **231**.71cd-78
- , effect(s) of donation(s) of **218**.24-28ab
- , effect(s) of eating of forbidden **223**.23-27
- , effect(s) of feeding of forbidden **220**.198-200ab
- , effect(s) of giving forbidden **220**.193cd-195ab
- , expiation for eating of forbidden **220**.200cd-203ab
- for ancestral rites, qualification(s) of **220**.178-185ab
- for Brahmins **216**.5-63; **219**.65cd-71ab
- for offerings **220**.43-48ab
- , forbidden **220**.195cd-197; **221**.56
- , four kinds of **61**.38
- of one's deities, maxim about **123**.173-175
- , origin of **1**.48cd-50ab
- , plants as **24**.19-25
- , praise of donation(s) of **218**.10cd-13ab
- , prescr. conc. leftovers of **221**.26-30
- , prescr. conc. purification of **221**.133cd-134ab
- , prescr. conc. salt in **221**.26-30
- , prescription(s) concerning **221**.47cd .57 .110
- , prescription(s) concerning forbidden **220**.189cd-204
- , prescription(s) concerning purification of **221**.123-125ab
- , punishment for eating of forbidden **214**.120-128; **215**.111cd-112ab .130cd-136ab; **220**.189ab .198 200ab
- , rebirth determined by **223**.23-27
- to ancestors, donation(s) of **219**.18-24
- to statue, offering of **67**.24-27
- , waters as origin of **126**.9-11
- with butter and honey **219**.65cd-71ab

food see also *eating, feeding*
food-balls, five **221**.138cd-139ab
fool, Brahmin as **228**.97-100ab
- reborn as Purūravas **228**.146-151
- , Urvaśī and the **228**.97-151

foot see also *step*
foot-lotus of Śiva **169**.1-2ab
forbidden animals, punishment for rearing of **22**.18cd-20
- food **220**.195cd-197; **221**.56
- food, effect(s) of eating of **223**.23-27
- food, effect(s) of feeding of **220**.198-200ab
- food, expiation for eating of **220**.200cd-203ab
- food, punishment for eating of **214**.120-128; **215**.111cd-112ab .130cd-136ab; **220**.189ab .198-200ab
- ingredients of ancestral rites, prescr. conc. **220**.168-177
- killing, punishment for **214**.120-128
- meat **220**.190cd-193ab

- meat, punishment for offering of **220**.193cd-195ab
- objects, stepping on **221**.24cd-25
- places for ancestral rites **220**.8-10ab
- sacrifice, performance of **228**.76-85
- sacrifice, punishment for **22**.15b: .17cd-18ab; **217**.40-42
- sexual intercourse, effect(s) of **225**.52
- sexual intercourse, punishment for **22**.12cd-13; **214**.120-128; **215**.72-77 .120cd-121ab; **217**.77cd-80ab
- sexual intercourse with wives, punishment for **22**.21-22
- things, punishment for selling of **22**.18cd -20

force, marriage by **111**.9-16; **199**.11-12
forest, departure for **7**.58cd-71ab .102cd-104ab; **8**.35-37; **10**.29cd-34ab; **12**.47-48; **13**.58-61 .127cd-132ab; **212**.93-94
- , king in **164**.7-9ab
- of Umā **108**.26-30

forests, four **18**.30
forgiveness, maxim about **87**.55-58ab
- , request for **202**.23-29; **203**.6-19; **204**.1-4

former existences, effect(s) of actions in **165**.23-26
- existences, memory of **111**.68cd-79; **164**.29-37; **204**.8-13ab; **228**.92cd-96; **229**.22-30 .72-86ab; **246**.30-33

former existences see also *rebirth*
forms of Gaṅgā, three **76**.8-10
- of Nārāyaṇa, four **61**.24
- of *puruṣa*, three **130**.7-14
- of *puruṣas* [souls?], three **175**.14cd-16
- of Śiva, eight **75**.4-13; **97**.20-23
- of Viṣṇu **49**.10-20
- of Viṣṇu allocated to body **184**.14-19
- of Viṣṇu, passions as **56**.27cd-30ab

forms see also *body, embodiment, incarnation, manifestation, shape*
formula, abbreviating **3**.78cd-80ab .89cd-90ab .102ab .106; **5**.3 .57cd-58ab; **13**.203-204; **14**.44; **18**.10; **21**.15-27; **25**.7-8ab; **27**.78cd; **41**.87; **45**.4; **46**.2; **54**.18-19; **55**.23cd-31; **64**.11-14; **65**.59-76ab .97-99; **68**.59cd; **70**.2cd; **79**.3-5ab; **174**.27cd-28; **175**.76-77; **176**.63; **177**.26 .27; **180**.39ab; **213**.165cd-168ab; **217**.115cd-116; **230**.9
- of blessing **13**.9-12ab
- of confirmation **70**.3ab
- of greeting **61**.26

forty-nine Maruts **3**.109cd-122; **124**.100-107
forward reference **3**.7cd-9; **5**.64; **12**.21cd; **34**.20a-d; **35**.60-63; **84**.19-20; **181**.26-31 .33-35; **190**.39-47; **193**.23; **199**.11-12; **232**.13
forward reference see also *anticipating summary, prediction, prophecy*
foster-child of Nanda, Baladeva as **184**.1-6
foster-parents, Pippala-tree(s) as **110**.78-80cd
foundation for Yogins, Vāsudeva as **180**.18cd-21ab
four arms of devotee **67**.58-60ab; **68**.29-32
- arms of Kṛṣṇa **192**.32-42; **211**.5-10
- arms of Vāsudeva **226**.30-41
- aspects of Nārāyaṇa **180**.17cd-18ab
- aspects of Viṣṇu **213**.124-126
- boons **13**.161-164
- castes **4**.115-121; **27**.71-72; **41**.28-29; **46**.7cd-10; **58**.59cd-64ab; **123**.2-7ab; **170**.69-74ab; **213**.145-153ab; **246**.18-19
- castes, creation of **45**.30-36
- castes, establishment of **213**.106-112
- castes of Krauñcadvīpa **20**.53cd-54ab
- castes of Kuśadvīpa **20**.38cd-40ab
- castes of Plakṣadvīpa **20**.16-17
- castes of Śākadvīpa **20**.65 .71-72ab
- castes of Śālmaladvīpa **20**.31
- castes, origin of **13**.32-35; **56**.22cd-23ab
- castes, professions of **19**.9; **27**.17-19ab
- castes, sons belonging to **11**.33-34ab; **13**.79
- directions **73**.63cd-65ab; **214**.107cd-128
- forests **18**.30
- forms of Nārāyaṇa **61**.24
- goals of life **27**.71-72; **58**.1-7; **88**.2-3 .10-15; **129**.101-124; **170**.32-36; **175**.14cd -16 .76-77; **246**.30-33
- heads of Brahman **113**.18-21
- incarnations of Viṣṇu **61**.39-40
- kinds of food **61**.38
- kinds of holy places **70**.16-29 .33-41; **175**.14cd-16
- kinds of speech **175**.14cd-16
- kinds of water **24**.12
- lakes **18**.31
- manifestations **61**.39-40
- manifestations of Viṣṇu **59**.34; **61**.7-12 .13; **192**.48-58

- methods of procreation **2**.50
- oceans **36**.63cd–70; **56**.27cd–30ab
- qualities **175**.14cd–16
- quarters of *dharma* **175**.17–24; **230**.8
- rivers, Gaṅgā divided into **18**.38cd–44ab; **73**.65cd–67
- stages of life **88**.10–15; **123**.2–7ab
- tusks, elephants with **202**.30–35
- Vedas **42**.38cd–42ab; **175**.14cd–16
- Vedas, origin of **56**.23cd–24ab
- Vidyuts **3**.60
- Yugas **19**.20; **27**.64cd; **175**.14cd–16 .29–32ab

four-*dvīpa*-theory **18**

four-eyed dogs dear to Yama **131**.2cd–4ab .31–39ab

fourfold knowledge **187**.42–54

freedom from death **7**.37a–d; **45**.59–67; **176**.33–34
- from fear **245**.44–47
- from harm by fire **125**.50–53
- from hunger and thirst **7**.37a–d
- from old age **7**.37a–d; **18**.24cd–28; **20**.86cd–87ab; **176**.33–34; **203**.24–25

freedom from see also *absence of*

friend and parents, *dharma* as **246**.37–38
- of devotees, Poverty as **137**.15–24
- of husband, wife as **129**.101–124; **167**.22–25
- of Indra, king as **168**.28cd–29
- of Indra, Maya as **124**.28cd–31
- of Indra, Pramati as **171**.44–46
- of Indra, Vṛṣākapi as **129**.99cd–100ef .101–124
- of Rāma, Vibhīṣaṇa as **157**.11–12ab
- of righteous people, Poverty as **137**.15–24
- of sinful Kṣatriyas, Lakṣmī as **137**.15–24
- , punishment for murder of **215**.105cd–107ab .114cd–115ab

friends and enemies, maxim about inheritage of **110**.80ef–86
- of Indra, Maruts as **124**.100–107 .137–139ab

friendship between Brahmin and Vaiśya **170**.2–5 .81–83
- between gods and demons **106**.2
- between pigeon and owl **125**.33–43
- , maxim about **124**.28cd–31; **170**.81–83
- with sun **16**.13–24

fruits, kinds of **220**.154–167 .168–177
- , list of **1**.3–9

fuel in sacrifice, summer as **161**.35cd–39ab

full moon **220**.10cd–11ab
- moon in simile **68**.43

functions at wedding-ceremony, ceremonial **72**.11cd–14
- of Agni **125**.16–17
- of Brahman **106**.19–22
- of Consciousness **237**.55 .57 .67–72 .73–75
- of manifestations of Viṣṇu **180**.17cd–42ab
- of Qualities **238**.3–4
- of senses **237**.76 .77; **240**.83–84
- of Viśvakarman **3**.42cd–46ab
- of women after marriage **144**.17–19

functions see also *attributes, description, epithets, qualities*

funeral rites for Kaṃsa **194**.10
- rites for Kṛṣṇa **212**.1–4

funeral see also *ancestral rites, cremation*

future, dream as prophecy of **205**.11–14 .15–22
- of world **1**.16–20

Gabhasti **20**.66–67; **110**.35–39ab

Gabhastihastin **31**.31–33ab

Gabhastimat **19**.6cd–7ab; **27**.14–16

Gabhastinī **110**.5–9 .124–130

Gabhastitīrtha, place of pilgrimage **25**.26

Gada **14**.45–46ab

gadā see *club*

Gadādhara **164**.51–53ab
- , place of pilgrimage **164**.53cd–54
- , Viṣṇu as **164**.1–2 .38–46

Gadātīrtha, place of pilgrimage **164**.38–46

Gādhi **10**.24–28ab .28cd–29ab .34cd–38ab .55–56; **13**.91
- , Indra born as **10**.24–28ab; **13**.88–90

Gail, A. **13**.161–198

Gālava **5**.44–45ab; **10**.57–60; **92**.2–11 .18cd–38 .39–47ab; **123**.77–81; **174**.2–5ab
- , place of pilgrimage **92**.48cd–49ef

gālava, etymology of **7**.105cd–109

Gālavas **10**.61–62; **13**.91

Gambhīrā **147**.9cd–13

gambling, dangers of **171**.27–39

game, coins as stake at **201**.10–22
- of dice **164**.17–28; **171**; **201**.10–22; **207**.28–43

game see also *play*

Gaṇḍa **165**.27–30ab

Gaṇḍakī, place of pilgrimage **64**.11–14

Gandhamādana **10**.5-8; **18**.21-23ab .32-36ab .44cd-45ab .46cd-50; **30**.49-52
- as place for asceticism **197**.4-5; **210**.33-35
- , place of pilgrimage **64**.8cd-9
- , sages residing on **226**.52-53
Gandhamādhana [forest] **18**.30
Gāndhāra **13**.148cd-151
- , horses from **13**.148cd-151
Gāndhāras **27**.43-50
Gāndhārī **13**.122; **14**.1-2ab; **16**.9-11
Gandharva [region] **19**.6cd-7ab
Gāndharva, place of pilgrimage **25**.23
- [region] **27**.14-16
Gandharva-knowledge **171**.44-46
- as stake at game of dice **171**.14-15
Gandharvas **3**.3-7ab; **10**.11-12; **13**.166-169; **18**.52-55; **20**.8-9 .36-38ab; **36**.21cd-22ab .22cd-23ab .63cd-70; **38**.17-19; **54**.16-17; **69**.12-43; **72**.11cd-14; **105**.8cd-11ab; **163**.3-6; **164**.3-6; **189**.10-12; **203**.45-62; **213**.60-65 .136-140; **214**.107cd-109; **239**.58-61
- , Citraratha as lord of **4**.2-9
- , gods and **141**.26-28
- , origin of **3**.104-105
- , Soma as lord of **105**.2
- , Soma taken away by **105**.3
- , world of **227**.16-32ab; **228**.146-151
Gāndharvatīrtha, place of pilgrimage **105**.22-26ab
Gāndī **17**.24-27
Gaṇḍikā **27**.25cd-27
Gaṇḍikī **27**.25cd-27
Gāndinī **14**.4-7 .8-10; **16**.50cd-54ab
Gāṇḍīva **212**.21-24
Gaṇḍūṣa **14**.14cd-20ab .29-31
Gaṇeśa **41**.88-90; **74**.13-22ab; **94**.15-21; **108**.26-30; **175**.33cd-35
- , advice by **74**.38cd-42
- as Ādideva **114**.2-5
- as Lambodara **114**.9-12
- as Lord of obstacle(s) **114**.13
- as narrator **175**.42-72
- , birth of **97**.20-23; **114**.9-12
- , boon by **114**.19-20
- , consecration of **114**.9-12
- disguised as Brahmin **74**.56-58
- , homage to **1**.1-2
- , hymn by gods to **114**.6-18
- , iconographic attributes of **114**.13
- invoked by Śiva **114**.6-8
- , obstacle(s) caused by **114**.2-5; **175**.73-74
- , Śiva and **110**.105-106
- , Umā and **175**.33cd-35 .36-41ef
- , Vighna as name of **175**.73-74
Gaṅgā **10**.9-10 .19cd-20; **13**.119; **18**; **21**.15-27; **27**.25cd-27; **39**.7-17ab; **69**.12-43; **71**.2-3; **72**.36; **73**.1; **74**.8-12; **82**.2-6; **89**.25cd-33; **109**.52-54; **110**.202-210; **123**.191-194; **158**.28-29; **163**.43-46; **208**.19-31
- and the triad of gods **73**.68-69ab; **175**.1-2ef
- and Yamunā, confluence of **129**.4-8
- as beloved of Śiva **74**.8-12; **158**.16-21; **175**.33cd-35
- as goddess **74**.1
- as Īśā **119**.13-17
- as tuft of hair of Śiva **75**.48
- , circumambulation of **76**.13-17; **78**.59-69
- , curse by **13**.82cd-87
- , descent of **8**.75cd-77ab; **73**.2-69; **75**.20; **78**.3-77
- divided into four rivers **18**.38cd-44ab; **73**.65cd-67
- , division of **76**.8-10
- drunk up by Jahnu **10**.15-18cd; **13**.82cd-87
- , Gautamī as southern **158**.28-29
- in hair of Śiva **119**.11
- in Veda(s) **76**.8-10
- , merit obtained at **75**.35-45
- , mouth of **64**.3-8ab
- [nether world], confluence of Gaṅgā [world of mortals] and **159**.46cd-48ab
- not removable from Śiva **175**.42-46ab
- originated from nether world **159**.46cd-48ab
- originated from step of Viṣṇu **18**.38cd-44ab; **150**.15-20
- , place of pilgrimage **64**.10 .11-14; **65**.84-96
- , prayer by Bhagīratha to **78**.59-69
- , prayer by Ciccika-bird to **164**.47-50ef
- , prayer-formula addressed to **164**.51-53ab
- , Śakti of **131**.29-30
- , Sāgaras purified by **78**.70-75ab
- , superiority of **75**.35-45
- , three forms of **76**.8-10
- , waters of heavenly **24**.13-18
- with ocean, confluence of **65**.84-96; **122**.3-7
Gaṅgā see also *Bhāgīrathī, Gautamī*

Gaṅgādhara, place of pilgrimage **25**.15
Gaṅgādvāra **39**.18cd-21; **77**.2-9ab
- as place for asceticism **147**.5-7
- , place of pilgrimage **25**.15; **64**.3-8ab; **65**.84-96
Gaṅgāhrada, place of pilgrimage **25**.54
Gaṅgās **27**.39cd-41ab
- , seven **172**.17cd-19ab
Gaṅgātīrtha, place of pilgrimage **25**.82
Gāṅgatīrtha, place of pilgrimage **85**.24
Gāṅgeya **82**.9-10
Gaṅgōdbhavasarasvatī, place of pilgrimage **25**.58
Gaṅgodbheda, place of pilgrimage **25**.32
Gaṇikā **86**.30-34 .35-39
Gaṇikāsaṃgama, place of pilgrimage **86**.2 .35-39
Gardabhākṣa **3**.64cd-70ab
gardens, celestial **203**.26-32
Garga **12**.11-17; **13**.62-63a; **184**.29-30
- , curse by **12**.9-10
- , Śeṣa as teacher of **21**.15-27
Gārgya, boon by Śiva to **196**.1-4
- , prophecy by **196**.23-29
Gārhapatya-fire **161**.30-33ab .54-58
Gariṣṭha **213**.81-104
garland, not withering **198**.15-17
- of svastikas **21**.15-27
garland-maker, boon by Kṛṣṇa to **192**.75-86
garment see *clothes*
Garuḍa **3**.95cd-96ab .97cd-98; **61**.13 .41-45ab; **65**.40-41; **69**.12-43; **90**.31-33; **131**.16-24; **136**.3cd-14ab .32-35ab; **159**.5 -11 .17-21 .41cd-46ab; **166**.8cd-11ab .11cd-13; **188**.24-28; **202**.13-15 .30-35; **203**.1-5 .33-37; **206**.10-13; **207**.13-24; **226**.62-65ab; **229**.37-43ab
- and Airāvata, fight between **203**.45-62
- and Kārttikeya, fight between **206**.24-30
- and snakes, fight between **206**.49-50
- as emblem **181**.20
- as golden bird **90**.34-35
- as lord of birds **4**.2-9
- , protection against **185**.50-51
- reproached by Kadrū **159**.28-31ab
- reproached by Vinatā **159**.31cd-35
- , snake imprisoned by **90**.5-8ab
- , snakes carried by **159**.22-24cd
- subordinate to snakes **159**.2-4
- , Tārkṣya as father of Aruṇa and **166**.2-4ab
- to Viṣṇu, complaint by **90**.12cd-19
- , Viṣṇu and **90**.20-30
Gāruḍatīrtha, place of pilgrimage **90**.1 .36
Garutmat **207**.13-24
gate(s) to city of Yama **214**.107cd-128; **215**.2-3
gāthā, vedic **120**.3ab .8-14
Gātravat **205**.1-6
Gaumatī **178**.7-11
Gaurī **7**.91-92; **20**.54cd-56ab; **71**.24-26; **205**.11-14
- , hymn to Śaṃkara and **108**.104-108
- , Śiva embraced by **119**.11
Gaurī see also *Devī, Durgā, Goddess, Pārvatī, Umā*
Gaurīpati **117**.16-17
Gaurīśikhara, place of pilgrimage **25**.74
Gautama **5**.34-35 .44-45ab; **70**.37cd-38; **74**.2-5 .24cd-30; **80**.1-3; **87**.2-34ab .34cd -59; **95**.12-15ab .15cd-17; **96**.8-10 .20-22ab; **107**.2-11 .17-18 .31-34 .35-40 .42-45; **145**.2cd-5ab; **152**.41; **174**.2-5ab
- and Śiva **175**.46cd-68
- as ideal ascetic **74**.22cd-38ab
- , ascetic power(s) of **74**.31-37
- , boon by Śiva to **75**.25-27
- , hymn by **107**.55-57
- , Indra as **87**.42-43
- , Indra cursed by **87**.58cd-59
- , Pippalāda married to daughter of **110**.225
- [son of Vṛddhakauśika] **170**
- to Śiva, hymn by **75**.4-24
- to Umā, hymn by **75**.4-24
Gautamairāvatītīrtha, place of pilgrimage **25**.59
Gautamas **13**.97
Gautameśvara, Liṅga named **174**.8-12ef
- , Śaṃkara as **91**.11cd-12
Gautamī **13**.97; **77**.2-9ab; **78**.77; **81**.13-15 .16-22ab; **82**.11-14; **83**.17-22; **84**.13-15; **85**.2-7; **86**.35-39 .43-46; **87**.39cd-41 .60-71 .66cd-69; **89**.25cd-33; **90**.31-33; **91**.6cd-11ab; **92**.12-18ab .18cd-38; **93**.5-11; **94**.37-42 .46-48ab; **95**.15cd-17 .31-32; **96**.20-22ab; **97**.15-17 .18-19; **99**.7cd-10; **100**.29cd-31ab; **101**.11cd-17ab; **104**.14cd-22ab .66-68 .86cd-87ab; **105**.4-8ab .11cd-13; **106**.31-36; **107**.48-52 .64ef-67ab; **108**.94-98 .99-102ab; **110**.87-97ef; **111**.68cd-79; **112**.20-22ab;

113.15; **114**.2-5; **115**.5-6ab; **116**.25c-f; **117**.2-5; **118**.2-9; **119**.4ef-8 .10; **120**.15 .16-18; **122**.63-67ab .67c-f .87-92; **123**.116-120 .121-128ab .191-194; **124**.87-93; **125**.44-49; **126**.30-32ab; **127**.35-47 .64a-f; **128**.1-2 .38-43 .77-81; **129**.65-67 .101-124 .125-127; **130**.17-21; **131**.31-39ab; **132**.3-5 .6; **134**.2-8ab; **135**.20-24; **136**.17-26 .27-31; **137**.25-28ab .28cd-30ab .30cd-39ab; **138**.20-21 .22-27; **139**.1-2ab .18; **140**.2-3ab .21ef-25 .31-34; **141**.2-5 .26-28; **142**.5-6ef; **144**.25-27; **146**.38-41; **148**.3cd-7 .27a-f; **149**.9cd-12; **150**.15-20; **151**.10-16; **152**.33; **154**.21cd-26 .32-34; **157**.2cd-7; **159**.41cd-46ab; **160**.13-16ef; **161**.21-23ef .64cd-65ab .72-78; **162**.2cd-6ab .31-33ef; **163**.3-6 .50-51; **164**.9cd-13 .38-46; **165**.37-44 .45-47ab; **166**.11cd-13; **167**.4-7 .26-28; **169**.2cd-3; **170**.49-50ef .54-63 .69-74ab; **171**.40-43; **172**.7cd-14 .15-17ab; **173**.3-6ab; **174**.27cd-28 .31-33; **175**.60-68 .73-74 .81cd-82; **178**.7-11
- and the triad of gods **175**.3-9ef
- as *brahman* **175**.3-9ef
- as Mother **157**.10
- as mother of rivers **160**.13-16ef
- as nectar of immortality, water of **133**.13-17
- as refuge **152**.31-32
- as Śakti of Śiva **123**.121-128ab
- as southern Gaṅgā **158**.28-29
- , bathing in **111**.80-82
- , boon by **85**.15-16
- , confluence of Kapilā and **155**.10cd-11ab
- , confluence of Phenā and **129**.82-93
- , confluence of Revatī and **121**.1 .24-25
- , confluence of Vidarbhā and **121**.1 .24-25
- , effect(s) of ancestral rites at **123**.128cd-139
- effecting release from hells **123**.121-128ab
- , Gautamī-Māhātmya as abridged, description of **175**.76-77
- honoured by Rāma **157**.30
- hostile to Poverty **137**.39cd-40ab
- , hymn by plants to **119**.9-12
- , island in **160**.13-16ef
- , Lakṣmī praised by **137**.30cd-39ab
- , merit obtained at **90**.31-33
- , merit of bathing in **80**.84-89
- obtained from Śiva **157**.12cd-13ab
- originated from bowl of Śiva **137**.25-28ab
- , praise of **175**.3-9ef
- praised by Kaṇva **85**.9-10
- praised by Rāma **157**.10-14
- , Rākṣasa sprinkled by water from **133**.18-23ab
- , Rāma at **123**.121-128ab .140-146; **154**.27-30ab
- , Rāma at source of **123**.207-213ab
- , Rāvaṇa killed by grace of **157**.11-12ab
- , Śiva and Nandin at **152**.42a-d
- , Śiva at **175**.55cd-59ef .69-72
- , sacrifice of Aṅgirasas at **155**.2-3ab
- , sacrifice of Rāma at **154**.32-34
- , sacrificial post thrown into **133**.18-23ab
- , sun at **158**.35cd-37ab
- , sun bathing in **86**.47-49ab
- , superiority of **77**.9cd-13; **88**.16-19; **129**.49-64; **175**.3-9ef .81-85
- , vedic sacrifice at **174**
- with ocean, confluence of **172**
- woshipped by monkeys **157**.15-18cd
- , Yama bathing in **86**.47-49ab

Gautamī see also *Gaṅgā, Godāvarī*

Gautamī-Māhātmya and Itihāsa-tradition **175**.76-77
- as abridged, description of Gautamī **175**.76-77
- as »summary« **174**.27cd-28

Gavākṣa **176**.37-51

Gavāṃbhavanatīrtha, place of pilgrimage **25**.38

Gavaya **176**.37-51

Gaveṣaṇa **14**.12-13

Gaya [demon] **70**.35cd-37ab
- , place of pilgrimage **64**.3-8ab
- [son of Havirdhāna] **2**.29-30ab
- [son of Puru] **2**.17-20ab
- [son of Sudyumna] **7**.17-19ab
- [son of Vitatha] **13**.62-63a

Gayā **7**.17-19ab; **220**.112cd-116ab
- , ancestral rites performed at **220**.30-31ab
- , place of pilgrimage **25**.10

Gayāśīrṣākṣaya-vaṭa, place of pilgrimage **25**.68

Gāyatrī **68**.56-59ab; **69**.12-43; **102**.2cd-5ab
- , place of pilgrimage **102**.1-2ab
- , recitation of **67**.15-18; **131**.39cd-51

Gāyatrīsthāna, place of pilgrimage **25**.80

Gāyatrī-verse, recitation of **60**.49-53; **107**.2-11
Geib, R. **43**.1-13
Geldner, K. F. **10**.1-14
genealogy of Bhojas and Kukkuras **15**
- of Kṛṣṇa **14**
- of Vāsudeva **226**.30-41
- of Vṛṣṇyandhakas **16**
generosity of Rāghavas **123**.86cd-96
- towards women, maxim about **123**.23-33ab
geography of India **19**; **27**.14-80
Ghaṇṭākarṇahrada, place of pilgrimage **25**.63
Ghargharikā-kuṇḍa, place of pilgrimage **25**.64
ghee for lamps **29**.35cd-36
ghee see also *butter*
Ghorā **214**.14-17
Ghoratīrtha, place of pilgrimage **25**.13
Ghoṣa **3**.30cd-33
ghosts, Śiva as lord of **4**.2-9
Ghṛtācī **32**.99cd-100; **41**.30-34ab; **68**.60-67; **178**.19-24
gift, consecration of sacrificial **155**.11cd
- , cows as sacrificial **13**.166-169
- , daughter as sacrificial **13**.142-146
- , earth as sacrificial **155**.2-3ab; **213**.114-122
- ending a vow, sacrificial **228**.127cd-145
- , exchange of sacrificial **155**.3cd-10ab
- , food as sacrificial **83**.23-29
- of cow **155**.12-13ab; **208**.8-18
- of ear of corn **136**.32-35ab
- of earth, hospitality equivalent to **163**.12cd-16
- of fearlessness **222**.46-54
- of land **51**.54-56; **73**.34-40; **155**.12-13ab
- of welcome **208**.8-18; **210**.50-52ab
- , prohibition of giving back a **35**.52-59
- , sacrificial **67**.39cd-45
- , silver as sacrificial **219**.71cd-86
- , three worlds as sacrificial **9**.13-16
- to Brahmins **47**.74-80ef .81-93ab .95c-f; **67**.39cd-45; **218**.8cd-9ab
- to priests **51**.48-53
- to teacher **51**.48-53; **67**.39cd-45 .46-48; **194**.23-31
gift see also *donation, reward*
Girikā **13**.109
Gītā **108**.113-115
Gītavana, place of pilgrimage **25**.69
gnashing of teeth, prohibition of **221**.70
Go **12**.3
goal of Yoga **243**.46-65
goals of life, body as means for **235**.11-12
- of life, contradictions among **221**.14-15
- of life, *dharma* as source of other **216**.73-80
- of life, four **27**.71-72; **58**.1-7; **88**.2-3 .10-15; **129**.101-124; **170**.32-36; **175**.14cd -16 .76-77; **246**.30-33
- of life, origin of three **129**.70-71
- of life, three **34**.29cd-32; **104**.10-14ab; **138**.10-13; **158**.30-35ab; **170**.8ef-13; **217**.4-11; **221**.10; **223**.41-52ab; **242**.25-26ab
goats, punishment for rearing of **22**.18cd-20
Gobhānu **13**.142-146
Gocapalā **13**.5-8
God, names of **241**.16cd-19ab
- , *puruṣa* and **243**.32-34
Godā **175**.69-72
Godāvarī **19**.12cd-13ab; **27**.35-36ab .43-50; **70**.33-35ab; **74**.24cd-30; **76**.18ab; **77**.9cd -13; **79**.5cd-6ab; **86**.8-9ab .20-21; **109**.46 -48; **122**.87-92; **123**.165-169; **129**.125-127; **141**.26-28; **148**.21-26; **160**.17-19; **161**.2cd -4ab; **167**.8-14; **173**.37-39; **175**.60-68 .83-84
- , hymn by Kaṇva to **85**.12-14
- , place of pilgrimage **64**.11-14
- , Rāma at the **157**.15-18cd
Goddess and Rāhu, fight between **106**.39-41
- as energy **131**.39cd-51
- as OM **161**.17-20
- , boon by gods to **106**.49cd-53ab
- , Gaṅgā as **74**.1
- , names of **106**.43-45ab
- , nectar of immortality swallowed by **106**.46cd
- , praise of **129**.75-78
- , prayer by Indra to **129**.79-80
- , Speech as **80**.46-55
- , useful things originated from sweat of **129**.75-78
Goddess see also *Devī, Durgā, Gaurī, Pārvatī, Umā*
Godhana **27**.20cd-24ab
gods afraid of ascetic **178**.12-18
- , Agni as messenger of **93**.12-24; **127**.29

-34; **128**.7-15
- , Agni as priest of **128**.3-6
- and ancestors, offerings to **221**.89-94
- and demons, assembly of **160**.6cd-9
- and demons, battle between **3**.109cd-122; **9**.23; **11**.4-7; **32**.9-11 .41cd-46; **97**.8-13ab; **106**.2; **109**.39cd-40; **112**.2-3; **123**.7cd-14ab; **142**.2-4; **160**; **162**.2cd-6ab
- and demons, competition between **11**.8-16
- and demons, consultation among **106**.3-7
- and demons, curse by **128**.29-37
- and demons, enmity between **97**.5cd-7
- and demons, friendship between **106**.2
- and demons, nectar of immortality obtained by **133**.13-17
- and Gandharvas **141**.26-28
- and sages, advice by **141**.23-25
- and sages, Śiva unknowable to **127**.48-53
- as lords of three worlds **32**.7-8
- at place of pilgrimage, triad of **174**.19-25ab
- , boar worshipped by **226**.59-61
- , boons by **127**.60-63; **141**.10-13
- born as sons of Atri, triad of **144**.2-4
- bound by actions **27**.69-70
- , Brahman as creator of **161**.43cd-50cd
- , Brahmins despised by **167**.8-14
- , caste regulations among **34**.33-38
- , chorus of **65**.23-26; **108**.71-74; **110**.183-187; **193**.57cd-60ab; **209**.21cd-22
- , classes of **5**.8-9ab .13ab .19cd .22ab .26 .30cd-31 .36-37ab; **213**.66-71
- , complaint by **73**.9-17
- , consultation among **106**.13-14
- descending on earth **160**.6cd-9
- , Devāpi as teacher of **13**.117ab
- , Dhanvantari as lord of **122**.44-47
- , eight mothers of **105**.8cd-11ab
- , embodiment of **3**.62-64ab
- encompassed by sun **110**.137-142 .219ef-224
- , energy of triad of **131**.39cd-51
- , enmity between Kaṃsa and **183**.1-7
- , fight between Kṛṣṇa and **203**.45-62
- , fire as mouth of **126**.4-8
- , Gaṅgā and the triad of **73**.68-69ab; **175**.1-2ef
- , Gautamī and the triad of **175**.3-9ef
- , Hari identical with **3**.125
- , hierarchy of **28**.40-41; **33**.13cd-14ab; **229**.8-13
- , holy places established by **70**.16-19
- , honouring of **216**.3-4
- , hospitality as satiation of **163**.17-22
- , Indra as lord of **131**.16-24
- , Indra expelled from lordship over **122**.48-49
- , intervention by **213**.60-65
- , jealousy of **123**.7cd-14ab
- , life-span of **5**.58cd-60
- , list of **65**.28-30; **191**.4-12
- , Manyu and **162**.13-19
- , Manyu as commander-in-chief of **162**.10cd-12
- , Manyu praised by **162**.20-27ab
- , Maruts as **124**.108-109
- obedient to hymns of Veda(s) **127**.29-34
- obtained by sacrifices to Viṣṇu, lordship over **191**.4-12
- , opposition of demons and **209**.2-11ab
- , origin of **1**.48cd-50ab; **3**.3-7ab; **161**.43cd -50cd; **213**.30-31
- , origin of enmity between Rākṣasas and **116**.20-22ab
- over demons, victory of **212**.72-85
- , partial incarnation of **181**.32
- , prescr. conc. offerings to **221**.21
- , punishment for hatred against **22**.14cd-15a
- , rebirth as **241**.45-47
- residing in body of Viṣṇu **226**.20cd-22ab
- , Śiva identical with **158**.22-27ef
- , Śiva praised by **37**; **113**.9 .15 .17; **160**.13-16ef
- , Śiva worshipped by **162**.6cd-10ab
- , sacrifice as support of **24**.19-25
- , *sattra*-rite of **114**.2-5
- seeking help from demons **116**.5cd-9
- , sun identical with triad of **168**.10-12
- [Sūrya, Viṣṇu, Śiva] at place of pilgrimage, three **166**.11cd-13
- taking refuge to Brahman **181**.15-19
- taking refuge to Viṣṇu **213**.66-71
- , thirteen **162**.10cd-12
- , thirty-three **3**.62-64ab
- , threat of curse against **127**.29-34
- , three kinds of **175**.14cd-16
- to demons, promise by **116**.5cd-9
- to Devakī, hymn by **182**.7-8
- to Gaṇeśa, hymn by **114**.6-18
- to Goddess, boon by **106**.49cd-53ab

- to Māṇḍavya, hymn by **96**.11-17
- to Mucukunda, boon by **196**.21-22
- to Pippalāda, boon by **110**.168-171
- to Pravarā, boon by **106**.54cd-56
- to Puruṣottama, hymn by **65**.21-22
- to Śiva, homage by **94**.46-48ab
- to Śiva, hymn by **37**.2-23; **71**.38-40ab; **94**.27-30; **110**.134-136; **112**.4-6
- to sun, hymn by **32**.89-90ab
- to Viṣṇu, hymn by **65**.49-51; **71**.7-12; **109**.41-42; **213**.72-73
- , triad of **71**.1; **178**.43-53
- , Vāsudeva identical with **226**.45cd-48ab
- , Vāyu as messenger of **123**.14cd-22
- , vehicles of **3**.42cd-46ab
- , Viṣṇu identical with **51**.1-8; **56**.13-15; **122**.68-73; **179**.72cd-75; **181**.15-19; **192**.48-58
- , Viṣṇu unknowable to **56**.51-54
- , wish for identity with **213**.53-57
- without sacrificial share **160**.2cd-6ab
- , world of **227**.16-32ab
gods see also *deities*
Godvīpa [island in the Godāvarī] **131**.26-28
Gograha, place of pilgrimage **42**.6-8
going everywhere, power of **140**.3cd-5ab
Gokarṇa, place of pilgrimage **25**.80; **64**.8cd-9
Gokula **184**.7-13
- , Baladeva in **197**.8-21
Golāṅgulas **27**.54-57
Golāṅgūlas **27**.54-57
gold, Agni as father of **148**.8-14ab
- as foundation of prosperity **128**.50-61
- identical with fire **148**.8-14ab
- named Jāmbūnada **18**.24cd-28
- originated from Agni and Śiva **128**.50-61
- praised by Śiva **128**.50-61
- , punishment for theft of **22**.9
- , purification by **128**.50-61
- , qualities of **128**.50-61
golden altars **13**.166-169
- area **20**.95cd-98ab
- bird, Garuḍa as **90**.34-35
- bow **213**.114-122
- cities **3**.80cd-83
- egg, origin of cosmos from **1**.39cd-42
- pillar, killing with **201**.23-26
- vessel, fire carried in **110**.202-210
Gomanta, place of pilgrimage **64**.8cd-9
Gomantha **27**.20cd-24ab
Gomatī **11**.41-43; **27**.25cd-27; **178**.7-11
- , place of pilgrimage **64**.10
Gomaya, place of pilgrimage **25**.68
Gomeda **20**.6-7
good conditions of life **152**.40
- people, Indra as protector of **140**.7-11
- people, maxim about contact with **163**.32-39
- qualities **167**.15-17; **222**.15-17
- qualities, list of **137**.30cd-39ab
- qualities of Viṣṇu **226**.23cd-25
goose, Self as **236**.33 .34
Gopālī [Apsaras] **14**.48-50ab
Gopatisthāna, place of pilgrimage **25**.80
Gopīs, Balarāma and **197**.19-21
- , love-play of Kṛṣṇa and **189**.14-45
Gopīs see also *cowherds*
Goprabhāva, place of pilgrimage **25**.24
Gorakṣa, place of pilgrimage **131**.29-30
Gosava-sacrifice **91**.6cd-11ab
Gotīrtha, place of pilgrimage **110**.216; **131**.25 .39cd-51; **155**.12-13ab
gourd, birth of **8**.65-68
- , sons born from **8**.69-72ab
Govara, place of pilgrimage **25**.24
Govardhana **189**.2-8; **190**.1-5; **193**.32-40
- lifted up by Kṛṣṇa **188**.17-19
- , place of pilgrimage **91**.11cd-12
Govardhanatīrtha, place of pilgrimage **91**.1-2ab
Govinda **16**.25-45ab; **20**.49cd-51; **60**.39-45; **61**.14-16; **86**.47-49ab; **184**.14-19; **187**.8-18; **196**.16-20; **206**.24-30; **211**.3-4
- , place of pilgrimage **122**.100-102
- , statue of Viṣṇu named **122**.100-102
- , world of **63**.18
Govinda see also *Kṛṣṇa, Viṣṇu*
Govinda, explanation of **122**.95-97ab; **188**.29-35
Govindasvāmin, Viṣṇu as **43**.77-82ab
grace of Viṣṇu, liberation by **178**.184-186; **239**.24-28
grain, kinds of **217**.62-65; **220**.154-167
grammatical order of cases represented in hymn **130**.23-31
grandson of Dakṣa, Nārada as **3**.7cd-9
- of moon, Dakṣa as **2**.51-53
grass, rainy season as sacrificial **161**.35cd-39ab
grass see also *Darbha-grass, Kuśa-grass*

Gṛdhrabhojāndhaka **16**.50cd-54ab
Gṛdhrakūṭa, place of pilgrimage **25**.69
Gṛdhras **3**.93cd-95ab
Gṛdhravaṭa, place of pilgrimage **25**.69
Gṛdhrī **3**.93cd-95ab
Gṛdhrikā **3**.92cd-93ab
Great Bear **2**.10-13; **5**.8-9ab; **23**.6-10
- Self, *puruṣa* as **245**.7
greatness of Anantavāsudeva **176**.3
- of Kṛṣṇa **185**.30-33
- of Puruṣottamakṣetra **177**
- of Śiva **41**.6-9
greatness see also *superiority*
greed see also *avarice*
greedy Brahmin **170**.17cd-22
- people, maxim about wrathful and **124**.68-73ab
greeting, formula of **61**.26
Gṛñjama **14**.14cd-20ab
Gṛñjima **14**.32cd
ground, circumference of sacrificial **161**.68-71
- , discussion about sacrificial **168**.2-5
Gṛtsamada **11**.32-33ab .33-34ab
Gṛtsamati **13**.63b-64ab .98-99
Grünendahl **223**
guardians of directions **4**.10; **6**.46cd-48ab; **18**.36cd-38ab; **28**.27; **61**.45cd-46; **72**.8; **123**.177cd-184; **154**.2-4; **160**.6cd-9; **162**.20-27ab; **174**.7; **175**.55cd-59ef
- of directions defeated by Rāvaṇa **143**.12-13
- of directions, homage to **61**.45cd-46
guardians of directions see also *lord of direction*
Guḍapākā **215**.121cd-122ab
Guḍivā **66**.1-2
- temple, procession to **66**
guest of Indra, Kṛṣṇa as **203**.24-25
guest see also *hospitality*
guest(s) at sacrifice **109**.13-20
- at wedding **72**.10cd-11ab
- , effect(s) of feeding of disqualified **220**.136-138
- granting access to heaven **163**.17-22
- , honouring of **1**.10-12; **47**.4-6 .63-67; **73**.58-63ab; **74**.31-37; **78**.8cd-11; **80**.46-55; **84**.5-8; **104**.3-4ef; **107**.42-45; **111**.48-51; **118**.2-9; **130**.2-6; **136**.3cd-14ab; **163**.17-22; **192**.1-4; **197**.8-18; **2C8**.8-18; **220**.121-123; **222**.32-35
- , maxim about **222**.36
Guha **206**.24-30
Guhāviṣṇupada, place of pilgrimage **25**.25
Guhyakas **39**.7-17ab
Guṇārṇavā **88**.2-3
Guṇḍīca-Mandapa **51**.32-45
Guṇḍikā **66**.1-2 .6-7ab
habitation, change of **231**.68-71ab
- during Kali-Yuga, places for **231**.4-41
- , prescription(s) concerning **221**.103-108
habitation see also *settlement*
Hacker, P. **23**.41-43; **213**.43-79
Hāhā **36**.63cd-70
Hāhās **32**.97cd-99ab
Haihaya **11**.44-48; **13**.69ab .154cd-155ab .155cd-156
Haihayas **8**.29-30 .31-32 .35-37 .42cd-43; **13**.203-204 .205-207ab; **213**.106-112
Haimavata **18**.18-20
Haimavatī **7**.90
hair, ceremony of parting the **100**.25-29ab
- , dragging by the **193**.67cd-76ab
- of Śiva, Gaṅgā as tuft of **75**.48
- of Śiva, Gaṅgā in **119**.11
- of Śiva, moon in **114**.9-12
- , prescr. conc. combing of **221**.21
- , pulling of **37**.2-23
Hairaṇyaka **18**.18-20
hairs of Viṣṇu, incarnation of two **181**.26-31
hair-styles **8**.44-51
Halāyudha **65**.10-11 .59-76ab; **209**.11cd-21ab
half of husband, wife as **161**.33cd-35ab
halves, killing by splitting in **190**.29-37; **202**.16-21
- of Brahman **161**.33cd-35ab
- of cosmic egg **1**.39cd-42
Haṃsa **18**.32-36ab
Haṃsalīlā **68**.60-67
Haṃsamārgas **27**.43-50
Haṃsapāda, place of pilgrimage **25**.31
Haṃsasthāna, place of pilgrimage **25**.40
hand as stake at game of dice, right **171**.6ef-9ef
- , churning of right **2**.21-24; **4**.48-52; **141**.10-13
- , killing by one stroke of **213**.74-79
- , right **221**.95-100

hand see also *palm*
hands as stake at bet **170**.37-38cd
- , eight pose(s) of **61**.52-55
- , pose(s) of **28**.28-29
- , prescr. conc. ritual use of **60**.54-65
Hanumat **154**.5-8ab .21cd-26; **157**.25cd-27ab; **176**.37-51
- , birth of **84**.9-12
- , mountain transported by **170**.54-63
- , Rāma and **157**.21cd-25ab
Hanūmata, place of pilgrimage **129**.1-2
Hanūmatatīrtha, place of pilgrimage **129**.9-10
happiness, righteousness as source of **170**.26a-f
happiness see also *enjoyment, pleasure, prosperity*
Hara **3**.46cd-49; **35**.4cd-10; **72**.23-25ab; **82**.9-10; **109**.43-45; **110**.87-97ef; **115**.12cd-15ab; **117**.2-5; **129**.49-64 .75-78; **130**.17-21; **135**.1-2ab; **143**.1; **205**.9-10
- , Hari and **135**.17-19
Hara see also *Śiva*
Hārabhūsikas **27**.43-50
hare, meat of **7**.48cd-51ab
Hari **3**.123-124; **5**.61-62; **8**.58-59ab; **9**.13-16; **12**.50; **13**.213c-f; **18**.57-58; **20**.41cd-42; **22**.37-41; **23**.36-37 .44; **42**.5 .11; **43**.6-9; **44**.8-9; **51**.42-45; **56**.61-66ab; **63**.1-7; **70**.3cd-8ab; **73**.48-51; **86**.27-29; **106**.23-26ab; **108**.68-70; **109**.1-3ab .13-20 .26cd-27 .28-29 .43-45 .49-50ef .52-54; **114**.2-5; **123**.121-128ab; **129**.49-64 .101-124; **135**.10cd-13cd; **136**.17-26; **149**.2-4ab .9cd-12; **150**.15-20; **153**.12; **156**.4-6; **160**.20; **161**.17-20; **163**.26-31 .47-49; **165**.45-47ab .47cd-48ef; **168**.10-12; **170**.40-43 .54-63 .69-74ab; **171**.1-2ab; **174**.5cd-6ab .7 .19-25ab; **178**.106-111 .112 .122-127; **179**.72cd-75; **181**.1; **182**.1-3; **184**.14-19; **185**.52-53; **188**.11-13; **194**.7-8; **195**.1-4; **196**.23-29; **197**.1-3; **199**.5-10; **201**.6-9; **203**.1-5; **204**.8-13ab; **205**.7-8; **206**.10-13 .14-19 .21-23 .31-38; **207**.13-24; **210**.44-46; **212**.8 .66-70; **216**.5-63 .87-89; **219**.30; **226**.11-12; **229**.15-18 .20; **233**.1-4 .43cd-46ab; **246**.34-35
- , absorption of cosmos in **5**.61-62
- and Hara **135**.17-19
- as Brahman **233**.1-4
- as creator **23**.36-37
- as *puruṣa* **3**.125
- as Soma **20**.19
- , homage to **1**.1-2
- identical with gods **3**.125
- in Jyeṣṭha, bathing of **65**.3
- [Indra] **93**.12-24; **108**.68-70; **122**.87-92; **124**.39cd-47; **129**.30-37 .82-93 .94-99ab; **140**.19cd-21cd .21ef-25; **171**.2cd-6cd; **178**.59-60
- , merit of listening to stories of **76**.18cd-23ab
- , merit of looking at discus of **51**.63-71
- [son of Parajit] **15**.1-12ab .12cd-13
- , *trimūrti*-functions of **1**.1-2
- , world of **227**.32cd-37ab
- , Yoga of **60**.1-6
Hari see also *Viṣṇu*
Haribhūṣikas **27**.43-50
Haridaśva **10**.65cd-67ab
Harigiri **20**.41cd-42
Harihara **160**.17-19
Harihaya **213**.81-104
Harikeśavana, place of pilgrimage **25**.62
Hariścandra **8**.24-28; **10**.65cd-67ab; **70**.39-40; **104**
- , place of pilgrimage **104**.1-2
Harita **8**.24-28; **20**.22-23 .29-30
Hārita **10**.57-60
Harivāhana **14**.4-7
Harivaṃśa **1**; **3**.7cd-9 .46cd-49; **5**.42-47; **8**.11-12; **12**.1-2 .9-10; **213**
Harivarṣa **18**.18-20
harm by fire, freedom from **125**.50-53
- by spell **58**.57
harmony between husband and wife **138**.10-13
Harṣaṇa **165**.30cd-36
- as ideal son **165**.37-44
- , Viṣṇu praised by **165**.45-47ab
Hartṛ **31**.31-33ab
Haryaṅga **13**.43-44 .45-48
Haryaśva **7**.87-88
Haryaśvas **3**.10-14 .16-18ab .19cd-23
Haryatvata **11**.27cd-31
Hasta **220**.33cd-42 .49cd-50ab
Hastināpura **208**.8-18 .19-31 .32-35
- , tilted position of **208**.38
hatred against ancestors, punishment for

22.14cd-15a
- against Brahmins, punishment for **22**.14cd-15a
- against gods, punishment for **22**.14cd-15a
- , maxim about **110**.121-123
hatred see also *disrespect, enmity, rival*
Havana **3**.46cd-49
Havidhra **5**.13cd-15ab
Havighna **5**.13cd-15ab
Havirdhāman **226**.30-41
Havirdhāna **2**.29-30ab .30cd-31ab
Havya **5**.9cd-10
Havyaghna, boon by Brahman to **133**.5-8
Haya **13**.154cd-155ab
Hayagrīva [demon] **213**.81-104
- killed by Kṛṣṇa **202**.16-21
Hayagrīva see also *Aśvaśīrṣan, Hayaśiras*
Hayamūrdhaka, place of pilgrimage **174**.8-12ef
Hayamūrdhan **70**.35cd-37ab; **174**.8-12ef
Hayapada, place of pilgrimage **25**.31
Hayarūpa **122**.68-73
Hayaśantika, place of pilgrimage **25**.68
Hayaśiras 3.74cd-78ab .80cd-83
- , Viṣṇu as **18**.57-58; **174**.8-12ef
Hayaśiras see also *Aśvaśīrṣan, Hayagrīva*
Hazra, R.C. **30**.40-41
head, cow-dung smeared on **184**.7-13
- , kissing of **9**.31-32
- of Brahman, Śiva freed from **229**.59-63
- , prescription(s) concerning washing of **221**.35
- , prohibition of scratching of **221**.34
heads of Ananta, three **226**.62-65ab
- of Brahman, five **113**.2-4 .22-23; **135**.10cd-13cd
- of Brahman, four **113**.18-21
- of fever, three **206**.14-19
- , Viṣṇu as Brahman with thousand **179**.22cd-26
heads see also *many-headedness*
healing by means of oblation **58**.48
- of birds burnt by sun **166**.6cd-8ab
- of blind princess **170**.74cd-76
- of humpbacked woman **193**.1-12
- of Rāma **170**.54-63
- of snakes **159**.39ef-41ab .41cd-46ab
healing see also *remedy*
heaven, ancestors fallen from **220**.193cd-195ab
- and hell **22**.44-47
- , ascension to **4**.48-52; **7**.21cd-22; **8**.20-21 .23; **80**.80-83 .90-91ef; **150**.15-20; **211**.5-10; **216**.67-72; **227**.32cd-37ab; **229**.72-86ab
- , conduct leading to **224**.9-14 .15-16ef
- , duration of sojourn in **67**.52-80; **110**.155 -156; **227**.16-32ab .32cd-37ab .42-47; **228**.86-91ab .146-151
- , fall from **219**.18-24; **220**.193cd-195ab
- , guest(s) granting access to **163**.17-22
- of Indra, Ātreya in **140**.5cd-6ef
- of Viṣṇu, adepts in **68**.43
- or hell, retribution in **165**.30cd-36
- , origin of rivers from **20**.68cd-70
- , rebirth in **197**.1-3; **225**.2-8
- , reward(s) in **215**.138cd-142
- , sojourn in **7**.85-86; **67**.64cd-75
- , suffering in **234**.50-54ab
- , welcome of Kṛṣṇa in **203**.1-5
heaven see also *city, world*
heavenly beings **68**.54-55
- chariot **12**.6cd-8 .11-17; **58**.70cd-77; **65**.46-47 .55-56; **66**.18-23; **67**.53-57; **68**.18-22; **110**.183-187; **227**.16-32ab
- conditions on earth **20**.85-86ab
- dance **32**.99cd-100
- enjoyments **68**.29-32
- Gaṅgā, waters of **24**.13-18
- music **7**.30-34 .74-77; **14**.14cd-20ab; **32**.97cd-103; **193**.57cd-60ab
- pleasures **58**.70cd-77; **59**.81-91
- sages **125**.1-2ab
- voice **7**.74-77; **32**.37-41ab; **78**.12-24; **83**.17-22; **97**.24-28; **104**.66-68; **123**.14cd -22 .82-83 .173-175 .177cd-184; **126**.28-29 .32cd-35; **135**.2cd-5ab; **138**.20-21; **148**.8-14ab .18cd-20; **160**.17-19; **161**.13-16 .17-20 .21-23ef .24-26 .39cd-43ab; **173**.29cd-33ab .33cd-34ab; **201**.10-22
- voice, dialogue between Brahman and **161**.11cd-26
- weapons, summoning of **195**.5-7
- worlds, descriptionof **23**
- worlds, distance of **23**.12-15
heavens, list of **54**.20-21
hell for unbelievers, threat of **49**.50cd-54ab
- , heaven and **22**.44-47
- , list of torments in **215**.84cd-136ab

- , Put as name of **4**.48-52
- , rebirth in **157**.21cd-25ab
- , retribution in heaven or **165**.30cd-36
- , sojourn of Daśaratha in **123**.109cd-115
- , son saving from **4**.48-52
- , torments in **123**.109cd-115; **234**.44-49

hells, description of **22**
- , Gautamī effecting release from **123**.121-128ab
- , list of **22**.7-27; **214**.14-17; **215**.84cd-136ab; **217**.80cd-86
- , names of **22**.2-6
- , number of **22**.28-29; **215**.78-80 .137cd-138ab
- , punishment in **22**.7-27; **215**.138cd-142
- , Yama as lord of **123**.121-128ab

help by Kṣatriya-woman in battle **123**.23-33ab
- from demons, gods seeking **116**.5cd-9
- from Kṛṣṇa, Balarāma asking for **187**.19-20
- in battle, promise of **123**.14cd-22

helpless people, punishment for killing of **215**.99-100ab
- persons, prescr. conc, treatment of **221**.44

Hemakūṭa **18**.16-17
Hemaparvata **20**.41cd-42
Hemaśaila **20**.41cd-42
herb as remedy **170**.54-63
heresies **230**.44-48; **231**.4-41; **242**.20cd-21ab
heretics see also *fallen people, Mlecchas, outcastes, unbelievers*
hermit killed by Daśaratha **123**.48cd-61ab
hermitage, description of **74**.24cd-30; **178**.7-11 .28-42
- of Vālmīki **154**.11cd-14ab
- of Vyāsa, description of **26**.3-17

hermits, boon by **118**.24cd-30
- , cremation of **123**.77-81
- , Daśaratha cursed by **123**.73cd-76

hero, observances for conception of a **125**.44-49
Heti and Agni **125**.18-21
- [pigeon] **125**.2cd-8
- to Agni, hymn by **125**.15-17

Hetyulūka, place of pilgrimage **125**.54-56
hiding of statue **45**.75-76
hierarchy of gods **28**.40-41; **33**.13cd-14ab; **229**.8-13
- of holy places **70**.16-19

hierarchy see also *comparison, superiority*
highest abode **23**.41-43; **24**.1-7ab
- deity, Mitra as **30**.49-52 .53-56
- deity, Śiva as **36**.44cd-48 .49-52ab
- deity, sun as **30**.7-13; **33**.13cd-14ab
- *dharma*, involvement as **240**.77-80
- principle, *puruṣa* as **1**.1-2; **161**.6cd-9
- reality, ignorance concerning **203**.6-19
- step in Yoga **235**.21-25
- step of Viṣṇu **42**.5; **51**.22-26 .57-58; **68**.4-5; **131**.39cd-51
- step of Viṣṇu, *brahman* as **234**.63cd-66ab
- truth, Vāsudeva as **44**.13

highest see also *absolute, brahman, transcendence*
hill as deity of cowherds **187**.42-54
- , circumambulation of **187**.42-54 .55-59ab
- , Kṛṣṇa embodied in **187**.59cd-61
- serving as umbrella **188**.11-13 .14-16

hills, description of **44**.76-77
Himācala **219**.25-29
Himālaya **19**.1 .10; **27**.25cd-27; **36**.1; **69**.12-43; **70**.22cd-23 .33-35ab; **78**.70-75ab .75cd-76; **108**.8-14ab .99-102ab; **161**.21-23ef; **174**.25cd-27ab; **219**.13-17 .18-24 .25-29 .113cd-115; **223**.4-6; **231**.68-71ab
- as lord of mountains **4**.2-9
- , description of **36**.90-93; **72**.1-4
- , place of pilgrimage **25**.12; **64**.8cd-9

Himavat **18**.16-17; **19**.10; **27**.65-66ab; **34**.39-41 .56-57 .73 .74-80; **35**.11-14; **36**.2-6 .54cd-57; **71**.19-23; **72**.1-4; **74**.13-22ab; **219**.18-24
- , boon by Brahman to **34**.74-80
- honoured by Viṣṇu **72**.7
- , three daughters of **34**.81

Hindolaka [Rāga] **86**.35-39
hindrance, Āṅgirasas pursued by **158**.8-15ef
hindrance see also *obstacle(s), Vighna*
Hiraṇmaya **18**.18-20
Hiraṇya [Daitya] **129**.11cd-16
Hiraṇyagarbha **5**.17a-c; **9**.13-16; **245**.31-41 .44-47
Hiraṇyaka **103**.2-6
- , place of pilgrimage **148**.21-26

Hiranyakaśipu **3**.64cd-70ab; **14**.20cd-24ab; **149**.2-4ab; **179**.18cd-22ab; **180**.24cd-38; **181**.36; **213**.43
- , boon by Brahman to **213**.44-52 .58-59

- , supremacy of **213**.53-57 .66-71
Hiraṇyākṣa **3**.64cd-70ab .72-73ab; **10**.57-60; **13**.91
- , place of pilgrimage **25**.11
Hiraṇyākṣas **10**.61-62
Hiraṇyaroman **4**.11-15; **5**.24cd-25
Hoffmann, K. **6**.5
holy cow **74**.59-67
- men, description of **46**.23
- places at Viraja **42**.6-8
- places, classification of **70**.16-29; **175**.29-32ab
- places, death at **35**.26cd-28
- places, *dharma* maintained at **175**.17-24
- places established by Asuras **70**.16-19
- places established by gods **70**.16-19
- places established by men **70**.16-19
- places established by sages **70**.16-19
- places, four kinds of **70**.16-29 .33-41; **175**.14cd-16
- places, hierarchy of **70**.16-19
- places, hundred and eight **146**.42-45
- places in Avantī **43**.65cd-85ab
- places, merit of bathing at **214**.114cd-119
- places, number of **41**.11-12; **62**.22cd-23; **77**.2-9ab; **89**.43-46ab; **94**.46-48ab; **96**.25cd-26; **98**.20-21ab; **106**.48cd-49ab; **108**.121-123; **110**.146c-f; **115**.20c-f; **116**.25c-f; **118**.31-32ef; **120**.16-18; **121**.26; **122**.104; **124**.140ef; **125**.54-56; **126**.1-2 .37-39; **127**.64a-f; **128**.77-81; **129**.125-127; **131**.52-53ab; **134**.15-16; **135**.27c-f; **136**.43; **137**.41c-f; **138**.39ab; **139**.20; **140**.35-38; **141**.29-30; **142**.14; **144**.25-27; **145**.14; **146**.42-45; **148**.1-3ab; **149**.16cd-19; **150**.21-22 .23; **151**.27cd-29; **152**.41; **153**.16cd; **154**.30cd-31; **155**.13cd-14ab; **159**.48cd-49ef; **160**.21-22ab; **161**.72-78; **175**.83-84
- rivers, twelve **70**.22cd-23
- texts, origin of sciences and **129**.75-78
- water **73**.58-63ab
holy see also *sacred*
holy places see also *place of pilgrimage*
homage by gods to Śiva **94**.46-48ab
- by Rāma to Viśvāmitra **93**.3-4
- by women **65**.76cd-77
- to Agni **126**.30-32ab
- to Brahman **131**.39cd-51
- to fig-tree, merit of **57**.17-19
- to Gaṇeśa **1**.1-2
- to guardians of directions **61**.45cd-46
- to Hari **1**.1-2
- to Prajāpati **24**.1-7ab
- to Śiva **79**.3-5ab
- to Śiva as Someśvara **122**.82
- to Thirst **139**.7cd-11
- to Vāsudeva **1**.1-2
- to water **126**.30-32ab
homage see also *veneration, worship*
homosexuality **225**.51
honey **219**.71cd-86; **220**.28cd-29
- , flesh of dog changed to **93**.12-24
- , food with butter and **219**.65cd-71ab
- , punishment for collecting of **22**.23ab
honour, maxim about loss of **146**.8cd-10
honouring of Brahmins **216**.3-4
- of Brahmins, prescr. conc. **76**.18cd-23ab
- of gods **216**.3-4
- of guest(s) **1**.10-12; **47**.4-6 .63-67; **73**.58-63ab; **74**.31-37; **78**.8cd-11; **80**.46-55; **84**.5-8; **104**.3-4ef; **107**.42-45; **111**.48-51; **118**.2-9; **130**.2-6; **136**.3cd-14ab; **163**.17-22; **192**.1-4; **197**.8-18; **208**.8-18; **220**.121-123; **222**.32-35
- of parents, maxim about **194**.1-5
- of teacher **216**.3-4; **221**.31 .32; **235**.4-5
- of teacher, prescription(s) concerning **221**.38
- of Viṣṇu, reciprocity of **226**.54-55
Hopkins, W. E. **3**.46cd-49
horse, demon as **190**.22-25
horse-headed form of Viṣṇu **18**.57-58; **178**.166cd-176
horses from Gāndhāra **13**.148cd-151
- of Varuṇa **213**.114-122
- , origin of **3**.93cd-95ab
- , punishment for selling of **22**.11
- , Uccaiḥśravas as lord of **4**.2-9
horse-sacrifice **43**.10-13; **73**.23-26; **104**.7cd-9; **127**.4cd-9ab .60-63; **131**.39cd-51; **144**.25-27; **154**.14cd-21ab; **175**.86-90
- as expiation for Brahmin-murder **12**.11-17; **123**.77-81
- , daughter obtained by means of **2**.7-8
- , description of **47**.50-98
- of Abhiṣṭut **168**
- of Indradyumna **47**.10-95
- of Rāma Jāmadagnya **213**.114-122

horse-sacrifice see also *sacrifice*
horse-sacrifices, hundred **8**.59cd-61
- , ten **213**.142-144
hospitality as satiation of gods **163**.17-22
- equivalent to gift of earth **163**.12cd-16
- , maxim about **163**.12cd-16; **172**.4-7ab .7cd-14
- of Maudgalya **136**.3cd-14ab
- , prescription(s) concerning **221**.85-86
hospitality see also *guest(s)*
hot water-spring, origin of **115**.15cd-16
Hotradhartis **27**.59cd-62ab
hour of death, Kṛṣṇa remembered at **192**.75-86
- of death, remembering of Viṣṇu at **229**.56-58 .64-67ab
hours, auspicious **221**.21
- for ancestral rites, auspicious **220**.120cd
hours see also *date(s), moment*
house of Kṛṣṇa, merit of looking at **212**.9-11
- , prescr. conc. cleaning of **221**.123-125ab
householder and ascetic **222**.32-35
- , duties of **221**.1-3; **222**.28-38
- , effect(s) of conduct of **222**.37-38
, importance of stage of **222**.32-35
- in simile, tree and **164**.9cd-13
- , stage of **88**.10-15
Hrada **3**.64cd-70ab .86cd-89ab
Hrāda **3**.64cd-70ab
Hṛdayā **17**.12-16
Hṛdīka **16**.4-6
Hrī **137**.8-14
Hṛṣīkeśa **50**.55-59; **60**.39-45; **184**.14-19; **213**.81-104; **226**.11-12 .65cd-67ab
Hūhū **36**.63cd-70
Hūhūs **32**.97cd-99ab
huṃ as Mantra **206**.24-30
human body, development of **179**.47cd-61
- flesh, eating of **186**.1-3
- life, suffering in **234**.9-42
- nature of Kṛṣṇa **189**.1-13; **195**.13-18; **204**.5-7
- nature of Kṛṣṇa, divine and **193**.80-87
- nature of Kṛṣṇa explained as Māyā **193**.80-87
- sacrifice **104**.89ab
human being birth of **217**.23-24
constituents of **217**.14-17
- demon as **187**.8-18
- rebirth as **19**.24; **27**.69-70; **216**.73-80; **229**.4-7; **241**.45-47
- river as **198**.12-14
- sixteen constituents of **236**.14; **237**.7-14; **240**.22cd-26
- Viṣṇu as **179**.62-64
human being see also *man*
human beings, classification of **237**.15-16
- , constituents of **237**.23-25
- , life-span of **20**.14-15 .80cd-82ab
Hūṇas **19**.18
Huṇḍa **3**.86cd-89ab
hundred and eight holy places **146**.42-45
- and eight names of Śiva **143**.2-5
- and eight names of sun **33**.33-46
- and eight years, worship during **176**.33-34
- horse-sacrifices **8**.59cd-61
- Rudras **3**.50
- sons of Danu **3**.73cd-74ab
- sons, religious practices for obtainment of **124**.132-136ab
- years, drought of **232**.14-23
- years, rain of **232**.30-40
hunger and thirst, affliction by **52**.11-15ab
- and thirst, freedom from 7.37a-d
- , boon by **85**.15-16
- , hymn by Kaṇva to **85**.12-14
- praised by Kaṇva **85**.9-10
hunter and Brahmin **169**
- as devotee of Śiva **169**.6cd-15 .39cd-43ab .43cd-45ef
- , description of **80**.6cd-9; **169**.25-32
- , Śiva as **102**.5cd
- , Umā and Śiva worshipped by **169**.16-22ab
hunters, punishment for **22**.25
hurting of cow **7**.43
- of tree, punishment for **215**.124cd-125ab
husband and wife as fire and water **144**.15-16 .20-22
- and wife, congruence of qualities of **165**.18-22
- and wife, harmony between **138**.10-13
- and wife, maxim about **80**.37-43; **109**.6cd -10; **128**.3-6; **129**.101-124
- and wife, punishment for separating of **215**.93cd-94ab .130cd-136ab
- as refuge, maxim about **111**.68cd-79
- , condemnation of self-choice of **219**.13-17
- , maxim about acceptance of **111**.57-60
- obtained according to merit **111**.57-60

- obtained by asceticism **2**.1-4; **15**.16-21; **71**.24-26
- of Mother of the world, Viṣṇu as **163**.43-46
- of plants, Soma as **119**.18-19
- , pleasing of **111**.64-68ab
- , Puruṣottama as **212**.72-85
- , wife as friend of **129**.101-124; **167**.22-25
- , wife as half of **161**.33cd-35ab

husbands, wives proud of **203**.64-69

Hutahavyavaha **3**.37-38cd

hymn by Aditi to Kṛṣṇa **203**.6-19
- by Aditi to sun **32**.12-16
- by Agni to Śiva **128**.44-45
- by Akrūra to Viṣṇu **192**.48-58
- by Aṅgiras to sun **32**.93cd-95ab
- by ancestors to Viṣṇu **219**.31-35
- by Āpastamba to Śiva **130**.23-31
- by Āsandiva to Viṣṇu **167**.30
- by Ātreya to Indra **140**.21ef-25
- by Bhagīratha to Śiva **78**.56-58
- by Bṛhaspati to Śiva **122**.74-82
- by Brahman to Śiva **36**.39cd-42
- by Brahman to Viṣṇu **181**.21-25
- by Dakṣa to Śiva **40**.2-100; **109**.30-35
- by Dattātreya to Śiva **117**.7-17
- by Death to Śiva **116**.15-16
- by Devāpi to Śiva **127**.48-53
- by Dhanvantari to Viṣṇu **122**.29-43
- by earth to Viṣṇu **202**.23-29
- by Gautama **107**.55-57
- by Gautama to Śiva **75**.4-24
- by Gautama to Umā **75**.4-24
- by gods to Devakī **182**.7-8
- by gods to Gaṇeśa **114**.6-18
- by gods to Māṇḍavya **96**.11-17
- by gods to Puruṣottama **65**.21-22
- by gods to Śiva **37**.2-23; **71**.38-40ab; **94**.27-30; **110**.134-136; **112**.4-6
- by gods to sun **32**.89-90ab
- by gods to Viṣṇu **65**.49-51; **71**.7-12; **109**.41-42; **213**.72-73
- by Heti to Agni **125**.15-17
- by Indra to Śiva and Umā **129**.68-81
- by Indra to Viṣṇu **122**.68-73
- by Indradyumna to Viṣṇu **49**.1-59; **51**.10-16
- by Kaṇḍu to Viṣṇu **178**.114-117 .128-177
- by Kaṇva to Godāvarī **85**.12-14
- by Kaṇva to Hunger **85**.12-14
- by Kaśyapa to Śiva **100**.19-21; **124**.94-99
- by Kubera to Śiva **97**.20-23
- by Lomaharṣaṇa to Viṣṇu **1**.21-29
- by Madhucchandas to Sūrya **138**.33-34
- by Mārkaṇḍeya to Viṣṇu **55**.11-35
- by Mucukunda to Kṛṣṇa **196**.30-45
- by Pailūṣa to Śiva **139**.13-17ef
- by Pippalāda to Śiva **110**.100-106
- by plants to Gautamī **119**.9-12
- by Rāma to Śiva **123**.195-206
- by Śeṣa to Śiva **115**.7-9
- by Śukra to Śiva **95**.18-21
- by Śveta to Viṣṇu **59**.34-72
- by sages to Śiva **116**.14
- by sages to Viṣṇu **126**.24-27
- by Ulūkī to Yama **125**.23-24ef
- by Viṣṇu to Śiva **109**.51
- by Vyāsa to Viṣṇu **180**.1-12
- , effect(s) of recitation of **75**.32
- from Ṛgveda, recitation of **60**.46-48; **219**.65cd-71ab
- , grammatical order of cases represented in **130**.23-31
- , Kaśyapa in vedic **174**.16
- , merit of recitation of **85**.19-23; **114**.21 -24; **124**.123-131; **125**.44-49 .50-53
- to Kṛṣṇa **57**.32-37
- to Śaṃkara and Gaurī **108**.104-108
- to Śiva, son obtained by **124**.136c-f
- to sun **33**.9-23
- to sun, merit of **31**.33cd-34

hymn see also *praise, prayer*

hymns of Veda(s), gods obedient to **127**.29-34
- , recitation of **50**.16-17; **51**.40-41; **67**.35cd -39ab

iconographic attributes of Balarāma **57**.20-28
- attributes of Gaṇeśa **114**.13
- attributes of Kṛṣṇa **50**.43cd-44ab; **53**.31-33; **57**.38-41; **192**.32-42
- attributes of Śeṣa **21**.15-27
- attributes of sun **28**.30-31; **33**.14cd-15ab
- attributes of Vāsudeva **44**.14-15; **50**.4-6; **207**.13-24
- attributes of Viṣṇu **49**.10-20; **51**.10-16; **59**.73-77; **61**.41-45ab .52-55; **68**.44-53; **79**.7cd-19; **109**.43-45; **122**.44-47; **126**.23; **136**.3cd-14ab; **145**.5cd-7; **156**.1-2ab; **163**.32-39; **176**.8-10 .21-25; **177**.1-2; **178**.122-127; **203**.6-19; **210**.47-48; **219**.31-35; **226**.22cd-23ab; **228**.8-14

ideal ascetic, Gautama as **74**.22cd-38ab

- conditions of life **74**.24cd-30; **153**.6cd-7
- king **44**.2-7
- king, Arjuna Kārtavīrya as **13**.172-173
- king, Rāma as **213**.145-153ab
- king, worship of Pṛthu as **4**.115-121
- kingdom **4**.58-59; **73**.2-6; **123**.2-7ab; **153**.6cd-7; **213**.145-153ab
- places for settlement **221**.103-108
- pupil **121**.10-12
- pupil, maxim about **121**.13-15
- son, Harṣaṇa as **165**.37-44
- son, maxim about **170**.8ef-13
identification by meditation **28**.26
identity of father and son **148**.8-14ab; **165**.5-17
- of individual and universal self **236**.21-23 .24-25 .54-56ab; **237**.17-19 .32; **245**.27-30
- of Kṛṣṇa and Śiva **206**.45-48
- of Sāṃkhya and Yoga **243**.20
- of Self and elements **237**.45
- of Viṣṇu and Ananta **226**.65cd-67ab
- of Viṣṇu and Śiva **56**.61-66ab .66cd-73
- with gods, wish for **213**.53-57
identity see also *absorption, oneness, union, unity*
idol see *image, statue*
ignorance concerning highest reality **203**.6-19
- , effect(s) of **206**.45-48
- in simile **244**.23-39
- in simile, knowledge and **234**.58-60ab
- , knowledge and **22**.48-49ab; **241**.21-22; **244**.2-9
- removed by power of holy place **130**.34
- , thirst caused by **139**.7cd-11
Ikṣu **20**.66-67
Ikṣvāku **5**.37cd-38ab; **7**.1-2 .19cd-21ab .44cd-45ab .48cd-51ab; **78**.3-8ab; **213**.158
- , descendants of **7**.44cd-109
ikṣvāku, etymology of **7**.44cd-45ab
Ikṣvāku-family **10**.50cd-53ab
Ila **108**
- and Yakṣas, fight between **108**.18-20ab
Ilā **7**.3-19ab; **9**.33-34; **13**.53; **72**.11cd-14; **108**; **113**.10-14; **226**.30-41
- [name of libation] **175**.60-68
Ilāsaṃgama, place of pilgrimage **105**.22-26ab
Ilātīrtha, place of pilgrimage **108**.1
Ilāvṛta **18**.18-20
- , extent of **18**.21-23ab
Ileśvara, Liṅga named **108**.121-123
illusion, actions ascribed to **193**.88-90
- destroyed by knowledge **139**.18
Ilvala **3**.74cd-78ab .86cd-89ab
image at Puruṣottamakṣetra, installation of **176**.52-56
- from ocean, emergence of **176**.52-56
- of Vāsudeva **176**.21-25
- of Vāsudeva, worship of **176**.12-15ab
- , theft of **176**.21-25
image see also *statue*
imitated world of Indra, destruction of **140**.31-34
immanence of Viṣṇu **179**.38-43ab
immaterial, material and **130**.17-21
- , superiority of the **130**.7-14
immobility of Liṅgas **157**.25cd-27ab
- of mind during meditation **237**.29-31
immortality caused by *amṛta* **104**.7cd-9
- caused by son **104**.7cd-9
- , clouds raining water of **93**.12-24
- , nectar of **106**.8-10ab; **140**.7-11; **142**.2-4; **159**.41cd-46ab
- , Soma as nectar of **119**.13-17
- , water of Gautamī as nectar of **133**.13-17
immortality see also *amṛta*
imperishable perishable and **241**.1-2 .34-36ab; **243**.37-40; **244**.11-42
- *prakṛti* as **244**.11-14ab
- Self, perishable and **236**.32 .35
importance of counteraction, maxim about **127**.16-22
- of Daṇḍaka-forest **161**.72-78
- of devotion **29**.15-17
- of feeding of Brahmins **123**.140-146
- of mother, maxim about **158**.4-7
- of plants **120**.9-13
- of saving one's life, maxim about **228**.44-46
- of son **104**.5-7ab; **220**.32cd
- of son, maxim about **108**.76cd-87
- of stage of householder **222**.32-35
- of Sunday **29**.31cd-32ab
- of teacher **158**.22-27ef
- of women **129**.49-64
- of Yogin at ancestral rites **220**.109cd-112ab
impossibility of description of Kṛṣṇa **65**.59-76ab
- of description of ocean **62**.22cd-23
- of looking at Kṛṣṇa **53**.39-40

- of looking at Śiva **162**.13-19
- of praise **49**.56cd-57ab; **55**.35ab; **185**.39-42 .44-49; **202**.23-29
- of revoking a given word **110**.191cd-194ab
impossibility of knowing see *unknowability*
impossibility of praise see also *abbreviating formula, unworthiness*
imprisonment of Devakī and Vasudeva **181**.33-35
impurity of dogs **221**.53-54
- , punishment for **22**.23cd-24ab
impurity see also *pollution, untouchability*
inability to praise see *impossibility of praise*
inadequacy of praise **55**.35c-f; **127**.48-53
inauspicious date(s) **221**.42
- events as omen(s) **184**.42cd-52ab
- moment, death at **228**.76-85
- persons **221**.77
incarnation of gods, partial **181**.32
- of Indra, Arjuna as partial **188**.39-41
- of Kāma, Pradyumna as **200**.23-28
- of sun, partial **32**.17-31
- of two hairs of Viṣṇu **181**.26-31
- of Viṣṇu, Buddha as **122**.68-73
- of Viṣṇu, Kṛṣṇa and Balarāma as partial **190**.10-19
- of Viṣṇu, Kṛṣṇa as partial **193**.32-40; **195**.13-18; **196**.23-29; **202**.23-29
- of Viṣṇu, purpose of **56**.35cd-38ab; **180**.24cd-38; **181**.1 .2-4; **185**.5-10; **187**.22-25; **188**.29-35; **193**.80-87; **202**.23-29; **210**.16-21; **212**.59-62
incarnation see also *aspects, body, forms, manifestation, shape*
incarnations of Viṣṇu **56**.39cd-42; **59**.35-64; **122**.68-73; **178**.166cd-176; **179**.2-75; **180** .24cd-38; **184**.14-19; **191**.4-12
- of Viṣṇu, four **61**.39-40
incarnations of Viṣṇu see also *Balarāma, boar, Buddha, dwarf, fish, Kṛṣṇa, man-lion, Rāma, Rāma Jāmadagnya, tortoise*
incense, offering of **67**.24-27
incest committed by Brahman **102**
- , punishment for **215**.130cd-136ab
incompleteness of *dharma* **122**.54cd-62
inconvenience(s) of Brahminhood **230**.66-69
- of wealth **230**.72-74
India, geography of **19**; **27**.14-80
India see also *Bhāratavarṣa*
indifference achieved by meditation **238**.31-33ab
- , maxim about **139**.2cd-7ab
- of outlook **236**.20
- , renunciation based on **153**.4-6ab
- towards women **81**.7cd-12
- towards worldly objects **122**.3-7
indifference see also *detachment, renunciation*
individual and universal self, identity of **236**.21-23 .24-25 .54-56ab; **237**.17-19 .32; **245**.27-30
- self, origin of **161**.6cd-9
Indra 3.53-58 .109cd-122; **7**.104cd-105ab; **8**.10cd .77cd-84ab; **10**.24-28ab .46cd-49ab; **11**.3 .24cd-26ab; **12**.6cd-8 .11-17; **13**.37-39 .109; **14**.4-7 .20cd-24ab; **17**.32-34; **18**.52-55; **30**.23-26 .28-39; **31**.17-18 .19-21 .22-26; **32**.90cd-91ab; **33**.9-13ab; **34**.42-45ab; **36**.23cd-24ab .31-36ab; **51**.1-8; **56**.13-15; **59**.1-2; **61**.45cd-46; **78**.12-24; **80**.46-55; **86**.11-16 .17-19 .20-21 .22-26 .27-29 .30-34 .47-49ab; **87**.66cd-69; **96**; **100**.4cd-6; **105**.11cd-13; **108**.116-118; **109**.13-20 .21-26ab; **110**.10-20; **122**.48-99 .68-73; **128**.29-37; **131**.10-15; **160**.6cd-9; **162**.20-27ab; **173**.29cd-33ab; **178**.12-18 .25-27 .59-60 .90-98; **179**.18cd-22ab .27-28; **191**.4-12; **192**.48-58; **213**.53-57 .81-104; **236**.9
- and Agni, rice-cake for **133**.2-4
- and Ahalyā **87**
- and Apsarases **147**.9cd-13
- and Bṛhaspati **122**.63-67ab .87-92
- and Diti **124**.87-140
- and Indrāṇī **129**.42-125
- and Maruts **168**.28cd-29; **171**.2cd-6cd
- and Maya **124**.33-48
- and Paulomī **129**.42-125
- and Pramati **171**
- and Soma **174**.18
- and Viśvāmitra **147**.17cd-20ab
- and Vṛṣākapi **129**.42-125
- , anger of **188**.1
- anointed by Bṛhaspati **122**.93-94
- , Arjuna as partial incarnation of **188**.39-41
- as cat **87**.50-52ab
- as falcon **93**.12-24
- as Gautama **87**.42-43

- as lord of gods **131**.16-24
- as lord of Maruts **4**.2-9
- as lord of rains **187**.35-40
- as lotus-filament **96**.2-5ab
- as name of Śiva **158**.22-27ef
- as offender against teacher's wife **96**.8-10
- as prisoner in nether world **129**.11cd-16
- as prisoner of Mahāśani **129**.20cd-29
- as protector of good people **140**.7-11
- as servant of Varuṇa **129**.38-41
- as slayer of Vṛtra **140**.19cd-21cd .21ef-25
- as son of Raji **11**.19cd-21ab
- , attendant(s) of **3**.109cd-122
- , Ātreya in heaven of **140**.5cd-6ef
- born as Gādhi **10**.24-28ab; **13**.88-90
- , Brahman as creator of **129**.30-37
- , city of **140**.7-11; **147**.5-7
- , clouds instructed by **188**.2-5
- consoled by Paulomī **129**.42-48
- , curse by **84**.13-15; **131**.10-15
- cursed by Agastya **124**.73cd-80
- cursed by Diti **124**.73cd-80
- cursed by Gautama **87**.58cd-59
- defeated by Kṛṣṇa **203**.45-62
- defeated by Mahāśani **129**.11cd-16
- defeated by Meghanāda **176**.19cd-20
- , description of splendour of **140**.7-11
- , destruction of imitated world of **140**.31-34
- disguised as Brahmin **87**.34cd-35; **124**.39cd-47
- , duplication of city of **140**.14-18ab
- , elephant of **13**.43-44
- , epithets of **140**.21ef-25
- expelled from lordship over gods **122**.48-49
- , fight between Kṛṣṇa and **203**.45-62
- , hymn by Ātreya to **140**.21ef-25
- imitated by Ātreya **140**.14-18ab
- in simile **43**.1; **123**.2-7ab; **146**.2-8ab; **189**.58c-f
- in womb of Aditi **179**.27-28
- in womb of Diti **124**.49-86
- , Kaśyapa as father of **124**.83-86
- , king as friend of **168**.28cd-29
- , kings in world of **171**.2cd-6cd
- , Kṛṣṇa and **188**; **194**.13-17
- , Kṛṣṇa anointed by **188**.36-37
- , Kṛṣṇa as guest of **203**.24-25
- , Kṛṣṇa praised by **203**.70-73
- , *lakṣmī* of **122**.8-20
- , lunar mansion sacred to **63**.22
- , Maruts as friends of **124**.100-107 .137-139ab
- , Maya as friend of **124**.28cd-31
- , Namuci killed by **124**.33-36ab; **129**.4-8
- , noose of **171**.10-13
- obedient to Kṛṣṇa **194**.13-17
- , obstacle(s) to consecration of **96**.8-10
- , obtained at place of pilgrimage, rank of **140**.35-38
- of demons, Prahlāda as **11**.8-16
- on earth **140**.19cd-21cd
- , opposition of Kṛṣṇa and **188**.11-13; **203**.26-73
- , origin of **161**.43cd-50cd
- , place of pilgrimage sacred to **168**.1
- , Pramati as friend of **171**.44-46
- , promise by Kṛṣṇa to **188**.42-47
- protected by Viṣṇu **179**.27-28
- , provocation of **187**.41
- , rank of **73**.52-55; **129**.101-124; **151**.27cd-29
- , rebirth as **27**.66cd-68
- , sacrifice to **174**.13-17
- , snakes healed by **159**.39ef-41ab
- , son like **10**.24-28ab; **13**.88-90; **124**.123-131
- , Sutrāman **110**.104
- taunted by Mahāśani **129**.30-37
- , thousand eyes of **87**.66cd-69; **124**.39cd-47
- to Goddess, prayer by **129**.79-80
- to Śiva and Umā, hymn by **129**.68-81
- to Viṣṇu, hymn by **122**.68-73
- , Vāsudeva worshipped by **176**.12-15ab
- , Viṣṇu praised by **129**.94-99ab
- , Vṛṣākapi as friend of **129**.99cd-100ef .101-124
- , world of **51**.29-31; **67**.64cd-75; **140**.5cd-6ef; **227**.16-32ab; **228**.146-151
- , world without **129**.20cd-29
- , Yoganidrā as sister of **181**.38-53

Indra see also *Hari, Śakra, Śatakratu, Sahasrākṣa, Vāsava*

Indradvīpa **19**.6cd-7ab; **27**.14-16

Indradyumna **43**; **44**; **45**; **47**; **48**; **49**; **50**; **51**; **66**.6-7ab; **70**.8cd-10
- [-lake], place of pilgrimage **45**.77-89
- , boon by Puruṣottama to **66**.7cd-13
- , boon by Viṣṇu to **49**.60; **50**.33-40; **51**.1-8

.22-45
- , statue consecrated by **51**.48-53
- to Viṣṇu, hymn by **49**.1-59; **51**.10-16
Indradyumna-Māhātmya **70**.11
Indradyumnasara, place of pilgrimage **25**.79
Indradyumnasaras, place of pilgrimage **25**.79; **63**.1-7
Indradyumna-tank **60**.11; **66**.6-7ab
- , bathing in **43**.14
- , merit obtained at **51**.29-31
Indra-festival **187**.31-34
Indragopa [mountain] **174**.25cd-27ab
Indrajit **3**.74cd-78ab; **176**.37-51
Indrajita, explanation of **176**.19cd-20
Indramārga, place of pilgrimage **25**.54
Indrāṇī, Indra and **129**.42-125
- , jealousy of **129**.99cd-100ef
Indranīla **46**.24-30
Indraprastha **212**.34
Indrasenā **13**.97
Indratāpana **3**.64cd-70ab; **213**.81-104
Indratīrtha, place of pilgrimage **87**.70-71; **96**.1; **122**.100-102; **124**.137-139ab; **129**.1-2; **168**.30
Indratīrtha see also *Aindratīrtha*
Indravajrā-metre **19**.25-27; **38**.17-19; **49**.68; **75**.4 .8 .9 .10 .19 .22 .23; **94**.27-30; **105**.18cd-19; **108**.105-106 .107-108; **116**.14; **138**.4-7; **175**.78; **191**.27-33; **213**.170; **220**.212; **238**.39
Indravaṃśā-metre **74**.88
Indreśvara, Liṅga named **129**.3
Indreśvaratīrtha, place of pilgrimage **129**.101-124
inequality of opponents **193**.42-49
inevitability of suffering **242**.34-39
infant(s), attempt of killing of **182**.27-30; **200**.2-10
- , exchange of **182**.19-26; **190**.1-5
- , killing of **181**.33-35 .38-53; **183**.1-7
infant(s) see also *child*
influence of planets **118**.24cd-30
information by means of meditation **87**.60-66ab
- provided by Nārada **78**.37cd-44; **109**.10cd-12; **181**.33-35; **190**.1-5; **196**.5-8; **200**.2-10 .23-28; **206**.10-13
information see also *knowledge*
ingredients of ancestral rites, prescription(s) concerning **220**.154-188
- of ancestral rites, prescr. conc. forbidden **220**.168-177
- of offerings to ancestors **220**.61cd-62ab
- of worship of Narasiṃha **58**.24-25
ingredients see also *constituents*
Iṅgudi-fruits, oil-cake from **123**.170-172
inhabitants of Avantī **43**.30-44
- of east **27**.51cd-53
- of Ekāmraka **41**.20-37ab
- of Meru **45**.5-7
- of middle region **27**.41cd-42
- of mountains **27**.62cd-64ab
- of north **27**.43-50
- of Puruṣottamakṣetra **44**.70-72; **46**.7cd-10
- of south **27**.54-57
- of Utkala **42**.32-33
- of Vindhya-mountains **4**.42-47; **27**.59cd-62ab
- of world of Viṣṇu **68**.23-27ab
inheritage of friends and enemies, maxim about **110**.80ef-86
initiation, liberation by **227**.6-7
- with sacred thread **107**.2-11; **111**.7-8
insect of womb see *womb-insect*
insects, liberation for worms and **161**.72-78
- , origin of worms and **161**.43cd-50cd
instability of meditation, death as result of **237**.28
installation of image at Puruṣottamakṣetra **176**.52-56
installation-ceremony **67**
- , merit of **67**.52-80
instruction by Brahmins **225**.54-55
- of Nārada **30**.45-86
instruments, musical **32**.102-103; **65**.12-16; **193**.24-31; **214**.110-114ab
- of oppression **225**.31-35 .36-41
intelligence of people, difference of **225**.46-52
intention, action and **173**.9-25
intercourse between mother and son, sexual **92**.2-11
- during ancestral rites, effect(s) of sexual **220**.106-109ab
- , effect(s) of forbidden sexual **225**.52
- , origin of sexual **45**.37-41
- , prescription(s) concerning sexual **221**.42 .71 .75
- , procreation by sexual **2**.50; **3**.3-7ab
- , punishment for forbidden sexual

22.12cd-13; **214**.120-128; **215**.72-77 .120cd-121ab; **217**.77cd-80ab
- through mouth, sexual **6**.41-43
- with daughter, punishment for sexual **22**.12ab
- with daughter-in-law, punishment for sexual **22**.12ab
- with sister, punishment for sexual **22**.10
- with teacher's wife, expiation for sexual **81**.16-22ab
- with teacher's wife, punishment for sexual **22**.10
- with wives, punishment for forbidden sexual **22**.21-22
interference by wife **125**.13-14 .22
intermediate space, origin of **161**.43cd-50cd
intervention by gods **213**.60-65
- by moon **2**.34-46
intoxication by liquor **137**.15-24
intoxication see also *drunkenness*
inverted worlds **22**.31
investiture ceremony for ancestors **220**.69cd -70
invincibility of Bali **13**.32-35; **73**.2-6
- of Candramas **152**.9cd-14
- of Kṛṣṇa **203**.22 .70-73
- of Kuvalāśva **7**.85-86
- of Narasiṃha **58**.26-27
invincible child **3**.109cd-122
- son, wish for **173**.6cd-8ef
invisibility of third eye of Śiva **110**.112-114
invitation of Brahmins for ancestral rites **220**.105
involvement as highest *dharma* **240**.77-80
Irā **3**.51-52 .104-105
iron, eating of powdered **196**.1-4
- tip of lance swallowed by fish **210**.11-14
Iṣa **5**.17d-19ab
Īśa **120**.3cd-5; **160**.20; **168**.10-12; **175**.1-2ef
- as name of Viṣṇu **171**.44-46
Īśā, Gaṅgā as **119**.13-17
Īśāna **61**.45cd-46; **123**.121-128ab; **131**.31-39ab; **139**.7cd-11
Īśāna see also *Śiva*
Īśānatīrtha, place of pilgrimage **25**.46
Īśānī **72**.9cd-10ab
island in Gautamī **160**.13-16ef
- , substitution of earth and **151**.22cd-24ab
Iṣutīrtha, place of pilgrimage **25**.80
Īśvara **3**.46cd-49; **33**.13cd-14ab; **56**.61-66ab; **139**.7cd-11 .12
Īṭāspada, place of pilgrimage **25**.41
Itihāsas **42**.38cd-42ab; **43**.85cd-88; **44**.10-12; **67**.35cd-39ab; **217**.33-35
- and Purāṇas, origin of **161**.27-29
Itihāsa-tradition, Gautamī-Māhātmya and **175**.76-77
Jābālā [wife of Maudgalya] **136**.1cd-3ab
- [wife of Maudgalya], request by **136**.14cd -16
Jābāli **91**.2cd-6ab; **123**.77-81; **145**.2cd-5ab; **174**.2-5ab
Jagannātha, Śiva as **109**.35; **110**.98-99ef
- , sun as **138**.35-38
- , Vāsudeva as **45**.16cd-17ef
Jagatī-metre **97**.20-23; **107**.41; **110**.21-70; **124**.3cd-6; **129**.30-37 .68-81; **140**.19cd-21cd; **150**.15-20; **157**.15-18cd .18ef-21ab; **174**.2-5ab .5cd-6ab; **191**.27 -33; **229**.37-88; **238**.12-14
Jagṛhu **14**.20cd-24ab
Jāhnavī **10**.9-10; **69**.12-43
Jāhnavī, explanation of **10**.18cd-19ab
Jahnu **5**.20cd-21; **10**.13-14 .15-20 .21-23; **13**.82cd-87 .88-90 .92ab
- , Gaṅgā drunk up by **10**.15-18cd; **13**.82cd -87
Jaigīṣavya **34**.92-93ab
Jaigīṣavyaguhā, place of pilgrimage **25**.62
Jaigīṣavyavana, place of pilgrimage **25**.62
Jaiminīyabrāhmaṇa **129**.4-8
Jaitra [chariot of Viṣṇu] **210**.47-48
Jalada **20**.59cd-61
Jaladhāra **20**.62-63
Jaleyu **13**.5-8
Jamadagni **5**.34-35; **10**.50cd-53ab .53cd-54; **13**.91
- , Bhārgava **10**.46cd-49ab
- , birth of **10**.28cd-50ab
Jāmadagnī [Gaṅgā] **173**.3-6ab
Jāmadagnya see *Rāma Jāmadagnya*
Jāmbavat **16**.25-45ab; **154**.8cd-11ab; **176**.37-51
Jāmbavatī **16**.25-45ab; **201**.3-5; **205**.1-6
Jambūdvīpa **18**; **19**.28 .29; **20**.1-2; **47**.62; **70**.20-22ab
Jambumārga, place of pilgrimage **64**.3-8ab
Jambūmārga, place of pilgrimage **25**.25
Jāmbūnada, gold named **18**.24cd-28
Jambūnadī **18**.24cd-28

Jambū-tree **18**.23cd-24ab
Janaka **30**.14-18; **83**.29; **88**.2-3 .4-7 .16-19 .21-26; **123**.97-105ab; **213**.142-144
- and Yājñavalkya, Varuṇa as teacher of **88**
Janaka see also *Karālajanaka*
Janakakūpa, place of pilgrimage **25**.71
Janakas **88**.21-26
Janaloka **23**.12-15 .16-20; **180**.24cd-38; **232**.28-29; **233**.5-6
Janamejaya **12**.9-10 .11-17; **13**.15cd-20ab .45-48 .109 .110-111 .112-113
- , Pārīkṣita **13**.123-124
Jānamejaya-power **13**.125
Janārdana **20**.40cd-41ab .56cd-57ab; **24**.1-7ab; **43**.6-9 .77-82ab; **50**.1-3; **56**.74; **86**.8-9ab; **109**.39cd-40; **122**.24cd-27; **129**.94-99ab; **151**.17-22ab; **161**.39cd-43ab; **163**.26-31 .40-42 .47-49; **165**.47cd-48ef; **170**.44-46; **171**.44-46; **178**.43-53; **181**.2-4; **184**.14-19; **189**.58c-f; **190**.9; **192**.43-47; **193**.24-31; **194**.18-22 .32; **207**.13-24; **216**.87-89; **219**.30 .52-60ab; **229**.37-43ab
- as Rudra **232**.30-40
Janārdana see also *Kṛṣṇa, Viṣṇu*
Janasthāna **89**.25cd-33; **92**.2-11; **213**.127-135
- , place of pilgrimage **88**.1 .21-26
Jāṅgalas **27**.43-50
Janoloka **23**.12-15
Jantu **13**.100-101
Jānudhi **18**.32-36ab
Jarā **210**.11-14
Jaras **210**.11-14; **211**.5-10
Jarāsaṃdha **12**.11-17; **195**; **196**.9-15; **199**.1-4 .5-10; **226**.42-45ab
- and Kṛṣṇa, battle between **195**.1-4
- , eighteen defeats of **195**.8-12
Jarāsaṃdha-episode **195**
Jārudhi **18**.46cd-50
Jaṭādharatīrtha, place of pilgrimage **100**.31cd
Jātaka **11**.51-53
Jātavedas, Agni **127**.29-34; **173**.26-28
- [brother of Agni], Agni and **98**
- killed by Madhu **98**.2-5
Jātavedasa, place of pilgrimage **98**.21cd-22
Jaṭāyu, Saṃpāti and **166**
Jaṭhara **18**.32-36ab .46cd-50
Jātīhrada, place of pilgrimage **25**.81
Jaya **10**.57-60; **11**.27cd-31
Jayā **109**.10cd-12 .13-20
- [daughter of Umā] **74**.13-22ab .59-67
- [wife of Ārṣṭiṣeṇa] **127**.2-4ab
Jayadhvaja **13**.199cd-202
Jayadratha **13**.45-48; **212**.12-17
Jayanta [Indra's son] **140**.7-11
Jayantī **215**.94cd-95ab
Jayatsena **11**.27cd-31
Jaya-verse **1**.1-2
jealousy, maxim about **152**.9cd-14
- of gods **123**.7cd-14ab
- of Indrāṇī **129**.99cd-100ef
- of Umā **74**.13-22ab
jewel named Syamantaka **16**.12-45ab; **17**
- , prosperity effected by magic **16**.13-24; **17**.24-27
jewels, punishment for faking of **22**.14cd-15a
Jīgarti [= Ajīgarti] **150**
Jīmūta **15**.24-28; **20**.22-23 .29-30
Jirikāvāsa, place of pilgrimage **25**.54
Jiṣṇu **212**.29-33
Jīva **95**.2-6
- [Bṛhaspati] **152**.2-4 .9cd-14 .26-28
Jñānatīrtha, place of pilgrimage **139**.19
Jñāneśvara, Liṅga named **117**.1
joy, son as source of **165**.37-44
jugglery, punishment for **22**.23cd-24ab
Juhu **13**.109
juice, punishment for selling of **22**.18cd-20
Jupiter and Leo, conjunction of **152**.37cd-39ef; **175**.83-84
Jupiter see also *Bṛhaspati*
Jyāmagha **15**.1-12ab .12cd-13
- and Śaibyā **15**.16-21
Jyeṣṭha **31**.19-21; **67**.2-5
- , auspiciousness of **45**.77-89; **63**.8-9 .11-16; **64**
- , bathing of Hari in **65**.3
Jyeṣṭhā **63**.22; **220**.33cd-42
Jyeṣṭhālika, place of pilgrimage **25**.71
Jyeṣṭhālikā, place of pilgrimage **25**.71
Jyeṣṭhasthānahrada, place of pilgrimage **25**.62
Jyotiḥsthala **39**.4-6
Jyotis **5**.13cd-15ab
Jyotiṣmat **5**.9cd-10; **20**.36-38ab
Kabandha **213**.136-140
Kaca [son of Bṛhaspati] **95**.28cd-30
Kacchapa **10**.57-60
Kadalīhrada, place of pilgrimage **25**.21
Kadamba-tree **18**.23cd-24ab; **185**.5-10
- , liquor flowing from **198**.4-6

Kādravā [river] **100**.1-3
Kādravāsaṃgama as place of pilgrimage **100**.1-3
Kadru **3**.51-52 .97cd-98
- , Nāgas as descendants of **3**.97cd-98
Kadrū **100**.4cd-6 .25-29ab .31cd
- and Vinatā **159**
- , Garuḍa reproached by **159**.28-31ab
Kaikeya **13**.25cd-27ab
Kaikeyas **13**.25cd-27ab; **27**.43-50
Kaikeyī **123**.2-7ab .84-86ab
- instigated by Mantharā **123**.105cd-109ab
- , three boons granted to **123**.23-33ab
Kailāsa **18**.46cd-50; **34**.1-6; **75**.2-3; **78**.47-54
- as abode of Śiva and Umā **143**.7-11
- in simile **21**.15-27
- , Śiva and Umā on **110**.102-103
- shaken by Rāvaṇa **143**.7-11
Kaiśika **15**.16-21
Kaiṭabha **4**.112; **118**.10-14
- , boon by Viṣṇu to Madhu and **213**.28-29
- killed by Viṣṇu, Madhu and **180**.24cd-38; **213**.28-29
Kaitava, place of pilgrimage **171**.47-49ef
Kākola **215**.109cd-110ab
Kakṣeyu **13**.5-8 .14cd-15ab
- , descendants of **13**.14cd-49
Kakudmat **20**.25-27
Kakudmin **7**.37ef-41
- , Raivata **7**.29cd
Kakutstha **7**.51cd-53; **12**.3
Kāla **3**.37-38cd .64cd-70ab; **13**.147-148ab; **59**.6-21
- , Viṣṇu as **56**.39cd-42
Kāla see also *date(s), time*
- see also *death, Yama*
Kālaka **213**.81-104
Kālakā **3**.80cd-83
Kālakeyas **3**.80cd-83 .84-86ab
Kālakopa **213**.81-104
Kālakūṭa [poison] **112**.4-6
Kālanābha **3**.72-73ab .86cd-89ab
Kālānala **13**.15cd-20ab
Kālanemi **179**.22cd-26; **181**.7-14 .26-31
- reborn as Kaṃsa **181**.7-14
Kālañjara **13**.37-39; **18**.32-36ab; **214**.114cd-119
- , Liṅga named **146**.1
- , place of pilgrimage **64**.8cd-9; **146**.42-45
- , Śiva as **147**.8-9ab
Kālarātrī **106**.43-45ab; **215**.45-55ab
Kālaśambara **200**.2-10
Kālasarpas **8**.44-51
Kālasūtra **215**.126cd-127ab
Kālatīrtha, place of pilgrimage **25**.76
Kālatīrthaka, place of pilgrimage **25**.77
Kālatoyadas **27**.43-50
Kālavadana **213**.81-104
Kālayavana **196**
- , birth of **14**.48-50ab
Kālayavana, explanation of **14**.50cd-56
Kali [brother of Havyaghna] **133**.5-8
Kālī **13**.120
Kālidhanas **27**.58cd
Kālikā **3**.80cd-83
Kālikāśrama, place of pilgrimage **25**.33 .49
Kālin **13**.109
Kālindī **201**.3-5; **205**.1-6
- [Yamunā] **185**.1-4
Kaliṅga **13**.30-31; **47**.7-9; **201**.10-22
Kaliṅgas **13**.36; **19**.16; **27**.41cd-42 .43-50 .54-57; **220**.8-10ab; **231**.68-71ab
Kāliya **189**.2-8; **190**.1-5; **193**.32-40
Kālīya, dance of Kṛṣṇa on **185**.34-38
- , defeat of **185**.34-38
- to Kṛṣṇa, prayer by **185**.44-49
Kālīya-episode **185**
Kali-Yuga **19**.20; **175**.17-24 .29-32ab .80
- , *adharma* in **56**.39cd-42
- , beginning of **212**.8
- , characteristics of **197**.4-5; **230**.44-48
- , conditions during **230**; **231**.47-79
- , effect(s) of religious practices in **230**.62-63
- , kingship during **231**.56-59
- , life-span during **230**.38-43
- , merit obtained in **230**.59
- , wish for living in **231**.1-2
Kalkin **122**.68-73
- , Viṣṇuyaśas **213**.164-165ab
Kalmāṣapāda, Saudāsa **8**.77cd-84ab
kalparāja [title of a text?] **58**.12-18
Kalpasaras, place of pilgrimage **25**.72
Kalpa-tree at Puruṣottamakṣetra **177**.16-19
Kāma **38**.1-13; **71**.27-37; **178**.25-27; **200**.23-28
- burnt by Śiva **38**.1-13; **71**.27-37
- , epithets of **38**.1-6
- , Pradyumna as incarnation of **200**.23-28
- , Śiva shot by arrow of **71**.27-37

Kāma see also *goals of life*
Kāmada, place of pilgrimage **25**.60
Kāmadambhaka **16**.4-6
Kāmadāyinī **77**.9cd-13
Kāmadohinī **72**.9cd-10ab
Kāmākhya, place of pilgrimage **25**.30
Kamalā **128**.50-61; **172**.7cd-14
- as name of Śrī **124**.137-139ab
- , place of pilgrimage **124**.137-139ab
- , Viṣṇu and **178**.166cd-176
Kāmālaya, place of pilgrimage **64**.3-8ab
Kāmalī **10**.50cd-53ab
Kāmāri [Śiva] **28**.27
Kāmarūpa **19**.16
Kāmatīrtha, place of pilgrimage **25**.76
Kambala **3**.99-101
Kambalabarhiṣa **15**.1-12ab; **16**.7
Kambhīpāka **214**.14-17
Kāmbojas **8**.35-37 .44-51; **27**.43-50
Kāmeśvara, place of pilgrimage **25**.39
Kaṃsa **15**.58cd-59; **176**.52-56; **177**.1-2; **181**.7-14 .33-35; **188**.42-47; **192**.67-68; **202**.3-12; **213**.159-163
- and gods, enmity between **183**.1-7
- , anger of **190**.1-5
- , funeral rites for **194**.10
- , Kālanemi reborn as **181**.7-14
- , killing of **193**.24-78ab
- , plans of **190**.6-8 .10-19; **193**.17-22
- warned by Yoganidrā **182**.31
Kaṃsā **15**.58cd-59
Kaṃsavatī **15**.58cd-59
Kāmyā **2**.5 .6
Kāmyaka, place of pilgrimage **25**.51
Kanaka **13**.157-159
Kanakas **27**.43-50
Kanakhala **70**.39-40
- as place of pilgrimage **64**.3-8ab
- , place of pilgrimage **25**.10
Kanavaka **14**.14cd-20ab .32ab
Kāñcana, place of pilgrimage **25**.76
Kāñcanaprabha **10**.13-14
Kāñcaneṣudhi **13**.27cd-29
Kaṇḍina **199**.1-4
Kaṇḍu **178**
- as author of *brahmapāra*-hymn **178**.112
- , boon by Viṣṇu to **178**.178
- , remorse of **178**.90-98
- to Viṣṇu, hymn by **178**.114-117 .128-177
- , Viṣṇu appearing to **178**.122-127
Kaṇḍu-episode **178**
Kane, P. V. **109**.55-57ab; **110**.226-228
Kaṅka **15**.58cd-59; **20**.25-27
Kaṅkā **15**.58cd-59
Kaṅkālinī [Rākṣasī] **167**.8-14
Kānti **21**.15-27; **68**.56-59ab; **181**.38-53; **198**.15-17
Kāntimatī **219**.6-12
Kaṇva **85**.2-7; **210**.6-10
- , Gautamī praised by **85**.9-10
- , Hunger praised by **85**.9-10
- to Godāvarī, hymn by **85**.12-14
- to Hunger, hymn by **85**.12-14
Kāṇva, Bāhlīka **148**
- , place of pilgrimage **148**.21-26
Kāṇvatīrtha, place of pilgrimage **85**.24
Kanyākumārikā, place of pilgrimage **25**.28
Kanyākuṇḍa, place of pilgrimage **25**.25
Kanyāsaṃvedha, place of pilgrimage **25**.72
Kanyāsaṃvetya, place of pilgrimage **25**.72
Kanyāśrama, place of pilgrimage **25**.25
Kanyāśramahrada, place of pilgrimage **25**.82
Kanyātīrtha, place of pilgrimage **25**.43 .45 .80
Kapālagautama, Śveta and **59**.6-21
Kapālamocana, place of pilgrimage **25**.51; **229**.59-63
Kapālin **3**.46cd-49
Kapardin **3**.46cd-49
Kapila **3**.74cd-78ab .99-101; **13**.62-63a; **18**.32-36ab; **20**.36-38ab; **69**.12-43; **78**.45-46; **141**.2-5 .23-25 .26-28; **213**.25-26; **240**.3-4 .51-52 .82
- , advice by **78**.47-54; **141**.6-9
- [caste] **20**.31
- , place of pilgrimage **25**.76
- sleeping in nether world **78**.24-31
- , Viṣṇu as **8**.54-57
Kapilā and Gautamī, confluence of **155**.10cd-11ab
- [river] **155**.11cd
Kāpila **20**.36-38ab
- , place of pilgrimage **41**.91; **42**.6-8
Kapilāhrada, place of pilgrimage **25**.69 .82
Kapilālohitārṇava, place of pilgrimage **25**.76
Kapilāsaṃgama, place of pilgrimage **141**.1 .29-30; **155**.14cd
Kapilatīrtha, place of pilgrimage **155**.1
Kapilātīrtha, place of pilgrimage **25**.38
Kapilāvana, place of pilgrimage **25**.50

Kāpilī, place of pilgrimage **25**.59
Kapīmada, place of pilgrimage **25**.47
Kapittha-tree **23**.22-27ab
Kapīvat **5**.20cd-21
Kapota, place of pilgrimage **125**.54-56
Kapotaroman **15**.46cd-48
Kapotatīrtha, place of pilgrimage **80**.5cd-6ab
Kāraka, place of pilgrimage **25**.20
Karāla **213**.81-104; **215**.130cd-136ab
Karālajanaka and Vasiṣṭha, dialogue between **241**; **243**; **244**; **245**
Karambha **15**.24-28
Karambhavālukā **215**.107cd-109ab
Karaṃdhama **13**.142-146
Karamodā **27**.30-32
Kāraṇḍava, place of pilgrimage **25**.42
Karatoyā **220**.8-10ab
- , place of pilgrimage **64**.11-14
Kāratoya, place of pilgrimage **25**.76
Kardama **2**.6; **4**.11-15
Kārīṣis **13**.91
Karkaśas **27**.59cd-62ab
Karki [son of Āpastamba] **130**.2-6
Karkoṭaka **3**.99-101; **13**.176cd-187ab
Karkoṭaka-vāpī, place of pilgrimage **25**.63
karman see also *actions, effect(s), retribution*
karman, Bṛhaspati as authority on **122**.50-54ab
Karṇa **208**.4-7 .8-18 .19-31; **212**.12-17
Karṇaprāvaraṇas **27**.62cd-64ab
Karṇikāsaṃgama, place of pilgrimage **105**.22-26ab
Kārta **13**.155cd-156
Kārtavīrya, Arjuna **3**.84-86ab .90cd-92ab; **13**.160 .161-198
- , boon by Brahman to **3**.84-86ab
Kārtavīrya see *Arjuna Kārtavīrya*
Kartṛ **31**.31-33ab
Kārttika **31**.19-21; **220**.55
Kārttikeya **3**.41ab; **41**.88-90; **81**.1; **82**.9-10 .11-14; **94**.15-21; **108**.26-30; **128**.7-15; **206**.21-23
- , fight between Garuḍa and **206**.24-30
- , origin of **128**.16-23
- , place of pilgrimage **81**.1
Kārttikeyatīrtha, place of pilgrimage **81**.22c-f
Karuṇas **27**.43-50
Kārupāvanatīrtha, place of pilgrimage **25**.45
Karūroma **13**.147-148ab
Karūṣa **7**.1-2 .25 .42
Kārūṣakas **10**.61-62
Karūṣas **14**.20cd-24ab
Kārūṣas **7**.25
- as Kṣatriyas **7**.42
Kāśa **11**.32-33ab .35
Kaseru **27**.14-16
Kaserumat **19**.6cd-7ab
Kasetumat **19**.6cd-7ab
Kāśeya **13**.64cd-67ab
Kāśi **11**.35; **13**.123-124; **14**.43cd; **16**.50cd-54ab; **194**.18-22
- and Vidarbha, battle between the kings of **229**.43cd-55
- burnt by discus of Viṣṇu **207**.28-43
- , decapitation of king of **207**.25-27
- , Dhanvantari as son of king of **11**.36-38
- , king of **13**.72cd-75ab; **207**.13-24
- , place of pilgrimage **64**.3-8ab
Kāśika **13**.63b-64ab .64cd-67ab
Kāśīras **27**.43-50
Kāśis **27**.41cd-42
Kaśmala **215**.127cd-128ab
Kāśmīris **231**.68-71ab
Kāṣṭhaka-vāpikā, place of pilgrimage **25**.63
Kāśya **11**.32-33ab .35; **15**.45cd-46ab
Kāśyā **13**.123-124; **15**.55
Kaśyapa **2**.47-49; **3**.25-28 .46cd-49 .53-58 .64cd-70ab .78cd-80ab; **5**.11cd-12 .34-35; **6**.1ab; **32**.3-6 .7-8 .34cd-35ab .37-41ab; **34**.42-45ab .56-57; **56**.13-15; **69**.12-43; **70**.37cd-38; **83**.2-5; **100**; **123**.77-81; **124**.87-93 .100-107; **166**.2-4ab; **221**.87-88; **226**.62-65ab
- as father of Indra **124**.83-86
- as teacher, superiority of **83**.13-16
- , descendants of wives of **3**.53-58
- , Diti and **124**.2cd-31
- in vedic hymn **174**.16
- , Mārīca **3**.109cd-122; **213**.114-122
- , sun as son of **89**.2ef-3
- to Diti, boon by **3**.109cd-122
- to Śiva, hymn by **100**.19-21; **124**.94-99
- , wives of **3**.51-52
Kāśyapa **5**.44-45ab; **11**.34cd
- as father of snakes **159**.28-31ab
Kaṭha **121**.6-9 .13-15 .16-18
- and Revatī, marriage of **121**.19-21ab
Kaṭha-Upaniṣad **7**.37a-d
Kati **10**.57-60; **13**.91
Kātyāyana **13**.91

Kātyāyanas, origin of **10**.57-60
Kātyāyanī **128**.72cd-76
Kauberahrada, place of pilgrimage **25**.80
Kaulikas **27**.54-57
Kaumāra **20**.59cd-61
- , place of pilgrimage **100**.1-3
Kaumodakī [club of Kṛṣṇa] **68**.44-53; **195**.5-7
Kaunteya [Arjuna] **212**.25-28
Kaurava, Bhīma **12**.11-17
Kauravas **12**.9-10; **13**.106-107; **212**.66-70
- , Balarāma and **208**
- , pride of **208**.19-31
Kauśalyā **15**.30-31; **123**.2-7ab .84-86ab
Kauśāmba, place of pilgrimage **25**.33
Kauśāmbī, place of pilgrimage **25**.33
Kauśika **5**.44-45ab; **7**.105cd-109; **8**.23; **10**.24-28ab .63; **13**.132cd-137; **14**.28c-f; **104**.83-86ab; **170**.2-5; **174**.2-5ab
Kauśikā **27**.25cd-27
Kauśikas **10**.61-62
- , clans of **10**.61-62; **13**.91
Kauśikāśrama, place of pilgrimage **25**.73
Kauśikī **68**.56-59ab; **231**.68-71ab
- , place of pilgrimage **25**.43; **64**.11-14
- [river], Satyavatī as **10**.49cd-50ab
Kauśikīdruma, place of pilgrimage **25**.75
Kauśikīhrada, place of pilgrimage **25**.75
Kauśikya, place of pilgrimage **25**.71
Kaustubha-Jewel **50**.43cd-44ab; **61**.41-45ab
Kavaṣa [father of Pailūṣa] **139**.7cd-11
- [son of Ailūṣa] in Aitareyabrāhmaṇa **139**
Kavaṣatīrtha, place of pilgrimage **139**.19
Kaverakā **20**.66-67
Kāverī **10**.19cd-20 .21-23; **19**.11-12ab
- cursed by Gaṅgā **13**.82cd-87
- , origin of **10**.19cd-20
- , place of pilgrimage **64**.11-14
Kāverīhrada, place of pilgrimage **25**.80
Kavi **2**.17-20ab
- [Agni] **82**.2-6
- [Śukra] **152**.18-20
- [Śukra] as son of Bhṛgu **95**.2-6
- [Śukra] as teacher of Daityas **95**.28cd-30
- [Śukra], curse by **152**.26-28
- [Śukra], oath by **152**.21-23
- [Śukra], Śiva pleased by **152**.24-25
Kāvya **5**.20cd-21
- [Uśanas] as name of Śukra **146**.19-25
Kedāra, place of pilgrimage **25**.11 .32 .40; **64**.3-8ab
Kerala **13**.147-148ab
Keralas **8**.44-51; **13**.147-148ab; **27**.43-50
Kesarin **20**.62-63; **84**.2-4 .5-8
Keśava **45**.53-56 .57-58; **51**.40-41 .42-45; **60**.39-45; **61**.14-16; **184**.14-19; **186**.1-3; **192**.71-74; **200**.29-30; **207**.13-24; **212**.9-11 .86; **213**.159-163; **219**.40-41; **229**.8-13 .20 .56-58
- , praise of **230**.64
Keśava see also *Kṛṣṇa, Viṣṇu*
Keśava, explanation of **190**.39-47
Keśin **177**.1-2; **181**.7-14; **183**.1-7; **188**.42-47; **190**.22-38; **193**.32-40; **202**.3-12; **213**.81-104 .159-163
- , fight between Kṛṣṇa and **190**.29-37
Keśin-episode **190**.22-38
Keśinī **8**.63-64 .65-68; **10**.13-14; **13**.81cd-82ab .82cd-87
Ketu **3**.74cd-78ab
Ketumāla **18**.29 .38cd-44ab .45cd-46ab .57-58
Ketumat **4**.11-15; **11**.39-40 .55-59; **13**.64cd-67ab; **213**.81-104
Ketuvīrya **3**.74cd-78ab
Kevalas **27**.54-57
Khaḍgapattra **157**.21cd-25ab
Khaḍgatīrtha, place of pilgrimage **139**.1-2ab .19
Khaladā **13**.5-8
Khaśā **3**.104-105
Khasā **3**.51-52
Khasas **27**.62cd-64ab
Khaṭvāṅga **8**.73cd-75ab
Khyāti **2**.17-20ab; **20**.54cd-56ab
Kila-hrada, place of pilgrimage **25**.47
killing by beating **189**.46-58ab
- by decapitation **207**.25-27
- by decapitation with hand **192**.71-74
- by mistake **123**.48cd-61ab
- by one stroke of hand **213**.74-79
- by splitting in halves **190**.29-37; **202**.16-21
- by sprinkling with water **168**.22-24
- by whirling around **193**.60cd-63ab
- of animals at water-place **123**.33cd-36ab
- of cow **8**.13-15b:
- of cow, punishment for **22**.7-8; **215**.84cd-136ab
- of demons **7**.82-84; **149**.4cd-9ab; **181**.38-53; **190**.29-37; **202**.16-21; **213**.136 -140

- of demons by Mothers **112**.20-22ab
- of elephant **123**.44-48ab; **193**.24-31
- of helpless people, punishment for **215**.99-100ab
- of infant(s) **181**.33-35 .38-53; **183**.1-7
- of infant(s), attempt of **182**.27-30; **200**.2-10
- of Kaṃsa **193**.24-78ab
- of Kṣatriya, punishment for **22**.10
- of Kṣatriyas **13**.64cd-67ab; **213**.114-122
- of Madhu and Kaiṭabha **213**.28-29
- of messenger, punishment for **22**.10
- of Mṛtyu **94**.2-14
- of one's brother, punishment for **124**.100-107
- of pupil, punishment for **217**.48
- of Sindhusena **122**.48-49
- of sleeping enemy **17**.29-31
- of teacher, punishment for **22**.7-8
- of unarmed person, punishment for **217**.100-104
- of Vaiśya, punishment for **22**.10
- of Vṛtra **122**.48-49
- of women, sin of **4**.74-80
- of Yādavas **210**.37-43
- permissible in battle **124**.53-67
- , punishment for **214**.88cd-96; **215**.130cd-136ab
- , punishment for forbidden **214**.120-128
- with brilliance **8**.54-57
- with curse **141**.2-5; **176**.15cd-19ab
- with discus **128**.63cd-70ab; **134**.12-14; **156**.4-6; **167**.31-32; **207**.13-24
- with Erakā-grass **210**.37-43 .44-46
- with fist **187**.26-28; **209**.11cd-21ab
- with foam **124**.33-36ab
- with golden pillar **201**.23-26
- with sound of conch **156**.4-6
- with spear **115**.10-12ab
- with spell-formula(s) **168**.22-24
- with *vajra* **129**.4-8

killing see also *burning, slaying*
Kiṃdāna, place of pilgrimage **25**.41
Kiṃjapa, place of pilgrimage **25**.41
Kiṃjaya, place of pilgrimage **25**.41
Kiṃnaras **18**.52-55; **36**.22cd-23ab .63cd-70; **86**.17-19; **105**.8cd-11ab; **123**.177cd-184
Kiṃpuruṣa [region] **18**.18-20
Kiṃpuruṣas **20**.36-38ab; **213**.53-57
Kiṃvāna, place of pilgrimage **25**.41

kindling of lamps **67**.24-27
kinds of actions, three **125**.44-49; **157**.13cd-14
- of actions, two **173**.9-25; **233**.40cd-43ab
- of beings, two **229**.15-18
- of clothes **242**.8-15ab
- of earth, five **221**.64cd-65ab
- of flowers **220**.154-167
- of food, four **61**.38
- of fruits **220**.154-167 .168-177
- of gods, three **175**.14cd-16
- of grain **217**.62-65; **220**.154-167
- of holy places, four **70**.16-29 .33-41; **175**.14cd-16
- of meat **220**.168-177
- of milk **220**.168-177
- of milk products **220**.154-167
- of pulses **220**.154-167 .168-177
- of scents **220**.154-167
- of speech, four **175**.14cd-16
- of spices **220**.168-177
- of sweets **220**.154-167
- of vegetables **220**.168-177
- of water, four **24**.12

kinds see also *classification*
kinds of see also *classes of, classification*
king and Vaiśya **170**.77-80ef
- , Arjuna Kārtavīrya as ideal **13**.172-173
- as creator of *dharma* **4**.35-41
- as father **44**.1
- as friend of Indra **168**.28cd-29
- , Brahmin as proxy of **8**.3-4
- compared with father **44**.41-43
- , consecration of **4**.16-17; **8**.22; **9**.13-16; **14**.33-34ab
- , duties of **4**.35-41; **7**.58cd-71ab; **222**.7-10
- , first **2**.21-24
- , ideal **44**.2-7
- in forest **164**.7-9ab
- , lament for dead **193**.76cd-78ab; **194**.7-8
- , maxim about **123**.33cd-36ab
- , maxim about vices of **108**.22-23ab
- , mocking at **168**.15-18ab
- of Cedi **12**.11-17; **14**.20cd-24ab
- of Kāśi **13**.72cd-75ab; **207**.13-24
- of Kāśi, decapitation of **207**.25-27
- of Kāśi, Dhanvantari as son of **11**.36-38
- of Laṅkā, Vaiśravaṇa as **97**.2-5ab
- of places of pilgrimage, ocean as **62**.1-4 .10-13ab

- of the earth, Pramati as **171**.2cd-6cd
- performing ancestral rites for subjects **220**.78cd-80ab
- , Pṛthu as first **4**.115-121
- , praise of **4**.61-65
- , punishment of **215**.55cd-64 .65-67 .68-69
- , qualities of **43**.2-5
- , Rāma as ideal **213**.145-153ab
- , rebirth as **28**.62cd-64ab; **60**.1-6; **67**.76-80; **228**.146-151
- rewarded by ascetic **7**.85-86
- , seven vices of **123**.33cd-36ab
- , snake as son of **111**.2-6
- , Soma addressed as **174**.15 .16
- , Vaiśya as **170**.84-88
- , voluntary death of **138**.22-27
- without children **78**.3-8ab
- without son **170**.69-74ab
- , worship of Pṛthu as ideal **4**.115-121
- , Yama as righteous **6**.46cd-48ab

king see also *lord*

kingdom as stake at game of dice **171**.20-24
- , division of **12**.18-21
- , ideal **4**.58-59; **73**.2-6; **123**.2-7ab; **153**.6cd-7; **213**.145-153ab
- , restoration of **122**.103; **171**.44-46
- restored by place of pilgrimage **140**.1
- without *dharma* **141**.2-5

kings in world of Indra **171**.2cd-6cd
- killed by Viṣṇu **226**.18
- , Kubera as lord of **4**.2-9
- , list of **70**.39-40

kingship during Kali-Yuga **230**.34-37; **231**.56-59
- of Ugrasena supported by Kṛṣṇa **194**.11-12
- , renunciation of **196**.5-8; **212**.91-92 .93-94
- , Yādavas deprived of **208**.8-18

kingship see also *royal power*

Kirātas **19**.8cd; **27**.17-19ab .43-50 .62cd-64ab; **220**.8-10ab

Kirfel, W. **1**; 3.7cd-9; **5**; **9**; **12**.1-2; **18**; **19**; **20**; **21**; **23**; **27**

Kīrti **34**.42-45ab; **68**.56-59ab; **137**.8-14; **181**.38-53

Kiṣkindhā **157**.2cd-7 .29

Kiṣkindhakas **27**.59cd-62ab

Kiṣkindhātīrtha, place of pilgrimage **157**.1-2ab .31

kissing of head **9**.31-32

Kīṭāda **214**.14-17

kneeling at sunrise **28**.32

knocking out of teeth **190**.26-28

knowledge, action and **145**.2cd-5ab; **237**; **238**.12-14
- and action **145**.8-11ab
- and ignorance **22**.48-49ab; **241**.21-22; **244**.2-9
- and ignorance in simile **234**.58-60ab
- as means of liberation **224**.5-8
- by means of meditation **33**.3-8; **74**.82-87; **87**.25-29; **114**.2-5; **131**.10-15
- by means of Yoga **6**.31-34ab .41-43; **10**.38cd-41ab; **17**.35-40
- , classification of **234**.58-60ab .61cd-63ab
- concerning livelihood, threefold **187**.42-54
- , differentiation destroyed by **158**.22-27ef
- , domains of **240**.5-16 .17-49
- , effect(s) of actions increased by **129**.49-64
- , five enemies of **139**.13-17ef
- , fourfold **187**.42-54
- , illusion destroyed by **139**.18
- in simile **246**.6-12
- , liberation by **237**.7-14; **238**; **240**.5-16; **243**.85-90; **244**.40-41; **245**.48-51
- , means of **231**.48-50
- obtained from Śiva **139**.12
- of astrology **21**.15-27
- of *brahman* **3**.42cd-46ab; **70**.3cd-8ab; **117**.2-5
- of *brahman*, liberation by **245**.42-43
- of *brahman*, Sāṃkhya as **240**.98-103
- of Daityas, personification of **206**.31-38
- of Kṣatriyas **108**.75-76ab; **123**.97-105ab
- of omen(s) **21**.15-27
- of Śiva **139**.7cd-11
- of Śiva, Veda(s) as authority on **139**.7cd-11
- of sages, supernatural **210**.6-10
- of Self **117**.18-19ab
- of Self, detachment due to **238**.5-6
- of self, *dharma* resulting from **231**.44-46
- of Self, effect(s) of **238**.24-25
- of self in simile **236**.24-25
- of Self, liberation by **238**.7-11
- of Self, qualification(s) for **236**.37cd-40ab
- of self resulting from disgust **231**.44-46
- , *puruṣa* and **241**.48
- , sacrifice and **233**.40cd-43ab
- , subjects and objects of **244**.4-9
- , two levels of **234**.61cd-63ab
- , value of **237**.33-40; **245**.31-41

knowledge see also *consciousness, information, perception, senses*
Kokā **219**.2-3 .98cd-107ab
- , merit of bathing in **219**.107cd-109ab
- , origin of **219**.13-17 .18-24
Kokā, explanation of **219**.6-12
Kokāmukha **219**.109cd-113ab
- , place of pilgrimage **25**.13; **64**.3-8ab; **219**.4-5; **228**.92cd-96; **229**.68cd-71 .72-86ab
Kokanada, place of pilgrimage **25**.20
Kokila, place of pilgrimage **25**.70
Kola **13**.147-148ab; **70**.35cd-37ab
Kolāhala **27**.20cd-24ab
Kolla **70**.35cd-37ab
Koṇāditya **28**.1-9 .11-18
Koṇāditya see also *sun*
Koṇārka **28**.11-65
Koṇārka see also *sun*
Koṇisarpas **8**.44-51
Koṅkanas **220**.8-10ab
Koraka, place of pilgrimage **25**.20
Kośala **47**.7-9
Kośalas **27**.41cd-42 .59cd-62ab; **231**.68-71ab
Koṭaraka, place of pilgrimage **25**.20
Koṭidruma, place of pilgrimage **25**.21
Koṭikṛta, place of pilgrimage **25**.41
Koṭikūṭa, place of pilgrimage **25**.41
Koṭīśvara, Śiva as **148**.1-3ab
Koṭitīrtha, place of pilgrimage **25**.12 .14 .15 .26 .36 .44 .55 .59; **64**.3-8ab; **148**.1-3ab .27a-f; **164**.53cd-54
Koṭitīrtha, explanation of **148**.21-26
Koṭitīrthasthalī, place of pilgrimage **25**.55
Krakaca **215**.120cd-121ab
Kramaṇa **15**.33
Kramu **20**.10-11; **27**.30-32
Kratha **13**.109; **15**.16-21; **213**.81-104
Krathas **220**.8-10ab
Kratu **1**.43-45ab; **2**.17-20ab; **5**.8-9ab; **34**.12cd-19; **174**.2-5ab
Kratulas **27**.41cd-42
Kratusthalā **68**.60-67
Krauñca **20**.49cd-51
Krauñcadvīpa **18**.11-12; **20**.46-58ab
- , four castes of **20**.53cd-54ab
- , mountains of **20**.49cd-51
- , regions of **20**.47cd-49ab
- , rivers of **20**.54cd-56ab
Krauñcī **3**.92cd-93ab .93cd-95ab
Kṛcchra **22**.23cd-24ab
Krimi **15**.33
Kriyā **27**.30-32
Kṛkaṇeyu **13**.5-8
Kṛmi [f.] **13**.20cd-22ab .22cd-23
- [m.] **13**.22cd-23
Kṛmibhakṣa **214**.14-17
Kṛmibhakṣya **22**.14cd-15a
Kṛmibhojana **22**.2-6
Kṛmilā [city] **13**.24-25ab
Kṛmilāśva **13**.93-96
Kṛmipūya **22**.18cd-20
Kṛmis **220**.8-10ab
Kṛmīśa **22**.2-6 .15b:
Kroḍatīrtha, place of pilgrimage **42**.6-8
Krodha **213**.81-104
Krodhahantṛ **213**.81-104
Krodhana **165**.27-30ab; **213**.81-104
Krodhavardhana **213**.81-104
Krodhavaśa **3**.102cd-103
Krodhavaśā **3**.51-52
Kroṣṭṛ **13**.153cd-154ab; **14**.1-2ab; **15**.1-12ab; **16**.9-11; **226**.30-41
Kṛpa and Kṛpī as twins **13**.97
Kṛpa, explanation of **13**.97
Kṛpī as twins, Kṛpa and **13**.97
Kṛpī, explanation of **13**.97
Kṛśarāsaṃgama, place of pilgrimage **105**.22-26ab
Kṛśāśva **3**.25-28 .61cd; **7**.89
Kṛṣṇa **3**.125; **14**.29-31 .42ab; **16**.8 .12-45ab; **17**; **22**.2-6 .37-41; **37**.2-23; **42**.35-36ab; **43**.10-13 .14; **49**.47cd-50ab; **62**.1-4; **163**.26-31; **226**.11-12; **246**.21-27
- , advice by **210**.33-35
- , Akrūra welcomed by **192**.1-4
- and Aditi **203**.1-24
- and Ariṣṭa, fight between **189**.46-58ab
- and Arjuna **188**.42-47
- and Baladeva, birth of **179**.6-10ab
- and Baladeva, Kuvalayāpīḍa killed by **193**.24-31
- and Balarāma as partial incarnation of Viṣṇu **190**.10-19
- and Balarāma, divinity of **191**.26
- and Balarāma, education of **194**.18-22
- and Balarāma, looking at **193**.41
- and Bāṇa, fight between **206**.31-38
- and Cāṇūra, fight between **193**.50-57ab
- and gods, fight between **203**.45-62

- and Gopīs, love-play of **189**.14-45
- and Indra **188**; **194**.13-17; **202**
- and Indra, fight between **203**.45-62
- and Indra, opposition of **188**.11-13; **203**.26-73
- and Keśin, fight between **190**.29-37
- and Pauṇḍraka, fight between **207**.13-24
- and Rukmiṇī, marriage of **199**
- and Rukmin, fight between **199**.5-10
- and Śiva, fight between **205**.7-8; **206**.21-23
- and Śiva, identity of **206**.45-48
- and Śiva, opposition of **207**.28-43
- anointed by Indra **188**.36-37
- , anointing of **193**.1-12
- appearing to Akrūra **192**.32-42 .43-47
- , Arjuna dependent on **212**.25-28 .42-53
- as *brahman* **192**.32-42
- as child **184**
- as fulfiller of wishes **227**.8-9
- as guest of Indra **203**.24-25
- as leader of Vṛṣṇyandhakas **14**.50cd-56
- as lord of cows **188**.29-35
- as partial incarnation of Viṣṇu **193**.32-40; **195**.13-18; **196**.23-29; **202**.23-29
- as Puruṣottama **57**.29-56
- as Rudra **232**.14-23
- as Vice-Indra, consecration of **188**.36-37
- as Viṣṇu **191**.4-12; **193**.80-87 .88-90; **195**.13-18; **196**.30-45; **202**.23-29; **203**.6-19 .70-73; **206**.39-44; **212**.63
- , Baladeva, Subhadrā **179**.4-5
- , Balarāma asking for help from **187**.19-20
- , Balarāma, Subhadrā **65**
- , battle between Jarāsaṃdha and **195**.1-4
- , birth of **182** .9-11
- , boon by Aditi to **203**.22
- bound by snakes **185**.11-17
- bound to mortar **184**.31-42ab
- , bow broken by **193**.13-16
- , brilliance of **196**.23-29
- , cart turned over by **184**.20-28; **190**.1-5
- [caste] **20**.31
- , Cāṇūra killed by **193**.60cd-63ab
- , cosmos as part of **185**.39-42
- , death of **211**
- , deeds of **193**.32-40; **202**.3-12
- , departure of **192**.14-31
- , departure of weapons of **210**.47-48
- , descendants of **205**.1-6
- , description of **44**.14-15; **57**.38-41; **179**.2-75; **191**.18-25; **193**.42-49
- , devotion of Akrūra to **191**
- , disrespect against **192**.71-74
- , divine and human nature of **193**.80-87
- , divine messenger sent to **210**.16-21
- , divinity of **203**.70-73
- , Dvaipāyana **13**.121; **26**.17; **235**.2
- , dyer killed by **192**.71-74
- , effect(s) of worship of **227**.6-7
- embodied in hill **187**.59cd-61
- , enemies killed by **213**.159-163
- , enmity between Śiśupāla and **199**.1-4
- entrusted to cowherds **182**.19-26
- , fight between bear and **16**.25-45ab
- , fighting as play of **193**.50-57ab .60cd-63ab; **199**.5-10; **206**.39-44
- for Satyabhāmā, love of **203**.26-32
- , four arms of **192**.32-42; **211**.5-10
- , funeral rites for **212**.1-4
- , genealogy of **14**
- , Govardhana lifted up by **188**.17-19
- , greatness of **185**.30-33
- , Hayagrīva killed by **202**.16-21
- , human nature of **189**.1-13; **195**.13-18; **204**.5-7
- , hymn by Aditi to **203**.6-19
- , hymn by Mucukunda to **196**.30-45
- , hymn to **57**.32-37
- , iconographic attributes of **50**.43cd-44ab; **53**.31-33; **57**.38-41; **192**.32-42
- identified with world **192**.62-66
- , impossibility of description of **65**.59-76ab
- , impossibility of looking at **53**.39-40
- in heaven, welcome of **203**.1-5
- , Indra defeated by **203**.45-62
- , Indra obedient to **194**.13-17
- , invincibility of **203**.22 .70-73
- , kingship of Ugrasena supported by **194**.11-12
- , Kubjā healed by **193**.1-12
- , liberation by devotion to **227**.6-7
- , liberation by looking at **177**.6
- , Māyā of **53**.34-38
- , meditation on **177**.4
- , merit of looking at **65**.83-99
- , merit of looking at house of **212**.9-11
- , miracle(s) worked by thoughts of **184**.42cd-52ab
- multiplying himself **204**.13cd-18
- , Mura killed by **202**.16-21

- , Muṣṭika killed by **193**.63cd-65ab
- , naked woman appearing to **206**.31-38
- [name of fig-tree] **60**.16-18
- , Naraka killed by **202**.16-21
- , omniscience of **191**.27-33; **192**.5-10; **210**.15 .22-27
- on earth, life-span of **210**.16-21
- on Kālīya, dance of **185**.34-38
- , origin of conch of **194**.23-31
- , Pañcajana killed by **194**.23-31; **202**.16-21
- , plans of **210**.22-27 .33-35
- , play of **186**.6-13
- praised by Indra **203**.70-73
- praised by the people **188**.17-19; **189**.58c-f; **190**.38
- , Pramathas defeated by **206**.10-13
- , prayer by Devakī to **182**.16 .17
- , prayer by Kālīya to **185**.44-49
- , prayer by snake wives to **185**.39-42
- , prayer by Vasudeva to **182**.14-15
- , refuge granted by **188**.17-19; **190**.22-25; **196**.30-45; **207**.28-43
- remembered at hour of death **192**.71-74 .75-86
- , Saṃkarṣaṇa, Subhadrā, looking at **177**.3 .8
- , Saṃkarṣaṇa, Subhadrā, remembering of **177**.7
- , search for **189**.22-25
- , separation from **189**.40-41; **192**.14-31
- , singing of **189**.14-17
- , singing of praise of **185**.54-56
- [son of Havirdhāna] **2**.29-30ab
- , statue of **50**.43cd-44ab .48-54
- , submission of Śiva to **206**.39-44
- submitting to fate **210**.15
- , summary of deeds of **226**.42-45ab
- , superiority of **207**.1-2; **229**.8-13
- , superiority of devotion to **49**.70
- taking away the Pārijāta-tree **203**.26-73; **204**
- , thunderbolt caught by **203**.45-62
- to Balarāma, advice by **187**.22-25
- to garland-maker, boon by **192**.75-86
- to Indra, promise by **188**.42-47
- to Mucukunda, boon by **197**.1-3
- to Nanda, advice by **187**.42-54
- to Pauṇḍraka, challenge of **207**.8-12
- to Śiva, boon by **206**.45-48
- to sixteen-thousand one hundred women, marriage of **204**.13cd-18
- , Tośalaka defeated by **193**.65cd-67ab
- , two Arjuna-trees felled by **184**.31-42ab; **190**.1-5
- , Utkala and **42**.35-36ab
- , Viṣṇu as **176**.52-56
- , weight of **193**.67cd-76ab
- , wives of **201**.3-5
- , worship of **57**.29-56; **59**.26-33
- , Yādavas killed by **210**.44-46
- , yellow clothes of **192**.71-74

Kṛṣṇa see also *Govinda, Hari, Janārdana, Keśava, Mādhava, Nārāyaṇa, Viṣṇu*

Kṛṣṇā **77**.2-9ab

Kṛṣṇasūtra **22**.2-6

Kṛṣṇatīrtha, place of pilgrimage **25**.30 .78

Kṛṣṇaveṇā **27**.35-36ab

Kṛṣṇaveṇī **19**.12cd-13ab

Kṛtācala **27**.20cd-24ab

Kṛtadāra **2**.32

Kṛtadhanvan **13**.157-159

Kṛtāgni **13**.157-159

Kṛtaka **13**.109 .117cd

Kṛtakarman **13**.157-159

Kṛtalakṣaṇa **14**.29-31

Kṛtālaya, place of pilgrimage **25**.47

Kṛtamālā **19**.13cd; **27**.36cd-37ab

Kṛtaśaila **27**.20cd-24ab

Kṛtaujas **13**.157-159

Kṛtavarman **16**.4-6; **210**.37-43

Kṛtavīrya **13**.157-159 .160

Kṛtayajña **13**.109

Kṛta-Yuga **19**.20; **43**.1; **142**.2-4; **156**.2cd-3; **175**.17-24 .29-32ab; **230**.4-7
- , return of **231**.44-46 .80-88

Kṛti **9**.13-16; **11**.27cd-31

Kṛttika, place of pilgrimage **25**.57

Kṛttikā **220**.33cd-42

Kṛttikās **3**.41ab; **82**; **128**.16-23

Kṛttikātīrtha, place of pilgrimage **82**.1 .15-16ef

Kṛtyā **110**.134-136 .137-142 .191cd-194ab .194cd-198ab .198cd-200cd
- and Death, marriage of **116**.22cd-24ab
- as mare **110**.124-130; **116**.22cd-24ab
- originated from sacrificial fire **207**.28-43

Kruśadaṇḍa, place of pilgrimage **25**.16

Kṣama, place of pilgrimage **25**.82

Kṣānti **68**.56-59ab; **109**.13-20

Kṣatravṛddha **11**.27cd-31 .32-33ab

- , descendants of **11**.32-61
Kṣatriya, punishment for killing of **22**.10
- represented by weapons **111**.39cd-47
Kṣatriyas **4**.115-121; **7**.25; **11**.33-34ab; **13**.63b-64ab .79 .91; **27**.43-50; **220**.3-4
- , begging not allowed for **168**.2-5
- , Brahmins and **10**.63; **13**.91
- , conduct of **223**.41-52ab
- , duties of **222**.7-10
- , education of **104**.22cd-37ab; **123**.97-105ab
- , Kārūṣas as **7**.42
- , killing of **13**.64cd-67ab; **213**.114-122
- , knowledge of **108**.75-76ab; **123**.97-105ab
- , Lakṣmī as friend of sinful **137**.15-24
- , loss of *dharma* of **8**.31-32 .44-51
- , maxim about truthfulness of Brahmins and **111**.39cd-47
- , origin of **161**.43cd-50cd
- , Śaryātas as **7**.37ef-41
- turning into Vaiśyas **7**.26ab
Kṣatriya-woman in battle, help by **123**.23-33ab
Kṣayā **27**.38cd-39ab
Kṣayāpalāsinī **27**.38cd-39ab
Kṣema **11**.55-59
Kṣemadhanvan **8**.84cd-92
Kṣemaka **20**.3-5
- [Rākṣasa] **11**.41-43 .54; **13**.72cd-75ab .75cd-77
Kṣemakarī **181**.38-53
Kṣemyā **181**.38-53
kṣetrajña, explanation of **30**.65-67
Kṣiprā **43**.75-76; **228**.15-21
- , place of pilgrimage **64**.11-14
Kṣīrakāvāsa, place of pilgrimage **25**.54
Kṣīrasaras, place of pilgrimage **25**.66
Kṣīraśrava, place of pilgrimage **25**.48
Kṣīreśvara, place of pilgrimage **25**.48
Kṣudhātīrtha, place of pilgrimage **85**.1 .24
Kṣuradhārā **215**.122cd-123ab
Kubera **36**.15cd-16ab; **56**.13-15; **69**.12-43; **72**.11cd-14; **97**; **128**.29-37; **157**.2cd-7; **176**.15cd-19ab; **192**.48-58; **213**.53-57
- as lord of kings **4**.2-9
- as lord of the north **97**.29
- as lord of wealth **97**.24-28
- in simile **209**.11cd-21ab
- , palanquin of **203**.45-62
- to Śiva, hymn by **97**.20-23
Kubera see also *Dhanada*
Kubjā healed by Kṛṣṇa **193**.1-12
Kubjāmbaka, place of pilgrimage **25**.49
Kubjavana, place of pilgrimage **25**.56
Kubjāvana, place of pilgrimage **25**.56
Kuḍmala **215**.110cd-111ab
Kuhakas **27**.43-50
Kuhara **3**.99-101
Kuhū **9**.13-16; **27**.25cd-27
Kukkuras, genealogy of Bhojas and **15**
Kukṣi **2**.6; **3**.64cd-70ab
Kukura **15**.45cd-46ab .46cd-48
Kukura-Andhakas **17**.32-34
Kukuras **15**.60ab
Kulakarṇahrada, place of pilgrimage **25**.75
Kulikas **27**.43-50
Kuliṅgaka, place of pilgrimage **25**.30
Kumāra **3**.39-40; **19**.14; **20**.59cd-61; **35**.64; **71**.27-37; **81**.1
- , birth of **3**.39-40
Kumāradhārā, place of pilgrimage **25**.74
Kumāraka **13**.127cd-132ab
- , place of pilgrimage **25**.66
Kumāras **27**.54-57
Kumāravāsa, place of pilgrimage **25**.75
Kumārī **20**.66-67; **27**.38cd-39ab
- , place of pilgrimage **64**.11-14
Kumārika, place of pilgrimage **25**.28
Kumbha **176**.37-51; **213**.81-104
- , place of pilgrimage **25**.65
Kumbhakarṇa **97**.2-5ab; **176**.37-51
Kumbhakarṇahrada, place of pilgrimage **25**.75
Kumbhanābha **3**.64cd-70ab
Kumbhāṇḍa **205**.15-22
Kumbhīpāka **215**.86cd-88ab
Kumuda **20**.25-27
Kumudamālyas **27**.41cd-42
Kumudottara **20**.59cd-61
Kumudvatī **20**.54cd-56ab; **27**.33-34
Kuñcakas **27**.62cd-64ab
Kundaka, place of pilgrimage **25**.82
Kuntakas **27**.62cd-64ab
Kuntalas **27**.41cd-42 .54-57
Kunti **14**.20cd-24ab; **15**.22-23; **188**.42-47
Kūpa, place of pilgrimage **25**.62 .65 .70 .73
Kupatha **213**.81-104
Kurarī **18**.32-36ab
Kūrma **18**.57-58
Kuru **13**.106-107 .108; **18**.45cd-46ab;

70.39-40
- [caste] **20**.16-17
Kurukṣetra **13**.106-107; **26**.3-17; **246**.21-27
- as place of pilgrimage **65**.84-96
- , place of pilgrimage **25**.4-6; **64**.3-8ab; **65**.84-96
Kurus **19**.15cd; **27**.62cd-64ab
Kurutīrtha, place of pilgrimage **25**.53
Kuśa **10**.21-23
- and Lava, Rāmāyaṇa recited by **154**.14cd-21ab
Kuśadhvaja, place of pilgrimage **25**.53
Kuśadvīpa **18**.11-12; **20**.35-45
- , four castes of **20**.38cd-40ab
- , mountains of **20**.41cd-42
- , regions of **20**.36-38ab
- , rivers of **20**.43-44
Kuśaga **20**.47cd-49ab
Kuśāgra **13**.109
Kuśa-grass **13**.102-105; **36**.130-134; **59**.81-91; **136**.3cd-14ab .17-26; **169**.36-39ab .43cd-45ef; **219**.42-47ab .71cd-86; **220**.61cd-62ab
- as emblem **20**.45
- as offering **219**.60cd-65ab
- in sacrifice **161**.35cd-39ab
- , origin of **219**.42-47ab
- , ring of **219**.52-60ab
- , satisfying by **161**.63-64ab
- used in sacrifice **161**.50ef-53
- , water purified by **161**.60-61ab
Kuśagrass see also *grass*
Kuśala **20**.47cd-49ab
Kuśāmba **10**.21-23
Kusamoda **20**.59cd-61
Kuśanābha **10**.21-23
Kuśaprathana, place of pilgrimage **25**.81
Kuśapravaṇa, place of pilgrimage **25**.81
Kuśasthalī [city] 7.28cd-29ab .30-34 .37ef-41
- , place of pilgrimage **25**.11
Kuśatarpaṇa, place of pilgrimage **161**.1-2ab .65cd-67
- superior to Vārāṇasī **161**.72-78
Kuśatarpaṇa, explanation of **161**.63-64ab
Kuśāvarta, place of pilgrimage **25**.67; **64**.3-8ab; **80**.1-3
Kuśāvila, place of pilgrimage **25**.30
Kuśeśaya **20**.41cd-42
Kuśika **10**.21-23 .24-28ab; **13**.88-90
Kuśodbhava, place of pilgrimage **25**.48
Kusumāsaṃgama, place of pilgrimage **105**.22-26ab
Kusumbhikā **105**.22-26ab
Kusumoda **20**.59cd-61
Kūṭaśālmalī **217**.80cd-86
Kutsa **2**.17-20ab
Kuvalāśva **7**.54-55 .57-86 .87-88
- and Dhundhu, fight between **7**.82-84
- , invincibility of **7**.85-86
Kuvalayāpīḍa **188**.42-47; **190**.10-19; **193**.17-22; **202**.3-12; **213**.159-163
- killed by Kṛṣṇa and Baladeva **193**.24-31
lac, punishment for selling of **22**.18cd-20
Lajjā **109**.13-20; **181**.38-53
lakes, four **18**.31
Lakṣmaṇa **123**.97-105ab .105cd-109ab .140-146 .170-172 .191-194; **154**.8cd-11ab; **176**.37-51; **213**.127-135
- and Śatrughna **123**.84-86ab
- , Liṅga worshipped by **123**.213cd-216
- , place of pilgrimage **123**.213cd-216
- , Rāma and **154**.14cd-21ab
- , Rāma, Sītā **123**.147-157
- , Sītā and **154**.11cd-14ab
- , Viśvāmitra as teacher of Rāma and **123**.97-105ab
Lakṣmaṇa see also *Saumitri*
Lakṣmaṇā **201**.3-5; **205**.1-6
Lakṣmī **9**.13-16; **18**.52-55; **69**.12-43; **109**.41; **122**.68-73; **128**.50-61; **129**.75-78; **174**.31-33; **198**.15-17
- and Poverty, dispute between **137**
- as friend of sinful Kṣatriyas **137**.15-24
- as Māyā **137**.30cd-39ab
- as principle of delight **137**.30cd-39ab
- as Śiva **137**.30cd-39ab
- as Sarasvatī **137**.30cd-39ab
- as Uṣas **137**.30cd-39ab
- in simile **111**.26-34; **127**.2-4ab
- , omnipresence of **137**.30cd-39ab
- praised by Gautamī **137**.30cd-39ab
- , Sītā as **213**.127-135
- sleeping in ocean, Viṣṇu and **172**.7cd-14
- , superiority of **137**.8-14
- , Viṣṇu and **68**.44-53; **80**.46-55; **144**.20-22
Lakṣmī see also *prosperity, wealth*
lakṣmī of Indra **122**.8-20
Lakṣmītīrtha, place of pilgrimage **137**.1
Lālābhakṣa **22**.2-6; **214**.14-17
Lālābhakṣya **22**.15cd-16a

Lambā **3**.29-30ab .30cd-33
Lambakas **27**.43-50
Lambodara, Gaṇeśa as **114**.9-12
lament for dead king **193**.76cd-78ab; **194**.7-8
- of Arjuna **212**.29-33
- of pigeon **80**.30-36
- of women **192**.14-31
Lampakas **27**.43-50
lamps, effect(s) of donation of **29**.35cd-42ab
- , kindling of **67**.24-27
- , prescr. conc. **29**.35cd-42ab
land and cow, substitution of **155**.12-13ab
- , effect(s) of donation(s) of **120**.3cd-5
- , gift of **51**.54-56; **73**.34-40; **155**.12-13ab
- granted by sun **168**.10-12
- of Pauras **12**.11-17
- of Uttarakurus **10**.5-8
- , punishment for annexation of **215**.86cd-88ab .122cd-123ab
- requested from ocean **196**.9-15
land see also *country, earth, field of action, region*
Lāṅgalinī **27**.37cd-38ab
Lāṅgulinī **27**.37cd-38ab
Laṅkā **97**.8-13ab; **143**.7-11 .14-16; **154**.2-4; **157**.11-12ab; **176**.21-25
- , Rākṣasas of **170**.54-63
- , Vaiśravaṇa as king of **97**.2-5ab
- , Vibhīṣaṇa as king of **170**.54-63
lap of father, son on **140**.7-11; **154**.14cd-21ab
- of Rāma, Sītā on **154**.8cd-11ab
laughing at Indra **171**.2cd-6cd
- at sages **100**.25-29ab; **132**.3-5
laughing at see also *mocking at*
laughter, offence by **201**.10-22
Lauhi **10**.67cd-68; **13**.92ab
Laukikas **27**.43-50
Lava, Rāmāyaṇa recited by Kuśa and **154**.14cd-21ab
Lavaṇa **70**.35cd-37ab; **213**.136-140
layers of elements, cosmic **23**.22-27ab
leaves, lotus of eight **61**.1-3
left, right and **2**.51-53; **45**.37-41; **219**.52-60ab; **220**.69cd-70
leftovers of food, prescr. conc. **221**.26-30
- of offerings **219**.60cd-65ab .71cd-86
leftovers see also *remnant*
Lekhas **5**.30cd-31
Leo, conjunction of Jupiter and **152**.37cd-39ef; **175**.83-84
leprosy **58**.44-46
- , Candramas afflicted with **152**.26-28
- , curse of **152**.26-28
levels of *brahman*, two **234**.61cd-63ab
- of knowledge, two **234**.61cd-63ab
libation(s), prescr. conc, daily **221**.20
liberation and suffering in simile **234**.54cd -57
- as merging in Viṣṇu **19**.25-27
- at Vārāṇasī **229**.64-67ab
- by absorption **237**.26-27
- by actions **26**.23-25
- by becoming, *brahman* **12**.3
- by death at Puruṣottamakṣetra **177**.24-25
- by devotion to Kṛṣṇa **227**.6-7
- by devotion to Śiva **94**.37-42
- by devotion to Viṣṇu **136**.17-26
- by grace of Viṣṇu **178**.184-186; **239**.24-28
- by initiation **227**.6-7
- by knowledge **237**.7-14; **238**; **240**.5-16; **243**.85-90; **244**.40-41; **245**.48-51
- by knowledge of *brahman* **245**.42-43
- by knowledge of Self **238**.7-11
- by looking at Kṛṣṇa **177**.6
- by remembering of Viṣṇu **229**.64-67ab
- by sojourn at Puruṣottamakṣetra **177**.28 .29-30
- by son **104**.10-14ab; **150**.15-20
- by union with Vāsudeva **227**.48-49
- by vision of the absolute **236**.69
- by worship of Viṣṇu **196**.30-45
- by Yoga **239**.11-23
- , conduct leading to **224**.5-8
- , constituents leading to **240**.20-22ab
- , *dharma* as means of **69**.12-43
- , discussion about means of **145**
- during life-time **136**.17-26
- , enjoyment and **88**.4-7; **136**.27-31 .37-40
- , enjoyment more difficult to obtain than **136**.17-26
- for ancestors **125**.44-49; **131**.39cd-51
- for animals **177**.16-19
- for evil-doers **216**.87-89
- for members of low caste **178**.184-186
- for renouncer **222**.55-56
- for women **178**.184-186; **238**.37cd
- for worms and insects **161**.72-78
- granted by Śiva, enjoyment and **130**.17-21
- , knowledge as means of **224**.5-8
- , means of **236**.3-5 .6

- , name of Vāsudeva as means of **22**.42-43
- of ancestors **79**.21cd-22
- of *puruṣa* **243**.84; **244**.20-22; **245**.25-26
- of twenty-sixth principle **245**.10cd-14ab
- of Yogin **227**.48-49; **235**.21-25 .26-27; **237**.82-86ab
- , path to **70**.3cd-8ab; **238**.56cd-57; **240**.69-75
- , qualification(s) for **236**.3-5
- , request for **178**.166ab
- , Śiva as **75**.23
- , voluntary **239**.39-41

liberation see also *release*
lies, maxim about telling of **135**.5cd-10ab; **228**.51
life, absence of bad conditions of **18**.24cd-28 .60-62ab; **20**.8-9 .65 .80cd-82ab .86cd-87ab; **68**.68-70; **164**.3-6
- as stake at bet **170**.47-48
- as stake at game of dice **171**.20-24
- , body as means for goals of **235**.11-12
- , contradictions among goals of **221**.14-15
- , *dharma* as source of other goals of **216**.73-80
- , duties of third stage of **222**.39-44
- , explanation for various conditions of **216**.73-80
- , four goals of **58**.1-7; **88**.2-3 .10-15; **129**.101-124; **170**.32-36; **175**.14cd-16 .76-77; **246**.30-33
- , four stages of **88**.10-15; **123**.2-7ab
- , ideal conditions of **74**.24cd-30; **153**.6cd-7
- , maxim about importance of saving one's **228**.44-46
- , prescr. conc. stages of **222**
- , stages of **1**.3-9; **57**.42-51; **242**.20cd-21ab
- , suffering in human **234**.9-42
- , three goals of **104**.10-14ab; **138**.10-13; **158**.30-35ab; **170**.8ef-13; **217**.4-11; **221**.10; **223**.41-52ab; **242**.25-26ab
- , transfer of **138**.22-27

life-giving effect of water in simile **107**.55-57
life-span, cosmic cycle as **23**.12-15
- during Kali-Yuga **230**.38-43
- of beings **18**.60-62ab
- of gods **5**.58cd-60
- of human beings **20**.14-15 .80cd-82ab
- of Kṛṣṇa on earth **210**.16-21

life-time, liberation during **136**.17-26
lifting of earth by boar **202**.23-29
- of sacrifice **79**

light, Śiva as **135**.2cd-5ab
- , Self as **237**.79-81

lightning, origin of **1**.48cd-50ab
Likhita **34**.92-93ab
Liṅga, circumambulation of **57**.6-8; **87**.17-20
- established at Adritīrtha **174**.25cd-27ab
- established by Agni **98**.21cd-22
- established by Death **116**.22cd-24ab
- established by Rāma **123**.191-194
- named Ādikeśa **169**.2cd-3 .6cd-15 .39cd-43ab
- named Bhāskareśvara **41**.75-81
- named Bhīmeśvara **173**.1-2
- named Brahmeśvara **174**.8-12ef
- named Cakreśvara **109**.1-3ab
- named Deveśvara **142**.12cd-13
- named Gautameśvara **174**.8-12ef
- named Ileśvara **108**.121-123
- named Indreśvara **129**.3
- named Jñāneśvara **117**.1
- named Kālañjara **146**.1
- named Madhyameśvara **100**.14-18
- named Mahānala **116**.1-2ab .22cd-24ab .24cd-25ab
- named Maheśvara **131**.39cd-51
- named Mārkaṇḍeyeśvara **57**.6-8
- named Nāgeśvara **111**.85cd-86
- named Śeṣeśvara **115**.19cd-20ab
- named Siddheśvara **122**.97cd-99 .100-102; **143**.1
- named Someśvara **97**.29; **174**.8-12ef
- named Vāgīśvara **135**.25-27ab
- named Vṛddheśvara **107**.1 .67cd-68ab
- named Yogeśvara **170**.1
- , Śiva as **128**.62-63ab
- talking to devotee **169**.22cd-24ef
- , worship of **41**.82-85; **56**.66cd-73; **97**.29
- worshipped by Lakṣmaṇa **123**.213cd-216
- , wound on **169**.36-39ab

Liṅgas, circumambulation of **157**.27cd-28
- , eighty thousand **160**.21-22ab
- established by monkeys **157**.21cd-25ab
- , immobility of **157**.25cd-27ab
- , number of **41**.11-12
- worshipped by Rāma **157**.27cd-28

lion killed by bear **16**.25-45ab
- , Prasena killed by **16**.25-45ab

lioness, earth as **155**.3cd-10ab
liquor flowing from Kadamba-tree **198**.4-6

- , intoxication by **137**.15-24
- , ocean of **18**.11-12; **20**.34
- , Vāruṇī as **198**.1-3
list of accomplishments **58**.12-18
- of animals **54**.4-7 .14; **178**.38-42; **220**.190cd-193ab
- of Apsarases **32**.99cd-100; **41**.30-34ab; **68**.60-67; **178**.19-24
- of bad qualities **137**.4-7
- of beings **1**.3-9; **22**.32; **39**.7-17ab; **42**.38cd-42ab; **45**.30-36; **51**.17-21; **54**.4-7; **56**.3-8; **89**.37-40ab; **105**.18cd-19; **152**.29-30; **214**.104-107ab .107cd-109; **241**.29-32
- of birds **41**.45-46; **42**.20-23; **43**.56-58ab; **44**.64-66ab; **45**.14cd-15ab; **178**.38-42
- of clean things **221**.120cd-122
- of confluences **105**.22-26ab
- of countries **27**.62cd-64ab
- of demons **70**.35cd-37ab; **181**.7-14; **188**.42-47; **213**.81-104
- of diseases **40**.113cd-118; **94**.15-21; **234**.2-4; **242**.5cd-7
- of drums **65**.12-16
- of enjoyments **21**.6cd-13ab
- of flowers **42**.24-26; **45**.13-14ab
- of fruits **1**.3-9
- of gods **65**.28-30; **191**.4-12
- of good qualities **137**.30cd-39ab
- of heavens **54**.20-21
- of hells **22**.7-27; **214**.14-17; **215**.84cd-136ab; **217**.80cd-86
- of kings **70**.39-40
- of lotuses **68**.13cd-14
- of Manus **5**.4; **65**.31-34
- of milking-vessels **4**.100-109
- of mountains **18**.16-17 .21-23ab .32-36ab; **19**.3; **27**.20cd-24ab; **54**.8-11; **56**.3-8; **64**.8cd-9; **65**.38cd-39ab
- of names of sun **33**.34-45
- of nether worlds **54**.20-21
- of peoples **19**.15cd-19; **27**.41cd-42 .43-50 .51cd-53 .54-57 .59cd-62ab .62cd-64ab; **54**.12-13; **56**.3-8; **220**.8-10ab
- of physical disabilities **225**.42-45
- of places of pilgrimage **25**.8cd-83ab; **65**.84-96
- of plants **41**.38cd-44; **42**.24-26; **44**.66cd-69; **68**.12-13ab
- of professions **44**.23-27ab .27cd-40
- of regions **18**.18-20
- of rivers **19**.11-12ab .12cd-13ab .13cd .14; **27**.25cd-27 .28-29 .30-32 .33-34 .35-36ab .37cd-38ab .38cd-39ab; **56**.3-8; **64**.10 .11-14; **70**.33-35ab; **105**.22-26ab; **161**.21-23ef
- of sins **212**.35-41; **214**.88cd-96; **215**.55cd-64 .72-77 .84cd-136ab; **223**.28-31; **228**.22-38; **240**.38-44
- of things cleaned with water **221**.113-114
- of torments in hell **215**.84cd-136ab
- of trees **1**.3-9; **26**.3-5; **28**.11-18; **42**.15-19; **43**.45-55; **44**.55-63; **45**.8-12; **51**.33-36; **68**.6-11; **178**.32-37
- of triads **179**.29-37
listener(s), admonition of **177**.29-30
- , comment by **69**.1-9
- , qualification(s) of **4**.24-26; **246**.16-17
- , request by **1**.16-20; **2**.51-53; **3**.1 .15; **4**.19-23; **5**.1-2; **7**.35-36 .56; **8**.33-34 .62; **13**.1; **18**.7-9; **23**.1-2; **25**.1; **26**.1 .18-25 .36; **27**.10-13; **28**.10; **29**.1-6; **30**.1-6 .45; **31**.28; **32**.1-2 .48; **33**.1-2 .32; **34**.7-8 .51-54; **38**.21; **39**.1-2; **41**.1-5; **43**.15-21; **45**.1-3; **46**.1; **48**.1-2; **51**.60-62; **58**.8-11; **59**.4-5 .22; **60**.7; **63**.10; **65**.1; **66**.3-5; **67**.1 .9; **68**.1-3; **70**.12 .14-15 .30-32; **71**.1; **73**.1; **74**.1 .6; **75**.1; **76**.1; **78**.1-2; **79**.1-2; **124**.32; **130**.15-16; **175**.1-2ef; **176**.1-2 .35-36; **178**.5; **179**.2-75; **200**.1; **205**.9-10; **207**.1-2; **208**.1-2; **210**.5; **213**.1-9; **214**.3-8; **215**.1; **217**.2-3 .12-13 .18 .22; **218**.1-2; **219**.1 .4-5; **220**.1 .68 .205 .207; **221**.4-5; **222**.1; **223**.1-3 .7-11; **224**.1-3 .27 .39-45; **225**.1 .42-45 .53 .57-59; **226**.4-6 .10; **227**.1-4; **228**.6; **229**.1-2 .14 .19; **230**.1-2 .8; **231**.3 .42-43; **232**.3; **235**.1; **236**.1-2; **237**.1-2 .43; **238**.15; **239**.1 .10 .42; **240**.1-2 .50 .77-80; **241**.1-2 .9-10; **243**.1-10
- , request to **67**.81; **70**.8cd-10
- , satisfaction of **179**.1
listening to Purāṇa **246**.34-35
- to Purāṇa, merit of **175**.86-90
- to stories of Hari, merit of **76**.18cd-23ab
livelihood granted by earth **2**.25-28ab; **4**.74-80
- granted by sun **31**.4-6
- , threefold knowledge concerning **187**.42-54
living, beings, classification of **241**.33
- in Kali-Yuga, wish for **231**.1-2

location of Bhāratavarṣa **27**.65-66ab
- of field of actions **161**.21-23ef
- of Puruṣottamakṣetra **45**.53-56

Lohākula, place of pilgrimage **25**.11
Lohakuṇḍa, place of pilgrimage **64**.3-8ab
Lohārgala, place of pilgrimage **25**.11; **64**.3-8ab
Lohika, place of pilgrimage **25**.70
Lohita **20**.29-30
Lohitārṇava, place of pilgrimage **25**.76
Lohitas **10**.61-62; **13**.91
Lokacakṣus **31**.31-33ab
Lokadvāra, place of pilgrimage **25**.38
Lokāloka **20**.95cd-98ab
Lokapāla, place of pilgrimage **25**.19
Lokapālatīrtha, place of pilgrimage **25**.23
Lokaprakāśaka **31**.31-33ab
Lokārohaṇa, place of pilgrimage **25**.32
Lokasākṣin **31**.31-33ab
Lolas **27**.58cd
Lomaharṣaṇa **1**.13-15; **235**.2
- as first-person narrator **246**.13-15
- as narrator **1**.31-32; **3**.2; **5**.3; **6**.1ab; **13**.2; **18**.10; **25**.2; **26**.2; **41**.1-5; **179**.1; **217**.1; **235**.2 .30; **246**.1-5
- , praise of **1**.16-20
- to Viṣṇu, hymn by **1**.21-29

Lomapāda, Daśaratha **13**.40-41
Lommel, H. **6**.44-45ab; **10**.65cd-67ab
looking at discus of Hari, merit of **51**.63-71
- at fig-tree **177**.26
- at house of Kṛṣṇa, merit of **212**.9-11
- at Kṛṣṇa and Balarāma **193**.41
- at Kṛṣṇa, impossibility of **53**.39-40
- at Kṛṣṇa, liberation by **177**.6
- at Kṛṣṇa, merit of **65**.83-99
- at Kṛṣṇa, Saṃkarṣaṇa, Subhadrā **177**.3 .8
- at Puruṣottama **177**.21
- at Puruṣottama, merit of **65**.76cd-77
- at Śiva, impossibility of **162**.13-19
- at sun **16**.13-24
- at sun, prohibition of **221**.20
- at sun, purification by **221**.26-30 .67cd-69 .136cd-137ab .140cd-141ab
- at wishing tree, merit of **60**.12-15
- at woman, Yoga destroyed by **219**.6-12

looks, burning by **8**.54-57; **38**.1-6; **71**.27-37; **78**.32-37ab, **118**.19-24ab; **196**.16-20
- , effect(s) of **225**.49

loop of Varuṇa **203**.45-62
Lopāmudrā **11**.51-53; **13**.72cd-75ab; **110**.5-9
lord of ancestors, Yama as **4**.2-9; **6**.46cd-48ab
- of ancestral rites, Vivasvat as **8**.95
- of Ādityas, Viṣṇu as **4**.2-9
- of birds, Garuḍa as **4**.2-9
- of castes, Soma as **4**.2-9
- of cows, bull as **4**.2-9
- of cows, Kṛṣṇa as **188**.29-35
- of demons, Prahrāda as **4**.2-9
- of *dharma*, Yama as **94**.31-36; **165**.30cd-36
- of elephants, Airāvata as **4**.2-9
- of Gandharvas, Citraratha as **4**.2-9
- of Gandharvas, Soma as **105**.2
- of ghosts, Śiva as **4**.2-9
- of gods, Dhanvantari as **122**.44-47
- of gods, Indra as **131**.16-24
- of hells, Yama as **123**.121-128ab
- of horses, Uccaiḥśravas as **4**.2-9
- of kings, Kubera as **4**.2-9
- of Maruts, Indra as **4**.2-9
- of mountains, Himālaya as **4**.2-9
- of Nāgas, Vāsuki as **4**.2-9
- of nether world, Śeṣa as **115**.2-4
- of obstacle(s), Gaṇeśa as **114**.13
- of plants, Soma as **4**.2-9; **9**.12; **120**.8; **174**.16
- of Prajāpatis, Dakṣa as **4**.2-9
- of rains, Indra as **187**.35-40
- of Rākṣasas, Meghahāsa as **142**.9-10ab
- of Rākṣasas, Śiva as **4**.2-9
- of rivers, ocean as **4**.2-9
- of sacrifice, Soma as **4**.2-9
- of sages, Soma as **9**.12
- of seeds, Soma as **9**.12
- of serpents, Takṣa as **4**.2-9
- of stars, Soma as **4**.2-9
- of the north, Kubera as **97**.29
- of the south, Agastya as **118**.2-9; **158**.8-15ef
- of the south, Yama as **125**.25-32; **131**.31-39ab
- of trees, fig-tree as **4**.2-9
- of Vasus, Agni as **4**.2-9
- of waters, Soma as **9**.12
- of waters, Varuṇa as **4**.2-9
- of wealth, Kubera as **97**.24-28
- of wild animals, tiger as **4**.2-9
- of Yakṣas, Śiva as **4**.2-9
- of Yoga, Viṣṇu as **170**.40-43 .54-63 .69-74ab .89a-f; **213**.170

lord see also *king*
lord of direction see also *guardians of directions*
lords of the earth **41**.60cd-71
- of three worlds, gods as **32**.7-8
lordship over gods, Indra expelled from **122**.48-49
- over gods obtained by sacrifices to Viṣṇu **191**.4-12
loss of Brahminhood **223**.28-31
- of *dharma* of Kṣatriyas **8**.31-32 .44-51
- of honour, maxim about **146**.8cd-10
- of memory **212**.21-24
- of memory during birth **234**.9-42
- of merit **178**.65-69
lotus as residence of Brahman **179**.22cd-26; **180**.24cd-38
- , Brahman originated from **161**.6cd-9
- , earth as **18**.13-15
- of eight leaves **61**.1-3
- originated from Viṣṇu and waters **161**.6cd-9
lotuses, list of **68**.13cd-14
- , white **59**.6-21
lotus-filament, Indra as **96**.2-5ab
lotus-flowers, worship of Śiva with **109**.46-48
lotus-position **110**.47cd-50; **235**.13-20 .28
love of Kṛṣṇa for Satyabhāmā **203**.26-32
love-play of Kṛṣṇa and Gopīs **189**.14-45
- of Śiva and Pārvatī **205**.11-14
low castes, wish-fulfilment for women and **227**.10-14
Lüders, H. **18**
lunar dynasty **9**.35ab; **10**; **11**; **12**; **13**; **14**; **108**.68-70 .119-120; **111**.2-6
- mansion **64**.1-2; **65**.3; **220**.10cd-11ab
- mansion sacred to Indra **63**.22
- mansions **23**.6-10; **24**.13-18; **26**.15; **220**.33cd-42 .118cd-120ab
- mansions in simile **68**.43
lunar mansion see also *Nakṣatra*
lust, creation of **1**.39cd-42
lustiness, punishment for **215**.95cd-98ab
lustre of Rāma **213**.156
lying down, prescription(s) concerning **221**.58ab
macro-microcosmic equivalences **56**.16-17ab .27cd-30ab
Mada **213**.81-104
Madgu **14**.8-10; **16**.50cd-54ab
Mādhava **5**.17d-19ab; **56**.58-60; **60**.39-45; **61**.14-16; **178**.178; **189**.30-33
- and Ramā **174**.8-12ef
- as fish **60**.1-6
- , statue of **59**.26-33
Mādhava see also *Kṛṣṇa, Viṣṇu*
Mādhavamāhātmya **59**.23-25
Mādhavas **13**.205-207ab
Madhu **4**.112; **5**.17d-19ab; **13**.205-207ab; **15**.24-28; **70**.35cd-37ab; **213**.136-140
- and Kaiṭabha, boon by Viṣṇu to **213**.28-29
- and Kaiṭabha killed by Viṣṇu **180**.24cd-38; **213**.28-29
- , Jātavedas killed by **98**.2-5
Madhucchandas **10**.57-60
- , advice by **171**.40-43
- as priest of Pramati **171**.25-26
- , boon by Sūrya to **138**.35-38
- , Śaryāti and **138**
- to Sūrya, hymn by **138**.33-34
Mādhucchandasa, place of pilgrimage **138**.39cd-40
Madhukaṇṭa, place of pilgrimage **25**.42
Madhukuṇḍa, place of pilgrimage **25**.19
Madhupadhvaja **13**.199cd-202
Madhusūdana **60**.39-45; **61**.14-16; **178**.118-121; **184**.14-19; **185**.5-10 .34-38; **188**.24-28; **194**.9; **207**.28-43
Madhusūdana see also *Kṛṣṇa, Viṣṇu*
Madhuvāhinī, place of pilgrimage **64**.11-14
Madhūvaṭa, place of pilgrimage **25**.42
Madhyadeśas **19**.15cd
Madhyakesara, place of pilgrimage **25**.15
Madhyameśvara, Liṅga named **100**.14-18
Madhyasthāna, place of pilgrimage **25**.81
Madirādi **14**.36-38
Madrā **13**.5-8
Madraka **13**.25cd-27ab
Madrakas **13**.25cd-27ab; **27**.43-50
Madras **19**.18; **27**.51cd-53
Mādrī **14**.1-2ab .3ab; **16**.9-11 .49cd; **205**.1-6
Maga [caste] **20**.71-72ab
Magadha **4**.67; **13**.109
Māgadha **195**.1-4
- [caste] **20**.71-72ab
- , origin of Sūta and **2**.25-28ab
- , Sūta and **4**.60-67
Magadha-forest, place of pilgrimage **25**.10
Magadhakas **27**.51cd-53
Magadhas **19**.16

Māgadhas **27**.43-50
Maghā **220**.31cd-32ab .33cd-42
Māgha **31**.19-21; **219**.109cd-113ab; **220**.56 .116cd-117ab
Maghavan **3**.74cd-78ab; **34**.42-45ab; **109**.13-20; **159**.39ef-41ab
magic jewel, prosperity effected by **16**.13-24; **17**.24-27
- of demons **78**.12-24
- power(s), fight by means of **200**.17-19; **206**.5-9
- power(s) obtained by asceticism **124**.36cd-39ab
- power(s), transfer of **200**.11-16
- use of Mantras **13**.43-44
- woman, Rākṣasas bewitched by **134**.8cd-11
magic see also *Māyā*
Mahābāhu **3**.74cd-78ab
Mahābala, place of pilgrimage **25**.12
Mahābhadra **18**.31
Mahābhārata **3**.46cd-49; **17**.8-11 .28; **18** .11-12 .13-15 .18-20 .44cd-45ab; **19** .3 .20; **20**.33 .36-38ab .41cd-42 .45 .47cd-49ab .49cd-51 .58cd-74ab .88ab; **65**.97-99; **78**; **95**.2-6; **97**.5cd-7; **128**; **146**; **159**; **211**.3-4; **212**.72-85; **217**; **218**; **223**; **224**; **225**; **226**; **236**; **237**; **238**; **239**; **240**; **241**; **242**; **243**; **244**; **245**
-, reference to battle of **188**.42-47; **212**.12 -17 .64-65
-, reference to Durvāsas-episode in **211**.3-4
-, Veda(s) and **246**.6-12
Mahābhīma **215**.111cd-112ab
Mahācaṇḍa **215**.65-67
Mahādeva **28**.56cd-62ab; **33**.9-13ab; **34**.90; **109**.6cd-10; **115**.5-6ab; **124**.132-136ab; **127**.35-47; **135**.2cd-5ab; **169**.1-2ab .43cd-45ef; **176**.26-32; **196**.1-4; **223**.4-6
Mahādeva see also *Śiva*
Mahādruma **20**.59cd-61
Mahāgaurī **27**.33-34
Mahāghora **214**.14-17
Mahāghorā **215**.130cd-136ab
Mahāhrada, place of pilgrimage **25**.58
Mahājihva **213**.81-104
Mahājvāla **22**.2-6 .12ab
Mahājvālā **215**.119cd-120ab
Mahākāla, Śiva as **43**.65cd-74
Mahākālavana, place of pilgrimage **25**.26
Mahākarṇa **3**.99-101
Mahākāśa **20**.59cd-61
Mahākāya, Śiva as **116**.15-16
Mahākuṇḍa, place of pilgrimage **25**.19
Mahālaya, place of pilgrimage **25**.12 .47
Mahālobha **22**.2-6
Mahālokas, seven **23**.21
Mahāmanas **13**.15cd-20ab
Mahāmārī **215**.45-55ab
Mahāmeru **20**.59cd-61
Mahānābha **3**.72-73ab
Mahānadī **20**.66-67; **27**.30-32
-, description of **46**.4-6ab
-, place of pilgrimage **25**.67; **64**.11-14
Mahānala, Liṅga named **116**.1-2ab .22cd-24ab .24cd-25ab
-, place of pilgrimage **116**.1-2ab
-, Śiva as **116**.15-16
Mahānīla **3**.99-101
Mahāpadma **3**.99-101
Mahāpāyin **215**.118cd-119ab
Mahāprabhā **215**.93cd-94ab
Mahāpreta **215**.130cd-136ab
Mahāpuṃs **20**.59cd-61
Mahāpura [city] **170**.69-74ab
Mahāpuruṣa **30**.69cd-70ab
Mahārāja [king] **170**.69-74ab
Mahārājahrada, place of pilgrimage **25**.82
Mahārāṣṭras **27**.54-57
Mahāraurava **215**.99-100ab
Maharloka **23**.12-15 .16-20; **232**.28-29
Mahāśāla **13**.15cd-20ab
Mahāśani as combination of Viṣṇu and Śiva **129**.94-99ab
- as son-in-law of Varuṇa **129**.17-20ab
-, Indra as prisoner of **129**.20cd-29
-, Indra defeated by **129**.11cd-16
-, Indra taunted by **129**.30-37
- slain by Abjaka [Vṛṣākapi] **129**.94-99ab
-, Varuṇa as father-in-law of **129**.20cd-29
Mahāśiras **3**.74cd-78ab
Mahāśrama, place of pilgrimage **25**.58
Mahāsrota, place of pilgrimage **25**.20
Mahāśrotra, place of pilgrimage **25**.20
Mahāsūtra, place of pilgrimage **25**.20
Mahāsvana **213**.81-104
Mahat **233**.12-29
Mahātāmisra **215**.102-103
Mahatī **8**.63-64
Mahātīrtha, place of pilgrimage **25**.67; **122**.87-92

Mahāvaṭa **215**.112cd-113ab
Mahāvīci **215**.84cd-136ab
Mahāvīta **20**.75cd-76
Mahendra **19**.3 .14; **27**.19cd-20ab .37cd-38ab
- as place for asceticism **213**.114-122
- , place of pilgrimage **64**.8cd-9
Māhendra, place of pilgrimage **25**.47 .79
Maheśa **158**.22-27ef
Maheśvara **3**.46cd-49; **31**.31-33ab; **33**.3-8; **41**.87; **78**.47-54; **82**.11-14; **94**.46-48ab; **97**.15-17; **100**.1-3 .14-18; **102**.6cd-8ab; **109**.3cd-6ab .10cd-12 .26cd-27 .36-39ab; **110**.87-97ef; **117**.2-5; **140**.3cd-5ab; **160**.13-16ef; **162**.2cd-6ab .6cd-10ab; **168**.1 .31-35; **225**.46-52; **226**.7-9; **229**.59-63
- , Liṅga named **131**.39cd-51
Maheśvara see also *Śiva*
Māheśvara, place of pilgrimage **25**.82
Maheśvaratīrtha, place of pilgrimage **168**.31-35
Māheśvarī **77**.9cd-13; **78**.75cd-76
Mahī **20**.43-44; **27**.28-29
- [mother of Sanājjāta] **92**
Mahiman as author of Mahimnastuti **153**.8-11
- [son of Prācīnabarhis] **153**.8-11 .15cd-16ab
Mahimnastuti, Mahiman as author of **153**.8-11
Mahiṣa **20**.25-27
Māhiṣakas **8**.44-51; **27**.54-57
Māhiṣikas **27**.54-57
Mahiṣmat **13**.157-159
Māhiṣmatī [city] **13**.176cd-187ab
Maināka **20**.49cd-51; **27**.20cd-24ab; **72**.7 .11cd-14
Maitra, place of pilgrimage **104**.1-2
Maitreyas **13**.97
Makara **69**.12-43
makha, explanation of **79**.7cd-19
Makhāntakas **27**.51cd-53
making of arrows, punishment for **22**.16b:
- of statue **50**.7-15 .29-32 .41-43ab .48-54
- of weapons, punishment for **22**.16cd-17ab
Maladā **13**.5-8
Maladas **27**.51cd-53
Mālāḍhya **176**.37-51
Malajas **27**.59cd-62ab
Mālava **43**.24
- , place of pilgrimage **96**.18-19
Mālavartikas **27**.51cd-53
Mālavas **19**.17; **27**.62cd-64ab
Malavya, place of pilgrimage **25**.24
Malaya **19**.3 .13cd; **27**.19cd-20ab .36cd-37ab
- , place of pilgrimage **64**.8cd-9
Malaya, explanation of **160**.10-12
male sex by bathing, restoration of **108**.113-115
Mālikāḍhya **176**.37-51
Mālinī **13**.127cd-132ab
- [city] **13**.43-44
Mālinī-metre **36**.71-79; **203**.70-73
Mālinītīrtha, place of pilgrimage **25**.76
Mallas **27**.51cd-53
Mālya, place of pilgrimage **25**.82
Mālyavat **18**.32-36ab .44cd-45ab
man disguised as woman **210**.6-10
manas see *mind*
Mānasa **20**.22-23 .29-30; **89**.1-2cd
- [caste] **20**.71-72ab
- , place of pilgrimage **25**.18
Mānasa-era **1**.53cd-54
Mānasa-lake **18**.31
Mānasottara **20**.77-80ab
Manastīrtha, place of pilgrimage **25**.45
Manasyu **13**.3-4
Mānavaka, place of pilgrimage **25**.53
Mānda **118**.15-18
Mandaga **20**.47cd-49ab
- [caste] **20**.71-72ab
Mandagāminī **27**.38cd-39ab
Māndaha [caste] **20**.38cd-40ab
Mandākinī **10**.5-8; **27**.30-32; **61**.29; **89**.1-2cd
Mandākinīhrada, place of pilgrimage **25**.82
Mandakrāntā-metre **36**.117
maṇḍala, prayer-formula allocated to **61**.20-22
- , prescr. conc. drawing of **61**.39-45ab
- , Viṣṇu allocated to **61**.19
Mandara **13**.176cd-187ab; **18**.21-23ab; **20**.41cd-42; **27**.20cd-24ab; **106**.8-10ab; **202**.3-12; **209**.11cd-21ab
- , place of pilgrimage **25**.11; **64**.3-8ab
Mandaradroṇī **178**.65-69
Mandatīrtha, place of pilgrimage **118**.1
Māṇḍavya **96**.11-17 .18-19
- , hymn by gods to **96**.11-17
Mandeha [caste] **20**.38cd-40ab
Māndhātṛ **7**.91-92 .93-95ab
Mandodarī **68**.60-67

Maṅgalā **68**.56-59ab
Maṅgalā, explanation of **122**.93-94
Maṅgalācaraṇam **1**.1-2
Maṅgalāsaṃgama, place of pilgrimage **122**.100-102
mango-tree **41**.11-12
Maṇi **3**.99-101
Maṇīcaka **20**.59cd-61
manifestation of Śiva, Umā as **75**.21
- of Viṣṇu in Puṣkara **213**.25-31
manifestation see also *aspects, incarnations*
manifestations, four **61**.39-40
- of Nārāyaṇa **181**.15-19
- of Vāsudeva, purpose of **213**.21-24
- of Viṣṇu **180**; **213** .25-26
- of Viṣṇu, characteristics of the **180**.17cd-42ab
- of Viṣṇu, four **59**.34; **61**.7-12 .13; **192**.48-58
- of Viṣṇu, functions of **180**.17cd-42ab
- of Viṣṇu, purpose of **213**.124-126
Maṇijalā **20**.66-67
Maṇikuṇḍala **170** .2-5 .8ef-13 .84-88
Maṇimanta, place of pilgrimage **25**.30
Maṇimat see *Maṇikuṇḍala*
Maṇimatta, place of pilgrimage **25**.30
Maṇināga **90**.2-4
Maṇipūra, place of pilgrimage **25**.31
Maṇipura-mountain, place of pilgrimage **25**.23
Maṇīraka **20**.59cd-61
Maṇiratnahrada, place of pilgrimage **25**.71
Maṇitīrtha, place of pilgrimage **25**.46
Maṇivāhaṇa **13**.109
Maṇivatī [city] **3**.90cd-92ab
Mañjūṣa **215**.90cd-91ab
man-lion, Viṣṇu as **179**.18cd-22ab; **180**.24cd -38; **184**.14-19; **191**.4-12; **213**.43-79
- , world of **227**.37cd-41
man-lion see also *Narasiṃha*
Manmatha **38**.1-13
Manmathadīpinī **68**.60-67
Manoharā **3**.38ef
Manojava **3**.39-40
- , place of pilgrimage **25**.42
Manojavā **20**.54cd-56ab
Manomaya, place of pilgrimage **25**.42
Manonuga **20**.47cd-49ab
mansion, lunar **64**.1-2; **65**.3; **220**.10cd-11ab
- sacred to Indra, lunar **63**.22
mansions in simile, lunar **68**.43
- , lunar **23**.6-10; **24**.13-18; **26**.15; **220**.33cd -42
Mantha, place of pilgrimage **25**.31
Mantharā, Kaikeyī instigated by **123**.105cd-109ab
Mantra, *huṃ* as **206**.24-30
Mantra see also *prayer-formula, spell-formula(s)*
Mantras as deity of Brahmins **187**.42-54
- as weapon **206**.24-30
- , magic use of **13**.43-44
Manu **2**.17-20ab; **6**.52cd-53; **7**.23 .44cd-45ab; **32**.58cd-63; **70**.37cd-38; **174**.2-5ab; **213**.27; **226**.30-41
- as authority on meat **220**.185cd-188ab
- as authority on truthfulness **228**.47-49
- as authority on Veda(s) **234**.60cd-61ab
- , Bhautya **5**.49-52
- , Bhāvya **5**.5cd-6ab
- , Cākṣuṣa **2**.16; **3**.53-58; **5**.4; **34**.26-29ab .29cd-32 .45cd-48
- , Raibhya **5**.5cd-6ab
- , Raivata **5**.4
- , Raucya **5**.5cd-6ab .49-52
- , Sāvarṇa **5**.49-52; **6**.18-20ab
- , Sāvarṇi **5**.5cd-6ab; **6**.48cd-50ab
- , Sāvarṇya **6**.18-20ab
- , Svārociṣa **5**.4
- , Svāyaṃbhuva **2**.1-4; **4**.96; **5**.4 .8-11ab
- , Tāmasa **5**.4
- , Uttama **5**.4 .17d-19ab
- , Vaivasvata **4**.16-17; **5**.5ab .49-52 .63; **6**.7 -8; **7**.1-2 .3-5ab; **34**.26-29ab .45cd-48; **89**.5a-c .37-40ab; **108**.2-7
Manu-era(s) **1**.53cd-54; **34**.42-45ab
- , duration of **5**.54cd-55ab
Manūgā **27**.38cd-39ab
Manuputra **5**.9cd-10
Manus, list of **5**.4; **65**.31-34
Manuvara, place of pilgrimage **25**.19
Manvantarā-days **220**.51cd-54
many-headedness of snakes **3**.96cd-97ab
- of Viṣṇu **122**.68-73
many-headedness see also *heads*
Manyu and gods **162**.13-19
- as commander-in-chief of gods **162**.10cd -12
- as Rudra **162**.27cd-30
- born from brilliance of Śiva **162**.10cd-12
- , description of **162**.20-27ab

- , omnipresence of **162**.20-27ab
- originated from third eye of Śiva **162**.20-27ab
- praised by gods **162**.20-27ab
- , Śiva as **162**.31-33ef
Manyu see also *anger, wrath*
Manyutīrtha, place of pilgrimage **162**.1-2ab .31-33ef
marble, white **59**.26-33
mare, birth of fire from **110**.131-133
- , changing into **6**.15-17; **32**.56-58ab
- , Kṛtyā as **110**.124-130; **116**.22cd-24ab
- pregnant with fire **110**.124-130
- , Uṣā as **89**.9cd-12
- [Vaḍavā], fire as son of **110**.198cd-200cd
- , Viṣṇu as **56**.19cd-22ab
Mārgaṇakeśatra, place of pilgrimage **25**.54
Mārgaśīrṣa **31**.19-21; **41**.54cd-57ab
Marīca **97**.8-13ab
Mārīca **3**.86cd-89ab; **213**.136-140
- , Kaśyapa **3**.109cd-122; **213**.114-122
Marīci **1**.43-45ab; **3**.80cd-83; **5**.8-9ab; **34**.12cd-19; **174**.2-5ab
- , advice by **4**.35-41
Mārīci **3**.74cd-78ab
Māriṣā **2**.34-46 .47-49; **34**.29cd-32 .45cd-48
- , birth of **178**.99-104
Mārjāra, place of pilgrimage **84**.19-20; **129**.9-10
Mārkaṇḍa, place of pilgrimage **145**.11cd-13
Mārkaṇḍeya **45**.77-89; **52**; **53**; **54**; **55**; **56**; **145**.2cd-5ab; **174**.2-5ab
- addressed as child **53**.18cd-20
- , boon by Viṣṇu to **56**.1-2 .51-54 .58-60
- , omniscience of **53**.34-38
- , place of pilgrimage **145**.1-2ab
- to Viṣṇu, hymn by **55**.11-35
- , Viṣṇu appearing to **54**; **55**.7-8; **56**.61-66ab
Mārkaṇḍeya-lake **57**.2-11; **60**.8cd-10
- , merit obtained at **57**.9-11
- , place of pilgrimage **56**.66cd-73
Mārkaṇḍeyapurāṇa **221**
Mārkaṇḍeya-tree **43**.14
Mārkaṇḍeyavana, place of pilgrimage **25**.78
Mārkaṇḍeyeśvara, Liṅga named **57**.6-8
marks of feet on hood of snake **185**.50-51
marriage by force **111**.9-16; **199**.11-12
- , functions of women after **144**.17-19
- , negotiation of **111**.35-39ab
- of Ahalyā **87**.25-29
- of Aniruddha **201**.6-9
- of Āsandiva and Brahmin girl **167**.18-21ef
- of boar and earth **219**.42-47ab
- of daughters of Dakṣa **2**.47-49; **3**.25-28
- of Kaṭha and Revatī **121**.19-21ab
- of Kṛṣṇa and Rukmiṇī **199**
- of Kṛṣṇa to sixteen-thousand one hundred women **204**.13cd-18
- of Kṛtyā and Death **116**.22cd-24ab
- of Viṣṭi and Viśvarūpa **165**.27-30ab
- , prescription(s) concerning age of **165**.5-17
- , qualification(s) for **107**.35-40
- , Rākṣasa way of **199**.11-12
- , rejection of **229**.22-30
marriage see also *self-choice, wedding*
marrying one's daughter, prescr. conc. **165**.23-26
Mārtaṇḍa **6**.1cd-2; **31**.14cd-16 .31-33ab; **32**.3-47
- , birth of **32**.37-41ab
- , demons burnt by **32**.41cd-46
- , Saṃjñā and **32**.49-107
mārtaṇḍa, etymology of **6**.5; **32**.37-41ab
Mārukas **19**.17
Marusthala, place of pilgrimage **64**.3-8ab
marut, etymology of **3**.109cd-122
Māruta **15**.1-12ab
Maruts **5**.36-37ab; **13**.148-150ab; **39**.22-27ab; **72**.8; **106**.26cd-30; **160**.6cd-9; **174**.1 .7 .8-12ef; **191**.4-12; **203**.45-62; **213**.66-71
- as friends of Indra **124**.100-107 .137-139ab
- as gods **124**.108-109
- , forty-nine **3**.109cd-122; **124**.100-107
- , Indra and **168**.28cd-29; **171**.2cd-6cd
- , Indra as lord of **4**.2-9
- , origin of **3**.109cd-122; **124**.68-73ab
- , rebirth as **27**.66cd-68
Marutta **13**.142-146
Marutvatī **3**.29-30ab .30cd-33
Marutvats **3**.30cd-33
Maśaka [caste] **20**.71-72ab
Maśakas **27**.41cd-42
Māsasaṃsaraka, place of pilgrimage **25**.40
Mataṅga, place of pilgrimage **25**.16
Mātaṅga **228**.22-38
Mataṅgahrada, place of pilgrimage **25**.70
Mātaṅgahrada, place of pilgrimage **25**.70
material and immaterial **130**.17-21

Māṭharas **27**.43-50
Mathurā **14**.50cd-56; **192**.5-10 .14-31 .67-68; **193**; **194**.32; **196**.5-8; **246**.21-27
- , place of pilgrimage **64**.3-8ab
- , siege of **195**.1-4
Māthura-Avatāra of Viṣṇu **180**.39cd
Mati **68**.56-59ab; **109**.13-20
Matināra **13**.51-52
Matitīrtha, place of pilgrimage **25**.70
mātṛ, etymology of **89**.17-21
Mātritīrtha [Mātṛtīrtha], place of pilgrimage **25**.39
Mātṛtīrtha, place of pilgrimage **25**.39; **112**.1 .23cd-24ab .24cd-26ab .28; **120**.16-18
Matsya **13**.109; **18**.57-58
Matsyamādhava **59**.3
- , worship of **60**.1-6
Matsyamādhava-Māhātmya **60**.1-6
Matsyas **27**.41cd-42
Matsyatila, place of pilgrimage **25**.17
Matsyodarī **228**.100cd-127ab
- , place of pilgrimage **25**.59
matter and spirit **23**.29cd-31ab; **130**.7-14; **161**.6cd-9; **237**.21-22
- and spirit in simile **23**.28cd-29ab .31cd-32ab; **237**.86cd-89
- , primordial **1**.33-34; **23**.22-27ab
matter see also *prakṛti, primordial matter*
Maudgalya **13**.97; **136**
- , hospitality of **136**.3cd-14ab
- , place of pilgrimage **136**.41-42
- , request by **136**.17-26
Maudgalyas **13**.91
Mauleyas **27**.54-57
Maulikas **27**.54-57
maxim about a reviler **163**.17-22
- about absence of enmity **106**.3-7
- about acceptance of husband **111**.57-60
- about anger **147**.14-17ab
- about attractiveness of women **147**.9cd-13; **151**.3-5ab; **152**.5-9ab
- about begging of Kṣatriyas **168**.2-5
- about Brahminhood **107**.2-11
- about clever people **124**.39cd-47
- about conduct **159**.31cd-35; **221**.161-169ab
- about conduct of the wise **212**.89-90
- about consolation by sons **154**.14cd-21ab
- about contact with good people **163**.32-39
- about demoralising effect of misfortune **150**.1cd-4ab
- about duties of son **108**.76cd-87
- about duty of father **111**.9-16
- about duty of wife **80**.71-77
- about effect(s) of actions **123**.177cd-184; **136**.17-26
- about enjoyment **140**.18cd-19ab
- about evil-doers **163**.32-39
- about failure due to delusion **72**.20-22
- about fate **123**.44-48ab; **159**.5-11; **171**.27-39
- about fickleness of women **151**.5cd-7ab
- about fleeing in battle **124**.73cd-80
- about food of one's deities **123**.173-175
- about forgiveness **87**.55-58ab
- about friendship **124**.28cd-31; **170**.81-83
- about generosity towards women **123**.23-33ab
- about guest(s) **222**.36
- about hatred **110**.121-123
- about honouring of parents **194**.1-5
- about hospitality **163**.12cd-16; **172**.4-7ab .7cd-14
- about husband and wife **80**.37-43; **109**.6cd-10; **128**.3-6; **129**.101-124
- about husband as refuge **111**.68cd-79
- about ideal pupil **121**.10-12 .13-15
- about ideal son **170**.8ef-13
- about importance of counteraction **127**.16-22
- about importance of mother **158**.4-7
- about importance of saving one's life **228**.44-46
- about importance of son **108**.76cd-87
- about indifference **139**.2cd-7ab
- about inheritage of friends and enemies **110**.80ef-86
- about jealousy **152**.9cd-14
- about king **123**.33cd-36ab
- about loss of honour **146**.8cd-10
- about means and ends **152**.15-17
- about misappropriation **140**.26-30
- about noble people **170**.81-83
- about noble young women **123**.165-169
- about old age **146**.11-14
- about pleasing one's beloved **108**.26-30
- about poverty and prosperity **137**.2-3
- about pride **110**.121-123
- about pride of women **203**.64-69
- about protection of the distressed **110**.147-154

- about refuge of enemies **152**.18-20
- about release of enemy **129**.20cd-29
- about respect **39**.27cd-28
- about rival **124**.3cd-6
- about rumours **154**.11cd-14ab
- about search for brother **3**.24
- about son **123**.36cd-43; **146**.26-27
- about submission to a rival **160**.13-16ef
- about teacher **107**.12-16
- about telling of lies **135**.5cd-10ab; **228**.51
- about time **236**.26
- about transitoriness **110**.61-66; **212**.89-90
- about trustful persons **167**.22-25
- about truthfulness of Brahmins and Kṣatriyas **111**.39cd-47
- about twice-born without ceremonies **111**.7-8
- about vices of king **108**.22-23ab
- about voluntary death **107**.31-34
- about wealth **170**.6-7ef
- about women **100**.9-13; **107**.47; **151**.10-16
- about women understanding women **137**.25-28ab
- about wrathful and greedy people **124**.68-73ab
- about youth **170**.6-7ef

Maya **2**.17-20ab; **160**.6cd-9
- , advice by **124**.49-52
- as friend of Indra **124**.28cd-31
- , Indra and **124**.33-48

Māyā **68**.56-59ab
- as yogic sleep of Viṣṇu **233**.5-6
- , effect(s) of **203**.6-19
- , human nature of Kṛṣṇa explained as **193**.80-87
- in simile **240**.54cd-68
- , Lakṣmī as **137**.30cd-39ab
- of Kṛṣṇa **53**.34-38
- of Viṣṇu **194**.1-5; **229** .43cd-67ab; **240**.54cd-68
- of Viṣṇu as dream **229**.88
- of Viṣṇu, Yoganidrā as **181**.37
- , world as **240**.54cd-68

Māyā see also *illusion, magic*

Māyāvatī **200**.2-10 .11-16 .17-19 .23-28

Māyāvidyodbhava, place of pilgrimage **25**.57

meaning of Purāṇa **174**.2-5ab
- of Veda(s) **158**.30-35ab; **161**.27-29

means and ends, maxim about **152**.15-17
- of dying **214**.27cd-31
- of knowledge **231**.48-50
- of liberation **236**.3-5 .6
- of liberation, discussion about **145**

meat **39**.59-66; **220**.185cd-188ab
- , classification of **220**.23cd-28ab
- , forbidden **220**.190cd-193ab
- , kinds of **220**.168-177
- , Manu as authority on **220**.185cd-188ab
- of dog, eating of **93**.5-11
- of hare **7**.48cd-51ab
- , offering of **187**.55-59ab
- , offering of wine and **181**.38-53
- , prescription(s) concerning eating of **221**.55 .111 .112
- , punishment for eating of **214**.88cd-96; **215**.127cd-128ab
- , punishment for offering of forbidden **220**.193cd-195ab
- , punishment for selling of **22**.18cd-20
- , purity of **221**.127cd-129ab

meat see also *flesh*

Medhā **68**.56-59ab; **102**.2cd-5ab
- , place of pilgrimage **102**.1-2ab

Medhātithi **5**.9cd-10; **20**.3-5

Medhāvina, place of pilgrimage **25**.82

Medhya **5**.9cd-10

medinī, etymology of **4**.112

meditation, constituents of **243**.47-48
- , death as result of instability of **237**.28
- , identification by **28**.26
- , immobility of mind during **237**.29-31
- in simile **237**.29-31
- , indifference achieved by **238**.31-33ab
- , information by means of **87**.60-66ab
- , knowledge by means of **33**.3-8; **74**.82-87; **87**.25-29; **114**.2-5; **131**.10-15
- on fire **61**.19
- on Kṛṣṇa **177**.4
- on moon **61**.19
- on Nārāyaṇa **60**.34-38
- on Puruṣottama **178**.187-190
- on Śiva **39**.90-91; **94**.2-14; **109**.52-54
- on sun **33**.27-31; **61**.19
- on Viṣṇu **45**.37-41; **80**.65-70; **86**.8-9ab
- , places for **58**.19-21ab
- , postures of **158**.28-29
- , prescription(s) concerning **243**.50-53
- with prayer-formulas **61**.23
- , Yoga of **20**.56cd-57ab; **52**.11-15ab

meditation see also *absorption,*

concentration, union
Medura **14**.8-10
Meghahāsa **142**
- as lord of Rākṣasas **142**.9-10ab
- , place of pilgrimage **142**.10cd-12ab
Meghanāda, Indra defeated by **176**.19cd-20
Meinhard, H. **75**.12
Mekhalā **15**.14-15
Melakas **27**.59cd-62ab
memory during birth, loss of **234**.9-42
- , loss of **212**.21-24
- of former existences **111**.68cd-79; **164**.29-37; **197**.1-3; **204**.8-13ab; **228**.92cd -96; **229**.22-30 .72-86ab; **246**.30-33
memory see also *remembering*
men, holy places established by **70**.16-19
Menā **34**.39-41 .81; **38**.22-40; **71**.19-23; **147**.5-7 .9cd-13
- , Śiva reproached by **38**.22-40
Menā see also *Menakā*
Menakā **13**.97; **32**.99cd-100; **41**.30-34ab; **68**.60-67; **86**.30-34; **178**.19-24
- and Viśvāmitra **147**.5-7
Menakā see also *Menā*
menstruation, prescr. conc, women during **221**.23 .75 .135cd-136ab .141cd-143ab .143cd-146ab
mental afflictions **234**.5-6
- worship **192**.59-61
Mercury see *Budha*
mercy, request for **206**.14-19 .39-44; **208**.32 -35; **211**.5-10
merit according to caste **28**.37-38
- , comparison of **25**.83cd-86ab; **28**.47-53ab .56cd-62ab; **29**.42cd-61; **33**.27-31; **41**.54cd-57ab .93; **57**.9-11 .17-19 .38-41 .42-51; **58**.70cd-77; **60**.46-48; **62**.16cd-22ab; **63**.1-7; **64**.1-2 .3-16; **65**.59-76ab .81-82 .83-99; **66**.18-23; **67**.52; **75**.35-45; **79**.21cd-22; **80**.84-89; **89**.1-2cd; **93**.25-26; **98**.20-21ab .21cd-22; **103**.8 .12c-f; **104**.89ab; **110**.216 .217-219cd .226-228; **111**.85cd-86; **118**.31-32ef; **119**.1; **128**.83-84; **132**.1-2; **134**.15-16; **138**.41; **144**.23-24 .25-27; **145**.1-2ab; **148**.18cd-20; **151**.27cd-29; **155**.13cd-14ab; **161**.61cd-62; **163**.12cd-16; **168**.26cd-28ab; **171**.1-2ab; **175**.60-68 .83-84 .86-90; **176**.57-62; **177**.9-15; **216**.64-66; **219**.116; **230**.59 .62-63; **246**.21-27
- gained by women **41**.86; **65**.76cd-77 .78-80
- , husband obtained according to **111**.57-60
- in Yugas, comparison of **230**.64
- , loss of **178**.65-69
- measured by sacrifice of cows **110**.216
- , multiplication of **40**.103-106; **41**.57cd-59ab; **62**.10-13ab; **148**.1-3ab .21-26; **149**.16cd-19; **154**.30cd-31; **164**.53cd-54
- obtained at auspicious date(s) **64**.3-16 .17-20
- obtained at bathing festival **65**.57-58
- obtained at Gaṅgā **75**.35-45
- obtained at Gautamī **90**.31-33
- obtained at Indradyumna-tank **51**.29-31
- obtained at Mārkaṇḍeya-lake **57**.9-11
- obtained at place of pilgrimage **28**.9 .11 -18; **35**.26cd-28; **41**.88-90 .91 .93; **42**.1-2 .6-8 .9 .13-14 .42cd-46ab; **43**.14 .65cd-74 .75-76 .77-82ab .83cd-85ab; **45**.53-56 .57-58; **51**.29-31 .63-71; **57**.9-11; **59**.81 -91; **62**.1-4 .13cd-15 .22cd-23; **63**.1-7; **70**.3cd-8ab; **81**.1 .22c-f; **82**.1 .15-16ef; **83**.29; **86**.1 .2; **88**.21-26; **89**.46cd; **91**.11cd -12; **93**.1-2; **94**.1 .48cd-50ab; **95**.1 .31-32; **96**.1 .25cd-26; **97**.1 .32cd-33; **98**.20-21ab .21cd-22; **99**.12a-f; **100**.1-3 .4ab .31ef; **101**.1; **102**.1-2ab .9cd-11ab .11c-f; **103**.12c-f; **105**.29cd-30ab; **106**.54cd-56; **108**.1 .121-123; **109**.1-3ab; **110**.166-167 .215 .226-228; **111**.85cd-86; **112**.1; **113**.1 .18-21 .22-23; **114**.21-24 .25; **115**.18-19ab .20c-f; **116**.24cd-25ab .25c-f; **117**.20c-f; **118**.31-32ef; **119**.1 .18-19; **120**.1 .16-18; **121**.24-25 .26; **122**.1-2 .87-92 .100-102 .104; **123**.1 .176-177ab .207-213ab; **124**.137-139ab; **125**.33-43 .54-56; **126**.1-2 .37-39; **127**.64a-f; **128**.77-81; **129**.1-2 .101-124 .125-127; **130**.1 .34; **131**.39cd-51 .52-53ab .54cd-57ef; **132**.1-2 .7-9ef; **133**.1 .23cd-25; **134**.15-16; **135**.1-2ab .25-27ab .27c-f; **136**.43; **137**.1 .40cd-41ab .41c-f; **138**.1 .39cd-40; **139**.19 .20; **140**.1 .35-38; **141**.29-30; **142**.14; **143**.17; **144**.23-24 .25-27; **145**.1-2ab .11cd-13; **146**.42-45; **147**.1-3 .20cd-23ab; **148**.1-3ab .21-26 .27a-f; **149**.13-16ab .16cd-19; **150**.21-22 .23; **151**.1-2 .22cd-24ab .27cd-29; **152**.40; **153**.13-15ab; **154**.1 .30cd-31; **155**.13cd-14ab; **156**.1-2ab .7-9ab;

157.1-2ab .29 .31; **158**.39cd-40ef; **159**.46cd-48ab .48cd-49ef; **161**.1-2ab .63-64ab .72-78; **162**.31-33ef; **163**.1-2 .52-53; **164**.1-2 .53cd-54; **165**.1 .47cd-48ef; **166**.1 .8cd-11ab .11cd-13; **167**.33; **168**.30 .36 .38; **169**.1-2ab .48-49cd; **170**.1 .89a-f; **171**.1-2ab .47-49ef; **172**.1 .19cd-20ef; **173**.34cd-35ef; **174**.25cd-27ab; **228**.92cd-96
- obtained at Puruṣottamakṣetra **43**.14; **177**
- obtained at Vārāhatīrtha **79**.21cd-22
- obtained by *stambha* **41**.92
- obtained in Kali-Yuga **230**.59
- of alms-giving **219**.107cd-109ab
- of ancestral rites **220**.43-48ab .48cd-49ab
- of asceticism **177**.9-15
- of bathing **228**.92cd-96
- of bathing at Agnitīrtha **125**.50-53
- of bathing at Ekāmraka **41**.93
- of bathing at holy places **214**.114cd-119
- of bathing at Viraja **42**.6-8
- of bathing in Gautamī **80**.84-89
- of bathing in Kokā **219**.107cd-109ab
- of bathing in Vaitaraṇī **42**.4
- of death at Puruṣottamakṣetra **177**.16-19
- of death at sun temple **28**.62cd-64ab
- of devotion to Ananta **176**.57-62
- of donation(s) **41**.57cd-59ab; **120**.3cd-5
- of donation(s) of plants **120**.6-7ab
- of donations **65**.59-76ab
- of drinking of Soma **119**.1
- of faithfulness of wife **80**.71-77
- of fasting **219**.107cd-109ab
- of feeding of Brahmins **218**.9-32
- of festival **66**.1-2
- of homage to fig-tree **57**.17-19
- of hymn to sun **31**.33cd-34
- of installation-ceremony **67**.52-80
- of listening to Purāṇa **175**.86-90
- of listening to stories of Hari **76**.18cd-23ab
- of looking at discus of Hari **51**.63-71
- of looking at house of Kṛṣṇa **212**.9-11
- of looking at Kṛṣṇa **65**.83-99
- of looking at Puruṣottama **65**.76cd-77
- of looking at wishing tree **60**.12-15
- of offerings **29**.42cd-61
- of pilgrimage **28**.53cd-54ab .54cd-56ab; **45**.77-89; **63**.19-20; **67**.2-5
- of praise of fig-tree **57**.15-16
- of prayer-formula **57**.30-31
- of procession **66**.15-17 .18-23
- of recitation of hymn **85**.19-23; **114**.21-24; **124**.123-131; **125**.44-49 .50-53
- of sacrifice **177**.9-15
- of sojourn at Puruṣottamakṣetra **177**.9-15; **178**.106-111
- of sojourn at Utkala **42**.42cd-46ab
- of vegetarianism **216**.64-66
- of voluntary death **110**.61-66
- of worship **51**.42-45; **57**.38-41 .42-51 .52-56 .59-61; **58**.1-7 .12-18 .59cd-77; **59**.81-91; **60**.1-6 .19-21; **61**.47-50; **66**.7cd-13; **68**.73
- of worship of Puruṣottama **178**.193-194
- of worship of Śiva **28**.56cd-62ab; **41**.60cd-71 .72-74 .88-90
- of worship of sun **28**.37-54ab .46 .47-53ab; **29**.7-61; **33**.27-31
- of worship of Varāha **219**.107cd-109ab
- of worship of Vārāhī **42**.11
- of worship of Virajā **42**.1-2
- of worship of Viṣṇu **42**.11
- , selling of **231**.4-41
- , transfer of **35**.46-51; **222**.36; **228**.62-73 .76-85 .86-91ab

meritorious observances **29**.1-6
- practices **27**.73-78ab
- practices, acceptability of **29**.15-17

Meru **10**.5-8; **18**.18-20; **30**.49-52; **38**.40; **39**.4-6 .17cd-18ab; **54**.4-7; **56**.3-8; **69**.12-43; **73**.63cd-65ab; **78**.70-75ab; **106**.3-7 .23-26ab; **112**.11-19; **161**.24-26; **181**.5-6 .32; **212**.72-85; **219**.6-12
- as pericarp **18**.13-15 .44cd-45ab
- as place for asceticism **5**.49-52; **6**.48cd-50ab; 7.30-34
- , description of **26**.28-30; **45**.5-16ab
- , extent of **18**.13-15

Merukuṇḍa, place of pilgrimage **25**.19
Merusāvarṇis **5**.5cd-6ab .49-52
Mesadhara, place of pilgrimage **25**.19
message, ambiguity of **207**.8-12
messenger of gods, Agni as **93**.12-24; **127**.29-34; **128**.7-15
- of gods, Vāyu as **123**.14cd-22
- , punishment for killing of **22**.10
- sent to Kṛṣṇa, divine **210**.16-21
- , Siddha as **228**.100cd-127ab
- , wind as **194**.13-17

messengers of Death **94**.2-14

- of Yama **214**.42cd-45
- of Yama, description of **214**.55-69
messengers of Yama see also *servants of Yama*
metals, prescr. conc, cleaning of **221**.125cd-127ab
methods of deposition of ancestral offerings **220**.149-151
- of procreation, four **2**.50
- of voluntary death **214**.114cd-119; **216**.5-63; **221**.152cd-154
metres as seven enclosure sticks in sacrifice **161**.35cd-39ab
middle region, inhabitants of **27**.41cd-42
Mihira **31**.14cd-16
milk, churning of ocean of **13**.176cd-187ab; **112**.4-6
- , kinds of **220**.168-177
- , ocean of **18**.11-12; **19**.29; **20**.73cd-74ab; **69**.12-43; **181**.15-19
- oozing from breasts **193**.32-40
- oozing from udders **188**.36-37
- , plants as **141**.23-25
- products, kinds of **220**.154-167
- , punishment for selling of **215**.115cd-116ab
- , Viṣṇu lying in ocean of **126**.23
milking of earth **2**.25-28ab; **4**.96-122; **141**.23-25 .26-28
milking-vessels, list of **4**.100-109
milk-products, offering of **187**.42-54 .55-59ab
milk-rice **220**.56
mind and Self in simile **236**.49cd-53
- and senses **236**.13 .48cd-49ab; **238**.17-19
- and senses in simile **236**.12; **237**.77
- , concentration of **243**.47-48
- , creation from **1**.43-45ab; **2**.47-49; **3**.3-7ab; **9**.1
- , creation of **1**.39cd-42
- during meditation, immobility of **237**.29-31
- , reality dependent from **22**.44-47
- , sons born from **158**.2-3
minister, qualities of **111**.26-34
miracle(s) worked by thoughts of Kṛṣṇa **184**.42cd-52ab
miraculous crossing of Yamunā **182**.19-26
misappropriation, maxim about **140**.26-30
misbehaviour of Satyavrata **7**.98-99
- of Veṇa **2**.21-24; **4**.28-34
miscarriage **181**.38-53
misfortune, maxim about demoralising effect of **150**.1cd-4ab
misfortune see also *calamity*
Miśraka, place of pilgrimage **25**.42
Miśrakeśī **68**.60-67; **178**.19-24
misuse of power **215**.55cd-64
Mithilā **17**.17-23 .28
Mithu killed by Nandin **127**.54-59
- [king of Dānavas] **127**.4cd-9ab
Mitra **3**.53-58; **8**.77cd-84ab; **30**.23-26 .28-39 .46-47ab; **31**.17-18 .19-21
- and Varuṇa, boon by **7**.9-14ab
- and Varuṇa, oblation to **7**.3-5ab
- as highest deity **30**.49-52 .53-56
- as name of Śiva **158**.22-27ef
- , asceticism practised by **30**.47cd-48
- , Nārada instructed by **30**.45-86
- , place of pilgrimage **30**.40-41
- , sun as eye of **30**.40-41
Mitratīrtha, explanation of **124**.137-139ab
Mitravala, place of pilgrimage **25**.33
Mitravana **30**.40-41
Mitravindā **201**.3-5
Mitrayu **13**.97
mixing of castes **223**.19-20
- of castes, punishment for **215**.121cd-122ab
Mleccha, rebirth as **217**.111cd-113ab
Mlecchas **27**.24cd; **231**.71cd-78
Mlecchas see also *casteless people*, unbelievers
mocking at deities **73**.48-51
- at Indra **171**.16-17ef
- at king **168**.15-18ab
- at unequal couple **107**.42-45
mocking at see also *laughing at*
Modaki **20**.59cd-61
Modakin **20**.59cd-61
modification of a prediction **10**.46cd-49ab
- of curse **6**.24-30; **32**.69-72; **146**.19-25; **147**.17cd-20ab; **212**.72-85
moment, death at inauspicious **228**.76-85
moment see also *date(s), hours*
monkey allies of Rāma **176**.37-51
monkeys, Gautamī woshipped by **157**.15-18cd
- , Liṅgas established by **157**.21cd-25ab
months, Ādityas and **31**.19-21
- , battle of ten **13**.148-150ab

moon as son of Atri **152**.2-4
- cursed by Śukra **152**.26-28
-, Dakṣa as father-in-law of **2**.51-53
-, Dakṣa as grandson of **2**.51-53
-, distance of **23**.5
-, full **220**.10cd-11ab
- in hair of Śiva **114**.9-12
- in simile **26**.15; **231**.80-88; **237**.15-16
- in simile, full **68**.43
- in simile, *puruṣa* and **242**.52cd-55ab .55cd -58ef
-, intervention by **2**.34-46
-, meditation on **61**.19
- nourished by sun **24**.8-11
-, origin of **161**.43cd-50cd
-, origin of spots in the **152**.26-28
-, phases of **44**.48-53ab
-, purification by sun and **221**.129cd-131ab
-, Rohiṇī and **144**.20-22
-, Śiva as **75**.7
-, tide caused by **20**.91cd-94ab
-, Viṣṇu worshipped as **20**.19
-, world of **227**.16-32ab
moon see also *Soma, Candramas*
moon-river **30**.28-39
morning worship, prescr. conc. **221**.18
mortar, Kṛṣṇa bound to **184**.31-42ab
mother and son, sexual intercourse between **92**.2-11
-, asceticism disturbed by **158**.8-15ef
-, attitude towards **81**.13-15
-, curse by **32**.73-75; **158**.4-7
-, curse by surrogate **6**.20cd-23; **89**.13-17ab
-, destruction by wrath of **13**.58-61
-, *dharma* as father and **170**.38ef-39
-, earth as **72**.27cd-34
-, Gautamī as **157**.10
- goddesses **42**.3; **43**.83cd-85ab
-, maxim about importance of **158**.4-7
- of Brahmin, Rākṣasī as surrogate **167**.8-14 .15-17
- of rivers, Gautamī as **160**.13-16ef
- of Rudras, cow as **74**.59-67
- of the world, Sītā as **154**.27-30ab
- of the world, Umā as **75**.17
- of the world, Viṣṇu as husband of **163**.43-46
- of Yoga, Ūrjā as **219**.91cd-98ab
-, procreation by father and **243**.1-10
-, respect for **38**.35-38
-, threat of curse against **9**.28-30
-, Umā named **108**.94-98
-, Virajā as **42**.1-2
-, wife as **144**.17-19
Mothers, Daityas and the **113**.2-4
-, demons killed by **112**.20-22ab
- of Brahman, plants as **119**.2-4cd
- of gods, eight **105**.8cd-11ab
- of world **34**.87-89
- originated from sweat of Śiva **112**.11-19
-, rivers as **27**.39cd-41ab
-, waters as **72**.27cd-34; **126**.9-11; **144**.15-16
-, worship of **112**.24cd-26ab
mountain, description of **164**.3-6
- transported by Hanumat **170**.54-63
mountain see also *hill*
mountains **4**.90
-, extent of **18**.16-17
-, Himālaya as lord of **4**.2-9
-, inhabitants of **27**.62cd-64ab
- levelled by Pṛthu **4**.90
-, list of **18**.16-17 .21-23ab .32-36ab; **19**.3; **27**.20cd-24ab; **54**.8-11; **56**.3-8; **64**.8cd-9; **65**.38cd-39ab
- of Krauñcadvīpa **20**.49cd-51
- of Kuśadvīpa **20**.41cd-42
- of Plakṣadvīpa **20**.6-7
- of Puṣkaradvīpa **20**.77-80ab
- of Śākadvīpa **20**.62-63
- of Śālmaladvīpa **20**.25-27
-, seven **18**.62c-f; **27**.19cd-20ab
mouth, birth from **89**.34-36
- of Balarāma, snake leaving from **210**.50-52ab
- of Gaṅgā **64**.3-8ab
- of gods, fire as **126**.4-8
- of Viṣṇu, sacrifice born from **79**.7cd-19
- of Viṣṇu, Sarasvatī in **122**.68-73
-, sexual intercourse through **6**.41-43
movement everywhere, unrestricted **58**.12-18
- of stars **24**.1-7ab
- through air **3**.96cd-97ab
Mṛga [lunar mansions] **65**.3
Mṛgapāda **213**.81-104
Mṛgapriya **213**.81-104
Mṛgaśiras **220**.33cd-42
Mṛgavyādha **3**.46cd-49
Mṛgavyādhatīrtha, place of pilgrimage **102**.11c-f
Mṛtasaṃjīvana, place of pilgrimage

138.39cd-40; 170.89a-f
Mṛtasaṃjīvanī [medicinal herb] 170.54-63
Mṛtasaṃjīvinītīrtha, place of pilgrimage 95.31-32
Mṛttikāvatī [city] 15.14-15
Mṛtyu, description of 215.45-55ab
-, killing of 94.2-14
Mṛtyuṃjaya, place of pilgrimage 42.6-8
Mucukunda 7.93-95ab; 196.16-20
-, boon by gods to 196.21-22
-, boon by Kṛṣṇa to 197.1-3
-, sleep of 196.21-22
- to Kṛṣṇa, hymn by 196.30-45
mud and water, cleaning with 221.116-117ab
Mudara 16.50cd-54ab
Mudgala 10.57-60; 13.93-96 .97; 136.1cd-3ab
Mudgalahrada, place of pilgrimage 25.71
Mudgalāśrama, place of pilgrimage 25.71
Mudgara 217.80cd-86
Muhūrtā 3.29-30ab .30cd-33
Muhūrtas 3.30cd-33
Muktakeśī [magic woman] 134.2-8ab
Mukuṭakulyas 27.41cd-42
Mūla 220.33cd-42
multiplication by ten millions 148.18cd-20
- of merit 40.103-106; 41.57cd-59ab; 62.10-13ab; 148.1-3ab .21-26; 149.16cd-19; 154.30cd-31; 164.53cd-54
- of oneself 204.13cd-18
multiplication of merit see also *comparison of merit*
Muni 3.37-38cd .51-52 .104-105; 20.47cd-49ab
Muñjavaṭa, place of pilgrimage 25.37
Muñjāvaṭaratha, place of pilgrimage 25.37
Muñjikasthalā 68.60-67
Mura killed by Kṛṣṇa 202.16-21
-, seven thousand sons of 202.16-21
Murāri 229.88
murder of friend, punishment for 215.105cd-107ab .114cd-115ab
- of parent, punishment for 215.104-105ab
murder of brahmin see *brahmin-murder*
Mūrti 5.13cd-15ab; 68.56-59ab
Mūrtimat 10.21-23
Mūṣaka 3.86cd-89ab
music 36.125-126
-, attraction of 189.14-17
-, heavenly 7.30-34 .74-77; 14.14cd-20ab; 32.97cd-103; 193.57cd-60ab
-, origin of dance and 129.75-78
musical instruments 21.6cd-13ab; 32.102-103; 65.12-16; 193.24-31; 214.110-114ab
- notes, five 228.8-14
- rhythms 32.97cd-99ab
- scales 32.97cd-99ab
musician, Cāṇḍāla as 228.8-14
Muṣikas 27.54-57
Muṣṭika 190.6-8; 193.17-22 .24-31 .42-49; 213.159-163
-, fight between Balarāma and 193.50-57ab .63cd-65ab
- killed by Kṛṣṇa 193.63cd-65ab
muttering of prayers 178.112
Nabha 5.13cd-15ab .17d-19ab .29cd-30ab; 8.84cd-92
Nābhāga 7.1-2 .24 .26ab .42; 8.77cd-84ab
Nabhasya 5.13cd-15ab .17d-19ab
Nāciketas 70.39-40
Nadīna 11.27cd-31
Naḍvalā 2.17-20ab
Nāḍvaleyas 5.32-33ab
Nāga 18.32-36ab
Nāga see also *Śeṣa*
Nāgadvīpa 19.6cd-7ab; 27.14-16
Nāgagiri 27.20cd-24ab
Nāgālaya [abode of snakes] 159.41cd-46ab
Nāgas 3.99-101; 13.176cd-187ab; 15.51cd-53; 21.2-5ab .15-27; 36.19cd-20ab .22cd-23ab .63cd-70; 213.60-65
- as descendants of Kadru 3.97cd-98
-, Vāsuki as lord of 4.2-9
Nāgatīrtha, place of pilgrimage 25.66; 111.1 .85cd-86; 115.18-19ab
Nāgavīthī 3.30cd-33
Nāgeśvara, Liṅga named 111.85cd-86
-, Śiva as 111.1
-, snake named 111.17-25
Nāgnajitī 201.3-5; 205.1-6
Nahuṣa 3.99-101; 11.1-2; 12.1-2; 70.39-40; 226.30-41
Nāhuṣa, place of pilgrimage 146.42-45
Naigameya 3.39-40
Naimiṣa 116.2cd-3ab
-, description of 1.3-9
-, place of pilgrimage 25.8cd; 64.3-8ab; 65.84-96
Naimiṣeya, place of pilgrimage 25.44
Nairṛta 61.45cd-46

Naiṣādi **14**.27cd-28ab
naked woman appearing to Kṛṣṇa **206**.31-38
nakedness, prescr. conc. **221**.23 .141cd-143ab
- , prescription(s) concerning **221**.34 .50cd -52
Nakṣatra see *lunar mansion*
Nakṣatras **69**.12-43
- as wives of Soma **2**.47-49
Nakula **208**.19-31
Nala **3**.86cd-89ab; **8**.77cd-84ab .84cd-92 .93
- [monkey] **176**.37-51
Nālābhakṣa **214**.14-17
Naladā **13**.5-8
Nalinī **20**.66-67
name of Śiva, Vṛṣākapi as **124**.100-107
- of Śrī, Kamalā as **124**.137-139ab
- of Vāsudeva as means of liberation **22**.42-43
name-giving ceremony **184**.29-30
names of Agni **98**.17cd-18ab
- of Brahman **241**.12-16ab
- of *brahman* **30**.58-61
- of Devī **181**.38-53
- of fig-tree **60**.16-18
- of God **241**.16cd-19ab
- of Goddess **106**.43-45ab
- of hells **22**.2-6
- of nether worlds **21**.2-5ab
- of Śiva **117**.16-17
- of Śiva, hundred and eight **143**.2-5
- of Śiva, thousand **40**.2-100
- of sages **26**.9-14; **65**.31-34; **70**.37cd-38; **145**.2cd-5ab
- of Skanda **82**.9-10
- of sun **31**.29-39
- of sun, hundred and eight **33**.33-46
- of sun, twelve **31**.14cd-16
- of Suvarṇā **128**.72cd-76
- of Viṣṇu **59**.35-64; **60**.39-45; **61**.14-16 .39-40; **65**.49-51; **184**.14-19; **192**.48-58
- of Viṣṇu, protection by **219**.31-35
- , thousand and eight **39**.96-97; **40**.2-100
Namuci **3**.86cd-89ab; **70**.35cd-37ab; **160**.6cd-9; **176**.12-15ab; **213**.81-104
- , brothers of **123**.23-33ab
- killed by Indra **124**.33-36ab; **129**.4-8
Nanda **182**.19-26; **187**.35-40; **188**.2-5; **190**.10-19; **193**.67cd-76ab; **197**.8-18
- , advice by Kṛṣṇa to **187**.42-54
- , Baladeva as foster-child of **184**.1-6
- to Viṣṇu, prayer by **184**.14-19
Nandā **72**.9cd-10ab; **77**.9cd-13
Nandana-forest **10**.5-8; **18**.30
Nandas **27**.51cd-53
Nāndīmukha-ancestors **220**.67a-f; **221**.95-100
Nandin **72**.20-22; **90**.8cd-12ab .20-30 .31-33; **91**.2cd-6ab .6cd-11ab; **94**.2-14 .15-21 .43-45; **108**.26-30
- at Gautamī, Śiva and **152**.42a-d
- , Mithu killed by **127**.54-59
Nandinī **72**.9cd-10ab; **109**.13-20
- [river] **128**.72cd-76
Nandinīsaṃgama, place of pilgrimage **128**.1-2
Nandīśvara **39**.7-17ab
Nandītaṭa, place of pilgrimage **152**.1
Nandītaṭa, explanation of **152**.42a-d
Nanditīrtha, place of pilgrimage **25**.74
Nara **10**.61-62; **70**.37cd-38
Nārada **21**.5cd-6ab; **30**.46-47ab; **32**.97cd-99ab; **36**.63cd-70; **39**.7-17ab; **69**.12-43; **70**.14-15 .30-32; **71**.1; **74**.1 .6; **124**.32; **174**.2-5ab; **175**.10-13; **210**.6-10; **229**.21; **245**.44-47
- , advice by **3**.7cd-9 .16-18ab .19cd-23; **14**.50cd-56; **82**.9-10; **200**.2-10
- and Parvata **104**.3-4ef
- , applause by **190**.39-47
- as famous bard **154**.14cd-21ab
- as grandson of Dakṣa **3**.7cd-9
- as Suśīlā **229**.43cd-55
- as woman **229**.43cd-67ab
- , birth of **3**.10-14
- , boon by Viṣṇu to **229**.56-58
- , Dakṣa as father of **3**.7cd-9
- , information provided by **78**.37cd-44; **109**.10cd-12; **181**.33-35; **190**.1-5; **196**.5-8; **200**.2-10 .23-28; **206**.10-13
- instructed by Mitra **30**.45-86
- [mountain] **20**.6-7
Naraka **3**.86cd-89ab; **181**.7-14; **188**.42-47; **209**.2-11ab; **213**.81-104 .159-163
- , Bhauma **202** .3-12; **219**.113cd-115
- killed by Kṛṣṇa **202**.16-21
- , raiding of residence of **202**.30-35; **204**.13cd-18
Naranārāyaṇa **197**.4-5; **210**.33-35
Narānta **16**.4-6
Narāntaka **176**.37-51

Narasiṃha **45**.77-89; **61**.14-16; **163**.26-31 .50-51; **213**.43-79
- , cave of **58**.32cd-49
- , invincibility of **58**.26-27
- , prescription(s) for adept of **58**.19-25
- , protection by **58**.29-32ab
- , terrible shape of **149**.4cd-9ab
- , Viṣṇu as **149**
- , worship of **58**
Nārasiṃha, place of pilgrimage **149**.13-16ab
Narasiṃha-Māhātmya **45**.77-89; **58**
Nārasiṃhatīrtha, place of pilgrimage **149**.1
Nārāyaṇa **1**.33-34; **5**.61-62; **8**.58-59ab .72cd -73ab; **12**.50; **22**.37-41; **24**.19-25; **34**.42-45ab; **59**.34; **60**.22-24; **61**.47-50; **62**.1-4; **68**.74-77ab; **70**.37cd-38; **163**.26-31; **167**.29 .30 .31-32; **176**.26-32; **179**.72cd-75; **181**.15-19; **184**.14-19; **216**.5-63 .82-86; **220**.43-48ab; **240**.20-22ab .69-75
- , Aniruddha as form of **180**.23cd-24ab
- as all **60**.25-33
- as boar **213**.1-9
- as Brahman **180**.17cd-18ab
- as Śiśumāra **24**
- as supporter of all **24**.19-25
- as teacher **181**.7-14
- , attainment of **239**.62
- , attributes of **56**.48cd; **240**.93-94
- , concentration on **240**.106-111
- , four aspects of **180**.17cd-18ab
- , four forms of **61**.24
- , manifestations of **181**.15-19
- , meditation on **60**.34-38
- , omnipresence of **180**.17cd-18ab
- , place of pilgrimage **167**.1 .33
- , Pradyumna as form of **180**.22cd-23ab .40-42ab
- , Śeṣa as form of **180**.21cd-22ab
- , *trimūrti*-functions of **240**.112
- , Vāsudeva as form of **180**.18cd-21ab
- , water as abode of **60**.34-38
- , world of **227**.42-47
- , worship of **61**.1-3
Nārāyaṇa see also *Viṣṇu*
Nārāyaṇa, etymology of **1**.38cd-39ab; **56**.12; **60**.25-33; **180**.16cd-17ab
Nārāyaṇāśrama, place of pilgrimage **25**.53
Nārāyaṇi **10**.61-62
Nārāyaṇī **68**.56-59ab
Nariṣyanta **7**.1-2 .26cd-27ab
Nāriṣyantas **7**.24
Narmadā **7**.95cd-97; **13**.176cd-187ab; **15**.14-15; **19**.11-12ab; **27**.30-32; **70**.33-35ab; **77**.2-9ab; **89**.25cd-33; **96**.11-17; **110**.202-210; **141**.26-28; **161**.21-23ef; **220**.8-10ab; **228**.97-100ab
- , place of pilgrimage **64**.11-14
Narmadātīrtha, place of pilgrimage **25**.27
Narmadobdheda, place of pilgrimage **25**.32
narrator, Brahman as **41**.10; **45**.77-89
- , Brahman as first-person **33**.3-8; **36**.8 .36cd-39ab .125-126; **39**.84-88ab; **42**.36cd-38ab; **59**.1-2; **72**.18-19; **73**.57cd .58-63ab; **83**.13-16; **87**.2-34ab; **91**.6cd-11ab; **94**.22-26; **96**.5cd-7; **97**.2-5ab; **101**.10-11ab; **106**.19-22; **108**.71-74; **110**.198cd-200cd; **112**.2-3; **113**.2-4; **115**.2-4; **119**.2-4cd; **122**.21-24ab .54cd-62; **123**.7cd-14ab; **124**.87-93; **126**.12-16ab; **128**.38-43; **134**.2-8ab; **135**.5cd-10ab .15-16; **137**.25-28ab; **143**.2-5; **145**.5cd-7; **156**.4-6; **158**.2-3 .35cd-37ab; **160**.2cd-6ab; **162**.2cd-6ab; **174**.8-12ef .19-25ab; **176**.4-7 .15cd-19ab
- , Gaṇeśa as **175**.42-72
- , Lomaharṣaṇa as **1**.31-32; **3**.2; **5**.3; **6**.1ab; **13**.2; **18**.10; **25**.2; **26**.2; **41**.1-5; **179**.1; **217**.1; **235**.2 .30; **246**.1-5
- , Lomaharṣaṇa as first-person **246**.13-15
- , Śiva as first-person **223**.55cd-56ab; **226**.20cd-22ab
- , Viṣṇu as **51**.60-62
- , Viṣṇu as first-person **45**.42-43 .68-70
- , Vyāsa as **26**.27; **41**.6-9; **177**.29-30; **212**.93-94
- , Vyāsa as first-person **212**.54; **220**.189ab
Nāsamaujas **16**.7
Nāsatya **6**.44-45ab; **8**.29-30
nāstika see *unbeliever*
natural omen(s) **182**.4-6
nature, disorder of **231**.4-41 .52-55
Nava **13**.22cd-23 .24-25ab
Navā **13**.20cd-22ab .22cd-23
Navagarbhā **68**.60-67
Navarāṣṭra **13**.24-25ab
Navaratha **15**.24-28
navel of Viṣṇu, Brahman residing in **226**.20cd-22ab
Nāveya **16**.48cd-49ab

nectar of immortality **106**.8-10ab; **140**.7-11; **142**.2-4; **159**.41cd-46ab
- of immortality obtained by gods and demons **133**.13-17
- of immortality, Soma as **119**.13-17
- of immortality, substitutes for **133**.13-17
- of immortality swallowed by Goddess **106**.46cd
- of immortality, water of Gautamī as **133**.13-17
nectar of immortality see also *amṛta, immortality*
negative description of body **227**.16-32ab
neglect of *dharma* **213**.106-112
negotiation of marriage **111**.35-39ab
nether world, cave as entrance to **112**.23cd-24ab; **115**.12cd-15ab
- world, entrance to **58**.37-40
- world, Gaṅgā originated from **159**.46cd-48ab
- world, Indra as prisoner in **129**.11cd-16
- world, Kapila sleeping in **78**.24-31
- world, Śeṣa as lord of **115**.2-4
- world, snakes healed by water from **159**.41cd-46ab
- world, water from **115**.12cd-15ab; **159**.36-39cd
- world, way to **58**.34cd-36
- worlds, colours of **21**.2-5ab
- worlds, description of **21**
- worlds, list of **54**.20-21
- worlds, names of **21**.2-5ab
- worlds, seven **23**.21
new-moon **220**.56
newmoon **220**.10cd-11ab
Nibiḍa **20**.49cd-51
Nidhirāmabhava, place of pilgrimage **25**.72
Nidrā **68**.56-59ab; **181**.36 .38-53
Nighna **8**.77cd-84ab; **16**.9-11
Nighnata **16**.9-11
night, duration of cosmic **233**.9
- , Yoga practised during **243**.50-53
Nīhāras **27**.62cd-64ab
Nikāśya **16**.4-6
Nikumbha **7**.87-88; **176**.37-51
- , curse by **11**.41-43
Nīla **13**.153cd-154ab
- [monkey] **176**.37-51
- [mountain] **18**.16-17 .44cd-45ab .46cd-50
Nīlagaṅgā, place of pilgrimage **80**.4-5ab
Nīlakālakas **27**.54-57
Nīlakaṇṭha **112**.4-6
Nīlakaṇṭhahrada, place of pilgrimage **25**.61
Nīlalohita **178**.43-53
Nīlamādhava, disappearance of **45**.1-76
Nīla-mountain **80**.4-5ab
Nīlaparvata, place of pilgrimage **25**.48
Nīlī **13**.81cd-82ab .93-96
Nīlinī **13**.93-96
Nimlocā **68**.60-67
Nimnabheda, place of pilgrimage **151**.1-2 .24cd-27ab
Nimnabhedatīrtha, place of pilgrimage **151**.27cd-29
nine gates, body as city of **236**.33
- parts of Bhāratavarṣa **27**.14-16
Nirāloka **215**.104-105ab
Nirmoha **5**.27-28
Nirṛti **28**.27; **84**.9-12 .13-15
Nirucchvāsa **215**.116cd-117ab
Nirukta **4**.48-52
Nirutsuka **5**.27-28
Nirvindhyā **19**.11-12ab; **27**.33-34
niṣāda, etymology of **4**.42-47
Niṣādas **14**.27cd-28ab
- , origin of **4**.42-47; **141**.6-9
Niṣadha **8**.84cd-92
- [mountain] **18**.16-17 .18-20 .32-36ab .44cd-45ab .46cd-50
Niśaṭha **14**.42cd
Niśaṭha **198**.18
Niścīvā, place of pilgrimage **25**.72
Niṣṭhīvā **27**.25cd-27
Niśumbha **181**.38-53
Nitala **21**.2-5ab
Nivāsapura, explanation of **106**.53cd-54ab
Nivātakavacas **3**.90cd-92ab
Nivṛtti **20**.28
noble people, maxim about **170**.81-83
nocturnal vigil **228**.8-14 .40-43
non-action, action and **88**.10-15
non-being being and **23**.41-43
non-existence, existence and **173**.9-25
non-violence, Brahman as authority on **224**.56c-f
- , effect(s) of **224**.47-52 .53-56ab
noon, worship at **192**.32-42
noose of Gaṇeśa **114**.13
- of Indra **171**.10-13
- of Yama **168**.25-26ab

nooses of Yama **125**.9-12 .22
north, inhabitants of **27**.43-50
- , Kubera as lord of the **97**.29
nose, birth from **6**.44-45ab
notes, five musical **228**.8-14
Nṛga **13**.22cd-23 .24-25ab
Nṛgā **13**.20cd-22ab .22cd-23
Nṛgadhūma, place of pilgrimage **25**.43
Nṛhari **149**.16cd-19
Nṛsiṃha **109**.42
Nṛsiṃhatīrtha, place of pilgrimage **149**.16cd-19
Nṛtyā **108**.113-115
number of cosmic eggs **23**.27cd-28ab
- of hells **22**.28-29; **215**.78-80 .137cd-138ab
- of holy places **41**.11-12; **62**.22cd-23; **77**.2-9ab; **89**.43-46ab; **94**.46-48ab; **96**.25cd-26; **98**.20-21ab; **106**.48cd-49ab; **108**.121-123; **110**.146c-f; **115**.20c-f; **116**.25c-f; **118**.31-32ef; **120**.16-18; **121**.26; **122**.104; **124**.140ef; **125**.54-56; **126**.1-2 .37-39; **127**.64a-f; **128**.77-81; **129**.125-127; **131**.52-53ab; **134**.15-16; **135**.27c-f; **136**.43; **137**.41c-f; **138**.39ab; **139**.20; **140**.35-38; **141**.29-30; **142**.14; **144**.25-27; **145**.14; **146**.42-45; **148**.1-3ab .27a-f; **149**.16cd-19; **150**.21-22 .23; **151**.27cd-29; **152**.41; **153**.16cd; **154**.30cd-31; **155**.13cd-14ab; **159**.48cd-49ef; **160**.21-22ab; **161**.72-78; **175**.83-84
- of invited, Brahmins **220**.60 .69cd-70
- of Liṅgas **41**.11-12
- of principles **243**.82-83
- of sunbeams of Ādityas **31**.22-26
Nyagrodha **15**.58cd-59
Nyagrodha-tree as emblem **20**.87cd
O'Flaherty, W. D. **40**.113cd-118
oath as guarantee for trustfulness **167**.8-14
- by Kavi [Śukra] **152**.21-23
- of revenge **110**.80ef-86
obedience to parents-in-law **111**.52-56
objects of knowledge, subjects and **244**.4-9
- , stepping on forbidden **221**.24cd-25
oblation, *amṛta* as **168**.26cd-28ab
- , healing by means of **58**.48
- in sacrifice, autumn as **161**.35cd-39ab
- to Mitra and Varuṇa 7.3-5ab
oblation see also *offerings, sacrifice*
obligations, three **99**.2-7ab .12a-f; **104**.7cd-9
obligatory rites, definition of **220**.81cd-82ab
obligatory rites, prescr. conc. **221**.146cd-149ab
observance of conventions **225**.60-62
- of *dharma* 7.9-14ab
- of *dharma* during Kali-Yuga **230**.78-81
- of *dharma* of caste **76**.18cd-23ab
observances during pregnancy **32**.32-34ab; **124**.19-28ab
- during vow **46**.24-30; **59**.26-33
- for conception of a hero **125**.44-49
- for worship of Śiva **168**.31-35
- , meritorious **29**.1-6
- of fasting **242**.15cd-20ab
- of purity for women **124**.19-28ab
- , Pāśupata **40**.107-111
- , purification by **136**.17-26
observances see also *conduct, practices, vow*
obstacle(s) caused by Gaṇeśa **114**.2-5; **175**.73-74
- , Gaṇeśa as Lord of **114**.13
- to consecration of Indra **96**.8-10
obstacle(s) see also *enemies, faults, hindrance, Vighna*
obstruction of earth by trees **2**.34-46
occupations of Apsarases **68**.60-67
ocean as king of places of pilgrimage **62**.1-4 .10-13ab
- as lord of rivers **4**.2-9
- as place for asceticism **7**.105cd-109
- as residence of snakes **185**.52-53
- , asceticism by standing in **2**.34-46
- , churning of **106**.8-10ab; **203**.33-37
- , confluence of Gaṅgā with **65**.84-96; **122**.3-7
- , confluence of Gautamī with **172**
- , description of **44**.44-47 .48-53ab; **172**.7cd-14
- drunk by fire **110**.202-210
- , eastern **172**.2-3
- , emergence of image from **176**.52-56
- , impossibility of description of **62**.22cd-23
- in simile **237**.67-72
- , land requested from **196**.9-15
- of butter **18**.11-12; **20**.45 .46-47ab
- of curds **18**.11-12; **20**.57cd-58ab
»ocean of *dharma*« **225**.63
ocean of liquor **18**.11-12; **20**.34
- of milk **18**.11-12; **19**.29; **20**.73cd-74ab; **69**.12-43; **181**.15-19
- of milk, churning of **13**.176cd-187ab;

112.4-6
- of milk, Viṣṇu lying in **126**.23
- of rebirth **57**.32-37; **59**.65-72
- of salt water **18**.11-12; **19**.29
- of sugarcane juice **18**.11-12; **20**.20 .24
- of water **18**.11-12; **20**.88cd-89ab
- , place of pilgrimage **44**.48-53ab; **45**.77-89; **62**.16cd-22ab; **172**.19cd-20ef
- , prayer-formula addressed to **62**.1-4
- , southern **70**.22cd-23
- , submersion of statue in **176**.37-51
- , submersion of world in **53**.12-14ab .14cd -18ab; **56**.51-54
- , superiority of **62**.16cd-22ab
- , Viṣṇu and Lakṣmī sleeping in **172**.7cd-14
- , worship of **62**.1-4

oceans, four **36**.63cd-70; **56**.27cd-30ab
- , seven **18**.11-12; **33**.3-8; **54**.1-3

Oḍradeśa see *Oṇḍradeśa*

offence against sages **210**.6-10
- by laughter **201**.10-22
- of ascetic **53**.21-24

offence see also *abuse, reproach*

offender against teacher's wife, Indra as **96**.8 -10

offering, fire as **126**.4-8
- of eye **109**.49-50ef
- of food to statue **67**.24-27
- of forbidden meat, punishment for **220**.193cd-195ab
- of incense **67**.24-27
- of meat **187**.55-59ab
- of milk-products **187**.42-54 .55-59ab
- of water on earth **60**.54-65
- of water with sesamum **57**.5; **60**.49-53
- of wine and meat **181**.38-53
- to Śiva **228**.76-85

offerings, deposition of **29**.42cd-61
- , food for **220**.43-48ab
- given to cocks **220**.149-151
- given to cows **220**.149-151
- given to crows **220**.149-151
- given to wife **220**.149-151
- , leftovers of **219**.60cd-65ab .71cd-86
- , merit of **29**.42cd-61
- , prescr. conc. **29**.42cd-61
- , prescription(s) concerning **221**.87-88
- , prescription(s) concerning distribution of **221**.89-94
- put in fire **220**.149-151
- put in water **220**.149-151
- , recompensation of **29**.42cd-61
- to ancestors **219**.52-60ab .60cd-65ab
- to ancestors, effect(s) of **220**.149-151
- to ancestors, ingredients of **220**.61cd-62ab
- to ancestors, pregnancy due to **219**.87-91ab
- to ancestors, prescr. conc. **60**.54-65
- to gods and ancestors **221**.89-94
- to gods, prescr. conc. **221**.21
- to various classes of beings **220**.89cd-97ab
- , worship of Śiva with sixteen **123**.191-194
- see also OBLATION, SACRIFICE **219**.60cd-65ab

offspring by churning of hand **2**.21-24; **4**.48-52; **141**.10-13
- by churning of thigh **4**.42-47; **141**.6-9

offspring see also *descendants*

oil, punishment for selling of **22**.18cd-20

oil-cake from Iṅgudi-fruits **123**.170-172

Ojasa, place of pilgrimage **25**.52

old age **234**.9-42
- age, curse of **146**.11-14
- age, destruction of **159**.41cd-46ab
- age, freedom from **7**.37a-d; **18**.24cd-28; **20**.86cd-87ab; **176**.33-34; **203**.24-25
- age, maxim about **146**.11-14
- age, transfer of **146**.28-31

old age see also *age*

Oldenberg, H. **125**.23-24ef

OM **235**.13-20
- , Goddess as **161**.17-20
- , sun as **32**.12-16

OM see also *sacred syllable*

omen(s), astrological **182**.4-6
- , auspicious **7**.74-77
- , bad **210**.29-30
- , inauspicious events as **184**.42cd-52ab
- , knowledge of **21**.15-27
- , natural **182**.4-6
- of war **206**.1-4

omnipresence of action **145**.8-11ab
- of fire **144**.15-16
- of Lakṣmī **137**.30cd-39ab
- of Manyu **162**.20-27ab
- of Nārāyaṇa **180**.17cd-18ab
- of Viṣṇu **202**.23-29

omnipresence see also *all*
- see also *all, all-comprehensiveness*

omniscience of Brahman **34**.93cd-99; **122**.50-54ab

- of Kṛṣṇa **191**.27-33; **192**.5-10; **210**.15 .22-27
- of Mārkaṇḍeya **53**.34-38
- of Śiva **162**.13-19
- of Vyāsa **26**.18; **223**.1-3; **239**.1; **240**.1-2; **246**.6-12
- of wives **129**.49-64

Oṇḍradeśa **28**.1-2
one-eyedness, curse of **100**.25-29ab
oneness of *puruṣa* **130**.7-14
- of Śiva **158**.22-27ef
- of Viṣṇu **49**.10-20

oneness see also *absorption, identity, union, unity*
only son of Brahmin **35**.32-38
opinions, difference of **220**.124-125ab; **238**.3-4; **239**.2 .6; **240**.3-4; **243**.36 .37-40; **244**.44-48
opponents, inequality of **193**.42-49
opposition of demons and gods **209**.2-11ab
- of Kṛṣṇa and Indra **188**.11-13; **203**.26-73
- of Kṛṣṇa and Śiva **207**.28-43

opposition see also *competition, enmity, rival*
oppression by taxes **231**.42-43 .60-67
- , instruments of **225**.31-35 .36-41

oppression see also *affliction, violence*
oral conception **6**.41-43; **82**.2-6
ordeal by fire **154**.2-4
origin of Agni **161**.43cd-50cd
- of all, fire as **126**.4-8
- of all, waters as **72**.27cd-34
- of *amṛta*, waters as **126**.9-11
- of animals **3**.102cd-103
- of Apsarases **3**.104-105
- of Apsaroyuga **147**.20cd-23ab
- of Aśvins **6**.44-45ab
- of asses **3**.93cd-95ab
- of bad qualities **129**.70-71
- of bards **4**.60-67
- of barley **219**.49-51
- of beings **2**.47-49; **32**.3-6
- of beings, body of Viṣṇu as **226**.13-14
- of beings, sun as **33**.9-13ab
- of beings, Viṣṇu as **196**.30-45
- of Bindusaras-lake **41**.50cd-54ab
- of birds **3**.93cd-95ab .102cd-103
- of Brahman **30**.78-79ab; **161**.6cd-9
- of Brahman, Viṣṇu as **161**.68-71
- of Brahmins **161**.43cd-50cd
- of brilliance **33**.3-8
- of buffaloes **3**.104-105
- of camels **3**.93cd-95ab
- of clouds **1**.48cd-50ab
- of conch of Kṛṣṇa **194**.23-31
- of constituents of sacrifice **161**.50ef-53
- of cosmos **1**.16-20; **33**.3-8
- of cosmos from golden egg **1**.39cd-42
- of cosmos, *puruṣa* as **161**.43cd-50cd
- of cows **3**.104-105
- of dance and music **129**.75-78
- of *dharma*, waters as **72**.27cd-34
- of directions **161**.43cd-50cd
- of discus of Viṣṇu **6**.50cd-51ab
- of domestic and wild animals **161**.43cd-50cd
- of earth **161**.43cd-50cd
- of embryo **217**.19-21
- of energy of Brahman **161**.13-16
- of enmity between Rākṣasas and gods **116**.20-22ab
- of fever **39**.74-89
- of food **1**.48cd-50ab
- of food and drink **129**.75-78
- of food, waters as **126**.9-11
- of four castes **13**.32-35; **56**.22cd-23ab
- of four Vedas **56**.23cd-24ab
- of Gaṅgā **150**.15-20; **159**.46cd-48ab
- of Gandharvas **3**.104-105
- of Gautamī **137**.25-28ab
- of gods **1**.48cd-50ab; **3**.3-7ab; **161**.43cd-50cd; **213**.30-31
- of gold **128**.50-61
- of horses **3**.93cd-95ab
- of hot water-spring **115**.15cd-16
- of individual self **161**.6cd-9
- of Indra **161**.43cd-50cd
- of intermediate space **161**.43cd-50cd
- of Itihāsas and Purāṇas **161**.27-29
- of Kārttikeya **128**.16-23
- of Kātyāyanas **10**.57-60
- of Kāverī **10**.19cd-20
- of Kokā **219**.13-17 .18-24
- of Kṛtyā **207**.28-43
- of Kṣatriyas **161**.43cd-50cd
- of Kuśa-grass **219**.42-47ab
- of lightning **1**.48cd-50ab
- of lotus **161**.6cd-9
- of Manyu **162**.10cd-12 .20-27ab
- of Maruts **3**.109cd-122; **124**.68-73ab
- of moon **161**.43cd-50cd

- of Mothers **112**.11-19
- of Niṣādas **4**.42-47; **141**.6-9
- of Paruṣṇī [river] **144**.23-24
- of Pārijāta-tree **203**.33-37
- of Phenā [river] **129**.4-8
- of places of pilgrimage **161**.60-61ab
- of plants **3**.104-105; **9**.9-10; **161**.43cd-50cd
- of plants, waters as **126**.9-11
- of pond **79**.7cd-19
- of Pṛthu **141**.10-13
- of purity, waters as **126**.9-11
- of *puruṣa* **161**.6cd-9
- of rain **1**.48cd-50ab
- of rain, sun as **31**.4-6
- of rain-bow **1**.48cd-50ab
- of Rākṣasas **3**.104-105; **156**.2cd-3
- of rivers from heaven **20**.68cd-70
- of Rudra **1**.45cd-46ab
- of Rudras **1**.46cd; **3**.46cd-49
- of Śūdras **161**.43cd-50cd
- of sacrifice, waters as **72**.27cd-34
- of sages **161**.43cd-50cd
- of Sādhyas **1**.48cd-50ab
- of sciences and holy texts **129**.75-78
- of semen **217**.19-21
- of senses **241**.26-27
- of sesamum **219**.42-47ab
- of sexual intercourse **45**.37-41
- of sky **161**.43cd-50cd
- of Soma **9**.2-5
- of spots in the moon **152**.26-28
- of sun **161**.43cd-50cd
- of Sūta and Māgadha **2**.25-28ab
- of third eye of Śiva **123**.195-206
- of three goals of life **129**.70-71
- of three Vedas **1**.48cd-50ab
- of thunder **1**.48cd-50ab
- of time, sun as **31**.7-10
- of two sexes **1**.51cd-52
- of Umā **75**.14
- of unbelievers **229**.15-18
- of Urvaśī **228**.100cd-127ab
- of useful things **129**.75-78
- of Vaiśyas **161**.43cd-50cd
- of Vālakhilyas **72**.18-19
- of Vāyu **161**.43cd-50cd
- of Vedadvīpa [island in the Gautamī] **151**.17-22ab
- of waters **161**.6cd-9
- of weapons **129**.75-78
- of wife of Brahman **161**.33cd-35ab
- of worms and insects **161**.43cd-50cd
- of Yakṣas **3**.104-105
- of Yakṣiṇī [river] **132**.3-5
- of Yoga **191**.4-12

origin see also *birth, creation, emanation, evolution*

ornaments, flowers as **221**.81cd-82ab
- of Balarāma **198**.15-17

outcastes, sacrificing for **22**.17cd-18ab
- , Vāsudeva worshipped by **227**.10-14
- , Yoga for women and **236**.68

overpopulation see *burdening of earth*

owl, pigeon and **125**

Pahlavas **8**.31-32 .35-37; **10**.24-28ab; **13**.88-90; **27**.43-50

Pailūṣa [son of Kavaṣa] **139**.2cd-7ab
- , thirst of **139**.7cd-11
- to Śiva, hymn by **139**.13-17ef

Pailūṣatīrtha, place of pilgrimage **139**.19

pain, prohibition of inflicting of **221**.74
- , women as cause of pleasure and **122**.21-24ab

painting of portraits **205**.15-22

Paippalādi **13**.132cd-137

Paiśāca, place of pilgrimage **84**.18; **150**.1ab

Paiśācatīrtha, place of pilgrimage **84**.1

Paitāmahatīrtha, place of pilgrimage **25**.29

Paiṭhīnasī [wife of Bharadvāja] **133**.2-4

Pākaśāsana **7**.104cd-105ab; **8**.10cd; **188**.24-28

palace of Viṣṇu **45**.71-73

Pālana **20**.36-38ab

palanquin of Kubera **203**.45-62

Palāśa-tree **103**.2-6

Palāśinī **27**.38cd-39ab

Pālita **15**.1-12ab .12cd-13

palm, sacred spots on the **221**.95-100

palm see also *hand*

Panasa **176**.37-51

Pañcadhāra, place of pilgrimage **25**.20

Pañcahrada, place of pilgrimage **25**.24

Pañcajana **8**.54-57 .65-68 .72cd-73ab .73cd-75ab; **13**.98-99; **194**.23-31; **202**.16-21
- killed by Kṛṣṇa **194**.23-31; **202**.16-21

Pāñcajanya [conch of Viṣṇu] **68**.44-53

Pāñcajanya see also *conch of* Kṛṣṇa

Pañcaka, place of pilgrimage **25**.51

Pañcakaṭaka, place of pilgrimage **25**.52

Pañcakūṭa, place of pilgrimage **25**.15

Pañcāla **14**.29-31
Pañcāla, etymology of **13**.93-96
Pañcālas **13**.93-96; **19**.15cd
Pañcanada **8**.54-57; **212**.12-17
- , place of pilgrimage **25**.29 .36
Pañcanadatīrtha, place of pilgrimage **25**.59
Pañcarātra **48**.12
Pañcaśikha, place of pilgrimage **25**.14
Pañcatīrtha, place of pilgrimage **25**.27 .38; **43**.10-13
Pañcatīrtha-Māhātmya **45**.77-89; **57**; **60**.8ab; **63**
Pañcatīrtha-pilgrimage **63**.19-20
Pañcavaṭaka, place of pilgrimage **25**.52
Pañcavaṭāśrama, place of pilgrimage **89**.43-46ab
Pañcayajñaka, place of pilgrimage **25**.46
Pāñcayajñika, place of pilgrimage **25**.46
Pāndarācala **27**.20cd-24ab
Pāṇḍava **212**.87-88
Pāṇḍavas **13**.119; **17**.8-11
- , birth of **14**.20cd-24ab
Pāṇḍu **13**.121 .123-124; **14**.20cd-24ab
Pāṇḍurācala **27**.20cd-24ab
Pāṇḍya **13**.147-148ab
Pāṇḍyas **13**.147-148ab
Pāṇikhāta, place of pilgrimage **25**.42
Pāṇins **10**.61-62; **13**.91
Paṇis, Saramā and the **131**
Pāṇiṣāta, place of pilgrimage **25**.42
Pañjiraka, place of pilgrimage **25**.28
Pāpa **22**.2-6
Pāpanāśana, place of pilgrimage **110**.215
Pāpanāśinī **27**.35-36ab
Pāpapramocana, place of pilgrimage **228**.92cd-96
Pāpapraṇāśana, place of pilgrimage **92**.1 .48cd-49ef
Pāradas **8**.31-32 .35-37 .44-51; **27**.43-50
paradise of Viṣṇu, Vaikuṇṭha as **161**.61cd-62
Parajit **15**.1-12ab
Parājitā [wife of Mahāśani] **129**.11cd-16
paralysis effected by Śiva **36**.31-36ab; **37**.2-23
Paramanyu **13**.14cd-15ab
Paramātman see *Supreme Self*
Parameśa **122**.68-73
Parameṣṭhin **3**.7cd-9; **32**.7-8
- , son of **124**.7-8
Paraṃtapa **5**.22cd-24
Parārdha **232**.1-2; **233**.46cd-49ab
- , definition of **232**.4-5
Parāśara **40**.135
Pārasīkas **19**.18
Paraśu [Rākṣasa] **163**
Paraśurāma **180**.24cd-38
Parāvatī **68**.60-67
parent, punishment for murder of **215**.104-105ab
parents, blessings by **110**.188-191ab
- , *dharma* as friend and **246**.37-38
- , maxim about honouring of **194**.1-5
- of Kṛṣṇa, death of **212**.1-4
- , punishment for annoying of **217**.51-52
- , punishment for beating of one's **217**.53-54
- , punishment for disrespect against **217**.49-50
- , Śiva as **122**.82
parents-in-law, obedience to **111**.52-56
Pārijāta-tree **109**.13-20; **110**.143-146ab; **208**.19-31; **212**.7
- , description of **203**.26-32
- , Kṛṣṇa taking away the **203**.26-73; **204**
- , origin of **203**.33-37
- , scent of **204**.8-13ab
Parīkṣit **12**.9-10; **13**.108 .109 .112-113 .123-124; **212**.93-94
Pārīkṣita, Janamejaya **13**.123-124
Parilumpa **215**.130cd-136ab
Pāriplava, place of pilgrimage **25**.35
Pāriplavas **5**.26
Paritāpa **215**.125cd-126ab
Pāriyātra **18**.46cd-50; **19**.3 .10 .17; **27**.19cd-20ab .28-29
- , place of pilgrimage **64**.8cd-9
Parjanya **4**.11-15; **5**.24cd-25; **13**.174-176ab; **30**.23-26 .28-39; **31**.17-18 .19-21 .22-26; **221**.89-94
- , rain sent by **159**.39ef-41ab
Parjanyatīrtha, place of pilgrimage **93**.27
Parṇāśā [river], Devāvṛdha and **15**.35-41ab
parrot, Agni as **128**.16-23
Pārśvaka **12**.1-2
Pārtha **212**.12-17
partial incarnation of gods **181**.32
- incarnation of Indra, Arjuna as **188**.39-41
- incarnation of sun **32**.17-31
- incarnation of Viṣṇu, Kṛṣṇa and Balarāma as **190**.10-19

- incarnation of Viṣṇu, Kṛṣṇa as **193**.32-40; **195**.13-18; **196**.23-29; **202**.23-29
parting the hair, ceremony of **100**.25-29ab
parts of Bhāratavarṣa, nine **27**.14-16
- of body **239**.39-41
Paruṣṇī [river], origin of **144**.23-24
Paruṣṇīsaṃgama, place of pilgrimage **144**.1 .25-27
Pārvaṇa **220**.64-66 .67a-f
Parvan-days **220**.58 .60
Parvata **39**.7-17ab
- , Nārada and **104**.3-4ef
Pārvatī **71**.27-37; **81**.4-7ab; **97**.20-23
- , love-play of Śiva and **205**.11-14
- , Śiva and **128**.7-15 .16-23
- , strategem of **81**.7cd-12
- to Uṣā, boon by **205**.11-14
- , wedding-ceremony of Śiva and **72**.11cd -14
Pārvatī see also *Devī, Durgā, Gaurī, Goddess, Umā*
passing of time, unawareness of **7**.30-34; **21**.6cd-13ab; **178**.65-69 .80-89
passions as forms of Viṣṇu **56**.27cd-30ab
- , five **56**.27cd-30ab
past events, summary of **110**.80ef-86
Pāśupata observances **40**.107-111
- Yoga **41**.60cd-71; **43**.65cd-74
Paśupati **3**.70cd-71; **39**.29-32; **192**.48-58
Paśupati see also *Śiva*
Pātāla **21**.2-5ab
Pātālaketu **70**.35cd-37ab
Pataṅga **18**.32-36ab
Patatritīrtha, place of pilgrimage **166**.1 .8cd-11ab
path leading to Yama **214**.11cd-103
- of *brahman* **223**.61cd-64ab
- to liberation **70**.3cd-8ab; **238**.56cd-57; **240**.69-75
patience of earth **108**.68-70
Pātin **2**.28cd
Paulastya **213**.127-135
- , place of pilgrimage **97**.32cd-33
Paulastyatīrtha, place of pilgrimage **97**.1
Paulikas **27**.54-57
Paulomas **3**.80cd-83 .84-86ab
Paulomī **129**.11cd-16 .42-48
- , Indra and **129**.42-125
Pauṇḍraka **199**.5-10
- , challenge of Kṛṣṇa to **207**.8-12
- , fight between Kṛṣṇa and **207**.13-24
- , Vāsudeva **207**.4-7
Pauṇḍras **19**.16
Paura, place of pilgrimage **146**.42-45
Pauras, land of **12**.11-17
Paurava **10**.63
Pauravas **12**.9-10; **13**.139-140 .142-146
Paurukutsā **10**.24-28ab
Paurvā **10**.24-28ab
Pauṣa **31**.19-21
Pauṣkara-manifestation **213**.25-31
Pautra, place of pilgrimage **148**.21-26
Pavamāna [king] **164**
Pāvamāna, place of pilgrimage **164**.53cd-54
pavamāna-hymn from Ṛgveda **174**.13-17
Pāvana, place of pilgrimage **25**.45 .46
Pavanas **27**.59cd-62ab
Pavitrā **20**.43-44
Pavitrāropaṇa **41**.72-74
Payoda **13**.153cd-154ab
Payoṣṇī **19**.11-12ab; **27**.33-34; **70**.33-35ab; **77**.2-9ab
- , place of pilgrimage **64**.11-14
peoples, list of **19**.15cd-19; **27**.41cd-42 .43-50 .51cd-53 .54-57 .59cd-62ab .62cd-64ab; **54**.12-13; **56**.3-8; **220**.8-10ab
perceptibility of deities **30**.19-20
- of *puruṣa* and *prakṛti* **243**.21-31
perception of self **236**.16cd-19
- , senses of **236**.10-11
perception see also *knowledge*
performance of forbidden sacrifice **228**.76-85
pericarp, Meru as **18**.13-15 .44cd-45ab
periods, change of cosmic **231**.93
- , conditions at end of cosmic **231**.4-41
- , cosmic **56**.39cd-42; **230**.4-7
perishable and imperishable **241**.1-2 .34-36ab; **243**.37-40; **244**.11-42
- and imperishable Self **236**.32 .35
person(s) at sacrifice **127**.60-63
- entitled to performance of ancestral rites **220**.76 .77-78ab .78cd-80ab
personification of fever **39**.74-81
- of knowledge of Daityas **206**.31-38
- of sacrifice, Viṣṇu as **73**.21-22
- of seasons **36**.63cd-70
- of wrath **39**.48-49; **162**.10cd-12
pestle as weapon of Baladeva **209**.11cd-21ab
- , birth of a **210**.11-14
- , curse of pregnancy with **210**.6-10

phalastuti **1**.31-32 .56; **2**.57; **3**.126; **4**.27; **5**.42-47 .47; **6**.54; **8**.95; **9**.35cd-36ab; **11**.26c-f; **12**.51; **13**.207cd-208ab .210-212ab .213c-f; **14**.35 .57; **15**.29 .60cd -61; **16**.58cd-59; **20**.10-11; **25**.83cd-86ab .86c-f; **27**.80; **30**.44 .89-91; **31**.35-36; **32**.108; **33**.48-49; **35**.64; **37**.29 .30; **40**.120 .121-134 .136-137; **49**.61-63 .68 .71; **70**.41a-f; **73**.69cd; **86**.49c-f; **89**.47; **94**.50c-f; **96**.27; **104**.89cd-90; **105**.30cd-31ab; **110**.229; **112**.28; **115**.19cd -20ab; **119**.20; **120**.14; **122**.103; **124**.1-2ab; **127**.1; **128**.1-2 .77-81; **131**.53cd-54ab; **136**.41-42; **152**.41; **157**.31; **168**.37; **172**.19cd-20ef; **173**.36; **175**.79; **178**.191; **206**.14-19; **213**.168cd-169ab .170; **219**.116; **220**.211; **246**.18-19 .21-35

Phālguna **31**.19-21; **212**.35-41

- , auspiciousness of **63**.18

Phālgunī **67**.2-5; **220**.33cd-42

phases of moon **44**.48-53ab

Phena **13**.27cd-29

Phenā and Gautamī, confluence of **129**.82-93

- [river], origin of **129**.4-8

Phenāsaṃgama, place of pilgrimage **84**.19-20; **129**.1-2

pigeon and owl **125**

- , lament of **80**.30-36

pilgrimage **10**.34cd-38ab

- as circumambulation of earth **228**.92cd-96
- at auspicious date(s) **41**.54cd-57ab
- , equivalence of self-control and **25**.4-6
- , merit of **28**.53cd-54ab .54cd-56ab; **45**.77 -89; **63**.19-20; **67**.2-5

pillar, killing with golden **201**.23-26

Pināka [Śiva's spear] **122**.1-2

Pinākin **3**.46cd-49

piṇḍa see *rice-balls, offerings, ancestral rites*

Piṇḍāraka **14**.39-41

- , place of pilgrimage **25**.24; **64**.3-8ab; **210**.6-10

Piṅgutīrtha, place of pilgrimage **25**.27

Piñjaraka, place of pilgrimage **25**.28

Pippala **174**.2-5ab

- , place of pilgrimage **118**.31-32ef
- [Rākṣasa] **118**.10-14

Pippalā [sister of Viśvāvasu] **132**

Pippalāda **110**.71-229

- , boon by gods to **110**.168-171
- , boon by Śiva to **110**.107-111 .165
- to Śiva, hymn by **110**.100-106

Pippalāda, explanation of **110**.78-80cd

Pippalādatīrtha, place of pilgrimage **110**.124-130

Pippalāda-trees **110**.158-159

Pippalatīrtha, place of pilgrimage **110**.1-4; **118**.1

Pippala-tree(s) **18**.23cd-24ab; **110**.166-167 .172-178 .219ef-224

- as foster-parents **110**.78-80cd

Pippaleśa, Śiva as **110**.226-228

Pippaleśvara, place of pilgrimage **110**.226-228

Piśāca, rebirth as **150**.1cd-4ab .6-9

Piśācamocana, place of pilgrimage **25**.61

Piśācas **39**.7-17ab

Piśācas see also *Dānavas, Daityas, demons, Rākṣasas*

Piśācikā **27**.30-32

Pīta [caste] **20**.31

Pitṛkūpa, place of pilgrimage **25**.70

Pitṛrūpa **3**.46cd-49

Pitṛsomarṣikulyā **27**.37cd-38ab

Pitṛtīrtha, place of pilgrimage **93**.1-2; **110**.217-219cd

Pitṛvana, place of pilgrimage **25**.78

Pīvara **20**.47cd-49ab

place, *dharma* in time and **175**.14-32ab

- for asceticism, Badarī as **210**.33-35
- for asceticism, Gaṅgādvāra as **147**.5-7
- for asceticism, Gandhamādana as **197**.4-5; **210**.33-35
- for asceticism, Mahendra as **213**.114-122
- for asceticism, Meru as **6**.48cd-50ab; **7**.30-34
- for asceticism, ocean as **7**.105cd-109

place(s) for depositing offerings to ancestors **220**.61cd-62ab

place of pilgrimage, Abjaka **128**.83-84; **129**.1-2

- , Abjakatīrtha **129**.11ab .101-124 .125-127
- , Adritīrtha **174**.25cd-27ab
- , Agnipada **25**.14
- , Agniprabha **25**.22
- , Agnitīrtha **98**.1 .19cd; **126**.37-39; **168**.26cd-28ab
- , Ahalyāsaṃgama **87**.70-71
- , Ailatīrtha **151**.24cd-27ab
- , Ainasa **25**.52
- , Aindava **104**.1-2

–, Aindra **104**.1-2
–, Aindratīrtha **93**.27; **174**.8-12ef
–, Aiśvara **104**.1-2
–, Aja **105**.22-26ab
–, Ajāmukharasa **25**.63
–, Ajāmukhasara **25**.63
–, Akhaṇḍitahrada **25**.83ab
–, Amarahrada **25**.44
–, Amarakaṇṭaka **25**.20; **64**.3-8ab
–, Amaravartanatīrtha **25**.82
–, Amṛta **120**.16-18
–, Aṅgāratīrtha **25**.82
–, Anaśana **25**.31
–, Anvindra **140**.1 .35-38
–, Apsarāsaṃgama **100**.1-3; **147**.1-3
–, Apsaroyuga **147**.1-3 .4
–, Arbuda **25**.27; **64**.8cd-9
–, Aruṇāspada **25**.60
–, Aruṇāvaruṇāsaṃgama **89**.1-2cd
–, Arundhatīvana **25**.56
–, Aśokavana **25**.60
–, Aśvadevī **25**.56
–, Aśvatīrtha **64**.3-8ab; **89**.43-46ab
–, Aśvattha **118**.31-32ef
–, Aśvatthatīrtha **118**.1 .24cd-30
–, Aśvavedī **25**.56
–, Auddālakatīrtha **25**.76
–, Aurvīśītīrtha **25**.75
–, Auṣadhya **120**.16-18
–, Auśana **104**.1-2
–, Auśanasa **25**.51
–, Avakīrṇa **25**.51
–, Avasarga **25**.79
–, Avedhya **25**.42
–, Avighna **114**.25
–, Avighnatīrtha **114**.1
–, Avimukta **25**.61; **113**.22-23; **229**.59-63
–, Āditya **155**.1
–, Ādityatīrtha **174**.19-25ab
–, Āgastya **118**.31-32ef
–, Āgneya **98**.21cd-22; **104**.1-2
–, Āgneyatīrtha **174**.19-25ab
–, Ālābu **42**.6-8
–, Āñjana **84**.18
–, Āṅgirasa **155**.1
–, Ānanda **152**.40
–, Āpastambatīrtha **129**.125-127; **130**.1 .34
–, Ārka **103**.9
–, Āśvina **104**.1-2
–, Āsīna **25**.37
–, Āspada **25**.41
–, Ātmatīrtha **117**.1 .20c-f
–, Ātreya **140**.1 .35-38
–, Ātreyatīrtha **140**.35-38
–, Babūravana **25**.37
–, Badarikāśrama **25**.77; **64**.3-8ab
–, Badarī **25**.17; **65**.84-96
–, Badarīhrada **25**.81
–, Badarīpāṭana **25**.54
–, Badarīpāvana **25**.54
–, Badarīśaila **25**.13
–, Badarīvana **25**.37
–, Barhapada **25**.32
–, Bāhukātīrtha **25**.58
–, Bāhutīrtha **25**.58
–, Bāṇatīrtha **123**.213cd-216; **131**.25 .39cd -51
–, Bārhaspatya **122**.100-102; **174**.19-25ab
–, Bhadra **105**.22-26ab
–, Bhadrabala **25**.33
–, Bhadrakarṇahrada **25**.50
–, Bhadrakālīhrada **25**.55
–, Bhadratīrtha **165**.1 .47cd-48ef
–, Bhadravaṭa **25**.26 .33 .49
–, Bhadrāvāsatīrtha **25**.66
–, Bhaktahrada **25**.66
–, Bharatatīrtha **25**.71
–, Bhartṛsthāna **25**.59
–, Bhaumasthāna **25**.40
–, Bhavābhatrana **25**.38
–, Bhānutīrtha **89**.43-46ab; **138**.2-3 .39cd -40; **168**.1 .13-14 .38
–, Bhāvatīrtha **153**.1-2ab .13-15ab .15cd-16ab
–, Bhillatīrtha **169**.1-2ab .48-49cd
–, Bhīma-forest **25**.11
–, Bhīmarathī **64**.11-14
–, Bhīmatāṇḍavavāmukha **25**.82
–, Bhṛgutīrtha **25**.48
–, Bhṛgutuṅga **25**.11
–, Bilvaprabha **25**.21
–, Bimbaprabha **25**.21
–, Brahma-Rudratīrtha **25**.28
–, Brahmabālukā **25**.30
–, Brahmahrada **25**.23
–, Brahmajña **25**.40
–, Brahmakuṇḍa **25**.17
–, Brahmaputra **64**.10
–, Brahmasara **25**.62 .65 .68
–, Brahmasaras **25**.65 .68 .73

– , Brahmasthāna **25**.45 .71
– , Brahmasthānavivardhana **25**.81
– , Brahmatīrtha **25**.35 .39 .45 .48; **101**.19cd -20; **102**.11c-f; **113**.1 .18-21 .22-23; **131**.39cd-51
– , Brahmatuṅga **25**.28
– , Brahmavāluka **25**.30
– , Brahmavīrāvakāpilī **25**.73
– , Brahmayoṇi **25**.48
– , Brahmāṇī **25**.58
– , Brahmāvarta **25**.39 .48 .56 .67
– , Brahmodumbara **25**.40
– , Brāhma **100**.1-3
– , Brāhma as **104**.1-2
– , Cakraprabha **25**.16
– , Cakratīrtha **25**.12 .21; **86**.1 .27-29; **109**.1-3ab .55-57ab; **110**.1-4 .87-97ef .143-146ab .217-219cd; **128**.70cd-72ab; **134**.1 .15-16
– , Cakṣustīrtha **170**.1 .89a-f
– , Campaka-forest **25**.9
– , Caṇḍeśvaratīrtha **25**.61
– , Caṇḍīśvaratīrtha **25**.61
– , Candrabhāgā **64**.11-14
– , Candrikā **25**.64
– , Carmaṇvatī **64**.11-14
– , Catuḥśṛṅga **25**.18
– , Catuḥśrotas **25**.18
– , Catuḥsāmudrika **25**.52
– , Cavarambana **25**.34
– , Cārunadī **25**.58
– , Chāyārohana **25**.32
– , Ciccika **164**.53cd-54
– , Ciccikātīrtha **164**.1-2
– , Citrakūṭa **64**.3-8ab
– , Daṃṣṭrākuṇḍa **25**.16
– , Dadhikarṇodapānaka **25**.67
– , Dadhikarṇodayātmaka **25**.67
– , Dadhīca **25**.55
– , Daiteya **140**.35-38
– , Dakṣiṇa **25**.68
– , Daṇḍaka-forest **25**.10
– , Daṇḍātmā **25**.76
– , Daśāśvamedha **25**.32 .40
– , Daśāśvamedhatīrtha **83**.29
– , Daśāśvamedhikatīrtha **25**.36; **83**.1
– , Daurvāsika **25**.28
– , Dāruvala **25**.32
– , death at **42**.10; **59**.81-91; **68**.74-77ab
– , Deva **25**.34
– , Devahradā **25**.21 .81 .82
– , Devakuṇḍa **25**.22
– , Devakūpa **25**.81
– , Devakūṭa **25**.73
– , Devaprabha **25**.22
– , Devapriya **160**.22c-f
– , Devasthāna **25**.47; **142**.1 .12cd-13
– , Devatīrtha **25**.43 .47; **98**.21cd-22; **105**.22-26ab; **127**.1 .60-63
– , Devāgama **160**.1-2ab .21-22ab .22c-f
– , Devītīrtha **25**.41
– , Dhaiṅuka **25**.69
– , Dhanada **97**.32cd-33
– , Dhanvaka **25**.70
– , Dhanyaka **25**.70
– , Dharma-forest **25**.9
– , Dharmatīrtha **25**.76
– , Dhautapāpa **92**.48cd-49ef
– , Dhānyatīrtha **120**.1 .15
– , Dhenuka **25**.9 .69
– , Dhenusaras **25**.14
– , Divākara **25**.33
– , Dīrghamanta **25**.31
– , Dīrghasattra **25**.31
– , Dṛṣadvatī **64**.11-14
– , Dṛṣṭakuṇḍa **25**.16
– , Drāvanāmita **25**.34
– , Durgātīrtha **132**.7-9ef
– , Dvādaśadhāraka-mountain **25**.18
– , Dvādaśavāraka-mountain **25**.18
– , Dvārakā **64**.3-8ab
– , Ekadhāra **25**.20
– , Ekarātra **25**.54
– , Ekāmraka **64**.3-8ab
– , Gabhastitīrtha **25**.26
– , Gadādhara **164**.53cd-54
– , Gadātīrtha **164**.38-46
– , Gaṅgōdbhavasarasvatī **25**.58
– , Gaṅgā **64**.10 .11-14; **65**.84-96
– , Gaṅgādhara **25**.15
– , Gaṅgādvāra **25**.15; **64**.3-8ab; **65**.84-96
– , Gaṅgāhrada **25**.54
– , Gaṅgātīrtha **25**.82
– , Gaṅgodbheda **25**.32
– , Gaṇḍakī **64**.11-14
– , Gaṇikāsaṃgama **86**.2 .35-39
– , Gandhamādana **64**.8cd-9
– , Gaurīśikhara **25**.74
– , Gautamairāvatītīrtha **25**.59
– , Gavāṃbhavanatīrtha **25**.38

-, Gaya **64**.3-8ab
-, Gayā **25**.10
-, Gayāśīrṣākṣaya-vaṭa **25**.68
-, Gālava **92**.48cd-49ef
-, Gāṅgatīrtha **85**.24
-, Gāndharva **25**.23
-, Gāndharvatīrtha **105**.22-26ab
-, Gāruḍatīrtha **90**.1 .36
-, Gāyatrī **102**.1-2ab
-, Gāyatrīsthāna **25**.80
-, Ghaṇṭākarṇahrada **25**.63
-, Ghargharikā-kuṇḍa **25**.64
-, Ghoratīrtha **25**.13
-, Gītavana **25**.69
-, Godāvarī **64**.11-14
-, Gograha **42**.6-8
-, Gokarṇa **25**.80; **64**.8cd-9
-, Gomanta **64**.8cd-9
-, Gomatī **64**.10
-, Gomaya **25**.68
-, Gopatisthāna **25**.80
-, Goprabhāva **25**.24
-, Gorakṣa **131**.29-30
-, Gotīrtha **110**.216; **131**.25 .39cd-51; **155**.12-13ab
-, Govara **25**.24
-, Govardhana **91**.11cd-12
-, Govardhanatīrtha **91**.1-2ab
-, Govinda **122**.100-102
-, Gṛdhrakūṭa **25**.69
-, Gṛdhravaṭa **25**.69
-, Guhāviṣṇupada **25**.25
-, Haṃsapāda **25**.31
-, Haṃsasthāna **25**.40
-, Hanūmata **129**.1-2
-, Hanūmatatīrtha **129**.9-10
-, Harikeśavana **25**.62
-, Hariścandra **104**.1-2
-, Hayamūrdhaka **174**.8-12ef
-, Hayapada **25**.31
-, Hayaśantika **25**.68
-, Hetyulūka **125**.54-56
-, Himālaya **25**.12; **64**.8cd-9
-, Hiraṇyaka **148**.21-26
-, Hiraṇyākṣa **25**.11
-, Ilāsaṃgama **105**.22-26ab
-, Ilātīrtha **108**.1
-, Indradyumna [-lake] **45**.77-89
-, Indradyumnasara **25**.79
-, Indradyumnasaras **25**.79; **63**.1-7
-, Indramārga **25**.54
-, Indratīrtha **87**.70-71; **96**.1; **122**.100-102; **124**.137-139ab; **129**.1-2; **168**.30
-, Indreśvaratīrtha **129**.101-124
-, Iṣutīrtha **25**.80
-, Īśānatīrtha **25**.46
-, Īṭāspada **25**.41
-, Jaigīṣavyaguhā **25**.62
-, Jaigīṣavyavana **25**.62
-, Jambumārga **64**.3-8ab
-, Jambūmārga **25**.25
-, Janakakūpa **25**.71
-, Janasthāna **88**.1 .21-26
-, Jaṭādharatīrtha **100**.31cd
-, Jātavedasa **98**.21cd-22
-, Jātīhrada **25**.81
-, Jirikāvāsa **25**.54
-, Jñānatīrtha **139**.19
-, Jyeṣṭhasthānahrada **25**.62
-, Jyeṣṭhālika **25**.71
-, Jyeṣṭhālikā **25**.71
-, Kadalīhrada **25**.21
-, Kaitava **171**.47-49ef
-, Kalpasaras **25**.72
-, Kamalā **124**.137-139ab
-, Kanakhala **25**.10
-, Kanakhala as **64**.3-8ab
-, Kanyākumārikā **25**.28
-, Kanyākuṇḍa **25**.25
-, Kanyāśrama **25**.25
-, Kanyāśramahrada **25**.82
-, Kanyāsaṃvedha **25**.72
-, Kanyāsaṃvetya **25**.72
-, Kanyātīrtha **25**.43 .45 .80
-, Kapālamocana **25**.51; **229**.59-63
-, Kapila **25**.76
-, Kapilatīrtha **155**.1
-, Kapilāhrada **25**.69 .82
-, Kapilālohitārṇava **25**.76
-, Kapilāsaṃgama **141**.1 .29-30; **155**.14cd
-, Kapilātīrtha **25**.38
-, Kapilāvana **25**.50
-, Kapīmada **25**.47
-, Kapota **125**.54-56
-, Kapotatīrtha **80**.5cd-6ab
-, Karatoyā **64**.11-14
-, Karkoṭaka-vāpī **25**.63
-, Karṇikāsaṃgama **105**.22-26ab
-, Kauberahrada **25**.80
-, Kaumāra **100**.1-3

–, Kauśāmba **25**.33
–, Kauśāmbī **25**.33
–, Kauśikāśrama **25**.73
–, Kauśikī **25**.43; **64**.11–14
–, Kauśikīdruma **25**.75
–, Kauśikīhrada **25**.75
–, Kauśikya **25**.71
–, Kavaṣatīrtha **139**.19
–, Kādravāsaṃgama as **100**.1–3
–, Kālañjara **64**.8cd–9; **146**.42–45
–, Kālatīrtha **25**.76
–, Kālatīrthaka **25**.77
–, Kālikāśrama **25**.33 .49
–, Kāmada **25**.60
–, Kāmatīrtha **25**.76
–, Kāmākhya **25**.30
–, Kāmālaya **64**.3–8ab
–, Kāmeśvara **25**.39
–, Kāmyaka **25**.51
–, Kāñcana **25**.76
–, Kāṇva **148**.21–26
–, Kāṇvatīrtha **85**.24
–, Kāpila **41**.91; **42**.6–8
–, Kāpilī **25**.59
–, Kāraka **25**.20
–, Kāraṇḍava **25**.42
–, Kāratoya **25**.76
–, Kārttikeya **81**.1
–, Kārttikeyatīrtha **81**.22c–f
–, Kārupāvanatīrtha **25**.45
–, Kāṣṭhaka-vāpikā **25**.63
–, Kāśi **64**.3–8ab
–, Kāverī **64**.11–14
–, Kāverīhrada **25**.80
–, Kedāra **25**.11 .32 .40; **64**.3–8ab
–, Khaḍgatīrtha **139**.1–2ab .19
–, Kiṃdāna **25**.41
–, Kiṃjapa **25**.41
–, Kiṃjaya **25**.41
–, Kiṃvāna **25**.41
–, Kila-hrada **25**.47
–, Kiṣkindhātīrtha **157**.1–2ab .31
–, Kokanada **25**.20
–, Kokāmukha **25**.13; **64**.3–8ab; **219**.4–5; **228**.92cd–96; **229**.68cd–71 .72–86ab
–, Kokila **25**.70
–, Koraka **25**.20
–, Koṭaraka **25**.20
–, Koṭidruma **25**.21
–, Koṭikṛta **25**.41
–, Koṭikūṭa **25**.41
–, Koṭitīrtha **25**.12 .14 .15 .26 .36 .44 .55 .59; **64**.3–8ab; **148**.1–3ab .27a–f; **164**.53cd–54
–, Koṭitīrthasthalī **25**.55
–, Kṛṣṇatīrtha **25**.30 .78
–, Kṛśarāsaṃgama **105**.22–26ab
–, Kṛtālaya **25**.47
–, Kṛttika **25**.57
–, Kṛttikātīrtha **82**.1 .15–16ef
–, Kroḍatīrtha **42**.6–8
–, Kruśadaṇḍa **25**.16
–, Kṣama **25**.82
–, Kṣiprā **64**.11–14
–, Kṣīrakāvāsa **25**.54
–, Kṣīraśrava **25**.48
–, Kṣīrasaras **25**.66
–, Kṣīreśvara **25**.48
–, Kṣudhātīrtha **85**.1 .24
–, Kubjavana **25**.56
–, Kubjāmbaka **25**.49
–, Kubjāvana **25**.56
–, Kulakarṇahrada **25**.75
–, Kuliṅgaka **25**.30
–, Kumāradhārā **25**.74
–, Kumāraka **25**.66
–, Kumāravāsa **25**.75
–, Kumārika **25**.28
–, Kumārī **64**.11–14
–, Kumbha **25**.65
–, Kumbhakarṇahrada **25**.75
–, Kundaka **25**.82
–, Kurukṣetra **25**.4–6; **64**.3–8ab; **65**.84–96
–, Kurukṣetra as **65**.84–96
–, Kurutīrtha **25**.53
–, Kuśadhvaja **25**.53
–, Kuśaprathana **25**.81
–, Kuśapravaṇa **25**.81
–, Kuśasthalī **25**.11
–, Kuśatarpaṇa **161**.1–2ab .65cd–67
–, Kuśāvarta **25**.67; **64**.3–8ab; **80**.1–3
–, Kuśāvila **25**.30
–, Kuśodbhava **25**.48
–, Kusumāsaṃgama **105**.22–26ab
–, Kūpa **25**.62 .65 .70 .73
–, Lakṣmaṇa **123**.213cd–216
–, Lakṣmītīrtha **137**.1
–, Lohakuṇḍa **64**.3–8ab
–, Lohakula **25**.11
–, Lohārgala **25**.11; **64**.3–8ab
–, Lohika **25**.70

- , Lohitārṇava **25**.76
- , Lokadvāra **25**.38
- , Lokapāla **25**.19
- , Lokapālatīrtha **25**.23
- , Lokārohaṇa **25**.32
- , Madhukaṇṭa **25**.42
- , Madhukuṇḍa **25**.19
- , Madhuvāhinī **64**.11-14
- , Madhūvaṭa **25**.42
- , Madhyakesara **25**.15
- , Madhyasthāna **25**.81
- , Magadha-forest **25**.10
- , Mahābala **25**.12
- , Mahāhrada **25**.58
- , Mahākālavana **25**.26
- , Mahākuṇḍa **25**.19
- , Mahālaya **25**.12 .47
- , Mahānadī **25**.67; **64**.11-14
- , Mahānala **116**.1-2ab
- , Mahārājahrada **25**.82
- , Mahāśrama **25**.58
- , Mahāśrotra **25**.20
- , Mahāsrota **25**.20
- , Mahāsūtra **25**.20
- , Mahātīrtha **25**.67; **122**.87-92
- , Mahendra **64**.8cd-9
- , Maheśvaratīrtha **168**.31-35
- , Maitra **104**.1-2
- , Malavya **25**.24
- , Malaya **64**.8cd-9
- , Maṅgalāsaṃgama **122**.100-102
- , Maṇimanta **25**.30
- , Maṇimatta **25**.30
- , Maṇipura-mountain **25**.23
- , Maṇipūra **25**.31
- , Maṇiratnahrada **25**.71
- , Maṇitīrtha **25**.46
- , Manastīrtha **25**.45
- , Mandara **25**.11; **64**.3-8ab
- , Mandatīrtha **118**.1
- , Mandākinīhrada **25**.82
- , Manojava **25**.42
- , Manomaya **25**.42
- , Mantha **25**.31
- , Manuvara **25**.19
- , Manyutīrtha **162**.1-2ab .31-33ef
- , Marusthala **64**.3-8ab
- , Mataṅga **25**.16
- , Mataṅgahrada **25**.70
- , Mathurā **64**.3-8ab
- , Matitīrtha **25**.70
- , Matsyatila **25**.17
- , Matsyodarī **25**.59
- , Maudgalya **136**.41-42
- , Mādhucchandasa **138**.39cd-40
- , Māhendra **25**.47 .79
- , Māheśvara **25**.82
- , Mālava **96**.18-19
- , Mālinītīrtha **25**.76
- , Mālya **25**.82
- , Mānasa **25**.18
- , Mānavaka **25**.53
- , Mārgaṇakeśatra **25**.54
- , Mārjāra **84**.19-20; **129**.9-10
- , Mārkaṇḍa **145**.11cd-13
- , Mārkaṇḍeya **145**.1-2ab
- , Mārkaṇḍeya-lake **56**.66cd-73
- , Mārkaṇḍeyavana **25**.78
- , Māsasaṃsaraka **25**.40
- , Mātaṅgahrada **25**.70
- , Mātṛtīrtha **25**.39; **112**.1 .23cd-24ab .24cd -26ab .28; **120**.16-18
- , Mātritīrtha [Mātṛtīrtha] **25**.39
- , Māyāvidyodbhava **25**.57
- , Medhā **102**.1-2ab
- , Medhāvina **25**.82
- , Meghahāsa **142**.10cd-12ab
- , merit obtained at **28**.9 .11-18; **35**.26cd-28; **41**.88-90 .91 .93; **42**.1-2 .6-8 .9 .13-14 .42cd-46ab; **43**.14 .65cd-74 .75-76 .77-82ab .83cd-85ab; **45**.53-56 .57-58; **51**.29-31 .63-71; **57**.9-11; **59**.81-91; **62**.1-4 .13cd-15 .22cd-23; **63**.1-7; **70**.3cd-8ab; **81**.1 .22c-f; **82**.1 .15-16ef; **83**.29; **86**.1 .2; **88**.21-26; **89**.46cd; **91**.11cd-12; **93**.1-2; **94**.1 .48cd-50ab; **95**.1 .31-32; **96**.1 .25cd -26; **97**.1 .32cd-33; **98**.20-21ab .21cd-22; **99**.12a-f; **100**.1-3 .4ab .31ef; **101**.1; **102**.1-2ab .9cd-11ab .11c-f; **103**.12c-f; **105**.29cd-30ab; **106**.54cd-56; **108**.1 .121-123; **109**.1-3ab; **110**.166-167 .215 .226-228; **111**.85cd-86; **112**.1; **113**.1 .18-21 .22-23; **114**.21-24 .25; **115**.18-19ab .20c-f; **116**.24cd-25ab .25c-f; **117**.20c-f; **118**.31-32ef; **119**.1 .18-19; **120**.1 .16-18; **121**.24-25 .26; **122**.1-2 .87-92 .100-102 .104; **123**.1 .176-177ab .207-213ab; **124**.137-139ab; **125**.33-43 .54-56; **126**.1-2 .37-39; **127**.64a-f; **128**.77-81; **129**.1-2 .101-124 .125-127; **130**.1 .34; **131**.39cd-51

.52-53ab .54cd-57ef; **132**.1-2 .7-9ef; **133**.1 .23cd-25; **134**.15-16; **135**.1-2ab .25-27ab .27c-f; **136**.43; **137**.1 .40cd-41ab .41c-f; **138**.1 .39cd-40; **139**.19 .20; **140**.1 .35-38; **141**.29-30; **142**.14; **143**.17; **144**.23-24 .25-27; **145**.1-2ab .11cd-13; **146**.42-45; **147**.1-3 .20cd-23ab; **148**.1-3ab .21-26 .27a-f; **149**.13-16ab .16cd-19; **150**.21-22 .23; **151**.1-2 .22cd-24ab .27cd-29; **152**.40; **153**.13-15ab; **154**.1 .30cd-31; **155**.13cd-14ab; **156**.1-2ab .7-9ab; **157**.1-2ab .29 .31; **158**.39cd-40ef; **159**.46cd-48ab .48cd-49ef; **161**.1-2ab .63-64ab .72-78; **162**.31-33ef; **163**.1-2 .52-53; **164**.1-2 .53cd-54; **165**.1 .47cd-48ef; **166**.1 .8cd-11ab .11cd-13; **167**.33; **168**.30 .36 .38; **169**.1-2ab .48-49cd; **170**.1 .89a-f; **171**.1-2ab .47-49ef; **172**.1 .19cd-20ef; **173**.34cd-35ef; **174**.25cd-27ab; **228**.92cd-96

- , Merukuṇḍa **25**.19
- , Mesadhara **25**.19
- , Miśraka **25**.42
- , Mitra **30**.40-41
- , Mitravala **25**.33
- , Mṛgavyādhatīrtha **102**.11c-f
- , Mṛtasaṃjīvana **138**.39cd-40; **170**.89a-f
- , Mṛtasaṃjīvinītīrtha **95**.31-32
- , Mṛtyuṃjaya **42**.6-8
- , Mudgalahrada **25**.71
- , Mudgalāśrama **25**.71
- , Muñjavaṭa **25**.37
- , Muñjāvaṭaratha **25**.37
- , Naimiṣa **25**.8cd; **64**.3-8ab; **65**.84-96
- , Naimiṣeya **25**.44
- , Nandinīsaṃgama **128**.1-2
- , Nanditīrtha **25**.74
- , Nandītaṭa **152**.1
- , Narmadā **64**.11-14
- , Narmadātīrtha **25**.27
- , Narmadobdheda **25**.32
- , Nāgatīrtha **25**.66; **111**.1 .85cd-86; **115**.18-19ab
- , Nāhuṣa **146**.42-45
- , Nārasiṃha **149**.13-16ab
- , Nārasiṃhatīrtha **149**.1
- , Nārāyaṇa **167**.1 .33
- , Nārāyaṇāśrama **25**.53
- , Nidhirāmabhava **25**.72
- , Nimnabheda **151**.1-2 .24cd-27ab
- , Nimnabhedatīrtha **151**.27cd-29
- , Niścīvā **25**.72
- , Nīlagaṅgā **80**.4-5ab
- , Nīlakaṇṭhahrada **25**.61
- , Nīlaparvata **25**.48
- , Nṛgadhūma **25**.43
- , Nṛsiṃhatīrtha **149**.16cd-19
- , ocean **44**.48-53ab; **45**.77-89; **62**.16cd-22ab; **172**.19cd-20ef
- , Ojasa **25**.52
- , Pailūṣatīrtha **139**.19
- , Paiśāca **84**.18; **150**.1ab
- , Paiśācatīrtha **84**.1
- , Paitāmahatīrtha **25**.29
- , Pañcadhāra **25**.20
- , Pañcahrada **25**.24
- , Pañcaka **25**.51
- , Pañcakaṭaka **25**.52
- , Pañcakūṭa **25**.15
- , Pañcanada **25**.29 .36
- , Pañcanadatīrtha **25**.59
- , Pañcaśikha **25**.14
- , Pañcatīrtha **25**.27 .38; **43**.10-13
- , Pañcavaṭaka **25**.52
- , Pañcavaṭāśrama **89**.43-46ab
- , Pañcayajñaka **25**.46
- , Pañjiraka **25**.28
- , Parjanyatīrtha **93**.27
- , Paruṣṇīsaṃgama **144**.1 .25-27
- , Patatritīrtha **166**.1 .8cd-11ab
- , Paulastya **97**.32cd-33
- , Paulastyatīrtha **97**.1
- , Paura **146**.42-45
- , Pautra **148**.21-26
- , Payoṣṇī **64**.11-14
- , Pāñcayajñika **25**.46
- , Pāṇikhāta **25**.42
- , Pāṇiṣāta **25**.42
- , Pāpanāśana **110**.215
- , Pāpapramocana **228**.92cd-96
- , Pāpapraṇāśana **92**.1 .48cd-49ef
- , Pāriplava **25**.35
- , Pāriyātra **64**.8cd-9
- , Pāvamāna **164**.53cd-54
- , Pāvana **25**.45 .46
- , Phenāsaṃgama **84**.19-20; **129**.1-2
- , Piñjaraka **25**.28
- , Piṅgutīrtha **25**.27
- , Piṇḍāraka **25**.24; **64**.3-8ab; **210**.6-10
- , Pippala **118**.31-32ef

– , Pippalatīrtha **110**.1-4; **118**.1
– , Pippalādatīrtha **110**.124-130
– , Pippaleśvara **110**.226-228
– , Piśācamocana **25**.61
– , Pitṛkūpa **25**.70
– , Pitṛtīrtha **93**.1-2; **110**.217-219cd
– , Pitṛvana **25**.78
– , Pṛthivī **25**.35
– , Pṛthukūṭa **25**.82
– , Pṛthutuṅga **64**.3-8ab
– , Pṛthūdaka **25**.35; **64**.3-8ab; **228**.86-91ab
– , Prabhava **25**.72
– , Prabhāsa **25**.10; **64**.3-8ab
– , Prabhāsana **25**.69
– , Prajādvāra **25**.49
– , Pramokṣa **25**.57
– , Praṇītāsaṃgama **161**.1-2ab .64cd-65ab .72-78
– , Pravara **25**.46
– , Pravarāsaṃgama **106**.1 .57-58ab
– , Prayāga **25**.4-6 .9 .25; **64**.3-8ab; **65**.84-96
– , Prācetasa **158**.1
– , Pretādhāra **25**.66
– , Priyasaṃjñaka **25**.27
– , Puṃnāga **25**.22
– , Pulomaka **25**.66
– , Puṇḍarīka **25**.31 .37
– , Puṇḍarīkahrada **25**.63
– , Puṇyaśata **25**.72
– , Puṇyatīrtha **124**.1-2ab
– , Puṇyāsaṃgama **96**.24cd-25ab
– , Puṇyāvartahrada **25**.77
– , Puṇyāvatīhrada **25**.77
– , Purūrava **151**.24cd-27ab
– , Purūravastīrtha **101**.1
– , Puṣkara **25**.4-6 .8cd; **64**.3-8ab; **65**.84-96
– , Puṣpanyāsa **25**.31
– , Puṣṭisaṃgama **105**.22-26ab
– , Putratīrtha **124**.1-2ab .137-139ab
– , Pūrṇatīrtha **122**.1-2 .100-102 .105
– , Pūrṇavat **25**.34
– , Pūrṇāhūti **105**.20
– , Pūrṇātīrtha **105**.22-26ab
– , Ṛṇamocana **25**.43
– , Ṛṇapramocanatīrtha **99**.1 .12a-f
– , Ṛṣabha **25**.77
– , Ṛṣakulyā **25**.57
– , Ṛṣikulyā **25**.57; **64**.11-14
– , Ṛṣisattra **173**.1-2
– , Ṛṣitīrtha **25**.28
– , rank of Indra, obtained at **140**.35-38
– , Ratnamūlaka **25**.37
– , Raudra **100**.1-3
– , Raudrapāda **25**.29
– , Rākṣasyatīrtha **25**.39
– , Rāmabhaṅgīkatīrthaka **25**.77
– , Rāmatīrtha **25**.78; **123**.1 .213cd-216 .217
– , Reṇuka **25**.52
– , Reṇukātīrtha **25**.29
– , Rohiṇīkūpa **25**.79
– , Rohita **104**.1-2
– , Rohitaka **25**.82
– , Rudrakoṭi **25**.34
– , Rudrakūpa **25**.34
– , Rudrapāda **25**.29
– , Rudratīrtha **25**.70; **113**.18-21
– , Rudrāraṇyaka **25**.82
– , Rudrāvarta **25**.50
– , Rudrāvāsatīrtha **25**.66
– , Rūpaśītika **25**.68
– , Rūpatīrtha **25**.12; **228**.127cd-145 .146-151 .152
– , Śaṃbhutīrtha **25**.14
– , Śaiva **103**.9
– , Śakrakarṇahrada **25**.50
– , Śakratīrtha **25**.29 .70 .82
– , Śamītīrtha **103**.1 .9
– , Śaṅkhahrada **156**.1-2ab
– , Śaṅkhaprabha **25**.22
– , Śaṅkhatīrtha **156**.7-9ab
– , Śaṅkhinī **25**.38
– , Śaṅkhuddhāra **64**.3-8ab
– , Śaṅkukarṇahrada **25**.50
– , Śanaiścara as **118**.31-32ef
– , Śatadru **64**.11-14
– , Śataki **25**.52
– , Śatasahasrikatīrtha **25**.59
– , Śatrukuṇḍa **25**.16
– , Śaukarava **228**.146-151
– , Śaukra as **146**.42-45
– , Śavatīrtha **123**.176-177ab
– , Śayana **25**.31
– , Śāṃbhava **171**.47-49ef
– , Śāṃkara **128**.70cd-72ab
– , Śākaṃbharī **25**.47
– , Śākhoṭaka **25**.13
– , Śālagrāma **25**.21; **64**.3-8ab; **65**.84-96
– , Śālatīrtha **105**.22-26ab
– , Śālitīrtha **25**.44
– , Śālīgrāma **25**.21

- , Śālvakūṭa **25**.82
- , Śārdūla **128**.1-2 .70cd-72ab .83-84
- , Śārmiṣṭha **146**.42-45
- , Śāryāta **138**.39cd-40
- , Śātavanatīrtha **25**.39
- , Śeṣatīrtha **115**.1
- , Śivakuṇḍa **43**.65cd-74
- , Śivoda **25**.59
- , Śivodbheda **25**.32
- , Śītavanatīrtha **25**.39
- , Śmaśānastambhakūpa **25**.65
- , Śmaśānastambha **25**.65
- , Śoka **25**.71
- , Śoṇa **25**.82
- , Śoṇodbhava **25**.77
- , Śṛṅgatīrtha **25**.67
- , Śraddhā **102**.1-2ab
- , Śreṣṭhasthānahrada **25**.62
- , Śrīdhārā **25**.74
- , Śrīkuñja **25**.44
- , Śrīnada **25**.79
- , Śrīnadī **25**.79
- , Śrīparṇāsaṃgama **105**.22-26ab
- , Śrīśaila **64**.8cd-9
- , Śrīśakrayajana **25**.30
- , Śrītīrtha **25**.10 .23 .79
- , Śrīvāsa **25**.75
- , Śrutatīrtha **25**.55
- , Śuddhikara **25**.12
- , Śuklatīrtha **133**.1
- , Śukratīrtha **25**.60; **95**.1 .31-32
- , Śuktimanta **64**.8cd-9
- , Śunaḥśepa **104**.1-2
- , Śūkara **25**.12; **64**.3-8ab
- , Śūkarava **25**.12; **228**.127cd-145
- , Śvakuṇḍa **25**.74
- , Śvetagaṅgā **59**.81-91
- , Śvetatīrtha **94**.1 .48cd-50ab
- , Śvetatīrthahrada **25**.64
- , Śyāmakūpa **25**.64
- , Śyenatīrtha **93**.27
- , Saṃdhyātīrtha **25**.76
- , Saṃtrāvanāsika as **25**.34
- , Saṃvarta **25**.81
- , Saṃyamanī **25**.34
- sacred to Agni **168**.1
- sacred to Indra **168**.1
- sacred to Śiva **132**.7-9ef; **168**.1
- sacred to Tvaṣṭṛ **168**.1
- sacred to Viṣṇu **136**.41-42
- sacred to Viṣṇu and Śiva **168**.36
- sacred to wife of Brahman **42**.1-11
- sacred to Yama **168**.1
- , Sadāprabha **25**.19
- , Sagara-forest **25**.10
- , Sahasrakuṇḍa **154**.1 .30cd-31
- , Sahasrika **25**.52
- , Sahya **64**.8cd-9
- , Saiṃhikeya **155**.1
- , Saindhava-forest **25**.9
- , Samudra **25**.62
- , Samyaktīrtha **124**.1-2ab
- , Saptadhāra **25**.20
- , Saptagodāvarīhrada **25**.81
- , Saptakuṇḍa **25**.71
- , Saptamāyuṣika **25**.14
- , Saptamāyuṣmika **25**.14
- , Saptarṣikuṇḍa **25**.41
- , Saptasārasvatatīrtha **25**.51
- , Sarasa **25**.40
- , Sarasvatī **25**.46; **64**.10; **102**.1-2ab
- , Sarasvatīsaṃgama **101**.19cd-20
- , Sarayū **64**.11-14
- , Sarpija **25**.36
- , Sarvadevavrata **25**.82
- , Satkāñcanasahasrika **25**.52
- , Sattratīrtha **126**.37-39
- , Satyapada **25**.17
- , Saugandhika **25**.46
- , Saugandhikavana **25**.46
- , Saukarava **228**.127cd-145
- , Saumya **100**.1-3; **103**.9; **120**.16-18
- , Saura **100**.1-3
- , Saurya **113**.18-21
- , Sāhoṭaka **25**.13
- , Sākoṭaka **25**.13
- , Sākṣida **25**.36
- , Sāmaga **118**.31-32ef
- , Sāmudra **172**.1
- , Sānugarta **25**.79
- , Sārasa **25**.40
- , Sārasvata **126**.37-39; **163**.52-53
- , Sārasvata-dvīpa **25**.34
- , Sārasvatatīrtha **163**.1-2
- , Sātīrtham **25**.23
- , Sāttrika **118**.31-32ef
- , Sāvitrī **102**.1-2ab
- , Sāvitrīhrada **25**.69
- , Siddhakeśvara **42**.6-8
- , Siddhatīrtha **143**.1

- , Siddhārtha **25**.57
- , Siddheśvara **25**.33; **128**.1-2; **157**.18ef-21ab
- , Siddhodbhava **25**.65
- , Sindhusāgara **64**.3-8ab
- , Sindhūdbhava **25**.65
- , Sindhūttha **25**.57
- , Sitoda **25**.59
- , Sītavana **25**.69
- , Sītā **123**.213cd-216
- , Skandāśrama **25**.14
- , Skandhāśrama **25**.14
- , Snānadaṇḍa **25**.25
- , Snānakuṇḍa **25**.25
- , Snānalomāpaha **25**.40
- , Soma **42**.6-8
- , Somaka **25**.66
- , Somakavana **25**.60
- , Somatīrtha **25**.13 .14 .37 .45 .55 .59; **64**.3-8ab; **105**.1 .22-26ab; **119**.1 .18-19; **174**.8-12ef .19-25ab
- , Somābhiṣecana **25**.19
- , Somāhva-mountain **25**.19
- , Somātri-mountain **25**.19
- , Someśvaratīrtha **129**.125-127
- , Sthalaśṛṅga **25**.18
- , Sthānutīrtha **25**.53
- , Sthūlaśṛṅga **25**.18
- , Subhadrāhrada **25**.61
- , Sudarśana **25**.35
- , Sugandhāśva **25**.50
- , Sujambuka **25**.41
- , Sukubjaka **64**.3-8ab
- , Sumanasa **25**.34
- , Sumālina **25**.70
- , Sundarikāśrama **25**.58
- , Suparṇāsaṃgamā **100**.1-3
- , Suprabha **25**.17
- , Sura **105**.22-26ab
- , Susaṃyata **25**.41
- , Sutīrtha **25**.28
- , Sutīrthaka **25**.39
- , Suvarṇa **25**.47
- , Suvarṇodapāna **25**.64
- , Sūkarava **228**.127cd-145
- , Sūryaprabha **25**.14 .19 .60
- , Sūryatīrtha **25**.38 .60
- , Svargadvāra **25**.49 .53; **45**.77-89; **161**.72-78
- , Svarlokadvārakatīrtha **25**.38
- , Svayaṃvaṭa **25**.33
- , Svāgatāsaṃgama **105**.22-26ab
- , Syamantapañcakatīrtha **25**.35
- , Tamasodbheda **25**.32
- , Tapastīrtha **126**.1-2 .37-39
- , Tapovana **128**.1-2 .72cd-76
- , Tapovana as **128**.83-84
- , Tāpī **64**.11-14
- , Tīrthabīja **25**.27
- , Tīrthavajra **25**.27
- , Tridhāraka **25**.20
- , Tripuruṣa **25**.82
- , Triśūladhāra **25**.47
- , Trisrotā **64**.11-14
- , Triviṣṭapa **25**.42
- , Tryambaka **79**.5cd-6ab
- , Tuṅgabhadrā **64**.11-14
- , Tuṅgakūṭa **25**.14
- , Tvaṣṭṛtīrtha **168**.22-24
- , Uddālakatīrtha **25**.76
- , Ullayāṅgopacāra **25**.34
- , Ulūka **125**.54-56
- , Urvaśī **25**.18
- , Urvaśītīrtha **171**.1-2ab .47-49ef
- , Urvīsaṃkramaṇa **25**.57
- , Utpalāvartaka **64**.3-8ab
- , Uttara **25**.68
- , Vaṃśagulma **25**.77
- , Vaḍavānala **116**.1-2ab
- , Vaḍavāsaṃgama **116**.24cd-25ab
- , Vahnikuṇḍa **25**.17
- , Vaiṇavīsaṃgama **105**.22-26ab
- , Vaiṣṇava **100**.1-3; **103**.9; **104**.1-2; **128**.70cd-72ab; **171**.47-49ef
- , Vaiśravasa **97**.32cd-33
- , Vaitaraṇī **64**.11-14
- , Vaitasikārūpa **25**.58
- , Vajratīrtha **25**.21
- , Vajrāyudha **25**.22
- , Vañjarāsaṃgama **159**.1 .48cd-49ef
- , Vanacaṇḍikātīrtha **25**.76
- , Varā **25**.59
- , Varusthāna **25**.38
- , Vasiṣṭhapada **25**.49
- , Vasiṣṭhāśrama **25**.72 .73
- , Vastrāpada **25**.32
- , Vasutīrtha **25**.28
- , Vaṭa **25**.54 .78
- , Vaṭamūlaka **25**.24
- , Vaṭāvaṭa **25**.33

- , Vālakhilyatīrtha **25**.82
- , Vāluka **25**.60
- , Vāmakara **25**.53
- , Vāmanaka **25**.60
- , Vāṇitīrtha **135**.1-2ab
- , Vāṇī **148**.21-26
- , Vārāha **25**.36
- , Vārāhatīrtha **79**.6cd-7ab .7cd-19; **122**.48-49
- , Vārṣabha **25**.80
- , Vārṣika **25**.28 .80
- , Vāruṇa **100**.1-3; **104**.1-2
- , Vāsavīsaṃgama **105**.22-26ab
- , Vāsiṣṭha **103**.9; **151**.24cd-27ab
- , Vāsiṣṭhakapilāhrada **25**.82
- , Vāsiṣṭhatīrtha **25**.27
- , Vāsuka **42**.6-8
- , Vāyukuṇḍa **25**.25
- , Vāyutīrtha **64**.3-8ab
- , Vedagāthā **120**.16-18
- , Vetasikārūpa **25**.58
- , Vidyādhara **25**.23
- , Vidyutprabha **25**.21
- , Vijaya **25**.34 .36
- , Vikarṇaka **25**.81
- , Vimaladaṇḍakuṇḍa **25**.61
- , Vimalaśoka as **25**.58
- , Vimocana **25**.52
- , Vināyakahrada **25**.65
- , Vindhya-mountains **64**.8cd-9
- , Vipāśā **64**.11-14
- , Vipratīrtha **167**.1 .33
- , Viraja **42**.1-11; **64**.3-8ab; **161**.2cd-4ab
- , Virajātīrtha **25**.78
- , Virūpākṣa **25**.48
- , Viṣayāntika **25**.36
- , Viṣṇuhrada **25**.21
- , Viṣṇukuṇḍa **25**.16
- , Viṣṇupada **25**.25 .43
- , Viṣṇuprabha **25**.21
- , Viṣṇupura **58**.1-7
- , Viṣṇutīrtha **25**.16; **136**.1ab; **219**.40-41
- , Viśva **25**.42
- , Viśvāmitra **104**.1-2
- , Viśvāmitratīrtha **93**.3-4 .27
- , Viśvāsa **25**.81
- , Viśveśvara **25**.53 .72
- visited by Siddhas **143**.17
- , Vitastā **25**.78; **64**.11-14
- , Vīra **25**.57
- , Vīradhāra **25**.20
- , Vīrapramokṣa **25**.57
- , Vīrāśrama **25**.73
- , Vṛddha **105**.22-26ab
- , Vṛddhāsaṃgama **107**.1 .68dc-69ab
- , Vṛṣākapa **129**.1-2
- , Vṛṣākapatīrtha **129**.11ab
- , Vyāsa **25**.31
- , Vyāsatīrtha **25**.13; **158**.1 .39cd-40ef
- , Yajana **25**.30
- , Yajñatīrtha **131**.26-28
- , Yakṣarājatīrtha **25**.39
- , Yakṣiṇīhrada **25**.36
- , Yakṣiṇīsaṃgama **132**.1-2 .7-9ef
- , Yamatīrtha **125**.1-2ab; **131**.1-2ab .39cd -51; **168**.25-26ab .30
- , Yamunā **64**.10; **65**.84-96
- , Yamunāprabhava **25**.56
- , Yayātipatana **25**.26
- , Yayātipattana **25**.26
- , Yājana **25**.30
- , Yājñika **118**.31-32ef
- , Yāmya **104**.1-2
- , Yāyāta **146**.1 .42-45
- , Yogatīrtha **25**.13
- , Yonidvāra **25**.69

place of pilgrimage see also *holy places*
places, classification of holy **175**.29-32ab
- , *dharma* maintained at holy **175**.17-24
- for ancestral rites **220**.5-7
- for ancestral rites, forbidden **220**.8-10ab
- for asceticism **242**.8-15ab
- for habitation during Kali-Yuga **231**.4-41
- for meditation **58**.19-21ab
- for religious practices **122**.3-7
- for settlement, ideal **221**.103-108
- for sojourn **242**.21cd-22
- for Yoga **236**.59cd-66
- forbidden for Yoga **235**.7-9
- , hundred and eight holy **146**.42-45
- of pilgrimage at Puruṣottamakṣetra, five **43**.10-13
- of pilgrimage, list of **25**.8cd-83ab; **65**.84-96

places, holy see *holy places*
places of pilgrimage, assembly of **105**.26cd-29ab; **152**.37cd-39ef; **175**.83-84
- , comparison of **43**.6-9; **69**.10-11; **70**.1-3ab; **75**.35-45; **77**.9cd-13; **88**.16-19; **149**.13-16ab; **161**.72-78; **177**.20
- honoured by Daityas **142**.14

- , ocean as king of **62**.1-4 .10-13ab
- originated from water-drops **161**.60-61ab
- , prescription(s) concerning bathing at **76**.18cd-23ab
Plakṣadvīpa **18**.11-12; **20**.3-21
- , four castes of **20**.16-17
- , mountains of **20**.6-7
- , regions of **20**.3-5
- , rivers of **20**.10-11
planet, ascension of Budha as **9**.31-32
- , Bṛhaspati as **175**.83-84
- , Rāhu as **142**.9-10ab
- , Śanaiścara as **6**.48cd-50ab .52cd-53
planets **220**.118cd-120ab
- , Bṛhaspati and the **174**.19-25ab
- , distance of **23**.6-10
- , influence of **118**.24cd-30
- , Rāhu as seizer of **106**.42
plans of Kaṃsa **190**.6-8 .10-19; **193**.17-22
- of Kṛṣṇa **210**.22-27 .33-35
plants, aquatic **178**.38-42
- as first of beings **119**.2-4cd
- as food **24**.19-25
- as milk **141**.23-25
- as mothers of Brahman **119**.2-4cd
- as queens of Soma **120**.6-7ab
- , *dharma* based on **119**.2-4cd
- , importance of **120**.9-13
- , list of **41**.38cd-44; **42**.24-26; **44**.66cd-69; **68**.12-13ab
- , merit of donation(s) of **120**.6-7ab
- , origin of **3**.104-105; **9**.9-10; **161**.43cd-50cd
- , promise by Brahman to **119**.4ef-8
- , rebirth as **27**.66cd-68; **229**.31-36ab
- , Soma as husband of **119**.18-19
- , Soma as lord of **4**.2-9; **9**.12; **120**.8; **174**.16
- swallowed by earth **141**.10-13
- to Gautamī, hymn by **119**.9-12
- , waters as origin of **126**.9-11
play of children **187**.8-18
- of Kṛṣṇa **186**.6-13
- of Kṛṣṇa, fighting as **193**.50-57ab .60cd-63ab; **199**.5-10; **206**.39-44
- of *puruṣa*, embodiment as **242**.29-33
- of Śiva, creation as **116**.14
- of Viṣṇu **195**.13-18; **212**.9-11 .66-70
- of Viṣṇu, fighting as **206**.20
play see also *game, love-play*
pleasing of ancestors **213**.168cd-169ab
- of husband **111**.64-68ab
- one's beloved, maxim about **108**.26-30
pleasure and pain, women as cause of **122**.21-24ab
- , asceticism destroyed by **178**.65-69
- , profit and **221**.11-16
- , suffering and **234**.50-54ab
pleasures, heavenly **58**.70cd-77; **59**.81-91
Pleiades **3**.41ab; **24**.13-18; **82**.15-16ef
plough as deity of farmers **187**.42-54
- as emblem **21**.15-27
plough-share, fight by means of **206**.24-30
ploughshare as weapon of Baladeva **195**.5-7; **208**.32-35
plurality, unity and **30**.76-77; **243**.37-40
plurality see also *differentiation*
poet(s) desirous of wealth **174**.17
poison destroyed by place of pilgrimage **166**.8cd-11ab
- swallowed by Śiva **112**.4-6
poisoning, punishment for **22**.21-22; **215**.125cd-126ab
Pole star **23**.6-10
pole star see also *Dhruva*
politeness, rules of **221**.39-40ab
politics **129**.75-78
- , rules of **106**.15-18; **111**.35-39ab; **195**.13-18
pollution according to caste, duration of **220**.63; **221**.146cd-149ab .155cd-158
- by a birth, prescr. conc. **221**.155cd-158
- by sight **221**.141cd-143ab
- by the dead **221**.135cd-136ab
- by touching **221**.143cd-146ab
- by touching of bones **221**.136cd-137ab
- by women **221**.135cd-136ab .143cd-146ab
- , prescr. conc. **221**.127cd-129ab
- , prescr. conc, duration of **221**.152cd-154
pollution see also *impurity, untouchability*
polyandry **84**.9-12
- , punishment for **215**.95cd-98ab
pond, origin of **79**.7cd-19
ponds, description of **41**.47-49ab; **42**.27-31; **43**.58cd-63ab; **44**.73-75
pores of Viṣṇu, stars as **56**.27cd-30ab
portraits, painting of **205**.15-22
pose(s) of hands **28**.28-29
- of hands, eight **61**.52-55
position of women **40**.136-137; **220**.3-4; **231**.4-41

position see also *rank*
post, sacrificial **161**.50ef-53
- thrown into Gautamī, sacrificial **133**.18-23ab
- , Time as sacrificial **161**.35cd-39ab .65cd -67
postponement of boon **37**.26-28
postures of meditation **158**.28-29
- of sitting, prescription(s) concerning **221**.47ab
- of standing, prescription(s) concerning **221**.43
- , yogic **242**.8-15ab
potsherds and cart, veneration of **184**.20-28
poverty and prosperity, maxim about **137**.2-3
- as friend of devotees **137**.15-24
- as friend of righteous people **137**.15-24
- destroyed by place of pilgrimage **137**.40cd -41ab
- , dispute between Lakṣmī and **137**
- , disrespect due to **137**.8-14
- , explanation for **225**.10-16
- , Gautamī hostile to **137**.39cd-40ab
- , superiority of **137**.15-24
power, misuse of **215**.55cd-64
- of going everywhere **140**.3cd-5ab
- , Sūrya as royal **168**.10-12
- , transfer of **110**.35-39ab
power(s), fight by means of magic **200**.17-19
- obtained by asceticism, magic **124**.36cd-39ab
- of asceticism **10**.46cd-49ab; **87**.45-48; **140**.3cd-5ab
- of Yoga **235**.21-25; **239**.24-28
- of Yoga, supernatural **176**.33-34; **205**.15-22; **206**.5-9
- , transfer of magic **200**.11-16
Prabhā **3**.80cd-83; **9**.13-16; **11**.1-2 .8-16; **68**.56-59ab
Prabhākara **13**.5-8 .9-12ab .12cd-14ab; **20**.36-38ab; **31**.14cd-16
Prabhāsa **3**.35cd-36 .42cd-46ab; **70**.37cd-38; **77**.2-9ab; **194**.23-31; **210**.29-30 .37-43
- as name of Somanātha **89**.42
- , place of pilgrimage **25**.10; **64**.3-8ab
- , temple of Somanātha at **110**.202-210
Prabhāsana, place of pilgrimage **25**.69
Prabhava, place of pilgrimage **25**.72
Prabhu **2**.6
Prabhūtas **5**.30cd-31
Pracetas **13**.152-153ab; **34**.29cd-32; **202**.3-12; **226**.30-41
Prācetasa, place of pilgrimage **158**.1
Pracetasas **2**.33 .51-53
Prācetasas **226**.30-41
Prācīnabarhis **2**.29-30ab .30cd-31ab .31cd; **34**.29cd-32 .45cd-48; **133**.5-8; **153**; **226**.30-41
- as founder of solar dynasty **153**.2cd-3
- , vow by **153**.4-6ab
Prācīnabarhiṣas **2**.33
practice, theory and **239**.7-9
practices, acceptability of meritorious **29**.15-17
- , comparison of religious **49**.70; **230**.64
- , effect(s) of religious **125**.33-43
- for obtainment of hundred sons, religious **124**.132-136ab
- for obtainment of son, religious **124**.123-131
- in Kali-Yuga, effect(s) of religious **230**.62-63
- , meritorious **27**.73-78ab
- of worship, prescr. conc. **28**.19-36
- of Yoga **39**.90-91; **110**.47cd-50 .115-120; **235**; **243**.46-65
- of Yoga, duration of **236**.59cd-66
- , places for religious **122**.3-7
- , religious **39**.42; **45**.44-46; **56**.30cd-35ab; **145**.8-11ab; **178**.65-69; **221**.6-7; **228**.1-5; **242**.23-24
practices see also *actions, conduct, deeds, observances*
Pradyumna **61**.39-40; **178**.158-165; **192**.48 -58; **199**.11-12; **205**.1-6 .15-22; **206**.10-13 .24-30; **210**.37-43
- , abduction of **199**.11-12
- and Śambara **200**
- as form of Nārāyaṇa **180**.22cd-23ab .40-42ab
- as incarnation of Kāma **200**.23-28
- , world of **227**.42-47
Prāgjyotiṣa **202**.3-12 .13-15; **219**.113cd-115
Prāgjyotiṣas **27**.51cd-53
Praharṣiṇī-metre **192**.48-58; **196**.30-45
Prahasta **176**.37-51
Prahlāda **11**.8-16; **69**.12-43; **213**.81-104
- as Indra of demons **11**.8-16
Prahrāda **3**.64cd-70ab; **11**.8-16
- as lord of demons **4**.2-9

praise by help of Sarasvatī **163**.47-49
 - , impossibility of **49**.56cd-57ab; **55**.35ab; **185**.39-42 .44-49; **202**.23-29
 - , inadequacy of **55**.35c-f; **127**.48-53
 - of Agni **126**.4-8
 - of Balarāma **187**.29-30; **209**.21cd-22
 - of Brahmins **28**.3-7
 - of donation(s) **216**.5-63
 - of donation(s) of food **218**.10cd-13ab
 - of fig-tree, merit of **57**.15-16
 - of Gautamī **85**.8; **157**.10-14; **175**.3-9ef
 - of Goddess **129**.75-78
 - of gold **128**.50-61
 - of Hunger **85**.8 .9-10
 - of Keśava **230**.64
 - of king **4**.61-65
 - of Kṛṣṇa **188**.17-19; **189**.58c-f; **190**.38; **203**.70-73
 - of Kṛṣṇa, singing of **185**.54-56
 - of Lakṣmī **137**.30cd-39ab
 - of Lomaharṣaṇa **1**.16-20
 - of Manyu **162**.20-27ab
 - of prosperity **137**.8-14
 - of question **240**.81
 - of Śiva **37**; **113**.9 .15 .17; **173**.29cd-33ab; **226**.4-6
 - of Sāṃkhya **240**.96-112
 - of sesamum **29**.37
 - of Soma **9**.7-8
 - of son **104**.10-14ab
 - of sun **31**.1-27 .29-39; **32**.88-95 .90cd-91ab .91cd-92ab
 - of teacher **1**.21-29
 - of Viṣṇu **129**.94-99ab; **161**.39cd-43ab; **165**.37-44 .45-47ab
 - of Viṣṇu, effect(s) of **216**.87-89
 - of Vyāsa **214**.1-2; **217**.2-3; **223**.1-3; **235**.30; **239**.1; **240**.1-2 .77-80; **241**.3-4; **246**.1-5 .6-12
 - of water **72**.27cd-34; **126**.9-11
 - with prayer-formulas **174**.2-5ab
 - with vedic verse(s) **174**.2-5ab
praise see also *homage, hymn*
praising of Viṣṇu, expiation by **22**.37-41
 - , son obtained by **182**.18
Prajādvāra, place of pilgrimage **25**.49
Prajāpati **2**.30cd-31ab; **3**.3-7ab .123-124 .125; **33**.9-13ab; **80**.46-55; **124**.7-8; **221**.87-88 .95-100; **234**.69cd-70ab
 - , Āpava **1**.50cd-51ab; **2**.1-4
 - , homage to **24**.1-7ab
 - , rank of **158**.30-35ab
 - , world of **67**.64cd-75; **227**.16-32ab; **230**.72-74
prajāpati, explanation of **5**.55cd-56
Prajāpatis **1**.43-45ab; **3**.123-124
 - , Āṅgirasas as **158**.16-21
 - , Dakṣa as lord of **4**.2-9
Prajñā **68**.56-59ab
Prakāśa **5**.27-28
Prakṛti **23**.22-27ab; **242**.29-33
 - as heavenly voice **161**.13-16
prakṛti see also *primordial matter, matter*
prakṛti and *puruṣa* in Viṣṇu, dissolution of **233**.38cd-40ab .43cd-46ab
 - as imperishable **244**.11-14ab
 - , dissolution in **243**.71-73
 - , perceptibility of *puruṣa* and **243**.21-31
 - , *puruṣa* and **161**.6cd-9; **242**.25-26ab .29-33 .43cd-48ab; **243**.1-10 .74-81; **244**.17-19
 - , Umā as **75**.14
Prakṛtis **5**.26
Pralamba **181**.7-14; **183**.1-7; **187**.8-30; **189**.2-8; **190**.1-5; **202**.3-12; **213**.81-104
Pramada **213**.81-104
Pramathas **206**.24-30; **207**.28-43
 - defeated by Kṛṣṇa **206**.10-13
Pramati **83**.2-5
 - as king of the earth **171**.2cd-6cd
 - , Indra and **171**
 - , Madhucchandas as priest of **171**.25-26
 - , Urvaśī and **171**.18-19
Pramlocā **41**.30-34ab; **68**.60-67; **178**.12-18 .19-24 .43-53 .54-58 .65-69 .90-98
Pramokṣa, place of pilgrimage **25**.57
Prāṃśu **7**.1-2 .26cd-27ab
Prāṇa **3**.38ef; **5**.11cd-12
Praṇītā [river] **161**.59
Praṇītāsaṃgama, place of pilgrimage **161**.1-2ab .64cd-65ab .72-78
Prapakṣa **205**.1-6
Prāpti **195**.1-4
Prasena **14**.11; **16**.9-11 .12 .13-24 .25-45ab; **17**.8-11
 - killed by lion **16**.25-45ab
Prasenajit **7**.90 .91-92; **16**.13-24
Prasvāpinī **16**.45cd-48ab
Pratardana **11**.49-50ab; **13**.67cd-68ab
Prathama **83**.2-5

Praticchatra **16**.4-6
Pratijayas **27**.51cd-53
Pratikṣatra **11**.27cd-31; **16**.4-6
Pratīpa **13**.114
Pratiṣṭhāna **7**.21cd-22; **10**.9-10; **111**.2-6 .48-51; **228**.146-151
- as abode of sun **110**.226-228
Pratiṣṭhāna, explanation of **110**.219ef-224; **112**.22cd-23ab
Pratīta **5**.13cd-15ab
Prātitheyī **110**.5-9 .67-70 .71-72 .121-123
Prativāha **14**.8-10; **16**.50cd-54ab
Pratyagratha **13**.109
Pratyalāvatī **27**.36cd-37ab
Pratyulūkakas **3**.93cd-95ab
Pratyūṣa **3**.35cd-36 .41cd-42ab
Prauṣṭha **31**.19-21
Prauṣṭhapadyā **220**.33cd-42
Pravara **13**.108
- , place of pilgrimage **25**.46
Pravarā **105**.30cd-31ab; **106**.45cd-46ab
- , Amṛtā as name of **106**.57-58ab
- , boon by gods to **106**.54cd-56
Pravarā, explanation of **106**.47-48ab
Pravaraka **20**.47cd-49ab
Pravarāsaṃgama named Suravallabha **106**.54cd-56
- , place of pilgrimage **106**.1 .57-58ab
Pravīra **13**.54-55
Prayāga **10**.9-10; **13**.106-107; **69**.1-9; **77**.2-9ab; **89**.1-2cd; **246**.21-27
- , place of pilgrimage **25**.4-6 .9 .25; **64**.3-8ab; **65**.84-96
prayer by Bhagīratha to Gaṅgā **78**.59-69
- by Ciccika-bird to Gaṅgā **164**.47-50ef
- by Devakī to Kṛṣṇa **182**.16 .17
- by Indra to Goddess **129**.79-80
- by Kālīya to Kṛṣṇa **185**.44-49
- by Nanda to Viṣṇu **184**.14-19
- by Rākṣasa to Sarasvatī **163**.43-46
- by snake wives to Kṛṣṇa **185**.39-42
- by Vasudeva to Kṛṣṇa **182**.14-15
- for protection **163**.26-31; **184**.14-19
- formulas **36**.63cd-70
- to Viṣṇu **67**.29cd-31ab
prayer see also *homage, hymn, praise*
prayer-formula **28**.33 .46
- addressed to fig-tree **57**.12-14
- addressed to Gaṅgā **164**.51-53ab
- addressed to ocean **62**.1-4
- addressed to Puruṣottama **67**.28-29ab .46-48
- addressed to Śiva **57**.2-4 .6-8; **143**.2-5
- addressed to Saṃkarṣaṇa **57**.20-28
- addressed to Subhadrā **57**.57-58
- addressed to sun **168**.6-9
- addressed to Viṣṇu **61**.51
- addressed to water **63**.1-7
- allocated to *maṇḍala* **61**.20-22
- , allocation of **60**.22-24 .34-38; **61**.4-6 .7-12
- , merit of **57**.30-31
- of eight syllables **60**.22-24; **61**.1-3 .7-12 .20-22
- of twelve syllables **57**.29; **59**.26-33; **61**.20-22
- , protection by **60**.39-45; **220**.141-145
- , repetition of **58**.21cd-23; **60**.49-53
- , sacrificial **104**.69-77
prayer-formula see also *spell-formula(s)*
prayer-formulas, consecration with **176**.11
- during ancestral rites **219**.52-60ab .71cd -86
- , meditation with **61**.23
- , praise with **174**.2-5ab
- , recitation of **72**.25cd-27ab
- , Śiva worshipped with vedic **168**.31-35
- , worship with **61**.24-38; **143**.14-16
prayers, muttering of **178**.112
precept of Vasiṣṭha **7**.21cd-22; **123**.97-105ab
preception of Vasiṣṭha **7**.48cd-51ab; **8**.44-51
preceptions, transgression of vedic **4**.28-34
- , vedic **67**.19
preceptor see also *teacher*
predetermination by fate **165**.23-26
prediction by Kṛṣṇa **192**.5-10
- , modification of a **10**.46cd-49ab
prediction see also *anticipating summary, foreward reference, prophecy*
- see also *anticipating summary, forward reference, prophecy*
pregnancy, brilliance of Devakī during **182**.4-6
- due to offerings to ancestors **219**.87-91ab
- , observances during **32**.32-34ab; **124**.19-28ab
- of earth **219**.113cd-115
- with pestle, curse of **210**.6-10
preparation of sacrificial ground **47**.35-41
prescr. conc, alms-giving **221**.159-160

- , ancestral rites **221**.149cd–155ab .159–160 .161–169ab
- , anointing **221**.21
- , bathing **57**.2–11; **60**.34–38 .46–48; **67**.12 –14; **221**.138cd–139ab
- , broken things **221**.31
- , castes **222**.2–21
- , cleaning of house **221**.123–125ab
- , cleaning of metals **221**.125cd–127ab
- , cleaning of teeth **221**.21 .48ab–49ab
- , combing of hair **221**.21
- , conduct **224**.4–16
- , contact **221**.139cd–140ab .140cd–141ab .141cd–143ab
- , daily libation(s) **221**.20
- , directions **124**.19–28ab; **221**.37
- , disposing of excrements **221**.137cd–138ab
- , drawing of *maṇḍala* **61**.39–45ab
- , duration of pollution **221**.152cd–154
- , evening worship **221**.18
- , forbidden ingredients of ancestral rites **220**.168–177
- , honouring of Brahmins **76**.18cd–23ab
- , lamps **29**.35cd–42ab
- , leftovers of food **221**.26–30
- , marrying one's daughter **165**.23–26
- , morning worship **221**.18
- , nakedness **221**.23 .141cd–143ab
- , obligatory rites **221**.146cd–149ab
- , offerings **29**.42cd–61
- , offerings to ancestors **60**.54–65
- , offerings to gods **221**.21
- , pollution **221**.127cd–129ab
- , pollution by a birth **221**.155cd–158
- , practices of worship **28**.19–36
- , purification of food **221**.133cd–134ab
- ritual use of hands **60**.54–65
- , salt in food **221**.26–30
- , simplification of worship **61**.57
- , sipping of water **221**.17 .26–30 .131cd–132ab
- , speech **224**.18–26
- , stages of life **222**
- , thoughts **224**.28–38
- , treatment of helpless persons **221**.44
- , urinating and defecating **221**.22 .26–30; **243**.49
- , vegetarian diet **58**.19–21ab
- , women during menstruation **221**.23 .75 .135cd–136ab .141cd–143ab .143cd–146ab
- , worship **61**
- , worship of sun **29**.7–61

prescription(s) concerning abstinence during ancestral rites **220**.106–109ab
- concerning age of marriage **165**.5–17
- concerning ancestral rites **220**; **221**.71 .95–100
- concerning anointing **221**.42
- concerning auspicious date(s) **221**.102
- concerning bathing **221**.50cd–52
- concerning bathing at places of pilgrimage **76**.18cd–23ab
- concerning carrying of fire and water **221**.101
- concerning circumambulation **221**.40cd–41ab
- concerning cleaning **221**.113–131ab
- concerning clothes **221**.33 .41cd .53–54 .81cd–82ab
- concerning conduct of Yogin **236**.43cd–44ab .59cd–66
- concerning conjugal privacy **128**.7–15
- concerning contact **221**.77 .78 .82cd–84 .85–86
- concerning daily routines **221**.17–112
- concerning date(s) for conception **221**.76
- concerning degrees of relation **221**.73
- concerning directions **221**.48ab–49ab .62cd–64ab .72 .89–94
- concerning distribution of offerings **221**.89–94
- concerning drinking of water **221**.102
- concerning earth for cleaning **221**.64cd–65ab
- concerning eating **221**.26–30 .48ab–49ab .56 .58cd–60ab
- concerning eating of meat **221**.55 .111 .112
- concerning expenditure of wealth **221**.11 –12
- concerning family life **221**.74
- concerning food **221**.47cd .57 .110
- concerning forbidden food **220**.189cd–204
- concerning habitation **221**.103–108
- concerning honouring of teacher **221**.38
- concerning hospitality **221**.85–86
- concerning ingredients of ancestral rites **220**.154–188
- concerning lying down **221**.58ab
- concerning meditation **243**.50–53
- concerning nakedness **221**.34 .50cd–52

- concerning offerings **221**.87-88
- concerning postures of standing **221**.43
- concerning postures of sitting **221**.47ab
- concerning purification **221**.65cd-67ab
- concerning purification of food **221**.123-125ab
- concerning purification of earth **221**.123-125ab
- concerning recitation **221**.36 .70
- concerning renunciation **153**.4-6ab
- concerning selection of bride **221**.73
- concerning sexual intercourse **221**.42 .71 .75
- concerning shaving **221**.79
- concerning shaving of beard **221**.72
- concerning sipping of water **221**.62cd-64ab .65cd-67ab .95-100
- concerning special cases of ancestral rites **220**.205-209
- concerning surviving ancestors **220**.148
- concerning teaching **221**.46cd
- concerning treatment of cows **221**.102
- concerning untouchability of Brahmin-murderer **123**.48cd-61ab
- concerning urinating and defecating **221**.37
- concerning vital spots **221**.44
- concerning washing of head **221**.35
- for adept of Narasiṃha **58**.19-25
- transgressed in danger **128**.7-15
Pretādhāra, place of pilgrimage **25**.66
pride attributed to Arjuna **212**.12-17
- , maxim about **110**.121-123
- of Kauravas **208**.19-31
- of wives **203**.64-69
- of women, maxim about **203**.64-69
priest at wedding-ceremony, Brahman as **72**.18-19
- of Ātreya, Agni as **140**.2-3ab
- of gods, Agni as **128**.3-6
- of Pramati, Madhucchandas as **171**.25-26
priests as protectors of sacrifice **127**.23-28
- as servants of Agni **127**.23-28
- at sacrifice, sixteen **168**.2-5
- , gift to **51**.48-53
- , seven **174**.14
- , threat of curse against **127**.23-28
primordial matter **1**.33-34; **23**.22-27ab
- Matter and Qualities **233**.33cd-35ab
- matter, Brahman originated from **30**.78-79ab
- matter, Viṣṇu as **23**.41-43
primordial matter see also *matter, prakṛti*
prince as serpent **111**
princess, blind **170**.69-74ab
- , dowry of **111**.48-51
principle of delight, Lakṣmī as **137**.30cd-39ab
- , *puruṣa* as highest **161**.6cd-9
principles in evolution, sixteen **243**.67-70
- , number of **243**.82-83
- , twenty-four **241**.28
priority of worship of sun **28**.40-41
prisoner in nether world, Indra as **129**.11cd-16
- of Mahāśani, Indra as **129**.20cd-29
privilege, worship of sun as **159**.12-16
Priya [mountain] **160**.22c-f
Priyā **5**.49-52
Priyadarśana **168**.2-5
Priyasaṃjñaka, place of pilgrimage **25**.27
Priyavrata **2**.5; **103**.2-6 .10-12ab
procession, merit of **66**.15-17 .18-23
- to Guḍivā temple **66**
procreation by father and mother **243**.1-10
- by sexual intercourse **2**.50; **3**.3-7ab
- , four methods of **2**.50
professions, list of **44**.23-27ab .27cd-40
- of four castes **19**.9; **27**.17-19ab
profit and pleasure **221**.11-16
progression of devotion **229**.8-13
prohibition of adultery **221**.60cd-62ab
- of begging **168**.2-5
- of blowing at fire **221**.102
- of defecating in water **221**.24ab
- of disrespect **221**.36
- of giving back a gift **35**.52-59
- of gnashing of teeth **221**.70
- of inflicting of pain **221**.74
- of looking at sun **221**.20
- of ridicule **221**.45cd-46ab .80-81ab
- of scratching of head **221**.34
- of sexual intercourse in water **221**.24ab
- of speaking to fallen persons **76**.18cd-23ab
- of stretching out of feet **221**.101
- of untruthfulness **221**.19
- of Yoga **235**.7-9; **243**.49
prohibition see also *forbidden ..., punishment*
promiscuity of Suvarṇa and Suvarṇā **128**.29

-37
promise by Brahman to plants **119**.4ef-8
- by gods to demons **116**.5cd-9
- by Kṛṣṇa to Indra **188**.42-47
- by Viṣṇu **73**.18-20
- , fire as witness of **140**.26-30
- of help in battle **123**.14cd-22
- of protection **188**.42-47
- to conceal true identity **6**.9-14
proper conduct see *conduct*
prophecy by Gārgya **196**.23-29
- by sages **2**.21-24
- by Viṣṇu **181**.38-53
- of future, dream as **205**.11-14 .15-22
- of future events by Brahman **213**.60-65
prophecy see also *anticipating summary, foreward reference, prediction*
prose **61**.13 .24-38; **65**.49-51
prosperity effected by magic jewel **16**.13-24; **17**.24-27
- , gold as foundation of **128**.50-61
- , maxim about poverty and **137**.2-3
- , praise of **137**.8-14
- , unjustice as source of **170**.23-25
prosperity see also *Lakṣmī, wealth*
prostitution of wives, punishment for **22**.21-22
protection against Garuḍa **185**.50-51
- by amulet **58**.44-46 .47
- by barley **219**.47cd-48 .49-51
- by *dharma* **228**.62-73
- by names of Viṣṇu **219**.31-35
- by Narasiṃha **58**.29-32ab
- by prayer-formula **60**.39-45; **220**.141-145
- by Soma **174**.14
- by spell-formula(s) **58**.29-32ab
- by sprinkling of water **168**.18cd-21
- of *dharma* by Viṣṇu **56**.35cd-38ab
- of subjects **7**.58cd-71ab
- of the distressed, maxim about **110**.147-154
- of worlds **5**.38cd-39
- , prayer for **163**.26-31; **184**.14-19
- , promise of **188**.42-47
protector of *dharma*, Śiva as **102**.5cd
- of good people, Indra as **140**.7-11
- , Śiva as **143**.2-5
- , Viṣṇu as **106**.23-26ab
protectors of sacrifice, priests as **127**.23-28
protectors of directions see *guardians of directions*
provocation of curse **34**.20a-d
- of Indra **187**.41
proxy of king, Brahmin as **8**.3-4
Pṛṣadhra **7**.1-2 .43
Pṛṣata **13**.100-101
Pṛthā **14**.14cd-20ab .20cd-24ab
Pṛthasaṃgama as place of pilgrimage **25**.27
Pṛthivī **108**.68-70; **181**.38-53
- , place of pilgrimage **25**.35
pṛthivī, etymology of **4**.113
Pṛthu **2**.21-24 -28; **3**.123-124; **4**.1 .28-122; **5**.20cd-21; **7**.51cd-53; **14**.12-13; **16**.56cd-58ab; **210**.37-43
- as first king **4**.115-121
- as ideal king, worship of **4**.115-121
- , consecration of **4**.53-57
- , earth and **141**.14-20
- , earth milked by **141**.23-25 .26-28
- , mountains levelled by **4**.90
- , origin of **141**.10-13
Pṛthūdaka, place of pilgrimage **25**.35; **64**.3-8ab; **228**.86-91ab
Pṛthukas **5**.30cd-31
Pṛthukīrti **14**.14cd-20ab .20cd-24ab
Pṛthukūṭa, place of pilgrimage **25**.82
Pṛthulākṣa **13**.42
Pṛthurukma **15**.1-12ab .12cd-13
Pṛthuśravas **15**.1-12ab; **99**.2-7ab .11
Pṛthutuṅga, place of pilgrimage **64**.3-8ab
pūjā see *homage, worship*
Pulaha **1**.43-45ab; **5**.8-9ab; **34**.12cd-19
Pulastya **1**.43-45ab; **5**.8-9ab; **13**.176cd-187ab; **34**.12cd-19; **97**.13cd-14 .15-17 .18-19; **143**.2-5
Pulindas **27**.54-57
Pulkasa **225**.17-23ab
Pulkasas **220**.97cd-98ab
pulling of hair **37**.2-23
Pulomaka, place of pilgrimage **25**.66
Puloman **3**.74cd-78ab .80cd-83; **213**.81-104
pulses, kinds of **220**.154-167 .168-177
Puṃnāga, place of pilgrimage **25**.22
Punarvasu **220**.33cd-42
Puṇḍarīka **8**.84cd-92
- , place of pilgrimage **25**.31 .37
Puṇḍarīkā **20**.54cd-56ab
Puṇḍarīkahrada, place of pilgrimage **25**.63
Puṇḍarīkavat **20**.49cd-51
Puṇḍra **13**.30-31

Puṇḍrakas **13**.36
punishment for abandoning of follower **22**.11
- for abduction **214**.88cd-96
- for absence of *dharma* **215**.136cd-137ab
- for abusing of Veda(s) **215**.130cd-136ab
- for accepting of bribes **215**.129cd-130ab
- for actors **22**.21-22
- for adultery **215**.94cd-95ab .130cd-136ab; **217**.66 .67 .68-71ab
- for afflicting a Brahmin **215**.130cd-136ab
- for annexation of land **215**.86cd-88ab .122cd-123ab
- for annoying of parents **217**.51-52
- for annoying of teacher **217**.51-52
- for arranging a remarriage **217**.71cd-73ab
- for arson **215**.100cd-101
- for astrologers **22**.17cd-18ab
- for beating of one's parents **217**.53-54
- for being double-faced **164**.17-28
- for Brahmin-murder **22**.9; **150**.10-14; **215**.86cd-88ab
- for breach of chastity **22**.27
- for breach of confidence **215**.104-105ab; **217**.59-61
- for breach of vow **22**.26
- for choice of wrong wife **22**.17cd-18ab
- for collecting of honey **22**.23ab
- for contact with fallen persons **217**.37-39
- for contact with sinners **22**.9
- for deceit **215**.72-77 .107cd-109ab
- for destruction of village **22**.23ab
- for disloyalty **217**.55-56
- for disrespect against teacher **22**.12cd-13
- for disrespect against Śiva **157**.21cd-25ab
- for disrespect against Brahmins **215**.29-38
- for disrespect against *dharma* **215**.72-77
- for disrespect against parents **217**.49-50
- for disrespect against brother **217**.75cd-77ab
- for drinking of alcohol **22**.9; **215**.92cd-93ab.127cd-128ab.130cd-136ab
- for eating before superiors **22**.15cd-16a
- for eating of forbidden food **214**.120-128; **215**.111cd-112ab .130cd-136ab; **220**.189ab .198-200ab
- for eating of meat **214**.88cd-96; **215**.127cd-128ab
- for eating sweets **215**.109cd-110ab
- for embezzlement **217**.57-58
- for embezzlement of trust **215**.86cd-88ab
- for embryo-murder **22**.7-8
- for evil thoughts **215**.119cd-120ab .130cd-136ab; **217**.45-47
- for exchange of sacrificial gift **155**.3cd-10ab
- for faking of jewels **22**.14cd-15a
- for false witness **22**.7-8; **214**.120-128; **215**.72-77 .88cd-90ab
- for felling of trees **22**.24cd
- for forbidden killing **214**.120-128
- for forbidden sacrifice **22**.15b: .17cd-18ab; **217**.40-42
- for forbidden sexual intercourse **22**.12cd-13
- for forbidden sexual intercourse with wives **22**.21-22
- for forbidden sexual intercourse **214**.120-128; **215**.72-77 .120cd-121ab; **217**.77cd-80ab
- for hatred against ancestors **22**.14cd-15a
- for hatred against Brahmins **22**.14cd-15a
- for hatred against gods **22**.14cd-15a
- for hunters **22**.25
- for hurting of tree **215**.124cd-125ab
- for impurity **22**.23cd-24ab
- for incest **215**.130cd-136ab
- for jugglery **22**.23cd-24ab
- for killing **214**.88cd-96; **215**.130cd-136ab
- for killing of cow **22**.7-8; **215**.84cd-136ab
- for killing of helpless people **215**.99-100ab
- for killing of Kṣatriya **22**.10
- for killing of messenger **22**.10
- for killing of one's brother **124**.100-107
- for killing of pupil **217**.48
- for killing of teacher **22**.7-8
- for killing of unarmed person **217**.100-104
- for killing of Vaiśya **22**.10
- for lustiness **215**.95cd-98ab
- for making of arrows **22**.16b:
- for making of weapons **22**.16cd-17ab
- for mixing of castes **215**.121cd-122ab
- for murder of friend **215**.105cd-107ab .114cd-115ab
- for murder of parent **215**.104-105ab
- for not giving alms **215**.116cd-117ab .117cd-118ab
- for not performing ancestral rites **215**.128cd-129ab
- for not performing rites **217**.73cd-75ab

- for not performing sacrifices **215**.110cd-111ab
- for offering of forbidden meat **220**.193cd-195ab
- for poisoning **22**.21-22; **215**.125cd-126ab
- for polyandry **215**.95cd-98ab
- for prostitution of wives **22**.21-22
- for rearing of birds **22**.18cd-20
- for rearing of boars **22**.18cd-20
- for rearing of cats **22**.18cd-20
- for rearing of cocks **22**.18cd-20
- for rearing of dogs **22**.18cd-20
- for rearing of goats **22**.18cd-20
- for robbery **215**.90cd-91ab
- for selling of daughter **165**.5-17; **214**.120-128; **215**.72-77 .112cd-113ab
- for selling of forbidden things **22**.18cd-20; **150**.6-9
- for selling of horses **22**.11
- for selling of juice **22**.18cd-20
- for selling of lac **22**.18cd-20
- for selling of meat **22**.18cd-20
- for selling of milk **215**.115cd-116ab
- for selling of oil **22**.18cd-20
- for selling of salt **22**.18cd-20
- for selling of son **150**.6-9
- for selling of sweets **22**.11
- for selling of Veda(s) **22**.12cd-13
- for separating of husband and wife **215**.93cd-94ab .130cd-136ab
- for sexual intercourse with sister **22**.10
- for sexual intercourse with teacher's wife **22**.10
- for sexual intercourse with daughter **22**.12ab
- for sexual intercourse with daughter-in-law **22**.12ab
- for shepherds **22**.25
- for sin against teacher **217**.43-44
- for speaking the untruth **22**.7-8
- for spying **22**.21-22
- for support by adulterine **22**.21-22
- for swallowing of semen **22**.23cd-24ab
- for teaching by sons **22**.27
- for theft **22**.14ab; **214**.88cd-96 .120-128; **215**.72-77 .102-103 .123cd-124ab .125cd-126ab .126cd-127ab .130cd-136ab; **217**.62-65 .87-99
- for theft of gold **22**.9
- for tormenting a Brahmin **215**.91cd-92ab
- for transgression against teacher's wife **217**.45-47
- for transgression of caste **22**.30
- for transgression of stage of life **22**.26 .30
- for untruthfulness **214**.120-128; **215**.118cd-119ab .130cd-136ab
- for untruthfulness, water-belly as **104**.39-43
- for violation of borders **22**.14ab .23cd-24ab
- for violation of vital spots **215**.130cd-136ab
- for violence **215**.72-77
- in hells **22**.7-27; **215**.138cd-142
- of evil-doers **215**
- of king **215**.55cd-64 .65-67 .68-69
- of pupil **221**.46cd
- of the wicked **215**.24-28
- of unbelievers **225**.10-16
- , unjustified **185**.44-49
- , Vasiṣṭha as authority on **215**.78-80

punishment see also *effect(s), rebirth, retribution, reward, sins, torments*
- see also *torments*

Puñjikasthalā **178**.19-24
Puṇyā **96**.22cd-24ab
Puṇyāsaṃgama, place of pilgrimage **96**.24cd-25ab
Puṇyaśata, place of pilgrimage **25**.72
Puṇyatīrtha, place of pilgrimage **124**.1-2ab
Puṇyatoya [river] **141**.26-28
Puṇyāvartahrada, place of pilgrimage **25**.77
Puṇyāvatīhrada, place of pilgrimage **25**.77
pupil, acceptance of **121**.10-12
- , ideal **121**.10-12
- , maxim about ideal **121**.13-15
- , punishment for killing of **217**.48
- , punishment of **221**.46cd
- , qualification(s) of **237**.33-40; **238**.34cd-35ab; **245**.31-41
- , teacher and **121**.16-18

Puraṃdhara **194**.13-17
Puraṃjaya **2**.14-15; **13**.15cd-20ab
Purāṇa **1**.43-45ab; **3**.50; **4**.18; **5**.11cd-12 .20cd-21 .22cd-24 .55cd-56; **27**.1; **42**.38cd-42ab; **43**.85cd-88; **44**.10-12; **48**.3; **62**.16ab; **67**.35cd-39ab; **70**.11; **121**.10-12; **145**.2cd-5ab; **173**.34cd-35ef; **175**.10-13; **177**.22-23; **213**.30-31; **235**.4-5; **240**.105
- and Epics **158**.30-35ab
- as written book **175**.86-90

- , Brahman as author of **1**.30
- , *dharma*-rules in **175**.78
- , listening to **246**.34-35
- , meaning of **174**.2-5ab
- , merit of listening to **175**.86-90
- , recitation of **246**.28-29
- told for the benefit of the world **175**.78
- , transmission of **1**.30
- , Veda(s) and **4**.24-26; **213**.165cd-168ab
Purāṇa-experts **15**.41cd-45ab; **121**.1
Purāṇapañcalakṣaṇa **1**; **3**.7cd-9; **5** .30cd-31 .42-47 .45cd-46; **8**.3-4; **10**.19cd-20 .61-62; **11**.27cd-31; **12**.1-2 .9-10 .11-17 .24-38; **13**.53 .97 .109 .152-153ab .157-159
Purāṇapuruṣa [name of fig-tree] **60**.16-18
Purāṇas, origin of Itihāsas and **161**.27-29
- , Veda(s) and **174**.29-30
Purāri, Śiva as **173**.37-39
purification by bathing **80**.84-89; **81**.16-22ab; **221**.79 .135cd-136ab
- by cow **221**.136cd-137ab
- by fasting **221**.134cd-135ab
- by fire and water **158**.35cd-37ab
- by gold **128**.50-61
- by looking at sun **221**.26-30 .67cd-69 .136cd-137ab .140cd-141ab
- by observances **136**.17-26
- by sipping of water **221**.67cd-69
- by sun and moon **221**.129cd-131ab
- by touching of water **221**.161-169ab
- by water **24**.13-18; **72**.27cd-34; **126**.32cd-35
- by water and earth **72**.23-25ab; **221**.132cd-133ab
- by wind **221**.132cd-133ab
- of body **61**.4-6
- of bones of Brahmin **110**.217-219cd
- of earth, prescription(s) concerning **221**.123-125ab
- of food, prescr. conc. **221**.133cd-134ab
- of food, prescription(s) concerning **221**.123-125ab
- of water **161**.60-61ab
- , prescription(s) concerning **221**.65cd-67ab
purification see also *cleaning, expiation*
purity for women, observances of **124**.19-28ab
- of meat **221**.127cd-129ab
- of Śūdras **223**.55cd-56ab
- , vow of **3**.109cd-122
- , waters as origin of **126**.9-11
Pūrṇā **105**.30cd-31ab
Pūrṇabhadra **13**.43-44
Pūrṇāhūti, place of pilgrimage **105**.20
Pūrṇas **27**.54-57
Pūrṇatīrtha, place of pilgrimage **122**.1-2 .100-102 .105
- , superiority of **122**.105
Pūrṇātīrtha, place of pilgrimage **105**.22-26ab
Pūrṇavat, place of pilgrimage **25**.34
purpose of incarnation of Viṣṇu **56**.35cd-38ab; **180**.24cd-38; **181**.1 .2-4; **185**.5-10; **187**.22-25; **188**.29-35; **193**.80-87; **202**.23-29; **210**.16-21; **212**.59-62
- of manifestations of Vāsudeva **213**.21-24
- of manifestations of Viṣṇu **213**.124-126
Puru **2**.17-20ab; **12**.5cd-6ab .18-21 .24-38
- , descendants of **13**.3-140
Pūru **12**.5cd-6ab .18-21; **146**.2-8ab .28-31 .32-34 .35-37
- , boon by Śiva to **146**.38-41
Purudvat **15**.24-28
Puruhūta **179**.18cd-22ab
Purujāti **13**.93-96
Purukutsa **7**.93-95ab .95cd-97
Purumīḍha **13**.80cd-81ab
Purūrava, place of pilgrimage **151**.24cd-27ab
Purūravas **7**.21cd-22; **9**.33-34; **108**.75-76ab .88-93 .94-98 .99-102ab .102cd-103 .107-108 .109-110; **226**.30-41
- and Sarasvatī **101**
- and Urvaśī **10**.1-14; **151**
- , birth of **7**.14cd-16
- , consecration of **108**.119-120
- , fool reborn as **228**.146-151
Purūravas, etymology of **108**.71-74
Purūravastīrtha, place of pilgrimage **101**.1
puruṣa see also *soul, spirit*
puruṣa and cognition **245**.7
- and God **243**.32-34
- and knowledge **241**.48
- and moon in simile **242**.52cd-55ab .55cd-58ef
- and *prakṛti* **161**.6cd-9; **242**.25-26ab .29-33 .43cd-48ab; **243**.1-10 .74-81; **244**.17-19
- and *prakṛti*, perceptibility of **243**.21-31
- and Qualities **244**.14cd-16; **245**.2-3
- as breath **243**.21-31
- as creator of Brahman **161**.43cd-50cd

- as Great Self **245**.7
- as highest principle **1**.1-2; **161**.6cd-9
- as origin of cosmos **161**.43cd-50cd
- as sacrificial animal **161**.39cd-43ab
- , description of **241**.37-44
- , differentiation of **30**.70cd-75
- , embodiment as play of **242**.29-33
- , etymology of **30**.68ab
- , Hari as **3**.125
- in Veda(s) **130**.7-14
- in Viṣṇu, dissolution of *prakṛti* and **233**.38cd-40ab .43cd-46ab
- , liberation of **243**.84; **244**.20-22; **245**.25-26
- , oneness of **130**.7-14
- originated from waters **161**.6cd-9
- , rebirth of **242**.52cd-55ab
- , three forms of **130**.7-14
- , Viṣṇu as **1**.1-2; **161**.6cd-9; **191**.4-12 .13-17; **226**.11-12

*puruṣa*s [souls?], three forms of **175**.14cd-16
Puruṣasūkta **1**.33-34; **45**.37-41; **161**.27-29 .39cd-43ab; **178**.137-157; **219**.65cd-71ab
Puruṣeśa **52**.15cd-19
Puruṣottama **42**.35-36ab; **57**.20-28
- , all-comprehensiveness of **42**.36cd-38ab .38cd-42ab
- as husband **212**.72-85
- as the absolute **177**.22-23
- , description of **42**.46cd-49ab
- , effect(s) of worship of **178**.1-4
- , hymn by gods to **65**.21-22
- , Kṛṣṇa as **57**.29-56
- , looking at **177**.21
- , meditation on **178**.187-190
- , merit of looking at **65**.76cd-77
- , merit of worship of **178**.193-194
- , prayer-formula addressed to **67**.28-29ab .46-48
- to Indradyumna, boon by **66**.7cd-13
- , Viṣṇu as **51**.1-8
- , worship of **43**.10-13; **67**.20-23

puruṣottama, explanation of **45**.51-52; **177**.22-23
Puruṣottamakṣetra as field of actions **178**.192
- , description of **44**.55-79; **46**.3-23
- , extent of **44**.78-79
- , five places of pilgrimage at **43**.10-13
- , greatness of **177**
- , installation of image at **176**.52-56
- , Kalpa-tree at **177**.16-19
- , liberation by death at **177**.24-25
- , liberation by sojourn at **177**.28 .29-30
- , location of **45**.53-56
- , merit obtained at **43**.14; **177**
- , merit of death at **177**.16-19
- , merit of sojourn at **177**.9-15; **178**.106-111
- , sojourn at **70**.3cd-8ab
- , superiority of **69**.10-11; **70**.1-3ab

Puruṣottamakṣetra-Māhātmya **69**; **70**.1-11
Pūrvacitti **68**.60-67; **178**.19-24
pus, rivers of **214**.14-17
Pūṣan **3**.53-58; **30**.23-26 .28-39; **31**.17-18 .19-21; **37**.2-23; **109**.13-20; **160**.6cd-9
- , breaking of teeth of **109**.21-26ab
- , Śiva and **190**.26-28

Puṣkala **213**.81-104
- [caste] **20**.53cd-54ab

Puṣkalas **27**.43-50
Puṣkara **69**.1-9; **70**.35cd-37ab; **220**.5-7; **246**.21-27
- [caste] **20**.53cd-54ab .56cd-57ab
- [demon] **213**.81-104
- , manifestation of Viṣṇu in **213**.25-31
- , place of pilgrimage **25**.4-6 .8cd; **64**.3-8ab; **65**.84-96

Puṣkaradvīpa **18**.11-12; **20**.74cd-95ab
- , mountains of **20**.77-80ab

Puṣkariṇī **2**.16
Puṣpa [demon?] **112**.4-6
Puṣpadaṃṣṭra **3**.99-101
Puṣpagiri **27**.20cd-24ab
Puṣpaka-chariot **143**.6 .7-11; **154**.8cd-11ab; **157**.2cd-7
Puṣpanyāsa, place of pilgrimage **25**.31
Puṣpavat **20**.41cd-42
Puṣpavatī **27**.36cd-37ab
Puṣpitāgra-metre **32**.108; **33**.47; **173**.36
Puṣpotkaṭa-range **163**.3-6
Puṣṭi **9**.13-16; **61**.41-45ab; **109**.13-20; **181**.38-53
Puṣṭimat **15**.58cd-59; **20**.41cd-42
Puṣṭisaṃgama, place of pilgrimage **105**.22-26ab
Puṣya **220**.33cd-42
Puṣyajā **27**.36cd-37ab
Put as name of hell **4**.48-52
Pūtanā **183**.1-7; **184**.7-20; **190**.1-5; **193**.32-40; **202**.3-12; **213**.159-163
Putra **2**.14-15
putra, etymology of **4**.48-52

Putrasaṃjñaka **5**.9cd-10
Putratīrtha, place of pilgrimage **124**.1-2ab .137-139ab
Pūyavaha **22**.2-6; **220**.198-200ab
qualification(s) for knowledge of Self **236**.37cd-40ab
- for liberation **236**.3-5
- for marriage **107**.35-40
- of Brahmins **67**.35cd-39ab; **107**.2-11; **220**.100cd-101ab .101cd-102ab .102cd .103-104
- of food for ancestral rites **220**.178-185ab
- of listener(s) **4**.24-26; **246**.16-17
- of pupil **237**.33-40; **238**.34cd-35ab; **245**.31-41
- of recipients of donation(s) **218**.29cd-31ab
- of teacher **107**.17-18; **223**.58cd-60ab
- of Vyāsa **238**.41
Qualities as ropes in sacrifice, three **161**.35cd-39ab
- , bondage by **242**.4-5ab
- , characteristics of **237**.58-61 .62-64
- , colours of **241**.45-47
- , dissolution of elements and **233**.12-29
- , four **175**.14cd-16
- , functions of **238**.3-4
- , good **167**.15-17; **222**.15-17
- , list of bad **137**.4-7
- , list of good **137**.30cd-39ab
- of actions, three **173**.9-25
- of Brahmin, bad **164**.17-28
- of gold **128**.50-61
- of husband and wife, congruence of **165**.18-22
- of king **43**.2-5
- of minister **111**.26-34
- of renouncer, bad **222**.46-54
- of Śiva, royal **130**.23-31
- of sage **178**.1-4
- of Viṣṇu, good **226**.23cd-25
- , origin of bad **129**.70-71
- , Primordial Matter and **233**.33cd-35ab
- , *puruṣa* and **244**.14cd-16; **245**.2-3
- , rebirth determined by **241**.45-47; **242**.40-43ab
- , Self and **237**.82-86ab
- , sixteen **236**.16ab
- , three **100**.19-21; **130**.7-14; **173**.9-25; **175**.14cd-16; **241**.37-44
quarters of *dharma*, four **175**.17-24; **230**.8
queens of Soma, plants as **120**.6-7ab
question, praise of **240**.81
- , rhetorical **41**.87; **42**.42cd-46ab; **49**.10-20 .54cd-56ab .56cd-57ab; **55**.35ab; **59**.1-2; **62**.22cd-23; **65**.59-76ab .97-99; **68**.59cd; **73**.9-17; **83**.23-29; **110**.146c-f; **112**.7-10; **114**.13; **119**.9 .10; **122**.1-2; **123**.44-48ab .121-128ab .165-169 .217; **124**.17-18; **129**.30-37; **142**.5-6ef; **147**.14-17ab; **152**.9cd-14 .24-25 .26-28; **153**.12; **157**.10; **160**.17-19; **161**.13-16; **167**.22-25; **169**.6cd -15; **170**.26a-f .64-68; **171**.27-39; **174**.31-33; **175**.75; **176**.63; **177**.26 .27; **178**.184-186; **203**.64-69 .70-73; **212**.35-41; **228**.44-46; **243**.21-31 .59-65
question see also *request*
quotation from Ṛgveda **120**.8-14; **129**.101-124; **140**.21ef-25; **152**.34-37ab
- from Rāmāyaṇa **123**.173-175
- from Veda(s) **129**.49-64
- of *subhāṣita* **138**.8-9ef
- of traditional verse(s) **2**.10-13; **11**.51-53; **12**.40-46; **13**.139-140 .170-171; **15**.41cd-45ab .49-50ab; **220**.112cd-116ab
Rāghavas, generosity of **123**.86cd-96
Raghu **8**.77cd-84ab .84cd-92
Rāhu **106**.26cd-30; **213**.81-104
- , advice by **106**.39-41
- as planet **142**.9-10ab
- as seizer of planets **106**.42
- [father of Meghahāsa] **142**.2-4
- , fight between Goddess and **106**.39-41
Raibhya, Manu **5**.5cd-6ab
Raibhyas **5**.26
raiding of residence of Naraka **202**.30-35; **204**.13cd-18
rain as support of beings **24**.19-25
- of flowers **14**.14cd-20ab; **65**.23-26; **74**.78-81; **75**.2-3 .49-50; **110**.183-187; **152**.33; **182**.9-11; **209**.21cd-22
- of hundred years **232**.30-40
- of seven days **188**.20-23
- of twelve years **53**.6-10ab
- , origin of **1**.48cd-50ab
- sent by Parjanya **159**.39ef-41ab
- , spell for **58**.50-55ab
- , sun as origin of **31**.4-6
rain-bow, origin of **1**.48cd-50ab
rain-god **3**.125
rains, Indra as lord of **187**.35-40

rainy season as sacrificial grass 161.35cd-39ab
- season, description of 36.71-79; 184.57cd-60
Raiva 7.28cd-29ab .29cd
Raivata 3.46cd-49; 27.20cd-24ab; 198.18; 209.11cd-21ab
- , Kakudmin 7.29cd
- , Manu 5.4
Raivata-era 5.24cd-28
Raivataka 20.62-63
Rājādhideva 16.1-3
Rājādhidevī 14.14cd-20ab
rājan, etymology of 4.53-57
rājasūya see *consecration*
Rājeya-power 11.3
Raji 11.1-2 .3-26
- , Indra as son of 11.19cd-21ab
Rākṣasa as Aśvattha-tree 118.10-14
- as Brahmin 118.10-14; 163.12cd-16
- , Cāṇḍāla as prey of 228.15-21
- , rebirth of Brahmin as 228.76-85
- , release for 163.50-51
- , shapes assumed by 163.7-12ab
- sprinkled by water from Gautamī 133.18-23ab
- to Sarasvatī, prayer by 163.43-46
- way of marriage 199.11-12
Rākṣasas 3.3-7ab; 7.37ef-41; 18.52-55; 36.63cd-70; 39.7-17ab; 69.12-43; 106.13-14 .26cd-30; 115.2-4; 116.17-19; 131.10-15; 140.19cd-21cd; 160.6cd-9
- and gods, origin of enmity between 116.20-22ab
- bewitched by magic woman 134.8cd-11
- , burning of 118.19-24ab
- killed by discus of Viṣṇu 134.12-14; 156.4-6
- killed by Rāma 176.37-51
- , Meghahāsa as lord of 142.9-10ab
- of Laṅkā 170.54-63
- , origin of 3.104-105
- originated from egg of Brahman 156.2cd-3
- , Śiva as lord of 4.2-9
- , Trikūṭa [mountain] belonging to 160.10-12
Rākṣasas see also *Dānavas, Daityas, demons, Piśācas*
Rākṣasī as surrogate mother of Brahmin 167.8-14 .15-17
- , Brahmin kidnapped by 167.4-7
- killed by discus of Viṣṇu 167.31-32
Rākṣasyatīrtha, place of pilgrimage 25.39
Raktākṣa 165.27-30ab
Ramā, Mādhava and 174.8-12ef
Rāma 5.43; 8.84cd-92; 59.1-2; 70.39-40; 122.68-73; 123.84-119ab .170-172; 180.24cd-38
- , Ahalyā redeemed by 123.97-105ab
- , allies of 157.2cd-7
- and Hanumat 157.21cd-25ab
- and Lakṣmaṇa 154.14cd-21ab
- and Lakṣmaṇa, Viśvāmitra as teacher of 123.97-105ab
- and Sītā 93.1-2
- as dutiful son 123.177cd-184 .187-190
- as ideal king 213.145-153ab
- at Gautamī 123.121-128ab .140-146; 154.27-30ab
- at Gautamī, sacrifice of 154.32-34
- at source of Gautamī 123.207-213ab
- at the Godāvarī 157.15-18cd
- , boon by Śiva to 123.207-213ab
- , bow broken by 213.142-144
- cured by herb 170.54-63
- , death of 213.157
- , demons killed by 123.116-120; 213.136-140
- , duration of reign of 213.153cd-154
- , exile of 123.105cd-109ab
- , Gautamī honoured by 157.30
- , Gautamī praised by 157.10-14
- Jāmadagnya 10.50cd-53ab; 13.187cd-189ab; 69.12-43; 122.68-73
- Jāmadagnya, horse-sacrifice of 213.114-122
- Jāmadagnya, Viṣṇu as 180.24cd-38; 213.113cd-123 .114-122
- , Liṅga established by 123.191-194
- , Liṅgas worshipped by 157.27cd-28
- , lustre of 213.156
- paying homage to Viśvāmitra 93.3-4
- , Rākṣasas killed by 176.37-51
- , Rāvaṇa killed by 154.2-4; 157.2cd-7
- , Śiva worshipped by 154.27-30ab; 157.18ef-21ab
- , Sītā abandoned by 154.11cd-14ab
- , Sītā, Lakṣmaṇa 123.147-157
- , Sītā on lap of 154.8cd-11ab
- to Śiva, hymn by 123.195-206

- , Vāsudeva worshipped by **176**.37-51
- , Vibhīṣaṇa as friend of **157**.11-12ab
- , Viṣṇu as **213**.124-158
Rāmā **68**.60-67
Rāma Baladeva see *Baladeva, Balarāma*
Rāmabhaṅgīkatīrthaka, place of pilgrimage **25**.77
Ramaṇa **3**.38ef
Ramaṇaka **18**.18-20
Rāmas **19**.18
Rāmaṭhas **27**.54-57
Rāmatīrtha, place of pilgrimage **25**.78; **123**.1 .213cd-216 .217
Rāmāyaṇa **4**.48-52; **8**.23 .29-72 .35-51; **11**.51-53; **35**.32-38; **78**; **93**.1-2; **97**.5cd-7; **108**; **123**.2-33ab .33cd-73; **124**.68-73ab; **128**; **143**; **146**; **154**; **166**
- , Ayodhyākāṇḍa of **123**.84-119ab
- , Bālakāṇḍa of **123**.84-119ab
- , quotation from **123**.173-175
- recited by Kuśa and Lava **154**.14cd-21ab
- , summary of **176**.37-51; **213**.127-135
Rambha **11**.1-2 .27ab
Rambhā **32**.99cd-100; **68**.60-67; **147**.9cd-13; **178**.19-24; **212**.72-85
Rāmeśvara, Śiva as **28**.56cd-62ab
Rāmopakhyāna **97**.5cd-7
Ramyaka **18**.18-20
Randhana **20**.36-38ab
rank determined by wealth during Kali-Yuga, social **230**.10-27
- of adherents of Sāṃkhya, social **240**.106-111
- of Brahman **2**.10-13; **236**.47-48ab
- of Indra **73**.52-55; **129**.101-124; **151**.27cd-29
- of Indra, obtained at place of pilgrimage **140**.35-38
- of Prajāpati **158**.30-35ab
rank see also *position*
Rasātala **21**.2-5ab
Rāṣṭrapāla **15**.58cd-59
Rāṣṭrapālī **15**.58cd-59
Rāṭadhānas **27**.43-50
Rathākāra **20**.36-38ab
rathaṃtara-melody **39**.43-45
Rathoddhatā-metre **238**.12-14
Rati **38**.1-6 .7-13; **97**.20-23
- , boon by Śiva to **38**.7-13
Ratiratha **13**.51-52
Ratnamūlaka, place of pilgrimage **25**.37
Rātri **20**.54cd-56ab; **68**.56-59ab
Raucya, Manu **5**.5cd-6ab .49-52
Raudra **214**.14-17
- , place of pilgrimage **100**.1-3
Raudrapāda, place of pilgrimage **25**.29
Raudrapuruṣa [name of Śiva?] **173**.29ab
Raudrāśva **13**.3-4 .5-8
Rauhiṇeya **185**.28-29
Raurava **22**.2-6 .7-8; **165**.5-17; **214**.14-17 .97-99; **215**.88cd-90ab; **220**.189ab .193cd-195ab
Rāvaṇa **13**.176cd-187ab; **97**.2-5ab; **143**; **157**.18ef-21ab; **176**.37-51; **213**.127-135 .158
- and Soma, fight between **143**.2-5
- and Vibhīṣaṇa **176**.15cd-34
- , boon by Brahman to **97**.8-13ab; **176**.15cd-19ab
- , boon by Śiva to **143**.12-13
- , description of **213**.127-135
- , guardians of directions defeated by **143**.12-13
- , Kailāsa shaken by **143**.7-11
- killed by grace of Gautamī **157**.11-12ab
- killed by Rāma **154**.2-4; **157**.2cd-7
- , Śiva and **110**.102-103
- , Śiva worshipped by **143**.14-16; **176**.26-32
Ravi **31**.14cd-16 .31-33ab; **138**.28-32; **168**.10-12 .13-14
Ravi see also *sun*
rays of sun, seven **232**.14-23
Ṛbhus **5**.30cd-31
Ṛceyu **13**.5-8 .51-52
- , descendants of **13**.50-140
Ṛcīka **5**.34-35; **10**.28cd-50ab .53cd-54; **13**.91
reality as consciousness **22**.48-49ab
- dependent from mind **22**.44-47
- , ignorance concerning highest **203**.6-19
realms, birth of **3**.30cd-33
- , distribution of **3**.123-124
realms see also *lord, sovereignties*
rearing of birds, punishment for **22**.18cd-20
- of boars, punishment for **22**.18cd-20
- of cats, punishment for **22**.18cd-20
- of cocks, punishment for **22**.18cd-20
- of dogs, punishment for **22**.18cd-20
- of goats, punishment for **22**.18cd-20
rebirth as animal **27**.66cd-68; **29**.40; **216**.81; **217**.33-35 .36-110 .55-56; **220**.87-89ab;

229.31-36ab; **240**.38-44 .106-111; **241**.45-47
- as Apsarases **27**.66cd-68
- as Brahman **27**.66cd-68
- as Brahmin **41**.60cd-71 .75-81; **43**.65cd-74 .77-82ab; **51**.42-45; **57**.9-11 .20-28 .52-56 .59-61; **58**.70cd-77; **59**.81-91; **62**.5-9; **64**.17-20; **66**.18-23; **67**.76-80; **176**.57-62; **227**.32cd-37ab; **228**.86-91ab .97-100ab; **229**.64-67ab
- as eunuch **225**.51
- as gods **241**.45-47
- as human being **19**.24; **27**.69-70; **216**.73-80; **229**.4-7; **241**.45-47
- as Indra **27**.66cd-68
- as king **28**.62cd-64ab; **60**.1-6; **67**.76-80; **228**.146-151
- as Maruts **27**.66cd-68
- as Mleccha **217**.111cd-113ab
- as Piśāca **150**.1cd-4ab .6-9
- as plants **27**.66cd-68; **229**.31-36ab
- as Vaiśya **229**.72-86ab
- as worm **155**.3cd-10ab
- as Yakṣas **27**.66cd-68
- as Yogin **13**.27cd-29; **28**.47-53ab; **43**.77-82ab; **70**.3cd-8ab; **227**.32cd-37ab
- caused by selfishness **244**.23-39
- , cycle of **216**.73-80; **242**.1-3 .34-39; **244**.23-39; **245**.48-51
- determined by actions **217**.29-31; **223**.52cd-54ab
- determined by food **223**.23-27
- determined by Qualities **241**.45-47; **242**.40-43ab
- determined by thoughts **34**.49-50
- in heaven **197**.1-3; **225**.2-8
- in hell **157**.21cd-25ab
- , ocean of **57**.32-37; **59**.65-72
- of Brahmin as bird **164**.29-37
- of Brahmin as Rākṣasa **228**.76-85
- of Dakṣa **34**.39-41 .45cd-48
- of *puruṣa* **242**.52cd-55ab
- of Satī **34**.39-41
- , release from **19**.25-27; **23**.12-15; **45**.18-20; **135**.25-27ab; **196**.30-45; **238**.37cd; **239**.54-56
- , suffering of **49**.23-47ab

recipients of ancestral offerings **220**.59
reciprocity of honouring of Viṣṇu **226**.54-55
recitation of Gāyatrī **67**.15-18; **131**.39cd-51
- of Gāyatrī-verse **60**.49-53; **107**.2-11
- of hymn, effect(s) of **75**.32
- of hymn from Ṛgveda **60**.46-48; **219**.65cd -71ab
- of hymn, merit of **85**.19-23; **114**.21-24; **124**.123-131; **125**.44-49 .50-53
- of hymns **50**.16-17; **51**.40-41; **67**.35cd-39ab
- of prayer-formulas **72**.25cd-27ab
- of Purāṇa **246**.28-29
- of Rāmāyaṇa **154**.14cd-21ab
- of stories **26**.16; **36**.63cd-70
- of stories on Vāsudeva **67**.31cd-35ab
- of texts **43**.85cd-88; **46**.11-12; **60**.49-53; **219**.65cd-71ab; **220**.212
- of Veda(s) **65**.12-16
- of vedic verse(s) **60**.49-53
- , prescription(s) concerning **221**.36 .70

recompensation by voluntary death **138**.22-27
- of offerings **29**.42cd-61

reference, backward **13**.58-61; **41**.1-5; **43**.82cd-83ab; **69**.1-9; **70**.8cd-10; **74**.8-12; **78**.1-2; **79**.3-5ab; **108**.76cd-87; **110**.87-97ef; **113**.18-21; **119**.12; **122**.48-49; **128**.24-28; **129**.9-10; **157**.8-9 .12cd-13ab .18ef-21ab; **172**.2-3; **175**.32cd -33ab; **185**.5-10; **189**.2-8; **190**.1-5; **193**.78cd-79 .88-90; **196**.23-29; **212**.59-62; **221**.89-94; **227**.1-4; **230**.77; **233**.10
- , forward **3**.7cd-9; **5**.64; **12**.21cd; **34**.20a-d; **35**.60-63; **84**.19-20; **181**.26-31 .33-35; **190**.39-47; **193**.23; **199**.11-12; **232**.13
- to battle of Mahābhārata **188**.42-47; **212**.12-17 .64-65
- to curse by Yayāti **194**.11-12
- to Durvāsas-episode in Mahābhārata **211**.3-4

reference see also *summary*

refrain **29**.9-14; **32**.12-16; **33**.16-21; **39**.33; **49**.1-8; **55**.12-17; **57**.42-51; **60**.25-33; **65**.59-76ab .84-96; **69**.12-43; **72**.27cd-34; **73**.9-17; **80**.30-36; **83**.23-29; **95**.18-21; **108**.104-108; **120**.8 -14 .9-13 .14; **126**.4-8; **130**.23-31; **174**.13 -17; **178**.128-136; **185**.44-49; **191**.2-17; **202**.23-29; **213**.145-153ab; **224**.9-14 .18-25 .30-37

refuge, Gautamī as **152**.31-32
- granted by Kṛṣṇa **188**.17-19; **190**.22-25; **196**.30-45; **207**.28-43

- , maxim about husband as **111**.68cd-79
- of enemies, maxim about **152**.18-20
- , Śiva as **111**.68cd-79
- to Brahman, gods taking **181**.15-19
- to Viṣṇu, ancestors taking **219**.30
- to Viṣṇu, gods taking **213**.66-71
- to Viṣṇu, Śuci taking **229**.22-30
- , Vāsudeva as **226**.48cd-50ab
regions, list of **18**.18-20
- of Krauñcadvīpa **20**.47cd-49ab
- of Kuśadvīpa **20**.36-38ab
- of Plakṣadvīpa **20**.3-5
- of Śākadvīpa **20**.59cd-61
- of Śālmaladvīpa **20**.22-23 .29-30
reign of Indradyumna, duration of **51**.22-26
- of Rāma, duration of **213**.153cd-154
rejection of alms **228**.97-100ab
- of *dharma* **237**.5
- of marriage **229**.22-30
rejuvenation by asceticism **178**.61-64
- by elixir **58**.37-40
- by water **159**.41cd-46ab
relation, prescription(s) concerning degrees of **221**.73
relatives, feeding of **228**.8-14
release for Rākṣasa **163**.50-51
- from rebirth **19**.25-27; **23**.12-15; **45**.18-20; **135**.25-27ab; **196**.30-45; **238**.37cd; **239**.54-56
- of ancestors **41**.92
- of ancestors from hell **34**.60-72
- of Ciccika-bird **164**.51-53ab
- of enemy, maxim about **129**.20cd-29
- of Sāgaras by Gaṅgā **78**.70-75ab
release see also *liberation*
religious practices **39**.42; **45**.44-46; **56**.30cd-35ab; **145**.8-11ab; **178**.65-69; **221**.6-7; **228**.1-5; **242**.23-24
- practices, comparison of **49**.70; **230**.64
- practices, effect(s) of **125**.33-43
- practices for obtainment of son **124**.123-131
- practices for obtainment of hundred sons **124**.132-136ab
- practices in Kali-Yuga, effect(s) of **230**.62-63
- practices, places for **122**.3-7
Remakī **13**.132cd-137
remarriage, punishment for arranging a **217**.71cd-73ab
remedy, branch of tree as **170**.64-68
- , herb as **170**.54-63
remedy see also *healing*
remembering of Kṛṣṇa **177**.5; **192**.71-74 .75-86
- of Kṛṣṇa, Saṃkarṣaṇa, Subhadrā **177**.7
- of Viṣṇu at hour of death **229**.56-58 .64-67ab
- of Viṣṇu by evil-doers **216**.87-89
- of Viṣṇu, expiation by **22**.37-41
- of Viṣṇu, liberation by **229**.64-67ab
remembering see also *memory, thoughts*
remnant see also *leftovers*
remnant-eaters as class of ancestors **220**.82cd-86
remorse of Ātreya **140**.31-34
- of Kaṇḍu **178**.90-98
renouncer after death, destiny of **222**.55-56
- , bad qualities of **222**.46-54
- , duties of **222**.45-54
- , liberation for **222**.55-56
Reṇu **10**.57-60; **13**.91
Reṇuka **10**.57-60
- , place of pilgrimage **25**.52
Reṇukā **13**.91; **20**.66-67
Reṇukātīrtha, place of pilgrimage **25**.29
renunciation based on indifference **153**.4-6ab
- of actions **237**.82-86ab
- of kingship **196**.5-8; **212**.91-92 .93-94
- , prescription(s) concerning **153**.4-6ab
renunciation see also *detachment, indifference*
Reṇus **10**.61-62
repentance and expiation **92**.39-47ab
- of sinner **150**.10-14
repentance see also *expiation, remorse*
repetition of prayer-formula **58**.21cd-23; **60**.49-53
reproach of Garuḍa by Kadrū **159**.28-31ab
- of Garuḍa by Vinatā **159**.31cd-35
- of Śiva by Brahmin **169**.25-32
- of Śukra by Yayāti **146**.15-18
- of teacher **95**.7-11
reproach see also *abuse, offence*
request by Jābālā [wife of Maudgalya] **136**.14cd-16
- by listener(s) **1**.16-20; **2**.51-53; **3**.1 .15; **4**.19-23; **5**.1-2; **7**.35-36 .56; **8**.33-34 .62; **13**.1; **18**.7-9; **23**.1-2; **25**.1; **26**.1 .18-25 .36;

27.10-13; **28**.10; **29**.1-6; **30**.1-6 .45; **31**.28; **32**.1-2 .48; **33**.1-2 .32; **34**.7-8 .51-54; **38**.21; **39**.1-2; **41**.1-5; **43**.15-21; **45**.1-3; **46**.1; **48**.1-2; **51**.60-62; **58**.8-11; **59**.4-5 .22; **60**.7; **63**.10; **65**.1; **66**.3-5; **67**.1 .9; **68**.1-3; **70**.12 .14-15 .30-32; **71**.1; **73**.1; **74**.1 .6; **75**.1; **76**.1; **78**.1-2; **79**.1-2; **124**.32; **130**.15-16; **175**.1-2ef; **176**.1-2 .35-36; **178**.5; **179**.2-75; **200**.1; **205**.9-10; **207**.1-2; **208**.1-2; **210**.5; **213**.1-9; **214**.3-8; **215**.1; **217**.2-3 .12-13 .18 .22; **218**.1-2; **219**.1 .4-5; **220**.1 .68 .205 .207; **221**.4-5; **222**.1; **223**.1-3 .7-11; **224**.1-3 .27 .39-45; **225**.1 .42-45 .53 .57-59; **226**.4-6 .10; **227**.1-4; **228**.6; **229**.1-2 .14 .19; **230**.1-2 .8; **231**.3 .42-43; **232**.3; **235**.1; **236**.1-2; **237**.1-2 .43; **238**.15; **239**.1 .10 .42; **240**.1-2 .50 .77-80; **241**.1-2 .9-10; **243**.1-10
- by Maudgalya **136**.17-26
- for boons **203**.20-21
- for forgiveness **202**.23-29; **203**.6-19; **204**.1-4
- for liberation **178**.166ab
- for mercy **206**.14-19 .39-44; **208**.32-35; **211**.5-10
- of ancestors **220**.31cd-32ab
- of listener(s) **178**.113
- to listener(s) **67**.81; **70**.8cd-10

request see also *question*
resemblance of father and son **200**.20-22
residence of Brahman, lotus as **179**.22cd-26; **180**.24cd-38
- of Naraka, raiding of **202**.30-35; **204**.13cd-18
- of Śiva and Śakti **106**.53cd-54ab
- of snakes, ocean as **185**.52-53
- of world-guardian(s) **227**.16-32ab

residence see also *abode, city, world*
respect, beings worthy of **221**.36
- for Brahmins **35**.46-51 .52-59
- for deities of others **29**.9-14
- for mother **38**.35-38
- for teacher **222**.22-27
- , maxim about **39**.27cd-28

respect see *honouring*
responsibility of creator **185**.44-49
restoration of kingdom **122**.103; **140**.1; **171**.44-46
- of male sex by bathing **108**.113-115
- of sacrifice **39**.92-95

restraining from curse **110**.61-66
restrictions on teaching **30**.87-88; **49**.64-66; **62**.16ab; **175**.86-90; **221**.170a-f; **245**.31-41 .53; **246**.39
- on use of vedic prayer-formulas **220**.3-4

retribution in heaven or hell **165**.30cd-36
- of actions **27**.69-70; **123**.140-146; **215**.55cd-64 .78-80 .138cd-142; **217**.4-11 .28 .33-35; **218**.3-5
- of donation(s) **216**.5-63
- of sins **214**.88cd-96 .120-128; **217**.36-110

retribution see also *effect(s), punishment, reward*
return of Kṛta-Yuga **231**.44-46 .80-88
- to *dharma* **231**.80-88

Revatī 7.30-34; **14**.42cd; **198**.18; **212**.1-4; **220**.33cd-42
- and Gautamī, confluence of **121**.1 .24-25
- , marriage of Kaṭha and **121**.19-21ab
- [river] **121**.21ab-22
- [sister of Bharadvāja] **121**.2-5

revenge for father as duty of son **142**.7-8ef
- , oath of **110**.80ef-86

reviler, maxim about a **163**.17-22
revivification by power of place of pilgrimage **138**.41
- of child **59**.6-21; **194**.23-31
- of Yama **94**.43-45
- , science of **95**.22-28ab
- , truth-spell used as means of **138**.22-27

revoking a given word, impossibility of **110**.191cd-194ab
reward for teacher **121**.16-18
reward(s) according to castes, classification of **218**.16cd-21ab
- distributed by Yama **216**.67-72
- for auspicious actions **214**.13cd
- in heaven **215**.138cd-142

reward(s) see also *effect(s), punishment, retribution*
reward for teacher see also *gift*
Ṛgveda **56**.22cd-23ab; **109**.13-20; **124**.53-67; **125**; **129**.4-8; **132**.3-5; **151**; **158**.22-27ef; **161**.35cd-39ab .43cd-50cd .68-71; **162**; **171**.27-39; **175**.14cd-16; **234**.61cd-63ab; **241**.12-16ab
- , Ākhyāna-hymn in **131**.1-2ab
- honoured by Brahman-sages **3**.61ab
- , *pavamāna*-hymn from **174**.13-17
- , quotation from **120**.8-14; **129**.101-124;

140.21ef-25; **152**.34-37ab
- , recitation of hymn from **60**.46-48; **219**.65cd-71ab
Ṛgveda see also *Veda(s)*
rhetorical question **41**.87; **42**.42cd-46ab; **49**.10-20 .54cd-56ab .56cd-57ab; **55**.35ab; **59**.1-2; **62**.22cd-23; **65**.59-76ab .97-99; **68**.59cd; **73**.9-17; **83**.23-29; **110**.146c-f; **112**.7-10; **114**.13; **119**.9 .10; **122**.1-2; **123**.44-48ab .121-128ab .165-169 .217; **124**.17-18; **129**.30-37; **142**.5-6ef; **147**.14-17ab; **152**.9cd-14 .24-25 .26-28; **153**.12; **157**.10; **160**.17-19; **161**.13-16; **167**.22-25; **169**.6cd-15; **170**.26a-f .64-68; **171**.27-39; **173**.29cd-33ab; **174**.29-30 .31-33; **175**.75; **176**.63; **177**.26 .27; **178**.184-186; **179**.2-3; **203**.64-69 .70-73; **212**.35-41; **228**.44-46; **243**.21-31 .59-65
rhinoceros-meat **220**.112cd-116ab
rhythms, musical **32**.97cd-99ab
rice-balls see also *offerings, ancestral rites*
rice-cake for Indra and Agni **133**.2-4
ridicule, prohibition of **221**.45cd-46ab .80-81ab
ridicule see also *laughing, mocking*
right and left **2**.51-53; **45**.37-41; **219**.52-60ab; **220**.69cd-70
- hand **221**.95-100
- hand as stake at game of dice **171**.6ef-9ef
- hand, churning of **2**.21-24; **4**.48-52; **141**.10-13
righteous king, Yama as **6**.46cd-48ab
- people, Poverty as friend of **137**.15-24
righteousness as source of happiness **170**.26a-f
- as source of unhappiness **170**.23-25
- , defeat of **170**.29-31
- , effect(s) of **170**.77-80ef
- , Vaiśya clinging to **170**.32-36
righteousness see also *auspicious actions, dharma, duty*
ring of Kuśa-grass **219**.52-60ab
Ripu **2**.14-15
Ripuṃjaya **2**.14-15
Riṣṭa **7**.1-2 .42
rites at wedding-ceremony **36**.130-134; **72**.15-17
- , definition of obligatory **220**.81cd-82ab
rites see *ancestral rites, funeral rites, obligatory rites, sacrifice*
ritual fire **58**.32cd-34ab
- food, division of **219**.71cd-86
rival, maxim about **124**.3cd-6
- , maxim about submission to a **160**.13-16ef
rival see also *competition, enmity, opposition*
river as human being **198**.12-14
- in simile **161**.61cd-62
- , Speech as **135**.15-16
- turning into woman **15**.35-41ab
- , Vṛddhā as **107**.63cd-64cd
rivers, Apsarases cursed to be **147**.17cd-20ab
- as mothers **27**.39cd-41ab
- , confluence of five **102**.9cd-11ab
- , earth milked at **141**.26-28
- , five **212**.12-17
- from heaven, origin of **20**.68cd-70
- , Gaṅgā divided into four **18**.38cd-44ab; **73**.65cd-67
- , Gautamī as mother of **160**.13-16ef
- , list of **19**.11-12ab .12cd-13ab .13cd .14; **27**.25cd-27 .28-29 .30-32 .33-34 .35-36ab .37cd-38ab .38cd-39ab; **56**.3-8; **64**.10 .11-14; **70**.33-35ab; **105**.22-26ab; **161**.21-23ef
- , ocean as lord of **4**.2-9
- of blood **214**.14-17
- of Krauñcadvīpa **20**.54cd-56ab
- of Kuśadvīpa **20**.43-44
- of Plakṣadvīpa **20**.10-11
- of pus **214**.14-17
- of Śākadvīpa **20**.66-67
- of Śālmaladvīpa **20**.28
- originating from tears of joy **128**.72cd-76
- , twelve holy **70**.22cd-23
Ṛkṣa **13**.102-105 .106-107 .110-111 .112-113
- [mountain] **19**.3 .11-12ab; **27**.19cd-20ab .30-32
Ṛkṣavat **19**.3
- [mountain] **15**.14-15
Ṛṇamocana, place of pilgrimage **25**.43
Ṛṇapramocanatīrtha, place of pilgrimage **99**.1 .12a-f
robbery, punishment for **215**.90cd-91ab
Rodha **22**.2-6
Rohiṇī **14**.36-38 .39-41; **181**.38-53; **182**.1-3; **184**.1-6 .31-42ab; **201**.3-5; **205**.1-6; **212**.1-4; **220**.33cd-42
- and moon **144**.20-22
Rohiṇīkūpa, place of pilgrimage **25**.79
Rohita **8**.24-28; **20**.22-23; **104**

- , place of pilgrimage **104**.1-2
Rohitaka, place of pilgrimage **25**.82
Romaka **13**.132cd-137
Romakī **13**.132cd-137
ropes in sacrifice, three Qualities as **161**.35cd-39ab
Rose, E. **40**.2-100
rose-apple-tree **18**.23cd-24ab .24cd-28
routines, prescription(s) concerning daily **221**.17-112
royal power, Sūrya as **168**.10-12
- qualities of Śiva **130**.23-31
- sages **12**.49
Ṛṣabha **13**.109; **18**.32-36ab
- , place of pilgrimage **25**.77
Ṛṣakulyā, place of pilgrimage **25**.57
Ṛṣikas **27**.54-57
Ṛṣīkas **231**.68-71ab
Ṛṣikulyā **19**.14
- , place of pilgrimage **25**.57; **64**.11-14
Ṛṣisattra, place of pilgrimage **173**.1-2
Ṛṣitīrtha, place of pilgrimage **25**.28
Ṛṣyamūka **27**.20cd-24ab
Ṛṣyaśṛṅga **123**.84-86ab
Ṛśyaśṛṅga **13**.40-41 .43-44
Ṛta **3**.46cd-49
Ṛtadhvaja **11**.50cd; **107**.19-30
Ṛtuparṇa **8**.77cd-84ab
rubbing, cleaning by **221**.117cd-120ab
Rucaka **18**.32-36ab
Rudhirāndha **22**.2-6 .21-22
Rudra **3**.46cd-49; **9**.21 .24-25; **10**.46cd-49ab; **34**.1-6 .29cd-32; **35**; **51**.1-8; **110**.98-99ef; **112**.11-19; **113**.18-21; **130**.17-21; **178**.137-157; **179**.72cd-75; **191**.4-12; **219**.98cd-107ab; **229**.64-67ab
- as all **158**.22-27ef
- as destroyer **21**.15-27
- as Yogin **20**.56cd-57ab
- , bow of **9**.21
- , Brahman as **158**.22-27ef
- in simile **8**.42cd-43
- , Janārdana as **232**.30-40
- , Kṛṣṇa as **232**.14-23
- , Manyu as **162**.27cd-30
- , origin of **1**.45cd-46ab
- , three worlds burnt by **232**.24-27
- to Aśoka-tree, boon by **35**.22-26ab
- , Viṣṇu worshipped as **20**.56cd-57ab
- , world of **67**.60cd-64ab
Rudra see also *Śiva*
Rudrakoṭi, place of pilgrimage **25**.34
Rudrakūpa, place of pilgrimage **25**.34
Rudrapāda, place of pilgrimage **25**.29
Rudrāraṇyaka, place of pilgrimage **25**.82
Rudras **1**.46cd; **5**.36-37ab; **39**.22-27ab .33 .53-58; **69**.12-43; **110**.10-20; **123**.177cd-184; **174**.7; **203**.45-62; **219**.60cd-65ab .98cd-107ab; **220**.118cd-120ab
- , cow as mother of **74**.59-67
- , eleven **3**.46cd-49; **39**.29-32
- , hundred **3**.50
- , origin of **1**.46cd; **3**.46cd-49
Rudratīrtha, place of pilgrimage **25**.70; **113**.18-21
Rudrāvarta, place of pilgrimage **25**.50
Rudrāvāsatīrtha, place of pilgrimage **25**.66
Rukmakavaca **15**.1-12ab
Rukmeṣu **15**.1-12ab .12cd-13
Rukmin **199**.1-4; **201**.6-9
- , breaking of teeth of **201**.23-26
- , fight between Kṛṣṇa and **199**.5-10
- killed by Balarāma **201**.23-26
Rukmiṇī **14**.29-31; **200**.20-22; **205**.1-6
- , abduction of **199**.5-10
- , marriage of Kṛṣṇa and **199**
- , sons of **201**.1-2
rules of politeness **221**.39-40ab
- of politics **106**.15-18; **111**.35-39ab; **195**.13-18
rumours, maxim about **154**.11cd-14ab
Ruṇḍikeras **27**.59cd-62ab
Rūpaśītika, place of pilgrimage **25**.68
Rūpatīrtha, place of pilgrimage **25**.12; **228**.127cd-145 .146-151 .152
Ruru **5**.32-33ab
Ruruka **8**.24-28
Śabala **22**.12cd-13
Śabalāśvas **3**.19cd-23
Sabhākṣa **16**.48cd-49ab
Sabhānara **13**.14cd-15ab .15cd-20ab
Śacī **3**.80cd-83; **34**.42-45ab; **86**.30-34; **140**.7-11
- , challenge of Satyabhāmā to **203**.38-44
- fabricated by Tvaṣṭṛ, artificial **140**.14-18ab
Śacīpati **188**.38
Śacīpati see also *Indra*
sacred spots on the palm **221**.95-100
- syllable **241**.16cd-19ab

- thread **61**.33; **220**.69cd–70
- thread, initiation with **107**.2–11; **111**.7–8
sacred see also *holy*
sacrifice, Agni as deity of the **127**.23–28
- and knowledge **233**.40cd–43ab
- as deer **39**.74–81
- as support of gods **24**.19–25
- at Gautamī, vedic **174**
- , boar as **213**.32–42
- born from mouth of Viṣṇu **79**.7cd–19
- , bricks for **148**.3cd–7
- , completion of **104**.78–81ab; **174**.18
- , constituents of **161**.35cd–39ab; **179**.29–37; **213**.12–20 .32–42; **242**.26cd–27
- , daughter born from **7**.3–5ab
- , Death as slaughterer at **116**.2cd–3ab
- , decapitation of **37**.2–23; **39**.68cd–69ab
- , destruction of **116**.5cd–9; **127**.4cd–9ab; **134**.8cd–11; **168**.15–18ab; **209**.2–11ab
- , disturbance of **100**.9–13; **103**.2–6; **114**.2–5
- disturbed by demon **127**.4cd–9ab
- , eating as **218**.28cd–29ab; **222**.55–56
- , effect(s) of **225**.46–48
- , energy of Brahman originated from **161**.13–16
- , faults of **83**.6–12; **122**.54cd–62
- for obtaining a son **7**.3–5ab
- , guest(s) at **109**.13–20
- , human **104**.89ab
- , Kuśa-grass used in **161**.50ef–53
- , lifting of **79**
- , merit of **177**.9–15
- of Aṅgirasas at Gautamī **155**.2–3ab
- of animals **187**.42–54
- of cows **131**.26–28; **187**.42–54
- of cows, merit measured by **110**.216
- of Dakṣa **109**.3cd–6ab .13–20
- of Dakṣa, completion of **109**.36–39ab
- of Dakṣa, destruction of **39**
- of own life by Śaryāti **138**.22–27
- of Rāma at Gautamī **154**.32–34
- of twelve days **228**.76–85
- of Viśvarūpa, terrible **173**.26–28 .34cd–35ef
- , origin of constituents of **161**.50ef–53
- , performance of forbidden **228**.76–85
- , person(s) at **127**.60–63
- , priests as protectors of **127**.23–28
- , punishment for forbidden **22**.15b. .17cd–18ab; **217**.40–42
- , restoration of **39**.92–95
- , Śiva as **75**.11
- , Śiva without share in **39**.34–39
- , sixteen priests at **168**.2–5
- , Soma as lord of **4**.2–9
- , Soma at **174**.13
- , son obtained by means of **13**.58–61
- , theft of **79**.7cd–19
- to Indra **174**.13–17
- , transitoriness of **113**.9
- , Viṣṇu as **23**.44; **56**.13–15; **161**.13–16 .17–20; **193**.80–87; **233**.40cd–43ab
- , Viṣṇu as creator of **179**.29–37
- , Viṣṇu as personification of **73**.21–22
- , Viṣṇu worshipped as **19**.22
- , waters as origin of **72**.27cd–34
- , witnesses of **127**.9cd–15
- , women interfering with **100**.9–13
sacrifice see also *horse-sacrifice, oblation, offering(s), sattra-rite*
sacrificer abducted by demon **127**.4cd–9ab
sacrifices directed to demons **213**.66–71
- , seven hundred **13**.166–169
- to Viṣṇu, lordship over gods obtained by **191**.4–12
sacrificial animal, *puruṣa* as **161**.39cd–43ab
- animal, Śunaḥśepha as **10**.65cd–67ab
- animal, theft of **78**.12–24
- animals **47**.74–80ef
- fire, creation of **161**.30–33ab
- fire, extinguishing of **148**.3cd–7
- fire, Kṛtyā originated from **207**.28–43
- fires, three **161**.54–58
- gift **67**.39cd–45
- gift, consecration of **155**.11cd
- gift, cows as **13**.166–169
- gift, daughter as **13**.142–146
- gift, earth as **155**.2–3ab; **213**.114–122
- gift ending a vow **228**.127cd–145
- gift, exchange of **155**.3cd–10ab
- gift, food as **83**.23–29
- gift, silver as **219**.71cd–86
- gift, three worlds as **9**.13–16
- grass, rainy season as **161**.35cd–39ab
- ground, circumference of **161**.30–33ab .68–71
- ground, description of **47**.51–58ab
- ground, discussion about **168**.2–5
- ground, preparation of **47**.35–41
- ground, selection of **47**.29cd–34
- post **161**.50ef–53

- post thrown into Gautamī **133**.18-23ab
- post, Time as **161**.35cd-39ab .65cd-67
- prayer-formula **104**.69-77
- share for Śiva **39**.84-88ab
- share, gods without **160**.2cd-6ab
- vessels **161**.50ef-53
- water **161**.59
sacrificing for fallen persons **217**.40-42
- for outcastes **22**.17cd-18ab
sadācāra see *conduct*
Sadāprabha, place of pilgrimage **25**.19
Sadherujā **27**.30-32
Sādhus, alms to **76**.18cd-23ab
Sādhyā **3**.29-30ab .30cd-33
Sādhyas **3**.30cd-33; **5**.36-37ab; **39**.7-17ab .22-27ab; **140**.5cd-6ef; **203**.45-62; **213**.66 -71
- , origin of **1**.48cd-50ab
Sagara **8**.29-72; **70**.39-40; **78**.3-8ab .37cd-44 .45-46 .47-54
- , birth of **8**.35-51
- , birth of sons of **8**.63-73
- , descendants of **8**.73cd-92
sagara, etymology of **8**.29-30 .39-40
sāgara, etymology of **8**.58-59ab
Sagara-forest, place of pilgrimage **25**.10
Sāgaras, burning of **78**.32-37ab
- purified by Gaṅgā **78**.70-75ab
sage as Cāṇḍāla girl **229**.68cd-87
- , boon by **78**.8cd-11
- , qualities of **178**.1-4
sages, adoption of seven **3**.107cd-109ab
- , advice by gods and **141**.23-25
- as authority **220**.153
- , curse by **116**.20-22ab; **132**.3-5
- , *dharma* spread by sons of seven **5**.38cd -39
- , dialogue between Śiva and **226**
- , discussion among **126**.3-11
- , divine **39**.7-17ab
- existing in body of Vāsudeva **226**.59-61
- , heavenly **125**.1-2ab
- , holy places established by **70**.16-19
- , laughing at **100**.25-29ab; **132**.3-5
- , names of **26**.9-14; **65**.31-34; **70**.37cd-38; **145**.2cd-5ab
- , offence against **210**.6-10
- , origin of **161**.43cd-50cd
- , prophecy by **2**.21-24
- residing on Gandhamādana **226**.52-53
- , royal **12**.49
- , Śiva as teacher of **145**.8-11ab
- , Śiva praised by **226**.4-6
- , Śiva unknowable to gods and **127**.48-53
- , *sattra*-rite of **116**.2cd-3ab
- , *sattra*-rite of seven **134**; **173**.3-6ab
- , seven **2**.10-13; **5**.8-9ab .11cd-12 .20cd-21 .29cd-30ab .34-35 .43 .44-45ab .58cd-60; **23**.6-10; **34**.29cd-32 .45cd-48; **82**.2-6; **172**.15-17ab; **213**.25-26
- , Soma as lord of **9**.12
- , supernatural knowledge of **210**.6-10
- to Śiva, hymn by **116**.14
- to Viṣṇu, hymn by **126**.24-27
- , Viṣṇu as creator of **226**.52-53
Saha **5**.17d-19ab
Sahadeva **11**.27cd-31; **13**.98-99; **208**.19-31
Sahadevā **14**.36-38
Sahajanyā **32**.99cd-100; **41**.30-34ab; **68**.60-67; **178**.19-24
Sāhañja **13**.155cd-156
Sāhañjanī [city] **13**.155cd-156
Sahasrada **13**.153cd-154ab .154cd-155ab
Sahasrāda **13**.153cd-154ab .154cd-155ab
Sahasrājit **15**.34
Sahasrākṣa **10**.24-28ab; **36**.9-10ab; **105**.11cd -13; **140**.5cd-6ef .21ef-25
Sahasrākṣa see also *Indra, thousand eyes*
sahasrākṣa, explanation of **87**.66cd-69
Sahasrakuṇḍa, place of pilgrimage **154**.1 .30cd-31
Sahasrakuṇḍa, explanation of **154**.32-34
Sahasrika, place of pilgrimage **25**.52
Sāhoṭaka, place of pilgrimage **25**.13
Sahya **19**.3 .12cd-13ab; **27**.19cd-20ab .35-36ab .43-50; **108**.116-118; **161**.2cd-4ab .21-23ef
- , place of pilgrimage **64**.8cd-9
Sahyadroṇī **108**.116-118
Śaibyā **15**.16-21; **205**.1-6
- , Jyāmagha and **15**.16-21
Saiṃhikeya, place of pilgrimage **155**.1
Saiṃhikeyas **3**.64cd-70ab .86cd-89ab
Saindhava-forest, place of pilgrimage **25**.9
Saindhavāyanas **10**.61-62; **13**.91
Śaiva, place of pilgrimage **103**.9
Śaivalā **27**.30-32
Śākadvīpa **18**.11-12; **20**.58cd-74ab; **32**.80-81
- , four castes of **20**.65 .71-72ab
- , mountains of **20**.62-63

- , regions of **20**.59cd-61
- , rivers of **20**.66-67
Śakala **13**.109
Śākala **19**.18
Śākalya **163**
Śākaṃbharī, place of pilgrimage **25**.47
Śakas **7**.24; **8**.31-32 .35-37 .44-51; **27**.54-57
Śākha **3**.39-40
Śākhoṭaka, place of pilgrimage **25**.13
Sākoṭaka, place of pilgrimage **25**.13
Śakra **3**.53-58; **10**.24-28ab; **11**.19cd-21ab; **12**.6cd-8; **13**.88-90; **36**.63cd-70; **42**.36cd-38ab; **43**.1 .83cd-85ab; **80**.46-55; **123**.2-7ab; **124**.53-67; **129**.11cd-16; **131**.10-15; **146**.2-8ab; **151**.27cd-29; **179**.27-28; **189**.1; **207**.1-2; **210**.16-21; **213**.81-104; **240**.17-19
Śakra see also *Indra*
Śakrakarṇahrada, place of pilgrimage **25**.50
Śakrāṇi **203**.23
Śakratīrtha, place of pilgrimage **25**.29 .70 .82
Sākṣida, place of pilgrimage **25**.36
Śakti **106**.43-45ab
- , Amṛtā as name of **106**.57-58ab
- as heavenly voice **161**.21-23ef
- of Gaṅgā **131**.29-30
- of Śiva **106**.37-38
- of Śiva, Gautamī as **123**.121-128ab
- of Śiva, Umā as **75**.15
- , residence of Śiva and **106**.53cd-54ab
- , unity of Śiva and **129**.81
Śakti see also *energy*
Śaktimatī **27**.30-32
Śakuni 3.72-73ab; 7.46cd-48ab; **15**.24-28
Śakunī **27**.30-32
Śakuntalā **13**.56-57
Śala **8**.84cd-92; **11**.32-33ab .34cd; **13**.116; **208**.19-31
Śalabha **213**.81-104
Śaladā **13**.5-8
Śālagrāma, place of pilgrimage **25**.21; **64**.3-8ab; **65**.84-96
Śālaṅkāyanas **10**.61-62; **13**.91
Śālatīrtha, place of pilgrimage **105**.22-26ab
Śālavatī **13**.91
Śālāvatī **10**.57-60
Śālavatyas **10**.61-62
Śālīgrāma, place of pilgrimage **25**.21
Śālitīrtha, place of pilgrimage **25**.44
Śalla **11**.32-33ab .34cd
Śālmala **214**.14-17; **215**.95cd-98ab
Śālmaladvīpa **18**.11-12; **20**.22-34
- , four castes of **20**.31
- , mountains of **20**.25-27
- , regions of **20**.22-23 .29-30
- , rivers of **20**.28
Śālmalī **215**.130cd-136ab
salt in food, prescr. conc. **221**.26-30
- , punishment for selling of **22**.18cd-20
salt water, ocean of **18**.11-12; **19**.29
Śālva **199**.5-10; **213**.159-163
Śālvakūṭa, place of pilgrimage **25**.82
Śālvas **19**.18
salvation see *liberation, release*
Śalya **3**.86cd-89ab
Samā **108**.8-14ab
Sāmaga, place of pilgrimage **118**.31-32ef
Śamakas **27**.41cd-42
sāman-melodies **39**.43-45; **65**.12-16
- , creation of **161**.50ef-53
- sung by Brahman **156**.2cd-3
Śamana **5**.45cd-46
sāman-melodies see also *Sāmaveda*
Samanyu **108**.8-14ab
Sāmaveda **109**.13-20; **168**.15-18ab
- , chanting of **118**.10-14
Sāmaveda see also *sāman-melodies*
Sāmba **205**.1-6; **208**; **210**.6-10 .11-14 .37-43
- cursed by Brahmins **210**.6-10
Śambara 3.74cd-78ab; **160**.6cd-9; **199**.11-12; **213**.81-104
- [lord of Daityas] **134**.8cd-11
- , Pradyumna and **200**
Sambara **213**.81-104
Śambhala **213**.164-165ab
Śāmbhava, place of pilgrimage **171**.47-49ef
Śambhu **2**.14-15; **3**.46cd-49; **35**.64; **40**.1; **71**.38-40ab; **81**.16-22ab; **90**.20-30; **91**.2cd-6ab; **95**.12-15ab; **102**.5cd; **106**.23-26ab .48cd-49ab; **107**.53-54; **108**.121-123; **109**.46-48 .52-54; **110**.131-133; **124**.108-109; **128**.50-61; **129**.101-124; **132**.7-9ef; **143**.12-13 .14-16; **150**.15-20; **158**.22-27ef; **168**.31-35; **169**.6cd-15; **171**.44-46; **205**.11-14; **241**.12-16ab
- , Yoga of **41**.75-81
Śaṃbhu see also *Śiva*
Saṃbhūta **7**.95cd-97
Śaṃbhutīrtha, place of pilgrimage **25**.14
Saṃdaṃśa **22**.2-6; **214**.14-17

Saṃdaṃśayātana **22**.26
Saṃdeva **15**.56-58ab
Saṃdhyā **20**.54cd-56ab; **133**.5-8
saṃdhyā-prayer **167**.8-14
Saṃdhyātīrtha, place of pilgrimage **25**.76
Sāṃdīpani **194**.18-22
Samerujā **27**.30-32
Saṃgrāmajit **205**.1-6
Saṃhara **213**.81-104
Saṃhatāśva **7**.89
Saṃhrāda **3**.64cd-70ab .90cd-92ab; **213**.81-104
Śamīka **14**.14cd-20ab .33-34ab
Śamin **16**.1-3 .4-6
Śamītīrtha, place of pilgrimage **103**.1 .9
Śamī-tree **103**.2-6; **136**.3cd-14ab; **230**.49-58
Saṃjaya **11**.27cd-31
Saṃjñā and Mārtaṇḍa **32**.49-107
- , Vivasvat and **6**
Saṃkalpa **3**.30cd-33
Saṃkalpā **3**.29-30ab .30cd-33
- , Suvarṇa and **128**.62-63ab
- , Suvarṇa married to **128**.24-28
Śaṃkara **28**.56cd-62ab; **34**.26-29ab; **35**.60-63; **39**.27cd-28 .29-32 .33; **69**.12-43; **78**.47-54; **81**.16-22ab; **90**.2-4 .31-33; **91**.6cd-11ab; **106**.31-36; **109**.21-26ab .28-29 .52-54; **110**.219ef-224; **117**.6 .16-17; **121**.19-21ab; **129**.101-124; **136**.17-26; **145**.5cd-7; **151**.10-16; **157**.21cd-25ab; **162**.20-27ab .31-33ef; **174**.7 .19-25ab; **205**.7-8; **206**.1-4 .21-23 .24-30 .45-48; **207**.28-43; **229**.8-13
- and Gaurī, hymn to **108**.104-108
- as Gautameśvara **91**.11cd-12
- , Yoga of **57**.9-11
Śaṃkara see also *Śiva*
Śāṃkara, place of pilgrimage **128**.70cd-72ab
Saṃkarṣaṇa **43**.10-13; **61**.39-40; **176**.52-56; **177**.3; **179**.6-10ab; **187**.8-18; **192**.48-58; **193**.67cd-76ab; **210**.22-27
- , prayer-formula addressed to **57**.20-28
- , world of **227**.42-47
- , worship of **57**.20-28
Saṃkarṣaṇa see also *Baladeva, Balarāma*
Sāṃkhya **23**.22-27ab; **33**.27-31; **37**.2-23; **43**.2-5; **55**.23cd-31; **60**.25-33; **181**.21-25; **243**.67-90
- and Yoga **40**.107-111; **236**; **244**.44-48
- and Yoga, difference between **239**.7-9
- and Yoga, identity of **243**.20
- as knowledge of *brahman* **240**.98-103
- , Brahman as authority on **245**.31-41
- , characteristics of **239**.4-5
- , praise of **240**.96-112
- , social rank of adherents of **240**.106-111
- , superiority of **240**.96-97 .98-103 .105
Saṃkṛti **11**.27cd-31; **13**.91
Sāṃkṛti **10**.57-60
Sāṃkṛtyas **10**.61-62
Saṃmati **20**.43-44
Saṃnati **11**.50cd .55-59; **181**.38-53
Saṃpāti and Jaṭāyu **166**
Saṃrāṭ **2**.6
Saṃsāra, description of **26**.19-22; **49**.23-47ab; **50**.33-40; **59**.65-72; **178**.179-183; **179**.6-10ab; **196**.30-45
Saṃsāra see also *existences, rebirth*
saṃsāra, wheel of **214**.9
Śaṃtanu **13**.97 .114 .115ab .118 .119 .120
Śāṃtanu **13**.114 .115ab .118 .119 .120
Saṃtrāvanāsika as place of pilgrimage **25**.34
Samudra **2**.32
- , place of pilgrimage **25**.62
Samudrā **7**.30-34
Sāmudra, place of pilgrimage **172**.1
Samudragās **27**.39cd-41ab
Samudrasnānamāhātmya **62**
Saṃvaraṇa **13**.106-107
Saṃvarta **13**.142-146; **83**.6-12
- , place of pilgrimage **25**.81
Saṃvartaka-clouds **188**.1
Saṃvartavasu **12**.9-10
Samyaktīrtha, place of pilgrimage **124**.1-2ab
Saṃyamanī, place of pilgrimage **25**.34
Saṃyatā **13**.142-146
Saṃyāti **12**.1-2
Sanādyata **92**.18cd-38
Śanaiścara **6**.18-20ab; **118**.15-18
- as place of pilgrimage **118**.31-32ef
- as planet **6**.48cd-50ab .52cd-53
- as son of Chāyā **165**.2-4
- disguised as Brahmin **118**.19-24ab
Sanājjāta **92**
Sanaka **233**.5-6
Sananda **23**.12-15
Sanātana **5**.22cd-24
Sanatkumāra **1**.45cd-46ab .47ab; **39**.7-17ab; **213**.27; **226**.52-53
Śani **89**.13-17ab

Śaṅkha **3**.99-101; **34**.92-93ab
Śaṅkhahrada, place of pilgrimage **156**.1-2ab
Śaṅkhakūṭa **18**.32-36ab
Śaṅkhapāda **4**.11-15
Śaṅkhapāla **3**.99-101
Śaṅkhaprabha, place of pilgrimage **25**.22
Śaṅkharoman **3**.99-101
Śaṅkhatīrtha, place of pilgrimage **156**.7-9ab
Śaṅkhinī, place of pilgrimage **25**.38
Śaṅkhuddhāra, place of pilgrimage **64**.3-8ab
Śaṅku **213**.81-104
Śaṅkukarṇa **3**.74cd-78ab; **213**.81-104
Śaṅkukarṇahrada, place of pilgrimage **25**.50
Sannateyu **13**.5-8
Śāntā **13**.40-41
Śāntabhaya **20**.3-5
Śāntavat **18**.32-36ab
Śānti **109**.13-20; **137**.8-14
Śāntideva **15**.51cd-53
Śāntidevā **14**.36-38 .45-46ab; **15**.56-58ab
Śāntijā **105**.22-26ab
Sānugarta, place of pilgrimage **25**.79
Saptadhāra, place of pilgrimage **25**.20
Saptagodāvarī, explanation of **173**.3-6ab
Saptagodāvarīhrada, place of pilgrimage **25**.81
Saptakuṇḍa, place of pilgrimage **25**.71
Saptamāyuṣika, place of pilgrimage **25**.14
Saptamāyuṣmika, place of pilgrimage **25**.14
Saptarṣikuṇḍa, place of pilgrimage **25**.41
Saptasārasvatatīrtha, place of pilgrimage **25**.51
Saptāśvavāhana **31**.31-33ab
Śarabha **213**.81-104
Śaradvat **5**.44-45ab; **13**.97
Śāradvatas **13**.97
Saramā and the Paṇis **131**
- bribed by demons **131**.4cd-6ab
Saramānas **3**.86cd-89ab
Śaraṇa **14**.39-41
Śāraṇa **14**.39-41
Sarasa, place of pilgrimage **25**.40
Sārasa, place of pilgrimage **25**.40
Sarasvat **101**.10-11ab
- , birth of **101**.2-9
Sārasvata, place of pilgrimage **126**.37-39; **163**.52-53
Sārasvata-dvīpa, place of pilgrimage **25**.34
Sārasvatatīrtha, place of pilgrimage **163**.1-2
Sarasvatī **68**.56-59ab; **102**.2cd-5ab .9cd-11ab; **107**.35-40; **109**.13-20; **110**.202-210; **163**.40-42 .50-51 .52-53; **236**.9
- , advice by **105**.4-8ab
- as heavenly voice **126**.32cd-35
- , exchange of Soma and **105**.4-8ab
- in mouth of Viṣṇu **122**.68-73
- in the words of a Brahmin **163**.43-46
- , Lakṣmī as **137**.30cd-39ab
- , place of pilgrimage **25**.46; **64**.10; **102**.1-2ab
- , praise by help of **163**.47-49
- , prayer by Rākṣasa to **163**.43-46
- , Purūravas and **101**
- [river] **27**.25cd-27; **70**.33-35ab; **77**.2-9ab; **89**.42; **127**.4cd-9ab; **141**.26-28
- [river], Speech as **135**.20-24
Sarasvatīs **27**.39cd-41ab
Sarasvatīsaṃgama, place of pilgrimage **101**.19cd-20
Saravas **27**.54-57
Sarayū, place of pilgrimage **64**.11-14
Śārdūla killed by Viṣṇu **128**.63cd-70ab
- , place of pilgrimage **128**.1-2 .70cd-72ab .83 84
Śārdūlavikrīḍitā-metre **1**.1-2; **36**.80-88; **178**.193-194; **246**.34-35
Saridvarā **27**.33-34
sarit, etymology of **219**.18-24
Śarmiṣṭhā **3**.80cd-83; **12**.4-5ab .5cd-6ab
- as slave of Devayānī **146**.8cd-10
- [daughter of Vṛṣaparvan] **146**.2-8ab
Śārmiṣṭha, place of pilgrimage **146**.42-45
Śārṅga [Viṣṇu's bow] **131**.16-24; **163**.50-51; **171**.1-2ab
Sarpija, place of pilgrimage **25**.36
Śarva **3**.46cd-49; **30**.58-61; **109**.3cd-6ab; **157**.15-18cd; **207**.1-2
Śarva see also *Śiva*
Sarvadevanamaskṛta **31**.31-33ab
Sarvadevavrata, place of pilgrimage **25**.82
Sarvajit **3**.74cd-78ab
Sarvakarman **8**.77cd-84ab
Śarvarī **109**.13-20
Sarvatra **30**.68cd
Śāryāta, place of pilgrimage **138**.39cd-40
Śaryātas as Kṣatriyas **7**.37ef-41
Śaryāti **7**.1-2 .27cd-28ab .35 36 .37cf-41; **12**.1-2
- and Madhucchandas **138**
- , sacrifice of own life by **138**.22-27

Śaśabindu **7**.93-95ab; **15**.1-12ab
Śaśāda **7**.51cd-53
śaśāda, etymology of **7**.48cd-51ab
Sasaka **15**.45cd-46ab
Śaśilekhā **68**.60-67; **178**.19-24
Śaśin **36**.16cd-17ab
Śāstras **42**.38cd-42ab; **44**.10-12; **217**.33-35
- as authority on expiation **123**.158-164
- , Veda(s) and **127**.4cd-9ab
Śāśvatas, Vāsudeva and **191**.13-17
Śatabhiṣaj **220**.33cd-42
Śatadhanvan **16**.4-6; **17**
Śatadru **19**.10; **27**.25cd-27
- , place of pilgrimage **64**.11-14
Śatadruha **13**.152-153ab
Śatadruhas **27**.43-50
Śatadyumna **2**.17-20ab
Śatahrada **3**.74cd-78ab
Śatājit **15**.34
Śataki, place of pilgrimage **25**.52
Śatakratu **11**.19cd-21ab .21cd-24ab; **78**.12-24; **124**.33-36ab; **171**.44-46; **174**.18
Śatānanda **13**.97
Śatapathabrāhmaṇa **129**.49-64; **161**.13-16 .33cd-35ab
Śatarūpā **2**.1-4 .5
Śatasahasrikatīrtha, place of pilgrimage **25**.59
Śātātapa **174**.2-5ab
Śātavanatīrtha, place of pilgrimage **25**.39
Śaṭha **14**.39-41
Satī **34**.9-50 .51-54; **109**.3cd-6ab
- , rebirth of **34**.39-41
- , voluntary death of **34**.20ef-25
satiation of ancestors, duration of **220**.22cd-31ab
- of gods, hospitality as **163**.17-22
Sātīrtham, place of pilgrimage **25**.23
satisfaction of Brahmins **220**.126
- of listener(s) **179**.1
satisfying by Kuśa-grass **161**.63-64ab
- of ancestors **80**.1-3 .4-5ab; **93**.1-2; **168**.30
Satkāñcanasahasrika, place of pilgrimage **25**.52
Satrājit **16**.9-11 .12-45ab .45cd-48ab; **201**.3-5
Śatrughna **14**.8-10 .27ab; **123**.97-105ab; **176**.37-51
- , Lakṣmaṇa and **123**.84-86ab
Śatruhan **16**.50cd-54ab
Śatrujit **11**.50cd; **16**.1-3
Śatrukuṇḍa, place of pilgrimage **25**.16
sattra-rite **1**.10-12; **98**.2-5; **100**.9-13; **126**.37-39
- , completion of **114**.19-20
- disturbed by demons **116**.5cd-9
- of Agastya **118**.2-9
- of Ātreya **140**.2-3ab
- of Ātreya, effect(s) of **140**.3cd-5ab
- of gods **114**.2-5
- of sages **116**.2cd-3ab
- of seven sages **134**; **173**.3-6ab
- protected by Śiva **116**.17-19
sattra-rite see also *sacrifice*
Sattratīrtha, place of pilgrimage **126**.37-39
Sāttrika, place of pilgrimage **118**.31-32ef
sattva and soul **237**.86cd-89
- , emanation from **238**.2
Saturn **6**.18-20ab .48cd-50ab .52cd-53; **23**.6 -10; **118**.15-18; **165**.2-4
Saturn see also *Śanaiścara*
Satvat **15**.24-28 .30-31
Sātvata **15**.30-31
Satyabhāmā **16**.45cd-48ab; **17**.2 .6-7; **202**.13 -15; **203**.26-32; **205**.1-6
- , boon by Aditi to **203**.24-25
- , love of Kṛṣṇa for **203**.26-32
- to Śacī, challenge of **203**.38-44
Satyadhṛti **13**.97
Satyaka **14**.24cd-25ab
Satyakarṇa **13**.126-127ab .127cd-132ab
Satyaketu **11**.55-59; **13**.75cd-77; **14**.43cd
Sātyaki **17**.8-11; **210**.37-43
Satyaloka **23**.12-15 .16-20
Satyanetra, Ātreya **5**.24cd-25
Satyapada, place of pilgrimage **25**.17
Satyarathā **8**.24-28
Satyas **5**.22ab
Satyavāk **2**.17-20ab; **5**.27-28
Satyavatī **10**.28cd-50ab .53cd-54; **13**.91 .120
- as Kauśikī [river] **10**.49cd-50ab
Satyavrata **7**.95cd-97 .98-109; **8**.1-23 .24-28
- , misbehaviour of **7**.98-99
Satya-Yuga **175**.29-32ab
Saubhāgyā **108**.113-115
Saudāmanī **68**.56-59ab
Saudāsa, Kalmāṣapāda **8**.77cd-84ab
Saugandhika, place of pilgrimage **25**.46
Saugandhikavana, place of pilgrimage **25**.46
Śaukara **22**.2-6
Śaukarava, place of pilgrimage **228**.146-151

Śaukarava, Saukarava see also *Śūkarava, Sūkarava*
Saukarava, place of pilgrimage **228**.127cd-145
Śaukra as place of pilgrimage **146**.42-45
Saumitri **123**.105cd-109ab .213cd-216; **157**.2cd-7; **176**.37-51
Saumitri see also *Lakṣmaṇa*
Saumya, place of pilgrimage **100**.1-3; **103**.9; **120**.16-18
- [region] **19**.6cd-7ab; **27**.14-16
Śaunaka **11**.33-34ab; **12**.11-17; **174**.2-5ab
Sauparṇikā [river] **100**.31cd
Saura, place of pilgrimage **100**.1-3
Saurāṣṭras **19**.17
Śauri **14**.28c-f .42ab; **202**.1-2; **206**.21-23; **207**.1-2
Sauri **23**.6-10
Saurya, place of pilgrimage **113**.18-21
Sauśravas **10**.61-62; **13**.91
Sauvīras **19**.18; **27**.43-50
Savaidūrya **18**.32-36ab
Savala **5**.9cd-10
Savana **20**.75cd-76
Savarṇā **2**.32 .33; **6**.9-14
Sāvarṇa **6**.52cd-53
- , Manu **5**.49-52; **6**.18-20ab
Sāvarṇa-era **5**.42-47
Sāvarṇi **89**.13-17ab
- , Manu **5**.5cd-6ab; **6**.48cd-50ab
Sāvarṇya **6**.18-20ab
- , Manu **6**.18-20ab
Śavatīrtha, place of pilgrimage **123**.176-177ab
Savitṛ **3**.53-58; **28**.62cd-64ab; **31**.14cd-16; **32**.9-11; **165**.2-4; **168**.6-9; **174**.19-25ab
Savitṛ see also *sun*
Sāvitra **3**.46cd-49
Sāvitrī **41**.88-90; **68**.56-59ab; **102**.2cd-5ab
- , place of pilgrimage **102**.1-2ab
Sāvitrīhrada, place of pilgrimage **25**.69
Śayana, place of pilgrimage **25**.31
saying see *maxim, subhāṣita*
scales, musical **32**.97cd-99ab
scent of Pārijāta-tree **204**.8-13ab
scents, kinds of **220**.154-167
science of revivification **95**.22-28ab
sciences and holy texts, origin of **129**.75-78
Scorpio **220**.49cd-50ab .50cd-51ab
scratching of head, prohibition of **221**.34
search for brother **3**.19cd-23
- for brother, maxim about **3**.24
- for Kṛṣṇa **189**.22-25
seasons, colours of sun according to **31**.12-14ab
- , cycle of **7**.37a-d
- for sacrifice, creation of **161**.35cd-39ab
- , six **36**.63cd-70 .71-124
seasons see also *autumn, rainy season, spring, summer, winter*
seat for ancestors **219**.71cd-86
secret teaching **30**.57 .85-86 .87-88; **33**.33; **40**.135; **56**.10-11; **152**.31-32; **161**.4cd-6ab; **175**.14ab .78; **237**.33-40; **238**.35cd-36ab
seduction of Ahalyā **87**.42-43
- of ancestors **219**.6-12
- of ascetic **122**.8-20; **147**.5-7 .14-17ab; **178**.43-53 .54-58
- of Yama **86**.35-39
seed and plant in simile **23**.38-40
seeds, Soma as lord of **9**.12
seizer of planets, Rāhu as **106**.42
selection of bride, prescription(s) concerning **221**.73
- of sacrificial ground **47**.29cd-34
selection see also *choice, self-choice*
Self and elements, identity of **237**.45
- and Qualities **237**.82-86ab
- as goose **236**.33 .34
- as light **237**.79-81
- , attributes of **240**.93-94
- , characteristics of **236**.27-31
- , detachment due to knowledge of **238**.5-6
- , *dharma* resulting from knowledge of **231**.44-46
- , distinction of several concept(s) of **238**.20-23
- , effect(s) of knowledge of **238**.24-25
- , identity of individual and universal **236**.21-23 .24-25 .54-56ab; **237**.17-19 .32; **245**.27-30
- in simile **236**.54-56ab; **238**.20-23 .24-25; **243**.59-65
- in simile, knowledge of **236**.24-25
- in simile, mind and **236**.49cd-53
- , knowledge of **117**.18-19ab
- , liberation by knowledge of **238**.7-11
- of the world, Śiva as **153**.1-2ab
- , origin of individual **161**.6cd-9
- , perception of **236**.16cd-19

- , perishable and imperishable **236**.32 .35
- , qualification(s) for knowledge of **236**.37cd-40ab
- , vision of **243**.59-65
self-accusation of ascetic **178**.90-98
self-castigation of devotee **169**.39cd-43ab
self-choice ceremony **201**.6-9; **208**.4-7
- of husband, condemnation of **219**.13-17
- of Umā **35**.11-14 .15-21; **36**
self-choice see also *choice, marriage, selection, wedding*
self-control and pilgrimage, equivalence of **25**.4-6
selfishness, rebirth caused by **244**.23-39
selling of daughter, punishment for **165**.5-17; **214**.120-128; **215**.72-77 .112cd-113ab
- of forbidden things **165**.5-17
- of forbidden things, punishment for **22**.18cd-20; **150**.6-9
- of horses, punishment for **22**.11
- of juice, punishment for **22**.18cd-20
- of lac, punishment for **22**.18cd-20
- of meat, punishment for **22**.18cd-20
- of merit **231**.4-41
- of milk, punishment for **215**.115cd-116ab
- of oil, punishment for **22**.18cd-20
- of salt, punishment for **22**.18cd-20
- of son **7**.105cd-109; **104**.44-59ab; **150**.1cd-4ab
- of son, punishment for **150**.6-9
- of sweets, punishment for **22**.11
- of Veda(s), punishment for **22**.12cd-13
semen, discharge of **13**.97
- , fire as **126**.4-8
- in water, creation from **1**.37cd-38ab
- of Brahman, discharge of **72**.18-19
- of Śiva **128**.16-23
- of Śiva, twins born from **128**.24-28
- , origin of **217**.19-21
- , punishment for swallowing of **22**.23cd-24ab
senses, absorption of **237**.53; **238**.17-19
- and organs of action, ten **241**.26-27
- and soul **240**.92cd
- , Consciousness and **237**.67-72
- , domains of **237**.51; **240**.17-19
- , five **179**.59-61; **236**.14
- , functions of **237**.76 .77; **240**.83-84
- in simile **240**.83-84
- in simile, mind and **236**.12; **237**.77
- , mind and **236**.13 .48cd-49ab; **238**.17-19
- of perception **236**.10-11
- , origin of **241**.26-27
separation from Kṛṣṇa **189**.40-41; **192**.14-31
sequence of evolution **243**.67-70
serpent, prince as **111**
serpents, Takṣa as lord of **4**.2-9
servant of Varuṇa, Indra as **129**.38-41
servants of Agni, priests as **127**.23-28
- of Yama **150**.6-9; **157**.21cd-25ab
- of Yama, advice by **123**.128cd-139
- of Yama, weapons of **215**.45-55ab .81-83ab
servants of Yama see also *messengers of Yama*
service as duty of women **230**.75-76
services of worship, five **67**.28-29ab
Śeṣa **3**.97cd-98 .125; **56**.19cd-22ab; **90**.2-4; **181**.38-53; **208**.3; **209**.23; **233**.1-4
- as form of Nārāyaṇa **180**.21cd-22ab
- as lord of nether world **115**.2-4
- as support of earth **21**.15-27
- as teacher of Garga **21**.15-27
- , Balarāma as **198**.1-3
- , blue clothes of **21**.15-27
- , breath of **232**.24-27
- , description of **21**.15-27
- , description of Balarāma as **192**.32-42
- , iconographic attributes of **21**.15-27
- to Śiva, hymn by **115**.7-9
- , Viṣṇu as **21**.13cd-15; **56**.19cd-22ab
- , Viṣṇu lying on **233**.1-4
- , yawning of **21**.15-27
Śeṣa see also *Nāga*
sesamum and butter, cows made of **216**.5-63
- as offering **219**.60cd-65ab
- , offering of water with **57**.5; **60**.49-53
- oil for lamps **29**.35cd-36; **67**.24-27
- , origin of **219**.42-47ab
- , praise of **29**.37
- , water with **28**.24; **219**.71cd-86
Śeṣatīrtha, place of pilgrimage **115**.1
Śeṣeśvara, Liṅga named **115**.19cd-20ab
- , Śiva as **115**.12cd-15ab
settlement, beginning of **4**.94-95
- , ideal places for **221**.103-108
settlement see also *habitation*
seven Ādityas **174**.14
- Brahmins **1**.43-45ab
- breaths **240**.22cd-26
- continents **4**.11-15; **12**.18-21; **13**.160

.166-169 .172-173 .189cd-197ab; **18**.11-12; **33**.3-8; **54**.1-3; **131**.39cd-51; **175**.60-68
- days, rain of **188**.20-23
- directions **174**.14
- enclosure sticks in sacrifice, metres as **161**.35cd-39ab
- Gaṅgās **172**.17cd-19ab
- hundred sacrifices **13**.166-169
- Mahālokas **23**.21
- mountains **18**.62c-f; **27**.19cd-20ab
- nether worlds **23**.21
- oceans **18**.11-12; **33**.3-8; **54**.1-3
- priests **174**.14
- rays of sun **232**.14-23
- sages **2**.10-13; **5**.8-9ab .11cd-12 .20cd-21 .29cd-30ab .34-35 .43 .44-45ab .58cd-60; **23**.6-10; **34**.29cd-32 .45cd-48; **82**.2-6; **172**.15-17ab; **213**.25-26
- sages, adoption of **3**.107cd-109ab
- sages, *dharma* spread by sons of **5**.38cd-39
- sages, *sattra*-rite of **134**; **173**.3-6ab
- steps at wedding ceremony **8**.5-8
- suns **232**.14-23
- thousand sons of Mura **202**.16-21
- vices of king **123**.33cd-36ab
- worlds **33**.3-8 .15cd
seven-*dvīpa*-theory **18**
sevenfold division of continents **20**
seventy Yugas **5**.54cd-55ab
seventy-one, Yugas **2**.1-4
sex, change of **108**.20cd-21 .113-115; **229**.43cd-55 .68cd-71
sexes, origin of two **1**.51cd-52
sexual intercourse between mother and son **92**.2-11
- intercourse during ancestral rites, effect(s) of **220**.106-109ab
- intercourse, effect(s) of forbidden **225**.52
- intercourse in water, prohibition of **221**.24ab
- intercourse, origin of **45**.37-41
- intercourse, prescription(s) concerning **221**.42 .71 .75
- intercourse, procreation by **2**.50; **3**.3-7ab
- intercourse, punishment for forbidden **22**.12cd-13; **214**.120-128; **215**.72-77 .120cd-121ab; **217**.77cd-80ab
- intercourse through mouth **6**.41-43
- intercourse with daughter, punishment for **22**.12ab
- intercourse with daughter-in-law, punishment for **22**.12ab
- intercourse with sister, punishment for **22**.10
- intercourse with teacher's wife, punishment for **22**.10
- intercourse with teacher's wife, expiation for **81**.16-22ab
- intercourse with wives, punishment for forbidden **22**.21-22
shadow as surrogate of wife **89**.6-9ab
shape, change of **187**.8-18
- of Narasiṃha, terrible **149**.4cd-9ab
- of Śiva, terrible **173**.36
- of Śiva, ugly **35**.4cd-10
- of sun **32**.47a-f
- of sun, unknown **174**.19-25ab
- of Viṣṇu, black **161**.54-58
- of Viṣṇu, white **161**.54-58
- of Viṣṇu, yellow **161**.54-58
shape see also *body, forms, incarnation, manifestation*
shapes assumed by Rākṣasa **163**.7-12ab
- of Viṣṇu, three **161**.68-71
share in sacrifice, Śiva without **39**.34-39
shaving of beard, prescription(s) concerning **221**.72
- , prescription(s) concerning **221**.79
shepherds, punishment for **22**.25
Śibi **13**.25cd-27ab
- , Auśīnara **13**.22cd-23
Śibis **13**.24-25ab
Siddha as messenger **228**.100cd-127ab
Siddhakeśvara, place of pilgrimage **42**.6-8
Siddhārtha, place of pilgrimage **25**.57
Siddhas **18**.52-55; **23**.16-20; **36**.63cd-70; **39**.7-17ab; **69**.12-43; **86**.17-19; **89**.37-40ab; **105**.8cd-11ab; **140**.5cd-6ef; **164**.3-6; **182**.32; **210**.50-52ab; **214**.107cd-109
- , place of pilgrimage visited by **143**.17
Siddhas see also *adepts*
Siddhatīrtha, place of pilgrimage **143**.1
Siddheśvara **101**.17cd-19ab .19cd-20; **106**.1
- , Liṅga named **122**.97cd-99 .100-102; **143**.1
- , place of pilgrimage **25**.33; **128**.1-2; **157**.18ef-21ab
Siddhi **68**.56-59ab

- as wife of Varuṇa **239**.58-61
Siddhodbhava, place of pilgrimage **25**.65
siege of Mathurā **195**.1-4
sight, pollution by **221**.141cd-143ab
Śikhā **20**.10-11
Śikhaṇḍinī **2**.29-30ab
Śikhī **20**.10-11; **105**.22-26ab
Śikhivāsa **18**.32-36ab
Siktā **96**.22cd-24ab
Śīlamaṇḍalā **201**.3-5
silk-cotton tree as emblem **20**.33
silver as sacrificial gift **219**.71cd-86
Siṃhikā **3**.64cd-70ab .86cd-89ab
- [Daitya-woman] **142**.2-4
- , descendants of **3**.86cd-89ab
similarity see also *resemblance*
simile, Agni in **146**.2-8ab
- , Amarāvatī [city of Indra] in **43**.85cd-88; **196**.9-15
- , Bali in **123**.2-7ab
- , body and soul in **242**.29-33
- , Brahmin and field in **223**.60cd-61ab
- , charioteer in **237**.21-22
- , concentration in **239**.54-56
- , deities in **108**.68-70
- , detachment in **237**.82-86ab
- , diamond in **163**.26-31
- , differentiation in **30**.70cd-75
- , dissolution of the world in **206**.21-23
- , dream in **35**.52-59
- , embodiment in **242**.4-5ab
- , evolution in **23**.32cd-35
- , faithfulness of wife in **80**.71-77
- , full moon in **68**.43
- , ignorance in **244**.23-39
- , Indra in **43**.1; **123**.2-7ab; **146**.2-8ab; **189**.58c-f
- , Kailāsa in **21**.15-27
- , knowledge and ignorance in **234**.58-60ab
- , knowledge in **246**.6-12
- , knowledge of self in **236**.24-25
- , Kubera in **209**.11cd-21ab
- , Lakṣmī in **111**.26-34; **127**.2-4ab
- , liberation and suffering in **234**.54cd-57
- , life-giving effect of water in **107**.55-57
- , lunar mansions in **68**.43
- , matter and spirit in **23**.28cd-29ab .31cd-32ab; **237**.86cd-89
- , Māyā in **240**.54cd-68
- , meditation in **237**.29-31
- , mind and Self in **236**.49cd-53
- , mind and senses in **236**.12; **237**.77
- , moon in **26**.15; **231**.80-88; **237**.15-16
- , ocean in **237**.67-72
- , *puruṣa* and moon in **242**.52cd-55ab .55cd-58ef
- , river in **161**.61cd-62
- , Rudra in **8**.42cd-43
- , Śiva in **147**.14-17ab
- , seed and plant in **23**.38-40
- , Self in **236**.54-56ab; **238**.20-23 .24-25; **243**.59-65
- , senses in **240**.83-84
- , slaying of Vṛtra in **189**.58c-f
- , snake in **57**.15-16
- , spider in **238**.2
- , subtlety of the absolute in **235**.21-25
- , sunrise in **58**.65cd-68ab
- , tortoise in **232**.14-23; **237**.53
- , tree and householder in **164**.9cd-13
- , tree in **23**.32cd-35 .36-37; **80**.18-21
- , unity and difference in **245**.23cd-24
- , Varuṇa in **146**.2-8ab
- , Vārāṇasī in **41**.11-12
- , Viṣṇu as boar in **49**.9
- , wheel in **237**.76
- , wish-fulfilment in **227**.8-9
- , wrath and fire in **108**.68-70
- , Yoga in **196**.16-20; **239**.50-52
- , Yogin in **239**.11-23 .31-38
simplification of worship, prescr. conc. **61**.57
sin against teacher, punishment for **217**.43-44
- of killing of women **4**.74-80
- , transfer of **123**.158-164; **163**.17-22
sin see also *bad evil expiation, purification, transgression, vices*
Sindhu **27**.25cd-27 .28-29
Sindhūdbhava, place of pilgrimage **25**.65
Sindhudvīpa **8**.77cd-84ab
- [hermit] **169**.4-6ab
Sindhus **27**.43-50
Sindhusāgara, place of pilgrimage **64**.3-8ab
Sindhusena **79**.7cd-19
- , killing of **122**.48-49
Sindhūttha, place of pilgrimage **25**.57
Śineyu **15**.1-12ab
sinful Brahmin, description of **164**.17-28
- Kṣatriyas, Lakṣmī as friend of **137**.15-24
singing, devotional **228**.8-14

- during love-play **189**.34–35
- during vigil **228**
- of Kṛṣṇa **189**.14–17
- of praise of Kṛṣṇa **185**.54–56
Śini **14**.24cd–25ab
Sinī **9**.13–16
Sinīvalī **27**.33–34
sinner, black **141**.6–9
- , repentance of **150**.10–14
sinners, punishment for contact with **22**.9
sins, classification of **218**.3–5
- comparable to Brahmin-murder **164**.29–37
- , expiation by confession of **218**.6 .7–8ab
- , expiation for **22**.35–36; **218**.16cd–21ab
- , list of **212**.35–41; **214**.88cd–96; **215**.55cd–64 .72–77 .84cd–136ab; **223**.28–31; **228**.22–38; **240**.38–44
- punished in hells **22**.7–27
- , retribution of **214**.88cd–96 .120–128; **217**.36–110
sipping of water **219**.71cd–86
- of water, prescr. conc. **221**.17 .26–30 .131cd–132ab
- of water, prescription(s) concerning **221**.62cd–64ab .65cd–67ab .95–100
- of water, purification by **221**.67cd–69
Śiprā **27**.28–29 .33–34; **43**.75–76
Siprā **27**.28–29 .33–34
Śiśira **3**.38ef; **18**.32–36ab; **20**.3–5
Śiśirāyaṇi **14**.46cd
sister of Indra, Yoganidrā as **181**.38–53
- , punishment for sexual intercourse with **22**.10
Śiśumāra, Nārāyaṇa as **24**
Śiśupāla **14**.20cd–24ab; **199**.5–10
- and Kṛṣṇa, enmity between **199**.1–4
Sītā **18**.38cd–44ab; **20**.66–67; **123**.105cd–109ab .140–146 .177cd–184 .191–194; **154** .5–8ab
- abandoned by Rāma **154**.11cd–14ab
- , advice by **123**.158–164
- and Lakṣmaṇa **154**.11cd–14ab
- as Lakṣmī **213**.127–135
- as mother of the world **154**.27–30ab
- , fire-ordeal of **154**.2–4
- , Lakṣmaṇa, Rāma **123**.147–157
- on lap of Rāma **154**.8cd–11ab
- , place of pilgrimage **123**.213cd–216
- , Rāma and **93**.1–2
- , wedding of **123**.97–105ab
Śītagiri **107**.12–16
Śītānta **18**.52–55
Sītavana, place of pilgrimage **25**.69
Śītavanatīrtha, place of pilgrimage **25**.39
Sitoda, place of pilgrimage **25**.59
sitting, prescription(s) concerning postures of **221**.47ab
Śiva **3**.64cd–70ab .70cd–71; **20**.3–5; **28**.27; **30**.19–20; **33**.13cd–14ab; **35**.4cd–10; **36**.2–6; **37**.1a–f; **38**.22–40; **39**.27cd–28 .69cd–73; **41**.50cd–54ab .88–90; **51**.1–8; **56**.13–15 .61–66ab; **70**.16–19; **71**.16–18; **90**.8cd–12ab .31–33; **91**.2cd–6ab; **94**.2–14 .31–36 .43–45; **95**.12–15ab; **97**.15–17; **100**.1–3 .14–18; **103**.2–6; **104**.69–77; **106**.1 .23–26ab .31–36; **107**.1 .53–54; **108**.26–30 .94–98 .111–112; **109**.1–3ab .3cd–6ab .10cd–12 .21–26ab .43–45 .46–48; **110**.168–171 .172–178; **113**.5–8ab .10–14 .18–21; **116**.10–13; **117**; **121**.19–21ab; **124**.87–140; **129**.49–64; **143**.1; **145**.5cd–7; **151**.10–16 .17–22ab; **156**.9cd–11ab; **163**.26–31; **166**.11cd–13; **171**.40–43; **203**.6–19; **219**.31–35; **226**.13–14; **239**.58–61
- , advice by **110**.137–142 .211–214, **129**.82–93
- , all-comprehensiveness of **130**.17–21
- and Bāṇa **110**.104
- and demons, fight between **112**.11–19
- and Gaṇeśa **110**.105–106
- and Nandin at Gautamī **152**.42a–d
- and Pārvatī **128**.7–15 .16–23
- and Pārvatī, love-play of **205**.11–14
- and Pārvatī, wedding-ceremony of **72**.11cd–14
- and Pūṣan **190**.26–28
- and Rāvaṇa **110**.102–103
- and Śakti, residence of **106**.53cd–54ab
- and Śakti, unity of **129**.81
- and sages, dialogue between **226**
- and Skanda **110**.105–106
- and Suvarṇā **128**.63cd–70ab
- and Umā **75**.24; **143**.12–13; **144**.20–22
- and Umā, dialogue between **223**; **224**; **225**
- and Umā, hymn by Indra to **129**.68–81
- and Umā, Kailāsa as abode of **143**.7–11
- and Umā on Kailāsa **110**.102–103
- and Umā, wedding of **36**.54cd–70 .125–136
- and Umā, worship of **169**.16–22ab
- and Viṣṇu at place of pilgrimage

174.8-12ef
- and Viṣṇu, temple of **122**.3-7
- , androgynous **110**.105-106
- appearing to Śveta **59**.6-21
- as all **75**.12; **158**.37cd-39ab
- as Ardhanārīśvara **110**.105-106
- as atmosphere **75**.9
- as Ādikeśa **169**.4-6ab .22cd-24ef
- as Bhīmanātha **173**.37-39
- as Bhīmeśvara **173**.34cd-35ef
- as Brahman and Viṣṇu **130**.17-21
- as *brahman* **158**.37cd-39ab; **173**.37-39
- as Cakreśvara **110**.87-97ef .226-228
- as Candramauli **123**.177cd-184
- as child **35**.32-64; **36**.27-30
- as creator of evil things **129**.70-71
- as darkness **112**.11-19
- as *dharma* **130**.23-31
- as earth **75**.5
- as epitome of beings **130**.23-31
- as existence and thought **153**.1-2ab
- as fire **75**.7
- as first-person narrator **223**.55cd-56ab; **226**.20cd-22ab
- as fulfiller of wishes **115**.5-6ab
- as highest deity **36**.44cd-48 .49-52ab
- as hunter **102**.5cd
- as Jagannātha **109**.35; **110**.98-99ef
- as Kālañjara **147**.8-9ab
- as Koṭīśvara **148**.1-3ab
- as liberation **75**.23
- as light **135**.2cd-5ab
- as Liṅga **128**.62-63ab
- as lord of ghosts **4**.2-9
- as lord of Rākṣasas **4**.2-9
- as lord of Yakṣas **4**.2-9
- as Mahākāla **43**.65cd-74
- as Mahākāya **116**.15-16
- as Mahānala **116**.15-16
- as manifestation of Viṣṇu **213**.25-26
- as Manyu **162**.31-33ef
- as moon **75**.7
- as Nāgeśvara **111**.1
- as parents **122**.82
- as Pippaleśa **110**.226-228
- as protector **143**.2-5
- as protector of *dharma* **102**.5cd
- as Purāri **173**.37-39
- as Rāmeśvara **28**.56cd-62ab
- as refuge **111**.68cd-79
- as Śeṣeśvara **115**.12cd-15ab
- as sacrifice **75**.11
- as self of the world **153**.1-2ab
- as Someśvara **116**.14; **174**.31-33
- as Someśvara, homage to **122**.82
- as sound **75**.10
- as sun **75**.7
- as teacher of sages **145**.8-11ab
- as terrible lord **173**.29cd-33ab
- as trident-bearer **112**.2-3
- as Tryambaka **110**.219ef-224
- as Vāgīśvara **135**.1-2ab
- as water **75**.6
- as wind **75**.8
- as Yakṣeśvara **132**.1-2
- at Apsarāsaṃgama **147**.20cd-23ab
- at Gautamī **175**.55cd-59ef .69-72
- at place of pilgrimage, Viṣṇu and **122**.1-2
- , attendant(s) of **3**.70cd-71; **41**.88-90
- , blue neck of **112**.4-6
- , boon by **37**.24-25; **75**.33; **81**.16-22ab; **95**.22-28ab; **97**.24-28; **100**.22-24; **112**.7-10; **124**.100-107; **130**.32-33; **152**.24-25; **153**.8-11; **162**.6cd-10ab; **169**.46-47 .49ef; **175**.46cd-47; **207**.28-43
- , boon by Kṛṣṇa to **206**.45-48
- , boon by Viṣṇu and **160**.20; **168**.31-35
- , Brahman and **129**.70-71
- , Brahman, Viṣṇu **33**.9-23; **74**.31-37; **123**.121-128ab; **129**.125-127; **130**.7-14; **131**.39cd-51; **144**.2-4; **158**.35cd-37ab; **175**.1-2ef; **213**.25-26; **219**.98cd-107ab; **226**.20cd-22ab .45cd-48ab
- , Brahmin as devotee of **169**.43cd-45ef
- , bull as emblem of **109**.52-54; **166**.11cd-13
- , city of **168**.37; **173**.37-39
- , compassion of **72**.23-25ab; **127**.48-53; **158**.37cd-39ab; **169**.6cd-15
- , compassion of Viṣṇu and **122**.87-92
- , conduct of **38**.35-38
- , constituents of worship of **43**.65cd-74
- , creation as play of **116**.14
- , curse by **111**.68cd-79
- , curse removed by **146**.38-41
- cursed by Dakṣa **34**.33-38
- , Dakṣa cursed by **34**.26-29ab .29cd-32
- [demon] **213**.81-104
- , description of **123**.195-206
- , devotion to **56**.61-66ab; **122**.75-80
- , discus of Viṣṇu swallowed by **109**.28-29

- , effect(s) of devotion to **214**.114cd–119
- , eight forms of **75**.4–13; **97**.20–23
- embraced by Gaurī **119**.11
- , enjoyment and liberation granted by **130**.17–21
- , epithets of **115**.7–9ab; **122**.74; **124**.132–136ab; **223**.7–11; **224**.1–3 .27; **226**.10
- establishing devotion to Vāsudeva **226**.59–61
- existing in body of Vāsudeva **226**.59–61
- , fearlessness granted by **90**.2–4
- , fever of **206**.14–19
- , fight between Kṛṣṇa and **205**.7–8; **206**.21–23
- , fire from third eye of **110**.115–120
- , foot-lotus of **169**.1–2ab
- freed from head of Brahman **229**.59–63
- , Gaṅgā as beloved of **74**.8–12; **158**.16–21; **175**.33cd–35
- , Gaṅgā as tuft of hair of **75**.48
- , Gaṅgā in hair of **119**.11
- , Gaṅgā not removable from **175**.42–46ab
- , Gaṇeśa invoked by **114**.6–8
- , Gautama and **175**.46cd–68
- , Gautamī as Śakti of **123**.121–128ab
- , Gautamī obtained from **157**.12cd–13ab
- , Gautamī originated from bowl of **137**.25–28ab
- , gold originated from Agni and **128**.50–61
- , gold praised by **128**.50–61
- , greatness of **41**.6–9
- , homage by gods to **94**.46–48ab
- , homage to **79**.3–5ab
- , hundred and eight names of **143**.2–5
- , hunter as devotee of **169**.6cd–15 .39cd–43ab .43cd–45ef
- , hymn by Agni to **128**.44–45
- , hymn by Āpastamba to **130**.23–31
- , hymn by Bhagīratha to **78**.56–58
- , hymn by Bṛhaspati to **122**.74–82
- , hymn by Brahman to **36**.39cd–42
- , hymn by Dakṣa to **40**.2–100; **109**.30–35
- , hymn by Dattātreya to **117**.7–17
- , hymn by Death to **116**.15–16
- , hymn by Devāpi to **127**.48–53
- , hymn by Gautama to **75**.4–24
- , hymn by gods to **37**.2–23; **71**.38–40ab; **94**.27–30; **110**.134–136; **112**.4–6
- , hymn by Kaśyapa to **100**.19–21; **124**.94–99
- , hymn by Kubera to **97**.20–23
- , hymn by Pailūṣa to **139**.13–17ef
- , hymn by Pippalāda to **110**.100–106
- , hymn by Rāma to **123**.195–206
- , hymn by Śeṣa to **115**.7–9
- , hymn by Śukra to **95**.18–21
- , hymn by sages to **116**.14
- , hymn by Viṣṇu to **109**.51
- identical with gods **158**.22–27ef
- , identity of Kṛṣṇa and **206**.45–48
- , identity of Viṣṇu and **56**.61–66ab .66cd–73
- , impossibility of looking at **162**.13–19
- in simile **147**.14–17ab
- , invisibility of third eye of **110**.112–114
- , Kāma burnt by **38**.1–13; **71**.27–37
- , knowledge obtained from **139**.12
- , knowledge of **139**.7cd–11
- , Lakṣmī as **137**.30cd–39ab
- laughing at Brahmin **169**.33–35
- , liberation by devotion to **94**.37–42
- , Mahāśani as combination of Viṣṇu and **129**.94–99ab
- , Manyu born from brilliance of **162**.10cd–12
- , Manyu originated from third eye of **162**.20–27ab
- , meditation on **39**.90–91; **94**.2–14; **109**.52–54
- , merit of worship of **28**.56cd–62ab; **41**.60cd–71 .72–74 .88–90
- , moon in hair of **114**.9–12
- , Mothers originated from sweat of **112**.11–19
- , names of **117**.16–17
- , observances for worship of **168**.31–35
- , offering to **228**.76–85
- , omniscience of **162**.13–19
- , oneness of **158**.22–27ef
- , opposition of Kṛṣṇa and **207**.28–43
- , origin of third eye of **123**.195–206
- , paralysis effected by **36**.31–36ab; **37**.2–23
- , place of pilgrimage sacred to **132**.7–9ef; **168**.1
- , place of pilgrimage sacred to Viṣṇu and **168**.36
- pleased by Kavi [Śukra] **152**.24–25
- , praise of **173**.29cd–33ab
- praised by gods **37**; **113**.9 .15 .17; **160**.13–16ef
- praised by sages **226**.4–6

- , prayer-formula addressed to **57**.2-4 .6-8; **143**.2-5
- , punishment for disrespect against **157**.21cd-25ab
- reproached by Menā **38**.22-40
- , royal qualities of **130**.23-31
- , Śakti of **106**.37-38
- , sacrificial share for **39**.84-88ab
- , *sattra*-rite protected by **116**.17-19
- scolded by Brahmin **169**.25-32
- , semen of **128**.16-23
- shot by arrow of Kāma **71**.27-37
- , snake as attribute of **111**.68cd-79; **116**.15-16
- , son born from third eye of **153**.8-11
- , son obtained by hymn to **124**.136c-f
- , spear obtained from **115**.10-12ab
- , Speech cursed by Viṣṇu and **135**.13ef-14
- , statue of Brahman, Viṣṇu **120**.3cd-5
- , sun superior to Viṣṇu and **28**.40-41
- , superiority of **153**.12
- , sweat of **39**.74-81
- , teeth of Pūṣan broken by **109**.21-26ab
- , temple of **41**.60cd-71
- , terrible shape of **173**.36
- , thirty-six parts of **123**.191-194
- , thousand names of **40**.2-100
- , three cities destroyed by **114**.6-8
- , three eyes of **110**.183-187
- to Agni, boon by **128**.46-49
- to Bāṇa, boon by **3**.70cd-71; **206**.1-4 .39-44
- to Bhagīratha, boon by **78**.59-69
- to Dakṣa, boon by **39**.90-91; **109**.36-39ab
- to Dattātreya, boon by **117**.18-19ab
- to Devāpi, boon by **127**.54-59
- to Gautama, boon by **75**.25-27
- to Gārgya, boon by **196**.1-4
- to Kṛṣṇa, submission of **206**.39-44
- to Pippalāda, boon by **110**.107-111 .165
- to Pūru, boon by **146**.38-41
- to Rati, boon by **38**.7-13
- to Rāma, boon by **123**.207-213ab
- to Rāvaṇa, boon by **143**.12-13
- to Śveta, boon by **59**.6-21
- to Umā, boon by **35**.60-63
- to Viṣṇu, boon by **109**.52-54
- , *trimūrti*-functions of **128**.44-45; **129**.68-69; **130**.17-21
- , twins born from semen of **128**.24-28
- , ugly shape of **35**.4cd-10
- , Umā and **35**
- , Umā as manifestation of **75**.21
- , Umā as Śakti of **75**.15
- unable to describe Gautamī **175**.76-77
- , union of Viṣṇu and **135**.10cd-13cd
- , union with **110**.166-167
- , unity of Viṣṇu and **109**.52-54
- , unknowability of **40**.83; **129**.68-69
- unknowable to Brahman and Viṣṇu **127**.48-53
- unknowable to gods and sages **127**.48-53
- , Veda(s) as authority on knowledge of **139**.7cd-11
- , Veda(s) subordinate to **127**.35-47
- , Viṣṇu and **90**.34-35 .36; **122**.63-67ab; **123**.7cd-14ab; **129**.101-124; **135**.5cd-10ab .17-19; **136**.17-26; **150**.15-20; **160**.17-19; **174**.5cd-6ab .7
- , Vṛṣākapi as name of **124**.100-107
- with lotus-flowers, worship of **109**.46-48
- with sixteen offerings, worship of **123**.191-194
- without share in sacrifice **39**.34-39
- , world of **41**.60cd-71 .75-81 .91 .92; **56**.66cd-73; **57**.9-11; **111**.80-82; **124**.132-136ab
- , worship of **59**.6-21; **169**.4-6ab .36-39ab; **216**.5-63
- , worship of Vāsudeva recommended by **226**.7-9
- , worship of Viṣṇu and **131**.31-39ab
- , worship of Viṣṇu recommended by **226**.67c-f
- worshipped by Abhiṣṭut **168**.31-35
- worshipped by gods **162**.6cd-10ab
- worshipped by hunter **169**.6cd-15
- worshipped by hunter, Umā and **169**.16-22ab
- worshipped by Rāma **154**.27-30ab; **157**.18ef-21ab
- worshipped by Rāvaṇa **143**.14-16; **176**.26-32
- worshipped by Viṣṇu and Brahman **153**.12
- worshipped with dancing **162**.6cd-10ab
- worshipped with vedic prayer-formulas **168**.31-35
- , Yoga of **28**.56cd-62ab

Śiva see also *Bhava, Hara, Īśa, Īśāna, Liṅga,* Maheśvara, Rudra, Śaṃbhu, Śaṃkara, Tryambaka

Śivā **3**.39-40; **20**.43-44; **128**.72cd-76
Śivakuṇḍa, place of pilgrimage **43**.65cd-74
Śivasahasranāmastotra **40**.2-100
Śivaśaryā **105**.22-26ab
Śivoda, place of pilgrimage **25**.59
Śivodbheda, place of pilgrimage **25**.32
six embryos **181**.36; **182**.1-3
- seasons **36**.63cd-70 .71-124
- tastes **20**.94cd-95ab; **61**.38
sixteen constituents of human being **236**.14; **237**.7-14; **240**.22cd-26
- offerings, worship of Śiva with **123**.191-194
- priests at sacrifice **168**.2-5
- principles in evolution **243**.67-70
- qualities **236**.16ab
sixteen-thousand one hundred women, marriage of Kṛṣṇa to **204**.13cd-18
Skanda **1**.47ab; **69**.12-43; **74**.13-22ab; **81**.1 .4-7ab .7cd-12; **94**.15-21; **228**.92cd-96
- as conqueror of Tāraka **82**.9-10
- , birth of **82**.2-6
- , names of **82**.9-10
- , Śiva and **110**.105-106
- , Yama killed by **94**.15-21
Skandāśrama, place of pilgrimage **25**.14
Skandhāśrama, place of pilgrimage **25**.14
sky, circumference of **23**.3-4
- , origin of **161**.43cd-50cd
- , sun falling from **13**.9-12ab
slaughterer at sacrifice, Death as **116**.2cd-3ab
slayer of Vṛtra, Indra as **140**.19cd-21cd .21ef -25
slaying of Vṛtra in simile **189**.58c-f
slaying see also *killing*
sleep and dream **240**.85-92ab
- of Brahman, cosmic **56**.55
- of Kapila **78**.24-31
- of Mucukunda **196**.21-22
- of Viṣṇu, cosmic **53**.12-14ab; **56**.49-50; **213**.25-26 .30-31
- of Viṣṇu, Māyā as yogic **233**.5-6
- of Viṣṇu, yogic **45**.29; **179**.22cd-26; **180**.24cd-38; **233**.8
sleeping enemy, killing of **17**.29-31
Śliṣṭi **2**.14-15
Śmaśānastambha, place of pilgrimage **25**.65
Śmaśānastambhakūpa, place of pilgrimage **25**.65
smell of blood **12**.11-17
smoke, demon born from **133**.2-4
smoke-drinker **39**.22-27ab
Smṛta **5**.13cd-15ab
Smṛti-literature **121**.10-12
snake as attribute of Śiva **111**.68cd-79; **116**.15-16
- as son of king **111**.2-6
- imprisoned by Garuḍa **90**.5-8ab
- in simile **57**.15-16
- leaving from mouth of Balarāma **210**.50-52ab
- , marks of feet on hood of **185**.50-51
- named Nāgeśvara **111**.17-25
- wives to Kṛṣṇa, prayer by **185**.39-42
snakes as fetters **206**.5-9 .49-50
- burnt by sun **159**.24ef-25ef
- carried by Garuḍa **159**.22-24cd
- , fight between Garuḍa and **206**.49-50
- , Garuḍa subordinate to **159**.2-4
- healed by Indra **159**.39ef-41ab
- healed by Vinatā **159**.36-39cd
- healed by water from nether world **159**.41cd-46ab
- , Kāśyapa as father of **159**.28-31ab
- , Kṛṣṇa bound by **185**.11-17
- , many-headedness of **3**.96cd-97ab
- , ocean as residence of **185**.52-53
- submitting to Arjuna Kārtavīrya **13**.176cd -187ab
snake-sacrifice **10**.15-18cd
Snānadaṇḍa, place of pilgrimage **25**.25
Snānakuṇḍa, place of pilgrimage **25**.25
Snānalomāpaha, place of pilgrimage **25**.40
sneezing, birth from **7**.44cd-45ab
Sneha [caste] **20**.38cd-40ab
social rank determined by wealth during Kali-Yuga **230**.10-27
- rank of adherents of Sāṃkhya **240**.106-111
sojourn at Puruṣottamakṣetra **70**.3cd-8ab
- at Puruṣottamakṣetra, liberation by **177**.28 .29-30
- at Puruṣottamakṣetra, merit of **177**.9-15; **178**.106-111
- at Utkala, merit of **42**.42cd-46ab
- for ten nights **108**.18-20ab
- in heaven **7**.85-86; **67**.64cd-75
- in heaven, duration of **67**.52-80; **110**.155-156; **227**.16-32ab .32cd-37ab .42-47; **228**.86-91ab .146-151
- of Daśaratha in hell **123**.109cd-115

- , places for **242**.21cd-22
Śoka, place of pilgrimage **25**.71
solar dynasty **7**; **8**; **108**.119-120; **123**.2-7ab
- dynasty, Prācīnabarhis as founder of **153**.2cd-3
soliloquy of soul **242**.34-39 .48cd-52ab; **244**.23-39
solstice **63**.17
Soma **3**.25-28 .35cd-36 .37-38cd; **4**.100-109; **7**.14cd-16; **13**.9-12ab .97; **33**.9-13ab; **36**.16cd-17ab; **56**.13-15; **69**.12-43; **103**.2-6; **106**.23-26ab .26cd-30; **108**.56-58; **110**.78-80cd; **219**.6-12 .60cd-65ab .98cd-107ab; **220**.112cd-116ab
- addressed as king **174**.15 .16
- , advice by **110**.87-97ef
- and Sarasvatī, exchange of **105**.4-8ab
- as deity of ancestors **219**.91cd-98ab
- as husband of plants **119**.18-19
- as lord of castes **4**.2-9
- as lord of Gandharvas **105**.2
- as lord of plants **4**.2-9; **9**.12; **120**.8; **174**.16
- as lord of sacrifice **4**.2-9
- as lord of sages **9**.12
- as lord of seeds **9**.12
- as lord of stars **4**.2-9
- as lord of waters **9**.12
- as nectar of immortality **119**.13-17
- at sacrifice **174**.13
- , descendants of wives of **3**.34-46ab
- , drinking of **13**.37-39; **82**.1
- , fight between Rāvaṇa and **143**.2-5
- , Hari as **20**.19
- , Indra and **174**.18
- , merit of drinking of **119**.1
- , Nakṣatras as wives of **2**.47-49
- , origin of **9**.2-5
- , place of pilgrimage **42**.6-8
- , plants as queens of **120**.6-7ab
- , praise of **9**.7-8
- , protection by **174**.14
- [son of Atri] **144**.2-4
- taken away by Gandharvas **105**.3
- , Tārā abducted by **9**.17-20
- , wives of **3**.59
- , world of **143**.2-5
Soma see also *moon*
Somābhiṣecana, place of pilgrimage **25**.19
Somadatta **13**.98-99 .116; **208**.19-31
Soma-drinker **39**.22-27ab
Somāhva-mountain, place of pilgrimage **25**.19
Somaka **13**.98-99 .100-101
- [mountain] **20**.6-7
- , place of pilgrimage **25**.66
Somakavana, place of pilgrimage **25**.60
Somanātha at Prabhāsa, temple of **110**.202-210
- , Prabhāsa as name of **89**.42
- [Śiva] **117**.16-17; **130**.23-31
Soma-sacrifice **175**.86-90
Somaśarman **228**.76-85
Somatīrtha, place of pilgrimage **25**.13 .14 .37 .45 .55 .59; **64**.3-8ab; **105**.1 .22-26ab; **119**.1 .18-19; **174**.8-12ef .19-25ab
Somātri-mountain, place of pilgrimage **25**.19
Soṁeśa **113**.10-14
Someśvara, homage to Śiva as **122**.82
- , Liṅga named **97**.29; **174**.8-12ef
- , Śiva as **116**.14; **174**.31-33
Someśvaratīrtha, place of pilgrimage **129**.125-127
son, acknowledgement of **9**.31-32; **154**.14cd-21ab
- , adoption of **2**.7-8; **10**.64-65ab; **11**.19cd-21ab; **13**.132cd-137; **14**.28c-f .29-31 .50cd-56; **104**.83-86ab
- , ancestors released by **34**.60-72
- as source of joy **165**.37-44
- , asceticism for obtaining a **13**.102-105; **128**.3-6; **196**.1-4
- born from third eye of Śiva **153**.8-11
- , exile of **7**.100-102ab; **78**.37cd-44
- , identity of father and **148**.8-14ab; **165**.5-17
- , immortality caused by **104**.7cd-9
- , importance of **104**.5-7ab; **220**.32cd
- , liberation by **104**.10-14ab; **150**.15-20
- like Indra **10**.24-28ab; **13**.88-90; **124**.123-131
- , maxim about **123**.36cd-43; **146**.26-27
- , maxim about duties of **108**.76cd-87
- , maxim about ideal **170**.8ef-13
- , maxim about importance of **108**.76cd-87
- obtained after twelve years **14**.48-50ab
- obtained by hymn to Śiva **124**.136c-f
- obtained by means of sacrifice **13**.58-61
- obtained by praising **182**.18
- obtained from Śiva **153**.15cd-16ab
- of Bhṛgu, Kavi [Śukra] as **95**.2-6

- of Kaśyapa, sun as **89**.2ef-3
- of king of Kāśi, Dhanvantari as **11**.36-38
- of king, snake as **111**.2-6
- of mare [Vaḍavā], fire as **110**.198cd-200cd
- of Parameṣṭhin **124**.7-8
- of Raji, Indra as **11**.19cd-21ab
- on lap of father **140**.7-11; **154**.14cd-21ab
- , praise of **104**.10-14ab
- , punishment for selling of **150**.6-9
- , Rāma as dutiful **123**.177cd-184 .187-190
- , religious practices for obtainment of **124**.123-131
- , resemblance of father and **200**.20-22
- , revenge for father as duty of **142**.7-8ef
- , sacrifice for obtaining a **7**.3-5ab
- saving from hell **4**.48-52
- , selling of **7**.105cd-109; **104**.44-59ab; **150**.1cd-4ab
- , sexual intercourse between mother and **92**.2-11
- , vow for obtaining a **124**.17-18
- , wish for **124**.12-16
- , wish for invincible **173**.6cd-8ef
son(s) obtained by asceticism **9**.2-5; **10**.24-28ab; **13**.20cd-22ab .88-90; **15**.35-41ab
Śoṇa, place of pilgrimage **25**.82
Śoṇā **27**.30-32
Śoṇaśva **16**.1-3
songs on Vāsudeva **67**.31cd-35ab
son-in-law of Varuṇa, Mahāśani as **129**.17-20ab
Śoṇitapura **206**.10-13
Śoṇodbhava, place of pilgrimage **25**.77
sons, adoption of **16**.8
- belonging to four castes **11**.33-34ab; **13**.79
- belonging to three castes **11**.60cd-61ab; **13**.63b-64ab
- born from gourd **8**.69-72ab
- born from mind **158**.2-3
- cursed by Viśvāmitra **104**.83-86ab
- , maxim about consolation by **154**.14cd-21ab
- of Atri, triad of gods born as **144**.2-4
- of Brahman **5**.8-9ab; **23**.12-15
- of Dakṣa, destruction of **3**.7cd-9; **158**.2-3
- of Danu, hundred **3**.73cd-74ab
- of Daśaratha, birth of **123**.84-86ab
- of Daśaratha, wedding of **123**.97-105ab
- of Mura, seven thousand **202**.16-21
- of Rukmiṇī **201**.1-2
- of Sagara, birth of **8**.63-73
- of Varuṇa **34**.45cd-48
- of Vasiṣṭha **5**.16cd
- , punishment for teaching by **22**.27
- , religious practices for obtainment of hundred **124**.132-136ab
sons-in-law of Dakṣa **34**.12cd-19
soul, body and **214**.46-51
- in simile, body and **242**.29-33
- , process of embodiment of **217**.26
- , *sattva* and **237**.86cd-89
- , senses and **240**.92cd
- , soliloquy of **242**.34-39 .48cd-52ab; **244**.23-39
soul see also *puruṣa, spirit*
sound of *brahman* **236**.59cd-66
- of conch, demons destroyed by **156**.4-6
- , Śiva as **75**.10
sounding of drums **14**.14cd-20ab
source of Gautamī, Rāma at **123**.207-213ab
south, Agastya as lord of the **118**.2-9; **158**.8-15ef
- as direction of ancestors **219**.71cd-86
- , inhabitants of **27**.54-57
- , Yama as lord of the **125**.25-32; **131**.31-39ab
southern Gaṅgā, Gautamī as **158**.28-29
- ocean **70**.22cd-23
sovereignties, distribution of **4**.1-17
sovereignties see also *realms*
sow, earth as **219**.113cd-115
space and time **23**.36-37
speaking to fallen persons, prohibition of **76**.18cd-23ab
spear, flaming **39**.7-17ab
- obtained from Śiva **115**.10-12ab
- of Śiva **122**.1-2
special body after death **214**.27cd-31 .46-51 .70-88ab
Speech as goddess **80**.46-55
- as river **135**.15-16
- as Sarasvatī [river] **135**.20-24
- as Vāṇī [river] **135**.20-24
- , creation of **1**.39cd-42
- cursed by Brahman **135**.15-16
- cursed by Viṣṇu and Śiva **135**.13ef-14
- , four kinds of **175**.14cd-16
- , prescr. conc. **224**.18-26
spell for rain **58**.50-55ab

- for wind **58**.55cd-56
- , harm by **58**.57
spell-formula(s) **123**.97-105ab; **168**.18cd-21
- and weapons **141**.10-13
- , killing with **168**.22-24
- , protection by **58**.29-32ab
spell-formula(s) see also *prayer-formula*
spells in worship of Narasiṃha **58**.50-59ab
spices, kinds of **220**.168-177
spider in simile **238**.2
spirit in simile, matter and **23**.28cd-29ab .31cd-32ab; **237**.86cd-89
- , matter and **23**.29cd-31ab; **130**.7-14; **161**.6cd-9; **237**.21-22
spirit see also *puruṣa, soul*
splendour of Indra, description of **140**.7-11
splitting in halves, killing by **190**.29-37; **202**.16-21
spots in the moon, origin of **152**.26-28
- on the palm, sacred **221**.95-100
spring as butter in sacrifice **161**.35cd-39ab
- , description of **36**.95-105ab
sprinkling of water, protection by **168**.18cd -21
- with consecrated water **65**.81-82; **110**.35-39ab
- with water, killing by **168**.22-24
spying, punishment for **22**.21-22
Śraddhā **68**.56-59ab; **102**.2cd-5ab; **109**.13-20
- , place of pilgrimage **102**.1-2ab
Śrāddhakalpa **220**.1
Śrāhuka **15**.46cd-48
Śrama **3**.37-38cd
Śrānta **3**.37-38cd
Śravaṇa **123**.36cd-43; **220**.33cd-42
Śravaṇā **14**.12-13; **16**.1-3 .56cd-58ab
Śrāvaṇa **31**.19-21; **41**.72-74
Śrāvasta **7**.51cd-53 .54-55
Śrāvasti **7**.51cd-53
Śraviṣṭhā **13**.132cd-137; **14**.12-13; **16**.1-3 .56cd-58ab
Śreṣṭhasthānahrada, place of pilgrimage **25**.62
Śrī **34**.42-45ab; **45**.4; **61**.41-45ab; **90**.20-30; **137**.2-3 .8-14
- , dialogue between Viṣṇu and **45**.16cd-89
- , Kamalā as name of **124**.137-139ab
- , Viṣṇu and **51**.10-16
Śrī see also *Lakṣmī*
Śrīdāman **187**.8-18
Śrīdevī **14**.36-38
Śrīdhara **60**.39-45
Śrīdhārā, place of pilgrimage **25**.74
Śrīgiri **167**.4-7; **169**.2cd-3
Śrīkuñja, place of pilgrimage **25**.44
Śrīmat **31**.31-33ab
Śrīnada, place of pilgrimage **25**.79
Śrīnadī, place of pilgrimage **25**.79
Śrīparṇāsaṃgama, place of pilgrimage **105**.22-26ab
Śrīparvata **27**.20cd-24ab
Śrīśaila, place of pilgrimage **64**.8cd-9
Śrīśakrayajana, place of pilgrimage **25**.30
Śrītīrtha, place of pilgrimage **25**.10 .23 .79
Śrīvāsa, place of pilgrimage **25**.75
Śrīvatsa-lock **45**.37-41; **49**.10-20; **50**.43cd-44ab .48-54; **53**.31-33; **61**.41-45ab .52-55; **68**.44-53; **176**.8-10; **182**.12-13; **193**.42-49; **207**.13-24
Sṛmaṇa **3**.74cd-78ab .86cd-89ab
Śṛṅgaka **70**.35cd-37ab
Śṛṅgatīrtha, place of pilgrimage **25**.67
Śṛṅgin **18**.16-17
Sṛñjaya **11**.27cd-31; **13**.15cd-20ab .93-96 .98-99
Sṛñjayī, Bāhyakā **15**.32 .33
- , Upabāhyakā **15**.32 .34
Śroṇi **20**.28
Śruta **8**.77cd-84ab; **205**.1-6
Śrutadevā **14**.14cd-20ab .20cd-24ab .27ab .27cd-28ab
Śrutasena **13**.109
Śrutaśravā **14**.14cd-20ab .20cd-24ab
Śrutatīrtha, place of pilgrimage **25**.55
Śrutavat **16**.50cd-54ab
Śrutāyu **10**.11-12
Śruti, advice by **152**.31-32
sruva, explanation of **79**.20-21ab
stage of householder **88**.10-15
- of householder, importance of **222**.32-35
- of life, duties of third **222**.39-44
- of life, punishment for transgression of **22**.26 .30
- of life, third **104**.10-14ab
stages of life **1**.3-9; **42**.32-33; **57**.42-51; **242**.20cd-21ab
- of life, duties common to all **222**.18
- of life, four **88**.10-15; **123**.2-7ab
- of life, prescr. conc. **222**
stake at bet, hands as **170**.37-38cd

- at bet, life as **170**.47-48
- at game, coins as **201**.10-22
- at game of dice, Gandharva-knowledge as **171**.14-15
- at game of dice, kingdom as **171**.20-24
- at game of dice, life as **171**.20-24
- at game of dice, right hand as **171**.6ef-9ef
- at game of dice, thunderbolt as **171**.10-13
- at game of dice, Urvaśī as **171**.6ef-9ef

staleness of food **221**.56
stallion, sun as **89**.22-25ab
Stamba **5**.11cd-12
stambha, merit obtained by **41**.92
standing, prescription(s) concerning postures of **221**.43
stars as pores of Viṣṇu **56**.27cd-30ab
- , movement of **24**.1-7ab
- , Soma as lord of **4**.2-9
- , world of **227**.16-32ab

statue, bathing of **67**.20-23
- consecrated by Brahman **176**.11
- consecrated by Indradyumna **51**.48-53
- , constituents of worship of **61**.24-38
- , fanning of **65**.17-18
- , hiding of **45**.75-76
- in ocean, submersion of **176**.37-51
- , making of **50**.7-15 .29-32 .41-43ab .48-54
- of Balarāma **50**.44cd-46ab .48-54
- of Brahman, Viṣṇu, Śiva **120**.3cd-5
- of Kṛṣṇa **50**.43cd-44ab .48-54
- of Mādhava **59**.26-33
- of Śvetamādhava **59**.4-5
- of Subhadrā **50**.46cd-47ab .48-54
- of Vāsudeva, stone **176**.4-7
- of Viṣṇu, blue **58**.1-7
- of Viṣṇu named Govinda **122**.100-102
- , offering of food to **67**.24-27
- , worship of **51**.37-39

statue see also *image*
statues, colours of **50**.48-54
- , worship of **51**.54-56

Stavarāja **31**.33cd-34
Staviṣṭhā [wife of Śaryāti] **138**.2-3
steam-drinker **39**.22-27ab
step in Yoga, highest **235**.21-25
- of Viṣṇu **172**.4-7ab; **246**.34-35
- of Viṣṇu, Gaṅgā originated from **18**.38cd-44ab; **150**.15-20
- of Viṣṇu, highest **42**.5; **51**.22-26 .57-58; **68**.4-5; **131**.39cd-51

step see also *foot*
stepmother, children treated unequal by **32**.58cd-63
stepping on forbidden objects **221**.24cd-25
steps at wedding-ceremony, seven **8**.5-8
- of Viṣṇu, three **73** .41-43cd .48-51; **179**.16cd-18ab; **213**.81-104

Sthalaśṛṅga, place of pilgrimage **25**.18
Sthaleyu **13**.5-8
Sthaṇḍileyu **13**.5-8
Sthāṇutīrtha, place of pilgrimage **25**.53
Sthūlaśṛṅga, place of pilgrimage **25**.18
stick of Yama **125**.22; **168**.25-26ab; **203**.45-62
stillbirth **221**.146cd-149ab
stone, statue of Vāsudeva **176**.4-7
stones from Vindhya-mountains **47**.7-9
stories of Hari, merit of listening to **76**.18cd-23ab
- on Vāsudeva, recitation of **67**.31cd-35ab
- , recitation of **26**.16; **36**.63cd-70
- told by Viṣṇu **136**.3cd-14ab

strategem of demons **78**.24-31
- of Pārvatī **81**.7cd-12

stretching out of feet, prohibition of **221**.101
Strīratnakūṭā **13**.5-8
student, duties of **222**.22-27
study of Veda(s) **111**.7-8; **217**.37-39
study see also *recitation*
Subāhu **13**.3-4 .51-52 .127cd-132ab; **14**.12-13; **16**.56cd-58ab; **213**.136-140
Subhadrā **13**.123-124; **14**.39-41 .43ab; **43**.10-13; **62**.1-4; **65**.57-58; **177**.3
- , Kṛṣṇa, Baladeva **179**.4-5
- , Kṛṣṇa, Balarāma **65**
- , prayer-formula addressed to **57**.57-58
- , statue of **50**.46cd-47ab .48-54
- , worship of **57**.57-61

Subhadrāhrada, place of pilgrimage **25**.61
Subhāhu **210**.37-43
Subhāṣaṇa **15**.58cd-59
subhāṣita, quotation of **138**.8-9ef
Śubhra **14**.39-41
- [mountain] **163**.3-6; **164**.1-2

subjects and objects of knowledge **244**.4-9
- , king performing ancestral rites for **220**.78cd-80ab
- , protection of **7**.58cd-71ab

submersion of Dvārakā **212**.9-11
- of earth, threat of **83**.23-29
- of statue in ocean **176**.37-51

- of world in ocean **53**.12-14ab .14cd-18ab; **56**.51-54
submission of Kṛṣṇa to fate **210**.15
- of Śiva to Kṛṣṇa **206**.39-44
- of snakes to Arjuna Kāratavīrya **13**.176cd-187ab
- to a rival, maxim about **160**.13-16ef
substances for bathing **67**.20-23
substitutes for nectar of immortality **133**.13-17
substitution of earth and island **151**.22cd-24ab
- of land and cow **155**.12-13ab
subtle body **217**.14-17
subtlety of the absolute in simile **235**.21-25
Sucāru **13**.127cd-132ab; **16**.8; **201**.1-2; **210**.37-43
success of rites, Umā as **75**.22
success see also *accomplishment, completion, perfection*
Succhāyā **2**.14-15
Sucetas **13**.152-153ab
Śuci **3**.92cd-93ab .93cd-95ab; **5**.17d-19ab; **31**.31-33ab; **229**.22-87
- , boon by Viṣṇu to **229**.37-43ab
- taking refuge to Viṣṇu **229**.22-30
Sudaṃśa **22**.2-6
Sudaṃṣṭra **16**.8
Sudānīrā **27**.28-29
Sudānta **16**.4-6
Sudarśana [discus of Viṣṇu] **68**.44-53; **167**.31-32; **206**.31-38 .39-44; **207**.28-43
- , place of pilgrimage **25**.35
Sudāsa **8**.77cd-84ab
Śuddhikara, place of pilgrimage **25**.12
Sudeṣṇa **14**.29-31; **201**.1-2
Sudevā **15**.56-58ab
Sudhā **182**.7-8
Sudhāman **5**.29cd-30ab; **20**.41cd-42
Sudhanus **13**.108
Sudhanvan **4**.11-15; **8**.84cd-92; **13**.3-4 .108 .109
Sudharmā [hall of Indra] **194**.13-17; **212**.7
Sudharman **14**.12-13
Śūdra **40**.136-137; **223**.23-27
- , curse of becoming a **7**.43
- regarded as Brahmin **223**.54cd-55ab .56cd-58ab
Śūdrā **13**.5-8
Śūdras **4**.115-121; **11**.33-34ab; **13**.79; **19**.17; **27**.43-50; **220**.3-4
- , blessings of **230**.66-71
- , Brahmins fed by **230**.70-71
- , conduct of **223**.32-36
- , duties of **222**.13-14
- , exclusion of women and **67**.19
- , origin of **161**.43cd-50cd
- , purity of **223**.55cd-56ab
- , twice-born without ceremonies compared to **111**.7-8
- , worship by **66**.7cd-13
Sudyumna **2**.17-20ab; **7**.9-14ab .17-19ab .19cd-21ab .21cd-22 .23; **226**.30-41
suffering and pleasure **234**.50-54ab
- , classification of **234**.1-8
- in heaven **234**.50-54ab
- in human life **234**.9-42
- in simile, liberation and **234**.54cd-57
- , inevitability of **242**.34-39
- of embryo **240**.27-32
- of rebirth **49**.23-47ab
- , three kinds of **100**.19-21
Sugandhāśva, place of pilgrimage **25**.50
sugarcane juice, ocean of **18**.11-12; **20**.20 .24
Sugrīva **154**.21cd-26; **176**.37-51; **213**.136-140
Sugrīvī **3**.92cd-93ab .93cd-95ab
Suhma **13**.30-31
Suhmakas **13**.36
Suhotṛ **13**.62-63a
Suhotra **10**.13-14; **13**.62-63a .63b-64ab .80cd-81ab .109
suicide, threat of **107**.31-34; **111**.9-16; **127**.9cd-15; **185**.18-27
suicide see also *voluntary death*
Sujambuka, place of pilgrimage **25**.41
Sujātas **13**.203-204
Śuka **30**.14-18
Sukanyā as twins, Ānarta and **7**.27cd-28ab
Śūkara **22**.2-6 .9
- [hell] **214**.14-17
- , place of pilgrimage **25**.12; **64**.3-8ab
Śūkarava, place of pilgrimage **25**.12; **228**.127cd-145
Śūkarava, Sūkarava see also *Śaukarava, Saukarava*
Sūkarava, place of pilgrimage **228**.127cd-145
Sukeśī **68**.60-67
Suketu **8**.54-57; **11**.55-59
Sukhodaya **20**.3-5
Śuklatīrtha, place of pilgrimage **133**.1

Śukra **5**.17d-19ab; **23**.6-10; **73**.23-26 .27-33; **146**.2-8ab; **152**.34-37ab
- , Aṅgiras as teacher of **95**.2-6
- , Bṛhaspati and **152**.18-20
- , Devayānī and **146**.8cd-10
- , Kāvya [Uśanas] as name of **146**.19-25
- , moon cursed by **152**.26-28
- reproached by Yayāti **146**.15-18
- [son of Havirdhāna] **2**.29-30ab
- to Śiva, hymn by **95**.18-21
- [Uśanas] **95**
- , Yayāti cursed by **146**.11-14
Śukra see also *Kavi*
Śukratīrtha, place of pilgrimage **25**.60; **95**.1 .31-32
Sukṛtā **20**.10-11
Sukṛti **5**.13cd-15ab
Śuktimanta, place of pilgrimage **64**.8cd-9
Śuktimat **19**.3 .14; **27**.19cd-20ab .38cd-39ab
Śuktimatī [city] **15**.14-15
- [river] **27**.30-32
Sukubjaka, place of pilgrimage **64**.3-8ab
Sukumāra **11**.55-59; **13**.75cd-77; **20**.59cd-61
Sukumārī **20**.66-67
Śūla **217**.80cd-86
Śūlapāṇin **14**.48-50ab
Śūlikas **27**.43-50
Sumālina, place of pilgrimage **25**.70
Sumanas **2**.17-20ab
- [mountain] **20**.6-7
Sumanasa, place of pilgrimage **25**.34
Sumati **5**.45cd-46
- [son of Pramati] **171**.25-26
Śumbha **181**.38-53
Sumeru **161**.21-23ef; **176**.4-7
Sumitrā **123**.2-7ab .84-86ab
summary, anticipating **43**.1-13; **45**.77-89; **210**.1-4 .22-27 .33-35 .52cd-58
- , concluding **41**.1-5; **43**.63cd-65ab; **56**.51-54; **69**.1-9; **70**.1-11 .8cd-10; **72**.36; **113**.16
»summary«, Gautamī-Māhātmya as **174**.27cd-28
summary of deeds of Kṛṣṇa **226**.42-45ab
- of past events **108**.76cd-87; **110**.80ef-86; **122**.54cd-62; **190**.1-5; **193**.32-40
- of Rāmāyaṇa **176**.37-51; **213**.127-135
summary see also *reference*
summer as fuel in sacrifice **161**.35cd-39ab
- , description of **36**.118-123
summoning of heavenly weapons **195**.5-7
Sumukha **3**.99-101; **90**
sun **3**.125
- , absorption of water by **24**.8-11
- according to seasons, colours of **31**.12-14ab
- and earth, equivalence of **29**.20-21
- and moon, purification by **221**.129cd-131ab
- appearing to Aditi **32**.17-31
- as creator **30**.7-13; **31**.1-3
- as eye of Mitra **30**.40-41
- as father and mother **30**.21-22
- as father of Yama **94**.22-26
- as fire **158**.22-27ef
- as highest deity **30**.7-13; **33**.13cd-14ab
- as Jagannātha **138**.35-38
- as OM **32**.12-16
- as origin of beings **33**.9-13ab
- as origin of rain **31**.4-6
- as origin of time **31**.7-10
- as son of Kaśyapa **89**.2ef-3
- as stallion **89**.22-25ab
- as teacher **30**.21-22; **159**.17-21
- as three Vedas **32**.12-16
- at Gautamī **158**.35cd-37ab
- bathing in Gautamī **86**.47-49ab
- , black shape of **6**.9-14
- , boon by **32**.17-31; **33**.24-26
- , circumambulation of **29**.20-21
- , curse by **89**.25cd-33
- , cutting of brilliance of **6**.34cd-40; **32**.80-81 .104-107; **89**.42
- , destruction of cosmos by **5**.58cd-60
- , devotion to **29**.9-14; **229**.8-13
- , distance of **23**.5
- , effect(s) of worship of **28**.42-45; **159**.12 -16
- falling from sky **13**.9-12ab
- , flying to **159**.22-24cd; **166**.4cd-6ab
- , friendship with **16**.13-24
- , gods encompassed by **110**.137-142 .219ef -224
- , healing of birds burnt by **166**.6cd-8ab
- , hundred and eight names of **33**.33-46
- , hymn by Aditi to **32**.12-16
- , hymn by Aṅgiras to **32**.93cd-95ab
- , hymn by gods to **32**.89-90ab
- , hymn to **33**.9-23
- , iconographic attributes of **28**.30-31; **33**.14cd-15ab

- identical with triad of gods **168**.10-12
- in Arka-plant **103**.2-6
- , land granted by **168**.10-12
- , livelihood granted by **31**.4-6
- , looking at **16**.13-24
- , meditation on **33**.27-31; **61**.19
- , merit of hymn to **31**.33cd-34
- , merit of worship of **28**.37-54ab .46 .47-53ab; **29**.7-61; **33**.27-31
- , moon nourished by **24**.8-11
- , names of **31**.29-39
- , origin of **161**.43cd-50cd
- , partial incarnation of **32**.17-31
- , praise of **31**.1-27 .29-39; **32**.88-95 .90cd-91ab .91cd-92ab
- , Pratiṣṭhāna as abode of **110**.226-228
- , prayer-formula addressed to **168**.6-9
- , prescr. conc. worship of **29**.7-61
- , priority of worship of **28**.40-41
- , prohibition of looking at **221**.20
- , purification by looking at **221**.26-30 .67cd-69 .136cd-137ab .140cd-141ab
- , Śiva as **75**.7
- , seven rays of **232**.14-23
- , shape of **32**.47a-f
- , snakes burnt by **159**.24ef-25ef
- superior to Viṣṇu and Śiva **28**.40-41
- thrown down by Vīrabhadra **109**.21-26ab
- , transcendence of **33**.16-21
- , *trimūrti*-functions of **138**.33-34
- , twelve names of **31**.14cd-16
- , twelve-fold shape of **30**.23-44
- , unknown shape of **174**.19-25ab
- , Uṣā as wife of **165**.2-4
- , Viṣṇu as **158**.22-27ef
- , world of **29**.22-27ab; **227**.16-32ab
- , worship of **28**.19-36; **60**.49-53; **67**.15-18; **131**.31-39ab; **138**.28-32
- , Yoga of **28**.62cd-64ab

sun see also *Āditya, Bhānu, Ravi, Sūrya*
Sunadya **10**.21-23
Śunaḥbhojana **214**.14-17
Sunahotra **11**.32-33ab
Śunaḥpuccha **10**.53cd-54
Śunaḥśepa **104**; **150**
- adopted by Viśvāmitra **104**.83-86ab
- , place of pilgrimage **104**.1-2
Śunaḥśepha **10**.53cd-54 .64-65ab; **13**.91
- as sacrificial animal **10**.65cd-67ab
Śunaka **11**.33-34ab
Sunāmā **14**.45-46ab
Sunāman **15**.58cd-59
- [brother of Kaṃsa] **193**.76cd-78ab
Sunāmnī **14**.36-38; **15**.56-58ab
Sunanda [club of Baladeva] **195**.5-7
Sunandā **72**.9cd-10ab; **77**.9cd-13
Śunaśokas **27**.43-50
sunbeams after death, existence in **30**.14-18
- of Ādityas, number of **31**.22-26
Sunda **3**.86cd-89ab; **181**.7-14
Sundarī **14**.8-10; **16**.50cd-54ab; **17**.34
Sundarikāśrama, place of pilgrimage **25**.58
Sunday, importance of **29**.31cd-32ab
Sunītha **11**.55-59
Sunīthā **2**.20cd; **4**.28-34
sunrise in simile **58**.65cd-68ab
- , kneeling at **28**.32
- , worship at **16**.13-24
Sūnṛtā **2**.7-8 .9
suns, seven **232**.14-23
sun temple, merit of death at **28**.62cd-64ab
Suparṇa **3**.97cd-98; **159**.17-21; **166**.11cd-13; **207**.13-24
Suparṇā **100**.4cd-6
- [river] **100**.1-3
Suparṇāsaṃgamā, place of pilgrimage **100**.1-3
Supārśva **18**.21-23ab
Supārśvaka **16**.56cd-58ab
superhuman beings **54**.16-17; **65**.31-34; **105**.8cd-11ab; **164**.3-6; **239**.58-61
superiority of action **88**.10-15; **145**.8-11ab
- of Agni **126**.4-8
- of Brahmapurāṇa **246**.20
- of conduct **221**.6-7
- of Daṇḍaka-forest **88**.16-19; **129**.49-64
- of devotion to Kṛṣṇa **49**.70
- of *dharma* **170**.77-80ef .84-88
- of fire **126**.16cd-19ab
- of Gaṅgā **75**.35-45
- of Gautamī **77**.9cd-13; **88**.16-19; **129**.49-64; **175**.3-9ef .81-85
- of Kaśyapa as teacher **83**.13-16
- of Kṛṣṇa **207**.1-2; **229**.8-13
- of Lakṣmī **137**.8-14
- of ocean **62**.16cd-22ab
- of Poverty **137**.15-24
- of Puruṣottamakṣetra **69**.10-11; **70**.1-3ab
- of Pūrṇatīrtha **122**.105
- of Śiva **153**.12

- of Sāṃkhya **240**.96-97 .98-103 .105
- of the immaterial **130**.7-14
- of Utkala **42**.42cd-46ab
- of Viṣṇu **149**.13-16ab .16cd-19; **226**.11-12
- of waters **126**.9-11 .19cd-22 .32cd-35

superiority see also *comparison, hierarchy*
- see also *greatness*

superiors, punishment for eating before **22**.15cd-16a

supernatural beings **3**.1; **18**.52-55; **21**.15-27
- beings, classes of **3**.3-7ab
- knowledge of sages **210**.6-10
- power(s) **140**.3cd-5ab
- power(s) of Yoga **176**.33-34; **205**.15-22; **206**.5-9

support by adulterine, punishment for **22**.21-22
- , earth as **126**.19cd-22
- of beings, rain as **24**.19-25
- of earth, Śeṣa as **21**.15-27
- of gods, sacrifice as **24**.19-25

supporter of all, Nārāyaṇa as **24**.19-25
- of all, Viṣṇu as **18**.59
- , Viṣṇu as **179**.38-43ab

supporter see also *trimūrti-functions*

Suprabha **20**.22-23 .29-30
- , place of pilgrimage **25**.17

Suprabhā **127**.2-4ab

Suprayogā **27**.35-36ab

supremacy of Hiraṇyakaśipu **213**.53-57 .66-71

Supreme Self [*paramātman*], Viṣṇu as the **233**.38cd-40ab

Śūra **13**.199cd-202; **14**.14ab; **226**.30-41

Sura, place of pilgrimage **105**.22-26ab

Surabhi **3**.46cd-49 .51-52 .104-105; **72**.9cd-10ab; **87**.17-20; **91**.2cd-6ab; **109**.13-20

Suramā **19**.11-12ab

Suras, twelve **3**.53-58

Surasa **27**.20cd-24ab

Surasā **3**.51-52 .96cd-97ab; **13**.5-8; **19**.11-12ab

Śūrasena **13**.199cd-202; **111**.2-6 .35-39ab .48-51

Suratha **13**.109 .110-111

Surathā **27**.30-32

Suravallabha, Pravarāsaṃgama named **106**.54cd-56

Sureṇu **6**.1cd-2

Sureśvarī **6**.1cd-2

Śūrpārakas **27**.58cd

surrogate mother, curse by **6**.20cd-23; **89**.13-17ab
- mother of Brahmin, Rākṣasī as **167**.8-14 .15-17
- of wife, shadow as **89**.6-9ab

surviving ancestors, prescription(s) concerning **220**.148

Sūrya **3**.64cd-70ab; **18**.52-55; **31**.14cd-16; **34**.42-45ab; **110**.137-142; **113**.18-21; **166**.8cd-11ab .11cd-13; **221**.89-94
- , advice by **131**.31-39ab
- as royal power **168**.10-12
- , hymn by Madhucchandas to **138**.33-34
- to Madhucchandas, boon by **138**.35-38
- , Viṣṇu worshipped as **20**.72cd-73ab

Sūrya see also *sun*

Sūryāpīḍa **13**.123-124

Sūryaprabha, place of pilgrimage **25**.14 .19 .60

Sūryatīrtha, place of pilgrimage **25**.38 .60

Susaṃyata, place of pilgrimage **25**.41

Suśānti **13**.93-96

Suṣeṇa **201**.1-2

Suśīlā, Nārada as **229**.43cd-55

Suṣmanta **13**.54-55

Śuṣmin [caste] **20**.38cd-40ab

Suṣumna **32**.32-34ab

Suśyāmā **107**.19-30

Sūta and Māgadha **4**.60-67

sūta, etymology of **4**.60

Sutala **21**.2-5ab

Sutanu **14**.36-38; **15**.58cd-59

Sutanū **15**.58cd-59

Sutapas **5**.22cd-24; **13**.27cd-29

Sutīras **27**.43-50

Sutīrtha, place of pilgrimage **25**.28

Sutīrthaka, place of pilgrimage **25**.39

Sutrāman, Indra **110**.104

Suvarṇa and Saṃkalpā **128**.62-63ab
- and Suvarṇā **128**.24-28
- and Suvarṇā, promiscuity of **128**.29-37
- married to Saṃkalpā **128**.24-28
- , place of pilgrimage **25**.47

Suvarṇā and Dharma **128**.62-63ab
- married to Dharma **128**.24-28
- , names of **128**.72cd-76
- , promiscuity of Suvarṇa and **128**.29-37
- , Śiva and **128**.63cd-70ab

- , Suvarṇa and **128**.24-28
Suvarṇodapāna, place of pilgrimage **25**.64
Suveśa **34**.60-72
Suvikālā **27**.38cd-39ab
Suvīra **13**.3-4 .25cd-27ab
Suvīras **13**.25cd-27ab
Suvrata **13**.22cd-23 .24-25ab
Suvratas **13**.203-204
Suyajña **15**.1-12ab
Suyāti **12**.1-2
Śvabhojana **22**.2-6 .27
Svadhā **182**.7-8; **219**.6-12 .25-29 .91cd-98ab .98cd-107ab
Svāgatāsaṃgama, place of pilgrimage **105**.22-26ab
Svāhā **182**.7-8
- , Agni and **128**.24-28
- as daughter of Dakṣa **128**.3-6
Svāhi **15**.1-12ab
Svairatha **20**.36-38ab
Śvajit **13**.91
Śvakuṇḍa, place of pilgrimage **25**.74
Svamiśra **213**.81-104
Svana **213**.81-104
Śvapāka **225**.17-23ab; **228**.40-43
Svapārśvaka **14**.12-13
Śvaphalka **14**.3cd .4-7 .8-10; **16**.50ab .50cd-54ab
Svarakalpa **3**.86cd-89ab
Svarbhānu **3**.74cd-78ab .80cd-83; **11**.1-2 .8-16; **13**.9-12ab
Svargadvāra **60**.19-21 .22-24; **70**.8cd-10
- , place of pilgrimage **25**.49 .53; **45**.77-89; **161**.72-78
Svargaratha **13**.37-39
Svarloka **23**.16-20
Svarlokadvārakatīrtha, place of pilgrimage **25**.38
Svārociṣa, Manu **5**.4
Svārociṣa-era **3**.107ab; **5**.11cd-15
Śvasana **28**.27
Svasṛma **3**.74cd-78ab
svastikas, garland of **21**.15-27
Svastyātreyas **13**.12cd-14ab
Svātī **220**.33cd-42
Svayaṃbhoja **16**.4-6
Svayaṃbhu **110**.107-111; **241**.12-16ab
Svayaṃbhū **1**.37cd-38ab; **3**.2; **34**.100-101
Svāyaṃbhuva, Manu **2**.1-4; **4**.96; **5**.4 .8-11ab
Svāyambhuva-era **5**.8-11ab
Svayaṃvaṭa, place of pilgrimage **25**.33
Śveta **18**.18-20; **20**.22-23 .29-30
- and Kapālagautama **59**.6-21
- , boon by Śiva to **59**.6-21
- , boon by Viṣṇu to **59**.73-77
- [Brahmin] **94**.2-14
- [mountain] **18**.16-17
- [palace of Viṣṇu] **45**.71-73
- to Viṣṇu, hymn by **59**.34-72
Śvetadvīpa **59**.3; **61**.47-50
Śvetagaṅgā **59**.3
- , place of pilgrimage **59**.81-91
Śvetakarṇa **13**.126-127ab
Śvetamādhava **59**.3; **70**.8cd-10
- , statue of **59**.4-5
Śvetamādhava-Māhātmya **45**.77-89; **59**
Śveta-mountain **163**.52-53; **164**.3-6
Śvetatīrtha, place of pilgrimage **94**.1 .48cd-50ab
Śvetatīrthahrada, place of pilgrimage **25**.64
swallowing of discus by Śiva **109**.28-29
- of nectar of immortality by Goddess **106**.46cd
- of plants by earth **141**.10-13
- of semen, punishment for **22**.23cd-24ab
sweat, birth from **178**.99-104
- of Goddess, useful things originated from **129**.75-78
- of Śiva **39**.74-81
- of Śiva, Mothers originated from **112**.11 -19
sweets, kinds of **220**.154-167
- , punishment for selling of **22**.11
swinging festival **63**.18
Śyāla **196**.1-4
Śyāma **14**.14cd-20ab .33-34ab; **20**.62-63
Śyāmakūpa, place of pilgrimage **25**.64
Syamantaka, jewel named **16**.12-45ab; **17**
Syamantapañcakatīrtha, place of pilgrimage **25**.35
Śyenatīrtha, place of pilgrimage **93**.27
Śyenī **3**.92cd-93ab .93cd-95ab
syllable, sacred **241**.16cd-19ab
syllables, prayer-formula of eight **60**.22-24; **61**.1-3 .7-12 .20-22
- , prayer-formula of twelve **57**.29; **59**.26-33; **61**.20-22
symptoms of anxiety **48**.4-11
Tāḍakā **3**.86cd-89ab
tail of a cow, waving the **184**.7-13

Tailapāka **215**.114cd-115ab
Taittirīyasaṃhitā **129**.49-64; **170**.64-68
Takṣa as lord of serpents **4**.2-9
Takṣaka **3**.97cd-98
Tāla **214**.14-17
Tālajaṅgha **13**.199cd-202
Tālajaṅghas **8**.29-30 .31-32 .35-37; **13**.199cd -202 .203-204
Tālakuṭas **27**.58cd
Talātala **21**.2-5ab
Tamas **22**.2-6
- [Asura] **122**.8-20
Tāmasa, Manu **5**.4
Tāmasa-era **5**.20-24ab
Tamasodbheda, place of pilgrimage **25**.32
Tāmisra **123**.109cd-115; **215**.100cd-101
Tamisrahan **31**.31-33ab
Tāmrā **3**.51-52 .90cd-92ab .92cd-93ab
Tāmraliptakas **27**.51cd-53
Tāmraparṇa **19**.6cd-7ab
Tāmraparṇī **19**.13cd; **27**.36cd-37ab
Tāmravarṇa **27**.14-16
Taṃsu **13**.53 .54-55
Tāna **22**.2-6
Taṅgaṇas **220**.8-10ab
Tantras **44**.10-12
Tantrija **14**.32ab
Tantripāla **14**.32ab
Tanūrja **5**.17d-19ab
Tanvin **5**.22cd-24
Tapana **31**.31-33ab
Tāpana **31**.31-33ab
Tapastīrtha, place of pilgrimage **126**.1-2 .37-39
Tapasvin **2**.17-20ab
Tapasya **5**.22cd-24
Tapatī **110**.202-210
Tāpī **19**.11-12ab; **27**.33-34; **70**.33-35ab; **89**.37-40ab .43-46ab; **161**.21-23ef
- , place of pilgrimage **64**.11-14
Tapobhūta **5**.22cd-24
Tapoloka **23**.12-15 .16-20
Taporati **5**.22cd-24
Tapovana as place of pilgrimage **128**.83-84
- , place of pilgrimage **128**.1-2 .72cd-76
Taptakuḍya **22**.2-6
Taptakumbha **22**.2-6 .10
Taptaloha **22**.11
Tāra abducted by Candramas **152**
Tārā **9**.24-25 .28-30
- abducted by Soma **9**.17-20
- [wife of Bṛhaspati] **152**.2-4
Tāraka **3**.74cd-78ab; **71**.4-6 .13-15; **81**.2-3; **128**.7-15
- , boon by Brahman to **71**.4-6
- , Skanda as conqueror of **82**.9-10
Tārakāmaya-battle **9**.23; **179**.22cd-26
Tārakāyaṇas **10**.61-62
Tārkṣya **109**.42
- as father of Aruṇa and Garuḍa **166**.2-4ab
tastes, six **20**.94cd-95ab; **61**.38
Tāṭakā [Rākṣasī] **123**.97-105ab
Tathās **5**.22ab
Tattvadarśin **5**.27-28
Tauṇḍikeras **13**.203-204
taxes, delivery of **182**.19-26; **184**.1-6
- , oppression by **231**.42-43 .60-67
teacher, Agastya as **158**.16-21
- and pupil **121**.16-18
- , choice of **107**.12-16
- , disrespect against **170**.44-46
- , gift to **51**.48-53; **67**.39cd-45 .46-48; **194**.23-31
- , honouring of **216**.3-4; **221**.31 .32; **235**.4-5
- , importance of **158**.22-27ef
- , maxim about **107**.12-16
- , Nārāyaṇa as **181**.7-14
- of Āpastamba, Agastya as **130**
- of Candramas, Bṛhaspati as **152**.2-4
- of Daityas, Kavi [Śukra] as **95**.28cd-30
- of Duryodhana, Baladeva as **17**.28
- of Garga, Śeṣa as **21**.15-27
- of gods, Devāpi as **13**.117ab
- of Janaka and Yājñavalkya, Varuṇa as **88**
- of Rāma and Lakṣmaṇa, Viśvāmitra as **123**.97-105ab
- of Śukra, Aṅgiras as **95**.2-6
- of Yoga, Dattātreya as **180**.24cd-38
- , praise of **1**.21-29
- , prescription(s) concerning honouring of **221**.38
- , punishment for annoying of **217**.51-52
- , punishment for disrespect against **22**.12cd-13
- , punishment for killing of **22**.7-8
- , punishment for sin against **217**.43-44
- , qualification(s) of **107**.17-18; **223**.58cd-60ab
- , reproach of **95**.7-11
- , respect for **222**.22-27

– , reward for **121**.16–18
– , sun as **30**.21–22; **159**.17–21
– , superiority of Kaśyapa as **83**.13–16
teacher see also *education, preceptor*
teacher's wife, expiation for sexual intercourse with **81**.16–22ab
– wife, Indra as offender against **96**.8–10
– wife, punishment for sexual intercourse with **22**.10
– wife, punishment for transgression against **217**.45–47
teaching by sons, punishment for **22**.27
– , prescription(s) concerning **221**.46cd
– , restrictions on **30**.87–88; **49**.64–66; **62**.16ab; **175**.86–90; **221**.170a–f; **245**.31–41 .53; **246**.39
– , secret **30**.57 .85–86 .87–88; **33**.33; **40**.135; **56**.10–11; **152**.31–32; **161**.4cd–6ab; **175**.14ab .78; **237**.33–40; **238**.35cd–36ab
– , tradition of **245**.44–47
teak tree as emblem **20**.64
tearing out of eyes **170**.49–50ef
– out of eyes of Bhaga **109**.21–26ab
tears of joy, rivers originating from **128**.72cd–76
teeth, knocking out of **190**.26–28
– of Pūṣan broken by Śiva **109**.21–26ab
– of Rukmin, breaking of **201**.23–26
– , prescr. conc, cleaning of **221**.21 .48ab–49ab
– , prohibition of gnashing of **221**.70
telling of lies, maxim about **228**.51
temple, construction of **43**.10–13; **47**.7–9; **56**.61–66ab .66cd–73; **59**.26–33
– , description of **68**.36–42
– of Śiva **41**.60cd–71
– of Śiva and Viṣṇu **122**.3–7
– of Somanātha at Prabhāsa **110**.202–210
– , worship in **228**.40–43
ten arms of Viṣṇu **226**.11–12
– directions **1**.39cd–42; **9**.2–5
– horse-sacrifices **213**.142–144
– millions, multiplication by **148**.18cd–20
– months, battle of **13**.148–150ab
– nights, sojourn for **108**.18–20ab
– senses and organs of action **241**.26–27
terrible lord, Śiva as **173**.29cd–33ab
– sacrifice of Viśvarūpa **173**.26–28 .34cd–35ef
– shape of Narasiṃha **149**.4cd–9ab
– shape of Śiva **173**.36
test of faithfulness of wife **138**.14–19
testimony, curse because of wrong **146**.15–18
texts, classes of **44**.10–12
– , recitation of **43**.85cd–88; **46**.11–12; **60**.49–53; **219**.65cd–71ab; **220**.212
theft of cows **131**.4cd–6ab
– of gold, punishment for **22**.9
– of image **176**.21–25
– of sacrifice **79**.7cd–19
– of sacrificial animal **78**.12–24
– of Soma **105**.3
– of Veda(s) **60**.1–6
– , punishment for **22**.14ab; **214**.88cd–96 .120–128; **215**.72–77 .102–103 .123cd–124ab .125cd–126ab .126cd–127ab .130cd–136ab; **217**.62–65 .87–99
theory and practice **239**.7–9
Thieme, P. **213**.43
thigh, churning of **4**.42–47; **141**.6–9
things, prescr. conc, broken **221**.31
third eye of Śiva, fire from **110**.115–120
– eye of Śiva, invisibility of **110**.112–114
– eye of Śiva, Manyu originated from **162**.20–27ab
– eye of Śiva, origin of **123**.195–206
– eye of Śiva, son born from **153**.8–11
– stage of life **104**.10–14ab
– stage of life, duties of **222**.39–44
third see also *three*
thirst, affliction by hunger and **52**.11–15ab
– caused by ignorance **139**.7cd–11
– , freedom from hunger and **7**.37a–d
– , homage to **139**.7cd–11
– of Pailūṣa **139**.7cd–11
thirteen gods **162**.10cd–12
thirty-six parts of Śiva **123**.191–194
thirty-three gods **3**.62–64ab
thought, Śiva as existence and **153**.1–2ab
thoughts, creation from **45**.37–41
– , effect(s) of **215**.119cd–120ab .130cd–136ab; **217**.45–47; **224**.28–29; **225**.50
– , fire produced from **34**.20ef–25
– of Kṛṣṇa, miracle(s) worked by **184**.42cd–52ab
– , prescr. conc. **224**.28–38
– , rebirth determined by **34**.49–50
thoughts see also *remembering*
thousand and eight names **39**.96–97; **40**.2–100
– arms of Arjuna Kārtavīrya **13**.160;

213.106-112
- arms of Bāṇa **205**.7-8; **206**.1-4
- arms of Viṣṇu **68**.44-53
- eyes of Indra **87**.66cd-69; **124**.39cd-47
- eyes of Viṣṇu **68**.44-53
- heads, Viṣṇu as Brahman with **179**.22cd-26
- names of Śiva **40**.2-100
- Yugas **3**.62-64ab; **5**.53-54ab .58cd-60
thousandfold appearance of Viṣṇu **181**.21-25
thread, initiation with sacred **107**.2-11; **111**.7-8
- , sacred **61**.33; **220**.69cd-70
threat of curse against gods **127**.29-34
- of curse against mother **9**.28-30
- of curse against priests **127**.23-28
- of hell for unbelievers **49**.50cd-54ab
- of reducing someone to ashes **87**.52cd-54; **96**.8-10 .11-17; **140**.12-13
- of submersion of earth **83**.23-29
- of suicide **107**.31-34; **111**.9-16; **127**.9cd-15; **185**.18-27
- of voluntary death **154**.21cd-26
three boons granted to Kaikeyī **123**.23-33ab
- castes, sons belonging to **11**.60cd-61ab; **13**.63b-64ab
- causes [*kāraṇa*] **173**.9-25
- cities destroyed by Śiva **114**.6-8
- colours of Viṣṇu **161**.54-58
- daughters of Himavat **34**.81
- divisions of time **161**.35cd-39ab
- eyes of Śiva **110**.183-187
- forms of Gaṅgā **76**.8-10
- forms of *puruṣa* **130**.7-14
- forms of *puruṣa*s [souls?] **175**.14cd-16
- goals of life **34**.29cd-32; **104**.10-14ab; **138**.10-13; **158**.30-35ab; **170**.8ef-13; **217**.4-11; **221**.10; **223**.41-52ab; **242**.25-26ab
- goals of life, origin of **129**.70-71
- gods [Sūrya, Viṣṇu, Śiva] at place of pilgrimage **166**.11cd-13
- heads of Ananta **226**.62-65ab
- heads of fever **206**.14-19
- impulses of action **237**.65
- kinds of actions **125**.44-49; **157**.13cd-14; **164**.17-28
- kinds of gods **175**.14cd-16
- kinds of suffering **100**.19-21
- obligations **99**.2-7ab .12a-f; **104**.7cd-9
- Qualities **100**.19-21; **130**.7-14; **173**.9-25; **175**.14cd-16; **241**.37-44
- Qualities as ropes in sacrifice **161**.35cd-39ab
- qualities of actions **173**.9-25
- sacrificial fires **161**.54-58
- shapes of Viṣṇu **161**.68-71
- steps of Viṣṇu **73** .41-43cd .48-51; **179**.16cd-18ab; **213**.81-104
- Vedas **109**.13-20; **131**.39cd-51; **213**.155; **233**.40cd-43ab
- Vedas, origin of **1**.48cd-50ab
- Vedas, sun as **32**.12-16
- virgins, asceticism of **34**.87-89
- worlds **6**.6; **23**.16-20; **100**.19-21
- worlds as sacrificial gift **9**.13-16
- worlds burnt by Rudra **232**.24-27
- worlds, gods as lords of **32**.7-8
- worlds, Viṣṇu identical with **122**.68-73
- years, drought of **14**.4-7
three see also *third, triad*
threefold Brahmin-murder **123**.147-157 .165-169
- knowledge concerning livelihood **187**.42-54
- transgression **8**.16-18
three steps see also *Trivikrama*
thumbs of Brahman, birth from **2**.51-53
thunder, origin of **1**.48cd-50ab
thunderbolt as stake at game of dice **171**.10-13
- caught by Kṛṣṇa **203**.45-62
thunderbolt see also *vajra*
tide caused by moon **20**.91cd-94ab
tiger as lord of wild animals **4**.2-9
Tilapākā **215**.113cd-114ab
Tiliri **15**.46cd-48
Tilottamā **32**.99cd-100; **41**.30-34ab; **68**.60-67; **147**.9cd-13; **178**.19-24; **212**.72-85
tilted position of Hastināpura **208**.38
time and place, *dharma* in **175**.14-32ab
- as sacrificial post **161**.35cd-39ab .65cd-67
- , creation of **1**.39cd-42
- , divisions of **31**.7-10; **65**.39; **179**.29-37; **230**.4-7; **232**.6-12; **241**.12-16ab
- , effect(s) of **212**.55-58 .64-65
- , maxim about **236**.26
- , space and **23**.36-37
- , sun as origin of **31**.7-10
- , three divisions of **161**.35cd-39ab

- , *trimūrti*-functions of **33**.9-13ab
- , unawareness of passing of **7**.30-34; **21**.6cd-13ab; **178**.65-69 .80-89
- , Viṣṇu identical with **55**.32ab
time see also *date(s), Kāla*
Tīrthabīja, place of pilgrimage **25**.27
Tīrthavajra, place of pilgrimage **25**.27
Tiśya [caste] **20**.53cd-54ab
Titikṣu **13**.15cd-20ab .27cd-29
- , descendants of **13**.27cd-49
Tittiri **15**.46cd-48
Tomaras **27**.43-50 .62cd-64ab
tonsure-ceremony **111**.7-8
tormenting a Brahmin, punishment for **215**.91cd-92ab
torments in hell **123**.109cd-115; **234**.44-49
- in hell, list of **215**.84cd-136ab
- of the deceased **214**.52-54 .70-88ab .97-99; **215**.4-23 .39-44 .70-71 .81-83ab
torments see also *punishment*
tortoise as base for steps of Viṣṇu **73**.48-51
- in simile **232**.14-23; **237**.53
- , Viṣṇu as **18**.57-58; **191**.4-12
Tośalaka defeated by Kṛṣṇa **193**.65cd-67ab
Toṣalas **27**.59cd-62ab
touching, conception by **202**.23-29
- of Aśvattha-tree **118**.24cd-30
- of bones, pollution by **221**.136cd-137ab
- of water **15**.35-41ab; **16**.13-24
- of water, purification by **221**.161-169ab
- , pollution by **221**.143cd-146ab
Toyā **20**.28; **27**.33-34
tradition, conformity to **220**.153
- of Āyurveda **11**.36-38
- of teaching **245**.44-47
traditional verse(s), quotation of **2**.10-13; **11**.51-53; **12**.40-46; **13**.139-140 .170-171; **15**.41cd-45ab .49-50ab; **220**.112cd-116ab
traditions, conflict of **2**.51-53; **3**.7cd-9
Traipuras **27**.59cd-62ab
Traiśaṅkava **8**.24-28
Traiśānu **13**.142-146
transcendence of sun **33**.16-21
- of Viṣṇu **23**.41-43; **178**.117; **192**.48-58; **202**.23-29
transcendence see also *highest absolute, brahman*
transfer of asceticism **35**.46-51 .60-63; **100**.4cd-6; **118**.15-18
- of bad actions **222**.36
- of life **138**.22-27
- of magic power(s) **200**.11-16
- of merit **35**.46-51; **222**.36; **228**.62-73 .76-85 .86-91ab
- of old age **146**.28-31
- of power **110**.35-39ab
- of sin **123**.158-164; **163**.17-22
transgression against teacher's wife, punishment for **217**.45-47
- of caste, punishment for **22**.30
- of stage of life, punishment for **22**.26 .30
- of vedic preceptions **4**.28-34
- , threefold **8**.16-18
transgression see also *breach, sin, violation*
transitoriness, maxim about **110**.61-66; **212**.89-90
- of sacrifice **113**.9
transmission of Purāṇa **1**.30
transmission see also *teaching*
Trasadasyu **7**.95cd-97
Trayyāruṇa **7**.95cd-97 .100-102ab
treacherous Brahmin **170**.14-17ab
treatment of cows, prescription(s) concerning **221**.102
- of helpless persons, prescr. conc. **221**.44
tree and householder in simile **164**.9cd-13
- as emblem **18**.23cd-24ab
- , circumambulation of **57**.12-14
- in simile **23**.32cd-35 .36-37; **80**.18-21
- , punishment for hurting of **215**.124cd-125ab
trees, deities hiding in **103**.2-6
- , description of **42**.20-23
- , fig-tree as lord of **4**.2-9
- , list of **1**.3-9; **26**.3-5; **28**.11-18; **42**.15-19; **43**.45-55; **44**.55-63; **45**.8-12; **51**.33-36; **68**.6-11; **178**.32-37
- , obstruction of earth by **2**.34-46
- , punishment for felling of **22**.24cd
Tretā-Yuga **19**.20; **175**.17-24 .29-32ab
triad of gods **71**.1; **178**.43-53
- of gods at place of pilgrimage **174**.19-25ab
- of gods born as sons of Atri **144**.2-4
- of gods, energy of **131**.39cd-51
- of gods, Gaṅgā and the **73**.68-69ab; **175**.1-2ef
- of gods, Gautamī and the **175**.3-9ef
- of gods, sun identical with **168**.10-12
triad of gods see also *Brahman, Viṣṇu, Śiva trimūrti*

triads, list of **179**.29-37
trident-bearer, Śiva as **112**.2-3
Tridhanavarjitas **13**.12cd-14ab
Tridhanvan **7**.95cd-97
Tridhāraka, place of pilgrimage **25**.20
Tridivā **27**.30-32 .37cd-38ab
Trikūṭa [mountain] **18**.32-36ab
- [mountain] belonging to Rākṣasas **160**.10-12
Trilocana **79**.3-5ab
Trilokeśa **31**.31-33ab
trimūrti see also *triad of gods*, Brahman, Viṣṇu, Śiva
trimūrti-functions of Hari **1**.1-2
- of Nārāyaṇa **240**.112
- of Śiva **128**.44-45; **129**.68-69; **130**.17-21
- of sun **138**.33-34
- of time **33**.9-13ab
- of Viṣṇu **56**.13-15; **73**.9-17; **167**.30; **179**.65-72ab; **181**.21-25; **185**.30-33; **193**.80-87; **202**.23-29; **203**.6-19 .70-73; **212**.63 .66-70; **226**.15-17
Tripura **70**.35cd-37ab; **206**.39-44
Tripuruṣa, place of pilgrimage **25**.82
Triśaṅku **8**.20-21
triśaṅku, etymology of **8**.19
Triśṛṅga **18**.46cd-50
Trisrotā, place of pilgrimage **64**.11-14
Triṣṭubh-Jagatī-metre **34**.100-101; **110**.5-70; **213**.27; **219**.31-35; **245**.31-41
Triṣṭubh-metre **33**.22-23; **107**.41; **110**.21-70 .100-106; **124**.3cd-6; **125**.23-24ef; **128**.29-37; **129**.30-37; **140**.21ef-25; **144**.17-19; **150**.15-20; **157**.15-18cd; **229**.37-88
- , irregular **125**.23-24ef
Triśūladhāra, place of pilgrimage **25**.47
Trivikrama **60**.39-45; **122**.68-73; **129**.1-2 .101-124
Trivikrama see also *three steps*
Triviṣṭapa, place of pilgrimage **25**.42
Triviṣṭapa-heaven **11**.21cd-24ab; **81**.2-3; **87**.34cd-35; **110**.137-142; **116**.3cd-5ab; **123**.23-33ab .128cd-139 .165-169; **157**.8-9
trust, punishment for embezzlement of **215**.86cd-88ab
trustful persons, maxim about **167**.22-25
trustfulness, oath as guarantee for **167**.8-14
truth and untruth **4**.91-93; **20**.83cd
- , world based on **228**.52-55
truthfulness as distinction of Brahmins **228**.56-59
- , Manu as authority on **228**.47-49
- of Brahman **135**.5cd-10ab
- of Brahmins and Kṣatriyas, maxim about **111**.39cd-47
- of Dilīpa **8**.73cd-75ab
truth-spell **178**.43-53 .117; **228**.22-38 .62-73
- used as means of revivification **138**.22-27
Tryambaka **3**.46cd-49; **34**.9-12ab .12cd-19 .20ef-25 .49-50; **77**.1; **79**.5cd-6ab
- , place of pilgrimage **79**.5cd-6ab
- , Śiva as **110**.219ef-224
Tumbaru **174**.2-5ab
Tumbūras **27**.59cd-62ab
Tumburu **32**.97cd-99ab; **36**.63cd-70; **174**.2-5ab
Tunduras **4**.42-47
Tuṅgabhadrā **27**.35-36ab; **70**.33-35ab; **77**.2-9ab
- , place of pilgrimage **64**.11-14
Tuṅgakūṭa, place of pilgrimage **25**.14
Tuṅgaṇas **27**.62cd-64ab
Tuṅganas **27**.62cd-64ab
Tuṅgaprastha **27**.20cd-24ab
Turvasu **12**.5cd-6ab .18-21; **13**.142-146; **146**.2-8ab .28-31
- , descendants of **13**.142-148ab
Tuṣamārgas **27**.62cd-64ab
Tuṣāras **4**.42-47; **27**.43-50
Tuṣitas **3**.53-58; **5**.13ab
tusks, elephants with four **202**.30-35
Tuṣṭi **109**.13-20
Tvaṣṭṛ **3**.46cd-49 .53-58; **6**.1cd-2 .15-17 .34cd-40 .50cd-51ab; **30**.23-26 .28-39; **31**.17-18 .19-21 .22-26; **32**.49-50; **89**.9cd-12 .37-40ab .40cd-41 .42; **110**.51-56ab .143-146ab; **140**.12-13 .31-34; **160**.6cd-9; **168**.22-24
- , advice by **6**.41-43; **168**.18cd-21
- , artificial Śacī fabricated by **140**.14-18ab
- , city of Indra duplicated by **140**.14-18ab
- , demons killed by **168**.22-24
- , place of pilgrimage sacred to **168**.1
- , Viśvakarman **32**.80-81; **72**.9ab; **109**.13-20
Tvaṣṭṛtīrtha, place of pilgrimage **168**.22-24
twelve Ādityas **3**.53-58; **30**.23-26; **31**.17-18
- days, sacrifice of **228**.76-85
- holy rivers **70**.22cd-23
- names of sun **31**.14cd-16

- Suras **3**.53-58
- syllables, prayer-formula of **57**.29; **59**.26-33; **61**.20-22
- years, drought of **7**.104cd-105ab; **8**.10cd
- years, rain of **53**.6-10ab
- years, son obtained after **14**.48-50ab
- years, vow of **8**.3-4 .13-15b:; **124**.12-16
twelve-fold shape of sun **30**.23-44
twenty-fifth and twenty-sixth principle **245**.17-23ab
twenty-four principles **241**.28
- years, drought of **74**.22cd-24ab
twenty-sixth principle **245**.8-10ab
- principle, liberation of **245**.10cd-14ab
- principle, twenty-fifth and **245**.17-23ab
twentysixth principle **245**.14cd-16
twice-born without ceremonies compared to Śūdras **111**.7-8
- without ceremonies, maxim about **111**.7-8
twins, Ānarta and Sukanyā as **7**.27cd-28ab
- born from semen of Śiva **128**.24-28
- , Kṛpa and Kṛpī as **13**.97
- , Yama and Yamunā as **6**.7-8
two Arjuna-trees felled by Kṛṣṇa **184**.31-42ab; **190**.1-5
- hairs of Viṣṇu, incarnation of **181**.26-31
- kinds of actions **173**.9-25; **233**.40cd-43ab
- kinds of beings **229**.15-18
- kinds of *dharma* **237**.6
- levels of *brahman* **234**.61cd-63ab
- levels of knowledge **234**.61cd-63ab
- sexes, origin of **1**.51cd-52
Uccaiḥśravas **65**.40-41; **69**.12-43
- as lord of horses **4**.2-9
- [elephant of Indra] **140**.14-18ab
Udayagiri **20**.62-63
Udbhida **20**.36-38ab
Uddālaka [desert] **7**.58cd-71ab
Uddālakatīrtha, place of pilgrimage **25**.76
Uddharṣiṇī-metre **203**.70-73
Uddhava **14**.25cd
Udumbara-wood **221**.125cd-127ab
ugliness of Revatī **121**.2-5
ugly shape of Śiva **35**.4cd-10
Ugra **213**.81-104; **223**.23-27
Ugragandha **215**.128cd-129ab
Ugrasena **15**.55 .58cd-59 .60ab; **60**.22-24; **181**.7-14; **190**.10-19; **192**.5-10; **194**.10; **197**.6-7; **208**.8-18 .19-31; **210**.11-14 .52cd-58; **212**.1-4
- , consecration of **194**.9
- supported by Kṛṣṇa, kingship of **194**.11-12
Ugrasenā **14**.11; **16**.55cd-56ab
Ugravyagra **213**.81-104
Ujjayinī **44**.16-40
Ukya **8**.84cd-92
Ullayāṅgopacāra, place of pilgrimage **25**.34
Ulmaka **198**.18
Ulūka, battle between Anuhrāda and **125**.9-12
- , enmity between Anuhrāda and **125**.2cd-8
- , place of pilgrimage **125**.54-56
Ulūkas **3**.93cd-95ab
Ulūkī, boon by Yama to **125**.25-32
- to Yama, hymn by **125**.23-24ef
Umā **34**.39-41 .42-45ab; **39**.34-39; **41**.88-90; **59**.6-21; **71**.24-26; **108**.26-30; **110**.172-178; **111**.68cd-79; **181**.38-53
- and Gaṇeśa **175**.33cd-35 .36-41ef
- and Śiva **35**
- and Śiva worshipped by hunter **169**.16-22ab
- and the crocodile **35**.32-64
- as manifestation of Śiva **75**.21
- as mother of the world **75**.17
- as *prakṛti* **75**.14
- as Śakti of Śiva **75**.15
- as success of rites **75**.22
- , asceticism of **34**.93cd-99
- , birth of **34**.55-101
- , boon by Śiva to **35**.60-63
- , descent of Gaṅgā caused by **75**.20
- , dialogue between Śiva and **223**; **224**; **225**
- , entertainment of **38**.24-27
- , epithets of **71**.19-23
- , forest of **108**.26-30
- , hymn by Gautama to **75**.4-24
- , hymn by Indra to Śiva and **129**.68-81
- , jealousy of **74**.13-22ab
- , Kailāsa as abode of Śiva and **143**.7-11
- named Mother **108**.94-98
- on Kailāsa, Śiva and **110**.102-103
- , origin of **75**.14
- , Śiva and **75**.24; **143**.12-13; **144**.20-22
- , self-choice of **35**.11-14 .15-21; **36**
- , wedding of Śiva and **36**.54cd-70 .125-136
- , worship of **110**.56cd-60
- , worship of Śiva and **169**.16-22ab
Umā see also *Devī, Durgā, Gaurī, Goddess, Pārvatī*

Umā, etymology of **34**.85-86
Umāvana **108**.20cd-21 .23cd-24ef .31-36ab .36cd-47 .48-51ef .59-61ab .94-98
umbrella, hill serving as **188**.11-13 .14-16
- of Varuṇa **202**.3-12 .30-35
unarmed person, punishment for killing of **217**.100-104
unawareness of passing of time **7**.30-34; **21**.6cd-13ab; **178**.65-69 .80-89
unbelievers, exclusion of **49**.64-66; **62**.16ab; **68**.72; **221**.170a-f; **245**.53
- , origin of **229**.15-18
- , punishment of **225**.10-16
- shunned by gods **29**.15-17
- , threat of hell for **49**.50cd-54ab
unbelievers see also *fallen people, heretics, Mlecchas, outcastes*
unhappiness, righteousness as source of **170**.23-25
union of Viṣṇu and Śiva **135**.10cd-13cd
- with *brahman* **10**.38cd-41ab; **110**.47cd-50
- with Śiva **110**.166-167
- with Vāsudeva, liberation by **227**.48-49
unity and difference in simile **245**.23cd-24
- and plurality **30**.76-77; **243**.37-40
- of Śiva and Śakti **129**.81
- of Viṣṇu and Śiva **109**.52-54
unity see also *identity, oneness, union*
universal self, identity of individual and **236**.21-23 .24-25 .54-56ab; **237**.17-19 .32; **245**.27-30
unjustice as source of prosperity **170**.23-25
unjustified punishment **185**.44-49
unknowability of fate **119**.10
- of Śiva **40**.83; **127**.48-53; **129**.68-69
- of Viṣṇu **55**.32cd-33ab; **56**.45 .51-54; **191**.4-12; **192**.48-58
unknown shape of sun **174**.19-25ab
Unnata **20**.25-27
unrestricted movement everywhere **58**.12-18
untimely death **35**.64; **59**.6-21; **86**.3cd-7; **217**.80cd-86
untouchability caused by Brahmin-murder **123**.73cd-76
- due to disrespect against *dharma* **170**.44-46
- of Brahmin-murderer, prescription(s) concerning **123**.48cd-61ab
untouchability see also *impurity, pollution*
untouchables, worship permitted to **58**.59cd-64ab
untruth permitted, five occasions for **228**.50
- , punishment for speaking the **22**.7-8
- , truth and **4**.91-93; **20**.83cd
untruthfulness, prohibition of **221**.19
- , punishment for **214**.120-128; **215**.118cd-119ab .130cd-136ab
- , water-belly as punishment for **104**.39-43
unworthiness of devotee **49**.57cd-59ab; **55**.35c-f; **117**.7-11 .13; **191**.27-33
Upabāhyakā, Sṛñjayī **15**.32 .34
Upadānavī **3**.80cd-83; **13**.54-55
Upadeva **14**.11; **15**.56-58ab; **16**.55cd-56ab
Upadevī **14**.36-38; **15**.56-58ab
Upadīpti **3**.80cd-83
Upajāti-metre **19**.25-27; **35**.64; **36**.7-24ab .24cd-26 .71-79 .89-94 .95-105ab .105cd-116 .124; **38**.20 .40; **39**.33 .42 .43-45; **49**.67 .69 .70 .71; **72**.36; **74**.88; **75**.5 .6 .7 .11 .12 .14 .15 .16 .17 .18 .20 .21 .24; **78**.56-58; **80**.46-55; **97**.20-23 .29; **100**.19 -21; **103**.8; **108**.104 .105-106 .107-108; **109**.41-42; **110**.87-97ef .100-106 .155-156 .158-159 .164 .166-167 .225 .229; **112**.4-6; **113**.9 .16; **114**.6-18; **117**.7-17; **119**.9-12; **122**.43 .74-82; **123**.195-206; **124**.2cd-3ab .7-8; **125**.15; **126**.24-27; **129**.68-81; **130**.23-31; **138**.4-7; **140**.7-11 .12-13 .14-18ab .18cd-19ab .19cd-21cd; **143**.6 .7-11 .12-13 .14-16 .17; **150**.21-22; **157**.10-14 .18ef-21ab .21cd-25ab .25cd-27ab .27cd-28 .29 .30 .31; **167**.8-14 .30; **173**.37-39; **174**.1 .2-5ab .5cd-6ab .29-30; **175**.75; **177**.5 .24-25; **178**.114-116; **179**.27-28; **181**.21-25; **182**.16; **191**.27-33; **219**.116; **222**.55-56; **228**.50 .152; **229**.37 -88; **239**.58-61; **240**.105-112; **246**.6-12 .37-38
Upalāvatī **27**.36cd-37ab
Upamadgu **14**.8-10; **16**.50cd-54ab
Upamanyu [father of Devāpi] **127**.35-47
Upaniṣads **72**.11cd-14; **175**.10-13; **177**.22-23; **237**.41-42ab
Uparathyā **105**.22-26ab
Upekṣa **16**.50cd-54ab
Upendravajrā-metre **25**.3; **36**.71-79; **75**.13 .48; **110**.163; **140**.14-18ab; **213**.141; **231**.93; **237**.20
Ūrdhvabāhu **5**.24cd-25
Ureṇu **6**.1cd-2

urinating and defecating, prescr. conc. **221**.22 .26-30; **243**.49
- and defecating, prescription(s) concerning **221**.37
urine of cow **220**.200cd-203ab
Ūrja **5**.13cd-15ab .17d-19ab
Ūrjā **5**.17a-c; **219**.6-12 .18-24 .98cd-107ab
- as mother of Yoga **219**.91cd-98ab
Ūrjas **5**.17a-c
Ūrṇas **27**.62cd-64ab
Urvaśī **9**.33-34; **10**.4; **32**.99cd-100; **41**.30-34ab; **68**.60-67; **101**.2-9; **147**.9cd -13; **178**.19-24
- and Pramati **171**.18-19
- and the fool **228**.97-151
- as stake at game of dice **171**.6ef-9ef
- , origin of **228**.100cd-127ab
- , place of pilgrimage **25**.18
- , Purūravas and **10**.1-14; **151**
Urvaśītīrtha, place of pilgrimage **171**.1-2ab .47-49ef
Urvīsaṃkramaṇa, place of pilgrimage **25**.57
Uṣā **89**.2ef-3
- , Aniruddha and **206**.5-9
- as mare **89**.9cd-12
- as wife of sun **165**.2-4
- , boon by Pārvatī to **205**.11-14
- [daughter of Bāṇa] **205**.7-8 .11-22
Ūṣā **205**.7-8
Uṣadgu **15**.1-12ab
Uṣadratha **13**.27cd-29
Uśanas **2**.10-13; **9**.21 .24-25; **12**.4-5ab; **23**.6-10; **34**.91; **39**.7-17ab; **69**.12-43
Uṣaṅgu **226**.30-41
Uṣas **34**.42-45ab; **109**.13-20; **221**.89-94
- , Lakṣmī as **137**.30cd-39ab
Uṣat **15**.1-12ab
Uṣata **15**.1-12ab
useful things originated from sweat of Goddess **129**.75-78
Uśīnara **13**.15cd-20ab .20cd-22ab; **14**.39-41
Uśira-plants **230**.49-58
Uṣṇa **20**.47cd-49ab
usurpation of emblems of Viṣṇu **207**.4-7
- of the epithet Vāsudeva **207**.4-7
Utkala **7**.17-19ab; **47**.7-9
- and Kṛṣṇa **42**.35-36ab
- , description of **42**.13-49ab
- , merit of sojourn at **42**.42cd-46ab
- , superiority of **42**.42cd-46ab
Utkalā **7**.17-19ab
Utpalā **27**.30-32
Utpalāvartaka, place of pilgrimage **64**.3-8ab
Uttama, Manu **5**.4 .17d-19ab
Uttama-era **5**.16-19
Uttamārṇas **27**.59cd-62ab
Uttānapāda **2**.5 .7-8 .9
Uttaṅka **7**.58cd-71ab .71cd-73
- , boon by **7**.85-86
Uttara, place of pilgrimage **25**.68
Uttarā Aṣāḍhā **220**.33cd-42
Uttarāhasta **220**.48cd-49ab
Uttarakuru **18**.18-20 .38cd-44ab .45cd-46ab .57-58; **32**.56-58ab; **89**.9cd-12
Uttarakurus **6**.15-17
- , land of **10**.5-8
Uttarā-Phālgunī **220**.33cd-42
Uttarā-Prauṣṭhapadyā **220**.33cd-42
Vācaspati **71**.27-37; **106**.19-22; **122**.50-54ab; **148**.21-26
Vaḍavā **14**.36-38; **110**.5-9
- as Kṛtyā **110**.124-130
- [river] **110**.198cd-200cd; **116**.22cd-24ab
Vaḍavānala, place of pilgrimage **116**.1-2ab
Vaḍavāsaṃgama, place of pilgrimage **116**.24cd-25ab
Vadhnya **13**.97
Vadhnyaśva **13**.97
Vāgīśvara, Liṅga named **135**.25-27ab
- , Śiva as **135**.1-2ab
Vāgīśvarī **75**.19; **107**.35-40
Vāhīkas **27**.43-50
Vāhlikas **27**.43-50
Vahni **13**.142-146
Vahnijvala **22**.2-6 .25
Vahnikuṇḍa, place of pilgrimage **25**.17
Vaibhaṇḍaki **13**.43-44
Vaibhrāja **20**.6-7; **27**.20cd-24ab
- [forest] **18**.30
Vaidarbhas **27**.54-57
Vaidarbhī **15**.24-28
Vaidyuta **20**.22-23 .29-30; **27**.20cd-24ab
Vaijayanta **27**.20cd-24ab
Vaikaṅka **18**.32-36ab
Vaikarṇa **13**.45-48
Vaikuṇṭha as paradise of Viṣṇu **161**.61cd-62
- [Viṣṇu] **61**.14-16; **127**.48-53; **179**.65-72ab
Vainateya, fig-tree **57**.12-19
Vaiṇavīsaṃgama, place of pilgrimage **105**.22-26ab

Vairāja **2**.17-20ab
Vairāja-gods **23**.12-15
Vairaṇī 3.25-28
Vairin **5**.45cd-46
Vairiṇī **2**.16
Vaiśākha **31**.19-21; **63**.21; **220**.55
Vaiśākhī **14**.36-38
Vaiśikyas **27**.54-57
Vaiṣṇava, place of pilgrimage **100**.1-3
- place of pilgrimage **103**.9; **104**.1-2; **128**.70cd-72ab; **171**.47-49ef
Vaiṣṇava see also *devotee of Viṣṇu*
Vaiṣṇavas after death, destiny of **227**
- in heaven, characteristics of **68**.29-32
Vaiṣṇavī **77**.9cd-13; **78**.75cd-76
Vaiśravaṇa **4**.2-9; **39**.7-17ab; **56**.13-15
- as king of Laṅkā **97**.2-5ab
- [hermit] **123**.36cd-43
Vaiśravasa, place of pilgrimage **97**.32cd-33
Vaiśvāmitrī **173**.3-6ab
Vaiśvānara **3**.74cd-78ab .80cd-83
Vaiśya **40**.136-137; **86**.3cd-7
- as king **170**.84-88
- , bet between Brahmin and **170**.27-28
- clinging to righteousness **170**.32-36
- , friendship between Brahmin and **170**.2-5 .81-83
- , king and **170**.77-80ef
- , punishment for killing of **22**.10
- , rebirth as **229**.72-86ab
Vaiśyas **4**.115-121; **11**.33-34ab; **13**.63b-64ab .79; **27**.43-50; **220**.3-4
- , conduct of **223**.37-40
- , duties of **222**.11-12
- , Kṣatriyas turning into **7**.26ab
- , origin of **161**.43cd-50cd
- turning into Brahmins 7.42
Vaitaṇḍya **3**.37-38cd
Vaitaraṇa **16**.4-6
Vaitaraṇī **22**.2-6 .23ab; **27**.33-34; **214**.14-17; **240**.27-32
- , merit of bathing in **42**.4
- , place of pilgrimage **64**.11-14
Vaitasikārūpa, place of pilgrimage **25**.58
Vaivasvata **78**.3-8ab; **88**.2-3
- , Manu **4**.16-17; **5**.5ab .49-52 .63; **6**.7-8; 7.1-2 .3-5ab; **34**.26-29ab .45cd-48; **89**.5a-c .37-40ab, **108**.2-7
- , Yama **4**.2-9; **194**.23-31
Vaivasvata-era **3**.53-58 .107cd-109ab; **4**.91-93; **5**.33cd-38ab; **34**.39-41; **39**.1-2
- , asceticism practised in **5**.40-41
Vājapeya-sacrifice **40**.103-106
Vājasaneya-Brahmins **231**.4-41
Vājin **5**.45cd-46
Vajra **205**.1-6; **210**.52cd-58; **211**.1-2; **212**.5-6 .34
vajra see also *thunderbolt*
vajra made of foam **129**.4-8
Vajrakapāṭā **215**.115cd-116ab
Vajrakuṭhārā **215**.124cd-125ab
Vajranābha **3**.74cd-78ab; **8**.84cd-92
Vajratīrtha, place of pilgrimage **25**.21
Vajrāyudha, place of pilgrimage **25**.22
Vāk **105**.4-8ab; **163**.52-53
Vākrūra **12**.11-17
Vālakhilyas **30**.14-18; **32**.92cd-93ab; **100**.4cd-6 .14-18
- , origin of **72**.18-19
Vālakhilyatīrtha, place of pilgrimage **25**.82
Vālin **176**.37-51; **213**.136-140
Vallakas **27**.51cd-53
Vālmīki, hermitage of **154**.11cd-14ab
value of knowledge **237**.33-40; **245**.31-41
Vāluka, place of pilgrimage **25**.60
Vālukā **217**.80cd-86
Vāmadeva **104**.69-77; **107**.42-45; **123**.77-81; **141**.2-5; **174**.2-5ab
Vāmadevī **173**.3-6ab
Vāmakara, place of pilgrimage **25**.53
Vāmana **60**.39-45; **73**
- [demon] 3.74cd-78ab
- [king of snakes] **65**.40-41
- [mountain] **20**.49cd-51
- [Nāga] 3.99-101
Vāmana see also *dwarf*
Vāmanā **68**.60-67; **178**.19-24
Vāmanaka **20**.49cd-51
- , place of pilgrimage **25**.60
Vāmaṅkurakas **27**.51cd-53
Vaṃśagulma, place of pilgrimage **25**.77
Vaṃśakarā **27**.37cd-38ab
Vaṃśasthavila-metre **33**.48-49; **36**.71-79 .105cd-116; **40**.120; **75**.6 .48; **85**.8; **119**.9 -12 .12; **236**.69
Vaṃśya **3**.86cd-89ab
Vanacaṇḍikātīrtha, place of pilgrimage **25**.76
Vanaduha **13**.152-153ab
Vanāyu **10**.11-12
Vaneyu **13**.5-8

Vaṅga **13**.30-31
Vaṅgas **13**.36; **27**.51cd-53; **231**.68-71ab
Vāṇī, place of pilgrimage **148**.21-26
- [river], Speech as **135**.20-24
Vāṇitīrtha, place of pilgrimage **135**.1-2ab
Vañjarā [river] **159**.41cd-46ab
Vañjarāsaṃgama, place of pilgrimage **159**.1 .48cd-49ef
Vāñjulā **27**.37cd-38ab
Vapuṣmat **20**.22-23
Varā, place of pilgrimage **25**.59
Varāha **60**.39-45; **61**.14-16
- , merit of worship of **219**.107cd-109ab
Varāha see also *boar*
Vārāha **18**.57-58; **163**.26-31
- [demon] **213**.81-104
- , place of pilgrimage **25**.36
Vārāha-manifestation **213**.32-42
Varāhapurāṇa **131**.2cd-4ab; **228**.8-91ab
Vārāhatīrtha, merit obtained at **79**.21cd-22
- , place of pilgrimage **79**.6cd-7ab .7cd-19; **122**.48-49
Vārāhī, merit of worship of **42**.11
Vārāṇasa **13**.126-127ab
Vārāṇasī **11**.39-40 .41-43 .44-48 .54; **13**.64cd-67ab .72cd-75ab .126-127ab; **34**.60-72; **41**.93; **100**.31cd; **128**.83-84; **207**.3; **228**.97-100ab
- in simile **41**.11-12
- , Kuśatarpaṇa superior to **161**.72-78
- , liberation at **229**.64-67ab
Vāraṇāvat **17**.6-7
Varcas **3**.37-38cd
Varcasvin **3**.37-38cd
Vardhanakā **20**.66-67
Variṣṭha **213**.81-104
varṣa see *region*
Vārṣabha, place of pilgrimage **25**.80
Varṣaketu **13**.75cd-77
Vārṣika, place of pilgrimage **25**.28 .80
Varuṇa **3**.53-58 .107cd-109ab; **13**.189cd-197ab; **30**.23-26 .28-39; **31**.17-18 .19-21 .22-26; **33**.9-13ab; **51**.1-8; **61**.45cd-46; **69**.12-43; **81**.7cd-12; **88**.2-3 .8 .10-15 .16-19; **89**.37-40ab; **104**.14cd-22ab .22cd-37ab .78-81ab; **122**.68-73; **128**.29-37; **158**.22-27ef; **160**.6cd-9; **162**.20-27ab; **171**.40-43; **173**.29cd-33ab; **192**.48-58; **198**.1-3; **213**.53-57
- as father-in-law of Mahāśani **129**.20cd-29
- as lord of waters **4**.2-9
- as teacher of Janaka and Yājñavalkya **88**
- , asceticism practised by **30**.47cd-48
- , boon by Mitra and **7**.9-14ab
- , horses of **213**.114-122
- in simile **146**.2-8ab
- , Indra as servant of **129**.38-41
- , loop of **203**.45-62
- , Mahāśani as son-in-law of **129**.17-20ab
- , oblation to Mitra and **7**.3-5ab
- , Siddhi as wife of **239**.58-61
- , sons of **34**.45cd-48
- , umbrella of **202**.3-12 .30-35
Varuṇā **89**.1-2cd .43-46ab
Vāruṇa **220**.33cd-42
- , place of pilgrimage **100**.1-3; **104**.1-2
- [region] **19**.6cd-7ab; **27**.14-16
Vāruṇī **21**.15-27
- as liquor **198**.1-3
Varusthāna, place of pilgrimage **25**.38
Vasantatilakā-metre **175**.78; **178**.177; **193**.88-90; **219**.36; **246**.36
Vasātapta **22**.2-6
Vaśāti **7**.46cd-48ab
Vāsava **4**.2-9; **202**.13-15; **203**.45-62; **213**.53-57
Vāsava see also *Indra*
Vāsavīsaṃgama, place of pilgrimage **105**.22-26ab
Vasiṣṭha **1**.43-45ab; **5**.8-9ab .34-35; **8**.3-4 .5-8 .9 .11-12 .16-18; **34**.12cd-19 .42-45ab; **70**.37cd-38; **71**.41-42; **96**.20-22ab; **103**.2-6 .7 .10-12ab; **104**.69-77; **107**.42-45; **108**.2-7 .116-118; **109**.13-20; **123**.2-7ab .77-81; **145**.2cd-5ab; **154**.32-34; **168**.2-5; **174**.2-5ab; **245**.44-47
- , advice by **78**.3-8ab; **123**.77-81 .86cd-96; **151**.10-16; **168**.6-9
- and Viśvāmitra, enmity between **147**.5-7
- as authority on punishment **215**.78-80
- as family-priest of Purūravas **151**.7cd-9
- , Āpava **13**.189cd-197ab
- , cow of **8**.13-15b:
- , curse by **13**.189cd-197ab
- , dialogue between Karālajanaka and **241**; **243**; **244**; **245**
- , precept of **7**.21cd-22; **123**.97-105ab
- , preception of **7**.48cd-51ab; **8**.44-51
- , sons of **5**.16cd

Vāsiṣṭha, place of pilgrimage **103**.9; **151**.24cd-27ab
Vāsiṣṭhā **173**.3-6ab
Vāsiṣṭhakapilāhrada, place of pilgrimage **25**.82
Vasiṣṭhapada, place of pilgrimage **25**.49
Vasiṣṭhaputra **5**.11cd-12
Vāsiṣṭhas **5**.16cd
Vasiṣṭhāśrama, place of pilgrimage **25**.72 .73
Vāsiṣṭhatīrtha, place of pilgrimage **25**.27
Vastrāpada, place of pilgrimage **25**.32
Vasu **3**.29-30ab .30cd-33; **5**.9cd-10 .45cd-46; **9**.13-16; **12**.9-10 .11-17; **13**.109; **15**.46cd -48
Vasudeva **7**.30-34; **14**.14cd-20ab .28c-f .36-38 .39-41 .42ab; **15**.56-58ab; **16**.55cd-56ab; **38**.7-13; **176**.52-56; **179**.6-10ab .10cd-16ab; **181**.26-31; **183**.8-11; **190**.10-19; **192**.5-10 .67-68; **193**.24-31 .67cd-76ab .78cd-79; **194**.1-5; **196**.23-29; **210**.52cd-58; **212**.1-4; **226**.30-41
- , advice by **184**.1-6
- , descendants of **14**.36-57
- , imprisonment of Devakī and **181**.33-35
- to Kṛṣṇa, prayer by **182**.14-15
- , wives of **14**.36-38
Vāsudeva **12**.11-17; **17**.34; **22**.37-41; **61**.13 .39-40; **191**.26; **192**.48-58; **207**.25-27 .28-43; **212**.95; **216**.82-86; **226**.30-41; **227**.1-4; **229**.8-13; **233**.5-6
- , absorption in **58**.37-40
- and Śāśvatas **191**.13-17
- as authority on *dharma* **226**.50cd-51
- as *brahman* **211**.3-4 .11-12
- as form of Nārāyaṇa **180**.18cd-21ab
- as foundation for Yogins **180**.18cd-21ab
- as highest truth **44**.13
- as Jagannātha **45**.16cd-17ef
- as means of liberation, name of **22**.42-43
- as refuge **226**.48cd-50ab
- as Viṣṇu **226**.11-67
- , devotion to **229**.4-7
- , divinity of **234**.71-75
- , effect(s) of worship of **227**.50
- , four arms of **226**.30-41
- , genealogy of **226**.30-41
- , homage to **1**.1 2
- , iconographic attributes of **44**.14-15; **50**.4-6; **207**.13-24
- identical with gods **226**.45cd-48ab
- , image of **176**.21-25
- in dream, vision of **50**.4-6
- , liberation by union with **227**.48-49
- , Pauṇḍraka **207**.4-7
- , purpose of manifestations of **213**.21-24
- , recitation of stories on **67**.31cd-35ab
- , Śiva establishing devotion to **226**.59-61
- , Śiva existing in body of **226**.59-61
- , sages existing in body of **226**.59-61
- , songs on **67**.31cd-35ab
- , stone, statue of **176**.4-7
- , Viṣṇu meditating on himself as **233**.5-6
- , worship of **226**.7-9
- worshipped by Indra **176**.12-15ab
- worshipped by outcastes **227**.10-14
- worshipped by Rāma **176**.37-51
- worshipped by women **227**.10-14
- , yellow clothes of **176**.8-10
Vāsudeva, etymology of **234**.68cd-69ab .70c-f
- , explanation of **179**.10cd-16ab
Vāsudeva-Māhātmya **226**.11-67
Vāsuka, place of pilgrimage **42**.6-8
Vāsuki **3**.97cd-98; **69**.12-43; **106**.8-10ab
- as lord of Nāgas **4**.2-9
Vasuṃdharā **16**.54cd-55ab
Vasumedha **16**.45cd-48ab
Vasurodha **13**.51-52
Vasus **3**.30cd-33; **5**.36-37ab; **39**.7-17ab .22-27ab; **69**.12-43; **174**.7; **191**.4-12; **213**.66-71; **219**.60cd-65ab .98cd-107ab; **220**.118cd-120ab
- , Agni as lord of **4**.2-9
- , eight **3**.35cd-36
Vasutīrtha, place of pilgrimage **25**.28
Vaṭa **60**.16-18
- , place of pilgrimage **25**.54 .78
Vāta **14**.20cd-24ab
Vāta see also *Vāyu*
Vātādhvaga **27**.20cd-24ab
Vātaghnī **27**.28-29
Vātaṃdhaya **27**.20cd-24ab
Vaṭamūlaka, place of pilgrimage **25**.24
Vātapati **16**.45cd-48ab
Vātāpi **3**.86cd-89ab
Vātāpī **213**.81-104
Vaṭa-tree **18**.23cd-24ab; **103**.2-6
Vaṭavaṭa, place of pilgrimage **25**.33
Vaṭeśvara **60**.16-18
Vatsa **11**.49-50ab .50cd .60ab; **13**.67cd-68ab

.78
Vatsabhūmi **11**.60ab; **13**.78
Vatsavat **14**.14cd-20ab .28c-f
Vatsāvat **14**.28c-f
Vāyu **5**.11cd-12 .22cd-24; **28**.27; **33**.9-13ab; **36**.13cd-14ab; **61**.45cd-46; **84**.9-12 .13-15; **124**.39cd-47; **126**.16cd-19ab; **128**.29-37; **178**.25-27; **221**.89-94
- as messenger of gods **123**.14cd-22
- [demon] **213**.81-104
- , origin of **161**.43cd-50cd
- , Viṣṇu worshipped as **20**.32
Vāyu see also *wind*
Vāyukuṇḍa, place of pilgrimage **25**.25
Vāyutīrtha, place of pilgrimage **64**.3-8ab
Veda [Brahmin] **169**.4-6ab .16-22ab .25-32 .36-39ab .43cd-45ef .49ef
Veda(s) **5**.55cd-56 .58cd-60; **24**.19-25; **33**.27-31; **40**.107-111; **43**.85cd-88; **67**.35cd-39ab; **72**.11cd-14; **80**.71-77; **99**.12a-f; **101**.1; **102**.1-2ab; **121**.10-12; **127**.2-4ab .60-63; **128**.38-43; **130**.2-6; **131**.39cd-51; **145**.2cd-5ab .8-11ab .14; **148**.3cd-7; **151**.22cd-24ab; **158**.4-7; **161**.4cd-6ab .9-11ab .24-26 .33cd-35ab .68-71; **163**.3-6; **164**.17-28 .29-37; **167**.2-3; **170**.44-46; **171**.27-39; **173**.29cd-33ab; **175**.10-13 .25-28 .36-41ef .78; **177**.22-23; **213**.12-20 .105; **219**.65cd-71ab; **220**.101cd-102ab; **234**.61cd-63ab; **235**.4-5; **240**.105
- , advice by **127**.35-47
- and Mahābhārata **246**.6-12
- and Purāṇa **4**.24-26; **213**.165cd-168ab
- and Purāṇas **174**.29-30
- and Śāstras **127**.4cd-9ab
- as authority **130**.7-14
- as authority on knowledge of Śiva **139**.7cd-11
- as *brahman* consisting of words **127**.35-47
- , disappearance of **213**.106-112
- , disrespect against **170**.44-46; **214**.41cd-42ab; **231**.4-41
- during Kali-Yuga, disrespect against **230**.10-27
- , Gaṅgā in **76**.8-10
- , gods obedient to hymns of **127**.29-34
- , Manu as authority on **234**.60cd-61ab
- , meaning of **158**.30-35ab; **161**.27-29
- , punishment for abusing of **215**.130cd-136ab
- , punishment for selling of **22**.12cd-13
- , *puruṣa* in **130**.7-14
- , quotation from **129**.49-64
- , recitation of **65**.12-16
- , study of **111**.7-8; **217**.37-39
- subordinate to Śiva **127**.35-47
- , theft of **60**.1-6
Vedadvīpa [island in the Gautamī] **151**.1-2
- [island in the Gautamī], origin of **151**.17-22ab
Veda-experts **99**.1; **120**.3ab
Vedagāthā, place of pilgrimage **120**.16-18
Vedagrabhā **181**.38-53
Vedaka **22**.16b:
Veda-knowledge granted by place of pilgrimage **151**.1-2
Vedāṅgas **40**.107-111; **42**.38cd-42ab; **44**.10-12; **145**.2cd-5ab; **148**.3cd-7; **158**.4-7; **164**.17-28
Vedānta **173**.37-39; **177**.22-23
- , Viṣṇu and **191**.13-17
Vedas, four **42**.38cd-42ab; **175**.14cd-16
- , origin of four **56**.23cd-24ab
- , origin of three **1**.48cd-50ab
- , sun as three **32**.12-16
- , three **109**.13-20; **131**.39cd-51; **213**.155; **233**.40cd-43ab
Vedaśiras **5**.24cd-25
Vedasmṛti **19**.10
Vedavatī **27**.28-29
vedic *gāthā* **120**.3ab .8-14
- hymn, Kaśyapa in **174**.16
- prayer-formulas, restrictions on use of **220**.3-4
- prayer-formulas, Śiva worshipped with **168**.31-35
- preceptions **67**.19
- preceptions, transgression of **4**.28-34
- sacrifice at Gautamī **174**
- verse(s), praise with **174**.2-5ab
- verse(s), recitation of **60**.49-53
- verse(s) sung by Āṅgirasas **158**.28-29
- verses, consecration by **58**.32cd-34ab
vedic verses see also *prayer-formula*
Vegavāhinī **27**.30-32
vegetables, kinds of **220**.168-177
vegetarian diet, prescr. conc. **58**.19-21ab
vegetarianism, merit of **216**.64-66
vehicles of gods **3**.42cd-46ab

Veṇa **2**.20cd .21-28
- , misbehaviour of **2**.21-24; **4**.28-34
Veṇā **27**.33-34
Vena **2**.20cd
- killed by curse **141**.2-5
venerability of Brahmins **104**.61-65
veneration of potsherds and cart **184**.20-28
veneration see also *homage, worship*
Veṇikā **70**.33-35ab
Veṇuhaya **13**.154cd-155ab
Veṇuhotra **11**.55-59
Veṇumaṇḍala **20**.36-38ab
Veṇumat **20**.36-38ab
Venus **9**.31-32; **23**.6-10
Veṇyā **27**.28-29
verse(s), praise with vedic **174**.2-5ab
- , quotation of traditional **2**.10-13; **11**.51-53; **12**.40-46; **13**.139-140 .170-171; **15**.41cd-45ab .49-50ab
- , recitation of vedic **60**.49-53
- sung by Āṅgirasas, vedic **158**.28-29
vessel, copper **28**.24
- , fire carried in golden **110**.202-210
vessels, sacrificial **161**.50ef-53
Vetasikārūpa, place of pilgrimage **25**.58
Vetravatī **27**.28-29 .30-32
Vibhāvasu **98**.18cd; **107**.35-40
Vibhīṣaṇa **59**.1-2; **97**.2-5ab; **154**.8cd-11ab .21cd-26; **157**.2cd-7 .18ef-21ab; **176**.37-51
- as devotee of Viṣṇu **176**.26-32
- as friend of Rāma **157**.11-12ab
- as king of Laṅkā **170**.54-63
- , Rāvaṇa and **176**.15cd-34
- [son of Vibhīṣaṇa] **170**.54-63
Vibhu **11**.55-59; **13**.75cd-77
Vibhūtaka-tree **219**.25-29
Vice-Indra, consecration of Kṛṣṇa as **188**.36 -37
vices of king, maxim about **108**.22-23ab
- of king, seven **123**.33cd-36ab
vices see also *bad evil sin*
Vicitravīrya **13**.120 .121
victory, exclamations of **108**.71-74; **110**.183-187; **152**.33
- of gods over demons **212**.72-85
- , wrath as means of **162**.27cd-30
victory see also *defeat, fight*
Vidarbha **8**.63-64; **15**.16-21 .22-23; **199**.1-4
- , battle between the kings of Kāśi and **229**.43cd-55
Vidarbhā and Gautamī, confluence of **121**.1 .24-25
Vidarbhā, explanation of **121**.23
Videhas **15**.12cd-13; **27**.51cd-53
Vidhātṛ **56**.13-15; **192**.48-58
Vidiśā **27**.28-29
Vidrāvaṇa **3**.74cd-78ab
Vidruma **20**.41cd-42
Vidura **13**.121
Vidūratha **13**.110-111; **16**.1-3; **199**.5-10
Vidyā **182**.7-8
Vidyādhara, place of pilgrimage **25**.23
Vidyādharas **32**.95cd-97ab; **38**.17-19; **39**.7-17ab; **50**.55-59; **58**.59cd-64ab; **214**.107cd-109
Vidyut **20**.43-44
Vidyutprabha, place of pilgrimage **25**.21
Vidyuts, four **3**.60
Vighna as name of Gaṇeśa **175**.73-74
Vighna see also *hindrance, obstacle(s)*
Vighna, explanation of **175**.73-74
Vighnakṛt **74**.68-75
Vighnarāṭ **74**.43-55
vigil, nocturnal **228**.8-14 .40-43
- , singing during **228**
Vijaya **8**.24-28; **11**.27cd-31; **14**.45-46ab; **111**.26-34 .39cd-47
- , place of pilgrimage **25**.34 .36
Vijayā **109**.10cd-12
- [daughter of Umā] **74**.59-67
Vikarṇa **13**.45-48
Vikarṇaka, place of pilgrimage **25**.81
Vikartana **31**.31-33ab
Vikramasvāmin, Viṣṇu as **43**.82cd-83ab
Vikṛti **15**.24-28
Vikṣara **213**.81-104
Vikṣobhaṇa **3**.74cd-78ab
Vikukṣi **7**.45cd-46ab .48cd-51ab
Vilepaka **215**.92cd-93ab
Vilepana **215**.130cd-136ab
village, punishment for destruction of **22**.23ab
Vimaladaṇḍakuṇḍa, place of pilgrimage **25**.61
Vimalaśoka as place of pilgrimage **25**.58
Vimocana, place of pilgrimage **25**.52
Vimocanī **20**.28
Vimoha **22**.14ab
Vimohana **22**.2-6; **214**.14-17
Vinatā **3**.51-52 .95cd-96ab; **32**.3-6

- , Garuḍa reproached by **159**.31cd-35
- , Kadrū and **159**
Vinatāśva **7**.17-19ab
Vināyaka **74**.13-22ab .38cd-42; **114**.2-5
Vināyakahrada, place of pilgrimage **25**.65
Vindhya-mountains **19**.3 .11-12ab; **27**.19cd-20ab .33-34 .59ab; **70**.22cd-23 .33-35ab; **78**.77; **89**.25cd-33; **161**.2cd-4ab .21-23ef .65cd-67; **228**.92cd-96
- , description of **118**.2-9
- , inhabitants of **4**.42-47; **27**.59cd-62ab
- , place of pilgrimage **64**.8cd-9
- , stones from **47**.7-9
violation of borders, punishment for **22**.14ab .23cd-24ab
- of vital spots, punishment for **215**.130cd-136ab
violation see also *breach, transgression*
violence, effect(s) of **224**.47-52
- , expiation for **218**.21cd-22ab
- , punishment for **215**.72-77
violence see also *affliction, oppression, torments*
Vipāpmā **27**.30-32
Vipāśā **20**.10-11; **27**.25cd-27 .30-32
- , place of pilgrimage **64**.11-14
Vipracitti **3**.64cd-70ab .74cd-78ab .78cd-80ab .86cd-89ab; **41**.30-34ab; **180**.24cd-38; **213**.81-104
Viprāsā **20**.10-11
Vipratīrtha, place of pilgrimage **167**.1 .33
Viprṭhu **14**.12-13; **16**.56cd-58ab; **210**.37-43
Vipula **18**.21-23ab
Vīra **2**.5 .14-15
- , place of pilgrimage **25**.57
Vīrabhadra **39**.51-52 .53-58 .67-68ab .69cd -73; **109**.21-26ab
- , eyes of Bhaga torn out by **109**.21-26ab
- , sun thrown down by **109**.21-26ab
Virādha **213**.136-140
Vīradhāra, place of pilgrimage **25**.20
Viraja, holy places at **42**.6-8
- , merit of bathing at **42**.6-8
- , place of pilgrimage **42**.1-11; **64**.3-8ab; **161**.2cd-4ab
Virajā **12**.1-2; **42**.1-2
- as Mother **42**.1-2
- , merit of worship of **42**.1-2
Virajas **5**.29cd-30ab
Virajātīrtha, place of pilgrimage **25**.78
Vīraṇa **3**.3-7ab .10-14
- [island] **159**.26-27
Vīrapramokṣa, place of pilgrimage **25**.57
Vīras **27**.43-50
Vīrasena **8**.93
Vīrāśrama, place of pilgrimage **25**.73
Virāśva **7**.51cd-53
Virāṭ **1**.53cd-54 .55; **2**.5 .6
virāṭ, Viṣṇu as **161**.68-71
virgins, asceticism of three **34**.87-89
Virgo **220**.43-48ab
Viriñci **241**.16cd-19ab
Virocana **3**.64cd-70ab; **213**.81-104
Vīru **14**.32cd
Virūpākṣa **3**.46cd-49; **228**.76-85
- , place of pilgrimage **25**.48
Viṣahara **15**.22-23
Viśākha **3**.39-40; **81**.4-7ab; **110**.105-106
Viśākhā **220**.33cd-42
Viśalyakariṇī [medicinal herb] **170**.54-63
Viśasana **22**.2-6 .16cd-17ab
Viṣayāntika, place of pilgrimage **25**.36
vision of Kṛṣṇa by Akrūra **192**.32-42 .43-47
- of naked woman by Kṛṣṇa **206**.31-38
- of Śiva **59**.6-21
- of Self **243**.59-65
- of sun by Aditi **32**.17-31
- of the absolute, liberation by **236**.69
- of Vāsudeva in dream **50**.4-6
- of Viṣṇu **54**; **55**.7-8; **56**.61-66ab
- of Viṣṇu by Kaṇḍu **178**.122-127
Viskara **213**.81-104
Viṣṇu **3**.53-58 .125; **10**.46cd-49ab; **13**.213c-f; **18**.52-55; **22**.37-41; **30**.19-20 .23-26 .28-39; **31**.17-18 .19-21 .22-26; **33**.3-8 .9-13ab; **34**.42-45ab; **36**.17cd-18ab .31-36ab; **38**.7-13; **39**.22-27ab .33; **43**.6-9; **44**.48-53ab; **56**.13-15; **60**.39-45; **61**.14-16; **69**.12-43; **70**.16-19; **71**.4-6 .16-18 .41-42; **72**.11cd-14; **103**.2-6; **104**.37cd-38; **106**.26cd-30; **107**.46 .53-54; **109**.1-3ab .13-20 .26cd-27 .28-29 .39cd-40 .49-50ef; **110**.10-20 .87-97ef; **122**.24cd-27; **129**.20cd-29 .49-64; **151**.10-16 .17-22ab; **163**.26-31 .52-53; **164**.51-53ab; **166**.8cd-11ab .11cd-13; **171**.40-43; **174**.31-33; **178**.106-111 .112; **184**.14-19; **207**.28-43; **219**.98cd-107ab; **220**.200cd-203ab; **239**.58-61
- , adepts in heaven of **68**.43

- , advice by **72**.15-17; **113**.5-8ab; **136**.27-31
- , all-comprehensiveness of **54**
- allocated to body, forms of **184**.14-19
- allocated to *maṇḍala* **61**.19
- , ancestors taking refuge to **219**.30
- and Ananta, identity of **226**.65cd-67ab
- and Brahman, Śiva worshipped by **153**.12
- and Garuḍa **90**.20-30
- and Kamalā **178**.166cd-176
- and Lakṣmī **68**.44-53; **80**.46-55; **144**.20-22
- and Lakṣmī sleeping in ocean **172**.7cd-14
- and Śiva **90**.34-35 .36; **122**.63-67ab; **123**.7cd-14ab; **129**.101-124; **135**.5cd-10ab .17-19; **136**.17-26; **150**.15-20; **160**.17-19; **174**.5cd-6ab .7
- and Śiva at place of pilgrimage **122**.1-2
- and Śiva, boon by **160**.20; **168**.31-35
- and Śiva, compassion of **122**.87-92
- and Śiva, identity of **56**.61-66ab .66cd-73
- and Śiva, Mahāśani as combination of **129**.94-99ab
- and Śiva, place of pilgrimage sacred to **168**.36
- and Śiva, Speech cursed by **135**.13ef-14
- and Śiva, sun superior to **28**.40-41
- and Śiva, union of **135**.10cd-13cd
- and Śiva, unity of **109**.52-54
- and Śiva, worship of **131**.31-39ab
- and Śrī **51**.10-16
- and Śrī, dialogue between **45**.16cd-89
- and Vedānta **191**.13-17
- and waters, lotus originated from **161**.6cd-9
- and world **180**.1-12
- appearing to Kaṇḍu **178**.122-127
- appearing to Mārkaṇḍeya **54**; **55**.7-8; **56**.61-66ab
- as Agni **60**.39-45
- as all **18**.57-58 .59; **55**.23cd-31; **56**.46ab-48ab; **126**.24-27; **181**.21-25; **189**.44-45; **191**.4-12; **193**.80-87; **196**.30-45; **202**.23-29; **203**.6-19 .70-73
- as Aśvaśīrṣan **178**.166cd-176
- as Aurva-fire **179**.18cd-22ab
- as bearer of earth **175**.60-68
- as Bhadrapati **165**.47cd-48ef
- as boar **18**.57-58; **42**.5; **56**.19cd-22ab; **79**.7cd-19; **179**.18cd-22ab; **180**.24cd-38; **191**.4-12; **213**.32-42; **219**.37-39; **226**.59-61
- as boar in simile **49**.9
- as boar, worship of **229**.86cd-87
- as Brahman **56**.51-54; **109**.41; **233**.10
- as Brahman with thousand heads **179**.22cd-26
- as *brahman* **23**.41-43; **178**.117
- as Brahmin **50**.25-28; **163**.32-39
- as Cakrapāṇi **174**.8-12ef
- as child **56**.49-50
- as creator **56**.56-57; **179**.29-37 .62-64; **233**.10
- as creator and destroyer **56**.38cd-39ab
- as creator of Brahman **45**.29
- as creator of sacrifice **179**.29-37
- as creator of sages **226**.52-53
- as Dattātreya **180**.24cd-38; **213**.106-112
- as destroyer **56**.26cd-27ab .39cd-42; **179**.16cd-18ab .43cd-44ab
- as dispenser of merit **56**.30cd-35ab
- as dream, Māyā of **229**.88
- as dwarf **73**; **179**.18cd-22ab; **180**.24cd-38; **184**.14-19
- as epitome **179**.44cd-47ab; **192**.48-58
- as fate **179**.38-43ab
- as father of Brahman **73**.58-63ab
- as fig-tree **57**.17-19
- as first-person narrator **45**.42-43 .68-70
- as fish **18**.57-58; **191**.4-12
- as Gadādhara **164**.1-2 .38-46
- as Govindasvāmin **43**.77-82ab
- as Hayaśiras **18**.57-58; **174**.8-12ef
- as human being **179**.62-64
- as husband of Mother of the world **163**.43-46
- as Kapila **8**.54-57
- as Kāla **56**.39cd-42
- as Kṛṣṇa **176**.52-56
- as lord of Ādityas **4**.2-9
- as Lord of Yoga **170**.40-43 .54-63 .69-74ab .89a-f; **213**.170
- as man-lion **179**.18cd-22ab; **180**.24cd-38; **184**.14-19; **191**.4-12; **213**.43-79
- as mare **56**.19cd-22ab
- as Narasiṃha **149**
- as narrator **51**.60-62
- as origin of beings **196**.30-45
- as origin of beings, body of **226**.13-14
- as origin of Brahman **161**.68-71
- as personification of sacrifice **73**.21-22
- as primordial matter **23**.41-43
- as protector **106**.23-26ab

- as *puruṣa* **1**.1-2; **161**.6cd-9; **191**.4-12 .13-17; **226**.11-12
- as Puruṣottama **51**.1-8
- as Rāma **213**.124-158
- as Rāma Jāmadagnya **180**.24cd-38; **213**.113cd-123 .114-122
- as Śeṣa **21**.13cd-15; **56**.19cd-22ab
- as sacrifice **23**.44; **56**.13-15; **161**.13-16 .17-20; **193**.80-87; **233**.40cd-43ab
- as sun **158**.22-27ef
- as supporter **179**.38-43ab
- as supporter of all **18**.59
- as the absolute **23**.41-43; **233**.35-38ab
- as the Supreme Self [*paramātman*] **233**.38cd-40ab
- as tortoise **18**.57-58; **191**.4-12
- as Vikramasvāmin **43**.82cd-83ab
- as *virāṭ* **161**.68-71
- , ascension to city of **176**.57-62
- at place of pilgrimage, Śiva and **174**.8-12ef
- , attributes of **55**.33cd-34; **56**.43-44
- , awaking of **67**.2-5
- , Āpastamba as devotee of **129**.82-93
- , black shape of **161**.54-58
- , blessing by **165**.45-47ab
- , blue statue of **58**.1-7
- , body of **56**.16-17ab
- , body protected by **163**.26-31
- , boon by **7**.58cd-71ab; **8**.58-59ab; **124**.36cd-39ab; **163**.47-49; **165**.45-47ab
- , boon by Śiva to **109**.52-54
- , bow of **131**.16-24; **163**.50-51; **171**.1-2ab
- , Brahman instructed by **161**.24-26
- , Brahman residing in navel of **226**.20cd-22ab
- , *brahman* as highest step of **234**.63cd-66ab
- , Buddha as incarnation of **122**.68-73
- , Cāṇḍāla as devotee of **228**.8-91ab
- , characteristics of the manifestations of **180**.17cd-42ab
- , chariot of **210**.47-48
- , city of **68**.68-70; **105**.30cd-31ab; **168**.37
- , colours of body of **56**.39cd-42
- , compassion of **122**.68-73; **164**.38-46
- , competition between Brahman and **135**.5cd-10ab
- , complaint by Garuḍa to **90**.12cd-19
- , conch of **68**.44-53
- , cosmic sleep of **53**.12-14ab; **56**.49-50; **213**.25-26 .30-31
- , day of **233**.46cd-49ab
- , demon as devotee of **73**.18-20; **149**.2-4ab
- , demons defeated by **206**.20
- , description of **126**.24-27; **178**.158-165; **179**.65-72ab; **191**.4-12; **196**.30-45; **202**.23-29
- , devotee identified with **61**.13 .17-18
- , *dharma* protected by **56**.35cd-38ab
- , dispute between Brahman and **135**.2cd-5ab
- , disrespect against **49**.50cd-54ab; **170**.44-46
- , dissolution of *prakṛti* and *puruṣa* in **233**.38cd-40ab .43cd-46ab
- , division of body of **181**.2-4
- , effect(s) of devotion to **216**.82-86 .87-89
- , energy of **23**.28cd-44 .29cd-31ab .31cd-32ab .38-40
- , entering of body of **53**.41-43; **56**.51-54
- , entourage of **68**.54-55
- , epithets of **45**.60-67; **55**.18-23ab; **180**.1-12; **213**.66-71; **233**.35-38ab
- , evil-doers thinking of **216**.87-89
- , expiation by praising of **22**.37-41
- , expiation by remembering of **22**.37-41
- , fever of **206**.14-19
- , fighting as play of **206**.20
- , forms of **49**.10-20
- , four aspects of **213**.124-126
- , four incarnations of **61**.39-40
- , four manifestations of **59**.34; **61**.7-12 .13; **192**.48-58
- , functions of manifestations of **180**.17cd-42ab
- , Gaṅgā originated from step of **18**.38cd-44ab; **150**.15-20
- , gods residing in body of **226**.20cd-22ab
- , gods taking refuge to **213**.66-71
- , good qualities of **226**.23cd-25
- , highest step of **42**.5; **51**.22-26 .57-58; **68**.4-5; **131**.39cd-51
- , Himavat honoured by **72**.7
- , horse-headed form of **18**.57-58; **178**.166cd-176
- , hymn by Akrūra to **192**.48-58
- , hymn by ancestors to **219**.31-35
- , hymn by Āsandiva to **167**.30
- , hymn by Brahman to **181**.21-25
- , hymn by Dhanvantari to **122**.29-43
- , hymn by earth to **202**.23-29

- , hymn by gods to **65**.49-51; **71**.7-12; **109**.41-42; **213**.72-73
- , hymn by Indra to **122**.68-73
- , hymn by Indradyumna to **49**.1-59; **51**.10-16
- , hymn by Kaṇḍu to **178**.114-117 .128-177
- , hymn by Lomaharṣaṇa to **1**.21-29
- , hymn by Mārkaṇḍeya to **55**.11-35
- , hymn by Śveta to **59**.34-72
- , hymn by sages to **126**.24-27
- , hymn by Vyāsa to **180**.1-12
- , iconographic attributes of **49**.10-20; **51**.10-16; **59**.73-77; **61**.41-45ab .52-55; **68**.44-53; **79**.7cd-19; **109**.43-45; **122**.44-47; **126**.23; **136**.3cd-14ab; **145**.5cd -7; **156**.1-2ab; **163**.32-39; **176**.8-10 .21-25; **177**.1-2; **178**.122-127; **203**.6-19; **210**.47-48; **226**.22cd-23ab; **228**.8-14
- identical with beings **196**.30-45
- identical with gods **51**.1-8; **56**.13-15; **122**.68-73; **179**.72cd-75; **181**.15-19; **192**.48-58
- identical with three worlds **122**.68-73
- identical with time **55**.32ab
- identical with world **23**.41-43; **179**.38-43ab
- , immanence of **179**.38-43ab
- in Puṣkara, manifestation of **213**.25-31
- , incarnation of two hairs of **181**.26-31
- , incarnations of **56**.39cd-42; **59**.35-64; **122**.68-73; **178**.166cd-176; **179**.2-75; **180**; **191**.4-12
- , Indra protected by **179**.27-28
- , inhabitants of world of **68**.23-27ab
- , Īśa as name of **171**.44-46
- , Kāśi burnt by discus of **207**.28-43
- killing with arrows **131**.16-24
- , kings killed by **226**.18
- , Kṛṣṇa and Balarāma as partial incarnation of **190**.10-19
- , Kṛṣṇa as partial incarnation of **193**.32-40; **195**.13-18; **196**.23-29; **202**.23-29
- , liberation as merging in **19**.25-27
- , liberation by devotion to **136**.17-26
- , liberation by grace of **178**.184-186; **239**.24-28
- , liberation by remembering of **229**.64-67ab
- , liberation by worship of **196**.30-45
- , lordship over gods obtained by sacrifices to **191**.4-12
- lying in ocean of milk **126**.23
- lying on Śeṣa **233**.1-4
- , Madhu and Kaiṭabha killed by **180**.24cd -38; **213**.28-29
- , manifestations of **180**; **213** .25-26
- , many-headedness of **122**.68-73
- , Māthura-Avatāra of **180**.39cd
- , Māyā as yogic sleep of **233**.5-6
- , Māyā of **194**.1-5; **229** .43cd-67ab; **240**.54cd-68
- meditating on himself as Vāsudeva **233**.5-6
- meditating on Śiva **109**.52-54
- , meditation on **45**.37-41; **80**.65-70; **86**.8-9ab
- , merit of worship of **42**.11
- named Govinda, statue of **122**.100-102
- , names of **59**.35-64; **60**.39-45; **61**.14-16 .39-40; **65**.49-51; **184**.14-19; **192**.48-58
- , omnipresence of **202**.23-29
- , oneness of **49**.10-20
- , origin of discus of **6**.50cd-51ab
- , palace of **45**.71-73
- , passions as forms of **56**.27cd-30ab
- , place of pilgrimage sacred to **136**.41-42
- , play of **195**.13-18; **212**.9-11 .66-70
- , praise of **165**.37-44
- praised by Brahman **161**.39cd-43ab
- praised by Dharma and Agni **128**.63cd-70ab
- praised by Harṣaṇa **165**.45-47ab
- praised by Indra **129**.94-99ab
- , prayer by Nanda to **184**.14-19
- , prayer to **67**.29cd-31ab
- , prayer-formula addressed to **61**.51
- , promise by **73**.18-20
- , prophecy by **181**.38-53
- , protection by names of **219**.31-35
- , purpose of incarnation of **56**.35cd-38ab; **180**.24cd-38; **181**.1 .2-4; **185**.5-10; **187**.22-25; **188**.29-35; **193**.80-87; **202**.23-29; **210**.16-21; **212**.59-62
- , purpose of manifestations of **213**.124-126
- , Rākṣasas killed by discus of **134**.12-14; **156**.4-6
- , Rākṣasī killed by discus of **167**.31-32
- , reciprocity of honouring of **226**.54-55
- remembered at hour of death **229**.56-58
- , Śārdūla killed by **128**.63cd-70ab
- , Śiva as Brahman and **130**.17-21
- , Śiva, Brahman **33**.9-23; **74**.31-37;

123.121-128ab; **129**.125-127; **130**.7-14; **131**.39cd-51; **144**.2-4; **158**.35cd-37ab; **175**.1-2ef; **213**.25-26; **219**.98cd-107ab; **226**.20cd-22ab .45cd-48ab
- , Śiva, statue of Brahman **120**.3cd-5
- , Śiva unknowable to Brahman and **127**.48-53
- , Śuci taking refuge to **229**.22-30
- , sacrifice born from mouth of **79**.7cd-19
- , Sarasvatī in mouth of **122**.68-73
- , stars as pores of **56**.27cd-30ab
- , step of **172**.4-7ab; **246**.34-35
- , stories told by **136**.3cd-14ab
- superior to Brahman **226**.11-12
- , superiority of **149**.13-16ab .16cd-19
- , temple of Śiva and **122**.3-7
- , ten arms of **226**.11-12
- , thousand arms of **68**.44-53
- , thousand eyes of **68**.44-53
- , thousandfold appearance of **181**.21-25
- , three colours of **161**.54-58
- , three shapes of **161**.68-71
- , three steps of **73** .41-43cd .48-51; **179**.16cd-18ab; **213**.81-104
- to ancestors, boon by **219**.98cd-107ab
- to Āsandiva, boon by **167**.31-32
- to Bali, boon by **73**.52-55
- to Dhanvantari, boon by **122**.44-47
- to directions, allocation of **61**.14-16
- to Indradyumna, boon by **49**.60; **50**.33-40; **51**.1-8 .22-45
- to Kaṇḍu, boon by **178**.178
- to Madhu and Kaiṭabha, boon by **213**.28-29
- to Mārkaṇḍeya, boon by **56**.1-2 .51-54 .58-60
- to Nārada, boon by **229**.56-58
- to Śiva, hymn by **109**.51
- to Śuci, boon by **229**.37-43ab
- to Śveta, boon by **59**.73-77
- , transcendence of **23**.41-43; **178**.117; **192**.48-58; **202**.23-29
- , *trimūrti*-functions of **56**.13-15; **73**.9-17; **167**.30; **179**.65-72ab; **181**.21-25; **185**.30-33; **193**.80-87; **202**.23-29; **203**.6-19 .70-73; **212**.63 .66-70; **226**.15-17
- , unknowability of **56**.45; **192**.48-58
- unknowable to Brahman **55**.32cd-33ab; **191**.4-12
- unknowable to gods **56**.51-54
- , usurpation of emblems of **207**.4-7
- , Vaikuṇṭha as paradise of **161**.61cd-62
- , Vāsudeva as **226**.11-67
- , Vibhīṣaṇa as devotee of **176**.26-32
- , wealth granted by **136**.35cd-36ef
- , weapons of **163**.32-39
- , white shape of **161**.54-58
- , wind originating from breath of **233**.1-4
- , world of **43**.77-82ab; **45**.57-58 .77-89; **49**.61-63; **51**.42-45 .63-71; **57**.17-19 .20-28; **58**.58-59ab .59cd-64ab .70cd-77; **62**.5-9; **63**.1-7 .11-16 .17 .22; **64**.17-20; **66**.18-23; **67**.2-5 .53-57; **68**; **121**.24-25; **128**.83-84; **150**.15-20; **163**.52-53; **175**.81cd-82; **227**.37cd-41; **246**.28-29
- , worship as ceremonial function of **72**.11cd-14
- , worship of **43**.82cd-83ab; **136**.3cd-14ab; **216**.5-63; **226**.56-57ab
- worshipped as Brahman **20**.40cd-41ab
- worshipped as moon **20**.19
- worshipped as Rudra **20**.56cd-57ab
- worshipped as sacrifice **19**.22
- worshipped as Sūrya **20**.72cd-73ab
- worshipped as Vāyu **20**.32
- worshipped by Yogins **56**.24cd-26ab
- , Yama protected by discus of **86**.27-29
- , yellow shape of **161**.54-58
- , Yoga as worship of **233**.40cd-43ab
- , Yoga of **43**.77-82ab; **57**.52-56 .59-61; **58**.70cd-77; **62**.5-9; **64**.17-20; **66**.18-23; **67**.76-80; **70**.3cd-8ab; **176**.57-62
- , Yoganidrā as Māyā of **181**.37
- , yogic sleep of **45**.29; **179**.22cd-26; **180**.24cd-38; **233**.8

Viṣṇu see also *Hari, incarnations, Janārdana, Kṛṣṇa, Nārāyaṇa, Vāsudeva*

Viṣṇudharma **223**

Viṣṇudharmottarapurāṇa **90**; **94**

Viṣṇuhrada, place of pilgrimage **25**.21

Viṣṇukuṇḍa, place of pilgrimage **25**.16

Viṣṇupada, place of pilgrimage **25**.25 .43

Viṣṇuprabha, place of pilgrimage **25**.21

Viṣṇupura, place of pilgrimage **58**.1-7

Viṣṇupurāṇa **181**.33-35; **182**.18; **188**.24-28; **189**.46-58ab; **190**.22-25; **222**; **230**; **232**; **233**; **234**

Viṣṇutīrtha, place of pilgrimage **25**.16; **136**.1ab; **219**.40-41

Viṣṇuyaśas, Kalkin **213**.164-165ab

Viśokā **70**.33-35ab
Viśravas **97**.2-5ab
Viśrutāśva **16**.54cd-55ab
Vistarāśva **7**.51cd-53
Viṣṭi **89**.13-17ab; **165**
- and Viśvarūpa, marriage of **165**.27-30ab
Viśva, place of pilgrimage **25**.42
Viśvā **3**.29-30ab .30cd-33
Viśvabādhi **13**.91
Viśvācī **12**.24-38; **32**.99cd-100; **41**.30-34ab; **68**.60-67; **178**.19-24
Viśvadhara **86**.3cd-7
Viśvakarman **3**.42cd-46ab; **32**.104-107; **45**.77-89; **72**.5-6; **83**.2-5; **136**.35cd-36ef; **176**.4-7 .8-10
- as Brahmin **50**.25-28
- , functions of **3**.42cd-46ab
- , Tvaṣṭṛ **32**.80-81; **72**.9ab; **109**.13-20
Viṣvaksena **14**.29-31
Viśvāmitra **5**.34-35; **7**.105cd-109; **8**.1-2 .13-15b: .22 .23; **10**.55-68a .63 .64-65ab .65cd-67ab .67cd-68; **13**.91; **93**.5-11 .12-24; **104**.69-77; **147**; **210**.6-10; **213**.142 -144
- , advice by **173**.9-25
- as teacher of Rāma and Lakṣmaṇa **123**.97-105ab
- , asceticism of **147**.14-17ab
- becoming a Brahmin **10**.55-56
- , boon by **8**.20-21
- , curse by **147**.17cd-20ab
- , Daśaratha and **123**.86cd-96
- , enmity between Vasiṣṭha and **147**.5-7
- , Menakā and **147**.5-7
- , place of pilgrimage **104**.1-2
- , Rāma paying homage to **93**.3-4
- , Śunaḥśepa adopted by **104**.83-86ab
- , sons cursed by **104**.83-86ab
Viśvāmitratīrtha, place of pilgrimage **93**.3-4 .27
Viśvaratha **10**.55-56
Viśvarūpa **3**.46cd-49; **18**.57-58; **30**.69ab
- , Bhadra as name of **165**.45-47ab
- [demon] **173**.6cd-8ef
- , demons detected by **168**.18cd-21
- , marriage of Viṣṭi and **165**.27-30ab
- [son of Tvaṣṭṛ] **160**.6cd-9
- [son of Viśvakarman] **83**.2-5
- , terrible sacrifice of **173**.26-28 .34cd-35ef
Viśvāsa, place of pilgrimage **25**.81
Viśvāvasu **39**.7-17ab; **132**.6 .7-9ef
- [lord of the Gandharvas] **171**.14-15
Viśvāyu **10**.11-12
Viśvedevas see *all-gods*
Viśveśvara, place of pilgrimage **25**.53 .72
Viśveśvarī, Yogamāyā as **131**.29-30
vital breath **214**.46-51
- breaths, five **179**.56cd-57ab .57cd-58
- spots, prescription(s) concerning **221**.44
- spots, punishment for violation of **215**.130cd-136ab
Vitala **21**.2-5ab
Vitastā **27**.25cd-27; **70**.33-35ab
- , place of pilgrimage **25**.78; **64**.11-14
Vitatha **13**.58-61 .62-63a
Vitatha, explanation of **13**.58-61
Vītihotras **13**.203-204
Vitṛṣṇā **20**.28
Vivasvan **3**.53-58
Vivasvat **5**.29cd-30ab .36-37ab; **16**.13-24; **28**.47-53ab; **30**.23-26 .28-39; **31**.17-18 .19-21 .22-26 .31-33ab; **33**.9-13ab; **36**.10cd-11ab; **102**.6cd-8ab
- and Saṃjñā **6**
- as lord of ancestral rites **8**.95
- , birth of **32**.3-47
Viviśva [caste] **20**.16-17
voice, dialogue between Brahman and heavenly **161**.11cd-26
- , heavenly **7**.74-77; **32**.37-41ab; **78**.12-24; **83**.17-22; **97**.24-28; **104**.66-68; **123**.14cd -22 .82-83 .173-175 .177cd-184; **126**.28-29 .32cd-35; **135**.2cd-5ab; **138**.20-21; **148**.8-14ab .18cd-20; **160**.17-19; **161**.13-16 .17-20 .21-23ef .24-26 .39cd-43ab; **173**.29cd-33ab .33cd-34ab; **201**.10-22
voluntary death **80**.65-70; **109**.6cd-10
- death, announcement of **110**.41cd-46ab .61-66
- death at place of pilgrimage **228**.146-151
- death by drowning **216**.5-63; **229**.72-86ab
- death by fasting **12**.47-48; **216**.5-63; **228**.86-91ab; **229**.72-86ab
- death, maxim about **107**.31-34
- death, merit of **110**.61-66
- death, methods of **214**.114cd-119; **216**.5-63; **221**.152cd-154
- death of king **138**.22-27
- death of Satī **34**.20ef-25

- death of widow **110**.67-70
- death, threat of **154**.21cd-26
- liberation **239**.39-41
voluntary death see also *suicide*
vow, breach of **3**.109cd-122
- by Prācīnabarhis **153**.4-6ab
- , conception after **124**.19-28ab
- for obtaining a son **124**.17-18
- , observances during **46**.24-30; **59**.26-33
- of chastity **81**.13-15
- of purity **3**.109cd-122
- of twelve years **8**.3-4 .13-15b:; **124**.12-16
- , punishment for breach of **22**.26
- , sacrificial gift ending a **228**.127cd-145
vow see also *observances, practices*
Vraja **2**.29-30ab; **187**.55-59ab
Vratinī **16**.45cd-48ab
Vṛddha, place of pilgrimage **105**.22-26ab
Vṛddhā as river **107**.63cd-64cd
Vṛddhagautama **107**.63cd-64cd
Vṛddhakauśika **170**.2-5 .84-88
Vṛddhāsaṃgama, place of pilgrimage **107**.1 .68dc-69ab
Vṛddhaśarman **11**.1-2 .27cd-31; **14**.20cd-24ab
Vṛddheśvara, Liṅga named **107**.1 .67cd-68ab
Vṛjinīvat **15**.1-12ab; **226**.30-41
Vṛka **8**.24-28; **205**.1-6
Vṛkadeva **14**.45-46ab
Vṛkadevī **14**.36-38 .45-46ab; **15**.56-58ab
Vṛkala **2**.14-15
Vṛkas **27**.41cd-42
Vṛkatejas **2**.14-15
Vṛndāvana, cowherds shifting to **184**.42cd-52ab
Vṛṣa **13**.205-207ab
Vṛṣadarbha **13**.25cd-27ab
Vṛṣadarbhas **13**.25cd-27ab
Vṛṣākapa, place of pilgrimage **129**.1-2
Vṛṣākapatīrtha, place of pilgrimage **129**.11ab
Vṛṣākapi **3**.46cd-49; **70**.39-40
- as friend of Indra **129**.99cd-100ef .101-124
- as name of Śiva **124**.100-107
- , Indra and **129**.42-125
Vṛṣala **3**.30cd-33
Vṛṣaṇa **13**.199cd-202
Vṛṣaparvan **3**.74cd-78ab .80cd-83; **12**.4-5ab
Vṛṣī **27**.28-29
Vṛṣṇi **12**.50; **13**.213c-f; **14**.3ab .3cd .24cd-25ab; **15**.30-31; **16**.49cd .50ab
Vṛṣṇis **5**.64; **13**.205-207ab; **14**.2cd .35
Vṛṣṇyandhakas **16**.13-24 .25-45ab; **17**.29-31; **205**.15-22
- , genealogy of **16**
- , Kṛṣṇa as leader of **14**.50cd-56
Vṛṣṭi **15**.46cd-48
Vṛtra **70**.35cd-37ab; **96**.2-5ab; **160**.6cd-9; **173**.29cd-33ab; **176**.12-15ab; **213**.81-104
- in simile, slaying of **189**.58c-f
- , Indra as slayer of **140**.19cd-21cd .21ef-25
- , killing of **122**.48-49
vultures, corpse abandoned to **216**.5-63
Vyāsa **5**.43; **26**.2; **30**.14-18; **40**.135; **41**.1-5; **69**.12-43; **245**.44-47
- , advice by **212**.91-92
- , Arjuna and **212**.35-94
- as first-person narrator **212**.54; **220**.189ab
- as narrator **26**.27; **41**.6-9; **177**.29-30; **212**.93-94
- as Yogin **235**.2
- , description of **26**.6-8
- , description of hermitage of **26**.3-17
- , omniscience of **26**.18
- , place of pilgrimage **25**.31
- , praise of **214**.1-2; **217**.2-3; **223**.1-3; **235**.30; **239**.1; **240**.1-2 .77-80; **241**.3-4; **246**.1-5 .6-12
- , qualification(s) of **238**.41
- to Viṣṇu, hymn by **180**.1-12
Vyāsas, Āṅgirasas as **158**.39cd-40ef
- of the future, Āṅgirasas as **158**.30-35ab
Vyāsatīrtha, place of pilgrimage **25**.13; **158**.1 .39cd-40ef
Vyaya **165**.27-30ab
Vyoman **15**.24-28
vyūha see *form, manifestations*
war, omen(s) of **206**.1-4
war see also *battle, fight*
warning of enemy **182**.31
washing of head, prescription(s) concerning **221**.35
water absorbed by sun **24**.8-11
- , Agni hidden in **98**.2-5
- and earth, cleaning with **221**.125cd-127ab
- and earth, purification by **72**.23-25ab; **221**.132cd-133ab
- as abode of Nārāyaṇa **60**.34-38
- , asceticism by standing in **178**.7-11; **212**.72-85
- , Ātreyī as **144**.20-22

- , cleaning with **221**.115
- , cleaning with ashes and **221**.117cd-120ab
- , cleaning with mud and **221**.116-117ab
- , consecration with **155**.11cd
- , cosmic **1**.37cd-38ab
- , creation from semen in **1**.37cd-38ab
- , cycle of **24**.8-11; **31**.4-6
- , donation(s) confirmed by **73**.34-40
- , earth resting upon **1**.39cd-42
- , effect(s) of consecrated **65**.78-80
- , equivalence of fire and **126**.12-16ab; **158**.22-27ef
- , four kinds of **24**.12
- from Gautamī, Rākṣasa sprinkled by **133**.18-23ab
- from nether world **115**.12cd-15ab; **159**.36-39cd
- from nether world, snakes healed by **159**.41cd-46ab
- , holy **73**.58-63ab
- , homage to **126**.30-32ab
- , husband and wife as fire and **144**.15-16 .20-22
- in simile, life-giving effect of **107**.55-57
- , killing by sprinkling with **168**.22-24
- , list of things cleaned with **221**.113-114
- , ocean of **18**.11-12; **20**.88cd-89ab
- of Gautamī as nectar of immortality **133**.13-17
- of immortality, clouds raining **93**.12-24
- , offerings put in **220**.149-151
- on earth, offering of **60**.54-65
- , praise of **72**.27cd-34; **126**.9-11
- , prayer-formula addressed to **63**.1-7
- , prescr. conc. sipping of **221**.17 .26-30 .131cd-132ab
- , prescription(s) concerning carrying of fire and **221**.101
- , prescription(s) concerning drinking of **221**.102
- , prescription(s) concerning sipping of **221**.62cd-64ab .65cd-67ab .95-100
- , prohibition of defecating in **221**.24ab
- , prohibition of sexual intercourse in **221**.24ab
- , protection by sprinkling of **168**.18cd-21
- , purification by **24**.13-18; **72**.27cd-34; **126**.32cd-35
- , purification by drinking of **72**.27cd-34
- , purification by fire and **158**.35cd-37ab
- , purification by sipping of **221**.67cd-69
- , purification by touching of **221**.161-169ab
- purified by Kuśa-grass **161**.60-61ab
- , rejuvenation by **159**.41cd-46ab
- , Śiva as **75**.6
- , sacrificial **161**.59
- , sipping of **219**.71cd-86
- , sprinkling with consecrated **65**.81-82
- , touching of **15**.35-41ab; **16**.13-24
- , weapons sprinkled with **110**.35-39ab
- with sesamum **28**.24; **219**.71cd-86
- with sesamum, offering of **57**.5; **60**.49-53

water-belly as punishment for untruthfulness **104**.39-43

water-drops, assembly of **41**.50cd-54ab
- , places of pilgrimage originated from **161**.60-61ab

water-jar, birth from **158**.8-15ef

water-place, killing of animals at **123**.33cd-36ab

waters, Agni born from **126**.32cd-35
- , ancestors lifted from **219**.37-39
- as first of beings **110**.200ef-201ef
- as mothers **72**.27cd-34; **126**.9-11; **144**.15-16
- as origin of all **72**.27cd-34
- as origin of *amṛta* **126**.9-11
- as origin of *dharma* **72**.27cd-34
- as origin of food **126**.9-11
- as origin of plants **126**.9-11
- as origin of purity **126**.9-11
- as origin of sacrifice **72**.27cd-34
- as prior to Brahman, earth and **137**.25-28ab
- , competition between Agni and **126**
- , lotus originated from Viṣṇu and **161**.6cd-9
- of heavenly Gaṅgā **24**.13-18
- , origin of **161**.6cd-9
- , *puruṣa* originated from **161**.6cd-9
- , Soma as lord of **9**.12
- , superiority of **126**.9-11 .19cd-22 .32cd-35
- , Varuṇa as lord of **4**.2-9

water-spring, origin of hot **115**.15cd-16

waving the tail of a cow **184**.7-13

way to nether world **58**.34cd-36

weakness of Arjuna **212**.21-24

wealth during Kali-Yuga, social rank determined by **230**.10-27

- granted by Viṣṇu **136**.35cd-36ef
- , inconvenience(s) of **230**.72-74
- , Kubera as lord of **97**.24-28
- , maxim about **170**.6-7ef
- , poet(s) desirous of **174**.17
- , prescription(s) concerning expenditure of **221**.11-12
wealth see also *Lakṣmī, profit, prosperity*
weapon, Erakā-grass as **210**.37-43
- , fever as **206**.14-19
- , foam as **124**.33-36ab
- made of foam **129**.4-8
- , Mantras as **206**.24-30
- named Brahmaśiras **9**.22
- of Agni **125**.9-12 .18-21
- of Baladeva, pestle as **209**.11cd-21ab
- of Baladeva, ploughshare as **195**.5-7; **208**.32-35
- of fire **8**.31-32 .41-42ab
- , yawning as **206**.24-30
weapon(s), elephant's teeth as **193**.24-31
weapons as deposit **110**.21-24
- at city of Yama **214**.120-128
- , Kṣatriya represented by **111**.39cd-47
- made from bones of Dadhīci **110**.51-56ab
- of demons **213**.81-104
- of Kṛṣṇa, departure of **210**.47-48
- of servants of Yama **215**.45-55ab .81-83ab
- of Viṣṇu **163**.32-39
- of Yama **125**.25-32; **168**.25-26ab
- , origin of **129**.75-78
- , punishment for making of **22**.16cd-17ab
- , spell-formula(s) and **141**.10-13
- sprinkled with water **110**.35-39ab
- , summoning of heavenly **195**.5-7
wedding, alms-giving at **72**.11cd-14
- , guest(s) at **72**.10cd-11ab
- of Śiva and Umā **36**.54cd-70 .125-136
- of Sītā **123**.97-105ab
- of sons of Daśaratha **123**.97-105ab
wedding see also *marriage, self-choice*
wedding-ceremony, absence of bridegroom in **111**.39cd-47
- , Brahman as priest at **72**.18-19
- , ceremonial functions at **72**.11cd-14
- , disturbance of **7**.98-99
- of Śiva and Pārvatī **72**.11cd-14
- , rites at **36**.130-134; **72**.15-17
- , seven steps at **8**.5-8
weight of Kṛṣṇa **193**.67cd-76ab
welcome, gift of **208**.8-18; **210**.50-52ab
- of Kṛṣṇa in heaven **203**.1-5
- offering **28**.33
welcome see also *honouring of guest(s), hospitality*
Weller, F. **10**.65cd-67ab
wheel in simile **237**.76
- of *saṃsāra* **214**.9
whirling around, killing by **193**.60cd-63ab
white and black **133**.18-23ab
- as auspicious colour **221**.81cd-82ab
- hair of Viṣṇu, black and **181**.26-31
- lotuses **59**.6-21
- marble **59**.26-33
- shape of Viṣṇu **161**.54-58
wicked, punishment of the **215**.24-28
wicked see also *evil-doers*
widow, burning of **8**.39-40; **110**.67-70; **212**.1-4; **229**.43cd-55
wife, abandoning of **82**.7-8; **154**.11cd-14ab
- , advice by **167**.26-28
- as fire and water, husband and **144**.15-16 .20-22
- as friend of husband **129**.101-124; **167**.22-25
- as half of husband **161**.33cd-35ab
- as mother **144**.17-19
- , fear of one's **15**.16-21
- , harmony between husband and **138**.10-13
- in simile, faithfulness of **80**.71-77
- , interference by **125**.13-14 .22
- , maxim about duty of **80**.71-77
- , maxim about husband and **80**.37-43; **109**.6cd-10; **128**.3-6; **129**.101-124
- , merit of faithfulness of **80**.71-77
- of Brahman, origin of **161**.33cd-35ab
- , offerings given to **220**.149-151
- , punishment for choice of wrong **22**.17cd-18ab
- , punishment for separating of husband and **215**.93cd-94ab .130cd-136ab
- , shadow as surrogate of **89**.6-9ab
- , test of faithfulness of **138**.14-19
wild animals at city of Yama **214**.120-128; **215**.4-23
- animals, origin of domestic and **161**.43cd-50cd
- animals, tiger as lord of **4**.2-9
Wilson, H. H. **24**.13-18
wind as messenger **194**.13-17

- , clouds destroyed by **53**.12-14ab
- originating from breath of Viṣṇu **233**.1-4
- , purification by **221**.132cd-133ab
- , Śiva as **75**.8
- , spell for **58**.55cd-56
wind see also *Vāyu*
wine and meat, offering of **181**.38-53
winter, description of **36**.89-94
wise, maxim about conduct of the **212**.89-90
wish for constant devotion **59**.78-80
- for daughter **144**.2-4
- for fearlessness **162**.2cd-6ab
- for identity with gods **213**.53-57
- for invincible son **173**.6cd-8ef
- for living in Kali-Yuga **231**.1-2
- for son **124**.12-16
- for the sake of others **125**.33-43
wish-fulfilment for women and low castes **227**.10-14
- in simile **227**.8-9
wish-fulfilment see also *boon*
wishing tree, merit of looking at **60**.12-15
wishing-cow **69**.12-43; **140**.14-18ab
- , circumambulation of **87**.17-20
wishing-tree **57**.12-19; **68**.74-77ab; **70**.8cd-10; **140**.14-18ab
witness of actions, elements as **217**.23-24
- of promise, fire as **140**.26-30
- , punishment for false **22**.7-8; **214**.120-128; **215**.72-77 .88cd-90ab
witnesses of sacrifice **127**.9cd-15
wives, disobedience of **100**.9-13
- of Ariṣṭanemin **3**.60
- of bad men, women as **217**.114cd-115ab
- of Dharma **3**.29-30ab
- of Kaśyapa **3**.51-52
- of Kaśyapa, descendants of **3**.53-58
- of Kṛṣṇa **201**.3-5
- of Soma **3**.59
- of Soma, descendants of **3**.34-46ab
- of Soma, Nakṣatras as **2**.47-49
- of Vasudeva **14**.36-38
- , omniscience of **129**.49-64
- proud of husbands **203**.64-69
- , punishment for forbidden sexual intercourse with **22**.21-22
- , punishment for prostitution of **22**.21-22
woman appearing to Kṛṣṇa, naked **206**.31-38
- as »field« **126**.4-8
- , demon as beautiful **122**.8-20
- , description of beautiful **122**.8-20
- , man disguised as **210**.6-10
- , Nārada as **229**.43cd-67ab
- , Rākṣasas bewitched by magic **134**.8cd-11
- , river turning into **15**.35-41ab
- , Yoga destroyed by looking at **219**.6-12
woman see also *widow, wife, mother, sister*
womb of Diti, Indra in **124**.49-86
»womb-insect« as abuse **170**.8ef-13
women, abduction of **7**.98-99; **9**.17-20; **152**; **202**.3-12; **208**.4-7; **212**.18-20 .25-28 .42-53
- after marriage, functions of **144**.17-19
- , ancestral rites for **220**.61ab .74 .75
- and low castes, wish-fulfilment for **227**.10-14
- and outcastes, Yoga for **236**.68
- and Śūdras, exclusion of **67**.19
- as cause of pleasure and pain **122**.21-24ab
- as wives of bad men **217**.114cd-115ab
- , beneficial effect(s) of noble **123**.165-169
- , blessings of **230**.72-76
- , creation of **2**.47-49
- , description of **41**.20-27 .30-34ab; **43**.36cd-44; **44**.23-27ab; **46**.13-22; **47**.68-70; **68**.23-27ab
- during Kali-Yuga **230**.10-27 .28-31
- during menstruation, prescr. conc. **221**.23 .75 .135cd-136ab .141cd-143ab .143cd-146ab
- , education of **108**.52-53ef
- , homage by **65**.76cd-77
- , importance of **129**.49-64
- interfering with sacrifice **100**.9-13
- , lament of **192**.14-31
- , liberation for **178**.184-186; **238**.37cd
- , marriage of Kṛṣṇa to sixteen-thousand one hundred **204**.13cd-18
- , maxim about **100**.9-13; **107**.47; **151**.10-16
- , maxim about attractiveness of **147**.9cd-13; **151**.3-5ab; **152**.5-9ab
- , maxim about fickleness of **151**.5cd-7ab
- , maxim about generosity towards **123**.23-33ab
- , maxim about noble young **123**.165-169
- , maxim about pride of **203**.64-69
- , merit gained by **41**.86; **65**.76cd-77 .78-80
- , observances of purity for **124**.19-28ab
- performing ancestral rites for brothers **220**.78cd-80ab

– , pollution by **221**.135cd–136ab .143cd–146ab
– , position of **40**.136–137; **220**.3–4; **231**.4–41
– , service as duty of **230**.75–76
– , sin of killing of **4**.74–80
– understanding women, maxim about **137**.25–28ab
– , Vāsudeva worshipped by **227**.10–14
– , worship by **41**.86; **66**.7cd–13
– , worship permitted to **58**.59cd–64ab
wooing of Śiva for Umā **35**.4cd–10
word, *brahman* as **234**.58–60ab
– , impossibility of revoking a given **110**.191cd–194ab
world, allegorical description of **238**.26–30
– as Māyā **240**.54cd–68
– based on truth **228**.52–55
– , emanation of **241**.11–36
– , future of **1**.16–20
– in ocean, submersion of **53**.12–14ab .14cd –18ab; **56**.51–54
– , Kṛṣṇa identified with **192**.62–66
– , mothers of **34**.87–89
– of Aniruddha **227**.42–47
– of boar **227**.37cd–41
– of Brahman **4**.68–73; **7**.30–34 .37a–d; **42**.1 –2 .6–8; **67**.60cd–64ab; **73**.48–51; **102**.8cd–9ab; **120**.6–7ab; **222**.55–56; **227**.16–32ab .32cd–37ab; **228**.86–91ab; **233**.5–6
– of cows **67**.64cd–75
– of Gandharvas **227**.16–32ab; **228**.146–151
– of gods **227**.16–32ab
– of Govinda **63**.18
– of Hari **227**.32cd–37ab
– of Indra **51**.29–31; **67**.64cd–75; **140**.5cd–6ef; **227**.16–32ab; **228**.146–151
– of Indra, destruction of imitated **140**.31–34
– of Indra, kings in **171**.2cd–6cd
– of man-lion **227**.37cd–41
– of moon **227**.16–32ab
– of Nārāyaṇa **227**.42–47
– of Pradyumna **227**.42–47
– of Prajāpati **67**.64cd–75; **227**.16–32ab; **230**.72–74
– of Rudra **67**.60cd–64ab
– of Śiva **41**.60cd–71 .75–81 .91 .92; **56**.66cd –73; **57**.9–11; **111**.80–82; **124**.132–136ab
– of Saṃkarṣaṇa **227**.42–47
– of Soma **143**.2–5
– of stars **227**.16–32ab
– of sun **29**.22–27ab; **227**.16–32ab
– of Viṣṇu **43**.77–82ab; **45**.57–58 .77–89; **49**.61–63; **51**.42–45 .63–71; **57**.17–19 .20–28; **58**.58–59ab .59cd–64ab .70cd–77; **62**.5–9; **63**.1–7 .11–16 .17 .22; **64**.17–20; **66**.18–23; **67**.2–5 .53–57; **68**; **121**.24–25; **128**.83–84; **150**.15–20; **163**.52–53; **175**.81cd–82; **227**.37cd–41; **246**.28–29
– of Viṣṇu, inhabitants of **68**.23–27ab
– of Yama **217**.33–35 .80cd–86
– of Yama, distance to **214**.11cd–12ab
– , Purāṇa told for the benefit of the **175**.78
– , Śiva as self of the **153**.1–2ab
– , Sītā as mother of the **154**.27–30ab
– , Umā as mother of the **75**.17
– , Viṣṇu and **180**.1–12
– , Viṣṇu identical with **23**.41–43; **179**.38–43ab
– without Indra **129**.20cd–29
world(s) of Yama **217**.80cd–86
world-guardian(s), residence of **227**.16–32ab
world-guardians see *guardians of directions*
worldly objects, indifference towards **122**.3–7
worlds burnt by Rudra, three **232**.24–27
– , distance of heavenly **23**.12–15
– , gods as lords of three **32**.7–8
– , inverted **22**.31
– , protection of **5**.38cd–39
– , seven **33**.3–8 .15cd
– , three **6**.6; **23**.16–20; **100**.19–21
– , Viṣṇu identical with three **122**.68–73
worm, rebirth as **155**.3cd–10ab
worms and insects, liberation for **161**.72–78
– and insects, origin of **161**.43cd–50cd
worship as ceremonial function of Viṣṇu **72**.11cd–14
– at noon **192**.32–42
– at sunrise **16**.13–24
– by Śūdras **66**.7cd–13
– by women **41**.86; **66**.7cd–13
– , collecting of flowers for **228**.15–21
– , concentration during **192**.59–61
– , constituents of **41**.60cd–71; **66**.7cd–13; **67**.24–27 .35cd–39ab; **228**.1–5
– during hundred and eight years **176**.33–34
– , five services of **67**.28–29ab
– in temple **228**.40–43
– , mental **192**.59–61
– , merit of **51**.42–45; **57**.38–41 .42–51 .52–56

.59-61; **58**.1-7 .12-18 .59cd-77; **59**.81-91; **60**.1-6 .19-21; **61**.47-50; **66**.7cd-13; **68**.73
- of Ādityas **155**.2-3ab
- of boar by gods **226**.59-61
- of Brahman **131**.31-39ab; **216**.5-63
- of Gautamī **157**.15-18cd
- of image of Vāsudeva **176**.12-15ab
- of Kṛṣṇa **57**.29-56; **59**.26-33; **187**.59cd-61
- of Kṛṣṇa, effect(s) of **227**.6-7
- of Liṅga **41**.82-85; **56**.66cd-73; **97**.29
- of Matsyamādhava **60**.1-6
- of Mothers **112**.24cd-26ab
- of Narasiṃha **58**
- of Nārāyaṇa **61**.1-3
- of ocean **62**.1-4
- of Pṛthu as ideal king **4**.115-121
- of Puruṣottama **43**.10-13; **67**.20-23
- of Puruṣottama, effect(s) of **178**.1-4
- of Puruṣottama, merit of **178**.193-194
- of Śiva **59**.6-21; **143**.14-16; **169**.4-6ab .36-39ab; **176**.26-32; **216**.5-63
- of Śiva and Umā **169**.16-22ab
- of Śiva by dancing **168**.31-35
- of Śiva, constituents of **43**.65cd-74
- of Śiva, description of **169**.6cd-15
- of Śiva, merit of **28**.56cd-62ab; **41**.60cd-71 .72-74 .88-90
- of Śiva, observances for **168**.31-35
- of Śiva with lotus-flowers **109**.46-48
- of Śiva with sixteen offerings **123**.191-194
- of Saṃkarṣaṇa **57**.20-28
- of statue **51**.37-39
- of statue, constituents of **61**.24-38
- of statues **51**.54-56
- of Subhadrā **57**.57-61
- of sun **28**.19-36; **60**.49-53; **67**.15-18; **131**.31-39ab; **138**.28-32
- of sun as privilege **159**.12-16
- of sun, effect(s) of **28**.42-45
- of sun, merit of **28**.37-54ab .46 .47-53ab; **29**.7-61; **33**.27-31
- of sun, prescr. conc. **29**.7-61
- of sun, priority of **28**.40-41
- of Umā **110**.56cd-60
- of Varāha, merit of **219**.107cd-109ab
- of Vārāhī, merit of **42**.11
- of Vāsudeva **227**.10-14
- of Vāsudeva, effect(s) of **227**.50
- of Vāsudeva recommended by Śiva **226**.7-9
- of Virajā, merit of **42**.1-2
- of Viṣṇu **43**.82cd-83ab; **136**.3cd-14ab; **216**.5-63; **226**.56-57ab
- of Viṣṇu and Śiva **131**.31-39ab
- of Viṣṇu as boar **229**.86cd-87
- of Viṣṇu, liberation by **196**.30-45
- of Viṣṇu, merit of **42**.11
- of Viṣṇu recommended by Śiva **226**.67c-f
- of Viṣṇu, Yoga as **233**.40cd-43ab
- of Yoganidrā as Devī **181**.38-53
- permitted to untouchables **58**.59cd-64ab
- permitted to women **58**.59cd-64ab
- , prescr. conc. **61**
- , prescr. conc. practices of **28**.19-36
- with dance **162**.6cd-10ab
- with prayer-formulas **61**.24-38; **143**.14-16
worship see also *homage, veneration*
wound on Liṅga **169**.36-39ab
wrath and fire in simile **108**.68-70
- as means of victory **162**.27cd-30
- , creation of **1**.39cd-42
- , fire of **39**.48-49
- of mother, destruction by **13**.58-61
- , personification of **39**.48-49; **162**.10cd-12
wrath see also *anger, Manyu*
wrathful and greedy people, maxim about **124**.68-73ab
written book, Purāṇa as **175**.86-90
wrong testimony, curse because of **146**.15-18
- wife, punishment for choice of **22**.17cd-18ab
Yādavas **7**.30-34; **13**.127cd-132ab .205-207ab; **210**.37-43
- deprived of kingship **208**.8-18
- , destruction of **210**
- , drunkenness of **210**.37-43
- , enmity between Kaṃsa and **190**.10-19
- killed by Kṛṣṇa **210**.44-46
- , killing of **210**.37-43
Yādavī **8**.38 .39-40
Yadu **12**.5cd-6ab .18-21 .24-38 .50; **146**.2-8ab .26-27 .28-31; **226**.30-41
- , descendants of **13**.153cd-204
Yadudhra **5**.24cd-25
Yajana, place of pilgrimage **25**.30
Yājana, place of pilgrimage **25**.30
Yajñadvīpa [= Vedadvīpa] **151**.17-22ab
Yajñaghna **133**.9-12
Yajñatīrtha, place of pilgrimage **131**.26-28
Yājñavalkya **88**.4-7 .8 .16-19 .21-26; **145**.2cd-5ab; **174**.2-5ab

- , Varuṇa as teacher of Janaka and **88**
Yājñika, place of pilgrimage **118**.31-32ef
Yājñyavālkyas **10**.61-62
Yajurveda **109**.13-20
Yakṣarājatīrtha, place of pilgrimage **25**.39
Yakṣas **3**.3-7ab; **18**.52-55; **20**.36-38ab; **36**.22cd-23ab .63cd-70; **50**.55-59; **51**.1-8; **54**.16-17; **69**.12-43; **105**.8cd-11ab; **189**.10-12; **214**.107cd-109; **219**.49-51; **237**.5
- , fight between Ila and **108**.18-20ab
- , origin of **3**.104-105
- , rebirth as **27**.66cd-68
- , Śiva as lord of **4**.2-9
Yakṣeśvara, Śiva as **132**.1-2
Yakṣiṇī, description of **108**.36cd-47
- [river], origin of **132**.3-5
Yakṣiṇīhrada, place of pilgrimage **25**.36
Yakṣiṇīsaṃgama, place of pilgrimage **132**.1-2 .7-9ef
Yama **7**.26cd-27ab; **22**.2-6; **32**.64-68; **36**.12cd-13ab; **37**.2-23; **45**.59-67; **51**.1-8; **56**.13-15; **59**.6-21; **61**.45cd-46; **65**.40-41; **69**.12-43; **70**.35cd-37ab; **86**.8-9ab; **89**.5a-c .13-17ab .17-21; **94**.15-21; **110**.10-20; **122**.68-73; **192**.48-58; **219**.60cd-65ab .98cd-107ab; **220**.49cd-50ab
- , abode of **123**.109cd-115
- , advice by **165**.37-44
- , advice by servants of **123**.128cd-139
- and Yamunā as twins **6**.7-8
- as crow **103**.2-6
- as lord of ancestors **4**.2-9; **6**.46cd-48ab
- as lord of *dharma* **94**.31-36; **165**.30cd-36
- as lord of hells **123**.121-128ab
- as lord of the south **125**.25-32; **131**.31-39ab
- as righteous king **6**.46cd-48ab
- , asceticism practised by **86**.43-46
- bathing in Gautamī **86**.47-49ab
- , boon by Agni and **125**.33-43
- , city of **214**.104-107ab
- cursed by Chāyā **6**.20cd-23; **32**.58cd-63
- , Daityas killed by **168**.25-26ab
- , description of **215**.45-55ab
- , description of messengers of **214**.55-69
- , discus of **168**.25-26ab
- , distance to world of **214**.11cd-12ab
- , entourage of **215**.45-55ab
- experienced as father **216**.67-72
- , four-eyed dogs dear to **131**.2cd-4ab .31-39ab
- , gate(s) to city of **214**.107cd-128; **215**.2-3
- , hymn by Ulūkī to **125**.23-24ef
- killed by Skanda **94**.15-21
- meditating on Viṣṇu **86**.8-9ab
- , messengers of **214**.42cd-45
- , noose of **168**.25-26ab
- , nooses of **125**.9-12 .22
- , path leading to **214**.11cd-103
- , place of pilgrimage sacred to **168**.1
- protected by discus of Viṣṇu **86**.27-29
- , revivification of **94**.43-45
- , reward(s) distributed by **216**.67-72
- seduced by Apsaras **86**.35-39
- , servants of **150**.6-9; **157**.21cd-25ab
- , stick of **125**.22; **168**.25-26ab; **203**.45-62
- stopped by effect(s) of place of pilgrimage **45**.59-67 .71-73
- , sun as father of **94**.22-26
- to Ulūkī, boon by **125**.25-32
- , Vaivasvata **4**.2-9
- Vaivasvata defeated by Baladeva **194**.23-31
- , weapons of **125**.25-32; **168**.25-26ab
- , weapons of servants of **215**.45-55ab .81-83ab
- , world of **217**.33-35 .80cd-86
- , world(s) of **217**.80cd-86
Yama see also *Death, Kāla*, time
Yāmabhūtas **13**.91
Yamadūtas **10**.61-62
Yamahasta **176**.37-51
Yamāntaka **176**.37-51
Yāmas **5**.8-9ab
Yamatīrtha, place of pilgrimage **125**.1-2ab; **131**.1-2ab .39cd-51; **168**.25-26ab .30
Yamī **6**.51cd-52ab
Yāmī **3**.29-30ab .30cd-33
Yamunā **6**.51cd-52ab; **27**.25cd-27; **32**.49-50; **70**.33-35ab; **77**.2-9ab; **89**.5a-c .37-40ab .43-46ab; **110**.202-210; **161**.21-23ef; **185**; **189**.22-25; **192**.32-42; **246**.21-27
- as twins, Yama and **6**.7-8
- , Balarāma and **198**
- , confluence of Gaṅgā and **129**.4-8
- , miraculous crossing of **182**.19-26
- , place of pilgrimage **64**.10; **65**.84-96
Yamunāprabhava, place of pilgrimage **25**.56
Yāmya, place of pilgrimage **104**.1-2
yantra, drawing of **28**.23; **61**.1-3

Yaśodā **181**.38-53; **182**.1-3; **184**.7-13 .20-28 .31-42ab; **185**.18-27 .28-29; **190**.1-5
Yati **12**.1-2 .3
Yāti **12**.1-2
Yatidharman **14**.8-10
Yātudhāna-Rākṣasas **219**.25-29
Yaudheyas **13**.24-25ab
Yauvanāśva **13**.148-150ab
Yavana **213**.159-163
Yavanas **8**.35-37 .44-51; **19**.8cd; **27**.17-19ab .43-50 .59cd-62ab
Yavīnara **13**.93-96
yawning as weapon **206**.24-30
- of Śeṣa **21**.15-27
Yayanta **3**.46cd-49
Yāyāta, place of pilgrimage **146**.1 .42-45
Yayāti **12**; **13**.139-140 .142-146; **146**; **226**.30-41
- cursed by Śukra **146**.11-14
- , reference to curse by **194**.11-12
- , Śukra reproached by **146**.15-18
Yayātipatana, place of pilgrimage **25**.26
Yayātipattana, place of pilgrimage **25**.26
years, drought of three **14**.4-7
- , drought of twelve **7**.104cd-105ab; **8**.10cd
- , drought of twenty-four **74**.22cd-24ab
- , rain of twelve **53**.6-10ab
- , son obtained after twelve **14**.48-50ab
- , vow of twelve **8**.3-4 .13-15b:; **124**.12-16
yellow clothes of Kṛṣṇa **192**.71-74
- clothes of Vāsudeva **176**.8-10; **207**.13-24
- shape of Viṣṇu **161**.54-58
Yoga **3**.42cd-46ab; **6**.41-43; **33**.27-31; **34**.87-89; **35**.4cd-10 .26cd-28; **37**.2-23; **43**.2-5; **45**.26-28 .44-46; **174**.2-5ab; **178**.112; **220**.89cd-97ab
- , abandoning of **219**.13-17; **239**.53
- , ancestors and **220**.109cd-112ab
- and ancestors **219**.13-17 .91cd-98ab .98cd -107ab
- as worship of Viṣṇu **233**.40cd-43ab
- , characteristics of **239**.3
- , circumstances forbidden for **243**.49
- , conditions forbidden for **235**.7-9
- , dangers of **239**.50-52
- , Dattātreya as teacher of **180**.24cd-38
- , death by means of **30**.14-18; **34**.20ef-25; **109**.6cd-10; **110**.47cd-50; **211**.3-4 .11-12
- , definition of **235**.28
- destroyed by looking at woman **219**.6-12
- , difference between Sāṃkhya and **239**.7-9
- , duration of practices of **236**.59cd-66
- , faults of **235**.11-12; **236**.40cd-43ab; **238**.44-51 .53-56ab; **239**.11-23 .47-49; **240**.53-54ab
- , five faults of **236**.37cd-40ab; **238**.52; **240**.51-52
- for women and outcastes **236**.68
- , goal of **243**.46-65
- , highest step in **235**.21-25
- , identity of Sāṃkhya and **243**.20
- in simile **196**.16-20; **239**.50-52
- , knowledge by means of **6**.31-34ab .41-43; **10**.38cd-41ab; **17**.35-40
- , liberation by **239**.11-23
- of Hari **60**.1-6
- of meditation **20**.56cd-57ab; **52**.11-15ab
- of Śambhu **41**.75-81
- of Śaṃkara **57**.9-11
- of Śiva **28**.56cd-62ab
- of sun **28**.62cd-64ab
- of Viṣṇu **43**.77-82ab; **57**.52-56 .59-61; **58**.70cd-77; **62**.5-9; **64**.17-20; **66**.18-23; **67**.76-80; **70**.3cd-8ab; **176**.57-62
- , origin of **191**.4-12
- , Pāśupata **41**.60cd-71; **43**.65cd-74
- , places for **236**.59cd-66
- , places forbidden for **235**.7-9
- , power(s) of **235**.21-25; **239**.24-28
- , practices of **39**.90-91; **110**.47cd-50 .115-120; **235**; **243**.46-65
- practised during night **243**.50-53
- , prohibition of **235**.7-9; **243**.49
- , Sāṃkhya and **40**.107-111; **236**; **244**.44-48
- , supernatural power(s) of **176**.33-34; **205**.15-22; **206**.5-9
- , Ūrjā as mother of **219**.91cd-98ab
- , Viṣṇu as Lord of **170**.40-43; **213**.170
Yogamāyā as Viśveśvarī **131**.29-30
Yoganidrā **181**.36 .38-53; **182**.1-3
- as Devī **182**.27-30
- as Devī, worship of **181**.38-53
- as Māyā of Viṣṇu **181**.37
- as sister of Indra **181**.38-53
- , benumbing by **182**.19-26
- , eight arms of **182**.27-30
- , Kaṃsa warned by **182**.31
Yogatīrtha, place of pilgrimage **25**.13
Yogeśvara, Liṅga named **170**.1
- [Viṣṇu] **170**.40-43 .54-63 .69-74ab .84-88

.89a-f
yogic postures **242**.8-15ab
- sleep of Viṣṇu **45**.29; **179**.22cd-26; **180**.24cd-38; **233**.8
- sleep of Viṣṇu, Māyā as **233**.5-6
Yogin **13**.27cd-29 .32-35 .172-173 .174-176ab; **224**.47-52
- absorbed in beings **239**.58-61
- absorbed in the imperishable **236**.56cd-57ab
- after death, destiny of **214**.107cd-109; **240**.69-75
- at ancestral rites, importance of **220**.109cd -112ab
- , Bali as **13**.32-35
- , concentration of **239**.31-38
- , conduct of **236**.45cd-46 .47-48ab
- , diet of **235**.6; **239**.43-46; **243**.50-53
- , distractions of **236**.57cd-59ab .67
- , education of **235**.4-5
- , fasting of **239**.43-46
- in simile **239**.11-23 .31-38
- , liberation of **227**.48-49; **235**.21-25 .26-27; **237**.82-86ab
- , prescription(s) concerning conduct of **236**.43cd-44ab .59cd-66
- , rebirth as **13**.27cd-29; **28**.47-53ab; **43**.77-82ab; **70**.3cd-8ab; **227**.32cd-37ab
- , Rudra as **20**.56cd-57ab
- , Vyāsa as **235**.2
Yogins, Vāsudeva as foundation for **180**.18cd-21ab
- , Viṣṇu worshipped by **56**.24cd-26ab
Yonidvāra, place of pilgrimage **25**.69
young women, maxim about noble **123**.165-169
youth, eternal **11**.51-53; **34**.87-89
- , maxim about **170**.6-7ef
Yuddhakāṇḍa of Rāmāyaṇa **154**.2-4
Yudhājit **14**.1-2ab; **16**.9-11 .49cd
Yudhiṣṭhira **14**.20cd-24ab; **188**.42-47; **208**.19-31; **212**.91-92 .93-94
Yugas, absence of **18**.60-62ab; **20**.14-15
- , castes in **175**.25-28
- , comparison of **230**.62-63 .78-81
- , comparison of merit in **230**.64
- , four **19**.20; **27**.64cd; **175**.14cd-16 .29-32ab
- , seventy **5**.54cd-55ab
- , seventy-one **2**.1-4
- , thousand **3**.62-64ab; **5**.53-54ab .58cd-60
Yugas see also *Dvāpara-Yuga, Kali-Yuga, Kṛta-Yuga, Satya-Yuga, Tretā-Yuga*
Yukta **5**.27-28
Yuvanāśva **7**.51cd-53 .91-92; **10**.19cd-20; **13**.82cd-87
Yuyudhāna **14**.24cd-25ab
zodiacal sign **64**.1-2